The
HANDBOOK *of* HUMANISTIC PSYCHOLOGY

This book is dedicated to our mentor and coeditor,
James Bugental. Jim's landmark work,
Challenges of Humanistic Psychology,
inspired the present volume.
His presence, patience, and clarity
inspire our lives.

KIRK SCHNEIDER

J. FRASER PIERSON

The
HANDBOOK *of*
HUMANISTIC
PSYCHOLOGY

Leading Edges in Theory,
Research, and Practice

Edited by
KIRK J. SCHNEIDER
JAMES F. T. BUGENTAL
J. FRASER PIERSON

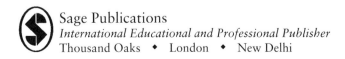
Sage Publications
International Educational and Professional Publisher
Thousand Oaks ◆ London ◆ New Delhi

For information:

Sage Publications, Inc.
2455 Teller Road
Thousand Oaks, California 91320
E-mail: order@sagepub.com

Sage Publications Ltd.
6 Bonhill Street
London EC2A 4PU
United Kingdom

Sage Publications India Pvt. Ltd.
M-32 Market
Greater Kailash I
New Delhi 110 048 India

Printed in the United States of America

Library of Congress Cataloging-in-Publication Data

The handbook of humanistic psychology: Leading edges in theory,
    research, and practice / [edited] by Kirk J. Schneider,
James F. T. Bugental, J. Fraser Pierson.
        p. cm.
    Includes bibliographical references and index.
    ISBN 0-7619-2121-4 (cloth: alk. paper)
    ISBN 0-7619-2782-4 (pbk.: alk. paper)
    1. Humanistic psychology. I. Schneider, Kirk J.
    II. Bugental, James F. T.   III. Pierson, J. Fraser.
    BF204 .H36 2001
    150.19'8—dc21   2001000095

This book is printed on acid-free paper.

    03 04 05 06 7 6 5 4 3 2

Acquisition Editor:	Jim Brace-Thompson
Editorial Assistant:	Karen Ehrmann
Production Editor:	Sanford Robinson
Editorial Assistant:	Candice Crosetti
Typesetter:	Marion Warren
Indexer:	Molly Hall
Cover Designer:	Michelle Lee

Contents

Part II. HUMANISTIC THEORY

META-THEMES

CONTEMPORARY THEMES

Part III. HUMANISTIC METHODOLOGY

Part IV. HUMANISTIC APPLICATIONS TO PRACTICE

Part V. HUMANISTIC APPLICATIONS TO BROADER SETTINGS

Part VI. EPILOGUE: HUMANISTIC PSYCHOLOGY IN THE NEW MILLENNIUM

Foreword

W E LIVE IN A TIME of enormous and pervasive change and challenge—a time of "raging chaos." It is clear that our old ways of being and doing no longer work and that our old myths neither hold our allegiance nor hold promise for solving our problems. As Albert Einstein once observed, "No problem can be solved from the same consciousness that created it. We must learn to see the world anew."

It is fitting, therefore, that a new book on humanistic psychology usher in our new millennium. It feeds our hunger for a new vision and a new way of being.

Humanistic psychology first came to my attention when my own pain and confusion shocked me out of my old beliefs and tested my sense of myself. I began a search for something to make sense of my life. That search led me to a series of workshops, during one memorable year, with Sidney Jourard, Abraham Maslow, James Bugental, James Fadiman, Rollo May, John Heider, and Carl Rogers. Those experiences saved my life, and they profoundly inform all of my social involvement and politics.

Futurist Willis Harman has identified three profound revolutions that shattered our old ways of being: (a) when Galileo and Copernicus recognized that the earth revolves around the sun (and not vice versa), (b) when Darwin recognized the evolution of species, and (c) when Freud recognized the internal dimensions within us humans. In each case, worlds came apart, we found ourselves in raging chaos, and then there arose a new order.

Today's "new Copernican revolution" amounts to a most profound shift in our view of our own selves, from a fundamentally negative view of human nature to a fundamentally positive one. In a break from the long traditions of original sin, where we needed to be tamed, we now sense ourselves alive with original grace, needing to be nurtured.

This radical idea upends all that has been constructed on the old foundation. It amounts to a total revolution. It was hinted at by Jourard, who proposed that we become "transparent selves." It gained credence with Bugental's observance of "the search for authenticity." It was given voice by Rogers in his famous aphorism: "I've been doing psychology for more than 50 years, and I've come to believe that we human beings are innately inclined toward becoming life affirming, constructive, responsible, and trustworthy." It was elaborated by May when he argued that the utterly free human will naturally be responsible. It was confirmed by Maslow when he identified our possible "democratic character structure" in which one's intellect, emotions, and body are liberated and altogether integrated into one's becoming a whole person.

What do these eloquent formulations amount to? A new revolution. Whereas the first American Revolution established our right to self-determination, this next revolution demands self-actualization. Simply said, the humanistic view of the self must become the organizing vision and ethic of our times and of our lives.

According to sociologist Paul Ray's book, *The Cultural Creatives*, fully one quarter of American adults already have enlisted themselves, however (un)consciously, in this revolution.

Humanistic psychology offers us the most faithful, hopeful, and loving human path toward our own wholeness and for addressing the most pressing social issues of our times. The present volume introduces us to ourselves and to visions and practices for our lives. Such visions and practices lead to engagements in social action that are grounded in faith, abound with hope, and relate in love.

There is almost nothing as powerful as an idea whose time has come, and this volume demonstrates that our time has come for humanistic psychology. May this book, comprised of the very latest in humanistic scholarship, serve to both enlighten and empower us. And may it lead us toward a fully realized human nature in our new millennium.

—JOHN VASCONCELLOS
California state senator

Preface

SOME 40 YEARS AGO, when I was studying psychology at the University of Chicago, I remember coming across a short article by Abraham Maslow, and for the first time in my graduate career, I felt a sense of confirmation—yes, it was worth toiling through the confusing morass of professional literature if one could end up writing like that. Afterward, I read most of Maslow's writings as well as those of Rogers and other exponents of the "third way." I took courses with Eugene Gendlin on Husserl, Heidegger, and Merleau-Ponty, and their thoughts became a part of my own thinking. At the same time, however, I also was exposed to the writings of Karl Popper and became persuaded that knowledge is best expressed by systematic propositions based on empirical evidence.

This autobiographical detail is intended to inform the reader that I am coming to the task of writing this preface as a sympathetic but critical fellow traveler. Most of the chapters in this volume deal with vital issues that psychology should be concerned with but rarely is. Amedeo Giorgi (Chapter 5) is completely on target when he claims that psychology has surrendered its agenda to other paradigms—neurology, cognitive science, and evolutionary perspectives—and that it is time for us to reclaim it. Arthur Lyons (Chapter 46) is equally on target with his call for humanistic psychology to address issues of positive social change. The themes most often repeated in the chapters in this volume—that we are responsible moral agents; that the self is real; that play, love, and wonder are important components of experience; and that authenticity is worth striving for—should indeed be cornerstones of psychology.

Clearly, the therapeutic applications of the humanistic perspective (which constitute the bulk of this volume) have been effective or else the whole enterprise would have foundered decades ago. But in terms of conceptual advances or the development of rigorous cumulative research findings, the yield has been far leaner. This makes me wonder whether the rejection of the hegemonic sway of the scientific methodology, which is perfectly understandable given the "dustbowl empiricism" in force when the founders were writing, has served humanistic psychology well in the long run. But as many of the contributors to this volume realize, method per se usually is more helpful than harmful. The challenge is to agree on a method that allows us to describe the phenomena of interest without trivializing them in the process.

Granted, much of the scientistic psychology spawned during the past century was not worth the pulp on which it was printed. The issue is not whether one uses the latest statistical fads and a fancy research design but rather whether one is willing to describe experience clearly and precisely so that others can build on one's observations. This type of attention to detail (according to some, the very abode of God) sometimes is a challenge in these writings, where insight is more readily apparent than is evidence.

Yet, the perspective on the human condition that humanistic psychology represents is too important to be ignored. If it is left out of the discourse of the social sciences, then we all will be the poorer for it. To join the parade and influence its direction and pace, one must show that one can follow the tune. In less metaphorical terms, sustained good work needs to be done.

Good work that stands the test of time never is easy, and it might require some compromise with a paradigm that is alien to many—some variant of the systematic work that has become known as the scientific method. Narrative methods are fine—I use them myself—but can we build a coherent human science on them? If so, then how? What should the units of analysis be? What degree of rigor should we expect so as to avoid vagueness and self-deception? Questions of this type are asked in this volume, but they will have to continue to be asked, and answers to them will have to be agreed on.

The humanistic approach is certain to survive either as a foundation for therapy and counseling or as an influence on other branches of psychology. The chapters assembled in this volume show the exuberant variety of applications of the humanistic perspective and the way in which these follow from previous insights into the nature of human beings—from those of Nietzsche, James, and Kierkegaard to those of Camus, Vigotsky, and Fellini.

There is no question that, now more than ever, we will need the insights into psychology that the humanistic perspective can provide.

At the start of this new millennium, our understanding of what it means to be human hangs in a precarious balance. Many of the conceptual pillars of what it means to be human—the self, consciousness, will, and freedom—are being rapidly deconstructed by the "hard" sciences, not to mention antiquated concepts such as "good" and "bad." The accounts offered by neurology, behavioral genetics, and computer science are compelling, and they threaten to reduce our view of the person to a bundle of loosely connected mechanisms thrown together by the necessity of survival over long eons of time.

On the other hand, there are signs that the spell of mechanistic approaches under which psychology has labored for so long is slowly breaking. Developmental psychology is relying on the notion of self-organization to explain individual growth over time. After being dealt an almost mortal blow during the 1970s, personology—the view that the individual possesses enduring traits and is not just responding to situational demands—is gaining new respectability. Some of the traits that are being investigated extensively—autonomy, love, spirituality, wisdom, humility, and forgiveness—depend on a paradigm that views people as purposive agents responsible to themselves and to the community.

Positive psychology, a rallying cry raised by Martin Seligman during his American Psychological Association presidency during 1998-1999, is another departure from psychology as practiced for most of the past century. Instead of focusing primarily on behavioral deficits, positive psychology starts with the assumption that virtues such as courage, altruism, and perseverance are just as genuine and important as the pathological conditions that traditionally have held center stage. Careful experiments and epidemiological studies show that patients who have hope recover more quickly, that optimistic persons tend to be more realistic, and that positive affect helps to negotiate complex existential problems.

The battle lines are being drawn. Will the contest end with an understanding of the person as nothing but a convenient placeholder for the intricate impulses programmed into the brain? Or, will we be able to provide a different picture, equally well based on evidence and reason, that will preserve a unique identity and power to the individual? Humanistic psychology has done much to clarify and anticipate the issues involved in this struggle. Directly or indirectly, it has provided some of the conceptual maps needed for its resolution. But the issue is far from settled. A great deal of good work—of systematic (and perseverant) thinking, observing, and recording—is needed if the humanistic perspective is to rival the reductionistic one in terms of influence. Let us hope that this collection of some of the best work will inspire others to engage in this enormously important task.

—MIHALY CSIKSZENTMIHALYI
Claremont Graduate University

Introduction

KIRK J. SCHNEIDER, JAMES F. T. BUGENTAL, AND J. FRASER PIERSON

> *In the history of science is the message of humanism—that we must think in the limited but positive terms of fulfillment, that true faith is a belief in the inherent potential of humanity. The telos is the eternal quest, the cosmos coming to know itself. To believe less—or to believe more—is to live in the shallows of what it means to be human.*
>
> —W. Wachhorst ("Touching the Sky," 1999)

WHAT IS THE NEXT STEP for psychology, and who or what will lead us into the beckoning age? Will it be the wizardry of artificial intelligence with its computerized models for living? The marvels of neuroscience with its brain-behavior correlations? Evolutionary psychology with its sociobiology of natural selection? Positive psychology with its "measurements" of "the good life" (Seligman, 1998)? The dizzying analyses of postmodernism with their culturally relative truths and patchwork quilt of meanings?

Although each of these paradigms is certain to have its place in the coming age, the reader is asked to envision an alternative scenario. What if psychology's next step were a holistic one, a rich mosaic consisting of each of the emerging trends but threaded throughout by the depth, breadth, and pathos of intimate human experience? What if artificial intelligence were complemented by poetic illumination, if neuroscience were supplemented by experiential inquiry, and if evolutionary psychology were matched by holistic reflection? What if positive psychology were linked with depth or philosophical investigation and if postmodernism were linked with personalism or transcendentalism?

If this amalgamated vision hints of familiarity, it should. For 40 years, humanistic psychology has grappled with this vision, and during more recent years, that struggle has intensified. The reasons for this intensification are many, but psychology's relentless yen for compartmentalizing—for fragmenting and subdividing knowledge—are surely at their core. In our haste to find mechanisms, abstractions, and formulas, are we neglecting the *being* to whom these modalities apply? Are we neglecting *lives*? Humanistic psychology poses the following overarching challenges to the study of conscious and nonconscious processes. (1) What does it mean to be fully experientially human? and (2) How does that understanding illuminate the fulfilled or vital life?

Say what one will about the trials and limitations of humanistic psychology's past; it is now a seasoned and multifaceted approach. Precisely at a time when technical models for living are on the ascendancy, humanistic psychology offers a poignant counterweight to those models and, thereby, a context through which they may become humanized. Humanistic psychology is a concerted brew of existential, transpersonal, and constructivist theorizing[1] and encompasses a breathtaking investigative range. Still, for all its variety, it converges on the profound and poignant wholeness of the human lot. Whereas there have been extremes within humanistic psychology (e.g., individualism, libertinism, spiritual and secular elitism), this volume reflects the leading edges and maturation of what we call *experiential humanism*. Experiential humanism embraces all modes of awareness and subawareness—individual, social, biological, and spiritual—but particularly as they resonate with lives. For example, neither aggregates nor abstractions are excluded from the experiential humanistic framework. But the question is, to whom and within what contexts do these formulations apply? And to the extent that they do not apply, how can we supplement them?

The contributors to this volume have a great deal to say about the living and breathing contexts for psychological inquiry. They have a great deal to convey about the methods and means by which to study such contexts, and they have even more to say about the applications that ensue from such study.

Before we expand on the aforementioned, however, let us briefly trace the lineage that led to its formation. (For a more formal exposition, see the chapter by Moss [Chapter 1] in this volume.) Contrary to popular belief, the roots of humanistic psychology are a diverse amalgam of secular, theistic, individualistic, and communalistic strands that, as suggested earlier, converge on two overarching themes: what it means to be fully experientially human and how that understanding illuminates the fulfilled or vital life.

The birth pangs of humanism are typically traced to 5th-century BCE Greece, during the period of the great philosophers and dramatists such as Socrates, Plato, and Sophocles (Garraty & Gay, 1972; Grondin, 1995). Classical humanism, as it has come to be known, was a turning away from the god-centered preoccupation of antiquity to that which concerned the distinctly "human." Following Socrates' famous dictum to "know thyself," humanistic thinkers elucidated themes such as personal responsibility, choice, love, and fear. According to such humanists, no longer could questions of motivation, morality, or truth be reducible to supernatural dogmas; instead, they required the complex applications of reason and reflection.

The second great flourishing of humanism occurred during the period of the Renaissance, approximately 400 to 600 years ago, when intellectuals such as Pico della Mirandola, DaVinci, and Erasmus rebelled against the strictures of the medieval Church and resurrected Greek humanism. The focus of these intellectuals was on human achievements or the *studia humanitatis* as opposed to the *studia divinitatis* (Grondin, 1995, p. 112). This curriculum emphasized "human artistry and culture in the original works of the Greek and Latin authors" (p. 112).

The third wave of humanism emerged during the Enlightenment of the 17th and 18th centuries. Two major branches reflecting earlier humanistic rifts characterized this wave. Rationalists represented the first branch, and romanticists represented the second branch. Rationalist-humanists, exemplified by thinkers such as Bacon, Newton, and Locke, held that cognition is what distinguishes the human being. The path to the fulfilled life for rationalists was prediction, control, and efficiency (Jones, 1969). On the other hand, romanticist-humanists, illustrated by such luminaries as Blake, Goethe, and Kierkegaard, believed that the heart (or emotions) is the distinguishing characteristic of humanity. To live with heart—with passion, intuition, and imagination—is to live the vital life, according to romanticists (Schneider, 1998).

The latest wave of humanism began at the turn of the 20th century. In psychology, such humanism emerged as a reaction to behaviorism and deterministic Freudianism. Early critics of these movements—William James (who, ironically, influenced behaviorism), Carl Jung, Otto Rank, Ludwig Binswanger, Medard Boss, and Henry Murray—protested the equation of human with animal or primate being.

By the late 1950s, the American humanistic psychology movement drew on all of the former sources of humanism but developed its own brand as well (DeCarvalho, 1991). The answer to the question "What makes us fully and optimally human?" was as varied as the American humanistic psychology movement itself. Given this caveat, however, authors as diverse as Abraham Maslow, Rollo May, Gordon Allport, Carl Rogers, Michael Polanyi, and James Bugental all coalesced with regard to one intertwining concern—the centrality of the personal. To the degree that American, and to a large extent European, humanistic psychologists turned to the personal or profoundly intimate as the fount of their investigative wisdom, they echoed the Enlightenment romantics to define their tradition. This lineage, which in turn echoed the biblical and Gnostic lineages of "knowledge or science of the heart" (Martinez, 1998, p. 100; Moyers, 1997), has two main emphases: a holistic or multilayered understanding of psychological phenomena and a valuing of tacit processes (affect, intuition, kinesthesia, and imagination) to both access and express that understanding (Schneider, 1998).

Today, humanistic psychology supposedly has fallen out of favor. Many in academia consider it obsolete (e.g., Sass, 1988). The question as to what is distinctively human and fulfilling is considered misguided at best or oppressive at worst (Sampson, 1993). The postmodern (or, more strictly speaking, poststructural) ethos, for example, militates against questions about global humanity. In poststructural circles, humanity is a social construction and fulfillment is a relative value. The rise in multicultural consciousness raises similar questions about humanistic precepts. There are as many "humanisms" for some multicultural thinkers as there are races, ethnic identities, and languages. Who can stand above them all and identify global human qualities? For some transpersonal and religious thinkers, on the other hand, humanism is shortsighted, indulgent, and devitalized. According to these thinkers, humanism is excessively preoccupied with individuals, personal achievements, and material realities. As a result, some transpersonal and religious thinkers accuse humanists of lacking faith, vision, and morality. Finally, technological thinkers accuse humanism of being fuzzy and impractical. Standardizing or technological psychologists (e.g., Salzinger, 1999), for example, tend to see humanists as undisciplined dreamers who consistently overestimate the value of feelings, intuition, and imagination while downplaying the corresponding value of logic, rationality, and systematization.

At the same time as humanistic psychology is being besieged, however, some segments of humanistic psychology are being absorbed and transformed. So-called relational theorists, for example, are drawing on humanistic concepts such as authenticity and the interpersonal field to reform conventional psychoanalytic theory (Portnoy, 1999; Stolorow, Atwood, & Brandchaft, 1994). Positive psychology is conveying key humanistic concepts to the mainstream (Seligman & Csikszentmihalyi, 2000).

Yet, humanism (and humanistic psychology in particular) is a great deal more complex than the conceptions of its detractors or even those of its transformers. As the contributors to this volume make clear, contemporary humanistic psychology has come a long way since the days of fuzzy-minded or idiosyncratic scholarship (to whatever extent those actually predominated). Now, it is a rich tapestry of diverse and reflective voices that often complement, inform, and even inspire their ostensible detractors. In this volume, for example, we see meditations on the humanistic contributions to cutting-edge research, discussions of the humanistic origins of postmodern narrative psychology, examinations of the complementarity between personal myths and contemporary physics, reflections on the place of humanistic psychology in cross-cultural studies, and considerations of the role of personalism in an era of "managed" mental health. We also see leading-edge formulations of humanistic ecology, peace, and gender studies along with many other traditional areas of inquiry.

The upshot of this elaboration is that contemporary humanistic psychology is an integrative psychology that addresses the most pressing issues of our times. What, then, does contemporary humanistic psychology offer that is distinctive, unique, or vital? In our view, contemporary humanistic psychology brings that which the earlier generation of humanistic psychologists also prized—the heart or personal dimension to which we earlier alluded. Unlike the previous generation, however, contemporary humanistic psychology has the benefit of incorporating a wealth of recent insight into its personalism, for example, a recognition of its significance for politics and culture as well as for individuals (see the chapters by O'Hara [Chapter 36] and Warmoth [Chapter 48] in this volume) and an increased openness to its spiritual implications (see the chapters by Elkins [Chapter 16], Krippner [Chapter 22], Pilisuk & Joy [Chapter 9], and Walsh [Chapter 45] in this volume). The poignancy of the tragic also is highlighted (see the chapters by Stern [Chapter 31], Heery [Chapter 34], Greening [Chapter 12], and Mendelowitz [Chapter 13] in this volume) along with traditional humanistic accents on hope. In short, the new personalism embraces experiences that *matter*—that have "resonance validity" (see the chapter on multiple-case depth research by Schneider [Chapter 23] in this volume), regardless of whether or not those experiences pertain to individuals or groups, persons or divinities.

Yet, it is precisely such experiences, and such openness, that psychology lacks today—on all of its major fronts. Consequently, it has withered, fragmented, and compartmentalized (Bevan & Kessel, 1994; Wertz, 1995). On the other hand, consider what the personal dimension (the intimate and resonant) could bring to psychology's various components—to the statistical mind-set of methodology, the standardization mentality of psychotherapy, the group consciousness of multiculturalism, the nihilism of poststructuralism, and the esoterics of transpersonalism.

Sixteen years ago, Carl Rogers issued a challenge: Can humanistic psychology, with all of its applied and philosophical richness, become a force in academia and science (Rogers, 1985)? We believe that it can, and we believe that this volume makes its appearance at a critical historical juncture. To the extent that psychology is fractured, rivalrous, and rife with tension, it is also abundant with possibility.

This volume, then, is a window on that possibility; it is a window on a larger view of science. Will the reader welcome this window? Indeed, we the editors believe that the reader will yearn to peer through.

One final note is in order. This volume represents a massive collective undertaking. It is the first time, to our knowledge, that the humanistic community has mobilized so comprehensively, and so devotedly, around its own distinctive vision.

There was, however, another time when the humanistic community undertook such a concerted project, and Bugental's (1967) *Challenges of Humanistic Psychology* was its embodiment. We are greatly indebted to both the participants in and the spirit of that trailblazer, and we bear its stamp with pride.

NOTE

1. These represent three basic emphases of contemporary humanistic psychology. Although these emphases overlap and sometimes are used interchangeably with one another (as well as with their umbrella context, i.e., humanistic psychology), they are generally considered to be separate yet historically linked (see the chapters by Moss [Chapter 1], Taylor & Martin [Chapter 2], Arons & Richards [Chapter 11], Josselson & Lieblich [Chapter 21], Leitner & Epting [Chapter 33], O'Hara [Chapter 36], Waddlington [Chapter 37], Walsh [Chapter 45], and Warmoth [Chapter 48] in this volume). Existential psychology emphasizes freedom, experiential reflection, and responsibility; transpersonal psychology stresses spirituality, transcendence, and compassionate social action; and constructivist psychology accents culture, political consciousness, and personal meaning.

REFERENCES

Bevan, W., & Kessel, F. (1994). Plain truths and home cooking: Thoughts on the making and remaking of psychology. *American Psychologist, 49,* 505-509.

Bugental, J. F. T. (Ed.). (1967). *Challenges of humanistic psychology.* New York: McGraw-Hill.

DeCarvalho, R. J. (1991). *The founders of humanistic psychology.* New York: Praeger.

Garraty, J. A., & Gay, P. (Eds.). (1972). *The Columbia history of the world.* New York: Harper & Row.

Grondin, J. (1995). *Sources of hermeneutics.* Albany: State University of New York Press.

Jones, W. T. (1969). *Kant to Wittgenstein and Sartre: A history of Western philosophy.* New York: Harcourt, Brace, & World.

Martinez, T. J. (1998). Anthropos and existence: Gnostic parallels in the early writings of Rollo May. *Journal of Humanistic Psychology, 38*(4), 95-109.

Moyers, B. (1997, May). *Baccalaureate address.* Paper presented at Brown University, Providence, RI.

Portnoy, D. (1999). Relatedness: Where humanistic and psychoanalytic psychotherapy converge. *Journal of Humanistic Psychology, 39*(1), 19-34.

Rogers, C. R. (1985). Toward a more human science of the person. *Journal of Humanistic Psychology, 25*(4), 7-24.

Salzinger, K. (1999). The loss of the romantic: A gain for science. *Journal of Humanistic Psychology, 39*(3), 30-37.

Sampson, E. E. (1993). Identity politics: Challenges to psychology's understanding. *American Psychologist, 48,* 1219-1230.

Sass, L. A. (1988). Humanism, hermeneutics, and the concept of the subject. In S. B. Messer, L. A. Sass, & R. L. Woolfolk (Eds.), *Hermeneutics and psychological theory: Interpretive perspectives on personality, psychotherapy, and psychopathology.* Brunswick, NJ: Rutgers University Press.

Schneider, K. J. (1998). Toward a science of the heart: Romanticism and the revival of psychology. *American Psychologist, 53,* 277-289.

Seligman, M. E. P. (1998, October). What is the "good life"? [president's column]. *APA Monitor.*

Seligman, M. E. P., & Csikszentmihalyi, M. (2000). Positive psychology: An introduction. *American Psychologist, 55,* 5-14.

Stolorow, R. D., Atwood, G. E., & B. Brandchaft. (1994). *The intersubjective context of intrapsychic experience: The intersubjective perspective.* Northvale, NJ: Jason Aronson.

Wachhorst, W. (1999, December). Touching the sky: How science lost its wonder . . . and what our schools can do about it. *San Francisco Magazine,* pp. 35-42.

Wertz, F. J. (1995). The scientific status of psychology. *The Humanistic Psychologist, 23,* 285-304.

Acknowledgments

THE BIRTHING OF A BOOK of this magnitude is essentially a labor of love from inspiration and conceptualization to actualization in the very tangible form that the reader holds in his or her hands. We are warmly appreciative of the authors who enthusiastically and generously contributed their current products in theory, research, and practice so that, collaboratively, we could offer a "handbook" of humanistic psychology. We also thank our forebears in philosophy and psychology, whose contributions to the movement of humanistic psychology are of such significance that their presence resonates to our generation and is expressed—sometimes between the lines—throughout the chapters of this volume. We especially acknowledge Søren Kierkegaard, Friedrich Nietzsche, William James, Martin Buber, Edmund Husserl, Otto Rank, Martin Heidegger, Paul Tillich, Jean-Paul Sartre, Maurice Merleau-Ponty, Gordon Allport, Charlotte Bühler, Erich Fromm, Henry Murray, Gardner Murphy, George Kelly, Abraham Maslow, Frederick Perls, Anthony Sutich, Rollo May, Carl Rogers, Virginia Satir, R. D. Laing, Sidney Jourard, and Ernest Becker.

We are indebted to our editors at Sage Publications, Jim Nageotte, Jim Brace-Thompson, and Sanford Robinson, who embraced our vision, encouraged us to expand it, and assisted us through every step of the publishing process. Thank you for such a congenial and fruitful relationship.

It is with joy and deepest love that we thank our spouses and dearest friends, Jūratė Elena Raulinaitis, Elizabeth Keber Bugental, and Jeff Hubbell, for the innumerable ways in which they have contributed to this grand adventure. Their loving presence is our greatest inspiration.

Part I

HISTORICAL OVERVIEW

Introduction to Part I

TO ILLUMINATE HUMANISTIC PSYCHOLOGY'S present, we must shed light on its past—and what a distinguished and colorful past it has been. What, then, were humanistic psychology's major battles, wounds, and inspirations? Who were the central figures in these scenarios, and how did they influence psychology? Finally, how do we assess the legacy of these pioneers and milestones? Where have they left us as a perspective? To bring these concerns into context, and to set the stage for the unfolding volume, we present four interweaving historical reflections on humanistic psychology.

Beginning with Chapter 1, Donald Moss provides a succinct and informative historical overview of humanistic psychology. From its rudiments in ancient Greece, to its emergence in Judeo-Christianity, to its flowering in the modern age, Moss's "road map" is both unique and foundational.

In Chapter 2, Eugene Taylor and Fred Martin reflect on humanistic psychology's recent lineage and arrive at some rather provocative conclusions. First, there is a window of opportunity for a humanistic reformation in psychology. Second, the question of whether this reformation actually will materialize remains open. Third, the revitalization of humanistic methodology, personology, and psychotherapeutic investigation is likely to bolster the chances of the reformation, whereas the overemphasis on humanistic folk psychology (e.g., meditative and somatic traditions) is likely to dampen these chances. The authors leave us with a challenge: Can humanistic psychology "articulate a phenomenological . . . epistemology" as the basis for a new experimental psychology and, beyond that, "a new experimental science," or will it go the way of disconnection from and resultant absorption by the positivistic mainstream?

In the next two chapters, the historical perspective shifts to two relatively hidden, if not neglected, humanistic legacies: women and multiculturalism. In Chapter 3, Ilene Serlin and Eleanor Criswell forcefully argue that although women's relationship to humanistic psychology has been complex, at the same time it has been integral, both practically and theoretically. The authors trace the entangled strands of humanistic psychology's approach to women, women's ambivalent reaction to those entangled strands, and the present challenge for both women and humanistic psychology. Finally, they address the many promising resonances between women and humanistic psychology such as the stress on holism, the prizing of interpersonal connection, and the concern with embodiment. The authors conclude that a revived humanistic psychology is contingent on a revived feminist humanism.

In Chapter 4, Adelbert Jenkins concludes this part of the volume with a focused discussion of humanistic psychology's multicultural legacy. He notes that although humanistic psychology began, and in many cases evolved, in concert with a multicultural consciousness in America, nonwhites tend not to identify with it. He goes on to examine this anomaly, tracing both the humanistic and multicultural bases for its emergence. The perception that humanistic psychology, like much of contemporary psychology as a whole, is the province of white privilege and European individualism has its validity, the author concludes. However, this perception tells only part of the story. He elaborates that humanistic psychology also is profoundly interpersonal and that its accent on the personal gives it a unique slant by which to apprehend the collective world. From this standpoint, the author concludes, culturally diverse populations might reassess their view of humanistic practices, and humanistic practices might undergo a reassessment of their own, becoming broader, deeper, and more sensitized as a result.

CHAPTER 1

The Roots and Genealogy of Humanistic Psychology

DONALD MOSS

THE HUMANISTIC movement in psychology has emphasized the search for a philosophical and scientific understanding of human existence that does justice to the highest reaches of human achievement and potential. From the beginning, humanistic psychologists have cared deeply about what it means to be fully human and have sought pathways and technologies that assist humans in reaching full humanness. Humanistic psychologists criticized the mainstream psychological schools of the first half of the 20th century for proclaiming a diminished model of human nature. Their strivings for a new and better concept of humanity provided much of the motivation for the early flourishing of humanistic psychology.

WHAT DOES IT MEAN TO BE FULLY HUMAN?

Concepts of Human Nature in Psychological Science

Articulate humanistic scholars such as Abraham Maslow and Rollo May criticized psychoanalysis and behaviorism for attempting to explain the full range of human nature in terms of mechanisms drawn from the study of neurotic patients and laboratory rats. Sigmund Freud wrote monographs about artists such as Michelangelo and Leonardo da Vinci and religious leaders such as Moses. Freud used the concepts of abnormal psychology to explain the lifetime artistic and spiritual achievements of these outstanding humans (S. Freud, 1953-1974, Vols. 11, 13, 23).

John Watson arrogantly proclaimed that, given the opportunity, he could condition any human infant to become either a criminal or a scientist by consistently applying the principles of modern behavioral theory (Watson, 1924, p. 82). Later, B. F. Skinner attacked concepts such as freedom and dignity and proposed reengineering human society by a process of instrumental conditioning (Skinner, 1971).

For humanistic psychology, this psychological reductionism presented a challenge. Can we study the higher reaches of human nature and discover a new basis for psychological science? Can we use the higher forms of human behavior to illuminate the lower ones instead of basing all psychological understanding on laboratory rats and the mentally ill? Authors as diverse as Straus (1930/1982), Maslow (1950/1973), and Csikszentmihalyi (1990) formulated this same challenge—to understand humans in terms of their highest potential and through the study of individuals who display the highest levels of human functioning.

Will Our Science Stifle or Nurture the Fulfilled Human Life?

The concern in humanistic psychology over inadequate scientific and philosophical models was not merely a matter of achieving a better understanding for the sake of understanding. Rather, reductionistic scientific theories of human behavior run the risk of constricting or reducing actual humans. If the prevailing understanding of humanness within science is narrow, then there is a risk that the same concepts will pervade popular culture as well and diminish the self-understanding and aspirations of the average human. Traditional "naturalistic" psychologies run the risk of harming humans by inviting them to lower their expectations of what is humanly possible.

A Prehistory and a History of Humanistic Psychology

This chapter provides a prehistory and a history of humanistic psychology. The *history* recounts those significant figures in modern psychology and philosophy who provided the foundational ideas and approaches making humanistic psychology what it is today. The *prehistory* examines the millennia before modern humanistic psychology and identifies *some* of the many antecedent figures who suggested more philosophically adequate concepts of being

human. This portion of the chapter must remain sketchy— leaping across centuries at a time—because of the enormous variety of philosophers, theologians, and literary figures who have contributed at least passing insights into what it means to be fully human. More time is spent on antiquity because foundations for later understanding were laid down then. Many Renaissance and modern efforts to restore a more adequate image of humanity have returned to early Greek and Christian texts for inspiration.

THE PREHISTORY OF HUMANISTIC PSYCHOLOGY

Classical Greece

Homer and the human journey. At the dawn of Western civilization, Homer's *Odyssey* created the image of the human individual as hero and of human life as a quest or an adventure. Odysseus, returning to Ithaca from the communal quest of the Trojan wars, is detained far from home by the nymph Calypso, the Sirens, and a variety of other dangers and distractions. In the course of the epic, Odysseus becomes an individual and a hero facing danger, battling adversaries, and savoring the adventures of the road. Finally, he returns to his home and family in Ithaca. The modern Greek poet C. P. Cavafy wrote of each human's journey to "Ithaca":

> Always keep Ithaca fixed in your
>   mind.
> To arrive there is your ultimate goal.
> But do not hurry the voyage at all.
> It is better to let it last for long years;
> And even to anchor at the isle when
>   you are old,
> Rich with all that you have gained on
>   the way,

*Not expecting that Ithaca will offer
you riches.* (Cavafy, 1961, p. 36)

Greek tragedy. The Greek dramatists portrayed human heroes struggling powerfully against fates that define the course of human lives. The protagonists are heroic and inhabit a world peopled with gods, demigods, and humans, but their pathways are defined in advance and end in tragedy. The fate of Oedipus is foretold by an oracle and is changed neither by his father Laius's actions nor by Oedipus's heroic struggles. The final words from Sophocles' drama, *Oedipus at Colonus*, express the tragic view of life: "Cease now and never more lift up these lamentations, for all this is determined."

Socrates (ca. 469-399 BCE) and Plato (ca. 427-347 BCE). Our image of Socrates is filtered largely through Plato, who recorded many of the Socratic dialogues decades later. Socrates left his heritage in the dialogues, dialectical conversations that sought deeper truths through examination of simple illustrations from daily life (Taylor, 1997). In the Socratic view, the *psyche* is the abode of character, intelligence, and virtue. Human well-being depends on the state of this psyche. Socrates' philosophy is ethical and personal. Socratic discourse perfects character and instills virtue through knowledge. Knowledge leads to good, and wrongdoing is involuntary and based on ignorance. In Socrates' view, no human would wish for anything less than true good and true happiness, but many individuals miscarry in their actions for lack of knowledge of the true good. Enlightenment by reason and dialogue leads to a correction of one's actions and a perfection of the human individual.

For Plato, this earthly life is but a dim likeness of the real and eternal life. A human lives as though in a cave without light, and by philosophical reflection the human gains a glimpse of the true *Eidos*, the transcendent essence of things as they are in truth (Plato, 1941). Plato's philosophy conveys a sense of values that we associate with Greek culture and with today's humanistic ideal. The true, the good, and the beautiful were elevated to the status of ends in themselves. The concept of an Eidos (or essence) reappeared in German phenomenological psychology when Straus (1930/1982) conceived of the essence of the person—the true self—as an Eidos that one sees actualized only in glimpses, in the course of existence, such as glimpses of light through a prism.[1]

Platonism survived many centuries after Plato himself, especially in the form of neo-Platonism. Plotinus (205-270 CE) and Proclus (410-485 CE) stand out as central neo-Platonists. Neo-Platonism portrayed each individual human life as a type of falling from an eternal origin in divine oneness, into earthly multiplicity. The task of human existence became a journey of inward reintegration, recovering lost oneness. This metaphysical schema of existence, in which the eternal origin is the true reality and all of life seeks restoration, lingered in the background through the early centuries of the Christian era and resurfaced to influence medieval and Renaissance views of life. For the neo-Platonists, philosophy remained a pathway for personal renewal through moral and intellectual self-discipline. The pathway of renewal took a mystical turn as an awakening from the normal human alienated state toward a mystical union with the one and the good.

Aristotle (384-322 BCE). Aristotle developed his own ethics and psychology, systematically defining the soul and its attributes. Of equal importance for psychological theory, however, Aristotle developed a systematic empirical approach to natural science. In combination with Christianity, this Aristotelian philosophy served as the framework for most of medieval scholastic philosophy, for example, in the works of Boethius and Aquinas. The empirical framework of scientific research in psychology reflects this Aristotelian heritage.

Stoicism. Stoicism as a philosophical movement commenced in Greece with Zeno (ca. 333-262 BCE). Stoicism became a widely taught approach to rational living, with influence on leading figures in Greece and Rome, through the time of the Stoic philosopher and Roman emperor Marcus Aurelius (121-180 CE). The Stoics advocated a thoughtful human life of self-cultivation, virtue, and wisdom (Inwood, 1985; Long, 1974). Philosophy for the Stoics was a love of wisdom (*philo-sophia*) and calls for a personal search for mastery over one's own life and emotions through reason. The Stoics developed confession or personal disclosure as a tool for increasing self-knowledge (Georges, 1995). The Stoics taught inward self-sufficiency through reason and wisdom regardless of how external tragedy might affect one's life. The Stoic philosopher Epictetus (born ca. 50 CE) anticipated the core of cognitive psychology when he wrote that it is not events that shape human life but rather the view that humans take of these events (Beck, Rush, Shaw, & Emery, 1979). Stoic values of self-examination, self-discipline, and self-determination are consistent with the theories of modern humanistic and cognitive psychologies. The Stoics' use of philosophy as a tool for living anticipated the present-day movement of philosophical psychotherapy.

Athens and a humanistic way of life. It was not only in epic, drama, and philosophy that Greek civilization conveyed an image of the human. Rather, the entire Athenian way of life, epitomized during the age of Pericles (443-429 BCE), was dedicated to stretching human capacities and talents to a higher level. Athens valued the pursuit of athletic prowess, intellectual competence, artistic gifts, political sophistication, and architectural beauty. The institution of democracy, the academies of philosophy, the flowering of literature, and the displays of art all were part of a public pursuit of higher levels of human potential. The Olympic games took this cultivation of perfection to the highest possible level.

Christian Authors in the Early Church

The life and teachings of Christ conveyed a new and different image of a perfected life. The Sermon on the Mount (Matthew 5: 3-11) and many other texts in the Christian scriptures provide specific values and guidelines for the would-be Christian. The early Christian image of the human placed less emphasis on reason and self-sufficiency than did Greek philosophy and placed more emphasis on an altruistic love for God, neighbor, and community. One early Christian philosopher, Aristides, writing circa 125 CE, described the Christian way of life in terms that still sound familiar today: "They walk in all humility and kindness, and falsehood is not found among them, and they love one another. They despise not the widow and grieve not the orphan. He that hath distributeth liberally to him that hath not" (cited in Foster, 1981, p. 69). This image of loving, communally oriented humans converges well with the communitarian movements in humanistic psychology (Moss, 1998b, pp. 76-78).

Some Christian authors, such as Kierkegaard (1844/1962a), saw the historical figure of Christ as symbolizing that the divine principle entered the human, elevating and glorifying the human. Saint Paul wrote of hearing creation groan in the process of giving birth to a new glorified human, liberated from enslavement to the law and made perfect in Christ (Romans 8). The early Christian writer Irenaeus wrote that the glory of God is a fully alive human (Roberts & Donaldson, 1953). Two and a half centuries after Aristides, during the time of Augustine, the neo-Platonic worldview was so pervasive as to redraw the Christian faith into a search for a return to one's origins. In his *Confessions*, Augustine expressed his deep yearning: "Our hearts are restless till they find rest in thee" (Augustine, 1980, Book 1, p. 3).

Other commentators, such as Nietzsche (1886/1966), read the same biblical texts yet accused the Christian religion of degrading the human to glorify God: "From the start, the Christian faith is a sacrifice, a sacrifice of all freedom, all pride, all self-confidence of the spirit [and,] at the same time, enslavement and self-mockery, self-mutilation" (p. 60).

Marx also labeled Christianity an "opium for the masses"; that is, he asserted that faith was a tool used by the wealthy to pacify and exploit the working class. Workers were promised a reward in the next world, thereby reducing their rebellion and discontent in this world.

Today's authors are perhaps accurate when they point to the history of Christian thought and the diversity of Christian theologies as showing that each generation interprets the historical phenomenon of Jesus in light of its own cosmology, ideologies, and need. Riley (1997) suggested that the initial gentile reception of Jesus was in terms of one more classical hero, such as Odysseus, wandering the earth and performing great feats. Riley showed that each age creates its own new image of Christ. The original scriptural message is filtered through the needs and understandings of the present age.

The Renaissance in Europe

The Renaissance began with a rediscovery of the learning of classical antiquity and a return to the original texts. Initially, this meant new translations and new access to Greek philosophy and literature. Later, it meant a return to biblical texts in their original languages, bypassing the versions of ancient knowledge mediated by the Catholic church and scholastic philosophy. In many cases, Platonic and neo-Platonic philosophy replaced the thought of Aristotle that had formed the basis of medieval scholasticism. The Greek idealization of earthly beauty and human perfection, and the Greek emphasis on the sensuality of the human figure, emerged during the Renaissance and remained a crucial strain in the humanism of the 15th and 16th centuries. A look at Renaissance philosopher Marsilio Ficino (1433-1499) illuminates this development.

Ficino's (1985) *De Amore* was written in the form of a commentary on Plato's symposium on love and highlights one of the essential shifts in thinking that influenced Renaissance art and learning. Ficino described love as fundamentally a longing for beauty. This is a marked difference from the traditional Christian definition of love in terms of selfless altruism. In neo-Platonic terms, all things—including humans—emanate from the original one, wherein lies beauty, truth, and goodness. Humans, in this framework, are attracted to their primordial origin in the one and are drawn by beauty and truth. Ficino suggested that earthly love, including attraction to sensual beauty, participates in metaphysical and divine love.

This new viewpoint "baptizes" a worshiping of human beauty, and the results are evident in Renaissance art. Renaissance statuary and art portray the sensual beauty of the human figure, and Renaissance portraiture portrays the complexity of human individuality. Both are ubiquitous in Renaissance churches.

Humanism and the Reformation

In northern Europe, the Renaissance took the direction of a humanism exemplified by the Dutch scholar Erasmus. At the same time, the breach with medieval tradition and authority took the form of the Protestant Reformation of the Christian church, nurtured by a return to the original scriptural texts.

Desiderius Erasmus (ca. 1469-1536). For Erasmus, the human is the center of creation. The measure of God's goodness is that God created a rich world to unfold the nature of the human. Man is a "noble animal, for whose sake alone God fashioned this marvelous contrivance of the world; he is the fellow citizen of the angels, son of God, heir of immortality" (*The Enchiridion,* cited in Augustijn, 1991, p. 53). Erasmus anticipated Kierkegaard in the former's emphasis on the human individual: "Man stands before God as an individual and takes counsel only of God and his own conscience. Man's responsibility and ability to live his own life receives all the emphasis" (p. 55). Erasmus's heated debate with Luther was triggered by Luther's critique of Erasmus's essay on *The Free Will.* Erasmus insisted on a role for the human will and personal responsibility, as well as God's grace, in achieving salvation. Luther, in turn, argued that grace alone provides salvation for the human.

The 19th Century

The 19th century saw the emergence of a number of key philosophical and literary movements with significance for modern humanistic psychology. This section reviews the works of Kierkegaard and Nietzsche. One also could highlight the movements of British and German romanticism in literature and Marxism in political economics.

Søren Kierkegaard: The dawning of existentialism. The Danish thinker Kierkegaard (1813-1855) wrote passionately about the existence of each human individual. He criticized the established church, philosophy, and society as lulling humans to sleep with a false sense of security. Kierkegaard believed that too many individual humans did not see any need to struggle with the direction of their personal existence. They assumed that they already were Christian and modern by birthright. He compared the average human's condition throughout life with that of a peasant who falls asleep in his cart while the horse pulls him home. Kierkegaard believed that philosophy should act like a mosquito and sting the complacent individual awake, to direct and experience the course of his or her own life or to awaken the individual and "oblige him to judge" (Kierkegaard, 1859/1962b, p. 35). Throughout his work, Kierkegaard confronted the myriad self-soothing defenses by which individuals preserve their sleepy complacency.

Was this your consolation that you said: One does what one can? Was this not precisely the reason for your disquietude that you did not know within yourself how much it is a man can do? . . . No earnest doubt, no really deep concern, is put to rest by saying that one does what one can.

(Kierkegaard, 1843/1959, pp. 347-348; see also Moss, 1998c, pp. 223-224)

Friedrich Nietzsche: Existentialism and the superman. Writing a generation later, Nietzsche (1844-1900) repeated Kierkegaard's emphasis on the individual. However, he saw Western civilization as degraded to the core and castigated Christianity as a distortion in humanity. He called for a "doctor of the soul" to tap his hammer and discover where the edifice of culture was rotten so that the wrecking process could begin. He called for a transformation in all values and created an image of a new individual, a "superman" (*Übermensch*) or "overman," who would create authentic values (Nietzsche, 1886/1966, 1892/1954). The superman would realize to a higher degree the human capacity to create the shape of one's own life. "Such a person, one might say, lives courageously by overcoming illusions and taking responsibility for his or her life" (Halling & Carroll, 1998, pp. 96-97).

The 20th Century

The 20th century produced breakthroughs in philosophy, psychiatry, and psychology, providing many of the foundations for a humanistic understanding of human existence. This section introduces briefly the phenomenological philosophers Husserl, Heidegger, and Merleau-Ponty, the phenomenological psychiatrists, and the unique dialogic theologian Buber (Halling & Carroll, 1998). Then, it reviews the contributions of Freud and his many followers within the psychoanalytic movement, who in several specific ways anticipated humanistic psychology.

Phenomenology in philosophy. Edmund Husserl (1859-1938) created the new movement of phenomenology in philosophy and psychology with his battle cry of returning "to the things themselves" (Halling & Carroll, 1998; Husserl, 1900/1970b). He encouraged philosophers and scientists to set aside theoretical assumptions and describe their immediate experiences of phenomena. He emphasized the *intentionality* of human mental activity. Psychic acts are intentional because they are oriented or directed toward some specific situation or object beyond themselves and can be meaningfully understood only by that context. Ultimately, this means that consciousness is not merely internal; rather, it is an involvement of the perceiving human with the object perceived.[2] Husserl (1936/1970a) emphasized the validity of the everyday "lifeworld," the world of immediate experience and life. He rejected the Cartesian scientific view that external reality consists only of internal mental representations. The human and the experiential world are interactive. Through intentionality, humans "cocreate" phenomena rather than just passively registering what is there. Husserl called for the development of a phenomenological psychology that would set aside the "naturalistic" modes of thinking used by medicine, biology, and physiology (Husserl, 1925/1977, p. 3; Kockelmans, 1967). Husserl's work parallels in its focus and approach the "radical empiricism" of the American psychologist and philosopher William James, and Husserl acknowledged James's work (Taylor, 1991).

Martin Heidegger (1889-1976), a German philosopher, combined Husserl's phenomenological method with existentialism. He turned from the study of mental acts to a detailed examination of the structure of human existence. In Heidegger's (1927/1962) landmark work, *Being and Time,* he described the human as a "being-in-the-world," that is, an entity whose very fabric involves an immersion in and openness to the surrounding world. Humans always discover themselves already thrown into a specific factual situation that defines them in their historicity. Heidegger studied the temporal organization of human life and found that humans discover their wholeness in an awareness of their own deaths. Humans also are truly metaphysical beings; they are the only beings that take their own being as a question to be pondered (Heidegger, 1927/1962).

The French philosopher Maurice Merleau-Ponty (1908-1961) drew on both Husserl and Heidegger and shifted the focus of phenomenological research to the structure of behavior. He understood behavior as intentionally directed toward a situation. Merleau-Ponty defined the "mental" as the organization or structure of behavior. In his principal works, *The Structure of Behavior* (Merleau-Ponty, 1942/1963) and the *Phenomenology of Perception* (Merleau-Ponty, 1945/1962), he used the evidence of the Gestalt psychologists, especially Kurt Goldstein's investigations of neurologically damaged individuals, to explore the organization of normal human movement and the embodied organism's relationship to the environment. For the phenomenologist, no human behavior and no neurophysiological process ultimately can be understood apart from its context and situation.

Phenomenology in psychiatry and psychology. Ludwig Binswanger (1881-1966) was a Swiss psychiatrist, as well as a lasting friend of Freud, who drew on the philosophy of both Husserl and Heidegger to find an alternative manner of understanding human existence, especially the experiencing of the mentally ill. Binswanger (1942, 1963) applied Heidegger's definition of the human as a being-in-the-world to psychiatry and mental illness. He emphasized the

existential significance of the *Mitwelt* (the social world shared with others), the *Umwelt* (the physical and biological environment), and the *Eigenwelt* (literally, the "own world" of identity and personhood). Binswanger described fundamental *existential a priori,* or existential structures, that shape human experiencing. He studied the worldviews, or patterns of experiencing, of disturbed individuals. Binswanger's case studies and essays on existential and phenomenological directions in psychology had a direct impact on humanistic psychology because of the 1958 publication of *Existence,* a collection of translations from Binswanger and other European phenomenological psychiatrists (May, Angel, & Ellenberger, 1958).

Medard Boss (1903-1991), who was also a Swiss psychiatrist, initially was trained in psychoanalysis. After World War II, he sought out the philosopher Heidegger and organized regular seminars with Heidegger and Swiss physicians seeking to apply the phenomenological perspective to rethink the foundations of both medicine and psychology (Boss, 1971/1979). Boss defined health as the total "haleness and wholeness" of the human. Health is characterized by an openness and flexible responsiveness to the world. In turn, he defined unhealthiness in human existence as "nothing but the privation, blocking, impairment, or constriction of this original openness and freedom" (Boss, 1988). He investigated psychosomatic illness as a means of jamming or blocking one's openness to the world and to specific threatening situations (Boss, 1971/1979; Moss, 1978).

Space allows for only a brief reference here to four additional 20th-century European figures who contributed to the modern humanistic understanding of human existence. The German psychiatrist Erwin Straus (1891-1975) proposed an anthropological and phenomenological psychology as an alternative to psychoanalysis and Pavlov's reflex theory (Moss, 1998a; Straus, 1966, 1930/1982). The Austrian Viktor Frankl (1905-1997) drew on his experience in the Nazi death camps to formulate logotherapy, a new existential psychotherapy (Frankl, 1963). Jan van den Berg (born 1914) developed a phenomenological and historical understanding or "metabletics" of the human's changing nature (van den Berg, 1963/1974). The British psychiatrist Ronald Laing (1927-1989) used the philosophy of Sartre (1943/1965) to illuminate the divided self of the schizophrenic patient (Laing, 1960). Straus, Frankl, van den Berg, and Laing all lectured in the United States during the 1960s and 1970s and directly influenced the first two generations of humanistic psychologists.

A philosophy of dialogue. Martin Buber (1878-1965) was a Jewish German theologian. His classic monograph *I and Thou* (Buber, 1923/1970) provided an appealing philosophy of the interpersonal that had a profound impact on the American humanistic psychologies of the 1950s and 1960s. Buber described reality as falling into two opposing realms. In the first authentic realm, an "I" addresses a "thou" in dialogue or in relationship. Within this unfolding relationship of an I to a thou, the human person is born and unfolds to its full potential. For Buber, the human self does not develop except in relationship or in dialogue: "It is from one man to another that the heavenly bread of self-being is passed" (Buber, 1965, p. 71). The opposing realm involves an I addressing an "it," that is, an object of practical utility. When one human addresses another human as an it, both the other and oneself are diminished.[3] This philosophy challenged and complemented the emphasis on self-actualization and the pursuit of self in much of American humanistic psychology. A classic 1957 dialogue between Buber and Carl Rogers highlighted the commonalities of Buber's philosophy and humanistic views, especially the emphasis on healing through a meeting of two persons, as well as their differing emphases on dialogue and self-actualization.

Sigmund Freud and psychoanalysis: A naturalistic humanism. Freud (1856-1939) has been criticized for interpreting human experiencing and behavior in terms of a biological instinct theory. In another sense, however, he laid down many of the foundations taken for granted by humanistic psychologists.[4] He showed, by his initial research on hysteria, that psychiatric symptoms can be understood as a language expressing the secret emotional life of the patient (S. Freud, 1953-1974). He showed, by his research on dreams and the "psychopathology of everyday life" (e.g., slips of the tongue), that every human action, however trivial, is meaningful and expresses parts of the individual's personal story not yet accessible to consciousness. He showed, by his research on the psychosexual stages of development, that the human personality is created and organized developmentally and is affected by troubled relationships and traumatic experiences at each critical juncture point in early development. Freud also showed that a "talking cure" can bring a disclosure and resolution of many of the conflicts within the person and within his or her intimate private life.

After Freud: A gifted cacophony of quasi-humanistic approaches. Freud formulated his new science in biological terms and sought a rigid orthodoxy in theory among his followers. He attracted a collection of brilliant young physicians and laypersons to his movement and then proceeded to alienate many of the brightest. Many of the dissenters from Freudian orthodoxy contributed to the emerging humanistic understanding of human nature.

Alfred Adler: Individual psychology. Adler (1870-1937) developed a psychology emphasizing that each individual creates a style of life reflecting the central "fiction" or goal around which the person organizes his or her life. Humans are socially embedded, and the development of a sense of social interest and community feeling is critical to human development. Human behavior is purposeful and future oriented, not merely driven by instinct and mechanism (Adler, 1969).

Carl Gustav Jung: A forerunner of transpersonal psychology. Jung (1875-1961) insisted on the validity of spiritual experience and explored the symbols and archetypes of human experience found in primitive peoples and the world's religions. He described the human life as a lifelong, never-completed process of psychological and spiritual individuation and integration (Jung, 1961). He described the self as a deeper and less rational structure than the ego and advocated that humans come to trust and accept the wisdom that emerges spontaneously from the self in dreams, images, and intuitions.

Otto Rank: The psychology of the will. Rank (1884-1939) formulated a psychology of the will that mirrored many of Nietzsche's themes (Rank, 1936, 1941/1958). He studied the process of artistic creation and concluded that all of human life, including neurosis, is a process of self-creation. Rank defined human heroism in terms of the larger and riskier stage on which one risks creating oneself. The neurotic makes other persons into gods and creates an individual

life guaranteed to please others. Most humans at times engage in such neurotic solutions to life, "tranquilizing" themselves with the trivial (Becker, 1973, pp. 178-179). The heroic human reaches for the broadest horizon, however unfamiliar, and lives more boldly (Becker, 1973; Rank, 1941/1958). Like Jung, Rank affirmed spirituality as one of the broadest stages on which the human can unfold an existence. Rank affirmed that the human is a "theological being" (Becker, 1973).

Wilhelm Reich: Character analysis and the body armor. Reich (1897-1957) was a gifted psychoanalyst who shifted the attention of psychotherapy toward an exploration of character and psychological defenses. Anna Freud's work on the ego and the mechanisms of defense developed from Reich's early research (A. Freud, 1936/1948). Later, Reich investigated the "body armor" or the muscular defenses against unacceptable feelings and impulses (Moss & Shane, 1998; Reich, 1949). Eventually, Reich and his student Alexander Lowen developed the bioenergetics approach, which applies a variety of techniques to facilitate a deep and systematic release of any muscular or bodily barriers against a full range of affective experiencing (Lowen, 1971). Bioenergetic therapy contributed to the humanistic emphasis on body therapies and the unity of body and mind.

THE HISTORY OF HUMANISTIC PSYCHOLOGY

The years 1954 to 1973 can be seen as the golden years of the humanistic psychology movement. Those dates were selected as follows. In the year 1954 Maslow developed a mailing list for correspondence with persons interested in "the scientific study of creativity, love, higher values, growth, self-actualization, [and] basic needs gratification" (Misiak & Sexton, 1973, p. 111). In the year 1973 Misiak and Sexton wrote their systematic academic book describing humanistic psychology as a complete movement.

Of immediate importance for their crucial role in influencing the key concepts and images of the humanistic viewpoint are two European imports, Goldstein (1939) and Angyal (1941), and several American psychologists, especially Allport (1955), Murray (Murray et al., 1938), and Murphy (1958). Their works commenced during the 1930s and 1940s and continued into the 1950s. They contributed a holistic understanding of the human personality, drawing on European Gestalt principles and giving attention to the human individual's spontaneous movement toward self-actualization and mastery of the environment. Goldstein was a German, and Angyal was a Hungarian who was educated in Austria and Italy. Allport, Murray, and Murphy were American but were influenced by the holistic psychologies of Europe during the 1930s.

Abraham Maslow and the birth of humanistic psychology. Abraham Maslow (1908-1970) is the single person most responsible for creating humanistic psychology. He translated the widespread yearning for a different type of psychological theory and practice into a cohesive viewpoint on humanistic psychology with journals, conferences, and formal organization. His theory of the self and of self-actualization served as a foundation for later humanistic psychologists. Rogers' client-centered or person-centered therapy and Sidney Jourard's psychology of self-disclosure are partially elaborations on the interpersonal condi-

tions most helpful in awakening and actualizing the inner self.

Maslow envisioned humanistic psychology as a psychology of the whole person based on the study of healthy, fully functioning, creative individuals. He criticized the psychologists of his time for spending too much time studying mentally ill and maladjusted humans and for seeking to explain higher levels of human experience by means of neurotic mechanisms. Maslow (1950/1973) proposed an investigation of "superior specimens" as a pathway to understanding the highest potentials of human nature. Maslow turned empirically to the study of self-actualized persons and the patterns of their lives, selecting both living and dead individuals who had strained their human nature to its highest limits. Maslow concluded that the highest reaches of human nature include the capacity for self-transcending altruism and for what he later would call *transpersonal experiencing*. During the early 1960s, Maslow, along with colleagues such as Anthony Sutich, founded the transpersonal psychology movement, a branch of humanistic psychology dedicated to the study of humans' highest potentials.

Carl Rogers: Client-centered therapy. Carl Rogers (1902-1987) provided the central clinical framework for the humanistic therapies. As a person, he provided leadership for three generations of humanistic clinicians. Rogers spent his early career identifying the "necessary and sufficient conditions" that enable humans to spontaneously grow and seek fulfillment. The conditions that define the core of his therapy are that (a) two persons are in emotional contact; (b) one of them, called the client, is troubled; (c) the other, called the therapist, shows genuineness and congruence in the relationship; (d) the therapist experiences and displays unconditional positive regard for the client; (e) the therapist achieves and expresses an empathic understanding of the client; and (f) the client perceives the genuineness, positive regard, and empathy of the therapist. Create these conditions, Rogers asserted, and the client will self-actualize in his or her own self-defined directions (Moss, 1998c, pp. 41-43; Rogers, 1957).

Frederick "Fritz" Perls: Gestalt therapy. Perls (1893-1970) was one of the many striking and memorable individuals of the humanistic movement. Trained as a psychoanalyst initially, Perls and his wife Laura, who was also an analyst, fled Nazi Germany and practiced in South Africa throughout World War II, then moved to the United States. His first book (Perls, 1947/1969) marked his migration away from Freud, and a subsequent fortuitous collaborative work, *Gestalt Therapy,* raised the banner of the new therapy (Perls, Hefferline, & Goodman, 1951). As the title implied, Perls drew on the holistic understandings of the German Gestalt psychologists. However, the new approach was equally indebted to Perls's past contacts with Wilhelm Reich and Karen Horney as well as to Perls's unique personality. Perls went "on the road" with the new therapy, conducting live demonstrations of bombastic body-oriented confrontations of volunteers' defenses (Shane, 1998). A classic video comparing Carl Rogers, Albert Ellis, and Fritz Perls served as the introduction to Gestalt therapy for several generations of graduate students.

The present history of humanistic psychology is all too brief. The roles of other major figures such as William James, James Bugental, Erich Fromm, Rollo May, George Kelly, Sidney Jourard, Amedeo Giorgi,

Erwin Straus, and Ken Wilber are described in Moss (1998c).

CONCLUSION: HUMANISTIC PSYCHOLOGY DURING THE 21ST CENTURY

The original inspiration of humanistic psychology unfolded its great momentum during the 1950s and 1960s. Students of Maslow, Rogers, Jourard, Perls, and others continue to teach today, and the students of these students, in turn, occupy faculty positions and fill the schedules at meetings of the Association for Humanistic Psychology. Each day, humanistically oriented psychotherapists assist troubled patients to discover their personhoods and renew paths of self-actualization. The recent movements of emancipatory, experiential, existential-integrative, transpersonal, and constructivist psychotherapy show the continued energies of humanism in psychotherapy (Schneider, 1998; see also the chapters by O'Hara [Chapter 36] and Watson & Bohart [Chapter 38] in this volume). Psychologists and therapists of all orientations, even the most behavioral ones, are more aware today of humanistic dimensions of personal change because of the lasting impact of humanistic psychology.

A challenge remains for all humanistically oriented psychologists: There is a continuing need to remind human society and the helping professions of the dignity and worth of humans (Moss, 1998c). The original humanistic vision must continue to be made relevant in each new generation. The world always will be in need of humanization. Psychology as a science and profession will need to be reminded in each generation of humanistic priorities and of the full breadth of human nature and human potential.

NOTES

1. Existential and phenomenological authors diverged considerably in this view of an unchanging essence in human existence, with Edmund Husserl showing that the human life world always is sedimented with the stuff of contemporary culture and Jean Paul Sartre declaring that the human's essence is his or her existence (i.e., human nature is redefined historically).

2. Intentionality also may involve the individual in an internal intending toward his or her own mental states—in self-reflection.

3. Buber described the realm of "I and it," self relating to object, as a universal dimension of human experience, not as something to be eradicated from life. On the other hand, he critiqued the more pervasive alienation during the modern era and other "sick ages." He described healthy ages as ones in which inspiration flows from "men of the spirit" to all people and there is an intermingling of the dimension of personal presence with the practical dimensions of life (Buber, 1923/1970, p. 102). Buber believed that personal dialogue can be renewing for all persons and all cultures.

4. Freud scholars have identified the complexity of Freud's work, which transcends his explicit instinctual, energetic, and hydraulic models of the mind. Sulloway (1979) elaborated Freud's intricate biological models. Fromm (1959) portrayed the implicit humanism in Freud's work. Rieff (1959) identified Freud as an ethical thinker. Ricoeur (1970) highlighted the hermeneutic-interpretive aspect of Freud's psychoanalytic work.

REFERENCES

Adler, A. (1969). *The practice and theory of individual psychology.* Patterson, NJ: Littlefield, Adams.

Allport, G. (1955). *Becoming: Basic considerations for a psychology of personality.* New Haven, CT: Yale University Press.

Angyal, A. (1941). *Foundations for a science of personality.* New York: Commonwealth Fund.

Augustijn, C. (1991). *Erasmus: His life, works, and influence* (J. C. Grayson, Trans.). Toronto: University of Toronto Press.

Augustine. (1980). The confessions of St. Augustine (J. G. Pilkington, Trans.). In W. J. Oates (Ed.), *Basic writings of St. Augustine* (Vol. 1, reprint ed., pp. 2-256). Grand Rapids, MI: Baker Book House.

Beck, A. T., Rush, A. J., Shaw, B. F., & Emery, G. (1979). *Cognitive therapy of depression.* New York: Guilford.

Becker, E. (1973). *The denial of death.* New York: Free Press.

Binswanger, L. (1942). *Grundformen und Erkenntnis menschlichen Dasein* (Basic forms and knowledge of human existence). Zurich, Switzerland: Niehans Verlag.

Binswanger, L. (1963). *Being-in-the-world: Selected papers of Ludwig Binswanger.* New York: Basic Books.

Boss, M. (1979). *Existential foundations of medicine and psychology.* Northvale, NJ: Jason Aronson. (Original work published 1971)

Boss, M. (1988). Recent considerations in *Daseinanalysis*. *The Humanistic Psychologist, 16*(1), 58-74.

Buber, M. (1965). *The knowledge of man* (M. Friedman, Ed.). New York: Harper & Row.

Buber, M. (1970). *I and thou* (Ich und Du; W. Kaufmann, Trans.). New York: Scribner. (Original work published 1923)

Cavafy, C. (1961). *The complete poems of Cavafy* (R. Dalven, Trans.). New York: Brace & World.

Csikszentmihalyi, M. (1990). *Flow: The psychology of optimal experience.* New York: HarperCollins.

Ficino, M. (1985). *De amore: Commentary on Plato's symposium on love* (S. Jayne, Trans.). Dallas, TX: Spring.

Foster, R. J. (1981). *Freedom of simplicity.* New York: Harper & Row.

Frankl, V. E. (1963). *Man's search for meaning.* Boston: Beacon.

Freud, A. (1948). *The ego and the mechanisms of defense.* London: Hogarth. (Original work published 1936)

Freud, S. (1953-1974). *The standard edition of the complete psychological works of Sigmund Freud* (24 vols., J. Strachey, Ed.). New York: Macmillan.

Fromm, E. (1959). *Sigmund Freud's mission.* New York: Harper.

Georges, E. (1995). A cultural and historical perspective on confession. In J. W. Pennebaker (Ed.), *Emotion, disclosure, and health* (pp. 11-22). Washington, DC: American Psychological Association.

Goldstein, K. (1939). *The organism: A holistic approach to biology derived from pathological data in man.* New York: American Book.

Halling, S., & Carroll. A. (1998). Existential-phenomenological psychology. In D. Moss (Ed.), *Humanistic and transpersonal psychology* (pp. 95-124). Westport, CT: Greenwood.

Heidegger, M. (1962). *Being and time.* New York: Harper & Row. (Original work published 1927)

Husserl, E. (1970a). *The crisis of European sciences and transcendental phenomenology* (D. Carr, Trans.). Evanston, IL: Northwestern University. (Original work published 1936)

Husserl, E. (1970b). *The logical investigations.* New York: Humanities Press. (Original work published 1900)

Husserl, E. (1977). *Phenomenological psychology* (J. Scanlon, Trans.). The Hague, Netherlands: Martinus Nijhof. (Original work published 1925)

Inwood, B. (1985). *Ethics and human action in early Stoicism.* Oxford, UK: Clarendon.

Jung, C. G. (1961). *Memories, dreams, reflections.* New York: Random House.

Kierkegaard, S. (1959). *Either/or* (Vol. 2, W. Lowrie, Trans.). Princeton, NJ: Princeton University Press. (Original work published 1843)

Kierkegaard, S. (1962a). *Philosophical fragments, or a fragment of philosophy* (D. F. Swenson, Trans.). Princeton, NJ: Princeton University Press. (Original work published 1844)

Kierkegaard, S. (1962b). *The point of view for my work as an author* (W. Lowrie, Trans.). Princeton, NJ: Princeton University Press. (Original work published 1859)

Kockelmans, J. J. (1967). *Edmund Husserl's phenomenological psychology.* Pittsburgh, PA: Duquesne University Press.

Laing, R. D. (1960). *The divided self.* London: Tavistock.

Long, A. A. (1974). *Hellenistic philosophy: Stoics, Epicureans, skeptics.* Berkeley: University of California Press.

Lowen, A. (1971). *The language of the body.* New York: Collier.

Maslow, A. H. (1973). Self-actualizing people: A study of psychological health. In R. J. Lowry (Ed.), *Dominance, self-esteem, self-actualization: Germinal papers of A. H. Maslow* (pp. 177-201). Pacific Grove, CA: Brooks/Cole. (Original work published 1950)

May, R., Angel, E., & Ellenberger, H. (Eds.). (1958). *Existence: A new dimension in psychiatry and psychology.* New York: Basic Books.

Merleau-Ponty, M. (1962). *Phenomenology of perception* (C. Smith, Trans.). London: Routledge and Kegan Paul. (Original work published 1945)

Merleau-Ponty, M. (1963). *The structure of behavior.* Boston: Beacon. (Original work published 1942)

Misiak, H., & Sexton, V. S. (1973). *Phenomenological, existential, and humanistic psychologies: A historical survey.* New York: Grune & Stratton.

Moss, D. (1978). Medard Boss and psychotherapy. In R. Valle & M. King (Eds.), *Existential-phenomenological alternatives for psychology* (pp. 308-323). New York: Oxford University Press.

Moss, D. (1998a). Erwin Straus: The individual, the senses, and the beloved earth. In D. Moss (Ed.), *Humanistic and transpersonal psychology: An historical and biographical sourcebook* (pp. 407-422). Westport, CT: Greenwood.

Moss, D. (1998b). The humanistic psychology of self-disclosure, relationship, and community. In D. Moss (Ed.), *Humanistic and transpersonal psychology: An historical and biographical sourcebook* (pp. 66-84). Westport, CT: Greenwood.

Moss, D. (1998c). *Humanistic and transpersonal psychology: An historical and biographical sourcebook.* Westport, CT: Greenwood.

Moss, D., & Shane, P. (1998). Body therapies in humanistic psychology. In D. Moss (Ed.), *Humanistic and transpersonal psychology: An historical and biographical sourcebook* (pp. 85-94). Westport, CT: Greenwood.

Murphy, G. (1958). *Human potentialities.* New York: Basic Books.

Murray, H. A., Barrett, W. G., Langer, W. C., Morgan, C. D., Homburger, E., & Others. (1938). *Explorations in personality.* New York: Oxford University Press.

Nietzsche, F. (1954). *Thus spoke Zarathustra* (W. Kaufmann, Trans.). New York: Viking. (Original work published 1892)

Nietzsche, F. (1966). *Beyond good and evil* (W. Kaufmann, Trans.). New York: Vintage Books. (Original work published 1886)

Perls, F. S. (1969). *Ego, hunger, and aggression.* New York: Vintage. (Original work published 1947)

Perls, F. S., Hefferline, R., & Goodman, P. (1951). *Gestalt therapy: Excitement and growth in the human personality.* New York: Julian.

Plato (1941). *The Republic of Plato* (F. M. Cornford, Trans.). London: Oxford University Press.

Rank, O. (1936). *Will therapy* (J. Taft, Trans.). New York: Norton.

Rank, O. (1958). *Beyond psychology.* New York: Dover. (Original work published 1941)

Reich, W. (1949). *Character analysis.* New York: Orgone Institute Press.

Ricoeur, P. (1970). *Freud and philosophy: An essay on interpretation* (D. Savage, Trans.). New Haven, CT: Yale University Press.

Rieff, P. (1959). *Freud: The mind of the moralist.* New York: Viking.

Riley, G. J. (1997). *One Jesus, many Christs: How Jesus inspired not one true Christianity, but many.* San Francisco: Harper San Francisco.

Roberts, A., & Donaldson, J. (1953). Fragments from the lost writings of Irenaeus. In A. Roberts & J. Donaldson (Eds.), *The ante-Nicene fathers* (Vol. 1, reprint ed., pp. 568-578). Grand Rapids, MI: William B. Eerdmans.

Rogers, C. (1957). The necessary and sufficient conditions of therapeutic personality change. *Journal of Consulting Psychology, 21*, 95-103.

Sartre, J.-P. (1965). *Being and nothingness* (H. Barnes, Trans.). New York: Citadel. (Original work published 1943)

Schneider, K. J. (1998). Toward a science of the heart: Romanticism and the revival of psychology. *American Psychologist, 53*, 277-289.

Shane, P. (1998). Gestalt therapy: The once and future king. In D. Moss (Ed.), *Humanistic and transpersonal psychology: An historical and biographical sourcebook* (pp. 49-65). Westport, CT: Greenwood.

Skinner, B. F. (1971). *Beyond freedom and dignity.* New York: Knopf.

Straus, E. (1966). *Phenomenological psychology: The selected papers of Erwin W. Straus.* New York: Basic Books.

Straus, E. (1982). *Man, time, and world* (D. Moss, Trans.). Pittsburgh, PA: Duquesne University Press. (Original work published 1930)

Sulloway, F. J. (1979). *Freud: Biologist of the mind.* New York: Basic Books.

Taylor, C. C. W. (Ed.). (1997). *From the beginning to Plato.* London: Routledge.

Taylor, E. I. (1991). William James and the humanistic tradition. *Journal of Humanistic Psychology, 31*(1), 56-74.

van den Berg, J. H. (1974). *Divided existence and complex society.* Pittsburgh, PA: Duquesne University Press. (Original work published 1963)

Watson, J. B. (1924). *Behaviorism.* New York: People's Institute.

CHAPTER 2

Humanistic Psychology at the Crossroads

EUGENE I. TAYLOR AND FREDERICK MARTIN

HUMANISTIC psychology today stands at a turning point in its history. Plans are under way for a series of major conferences assessing the past, present, and future of the movement. The American Psychological Association (APA, 2000) is poised in at least one of its many study groups to recognize the legitimacy of the existential-humanistic approach in its "criteria" for psychotherapeutic guidelines. The prestigious *American Psychologist* even has consented to publishing the existentialists' call that we return to the romantic as a still-missing piece of the puzzle of what it means to be human (Schneider, 1998). Indeed, mainstream academics who have launched their own form of positive psychology have invited humanistic thinkers to publicly debate the issue. Is positive psychology, as many humanistic psychologists contend, a usurper of an already established venue? Or, is positive psychology, as many cognitive psychologists would have it, a more superior development to its human-

istic forebears, given that this newer form is more experimental?

One easily could interpret these developments as destiny at the crossroads. Or, to put the question in another way, 40 years after its heyday, will humanistic psychology finally, and quietly, slip into oblivion by being absorbed into the mainstream—gone with nothing more than a whimper instead of a bang, its votaries once having been full of sound and fury but now signifying nothing? Or, is the long-awaited era of its maturity finally at hand, what has gone on in the past being but a prelude of what is to come?

The authors (Taylor, 1999a) are responding to the future of the humanistic movement with guarded optimism. Our only caveat is that humanistic psychology may be able to resurrect itself within the larger field of American academic psychology, but only under a set of specific conditions informed by its own history. Although the humanistic movement is generally associated with the field of psychology per se, over the past 50 years, it has come to influence a variety of fields beyond the social sciences—medicine, law, dentistry, nursing, and business administration, to name but a few. Recent historical scholarship, however, reaffirms what the founders already knew but many today forget—namely, that humanistic psychology did not just appear out of nowhere. It originally was an outgrowth of personality, social, abnormal, and motivation—those subfields of academic psychology long considered to be the so-called soft sciences (Taylor, 2000).

While reductionistic behaviorism had maintained an ideological stranglehold in academic departments of psychology, especially since the 1930s, psychoanalysis came to control clinical teaching in psychology and psychiatry during the same period. Within the academic arena, however, the more overtly reductionistic subfields such as learning, sensation and perception, mathematical, and physiological psychology that dominated the laboratory scene were challenged by the rise of the macropersonality theorists. Researchers such as Henry A. Murray, Gordon Allport, and Gardner Murphy rejected the reductionistic atomism of experimental psychologists whose main focus was the study of the white rat. They argued instead for psychology as a person-centered science. These voices then became the grandfathers and -mothers of the humanistic movement in psychology that first appeared during the 1940s, when Carl Rogers articulated his client-centered therapy, and grew to a crescendo during the 1950s, when Rollo May and others introduced the existential and phenomenological viewpoint into psychology and psychiatry and Abraham Maslow defined the self-actualizing personality. After that, a period of institutionalization began.

The *Journal of Humanistic Psychology* was officially launched in 1961, followed by the founding of the American Association for Humanistic Psychology a year later. In November 1964, the historic First Old Saybrook Conference was held, at which Murray, Allport, Murphy, and Kelly passed the torch to Maslow, Rogers, and May, legitimizing the humanistic movement as a viable form of discourse within academic psychology. The Humanistic Psychology Institute, soon the first Ph.D. program of the movement, began in 1971, and the Division of Humanistic Psychology was launched within the APA in 1973 (Taylor & Kelley, 1998). For all intents and purposes, it looked outwardly like the field was well launched, and the expectation by deans and college presidents was that it soon would usher in a new dialogue between science and the humanities, healing the historic rift between C. P. Snow's two cultures.

It was a revolution within the academy whose time, however, had not yet come. Abraham Maslow and Anthony Sutich, two of the most influential founders of the movement, were emblematic of the currents at work during that period. With Sutich as founding editor and Maslow as contributor and national point man, the *Journal of Humanistic Psychology* soon came to represent a new emphasis in psychology on the experience of the fully functioning person; on emotional maturity and interaction in relationships; and on values in science, especially the psychology of the science-making process. Its original home was Brandeis University, and its editorial board included influential figures in academic and clinical psychology as well as other disciplines. Furthermore, it was buttressed by the inclusion of the existential and phenomenological perspective, flourishing at the time as a growing cultural force but with no direct venue into psychology until the humanistic movement came into being and remolded it as a form of psychotherapy. Along these lines, humanistic psychology became a force for cultural change by focusing on significant dimensions of personality left unexplored by the experimental reductionists' methods.

Maslow and Sutich, however, quickly became dissatisfied with experiential and social transformation that left the spiritual quite out of the picture (Sutich, 1976). They conspired self-consciously to introduce this dimension back into psychology by bolting from the editorial and organizational positions they had made for themselves in the humanistic movement and, in 1969, founding in their place the *Journal of Transpersonal Psychology* and its attendant organization, the Association for Transpersonal Psychology. The spiritual dimension of experience, the actualization of self and being, metavalues, meditation, and higher states of consciousness became the new foci of their efforts.

By making this abrupt transition, Maslow and Sutich effectively took most of the leaders of the humanistic movement at the time with them. One unintended consequence, however, was a dramatic shift in emphasis away from psychology in the academy to psychology in culture-at-large. The counterculture psychotherapeutic movement was fully under way by that time, fueled in part by the advances of humanistic psychology but also by widespread experimentation with psychedelics, rising interest in religious movements from Asian cultures, the antiwar movement, the rise of feminism and radical gender politics, a new anti-intellectual culture of the body, and a period of sexual experimentation and new definitions of the family unprecedented during the modern era.

Humanistic psychology became transformed into something else overnight, virtually indistinguishable from its new, myriad, and more radical forms. The forms themselves, however, are readily identifiable. When humanistic psychology became absorbed into the psychotherapeutic counterculture, it effectively fractionated into three separate and unintegrated streams, none of which had any venue into the academic university environment. The first was meditation and altered states of consciousness, the second was experiential body work and group dynamics, and the third was human science. Meditation and altered states of consciousness have persisted as transpersonal psychology. Experiential bodywork, still expanding in its old forms, also has evolved into therapeutic touch, Reiki healing, and shamanic journeying, whereas group dynamics has moved from the churches into the corporate boardrooms. Human science has come to encompass political psychology, gender studies, social criticism, and all forms of postmodernism, from constructivism to deconstructionism and contextualism.

Yet, while the influence of humanistic psychology suddenly became subterranean, its newly launched institutions remained visible within the dominant culture, proceeding along a relatively unchanging course that continues to be defined by issues and personalities from the 1960s and early 1970s. In these more visible forms, humanistic psychology today looks like a persistent throwback to that era. In its invisible form, however, it has evolved through a series of cultural phases, from sensitivity training, growth groups, and therapeutic massage to biofeedback and meditation, socially engaged spirituality, psychotherapy and shamanism, and now alternative and complementary therapies. It now has surfaced reincarnated, more pervasively 50 years later, in the form of a shadow culture that is transforming the dominant culture at nearly every niche from the bottom up (Taylor, 1999b). The old humanistic psychologists still are there, but they now call themselves transpersonalists, Gestalt therapists, psychophysiologists, integral psychologists, mind/body practitioners, postmodernists, and human (as opposed to natural) scientists.

Psychology in the academy, meanwhile, became somewhat more humanistic, but not by that name. Behaviorism, which had dominated the laboratory science of psychology since the 1930s, gave way to cognitive psychology, which in turn was quickly absorbed into the newly developing disciplines of the cognitive neurosciences. Mainstream science, previously driven by physics and mathematics and their subordinate sciences, suddenly became more biological as well, leading to the present-day interdisciplinary emphasis at the nexus of fields such as molecular genetics, neurology, endocrinology, immunology, and psychiatry.

Psychology has participated significantly in these endeavors, primarily because the neuroscience revolution is all about the biology of consciousness. Artificial intelligence, parallel distributive processing models of cognition, and MRI scanning of mental processes from abstract problem solving to mental imaging have come into vogue. As a result, clinical psychology has become more medicalized. Clinicians are called on to perform almost the same diagnostic functions as are psychiatrists when mental illness is the primary issue, prescription privileges for psychologists already have been instituted in the military on a limited scale, psychologists have almost totally colonized psychoanalysis (a field previously controlled exclusively by physicians), and psychologists and psychiatrists remain embroiled together in the fate of managed care.

At the same time as it has become more biological, however, mainstream psychology also has become more philosophical, commensurate with a similar expansion in disciplines associated with the neurosciences. Questions about the relation of the brain to our experience, long banned as unscientific, now are at the center of discussions about the nature of consciousness. The facts of science now are being discussed in terms of their context. The language of behaviorism has been transformed into the more cognitive language of mentalism. And the whole issue of values in science once again is on the table, as experimental psychologists tout the benefits of promoting what Seligman (1990, 1993) called a "positive psychology," the study and application of science to positive, growth-oriented outcomes. Cloninger's seven-factor theory of personality even has developed a transpersonal scale to measure religiosity as it emerges in later life (Cloninger et al., 1998).

The question now before us, however, is the following: Where does humanistic psychology fit into this picture? Today, the Humanistic Psychology Institute has become Saybrook Graduate School and Research Center, a fully accredited-at-a-distance Ph.D. program, but dominated more by human science than by humanistic or transpersonal psychology. Division 32 within the APA stands by itself as one of the smaller but still functioning divisions except that its journal, *The Humanistic Psychologist,* never has been able to widen its subscription base enough to make it financially viable. The Association for Humanistic Psychology remains active but represents only a small core of primarily the psychotherapeutic counterculture and, as such, has practically no venue into academic psychology. Its main organ, the *Journal of Humanistic Psychology,* no longer is owned by the association but rather operates independently due to financial constraints. And although the majority of psychologists in the APA might consider themselves person centered, nondirective, and even growth oriented, only the smallest fraction would use the term *humanistic* to describe their orientation.

Mainstream psychologists, if they have any name recognition at all when asked about the movement, think of humanistic psychology as unscientific, guilty of promoting the cult of narcissism, and a thing of the past. Transpersonal psychologists are convinced that because humanistic psychologists study existential states and transpersonalists study spiritual ones, and because spiritual states are superior to existential ones, transpersonal has superseded humanistic (see, e.g., the chapter by Walsh & Schneider [Chapter 45] in this volume). Bodyworkers and those advocating group dynamics tend to remain distant from the intellectual milieu that connects the humanistic tradition to the disciplines of higher learning, whereas the votaries of human science have been swamped by a radical Marxist ideology that has managed to colonize every liberal niche created by the humanistic movement in psychology in the United States since the 1960s.

Humanistic psychologists, meanwhile, generally have bought into postmodernism and its ideology, believing human science to be a more general rubric that differentiates a mechanistic approach to science from a more person-centered one. This appears somewhat of a false dichotomy given that human science as a field of study has been completely overrun by radical trends in European social criticism that have little direct relevance to humanistic and transpersonal psychology and, in fact, represent forces hostile to it. At the same time, the humanistic movement has spread its meager resources out over a vast terrain, aiming at business, law, medicine, the arts, and culture in a way that has quite obscured its origins in psychology. Psychology, meanwhile, has become more humanistic, but its more liberal transformation has not gone by that name.

So, we now are able to sharpen the question considerably by re-asking it in a different but more historically informed way: What is the potential future of humanistic psychology within psychology? Will it be absorbed into the mainstream? Or, will it awaken psychologists to the construction of a new science that finally addresses the full spectrum of human experience, thus potentially transforming the other sciences through psychology and, at the same time, opening a new dialogue between science and the humanities?

If humanistic psychologists continue to proceed along their present course, dissipating their attention across too many subject areas and believing that their future lies in propounding the already outmoded theories of postmodernism while forgetting their basic roots in psychology, then the answer is that their basic contributions are destined to be co-opted by mainstream psychologists, and their fate will be similar to that of the experimental Gestalt psychologists of the 1930s. Gestalt psychology was the first uniquely experimental laboratory challenge to the Wundtian atomism that has always dominated American experimental laboratories because Gestalt was holistic at the same time as it remained scientific and experimental. American experimental psychologists effectively neutralized its epistemological challenge, however, by co-opting its major ideas of figure-ground, closure, contrast, continuity, and the like into the flow of general psychology textbooks without having to confront the metaphysical questions it raised about the way in which basic science is conducted. American psychology then went on being behavioral and reductionistic. Humanistic psychology now appears to be undergoing a similar assimilation.

If humanistic psychology decides to focus its attention back on the discipline of psychology, however, then an entirely different outcome might ensue that could place the humanistic movement at the forefront of not only a sea change in psychology but also a major transformation of the social and natural sciences. But certain new conditions would have to be established for a change of this magnitude to take place. We have already provided (1999a) the details of this proposal, so the present chapter is confined to just the bare outlines.

To regain its stature in the visible halls of academia, humanistic psychology would have to temporarily distance itself from its more radical offspring long enough to reclaim its historical position among the soft sciences and to engage psychologists as scientists, clinicians, and administrators in terms useful to their own endeavors. It also would have to be led by voices of significant stature who self-consciously identify themselves with the movement.

To do this, humanistic psychology temporarily would have to become less transpersonal, less experiential, and less political and, in exchange, return to being more psychological. For example, it could constructively embrace Seligman's positive psychology at the same time that it could promote Cloninger's seven-factor theory over the five-factor theory now in vogue. It could prepare itself to become more of a viable interpreter of the humanistic implications of the neuroscience revolution, particularly regarding the problem of consciousness. It could bring psychologists to a renewed focus on the need for a more person-centered science, that is, a science of psychology that focuses on the person as its primary subject matter.

Our contention is that humanistic psychology, by claiming its legitimate place in the history of American psychology as the offspring of personality, social, abnormal, and clinical, could resurrect the dialogue with psychologists about the growth-oriented dimension of personality; it could reorient the training of clinicians toward education for transcendence instead of a psychology of the neurosis; and it could reemphasize the existential nature of the psychotherapeutic hour as not only the crucible for personality transformation but also the laboratory for a new type of experimental psychology. Concretely, humanistic psychologists also could focus the precious resources of the movement on Division 32 in the APA, which needs a serious infusion of financial support, more members, and more subscribers to its journal.

By instituting such changes within their own ranks, humanistic psychologists might immediately garner the attention of mainstream psychologists. The next question, however, is more crucial: What will humanistic psychologists tell their mainstream counterparts if they actually could get their attention?

In our opinion, the single most important contribution that humanistic psychologists have to make to modern psychology is to bring the attention of the experimentalists to focus on the phenomenology of the science-making process and, once the attention of the discipline is focused on that point, to articulate a phenomenological (rather than a positivistic) epistemology as the basis for a new experimental science.

Such a science is not new; we have heard a similar call in James's radical empiricism and from depth psychologists such as Jung and Freud and theologians such as Paul Tillich. Maslow (1966) pointed in that direction with his *Psychology of Science*, and it also was the basis for Giorgi's (1970) interpretation of Husserl and Merleau-Ponty in *Psychology as a Human Science*. It is also the foundation of Dignaga's Buddhist theory of perception. At any rate, it is a scientific psychology that would address the full range of human experience while at the same time accommodate non-Western epistemologies, two key conditions not presently fulfilled by contemporary positivistic epistemology. What implications such a new science would have for the social and behavioral sciences, and even for physics and biology, would remain to be worked out. But even established in its most primitive form, it would more than adequately fulfill the original agenda of those who founded humanistic psychology in the first place.

REFERENCES

American Psychological Association. (2000, March). *Criteria for evaluating treatment guidelines* (draft, Template Implementation Work Group). Washington, DC: Author.

Cloninger, C. R., Bayon, C., & Svrakic, D. M. (1998). Measurement of temperament and character in mood disorders: A model of fundamental states as personality types. *Journal of Affective Disorders, 51*(1), 21-32.

Giorgi, A. (1970). *Psychology as a human science.* New York: Basic Books.

Maslow, A. H. (1966). *The psychology of science: A reconnaissance.* New York: Harper & Row.

Schneider, K. J. (1998). Toward a science of the heart: Romanticism and the revival of psychology. *American Psychologist, 53,* 277-289.

Seligman, M. (1990). *Learned optimism.* New York: Knopf.

Seligman, M. (1993). *What you can change and what you can't: The complete guide to successful self-improvement.* New York: Knopf.

Sutich, A. (1976). *The founding of humanistic and transpersonal psychology: A personal account.* Unpublished doctoral dissertation, Humanistic Psychology Institute.

Taylor, E. I. (1999a). An intellectual renaissance of humanistic psychology? *Journal of Humanistic Psychology, 39*(2), 7-25.

Taylor, E. I. (1999b). *Shadow culture: Psychology and spirituality in America.* Washington, DC: Counterpoint.

Taylor, E. I. (2000). What is man, psychologist, that thou art so unmindful of him? Henry A. Murray on the historical relation between classical personality theory and humanistic psychology. *Journal of Humanistic Psychology, 40*(3), 29-42.

Taylor, E. I., & Kelley, M. (1998). Historical outline of humanistic psychology. In *History and systems of psychology course guide.* San Francisco: Saybrook Graduate School.

CHAPTER 3

Humanistic Psychology and Women
A Critical-Historical Perspective

ILENE SERLIN AND ELEANOR CRISWELL

T HE ROLE OF WOMEN in humanistic psychology is complex. On the one hand, much of humanistic thought, especially with regard to the centrality of personal experience and holistic and tacit ways of knowing (Polanyi, 1958), has much in common with feminist theories of intersubjectivity (Chodorow, 1978; Jordan, 1991), personal knowledge, and the importance of finding one's own voice (Gilligan, 1982; Heilbrun, 1988; Woolf, 1929/1989). On the other hand, existential, humanistic, and transpersonal psychologies all have been subject to feminist critiques that these perspectives privilege the sole self-evolving individual on a solitary and heroic journey of self-discovery (Crocker, 1999; Wright, 1995). This journey is characterized by subduing nature; overcoming matter; transcending the body (Wilber, 1986); and promoting individuation, differentiation, and abstraction. It is filled with masculine terms of agency, control, and self-sufficiency (Crocker, 1999). Humanistic

psychology, these critics charged, had forgotten the body and nature (Starhawk, 1988; Wright, 1995). In fact, existential humanism was based on the experience of the modern, alienated, urban white European male (Roszak, 1992), thereby leaving out relevant experiences of women, children, and indigenous peoples. Even the postmodern trend in humanistic psychology also can be critiqued as sharing "modernity's groundlessness" (Weil, 1999), being disembodied, and lacking a sense of place and body. A truly radical feminist postmodern humanistic psychology, therefore, would have to be grounded in an "ecosocial matrix" (Spretnak, 1997) that restored elements of earth, body, and community. Finally, a feminist perspective on humanistic psychology can itself be critiqued as being insensitive to issues of power and social context. "Womanist" philosophy extends the themes of feminist psychology through its focus on concrete and social-political activism. This activism is expressed through the practice of mutual caring in community and through the centrality of the family. It challenges psychologists to move beyond individualized experience to liberation and transformation (Cannon, 1995; Jacklin, 1987; Leslie, 1999). Although these criticisms are true for only part of humanistic psychology, as challenges, they are important reminders for the field.

THE ROLE OF WOMEN IN HUMANISTIC PSYCHOLOGY

Whereas the "third force" or humanistic orientation to psychology was fathered by men such as Abraham Maslow, Carl Rogers, Rollo May, and Sidney Jourard, many women served as the mothers of humanistic psychology. Humanistic psychologists believed that all humans are basically creative and behave with intentionality and values. Their focus was on the experiencing person and the meaning of experience to the person, they emphasized the human qualities of choice and self-realization, they were concerned with problems that are meaningful to humans, and their ultimate concern was with the dignity and worth of humans and an interest in the development of the potential inherent in every person (Krippner & Murphy, 1973). During the late 1960s and 1970s, many women were attracted to humanistic psychology because of its philosophy, practices, and promises of self-fulfillment.

At approximately the same time, parallel social movements were beginning. For example, during the late 1950s, the women's liberation movement led by Betty Freidan championed similar humanistic principles and rights. The world of humanistic psychology was a favorable environment for women. Many women attended workshops in growth centers throughout the country, and these continue to be char-

acterized by a great deal of exploration, experimentation, and creativity. The Humanistic Psychology Institute (now Saybrook Graduate School and Research Center) was founded by Eleanor Criswell from the Association for Humanistic Psychology (AHP) in 1970 as its academic arm—as a place for training humanistic psychologists, both men and women.

The humanistic psychology movement and the human potential movement were not identical but were mutually supportive. Many women answered the call to human potential events. Therefore, their spirit of coming closer with others, the hallmark of women's ways of being and knowing, was significant in the zeitgeist of humanistic psychology.

During the 1970s, the second contemporary wave of the women's movement, led by Gloria Steinem and others, arrived. Women in the AHP began to assert their feelings about not having enough of a voice, were encouraged to move into leadership positions in the organization, and were given more program time devoted to women's issues. Up to 1976, there were 3 female AHP presidents—Charlotte Buhler, Norma Lyman (the first organizational secretary of the AHP), and Eleanor Criswell—in contrast to the 11 male presidents. After 1976, there were 13 female presidents and 12 male presidents. On two occasions, there were male and female co-presidents. Women presidents after 1976 were Jean Houston, Jacquelin L. Doyle, Virginia Satir, Peggy Taylor, Lonnie Barbach, Frances Vaughan, Elizabeth Campbell, Maureen O'Hara, Sandy Friedman, Ann Weiser Cornell, M. A. Bjarkman, Jocelyn Olivier, and Katy Brant. The AHP conventions always were highly experiential and featured women's issues, community issues, relationship concerns, somatic practices, and environmental concerns.

Both inside and outside the AHP and American Psychological Association (APA), there have been other outstanding women humanistic psychologists and therapists. For example, Laura Perls, who with Fritz Perls brought individual responsibility into an active experiential process (Serlin, 1992), and Virginia Satir, the founder of conjoint family therapy, both were well known in their days. Stella Resnick, Ilana Rubenfeld, and Natalie Rogers were active in AHP conventions. Charlotte Bühler, a personality theorist, met with the others in Old Saybrook, Connecticut, in November 1964, a seminal gathering for the founding of the humanistic psychology field. Carol Guinn was the longtime editor of the AHP newsletter, an important voice in the field. Some women were active in their humanistic institutions of higher education including Anne Richards (State University of West Georgia) and Nina Menrath, Norma Lyman, and Eleanor Criswell (Sonoma State University). There have been many unsung women in humanistic psychology. Some of them are the wives of founding fathers Carl Rogers, Abraham Maslow, and Sidney Jourard— Helen Rogers, Bertha Maslow, and Antoinette (Toni) Jourard. It is interesting that all of them were (are) artists. Helen Rogers was a painter, Bertha Maslow was a sculptor, and Antoinette Jourard is a photographer. All were (are) deeply self-actualizing persons, fully functioning and inspiring to their husbands as well as to others.

Although the leadership of the AHP included many women, the leadership of Division 32 (Humanistic Psychology) of the APA did not. Division 32 was founded to bring humanistic psychology specifically into academic and professional psychology organizations.

The perspective of humanistic psychology was officially born in [the] APA with the establishment of Division 32 [Humanistic Psychology] in 1971. Its credo was to apply "the concepts, theories, and philosophy of humanistic psychology to research, education, and professional applications of scientific psychology" and to ensure "that humanistically oriented ideas and activities operate within [the] APA and some of its divisions." (Serlin, 1997, pp. 6-7)

A number of women participated in the founding of Division 32. For example, Joyce Howard, Louise Riscalla, and Constance Moerman attended the founding meeting of Division 32, and Gloria Gottsegen was named its acting secretary. During the first Division 32 election, Elizabeth Mintz, Joen Fagen, and Janette Rainwater were elected members-at-large of the executive board. Karen Goodman and Marta Vargo helped to run the hospitality suite during the APA conventions, and this started the general APA tradition that hospitality suites host the more experiential programs at APA. Zaraleya was named the newsletter editor, and Nora Weckler, a California psychologist, also was active in the governance of Division 32. Past presidents include Gloria Gottsegan and Mary Jo Meadow. Contemporary women humanistic psychologists active in the division include Eleanor Criswell, president (Sonoma State University); Constance Fischer, president-elect (Duquesne University); Ilene Serlin, past president and APA council representative (Saybrook Graduate School faculty member); Ruth Heber, past president; Mary Anne Siderits, newsletter editor (Marquette University); and Maureen O'Hara, member-at-large (Saybrook Graduate School president). Despite the involvement of women members, however, the leadership has been predominantly male. Compared to 38.5% women among all members of the APA, Division 32 is close to average with 30.1%

female membership. Statistics on the percentages of women officers in divisions, however, shows the Humanistic Psychology division to have only 16.6% women officers; this compares to 42.8% women officers in the Theoretical and Philosophical Psychology division, 46.6% in the Psychotherapy division, 33.3% in the Psychology of Religion division, and 38.8% in the Psychoanalysis division (APA, 1999). This trend may be changing, with four women elected president during recent years: Ruth Heber (1993-1994), Ilene Serlin (1996-1997), Eleanor Criswell (1999-2000), and Constance Fischer (2000-2001).

WOMEN'S WAYS OF KNOWING AND HUMANISTIC PSYCHOLOGY

In a recent sequel to the now well-known *Women's Ways of Knowing* (Belenky, Clinchy, Goldberger, & Tarule, 1986), this same group of women extended their epistemological analysis to *Knowledge, Difference, and Power* (Goldberger, Tarule, Clinchy, & Belenky, 1996). The position that they laid out echoes core values of humanistic psychology (p. 205).

In their opening chapter to *Knowledge, Difference, and Power,* Goldberger and colleagues (1996) framed their argument with a statement that the discussion would be in terms of gender roles and the archetypally feminine, not in terms of real complex women and men. In the same way, the distinctions that we make here about women's versus men's ways of knowing, and about experiential versus cognitive approaches to humanistic psychology, are simply helpful conceptual tools. Because society always has "genderized" knowledge, understanding women's ways of knowing can raise our consciousness to include "the situational and cultural determinants of knowing" and

"the relationship between power and knowledge" (p. 8), "standpoint epistemologies" (Harding, 1986; Jagger, 1983), and "social positionality and situated knowledge" (Collins, 1990; de Laurentis, 1986; Haraway, 1991; hooks, 1983).

Therefore, the key concepts of those women's ways of knowing are the following.

Connectedness. In contrast to the separate male way of knowing that emphasizes separation and individuation, critical analysis, rational debate, and detachment, and whose mode of discourse is the argument and is hostile to new ideas (Goldberger et al., 1996, p. 207), connected knowing draws on empathy and intuition, is receptive to new ideas, and seeks collaboration with others.

Women's epistemology of connected knowing is supported by their physiology of connected knowing. Brain research shows that women tend to be less lateralized, that is, less biased in one cerebral hemisphere (Springer & Deutsch, 1993). Women have larger corpora callosa than do most men, especially the posterior part of the corpus callosum that connects the two occipital lobes. Because the corpus callosum is the bridge of neuron axons that connects the two brain hemispheres, women appear to have more integrated cerebral functions as a biological condition.

Connected knowing also is closely related to the humanistic psychology concept of empathy. Rogers, the main theorist on empathy, described empathy as a way of knowing another person through connection, that is, through taking on that person's frame of reference so as to fully experience his or her world. Humanistic psychotherapists sense their clients' worlds by being open to them, being transparent to themselves, and laying "aside all perceptions from the external frame of reference" (Rogers, 1951, p. 29; see also the chapter by O'Hara [Chapter 36] in this volume).

Social construction of methodologies. Whereas separate knowing is concerned with the discovery of truth, connected knowing is concerned with the discovery of meaning (Lather, 1991; Maguire, 1987; Reinharz, 1992). Whereas separate knowing uses rational debate to validate truth, connected knowing, as it informs humanistic research methods, looks for validity in the empathic resonance (Hare-Mustin, 1983; Howard, 1991) and the meaning it awakens in the other (Buber, quoted in Friedman, 1985, p. 4). Qualitative research is concerned with quality rather than numbers and is descriptive rather than prescriptive. Feminist research, as a form of qualitative research, is "passionate" and is "communal rather than hierarchical" (Smith, 2000, p. 19). It seeks meaningful patterns in experience, not for prediction or control (see also the chapters by Wertz [Chapter 18] and Leitner & Epting [Chapter 33] in this volume).

The self. In connected knowing, the self is not experienced in isolation but rather is known through interaction with others and "self-insertion" into experience (Elbow, 1973, p. 149). Feminist psychology shares, with humanistic psychology, a view that the self is not a solitary entity but rather is known only in relationship. The self itself is the instrument in psychotherapy and in research. It is used as an instrument of knowing both in the experience of everyday life and in participatory research methodologies. In contrast to the more rigid boundaries of separate knowing, its boundaries are flexible and sometimes permeable (Buber, 1985; Perls, 1992; Rogers, 1980; Serlin & Shane, 1999), demonstrating the "paradox of separateness within connection" (Jordan, 1991, p. 69). Finally, not a static object, the self is a "self-in-process," collaboratively created and re-created in the context of relationships (see also the chapter by Polkinghorne [Chapter 8] in this volume).

Dialogic knowing. In connected knowing, the "I" transforms an "it" into a "thou" (Goldberger et al., 1996, p. 221). Meaning is found in the intersubjective space between the two so that the act of interpretation is dialogic (Friedman, 1985, p. 4; see also the chapters by Friedman [Chapter 26] and Sterling [Chapter 27] in this volume). Dialogic knowing characterizes humanistic theory, therapy, and research, and it transpires between speaker and listener, between reader and text (Ricoeur, 1976), and between researcher and coresearcher (Polkinghorne, 1988).

Feeling. In connected knowing, thinking is inseparable from feeling. It is feeling that allows one to feel oneself into the world of the other (Goldberger et al., 1996, p. 224), to differentiate the particularities of his or her unique experience, in contrast to the abstract, categorical, and generalized thinking of separate knowing. Psychological research shows that women are emotionally expressive, whereas brain research suggests that women have greater metabolic activity in the emotional areas of the brain than do men (Gur et al., 1995) and that women are more empathic and more concerned with communication and relationships than are men.

It could be said that there is a masculine version and a feminine version of humanistic psychology. The masculine version deals mainly with intellectual conceptions, perhaps explaining why Division 32 is male oriented. The feminine version is concerned with the experiential aspects of relationship and nurturing the development of the person, perhaps explaining why the AHP is more female oriented.

Both the masculine and feminine approaches to humanistic psychology are important. The theoretical understandings are important for the foundations of the field, and the experiential aspects are important for the implementation of humanistic perspectives in life.

CONCLUSION

On the one hand, categories of feminist epistemologies are close to humanistic values of holism, subjectivity, and the centrality of the experiencing human (Bugental, 1976; Maslow, 1962; May, 1953; Yalom, 1980) and "experiential humanism" (Schneider, 1998; see also the introduction to this volume). On the other hand, feminist values can help to bring humanistic theory back down to earth, to matter and flesh, and to connection with other humans, other species, and nature (see also the chapter by Pilisuk & Joy [Chapter 9] in this volume).

What can humanistic psychology offer women in the future? One of the trends that emerged over the years, encouraged by humanistic psychology, is the greater actualization of potential for all. Women have been allowed and encouraged to develop more of their potential. This also is true for men; they have been allowed to become more emotionally expressive and to embrace life. These advances in gender role expansion need to be maintained and further developed. After differentiation comes integration. Perhaps it is time for gender transcendence without losing the richness of gender differences. As humanistic psychologists, we have a concern for all persons and their basic human rights—the right to be treated as individuals with worth and dignity, the right to the primacy of their experiences, the right to the holistic development of their various talents and capacities, and the right of society to receive the contributions of all individuals toward the cultural evolution of humankind. This is a fertile ground for the continued development of all toward global and environmental well-being.

REFERENCES

American Psychological Association. (1999). *Report on the status of women in psychology*. Washington, DC: Author.

Belenky, M., Clinchy, B., Goldberger, N., & Tarule, J. (1986). *Women's ways of knowing: The development of self, voice, and mind*. New York: Basic Books.

Buber, M. (1985). *Between man and man*. (R. G. Smith, Trans.). New York: Macmillan.

Bugental, J. F. T. (1976). *The search for existential identity*. San Francisco: Jossey-Bass.

Cannon, K. G. (1995). *Katie's canon: Womanism and the soul of the black community*. New York: Guilford.

Chodorow, N. (1978). *The reproduction of mothering.* Berkeley: University of California Press.

Collins, P. H. (1990). *Black feminist thought: Knowledge, consciousness, and the politics of empowerment.* Cambridge, MA: Unwin Hyman.

Crocker, R. (1999). *Women, freedom, and responsibility: A comparison of the existentialist thought of Irvin Yalom and James Bugental.* Unpublished manuscript, Saybrook Graduate School.

de Laurentis, T. (1986). Feminist studies/critical studies: Issues, terms, and context. In T. de Laurentis (Ed.), *Feminist studies/critical studies* (pp. 1-19). Bloomington: Indiana University Press.

Elbow, P. (1973). Appendix essay: The doubting game and the believing game—An analysis of the intellectual enterprise. In *Writing without teachers.* London: Oxford University Press.

Friedman, M. (1985). *The healing dialogue in psychotherapy.* Northvale, NJ: Jason Aronson.

Gilligan, C. (1982). *In a different voice.* Cambridge, MA: Harvard University Press.

Goldberger, N., Tarule, J., Clinchy, B., & Belenky, M. (1996). *Knowledge, difference, and power.* New York: Basic Books.

Gur, R. C., Mozley, L. H., Mozley, P. D., Resnick, S. M., Karp, J. S., Alvi, A., Arnold, S. E., & Gur, R. E. (1995). Sex differences in regional cerebral glucose metabolism during a resting state. *Science, 267,* 528-531.

Haraway, D. (1991). Situated knowledges: The science question in feminism and the privilege of partial perspectives. In D. Haraway (Ed.), *Simians, cyborgs, and women.* New York: Routledge.

Harding, S. (1986). *The science question in feminism.* Ithaca, NY: Cornell University Press.

Hare-Mustin, R. (1983). An appraisal of the relationship between women and psychotherapy. *American Psychologist, 8,* 593-601.

Heilbrun, C. (1988). *Writing a woman's life.* New York: Random House.

hooks, b. (1983). *Feminist theory: From margin to center.* Boston: South End Press.

Howard, G. (1991). Cultural tales: A narrative approach to thinking, cross-cultural psychology, and psychotherapy. *American Psychologist, 46,* 187-197.

Jacklin, C. N. (1987). Feminist research and psychology. In C. Farnham (Ed.), *The impact of feminist research in the academy* (pp. 95-110). Bloomington: Indiana University Press.

Jagger, A. (1983). *Feminist politics and human nature.* Totowa, NJ: Rowman & Allenheld.

Jordan, J. (1991). Empathy and self-boundaries. In J. V. Jordan, A. G. Kaplan, J. B. Miller, I. P. Stiver, & J. L. Surrey (Eds.), *Women's growth in connection: Writings from the Stone Center* (pp. 67-80). New York: Guilford.

Krippner, S., & Murphy, G. (1973). Humanistic psychology and parapsychology. *Journal of Humanistic Psychology, 13*(4).

Lather, P. (1991). *Getting smart: Feminist research and pedagogy with/in the postmodern.* New York: Routledge.

Leslie, E. (1999). *Narratives from a womanist perspective: African American women ministers in the church.* Unpublished manuscript, Saybrook Graduate School.

Maguire, P. (1987). *Doing participatory research: A feminist approach.* Amherst: University of Massachusetts, Center for International Education.

Maslow, A. H. (1962). *Toward a psychology of being.* New York: Van Nostrand Reinhold.

May, R. (1953). *Man's search for himself.* New York: Van Nostrand Reinhold.

Perls, L. (1992). *Living at the boundary* (J. Wysong, Ed.). Highland, NY: Center for Gestalt Advancement.

Polanyi, M. (1958). *Personal knowledge: Towards a post-critical philosophy.* Chicago: University of Chicago Press.

Polkinghorne, D. E. (1988). *Narrative knowing and the human sciences.* Albany: State University of New York Press.

Reinharz, S. (1992). *Feminist methods in social research.* New York: Oxford University Press.

Ricoeur, P. (1976). *Interpretation theory: Discourse and the surplus of meaning.* Fort Worth: Texas Christian University Press.

Rogers, C. R. (1951). *Client-centered therapy.* Boston: Houghton Mifflin.

Rogers, C. R. (1980). Empathic: An unappreciated way of being. In C. R. Rogers (Ed.), *A way of being* (pp. 137-162). Boston: Houghton Mifflin.

Roszak, T. (1992). *The voice of the earth.* New York: Simon & Schuster.

Schneider, K. J. (1998, March). Toward a science of the heart: Romanticism and the revival of psychology. *American Psychologist, 53,* 277-289.

Serlin, I. A. (1992). In memoriam of Laura Perls. *The Humanistic Psychologist, 19*(1), 105-113.

Serlin, I. A. (1997, August). *Presidential talk: The history and future of humanistic psychology.* Paper presented at the annual meeting of the American Psychological Association, Chicago.

Serlin, I. A., & Shane, P. (1999). Laura Perls and Gestalt therapy: Her life and values. In D. Moss (Ed.), *Humanistic and transpersonal psychology: A historical and biographical sourcebook* (pp. 374-384). Westport, CT: Greenwood.

Smith, H. (2000). *Research practicum.* Unpublished manuscript, Saybrook Graduate School.

Spretnak, C. (1997). *The resurgence of the real: Body, nature, and place in a hypermodern world.* Reading, MA: Perseus.

Springer, S. P., & Deutsch, G. (1993). *Left brain, right brain* (4th ed.). New York: Freeman.

Starhawk. (1988). *Dreaming the dark: Magic, sex, and politics.* Boston: Beacon.

Weil, L. (1999, March). Leaps of faith. *Women's Review of Books,* pp. 21-22.

Wilber, K. (1986). *Transformations of consciousness.* Boston: Shambhala.

Woolf, V. (1989). *A room of one's own.* New York: Harcourt Brace Jovanovich. (Original work published 1929)

Wright, P. (1995). Bringing women's voices to transpersonal theory. *ReVision: A Journal of Consciousness and Transformation, 17,* 3-11.

Yalom, I. D. (1980). *Existential psychotherapy.* New York: Basic Books.

CHAPTER 4

Humanistic Psychology and Multiculturalism

A Review and Reflection

ADELBERT H. JENKINS

ONE OF THE MOST prominent African American intellectuals of the past century, W. E. B. Du Bois, noted nearly 100 years ago, "The problem of the twentieth century is the problem of the color line—the relation of the darker to the lighter races of men in Asia and Africa, in America and the islands of the sea" (DuBois, 1903/1994, p. 9). As we enter the new century, the relations among the different cultures of the world clearly still are a major problem for modern civilization. With respect to the United States, during the previous two centuries through its importing of slaves, through its colonization of native people, and as a result of the stream of immigration from all over the world, this country has become a special proving ground for ethnic group relations. Demand for full access to the opportunities offered to some by the society has been expressed in sharp but scattered protests throughout American history. However, during the latter half of the 20th century, these calls for justice burst into explicit and collective expression by the masses of people of color in the United States.

It is interesting to note in this regard that the humanistic approach to psychology evolved as a major theoretical approach during the latter half of the 20th century as well. Humanistic psychology, in its theory and therapeutic techniques, always has emphasized the human individual's capacity for choice, freedom, and self-development. With these as principal concerns, one might think that this approach would have much to offer people of color in America. By and large, however, psychologists of color have not flocked to humanistic psychology as a champion of their cause, and some have questioned the relevance of the humanistic position to the situation of people of color (Carter, 1995).

At the start of the new century, the country is rapidly becoming a multicultural society. It is particularly appropriate for the human potential movement to consider why ethnic communities of color have not seen humanism's body of theory and practice as particularly relevant. Does a humanistic approach to psychology, broadly considered, have something useful to contribute to psychological understanding in our increasingly pluralistic social milieu? I think that it does, and after a brief discussion of what might seem to be problematic issues in the humanistic position, I try to articulate the applicability of such a view (see also the chapter by Vontress & Epp [Chapter 29] in this volume).

There are a number of vantage points from which one could characterize the humanistic position. As we know, historically the humanistic view in psychology was posed as a "third force" (Maslow, 1968) to counter the behavioristic and psychoanalytic views. In so doing, it puts an emphasis on the individual and his or her capacities for growth. Chein (1972) noted that a humanistic position in psychology typically seeks to characterize the person as "an active, responsible agent, not simply a helpless, powerless reagent" (p. 6). The human in this image is one

> who actively does something with regard to some of the things that happen to him or her . . ., a being who seeks to shape [the] environment rather than passively permit [himself or herself] to be shaped by the latter, [and thus] a being . . . who insists on injecting [himself or herself] into the causal process of the world around. (p. 6)

As another humanistic writer put it, broadly speaking, it could be said that "the tie binding all humanists is [the] assumption that the individual 'makes a difference' or contributes to the flow of events" (Rychlak, 1976, p. 128).

DILEMMAS FOR THE HUMANISTIC APPROACH

Culture and "Informal Assessment"

There are two issues that I highlight as possibly problematic for humanistic psychology historically with respect to its attractiveness to people of color. It shares the first dilemma with all of American psychotherapy and psychology, and it follows on my opening reference to DuBois. It has to do with the nature of what Korchin (1976) might call the "informal assessment" activities of the clinician.[1] Informal assessment refers to the activities of person perception characteristic of all humans as they form impressions of others. As professionals and laypersons, in our daily lives we are continually involved in making judgments as to whether others are friendly or antagonistic, sad or happy, honest or deceitful. Empathic ability, or the capacity to "feel one's way into" another's emotional position, derives partly from these activities. The formal assessment activities of the clinician "involving interviews, tests, and systematic observation builds on, extends, and sharpens informal assessment, but it does not replace it" (p. 144).

The relevance of these considerations here is that, in considering clinical work with people of color in America, we need to remind ourselves that how we function as clinicians is related to who we are as people, over and above our training. The capacity to be empathic with clients of color is affected by the informal judgment processes that we bring to our work. Our informal assessment activities, on which our professional work rests, develop within a sociocultural framework. Formal assessment and therapy activities are bound to be influenced by the social and historical contexts in which they have developed. Humanistic therapists, like most psychologists, have been persons of European and Euro-American backgrounds and, like all persons, have been people of their cultures. As Jones (1985) noted regarding work with African American patients, whereas

> any client can invoke in a therapist an unhelpful emotional response . . . black patients may evoke more complicated countertransference reactions and [do so] more frequently. The reason for this seems to be that social images of blacks still make them easier targets for therapists' projections and that the culturally different client provides more opportunities for empathic failures. (p. 178)

This, of course, is not a particular indictment of humanistic therapists. In fact, many within the humanistic camp have been particularly progressive in their social perspectives. They have, nonetheless, tended to operate from a Western (European/ Euro-American) cultural understanding that might have seemed somewhat limiting to a non-Western view. In general, persons of color, especially those of working-class status, generally have not availed themselves of psychotherapy as readily as have white and middle-class persons (Sue, 1977). Humanistic therapists do not seem to have been more effective than other mainstream clinicians in reaching out to these groups.

Differences in the Sense of Individuality

The second issue has more to do with the Western conceptual perspective on personality and the sense of self than with practitioners as persons. The primary focus of mainstream psychotherapeutic viewpoints during the 20th century tended to be on the improved psychological functioning of the *individual* person. Such a way of addressing psychological problems can be seen to be an outgrowth of the particular indigenous view of the nature of individuality characteristic of Western societies. However, because the self can be seen to reflect "the shared moral understandings within a particular culture of what it means to be human" (Cushman, 1995, p. 23), the Western view on this topic is one that is not necessarily shared by other cultures.

A number of recent scholars have suggested that the cultural ideal for the self identified in the industrialized West (as represented especially by white, urban, middle-class males in the United States) puts an emphasis on autonomy and the uniqueness of the individual. Sampson (1988) called this "self-contained individualism." Such an orientation is characterized by *firm boundaries* demarcating the sense of self from *nonself other,* an emphasis on *personal control* and independence, and an *exclusionary* singular conception of the self (p. 16). Landrine (1992), in her discussion of cultural differences in the self concept, suggested that this mode of individuality, the "referential" self, is one in which the self's relationships to others are secondary and derivative. (Those writing on this topic recognize that many people in a given culture do not necessarily exemplify the major features of the dominant cultural frame and, in fact, may resist it in various ways. Thus, "many Americans would not claim that they are independent, autonomous entities; rather, they experience themselves as interdependent, highly social, and affiliative. Yet, they are constantly exposed to the individualist idea and its related practices because they live within a society created by and based on it" [Markus & Kitayama, 1994, p. 97].)

By contrast, the native construction of the ideal for personhood more frequently seen around the world is a sense of self-defined in *apposition* to, not in *opposition* to, others (Nobles, 1973). This is epitomized in the African worldview, which "suggests that 'I am because we are, and because we are therefore I am.' In so emphasizing, this view makes no real distinction between self and others" (pp. 23-24). Sampson's (1988) term for this conception of self is "ensembled individualism." Landrine (1992) labeled this construction of individuality the "indexical" self. In her view, the features of the indexical self may manifest in one of two ways depending on the particular societal context. The first is *self-as-social role*. Here, the self is defined by the way in which it fulfills the role prescriptions of the family and/or community. A second manifestation of the indexical self is *self-as-illusion* or *self-as-receptacle*. In this particular manifestation of individuality, the person is seen as a mere vessel through which immaterial forces, such as the spirits of one's ancestors or some vastly larger spiritual force, may act. In neither of these indexical conceptions is the self thought to be the primary source of action. "Instead, relationships, situations, and immaterial . . . forces are the culturally constituted and culturally acceptable explanations for one's 'own' thoughts, feelings, goals, fears, and behaviors" (p. 411).

Some of the writing on psychotherapy in multicultural contexts suggests that these latter types of sociocentric themes are likely to be more important to the worldview of many people of color living in America. Thus, for those persons of color who are recent immigrants or of lower/working-class backgrounds, and who therefore might be less acculturated to main-stream American society, thought needs to be given to the type of intervention technique chosen (Landrine, 1992). Modalities that are more consistent with features of these persons' cultural backgrounds, such as family and network therapies, might be more appropriate. Such methods do not emphasize the individual's autonomy and separateness in the handling of issues in life. This would seem not to be the focus of the more person-centered orientation of humanistic therapies.

However, there are broader political considerations that bear on these issues as well. The problem for ethnic minorities generally has not been that they have not known *how* to achieve individual development as persons. The problem has been that their opportunities to do so have been blocked. Throughout their history in America, for example, African Americans have thrilled to the principles of individual and human rights as expressed in the Declaration of Independence and the Constitution. They have subscribed to the idea that one improves one's status and that of one's ethnic group by improving oneself as an individual. For at least some in the African American community, one major way of doing so was through education, thereby making themselves ready to participate in the technological developments occurring in the nation during the late 19th and 20th centuries. But as prejudice and systematic discrimination steadfastly continued to place formidable obstacles in the way of their efforts, many African Americans came to abandon the idea that they could advance themselves by only working on themselves *as individuals*. During the height of the civil rights movement of the 1960s in particular, many African Americans began to espouse the notion that an individual's status was necessarily tied to that of his or her ethnic group and that the best way in which to make progress as an individual was through collective action that would promote *group* advancement. This tended to heighten ethnic consciousness even among some of those in the African American community whose individual efforts had made them relatively successful economically. Again, it would seem that the conceptual orientation of the developing human potential movement during the 1960s, although being led by progressive and fair-minded persons, might not have been seen as relevant to these types of goals.

To summarize the discussion so far, I have been saying that the humanistic movement, in its laudable effort to "recover the person in psychology" (Aanstoos, 1994), nevertheless has had certain difficulties in addressing the psychological situation of some cultural groups in the United States. For one thing, the humanistic movement has been led by men and women of Euro-American backgrounds who have at least partly been heirs to the privilege of a society that is culturally biased and often has been oppressive to the interests of people of color. This has been so even though humanists themselves usually did not consciously hold prejudicial views. Because our society has not been open to the perspectives of its many ethnic groups, the humanistic movement has not necessarily understood the cultural views of people of color in the United States. Specifically, the emphasis on *individual* choice and agency seems to run counter to an important aspect of the cultural traditions from which many people of color come, and this might have made the humanistic movement seem irrelevant to these people. However, it is my view that a closer consideration of some of the conceptual bases of the humanistic position on individuality may reveal that there is no necessary conflict

with the legitimate interests of people of color. I turn my attention to these issues in the remainder of the chapter.

THE CASE FOR HUMANISM IN A MULTICULTURAL PSYCHOLOGY

The orientation toward humanistic psychology that I draw on to support this idea is defined through a particular position toward the person as a psychological agent. In the view I am using here, an agent is a being who can behave so as to go along with, add to, oppose, or disregard sociocultural and/or biological stimulations (Rychlak, 1988). Agency is particularly reflected in the human capacity to exercise "dialectical" imaginative processes of human mentality in formulating meaning in life situations (Rychlak, 1994). This notion recognizes that an item or event in experience can be defined not only in exclusive regard to a specific referent ("demonstrative" thinking, in Aristotelian terms) but also by its simultaneous conceptual relation to the opposite of this referent. Dialectical mentality refers to the ability to appreciate the alternative ways—in fact, the opposite ways—of construing what seems to be a firmly structured social or physical circumstance. Although most of us like to deal with well-defined situations in our lives most of the time, in fact a number of options always are potentially available for characterizing any given event.

> [There is always a] quality of open alternatives in experience [that] demands that the human being affirm some . . . meaning at the outset for the sake of which behavior might then take place. . . . This affirmative necessity is another one of those *active* roles assigned to mind by humanists, because which pole of a bipolarity is affirmed

. . . is up to the individual and *not* to the environment. (Rychlak, 1988, p. 295, italics added)

Such a capacity involves being able to see things as they are (conventionally) presented and, at the same time, imagining how they might be different. The actor can set intentions that guide actions, perhaps in accord with or perhaps in opposition to received wisdom. However, within these constraints, there always are options for how one can conceive (construe or mentally construct) a situation.

This basic human dialectical symbolizing capacity sets the psychological basis for individual freedom of the will. It is the ability to contribute a necessary component of the conceptual grounds for defining the meaning of a situation by taking a stand or making a choice. In this view, the "freedom" in the *free will* term is the option for alternative conceptions of the given experience *prior to* the agent's affirmation that *this* as opposed to *that* is so. Having decided, the individual proceeds to act "willfully" or intentionally (i.e., "for the sake of"), furthering the meanings of such a conception. The apparent problem here is that it seems as if this conception of agency emphasizes the autonomy and independence of the individual self. This would make this notion appear to be irrelevant to those societies, organized along more collectivistic lines, in which individuality seems to be subordinated to the influence of the cultural context. However, this apparent contradiction can be resolved.

Individuality in the Collective

As Jenkins (in press) indicated, although it may be correctly argued that Westerners overvalue the importance of unique and masterful individuality, the recognition of the relational quality of non-Western cultures may incorrectly ignore the importance of individual agency in such societies. Whereas it is not possible to develop one's humanity except in a sociocultural context, it also is not possible to understand human experience and behavior without an understanding of irreducibly individual features of human action within those settings. The dialectic features of human agency provide an example. For example, the Confucian system has been a principal ethical scheme in cohesive, essentially sociocentric Asian societies for thousands of years. The Confucian scholar Tu Wei-ming (1985) noted that in this ancient perspective, the development of self "is a lifelong commitment which necessitates a ceaseless process of learning . . . through the disciplining of the body and mind . . . as an *active participant* in the living community—the family, the province, the state, and the world" (p. 232, italics added). So, for example, a primary life task of a man's self-development occurs within the framework of binding obligations to honor and respect his father. But paradoxically, for the sake of the group's survival, this maxim cannot be carried out through mere blind obedience. Patriarchs throughout history have been known to be fallible. Thus, sustaining the filial piety mandate involves the exercise of judgment and requires the son's "willing participation . . . socialized by a long and strenuous education supported by the community and sanctioned by the political leadership" (p. 234).

Tu (1985) recounted a legend from Confucian lore to illustrate the point. A young man, Shun, was confronted by a brutish father who plotted with Shun's stepmother and stepbrother to murder him. As he became aware of the various snares set for him, he did not capitulate to his father's treacherous intentions toward him. At the same time, however, he diligently acted in whatever ways he could fashion to sustain the father's honor and dignity. Shun recognized that a son's duty is to act so as not only to enhance his father as a living person but also to amplify the father's "ego ideal," that is, act in ways that would help the father to be the type of father he *should* be—in this case, a father who did not defile himself by murdering his son. This called for creative and thoughtful consideration of alternatives. Although this obviously is a heroic and perhaps fabled example, it need not overshadow the idea that the use of dialectically imaginative thinking, or psychological agency, is a necessary part of adapting to the more mundane challenges of daily living, even in sociocentric societies.

Similarly, Ramirez (1998) noted that among many North American Indian peoples, the central importance of community identity and responsibility to the group led each individual to feel himself or herself to be a representative of his or her assemblage. "I am the people" was typical of this sentiment. Yet at the same time, the people living in this tradition were expected to educate themselves and nurture their individual skills to the fullest. They were expected to develop their *free will*, or the capacity to recognize and choose among alternatives, by training themselves to be able to rise above selfish promptings and environmentally posed hardships so that they could make choices that were in the best interests of the group.

CONCLUSION

The humanistic perspective argues that all persons in whatever cultural context they find themselves make use of processes of individual agency in their daily living. These capacities, such as the ability to think dialec-

tically, cannot be understood as referable *to* the cultural context if one is to fully comprehend people's behavior in their social settings. In the humanistic account as presented here, the human being brings an evaluating mentality to the process of living within the proscriptions of a sociocultural context. The individual develops and functions through the personal constructions—the meanings—that he or she places on what is presented. The person's way of living in any cultural setting cannot be accounted for by the environment or biological factors alone. To say that the larger Gestalt of culture shapes individual functioning is to say, to some extent, that the social context serves as the grounds, or the basis, for the individual's self-conceptualizing. At the same time, the humanistic view is very much open to a multicausal perspective for accounting for human events. Thus, the development of one's human agency and personal uniqueness, or one's *humanness*, can occur only within the delimiting and nurturing context of the physical and sociocultural world in which the individual lives. This is a world that the individual strives to develop further through active engagement with it. Within the broad context of citizenship in the American nation, the humanistic view argues that cultural traditions will propose different ways of living out one's individuality. Particular cultural expressions in one group may be instructive to other groups within the larger society and come to have an influence on institutional change. For example, the attitudes that some more collectivistic societies have toward their elders may become a spur for rethinking how we provide economically and socially for the increasing numbers of elderly in our society as a whole. In principle, a humanistic psychological approach is fully compatible with multicultural differences. It acknowledges that the person, insisting on "injecting [himself or herself] into the causal process of the world around" (Chein, 1972, p. 6), does so in a cultural context to which he or she is fully committed.

NOTE

1. Assessment, in Korchin's (1976) view, refers to the clinician's efforts to gather information about the client so as to be of help to him or her. The humanistic clinician engages in assessment in the broader sense of trying empathically to enter the client's world so as to gain understanding of his or her experience and worldview.

REFERENCES

Aanstoos, C. M. (1994). Mainstream psychology and the humanistic movement. In F. Wertz (Ed.), *The humanistic movement: Recovering the person in psychology* (pp. 1-12). Lake Worth, FL: Gardner.

Carter, R. T. (1995). *The influence of race and racial identity in psychotherapy: Toward a racially inclusive model*. New York: John Wiley.

Chein, I. (1972). *The science of behavior and the image of man*. New York: Basic Books.

Cushman, P. (1995). *Constructing the self, constructing America: A cultural history of psychotherapy*. Reading, MA: Addison-Wesley.

Du Bois, W. E. B. (1994). *The souls of black folks*. New York: Dover. (Original work published 1903)

Jenkins, A. H. (in press). Individuality in cultural context: The case for psychological agency. *Theory and Psychology*.

Jones, E. E. (1985). Psychotherapy and counseling with black clients. In P. Pedersen (Ed.), *Handbook of cross-cultural counseling and psychotherapy* (pp. 173-179). Westport, CT: Greenwood.

Korchin, S. J. (1976). *Modern clinical psychology*. New York: Basic Books.

Landrine, H. (1992). Clinical implications of cultural differences: The referential versus the indexical self. *Clinical Psychology Review, 12,* 401-415.

Markus, H. R., & Kitayama, S. (1994). The cultural construction of self and emotion: Implication for social behavior. In S. Kitayama & H. R. Markus (Eds.), *Emotion and culture: Empirical studies of mutual influence* (pp. 89-130). Washington, DC: American Psychological Association.

Maslow, A. H. (1968). *Toward a psychology of being* (2nd ed.). New York: Van Nostrand Reinhold.

Nobles, W. W. (1973). Psychological research and the black self-concept: A critical review. *Journal of Social Issues, 29*(1), 11-31.

Ramirez, M. (1998). *Multicultural/multiracial psychology: Mestizo perspectives in personality and mental health* (2nd ed.). Northvale, NJ: Jason Aronson.

Rychlak, J. F. (1976). Is a concept of "self" necessary in psychological theory, and if so why? A humanistic perspective. In A. Wandersman, P. J. Poppen, & D. F. Ricks (Eds.), *Humanism and behaviorism: Dialogue and growth* (pp. 121-145). New York: Pergamon.

Rychlak, J. F. (1988). *The psychology of rigorous humanism* (2nd ed.). New York: New York University Press.

Rychlak, J. F. (1994). *Logical learning theory: A human teleology and its empirical support.* Lincoln: University of Nebraska Press.

Sampson, E. E. (1988). The debate on individualism: Indigenous psychologies of the individual and their role in personal and social functioning. *American Psychologist, 43,* 15-22.

Sue, S. (1977). Community mental health services to minority groups: Some optimism, some pessimism. *American Psychologist, 32,* 616-624.

Tu Wei-ming. (1985). Selfhood and otherness in Confucian thought. In A. J. Marsella, G. DeVos, & F. L. K. Hsu (Eds.), *Culture and self: Asian and Western perspectives* (pp. 231-251). London: Tavistock.

Part II

HUMANISTIC THEORY

Introduction to Part II

HUMANISTIC THEORY has one overriding mission: to unveil the "guts," core, or essence of what it means to be vitally human. At the same time that it engages this mission, however, it also is cognizant of an irony—the mission's futility. Although this qualification might sound odd, it is not particularly so for humanists. This is because, for humanists, the guts, core, and essence of anything is ever evolving, ever eluding our grasp, and ever transforming our assumptions. Yet, it is all worth the effort, according to humanists— even, and perhaps especially because of, its puzzlement.

Each generation of humanists, then, returns to the Quixotic quest in full awareness of its incomplete and provisional nature yet also, at the same time, in full awareness of its compelling and edifying nature. This part of the volume explores 11 contemporary angles on what it means to be vitally human. Beginning with 4 broad "Meta-Themes," this part then funnels into 7 narrower domains that both dovetail with and draw on the aforementioned themes.

In Chapter 5, an American pioneer of phenomenological psychology, Amedeo Giorgi, asks what happened to the psyche in psychology and how it can be restored to its rightful place. In response, he concludes that although the psyche is very much alive in humanity, in academic psychology it has been critically injured. "I am not arguing against inter-disciplinary studies such as neuropsychology or psychopharmacological analyses," he states. "What I am arguing is that there should be stronger psychological contributions to such studies and that psychology should not be riding on the coattails of the disciplines with which it is dialoging."

Precisely at a time when managed care, standardization, and medicalization threaten to extinguish the rich legacy of romanticism in psychology, in Chapter 6, Kirk Schneider argues for a return to such romanticism. Echoing Giorgi and augmenting his 1998 *American Psychologist* article, Schneider advocates a revival of the romantic heritage of Goethe, Blake, and others to resuscitate the promise of psychology.

In Chapter 7, prominent social critic Thomas Szasz turns his attention to the moral dimensions of the current psychological ethos. Specifically, he argues for a recognition of the authority of persons—as opposed to institutions—in the clarifying, formulating, and determining of their mental well-being. To the extent that this authority is endangered, humanity also is imperiled, he challenges.

Pursuing a separate but related line of inquiry in Chapter 8, the chair of humanistic psychology at the University of Southern California, Donald Polkinghorne, investigates contemporary conceptions of the self. In this authoritative commentary, he shows how contemporary perspectives on the self broaden but do not necessarily deepen psychological understanding. Despite the stereotypes about isolated individualism, Polkinghorne elaborates, humanistic psychology offers a dimension of intimacy and embodiment to the study of the self with profound interdisciplinary implications.

Marc Pilisuk leads off the "Contemporary Themes" section with two cutting-edge presentations on humanistic psychology and ecology (with co-author Melanie Joy) and humanistic psychology and peace. Pilisuk and Joy (Chapter 9) and Pilisuk (Chapter 10) challenge the assumption that humanism has little to contribute to either the community or the environment but also, equally, that humanism can stand alone within these contexts. They suggest that whereas humanistic psychology offers a keen personal angle on peace and the environment, there are broader issues at play. For example, when many people think of humanistic applications to peace, they immediately flash on that poignant moment when President Jimmy Carter connected personally with Menachem Begin and Anwar Sadat at the Camp David peace conference. When they think of humanizing the ecosystem, they envision beautifying a city housing project or pausing to marvel at a sunset. But the authors show that, in addition to these moving applications, humanistic psychology also must scrutinize the government policies that lead to the need for peace conferences and the corporate policies that eventuate in beautification projects. They conclude that only an amalgamated humanistic vision—personal, political, and spiritual—will humanize as intended.

In Chapter 11, Mike Arons and Ruth Richards plumb humanistic psychology's "bread-and-butter" issue—creativity. The chapter opens dramatically with the story of two related "insurgencies": humanistic psychology and creativity research. Conceived just 50 years ago, these parallel movements rocked the psychological world. In a personal and moving historical memoir, Arons and Richards animate the main inspirations for the humanistic-creativity insurgency: Abraham Maslow and

J. P. Guilford. But they do not stop there. Shifting to the contemporary scene, Arons and Richards then focus on the relevance of the insurgency legacy for three emerging concerns: chaos theory and modern science, health and healing, and everyday or "ordinary" creativity (i.e., the mead of life).

In the subsequent special section chapters, Thomas Greening and Edward Mendelowitz illuminate the rich and underappreciated seedbed of humanistic inquiry—the literary arts. In his opening section, Greening (Chapter 12) taps the linchpin of humanistic literary appreciation—intentionality. The humanistic investigator concerns himself or herself not only with the dynamics of a character's tragic past but also with the character's unfolding present, Greening proposes. Above all, Greening stresses, literature reminds "us that we are in the midst of the most powerful drama we will ever know personally and for which we have responsibility—our own lives." He then goes on to illustrate his thesis with analyses of three Albert Camus parables: *The Plague, The Fall,* and *The Stranger.*

Drawing on Federico Fellini's cinematic masterwork, *Ginger and Fred,* Mendelowitz (Chapter 13) also vivifies Greening's axioms. Hope and despair, folly and arrogance, denial and responsibility—they all are there in the film, which is a mirror of our times. Through Fellini's festival of life, Mendelowitz anatomizes culture, personality, and spirit. He leaves us with a caveat: "The filmmaker has much to teach us about the world we inhabit and share and the incompleteness we mostly embody and still long to surpass, about the sheer madness and mystery of being in a new millennial landscape and terrain." *Ginger and Fred,* Mendelowitz concludes evocatively, "is the artist's peek behind the proscenium arch. . . . It is psychology."

In Chapter 14, Gayle Privette transports us to the passionate science of peak performance and peak experience. Following the lead of Maslow as well as her own extensive investigations, she considers "peak" dimensions across numerous spheres of functioning—from daily life, to recreational activity, to work and home environments, to interpersonal relationships, to love. Although peak performers and experiencers are not always wise, graceful, or even competent, Privette shows, they almost invariably are engaged. This engagement pays off big, she concludes, as lives are transformed in its wake.

Opening the "Emergent Trends" section, David Feinstein (Chapter 15) presents a groundbreaking theory of personal myths. Personal myths are "organizing models that shape perception, understanding, and behavior." Combining these internalized models with field theories of nonlocal physics, Feinstein formulates his concept of "mythic fields" and then leads us on a most fascinating tour of anomalous human experiences—at-a-distance healing, "energy" medicine, "idio-savant" phenomena, and "psychotherapeutic resonance." He concludes that with a more precise understanding of the operation of mythic fields, it will be much more possible to "tailor" healing modalities.

In Chapter 16, David Elkins provides an intimate humanistic reflection on spirituality. Although "spirit" and "humanism" might at first seem antithetical, he shows how they can intricately meld. Drawing on his own hard-won experiences as well as those of existential-theological scholars, Elkins evokes a spirituality of awe. This is a spirituality that too often is overlooked today but that has a time-honored lineage. Like Buber, Otto, Tillich, and many before them, Elkins responds to the question "What does it mean to be fully experientially human?" with both humility and boldness and both conviction and doubt. He translates this sensibility to his philosophy, his theology, and his practice.

In Chapter 17, Chris Aanstoos rounds out this section with a humanizing reflection on technology. Beginning with the challenges to humanistic psychology posed by cognitive science, he moves on to the more general concerns raised by technology. By tracing the historical and psychological roots of these movements, Aanstoos illuminates not only their appeal but also their perniciousness. In the balance of his commentary, he highlights humanistic psychology's critical role, not just as an adversary of these burgeoning trends but also as a constructive respondent.

CHAPTER 5

The Search for the Psyche
A Human Science Perspective

AMEDEO GIORGI

THE PURPOSE of this chapter is to confront an intrinsically difficult and often bypassed question: What is the meaning of the psyche? I approach the question with modest ambitions. I do not expect to give a full answer; rather, I hope to revive and restore its legitimacy and perhaps move the discussion of it forward a bit. After all, the founders of our discipline were forced to answer the question because they were claiming to found a new science, and one can hardly make that claim without articulating, to some degree, what the new science is all about. The only trouble was that the founders of our discipline did not always agree on the subject matter, the approach to it, the methods to be employed, or even the value of the knowledge gained.

I am aware, of course, that the psyche, as the phenomenon to be explored by psychology, has been denied. The claim is made that the name represents an anachronism. Nevertheless, I do believe that the term has staying power and connotes a uniqueness not contained in its competitors—consciousness, the unconscious, behavior, and experience. Better yet, one way of responding to the challenge is to show how the term *psyche* can incorporate each of the four competing terms. The deeper challenge is to be able to discern accurately and articulate well the specific unique connotations of the psyche.

BIOGRAPHICAL ROOTS OF THE "SEARCH FOR THE PSYCHE"

I was a graduate student during the 1950s, and I followed an experimental program. I was trained as a psychologist specializing in the field of visual perception. However, I would say that the guiding idea of my training was *how to be scientific*. Indeed, how to become a scientist was enforced more vigorously than was sensitivity to psychological manifestations. This fact, in and of itself, could have been a great benefit if the balance between scientific emphasis and psychological sensitivity was proportional or if the sense of science being pursued was more in tune with the nature of psychological reality. However, neither desideratum actually was experienced by me. To be excellently scientific was the alpha and omega of all of my psychological education.

Now, I have to state another personal fact. The reason that I chose psychology as a career was because I read William James. I read the *Principles of Psychology* (James, 1890/1950) primarily, and I was especially attracted to the chapters that described the major characteristics of consciousness—that it was like a stream with substantive and "fringelike" parts, that it always was personal and selective, that consciousness is changing constantly even though organized, and that it deals with objects that are independent of it. These were the issues that I was interested in exploring and this was why I chose psychology as a profession, and I was keenly interested in knowing how knowledge about such themes had developed during the roughly half century since James had penned those words.

Needless to say, none of those themes were touched on during my entire psychological training, nor were there specialists where I studied who could guide readings in those areas. However, that disappointment is only part of the story. After all, I was only a student, and there was much about humans that I did not know, so I tried to appropriate as much knowledge as I could, arguing to myself that it never hurts to have general background knowledge about humans. However, I was curious about how the understanding of psychology evolved. I did not know what the psyche was, and I was hoping that somebody would tell me so

that I would have a better understanding of my own field.

Perhaps it was because I had this expectancy that I noticed something else about my education: It was dispersed and not unified. By this assertion, I mean something specific and concrete. If I wanted to know something more detailed about the stimulus that triggered off vision, then I went to the physics section of the library and read articles about the characteristics of light. If I wanted to know more about the receptor for vision, then I went to the biology or physiology section of the library to read about the anatomy of the eye or the retina. If I wanted some more nitty-gritty understanding of the visual process, then I also went to the chemistry section of the library to learn about the characteristics of rhodopsin or iodopsin. If I wanted to become methodologically sophisticated and learn about statistics and probability theory, then I found myself in the mathematics section of the library. Finally, if I reverted to my original interest in consciousness, then I read philosophers because psychologists had basically ceased talking about it. The ultimate irony for me, then, was that I was preparing for a career in psychology but rarely was in the psychology section of the library. It seemed to me that I was confronting a certain void. Where was psychology? Why did it seem so hidden? It was imaginable, of course, that psychology could be spread across all of these disciplines, but should it not at least contribute a unifying perspective? There was none that I could see.

Now, one could argue that perhaps my experiences were due to the subject matter that I chose to study—vision, a sensorial process heavily dependent on physical stimuli and the body. There is some truth to this, but it cannot be the whole story. That is because it never was made clear just how psychology unified the various perspectives. It seemed redundant. It was as though the visual experiences could be explained by an amalgamation of all of the other disciplines. I kept wondering why the consciousness that motivated me to become a psychologist was so assiduously avoided.

BENTLEY'S LAMENT

I tried to share my concerns about the gap in the center of the field with my peers, as well as with the few professors I knew well enough, but none seemed to share my concerns. Nevertheless, I carried these concerns with me throughout my studies and during my whole professional career. I read rather thoroughly in the history of psychology, and one day I came across a psychologist who saw exactly the same problem and, mirabile dictu, was even worried about it.

The psychologist was Madison Bentley, a student of Titchener who also taught at Cornell University. It is not surprising, perhaps, that he was sensitive to this issue given that his teacher was one of the psychologists most responsible for attempting to give psychology a unified definition, even in terms of consciousness. Bentley wrote an article titled "A Psychology for Psychologists" in 1930. Forgive me for using a long quotation from this article, but I do so because I do not think that the situation has changed today even though Bentley's (1930) article was written more than 70 years ago. That is, the content is somewhat dated, but the dynamics that created Bentley's lament still are alive and well.

> So we add one more photographic presentation of our common array of psychological facts and objects, leaving the unfortunate reader to create his own clear perspective out of many limited and divergent views.
>
> Our main and underlying contention will be that the present confusion of tongues, now widely deplored, is chiefly due to the fact that outside concerns and foreign interests have played too great a part in shaping and defining our field. The result is that we tend artificially to maintain our identity by virtue of the common label "psychology." Really psychological points of view and interests have been made secondary to evolutionism, the doctrine of heredity, zoological hypotheses, clinical medicine, psychiatry, theory of knowledge, the training of infants, educational doctrines, sociology, anthropology, propaganda for "efficiency," and amateurish conceits about "human nature." Were you to hold to the light any one of the many proposals for a "new psychology" and to look steadily through it, you would almost certainly see the obscuring shadow of one or another of the extra-psychological subjects named in this long list. And the main reason why so many persons are now ambitious to wear the badge and to speak a dialect of psychology is that practically all men can thereby serve some extraneous interest. A few terms borrowed from one of these outside sources—such terms as conditioning, instinct and habit, mental evolution, original nature, reflexes, learning, the unconscious, introversion, inferiority, intelligence, social responses, primitive man, and achievement test—are enough to give [an] air of scientific sophistication and to suggest the epithet "psychology." But practically all such terms are imports from without. Insofar as they are assimilated at all, they are assimilated not to psychology but to that particular brand of the subject which has derived from, and has been fashioned to serve, the context which the given

term implies. It is inevitable, therefore, that we should now possess multiple psychologies reducible to no common denominator; psychologies pluralized not in the sense of many envisagements of one and the same universe of facts and principles but in the sense of a common name for many diverse and divergent undertakings. (pp. 95-96)

After this long description about external influences on psychology, Bentley (1930) reduced the number of primary determiners to three: biology, medicine, and education (p. 96). I would say that psychology still is being largely determined by outside factors, but the top three today would be medicine, neurology, and cognitive sciences. Of course, with practitioners, managed care also has emerged as a determining factor. But none of this would be possible, of course, if we had a clearer idea of what we meant by psyche, clearly demarcating its essence and variations and establishing a good sense of its boundaries. Until we do that, we really can only expect more of the same.

Another manifestation of the fragmentation of psychology can be seen in the number and types of divisions that the American Psychological Association sponsors. There now are 52 divisions reflecting psychological interests, but the relationship among the divisions is totally a "chance" one. It is a type of relationship that Gestalt psychologists called *und-verbindungen* or a mere side-by-sideness. It reflects the fact that psychology has grown more by proliferation and extensiveness than by depth of knowledge in terms of the reduction of multifarious facts to basic principles or theoretical organization.

CONTEMPORARY EXAMPLES OF BENTLEY'S LAMENT

I now demonstrate that Bentley's perspicacious point about how psychology is driven by external factors still persists today. Many books concerning the mind and/or therapy were published during the 1990s that have stirred the popular imagination to some extent, and I use these more popular books to indicate the cultural expectations that currently exist, although psychologists' works are heavily referenced in all of these publications. The three books I have chosen as examples, all of which were reviewed in prestigious sources, are as follows: *The User Illusion: Cutting Consciousness Down to Size,* by Tor Norretranders, a Danish science journalist (Norretranders, 1991); *How the Mind Works,* by Steven Pinker, a cognitive scientist (Pinker, 1997); and *The Talking Cure: The Science Behind Psychotherapy,* by Susan Vaughan, a psychiatrist (Vaughan, 1997). First I cite some of the claims and statements made by these authors, and then I comment on them.

Pinker's (1997) book was written in such a way that one could easily believe that it was written to exemplify Bentley's point. Pinker states that he believes that the problems of the mind can be solved through the twin perspectives of cognitive science and evolutionary psychology. His strategy is to use "reverse engineering, i.e., the attempt to discover the functions of organs," with Pinker arguing that this "is what one should be doing to the human mind" (p. 165). Natural selection is used as a basic metaphysical principle; it explains "the appearance of design without a designer, using ordinary forward causation as it applies to replication" (p. 157). However, "the original molecule was not a product of natural selection (for that would lead to an infinite regress) but [rather] of the laws of physics and chemistry. Nevertheless, these replicators are wont to multiply, and over time, changes that are for the better will be accumulated" (p. 158). Pinker admits that "natural selection is not the only process that changes organisms over time, but it is the only process that seemingly *designs* organisms over time" (p. 158). An organism, for Pinker, is a "replicator with a well-engineered body" (p. 158). Indeed, Pinker writes that "organisms are not just cohesive blobs or pretty spirals or orderly grids. They are machines, and their 'complexity' is *functional adaptive* design: complexity in the service of accomplishing some interesting outcome" (pp. 161-162). Pinker asserts that the study of the modern mind is being accomplished by cognitive science. "What makes humans unusual, in addition to upright posture and precision manipulation, is our behavior and our mental programs that organize it" (p. 187).

As Bentley stated, the external interests are dominant here. Mind will be understood by cognitive science, and psychology will be understood in terms of the principles of evolution. In this scenario, does psychology have the right to make a discovery that might challenge its framework? Will the framework allow it?

Vaughan's (1997) approach is different, but the consequences for psychology are similar. She is a practicing psychoanalyst, but she feels compelled to ground psychoanalysis scientifically through neurology.

In this book, I present evidence that shows how psychotherapy literally changes the structure of your brain. It actually can alter the web of interconnecting neural cells found in the gray matter of the cerebral cortex. Taken together over time, these physical changes in how neurons are connected help us to produce new internal representations of self and other, changing the ingrained neural patterns about relationships that were laid down during early childhood development. The techniques of psychodynamic psychotherapy—from the use of free association and the exploration of dreams to the probing of the evolving patient-therapist relationship itself—make

sense in neuronal terms. I believe that the new evidence explains how and why the "talking cure" works at the cellular level. I hope to put neuron back into neurosis. (pp. 4-5)

Throughout the book, Vaughan (1997) first describes her relationship to a client and presents some of the dialogue, and then she departs from the level of experience and behavior to give interpretations of brain activity that could account for why the client was experiencing things or behaving the way in which he or she was behaving. It is as though understanding the experience or behavior itself was not sufficient and that only understanding pathologies in terms of neural activity could truly matter. Indeed, the talking cure is not reliable in and of itself; the scientific basis for its workability has to be established, and that comes from the activity of the brain.

Norretranders's (1991) perspective is that of science and technology, and by taking an objective perspective toward persons, he argues that the reality that consciousness gives us is much less than what the body as a whole receives. He places great stock in unconscious processing and believes that it is a source of richness that too often is discarded in contemporary culture. Thus, he speaks of our consciousness as a "user illusion," the term coming from computer design technology whereby the user of a computer is led to believe that the computer functions in terms of the symbols on the screen, whereas the engineer knows that a sequence of binary choices are being processed. In Norretranders's own words,

The user illusion, then, is the picture the user has of the machine. [The computer designers] realized that it does not really matter whether this picture is accurate or complete, just as long as it is coherent and appropriate. So, what matters is not explaining to the user how the computer works but [rather] the creation of a myth that is consistent and appropriate—and is based on the user, not the computer. (p. 291)

From this understanding, Norretranders (1991) goes on to make a series of significant statements:

▶ "The *I* experiences that it is the *I* that acts; that it is the *I* that senses; that it is the *I* that thinks. But it is the *ME* that does so. *I am my user illusion of myself*" (p. 292).

▶ "Just as the computer contains loads of bits that a user is not interested in, the *ME* contains loads of bits [that] the *I* is not interested in" (p. 292).

▶ "But it is not only the *I* experienced as our personal identity and active subject that is an illusion. Even what we actually experience is a user illusion. The world we see, mark, feel, and experience is an illusion" (p. 293).

▶ "There are no colors, sounds, or smells *out there* in the world. They are things we experience. This does not mean that there is no world, for indeed there is. The world just *is*. It has no properties until it is experienced. At any rate, not properties like color, smell, and sound" (p. 293)

▶ "I see a panorama, a field of vision, but it is not identical with what arrives at my senses. It is a reconstruction, a simulation, a presentation of what my senses receive. An interpretation, a hypothesis!" (p. 293).

As one commentator put it,

Seizing on the importance of discarded information as his reigning metaphor, [Norre-

tranders] moves from physics to psychology, steadily whittling down consciousness. It is estimated that of the millions of bits of information flooding through the senses at any moment, most [are] thrown away, and only a tiny fraction enter into human awareness. From this thin stream of data (engineers call it a low-bandwidth signal), the brain creates a picture—a simulation that we mistake for reality. (Johnson, 1998, p. 35)

Note how all three authors share a common theme, that which is the basis of Bentley's lament. Norretranders (1991) approaches the understanding of persons from the perspective of the physical sciences, computer design, and technology. He grants that there is consciousness, but it is simply brain activity, and it is not even as good as brain activity given that the brain receives so much more than consciousness apparently can appropriate. Vaughan (1997) practices psychoanalysis but, as a psychiatrist, believes that experiential-behavioral pathologies can be scientifically understood only in terms of neural processes. Because neural activity apparently participates in some of the dynamics of our experiential, meaningful world, one can use it to explain why we experience what we do. Finally, Pinker (1997) is a cognitive scientist who believes that principles of software design, plus principles of evolution, can totally account for human behavior. He grants that this total understanding is a long way off, but comprehension eventually will yield to those principles. So, physical science, neurology, evolutionary theory, and cognitive science can basically do the job that psychology was called to do. My argument is that this is not possible. But as Bentley said, there are psychologists who lend their labels to such external views. However, they are looking for the psyche in all the wrong places. Do they not realize that they are in the process of undermining their own field?

Now, specifically with respect to the point that Norretranders (1991) makes about consciousness, it is in a way ironic that he tries to diminish consciousness and sees its narrowness as a limitation and it as illusory. After all, it is this so-called illusory consciousness that has established the effectiveness of the unconscious achievements. All science, after all, is performed with waking consciousness. Second, there is a strong metaphysical assumption that the world is organized according to our understanding of physical nature, that the "really real" is all that information that arrives in bits. Yet, when Norretranders calls our consciousness illusory, he really is acknowledging that conscious awareness does not follow the bits in any literal way. As Gestalt psychology showed long ago, consciousness organizes and thematizes what it receives and makes a contribution to awareness. Thus, the assumption that consciousness should follow the inputs of bits in a passive way is not at all in accord with our experience of the world. Finally, Norretranders seems not to take seriously the fact that the unconscious is a mode of consciousness and, therefore, may well begin the transformation processes that he calls illusory and that we would call phenomenal.

With respect to Vaughan (1997), it is not at all clear why a demonstration that neurons can do what the organization of experience or behavior already does is an advantage for understanding neuroses or even more severe pathologies. It is not at all clear why remaining at the level of experience or behavior is less satisfying. We find in Vaughan passages such as the following:

> But Alice's networks, with their built-in association, have been organized since early childhood in the absence of this information. Once she learns about Max, it is too late for her to go back and reorganize all those interconnected themes on her own. Her networks already have evolved in a particular way. The new information gets stuck onto Alice's networks the way a wad of chewing gum is stuck to the theater seat.
> . . .
> Part of our task in psychotherapy is to reach into Alice's adult networks and disconnect those neurons that link growing up with sadness. This reexamination and reshaping of networks laid down in early life is probably the neurobiological equivalent of what analysis terms "working through." (pp. 45-46)

If the neural dynamics are merely equivalent to the experiential ones, then what is the gain? Is it really more empirical to speak about sad neurons than about sad persons? Do we really feel more enlightened if we know that the reconnecting of neural patterns is the basis of working through? Why is this redundancy in physical terms necessary? And is the neural explanation not dependent on the experiential given that it is only through consciousness (experience) that changes announce themselves? Is it not psychology's task to develop the understanding of those experiential-behavioral patterns?

With respect to Pinker's (1997) work, one can easily grant that cognitive science might account for cognition, but are psychological experiences and cognitive experiences identical? Is it not true that affects and desires cannot be exhausted by a cognitive approach even if we grant some cognitive dimensions of those experiences? And there are many criticisms of natural selection as a universal principle of selection even if it is partially successful.

So, let us ask the key question: Why is psychology so prone to be externally driven?

For one thing, because there is a lack of clarity with respect to the meaning of the psyche, many pretenders are quite eager to rush in. The "void" invites all sorts of analogical speculation. In addition, psychology's desire to be and look scientific is a big factor. One way in which a person can demonstrate that he or she is scientific is by using the language of science or terms that are in harmony with it. (Of course, when I use the term *science* without qualifiers, I mean natural science.) This motivates a type of languaging that could be detrimental to the clarification of psychological reality. Here, I need to make an additional point regarding psychological perspectives. We have heard that the cognitive perspective brought about a revolution in psychology from its behavioral past. However, from my perspective, the shift to the cognitive perspective is only a shift in content and not a true revolution. Indeed, I would argue that cognitive psychology is doing precisely what it is necessary to do so as to preserve the natural science paradigm in psychology and study cognitive processes. Moreover, its advance undoubtedly was aided by the development of the computer and various software programs.

This leads me to another critical point. Psychology seems to be fascinated by technology and pragmatism. Roback (1952) noted long ago that psychology in the United States, as opposed to that in Germany, was practical and technical. This certainly was true of the behavioristic era. Skinner admitted not only that he did not know what behavior was but also that he did not care. What he wanted to do was shape it. Much of cognitive psychology seems to be inspired along the same lines. Questions about cognition often are couched in terms that make certain practical functions possible rather than intrinsic questions about the phenomena as such. All of these factors tend to keep our languaging of the psyche away from essential description.

WHAT IS NOT MEANT BY MY COMMENTS

I have been making some strong assertions, and precisely because they are strong, I want to be sure that I am clearly understood. First, I am not saying that neurology, cognitive science, and evolutionary biology are not legitimate sciences. They are. I am only saying that they are not psychology. Second, I am not arguing against interdisciplinary studies such as neuropsychology and psychopharmacological analyses. What I am arguing is that there should be stronger psychological contributions to such studies and that psychology should not be riding on the coattails of the disciplines with which it is dialoguing. Third, I am not saying that a person who was trained as a psychologist cannot change interests and begin to function as another type of scientist. Clearly, one can, but then the psychological training may be incidental to the new effort, and that should be made clear. Fourth, I am not saying that there cannot be an applied psychology. I am only saying that the clearer we are about what is unique about the psychological approach, the better the applications will be. Fifth, I am not saying that analogical models for psychological phenomena cannot be used. I am only saying that we should remember that fact and not take them literally. Every analogy has unlike characteristics as well as like ones. Finally, to argue for a unique perspective for psychology is not to make it unique science in any special sense but only in the ordinary sense that every science has an irreducible perspective. Otherwise, it should not exist as a separate science.

TOWARD THE MEANING
OF THE PSYCHE

I do not pretend to have solved all of the problems surrounding the discrimination of psychical processes (Giorgi, 1982, 1986), but I would like to see in psychology types of thinking other than the type that I have been criticizing. My own perspective depends on the phenomenological approach, and the few things I say here depend on scholars writing within that approach (Giorgi, 1981).

The first thing that one can say is that the psyche does offer special problems for investigators because our subject matter is not clearly and noncontroversially delineated. This fact immediately forces the issue of perspective. One cannot say that the whole person—or the whole organism—purely and simply is what psychology seeks, for one can adopt many perspectives toward persons. Moreover, neither can one say that it is the person as such that is the subject matter of psychology (i.e., from the skin inward) because the person must relate to the environment or to his or her situation. And of course, this interaction is dialectical. That is, what is important for whatever we call *psychology* is the fact that the environment impinges on a person, and the human person initiates actions toward the world. Again, however, many disciplines take into account this double interaction, so the issue of perspective comes up again. How do we delineate the content to be called psychology? What phenomenon presents itself to the consciousness of the psychologist when he or she looks for psychological reality?

One way in which to look at this issue is to see what the quality of entities is like. We know that there are physical things without consciousness, and we also know that there are entities with the dimension of life. The latter are the subject matter of biology. What quality is added to "bios" for the psyche to appear? Following Straus (1956/1963), I would say *worlds*. Worlds are correlated with entities—or organisms—that have sensoriness and motility. That is, psychology emerges with beings that are capable of receiving impingement from the world and move about in it. So far, then, the psyche would refer to a functioning that would include worlds, and here I would add a further restriction: Psychology has to do with individuated worlds, although these could be generalized into types such as the world of the rat, the world of the pigeon, and the differentiated worlds of humans (e.g., entertainment, finance).

If there is a psyche, then it always is attached to an entity that has bios or an organism. Psyches never appear isolatedly, nor do they attach themselves to physical things. That is why a mechanistic approach to a human or to psychological reality, understood literally, always falsifies. Mechanistic thought can be applied to the human psyche only analogically. That is why a computer model of mind can, at best, be only an analogy. The basic practical proof is the fact that any machine made by humans can be taken apart, the parts all can be laid down side by side, they then can be put back together, and the machine can function again. No attempt to keep the entity alive is necessary, as with organisms. That is because a machine is grounded by the principle of *partes extra partes*, that is, by external relations. Entities manifesting life have different organizing principles, and so would entities capable of bearing psychological life.

I have argued that the psyche extends bios by establishing relationships with a world within which it can act and react, against which it can resist, or with which it can harmonize. But how does it do this? We have to answer *through consciousness and bodies.* I offer the suggestion that the psyche refers to a level of integration of mind and body with horizontal relations to the world and vertical relations with itself. However, psychology would be interested in only a certain level of integration of consciousness-body. Not every relation between consciousness and body would be psychological, and this thought again implies perspective. That is, there are certain levels of conscious functioning that would not be of interest to psychology, such as logical and mathematical thinking. Similarly, there would be aspects of the body that would not be of direct interest to psychology, such as anatomy and neurology. Rather, psychology would be directed toward the integrated functioning of consciousness-body that we could call *subjectivity.* This calls for a little elaboration.

It is important to bear in mind that in the phenomenological tradition, the essence of consciousness is intentionality, not awareness. *Intentionality* means that consciousness always is directed to an object that transcends the act in which it appears. Basically, this means that consciousness is a principle of openness. By means of it, we are open to a world. The body shares the intentionality of consciousness. It partakes of the directedness toward the world, and so does the unconscious, only awareness often does not accompany this directedness. Nevertheless, all those achievements that Norretranders (1991) speaks about that he assigned to a "ME" still are achievements of what we call consciousness, but they are not accompanied by awareness. However, reflection on such unaware achievements also belong to consciousness, so some access to them is possible. The point here is that the body as a subjectivity directed toward the world is the sense of the psychological body. But in this sense, the body shares subjectivity with a series of conscious acts that are not necessarily acted out bodily.

Psychology, then, is interested in a subjectivity engaged with a world in an individualistic way and with the interpreted sense-makings of the world as constituted by individuals. Because the body acts, behavior is involved, and because of impingements from and openness to the world, experience is included. Because of bodily engagements with the world and others without awareness, the unconscious is included, and because of spontaneity and acts of deliberate initiative, consciousness is included. The psyche then would be a certain perspective on the integrated functioning of all of them. But psychology does not exhaust those four topics. There always is some remainder that belongs to each of them that offers itself for analysis for other disciplines.

So far as the scientific study of the psyche is concerned, another degree of complexity enters, a complexity articulated best by the French philosopher Maurice Merleau-Ponty. Merleau-Ponty (1942/1963) pointed out that Western scholarly traditions have been very good with two types of objects: Philosophers developed expertise in dealing with ideas, and scientists developed expertise in dealing with things. Merleau-Ponty made the point that behavior (and I would say the psyche) is neither thing nor idea, and that is one reason why we have problems delineating and comprehending it. Moreover, behavior and the psyche present themselves primarily to perceptual consciousness, which is a level of consciousness that is nontransparent. So, the opacity of the psyche is offered to nontransparent perceptual consciousness, and this relationship does not fall neatly into the traditional categories of knowledge. That is another reason why psychological reality has eluded sharp analyses and why progress within psychology has been slow.

Certain other characteristics of the psyche need to be mentioned even though the context does not allow sufficient time for me to provide arguments. An argument can be made that the psyche is guided primarily by interests rather than truths or, in other words, by "truths for me." Its structures are primarily para-rational or para-logical. The norms it produces are contingent norms (Giorgi, 1993). That is, they could be other than what they are. The objects constituted by the psyche are para-objective, and this also implies that a level of intentional functioning has to be discerned that is other than that of the objective intentionality articulated by Husserl. Indeed, psychic life is a contingent life. It is a life of making sense of many situations that are not of our making, which is why access to the psychological should be through the meanings lived by engaged embodied subjectivities.

If what I am saying about the psyche is at least partially true, then what is called for—what these phenomena demand—are genuinely new rigorous approaches to study them. We are encountering qualities and types of phenomena that are not directly confronted by other disciplines. We certainly can benefit from past scientific achievements, but we also must learn how to discern and respect the uniqueness of our own phenomena. However, an original approach can emerge only if psychology dares to break from the natural scientific tradition and its technological offshoots. Rather, philosophers of science concerned about psychological science should be asking what framework is required for psychological science given its ambivalent phenomena. We should be asking what would do for psychology that technology does for natural science instead of seeking technological solutions to problems of psychology. Let us not be afraid to depart from the known realities of physical nature or things to deal with the psyche, for the psyche offers scientific consciousness peculiar characteristics not found in nature or ideas such as intentionality and meanings. Let us not be afraid to pursue phenomena and modes of understanding that might upset the status quo. I do not mean anything exotic by the latter statement. I simply mean the pursuit of "psycho-logic" to wherever it leads. Let us seek the psyche where it lives, with the human—or other organism—in its lived relationship with others and the world.

REFERENCES

Bentley, M. (1930). A psychology for psychologists. In C. Murchisin (Ed.), *Psychologies of 1930* (pp. 95-114). Worcester, MA: Clark University Press.

Giorgi, A. (1981). Ambiguities surrounding the meaning of phenomenological psychology. *Philosophical Topics, 12,* 89-100. (Special supplement to *Phenomenology and the Human Sciences*)

Giorgi, A. (1982). Issues relating to the meaning of psychology as a science. In G. Floistad (Ed.), *Contemporary philosophy: A new survey* (Vol. 2, pp. 317-342). The Hague, The Netherlands: Martinus Nijhoff.

Giorgi, A. (1986). The meaning of psychology from a scientific phenomenological perspective. *Études Phenomenologiques, 2*(4), 47-73.

Giorgi, A. (1993). Psychology as the science of the paralogical. *Journal of Phenomenological Psychology, 24,* 63-77.

James, W. (1950). *Principles of psychology.* New York: Henry Holt. (Original work published 1890)

Johnson, G. (1998, May 3). This is a simulation [review of *The User Illusion* by Tor Norretranders]. *New York Times Book Review,* p. 35.

Merleau-Ponty, M. (1963). *The structure of behavior* (A. Fisher, Trans.). Boston: Beacon. (Original work published 1942)

Norretranders, T. (1991). *The user illusion: Cutting consciousness down to size* (J. Sydenham, Trans.). New York: Viking.

Pinker, S. (1997). *How the mind works.* New York: Norton.

Roback, A. A. (1952). *Hisory of American psychology.* New York: Library Publishers.

Straus, E. (1963). *The primary world of senses.* Glencoe, IL: Free Press. (Original work published 1956)

Vaughan, S. (1997). *The talking cure: The science behind psychotherapy.* New York: Putnam.

CHAPTER 6

The Revival of the Romantic Means a Revival of Psychology

Kirk J. Schneider

> *Psychology, or at least American psychology, is a second-rate discipline. The main reason is that it does not stand in awe of its subject matter.*
>
> —J. J. Gibson
> (cited in Reed, *James J. Gibson
> and the Psychology of Perception,* 1988)

> *St. Peter to a psychologist at the Pearly Gates: "We sent you to earth for 72 years to a Dantean circus and you spent your days and nights at sideshows!"*
>
> —R. May (*Psychology
> and the Human Dilemma,* 1967)

ROMANTICISM is an artistic and intellectual movement that originated during the late 18th century. Although romanticism rebelled against formal (technical) reason, it was not, for the most part, an irrational movement (Jamison, 1993; Jones, 1969). To the contrary, romanticism attempted to broaden rationality, fortify it with affect and intuition, and relate it to the most puzzling problems of life—love, freedom, and fear (Jones, 1969). In short, romanticism addressed what it viewed as our fundamental relationship to being or the universe and not merely to part-

AUTHOR'S NOTE: This chapter is dedicated to the passion, spirit, and romantic realism of Rollo May. It is adapted from my article of the same title that appeared in a 1999 issue of the *Journal of Humanistic Psychology* (Vol. 39, No. 3, pp. 13-29). A more comprehensive version of the article was published in the March 1998 issue of *American Psychologist* (Vol. 53, pp. 277-289).

processes such as physiology, behavior, and mentation[1] (Barrett, 1958; Jones, 1969; Tillich, 1952).

Although romanticism had its excessive sides, such as idealization and melodrama (Kaufmann, 1968), it also nourished psychological insight (Barrett, 1978; Tillich, 1952). Some of the most prominent thinkers and artists in history have attested to this contention (Jamison, 1993), as have pioneering psychologists (e.g., James, 1902/1936).

Despite these facts, a split has occurred in American psychology. Four decades after Hebb (1960) urged a "thoroughgoing behavioristics of the thought processes" (p. 736), and during the past 20 years in particular, American psychology has conspicuously distanced itself from its romantic roots. Since about 1975, the most prominent manifestation of these roots, the humanistic psychology movement,[2] has been relegated to a quaint afterthought in the curriculum of most American Psychological Association (APA)-accredited doctoral programs in psychology (Giorgi, 1987; Mayne, Norcross, & Sayette, 1994; Wertz, 1992). At the undergraduate level, humanistic psychology receives slightly more acknowledgment, but mainly with regard to the works of Abraham Maslow and Carl Rogers and not those of the more philosophically inclined existential-humanistic thinkers such as Rollo May, R. D. Laing, Ernest Becker, and James Bugental (Churchill, 1988).

ROMANTICISM ON THE ROPES

In this chapter, I propose that existential-humanistic psychology is the latest and most prominent successor to the romantic psychology embodied in the works of American thinkers such as Henry David Thoreau and Ralph Waldo Emerson at the end of the 19th century and carried on by America's seminal psychologist and philosopher William James (Leary, 1992; Taylor, 1992). This thread then was revived and strengthened with the publication of May, Angel, and Ellenberger's (1958) landmark work, *Existence: A New Dimension in Psychiatry and Psychology*, which imported the European version of existential-humanistic psychology to America.

As indicated previously, however, existential-humanistic inquiry has been declining within mainstream psychology. It has been usurped by a preoccupation with "environments," measurable and overt behaviors, physiological substrates, and schematic explanations of nonschematic human experiences. Let us look more closely at these problems and the consequences that they have wrought.

DISCARDING THE ROMANTIC AND ITS PRICE

In my own field of clinical psychology, traditional approaches have converged on information processing, psychopharmacology, and short-term modalities to transform dysfunctional behavior (Norcross, Alford, & Demichele, 1992). The APA has launched a bold new program aimed at standardizing clinical training—the "National College"—and Division 12 of the APA has formed a task force to consider "manualizing" clinical practice (Stern, 1994-1995; Task Force on Promotion and Dissemination of Psychological Procedures, 1995).

The central question, however, is the following: Are we *prepared* for such developments? That is, are we prepared to trade centuries of investigation that stress qualitative, holistic, and idiographic features of human functioning (Allport, 1961) for a positivistic-experimental tradition empha-sizing quantitative, atomistic, and nomothe-tic features of human functioning? Are we prepared, for all practical purposes, to sever our ties with the arts and humanities, virtu-ally banishing them from the education of our trainees? Are we prepared to lose artis-tic and philosophically inclined graduates in psychology and psychotherapy? In short, do we see where we are headed?

I do not believe that we fully perceive the implications of our redirection in psychol-ogy. Indeed, it seems painfully evident that mainstream psychology's own findings bode ill for its aims.

Consider, for example, the evident incon-sistency and disarray in the field of psycho-therapy outcome research. The meta-analytic finding that the leading therapeutic orientations achieve equivalent efficacy (Lipsey & Wilson, 1993; Smith, Glass, & Miller, 1980) seems adequate in itself to dis-courage the standardizing of therapeutic practice, but there are many more problems that such research has unveiled. One of the most glaring problems is defining the terms of therapeutic efficacy. Is it symptom based, internal or subjective, or physiologically measurable (Garfield & Bergin, 1986)? Who is in the best position to judge thera-peutic effectiveness—the therapist, an out-side "expert," a family member, or the cli-ent? (Interestingly, it is *clients'* judgments of therapeutic processes that correlate best among the disparate evaluators with regard to therapeutic outcome [Lambert, Shapiro, & Bergin, 1986], and it is a glaring feature of that client-based perspective that "non-specific" factors such as warmth and genu-ineness are cited by clients as the most thera-peutically salient, whereas technical and professional variables are viewed as second-ary [Duncan & Moynihan, 1994; Lambert & Bergin, 1994]. Recent survey data, more-over, indicate that clients prefer long-term, "growth"-oriented therapy over short-term, "medicalized" approaches ["Mental Health," 1995].)

In addition to the perplexities just cited, there has been a paucity of studies examin-ing alternative therapeutic modalities such as that of existential therapy (for excep-tions, see Mahrer, Fairweather, Passey, Gingras, & Boulet, 1999, and Norcross, 1987). This limited research output is attributable, in part, to alternative thera-pists ourselves, but it also surely is due to the reluctance on the part of mainstream psy-chology to accept the qualitative, phenome-nologically based research that we deem to be appropriate to our inquiries (Giorgi, 1970; Norcross, 1987).

In light of this background, psychology's move to standardize therapeutic procedures and the methods designed to evaluate them seems misguided. It also does not seem pru-dent to discard the romantic (idiographic, qualitative) element in such research, which presses for acknowledgment at every turn:

> Technical requirements have led us to quantify and calculate a great many more parts of life; but preoccupied as we may be with objects and data, the human subject is still there, restless and unappeased, haunt-ing the edges of the technical world. (Barrett, 1978, pp. 240-241)

The consequences of discarding the ro-mantic in psychology are further damaging in the domains of personality and psychopathology. How many more studies of symptom clusters and of diagnostic and prognostic profiles do we need? Can norma-tive data assist us in understanding *indi-viduals'* needs, desires, and conflicts? Can diagnostic groups reveal *individuals'* dispo-sitions, requirements for treatment, or propensities for success? To what extent do these groups truncate our understanding of individual lives or of experiences that cannot be quantified or objectified?

What is the price for suppressing the artist's eye, our intuitions and imaginations, and our palpable contacts with subjects in psychology? To illustrate this problem, I present two different versions of psychological inquiry. The first is from Bergmann and Spence's (1944) classic experimental approach, and the second is from Vincent Van Gogh:

> Scientific empiricism holds to the position that all sciences, including psychology, deal with the same events, namely, the . . . perceptions of the scientist himself. . . .
>
> The empiricist should . . . not (in reporting responses of subjects) . . . use any mentalistic terms which have not been introduced from a physicalistic meaning basis. (Bergmann & Spence, 1944, pp. 3-4)

> Standing behind many pictures of almost unknown artists, one feels that they are made with a will, a *feeling*, a passion, and love. . . . Am I then so far wrong when I criticize . . . those critics who in these days talk humbug about this so often misused word, "technique." . . .
>
> To paint direct from life means to . . . be in the fields as are the peasants; in summer to stand the heat of the sun, in winter to suffer from snow and frost, not indoors but outside, and not just during a walk, but day after day like the peasants themselves. (Van Gogh, cited in Stone, 1833/1937, p. 299)

According to Van Gogh, then, psychological (and artistic) inquiry begins with passion, feeling, and love; it does not, as Bergmann and Spence (1944) imply, start with the sense perceptions of the investigator. Moreover, according to Van Gogh, to understand the subject, the investigator needs to experience him or her, not merely observe the individual at a distance as if he or she were a thing.

Elsewhere, Van Gogh writes,

> I see in my work an echo of what struck me; I see that nature has told me something, has spoken to me, and that I have written it down in shorthand. In my shorthand may be words that cannot be deciphered, mistakes and deficiencies, but there is something in it of what the forest, beach, or figure told me, and it is not a tame or conventional language. (cited in Graetz, 1963, p. 50)

The final difference between Van Gogh and Bergmann and Spence, then, is the use of the investigator's "language"—the degree to which it reflects the *subject's* position, explicates the *subject's* concerns, and unveils the *subject's* depths.

Returning to the areas of personality and psychopathology, what is the specific impact of the Bergmann and Spence (physicalistic) inquiry process? Again, I answer with a series of vignettes. The first set of vignettes concern clinical states of depression. Two are drawn from mainstream psychology (i.e., the *DSM-IV* [*Diagnostic and Statistical Manual of Mental Disorders*; American Psychiatric Association, 1994] and cognitive psychology), and two are drawn from literary narratives.

Consider, then, a *major depressive episode* as defined by the *DSM-IV*:

> (1) depressed mood . . . most of the day, nearly every day, as indicated by either subjective report (e.g., feels . . . empty) or observation made by others (e.g., appears tearful). (2) markedly diminished interest in all, or almost all, activities . . . (as indicated either by subjective account or obser-

vations by others. . . . .). (3) significant weight loss . . . or weight gain (e.g. , a change of more than 5 percent of body weight in a month). . . . (4) insomnia or hypersomnia nearly every day. (5) psychomotor agitation or retardation. . . . (6) fatigue or loss of energy. . . . (7) feelings of worthlessness. . . . (8) diminished ability to think or concentrate. . . . (9) recurrent thoughts of death. (American Psychiatric Association, 1994, p. 327)

Now, consider this description of depression by Goethe (1790/1961) from his classic drama *Faust*:

Faust:
I shall not cease to feel in all attires,
The pains of our narrow earthly day,
I am too old to be content to play,
Too young to be without desire,
What wonders could the world reveal?
You must renounce! You ought to yield!
That is the never-ending drone
Which we must, our life-long hear
Which hoarsely, all our hours intone
And grind into our weary ears.
Frightened I waken to the dismal dawn,
Wish I had tears to drown the sun
And check the day that soon will scorn
My every wish and not fulfill one. . . .

When night descends at last, I shall recline
But anxiously upon my bed;
Though all is still, no rest is mine
As dreams enmesh my mind in dread. . . .

And thus existence is for me a weight,
Death is desirable, and life I hate.
(p. 175)

Next, let us compare a cognitive description of depression to a literary one. Here is what Beck (1976) has to say:

The thought content of depressed patients centers on significant loss. The patient perceives that he has lost something he considers essential to his happiness or tranquility; he anticipates negative outcomes from any important undertaking; and he regards himself as deficient in the attributes necessary for achieving important goals. (p. 84)

Now, consider what Rilke (1904/1993) has to say about depression in his *Letters to a Young Poet*:

Dear Mr. Kappus . . . You have had many and great sadnesses. . . . But, please, consider whether these great sadnesses have not rather gone right through the center of yourself? Whether much in you has not altered, whether you have not somewhere, at some point of your being, undergone a change while you were sad. . . . We must assume our existence as *broadly* as we in any way can; everything, even the unheard-of, must be possible in it. That is at bottom the only courage that is demanded of us: to have the courage for the most singular and the most inexplicable that we may encounter. (pp. 63, 67)

Finally, let us consider two versions of the dynamics of *neurotic anxiety*. The first is a Freudian version, likely to be used in any basic primer on Freudian psychology, and the second is from William Shakespeare's *Macbeth*:

Neurotic anxiety is aroused by a perception of danger from the instincts. It is a fear of what might happen should the anti-cathexes of the ego fail to prevent the instinctual object-cathexes from discharging themselves in some impulsive action. (Hall, 1954, pp. 64-65)

To-morrow, and to-morrow, and to-
  morrow,
Creeps in this petty pace from day to
  day,
To the last syllable of recorded time;
And all our yesterdays have lighted
  fools
The way to dusty death. . . .
Life's but a walking shadow; a poor
  player,
That struts and frets his hour upon
  the stage,
And then is heard from no more: it is
  a tale
Told by an idiot, full of sound and
  fury,
Signifying nothing. (Shakespeare,
  1975b, p. 1068)

What then, do these vignettes convey to us? What do they inform us about the price of discarding the romantic? First, they inform us about how mechanistic traditional psychology has become. A brief comparison of the language styles used in the respective vignettes readily elucidates this point. The *DSM-IV* vignette, for example, uses arid objectivistic language. Its focus is on the measurable (i.e., discretely categorizable) features of depression. The Goethe vignette, on the other hand, uses a rich and connotative language. Its focus is on the experience

of depression, its internal sense, and its affective and bodily components (e.g., "tears to drown the sun," "existence is for me a weight"). The cognitive description of depression highlights the intellectual distortion that occurs following loss (e.g., "negative" schemata). Rilke's description, on the other hand, highlights the experiential component of sadness (it goes "right through the center," he says). He also highlights the multidimensionality of depression ("everything, even the unheard-of, must be possible in it"). The Freudian perspective on anxiety, finally, employs an arcane and all-too-familiar psycho-jargon. The interplay of drives, objects, and prohibitions *atomizes* psychological functioning and begs the question: Where is the *person* in this formulation (May, 1983)? Shakespeare's rendering of anxiety, by contrast, *embodies* the phenomenon ("all our yesterdays have lighted fools The way to dusty death") and takes us to the core of anxiety ("Life's but a walking shadow . . . That struts and frets his hour upon the stage").

To summarize, the problem of traditional psychology is one of scale. The *DSM-IV* locates dysfunctional behavior in overt and measurable symptoms, cognitive psychology locates it in expectations and schemata, and psychoanalysis locates it in sexual-aggressive conflicts. The romantic genre, however, validates our *holistic* sense of dysfunctional experience. It locates dysfunctional (as well as functional) experience, not only in the part-processes of traditional psychology but also (and more importantly) in people's relation to being, creation, and existence.

The great problem, of course, is how to translate these pithy narratives—how to draw on them for practical psychological application. That this was a problem engaged with relish by America's "founding" psychologist, James, is no small testament to its significance (Leary, 1992, p. 152).

James's "system of thought," he elaborated, was "romantic" rather than "classic." It was "concrete, uncouth, complex, overflowing, open-ended, and incomplete" (quoted in Leary, 1992, pp. 158-159). It emphasized the "more" of human experience "that continuously supersedes [itself] as life proceeds" (James, 1904/1987, p. 1173). Finally, it gave impetus to "radical empiricism," which "neither admit[s] into its constructions any element that is not directly experienced nor exclude[s] from them any element that is directly experienced" (p. 1160; see also Leary, 1992).

The price for discarding the romantic in psychology, therefore, is precisely that we discard James's radical empiricism and its enveloping "more." It is precisely that we delimit affects, intuitions, and the copious discoveries of literature, which even Freud (1926/1959), in his more humanistic moments, prized above all other forms of psychoanalytic education (see also Hillman, 1975; May, 1985, 1991; Schneider, 1993; Schneider & May, 1995). Yet, I ask my colleagues: Where, but from the romantic stirrings of artists (or the artistically minded), is subjectivity so well articulated (e.g., as in Van Gogh), or affect (as in Goethe), or kinesthesia (as in Fitzgerald), or symbolism (as in Poe), or being (as in all four)? Where, but from the romantic stirrings of artists, are the "possibilities" in sadness (Rilke, 1904/1993, p. 64); the "intelligence" in madness (Poe, 1842/1981, p. 301); the "health" in disease (Eliot, 1970, p. 187); and the cosmological illuminations in bereavement (Shakespeare, 1600/1975a), love (Whitman, 1855/1959), ambition (Shelley, 1818/1981), and human development (Pascal, 1654/1991) as eloquently wrought?

Moreover, who but the most aristically minded psychologists would venture to draw on these rich portrayals? Consider, for example, the works of Giorgi (1970), Polkinghorne (1983), and Van Kaam (1966) in the area of methodology; Barron (1963) and Jamison (1993) in the area of creativity; Becker (1973), Greening (1965), Laing (1969), Maslow (1968), May (1981), and Schneider (1993, 1999) in the areas of personality and psychopathology; Kobasa (1979) in the area of psychophysiology; and Kierkegaard (1844/1957) and Vandenberg (1991) in the area of human development.

The problem is that we are in danger of losing these existential-humanistic threads in psychology. Managed care, corporate funding, the growing enchantment with psychotropic drugs, and the traditional bias against subjectivity in our profession are making it increasingly difficult for such applications to survive (Breggin, 1991; Giorgi, 1987).

On the other hand, Bugental and Bracke (1992) pointed out that there may be a backlash against this menacing trend. They reasoned from the standpoint of psychotherapy that if standardized approaches disappoint enough people, then romantic alternatives will be viewed as more appealing. Furthermore, they argued, standardized approaches will be viewed as entrées or stepping-stones for many clients to deeper and fuller engagements. Although I am encouraged by Bugental and Bracke's perspective, in my view, many more crises might have to be endured before that perspective is widely and concretely realized.

THE POSTMODERN "ALTERNATIVE"

Another prominent counterbalance to the standardization of psychology is postmodernist philosophy (Berger & Luckmann, 1966; Cushman, 1990; Gergen, 1994;

Sampson, 1993). Postmodern philosophy holds three essential tenets: There are no absolute truths, all realities are socially constructed, and fluidity among realities is desirable (O'Hara & Anderson, 1991). To put it succinctly, postmodernism abandons "representationalism" in philosophical discourse, that is, "the assumption that there is (or can be) a determinant (fixed or intrinsic) relationship between words and world" (Gergen, 1994, p. 412).

This deconstruction of mainstream reductionistic psychology is welcome news to those of us calling for a romantic psychological revival. To the degree that postmodernism curbs the conventional trend toward objectifying (and quantifying) psychological data and upholds the sanctity of unique and alternative discourses, the postmodernist position is compatible with the romantic.

However, to the degree that postmodernism makes a "shrine" of those disparate discourses, approaches them as selfsealing doctrines, and forgets our collective (i.e., human) situation on this planet, postmodernism cultivates its own reductionism and runs directly counter to the romantic sensibility. This is because romanticism goes beyond the unique viewpoints of subjects and cultures and attempts to understand their common conditions.

Drawing on feeling and intuition, romanticism attunes to the life that we share—our awareness of death, our journey through creation, our urges to love and be loved—*as well as* our unique interests, conflicts, and concerns. Postmodernism, however, sometimes obscures these global conditions and exalts the unbridgeable distinctions among individuals and communities (Sampson, 1993).

I concur with Smith (1994) that a "pragmatic" and "provisionally" forged consensus about reality is a highly useful aim (p. 408). If we abandon our sense of commonality on this planet, then we abandon the ties that help us to intercommunicate, to broaden our outlooks, and ultimately to coexist. "Each of us . . . contains the other," Styron (1995) recently quoted fellow author James Baldwin. Male and female, black and white, we all are part of each other, Styron intimated. It is the "duty" of the artist (and of the sensitive psychologist, I might add) to explore and "dignify" these perceptions.

SUMMARY AND CONCLUSION: WHITHER THE ROMANTIC?

When the 1994 president of the APA, Frank Farley, suggested that we psychologists "stand very close to being a discipline concerned with superficial problems" and that spirituality, "deep feelings about soul and eternity . . ., a psychology of meaning in the broadest sense . . ., placing the mystery of life in context, and most importantly, showing the road to generosity and love" will "become increasingly important" (quoted in Martin, 1994, p. 12), he was sounding a romantic chord.

In this chapter, I have argued that mainstream psychology is increasingly abandoning its romantic roots. This development is based on many factors, but the increasing reliance on managed care, corporate funding, technocratic models for living, and psychopharmacology are among the most salient. (See, e.g., the heavy reliance on terms such as *treatment, objectivity,* and *balance* in a recent brochure disseminated to the public by the APA [1998] titled *How Does Therapy Work?*)

I have further proposed that there is a formidable price to be paid for abandoning our romantic roots that includes dissociation from the arts and humanities, alienation of artistically and creatively minded graduate students, depersonalization of clients and experimental subjects, restriction of applied and basic research, reductionism of psychological understanding, and increasing multicultural strife.

The postmodernist influence is a liberating counterweight to these developments, but ironically, it also can reinforce the growing fragmentation, and to the extent that it does this, it defeats its own ends.

The romantic psychology I have offered as an alternative to these disturbing scenarios is not a panacea. I recognize this. As I have suggested, it too can have its excessive and reductionistic sides, and it too can fractionate psychology (see discussions of romantic excesses in the transpersonal movement in Schneider, 1987, 1989, 1996). However, if I stress romanticism at this juncture of our history, it is because psychology is so antiromantic and so unbowed in its objectivizing quest. I am partially sympathetic with this trend; social and economic pressures are promoting it. Yet, what I am unsympathetic toward is its domination, my colleagues' mass capitulation to its dictates, and their blindness as to its effects.

NOTES

1. I acknowledge the complex and controversial nature of the so-called romantic movement in the arts and philosophy. The term has many connotations and many historical antecedents (Jones, 1969). However, I have distilled in this definition what I believe to be the relevant features of this movement for contemporary psychology.

2. Although humanistic psychology and its existential-phenomenological philosophical base are not synonymous with romanticism, they do share many features in common (see, e.g., May, 1985, 1991, and Tillich, 1952). I acknowledge, moreover, the many other psychological orientations that share features in common with romanticism (e.g., aspects of Jungian psychology, Freudianism, and neo-Freudianism), but existential-humanistic psychology, it seems to me, is the one most closely allied with the romantic movement (Barrett, 1958), and that is why I highlight it here.

REFERENCES

Allport, G. (1961). *Pattern and growth in personality.* New York: Holt, Rinehart & Winston.

American Psychiatric Association. (1994). *Diagnostic and statistical manual of mental disorders* (4th ed.). Washington, DC: Author.

American Psychological Association. (1998). *How does therapy work?* [brochure]. Washington, DC: Author.

Barrett, W. (1958). *Irrational man.* Garden City, NY: Doubleday.

Barrett, W. (1978). *The illusion of technique.* Garden City, NY: Doubleday.

Barron, F. (1963). *Creativity and psychological health.* New York: Van Nostrand Reinhold.

Beck, A. (1976). *Cognitive therapy and the emotional disorders.* New York: New American Library.

Becker, E. (1973). *The denial of death.* New York: Free Press.

Berger, P., & Luckman, R. (1966). *The social construction of reality.* Garden City, NY: Doubleday.

Bergmann, G., & Spence, K. W. (1944). The logic of psychophysical measurement. *Psychological Review, 51*, 1-24.

Breggin, P. (1991). *Toxic psychiatry.* New York: St. Martin's.

Bugental, J. F. T., & Bracke, P. (1992). The future of existential-humanistic psychotherapy. *Psychotherapy, 29*, 28-33.

Churchill, S. D. (1988). Humanistic psychology and introductory textbooks. *The Humanistic Psychologist, 16*, 341-357.

Cushman, P. (1990). Why the self is empty: Toward a historically situated psychology. *American Psychologist, 45*, 599-611.

Duncan, B. L., & Moynihan, D. W. (1994). Applying outcome research: Intentional utilization of the client's frame of reference. *Psychotherapy, 31*, 294-301.

Eliot, T. S. (1970). *T. S. Eliot: Collected poems—1909-1962.* New York: Harcourt, Brace, & World.

Freud, S. (1959). The question of lay analysis. In J. Strachey (Ed.), *The standard edition of the complete psychological works of Sigmund Freud* (Vol. 20, pp. 183-258). London: Hogarth. (Original work published 1926)

Garfield, S. L., & Bergin, A. E. (1986). Introduction and historical overview. In S. L. Garfield & A. E. Bergin (Eds.), *Handbook of psychotherapy and behavior change* (pp. 3-22). New York: John Wiley.

Gergen, K. J. (1994). Exploring the postmodern: Perils or potentials? *American Psychologist, 49*, 412-416.

Giorgi, A. (1970). *Psychology as a human science.* New York: Harper & Row.

Giorgi, A. (1987). The crisis of humanistic psychology. *The Humanistic Psychologist, 15*, 5-20.

Goethe, J. W. V. (1961). *Goethe's Faust* (W. Kaufmann, Trans.). Garden City, NY: Doubleday. (Original work published 1790).

Graetz, H. R. (1963). *The symbolic language of Vincent Van Gogh.* New York: McGraw-Hill.

Greening, T. (1965). Candid: An existential dream. *Journal of Existentialism, 5*, 413-416.

Hall, C. S. (1954). *A primer of Freudian psychology.* New York: Signet.

Hebb, D. O. (1960). The American revolution. *American Psychologist, 15*, 735-745.

Hillman, J. (1975). *Revisioning psychology.* New York: Harper & Row.

James, W. (1936). *The varieties of religious experience.* New York: Modern Library. (Original work published 1902)

James, W. (1987). A world of pure experience. In *William James: Writings 1902-1910* (pp. 1159-1182). New York: Viking. (Original work published 1904)

Jamison, K. R. (1993). *Touched by fire: Manic-depressive illness and the artistic temperament.* New York: Free Press.

Jones, W. T. (1969). *Kant to Wittgenstein and Sartre: A history of Western philosophy.* New York: Harcourt, Brace, & World.

Kaufmann, W. (1968). *Nietzsche: Philosopher, psychologist, Antichrist.* New York: Random House.

Kierkegaard, S. (1957). *The concept of dread* (W. Lowrie, Trans.). Princeton, NJ: Princeton University Press. (Original work published 1844)

Kobasa, S. (1979). Stressful life events, personality, and health: An inquiry into hardiness. *Journal of Personality and Social Psychology, 37*, 1-11.

Laing, R. D. (1969). *The divided self: An existential study in sanity and madness.* Middlesex, UK: Penguin.

Lambert, M., & Bergin, A. (1994). The effectiveness of psychotherapy. In A. Bergin & S. Garfield (Eds.), *Handbook of psychotherapy and behavior change* (pp. 143-189). New York: John Wiley.

Lambert, M., Shapiro, D., & Bergin, A. (1986). The effectiveness of psychotherapy. In A. Bergin & S. Garfield (Eds.), *Handbook of psychotherapy and behavior change* (pp. 157-212). New York: John Wiley.

Leary, D. E. (1992). William James and the art of human understanding. *American Psychologist, 47,* 152-160.

Lipsey, M. W., & Wilson, D. B. (1993). The efficacy of psychological, educational, and behavioral treatments: Confirmation from meta-analysis. *American Psychologist, 48,* 1181 -1209.

Mahrer, A., Fairweather, D., Passey, S., Gingras, N., & Boulet, D. (1999). *Journal of Humanistic Psychology, 39*(1), 35-53.

Martin, S. (1994, October). Farley sums up his 1993-1994 presidential year. *APA Monitor,* p. 12.

Maslow, A. (1968). *Toward a psychology of being.* New York: Van Nostrand Reinhold.

May, R. (1967). *Psychology and the human dilemma.* New York: Van Nostrand Reinhold.

May, R. (1981). *Freedom and destiny.* New York: Norton.

May, R. (1983). *The discovery of being.* New York: Norton.

May, R. (1985). *My quest for beauty.* Dallas, TX: Saybrook Graduate School.

May, R. (1991). *The cry for myth.* New York: Norton.

May, R., Angel, E., & Ellenberger, H. (1958). *Existence: A new dimension in psychiatry and psychology.* New York: Basic Books.

Mayne, T. J., Norcross, J. C., & Sayette, M. A. (1994). Admission requirements, acceptance rates, and financial assistance in clinical psychology programs. *American Psychologist, 49,* 806-811.

Mental health: Does therapy help? (1995, November). *Consumer Reports,* pp. 734-739.

Norcross, J. C. (1987). A rational and empirical analysis of existential psychotherapy. *Journal of Humanistic Psychology, 27*(1), 41-68.

Norcross, J. C., Alford, B. A., & Demichele, J. T. (1992). The future of psychotherapy: Delphi data and concluding observations. *Psychotherpy, 29,* 150-158.

O'Hara, M., & Anderson, W. (1991, September). Welcome to the postmodern world. *Networker,* pp. 19-25.

Pascal, B. (1991). Penseés. In M. Friedman (Ed.), *The worlds of existentialism* (pp. 38-41). Amherst, NY: Humanity Books. (Original work published 1654)

Poe, E. A. (1981). Eleonora. In *The complete Edgar Allen Poe tales* (pp. 301-304). New York: Crown. (Original work published 1842)

Polkinghorne, D. E. (1983). *Methodoloqy for the human sciences: Systems of inquiry.,* Albany: State University of New York Press.

Reed, E. S. (1988). *James J. Gibson and the psychology of perception.* New Haven, CT: Yale University Press.

Rilke, R. M. (1993). *Letters to a young poet* (M. Horter, Trans.). New York: Norton. (Original work published 1904)

Sampson, E. E. (1993). Identity politics: Challenges to psychology's understanding. *American Psychologist, 48,* 1219-1230.

Schneider, K. J. (1987). The deified self: A "Centaur" response to Wilber and the transpersonal movement. *Journal of Humanistic Psychology, 27*(2), 196-216.

Schneider, K. J. (1989). Infallibility is so damn appealing: A reply to Ken Wilber. *Journal of Humanistic Psychology, 29*(4), 495-506.

Schneider, K. J. (1993). *Horror and the holy: Wisdom-teachings of the monster tale.* Chicago: Open Court.

Schneider, K. J. (1996). Requiem for an enigma [Review of *The Ego and the Dynamic Ground*]. *San Francisco Jung Institute Journal, 15*(1), 75-78.

Schneider, K. J. (1999). *The paradoxical self: Toward an understanding of our contradictory nature* (2nd ed.). Amherst, MA: Humanity Books.

Schneider, K. J., & May, R. (1995). *The psychology of existence: An integrative clinical perspective.* New York: McGraw-Hill.

Shakespeare, W. (1975a). Hamlet, prince of Denmark. In *The complete works of William Shakespeare* (pp. 1071-1112). New York: Crown. (Original work published 1600)

Shakespeare, W. (1975b). Macbeth. In *The complete works of William Shakespeare* (pp. 1045-1070). New York: Crown. (Original work published 1606)

Shelley, M. (1981). *Frankenstein.* New York: Bantam Books. (Original work published 1818)

Smith, M. B. (1994). Selfhood at risk: Postmodern perils and the perils of the postmodern. *American Psychologist, 49,* 405-411.

Smith, M. L., Glass, G. V., & Miller, T. I. (1980). *The benefits of psychotherapy.* Baltimore, MD: Johns Hopkins University Press.

Stern, E. M. (1994-1995, Winter). August 1994 APA council session. *Division 32 Newsletter,* pp. 3-4.

Stone, I. (1937). *Dear Theo: The autobiography of Vincent Van Gogh.* New York: Signet. (Original work published 1883)

Styron, W. (Speaker). (1995, February). *Interview with William Styron.* San Francisco: KQED Radio.

Task Force on Promotion and Dissemination of Psychological Procedures. (1995). Training and dissemination of empirically-validated psychological treatments: Report and recommendations. *Clinical Psychologist, 48,* 3-23.

Taylor, E. (1992). William James and the humanistic tradition. *Journal of Humanistic Psychology, 31*(1), 56-74.

Tillich, P. (1952). *The courage to be.* New Haven, CT: Yale University Press.

Vandenberg, B. (1991). Is epistemology enough? An existential consideration of development. *American Psychologist, 46,* 1278-1286.

Van Kaam, A. (1966). *Existential foundations of psychology.* Pittsburgh, PA: Duquesne University Press.

Wertz, F. (1992). Representations of the "third force" in the history of psychology textbooks. *The Humanistic Psychologist, 20,* 461-476.

Whitman, W. (1959). *Walt Whitman's leaves of grass* (M. Cowley, Ed.). New York: Penguin. (Original work published 1855)

CHAPTER 7

The Person as Moral Agent

Thomas Szasz

IT SEEMS LIKELY that once pre-humans became "human," they began to observe and form an understanding of themselves. Intuitively, we regard this effort at self-observation and self-understanding as intrinsic to what we mean by being human. Less obviously, the effort to understand ourselves merges into the effort to understand human nature or the mind.

Before long, the tendency toward role specialization, inherent in the social nature of human life, led to certain persons becoming accredited as experts in understanding humans (e.g., psyche, soul, mind). The first authorities, called *priests,* soon were followed by philosophers and playwrights. From antiquity until the end of the 18th century, the members of these three groups were the acknowledged experts on human nature. Attributed to divine sources, the authority of the priesthood was unquestioned and unquestionable and was inseparable from the authority of the "state" (as the executive arm of the "church").

With the advent of modernity, the authority of religion to legitimize the state in general, and social sanctions in particular, gradually declined and was replaced by the authority of reason. We call the result of this metamorphosis the Enlightenment and attribute its authority to science. By the end of the 19th century, moral-philosophical explanations of personal conduct were replaced by psychological and sociological explanations of it. Today, the familiar psychoanalytic "psychobabble," parading as psychological science, is being refurbished with so-called neurophilosophical accounts of mind-as-brain. As a result, the study of the human as moral agent became "unscientific" and unfashionable and was replaced by the "scientific" study of the human as (mental) patient whose behavior is determined by the chemicals in the person's brain and the genes in his or her body. Moral philosophers, therefore, ceded their mandate to the experts in neuroscience; respect, justice, and the rule of law were replaced by compassion, tort litigation, and medical ethics;

and the welfare state was absorbed into the therapeutic state.

Not surprisingly, the results still fall short of utopia. It is one thing to understand the structure of DNA or control a dog in a kennel. It is a very different thing to understand human behavior, much less to control a person possessing rights in a society ostensibly committed to respecting "human rights." As I show, modern experts' inability or unwillingness to concede this difference is regularly accompanied by their inability or unwillingness to acknowledge the conceptual primacy of the person as moral agent, that is, the cognitive absurdity and moral impropriety of reducing a person to his or her body, mind, or soul.

I daresay that there is something bizarre about the materialist-reductionist's denial of persons. To be sure, brains in craniums exist, and so do persons in societies. The material substrates of a human—a person—are organs, tissues, cells, molecules, atoms, and subatomic particles. The material substrates of a human artifact—say, a wedding ring—are crystals, atoms, electrons in orbits, and so forth. Scientists do not claim to be able to explain the economic or emotional value of a wedding ring by identifying its material composition, nor do they insist that a physicalistic account of its structure is superior to a cultural and personal account of its meaning. Yet, many scientists, from physicists to neurophysiologists, claim that they can explain choice and responsibility by identifying its material substrate—that "life can be explained in terms of ordinary physics and chemistry" (Stent, 1974, p. 780). Indeed, during recent decades, the canons of respectable scholarship and journalism alike have virtually mandated that we view only biological-reductionistic explanations of human behavior as scientific. The following statement by Steven Weinberg, a Nobel laureate and professor of physics at the University of Texas, is typical:

> There are no principles of psychology that are free-standing, in the sense that they do not need ultimately to be understood though the study of the human brain, which in turn must ultimately be understood on the basis of physics and chemistry. . . . Of course, everything is ultimately quantum-mechanical; the question is whether quantum mechanics will appear directly in the theory of the mind and not just in the deeper-level theories like chemistry on which the theory of the mind will be based. (Weinberg, 1995, pp. 40-41)

Socrates' dialogues—called *elenctic* (from the Greek *elenchus*, meaning to refute)—epitomize rational skepticism aimed at questioning a widely held misconception. The inexcusable conceit of the contemporary debate about the mind is that, a priori, it illegitimizes such skepticism. Dismissively, Weinberg (1995) wrote, "Many of our fellow citizens still think that George [a hypothetical actor] behaves the way he does because he has a soul that is governed by laws quite unrelated to those that govern particles or thunderstorms. But let that pass" (p. 40). My aim in this chapter has been to prevent such reductionism from passing as self-evident.

In view of the postwar popularity of "atheistic" existentialism, it is surprising that many scientists continue to maintain that viewing a person as a responsible agent is tantamount to believing that the person has a soul (that, moreover, governs his or her behavior). Nevertheless, the acceptance of this canard—illustrated by Weinberg's (1991) remark, which could easily be multiplied—has become de rigueur in current debates about the mind.

Neither Camus nor Sartre can be accused of believing in the existence of souls (in the same sense as medieval churchmen believed in them or, for that matter, in any other sense). In fact, both fought tirelessly—albeit in very different ways—to restore agency, liberty, and responsibility to the human as person. "The aim of a life," declared Camus (1957/1961), "can only be to increase the sum of freedom and responsibility to be found in every man and in the world. It cannot, under any circumstances, be to reduce or suppress that freedom, even temporarily" (p. 240). Sartre was equally emphatic that we must view the person as a responsible agent. Apropos of the situation of the draftee conscripted into fighting a war that he considers evil, Sartre (1956) wrote, "I deserve it [my fate] because I could always get out of it by suicide or by desertion. . . . For lack of getting out of it, I have chosen it" (p. 554). Sartre dismissed the objection that "I did not ask to be born" with the following rejoinder: "I am responsible for everything, in fact, except for my very responsibility, for I am not the foundation of my being" (p. 555).

It is ironic that the atheists Camus and Sartre adhered to the classic Judeo-Christian view of the human as a morally responsible being more faithfully than do the representatives of modern Judaism and Christianity. I believe that they could do so with relative ease because Camus and Sartre, unlike the Jewish and Christian clergy, rejected the modern medicalized abhorrence of suicide and its attribution to mental illness (Szasz, 1996). In fact, Sartre explicitly spurned the metaphors of psychiatry and psychoanalysis as semantic tricks for lifting the burden of freedom-as-responsibility from our shoulders. In one of the pithiest and most incisive criticisms of Freud, Sartre (1956) wrote, "Thus psychoanalysis substitutes for the notion of bad faith, the idea of a lie without a liar" (p. 51). "Bad faith" is Sartre's term for self-deception, the "I" lying to the "me." Sartre continued, "If we reject the language and the materialist mythology of psychoanalysis, . . . we are compelled to admit that the censor must choose and in order to choose must be aware of so doing" (p. 52).

Fundamental to Sartre's perceptive analysis is the twinned idea of truth-lie. But what is *truth*? The word has two different uses and meanings. One is pragmatic (truth is what works best), and the other is social (truth is what convention legitimizes as factual). As human history (especially the history of religion) tells us, the word *truth* is a dangerously intolerant term. It allows no disagreement. Who can be against the truth? The word *understanding* is more hospitable and tolerant. It implies a dialectic and the possibility of misunderstanding. "Understanding," Oakeshott (1933/1985) observed, "is not such that we either enjoy it or lack it altogether. . . . To be human and to be aware is to encounter only what is in some manner understood" (p. 1).

In other words, everyone, at all times, has some understanding of everything in his or her life. At the same time, just as every person's fingerprint is different from that of every other person, so too is every person's understanding of himself or herself and the world different from that of every other person. This virtually limitless variety of personal insights and outlooks is why society rightly values agreement and harmony more highly than it does accuracy and disputation. "An ounce of loyalty," Arthur Koestler once aptly remarked, "is worth a pound of brains."

The proverb "When in Rome, do as the Romans do" reminds us that social cooperation requires compliance with custom. In real life—the scientific enterprise included—only the legitimate can be right. Illegitimate behavior, by definition, is behavior that society deems wrong and stigmatizes as either crime or mental illness. An illegitimate idea—spoken or written—is a type of behavior that society treats similarly.[1] For illegitimate ideas—be they delusions or discoveries—the only safe domain is the mind as the dialogue within.

NOTE

1. I believe that this is why some creative persons—Mark Twain and Franz Kafka, for example—have withheld some or all of their works from publication during their lifetimes (and instructed their executors to destroy their unpublished works). These considerations also help to dispel the seemingly mysterious, but actually socially constructed, connections between genius and madness.

REFERENCES

Camus, A. (1961). The wager of our generation. In *Resistance, rebellion, and death* (J. O'Brien, Trans.). New York: Knopf. (Original work published 1957)

Oakeshott, M. (1985). *Experience and its modes.* New York: Cambridge University Press. (Original work published 1933)

Sartre, J.-P. (1956). *Being and nothingness* (H. Barnes, Trans.). New York: Philosophical Library.

Stent, G. S. (1974). Molecular biology and metaphysics. *Nature, 248,* 779-781.

Szasz, T. (1996). *The meaning of mind: Language, morality, and neuroscience.* New York: Praeger.

Weinberg, S. (1995, October 5). Reductionism and redux. *New York Review of Books,* pp. 39-42.

CHAPTER 8

The Self and Humanistic Psychology

DONALD E. POLKINGHORNE

ONE SIGNIFICANT contribution of the founders of humanistic psychology was reintroducing the self into the conversation of psychology. Since the time when the founders wrote, significant changes have taken place in psychological and philosophical theory. As the founders of humanistic psychology engaged the behavioral and psychoanalytic views of their day, current humanistic psychologists need to engage present-day academic psychology and philosophy. The insights of the founders need to be reformulated in light of the contemporary opposition to the humanistic understanding of the self and its actualization. This chapter presents the rudiments of such an engagement and reformulation. The introductory section presents a brief formulation of the founders' understanding of the self. The subsequent section outlines the absence of the self in current academic psychological research and in current philosophical theory. The concluding section introduces several contemporary theorists whose ideas can be helpful in the develop-

ment of a present-day formulation of the founders' view of the self.

THE FOUNDERS' VIEW OF THE SELF

The self was an important topic during the early period of the history of psychology, and it held a central position for writers such as James (1890) and Baldwin (1916). However, with the advent of behaviorism during the 1920s, the discipline abandoned its concern with the self (Epstein, 1980). Thereafter, American academic psychology left further development of the notion of self to sociologists such as Cooley, Mead, and Goffman (Danziger, 1997). Thus, when humanistic psychologist Allport (1955) made his call for readmitting the self into psychology, it was not a call for a continuation of work on the self that had been under way in psychology but rather a call to introduce a new concern for the self back into psychology. Allport wrote,

Until about 1890, certain American writers, including Dewey, Royce, [and] James, continued to regard self as a necessary concept. They felt that the analytical concepts of the New Psychology lost the manifest unity of mental functioning. But for the ensuing fifty years, very few American psychologists made use of it . . . and none employed "soul." (p. 36)

Other founders of humanistic psychology, such as Maslow, Rogers, May, and Bugental, also held that it was necessary to reintroduce the idea of self into psychological theory so as to understand people's lives. The self became a cornerstone in their view of the development of the inherent possibilities of human existence and of the process through which positive changes occurred in their psychotherapeutic work with clients.

The Self as the Tendency for Growth

The founders' view of the self is that it is a pattern of change. Rogers held that all living things have an essential pattern of dynamic change that serves to move them toward their full and mature development. In a human, this innate pattern of growth toward full development includes not only the physical growth of the body but also the psychological growth to the full unique potential inherent in the person. The self is this natural tendency or force to actualize the fullness of an individual's personhood. Rogers (1986) gave the following description of this actualizing tendency:

The person-centered approach depends on the actualizing tendency present in every living organism—the tendency to grow, to develop, to realize its full potential. This way of being trusts the constructive directional flow of the human being toward a more complex and complete development. (p. 200)

The founders varied in their understanding of the role of personal will in actualizing the self or tendency toward growth. On the one hand, Rogers viewed the actualization of one's human potential as a natural process that would culminate in a fully functioning person unless thwarted by environmental constraints such as lack of positive regard from one's parents. On the other hand, more existentially influenced humanistic psychologists stressed the idea that actualization of one's potential required personal courage and will. Maslow (1968) suggested that Rogers had "perhaps understressed the factors of will, of decision, and of the ways in which we do make ourselves by our choices" (p. 17).

The founders understood self not as mind or a thing but rather a propensity. It is a "pure process, pure subject *I* [self]" (Bugental, 1965, p. 213), or a becoming (Allport, 1955), not a static and unchanging structure. One's self is the urge to develop the fullness inherent in one's existence, in other words, the drive (not in Freud's sense) to become the person one truly and authentically can be. Thus, the essence of self is a tendency to grow to fullness, and it is the essential characteristic of humans.

The revolutionary impact of the humanistic idea of the self reflected in the writings of the founders can be seen against the background of the other operating views of the nature of self. The humanistic view was that the self is the intrinsic innate tendency to actualize one's unique potential for full human existence. The founders differentiated their view of the self from that of the psychoanalytic ego. May (1958) wrote, "The 'I-am' experience must not be identified with what is called in various circles the 'functioning of the ego' " (pp. 45-46). Freud conceived the ego as a relatively weak, passive, and derived agent that was an epiphenomenon of id drives. It functioned to negotiate between internalized societal restraints (superego) and the need to reduce the tensions built up from unreleased id forces. May acknowledged that developments in psychoanalytic theory, such as ego psychology by Anna Freud, gave an increased importance to the ego in personality. However, her emphasis was primarily on an expanded understanding of the role of the ego in developing and maintaining defense mechanisms, not on the positive tendency toward growth, which was the central characteristic of the self.

The founders' idea of the self also differed from a Cartesianlike notion that the self is a type of mental or material substance whose function is simply to serve as a person's executive, taking in information and initiating bodily actions to affect the environment. In its executive function, the self was held to be the seat of reason and thought of as an observer of representations of objects produced by the body's senses. In this view, the self was held to be a nonmaterial psyche or mindlike homunculus, residing inside the bodily person and with the power to direct the body's movements. In addition, the founders' notion of the self as innate did not concur with Mead's (1934) view that the self is something that has to be constructed by society after birth out of an essentially receptive and formless organism.

Allport (1955), recognizing that the term *self* had so many confusing meanings, suggested that humanistic psychology select another term (his proposal was *proprium*) to emphasize the uniqueness of the humanistic understanding of the self as a tendency rather than a thing. "Psychologists who allow for the proprium use both the term[s] 'self' and 'ego'—often interchangeably— and both terms are defined with varying degrees of narrowness or comprehensiveness" (p. 40).

The Self Versus the Self-Concept

In their view of the self, the founders made a crucial distinction between the actual self and the understandings that people have about the self. People's understanding of who and what they are is called *self-concept*. The significance of the distinction between self and self-concept derives from the founders' position that people act and respond on the basis of their understandings of how things are rather than how things actually are. They held that people are guided in their behavior by their implicit understandings and theories of reality (Gopnik & Meltzoff, 1997). Rogers said that people act out of their "internal frame of reference" (Rogers, 1959, p. 213) and that "I do not react to some absolute reality but [rather] to my perception of this reality. It is this perception which for me *is* reality" (Rogers, 1951, p. 484).

The conceptual understandings that people have of the world, others, and the self serve not only to highlight and give meaning to some experiences but also to cover over and make inaccessible other experiences. The voice of one's actual self as a force or growth and actualization of positive possibilities can be drowned out by conceptual schemes imposed by society and enforced by significant people in one's life. These schemes often can lead people to understand their selves as static and unchangeable things that do not measure up to social expectations; they appear as being stuck in their present conditions and without possibilities. However, the realization that the socially imposed notions of their selves do not represent who and what people really are frees them to turn their attention to the submerged voices of their selves. If one's conceptual schemes are open enough, then they can allow the real self beneath the distorting understandings to be directly felt. Stagner (1961) stated that the experience of the self is a

> kind of primitive experience about which communication is virtually impossible. . . . One can experience self, but this experience must be uniquely personal. . . . "I am what I am" is the succinct biblical assertion that selfhood cannot be further defined but must be experienced. (p. 185)

May (1958) described the coming to experience the real self as an "I am" experience or "a sense of being" (p. 43).

People often are aware of a tension between the felt experience of their selves and the conflicting conceptual understandings they have of the self. The awareness of a division between the experienced self and the self-concept was described by Laing (1960) as a "divided self." Rogers (1961), in discussing this experience, wrote, "When there is no relationship in which we are able to communicate both aspects of our divided self—our conscious facade and our deeper level of experiencing—then we feel the loneliness of not being in real touch with any human being" (p. 94).

The unmediated experience of the self can serve to correct a person's understanding of who and what he or she is. The experience can re-form the imposed concept of self into one that displays self as a basic tendency to fully actualize the possibilities inherent in being a person. When the self-concept accurately depicts the self, it is said

to be *congruent*. When it inaccurately depicts the self, it is said to be *incongruent*.

Actualization of the Self

For the founders, the goal of human existence is to fully actualize the potential inherent in one's humanness. The means to achieving this goal is to gain access to the inherent force that impels growth to full humanness. One gains access to this force when the self-concept allows its presence into awareness. The founders emphasized that the real self has to appear or be accurately depicted in conscious awareness if it is to affect behavior. When conscious thought displays the real self, a person is most free to become fully functioning. The person is able to make choices that express his or her authentic values and to have available the undistorted full range of his or her life possibilities. The ideal, fully functioning person is in a state of congruence; that is, no disharmony exists between the self-concept and the actualizing tendency.

The concept of the actualized or fully functioning person is an ideal that represents the ultimate actualization of the human organism. In life, a person does not achieve this absolute state. Actualization is not a static and stable condition that one becomes. In life as lived, people are fully functioning in relative terms—some more so, some less so. Self-actualization is a process in which a person grows toward the ideal. Thus, Maslow preferred to use a verb form—self-actualiz*ing*. Authentically being human involves the movement toward, not the achievement of, the full actualization of the potential that is inherent in humans. As a process on the way, one experiences the self as a history, a story of the temporal movements toward and retreats from realization of one's full potential. May (1958) captured the dynamic nature of the self in his description of a "human being":

> The full meaning of the term "human being" will be clearer if the reader will keep in mind that "being" is a participle, a verb form implying that someone is in the process of *being something*. It is unfortunate that, when used as a general noun in English, the term "being" connotes a static substance, and when used as a particular noun such as a being, it is usually assumed to refer to an entity. . . . Rather, "being" should be understood, when used as a general noun, to mean *potentia*, the source of potentiality; "being" is the potentiality by which the acorn becomes the oak or each of us becomes what he truly is. And when used in a particular sense, such as a human being, it always has the dynamic connotation of someone in process, the person being something. Perhaps, therefore, *becoming* connotes more accurately the meaning of the term in this country. We can understand another human being only as we see what he is moving toward, what he is becoming; and we can know ourselves only as we "project our *potentia* in action." The significant tense for human beings is thus the *future*—that is to say, the critical question is what I am pointing toward, becoming, what I will be in the immediate future. (p. 41)

In summary, the founders of humanistic psychology held that the move to authenticity involved the development of concepts about the self that truly reflect people's tendency to actualize their human potential. The need for acceptance by others and the press of social conformity produce self-concepts that distort and hide aspects of people's true selves. Because it is the concepts about the self that guide people's actions and interactions, when they are incongruent with people's real selves, people are not able to actualize who they really are; rather, they are directed by socially presented distortions of who they are. When people's self-concepts are in tune with their real selves, they are free to let their human potential manifest itself. The move toward congruence is a move to a more fully functioning and psychologically healthy person.

NEW CHALLENGES FOR UNDERSTANDING THE SELF

In the four decades since the founders of humanistic psychology introduced their ideas of the self, academic psychology has turned its attention to mental functioning and cognition, and philosophy has taken up postmodern themes. There is a need to translate the humanistic ideas about the self and actualization into contemporary idioms and to reshape arguments that address the concerns of current audiences.

In the main, contemporary academic psychology and philosophy are as antagonistic to the humanistic notion of the self as were the psychology and philosophy of the founders' time. Cognitive psychology avoids the idea of self, although it is concerned with self-concept. Postmodern philosophy dismisses the idea of self, although it has much to say about what is wrong with the idea. However, if humanistic psychology is to launch a renaissance (Taylor, 1999), then it will need to confront these current psychological and philosophical views. As the founders had turned to the ideas of existential and phenomenological writers for support in their clash with behaviorism and psychoanalysis, there are ideas of present-day theorists that can offer support for the humanistic psychology idea of the self. Four of these ideas are Neisser's sources of knowledge of self, Gendlin's understanding of self as intricacy, Lakoff's philosophy of the flesh, and Ricoeur's narrative conception of self.

This section first describes the absence of the self in current approaches in psychology and philosophy and then discusses the four ideas that can serve as contemporary vehicles for the expression of a renewed humanistic account of the self.

Absence of the Self in Current Academic Psychology

Focus on the self continues to remain central to the practice of some psychotherapies such as the humanistic psychotherapies (May, 1958; Rogers, 1959), self psychology (Kohut, 1977), and narrative-informed psychoanalysis (Schafer, 1992). However, attention to the self per se has been absent in academically based psychology, and the more recently academically derived psychotherapies focus on changing behavior through altering environment stimuli or altering thoughts; these include behavioral therapy (Spiegler & Guevremont, 1998) and cognitive-behavioral therapy (Beck, 1967).

Current academic psychology does not include inquiries about the character or function of the self, nor does it explore the self's role in people's psychological lives. Its interest is limited to the ideas or beliefs that people have about their selves, that is, their self-concepts. During its cognitive turn, academic psychology came to accept data about people's subjective experiences and beliefs into its studies. The move to include people's beliefs had been one advocated by the founders of humanistic psychology (e.g., Combs & Syngg, 1959). The founders' understandings of the functions of the subjective realm were based on an organic metaphor and included growth, change, and purposive action. However, mainstream academic psychology has based its understanding of the subjective realm on a computer metaphor. Mental operations are seen as analogous to or isomorphic of computer operations, and the notion of self has been replaced by the idea of a mental executive or synthesizing function.

Viewing the operation of the mental realm as computerlike has allowed psychology to continue to rely on research designs left over from logical positivism. Thus, studies of the subjective realm are limited to correlations between people's self-reported beliefs and their behavior. Among these studies are those that focus on people's beliefs about their selves (rather than on concepts about the world or others). Osborne (1996), who reviewed the recent psychological research on the self-concept, identified more than 400 such studies. These studies were of three types: (a) those that investigated the type of information that the self-concept includes, (b) those that examined the stages of development of the self-concept during childhood (an area previously investigated by Rogers, 1951, and Sullivan, 1953), and (c) those that studied how variations in people's self-concepts correlate with variations in their behavior.

The majority of studies are of the third type. They include studies of self-esteem in which the focus is on the aspect of people's self-concepts that is related to the evaluation or esteem of their selves. They attempt to show that the more positive evaluations people's self-concepts have of their selves, the better they will perform on various tasks. These studies have given impetus to a misplaced fascination with programs designed to increase self-esteem so as to increase performance, especially school performance (Hewitt, 1998). Another focus of this third type of studies has investigated variations in self-efficacy, that is, beliefs about how well one can perform a task and how well one actually performs it. Studies have focused on the effect of various other aspects of people's concepts about the self on performance, perception, and interpretation of new information (see, e.g., Klein & Loftus, 1988).

The founders distinguished between ideas or concepts people have about their selves and their actual selves. A concept about the self is a mental representation of one's self. One's self-concept can be an accurate representation (congruent) or a misrepresentation (incongruent). The founders' concern was with the relationship between people's ideas and the referent of those ideas—the actual self. The attention of current academic psychology has focused on the relationship between variations in people's thoughts about their selves and variations in their behaviors. The founders' attention was focused on the relationship between people's thoughts about their selves and their actual selves. The absence of the actual self in academic psychology is implied by the neglect to include it in its research programs. However, the absence of the self is explicitly declared by postmodernist philosophy.

The Absence of the Self in Postmodern Philosophy

Prior to postmodernism, the self had a central place in the theological and philosophical views of the West. Postmodernist writers have attacked the idea of self and hold that the notion of the existence of self was a philosophical mistake. The mistake came from erroneously assuming that, because in the grammar of Western languages verbs (action words) require nouns or agents as the subjects that perform the actions, there must be a self or subject that is the causal author of these actions. The postmodernist view is that although a person has a concept of self, there is nothing to which the concept refers; that is, the self is an empty concept.

The idea of self assaulted by postmodern writers had been worked out by Descartes during the early 1600s. Descartes had translated the medieval theological notion of the soul into a modern philosophical notion of mind or self. Western religious thought held that a human was made up of two parts: the soul and the physical body. The essence of a person was his or her soul, and the soul was one's true self. The physical body was but a temporary vehicle in which the soul resided until the body perished. Once created, the soul existed eternally, and after its sojourn in a physical body, it ascended to heaven or descended to hell, where it remained until the Second Coming. The soul had a spiritual (not physical) existence, and it was invested with freedom so that its bearer had personal responsibility for choosing good or evil.

The emerging scientific view challenged, and eventually overthrew, the medieval view of the world. Aided by the breakup of the unified church by the Protestant Reformation and the subsequent disruptions of the Thirty Years' War (Toulmin, 1990), the hegemony of the medieval view of the world was fractured. Whereas the medieval view saw the world as a stage for God's activities and held that events in the world were mysterious expressions of God's interventions, the scientific view saw the world as ordered and lawful and without mystery. The scientific view saw the world as disenchanted.

It was Descartes's task to reformulate the medieval view into one that retained the spiritual dimension while, at the same time, accepting the scientific view of an ordered and lawful world. The new formulation developed by Descartes has, in the main, held sway in philosophy for more than three centuries. It has served as the framework for what is termed the *modern period*. Descartes began by depicting the physical world (which included people's bodies) as consisting of causally ordered mechanical relationships among objects (whose basic property was extension in space). These relationships could be known through scientific investigation, and this knowledge could be used to achieve power over nature. However, this view of the world left out the knower, that aspect of reality that knows about and directs the body's actions in the world. Descartes called this aspect *mind* or *self*. Its basic property had to be other than what held for physical reality. Thus, he described it as lacking extension in space.

The modern philosophical view of the self has continued to rely on Descartes's original formulation. The mind, which does not have physical properties, functions as the aspect of a person that knows, thinks, and directs the movement of the body. The mind comes to know in two ways: (a) through the information it receives from the body's senses and (b) through its use of reason. The mind learns about the world through the body but learns about eternal truths, such as the truths of mathematics and geometry, through the exercise of its reasoning capacity. It is only through this second way of knowing that the mind can come to certain knowledge. In Descartes's famous description of methodical doubt, he described how all that he thinks he knows can be doubted except his existence as mind or self. On this certainty of his existence as mind, he could rebuild his faith in the rest of his mind's knowledge.

It is this modern view of mind or self (a nonphysical thing that knows, thinks, and directs the body's motion) that postmodernism rejects. Postmodern writers follow in the skeptical steps of Hume, who said that when he examined his thoughts, he could not find a thinker who thought them. The postmodernists do not accept Descartes's rationally derived proof that if there are doubts (or thoughts), then there must be something that is doing the doubting (or thinking). Postmodern phrases, such as *decentering the self* and *the death of the subject,* are slogans aimed against Descartes's modernistic formulation of a self or subject as that aspect of a person that knows. Postmodern writers agree with Ryle's (1949) statement that there is no "ghost in the machine"; they have abandoned the notion of self (Anderson, 1997).

A central theme of postmodern thought is that thoughts are not simple mirrored representations of worldly objects (Rorty, 1979). Rather, thinking is done in words, and because there is an arbitrary relation between words *(signifiers)* and the things to which they refer *(the signified)*, thoughts are reflections of one's language, not of the objects of an independent world. Because different languages divide up the world differently, peoples of different cultures and languages think about the world differently. Because thought is mediated by language and because there is no universal reason, one cannot know for certain whether one's thoughts accurately correspond to what is thought about.

Thus, just because there is a word *self* (a signifier) in our language does not imply that there is such a thing as a self. Postmodern theory, in its position on the existence of a self, neglects its general skeptical position and takes the stand that there is no such thing as a self that is the referent of the word *self*. The concept of self is held to be a fictional creation of Western grammar and cognitive schemes. There is no self, so the concept is not informed by a real referent, nor is it susceptible to correction. The humanistic idea that the concept of self can be congruent or incongruent with one's actual self is dismissed because there is no actual self.

The concept of self is a creation of Western culture and may serve psychological functions within that culture, but just because it may have psychological benefits does not mean that it exists. In arguing for the cultural creation of the concept of self, some postmodern writers have pointed out that not all cultures include a belief in the self; for example, Buddhists believe in a nonself (Varela, Thompson, & Rosch, 1991).

With no actual self to inquire about, postmodern writers, like contemporary academic psychologists, have limited their concern to the function of people's concepts about the self. Because self-concepts are a cultural product, they vary according to the historical period and local culture in which people live. German philosophers of the 19th century had developed the notion that people living during different historical periods had dissimilar cognitive frames, and anthropologists had reported that the cognitive frames of different cultures also were dissimilar. From these findings, postmodernists propose that concepts about the self share no universal characteristics but are completely relative. People's understandings of the world, others, and themselves are a function of their different culturally given interpretative schemes, and their thoughts and actions always are mediated and constructed through the lens of these schemes. The modernist idea that we could progressively come to a more truthful understanding of the world and self was wrong. Instead, the diverse understandings of people are simply different, and one conceptual framework is not more truthfully revealing than are others.

The heyday of postmodernism is drawing to a close. Its relativistic skepticism appears now as an overreaction to the recognition that science does not produce absolutely certain truths (Anderson, 1990). Philosophical efforts have moved on to investigate how people can pragmatically guide their lives and solve the problems they encounter. Rather than accepting a dichotomy between certain truth and no truth, philosophers have turned to the idea of "good enough" knowledge. Without the assurance that understanding is totally true, one can know enough to accomplish daily tasks and live a meaningful life. Within this context, theorists are beginning to reconsider the postmodernists' rejection of the self and to look again at its role in human existence.

CONTEMPORARY VEHICLES FOR HUMANISTIC VIEWS OF THE SELF

Current philosophical theories are being constructed that take account of the postmodernists' critique of modernist assumptions but move beyond them. These theories reach conclusions about knowledge of the self that differ from the skeptical and cynical deductions of postmodern writers. Some of these theories are compatible with the ideas and values of the humanistic founders and offer possible frameworks for communicating humanistic ideas to contemporary audiences. The rest of the chapter is devoted to a brief exposition of Neisser's self-knowledge, Lakoff's philosophy of the flesh, Gendlin's experiencing, and Ricoeur's narrative conception of the self.

Neisser's Self-Knowledge

Neisser's theory (Neisser, 1988, 1993a; Neisser & Fivush, 1994; Neisser & Jopling, 1997) agrees with postmodernism in rejecting the idea that there is "an inner self of some kind, a 'real me' who is (or should be) ultimately responsible for behavior" (Neisser, 1993b, p. 3). Neisser says that he is in full agreement with contemporary philosophy, as well as with neuroscience, that "the brain is not organized by any Cartesian flow toward and from some inmost center" (p. 4). However, this position does not lead Neisser to reject the idea of a self. Instead, he views the self not as a special part of a person but rather as the whole person considered from a particular point of view. I think that humanistic psychology's founders' position that the self is a developmental tendency or inclination, and not a core homunculus, could accommodate Neisser's proposition by regarding the self as a tendency affecting the whole person. Maslow's (1954, 1968) inclusion of accomplishment of multiple needs implies that the self is directed to the development of all aspects of a person.

Neisser's work understands the self as a more general notion than the founders' view that the self is the actualizing tendency. He employs the term *self* in a way that is similar to Allport's (1937, 1955) use, that is, referring to all of the various aspects of one's personhood or personality that an individual would identity as his or her own. The focus of Neisser's work is the different forms of information that contribute to the experience of one's self. He identifies five aspects of self that are informed by five types of self-specifying information: the ecological self, the interpersonal self, the extended self, the private self, and the conceptual self. The first two types of information are directly perceived, not mediated through conceptual frameworks (the postmodern position). The *ecological self* is experienced as the perceiver of the environment in the sense of Gibson's (1979) visual kinesthesis theory. According to Gibson, changing perceptions of worldly objects include perceptions of one's own movement and posture. The ecological self is the self perceived in relation to the physical envi-

ronment and the effect that one has on this environment. "I am the person here in this place, engaged in this particular activity" (Neisser, 1988, p. 36). Knowledge of the *interpersonal self* is informed by the directly experienced emotional rapport and face-to-face communicative interaction with others.

Neisser draws on recent research on early childhood as the basis for his assertion that a person's experience of being located in and acting on the world and the experience of being in relation to other people are directly perceived. Neisser (1993b) says, "We can see and hear and feel what we are doing, both ecologically and interpersonally" (p. 4). His view provides an opening for the founders' notion that aspects of the self, in particular the self as tendency, are not simply an illusory projection of self-concept but rather are directly available to experience. Thus, these direct experiences of the self can serve as corrections to beliefs about one's self that are produced by culturally imposed distortions. The ecological and interpersonal experiences continue to inform people throughout their lives. They are not discarded and replaced by conceptually interpreted experience when children learn to use the mediating conceptual categories that come with language acquisition (McIntosh, 1995).

The remaining three types of information used to specify one's self differ from the directly experienced ecological and interpersonal. They are available only through reflective thinking about one's self. The *extended self* is based on personal memories and imagined futures. It is a reconstruction derived from remembered ecological and interpersonal experiences. The *private self* represents the conclusion that some of one person's experiences are not directly shared by other people and that this person is the only person who feels, for example, this unique and particular pain. Neisser's fifth self, the *conceptual self* or self-concept, is similar to the founders' view of the self-concept and consists of people's beliefs about themselves. Neisser (1988) says, "There is a remarkable variety in what people believe about themselves, and not all of it is true" (p. 36). Thus, like the founders, Neisser holds that one's self-concept can distort and hide aspects of who one "really is."

Lakoff and Johnson's Philosophy of the Flesh

Lakoff and Johnson (Lakoff, 1987; Lakoff & Johnson 1980, 1981, 1999) distinguish two generations in the development of cognitive science. The first generation, which evolved during the 1950s and 1960s, was begun, like humanistic psychology, as a movement to correct psychology's overdependence on behavioristic understanding of humans. However, it changed direction when its approach took up the newly available computer as its model of mental functioning (Gardner, 1985). The computer model fit well with the view of Anglo-American analytic philosophy that mental reasoning, like computers, functioned by logically manipulating symbols. Lakoff and Johnson (1999) say the following of the first generation of cognitive scientists: "It seemed natural [to them] that the mind could be studied in terms of its cognitive functions, ignoring any ways in which those functions arise from the body and brain" (p. 75).

The second generation of cognitive scientists, which arose during the late 1970s, called into question the notion that thought was unaffected by the body and was ordered according to the patterns of formal logic. The second-generation view was derived from research findings showing that (a) there is a strong dependence of concepts and reasoning on the body and that (b) "imaginative processes, especially metaphor, imagery, metonymy, prototypes, frames, mental spaces, and radical categories" (Lakoff & Johnson, 1999, p. 77) were central to conceptualization and reason.

The focus of Lakoff and Johnson's work is on the source of concepts that people use to interpret and make sense of the world, others, and the self. The traditional view was that the source of the concepts that we use to organize experience is the world itself; that is, our concepts are simply representations of the natural types of things in the world. As stated previously, postmodernism argued against this view and held, in its place, the notion that the world lacked a permanent order. It held that any order of sense that was made of the world was a misleading human construction. The types of sense that one made of the world were a function of the conceptual furniture supplied by one's particular culture, not a reflection of an actual order. Against this postmodern position, Lakoff and Johnson propose that the type of conceptual order that humans make is based on basic-level bodily experiences. These bodily experiences are metaphorically extended to supply structural models of higher level experiences. Lakoff and Johnson (1999) hold that the conceptual metaphor is one of our central intellectual tools. "[Conceptual metaphor] is the principal instrument of abstract reason, the means by which inferential structures of concrete domains are employed in abstract domains" (p. 155). For example, time is understood through the metaphor of "motion of objects past an observer" (p. 141).

In concert with the proposition that abstract concepts are largely metaphorical, Lakoff and Johnson hold that the mind is inherently embodied and that thought is mostly unconscious. They hold that thought does not take place in a disembodied realm of reason (an idea left over from Descartes's notion of mental substance); rather, it is an activity of the body itself. The idea of embodiment, including the idea that the self is embodied, was not foreign to humanistic psychology's founders. They did not conceive of the actualizing tendency as located in a disembodied realm of thought; rather, it was a tendency toward growth and maturity that was present in all living things. Rogers explicitly held an organic understanding of the self. Allport included in his list of the aspects of one's own personhood the notion of the bodily sense. Neisser also recognized the embodied nature of the ecological self. Thus, Lakoff and Johnson's theories, along with Merleau-Ponty's (1968) idea of the body-subject and "the flesh" and Varela and colleagues' (1991) notion of an embodied mind, can provide humanistic psychology support in emphasizing the bodily character of the self.

Lakoff and Johnson's view that thought occurs mostly out of awareness is aligned with Rogers's view that the operation of the tendency for growth is not under conscious control. Instead, its operation depends on clearing away distorted blocking beliefs about one's self by providing an environment of positive regard. Existential humanists, although emphasizing the conscious responsibility to choose to act in ways consistent with the actualizing tendency, can locate the experience of self below the level of conscious awareness.

Gendlin's Intricacy and Self

Gendlin (1962, 1997; see also Levin, 1997) is a psychotherapist and philosopher. He worked with Rogers when the latter was at the University of Chicago, and his theories have special relevance for humanistic psychology. Like Neisser and Lakoff and Johnson, Gendlin's work concerns the rela-

tionship between experience and the concepts we use to order experience. In opposition to postmodernists, he holds that experience is not a construction of culturally imposed structures; rather, experience is the result of a more fundamental interaction between a person and the world. Gendlin's basic thesis is that the source of speech and action is experience (or *experiencing,* a term he uses to emphasize that experience is an ongoing process, not a thing). Experiencing is our interaction with life situations and the bodily felt meanings that these situations have for us. It consists of a more complex and intricate order than the concepts and distinctions that inhere in language. Speech and action are partial expressions of the intricate multiplicity of experiencing. Experiencing has a more complex order than does language and remains in excess of what one says. Words become meaningful as they are used to communicate and reflect on an aspect of one's felt experience. Gendlin's theory of felt meaning reverses the notion that conceptual distinctions and structures are the determinants of speech and actions. Instead, he holds that words and phrases are drawn out of experiencing and that words retain flexibility in use to express new meanings and concepts. He lends support to the view held by Lakoff and Johnson that conscious deliberation does not decide most human activity; rather, it flows directly from felt meaning.

In his *Experiencing and the Creation of Meaning,* Gendlin (1962), like the founders, argues that his theory of felt meaning was an alternative to the logical positivists' view of the workings of language. During the nearly four decades since its publication, the philosophical landscape has changed. Postmodernists, in addition to discarding the self, dismantled positivism's epistemological claims to produce certain knowledge. Levin (1985) writes that Gendlin's more recent position regarding language takes a middle road between the empiricist-rationalist tradition and the structural and poststructural traditions. The empiricist-rational tradition, which maintained Descartes's mind-body distinction, held that representations of objects in the world were created in the mind by the association of sense data and/or clear and distinct ideas. Inherent in this position was the question of how one can be certain that the mental representations are accurate reflections of objects in the "external" world. Language was either understood to be a simple tool to communicate one's mental representations or understood to consist of a series of propositions representing the states of affairs in the world. Structuralism changed the focus of philosophy from a subject's mental representations to the language system in which he or she spoke and wrote. The conceptual network of a particular language was held to determine the forms and categories through which one experienced the world. Poststructuralists and postmodernists attacked the sign-signified connection and posed that one cannot use language to think outside language, and therefore, one cannot guarantee the meanings of words. They held that there is no such thing as objective meanings and that attaching particular meanings to words always is arbitrary and dictated by politics or power and not by the words themselves. The notion that there is a disconnect between words and objects has gained further support from a relativistic reading of hermeneutics. Nietzsche held that *all is interpretation* (i.e., there is no epistemological foundation for the conceptual network exhibited in a language), and Heidegger (1962) proposed that how one understood the world was a function of the historical and cultural tradition in which one stood. Thus, there is no direct access to the things in themselves. The postmodernists extended the implications of the word-world disconnect into an extreme skepticism and relativism.

Gendlin provides a viable alternative to the empiricist-rationalist philosophies based on the discredited subject-object dichotomy and to the relativism of postmodernism. Gendlin turns attention to what had been neglected by these positions—the bodily felt meaning. Because felt meaning is more intricate than can be expressed through the concepts and formations of language, Gendlin uses the sign ". . . ." to refer to felt meaning. The ". . . ." is the source of the creation of meaning. Felt meaning is not an inner representation of outside objects; instead, it consists of people's responsive interplay with the situated thickness in which they live.

Gendlin opens up the space in which the experiencing of the self takes place. Knowledge of the self is, first, a bodily felt knowing, not a conceptual construction. The self is complexly interwoven within a person's experiencing of the situational interactions that exist between the person and the world, others, and the self. The self and its intricate relations within experience cannot be abstracted out into the conceptual forms of language without distortion. However, languaged descriptions of the self can be judged as more or less congruent with the self as it is present in one's experiencing. Gendlin's work leads humanistic psychology to an understanding that the self exists beyond the imagined image that is constructed by culturally provided categories. The acceptance of a preverbal sense of the self that continues to exist after the development of the capacity to conceive of the self in language "call[s] us to conceive of a primordial, interpersonal, and meaningful relationship with the world that grounds our adult conceptions in an innocent and direct engagement of body and world" (Simms, 1993, p. 39).

Ricoeur's Narrative Conception of the Self

Ricoeur (1984, 1991, 1992), like the other theorists just described, is primarily concerned with the conceptual forms used to understand and give sense to one's experiential complex. His philosophical work is based on his continuing interest in the negotiation between "living experience and [languaged] conceptualization" (Ricoeur, 1995b, p. 123). He accepts the idea that there is a realm of human life that is outside language to which language can refer; this acceptance differentiates him, as it did Gendlin, from the postmodernists. He also proposes that the structure and conceptual network of a language does not produce a mirrored literal description of the realm of human experiencing. He believes that the intricate and complex structuring present in lived experience differs from the literal meanings and structures of language. Thus, Ricoeur turns to language's capacity to be used artistically to reveal structures that would have remained unrecognized without art (Carr, Taylor, & Ricoeur, 1991). Ricoeur, before his investigation of narrative identity, had rejected Husserl's assumption that reflection on one's own consciousness was the privileged way to truth. In his explorations in *The Symbolism of Evil* (Ricoeur, 1969) and *Freud and Philosophy* (Ricoeur, 1970), he comes to appreciate that some aspects of experiencing cannot be brought directly to awareness. Merleau-Ponty (1962) said that reflecting on one's experience is like looking down a well; the light only reaches so far, and beyond that is the darkness. Thus, Ricoeur supports Lakoff and Johnson's position that much of experiencing and responding happens outside awareness and that literal language is unable to describe life's deepest experiences.

Ricoeur proposes that although language neither describes reality nor is severed from reality, it does serve to redescribe reality. In his "Intellectual Autobiography," Ricoeur (1995) says that he remembers having raised the questions "Was the distinction between sense and reference still valid in the case of metaphorical statements?" and "Could one say of metaphor that it uncovered aspects [or] dimensions of the real world that direct discourse left hidden?" (p. 28). He reaches the conclusion that "it is the language freest of all prosaic constraints . . . that is most available to express the secret of things" (p. 28). Thus, for Ricoeur, aspects of the experiential complex are best displayed through the figural functioning of concepts rather than the literal functioning. It is the configural operations of metaphors and narratives (stories) that allow the complex of experience to show itself.

Ricoeur points out that different types of concepts account for their referents in different ways. The two major types of concepts are paradigmatic and narrative concepts (Bruner, 1986). Paradigmatic concepts depict their referents as a type of something, for example, the conceptual understanding of one's self as male or female, tall or short, good or bad, and so on. Paradigmatic concepts limit the display of what is referred to as an instance of some stable category. Narratively structured concepts display processes and changes that occur over time (Polkinghorne, 1988). The founders held that the essence of self was a process or pattern of change, not a type of matter or form. Because of this, paradigmatic concepts, which are able to present something only as an instance of a category (i.e., as an instantiation of a type or form), cannot display the self as the process it essentially is (Polkinghorne, 1991). Because the founders viewed the self as an activity or process of change guided by the tendency to actualize an inherent potential, narrative concepts come closer than paradigmatic concepts to exhibiting the self as process.

Narrative is a special type of discourse production. Narratives configure happenings and actions into coherent wholes by means of emplotment. A plot is a type of conceptual frame through which the contextual meaning of and connections among events can be displayed. A simple story, "The king died and the prince cried," illustrates the power of narrative form to give relational meaning to seemingly independent happenings. In isolation, the two happenings are simply the description of two independent events. When composed into a story, the happenings become parts of a drama. The prince's crying shows up as a response to his father's death.

The primary dimension of the living person is temporal, not spatial. The founders understood *human being* as an activity, that is, as human be-*ing* or becoming (Allport, 1955), not as a nounlike substance. May (1958) wrote,

> [Existentialists] are struck by the fact that the most profound human experiences, such as anxiety, depression, and joy, occur more in the dimension of time than in space. They boldly place time in the center of the psychological picture and proceed to study it not in the traditional way as an analogy to space but [rather] in its own existential meaning for the patient. (p. 65)

Ricoeur proposes that narrative or story is the linguistic form that least distorts temporal experience. From the perspective of humanistic psychology, the basic plot of people's life stories is about their struggles to actualize their inherent potentials.

Some philosophers of narrative (Carr, 1986; MacIntyre, 1981) have proposed that experiencing itself has a narrative form. For example, Carr (1986) stated that he has been "urging that narration is not only a mode of discourse but more essentially a mode, perhaps *the* mode of life" (p. 173), and MacIntyre (1981) stated, "We all live out narratives in our lives and . . . we understand our own lives in terms of the narrative[s] that we live out" (p. 212). The position that experiencing itself has a narrative form is called the *life as narrative* position. Other philosophers (Neisser, 1994; Sass, 1992; White, 1978) hold a view, similar to postmodernism, that experiencing is unorganized and has no discernible structure. For them, the narrative form is an imposition of the languaged narrative structure on what is actually unstructured and fragmented. This position is called the *life versus narrative* position.

Ricoeur thinks that these two positions exaggerate the relation of narrative structure to experiencing. Ricoeur believes that a dynamic relation holds between life as narratively emplotted and life as lived. He proposes that narrative configuration moves through three stages. The first stage involves a return to the original or prelinguistic felt sense of human action. He holds that our primordial experiences of ourselves and others have a "pre-narrative quality" and are inchoate or incipient narratives. His position is that this characteristic of our prenarrative awareness of human conduct, on reflection, appears as unfinished and "constitutes a demand for narrative" (Ricoeur, 1984, p. 74). Our prefigured experiencing calls for a reflective review that can consider the unintentional (as well as intentional) effects of our actions, the consequences of which we could not be aware at the time of the actions. The reflective review integrates the pre-narrative understandings we had at the time of the actions and happenings with understandings that we have gained from the perspective of hindsight.

The second stage consists of a narrative composition in which experienced actions are linked together as contributors to or detractors from achieving an intended purpose. By configuring lived actions into meaningful wholes, an order and coherence is unveiled that did not previously appear in life as lived. The construction of a narrative story consists of more than simply gathering the discordant elements uncovered in the first stage and placing them in chronological order. Merleau-Ponty (1962) wrote that we are not "a succession of 'psychic' acts, . . . but [rather] one single experience inseparable from itself, one single 'living cohesion' " (p. 407). Narrative structuring serves to accomplish the move to a unified identity that is inherent, but not yet accomplished, in our pre-narrative existence.

The third stage consists of the new actions that are the result of the renewed lived understanding of who we are that has been brought about by the second stage narrative composition. These new actions fold back into the first stage as additional components of one's lived experiencing. These continuing changes in experiencing lead to continual revisions in the composed story of one's life. Thus, one's narrative understanding of one's life is constantly under revision as one circles through the three stages of the narrative process.

Ricoeur's formulation of the relationship among experiencing, the narrative configuration of experiencing, and changes in actions provides a format for describing the operation of the humanistic notion of the actualizing tendency. The self becomes manifest in a person's actions as the person evolves his or her life stories toward one in which the experienced inherent potential is displayed in the person's actions.

At the time when the founders of humanistic psychology wrote, academic psychology had no place for the self in its stimulus-response paradigm, and mainstream philosophy had not yet moved beyond a Cartesian view of the self as an immaterial soullike substance. In their clinical experiences, the founders encountered in their clients a propensity to actualize their potential to become fully developed humans. From this encounter, the founders developed the innovative and insightful notion that this propensity was the core of humanness; that is, it is the self. During the four decades since the founders wrote, their understanding of the self has become integral to many approaches to psychotherapy. However, neither academic psychology nor philosophy has, as yet, incorporated the founders' perceptive understanding of the self. Because psychology and the philosophical context have undergone immense changes since the founders wrote, affecting these disciplines' understanding of the self requires their restatement in a contemporary idiom. I have described four contemporary theories—Neisser's self-knowledge, Lakoff's philosophy of the flesh, Gendlin's experiencing, and Ricoeur's narrative conception of the self—that capture the view of self as an embodied tendency to become what is inherently intended for authentic human existence. These theories can provide entry into contemporary psychology and philosophy of the founders' view of the self.

REFERENCES

Allport, G. W. (1937). *Personality: A psychological interpretation.* New York: Henry Holt.

Allport, G. W. (1955). *Becoming: Basic consideration for a psychology of personality.* New Haven, CT: Yale University Press.

Anderson, W. T. (1990). *Reality isn't what it used to be.* New York: Harper & Row.

Anderson, W. T. (1997). *The future of the self: Inventing the postmodern person.* New York: Tarcher.

Baldwin, J. M. (1916). *The story of the mind.* New York: D. Appleton.

Beck, A. T. (1967). *Depression: Clinical, experimental, and emotional aspects.* New York: Harper & Row.

Bruner, J. (1986). *Actual minds, possible worlds.* Cambridge, MA: Harvard University Press.

Bugental, J. F. T. (1965). *The search for authenticity: An existential-analytic approach to psychotherapy.* New York: Holt, Rinehart & Winston.

Carr, D. (1986). *Time, narrative, and history.* Bloomington: University of Indiana Press.

Carr, D., Taylor, C., & Ricoeur, P. (1991). Discussion: Ricoeur on narrative. In D. Wood (Ed.), *On Paul Ricoeur: Narrative and interpretation* (pp. 160-187). London: Routledge.

Combs, A. W., & Syngg, D. (1959). *Individual behavior: A perceptual approach to behavior* (rev. ed.). New York: Harper & Row.

Danziger, K. (1997). The historical formation of selves. In R. D. Ashmore & L. Jussim (Eds.), *Self and identity: Fundamental issues* (pp. 137-159). New York: Oxford University Press.

Epstein, S. (1980). The self-concept: A review and the proposal of an integrated theory of personality. In E. Staub (Ed.), *Personality: Basic aspects and current research* (pp. 81-132). Englewood Cliffs, NJ: Prentice Hall.

Gardner, H. (1985). *The mind's new science.* New York: Basic Books.

Gendlin, E. T. (1962). *Experiencing and the creation of meaning.* Glencoe, IL: Free Press.

Gendlin, E. T. (1997). How philosophy cannot appeal to experience, and how it can. In D. M. Levin (Ed.), *Language beyond postmodernism: Saying and thinking in Gendlin's philosophy* (pp. 3-41). Evanston, IL: Northwestern University Press.

Gibson, J. J. (1979). *The ecological approach to visual perception.* Boston: Houghton Mifflin.

Gopnik, A., & Meltzoff, A. N. (1997). *Words, thoughts, theories.* Cambridge, MA: MIT Press.

Heidegger, M. (1962). *Being and time* (J. Macquarrie & E. Robinson, Trans.). New York: Harper & Row.

Hewitt, J. P. (1998). *The myth of self-esteem: Finding happiness and solving problems in America.* New York: St. Martin's.

James, W. (1890). *Principles of psychology.* New York: Holt.

Klein, S. B., & Loftus, J. (1988). The nature of self-reference encoding: The contributions of elaborative and organizational processes. *Journal of Personality and Social Psychology, 55,* 5-11.

Kohut, H. (1977). *The restoration of the self.* Madison, CT: International Universities Press.

Laing, R. D. (1960). *The divided self.* Chicago: Quadrangle Books.

Lakoff, G. (1987). *Women, fire, and dangerous things: What categories reveal about the mind.* Chicago: University of Chicago Press.

Lakoff, G., & Johnson, M. (1980). *Metaphors we live by.* Chicago: University of Chicago Press.

Lakoff, G., & Johnson, M. (1981). The metaphorical structure of the human conceptual system. In D. A. Norman (Ed.), *Perspectives on cognitive science* (pp. 193-206). Norwood, NJ: Ablex.

Lakoff, G., & Johnson, M. (1999). *Philosophy in the flesh: The embodied mind and its challenge to Western thought.* New York: Basic Books.

Levin, D. M. (1985). *The body's recollection of being: Phenomenological psychology and the deconstruction of nihilism.* London: Routledge.

Levin, D. M. (Ed.). (1997). *Language beyond postmodernism: Saying and thinking in Gendlin's philosophy.* Evanston, IL: Northwestern University Press.

MacIntyre, A. (1981). *After virtue: A study in moral theory.* Notre Dame, IN: University of Notre Dame Press.

Maslow, A. H. (1954). *Motivation and personality.* New York: Harper & Row.

Maslow, A. H. (1968). *Toward a psychology of being* (2nd ed.). New York: Van Nostrand Reinhold.

May, R. (1958). Contributions of existential psychotherapy. In R. May, E. Angel, & H. Ellenberger (Eds.), *Existence: A new dimension in psychiatry and psychology* (pp. 37-91). New York: Basic Books.

McIntosh, D. (1995). *Self, person, world: The interplay of conscious and unconscious in human life.* Evanston, IL: Northwestern University Press.

Mead, G. H. (1934). *Mind, self, and society.* Chicago: University of Chicago Press.

Merleau-Ponty, M. (1962). *Phenomenology of perception* (C. Smith, Trans.). New York: Humanities Press.

Merleau-Ponty, M. (1968). *The visible and the invisible* (A. Lingis, Trans.). Evanston, IL: Northwestern University Press.

Neisser, U. (1988). Five kinds of self-knowledge. *Philosophical Psychology, 1*(1), 35-59.

Neisser, U. (Ed.). (1993a). *The perceived self: Ecological and interpersonal sources of self-knowledge.* Cambridge, UK: Cambridge University Press.

Neisser, U. (1993b). The self perceived. In U. Neisser (Ed.), *The perceived self: Ecological and interpersonal sources of self-knowledge* (pp. 3-21). Cambridge, UK: Cambridge University Press.

Neisser, U. (1994). Self-narrative: True and false. In U. Neisser & R. Fivush (Eds.), *The remembering self: Construction and accuracy in the self-narrative* (pp. 1-18). Cambridge, UK: Cambridge University Press.

Neisser, U., & Fivush, R. (Eds.). (1994). *The remembering self: Construction and accuracy in the self-narrative.* Cambridge, UK: Cambridge University Press.

Neisser, U., & Jopling, D. A. (Eds.). (1997). *The conceptual self in context: Culture, experience, and self-understanding.* Cambridge, UK: Cambridge University Press.

Osborne, R. E. (1996). *Self: An eclectic approach.* Boston: Allyn & Bacon.

Polkinghorne, D. E. (1988). *Narrative knowing and the human sciences.* Albany: State University of New York Press.

Polkinghorne, D. E. (1991). Narrative and self-concept. *Journal of Narrative and Life History, 1*(2-3), 135-153.

Ricoeur, P. (1969). *The symbolism of evil* (E. Buchanan, Trans.). Evanston, IL: Northwestern University Press.

Ricoeur, P. (1970). *Freud and philosophy* (D. Savage, Trans.). New Haven, CT: Yale University Press.

Ricoeur, P. (1984). *Time and narrative* (Vol. 1, K. McLaughlin & D. Pellauer, Trans.). Chicago: University of Chicago Press.

Ricoeur, P. (1991). Narrative identity. In D. Wood (Ed.), *On Paul Ricoeur: Narrative and interpretation* (pp. 188-199). London: Routledge.

Ricoeur, P. (1992). *Oneself as another* (K. Blamey, Trans.). Chicago: University of Chicago Press.

Ricoeur, P. (1995a). Intellectual autobiography. In L. E. Hahn (Ed.), *The philosophy of Paul Ricoeur* (pp. 3-53). La Salle, IL: Open Court.

Ricoeur, P. (1995b). Reply to David Pellauer. In L. E. Hahn (Ed.), *The philosophy of Paul Ricoeur* (pp. 123-125). La Salle, IL: Open Court.

Rogers, C. R. (1951). *Client-centered therapy: Its current practices, implications, and theory.* Boston: Houghton Mifflin.

Rogers, C. R. (1959). A theory of therapy, personality, and interpersonal relationships, as developed in the client-centered approach. In S. Koch (Ed.), *Psychology: A study of a science* (Vol. 3, pp. 184-256). New York: McGraw-Hill.

Rogers, C. R. (1961). *On becoming a person.* Boston: Houghton Mifflin.

Rogers, C. R. (1986). A client-centered/person-centered approach to therapy. In I. Kutash & A. Wolf (Eds.), *Psychotherapist's casebook* (pp. 197-208). San Francisco: Jossey-Bass.

Rorty, R. (1979). *Philosophy and the mirror of nature.* Princeton, NJ: Princeton University Press.

Ryle, G. (1949). *The concept of mind.* London: Hutchinson.

Sass, L. A. (1992). The epic of disbelief: The postmodernist turn in contemporary psychoanalysis. In S. Kvale (Ed.), *Psychology and postmodernism* (pp. 166-182). London: Sage.

Schafer, R. (1992). *Retelling a life: Narration and dialogue in psychoanalysis.* New York: Basic Books.

Simms, E.-M. (1993). The infant's experience of the world: Stern, Merleau-Ponty, and the phenomenology of the preverbal self. *The Humanistic Psychologist, 21,* 26-40.

Spiegler, M. D., & Guevremont, D. C. (1998). *Contemporary behavior therapy* (3rd ed.). Pacific Grove, CA: Brooks/Cole.

Stagner, R. (1961). *Psychology of personality.* New York: McGraw-Hill.

Sullivan, H. S. (1953). *The interpersonal theory of psychiatry.* New York: Norton.

Taylor, E. (1999). Renaissance of humanistic psychology? *Journal of Humanistic Psychology, 39*(1), 7-25.

Toulmin, S. (1990). *Cosmopolis: The hidden agenda of modernity.* Chicago: University of Chicago Press.

Varela, F. J., Thompson, E., & Rosch, E. (1991). *The embodied mind: Cognitive science and human experience.* Cambridge, MA: MIT Press.

White, H. (1978). *Tropics of discourse: Essays in cultural criticism.* Baltimore, MD: Johns Hopkins University Press.

CHAPTER *9*

Humanistic Psychology and Ecology

MARC PILISUK AND MELANIE JOY

> *The whole universe together participates in the divine goodness more*
> *perfectly and represents it better than any single creature whatever.*
>
> —Saint Thomas Aquinas (*Summa Theologaie*,
> Part One, Question 4, Article I)

IN THE DEEP RECESSES of our minds, we are aware that the threats to our environment are serious. The rays of the sun passing through gaps in the ozone layer are dangerous. The food chain is contaminated with pesticides, additives, and wastes. Water sufficiently pure to safely drink often is not available. Climate change has begun to wreak havoc with weather patterns as a small warning of what is in store for a planet overheated by greenhouse gases. The air we breathe, both indoors and outdoors, is saturated with harmful chemicals (Lappe, 1991). Even as these chemicals affect individual fertility, we continue to overproduce humans by offering no security and no hope for poor women other than the allegiance of their offspring.

We continue to kill 9 billion animals per year for domestic consumption in the United States and to diminish and extinguish countless rare species in wild habitats. We do this while conveniently ignoring that the practice probably is our single greatest cause of water pollution, waste accumulation, deforestation, and ozone depletion (Stepaniak, 1998). Rainforests and coral reefs, the remaining sources of protection for the diverse species that have made complex forms of life possible, are rapidly being contaminated and destroyed. We know that we have too many people for the resources of this planet to support in a way deemed the model for a successful style of life. We know that our inability to manage the wastes of our appetites and our greed are being borne disproportionately by people of color and people who are poor (Bullard, 1995). Yet, the cancer prevalence rates tell us that even wealth cannot protect us. We also know that the settings of beauty that are a source of our spiritual renewal are being lost. We are able to move mountains and change the course of rivers, to venture into space, to turn the genetic blueprints of living things into salable commodities, and to unleash the power of the nuclear genie in ways that can end all of civilization and all of life. We can incarcerate millions and control the behavior of large segments of our population. However, none of these products of our ingenuity and our avarice has made us feel safe or made us accepting and appreciative of our place in the universe (Gottlieb, 1999).

That place is offered by Gaia theory, a model of how the planet works. Lovelock (1979) hypothesized that the earth's highly reactive mix of carbon dioxide, nitrogen, and oxygen could be retained only through the continuing activity of living organisms. Life, in fundamental ways, influences its own environment. With this hypothesis, we may examine the "vital signs" of the planet, note the imbalances, and act as stewards in its restitution. That role of steward is honored more in the breach than in the observance.

Deep down, we are aware that the social constructions we have created to tell us what is real and what is of worth describe a world that holds little promise to nurture either human or nonhuman well-being. This is so precisely because the constructed patterns of thought permit abuse of the settings that should be cherished if they are to remain a source of renewal.

PERSON AS PRIORITY OR AS INSEPARABLE

Humanistic psychology has had an unclear relation to ecological psychology. On the one hand, humanistic psychology places a predominant value on the potential for individual development. It values the diverse human experience and the ability of the human mind to transcend its mundane surroundings in creative and profound ways. So deep is the regard in humanistic psychology for human experience and development that it has sounded the call for new methods of study distinct from those considered acceptable to study all nonhuman forms. So constraining has the earlier scientific effort been on the study of human behavior that the humanists have called for distinct methods (i.e., human sciences) to capture experience in all of its subjective splendor. This has led to an emphasis on a variety of phenomenological methods aimed at getting, as closely as possible, inside the shoes of other humans. Humanistic psychology has, by default, left the study of all nonhuman forms under the rubric of objective science.

Ecological psychology, on the other hand, looks on the separation of humans from other plants, animals, and the material world as artificial, misleading, and not prudent. From the ecological view, the most universal and highly valued symbols and images of the human mind derive from our capacity to glean, in small measure, the marvels and beauty of a sustaining universe and of our own particular niche within it. If these symbolic representations are an essential aspect of human fulfillment, then it is useful to consider an "ecological self" that embraces all forms of life and the feelings of unity that accompany such a self (Naess, 1986, 1989). Currently, psychologists' offices are flooded with anxious, depressed, confused, and lonely individuals who are seeking some explanation for their sense of isolation and despondency. The contemporary workplace, with its emphasis on incessant technological development, fierce competition, and individualism, has created countless victims. Such victims present a loss of existential meaning as well as physical health concerns due to the dramatic increase in toxic occupational environments (Edelstein, 1988). Traditionally, these people have been treated by well-intentioned yet uninformed psychotherapists. Therapists often exacerbate client suffering by addressing only individual and personal concerns. They fail to focus on ways in which clients may be reconnected to the broader human community and the natural environment so as to effect more sustaining and fulfilling ways of life. A few therapists have found the reintegration of clients into natural settings to be a powerful force, diminishing the emptiness provided by the popular culture and rediscovering an abundant resource for health (Kanner & Gomes, 1995).

To the ecopsychologist, there is a hubris or arrogance to the assumption that humans stand on a separate and raised pedestal. The posture of being separate and superior presents, at best, an incomplete picture, concealing the interdependence of humans with the environment. Such separation also continues to help individuals relate to their environment as if the problems we bring to it do not require a dramatically different way of conducting our transactions with the natural order. If we will have to learn to live with significantly less consumption of meat, plastics, or fossil fuels; if we will have to be accountable for toxic radioactive or chemical wastes before we are permitted to produce them; and if we are to ensure that every person and community has the means to sustain itself before others are allowed to accumulate great wealth by exploiting matter and labor from distant sources, then we are envisioning more than a passive change in beliefs. We are envisioning a recovery from our addiction to modern society. Chellis Glendinning noted this well in her book, *My Name is Chellis and I'm in Recovery From Western Civilization* (Glendinning, 1994). Humanistic psychol-

ogy needs a significant greening if it is to carry its weight in this transformation.

ECOLOGICAL SEEDS IN THE HUMANISTIC PSYCHOLOGY TRADITIONS

The seeds of this shift have been present in the vision of founding figures of humanistic psychology. Buber identified the "I-thou" relationship in which the recognition of the genuine value of the other contributes to the authenticity of the self (Friedman, 1983). For Buber, such encounters extended beyond human interaction. Buber's animism held that, ideally, one would relate to all of nature as though it were animated in a personal and sacred manner (Anderson, 1973).

The link between involvement with the outside world and optimal development of the self was hinted at in Maslow's (1971) description of the self-actualizing person: "Self-actualizing people are, without one single exception, involved in a cause outside of their own skin, in something outside of themselves" (p. 43). Deep respect for what is natural also was noted in Maslow's (1976) work:

> One finds what is right for oneself by listening. Similarly, one finds out what is right to do with the world by the same kind of listening to its nature and voices; by being sensitive to its requiredness and suggestions; by hushing so that its voices may be heard; by being receptive, noninterfering, nondemanding, and letting be. (p. 119)

Moustakas (1985) carried this theme by describing his meaning of *humanistic* to include "an authentic relationship to myself, to other human beings, to nature and the universe" (p. 5). The direction is carried further still in ecological psychology. Metzner

(1999) described an ecopsychological worldview that values sustainability "of all forms of life and habitats, not just those of humans or one group of humans" (p. 3).

One stream of humanistic psychology has focused less on the separateness of human thoughts and feelings and more on the artificiality of the link between mind and body. Bodily functions now are clearly understood to be inextricably linked to mental ones. The healing power of potions, postures, and rituals now contribute to holistic health in the practices of even the more traditional deliverers of medical services. The popularity of such beliefs about healing also may contribute, in some collective way, to undermine the concerns of ecological psychology. Poverty, chemical carcinogens in the air and water, and patterns of work that induce excessive stress and preclude renewing experience with the natural environment all are matters that are not curable solely by the mental powers of the individual. Such phenomena are products of our collective activity and may be addressed only by our collective efforts.

THE SHARED CRITIQUE OF OBJECTIFICATION

There are, however, important places in which humanistic and ecological psychologies have formed common ground. One is in the critique of the ways in which science and technology have evolved. Whatever marvels they have created, science and technology have been used primarily to extend our mastery of an objectified nature. Every atom, cell, molecule, neuron, person, life form, acre of ground, and portion of the infinite universe is, for science, an object to be isolated, named, and harnessed for the purposes of those who sponsor the scientific enterprise. The enterprise has done well to establish the veracity of specific and invariant relationships among specific bounded things. It has done less well with the intricate interdependencies by which all things are interrelated to each other across time and space. Appreciation of such complexities more commonly lies in the world of the spirit. Such intricate systems still are matters for reverence more than for immediate dissection, cataloguing, and control. The reverence is more readily recognized in cultures other than our own.

When Chief Seattle reluctantly accepted the Port Elliot treaty moving the Duwamish of Puget Sound to a reservation, he affirmed a spiritual conviction:

> Every part of this soil is sacred in the estimation of my people. Every hillside, every valley, every plain and grove has been hallowed by some sad or happy event in days long vanished. Even the rocks, which seem dumb and dead as they swelter in the sun along the silent shore, thrill with memory of stirring events connected with the lives of my people. (quoted in Vanderworth, 1971, p. 21)

Contemporary psychology has made little room to accommodate sacred experience. But Metzner's (1999) *Green Psychology* takes all of the license afforded by humanistic and transpersonal inquiry to reweave a psychology that is consonant with the human relationship to the earth. Winter (1996) took on the more daunting task of rewriting the existing field of psychology to embed it in an environmental context. But these are exceptions. Psychology has, for the most part, reflected and contributed to a self-centered and objectified view of people that exists in the dominant culture.

THE PURPOSE OF LIFE

For the mainstream of contemporary culture, the purpose of life is development, growth, and mastery. The contribution of such attainments to individual fulfillment is not frequently questioned but surely is questionable. Those who have acquired great affluence do, in general, enjoy an advantage in better health and control of their lives compared to others (Adler et al., 1994; Marmot et al., 1991). However, the advantage is not ensured and, in fact, comes with a cost of denying how one's advantages contribute to the devastation of other persons and the planet. The advantage of well-being also requires a continued dedication to maintaining the dominant goals. They must be persistently pursued because no degree of attainment or acquisition is sufficient to ensure one's position among potential competitors. The goals are maintained not only for oneself but also for all others who cannot attain these goals and feel only the intense pressure to strive for them and the dissatisfaction with their own attainments. For the poor, this often is accompanied by the scorn of others and the internalized scorn of oneself for failure to achieve the goals of consumption promoted constantly within the larger culture (Pilisuk, McAllister, & Rothman, 1996).

A competing worldview has persisted, not only in indigenous regions but also among dissidents who find the dominant course to estrange them from their communities (both human and natural). Those special connections have, throughout history, been considered more a part of the sacred world than of the secular world, for outside of the dominating addictive pressures to consume and compete, humans find a need to contemplate what is magnificent in the universe and in the miracle of life. For many, the purpose of human life has less to do with achieving higher productivity and consumption than with the contemplative wonder, love, and joy in the presence of what feels sacred (Cummings, 1991; see also the chapter by Elkins [Chapter 16] in this volume).

THE DEPTH OF OUR CONNECTIONS

We have evolved from living and nonliving materials. We know that our bodies bear the imprints of a material universe older and more dispersed than we are able to experience directly. This understanding has grown to include the minute components of the atom; the workings of the cell; and the effects of microbes, neurotransmitters, background radiation, geologic formations, and beyond our solar system to the understanding of quasars, pulsars, and the recent discoveries of stars in other galaxies with planets surrounding them. Although our comprehension of this universe is increasing, our understanding remains modest. Cognitive comprehension is a rather recent arrival in the scheme of an evolving universe. Our more sensory, more affective, and more instinctual attributes, however, contribute to a capacity for the appreciation of the grandeur of the natural design. Seasons bring rains and harvests, and sunlight brings warmth and nurturance. Members of living species reproduce themselves, consume resources, and provide resources for other forms of life. Injuries heal. The sounds of the oceans and wild rivers, of wolves and songbirds, touch us deeply. Clouds, flowers, and the setting sun, in all their beauty, are recognized as gifts that rejuvenate the human spirit. It is perhaps paradoxical that the increasing complexities of modern life call on ever greater development of our capacities to categorize and to use our rational capacities to understand, master, and control our environment. At the same time, major segments of our life experience are further removed from their primordial roots. Freud (1962) noted this clearly:

> Originally, the ego includes everything, [and] later it separates off an external world from itself. Our present ego-feeling is, therefore, a shrunken residue of a more inclusive, indeed all-embracing, feeling which corresponded to a once intimate bond between the ego and the world about it. (pp. 15-16)

Whereas Freud saw this limitation as the necessary price for sanity in a civilized world, Jung (1971) observed this same phenomenon more positively:

> The more civilized, the more unconscious and complicated a man is, the less he is able to follow his instincts. His complicated living conditions and the influence of his environment are so strong that they drown out the quiet voice of nature. (cited in Campbell, 1971, p. 160)

HARMONY AND DESTRUCTIVENESS

Whereas our symbolic and often unconscious images provide an avenue toward appreciation of our connection to nature, Jung made another important contribution to our understanding of what the psyche brings to the environmental problem. What was and is natural in human nature is not entirely benign. The psyche includes attributes other than those that might cause us to live more harmoniously with our fellow humans or our environs. The concept of the shadow that Jung described represents a potential for destructive or selfish activity that is as fundamental a part of the human condition as is the capacity to care (Jung, 1969). The theme is elaborated in May's concept of the "daimonic," which is seen to underlie human potential both for creativity and for evil. We are indeed better able to deal with our knowing destruction of our ecology if we recognize that the roots of our destructiveness lie not only in our ignorance of what is required to survive but also in our penchants to thwart what we understand to be moral constraints.

In his dialogue with Rogers, May (1984) confronted the Rogerian image of a better world. For Rogers (1984), the increasing unfolding of self-awareness went hand in hand with progress in building a more life-enhancing world. For May (1984), awareness included acknowledgment of our daimonic selves and the necessity to deal with such potentials rather than to hope for a utopian world in which only the potential for goodwill flourishes. The implication for ecopsychology is that survival of our species will take more than a realization, even more than an appreciation, of our great interconnection with our ecology. Surely, more of us will have to develop ecological selves in which the pain of the contaminated world is our own pain and the preservation of life in general gives meaning to our own lives. Even if we were able to reconnect to the joys and wonders of the natural world, the daimonic potential still would be part of us. Hence, we still are likely to always need institutions that hold us accountable for the damage we do to our world and to each other, just as we always will need institutional practices to heal and forgive those who have contributed so strongly to the devastation of the planet.

TRANSFORMATION OF CONSCIOUSNESS AND SOCIETY

The issue of what social changes are necessary for survival needs integration into the mainstream of humanistic psychology. It is too easy to join in the belief that we—our selves and our communities—are part of nature in the most profound way. It is immediately rewarding to touch the natural world and be touched by it. It is satisfying to engage in the effort to preserve one species of bear or one shoreline or to recycle one's newspapers and believe that our awareness is saving the environment. Such awareness may be necessary but not sufficient to avoid the horrors we would hope to avoid. Marien (1984) likened much of New Age awareness to a sandbox for adults, serving to remove them effectively from the need to engage in a political process. The lure of the sandbox is particularly great when the systems that perpetuate the destruction of our environment are entrenched, ubiquitous, and powerful. They include not only a global corporate decision-making process but also individual decisions to follow the daimonic and do less than we might do as actualized individuals.

The transition in consciousness and action to be bridged is at a point where humanistic and ecological psychologies converge. It is in the challenge to the basic assumptions about the world order that we have created. We still live in the shadow of the 17th-century philosopher Francis Bacon, who asserted, "The world is made for man, not man for the world" (quoted in Dumanoski, 1999, p. 7).

Our counterforce has derived from the romantic tradition, preserved by poets and artists who loved the redemptive power of nature but disdained the struggle to plan for the future. But the bomb, the domination of synthetic chemicals, and the degraded global environment are signs of an accelerating treadmill leading to dire consequences. Something more is required. The nature we have left to preserve is something different from the pristine world of the romantics. It is a nature that must find a

way in which to survive with an already gross overpopulation. The debates between anthropocentrism and biocentrism do not engage the full social and political reality. We lack a coherent and compelling vision of a sustainable world order. We surely are in need of a vision of what science, technology, and business would look like. We also are in need of an ethic to replace rampant individualism. The pursuit of happiness needs to be replaced by the pursuit of compassion. Surely, the protection of individual freedoms has been wrongly applied to the protection of massive corporations to engage in free trade even as it prevents cultural preservation and environmental protection. We face the impact of global forces that curtail diversity and produce a "monoculture of the mind" (Shiva, 1994). If the machinery designed for the accumulation of wealth and subjugation of nature also is the fiscal monitor of political succession and public information, then the task of creating a new vision is large. If the self, wonderful and imperfect as we know it to be, is to have an actualized future, then it will have to be found in the effort to bring about this new vision.

The efforts of contemporary civilization have modified the face of this planet more during the past 200 years than all forces of nature have done during the past 2 million years. Indigenous peoples have lived in barely changing environments, and their lifestyles both required and reflected a more harmonious accommodation to forces of nature. The Miwok clan along the northern California coast lived with primitive tools to grind acorns into flour and to catch the abundant shellfish. They shared their temperate region with the giant redwoods, the salmon, the shorebirds, the gray fox, the grizzly bear, and the field mouse. Like these other residents with whom they shared the hospitality of the earth, they used it sparingly and peaceably with neither a word nor a concept of what later civilization has called *warfare*. And like the stunted pygmy forests just north of them, their successive generations came and went with a measured stability.

> Civilizations came into being in Sumer, Babylon, and all other ancient places of the earth, only to recede into dust and forgotten decay. Troy, Mycenea, Athens, and Rome rose, flourished, and collapsed. Still the people along the shores of California lived out the measured, undisturbed course of their days. (Crouch, 1973, p. 16)

This extended stability reflected the inability to accumulate surplus and, thereby, to permit differences in wealth. It likely owed much to the benefits of cooperation in a hunting-and-gathering society, to the ritual reaffirmations of the bonds of people to their kin, and to their special niche in the ecology. Whatever its advantages or lessons for the rest of us, the arrangements proved fragile when the Spaniards arrived and corralled the Indians into large missions. The zealous effort to save their souls ensured the obliteration of the Indian way of life. Within a hundred years, it was gone.

POWER AS A FACTOR IN THE HUMAN POTENTIAL

Rogers (1986), May (1981), and (to a lesser degree) Maslow (1971) all were critics of the effort to aggrandize power and of zealotry. During his later years, Rogers saw with increasing clarity the need to prevent concentrations of power from precluding the opportunities for an unfolding of the human potential. After taking part in the Rust Conference—an international workshop created to extend the person-centered approach to

political powers—Rogers suggested that the person-centered approach might be used to work against disempowering conditions. The person-centered approach, in his view, should be a catalyst with applications toward long-lasting solutions to problems of the political world (Rogers, 1986). During the present era of globalization, the concentration of power and its reach over every aspect of personal and community life have reached unprecedented extremes.

Life moves with a stressful speed. More and more time is spent in accommodation to the technologies we have created (Berry, 1983). We depend on technical experts for our food, transportation, and communication. The ideas we hold reflect the filtered flow of massive quantities of information released by powerful corporate sources. We are driven to be competitive so as to be part of an expanding economy that uses the earth in wasteful and hazardous ways. In valuing people only for what they produce and consume, we exploit both people and regions mercilessly. The example of the rainforests is helpful.

The great forests of Europe and North America have been destroyed. Remaining rainforests are the lungs of our planet that, along with the dwindling coral reefs, provide home to the diverse life forms that are part of the miracle of continuing evolution. Although our scientists can—and some do—tell us of the rainforests' importance (and of their jeopardy), our ability to comprehend the urgency appears to require a willingness to hear the voices of others who live with a different cosmology.

For thousands of years, indigenous communities of Borneo have cared for their homes in the world's oldest rainforest. The forest has, in turn, provided them with the resources needed to survive. The complex relationships of this fragile ecosystem are endangered. Logging and oil palm plantations, ignoring traditional land claims of native peoples, are clear-cutting the forest at an unprecedented rate. The costs in depletion of the earth's oxygen and extinction of medicinal plant species are impossible to estimate. The costs to the inhabitants are apparent. Contaminated river systems and degraded forests have eroded the abundant resource base on which a resourceful people have depended for the past millennium. The local people of Uma Bawang have combined forces with an organization in Berkeley, California, to form the all-volunteer Borneo Project. It is using citizen diplomacy, outreach, direct assistance, and cultural exchange to monitor violations of human rights and land rights by networking with other international associations (Pilisuk, 1998). Mutang Urad, a leader of the Kelabit tribe in Sarawak, explained the importance of the approach:

> In our race to modernize, we must respect the ancient cultures and traditions of our peoples. We must not blindly follow the model of progress invented by European wealth; we must not forget that this wealth was bought at a very high price. The rich world suffers from so much stress, pollution, violence, poverty, and spiritual emptiness. The wealth of the indigenous communities lies not in money or commodities but [rather] in community, tradition, and a sense of belonging to a special place. (Earth Island Institute, 1997)

The model provided by this and other projects focuses on the preservation and rediscovery of what is sacred in the relation between the person and the planet. It should be seen as a current and appropriate model for meaningful self and community actualization. It provides an opportunity both for saving our planet and for finding our souls through a reconnection to the vast unfolding world in which our special gifts of understanding and compassion are needed (see also the chapter by Lyons [Chapter 46] in this volume).

CANCER: THE CASE OF GREENING THE HUMANISTIC APPROACH

The case of breast cancer offers a metaphor for understanding the overlapping terrain of humanistic and ecological psychology. Breast cancer will affect 175,000 women in the United States in 1999 and will kill 43,000. The rates have been rising rapidly. Women born between 1947 and 1958 are three times more likely to get breast cancer than were their great-grandmothers at the same age (Batt & Gross, 1999). Humanistic psychology has provided a freedom to look at the nature of lived experiences that affects the maintenance or the breakdown of human health. It has contributed to a type of treatment that makes some women better able to confront this awful disease and retain a decent quality of life while pursuing treatment. The images we hold apparently affect the workings of our bodies and our capacities to cope. They can be directed to healing and humanistically oriented programs, and they have become critical parts of cancer treatment (Robbins, 1998). Humanistic psychology has contributed the compassion. But something is missing. This missing element is a subject of ecopsychology that is less present in humanistic psychology. The rates continue to increase.

The reasons clearly are linked to the presence of pollution, estrogenic medications, toxins in consumer products, and carcinogens in the workplace. Breast cancer mortality in New Jersey was associated with closeness of residence to one of the state's 111 superfund sites. Breast cancer mortality rates in Israel increased every year for 25 years until 1978, when the government banned DDT, benzene hexachloride, and lindane. By 1986, the rate had dropped by a third for women in the 25- to 34-year age range. The first warnings of the current environmental disaster appeared in Rachel Carson's *Silent Spring* during the early 1960s (Carson, 1962). Carson died of breast cancer 18 months after its publication, and others are carrying her message.

General Electric, which manufactures X-ray machinery, supports early detection and mammography. The company also has been a major polluter. When it administered the Hanford nuclear weapons facility, General Electric released large amounts of radioactive wastes into the atmosphere and into the Columbia River. The company also was responsible for the massive release of PCBs into the Hudson River. The paradox of a company profiting both from activities that cause cancer and from the treatment of cancer is a repeated pattern. Breast Cancer Awareness Month was created by Astra-Zeneca in 1985. AstraZeneca is the world's third-largest drug corporation. Its message is "Get a mammogram." The British-owned multinational corporation is the producer of Tomaxafin, widely used in breast cancer treatment, and is the owner of the Salick chain of cancer treatment centers. Astra-Zeneca also produces herbicides and fungicides including the carcinogen acetechlor. Its subsidiary chemical plant in Ohio is the third-largest source of potential carcinogenic pollution in the United States. At the time when Breast Cancer Awareness Month was created, AstraZeneca was owned by Imperial Chemical Industries, a multi-billion-dollar producer of pesticides and plastics that was charged by state and federal authorities with the dumping of DDT and PCBs into California harbors long after both substances had been banned.

Samuel Epstein, of the University of Illinois School of Public Health, noted the conflict of interest when a company that is a spin-off of one of the largest manufacturers of cancer-causing chemicals is in control of the treatment centers and the funding of cancer research (Epstein, 1979, 1998). Ranking officials of the National Cancer Institute often accept lucrative posts from the cancer drug industry. The American Cancer Society has, among its trustees, the president of a major drug company. It also has, on its board of directors, the vice president of American Cyanamid, and others on the board have ties to Dupont, CBS, Disney, and Boeing. In 1990, Armand Hammer served as chair of a presidential cancer advisory committee that advocated a drive to add $1 billion to the National Cancer Institute budget to help find a cure for cancer within 10 years. At the time, he also was the chair of Occidental Petroleum, which would have to pay millions of dollars to the federal government and to New York State for its culpability in the environmental disaster at Love Canal (Epstein, 1979, 1998; Proctor, 1996). The highly respected *New England Journal of Medicine* ran a position paper by toxicologist Stephan Safe belittling the evidence linking chemical residues to cancer without noting that Safe recently had received research funds from the Chemical Manufacturers Association (Safe, 1997). The journal subsequently reviewed Sandra Steingraber's book, *Living Downstream* (Berke, 1997; Steingraber, 1997). This book by a cancer survivor and scientist was labeled "an obsessive concern with environmental causes of cancer." The article did not note that the reviewer was a senior official of the chemical giant W. R. Grace, which was forced by the Environmental Protection

Agency to pay millions of dollars for the cleanup of contaminated wells in Woburn, Massachusetts. The attention to Woburn, as to Love Canal, came only after the cries and organizing efforts in the local communities were sufficient to overcome the denials of both authorities and the corporate polluters (Brown, 1989). The struggle has been, as it has been for much of humanist psychology, how to contest a prevailing standard of scientific, technical, and corporate reality and expand it to include one reflecting the human experience. Kanner and Gomes (1995) took this issue one step further to challenge the role of psychologists in an increasingly consumerist society:

> When psychologists offer their services to corporations, their statistical skills and therapeutic insights are used to manipulate people for economic gain rather than to foster well-being. Yet, consumerism is so ingrained in American society that this outright abuse of psychological expertise receives no mention in the ethical code of the American Psychological Association. (pp. 82-83)

For ecopsychology, the reflection of human experience includes the fears for our children, the observations of bad air, the ability to see links between the odor of our water and the ailing pets and children, and the willingness to decide that assurances of acceptable risk should come with the question, "Acceptable to whom?" Steingraber, now a mother as well as a biologist and cancer survivor, advises women to breast-feed their infants. Nonetheless, she notes that this magical holy water filled with antibodies has more PCBs and more DDT and fat-soluble pesticides than would be allowed in other foods (Gross, 1999).

Terry Tempest Williams is a "downwinder," that is, a person who lived downwind from the site of nuclear weapons tests and, therefore, was subject to radiation exposure. She is a cancer survivor in Utah, where nuclear weapons tests at the Nevada site have left a trail of illness and deformity. Her writing on the clan of the one-breasted women confronted the official assurances with the reality of the experience of people who have been affected (Williams, 1998). She described the inner reality of her own surgery to remove a cancer of the breast. Her dreams compare the clear-cut forests with the breasts removed by the knives of surgeons:

> Where do the trees go? Where do the clear-cut breasts of women go? . . . Frozen sections are placed under a microscope while frightened humans await the word—malignant or benign. We emerge from close calls with mortality with an acute awareness of how much we want to live, to love, and to have more time on earth. But what disappears or dies, whether trees or breasts, is part of our story. . . . What do I do now with the open space in front of my heart? (Williams, 1999, p. 43)

The breast, a symbol across cultures of fertility and nurturance, provides the infant's starting relationship with its environs. That we have contaminated this fountain should provide a symbolic warning of what we must do to reaffirm our place in the larger ecology. There is no way in which to protect this milk, or our air, water, and food chain, by individual changes of diet or by placing filters on our water taps and heat ducts. There is no way in which to prevent the environmental harm we cause to ourselves and other species by individual actions alone. However, it is not from fear alone that we must take part in a cooperative transformation of the destructive institutions of society. It also is to find joy in the actualization of our potential to survive and thrive for generations to come. The mission taps our spiritual needs (Warner, 1988-1989). Ecological psychology reminds us that our participation in this effort can provide the experience of awe, reverence, and connection to the surroundings of which we are a part.

REFERENCES

Adler, N. E., Boyce, T., Chesney, M. A., Cohen, S., Folkman, S., Kahn, R. L., & Syme, E. L. (1994). Socioeconomic status and health: The challenge of the gradient. *American Psychologist, 49,* 15-24.

Anderson, W. (1973). *Politics and the new humanism.* Pacific Palisades, CA: Goodyear Publishing.

Batt, S., & Gross, L. (1999, September-October). Cancer, Inc. *Sierra,* pp. 36-63.

Berke, J. H. (1997). Living downstream: An ecologist looks at cancer and the environment [Book review]. *New England Journal of Medicine, 337,* 1562.

Berry, T. (1983). Technology and the nation-state in the ecological age. In *Riverdale papers VIII, 4.* Riverdale, NY: Riverdale Center for Religious Research.

Brown, P. (1989). Popular epidemiology: Community response to toxic waste-induced disease in Woburn, Massachusetts. In P. Brown (Ed.), *Perspectives in medical sociology* (pp. 617-631). Belmont, CA: Wadsworth.

Bullard, R. (1995). Decision making. In L. Westra & P. Wenz (Eds.), *Faces of environmental racism* (pp. 3-28). Totowa, NJ: Rowman & Littlefield.

Campbell, J. (Ed.). (1971). *The portable Jung* (R. F. C. Hull, Trans.). New York: Viking.

Carson, R. (1962). *Silent spring.* Boston: Houghton Mifflin.

Crouch, S. (1973). *Steinbeck country.* New York: Crown.

Cummings, C. (1991). *Eco-spirituality: Toward a reverent life.* Mahwah, NJ: Paulist Press.

Dumanoski, D. (1999, Autumn). Rethinking environmentalism. *Conservation Matters,* pp. 4-9. (Boston: Conservation Law Foundation)

Earth Island Institute. (1997). *Why Borneo? The Borneo Project* [online]. Available: www.earthisland.org/berkborn.html

Edelstein, M. (1988). *Contaminated communities: The social and psychological effects of residential toxic exposure.* Boulder, CO: Westview.

Epstein, S. (1979). *The politics of cancer.* New York: Doubleday.

Epstein, S. (1998). *The politics of cancer revisited.* New York: East Ridge Press.

Freud , S. (1962). *Civilization and its discontents.* New York: Norton.

Friedman, M. (1983). *The confirmation of otherness in family, community, and society.* New York: Pilgrim Press.

Glendinning, C. (1994). *My name is Chellis and I'm in recovery from Western civilization.* Boston: Shambhala.

Gottlieb, R. S. (1999). Seeing in the dark: Facing ecocide. *ReVision: A Journal of Consciousness and Transformation, 22,* 42-48.

Gross, L. (1999, September-October). Rachel's daughter. *Sierra,* pp. 38-39.

Jung, C. G. (1969). *The structure and dynamics of the psyche: Collected works.* Princeton, NJ: Princeton University Press.

Jung, C. G. (1971). Aion: Phenomenology of the Self, The Ego and The Shadow, and The Syzgy—Aninma/Animus. In J. Campbell (Ed.), *The portable Jung* (pp. 139-162). New York: Viking.

Kanner, A., & Gomes, M. (1995). The all-consuming self. In T. Roszak, M. Gomes, & A. Kanner (Eds.), *Ecopsychology* (pp. 77-91). San Francisco: Sierra Club Books.

Lappe, M. (1991). *Chemical deception: The toxic threat to health and the environment*. San Francisco: Sierra Club Books.

Lovelock, J. (1979). *Gaia: A new look at life on earth*. Oxford, UK: Oxford University Press.

Marien, M. (1984). The transformation as sandbox syndrome. In T. Greening (Ed.), *American politics and humanistic psychology* (pp. 52-58). San Francisco: Saybrook Publishing.

Marmot, M. G., Smith, G. D., Stanfeld, S., Patel, C., North, F. O., Head, J., Whitre, I., Brunner, E., & Feeney, A. (1991). Health inequalities among British civil servants: The Whitehall II study. *Lancet, 37*, 1387-1393.

Maslow, A. H. (1971). *The farther reaches of human nature*. New York: Viking.

Maslow, A. H. (1976). *Religions, values, and peak experiences*. New York: Penguin.

May, R. (1981). *Freedom in destiny*. New York: Norton.

May, R. (1984). The problem of evil: An open letter to Carl Rogers. In T. Greening (Ed.), *American politics and humanistic psychology* (pp. 12-23). San Francisco: Saybrook Publishing.

Metzner, R. (1999). *Green psychology: Transforming our relationship to the earth*. Rochester, VT: Park Street Press.

Moustakas, C. (1985). Humanistic or humanism? *Journal of Humanistic Psychology, 25*(3), 5-11.

Naess, A. (1986). The deep ecological movement: Some philosophical aspects. *Philosophical Inquiry, 8*, 10-13.

Naess, A. (1989). *Ecology community and lifestyle: Outline of an ecosophy*. Cambridge, UK: Cambridge University Press.

Pilisuk, M. (1998). The hidden structure of contemporary violence. *Peace and Conflict: Journal of Peace Psychology, 4*, 197-216.

Pilisuk, M., McAllister, J., & Rothman, J. (1996). Coming together for action: The challenge of contemporary grassroots community organizing. *Journal of Social Issues, 52*(1), 15-37.

Proctor, R. (1996). *Cancer wars: How politics shapes what we know and don't know about cancer*. New York: HarperCollins.

Robbins, J. (1998). *Reclaiming our health: Exploding the medical myth and embracing the source of true healing*. Tiburon, CA: H. J. Kramer.

Rogers, C. R. (1984). Notes on Rollo May. In T. Greening (Ed.), *American politics and humanistic psychology* (pp. 11-12). San Francisco: Saybrook Publishing.

Rogers, C. R. (1986). An international workshop. *Journal of Humanistic Psychology, 26*(3), 24-45.

Safe, S. H. (1997). Xenoestrogens and breast cancer. *New England Journal of Medicine, 337*, 1303-1304.

Shiva, V. (1994). *Monocultures of the mind*. London: Zed Books.

Steingraber, S. (1997). *Living downstream: An ecologist looks at cancer and the environment*. Reading, MA: Addison-Wesley.

Stepaniak, J. (1998). *The vegan sourcebook*. Los Angeles: Lowell House.

Vanderworth, W. C. (Ed.). (1971). *Indian oratory: Famous speeches by noted Indian chieftains*. Norman: University of Oklahoma Press.

Warner, G. (1988-1989, Winter). Ecology is the contemporary religion. *Earth Island Journal*, pp. 3-7.

Williams, T. T. (1998). The clan of the one-breasted women. *The Ecologist, 28*(22), 110.

Williams, T. T. (1999, September-October). Clearcut. *Sierra,* pp. 42-43.

Winter, D. (1996). *Ecological psychology: Healing the split between planet and self.* New York: HarperCollins.

CHAPTER 10

Humanistic Psychology and Peace

MARC PILISUK

PEACE is surely more than the absence of war. It is a state of the community and of the world in which healthy human development can take place. Humanistic psychology has something vital to say about the transformation to peace. However, because both humanistic psychology and peace psychology have weighed in most strongly with their concerns about war (White, 1986), this is a good place to start. War is but one of the ways in which we inflict violence on one another. Among all forms of destructiveness, war is special mainly in the ways in which it is justified. A declaration of war gives a state the recognized right to order people to conquer, destroy, and kill. Why do we do it?

The answer begins with an observation on war that is well documented in Tuchman's (1984) *The March of Folly: From Troy to Vietnam.* Tuchman's book details a history of the human propensity to engage in violent wars including numerous cases in which the potential gains for any of the participants were small compared to the costs. Examples of societies that have been relatively free of violent wars for long periods of time are few and lie mostly outside of the dominant societies modernized in the Western image. The exceptions, although rare, are important given that they bear on critical questions debated within humanistic psychology. What does such recurrent violence have to say about human nature? Are the cruel, selfish, and violent activities as fundamental a part of human nature as the creative, caring, and cooperative actions? If so, do such instinctive aggressive inclinations mean that wars are inevitable?

Humanistic psychology was begun by persons whose appreciation for the richness of human experience and for its value convinced them that the psychology of their day gave too little opportunity for the human potential to thrive. It should be of no surprise that many of these same people were equally concerned about the threat posed by war to diminish not only the hopes of humankind but also the possibilities for its survival, for what does it mean to cherish the individual human while ignoring the human-created cloud that might bring all life to an end?

Many of the legendary figures of humanistic psychology have spoken to the issues of war and peace. Before the advent of two world wars and the development of nuclear weapons, James (1910/1995) contemplated the psychological alternatives to war. Murphy (1945), whose holistic approach to human personality was prophetic for humanistic psychology, sought to mobilize the strengths of psychology and social science to the prevention of war. Frank (1982, 1986) and Fromm (1961) were pioneers in relating the depth of human experience to the waging of war. Lifton (1967) explained the psychic numbing that occurs as we contemplate mass destruction, and Macy (1983) explored the path to overcome such detachment and despair through supportive action. Profound insights about the relation of the nuclear threat to denial, apocalyptic thinking, pride, gender, and mourning have since been added from depth psychology (Levine, Jacobs, & Rubin, 1988). Friedman (1984) considered the depth of the human commitment to the "other" as a factor critical to avoiding nuclear war. The passion for peace within humanistic psychology has been well documented (Greening, 1986). Well before peace psychology had established its own organization and journal, Greening had presented both an edited volume relating American politics to humanistic psychology (Greening, 1984) and two editions of the *Journal of Humanistic Psychology* devoted completely to the topic of peace. Maslow (1984) spoke of the dangers of exclusive values, including sovereignty, as a source of intergroup hatred and an obstacle to peace. Particularly during his later years, Rogers saw, with increasing clarity, the need to prevent concentrations of power from precluding the opportunities for an unfolding of the human potential. He was outspoken in opposing the nuclear arms race. Reflecting on the Rust Conference, an international workshop created to extend the person-centered approach to political powers, Rogers (1986) noted, "The person-centered approach might be the catalyst of a long-lasting peace process and should also be applied to other politically explosive zones of the world."

Although both Rogers and Maslow recognized that society needed to be more inviting to the development of caring and concerned individuals, both placed the major emphasis on the unfolding of the individual potential for caring engagement with the world beyond the ego (Rogers, 1984). By partial contrast, May saw a darker side to human nature that made the unfolding of the human potential for caring more difficult. He believed that movement toward freedom, toward participation and caring, was most realistic when it recognized the constraints of destiny. For May (1984), these included a "daimonic" human quality that was the source of both creativity and destructiveness. May's recognition of the destructive potential is a major contribution to the debate on what is needed for peace. Indeed, it is this juxtaposition between the commitment to fulfillment of the human potential and the realization of the human capacity for violence and destruction that has led to one of the most important dialogues about human nature. If people cannot always be counted on to restrict their own belligerent inclinations, then the unfolding of human potential will have to be accompanied by the creation of human institutions that hold us accountable to some greater good.

WHY WAR

There are many psychological explanations for why humans engage in organized mass killing of each other with such apparent frequency and with approval and even acclaim by others. These surely include the psychological contributions of Freud (1962), Fromm (1964), and Frank (1982) as well as James's (1910/1995) essay on the moral equivalent of war. Recent comments of the Dalai Lama on warfare capture the basic concern:

> The unfortunate truth is that we are conditioned to regard warfare as something exciting and even glamorous: the soldiers in smart uniforms (so attractive to children) with their military bands playing alongside them. We see murder as dreadful, but there is no association of war with criminality. On the contrary, it is seen as an opportunity for people to prove their competence and courage. We speak of the heroes it produces, almost as if the greater the number killed, the more heroic the individual. And we talk about this or that weapon as a marvelous piece of technology, forgetting that when it is used it will actually maim and murder living people. Your friend, my friend, our mothers, our fathers, our sisters and brothers, you and me.
>
> What is even worse is the fact that in modern warfare, the roles of those who instigate it are often far removed from the conflict on the ground. At the same time, its impact on noncombatants grows even greater. Those who suffer most in today's armed conflicts are the innocent—not only the families of those fighting but, in far greater numbers, civilians who often do not play a direct role. Even after the war is over, there continues to be enormous suffering due to land mines and poisoning from the use of chemical weapons. (Bstan-'dzin-rgya-mtsho, Dalai Lama, 1999, pp. 204-205)

The Dalai Lama also noted the effects on the dispersion of destruction. War brings a destruction of infrastructure—roads, bridges, housing, farmlands, electricity, and medical facilities—as well as a general economic hardship. This means that, with increasing frequency, women, children, and the elderly are among its prime victims. The history of sacrifice and sexual abuse of women in war is well documented (Elshtain, 1987; Nikolic-Ristanovic, 1996). Similarly, the Graca Machel report to the United Nations on the effects of war on children documents the disastrous effects on young people. These include the loss of young lives clearly not at fault, the mutilations, the separations from family, the forced child soldiers and child sex slaves, the fear, the trauma, and the unresolved anger that later will influence survivors' own propensity to be perpetrators or victims of violence (Wessells, 1998). The Dalai Lama also addressed the impersonality of destruction:

> The reality of modern warfare is that the whole enterprise has become almost like a computer game. The ever-increasing sophistication of weaponry has outrun the imaginative capacity of the average layperson. [Its] destructive capacity is so astonishing that whatever arguments there may be in favor of war, they must be vastly inferior to those against. We could almost be forgiven for feeling nostalgia for the way in which battles were fought in ancient times. At least then, people fought one another face-to-face. There was no denying the suffering involved. And in those days, it was usual for rulers to lead their troops in battle. If the ruler was killed, that was generally the end of the matter. But as technology improved, the generals began to stay farther behind. Today they can be thousands of miles away in their bunkers underground. (Bstan-'dzin-rgya-mtsho, Dalai Lama, 1999, p. 205)

War, however destructive, always is justified by its antagonists and typically is honored. James (1910/1995) noted, however, that the sentiments tapped by war are not all bad: "Indeed, they represent the more virtuous dimensions of human existence: conceptions of order and discipline, the tradition of service and devotion, of physical fitness, of unstinted exertion, and of universal responsibility" (p. 26).

More recently, Ehrenreich (1997) placed mystical experience at the core of her theory of war. Her claim was that war is a sacrament, a blood ritual that draws on humankind's oldest and deepest impulses. In the Seville statement on war, a multidisciplinary group of distinguished scholars stated clearly that war (and, by implication, the preparation to wage war) cannot be explained as a human instinct. Although militarism is not instinctual, the religious sentiment underlying it shows characteristics of primitive programmed reactions. History provides numerous instances of the religious passions of war. The Crusades and the Islamic *jihad* elicited spiritual strengths of self-sacrifice, courage, and honor. During the 20th century, nationalism provided an illustration of the same religious zeal. In Nazism, where religious rituals were specifically incorporated (but also in World War II generally), the absolute righteousness of the participants was paramount. Ehrenreich observed that "the passions of war are among the 'highest' and finest passions humans can know: courage, altruism, and the mystical sense of belonging to 'something larger than ourselves' " (p. 238).

Such motivations reflect a potential that humanistic psychology has sought to encourage in people. Yet, with such sentiments, whole societies may be swept up into an altered state of consciousness marked by emotional intensity and a fixation on the collectivity. For example, World War I brought on the ecstasy of taking part in great events and joy of overcoming the fear of death. People became socially intoxicated with the feeling that they were a part of something greater and with the sense of being lost in that greater whole (Partridge, 1919). The institution of war clearly is enabled by those who can be mobilized at each clarion call to stand up, militarily, to the currently popularized despot.

Although the individual capacities that enhance human willingness to engage in war are important, they are not sufficient to explain it. War and its preparedness are institutions of society. Even in World War II, which was fought with a righteous belief in the cause, soldiers still were in service mainly because they were drafted. They served in combat duty only for as long as their assignments required. Studies show that they were fighting more for their loyalty to their immediate squadrons than to their country (Stouffer, 1965). The morale needed to bear the sacrifices involved—for soldiers and for the nation—had to be promoted. This war, like most, was sustained by propaganda, demonizing the enemy, and extolling the virtues of our effort.

The image of a hostile enemy is a precursor to war (Reiber, 1991). The period of the cold war demonstrated the continuing power of a military and economic elite, on both sides, to create so awesome an enemy (Bronfenbrenner, 1961) that its containment could justify great sacrifices to freedom and well-being at home. In the proxy wars fought in Angola, Korea, Vietnam, Panama, Afghanistan, El Salvador, and Iran, the public typically was treated to televised vilifications of individuals and displays of war that concealed its atrocities and costs. Even then, extended war has been unpopular.

Humanists are people who value all human life. But even for ordinary people both in and out of uniform, for people whose information comes from a mass media relying mainly on reports from the press rooms of government agencies and large corporations, war still is a horror. The images of dedication, purpose, and belonging that it brings forth often are short-lived. This fact alone should be somewhat heartening to those who would seek to build a less violent and more caring society. That task is shared by humanistic and peace psychology.

BUILDING PEACE

To appreciate the many ways in which peace can be approached, it is necessary to start with a positive definition of peace, one that goes well beyond the absence of war. A world at peace is one in which people use other means than violence or the threat of violence to achieve objectives. It is a world in which conflicts are settled peaceably and where the conditions of gross inequality of power and privilege that underlie much of mass violence are changed to conditions of equal opportunity. It is a society that ensures the requisites for a positive identity for all people. It is a world in which the security of one's surroundings allows for the attention to other levels of development. Peace means an environment in which the fulfillment of the human potential of some does not come at the expense of others. Harmon (1984) noted,

> The goal of sustained world peace is the goal of a global commonwealth in which war has no legitimacy anywhere; in which every planetary citizen has a reasonable chance to create through his or her own efforts a decent life for self and family; in which men and women live in harmony with the earth and its creatures, cooperat-

ing to create a wholesome environment for all; in which there is an ecology of different cultures, the diversity of which is appreciated and supported; in which there is a deep and shared sense of meaning in life itself—meaning that does not have to be sought in mindless acquisition and consumption. (p. 79)

Peace psychology and humanistic psychology have spoken with similar voices on the contribution of the human psyche to violent behavior and participation in war. However, humanistic psychology has adhered closely to understandings and solutions that involve individual attributes and has, by and large, left the political and societal contributions to war to others. The gap is important. Those who now plan and justify excessive efforts for military preparedness, and those whose work depends on this effort, are not rabid militarists, nationalists, or religious crusaders. Some who work most directly within the classified and secret subculture of nuclear weapons, with their godlike power to destroy, show clear signs of addictive attachment and cultlike ritual in their work (Gusterson, 1991; Pilisuk, 1999). A similar case for the addictive attachment to cultural scapegoating has been used to explain tolerance for the Gulf War and for the devastating effects of the postwar embargo on civilians (Harak, 1992). Surely, war and its preparation do contain addictive aspects. However, most people employed in the defense sector are indistinguishable from others working in large competitive corporations. The madness of mass killing lies in the system.

STRUCTURAL VIOLENCE

The broader definition of peace requires us to examine aspects of violence that go beyond overt warfare. Ramphal (1982) reminded the United Nations of the following:

> It does the cause of human rights no good to inveigh against civil and political rights deviations while helping to perpetuate illiteracy, malnutrition, disease, infant mortality, and a low life expectancy among millions of human beings. All the dictators and all the aggressors throughout history, however ruthless, have not succeeded in creating as much misery and suffering as the disparities between the world's rich and poor sustain today. (p. 1)

Humanistic psychology always has looked on the development of individuals whose respect for others would not permit them to engage directly in unwarranted acts of violence. This is essential in the promotion of peace. It also is not enough. The concept of structural violence helps to define the broader domain of peace psychology. Violence is present when an individual or a group of people die or suffer from the preventable actions of others. In structural violence, these actions are not direct but rather lie in the institutionalized behaviors that make violent outcomes inevitable (Christie, 1997; Galtung, 1996; Pilisuk, 1998). The perpetrator clearly is identifiable in incidents of premeditated murder or rape, in certain hate crimes, and in the shootings of high school children. In acts of war, the sources often are more complex, but we still think that we can attribute responsibility.

In the most frequent forms of violence, the sources are more difficult to identify. Between 1950 and 1997, the world economy grew sixfold, to a total of $29 trillion. But each year, 12 million children under 5 years of age die—33,000 per day—the overwhelming majority from preventable condi-

tions. An equal number survive with permanent disabilities that could have been prevented.

In 1997, 250 million children were working. That year, 110 million did not attend primary school, and 275 million failed to attend secondary school. Fully 2 million girls become prostitutes each year. Approximately 585,000 women died during pregnancy or childbirth in 1996. A total of 1.33 billion people live in absolute poverty, receiving less than $1 per day (Bellamy, 1997). This violence is attributable to the ways in which many people, often distant from the victims, conduct their daily lives.

Particularly when we consider structural violence, the distinction between perpetrators and bystanders is diminished. The corporations that buy the land and resources that once sustained viable communities are perpetrators. The World Bank and the International Monetary Fund, which have loaned money for projects that exploited poor countries and left them with enormous debt, are perpetrators. The economic arrangement that leaves some people too impoverished to secure food or inoculations for their children is a perpetrator of structural violence. The government leaders who have not required that a living wage be paid and a safe environment be maintained by companies permitted to locate anywhere also are to blame. Responsibility falls on those who exploit indigenous workers and their environments. It extends to those who maintain such exploitation by providing arms to national rulers who suppress efforts to obtain a living wage. The net of culpability is even greater. What of the stockholders and those people whose pension plans support the exploiting companies? What of the people whose standard of living is elevated by a global economy, the people who purchase the food, clothing, sound systems, and computers at "competitive" prices that have been lowered by the exploitation of child workers and their teenage parents? Are we ordinary people, however self-actualized, also perpetrators of this structural violence that kills and maims in numbers greater by far than all identified wars in all time?

TRANSFORMATIVE CHANGE

To build peace, as opposed to merely wishing for it, profound changes will be required by many including those who already are aware of the need for transformation. Even those who believe that transformation to a peaceful world is essential but beyond their own efforts are part of a system whose properties must be changed. Humanistic psychology offers an optimistic view of the capacities for human transformation that begins with awareness. The awareness must include present realities. Peace psychology tries to enlarge the view of what must be transformed and how it must be transformed if a world that sustains life and enriches the human experience is to survive. It confronts us repeatedly with facts that, if not faced, will return to haunt us:

▶ More resources now are committed to the development and testing of nuclear weapons than were spent (using constant dollar comparisons) at the height of the cold war (Schwartz, 1998). The dangers of this activity are protected by a culture of secrecy at the weapons laboratories (Gusterson, 1991).

▶ Professional activities of those who develop and rationalize weapons of mass destruction provide extensive financial rewards. These, in turn, ensure inordinate influence on policy.

The vocations also provide gratification for masculine identities that play with a godlike power sufficient to destroy the planet. Such activities often are pursued without conscious awareness of an underlying preoccupation with the subjugation of the weak and feminine (Cohn, 1987; Pilisuk, 1999).

▶ Military production is associated with the largest and most powerful of the world's corporate giants including exorbitant amounts spent on lobbying and political campaigns (Buzuev, 1985).

▶ Nuclear weapons are proliferating. The number of nations that now have, or are capable of developing, nuclear weapons makes the risk of their use quite high (Renner, 1990). Despite a public willingness to view the threat as past, failures to curtail the development and proliferation of nuclear weapons and to move toward nuclear disarmament leave humanity vulnerable to its own rapid extinction (Wessells, 1995).

▶ The world market in weapons trade is extensive and provides the means by which ethnopolitical wars are being fought (Greider, 1998; Renner, 1998).

▶ The global economy is creating populations with no measure of control over the local material and human resources they need to survive (Korten, 1998).

▶ World Bank and International Monetary Fund policies have left the poorer countries so deep in debt that they have no choice but to allow international commerce to exploit their natural resources, pay their workers at poverty levels, and accept the toxic wastes of the developed world (Bello, 1994).

▶ The capacity to wage biological warfare is widespread, and clandestine forms of transmission can protect its users from detection (Barnaby, 1999; Wright, 1990).

▶ The information technologies so central to command and control of dangerous weapons often are penetrated by unauthorized sources (Center for Defense Information, 1996).

▶ Violence by ever younger individuals and groups indicates disconnection and alienation (National Health Information Center, 1995; Osofsky, 1995). These conditions provide rich soil both for hate groups and for mobilization of support for militaristic activity by the scapegoating of enemies (Lamy, 1996).

▶ Military force is considered appropriate for the protection of national interests. Such interests typically are identified as the right to exploit the resources of other countries (Chomsky, 1988, 1991).

LIGHTING A HUMANISTIC PATH TO PEACE

Smith (1992) suggested a war to preserve nature as an appropriate cause that might become the new moral equivalent to war. Smith noted the political problem in this goal as

> how to advance the objectives of obtaining a sustainable ecology while enlisting the support of the have-not blue-collar workers (and the increasing underclass) in our own nation and of the have-not nations so crucially involved. Real sacrifice must

eventually be expected on the part of us affluent [people and countries]. The kind of discipline that William James wrote of may be required of us. (p. 89)

Smith (1992) saw the common enemy as our own unsustainable economic practices. The political agenda he noted is far beyond the competence of psychology, but psychology knows much about changing behavior. There has been a strong and justifiable caution among humanistic psychologists to seeing all that we psychologists know applied to monitoring people's behavior. It smacks of the Skinnerian worldview in which some informed elements of the society intentionally control the behavior and development of others. Rogers, whose life work focused on allowing the potential of the individual to unfold, persistently raised the question of whose values would define the goals of such intervention. Moreover, psychology, as both a profession and a science, has tried to avoid most political agendas (except perhaps the self-serving agenda of getting more funds for psychological research and services). An ethical issue is raised here. Do we overstep our boundaries by political advocacy even if such advocacy is intended to influence the behavior of others in ways that we perceive are vital for survival. This issue is not fully resolved in either humanistic psychology or peace psychology.

There are two profound messages prominent in humanistic psychology that appear essential for peace. The first is an ethical view promulgating the value of all people. There no longer is any meaningful ethic of self-interest, and there no longer is any meaningful nationalism. Our collective survival requires appreciation of a "community of otherness" in which acceptance and willingness to dialogue comes without regard to our perceived differences (Friedman, 1983,

1984). Peace psychology has brought forward the means for such dialogue in forms of dispute resolution that can be applied even under conditions of deadlocked distrust and ideological intransigence (Deutch, 1994; Kelman, 1999; Osgood, 1962; Pilisuk, 1997; Pilisuk, Kiritz, & Clampitt, 1971; Rapoport, 1960; Sherif & Sherif, 1969).

A second essential teaching from humanistic psychology regards the capacity for involvement in social action on behalf of peace. Humanistic psychology has long stressed the need for the fulfilled human to identify with causes beyond the self (Maslow, 1971, 1984). What causes and courses of action have been less clear, but building of peace must be high on the agenda given that destructive paths threaten to obliterate the entire experiment of life on earth. The agenda must include awareness of the harsh facts that jeopardize peace but must not allow us to be paralyzed by them.

Small causes with clearly achievable ends, such as providing therapy and hope to victimized individuals, surely are more comforting in the short term than is something so grand as building a peaceful world. But often these highly human efforts to improve the quality of lives leave untouched the underlying causes of massive suffering. The effort needs to be linked to a larger vision. On the other hand, writing about grand transformational visions and contemplating them, however essential, might make us part of a self-congratulatory elite detached from the pain of ordinary people. The paradox points to some important lessons. First, everyone has value, and all people must be included. Those who have been subjected to inhumane treatment are in the greatest need of opportunity to express their potential. Their participation is vitally needed if large-

scale change is to occur. Second, no analysis of a broad social problem is complete if it ends with what must be done. The analysis also must include what we ourselves must do.

Campbell (1984) asked just what the business of humanistic psychology is:

> To reconceptualize our role in society . . . , we must start with conscious self-evaluation and learn to take responsibility for the effects of our actions. I believe our major challenge, our business, is to apply the skills and resources accumulated in humanistic psychology in the broad arena of social change. (p. 202)

Activities to address the transition to a peaceful world can appear demanding and draining. Here, Macy (1984) offered a mind-set that could help to sustain such activity:

> The action is not a burden that we nobly assume: "I am going to go out and save the world." That's very boring, very tedious. But when you experience it as being liberated into your true nature, which is inextricably interwoven with that of every other being, then your conceptual structure of reality and your response to it are inseparable. Each act then becomes a way of affirming and knowing afresh the reality to which the doctrine gives form. (p. 118)

In the final analysis, we have no way of knowing whether we will be able to increase our involvement sufficiently to bring about a transformation to a world at peace. We do not know whether our practices to find deeper awareness or inner peace will help us to attain this end. Nor do we know whether we will be able to build institutions within which the potential for both direct and structural cruelty will be seriously lessened and the potential for goodness will be mark- edly enhanced. We do know that if we love and honor life, then we must try.

REFERENCES

Barnaby, W. (1999). *The plague makers: The secret world of biological warfare.* London: Vision.

Bellamy, C. (Ed.). (1997). *The state of the world's children, 1996* (UNICEF report). Oxford, UK: Oxford University Press.

Bello, W. (1994). *Dark victory: The United States, structural adjustment, and global poverty.* Oakland, CA: Food First.

Bronfenbrenner, U. (1961). The mirror image in Soviet-American relations: A social psychologist's report. *Journal of Social Issues, 17*(3), 45-56.

Bstan-'dzin-rgya-mtsho, Dalai Lama. (1999). *Ethics for the new millennium: His Holiness the Dalai Lama XIV.* New York: Riverhead Books.

Buzuev, A. (1985). *Transnational corporations and militarism.* Moscow: Progress Publishers.

Campbell, E. (1984). Humanistic psychology: The end of innocence. In T. Greening (Ed.), *American politics and humanistic psychology* (pp. 183-203). San Francisco: Saybrook Publishing.

Center for Defense Information. (1996). Nuclear leakage: A threat without a military solution. *The Defense Monitor, 25*(6), 1-7.

Chomsky, N. (1988). *The culture of terrorism.* Boston: South End.

Chomsky, N. (1991). *The new world order.* Westfield, NJ: Open Media.

Christie, D. J. (1997). Reducing direct and structural violence: The human needs theory. *Peace and Conflict: Journal of Peace Psychology, 3,* 315-332.

Cohn, C. (1987). Sex and death in the rational world of the defense intellectuals. *Journal of Women in Culture and Society, 12,* 687-718.

Deutch, M. (1994). Constructive conflict resolution: Principles, training, and research. *Journal of Social Issues, 50*(1), 13-32.

Ehrenreich, B. (1997). *Blood rites: Origins and history of the passions of war.* New York: Metropolitan Books.

Elshtain, J. B. (1987). *Women and war.* New York: Basic Books.

Frank, J. D. (1982). *Sanity and survival in the nuclear age.* New York: Random House.

Frank, J. D. (1986). The role of pride. In R. J. White (Ed.), *Psychology and the prevention of nuclear war* (pp. 220-226). New York: New York University Press.

Freud, S. (1962). *Civilization and its discontents.* New York: Norton.

Friedman, M. (1983). *The confirmation of otherness: In family, community, and society.* New York: Pilgrim.

Friedman, M. (1984). The nuclear threat and the hidden human image. *Journal of Humanistic Psychology, 24*(3), 65-76.

Fromm, E. (1961). *Escape from freedom.* New York: Holt, Rinehart & Winston.

Fromm, E. (1964). *Escape from freedom.* New York: Holt, Rinehart & Winston.

Galtung, J. (1996). *Peace by peaceful means: Peace and conflict, development, and civilization.* London: Sage.

Greening, T. (Ed.). (1984). *American politics and humanistic psychology.* San Francisco: Saybrook Publishing.

Greening, T. (1986). Passion bearers and peace psychology. *Journal of Humanistic Psychology, 26*(4), 98-105.

Greider, W. (1998). *Fortress America: The American military and the consequences of peace.* New York: Public Affairs.

Gusterson, H. (1991). *Rituals of renewal among nuclear weapons scientists.* Washington, DC: American Association for the Advancement of Science.

Harak, G. S. (1992). After the Gulf War: A new paradigm for the peace movement. *Journal of Humanistic Psychology, 32*(4), 11-40.

Harmon, W. (1984). Peace on earth: The impossible dream becomes possible. *Journal of Humanistic Psychology, 24*(3), 77-92.

James, W. (1995). The moral equivalent of war. *Peace and Conflict, 1*(1), 17-26. (Original work published 1910)

Kelman, H. (1999). Interactive problem-solving as a metaphor for international conflict resolution. *Peace and Conflict: Journal of Peace Psychology, 5,* 201-218.

Korten, D. C. (1998). *Globalizing civil society.* New York: Seven Stories.

Lamy, P. (1996). *Millennium rage: Survivalists, white supremacists, and the doomsday prophecy.* New York: Plenum.

Levine, H. B., Jacobs, D., & Rubin, L. J. (1988). *Psychoanalysis and nuclear threat: Clinical and theoretical studies.* Hillsdale, NJ: Analytic Press.

Lifton, R. J. (1967). *Death in life: Survivors of Hiroshima.* New York: Simon & Schuster.

Macy, J. (1983). *Despair and personal power in the nuclear age.* Philadelphia: New Society.

Macy, J. (1984). Buddhist approaches to social action. *Journal of Humanistic Psychology, 34*(3), 117-129.

Maslow, A. H. (1971). *The farther reaches of human nature.* New York: Viking.

Maslow, A. H. (1984). Politics. In T. Greening (Ed.), *American politics and humanistic psychology* (pp. 80-96). San Francisco: Saybrook Publishing.

May, R. (1984). The problem of evil: An open letter to Carl Rogers. In T. Greening (Ed.), *American politics and humanistic psychology* (pp. 12-23). San Francisco: Saybrook Publishing.

Murphy, G. (1945). *Human nature and enduring peace.* Ann Arbor, MI: Society for Psychological Study of Social Issues.

National Adolescent Health Information Center. (1995). *Fact sheets on adolescent homicide, mortality, suicide, and injury.* San Francisco: Author.

Nikolic-Ristanovic, V. (1996). War and violence against women. In J. Turpin & L. A. Lorentzen (Eds.), *The gendered new world order* (pp. 195-210). New York: Routledge.

Osgood, C. (1962). *An alternative to war or surrender.* Urbana: University of Illinois Press.

Osofsky, J. D. (1995). The effects of exposure to violence on young children. *American Psychologist, 50,* 782-788.

Partridge, G. E. (1919). *The psychology of nations: A contribution to the philosophy of history.* New York: Macmillan.

Pilisuk, M. (1997). Resolving ideological clashes through dialogue: Abortion as a case study. *Peace and Conflict: Journal of Peace Psychology, 3,* 135-137.

Pilisuk, M. (1998). The hidden structure of contemporary violence. *Peace and Conflict: Journal of Peace Psychology, 4,* 197-216.

Pilisuk, M. (1999). Addictive rewards in nuclear weapons development. *Peace Review: A Transnational Journal, 11,* 597-602.

Pilisuk, M., Kiritz, S., & Clampitt, S. (1971). Undoing deadlocks of distrust: Hip Berkeley students and the ROTC. *Journal of Conflict Resolution, 15*(1), 81-95.

Ramphal, S. (1982, February). *Address to the United Nations.* New York: United Nations.

Rapoport, A. (1960). *Fights, games, and debates.* Ann Arbor: University of Michigan Press.

Reiber, R. W. (Ed.). (1991). *The psychology of war and peace: The image of the enemy.* New York: Plenum.

Renner, M. (1990). Converting to a peaceful economy. In L. Brown (Ed.), *State of the world, 1990* (pp. 154-172). New York: Norton.

Renner, M. (1998). Curbing the proliferation of small arms. In L. R. Brown, C. Flavin, & H. French (Eds.), *State of the world, 1998* (pp. 131-148). New York: Norton.

Rogers, C. (1984). Notes on Rollo May. In T. Greening (Ed.), *American politics and humanistic psychology* (pp. 11-12). San Francisco: Saybrook Publishing.

Rogers, C. (1986). An international workshop. *Journal of Humanistic Psychology, 26*(3), 24-45.

Schwartz, S. I. (Ed.). (1998). *Atomic audit: The costs and consequences of U.S. nuclear weapons since 1940.* Washington, DC: Brookings Institution.

Sherif, M., & Sherif, C. (1969). *Social psychology.* New York: Harper & Row.

Smith, M. B. (1992). Nationalism, ethnocentrism, and the new world order. *Journal of Humanistic Psychology, 32*(4).

Stouffer, S. A. (1965). *The American soldier.* New York: John Wiley.

Tuchman, B. W. (1984). *The march of folly: From Troy to Vietnam.* New York: Random House.

Wessells, M. G. (1995). Social-psychological determinants of nuclear proliferation: A dual-process analysis. *Peace and Conflict: Journal of Peace Psychology, 1,* 49-65.

Wessells, M. G. (1998). The changing nature of armed conflict and its implications for children: The Graca Machel UN study. *Peace and Conflict: Journal of Peace Psychology, 4,* 321-334.

White, R. K. (Ed.). (1986). *Psychology and the prevention of nuclear war.* New York: New York University Press.

Wright, S. (Ed.). (1990). *Preventing a biological arms race.* Cambridge, MA: MIT Press.

CHAPTER 11

Two Noble Insurgencies
Creativity and Humanistic Psychology

MIKE ARONS AND RUTH RICHARDS

CREATIVITY as a discipline and humanistic psychology as the "third force" both emerged a half century ago as two insurgencies. They emerged along with resurgent interest in classical subjects challenging a psychology preoccupied more with its method than with its subject. This preoccupation associated with an American postwar social climate characterized as conformist, depersonalized, compartmentalized, and materialistic (Arons, 1994). Starting independently, both insurgencies inquired into what is most unique and valued in being human, heedless of whether it was the most easily standardizable or measurable and not limited by the then dominant "homeostatic" model of psychological health. Although both insurgencies at first focused on special individuals (i.e., the creatively gifted and the self-actualizing), their crossing and merging paths, as well as their massive impact on the culture, led to important implications for all persons and a profound intimation of what is essentially human.

To gain a historical focus on the merging of these insurgencies, this chapter spotlights two leaders: J. P. Guilford and A. H. Maslow. Both Guilford and Maslow were consummate insiders whose influence spread so "far out" of the confines of their field as to significantly energize a cultural, institutional, and spiritual revolution. The emerging vision reveals creativity in the texture of everyday experience while also bringing everyday experience to its fullest spiritual purpose: The vision is a holistic, dynamic, and integrative picture of psychological health and development that, through content more than method, shows promise of bringing psychology and the other sciences closer to a long sought unity. We begin with history and then look at a few points of contemporary impact relative to three areas: chaos theory and modern science, health and healing, and issues of spirituality in a troubled world.

CREATIVITY AND HUMANISTIC PSYCHOLOGY: WORKING DEFINITIONS

Leaning on Barron (1969), we define creativity broadly and yet, in our dual insurgency context, with pointed relevance. Creativity involves both *originality* and *meaningfulness*. In the simplest terms, a creative product (be it an object, an idea, or a behavior) is original; that is, it is new or departs from the conventional in some major aspect. Furthermore, it also communicates; it is meaningful to others. Simple, yes, but this definition also speaks a modest magnificence. Both terms generically implicate creativeness as a uniquely human and valued quality—a necessary ingredient of psychological health—while, at the same time, subsuming its varied forms of manifestation and expression such as *eminent, talent-centered, self-actualizing, inventive,* and *everyday* creativity.

Here, we define humanistic psychology as an orientation with a model of human psychological health based on the fullest realization and actualization of self. This "self" is not a static object but rather is, at once, both an agency for and a renewing product of meaningful change. It is self-organizing, open, and responsive (Richards, 1996). This self is by nature creative, conscious, and dynamically transforming.

In the context of mid-20th-century psychology, both creativity and humanistic psychology starkly distinguished themselves from the "human" model held by a psychology that proclaimed itself to be objective and value free. Yet, one should note well that this was a mainstream psychology whose supreme value was to predict and control. By contrast, originality—by definition new and unique—lends itself to neither of these positivistic ambitions.

Dual Insurgencies

The resurgence of interest in the subject of creativity in psychology dates back half a century, and in that time frame it roughly coincides with the emergence of the third force that came to be called humanistic psychology. Although the two insurgencies began independently, they progressively have merged. Little wonder. In the tradition of William James, both viewed one's inner subjective reality as essential to the fullest understanding of human possibility, looking where necessary beyond those "outside" objective variables that could be laboratory quantified. Both insurgencies bridged logical dichotomies, revealing that these were transcended in the subjects they were studying, including polarities of convergent-divergent, mind-body, conscious-unconscious, masculine-feminine, and personal-transpersonal. Both viewed humans in holistic terms—as growing, changing, and (for some theorists) unfolding toward a higher spiritual purpose—rather than as predictable organisms geared toward a stable and homeostatic quiescence (i.e., a Freudian dynamic of psychological "health"). Both not only spoke to the serious lacks but also added new hope, feeding a social hunger in their day—not for bread during those prosperous times but rather for self-understanding, spiritual connection, and full and empowered humanness. Both were expressions of and a sustaining force for the cultural, consciousness, and spiritual revolutions that would erupt during the 1960s and of and for the aftershock convulsions that would continue to transform the cultural landscape.

GUILFORD AND MASLOW: FAR OUT INSIDERS

Guilford's works crossed the areas of psychometrics, cognitive psychology, and nonintellective factors in creativity (Guilford, 1968), overlapping in many ways with Maslow's interests despite very different approaches. Both Guilford and Maslow were consummate insiders who had been elected presidents of the American Psychological Association (APA). The works of each had an immediate and enduring impact both within and outside of the field. Prior to Guilford's famous 1950 APA presidential address, only 186 psychology studies referring to creativity were recorded. By contrast, during just the decade that followed, 800 such publications had piled their way into that literature (Arons, 1965). For his part, Maslow's (1962) *Toward a Psychology of Being* had sold more than 200,000 copies before the trade edition had even come out (Hoffman, 1996).

Both men helped to spark insurgencies that to this day put to the ultimate test psychology's methods and paradigm. These insurgencies have transformed institutions with insights that reach so deeply into the humanities that they tap the core of the perennial wisdom and yet have so ingrained themselves in the public consciousness as to have inspired the most popular motto the U.S. Army has ever employed: "Be all that you can be . . . in the army."

Guilford's (1950) presidential address pointed to how mid-century psychology had largely reduced the creative capacity to a score on a standardized IQ test or to a learned response or defense mechanism—*sublimation*. For his part, Maslow, reflecting on the sterilized model of the human at mid-century, pointed to "a huge gaping hole in psychology." "Where," he asked, "was goodness, nobility, reason, loyalty, courage, and (even) science?" (quoted in Bennis, 1969). In its push to become a behavioral science, psychology had deleted consciousness after having expunged much of the rest of the "psyche" along with the creative source and value ends of science itself. The discarding of all that was not measurable was made by psychology in its attempt to join the hard sciences. That is, under the rubric of scientific monism, there historically has existed the presumption that, ultimately through the same methods, the subject matter of psychology could be reduced to that of physics.

Yet, how ironic that this attempt to unify psychology now is taking place, albeit not as a physical science, thanks to the humanistic psychology and creativity insurgencies, but as a reaffirmation of consciousness and creativity at the level of the human participant. As we indicate later, the psychology of consciousness and creativity and the physics of quantum and particularly chaos theory currently are in a heated heuristic dialogue. Moreover, the issues that these insurgencies tapped in exploring the "farther reaches of human nature" (Maslow, 1971) also join psychology with fields such as philosophy and theology, touching as they do the core of eternal questions such as the one and the many, chaos and order, and mind and body. All of these are classical questions now, in our day, centrally preoccupying psychology, philosophy, theology, and the physical and biological sciences by terms such as *chaos theory* and *holistic* or *alternative medicine*.

J. P. Guilford

Guilford's (1950) mid-century presidential address to the APA, bemoaning the paucity of research into creativity, proposed a three-dimensional, 120-ability, structure-of-intellect model, a true tribute to the diversity of human potential. Included among five options within his "operations" dimension was "divergent production." Unlike "convergent production," Guilford's divergent production implied that a question need not have only one answer. Indeed, the most divergent and unanticipated answer (or even a different question) can turn out to have the greatest value. Such originality is the hallmark of creativity. By contrast, the IQ tests of Guilford's day—indeed, the whole standardized testing format with its one correct answer structure—gave greatest credence to convergent thinking. High scores on such IQ tests had come to be judged as the mark of genius. Against this limited and discriminatory view, in academia and elsewhere, Guilford's contribution opened consideration of the human capacity to everything and anything—to whatever is creatively possible. Reciprocally, he also opened the notion of intelligence to include non- and supra-intellectual capacities (Gardner, 1995)—heralding what would come to be called *emotional intelligence* (Goleman, 1995). All of this drew closer the link between creative output and a fuller and more ongoing view of human development.

Guilford's opening of the creativity-human potential link roughly corresponds to the early writings of Maslow, Rogers, May, and Moustakas, among those credited with founding humanistic psychology and who, starting from the human potentials end, came in time to appreciate the essential role of creativity. For Maslow (1968, 1971), creativity was important for all persons as an enabling process for growth. As further interpreted by Rhodes (1990), creativity became integrally involved in Maslow's needs hierarchy, especially for self-actualization and beyond (Maslow, 1968, 1971).

The creativity research, overlapping and merging with humanistic psychology insights, entered into the bloodstream of the 1960s cultural revolution, notably with its stress on creative empowerment. It helped to inspire the civil rights movements while challenging, at their core, institutions such as education (Getzels & Jackson, 1962; Torrance, 1995) and the industrial-organizational infrastructure (Maslow, 1965; McGregor, 1960). This creativity-humanistic psychology conjunction, in its radical questioning of models and methods used in understanding humans, also helped to support a poststructuralist cultural critique. This has transformed the humanities and, even more radically, has questioned the underpinning of the modern epoch in toto including the modernistic scientific metaphysics. It also has been critical of the autonomous self that, interestingly, some (e.g., Gergen, 1985) associate with humanistic psychology. Yet, one can appreciate the depth of human experience while also attending well to the contextual forces and constructions that help to shape it. Similar to the insights of the dual insurgencies, those of this postmodern inquiry owe much to a range of human science research methods such as phenomenology, hermeneutics, and narrative research approaches. Little wonder given the indigenous familiarity with the creative and self-actualizing process of the divergent-convergent, deconstructive-reconstructive, and intellective-nonintellective interplay (Anderson, 1998; Kelly, 1955).

A. H. Maslow

In formulating his psychology of self-actualization, Maslow ranged broadly, joining empirical observation to literature, animal studies to human studies, and the personal to the transpersonal. He synthesized these observations with writings that crossed over the humanities, the social and biological sciences, the esoteric wisdom literature, and a potpourri of trends from psychology itself. He drew from ancient philosophy, 19th- and 20th-century European existentialism and phenomenology, and other philosophical sources such as Bergson, Buber, and Hartman. He also drew from anthropology (Benedict, 1970; Lee, 1959) and general semantics (Hayakawa, 1942) as well as from the Jungians and neo- and post-Freudians such as Rank, Adler, and Horney. He discerned unifying themes from apparently disparate sources such as Goldstein's (1939) organismic physiology, which helped to inspire his notion of holistic psychology, and he gleaned key insights from the esoteric wisdom literature of both the East and the West (Laski, 1961) that led him to the threshold of a transpersonal psychology.

Maslow found intellectual kinship in contemporaries such as Allport, Rogers, May, Moustakas, Kelly, and Klee. Their emerging-converging vision(s) formed the third force in psychology, an orientation radically distinguishing itself from behaviorism and psychoanalysis while also subsuming their limited premises (Wertz, 1994). Like others at the time, Maslow started with animal subjects, but these for him ironically suggested, by both their limits and their implications, further inquiry into the healthy human personality. This inquiry, in turn, led him to a "fourth force," transpersonal psychology, that engendered its own multiple paths of exploration, subsequently trekked by a growing number of thinkers, including Wilber, Grof, Tart, Huston Smith, Capra, Bohm (Walsh & Vaughan, 1998), Metzner (1994), and Deikman (1982). These paths have wended their way through the thickets and clearings of consciousness, to the singular origin of all, elucidated by art, science, and everyday creativity.

WISDOM OF THE BODY: THE INSTINCTOID

One example of Maslow's early animal research involved a "cafeteria-feeding" experiment (Maslow, 1933). Maslow noted that a minority of his animal subjects had given priority to nutrition over taste of food, and he called these animals "good choosers." Based on such studies, he formed the notion of the "wisdom of the body," an instinctual wisdom he also identified in humans. However, human wisdom was far from reducible to this. For humans, he evolved the word "instinctoid" (Maslow, 1970). Instincts were an inner "calling" both to survival and to the fullest species identity. Unlike animal instincts, those of humans were fragile and easily overcome by counter-pulls.

Reversing the dominant trend in psychology to concentrate on the methodologically quantifiable, or on pathology, Maslow began to study the complexity of human participants by focusing on the best of humanity, selecting individuals who shared qualities, capacities, and virtues that had been classically recognized as noble and even saintlike. He called these persons self-actualizers (e.g., Albert Schweitzer, Eleanor Roosevelt). He came to see these individuals not as superhuman but rather as more fully human, being on a path toward realizing their own talents and unique and species-best potentials. If these were "elite" persons, then their self-actualizing destiny was possible for any human.

In his needs hierarchy, Maslow noted that humans are drawn by this "wise" instinctoid calling to care for their needs in hierarchical order, from the most "basic" or deficiency needs (e.g., thirst, hunger, and safety needs) to the "being" needs (e.g., self-actualization, self-transcendence; Maslow, 1968, 1971). Much of the psychology of his day had presumed the basic needs as the prime, if not only, motivator. Each need level satisfied, then, opened a different set of insights, possibilities, and interests and led to a different value outlook. Maslow (1968) would describe his self-actualizers as open to experience, transcending polarities, being centered on ends (what is valued) rather than on means (what is instrumental to that valued end), and being problem-centered rather than self-centered. They identified with species interests and beyond. Yet, even here was a paradox, for both ends of each of these polarities were necessarily implicated, albeit in new ways, at the next step. For example, in species interests, we ultimately also find self-interests (Maslow, 1968).

Unlike other species, whose behavior is largely determined by instinct and conditioning, the humanly instinctoid could be easily intimidated and overridden, socially or otherwise, or could be repressed or denied. This made self-actualization an existential choice requiring the courage to be— the courage to authentically realize one's creative nature (May, 1975) and one's unique and species being. This stress on authenticity and courage to be, among other points of convergence, brought Maslow's biologically based theory into partial alignment with writings of European existentialists, such as Sartre, who saw the biological and social (and even one's inevitable death) not as prime determinants but rather as coexistent "givens"—marks and resources of the existential condition—with, by, and through which one's authentic engagement could be realized. Consequently, human meanings, problems, pathologies, and possibilities were not adequately understandable without systematic descriptions of experiences of the lived world. Description of the lived world is the central focus of phenomenology (Giorgi, 1970) and most other human sciences that have evolved together

with existential, humanistic, and post-structuralist inquiries (Denzin & Lincoln, 1994). Such descriptions have more access to the fuller range of experience that scientific psychology had abandoned.

Maslow also found that his self-actualizing individuals manifested in their ongoing lives an everyday creativeness. This was not necessarily associated with talent or an acclaimed product but rather involved a way of being. These individuals also reported peak or unitary and transcendent experiences more frequently than did the average person. As a consequence, they lived their everyday lives more creatively and more frequently at a higher plateau than did the average person (Maslow, 1968).

SELF-ACTUALIZING, EMINENT, AND EVERYDAY CREATIVITY

Maslow (1962, 1971) saw similarities between reported experiences of eminent creative geniuses across time and culture— at the heart and in the heat of their creative process—and those of his self-actualizing individuals. His self-actualizers were creatively engaged in the tasks of daily life rather than in monumental works in the arts, sciences, or technology, but with passionate involvement, full use of their capacities, and aliveness in the moment. Maslow's descriptions also were strikingly familiar to experiences reported across the literature intimating "flow" or optimal functioning. Csikszentmihalyi (1991) and others would expand on this theme in the context of the creativity literature. Of this genre of experience, Maslow (1971) wrote,

> One is in the moment, fully in the present, in the NOW. There is a loss of self, or ego, or sometimes a transcendence of self. . . . Actually the two, self and selfless, become a

single unity. . . . A formerly hidden truth, a revelation, is stripped of its veils and finally, almost always, there is the experience of bliss, ecstasy, rapture, [and] exhilaration. (p. 62)

Such experiences, for Maslow, often were gateways to what he called "being cognition" (later developed by Rhodes [1990] as "being creativity").

The creative experiences of self-actualizers and the plateaus at which they lived had striking resemblance to reported creative moments of genius. But these experiences also were familiar to nearly everybody at certain peak moments such as those involved in love, in witnessing sunsets, or in undergoing religious and spiritual transformations. The sense of absorption in the now, spontaneity, playfulness, and exhilaration also were marks of the child's experience. However, these self-actualizers were not children or childish; rather, they were "childlike." They had very strong egos, but having taken care of their ego needs, they were capable of experiencing a *deuxieme naïveté* (a newly innocent look), a concept also central to phenomenology and other human sciences. They could operate intrinsically rather than defensively, manipulatively, or stereotypically (Maslow, 1971).

Little wonder that Maslow would find his own insights comingling with a range of others. One comparable notion would appear in the creativity literature as "regression in the service of ego" (Kris, 1952), where ego strength, as with a martial arts master in which all situations are manageable, allows for a suspension of everyday reality in the interest of a glimpse of a fuller possibility. That fuller possibility now experienced intrinsically, for its own sake with childlike wonder, shows unity—even a variety of possible unities—of what the instru-

mental, defensive, or overrational mind had compartmentalized.

Moreover, such ego-transcending and naïve openness to the object—being with "it" spontaneously, experiencing it freshly, being absorbed with it fully and on its own terms—also is an experience inherent to Buber's (1958) "I-thou," as it is to the client-centered therapy of Rogers (1961) under his term *unconditional positive regard*. And again, this experience of openness to the object is foundational to Husserl's (1962) phenomenology, the prime dictum of which is "let the object speak," in all its inherent richness and complexity, holistically, on its own terms, in its own way—a quite different understanding of objectivity. Nor is this experience completely alien to the philosophical axioms underpinning empirical science. After all, we are speaking, in James's terms, of a *radical empiricism*. Or, on another plane, as the existentialists put it, *existence precedes essence,* or more radically, as Heidegger meant it, *being precedes the world of beings.* Such ego "surrender" and childlike experiences also are mindful of the most profound insights gleaned from the heart of religious traditions worldwide (e.g., "be as a child," the "beginner's mind") and at the beginnings of paradigm shifts (e.g., the big picture seen freshly).

Of the premiere (or child's) naïveté, the phenomenologist-existentialist Merleau-Ponty coined the notion *le monde d'ultrachoses* (i.e., world of ultra things) in taking issue with rationalist Piaget, who conceived of the child's experience as a blooming state of chaos and disorder. The child's world, Merleau-Ponty insisted, is open-ended. It is a lived world in which things are not boxed in by a given definition or function but rather have horizons, with each horizon open to others and all open to intriguing, exhilarating, and endless possibilities.

Should we be surprised, then, that the adult who is just that, in the fullest sense of having a strong ego (having mastered basic needs) and confident in handling instrumental and definable reality, should naturally (instinctoidly) suspend or "bracket" that premapped conventional reality? And seeing it freshly as a child, be able then to draw new insights from the experience? And from that second naïveté, with the skills, talents, or disposition of the adult, be able to creatively incarnate the insights drawn from the childlike experience into the flesh of that adult consensual reality—this in the form of, say, a novel product, or a personal or social achievement, or a lifestyle, or even a personal transformation? Given such "excursions" into the fresh and undefined, their blending of child and adult, should we be surprised that creative individuals, like Maslow's self-actualizers, are in person and in process characterized by their "tolerance for ambiguity" and "chaos," their "trust of intuition," and their "fascination with apparent opposites, anomalies, paradoxes, and contradictions" (Barron, 1968, p. 224). Should we be surprised at Barron's (1968) following description?

> Thus, the creative genius is at once naive and knowledgeable, being at home equally to primitive symbolism and to rigorous logic. He is both more primitive and more cultured, more destructive and more constructive, occasionally crazier and, yet, adamantly saner than the average person. (p. 224)

In describing genius, Barron (1968) carefully used the phrasing *more than*, as opposed to *distinct from*, the average person. He knew that there are creative child's doodles, as there is playful scientific research. Maslow would more fully reopen the path followed by Dewey from eminent creativity

to the everyday. In the next section, let us move to today and consider how the tandem creativity-humanistic psychology insurgencies of the mid-century might be leading us closer to a unity of some apparent opposites that have particularly compartmentalized our Western consciousness. These apparent opposites include the everyday, the creative, the spiritual, health, and the cutting edges of science.

CHAOS, COCREATION, AND EVERYDAY CREATIVITY: A CONTEMPORARY LOOK

What are some modern outcomes of the humanistic psychology–creativity insurgency? In what follows, we discuss three areas that carry the legacy of humanistic psychology and the earliest studies of creativity: modern science (and chaos theory), new visions of health and healing, and issues of spirituality in a troubled world.

Modern Science

For years, the creativity of everyday life has been formally studied by theorists as diverse as Dewey (see Richards, 1999), Guilford (1950), and Maslow (1968). Creative accomplishment can be formally assessed within virtually any activity of daily life, at work or at leisure (Kinney, Richards, & Southam, in press; Richards, 1998). For example, the dual criteria of originality and meaningfulness (Barron, 1969) can be perceived in one's teaching or counseling activities, in doing landscaping, in singing in a church choir, in making home repairs, or in planning an organizational campaign (Kinney et al., in press; Richards, 1998). Our everyday creativity is anything but a frill or an extra. It helps us to adapt to changing conditions, may keep us alive, and show us just what we are living for

(Maslow, 1971; Miller & Cook-Greuter, 2000; Richards, 1999).

Now, enter modern mathematics and hard science, which often appear much closer to humanistic psychology than to mainstream psychological science. Krippner (1994) noted that nonlinear dynamical systems (chaos) theory (Briggs & Peat, 1989) has a rather natural affinity with humanistic psychology. This affinity includes its holistic, complex, evolving, and often unpredictable nature. Chaos theory helps us to see the world, and ourselves in it (metaphorically at the very least), in terms of ongoing flux and "far from equilibrium" conditions that, at key moments, can change in a heartbeat (and dramatically). In the fabled "butterfly effect" (Briggs & Peat, 1989), a butterfly flapping its wings in Moscow could, under the right conditions, cause a storm system to erupt over New York City. Here, the weather (a complex evolving whole) has reached a critical juncture, and the butterfly (or its puff of air) merely pushes things over the edge. The nonlinear response exceeds all expectations.

Little wonder the weather can be so hard to predict. Yet, this is not just about the weather. Such sudden reconfigurations have been linked to human phenomena, notably those including creative insight (Abraham, 1996; Richards, 1996). A potential role arises for quantum mechanics as well in collapsing the uncertainty of multiple possibilities prior to creative breakthrough and in opening the creator to transpersonal sources of inspiration (Cook & Miller-Greuter, 2000). Such events may be linked to findings in physics consistent with nonlocality (Goswami, 1999; see also Bohm & Peat, 1987), which might help to explain other, more anomalous phenomena as well (Laszlo, 2000). Over longer periods, even months or years, chaos theory also has helped us to understand individuals' artistic career patterns, including changes during times of illness or strife, and has illuminated certain group processes (Schuldberg, 1999; Tarlow-Marks, 1995).

There also is the holistic issue of self in culture. Using a chaos theory model, we can appreciate our "selves" as open evolving systems in ongoing interchange with a profoundly interconnected environment. We are not the same in this setting as we would be in that one, and in either place we are constantly changing. This "metabolism of the new" (Richards, 1996) constantly calls on the everyday creativity of each one of us. We all continue to improvise in our ongoing *re-creation*. We change the instant we see others smile or hear others speak; our brains, and our totality as humans, never will be the same again (Richards, 1996).

Gone is the myth of the "Lone Genius," the autonomous self, or indeed the fixed identity (Arons, 1999; Richards, 1996). We live in the ever-evolving realm of interbeing (Nhat Hanh, 1998) and the ongoing flux of cocreation (Bohm & Peat, 1987). None of us is a static thing, a picture, or even a *noun*. Each of us is a process in motion with his or her own characteristic signature, to be sure, yet always in a flurry of change. One surely cannot step into this river twice.

New awareness of our dynamic and coevolving creativity is reaching the mainstream along with a celebration of our roles. For example, a 1999 art show called "What Is Art For? William T. Wiley and Mary Hull Webster and 100 Artists," at the Oakland Museum of California, brought together artists, community-based groups, and collaborative teams presenting a series of artworks and installations, live performances, and special events celebrating the art we all make and share. The second author (Ruth Richards), along with a talented multidisciplinary team, presented "Creating in Spite of Ourselves: Evolving at the Edge of Chaos," a talk, continuous slides, an ongoing dance improvisation, and periodic demonstrations of everyday creation from humorists, persons who had coped with adversity through arts, experts in child creativity, and others including the remarkable artists of the National Institute of Art and Disabilities in Richmond, California. These developmentally disabled artists show us that *we* might be the ones who are disabled—who have lost the freshness of wonder and forgotten how to see.

Reproduced here (Figure 11.1) is a 140-word "answer" by Richards to *What Good Is Art?,* a book edited by Nissen (1999) that accompanied the show. This statement never would have taken its present form, however, without the collaboration of Richards's then 8-year-old daughter, Lauren Richards-Ruby, who inspired the bold-lettered supertext and parts of the fractal drawing and whose picture adorns the lower right corner (clearly in touch with all of infinity). How continually we draw from those around us, in our ongoing webwork of innovation. Let us not lock away our human birthright of creativity, assigning its exercise to elite professionals and its products to special viewing rooms. Let us see its wonders everywhere. Does this sound like the humanistic psychology of the 1950s and 1960s? Of course it does.

New Visions of Health and Healing

Some persons still doubt the unity of mind and body but are brought up short by results such as those of Pennebaker, Kiecolt-Glaser, and Glaser (1988). Imagine writing privately and creatively about a traumatic incident that you had kept secret, writing for 20 minutes a day for only 4 consecutive days. Meanwhile, a control group writes about something bland. Can such cathartic creative writing be good for you? The answer is a resounding *yes.* Cathartic writ-ers not only showed greater well-being (at 6 weeks follow-up, if not immediately) but also had fewer health center visits and stronger quantitative indexes on two types of T-cell function. Here is hard data indeed; even their white blood cells—their immune systems—knew the difference.

At the other extreme, if we keep psychological conflict from our conscious minds (as Wickramasekera [1995] and others have shown), then we can put our physical and psychological health at risk. Barron (1969), Richards (1998), and others (see Runco & Richards, 1997) have indicated the healing qualities of creative openness. Achterberg, Serlin, and Zausner (see Richards, 1998), Gedo (1990), Ostwald (1997), and others (see Runco & Richards, 1997) have presented powerful evidence of uses of visualization, visual arts, music, movement, and other modalities in the healing process for people with cancer and other physical and psychological ailments. We see the unity of mind-body-spirit and the healing power of prayer (Miller, 1999).

Does the mainstream finally take notice when it can benefit so greatly? Consider an influential report, *Alternative Medicine: Expanding Medical Horizons* (National Institutes of Health, 1992), on alternative medical systems and practices in the United States. The whole face of health care is changing; it is broadening along with our views of ourselves. Included is a widely available medicine, one known to us all, and it is free—our creativity.

Creativity can help to make us whole, be this from trauma or from the false dichotomies of a culture for which, as O'Hara (1994) stated, "the image of psychological health enshrined within the mental health community is actually deeply sick" (pp. 322-323). Humanistic psychologists always have looked at broader definitions of psychological health. For example, consider *creative personality,* where the rigid stereo-

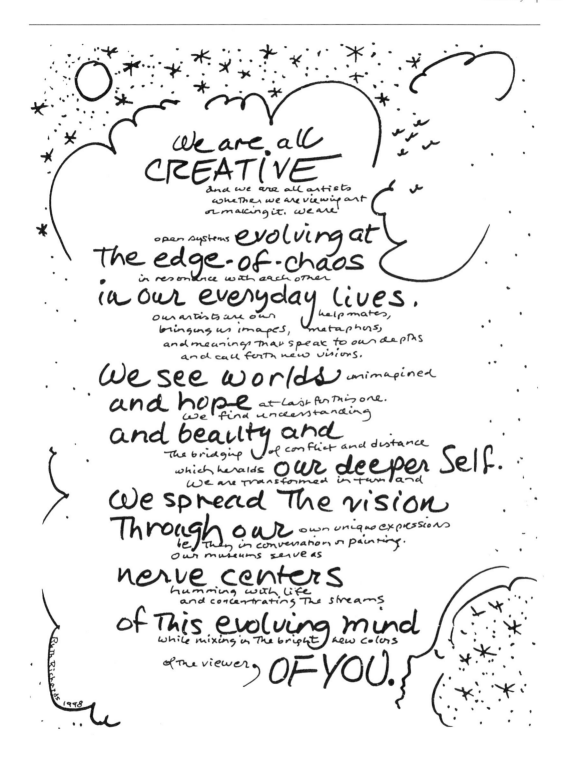

Figure 11.1. Richards's Contribution to *What Good Is Art?*
SOURCE: Nissen (1999).

types of gender are bridged toward a more androgynous creator, both sensitive and dominant, intuitive, and outspoken. Creative people can "have it all." Creativity also leaves affect and intellect more naturally intertwined (Damasio, 1994; Richards, 1997); honors the variety of altered states in our waking and dreaming reality; and values conscious awareness, aesthetic response, transpersonal potential, deeper knowing, and dynamic flow states required for the fullest creativity (see, e.g., Krippner, 1994; Miller & Cook-Greuter, 2000; Richards, 1999).

Let us note further the recasting of normality and abnormality in a culture that is discovering that what is abnormal is not necessarily pathological. Conformists beware. Converging evidence indicates that creativity is enhanced in individuals carrying both familial and individual risk for bipolar mood disorders. This even affects certain normal relatives and many more individuals with "spectrum" disorders involving pure unipolar depressions or dysthymias as well as bipolar patterns (Richards, 1997, 1998; see also others in Runco & Richards, 1997). This finding does not concern only some occasional person. As much as 4% to 5% of the population may have bipolar spectrum disorders, and if each has one normal relative, then we might be talking as much as 10% of the population. Why, one might ask, are rates so high, and have these disorders not been selected against down through evolution? Some have proposed evolutionary effects consistent with a model of "compensatory advantage" (Richards, 1997). Beyond this, we all can learn from such findings. Similar but more muted patterns of mood swings are found in all of us (Richards, 1997). Among the many lessons here is to avoid pathologizing something just because it is different and to broaden our acceptable limits of normality to encompass all the healthy diversity that we, as unique individuals, are able to bring (Richards, 1996, 1998).

What the World Needs Now

Many agree that we live in a time of environmental degradation, overpopulation, and escalating conflict, with little time remaining to turn the tide (Laszlo, 2000; Richards, 1997). According to philosopher and futurist Peter Russell,

> The root of the problem lies in our thinking, our attitudes, and our values. . . . We continue to consume and despoil the planet in the vain hope that if only we had enough of the right things, we would find fulfillment. Today it is our collective survival that is at stake. And it is our inner, spiritual well-being that most urgently needs our care and attention. This is the challenge of the early 21st century. It is the exploration of inner space—the development of human consciousness. (quoted in Laszlo, 2000, p. 115)

In fact, humanistic psychologists have fearlessly been forging this path for several decades through both the so-called third and fourth forces of psychology. Consider, for example, Maslow's (1971) Theory Z people, those self-actualizers with transcendent and mystical understandings who move beyond basic and deficiency needs to the generation of being values. They bring their creativity along on the self-same voyage, where it blossoms into being creativity (Gruber, 1997; Rhodes, 1990; Richards, 1997) and "creative altruism," with an expanding wish to help others as the modern Bodhisattvas they are becoming (Kotler, 1996). These individuals show us a different set of priorities focused on the sacred, on beauty, on fullness of the moment, and on a helping and holistic synergic involvement with a greater whole and with a greater transcendence of ego (Maslow, 1971).

As they continue their development, these people do not deny the unique individual but rather see him or her as a process-in-motion, in interdependent and dynamically evolving connection with a whole that needs reverence and care (Miller & Cook-Greuter, 2000; Nhat Hanh, 1998; Richards, 1996). Their concerns are spiritual rather than materialistic, and they resonate with a Taoistic flow and dynamic participation in life that, in turn, furthers their fullest creativity (Maslow, 1971; Miller & Cook-Greuter, 2000; Richards, 1999). They tread a path toward transforming "end experiences (of suchness)" (Maslow, 1971, p. 282) and see the needed voyage within (Goswami, 1999). Yet, at the same time, they bring skillful means and socially engaged spirituality to the pain of the world (Kotler, 1996). In their greater purpose, they readily "go beyond self-actualization" and, at the same time, very much "know who they are" (Maslow, 1971, p. 282).

A NEWLY GLIMPSED HUMAN SUBJECT WAITING FOR ITS PSYCHOLOGY TO CATCH UP

For more than 50 years, humanistic psychology, as the third or fourth force in psychology, has led boldly into the fullest realization of our human potential, and our healthiest development, hand in hand with the psychological study of creativity. As per Taylor (1994), the field of humanistic psychology—and also, we would say, the psychology of creativity—has introduced to psychology and the mainstream multiple qualitative methods, a revised value base for science, and a need to stress interdisciplinary inquiry. These two insurgencies have further united or reunited psychology with modern physical and biological science and with both ancient Eastern wisdom traditions and modern socially engaged spirituality. They have produced new models of health, of human development, and of spiritual transformation and participation. These insurgencies have helped to spark mainstream movements (e.g., positive psychology) while rejoining the interests of psychology and the humanities. Indeed, one may think of creativity as the dominant life force in the universe and the source of all being, growth, and transformation (Barron, 1969; Wilber, 1995). Creativity joins humanistic psychology in its greater mission, and in its expansive methods (Arons, 1994, 1999), at a time in human history when the challenges never have been greater.

REFERENCES

Abraham, F. (1996). The dynamics of creativity and the courage to be. In W. Sulis & A. Combs (Eds.), *Nonlinear dynamics in human behavior* (Vol. 5, pp. 364-400). Singapore: World Scientific.

Anderson, W. T. (1998). *The future of self: Inventing the postmodern person.* Los Angeles: Tarcher.

Arons, M. (1965). *Le problème de la creaviié: Discussion méthodologique, réactions dans la psychologie américaine* (The problem of creativity: Methodological discussion—Reactions in American psychology). Unpublished dissertation, Library of the Sorbonne, Paris.

Arons, M. (1994). Creativity, humanistic psychology, and the American zeitgeist. In F. Wertz (Ed.), *The humanistic movement* (pp. 45-61). Lake Worth, FL: Gardner.

Arons, M. (1999, August). *Self, multiple selves, and the illusion of separate selfhood.* Invited address, Abraham H. Maslow Award, Division 32, American Psychological Association, Boston.

Barron, F. (1968). *Creativity and personal freedom.* New York: Van Nostrand Reinhold.

Barron, F. (1969). *Creative person and creative process.* New York: Holt, Rinehart & Winston.

Benedict, R. S. (1970). Synergy: patterns of the good culture. *American Anthropologist, 72,* 320-333.

Bennis, W. (1969). *Being Abraham Maslow: An autobiographical film portrait (an interview with Warren Bennis)* [Video]. (Filmmaker's Library, 124 E. 40th St., New York, NY 10016)

Briggs, J., & Peat, F. D. (1989). *Turbulent mirror.* New York: Harper & Row.

Bohm, D., & Peat, F. D. (1987). *Science, order, and creativity.* New York: Bantam Books.

Buber, M. (1958). *I and thou.* New York: Scribner.

Csikszentmihalyi, M. (1990). *Flow: The psychology of optimal experience.* New York: Harper & Row.

Damasio, A. R. (1994). *Descartes' error: Emotion, reason, and the human brain.* New York: Grossett/Putnam.

Deikman, A. (1982). *The observing self: Mysticism and psychotherapy.* Boston: Beacon.

Denzin, N. K., & Lincoln, Y. S. (Eds.). (1994). *Handbook of qualitative research.* Thousand Oaks, CA: Sage.

Gardner, H. (1995). *Multiple intelligences: The theory in practice.* New York: Basic Books.

Gedo, J. E. (1990). More on the healing power of art: The case of James Ensor. *Creativity Research Journal, 3*(1), 33-57.

Gergen, K. J. (1985). The social constructionist movement in modern psychology. *American Psychologist, 40,* 266-275.

Getzels, J., & Jackson, P. (1962). *Creativity and intelligence: Explorations with gifted students.* New York: John Wiley.

Giorgi, A. (1970). *Psychology as a human science: A phenomenologically based approach.* New York: Harper & Row.

Goldstein, K. (1939). *The organism.* New York: American Books.

Goleman, D. (1995). *Emotional intelligence: Why it can matter more than I.Q.* New York: Bantam Books.

Goswami, A. (1999). Quantum theory of creativity. In M. Runco & S. Pritzker (Eds.), *The encyclopedia of creativity* (Vol. 2, pp. 491-500). San Diego, CA: Academic Press.

Gruber, H. E. (1997). Creative altruism, cooperation, and world peace. In M. Runco & R. Richards (Eds.), *Eminent creativity, everyday creativity, and health* (pp. 463-479). Norwood, NJ: Ablex.

Guilford, J. P. (1950). Creativity. *American Psychologist, 5,* 444-454.

Guilford, J. P. (1968). *The nature of human intelligence.* New York: McGraw-Hill.

Hayakawa, S. I. (1942). *Language in action.* New York: Harcourt Brace.

Hoffman, E. (1996). *Future visions: The unpublished papers of Abraham Maslow.* Thousand Oaks, CA: Sage.

Husserl, E. (1962). *Ideas.* New York: Collier.

Kelly, G. A. (1955). *The psychology of personal constructs.* New York: Norton.

Kinney, D. K., Richards, R., & Southam, M. (in press). Everyday creativity, its assessment, and the Lifetime Creativity Scales. In M. Runco (Ed.), *The handbook of creativity*. Creskill, NJ: Hampton.

Kotler, A. (Ed.). (1996). *Engaged Buddhist reader*. Berkeley, CA: Parallax Press.

Krippner, S. (1994). Humanistic psychology and chaos theory: The third revolution and the third force. *Journal of Humanistic Psychology, 34*(3), 48-61.

Kris, E. (1952). *Psychoanalytic explorations in art*. Madison, CT: International Universities Press.

Laski, M. (1961). *Ecstacy*. London: Crosset.

Laszlo, E. (2000). *Macroshift 2001-2010: Creating the future in the early 21st century* [Online]. Available: www.iuniverse.com

Lee, D. (1959). *Freedom and culture*. Englewood Cliffs, NJ: Prentice Hall.

Maslow, A. H. (1933). Food preferences of primates. *Journal of Comparative Psychology, 6*, 187-197.

Maslow, A. H. (1962). *Toward a psychology of being*. New York: Van Nostrand Reinhold.

Maslow, A. H. (1965). *Eupsychian management: A journal*. Chicago: Irwin Dorsey.

Maslow, A. H. (1968). *Toward a psychology of being* (2nd ed.). New York: Van Nostrand Reinhold.

Maslow, A. H. (1970). *Motivation and personality* (2nd ed.). New York: Harper & Row.

Maslow, A. H. (1971). *The farther reaches of human nature*. New York: Penguin.

May, R. (1975). *The courage to create*. New York: Norton.

McGregor, D. (1960). *The human side of enterprise*. New York: McGraw-Hill.

Metzner, R. (1994). *The well of remembrance*. Boston: Shambhala.

Miller, M. E., & Cook-Greuter, S. R. (Eds.). (2000). *Creativity, spirituality, and transcendence: Paths to integrity and wisdom in the mature self*. Norwood, NJ: Ablex.

Miller, W. R. (Ed.). (1999). *Integrating spirituality into treatment: Resources for the practitioner*. Washington, DC: American Psychological Association.

National Institutes of Health. (1992). *Alternative medicine: Expanding medical horizons*. Washington, DC: Government Printing Office.

Nhat Hanh, T. (1998). *The heart of the Buddha's teaching: Transforming suffering into peace, joy, and liberation*. Berkeley, CA: Parallax Press.

Nissen, D. (Ed.). (1999). *What good is art?* Oakland, CA: Oakland Museum of California.

O'Hara, M. (1994). Relational humanism: A psychology for a pluralistic world. In F. J. Wertz (Ed.), *The humanistic movement: Recovering the person in psychology* (pp. 322-329). Lake Worth, FL: Gardner.

Ostwald, P. (1997). The healing power of music: Some observations on the semiotic function of the transitional objects in musical communication. In M. Runco & R. Richards (Eds.), *Eminent creativity, everyday creativity, and health* (pp. 213-229). Norwood, NJ: Ablex.

Pennebaker, J. W., Kiecolt-Glaser, J. K., & Glaser, R. (1988). Confronting traumatic experience and immunocompetence. *Journal of Consulting and Clinical Psychology, 56*, 638-639.

Rhodes, C. (1990). Growth from deficiency creativity to being creativity. *Creativity Research Journal, 3*, 287-299.

Richards, R. (1996). Does the Lone Genius ride again? Chaos, creativity, and community. *Journal of Humanistic Psychology, 36*(2), 44-60.

Richards, R. (1997). The full reference is when illness yields creativity. In M. Runco & R. Richards (Eds.), *Eminent creativity, everyday creativity, and health* (pp. 485-540). Norwood, NJ: Ablex.

Richards, R. (1998). Everyday creativity. In H. Friedman (Ed.), *Encyclopedia of mental health* (pp. 619-633). San Diego, CA: Academic Press.

Richards, R. (1999). The subtle attraction: Beauty as a force in awareness, creativity, and survival. In S. W. Russ (Ed.), *Affect, creative experience, and psychological adjustment* (pp. 195-219). New York: Brunner/Mazel.

Rogers, C. R. (1961). *On becoming a person.* Boston: Houghton Mifflin.

Runco, M., & Richards, R. (Eds.). (1997). *Eminent creativity, everyday creativity, and health.* Norwood, CT: Ablex.

Schuldberg, D. (1999). Chaos theory and creativity. In M. Runco & S. Pritzker (Eds.), *The encyclopedia of creativity* (Vol. 1, pp. 259-272). San Diego, CA: Academic Press.

Tarlow-Marks, T. (1995). The fractal geometry of human nature. In R. Robertson & A. Combs (Eds.), *Chaos theory in psychology and the life sciences* (pp. 275-284). Hillsdale, NJ: Lawrence Erlbaum.

Taylor, E. T. (1994). Transpersonal psychology: Its several virtues. In F. J. Wertz (Ed.), *The humanistic movement: Recovering the person in psychology* (pp. 170-185). Lake Worth, FL: Gardner.

Torrance, E. P. (1995). *The creativity man.* Norwood, NJ: Ablex.

Walsh, R., & Vaughan, F. (Eds.). (1998). *Paths beyond ego: The transpersonal vision.* New York: Putnam.

Wertz, F. (Ed.). (1994). *Humanistic movement: Recovering the person in psychology.* Lake Worth, FL: Gardner.

Wickramasekera, I. (1995). Somatization: Concepts, data, and predictions from the high risk model of threat perception. *Journal of Nervous and Mental Disease, 183,* 15-23.

Wilber, K. (1995). *Sex, ecology, spirituality.* Boston: Shambhala.

CHAPTER **12**

Becoming Authentic

An Existential-Humanistic Approach to Reading Literature

THOMAS GREENING

THIS CHAPTER offers an existential-humanistic view of the writing and reading of fiction and illustrates this view with a discussion of three novels by Albert Camus, especially *The Fall* (Camus, 1956).

Freudian analyses of literature typically focus on writers' unresolved unconscious needs, conflicts, and defenses that manifest themselves in disguised forms containing symbols and the return of the repressed. Writing from such motivation, and reading the resulting writing, may benefit the writer and reader by sublimating drives and conflicts and by vicariously reducing defenses, resulting in greater awareness (Lesser, 1957). But Freudian analyses have become notorious for their reductionism. Freud repeatedly focused on psychopathology as manifested in creative expressions and insisted that literature (as well as art) is the product of blocked libido being sublimated. Note the

absence of an affirmative view of the artist's journey in the following quotations:

> An artist is . . . an introvert, not far removed from neurosis. He is oppressed by excessively powerful instinctual needs. He desires to win honor, power, wealth, fame, and the love of women, but he lacks the means for achieving these satisfactions. Consequently, like any other unsatisfied man, he turns away from reality and transfers all his interest, and his libido too, to the wishful constructions of his life of phantasy, whence the path might lead to neurosis. (Freud, 1917/1958b, p. 376)

> An artist is originally a man who turns away from reality because he cannot come to terms with the renunciation of instinctual satisfaction which it at first demands, and who allows his erotic and ambitious

wishes full play in the life of phantasy. (Freud, 1911/1958a, p. 224)

In response to such pathologizing, Jung (1966) wrote, "The reductive method of Freud is a purely medical one. . . . The golden gleam of artistic creation is extinguished" (pp. 68-69). In addition, Hillman (1994) introduced the contrasting concept of "psychopoiesis" or soul-making.

Sackett (1995) also offered an alternative humanistic approach focused on authenticity and growth in an article titled "The Application of Rogerian Theory to Literary Study." His study of literary characters proceeded "by recognizing incongruence between the character's internally experienced reactions and those the character feels obligated to have because of pressures from the environment" (p. 141). He also argued that, in addition to unconscious conflicts, "a literary work contains a system of values that can be apprehended by the reader through his or her emotional responses to the work" (p. 140). This focus on values and growth is more in line with humanistic psychology; struggle and redemption in the face of the absurd and tragic add an existential theme.

Sackett (1995) stressed that reading benefits the reader because it "increases awareness of the reader's own organismic experience" (p. 141). So, to values, he has added the reward of heightened awareness, not just a cognitive or verbal awareness but rather an "organismic experience," and not just awareness of negative psychological forces but rather of positive, life-affirming, growth-seeking ones.

Rogers (1961) described the creative process as "the emergence in action of a novel relational product, growing out of the uniqueness of the individual, on the one hand, and the materials, events, people, or circumstances of his life, on the other" (p. 350). Note the reference to context and

the "relational." Although some writers work in isolation from deep personal suffering, the act of writing, and certainly of publishing, is a relational outreach. And although the sources may grow "out of the uniqueness of the individual," Rogers insisted that the most personal also is the most universal.

Rogers (1961) emphasized "man's tendency to actualize himself, to become his potentialities" (p. 351). From this vantage point, we can ask not only what are a literary character's conflicts and defenses but also what are his or her growth strivings, visions of the good life, courageous ventures, and explorations into self-actualization. Rogers wrote about a person who is open to experience. "Instead of perceiving in predetermined categories . . ., the individual is aware of this existential moment as it is, thus being alive to many experiences which fall outside the usual categories" (p. 353). In this view, writing, and potentially the reader's response, expresses health and openness rather than pathology, sublimation, and defense. "In the depths of winter," Camus once stated, "I finally learned that within me there lay an invincible summer."

Rogers, as well as Sackett in his article, discusses artistic creation as playing, toying, exploring, juggling, and experimenting with ingredients, some of them "explosive" or "tainted," with the eventual goal of producing a product with communal value. One thinks of how the street entertainer juggling chain saws proceeds from what a psychoanalyst might interpret reductionistically as defensive managing of castration anxiety through repetition compulsion, to entertainment of others, a source of income, and even a sort of balletic art.

In a humanistic approach to literature, therefore, the focus is on intentionality, a process not only leading to present results but also evolving into the future, in contrast to a static retrospective analysis of past problems leading up to present character and drama. We ask not only "Where have this character and his or her actions come from, and what pathology do they manifest?" but also "What strengths and self-actualizing vision and drive do this character and his or her actions reveal in spite of all the internal and external obstacles?" What grounds for hope and guidance may we find in this story, even if it contains flawed characters and tragic events? King Lear is broken and humbled, but he emerges from illusions and nightmares that were not livable.

As Rogers has emphasized repeatedly, full honest experiencing often is costly and painful, but the alternative is a life of accumulating inauthenticity leading to partial, and in some cases total, deadness. Rogers' (1980) analysis of the case of Ellen West and her suicide is one of his most existential pieces of writing and can be interpreted as warning us to "grow or die."

Fiction, then, can serve as a goading and facilitating therapist, stirring up feelings, confronting us with our blind spots, warning us of consequences, showing us paths, offering us values and identification models, highlighting choices, and (above all) reminding us that we are in the midst of the most powerful drama we will ever know personally and for which we have responsibility—our own lives.

The life of Camus and the lives of the fictional characters he created in *The Stranger* (Camus, 1954), *The Plague* (Camus, 1948), and *The Fall* (Camus, 1956) vividly portray deep inner conflicts between emotional relatedness and despairing isolation at the interpersonal level and between personal authenticity and deluded self-alienation at the intrapsychic level. These same conflicts have been addressed in the writings of existential-humanistic psychologists. For example, Bugental (1965) has written eloquently about our inner authenticity and outward relatedness from an existential-analytic viewpoint. The fourth ontological fact, according to Bugental, is that we are separate from, yet related to, others. He spoke of "the deep satisfactions of intimacy with another and the continuing frustration of being always caught within the envelope of our own individuality" (p. 39). Buber (1937) and Jourard (1964) are other examples of theorists who have been especially concerned with our efforts to know ourselves and to build relationships on authentic sharing of that being in spite of the barriers within and around us.

Nonfiction studies can do part of the job of helping us to confront our human condition. However, fiction such as that of Camus reaches us at another level (Lesser, 1957) and, therefore, is an indispensable partner in this enterprise.

Psychological exploration of literature can catalyze the partnership of psychology and literature into yielding its fullest measure of insight. Humanistic psychology needs studies of great literature and its authors to enrich our perspective on the human experience—on what it really feels like to live a human life in this century—and to try to actualize our positive potentials in the face of much negativity. Our own phenomenological experience can give us an individual vision of the human venture but may be limited by our external circumstances and internal repressions. Great writers can distill and express core themes of life in ways that reflect clearer light back on our own dim and provincial musings. In this chapter, I suggest that Camus can teach us much about ourselves if we can see that all of us have walked the streets of Algiers, Oran, and Amsterdam with Meursault, Dr. Rieux, and Clamence and that our footsteps have traced a pattern that unites us as humans in our flawed and faltering struggle to live authentically.

Camus as a political man of action, essayist, and fiction writer captured the public imagination and became a hero. Or, if our age is too jaded for heroes, at least he has become a central figure in our modern drama, symbolizing through his life and writings basic themes in the lives of we who now survive him. Camus confronted physical illness, fascism, helplessness, contingency, absurdity, chaos, anomie, and estrangement. In spite of these forces, he struggled to live a life of action, creation, commitment, involvement, and relatedness. During his youth, he was an athlete. At 17 years of age, he began a lifelong battle with tuberculosis (a disease that also had a formative impact on Rollo May). He opposed the Germans as editor of the underground newspaper *Combat,* and he worked to rebuild his country during the chaos, rancor, and frustration of postwar French politics. He was noted for his personal charm. In addition to his career as a novelist, he was active as a journalist, political spokesman, playwright, producer, and theater director. Nevertheless, Camus was tormented by a sense of passivity, estrangement, and "unbearable solitude." "Only by a continual effort can I create. My tendency is to drift toward immobility. My deepest, surest inclination lies in silence and the daily routine" (Camus, 1965b, p. 120).

The same duality predominates in his fictional characters. Meursault, in *The Stranger* (Camus, 1954), is the ultimate of passivity, boredom, detachment, and emotional flatness. He is overtly unmoved by his mother's death, his boss's offer of a promotion to a job in Paris, his mistress Marie's love, and his own violent murder of an Arab. Meursault, his mother, Marie, Raymond (a friend), and Salamano (a neighbor) and Salamano's dog all drift about seeking

and repelling intimacy. As discussed later in this chapter, similar ambivalent approach-avoidance feelings about closeness pervade *The Plague* (Camus, 1948), *The Fall* (Camus, 1956), and his personal notebooks (Camus, 1965a, 1965b). But given that Meursault could be considered an antihero, why focus on him?

> The anti-hero of modern times seems to relate very directly to the negative and reductionist Freudian and behaviorist images of man. . . . The anti-hero of the intensely ironic, absurd, modern tragic vision is a victim in a meaningless reality in which no catharsis is possible to relieve the polarized tensions. (Heitner, 1978, pp. 7-8)

As we will see, however, there is more to Meursault and Camus than the antihero. Meursault's slow awakening begins, ironically, in response to a dog. Salamano's dog in *The Stranger* (Camus, 1954) is perhaps one of the most pathetically expressive symbols in Camus's work. The intensely ambivalent attachment of Salamano to his "wretched spaniel" is one of the few examples in this novel of any lasting, deep relationship between two creatures. Salamano got the dog soon after his wife's death to help fill the gap in his life. "For eight years the two had been inseparable" in spite of constant battling. Meursault's mother had been fond of the dog, and the implication seems to be that the dog, Salamano, the mother, and Meursault are variations on the same theme of ambivalent relatedness and bedraggled loneliness, with the dog having a slight edge so far as its capacity to provide emotional involvement and win loyalty. In Camus's world, all closeness ends in loss, so Salamano loses his dog and weeps. Meursault, who is unable to experience grief at the death of his mother, makes the following comment after hearing Salamano weep for his lost dog: "For some reason, I don't know what, I began thinking of mother" (p. 50). He does not pursue his thoughts and quickly goes to sleep. He cannot consciously acknowledge that he needs Salamano to do his weeping for him or that he is losing his hold on life just as Salamano has lost his dog. Authenticity still eludes him until further events unfold.

In *The Plague* (Camus, 1948) and *The Fall* (Camus, 1956), Camus also introduces dogs at critical points to dramatize loss and alienation and to provide poignant reminders of our flawed and often disguised, displaced, or even betrayed search for authentic relatedness. In *The Fall,* Clamence describes a critical encounter with a dog on a subway platform during the German occupation:

> Big, wiry-haired, one ear cocked, eyes laughing, he was cavorting and sniffing the passing legs. I have a very old and very faithful attachment for dogs. I like them because they always forgive. I called this one, who hesitated, obviously won over, wagging his tail enthusiastically a few yards ahead of me. Just then, a young German soldier, who was walking briskly, passed me. Having reached the dog, he caressed the shaggy head. Without hesitating, the animal fell in step with the same enthusiasm and disappeared with him. (Camus, 1956, pp. 121-122)

Dependable, authentic relationships—with dogs or people—are hard to come by in the alienated realm that Camus portrays in these novels. Dogs disappear, get shot by misanthropes, or desert to the enemy, demonstrating that in Camus's world one can count neither on people nor on man's best friend. But the characters continue searching.

The first line of *The Stranger* announces a loss: "Mother died today" (Camus, 1954). Yet, Meursault then proceeds through apathetic words and listless deeds to act as if he feels no loss. He uses the psychoanalytic defenses of denial and isolation of affect. In classic psychoanalytic fashion, Fenichel (1953a, 1953b; see also Leites, 1957) described such symptoms and possible unconscious sources but left us at a loss for a way out. Tragically, Meursault plunges deeper before he arrives at an existential breakthrough. Repeated references to the glare of the sun and the oppressiveness of the heat provide external symbolic cues to Meursault's repressed feelings. The day after his mother's funeral, with Meursault's characteristically studied casualness, he decides to swim, meets Marie at the pool, and begins an affair—a mother lost, a mistress gained. Marie soon decides that she loves him. Meursault has no reaction. Marie tells him that she wants to marry him. Meursault, persisting in his affectlessness, says that he does not mind. One weekend at the beach, Meursault and Marie become emotionally close, swimming happily together in the sea and embracing. Meursault seriously thinks that he will marry Marie and actually feels "pleasant," but he withdraws into sleep. Then he eats and takes a walk with Raymond in the hot sun. "It was just the same sort of heat as at my mother's funeral, and I had the same disagreeable sensations" (p. 75). Moments later, Meursault—confused and tense—impulsively kills an Arab and, thereby, unconsciously ensures his separation from the blessings but challenges of intimacy with Marie.

This is a vivid description of inauthenticity. Can Meursault move beyond it? He is by no means a simple and uncomplicated person, free from unconscious motivation and intense affect, even though Camus presents him as such in the beginning of the novel. Instead, Meursault must be regarded as the most dangerous and blind type of inauthentic and unrelated man, the type who claims to know himself and to be content with his relationships. He is, therefore, unaware of the self-alienation and loneliness that really drive him, and when his defenses finally crumble, his pent-up rage and frustration explode with lethal force:

> Then everything began to reel before my eyes; a fiery gust came in from the sea, while the sky cracked in two, from end to end, and a great sheet of flame poured down through the rift. Every nerve in my body was a steel spring, and my grip closed on the revolver. The trigger gave. . . . And so, with that crisp, whip crack sound, it all began. . . . I fired four more shots into the inert body. . . . And each successive shot was a loud, fateful rap on the door of my undoing. (Camus, 1954, p. 76)

This concludes the first half of *The Stranger* (Camus, 1954). The second half of the novel is devoted to Meursault as a prisoner. He begins to change, but within terrible finite limits. At first, he still does not really face the fact that he is in prison and probably will be condemned to death—until his one and only visit from Marie. "I was hardly conscious of being in prison. I had always a vague hope that something would turn up, some agreeable surprise" (p. 89). Marie comes to see him, and the scene is an epitome of blocked communication and frustrated attempts at closeness. Marie and Meursault face each other across a space of 30 feet, separated by iron grills. A dozen other prisoners are in Meursault's compartment. Meursault and Marie shout to each other, fall silent, shout inanities again, and are drowned out. Finally, the jailer takes Meursault away. Soon after, he receives a letter from Marie saying that she is not al-

lowed to visit him again. "It was from that day that I realized that this cell was my last home, a dead end, so to speak" (p. 89). Meursault now begins to experience intense feelings about the very life from which he has cut himself off. He moves from his apathetic detachment toward an open avowal of emotion, an assertive commitment to action, and a direct search for contact with the human race. His transition from passive confusion to active engagement parallels the development of his French ancestor, Candide (Greening, 1965). He hopes that the lawyer will like him, he becomes enraged at a meddlesome priest, he experiences a welling up of nostalgic feelings for Marie, he takes pleasure in the realization that his mother had found some happiness in a love affair just before her death, and he experiences deep happiness on the eve of his execution.

Meursault has lost his mother, his mistress, and his friends. He is alone at last. He sleeps and awakens. In his final hours, he allows himself to experience a wish for the only form of doomsday relatedness he dares trust. The closing lines of the novel are as follows: "All that remained to hope was that on the day of my execution there should be a huge crowd of spectators and that they should greet me with howls of execration" (Camus, 1954, p. 154). For this lonely, confused, and distrustful man, execution holds out the one hope for reunion and contact with the human race. Joseph K, in Kafka's (1956) *The Trial*, also finds some ironic solace for his confusion and loneliness in the final scene of execution, where he at last establishes contact with his persecutors and receives a "reassuring pat on the back" (p. 284).

Both the fictional character Meursault and the author Camus exemplify a dangerous inauthenticity and isolation. There is evidence that Camus did not understand the unconscious self-alienation of the character he had created in *The Stranger* and that only later, in writing *The Fall*, did he demonstrate insight into the self-deluding capacity of an "honest" man. Camus wrote the following in a preface for a new edition of *The Stranger*:

> We will have a better idea of, or at least one in conformity with, the intentions of the author if we ask ourselves in what way Meursault refuses to play the game. The answer is simple: He refuses to lie. Now, lying is not only saying what is not. It's also saying more than is and, in matters of the human heart, more than we feel. (Camus, 1957, p. 355)

Camus (1957) describes Meursault as having "a passion for the absolute and the truth . . . the truth of being and feeling" (p. 356). In my perspective, while Meursault may have had a passion for honesty, he has lost contact with his true feelings. Thus, in spite of Meursault's and Camus's well-intentioned attempts at authenticity, psychological analysis of Meursault's supposed "truth of being and feeling" inevitably leads us to the same conclusion as that voiced by the profound pre-existentialist philosopher W. C. Fields, who warned, "Never trust an honest man."

Several of the characters in Camus's (1948) *The Plague* also act out variations on the themes of separation and reunion, despair and hope, and detachment and involvement. In this novel, as in *The Stranger,* the source of human distress is seen by the characters as external, not self-imposed. Just as Meursault blinded himself to his own inner disease of emotional isolation by focusing on his mother, the sun, an Arab, and a priest as causes of his aggravation, so do the characters in *The Plague* experience the plague as causing the frustra-tion of their inner happiness and their isolation from loved ones who are outside the city. Dr. Rieux uses work to avoid confronting his loneliness. He achieves a high degree of existential commitment to involvement and action in the face of estrangement and contingency. He retains his belief in the fundamental importance of personal relationships (Greening, 1963b). At the end, however, his wife and his friend Tarrou are dead, Rambert and his mistress are reunited, and Rieux is alone except for his mother.

In *The Fall* (Camus, 1956), a haunting novel published at the peak of Camus's career and three years before his death, he finally presents us with a protagonist, Clamence, who openly epitomizes the inauthenticity and loneliness that Meursault denied through repression and that Rieux tried to surmount through hard work. It takes no psychological analysis of Clamence or debunking of a Camus preface for the reader to see the dishonesty and isolation of Clamence's life because the book is a monologue by Clamence describing his life in just those terms. Camus clearly has gained insight into the darker regions of himself and the rest of us, and has undertaken to create a protagonist far more complex than a simple, honest Algerian clerk mistreated by society or a dedicated doctor fighting the plague.

Elsewhere (Greening, 1963a) I presented the theory that, in creating Clamence, Camus's long-standing pessimism and bitterness were emerging from beneath a lifetime of attempted repression and that, as a result of this emergence, Camus may have committed a "subintentioned suicide" (Shneidman, 1963; Tabachnick & Litman, 1966). Despite our admiration for Camus, we would not enhance his value or the value he placed on honesty if we allowed our admiration of him to blind us to the strong indication that he may have fallen victim to the inauthenticity that he fought against for so long.

In *The Fall*, his final novel, Camus (1956) reveals an awesome insight into the entanglements of self-deception, false relatedness, and the desperate cry for contact and authenticity. From the first paragraph, the reader is assaulted by Clamence's gracious, intrusive, wheedling, deferent, insistent attempt to reach out and establish a bond. Clamence, weighted down with his albatross of guilt, has wandered like a modern mariner to a seaman's bar in the port of Amsterdam and is driven to pour out his tale to a stranger. Why? Clamence is lonely and devious. Only as his tale unfolds does his goal gradually become apparent.

In Clamence, Camus presents a thorough portrayal of a phony humanist. Clamence was all things good—at least in his conscious mind and his public image. He was a successful attorney, the champion of innocent victims, and a gracious and beloved social companion.

> I had a specialty: noble cases. Widows and orphans. . . . My heart was on my sleeve. You would really have thought that justice slept with me every night. I am sure you would have admired the rightness of my tone, the appropriateness of my emotions, the persuasion and warmth, the restrained indignation of my speeches before the court. (Camus, 1956, p. 17)

But in contrast to *The Stranger*, where Camus and his creation, Meursault, both remain unaware of Meursault's inner dishonesty and see society as the source of evil and absurdity, and in contrast to *The Plague*, where Rieux fights against an external enemy (the plague), in *The Fall* Camus seems at last to have evolved a protagonist who directly confronts himself as the prime source of the evil in his world (Thody, 1957). At a

crucial moment in *The Fall*, Clamence betrayed himself and all that he thought he stood for. His sin is the same as Meursault's in *The Stranger*—indifference and inaction in response to a woman's death.

Clamence is forced by his sudden unexpected treachery against himself and humanity to admit painfully and inescapably that he is not what he seemed to be. He speaks of how he learned "to see clearly within me and to discover at last that I was not simple" (Camus, 1956, p. 84). He finally confronts the full extent of his inauthenticity and concludes, "After profound research on myself, I brought out the fundamental duplicity of the human being" (p. 84). "I was absent at the moment when I took up the most space" (p. 87).

Two decades earlier, Camus (1965a) struggled against this pressure toward role-playing and wrote despairingly in his journal, "I waste my time all day long, while other people say that I do a great deal" (p. 9). In the same vein, at the time his first marriage ended Camus wrote, "One goes back into the game. And, without believing in them, everyone smiles at appearances and pretends to accept them" (p. 17). Through Clamence, Camus pursues this conflict to an attempted resolution. Clamence decides to confess:

> A ridiculous fear pursued me, in fact: One could not die without having confessed all one's lies. Not to God or to one of his representatives; I was above all that, as you well imagine. No, it was a matter of confessing to man, to a friend, to a beloved woman, for example. (Camus, 1956, pp. 89-90) . . .
>
> I wanted to upset the game and above all to destroy that flattering reputation, the thought of which threw me into a rage. (p. 93) . . . In order to reveal to all eyes what I was made of, I wanted to break

open the handsome wax figure I presented everywhere. (p. 94)

Clamence was embarked on his "search for authenticity" (Bugental, 1965). But he is not content to admit his guilt to himself, to confess to others, and to seek forgiveness or punishment. His goal is relatedness, not absolution. He prefers fraternity in hell to honor in life or forgiveness in heaven. Clamence wants to rejoin the human race. He is so obsessed with his own inauthenticity and guilt, however, that he believes the only true fraternity is that of the condemned. He points to himself and, in effect, says, "There, without the grace of God, go all men." Here is a Raskalnikov, an ancient mariner, or a Joseph K, who will not suffer alone and who insists on drawing his accusers and even indifferent spectators into complicity.

> When we are all guilty, that will be democracy. . . . Death is solitary, whereas slavery is collective. The others get theirs, too, and at the same time as we—that's what counts. All together at last, but on our knees and heads bowed. (Camus, 1956, p. 136)

Clamence chooses a bar in Amsterdam as the setting for his confession and his reunion with humanity. The nearby Zuider Zee is "a soggy hell. . . . Space is colorless, and life [is] dead" (Camus, 1956, p. 72). "For we are at the heart of things here. Have you noticed that Amsterdam's concentric canals resemble the circles of hell?" (p. 14). He believes that all of us sometime must pass through this disreputable seaport bar. He strikes up a conversation with us, his readers. As he nears the end of his tale, he tells us,

> Covered with ashes, tearing my hair, my face scored by clawing, but with piercing eyes, I stand before all humanity recapitulating my shames without losing sight of the effect I am producing, and saying: "I was the lowest of the low." Then imperceptibly I pass from the "I" to the "we." . . . Ah, *mon chere*, we are odd, wretched creatures, and if we merely look back over our lives, there's no lack of occasions to amaze and horrify ourselves. Just try. I shall listen, you may be sure, to your own confession with a great feeling of fraternity. (p. 140)

Now it is our turn, if Camus and Clamence have succeeded. We may put down the book, turn away from this raving barfly, and even wonder whether perhaps Camus had sunk into some private pathology. But the voice of Clamence pursues us: "Admit, however, that today you feel less pleased with yourself than you felt five days ago? Now I shall wait for you to write me or come back. For you will come back, I am sure!" (p. 141).

And we do come back to Camus, for, as does the penitent Clamence, he shows us what we fear, deny, and then reluctantly confront in ourselves so as to grow. We must acknowledge our self-alienation and isolation so as to begin our search for authenticity and relatedness. Let us hope that we do not wait, as did Meursault, until the eve of our execution or, as did Rieux, until solitary work amid separations and deaths caused by a plague has worn us down or, as did Clamence, to incur still more existential guilt in an Amsterdam fog. In these three novels, Camus showed us some varieties of alienation in vivid stories and characters. In his own life, he sketched some visions of authenticity, and then he died young in a senseless car accident. It becomes our task to learn from him and his fictional characters and to create our own paths to authenticity.

REFERENCES

Buber, M. (1937). *I and thou.* New York: Scribner.

Bugental, J. F. T. (1965). *The search for authenticity.* New York: Holt, Rinehart & Winston.

Camus, A. (1948). *The plague* (S. Gilbert, Trans.). New York: Modern Library.

Camus, A. (1954). *The stranger* (S. Gilbert, Trans.). New York: Vintage.

Camus, A. (1956). *The fall* (J. O'Brien, Trans.). New York: Vintage.

Camus, A. (1957, November 16). Preface to *The Stranger* (V. Hall, Jr., Trans.). *The Nation,* pp. 355-356.

Camus, A. (1965a). *Notebooks: 1935-1942* (P. Thody, Trans.). New York: Modern Library.

Camus, A. (1965b). *Notebooks: 1942-1951* (J. O'Brien, Trans.). New York: Knopf.

Fenichel, O. (1953a). An infantile, preliminary phase of "defiance by lack of affect." In *The collected papers of Otto Fenichel, first series.* New York: Norton.

Fenichel, O. (1953b). On the psychology of boredom. In *The collected papers of Otto Fenichel, first series.* New York: Norton.

Freud, S. (1958a). Formulations on the two principles of mental functioning. In S. Freud (Ed.), *The case of Schreber: Papers on technique and other works* (12th standard ed., pp. 218-226). London: Hogarth Press and Institute of Psycho-Analysis. (Original work published 1911)

Freud, S. (1958b). The paths to the formation of symptoms, Lecture 23: General theory of the neuroses. In S. Freud (Ed.), *Introductory lectures on psycho-analysis* (Part 3, 16th standard ed., pp. 358-377). London: Hogarth Press and Institute of Psycho-Analysis. (Original work published 1917)

Greening, T. (1963a, December). *Camus' unconscious guilt as a factor in his life, death, and fiction.* Paper presented at the meeting of the California State Psychological Association, San Francisco.

Greening, T. (1963b). Existential fiction and the paradox of ethics. *Antioch Review, 23,* 93-107.

Greening, T. (1965). Candide: An existential dream. *Journal of Existentialism, 5,* 413-416.

Heitner, J. (1978). *The search for the real self: Humanistic psychology and literature.* Washington, DC: University Press of America.

Hillman, J. (1994). *Healing fiction.* Dallas, TX: Spring.

Jourard, S. (1964). *The transparent self.* New York: Litton Educational Publishing.

Jung, C. G. (1966). The spirit in man, art, and literature. In C. G. Jung (Ed.), *Collected works* (Vol. 15, pp. 68-69). Princeton, NJ: Princeton University Press.

Kafka, F. (1956). *The trial* (W. Muir & E. Muir, Trans.). New York: Modern Library.

Leites, N. (1957). The stranger. In W. Phillips (Ed.), *Art and psychoanalysis* (pp. 247-267). New York: Criterion Books.

Lesser, S. G. (1957). *Fiction and the unconscious.* Boston: Beacon.

Rogers, C. R. (1961). Toward a theory of creativity. In C. Rogers, *On becoming a person.* Boston: Houghton Mifflin.

Rogers, C. R. (1980). *A way of being.* Boston: Houghton Mifflin.

Sackett, S. J. (1995, Fall). The application of Rogerian theory to literary study. *Journal of Humanistic Psychology, 35*(4), 140-157.

Shneidman, E. S. (1963). Orientations toward death. In R. W. White (Ed.), *The study of lives* (pp. 201-227). New York: Atherton.

Tabachnick, N., & Litman, R. E. (1966). Character and life circumstance in fatal accident. *The Psychoanalytic Forum, 1,* 66-74.

Thody, P. (1957). *Albert Camus: A study of his work.* London: Hamish Hamilton.

CHAPTER 13

Fellini, Fred, and Ginger
Imagology and the Postmodern World

EDWARD MENDELOWITZ

> *Our danger is that, invaded by the external, we may be driven out of ourselves, left with our inner selves empty, and thus become transformed into gateways on the highway through which a throng of objects come and go.*
>
> —J. Ortega y Gasset (*Meditations on Quixote*, 1961)

THE BRITISH PLAYWRIGHT George Bernard Shaw once quipped that all professions were conspiracies against the laity. A bit of hyperbole perhaps, the remark is nonetheless instructive. Our own guild suffers the same commercial pressures and varieties of professional demarcation as do the others, with insiders very often the last to find out. In this chapter, I offer a corrective and recompense in the consideration of one example of would-be "being-in-the-world" using filmmaker Federico Fellini's astonishing *Ginger and Fred* as text and gospel. Fellini's interest in psychology was prodigious, as was his fascination with humanity's success and failure at finding itself in a disjointed location in time. For him, life inhered in neither ideology nor the empirical but rather in wonder and transience, humor and poignancy, sadness and love. The filmmaker has much to teach us about the world we inhabit and share and the incompleteness we mostly embody and still long to surpass, about the sheer madness and mystery of being in a new millennial landscape and terrain. It is the artist's peek behind the proscenium arch. In other words, it is psychology.

Amid a proliferation of strategies of psychotherapeutic endeavor and an ever-increasing influx of information bits, the psychologist today stands in Kafkaesque perplexity before a deafening surfeit. It is not so different, really, from the way in which the rest of the world feels—deluged, jaded, confused. Consider: The overwrought layperson consults an overwrought psychologist to secure a bit of respite in an overwrought world. What that person finds, inexorably, are leveling reductions, formulaic responses, and specious techniques—all masquerading as truth. Take our professional curricula or, for example, our annual pageants and conventions. Which door to choose, which lecture hall, which rally cry? By all means, we must stay current. Truth is fashion, and fashion is what sells in the marketplace of commerce and experience. The Czech writer Milan Kundera—the very same one who has coined our word "imagology" and whose novels are psychologically stunning—has stated the problem with grave precision: In the age of speed and expedience, it is requisite, as Rimbaud had already admonished, that we remain "absolutely modern." But just what does it mean to be absolutely modern, and what, God help us, is the price tag? It is a strange world out there and, I sometimes think, even stranger here within our professional divisions and cliques with our comforting shibboleths and statutes and theoretical watering holes. It is stranger perhaps for the very lack of correspondence between so much that goes on in our offices and heads and what it means to be alive on a teetering planet in the dawning moments of a postmodern millennium. "To be absolutely modern," Kundera (1991) laments with all the solemnity of a eulogy, "means to be the ally of one's gravediggers" (p. 141).

We psychologists are the worse for our overspecializations and frantic routines, accoutrements that too rarely let in the greater light. We have detached ourselves from the source and do not know how it is that we have become so threadbare. Rollo May said it was because we had lost touch with what it might mean to be fully human, with wonder and what Goethe called "the All." Having cut our cords with the motherland, we no longer are able to hear the music of the spheres (a very different type of chord) or the reverberations of our own heartstrings. We have become purveyors of flatness and representation, system and certainty, rotation and sham. Cords versus chords? This is our question.

Lately I have been watching the films of Federico Fellini, many viewings apiece for they are fathomless in their scrutiny and depth. An amazing psychologist and brilliant articulator of the complexities of the self and the vagaries of postmodern existence, the Italian maestro is almost too shrewd for us. The general practitioner is quite baffled by the subtlety and scope of the artistry and insight and so bids a crude and hasty retreat into safe havens of diagnosis and dismissal. But how to diagnose genius? See how we retreat from the vastness of our subject. One film in particular interests me for its very depiction of a world gone wrong and the near impossibility of finding oneself amid a morass of sound bites, information streams, and video monitors where all is simulation, packaging, and artifice. *Ginger and Fred* (Fellini, 1985) is an unflinching depiction of an uncanny time, one in which image is everything. Reflected here is a world of superfluity and void, a static drama of boredom and titillation, a fascination with the odd and grotesque so as to conceal perpetual inner emptiness and outer vacuity.

From the opening scenes and thereafter, we are besieged with advertising and stridency and commercials, with the television monitor never far from view. "YOU'LL BE BETTER-LOOKING, STRONGER, AND RICHER WHEN YOU USE . . ." reads the billboard ad at the train station in downtown Rome where the story begins. We know psychologists and pharmaceutical houses who use more or less the same line. And the crowds! Who are these multitudes, and just where do they think they are going? They scurry back and forth in search of vocation and author, all waiting to play bit parts in a holiday gala to be aired on television. The world has become a tentacular broadcasting station whose insidious reach now ensnares all, an electronic shopping mall of hype and Hollywood, an Internet of the inane. Mediocrity tops the postmodern hegemony; you will not find an individual in sight.

The protagonists are, in fact, not Ginger and Fred but rather Amelia and Pippo, dancers from a bygone era who once had made a name for themselves (and a living as well) impersonating the more famous couple. And just whom have they copied but Hollywood stars who themselves were not what they seemed and had, in fact, changed their own names even further back so as to pander to audiences wanting only to be entertained and thereby let off the cross of self-consciousness for a spell? Fred Astaire and Ginger Rogers, icons of flash selling American dreams with their tiresomely happy endings. And indeed, the States, with our incessant ebullience and our penchant for packaging, hover ominously over Fellini's film like a dark and foreboding postmodern cloud. "It's important," observes Amelia, "to have an American name."

Amelia and Pippo have come out of retirement to dance once more for old time's sake. They are to be the nostalgia act in the incessantly promoted television extravaganza. Amelia has been coaxed by family and friends. Pippo seems to need the money and will confess, in a moment of weakness, that he has been reduced to selling encyclopedias on the sly. They have not seen each other for 30 years and are by no means the only copyists. There will be a part of the show given to look-alikes, and doubles are seen flitting about everywhere—Clark Gable, Marcel Proust, Sitting Bull, Brigitte Bardot, Ronald Reagan ("Where is your cowboy suit?" we hear somebody shout), and Woody Allen (who has, of course, been copying himself for years). "Kafka has arrived!" says the gum-chewing chauffeur. The situation is Kafkaesque indeed. Clark Gable mistakes Amelia for Bette Davis while introducing her to Proust. "He's a big French writer," he points out. "I'm not anyone's look-alike," protests the Italian dancer with the American name.

Let us take a closer look at postmodernity's lineup, for we find, unremittingly, the counterparts filling up the ranks of our own profession as well. There is the transvestite Evelina Pollina, quintessential exhibitionist who offers herself as a Madonnalike pinup to all of Italy's prison inmates. It is a ball pitched, according to Kundera (1991), "to the lowest ontological floor" (p. 111). "I'm in such agony over those poor boys," the transvestite sighs. "Shouldn't somebody care?" Amelia thinks for a moment that she has met some overcoifed acolyte of Mother Teresa who has taken a wrong turn somewhere and wound up in Bloomingdales or the boutiques of Milan. "I felt a calling, a true vocation," Evelina proclaims. It is more likely that this calling has been preceded by dread and impoverishment, by the harrowing prospect of having to survive in a world now defined by image and chip and by a populace weaned on the commonplace.

We next observe a most touching character, a retired admiral, a military hero said to have once saved a ship and perhaps a city with his valorous exploits, although all details are lacking in an ambiguous age. The admiral is now old and bent, the event for which he will be remembered having occurred half a century ago whatever it was, a hazy story about a faded snapshot taken long ago. "I love artists," says the admiral with all graciousness and dignity on meeting Amelia. "They are the benefactors of humanity." Rilke and Proust, of course, had said it as well, and I suggest that we write it down on our organizational shirtsleeves before it is lost forever beneath a deluge of sophomoric techniques and humorless technicians who look too much like foot soldiers but lack the admiral's blossoming quietude and consciousness even as the body declines. With senility comes release from conformity and spectacle, from the oppressive need to keep up and hang on and in. The admiral is less a serviceman than the teeming imagologists who surround him and many psychologists as well.

But wisdom is fleeting in the new-millennial landscape, and we proceed straightaway to an oddball mother-and-son duo who record voices from the stratosphere and beyond on their tape recorder. "The dead," rants the mother. "They're so happy, so festive." "A kind of murmur," the son concurs. "It's all been tested by experts, no tampering." It is New Age proof of the soul's immortality though, to be sure, what cannot survive here will not be found there. Tested by experts, like antidepressants and American Psychological Association-sanctioned training, like rote psychotherapy and the *management* of *care*—tested by experts, no tampering.

Conventional religion has no place in the marketplace of novelty: the post-theological age will require a trick. And so the Church's sole representative to the garish festivities is a priest who is able to levitate! The master of ceremonies tries to coax the "flying monk" into demonstration—"a miracle to open the audience to the hope of life everlasting." "Everything in life is a miracle," says the priest. "It's up to us to discern it in all we survey." It is one of those hallowed moments when the prankish director lays down his arms and discloses his hand. "We are not small enough to understand the big things," says the priest. And indeed we are

not, for the bloated ego precludes wonderment. Write it down on your shirtsleeves: it is manna from heaven courtesy of a Zen master that you will find nowhere in the District of Columbia or Babylon.

Next comes a *mafioso* resplendent with Italian tailoring and youthful good looks, one whose style and story will make equally good press. But despite Mediterranean machismo, the apprehended gangster is, in the end, one more copyist. We can trace his vintage back to Godard's *Breathless* (where Belmondo copies Bogart) or Brando's Don Corleone. Indeed, the gangster is no better or worse than anyone else in a world that exists now in a zone far beyond good and evil. The laws of the marketplace dictate the postmodern ethos and guideposts. Those Italians know how to dress, and the hit man should score high.

And now, perhaps, the ultimate in postmodern feminism—a woman who has abandoned her family and home and has married an alien. "He understands me!" she muses in the obligatory television interview, this contrived format having long since eclipsed human encounter in import and valence. This woman is beyond men, beyond women, and yet (in her inability to get beyond staging and self-interest and stratagem) fails like the rest in glimpsing the mystery is not small enough to embrace the beyond. The camera-ready plastic surgeon, with his entourage of testimonials, is all but predictable, one more instance of postmodern fundamentals: "YOU'LL BE BETTER-LOOKING, STRONGER, AND RICHER . . ." And we move quickly along (for slowness is postmodern heresy) to a housewife who, driven like the rest by the transfixing spotlight, has agreed to the ultimate in sacrifice in forgoing television for a godforsaken month. She is tearful and shaken after her ordeal, the quintessence of suffering in an age without interiority or substance. Postmodern posttraumatic stress disorder! "Never again! Never again!" cries our postmodern saint. Words once uttered in prayer before the ashes of millions of gypsies and Jews and Proustian inverts and the few individuals they managed to find who went up in flames in the death camps of Europe now express the misery of the unplugged! But God forbid that we who sit back and laugh give up our own currencies and jargons, our degrees and positions and fine opinions of ourselves, and throw ourselves back on ourselves. Try finding yourself in the world where we live. It's important to have an American name.

There are two participants in this televisual chaos and bedlam who are real: two bona fide vagrants, although Pippo mistakes them for look-alikes. The vagabonds are real! *Lei capisce?* This is what we all are when we crack the code and cut to the chase. The charade lies in mistaking ourselves for the images projected. Beckett (1954) gained fame for his depictions of bums who reminded us uncomfortably of ourselves, wrote an essay on Proust, and spent a lifetime pondering "the suffering of being" and the problem of "accursed time." He could have dissected each act on our list with more skill than a surgeon, exposing the hobo at the existential core. "We're incapable of [silence]," says Estragon. "We're inexhaustible," agrees Vladimir. The punch line is Estragon's: "It's so we don't think."

It is all, gasps Amelia, a "spectacle" and "circus"—the doubles, the monk, "and, of course, the admiral." In the background, a line from Dante markets alkaline batteries. Backstage, Pippo laughs it up with a chimpanzee. "Boy, you're a mess," he thinks he hears the chimp say. It is one of the more perceptive appraisals that we have in fact heard. More copies of copies, such as Belmondo and Bogart, and copyist audiences too. All the world is a stage. We all are understudies awaiting our 15 minutes of fame and perhaps fortune, a Proustian moment in the postmodern sun.

Mimicry and commerce, simulacra and gimmick. Reality manufactured by God knows who and fed back to us in cathode ray tubes and billboard ads, professional lexicons and manuals tested by experts, no tampering. "An obsession," observes Salman Rushdie, "with flimflam." "I am Pippo Botticelli, stage name Fred. I imitate anything!" says Marcello Mastroianni, who indeed *could* and *did*, although nothing so flawlessly as humankind's puzzlement at finding itself here in the first place. "Bravissimo!" is Amelia's adoring response. But really, it is the (genuinely) inimitable Giulietta Masina who also could and did. Hard to talk of self and encounter and the old "I-thou" and still keep a straight face in this wasteland of assemblage and glitter. There is no figure-ground here, no touchstone for our valuations. Only imitations of imitations, and psychologists would do well to take note. It is a madhouse, no doubt, yet more accurate by far than our organizational platitudes and technical truths, our protocols of "treatment" with their childish mathematics, our templates and theories with their bizarre reductions and symmetrical cures.

Appearances though they may be, Ginger and Fred yearn nonetheless for the real. "We're professionals, you know," complains Amelia. "We're surrounded by dilettantes," echoes Pippo, who also takes his craft seriously in the end. And it is in this foundering relationship between two worn-out souls that we find a shimmering of postmodern redemption. Pippo is forever the clown but intent and earnest in guiding Amelia on fine points of nuance and dance: "You always got this part wrong. It should be much more subtle. Here the melody ends, embracing, oblivious, like a dream. Do you understand?" And do you, you psychologists? For we also have got it all wrong. That is what William James had said. I am only the reminder and gadfly, epitaph to genius and history.

It is not for nothing that Pippo and Amelia are dancers. There they intuit something of the ineffable mystery almost in spite of themselves, speak in hushed and reverent tones of movement and tap dance and roots. "It's not just a dance," says Pippo. "It's much, much more. The Morse code of slaves, a wireless telegraph, the language of love and death." Do you see? A stab at the real, possibility, encounter so as to counterpose the postmodern worm at the core. There is the remnant of prophecy in this Italian joker despite his buffoonery, no matter that he mistakes Reagan for Sitting Bull!

And, indeed, it is in the moment of Indian-like stillness just at the start of Ginger and Fred's performance, before the gaping audience and its canned applause (when the blackout occurs and the transmitting devices and deities are suddenly silenced), that the voices of reason and soul call out to man and woman once more. We see for just an instant the motionless broadcasting tower, that postmodern cross of the New. And now quickly follows the epiphany of dancers:

Amelia: What did we come here for? We must be completely out of our minds!

Pippo: A giant with feet of clay. It's like a dream, far from reality. You have no idea where you are. . . . We're phantoms, Amelia. We arise from the darkness and vanish into darkness.

Amelia: I was looking forward to seeing you again.

Pippo: *Molto romantico!* I was looking forward to seeing you too.

Pippo urges Amelia to flee with him into the darkness, escape to something more solid than the ephemera of airwaves and anonymous praise. But power is restored at this very instant, and Ginger and Fred complete their routine—a final waltz for the crowd, a wireless telegraph, a two-step and shadow dance of love and death. "Pippo, we made it!" exclaims Amelia at the end. And who among us could say more? For here the melody ends, embracing, oblivious, a spiritual flash in the postmodern sky.

The parting at the station where it all began is poignant enough, the two old copyists ever at a loss for what to do in real life. Some youths ask for their autographs: they have seen a nostalgia act on television. Amelia loans Pippo some money, and the couple bid farewell through the hackneyed reenactment of a scene from their Astaire-Rogers routine. It is moving, because so empty, in the extreme. As Amelia's train departs, Pippo disappears into a cafe. He has decided to stay in Rome for a while and try his hand at the television game. Before a monitor on the platform, a solitary figure dances a few desolate schizophrenic steps with himself, one more shiftless creature mesmerized by the artificial light and chasing after postmodern dreams.

Long before making *Ginger and Fred,* Fellini (1974/1976) wrote,

Our trouble, as moderns, is loneliness. . . . No public celebration or political symphony can hope to be rid of it. Only . . . through individual people can a kind of message be passed, making [us] understand—almost *discover*—the profound link between one person and the next. (p. 61)

There are, no doubt, other voices with something important to say:

We stumble from one false perspective into another, the bewildered victims of false prophets and charlatans whose recipes for happiness only close one's eyes and ears, so that we fall through the mirrors, like trap doors, from one disaster to another. (Kafka, cited in Janouch, 1985, p. 73)

Our vanity, our passions, our spirit of imitation, our abstract intelligence, our habits have long been at work, and it is the task of art to undo this work of theirs, making us travel back in the direction from which we have come to the depths where what has really existed lies unknown within us. (Proust, cited in de Botton, 1997, p. 103)

You have taken our land and made us outcasts. (Tatanka Iyotake [Sitting Bull], cited in Brown, 1970, p. 426)

And here the melody ends, embracing, oblivious. Fragmentation and chaos, memory and speed. Sheep without shepherd, pretense and travesty. Dance and embrace. Time lost and never recovered. As for paradise, it is irreparably the same. Dance and embrace. Anxiety. Acceptance. Reality. Awe. A postmodern nightmare and love story, a tap dance of sublimity and prescience has been captured on celluloid and tape.

REFERENCES

Beckett, S. (1954). *Waiting for Godot.* New York: Grove Press.
Brown, D. (1970). *Bury my heart at Wounded Knee: An Indian history of the American West.* New York: Henry Holt.
de Botton, A. (1997). *How Proust can change your life.* New York: Random House.
Fellini, F. (1976). *Fellini on Fellini* (I. Quigley, Trans.). New York: Delacorte Press. (Original work published 1974)
Fellini, F. (Director). (1985). *Ginger y Fred* (Ginger and Fred) [Film]. Rome: PEA/RAI.
Janouch, G. (1985). *Conversations with Kafka.* London: Quartet Books.
Kundera, M. (1991). *Immortality* (P. Kussi, Trans.). New York: Grove.
Ortega y Gasset, J. (1961). *Meditations on Quixote.* New York: Norton.

CHAPTER 14

Defining Moments of Self-Actualization
Peak Performance and Peak Experience

GAYLE PRIVETTE

*P*EAK PERFORMANCE, the perfect moment when mind, muscle, and movement come together, and *peak experience,* a precious moment of highest happiness and joy, are personally valued experiences. We cherish these times, enjoy remembering them, and intuitively expect that they can enlighten our lives. These cherished personal experiences also are significant constructs in humanistic psychology.

Peak performance is releasing latent powers through skill in an athletic contest, artistic expression, physical strength in a crisis, intellectual prowess, rich interpersonal relationships, moral courage, or excellence in any activity. *Peak experience* is intense joy or ecstasy that stands out perceptually and cognitively among other experiences. Pervasive personality characteristics related to excellence and joy are identified in self-actualizing people. It is within the spirit of Maslow's thinking to consider the frequent occurrence of peak performance and peak experience as a partial operational definition of self-actualization.

Intuitively, experience makes more sense than behavior as a core unit of personality. It is the stuff of our lives and the base of personal identities. As subjects of inquiry, peak performance and peak experience emphasize the experiential rather than the behavioral, the positive rather than the pathological, the integrative rather than the reductionistic, and the idiosyncratic rather than the normative. Following the pioneer work of Rogers (1961), May (1953), and Maslow (1962), experience, the positive in human character, holism, and uniqueness have been recognized as significant or too important to ignore or trivialize with reductionistic methods.

The three major approaches to positive aspects of human life focus on personality, behavior, and experience. Maslow's self-actualization and Bugental's (1965) authenticity are notable examples of personality study. Jourard's (1968) self-disclosure exemplifies study of one type of behavior. The approach that we choose emphasizes experience. Experience is less global than personality and more comprehensive than behavior. My work is among humanistic studies establishing that experience is accessible, the positive is illuminating, and self-report can be trusted.

My long-term interest in peak performance has its roots with Sid Jourard, Ted Landsman, and David Lane at the University of Florida during the 1960s. They were awesome mentors. Jourard helped me to tease out the question, "What releases latent power for transcendent functioning?" Landsman gave his vision of the beautiful and noble person, his phenomenological perspective, and his demand for rigor. Finally, Lane helped to put this into psychotherapy. In our first studies, we made inferences from self-reports using computer technology that was innovative at the time, anticipating a model defined by experiential processes. These studies featured positive experiences and derivative negative experiences, a shift from conventional psychological approaches (Privette, 1964, 1965, 1968; Privette & Landsman, 1983).

Four decades ago, Landsman (1961) asked, "Is experience important in the affairs of men? Are joy and exhilaration, depression, or blinding hostility of consequence in reality, or are such matters for poets and philosophers alone?" (p. 42). My colleagues, graduate students at several universities, and I have studied experiences that engage enduring human questions rather than those most accessible to empirical research (Bugental, 1967). We found experience to be no more complicated than complex behavior, which comprises most human behavior. With attention to rigor, we applied the perspective of humanistic psychology because we believe that experience is not just the purview of poets and philosophers.

As self-actualization is prototypic of healthy personality, peak performance and peak experience are prototypic of positive experiences. Optimal moments are interesting in their own right and, as pole stars, give direction for our human possibilities. These experientially defined constructs illuminate a range of questions about human performance and feeling, and they provide building blocks for personality constructs.

In this chapter, I describe experiences as they emerged from our research, with peak performance, peak experience, misery, and failure as extremes of performance and feeling and with commonplace events and sport as anchors for the extremes. Peak performance, my long-term focus, is featured. A discussion of the experience model and some applications follow. Prospective directions are submitted in the final section.

EXPERIENTIAL CONSTRUCTS

In our research, we found that the experiential constructs were stable and that each was characterized by a constellation of inner processes. I introduce these experiential constructs with the portrayals of peak performance found in personal stories of people using the vernacular of their own activities.

Peak Performance

Peak performance can happen in any endeavor. It is functioning that is more efficient, more creative, more productive, and in some way better than one's habitual behavior. Moments of peak performance validate our intuitive belief in extraordinary powers. In our research, we found that inner processes formed a recognizable core of peak performance, beginning with clear focus. A musician illustrated these processes in his saxophone recital when everything important came together and everything extraneous faded away. He felt a sudden narrowing of focus, and only he and the music existed in his world. He said,

> I was really quite frightened when I walked on the stage, and my nerves didn't calm down til I played about eight measures of the piece. *Then all of a sudden, nothing seemed to matter except the music. It just came out naturally. All I thought about* was expressing myself the way I thought the piece should sound. *I never noticed* the audience after the first eight bars. (italics added)

An athlete told of her peak basketball performance against a team that outranked hers. In spite of outer differences from the saxophone recital, she reported inner processes remarkably like those of the musician:

> *My concentration on the game was so intense, I don't believe I would have heard a bomb outside.* I felt—really felt—I could do no wrong, that I had boundless energy, that I could outsmart and outwit my opponent, and that I would *not* be moved. I played like this. I was all over the court at once. I marveled at my own agility and speed. The gym, fans, noises, [and] distractions were only background. *Only my activities are vivid.* None of the fans believed what they had seen. It was near perfect playing, and I wasn't even tired after the hardest game I had ever played in my life. (italics added)

Peak performance of a different type was described by a law enforcement officer when he responded to another person at the scene of a double-fatality traffic accident:

> Blood and death per se I had been exposed to in war and other accidents, but I did not know how I would react in an intimate situation. Always my feelings had been objective, but this time they weren't. I didn't know the victims, but one bloody mess that hardly looked human called to me and, out of what was once a face, appealed for help. He did not want physical assistance, but some close personal contact, some love and affection. He knew he was going to die, he said, but was lonely. For an instant, I felt repulsed, then I knelt and placed his head in my lap and held his hand. This grip was the answer. I had given him what he needed. The episode was short, but I remember the compassion I felt for him and then the anger at this needless waste of life and potentiality of living. Shortly thereafter, he died, [and] the ambulance came and took him away. I felt sad, then lonely. Then objectivity returned and the continuance of my function as an officer. Feelings were flashes, not long moments in time of minutes but [rather] short. Until then, I didn't think it [was] possible for me to become personally involved in this manner. I don't know if I could again. It is hard to say.

Another peak performance in crisis was described by a hunter. His reflexive response, although very different from the deeply personal one of the law enforcement officer, was clearly focused:

> While in the foothills of the Smoky Mountains, three other hunters and I saw the opening of a cave. After swinging in, I made the eight-foot drop. Just as I landed, I heard a sickening sound. I had hit in the middle of a rattlesnake den. I don't know, to this day, how I got up eight feet of rock wall and out a small opening. My thick leather boots had five bites, and I had one on my shoulder. The thing I emphasize is the strength I had to get out of the cave under these circumstances.

Peak performance dyad. Throughout our studies, inner processes of peak performance were unlike processes at a typical level in the parallel activities of discrete groups of participants (Privette, 1981a; Privette & Bundrick, 1987). The identifying processes—full, clear focus on object and self—comprised a peak performance dyad, which was pivotal in all optimal performances. The dyad involved absorption, yet it was more than absorption. I labeled it *clear focus* because this term requires something beyond self—another person, a situation, a value, even an idea—yet it also requires self. Clear focus initiates responses and accommodates interactive processes. I feel limited in portraying this synergistic process as holistically as I believe performers experienced it. To discuss clear focus as comprehensively as possible, I bracket various elements to examine each one at a time and, later, bring each back into the whole.

Clear focus, simply put, is seeing what is there without obstruction. In perceptual terms, clear focus brings figure into bold contrast to ground, extending phenomenological and Gestalt theories in which the figure-ground interaction has been the subject of theoretical and experimental studies (Combs & Snygg, 1959). Heightened perception resembles a creative incident of tunnel vision, which is a caricature of the integrated focus on object, self, and relationship that elicits peak performance. In peak performance, goal-directed absorption seemed to "click" spontaneously along with clarity about oneself in the situation. Clarity and sharpness of focus were critical to efficiency of performance. A curious research result was that the most negative scoring on focus was found not in failure but rather in commonplace events, and it was neither clear nor full.

The preceding research participants described a solo music performance, a team

sport, and traumatic crises. Their tasks, or objects of focus, were different, yet their absorbed concentration was similar. In these peak performances, figure was sharp; task, value, or goal stood out clearly. Each person was not submerged in the object of focus but rather was strong and aware of a unique self-identity. Both self and other were completely necessary and, when left unobstructed, were most free to come together in a meaningful relationship. Buber's (1970) profound thought on the "I-thou" relationship speaks to this aspect of peak performance. For Buber, self and other are separate yet meaningfully related to one another.

Because people react to everything that has existential reality for them, bringing an object into full focus commands full response. A process of clear focus becomes channeled between person and other and seems effortless and graceful. Peak performance often is described by words such as "spontaneous" and comments such as "it just came out naturally." The process is like a river flowing channeled within its banks toward the sea. It fits its course not necessarily in a straight line but without hesitation. By contrast, water in a bog spreads—not flowing, not channeled, and not moving forward. When clear focus happened, self and other came together as subject-to-subject or I-to-thou. A person had full commitment to the other, and equally essential, the person was not lost in the other but had a strong sense of identity. Such *clear focus on object and self is the necessary precondition of peak performance* and comprises the peak performance dyad.

Attributes of peak experience in peak performance. In our studies, many peak performances also had attributes of peak experience. For example, the musician and athlete reported such qualities. Features of the peak experience are examined shortly in another section. The interplay between peak performance and peak experience is explored later. (White, 1989.)

Other studies. Peak performance constructs and methods have been used to study performance-based activities. The most conspicuous of these is sport, elaborated in a later section. Peak performance has been studied with other samples as well. Atkins (1990), for example, studied peak performance of actors, and Fobes (1986) did similar research for the military. Irizarry (1988); Quinn, Spreitzer, and Fletcher (1991); and Thornton, Privette, and Bundrick (1999) did research on business.

Peak Experience

A second experience in our studies is at the positive extreme of feeling. Maslow (1971) called the peak experience simply a moment of highest happiness. He threw down the gauntlet challenging human scientists to come to grips with enduring questions of human life. In what probably was the first doctoral dissertation exploring peak experiences, Leach (1962) defined the peak experience as a "highly valued experience which is characterized by such intensity of perception, depth of feeling, or sense of profound significance as to cause it to stand out, in the subject's mind, in more or less permanent contrast to the experiences that surround it in time and space" (p. 11). Laski (1962) described *transcendent ecstasy* as "joyful, transitory, unexpected, rare, valued, and extraordinary to the point of often seeming as if derived from a praeternatural source" (p. 5).

In our studies, we first included peak experience to clarify peak performance and differentiate the two constructs. We analyzed related literature available during the early 1980s, adding Csikszentmihalyi's

(1975) *flow,* which is not defined by a specific gradient of performance or feeling but often involves some level of positive performance and feeling. With descriptors from the literature, we elicited phenomenological accounts, many of which were both peak experiences and peak performances—moments of highest happiness *and* superior performance. Still, we were able to tease out independent processes of peak experience, unless one regards superior perception and openness as peak performance, as Schachtel (1959) suggested (Privette, 1983, 1984; Privette & Bundrick, 1991; Privette & Sherry, 1986). Following are examples of peak experiences that were not accompanied by peak performance.

One young woman in our studies described her own peak experience as follows:

> An incident of highest happiness in my life was the birth of my daughter. I had had a miscarriage before. Early in this pregnancy, I was told I would likely miscarry again. I didn't, and when she was finally born a beautiful, healthy girl, I was extremely happy. I remember watching her for hours in amazement, almost as if I were watching the scene from somewhere else. I just couldn't believe that such a miracle had happened and I had had a part in it.

Another research participant described an "amazing" experience in a very different context:

> I went walking with a friend, and after lunch, atop a lovely fell in Scotland, I stretched out on a clear space. When I woke up, I truly had forgotten where I was and how I'd gotten there. The beauty bombarded my senses; every breath was an experience. Suddenly, fear invaded. I was completely alone—on top of the world.

Where was Becky? At that very moment, I heard her and saw her outline on the next peak, arms outstretched to the sky, head back, and a newer fuller feeling took over. The world was exquisitely beautiful—and I was not alone. I saw the wonder of aloneness, its beauty—and the joy of sharing, of true companionship. A very powerful moment!

Maslow suggested music and sex as frequent contexts for peak experience. In our studies, as well as in Laski's and Leach's studies, peak experiences were described in relationships including sexual love and childbirth, art and creative work, appreciation of nature, religious experience, sport, and assorted other situations.

Landsman (1961) described the capacity of human relationship experiences to magnify as follows:

No sunset is greater than human love, nor can it substitute for human love. . . . And of the human relationship experiences, perhaps none compares with the one where you reach out, tentatively, hardly hopefully, terribly needfully for a particular person—to discover by a few words or a touch of fingers that the same person was reaching out tentatively, hardly hopefully, and terribly needfully for you. Beyond the power of human relationship itself is its potential for the magnification of any experience. There is such a thing as the walking alone in sand by the sea shore. But it is another thing to be walking hand in hand by that same sea shore with the cared-for person. There is such a thing as sitting upon a small cliff overlooking a clear lagoon. Above rise tall pines and oaks to a flawless sky, before you is the foliage of early fall, below in green clear water, unruffled, small groups of fish swim and play. You might think such beauty were unsurpassed—until you might sit upon that same cliff beside the cared-for person. I am reminded of Aiken's poem, "Music I heard with you was more than music. . . ." This will surely provide an intriguing measurement problem, for unlike the sharing of bread, the sharing of experience does not diminish each person's share but [rather] increases it. (p. 50)

Qualities of peak experience: fulfillment, significance, and spirituality. Among humanistic psychologists and educators, literature regarding peak experience has grown since the early works of Maslow, Laski, and Leach. Our participants validated many initial ideas about peak experience as profound, with a special flavor of awe, transcending usefulness. Leach (1962) found that most mentioned was a "sense of being fortunate, blessed, or enriched by it" (p. 81) and that peak experiences, rather than defining a personality characteristic, portray "the desire, the expectation, [and] the willingness to behold the wondrous commonplaces of life" (p. 84). Our participants called their peak experiences fulfilling and distinguished them by feelings of joy and ecstasy that continued after the moment. Peak experiences were viewed as significant, personally meaningful, valuable, and expressive. Many respondents—but not all—called their own peak experiences turning points in their lives. They endorsed Maslow's idea of transcendence of boundaries with qualities of spirituality. Many people simply said that their experiences were ineffable or beyond words. The most intriguing exception to prediction based on Maslow's ideas was participants' support of sense of self and denial of loss of self. Whether the differences are conceptual, semantic, or a questionnaire artifact remains to be tested.

Other studies. In two theses, peak experiences of artists and realtors were studied.

Significance, fulfillment, and spiritual qualities were cited by demographically diverse participants across contexts. Participants called their peak experiences significant or turning points in their lives and validated lasting effects (Lanier, Privette, Vodanovich, & Bundrick, 1996; Yeagle, Privette, & Dunham, 1989).

Negative Events

Misery. When asked about negative extremes of feeling, participants responded with surprising candor, disclosing very personal experiences. Many told of death, sickness, and relationship endings as the contexts for their misery, which, along with peak experiences, they considered as their most significant times. Misery was characterized as intense, overwhelming other senses and thoughts, not sociable but painfully interpersonal. The contrast between identity confusion in misery and sense of self in peak performance was marked. Participants described misery as beyond words and more spiritual than any other experience. Posey (1989) caught this ineffable sense in her poem, "for billy":

> i want to name your pain/ call it out of you/
> wrap it up/ row it out to sea (pp. 106-107)

We were quite moved that people participating in the research project of strangers would share their deeply personal and deeply painful moments. They seemed to do this with awareness of the uniqueness yet the universality of their personal experiences, once again validating Sullivan's belief that "we are all much more simply human than otherwise" (cited in Chapman, 1976, p. 264).

Failure. Failure is the negative extreme of performance. Work and school were frequent contexts for our participants' failures, followed by relationships and assorted other activities. Research respondents characterized their failures as consistent with tunnel vision with focus centered on a threatened, disabling, and intensified concentration along with personal identity confusion. Tunnel vision resulted in paralysis, self-defeating behavior, and inability to meet desperate needs. Participants saw failure as personal and serious, and they described an ineffable sense of loss of self and orientation. This was illustrated by an emergency medical technician who found the body of a 12-year-old lying next to a 12-gauge shotgun:

> Just as I turned to get a body bag, his mother walked through the back door. The look she gave me was heart wrenching. She looked at me and said, "Help him, please don't let him die." There was nothing I could do. The feeling of helplessness makes this stick in my mind.

Anchors

Commonplace events. We identified an anchor, commonplace events, by time frame. When asked to identify an experience from the previous afternoon, our participants described activities at work, school, or recreation. In commonplace events, participants assessed their performance as between inefficiency and effectiveness and assessed their feeling as between boredom and enjoyment. They reported moderately structured and sociable activities, not significant or particularly fulfilling and, overall, not remarkable. What was remarkable was their report of focus as significantly less clear in commonplace events than in any other experience, differing from both full focus of peak performance and tunnel vision of failure and misery. In commonplace events, figure and ground blurred, reminiscent of a photograph snapped with an improperly adjusted lens. Normally, focus seems divided among a number of things besides the one that is ostensibly in the foreground. Diffuse focus extends to blur personal identity, and the self-object contact boundary is vague. Responding with a fuzzy identity to blurred awareness results in ineffective behavior (Privette & Bundrick, 1987).

Sport. For perspective, we added sport as an anchor because, although it is not gradient specific, it is performance based and typically taps a range of feeling. Research participants, who were not elite athletes, reported peak, average, and failing performance in sport, and we found processes that distinguished these performance levels (Privette & Bundrick, 1997). Assessing the impact of psychological processes on sport performance is a challenge for athletes and sport researchers. McInman and Grove (1991), in their overview of peak moments in sport, reviewed our early work and tied our experience model to sport performance so as to illustrate the bond between sport behavior and psychological processes. Our methods and constructs have been used in our own studies of peak sport performance and by other researchers (Grove & Lewis, 1996; Jackson, 1988; Privette, 1981b, 1982b; Waller, 1988; Young, 1994).

In sport, we found a strong association between focus and process; focus on game tasks extended to behavior. Optimal performance featured the peak performance dyad—clear focus with a strong sense of self—which may be the margin of victory between well-matched competitors. The focus-process dyad in failure was tunnel vision with fragmented and constrained processes. And in average performance, the focus-process dyad included clarity of self but lacked intensity and absorption. Focus was blurred, diffused by distracting stimuli; the edge was not there.

Feeling was linearly related to self-assessed performance; the better one perceived performance, the more fulfilling the experience, whereas the more poorly one assessed performance, the less fulfilling the experience. Peak performance was set apart by ecstasy, average performance by enjoyment or neutrality, and failure by boredom or worry. These feeling trends carried over after sport events as well.

Consistent with Csikszentmihalyi's (1975, 1992) study, sport, which is a frequent flow activity, was playful and sociable when performance was average or peak. Sport can be fun with or without superior performance. Failing in sport, however, was not fun, playful, or companionable. Our study raised questions for elite athletes. Do they experience sport as playful, fun, and companionable, as do nonelite athletes? Generally, in our cross-disciplinary studies, peak performance was not viewed as playful and others were not seen in convivial ways in events involving peak performance.

Cross-Cultural Studies

Since the beginning of our peak performance studies, we have had communication from researchers and others from many parts of the world expressing interest in experiential constructs and the desire to study them. Maslow's speculations about the universality of peak experiences stands as a challenge to explore experiential dimensions among people with different cultural influences. In a comparative study, we examined constructs among Taiwanese to consider their correspondence with descriptions from our American samples.

Constructs. In our studies with Americans and Taiwanese, constructs had both generality and cultural sensitivity. All in all, construct effects were conspicuously stronger than effects of sample, age, or sex. The cross-cultural stability and sensitivity of the two positive experiences—peak performance and peak experience—were of central interest to us. Peak performance was unambiguous with only minor sample differences. Both groups recognized and endorsed the peak performance dyad. Peak experiences, however, had sample differences with Americans more enthusiastic in general and more supportive of qualities of significance, fulfillment, and spirituality. Taiwanese, but not Americans, moderately endorsed receptivity, an attribute that Maslow thought to be essential to the experience. Negative events differed in magnitude more than in pattern. Americans considered misery more serious and spiritual than did Taiwanese, who found intrinsic reward in these most unhappy moments. Americans, but not Taiwanese, described identity confusion in misery. Failure was the most culturally disparate event in our studies, but again, most differences were of magnitude, not pattern. A striking difference was that Taiwanese, but not Americans, endorsed the significance of their failures. Cultural influences on sport were noted. Whereas Americans viewed sport as playful and sociable, Taiwanese viewed it as serious, somewhat significant, and invested with personal meaning. Taiwanese and Americans described commonplace events in essentially identical ways.

Processes. Experiential processes were found to be accessible, cogent data units that also exhibited stability and cultural sensitivity. Processes of particular interest are focus, self, and significance. Focus was similar within each sample—full focus in peak performance, tunnel vision in misery and failure, and blurred vision in commonplace events. The dimension of self showed generality yet diverged in negative events, as Americans cited identity confusion and disorganization, whereas Taiwanese sustained a consistent sense of self. Cultural variations were seen in the sources of significance, as both samples denied the significance of commonplace events and endorsed it in misery, peak performance, and (with differences) peak experience. Americans denied the significance of sport more than did Taiwanese. Taiwanese, but not Americans, endorsed the significance of their failures (Privette, Hwang, & Bundrick, 1997).

MODEL OF EXPERIENCE: DIMENSIONS OF PERFORMANCE AND FEELING

From our studies, we saw that at least some events are most meaningfully defined experientially or by inner processes. Conventionally, human affairs are defined by behavior, environment, or activity. We found that activities—work, relationships, crises, spiritual moments, and sport—influenced processes but were not primary identifying aspects of events. A sunset may be just a sunset, or it may be a nuisance to a westbound driver, yet a peak experience is a precious moment whether it is watching a sunset, hearing a symphony, or catching a fleeting smile on the face of a loved one. It is clear that a peak experience is a meaningful unit of human life and that inner processes—not behavior, environment, or activity—are the defining aspect of the event in which it occurs (Privette & Bundrick, 1989).

Operational Definition of an Event

To extend the usefulness of our research for our ongoing studies and those of others, we organized our findings in a comprehensive pattern. We operationally defined an event as consisting of the following:

▶ An activity (the context in which experience occurs) such as playing a sport, preparing dinner, participating in a staff meeting, mowing the lawn, or conducting an orchestra

▶ A level of performance ranging from peak performance, to mediocrity, to failure

▶ A level of feeling ranging from peak experience, to neutrality, to misery

▶ Many correlates, or catalysts, such as the following: personality, developmental (enduring qualities; e.g., intelligence, introversion, middle age, industry, ego strength, sociopathy, need for approval, self-actualization); neurophysiological (e.g., heart rate, beta activity, adrenalin flow, genetic determinants, anxiety); behavioral (e.g., running, painting, talking, laughing, eye blinking); environmental (e.g., sociocultural, geographic and ambient contexts, urban smog, an uncomfortable chair, a hostile crowd, a snowstorm, a forest by a stream, stress, quiet); experiential (inner processes; e.g., feeling, deciding, valuing, thinking, spirituality, sense of self, including interpreting other correlates)

In our research, we identified events by gradient of performance or feeling, for example, extreme negative feeling (misery) or extreme positive performance (peak performance). Contextual activities and correlates are of interest, but we targeted experiential correlates because they are important in their own right and include interpretation and symbolization of environmental, developmental, and neurophysiological influences. A basic concept in our studies is that experiential processes—thinking, feeling, interpreting, valuing, and decision making—have logical lawful relationships to behavior and to patterns in personality.

In Figure 14.1, experiential events, identified by gradient-specific performance or feeling level and defined by experiential processes, are illustrated (Privette, 1985a, 1985b). The figure suggests several interrelations between feeling and performance with implications for important behaviors and personality characteristics. Each quadrant, for example, shows a particular relation between the two dimensions.

Negative Feeling/Negative Performance

Negative feeling and negative performance are typified in the lower left quadrant of Figure 14.1, with extremes the focus of psychopathology and criminology. This quadrant encompasses defeat and its aftermath in all aspects of life. Poor performance and the disappointment of losing a game are commonplace and often inconsequential occurrences. More seriously, this quadrant charts the failure and misery of disability, substantive losses, the cumulative traumatic stress of burnout, and mental illness of all types and degrees of severity. Extreme experiences are misery and failure, and homicidal and suicidal behavior and personality decompensation are manifestations of their prolonged unyielding fusion. The performance-feeling interaction found in this quadrant has far-reaching personal and societal consequences.

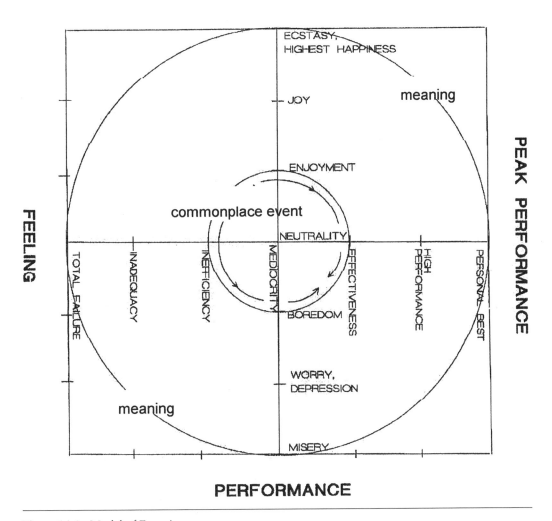

Figure 14.1. Model of Experience
SOURCE: Reprinted with permission from *Psychological Reports*, 1985, Vol. 56, p. 264.

Positive Feeling/ Negative Performance

The upper left quadrant of Figure 14.1 represents elevated feeling coupled with poor performance. Occasionally in sport, a losing team captures the heart and brings pleasure to fans and themselves. More often, fans vicariously experience ecstasy with a winning team or player. There is no question that Michael Jordan and Tiger Woods have stimulated myriad moments of awe. Spectator activities strive to maximize positive feeling with least effort. Channel surfing surely qualifies. The pleasure-failure interaction is exemplified in noninstrumental responses aimed at disguising or denying the pain of failure such as the abuse of mind-altering substances or escapist activities. Waller (1988) used our questionnaire to compare altered awareness in sport to that following ingestion of a mind-altering drug, Ecstasy. Mogar (1967) defined alcoholism as a disease of boredom that leads to comprehensive failure. He treated alcoholism by inducing peak experiences to provide meaning as an antidote to boredom. This research suggests intriguing possibilities for ameliorating serious or chronic failure.

Positive Performance/ Negative Feeling

High performance coupled with negative feeling is found in the lower right quadrant of Figure 14.1. Atkins (1990), studying peak performance among actors, found that many actors reported simultaneous peak experiences, whereas others did not. In fact, some actors reported very negative feeling processes during their outstanding acting performances. Only afterward did they feel satisfaction or joy. Atkins postulated that for these actors, misery might have had a motivating effect that parallels the motivation of ecstasy for others including the other group of actors in his study.

Turning points. Fuerst's (1965) dissertation on turning point experiences anticipated the interrelation of negative feelings and positive performance. Many of his respondents reported negative life events—even serious illness or death—that had a long-lasting and significant positive impact. A participant in our peak performance studies told of how her encounter with the possibility of imminent death led her to a turning point, daily actualizing many potentials she had not used before:

I lived in a rut—not the depths of depression, just a rut. I had been divorced for several years and occasionally patted myself on the back for holding down a responsible job, having time for my son, keeping at least 1 day ahead of the ironing. Then I found a lump in my breast, and almost the next thing I knew, I was in intensive care—without my right breast. I don't remember how my thoughts and feelings progressed, but I remember looking out the window to an early spring day and being filled with life—alive!—of feeling grateful to be alive. I had wanted to write. Now, I wake before 5 [o'clock] each morning, ready to write a few hours before work. My writing absorbs me. My house isn't spotless, but housework done is without the added strain of resistance. I spend time with people I enjoy and take a creative writing class—yes! Boredom is a thing of the past. Facing death made me alive.

Yalom (1980) succinctly pointed out that whereas the physicality of death destroys, the idea of death makes it possible to live life in an authentic fashion.

Victorious personality. In her description of the victorious personality, Sheehy (1986) introduced an intriguing personality dimension that is parallel to this experiential quadrant. Sheehy wrote of her adopted daughter, Mohm, who as a young child experienced the atrocities of Pol Pot in Cambodia. It is well known that many, if not most, people are permanently disabled by such devastating situations. Mohm not only survived but, with careful nurturing, later thrived, impelling Sheehy to write of this "spirit of survival" that was urged on by the victorious personality. Sheehy described the victorious personality as a kernel within that, for some people, evokes heroic courage, a sense of meaning, and vitality that energizes life activities and relationships. Frankl (1966) and Wilson (1972), in their reports of people in concentration camps, corroborated this victorious response to traumatically stressful events. Sumerlin (1995) explored similar attributes among homeless men in America. The annals of great individual achievement authenticate this peak performance-misery relationship. Beethoven's Ninth Symphony epitomizes the victorious personality emerging from isolation and misery. It has been suggested that Beethoven's phenomenal late achievement might be attributed to his intense focus on composing after deafness curtailed his virtuosity.

As the Chinese character for "crisis" implies both danger and opportunity, or coexisting possibilities of destructiveness and creativity, so do aspects in this quadrant signify coexisting possibilities. A psychotherapist can use this perspective to authentically validate a client's personally negative and destructive experiences while also vigorously encouraging coexisting creative possibilities for heroic responses by that inner kernel of the victorious personality.

Positive Performance/ Positive Feeling

Happy productive functioning is shown in the upper right quadrant of Figure 14.1, capped by moments of peak performance that also are peak experiences. These often, but not necessarily always, occur together. A familiar activity in this quadrant, not always at peak, is flow, described by Csikszentmihalyi (1975) as an intrinsically rewarding experience. Berretta (1971) found a strong association between play and creative thinking in children. Ravizza

(1977) reported peak experiences in great moments of sport, and Sachs (1984) added research on the runner's high. Murphy and White (1978) broadly documented this link in sport. Atkins (1990) found that many actors reported peak experiences accompanying performances they considered great. The interrelation of peak performance and peak experience appears to be reciprocal and significant.

This synergistic interrelation of power and joy is an intriguing puzzle at the heart of humanistic psychology. Many experiences that fit into this quadrant have been addressed by humanistic study and discourse, harking back to the parent anthology of the present volume (Bugental, 1967). The magnifying effect of power and joy is seen most pervasively and dramatically in self-actualizing people.

Self-actualization. Self-actualization, of course, is a personality dimension parallel to this quadrant. Maslow (1971) also associated peak experience and optimal functioning with self-actualization and related these experiences to each other. For example, Maslow thought that optimal achievement triggered peak experience and that, correspondingly, peak experiences may trigger optimal performance. People whom Maslow identified as probably self-actualizing were noted for optimal functioning in some aspects of their lives. Many, but not all, were thought to have frequent peak experiences.

Considering frequent occurrences of peak performance and peak experience as a partial operational definition of self-actualization offers an opportunity to extend our understanding of optimal personality. Because experience is more specific and measurable than personality attributes, the study of key experiences can provide relevant and fundamental data (Sumerlin, Berretta, Privette, & Bundrick, 1994).

Power and joy. Linking power and joy reduces both the threat of power and the frivolity of joy. The magnifying quality of power and joy are seen in Mogar's (1967) use of induced meaning, peak experience, to enhance performance and in programs such as Outward Bound that induce peak performance to enhance meaning. In his warning about the Jonah complex, or our tendency to demean the best in ourselves and others, Maslow (1971) again challenged us, this time to protect the precious aspects of our lives illustrated in this quadrant. Merging of transpersonal and humanistic approaches in this quadrant may be positively mutative, transforming us to higher levels in both our inner and outer endeavors. Our peaks may enlighten the commonplace—our plateaus and plains—and, as beacons, guide us to be more joyous and powerful in our daily lives, in business, in education, and in our community activities.

Perimeter Events

Perimeter events, or performance and feeling at positive and negative poles, are in some respects opposites. For example, fulfillment is linearly related to both performance and feeling. In other ways, perimeter events are contrasted with commonplace events, as in sense of meaning. We examined crises as perimeter events with both superior performance with positive outcomes and ineffectiveness with worry or misery.

The focus-process dyad, above all, was associated with crisis outcome. In peak performance, actions or thoughts seemed to emerge spontaneously, and participants expressed wonder at their own knowledge, strength, or courage. In failure, intense focus, marred by a sense of powerlessness

and confusion, became tunnel vision. The peak performance dyad and tunnel vision both contrasted with the blurred vision typical of commonplace events. A parallel in personality theory may be seen in Rank's (1945) concepts of the *average person,* the *neurotic person,* and the *artist.* Among these personality types, average is different from optimal in critical ways, and the negative is a distortion of the optimal.

Participants saw all trauma as significant, serious, solitary, and noncompanionable; two thirds of them said that aftereffects were significant or a turning point. Inadequacy and negative feelings had a long-lasting impact, undermined future effectiveness, and predisposed participants toward burnout and trauma-based disorders. Likewise, peak crisis responses had a long-term positive impact. The law enforcement officer at the traffic fatality long remembered his profound, albeit brief, encounter. Coincidentally, perhaps, he later became a professional counselor. He embodied the victorious personality, emerging with self-awareness from trauma.

Unlike commonplace events, trauma tapped personal meaning and expression, even when the expression was reflexive behavior such as lifting a heavy object off a trapped child. Some participants called their experiences "spiritual," some "mystical," and some "loss of self," but all agreed that the state of awareness was beyond words. No matter how often it happened, crisis awareness was not an "everyday" state of mind. Examining data with meaning specifically in mind, we found that peak experience, misery, peak performance, and (for Taiwanese participants) failure signified great personal meaning, especially when these experiences occurred in relationships and work. (See Privette & Bundrick, 1992.)

As humanistic or existential psychologists, we support the tenet compellingly articulated by Frankl (1966) that humans search for meaning, surviving with it or perishing without it. Perimeter events signal meaning and provide a window for discovery. I am among those who trust that we never will be mostly predictable, or peak moments available on command. Understanding these cherished moments/experiential constructs, however, can illuminate our own evolution and that of people with whom we live and work. And we can hope to attain "the desire, the expectation, the willingness to behold the wondrous commonplaces of life," as Leach (1962, p. 84) concluded about the peak experience. (See Privette, 1982a.)

Applications of the Experience Model

There are many applications of the experience model. Human relationships have been mentioned throughout this chapter and are of central concern to humanistic psychologists, and counseling is among our most important professional relationships. Here, I mention a few implications of our research for counseling and also tie research implications to a second domain, sport, the performance endeavor par excellence.

Counseling. Several aspects of peak performance complement comprehensive humanistic models of counseling and personality held by counselors. The peak performance dyad supports the therapist's clear focus on a client's feelings and meanings. Focusing on a client as an experiencing person enables the client, in turn, to focus on the personal meanings and values in the situation (Baggett, 1967; Gendlin, 1981). A sense of self as powerful and confident frees a counselor from distracting needs for reassurance, dominance, or overidentification. This strong sense of self promotes a full, clear focus on the client that becomes what

Rogers (1961) called the "as if" quality of empathy. In a relationship, the peak performance dyad is the subject-to-subject or I-thou encounter described by Buber (1970) that allows response to flow spontaneously. Spontaneity in counseling is not impulsivity but rather the use of previously acquired knowledge and skills freed from undue attention to techniques, details, fragmented behaviors, and extraneous thoughts (see a model for counseling homeless men, a population living with stress on a daily basis, in Sumerlin & Privette, 1994).

The peak performance dyad makes it possible for a counselor to perceive a client's painful experiences and validate them. Counselor validation means communicating an understanding of the inner view and acceptance of that view as legitimate. Only after validation is incorporated can a client be open to a counselor's efforts to help reframe these experiences. Reframing, then, does not deny the negative, but alongside these painful and destructive experiences, it may point to genuine coexisting creative possibilities for heroic responses. Through this sequence, a counselor may invoke that inner kernel of the victorious personality. In personality growth and therapeutic relationships, the synergistic effect of power and joy may become a positive spiral and enhance a person's movement in the self-actualizing process.

Why not a humanistic sport psychology? Humanistic psychology emphasizes issues that are important for a psychology of sport. Our research, and that of many other humanistic psychologists, confirms that experience is not simply "warm fuzzy feelings" but also complex inner processes that are significantly connected to performance, accessible to research, and amenable to organization. A positive, integrative, and idiosyncratic orientation is more compatible with sport than is a negative orientation or one geared toward norms. Sport targets superior performance and the ecstasy of victory while, at the same time, acknowledging the misery of defeat. The lessons of self-actualizing people are more relevant than psychopathology for both elite and nonelite athletes. These links suggest that a humanistic sport psychology, more than any other approach, is a natural fit for addressing sport issues.

PROSPECTIVE

In this chapter, I have tracked my long-term studies beginning with fascination of the full use of human potential—peak performance. Throughout my work, phenomenological and technological methods were intertwined. My emphasis was on experiential qualities—feelings as well as thoughts—associated first with peak performance and later extended to other events identified by positive and negative extremes of feeling or performance. From studying these experiential constructs, a model of experience emerged that accommodates the broad study of human life including activities such as sport and counseling relationships, developmental and personality issues, and impact of culture. From my research perspective, two challenges for humanistic psychology in the new millennium emerged: a global humanistic psychology and leadership vis-à-vis technology.

A Global Humanistic Psychology

Humanistic psychology is singularly suited to a global psychology because of its unique viewpoint and its methodology. The forerunners Fromm (1961), Jung (1958), and Watts (1961) emphasized a cross-cultural perspective bridging Western psychology and Eastern thought, and we found that self-report and techniques of inference, as well as our experiential subject matter, accommodated an Asian culture. These and other humanistic methods, including qualitative research, are not geared toward predicting behavior or superimposing single-culture constructs. Instead, they are intended to increase understanding in ways that open possibilities for developing potentials and engaging in meaningful relationships.

In the spirit of Maslow's fascination, we can question the universality of peak performance and peak experience. These and other experiences may be operationally defined by dimensions such as the performance and feeling dimensions we used. We can raise questions in any culture. What is the felt experience of highest happiness? What is the focus-process mode in optimal functioning? In failure? What significance is attached to failure? Highest happiness? How is self perceived in highest happiness, optimal functioning, and failure? How do the processes of perimeter events influence sensitivity to the commonplace? The humanistic preference for the idiosyncratic rather than the normative supports decentered concepts that are essential to a global psychology. Likewise, the humanistic emphasis on integration and holism instead of reductionistic methods sets a tone of inclusion that accommodates and values both commonalities and cultural variations.

Research that considers life-span experiential data across cultures can enable mapping core human experiences with cultural, developmental, and individual variations. Such research may contribute to manageable exploratory probes and demystify major theoretical concepts such as the collective unconscious. Because experience marks the person-situation juncture and bridges behavior, personality, development, and culture, it can be used as a basic data unit, for an integrated science in the study of persons. Humanistic psychology offers the only approach that is inclusive enough and has the scope to encompass an integrative global psychology.

Humanistic Psychology and Technology

My research began with cutting-edge computer technology for experiential inference. A room-size computer calculated a previously insurmountable factor analysis for a 40 × 40 matrix in less than an hour. The dazzling rate of acceleration of technology, from the first steps into space during the 1960s to cyberspace in many households before 2000, forecasts the penetration of technology into our lives. The character of technology is in a formative stage, and humanistic psychology has the perspective,

core of knowledge, and professional underpinnings to influence its development and uses (see also the chapter by Aanstoos [Chapter 17] in this volume). Our leadership must include objecting to uses of technology that are intrusive or that distort and trivialize important human values. We also may offer proactive guidance toward pursuits of "beautiful and noble" human goals.

We must not discount technology; instead, we must embrace it. We have a special obligation to communicate humanistic priorities to help society-at-large find a balance, to get online without losing our human values—the primacy of the person, actualizing meaning, experiencing highest happiness or the excellence of focused performance, validating our grief, sharing experience with a loved one. Our challenges today are no less daunting than were those of the new humanistic psychology in 1967.

REFERENCES

Atkins, C. (1990). *A comparative analysis of peak experience performance and non-peak experience performance in professional actors and actresses.* Doctoral dissertation, U.S. International University. (*Dissertation Abstracts International, 51*-04B, 2096; University Microfilms No. 9025205)

Baggett, R. L. (1967). *Behaviors that communicate understanding as evaluated by teenagers.* Doctoral dissertation, University of Florida. (*Dissertation Abstracts International, 29*-01A, 0115; University Microfilms No. 68-9509)

Berretta, S. (1971). *Comparative effects of play on creative thinking: The immediate influence of art, drama, and playground experiences on children.* Doctoral dissertation, University of Southern Mississippi. (*Dissertation Abstracts International, 32*-B, 2981; University Microfilms No. 71-28,824)

Buber, M. (1970). *I and thou* (W. Kaufmann, Trans.). New York: Scribner.

Bugental, J. F. T. (1965). *The search for authenticity: An existential-analytic approach to psychotherapy.* New York: Holt, Rinehart & Winston.

Bugental, J. F. T. (Ed.). (1967). *Challenges of humanistic psychology.* New York: McGraw-Hill.

Chapman, A. H. (1976). *Harry Stack Sullivan: His life and his work.* New York: Putnam.

Combs, A. W., & Snygg, D. (1959). *Individual behavior: A perceptual approach to behavior.* New York: Harper & Row.

Csikszentmihalyi, M. (1975). Play and intrinsic rewards. *Journal of Humanistic Psychology, 15,* 41-63.

Csikszentmihalyi, M. (1992). *Flow: The psychology of happiness.* New York: HarperCollins.

Fobes, J. L. (1986). *Training lessons learned from peak performance episodes.* Report No. ARI-TR-711, Army Research Institute for the Behavioral and Social Sciences Field Unit, Presido of Monterey, CA.

Frankl, V. E. (1966). *Man's search for meaning.* New York: Washington Square.

Fromm, E. (1961). Psychoanalysis and Zen Buddhism. In D. T. Suzuki, E. Fromm, & R. DeMartino (Eds.), *Zen Buddhism and psychoanalysis* (pp. 134-141). New York: Harper & Row.

Fuerst, R. (1965). *Turning-point experiences.* Doctoral dissertation, University of Florida. (*Dissertation Abstracts International, 26*-10, 5863; University Microfilms No. 66-2022)

Gendlin, E. (1981). *Focusing.* New York: Bantam Books.

Grove, J. R., & Lewis, M. A. E. (1996). Hypnotic susceptibility and the attainment of flowlike states during exercise. *Journal of Sport and Exercise Psychology, 18,* 380-391.

Irizarry, J. (1988). *The relationship of self-perceived peak performer attributes to job performance.* Doctoral dissertation, University of Massachusetts. (*Dissertation Abstracts International, 49*-12B, 5214; University Microfilms No. 8906295)

Jackson, S. (1988). *Positive performance states of athletes: Toward a conceptual understanding of peak performance.* Unpublished master's thesis, University of Illinois at Urbana-Champaign.

Jourard, S. (1968). *Disclosing man to himself.* New York: Van Nostrand Reinhold.

Jung, C. G. (1958). *Psychology and religion: West and East* (H. Read, M. Fordham, & G. Adler, Eds., Collected Works of C. G. Jung, Bollingen Series, Vol. 11). New York: Pantheon.

Landsman, T. (1961). Human experience and human relationship. In A. W. Combs (Ed.), *Personality theory and counseling practice* (pp. 42-52). Gainesville: University of Florida Press.

Lanier, L., Privette, G., Vodanovich, S., & Bundrick, C. M. (1996). Peak experiences: Lasting consequences, and breadth of occurrences among realtors, artists, and a comparison group. *Journal of Social Behavior and Personality, 11,* 781-791.

Laski, M. (1962). *Ecstasy: A study of some secular and religious experiences.* Bloomington: Indiana University Press.

Leach, D. (1962). *Meaning and correlates of peak experience.* Unpublished doctoral dissertation, University of Florida.

Maslow, A. (1962). *Toward a psychology of being.* New York: Van Nostrand Reinhold.

Maslow, A. (1971). *The farther reaches of human nature.* New York: Viking.

May, R. (1953). *Man's search for himself.* New York: Norton.

McInman, A. D., & Grove, J. R. (1991). Peak moments in sport: A literature review. *Quest, 43,* 333-351.

Mogar, R. (1967). Psychodelic (LSD) research: A critical review of methods and results. In J. Bugental (Ed.), *Challenges of humanistic psychology* (pp. 135-146). New York: McGraw-Hill.

Murphy, M., & White, R. (1978). *The psychic side of sports.* Reading, MA: Addison-Wesley.

Posey, E. C. (1989). for billy. In R. B. Cannon (Ed.), *Emerald Coast review* (premier ed., pp. 106-108). Pensacola, FL: West Florida Literary Federation.

Privette, G. (1964). *Factors associated with functioning which transcends modal behavior.* Doctoral dissertation, University of Florida. (*Dissertation Abstracts International, 25,* 3406; University Microfilms No. 64-11552)

Privette, G. (1965). Transcendent functioning. *Teachers College Record, 66,* 733-737.

Privette, G. (1968). Transcendent functioning: Full use of potentialities. In H. Otto & J. Mann (Eds.), *Ways of growth* (pp. 213-223). New York: Grossman.

Privette, G. (1981a). Dynamics of peak performance. *Journal of Humanistic Psychology, 21*(1), 57-67.

Privette, G. (1981b). The phenomenology of peak performance in sports. *International Journal of Sport Psychology, 12,* 51-60.

Privette, G. (1982a). Peak performance in the death crisis. In R. Pacholski & C. Corr (Eds.), *Priorities in death education and counseling* (pp. 7-16). Arlington, VA: Forum for Death Education and Counseling.

Privette, G. (1982b). Peak performance in sports: A factorial topology. *International Journal of Sport Psychology, 13,* 244-249.

Privette, G. (1983). Peak experience, peak performance, and flow: A comparative analysis of positive human experiences. *Journal of Personality and Social Psychology, 45,* 1361-1368.

Privette, G. (1984). *Experience questionnaire.* Pensacola: University of West Florida.

Privette, G. (1985a). Experience as a component of personality theory. *Psychological Reports, 56,* 263-266.

Privette, G. (1985b). Experience as a component of personality theory: Phenomenological support. *Psychological Reports, 57,* 558.

Privette, G., & Bundrick, C. (1987). Measurement of experience: Construct and content validity of the Experience Questionnaire. *Perceptual and Motor Skills, 65,* 315-332.

Privette, G., & Bundrick, C. (1989). Effects of triggering activity on construct events: Peak performance, peak experience, flow, average events, misery, and failure. *Journal of Social Behavior and Personality, 4,* 299-306.

Privette, G., & Bundrick, C. M. (1991). Peak experience, peak performance, and flow: Correspondence of personal descriptions and theoretical constructs. *Journal of Social Behavior and Personality, 6,* 169-188.

Privette, G., & Bundrick, C. M. (1992). Meaning-constellating processes in experientially defined human events. In M. Stamenov (Ed.), *Current advances in linguistic theory* (pp. 143-150). Philadelphia: John Benjamins.

Privette, G., & Bundrick, C. M. (1997). Comparison of psychological processes of peak, average, and failing sport experiences. *International Journal of Sport Psychology, 28,* 323-334.

Privette, G., Hwang, K. K., & Bundrick, C. M. (1997). Cross-cultural measurement of experience: Taiwanese and American peak performance, peak experience, misery, failure, sport, and average events. *Perceptual and Motor Skills, 84,* 1459-1482.

Privette, G., & Landsman, T. (1983). Factor analysis of peak performance: The full use of potential. *Journal of Personality and Social Psychology, 44,* 195-200.

Privette, G., & Sherry, D. (1986). Reliability and readability of questionnaire: Peak performance and peak experience. *Psychological Reports, 58,* 491-494.

Quinn, R. E., Spreitzer, G. M., & Fletcher, J. (1991). *The hero in the hierarchy: An analysis of managerial performance myths.* Unpublished manuscript, University of Michigan.

Rank, O. (1945). *Will therapy and truth and reality.* New York: Knopf.

Ravizza, K. (1977). Peak experiences in sport. *Journal of Humanistic Psychology, 17*(4), 35-40.

Rogers, C. R. (1961). *On becoming a person.* Boston: Houghton Mifflin.

Sachs, M. L. (1984). The runner's high. In M. L. Sachs & G. W. Buffone (Eds.), *Running as therapy*. Lincoln: University of Nebraska Press.

Schachtel, E. G. (1959). *Metamorphosis: On the development of affect, perception, attention, and memory*. New York: Basic Books.

Sheehy, G. (1986). *Spirit of survival*. New York: William Morrow.

Sumerlin, J. R. (1995). Adaptation to homelessness: Self-actualization, loneliness, and depression in street homeless men. *Psychological Reports, 77,* 295-314.

Sumerlin, J. R., Berretta, S. A., Privette, G., & Bundrick, C. M. (1994). Subjective biological self and self-actualization. *Perceptual and Motor Skills, 79,* 1327-1337.

Sumerlin, J. R., & Privette, G. (1994). Humanistic constructs and counseling homeless men. *Psychological Reports, 75,* 611-626.

Thornton, F., Privette, G., & Bundrick, C. M. (1999). Peak performance of business leaders: An experience parallel to self-actualization theory. *Journal of Business and Psychology, 14,* 253-264.

Waller, S. (1988). *Alteration in consciousness in peak performance*. Doctoral dissertation, Saybrook Graduate School. (*Dissertation Abstracts International,* 49-10B, 4585; University Microfilms No. 8827944)

Watts, A. W. (1961). *Psychotherapy East and West*. New York: Pantheon.

White, R. (Ed.). (1989). *Annotated bibliography on peak and mystical experiences*. Dix Hills, NY: Parapsychology Sources of Information Center.

Wilson, C. (1972). *New pathways in psychology: Maslow and the post-Freudian revolution*. New York: Taplinger.

Yalom, I. D. (1980). *Existential psychotherapy*. New York: Basic Books.

Yeagle, E., Privette, G., & Dunham, F. (1989). Highest happiness: Analysis of artists' peak experience. *Psychological Reports, 65,* 523-530.

Young, J. A. (1994). *Perceptions of attentional skills of elite junior tennis players: Toward a conceptual understanding of peak performance*. Unpublished honour's thesis, Monash University, Australia.

CHAPTER 15

At Play in the Fields of the Mind
Personal Myths as Fields of Information

DAVID FEINSTEIN

> *Mythological symbols touch and exhilarate centers of life beyond the reach of the vocabularies of reason and coercion.*
>
> —J. Campbell (*Creative Mythology*, 1968)

THE RECOGNITION that *personal* myths shape individual behavior in a manner analogous to the way in which *cultural* myths influence social behavior has been gaining currency within psychology (Bagarozzi & Anderson, 1989; Feinstein, 1979, 1997; Gullestad, 1995; Hartocollis & Graham, 1991; Krippner, 1990, 1994; Larsen, 1976, 1990; Lukoff, 1997; McAdams, 1993). A comprehensive theory of human development based on the individual's evolving mythology potently integrates the cultural and spiritual dimensions of experience into the biological and psychodynamic foundations of human behavior. Such a mythically

informed psychology is decidedly humanistic. Specifically, this framework is capable of accommodating the farther and more noble "reaches of human nature" (Maslow, 1971) that conventional psychology has tended to neglect but humanistic psychology has tended to embrace, including scientifically slippery areas such as consciousness, values, love, identity, freedom, will, and self-transcendence.

Myth is grounded in the quintessential human ability to address the large questions of existence using symbolism and narrative. Whereas a myth—to be plausible for contemporary individuals—must be aligned with our capacity for rational thought,

AUTHOR'S NOTE: This chapter is an abridged version of an article with the same title that appeared in the *Journal of Humanistic Psychology*, Vol. 38, No. 3, pp. 71-109.

myth making is as much with us today as it was thousands of years ago. The symbolism of an individual's guiding mythology can, in fact, be discerned using established psychological techniques for uncovering unconscious processes, including interviews, dream analysis, free association, structured fantasy, and projective instruments (Feinstein & Krippner, 1997; McAdams, 1993).

This chapter introduces and expands the personal mythology construct, suggesting that personal myths function not only as biochemically coded models of reality but also as *fields of information*—natural albeit nonvisible elements of the physical universe—that affect consciousness and behavior. Just as some neurologists have proposed that "mental fields" complement brain activity in unifying experience and some biologists have proposed that "morphic fields" complement the action of the gene in giving form to an organism, this chapter develops the thesis that myth-carrying fields of information complement the physiological bases of consciousness in storing symbolic content and maintaining psychological habits.

THE NATURE OF PERSONAL MYTHS

Personal myths are organizing models that shape perception, understanding, and behavior. They emerge from four sources: biology, personal history, culture, and transcendent experiences (Feinstein, Krippner, & Granger, 1988). Comprised of postulates about oneself, one's world, and the relationship between the two, personal myths are *internalized models of reality* that explain the external world, guide individual development, provide social direction, and address spiritual questions in a manner that

is analogous to the way in which cultural myths carry out those functions for entire societies. These internalized guiding models address both immediate and eternal concerns, and they are both descriptive (furnishing explanations) and instructive (generating motivation).

As organizing models, personal myths are continually being compared to experience. When a mismatch is detected between an inner model and an experience, perceptions may be changed to match the model (Piaget's [1977] assimilation), or the model may be changed to match the experience (Piaget's accommodation). The evolution of internal models, a process that occurs largely outside the individual's awareness, is a primary focus of psychotherapeutic intervention. By framing internal models as *personal myths*, the dynamic, "storied nature" (Sarbin, 1986) of human cognition comes to the foreground. In addition, recognizing the essential mythological nature of the psyche extends the boundaries of scientific language, allowing it to more readily incorporate the larger cultural and spiritual dimensions of human experience (Feinstein, 1997).

Like beliefs and attitudes, personal myths are rooted in the individual's biochemistry. They are biochemically coded models of reality. This chapter considers evidence that biochemical theories of information storage and retrieval are not sufficient in themselves for explaining the way in which personal myths function. It develops the hypothesis that personal myths, in addition to their biochemical infrastructure, are embedded in fields that store information and maintain habits.

FIELDS OF INFORMATION

A field is a *domain of influence*, presumed to exist in physical reality, that cannot be observed directly but that is inferred through its effects. Although they elude direct inspection, the four established fields of physics—gravitational fields, electromagnetic fields, strong quantum matter fields, and weak quantum matter fields—are known to exist because of phenomena that *can* be observed. They are understood as material albeit elusive forces in the physical universe.

Findings from several areas of science are converging to cause some investigators to postulate a variety of fields that are different in nature from the four established fields of physics but similar to one another in that each is conceived of as carrying information that influences consciousness and behavior. Neurologists, for example, have proposed that previously undetected fields may be involved in brain function. The ability of neurons to broadcast signals to one another was identified by Schuman and Madison (1994) at Stanford Medical School. Their "neural broadcasting" theory suggests that information can be transmitted from a single neuron to neighboring neurons that are not electrochemically connected by way of axon and dendrite. "The formation of synaptic changes previously thought to be restricted to synapses onto a single cell can also result in synaptic changes at nearby synapses" (p. 535). The investigators speculated that "the presence of synaptic activity may work in concert with other factors" (p. 535), and it is entirely plausible that these unidentified "other factors" involve the influence of neural fields. Lipet (1994), another prominent neurologist, has in fact hypothesized a *mental field* "which is produced by, but is biologically distinct from, brain activity" (p. 119). It is formulated as a "testable field theory of mind-brain interaction." These mental fields "cannot be observed directly by external physical means" (p. 121), and their properties differ significantly from those of any currently known physical field in dimensions, such as their ability to alter neuron function and to unify subjective experience.

Physicists have been discussing correspondences between consciousness and quantum fields for well over half a century (Bohm, 1951; Edington, 1929). Penrose (1994), for example, holds that many of the brain's capacities can best be explained by postulating that consciousness operates according to the principles of quantum mechanics. Although quantum theories of consciousness might place many difficult questions about the brain and the mind into a compelling new context (Friedman, 1994; Wolf, 1994; Zohar & Marshall, 1994), the question of whether parts of the brain small enough to be governed by the laws of quantum mechanics could be complex enough to exert a discrete influence on consciousness remained unanswered.

Hameroff (1994), an anesthesiologist, proposed that the microtubule is the brain component that operates at the quantum level while affecting consciousness. A microtubule is composed of long, thin, hollow tubes of protein about one 10-millionth of an inch in diameter that form meshlike networks throughout each cell. A single electron sliding back and forth along the microtubule's length determines the microtubule's configuration and function. Significantly, the action of anesthetics, such as ether and halothane, is that they temporarily incapacitate the microtubules, turning off consciousness with minimal disruption to other brain functions. Because microtubules are small enough to operate according to quantum principles and are directly involved with consciousness, Hameroff holds that they are the link between consciousness and quantum mechanics.

According to Hameroff (for a rebuttal that highlights existing controversies, see Grush & Churchland, 1995),

> Quantum field theory describes the underlying reality of everything in the universe (including consciousness) as consisting of three components: the *vacuum*, space, and time. A "field of fields" which contains no particles, the vacuum gives rise to quantum wave/particles as excitations or energy fluctuations within it. (Hameroff, 1994, p. 103)

Tiller (1993), a physicist in the Department of Materials Science and Engineering at Stanford University, surveyed a set of anomalous phenomena, such as remote viewing experiments and the feats of remarkable strength sometimes exhibited by hypnosis participants, and also postulated a domain of subtle energy emerging from the quantum vacuum state. The quantum vacuum also is the basis of a fifth physical field as formulated by Laszlo (1995), a systems theorist, to account for the transmission of information beyond the limits of space and time as understood in electromagnetic and gravitational fields and beyond the microprocesses governed by strong and weak quantum matter fields. Laszlo argued that the quantum vacuum functions as an "information-rich" (p. 28) holographic field that would allow a thought to be simultaneously available at distant locations.

In addition to these complementary theories emerging from neurology, physics, anesthesiology, and systems theory, engineers (Jahn & Dunne, 1989), biologists (Sheldrake, 1988; Weiss, 1939), physiologists (Hunt, 1995), neuroanatomists (Burr, 1972), physicians (Gerber, 1996), psychologists (Gallo, 1998; Larson, 1987), and nontraditional healers (Eden, 1999) have postulated the existence of information fields that might influence consciousness and behavior based on findings from within their respective disciplines. Beyond such scientific speculation, a number of time-honored traditions in both the East and the West refer to a more subtle counterpart to the material body, referred to variously as the "aura," "subtle body," "pranic body," or "etheric body." I next consider the empirical evidence that has bearing on the question of whether these ancient terms and concepts, as well as the more contemporary ones, might refer to fields of information that influence consciousness and behavior.

SIX ANOMALIES IN SEARCH OF A THEORY

Because fields cannot be *directly* measured through existing physical instrumentation, they are inferred by their apparent effects on what can be observed. The inference that a field is operating must meet the basic criterion that there is not a more parsimonious, nonreductionistic explanation for a set of empirically observed phenomena.

A range of anomalies about consciousness and behavior would be parsimoniously and nonreductionistically explained if a field of information is inferred. For example, it now is documented, under controlled conditions, that focused visualization by one person about a second person, any distance away and unaware of the first person, may measurably influence the second person's electrodermal activity (Braud, 1992). Such anomalies are flash points in the natural world where observations elude conventional scientific understanding, where empirical data contradict the culture's dominating mythology, and where this understanding and mythology are challenged to expand. Following is a survey of anomalies that have a substantial empirical basis and that no longer would be considered anomalies if previously undetected fields that affect consciousness were shown to carry information over distance.

Effects of Human Activity on Distant Mechanical Devices

An enduring enigma in quantum mechanics is that if two paired photons are separated, regardless of the distance that might come between them, a change in one appears to create a simultaneous change in the other (quantum coherence). These distant effects at the nuclear level are difficult to explain, but they are no more mysterious than the accumulation of evidence that human thought and activity can, from a distance, influence mechanical devices.

Numerous anecdotes describing how an old clock stopped at the moment its owner died, for example, have been documented (Cano, 1996). Several meticulously designed studies have demonstrated that certain individuals, by focusing their attention, can reliably influence mechanical systems such as random number generators (Jahn & Dunne, 1989). Researchers in the School of Engineering at Princeton University found that the output of random event generators also was affected when the devices were simply placed in the presence of an organized group of people. The effect was strongest during periods when a group's attention was focused, when a group's cohesion was high, and when a group's members were sharing a common emotional experience. In experiments at 10 separate gatherings ranging from business meetings, to scientific research conferences, to ritual religious events, the effect of a group's collective behavior, although slight, was so consistent that the odds against its having occurred by chance were about 5,000 to 1. The researchers concluded, "If sustained over more extensive experiments, such ef-

fects could add credence to the concept of a consciousness 'field' as an agency for creating order in random physical processes" (Nelson, Bradish, Dobyns, Dunne, & Jahn, 1996, p. 111). At least a dozen other studies of interactions between fields and consciousness lend support to these findings (cited in Radin, 1997).

Distant Effects of Visualization, Prayer, and Meditation

Numerous laboratory experiments have demonstrated that some people can mentally influence the growth of plants, fungi, and bacteria (Benor, 1993). Experimental participants, after being instructed in how to use visualization to inhibit the breakdown of red blood cells in a test tube located in a different room, achieved statistically significant results in their efforts to slow the rate of cell deterioration (Braud, 1990). Well-controlled studies also have demonstrated, at an extraordinarily high significance level (2.6×10^{-14}), that some people can, through the use of calming or activating imagery, influence the relaxation or anxiety levels of targeted individuals, unawares and in other locations, as gauged by spontaneous changes in their electrodermal activity (Braud, 1992).

Numerous investigations support the efficacy of prayer in physical recovery (Dossey, 1993). Of 131 studies that calculated probability values of the effects of prayer on healing published up to 1993, 77 reported statistical significance—56 at the .01 level and 21 at the .05 level (Benor, 1993).

Groups of people meditating together appear to have positively affected nearby nonmeditators with whom they have had no physical contact. For example, a series of well-designed and replicated, albeit still controversial, large-scale studies showed that crime rates decreased significantly in cities where transcendental meditation was being practiced by an infusion of meditators, as compared to crime rates in matched control cities (Dillbeck, Cavanaugh, Glenn, Orme-Johson, & Mittlefehldt, 1987) and that other quality-of-life indicators improved as well (Assimakis & Dillbeck, 1995).

Prodigies and Savants

Prodigies such as Mozart, who composed elegant symphonies while a child, and instances of the idio-savant, as portrayed by Dustin Hoffman in the film *Rain Man,* also are among the psychological anomalies that could be explained by the existence of information fields. At least 100 savants with prodigious mental abilities were documented during the past century (Treffert, 1989). A boy diagnosed as illiterate and ineducable, and with a conversational vocabulary of some 58 words, could accurately answer inquiries as to the population of every major city and town in the United States; its distance from the largest city in its state; the names, number of rooms, and locations of its leading hotels; and statistics on thousands of mountains and rivers (Treffert, 1989). A well-known blind musical savant could "repeat, on the piano, a complex piece heard only once, in a perfect mirroring, including every emotional nuance of expression" (Pearce, 1992, p. 4). During World War II, the British government employed two mathematical savants to serve, essentially, as computers (p. 4).

Although attempts have been made to explain the special abilities of the prodigy and the savant within conventional frameworks—including favorable genetic quirks, highly specialized neurological pathways, and unusually efficient information processing strategies—these explanations raise more questions than they answer

(Treffert, 1989). Some investigators have speculated that prodigies, savants, and others with exceptional abilities are tuning into existing fields of information (Laszlo, 1995; Moss, 1974; Pearce, 1992).

Inspiration that seems to be derived from beyond oneself is well recognized in the study of creativity. The German word *Einfal* refers to a sudden and spontaneous intuition leading to a conceptual or aesthetic breakthrough (Laszlo, 1995, p. 130; see also Chapter 11, by Arons & Richards, this volume). Individuals such as Mozart, Michelangelo, and Shakespeare were distinguished for remarkable creative perceptions apparently "falling" into their awareness. Laszlo reflected that, in addition to such giants,

> Sometimes, otherwise entirely unremarkable individuals display astonishing, seemingly inborn, capacities in specific fields, especially in music and in mathematics. To call such individuals "gifted" and their achievements "works of genius" is not to explain their abilities but [rather] only to label them. An explanation involves answering questions regarding the origins of their unusual accomplishments. Are they possessors of a specially fortunate combination of genes? Or, did they receive their gifts from a higher source? (p. 130)

Systematic Investigations of Telepathy

Many stories exist that purport spontaneous telepathic communication between people with emotional or genetic ties, particularly under conditions of crisis or trauma. How can a twin know her sister is in danger some 1,000 miles away? Why would a woman wake up with a shock in the middle of the night at the moment her husband has just died in a plane crash? What causes a father to dream about his daughter's terror while at that very moment she is fending off an attacker? Although an abundance of anecdotal reports, observations by anthropologists studying indigenous cultures, and sophisticated laboratory studies provide substantial evidence for the existence of telepathy (Laszlo, 1995, pp. 88-90), a physical basis for it has not been established. Still, the evidence is compelling.

Here is a single dramatic example. In 1970, Jerry Garcia asked Stanley Krippner, a personal friend and leading parapsychology researcher, whether Krippner thought that the Grateful Dead's music could boost the transmission of telepathic messages. At 11:30 p.m. on February 19, 1971, some 2,000 concert fans, in various music and otherwise-induced nonordinary states of consciousness, at the Capitol Theater in Port Chester, New York, participated in a pilot study. They attempted to transmit an image to Malcolm Bessent, a "sensitive" who was sleeping in a dream research laboratory some 50 miles away. The randomly selected image of Scralian's painting *The Seven Spinal Chakras* was projected from a slide onto the theater screen while the band played on. The audience members were told that they were taking part in an ESP experiment and were instructed to "try using your ESP to 'send' this picture to Malcolm Bessent," who was sleeping "at the Maimonides Medical Center in Brooklyn" (where Krippner was the director of the Dream Research Laboratory). The painting, which was shown for about 15 minutes, depicts a man in a lotus position with all seven chakras—the energy centers along the spine and head—illuminated. The ground the man is sitting on is not depicted in the painting. Bessent's dream report that night included an image of a man "suspended in mid-air," thoughts about "a spinal column," and an interest in "using natural energy" (Krippner, 1975, pp. 90-93).

Although rigorous experimental procedures were observed, most psychologists are not impressed with such stories. Only 34% of the psychologists responding to a survey of 1,100 college professors said they believed that ESP is an established fact or a likely possibility. This low percentage contrasts with 55% of those in the natural sciences; 66% of other social scientists; and 77% of those in the humanities, art, and education who reported that belief. On the other side of the spectrum, an equal percentage of psychologists—34%—declared ESP to be an impossibility, as contrasted with 3% of the natural scientists and none of the 166 professors in the other social sciences (Wagner & Monnet, 1979). An *American Psychologist* article used the Maimonides Medical Center's 10-year research program demonstrating dream telepathy as the case study in tracing the systematic bias, in professional psychological organs, against anomalous observations such as ESP (Child, 1985). Child (1985) concluded that, although the Maimonides research is "widely known and greatly respected" among scientists active in parapsychology, the experiments have received no mention in reviews to which they are clearly pertinent or have been condemned based on entirely erroneous assertions. "Insofar as psychologists are guided by these reviews," Child observed, "they are prevented from gaining accurate information about research" that might significantly affect their worldview (p. 1219). Although this trend may be changing, discussions of parapsychological research still are being de facto excluded from most mainstream psychological journals and textbooks.

Nonetheless, research in parapsychology, partly because it is so exposed to attack, often is conducted with more meticulous experimental standards than is research on less controversial topics, and evidence supporting parapsychological phenomena continues to mount (Bem & Honorton, 1994; Radin, 1997: Targ & Katra, 1998). Findings that do not conform to established paradigms (i.e., that buck the prevailing mythology), however, are systematically relegated to the purgatory of scientific investigation. In short, if the evidence supporting the enigmatic "information transfer" produced by the Maimonides research and in other well-designed parapsychology experiments fell within a conventional area of investigation, then the burden of proof would be on those wanting to discredit the reality of the phenomenon.

Similarities in Myths and Symbols Across Cultures

A debate persists among archaeologists regarding whether curious similarities in sculpture, painting, and architecture (Schuster & Carpenter, 1996) are "transmitted" by travelers or, because of shared genetic coding within the human nervous system, are independently generated by different societies. In addition to the similar figures and symbols found by archaeologists across cultures, parallel myths in societies that had no knowledge of one another are well documented in the works of comparative mythologists such as Campbell, Cassirer, Eliade, Frazer, Graves, and Lévi-Strauss (Bierlein, 1994). Symbols such as the "great earth mother," the "eternal child," the "hero's journey," the "mandala," and the "shadow" frequently appear worldwide in classical myths and historical artwork as well as in contemporary Western literature, drama, and film productions. Jung (1934/1968a), who spoke of these universal symbols as archetypes, believed that they represent structures within the psyche that unfold according to an inborn maturational plan determining the essential

form and developmental path of consciousness.

Although the role of archetypes in human experience generally has been discounted in mainstream scientific circles, the idea has prevailed, in part because researchers in disciplines such as anthropology, archaeology, ethology, and linguistics keep rediscovering the concept and renaming it in their own terms (Stevens, 1993). Most recently, evolutionary psychologists have been making a case for the "evolved deep structure of the psyche" (Slavin & Kriegman, 1992, p. 68). Beyond the well-established innate structures underlying linguistic abilities, a "complex preexisting psychic architecture . . . regulates many of our key interactions with the world and guides the process of organizing experience" (p. 69). The human mind, from this perspective, "consists of a set of evolved information-processing mechanisms instantiated in the human nervous system [that are] functionally specialized to produce behavior that solves particular adaptive problems such as mate selection, language acquisition, family relations, and cooperation" (Tooby & Cosmides, 1992, p. 24). Some anthropologists, in fact, take the position that, *across cultures*, "once one gets behind the surface manifestations, the uniformity of human social arrangements is remarkable" (Fox, 1989, p. 34).

Although the expression of *any* innate behavior in humans varies so greatly from one person to the next and from one culture to another that the existence of universals still is debatable (Brown, 1991), prototypes of the archetype are common in the animal kingdom and may shed light on underlying mechanisms. For example, when a wooden model of a flying hawk is pulled over the head of a newly hatched chick, the chick will crouch down and emit cries of alarm. Even if the next 10 generations never are exposed to a hawk, the moment a real or wooden hawk comes into view, the chick's descendants still will cringe (Stevens, 1982). Using this response to illustrate the concept of the archetype, Stevens (1982) concluded, "The 'predator archetype' had lain dormant in the 'collective unconscious' of these birds" (p. 48) for generations.

The counterargument to the position that the appearance of similar archetypal symbolism across cultures is inherited from past ages is summarized by Wilber (1995). Archetypes can be seen as "secondary byproducts of cognitive structures which themselves are similar wherever they appear and which, in interpreting a common physical world, generate common motifs" (p. 220). Thus, the commonalities found in disparate cultures, such as the hero's journey, the great earth mother, and parallel representations of birth, death, and rebirth, can be explained not as inherited imagery but rather as products of similar neurological structures spontaneously encoding common features of human experience (e.g., cycles of the seasons, infant's extended dependence on the mother, mating, food procurement).

Although this spontaneous generation of imagery and adaptational strategies no doubt accounts for some of the thematic parallels across cultures, the more *specific* and *complex* the parallel images, the more likely that other influences are involved. The finch's response to a highly specific shape it never has encountered, or the honeybee's complex communication dance, clearly invites explanations that presuppose an inherited rather than spontaneously generated response set. For humans, the immense number of variables that must be tracked in trying to settle the controversy obscures the underlying processes, but people who have been observed in clinical settings or while in nonordinary states of consciousness provide a natural laboratory for further considering the question.

Parallel Symbolism Found in Psychotherapy and in Nonordinary States of Consciousness

Jung was not the only psychiatrist of his era to speculate about inherited imagery. Freud also was impressed by his observation that individuals in therapy kept reproducing essentially similar themes. Freud (1924/1953) wondered,

> How is it to be explained that the same phantasies are always formed with the same content? I have an answer to this which I know will seem to you very daring. I believe that these *primal phantasies* . . . are a phylogenetic possession. In them, the individual . . . stretches out to the experiences of the ages. (p. 380)

Campbell, who examined the hero's journey in depth, also noted his "amazement" on reading of Perry's (1976) work with psychosis and discovering that sometimes "the imagery of schizophrenic fantasy perfectly matches that of the mythological hero journey" (Campbell, 1972, p. 208) as Campbell had outlined it more than two decades earlier.

Contemporary consciousness research corroborates these impressions. Consider, for example, the following extraordinary but carefully documented observations by Grof (1992) based on his extensive clinical research using psychedelic substances and breath-oriented psychotherapeutic techniques:

> It has been remarkable to find that people raised in one culture, or belonging to a particular race, are not limited to the archetypes of that culture or race. In our research, we have seen, for example, that white, urban, middle-class Americans can have meaningful encounters while in

nonordinary states of consciousness with such legendary heroes as the Polynesian Maui or Shango, the Bantu god of sex and war. Over the years, I have, on many occasions, witnessed European and American women who became the Hindu Goddess Kali, taking on the traditional facial expressions of that figure, with the tongue[s] stretched far out of their mouth[s], even though they had no previous knowledge about that figure. Conversely, during workshops in Japan and India, we witnessed several participants, born and raised in those traditions, who had powerful identifications with Christ. . . .

It is particularly interesting to note that in many cases, where people had no previous knowledge of certain mythological figures, they were not only able to *experience* them accurately and with great detail, but they [also] were able to draw pictures with details that perfectly matched ancient descriptions of those figures. (p. 161)

Repetitive symbols and themes also have been identified in both large-scale (Hall & Norby, 1972) and cross-cultural (Griffith, Miyagi, & Tago, 1958) dream studies. For example, Hall and Norby (1972), in a content analysis of more than 50,000 dreams, identified "typical dreams" that "express the shared concerns, preoccupations, and interests of all dreamers. They may be said to constitute the universal constants of the human psyche" (p. 35). Stevens (1993) concluded from such findings that dreams are "the means by which the entire behavioral repertoire of the species is integrated with the recent experience of the individual, thus promoting its capacity to survive the demands and exigencies of the following day" (p. 24). This hypothesis, he noted, is in close accord with the "ethological view that dreaming sleep is necessary for an animal to update its strategies for survival by integrating the ethogram (the total behavior repertoire of the species encoded in the brain) with the recent experience of the individual" (p. 37).

Are the common images and themes found among cultures widely separated by time and space, as well as in the fantasies and dreams of individuals, precoded genetic proclivities? Evolutionary psychologists believe that "content-specific information-processing mechanisms," produced by natural selection, "generate some of the particular content of human culture including certain behaviors, artifacts, and linguistically transmitted representations" (Tooby & Cosmides, 1992, p. 24). The manner by which genes might govern such content-specific symbolism, however, is unmapped and unknown. According to some biologists, in fact, attributing to genes the instinctive cooperative behavior of honeybees, no less the parallel symbolism found in human cultures, still is more a matter of faith than a matter of fact. Sheldrake (1988), for example, argued, "The role of genes is inevitably overrated, and properties are projected onto them that go far beyond their known chemical roles" (p. 158).

The Hypothesis to Which the Six Anomalies Lead

This line of reasoning suggests that genes are supplemented by other mechanisms in organizing certain inherited psychological characteristics and behavioral patterns. The debate distills down to the tension between parsimony and reductionism. Parallel symbolism has been documented across diverse psyches as well as unrelated societies. Some (e.g., Neher, 1996) believe that, to the extent that parallel symbolism is conclusively documented, a parsimonious explanation for it will be found in genetics. Others (e.g., Sheldrake, 1988) believe that it is blatantly reductionistic to suggest that DNA can actually encode the immense folio of specific, complex mythological figures and motifs that spontaneously appear in dreams, nonordinary states, and artistic and other cultural expressions. Jung, who initially believed that archetypes are genetically coded, later came to the conclusion that genes alone cannot explain the range of parallel symbolism he had observed in his lifetime (Jung, 1952/1968b). But if not genetic coding, then what mechanisms might account for such parallels? A number of investigators have proposed a field of information explanation for the archetype (Feinstein, 2000; Laszlo, 1995; Laughlin, 1996). Could informational fields—repositories of images independent of the central nervous system—influence an individual's "spontaneously generated" thought and behavior?

Several features are shared by reports of (a) human activity influencing mechanical devices from a distance; (b) distant effects of visualization, prayer, and meditation on consciousness, healing, and even the activity of blood cells in test tubes; (c) the extraordinary mental abilities of prodigies and savants; (d) systematic investigations of telepathy; (e) similarities in myths and symbols across cultures; and (f) the parallel symbolism observed in clinical situations and in nonordinary states of consciousness:

▶ Evidence suggesting the existence of each of these phenomena, although not always unequivocal, has been accumulating.

▶ Each seems to involve the procurement of information in a manner whose mechanisms are difficult to explain in terms of known physiological structures.

▶ The effects observed are consistent with a field of information hypothesis.

SHELDRAKE'S MORPHIC FIELD HYPOTHESIS

Various field theories and related models have intrigued modern consciousness researchers, from neuropsychologist Pribram's (1971) holographic brain to nuclear physicist Bohm's (1980) holographic universe. The one that seems formulated in a manner that offers the greatest explanatory power relative to my own observations about a structure-field complementarity in the personal myth is Sheldrake's (1981, 1988) controversial hypothesis of the morphic field.

Sheldrake, who holds a doctorate in biochemistry from Cambridge University and was a Rosenheim research fellow of the Royal Society and a Frank Knox fellow at Harvard University, believes that every natural system—atom, molecule, crystal, living organism, society, custom, habit of mind—is associated with a field of information or a morphic field that interacts with observable matter. Morphic fields organize the structure of natural systems as well as their patterns of activity. Sheldrake (1988) indicated that morphic fields "are physically real in the sense that gravitational, electromagnetic, and quantum matter fields are physically real" (pp. 107-108). His formulations have earned his work both favorable comparisons with Darwin and the suggestion, in an editorial of the prominent journal *Nature*, that by being so facile in presenting such a misleading theory, this may be a "book for burning" (Editorial, 1981, p. 245).

For Sheldrake, every living system and every unit of the physical world, from the molecule to the mind, has its own unique field, an inherent vibration that holds information about the system's potential form and behavior, analogous to genetic information. Such fields store and transmit information from one generation to the next. Each field *attracts* the system with which it is associated toward its mature form, and it arouses behavior in that system. The morphic field of the tadpole encodes the physical form and instinctive behavior of the mature frog. According to Sheldrake, it is the *field*, as well as the *gene*, that stores at least some of the information for the complex patterns that comprise a system's form.

Sheldrake (1988) has described morphic fields as purposive, goal-directed "attractors" (his use of the term is akin to its use in dynamic systems theory) that guide "the systems under their influence toward characteristic patterns of organization" (p. 101). Sheldrake's hypothesis also is consistent with the view emerging from modern physics (Sheldrake & Bohm, 1982). In quantum theory, every subatomic particle has its own field, and Sheldrake (1988) indicated that "morphic fields may indeed be comparable in status to quantum matter fields" (p. 119) while postulating that morphic fields also influence larger systems than the microsystems governed by quantum fields. Sheldrake's notion of a parallel between morphic fields and quantum fields, which is consistent with the hypotheses of Hameroff (1994), Laszlo (1995), and Tiller (1993) that nature's "fifth field" emerges from the quantum vacuum, could account for several properties that Sheldrake attributes to the morphic field. For example, morphic fields appear to be "nonlocal," possessing the quantum property where an effect is *instantaneous* and *unaffected by distance*.

Morphic fields purportedly provide information that is transmitted through resonance or attunement *rather than* an exchange of energy where one entity gains what the other expends. Not only does Sheldrake (1988) believe that morphic fields guide the development of a member of a species toward its mature form, he suggests that morphic fields *themselves* evolve in the process. Because the laws of nature operate independently of what they govern, Sheldrake challenges the Platonic notion that nature's laws are fixed and eternal, pointing out that this assumption presumes that the laws governing the formation of sugar crystals, for example, existed before "the first sugar molecules arose anywhere in the universe. Indeed, they existed before there was a universe at all" (p. 11). Sheldrake asserts, instead, that the morphic fields that hold the organizing principles of the physical universe themselves *evolve*. "Not only does the world evolve in space and time, but these immanent organizing principles themselves evolve. (p. 313) . . . We find ourselves in an evolving universe whose organizing principles are evolving with it" (p. 316).

MYTHIC FIELDS

My core thesis is that mythic fields are a subset of Sheldrake's morphic fields. They become established when new patterns of understanding and motivation are initiated and repeated. Once established, they tend to maintain the psychological habits that typify the individual—the person's characteristic *forms* of emotion, thought, and behavior. The influence is bidirectional; field follows form *and* form follows field. Psychophysiological forms and mythic fields are linked by resonance. Sheldrake (1988) explained that "characteristic rhythmic patterns of activity within the nervous system" (p. 151) may enter into resonance with a morphic field. Interestingly, when a group of neurons becomes linked through mental activity, the neurons themselves behave like a "field" (Pearce, 1992, p. 16), with all the cells vibrating as a single frequency or "phase-coherent oscillation" (Edelman, 1992, p. 95). The individual's mythic field presumably resonates with these neurons in a process of mutual influence.

Adults in nonordinary states of consciousness (induced, e.g., by abreaction, hypnosis, or psychedelics) sometimes have the sense of reliving their own births or even prenatal events, including details about which they never had been informed (e.g., an attempted abortion). In some instances, idiosyncratic details subsequently have been verified with parents or by other means, suggesting that the memories were accurate (Chamberlain, 1990; Cheek, 1980). When such experiences occur in clinical settings, striking parallels have on occasion been observed between the circumstances of the birth and patterns in the person's life (Grof, 1985). However, the cerebral cortex of the newborn, lacking the needed myelin sheaths on its neurons, is not well enough developed to code such experiences (Grof, 1985). Thus, memories of one's birth or of prenatal events—if their accuracy is confirmed in cases where the details recalled had not previously been available to the person—would be another anomaly that could be explained by the existence of information fields that code experience.

In my own formulation, I first conceived of the mythic field as a subtle form of energy that exists within the dimensions of Newtonian space-time. More recently, in trying to account for the anomalies described earlier, I have come to believe that mythic fields sometimes must embody properties that are associated with quantum fields such as nonlocality.

Even without visual or auditory cues, a sensitive individual often can detect changes in another person's mythic field, experienced as an altered "energy" or "vibration" (e.g., "Before I even pulled into the driveway, I could feel that he was angry"). People who work in the "new" discipline of energy medicine are particularly attuned to this realm. The following is excerpted from an interview I conducted with my partner, Donna Eden, a mind/body healer known for her ability to see and feel the body's energies and, based on what she sees and feels, to identify physical problems in a manner that reliably corresponds with medical diagnoses. She described the way in which she experiences what I refer to as personal myths and personal fields of information:

> In shifting from one myth into another, the vibration of the person's field changes and the field's colors change. When a person is under emotional stress, the energy tends to take on the stamp of an old myth that is oriented toward emotional or physical survival, usually some version of fight or flight. When one of these survival-oriented myths is activated, I see its energy originating in the root chakra. The old myth sits like a fountain in the root chakra, with the field that comes out from this fountain surrounding the person's body.
>
> At other times, the old myth quiets down. While I can still see its energy, I can also see the energy of other myths come in. When a new myth has become more than an idea and has begun to take a stable physical form, it begins to infiltrate the auric bands, changing some of their colors. Its energy will be less dense and move more quickly than the energy of the old myth. As a new myth begins to take hold, at first it looks faint to me, but with time it becomes more distinct.

What you call the conflict between an old myth and an emerging myth often isn't so much that the two fight one another but [rather] that the old myth is simply fighting for its survival. When a myth doesn't work anymore, a point is reached where its energy gets very murky. I can see the energy of an old myth doing all it can to hold on, like hot tar. If it gets stuck that way for a long period, physical illness often follows. (personal interview, February 28, 1995)

A small body of evidence suggesting a relationship between subtle vibrational patterns in the body and disease states is, in fact, accumulating (Hunt, 1995), and the paradigm underlying energy medicine (Eden, 1999; Gerber, 1996) complements the line of reasoning presented here.

CLINICAL IMPLICATIONS: SHIFT THE FIELD, CHANGE THE MYTH

More than half a century ago, May (1939/1989) observed, "Both the counselor and the counselee are taken out of themselves and become merged in a common psychic entity. The emotions and will of each become part of this new psychic entity" (p. 67). One of May's students, Larson (1987), a psychologist who has studied this "new psychic entity," described a striking incident from her own clinical work:

A new client entered my office for the first appointment. I spontaneously began experiencing very subtle unusual sensations in my own lower torso. Prior to this appointment, I had completed a deep relaxation exercise, so I was quite aware when the subtle tingly sensations began. I first reflected inwardly, trying to discover the source of the mysterious sensations. I asked myself if the new client reminded me of someone I had previously known. I searched

myself to ascertain if my own personal memories were related to the tingly sensations. Then I bracketed the experience, noting it, watching it, and reflecting further upon it. Finally, my curiosity was overpowering. At a seemingly appropriate point, I described my experience to the young woman client and asked if my experience had some meaning for her. The young woman immediately replied, "Oh yes, I have cancer of the cervix, and I've been having chemotherapy there." (p. 323)

Investigating this phenomenon, which she termed *psychotherapeutic resonance,* Larson found that many therapists report a momentary merging of the boundary between themselves and a client that, in its intensity, exceeds empathy and rapport (see also Sterling & Bugental, 1993, on the "meld" experience of therapist with client). In psychotherapeutic resonance, the therapist evidences immediate nonverbal understanding of feelings that the client has not acknowledged, the therapist may directly experience physical sensations that the client is experiencing, and the therapist and client become synchronized in even tiny movement patterns. Is the therapist unconsciously tuning into a subtle field of information carried by the client?

Early in my career, I had the good fortune of observing firsthand the therapeutic mastery of Milton Erickson, Alexander Lowen, Peg Mayo, Carl Rogers, and Virginia Satir. I often was present when one of these gifted clinicians would provide a demonstration for trainees. Their skills sometimes seemed uncanny. How did they *know* what a person needed? I would study transcriptions of their clinical work, hoping to discern their secrets. The most interesting pattern I could detect was their ability to offer a creative and unexpected intervention at the moment of therapeutic opportunity, impossible to acquire by studying transcripts and often quite different from their trademark techniques, yet strikingly attuned, plausibly through resonance, to the client's unique needs. I have witnessed Rogers being decidedly directive (e.g., "Steven, I don't think you should marry her"), Satir cutting to the core of a psychodynamic conflict with no reference to the person's family or family of origin, and Lowen getting to the heart of a problem with no mention of the person's posture or bodily tensions. I wondered, if their interventions were not based on their established clinical approach, then to what were they attuning themselves? I have come to think of this elusive "what" as the client's mythic field. I believe, in fact, that many effective therapists are high in psychotherapeutic resonance, able to spontaneously attune themselves to a client's field, accurately obtaining information that is not transmitted through even the most subtle sensory cues.

Many phenomena that are difficult to account for in psychotherapy, such as the enormous power of projective identification (e.g., a seasoned child psychiatrist observing that she knows she is dealing with a victim of child abuse when she experiences an irrational "impulse to abuse the child" [cited in Gabbard, 1994, p. 71]) have been attributed to subtle sensory cues. I would reverse the argument; wherever subliminal sensory cues are the explanation of last resort, consider the possibility that a field of information also is involved. I myself have learned, when in a clinical situation and unsure about what I should do next, to quiet my inner chatter, shift my attention to the field that the client brings into the room, and allow it to inform my responses. This often results in the subjective experience that I am tuning into a normally imperceptible atmosphere carried by the client. After consciously shifting my attention to the client's hypothetical field,

new understanding and interventions may come in a flash. Such moments of insight sometimes seem to tap into information about the client to which I do not have any apparent access but that subsequently is confirmed (see also the second chapter by Schneider [Chapter 23] in this volume). Whether shifting my attention to the client's field is a way of actually attuning myself to a dimension of the clinical situation that transcends sensory cues or is just a helpful bit of self-deception, I believe that the maneuver makes me a better therapist.

Focused imagery that brings a person into the past to rework early emotional distress and trauma can be designed to mimic some of the healing functions of dreams and to help transform the psychodynamic bedrock of a dysfunctional myth. A man was able to trace his abusive impulses toward his son back to his own experiences of abuse. He was guided to visualize himself as a child in his primal drama with his own father. In this rendition, however, his adult self also was there. The adult self persuaded the father to shower his son with the love and emotional support that the father at some level—buried beneath his own conflicts—held but did not express. (In extreme cases, the person's fantasy might have to eliminate the parent altogether and have the adult self provide the parenting directly. In any case, coming to a productive scenario is a significant piece of the therapeutic work.) In the presence of that imagined emotional support, he could sense a shift, the genesis of the field that might have existed if he actually had received the love being fantasized. This is a procedure for deep transformation that I call *rewriting history through the emotionally corrective daydream*. A daily ritual to strengthen the father's new personal myth, and the field associated with it, might project him into an imagined future where he is living from a guiding myth that supports constructive responses to his son at the moments of greatest stress. Because repetition increases the strength of a field (according to Sheldrake, 1988), by frequently evoking in his imagination the sensations and images associated with his new myth, the father presumably can increase the habit strength of this fledgling myth until it becomes readily accessible.

Based on preliminary clinical observations (Feinstein & Krippner, 1997), therapeutic rituals for directly embedding a new mythology can be designed around the presumed influence on mythic fields on each of the following:

▶ Setting an intention to initiate constructive change

▶ Imagery journeys to the past that psychodynamically rework dysfunctional myths

▶ Imagery journeys that seed the future with a more constructive guiding mythology

▶ Visualizing the qualities of this new myth

▶ Shifting internal speech to support the new myth

▶ Behavioral rehearsal to anchor the new myth

CONCLUSION

The evidence for telepathy, the distant effects of visualization, and the other anomalies summarized in this chapter suggests that consciousness is not just an epiphenomenon emerging from biochemical events any more than the evening news originates only in the television set. The news is produced by both the television set (a "bottom-up" influence) and the television signal (a "top-down" influence). Personal myths also are produced by bottom-up and top-down influences. Neurons, like the television components, exert a bottom-up influence, from the brain *up* to the developing story. Fields of information, like the television signals, exert their influence from the top *down* to the developing story. Neurons and fields seem to operate in tandem like the television set and the signal. Personal myths reflect both the brain and the field, just like the television program is a reflection of both the television set and the signal. Personal myths, *as biochemically coded organizing models*, exert a bottom-up influence on - consciousness and behavior. Personal myths, *as fields of information*, exert a top-down influence.

The hypothesis that mythic fields influence feelings, thoughts, and behavior, if supported, would hold far-reaching implications. Although we know with relative certainty that Lamarck was wrong to believe that a person's experiences create biological changes that are then passed along through the genes, the possibility that those experiences create changes in a field of information that is part of the child's intellectual "amniotic fluid" gives a new twist to Lamarckian interpretations. An understanding of the way in which mythic fields act on the psyche would make it possible to tailor more proficiently, for desired change, techniques that use ritual, visualization, focused intention, and behavioral enactments. An understanding of the more subtle physical realms that influence mental structures also would provide a stronger empirical foundation for investigating the higher mental processes that have long been the concern of humanistic psychologists. More dramatically, the idea that fields of information affect consciousness would augment our understanding of collective myth making, suggesting in fact a physical infrastructure for the fashionable idea that a "global brain" (Russell, 1995) now is emerging.

Given that experimental evidence has linked mental activity with nonlocal fields of information, it is not a huge leap to postulate that, just as two aligned magnets form a shared field, an idea that is held by many people would exist in concert with a *collective* field of information. Such a collective field presumably would intensify if the num-

bers holding the idea increased, as when an image is multiplied by way of satellite (Feinstein, Mortifee, & Krippner, 1998). With electronic communications media, we are in fact able to interact more consciously than ever before with the fields that underlie our collective thoughts, to recognize them as tangible albeit subtle entities, and to open to novel approaches for participating in their evolution.

REFERENCES

Assimakis, P. D., & Dillbeck, M. C. (1995). Time series analysis of improved quality of life in Canada: Social change, collective consciousness, and the TM-Sidhi program. *Psychological Reports, 76*, 1171-1193.

Bagarozzi, D. A., & Anderson, S. A. (Eds.). (1989). *Family myths: Psychotherapy implications*. New York: Haworth.

Bem, D. J., & Honorton, C. (1994). Does psi exist? Replicable evidence for an anomalous process of information transfer. *Psychological Bulletin, 115*, 4-18.

Benor, D. J. (1993). *Healing research: Holistic energy medicine and spiritual healing*. Munich: Helix Verlag.

Bierlein, J. F. (1994). *Parallel myths*. New York: Random House.

Bohm, D. (1951). *Quantum theory*. London: Constable.

Bohm, D. (1980). *Wholeness and the implicate order*. London: Routledge.

Braud, W. G. (1990). Distant mental influence of rate of hemolysis of human red blood cells. *Journal of the American Society for Psychical Research, 84*, 1-24.

Braud, W. G. (1992). Human interconnectedness: Research indications. *ReVision: A Journal of Consciousness and Transformation, 14*, 140-149.

Brown, D. E. (1991). *Human universals*. Philadelphia: Temple University Press.

Burr, H. S. (1972). *The fields of life*. New York: Random House.

Campbell, J. (1968). *The masks of god: Vol. 4. Creative mythology*. Garden City, NY: Doubleday.

Campbell, J. (1972). *Myths to live by*. New York: Bantam Books.

Cano, J. L. (1996, July). The secret life of objects. *Ano Cero*, pp. 84-88.

Chamberlain, D. B. (1990). *Babies remember birth*. New York: Random House.

Cheek, D. B. (1980). Ideomotor questioning revealing an apparently valid traumatic experience prior to birth: A clinical note. *Australian Journal of Clinical and Experimental Hypnosis, 8*(2), 65-70.

Child, I. L. (1985). Psychology and anomalous observations: The question of ESP in dreams. *American Psychologist, 40*, 1219-1230.

Dillbeck, M. C., Cavanaugh, K. L., Glenn, T., Orme-Johnson, D. W., & Mittlefehldt, V. (1987). Consciousness as a field: The transcendental meditation and TM-Sidhi program and changes in social indicators. *Journal of Mind and Behavior, 8*(1), 67-104.

Dossey, L. (1993). *Healing words: The power of prayer and the practice of medicine*. New York: HarperCollins.

Edelman, G. M. (1992). *Bright air, brilliant fire: On the matter of the mind*. New York: Basic Books.

Eden, D. (1999). *Energy medicine*. New York: Penguin.

Edington, A. (1929). *The nature of the physical world*. London: Dent.

Editorial: A book for burning? (1981). *Nature, 293*, 245-246.

Feinstein, D. (1979). Personal mythology as a paradigm for a holistic public psychology. *American Journal of Orthopsychiatry, 49*, 198-217.

Feinstein, D. (1997). Personal myths and psychotherapy: Myth-making in psychological and spiritual development. *American Journal of Orthopsychiatry, 67*, 508-521.

Feinstein, D. (2000). Archetypes. In A. E. Kazdin (Ed.), *Encyclopedia of psychology*. New York: Oxford University Press.

Feinstein, D., & Krippner, S. (1997). *The mythic path*. New York: Tarcher.

Feinstein, D., Krippner, S., & Granger, D. (1988). Myth-making and human development. *Journal of Humanistic Psychology, 28*(3), 23-50.

Feinstein, D., Mortifee, A., & Krippner, S. (1998). Waking to the rhythm of a new myth. *World Futures, 52*, 187-238.

Fox, R. (1989). *The search for society*. New Brunswick, NJ: Rutgers University Press.

Freud, S. (1953). *A general introduction to psychoanalysis* (J. Riviere, Trans.). New York: Permabooks. (Original work published 1924)

Friedman, N. (1994). *Bridging science and spirit*. St. Louis, MO: Living Lake Books.

Gabbard, G. O. (1994). *Psychodynamic psychiatry in clinical practice*. Washington, DC: American Psychiatric Press.

Gallo, F. P. (1998). *Energy psychology: Explorations at the interface of energy, cognition, behavior, and health*. Boca Raton, FL: CRC Press.

Gerber, R. (1996). *Vibrational medicine*. Santa Fe, NM: Bear.

Griffith, R. M., Miyagi, O., & Tago, A. (1958). The universality of typical dreams: Japanese versus Americans. *American Anthropologist, 60*, 1173-1178.

Grof, S. (1985). *Beyond the brain: Birth, death, and transcendence in psychotherapy*. Albany: State University of New York Press.

Grof, S. (1992). *The holotropic mind: The three levels of human consciousness and how they shape our lives*. New York: HarperCollins.

Grush, R., & Churchland, P. S. (1995). Gaps in Penrose's toiling. *Journal of Consciousness Studies, 2*(1), 10-29.

Gullestad, S. E. (1995). The *personal myth* as a clinical concept. *International Journal of Psycho-Analysis, 76*, 1115-1166.

Hall, C. S., & Norby, V. J. (1972). *The individual and his dreams*. New York: New American Library.

Hameroff, S. (1994). Quantum coherence in microtubules: A neural basis for emergent consciousness? *Journal of Consciousness Studies, 1*(1), 91-118.

Hartocollis, P., & Graham, I. D. (Eds.). (1991). *The personal myth in psychoanalytic theory*. Madison, CT: International Universities Press.

Hunt, V. (1995). *Infinite mind: The science of human vibrations*. Malibu, CA: Malibu Publishing.

Jahn, R. G., & Dunne, B. J. (1989). *Margins of reality: The role of consciousness in the physical world*. Orlando, FL: Harcourt Brace.

Jung, C. G. (1968a). *Archetypes of the collective unconscious* (Collected Works, Vol. 9, Part 1, 2nd ed.. R. Hull, Trans.). Princeton, NJ: Princeton University Press. (Original work published 1934)

Jung, C. G. (1968b). *Synchronicity: An acausal connecting principle* (Collected Works, Vol. 8, 2nd ed., R. Hull, Trans.). Princeton, NJ: Princeton University Press. (Original work published 1952)

Krippner, S. (1975). *Song of the siren: A parapsychological odyssey*. New York: Harper & Row.

Krippner, S. (Ed.). (1990). Personal mythology: Psychological perspectives [Special issue]. *The Humanistic Psychologist, 18*(2).

Krippner, S. (Ed.). (1994). Mythology and psychology [Special theme section]. *The Humanistic Psychologist, 22,* 122-227.

Larsen, S. (1976). *The shaman's doorway: Opening the mythic imagination to contemporary consciousness.* New York: Harper & Row.

Larsen, S. (1990). *The mythic imagination: Your quest for meaning through personal mythology.* New York: Bantam Books.

Larson, V. A. (1987). An exploration of psychotherapeutic resonance. *Psychotherapy, 24,* 321-324.

Laszlo, E. (1995). *The interconnected universe: Conceptual foundations of transdisciplinary unified theory.* London: World Scientific.

Laughlin, C. D. (1996). Archetypes, neurognosis, and the Quantum Sea. *Journal of Scientific Exploration, 10,* 375-400.

Libet, B. (1994). A testable field theory of mind-brain interaction. *Journal of Consciousness Studies, 1*(1), 119-126.

Lukoff, D. (1997). The psychologist as mythologist. *Journal of Humanistic Psychology, 37*(3), 34-58.

Maslow, A. H. (1971). *The farther reaches of human nature.* New York: Viking.

May, R. (1989). *The art of counseling* (rev. ed.). New York: Gardner. (Original work published 1939)

McAdams, D. P. (1993). *Stories we live by: Personal myths and the making of the self.* New York: William Morrow.

Moss, T. (1974). *The probability of the impossible: Scientific discoveries and explorations in the psychic world.* Los Angeles: Tarcher.

Neher, A. (1996). Jung's theory of archetypes: A critique. *Journal of Humanistic Psychology, 36*(2), 61-91.

Nelson, R. D., Bradish, G. J., Dobyns, Y. H., Dunne, B. J., & Jahn, R. G. (1996). FieldREG anomalies in group situations. *Journal of Scientific Exploration, 10,* 111-141.

Pearce, J. C. (1992). *Evolution's end: Claiming the potential of our intelligence.* New York: HarperCollins.

Penrose, R. (1994). *Shadows of the mind: A search for the missing science of consciousness.* New York: Oxford University Press.

Perry, J. W. (1976). *Roots of renewal in myth and madness: The meaning of psychotic episodes.* San Francisco: Jossey-Bass.

Piaget, J. (1977). *The development of thought: Equilibrium of cognitive structures* (A. Rosin, Trans.). New York: Viking.

Pribram, K. H. (1971). *Languages of the brain.* Englewood Cliffs, NJ: Prentice Hall.

Radin, D. (1997). *The conscious universe: The scientific truth of psychic phenomena.* New York: HarperCollins.

Russell, P. (1995). *The global brain awakens: Our next evolutionary leap.* Palo Alto, CA: Global Brain.

Sarbin, T. R. (Ed.). (1986). *Narrative psychology: The storied nature of human conduct.* New York: Praeger.

Schuman, E., & Madison, D. (1994). Locally distributed synaptic potentiation in the hypocampus. *Science, 263,* 532-536.

Schuster, C., & Carpenter, E. (1996). *Social symbolism in ancient and tribal art.* New York: Abrams.

Sheldrake, R. (1981). *A new science of life: The hypothesis of formative causation.* Los Angeles: Tarcher.

Sheldrake, R. (1988). *The presence of the past: Morphic resonance and the habits of nature.* New York: Random House.

Sheldrake, R., & Bohm, D. (1982). Morphogenic fields and the implicate order: A conversation between Rupert Sheldrake and David Bohm. *ReVision, 5*(2), 41-48.

Slavin, M. O., & Kriegman, D. (1992). *The adaptive design of the human psyche: Psychoanalysis, evolutionary biology, and the therapeutic process.* New York: Guilford.

Sterling, M. M., & Bugental, J. F. T. (1993). The meld experience in psychotherapy supervision. *Journal of Humanistic Psychology, 33*(2), 38-48.

Stevens, A. (1982). *Archetypes: A natural history of the self.* New York: William Morrow.

Stevens, A. (1993). *The two million-year-old self.* College Station: Texas A&M University Press.

Targ, R., & Katra, J. (1998). *Miracles of mind: Exploring nonlocal consciousness and spiritual healing.* New York: New World Library.

Tiller, W. A. (1993). What are subtle energies? *Journal of Scientific Exploration, 7,* 293-304.

Tooby, J., & Cosmides, L. (1992). The psychological foundations of culture. In J. Barkow, L. Cosmides, & J. Tooby (Eds.), *The adapted mind: Evolutionary psychology and the evolution of culture* (pp. 19-136). New York: Oxford University Press.

Treffert, D. (1989). *Extraordinary people: Redefining the "idio-savant."* New York: Harper & Row.

Wagner, M. W., & Monnet, M. (1979). Attitudes of college professors toward extrasensory perception. *Zetetic Scholar, 5,* 7-16.

Weiss, P. (1939). *Principles of development.* New York: Henry Holt.

Wilber, K. (1995). *Sex, ecology, spirituality.* Boston: Shambhala.

Wolf, F. A. (1994). *The dreaming universe: A mind-expanding journey into the realm where psyche and physics meet.* New York: Simon & Schuster.

Zohar, D., & Marshall, I. (1994). *The quantum society: Mind, physics, and a new social vision.* New York: William Morrow.

CHAPTER 16

Beyond Religion

Toward a Humanistic Spirituality

DAVID N. ELKINS

HUMANISTIC PSYCHOLOGY has no manifesto and, therefore, no official position in regard to spirituality. For more than 40 years, the humanistic movement has provided an open arena for discussions about spirituality, refusing to institutionalize any particular point of view. In my opinion, this open attitude is one of the movement's greatest contributions to the study of spirituality. This chapter, despite its appearance in a humanistic psychology handbook, is not intended to be a statement of humanistic psychology's position on the topic. Rather, it is simply my personal contribution to these ongoing discussions.

SPIRITUALITY IN THE HUMANISTIC MOVEMENT

Importance of Spirituality

Spirituality always has been an important topic in the humanistic psychology movement. Humanistic psychology writers have published numerous books on the subject, articles on spirituality frequently appear in the journals and newsletters of the movement, and spirituality is a common theme at professional conferences and other gatherings of humanistic psychologists. A recent survey by Elkins, Lipari, and Kozora (in press) provided empirical confirmation of this widespread interest. A 71-item questionnaire, which contained one section of items related to spirituality, was mailed to all 615 members of Division 32 (Humanistic Psychology) of the American Psychological Association (APA). Of the 230 members who completed and returned the questionnaire, 77% said that spirituality is "important" or "very important" in their lives. In addition, 75% said that they believe in some type of higher power or transcendent force, and 43% professed faith in a personal god. When asked to select the statement that best describes their spiritual orientation, 55% chose "I am spiritual but not religious," and

32% chose "I am both religious and spiritual." Only 6% chose "I am neither religious nor spiritual."

Abraham Maslow and Spirituality

Abraham Maslow, whose writings helped to lay the theoretical foundations of the humanistic psychology movement, considered spirituality to be a major component of the humanistic vision. Instead of pathologizing religious needs, Maslow (1962) said, "The human being needs a framework of values, a philosophy of life, a religion or religion surrogate to live by and understand by, in about the same sense he needs sunlight, calcium, or love" (p. 206). Maslow (1976) also said, "Humanistic psychologists would probably consider a person sick or abnormal in an existential way if he were not concerned with these 'religious questions' " (p. 18).

Maslow made a distinction between organized religion and personal spirituality. In *Religions, Values, and Peak Experiences,* Maslow (1976) stated his position as follows:

> I want to demonstrate that spiritual values have naturalistic meaning, that they are not the exclusive possession of organized churches, that they do not need supernatural concepts to validate them, that they are well within the jurisdiction of a suitably enlarged science, and that, therefore, they are the general responsibility of all mankind. (p. 33)

Maslow was not opposed to organized religion per se, nor did he believe that a nontheistic view was the only viable philosophical perspective. In fact, Maslow (1976) said that the "essential core-religious experience may be embedded in either a theistic, supernatural context or a nontheistic context" (p. 28). Nevertheless, he viewed spirituality as a universal human phenomenon that did not belong exclusively to any church or religious group. By emphasizing its human character, Maslow placed spirituality in the domain of the human sciences where it could be studied naturalistically.

For Maslow, spirituality was intimately connected with "peak experiences" or mystical encounters characterized by feelings of intense awe, reverence, bliss, and ecstasy. He believed that religion had its origin in such mystical experiences. Maslow (1976) wrote, "The intrinsic core, the essence, the universal nucleus of every known high religion . . . has been the private, lonely, personal illumination, revelation, or ecstasy of some acutely sensitive prophet or seer" (p. 19). However, as Maslow pointed out, this mystical vision tends to become institutionalized as the prophet's followers codify the teachings and standardize the religious practices. Ironically, orthodox religion may then suppress those claiming direct religious experiences. As Maslow put it, "Conventional religions may even be used as defenses against and resistances to the shaking experiences of transcendence" (p. 33).

Maslow believed that peak experiences, although universal, always are interpreted within the framework of a particular cultural or personal belief system. For example, a Christian will describe the experience using the language and symbols of Christianity, a Hindu will use Hindu terms and symbols, and a Buddhist will use the language of that tradition. An individual who does not subscribe to any religious system may use psychological or neurological models to explain the experience. So, whereas peak experiences constitute the universal core of religion, these experiences always are dressed in the symbolic and linguistic clothing of a particular time, place, culture, and belief system.

Maslow believed that peak experiences transport us out of ordinary consciousness into a higher dimension of being, providing us with glimpses of a transcendent reality and allowing us to touch ultimate values such as truth, beauty, goodness, and love, which Maslow called "being-values." Mystical moments give us a taste of what it would be like to live at the highest level of actualization. The poet William Blake said, "If the doors of perception were cleansed, everything would appear to man as it is, infinite" (Blake, 1977, p. 188). This is the way things look in the realm of being.

Maslow viewed peak experiences as an important component of psychological health. In his psychological theory, he divided human needs into basic needs and higher needs. Basic needs have to do with our physical survival and include our need for food, shelter, security, and social connections. Higher needs have to do with being-values including our need for truth, beauty, goodness, and love. If deprived of these higher values, we tend to fall into what Maslow called *metapathology*, a pathology that is a direct result of deprivation at the spiritual level. The best cure for this malady is renewed contact with the realm of being, to which peak experiences are the "royal road." Although Maslow recognized that we cannot have peak experiences at will, he nevertheless believed that it was possible to learn what he called "being-cognition." Being-cognition is the capacity to open one's heart to the sanctity of everyday experiences or to view one's mate, children, friends, and daily life under the aspect of eternity.

Transpersonal Psychology

The emergence of transpersonal psychology is a major part of the history of the humanistic movement. In *Shadow Culture*,

Taylor (1999) pointed out that from 1941 to 1969, humanistic psychology thrived as a respected alternative point of view within the academic community, but that during the late 1960s, the intellectual focus of the movement was overshadowed by the political and social ferment of that period and humanistic ideals were preempted by the counterculture. Taylor described what happened at that point:

> Within this flood tide, between 1967 and 1969, humanistic psychology split into at least three parts. The first was transpersonal psychology, with its emphasis on spiritual practice, meditation, and higher states of consciousness. The second was experiential encounter, which emphasized emotional relationships, cultivation of sensory experience, and a greater awareness of the body. Finally, there was radical therapy, a catch-all term referring to the marriage of psychology and radical political action in such divergent areas as militant feminism, the antipsychiatry movement, critical thinking, and what has come to be called human science. (p. 274)

Taylor (1999) went on to say that the emergence of transpersonal psychology was due, in large measure, to the influence of Maslow, who was convinced that mystical states represented a new frontier for psychology. Anthony Sutich, the first editor of the *Journal of Humanistic Psychology*, shared Maslow's enthusiasm. According to Taylor, at a workshop at the Esalen Institute in 1966, the two friends became convinced that a major new thrust was needed in the humanistic movement, one that would focus on mystical states and spiritual values. In 1967, Maslow first announced the emergence of a "fourth force" in American psychology in a lecture he delivered in San Francisco for the Esalen Institute. In 1969,

Sutich turned over the editorship of the *Journal of Humanistic Psychology* to Miles Vich and launched a new publication called the *Journal of Transpersonal Psychology*. In the first issue, Sutich (1969) defined transpersonal psychology as

> an emerging force in the psychology field by a group of psychologists and professional men and women from other fields who are interested in those ultimate human capacities and potentialities that have no systematic place in positivistic or behavioristic theory ("first force"), classical psychoanalytic theory ("second force"), or humanistic psychology ("third force"). (pp. 15-16)

Sutich (1969) went on to describe this new movement as the fourth force in psychology and gave a long list of topics with which it was concerned. The list included things such as ultimate values, unitive consciousness, ecstasy, mystical experience, awe, bliss, wonder, ultimate meaning, cosmic awareness, and the sacralization of everyday life. In 1971, Sutich organized the American Association of Transpersonal Psychology, later renamed the Association for Transpersonal Psychology. For the past 30 years, transpersonal thinkers such as Tart (1975a, 1975b, 1989), Wilber (1977, 1980, 1981, 1995, 1997), Vaughan (1979, 1986), Walsh (1990, 1995), and Washburn (1988) have made major contributions to our understanding of spirituality, demonstrating the relevance of the spiritual dimension to clinical theory and practice and to a fuller understanding of the human.

Frager (1989), acknowledging his debt to Hastings for the model, suggested that the field of transpersonal psychology can be divided into three major domains: "the psychology of personal development, the psychology of consciousness, and spiritual psychology" (p. 289). According to Frager, the psychology of personal development has to do with the theoretical formulations and practical applications of therapeutic approaches designed to promote individual growth; the psychology of consciousness is concerned with various states of consciousness including meditation, dreams, drug states, and parapsychology; and spiritual psychology includes the study of the world's religious traditions and the integration of spiritual knowledge into psychological theory. Frager emphasized that transpersonal psychology should not be limited to the content of these three domains given that it is a point of view that can be applied to various disciplines related to human behavior. Nevertheless, these three domains help to organize the field of transpersonal psychology and provide a way in which to examine the contributions that have been made in each area.

As Hastings (1999) pointed out, humanistic psychologists tend to place transpersonal psychology under the general umbrella of humanistic psychology. By contrast, those associated with transpersonal psychology tend to view it as a distinctive fourth force and seek to have its independent status acknowledged. This disagreement took on a concrete form during the 1980s when transpersonal psychologists sought to form a Transpersonal Psychology division in the APA. Rollo May, along with some other humanistic and existential psychologists, opposed the forming of the new division, arguing that the proper home for transpersonal psychologists was Division 32 (Humanistic Psychology) of the APA. This issue came up again during the late 1990s when some members of the Division 32 executive council suggested that the name of Division 32 be changed from Humanistic Psychology to Humanistic and Transpersonal Psychology. However, when

Division 32 members were surveyed on this issue, 69% opposed the name change (Elkins et al., in press).

Humanistic and transpersonal thinkers also have had their share of disagreements in the theoretical arena. For example, Schneider (1987, 1989) raised concerns about transpersonal models that seem to imply that individuals struggling with humanistic and existential issues are at a lower level of spiritual development than those who are at the transpersonal level. Schneider disagreed with such hierarchical thinking and argued that such transpersonal theory is at risk of losing its earthy grounding in human experience. (For an example of this debate, see the exchange between Schneider and Walsh [Chapter 45] in this volume.)

Despite such disagreements and occasional conflicts, humanistic and transpersonal psychologists generally are supportive of each other. The *Journal of Humanistic Psychology* publishes articles on transpersonal themes, and Division 32 has a transpersonal psychology section and sponsors presentations on transpersonal topics at the annual meetings of the APA. Disagreements between transpersonal and humanistic psychologists tend to be viewed as family feuds, with members of the same family debating their differences yet ultimately supporting each other in the broader arena of American psychology and culture.

Unfortunately, mainstream American psychology, with its materialistic assumptions and scientist bias, has tended to marginalize the contributions of transpersonal psychology. Nevertheless, the fourth force continues to attract a wide range of students, clinicians, researchers, and professors. The Institute of Transpersonal Psychology in Menlo Park, California, is specifically devoted to training students in this discipline.

MY PERSONAL STORY

Although I respect the work of transpersonal psychologists, my own approach to spirituality has been informed not so much by contemporary transpersonal thinkers as by individuals such as Otto (1923), Eliade (1959), James (1902), Tillich (1957), Buber (1970), Frankl (1963), Fromm (1950), Hillman (1975), Jung (1933, 1964), and Maslow (1962, 1971, 1976).

Because I believe that knowledge always is embedded in a personal context, I would like to describe my own spiritual journey before turning to the more theoretical aspects of my views. I was born in the foothills of the Ozark Mountains in northeastern Arkansas. This area of the country is part of the Bible Belt, and my family was very religious. As a young boy, I decided that I wanted to become a minister. After graduating from high school, I attended a church-related college near Little Rock, and in 1966 I was ordained as a minister. Shortly thereafter, my young family and I moved to Flint, Michigan, where I became the minister of a church composed primarily of transplanted Southerners who had gone north to work in the automobile factories. My church was conservative, holding fundamentalist views on most Christian topics. As a result of my theological training and my own studies as a young minister, I began to question some of the conservative doctrines of my church. Eventually, I came into conflict with the leaders of my congregation. In 1968, I was fired and excommunicated by the board of elders of my congregation because of my "liberal" views. With my ministerial career at an end, I returned to graduate school to study psychology, eventually graduating with a Ph.D. This is where I first was exposed to humanistic and existential psychology. Viktor Frankl was one of my doctoral professors.

After being expelled as a minister, I was wary of organized religion and sometimes thought that my spiritual life had come to an end. Then in 1976, I went into therapy with a Jungian analyst who helped me to see that religion and spirituality are not the same. Serving as my spiritual mentor, this old gentleman showed me how to nourish my soul and develop my spiritual life outside the walls of traditional religion. The seeds that were planted during that therapy experience, cultivated by my own studies of spirituality during the past 20 years, now have grown into my own vision of spirituality.

AN ACCESSIBLE MODEL OF SPIRITUALITY

I am a clinician at heart, and my own theoretical work has focused on developing an accessible model of spirituality that can be used to show clients and others how to nourish their souls and develop their spiritual lives. My approach to spirituality comprises three major constructs: the soul, the sacred, and spirituality itself. I provide a brief discussion of the three constructs and show how they relate to one another. (For a more complete discussion of this model, see my book, *Beyond Religion* [Elkins, 1998].)

The Soul

The word *soul* comes from the Old English word *sawol* or the Anglo-Saxon *sawal,* words that referred to the breath or life force. In Latin, the word for soul is *anima*; in Greek, it is *psyche.*

It is not easy to define the word *soul.* As Hillman (1975) said, "The soul is immeasurably deep and can only be illumined by insights, flashes in a great cavern of incomprehension" (p. xvi). The word *soul* is not intended to point to a tangible reality.

Rather, *soul* is a construct or an abstract word that serves as an umbrella term for certain aspects of human experience, helping us to identify and organize those experiences. As Moore (1992) said, " 'Soul' is not a thing but [rather] a quality or a dimension of experiencing life and ourselves. It has to do with depth, value, relatedness, heart, and personal substance" (p. 5). Soul points to the mystical and imaginal dimensions of human experience. It has to do with awe, wonder, and reverence. These experiences can occur in almost any setting but seem especially associated with things such as music, literature, poetry, ceremony, symbol, religion, being in nature, intimate relationships, and other activities that open our hearts to the mystical imaginal world. If individuals in all cultures look up in wonder and awe, then the word *soul* points to that within us that makes such experiences possible. The soul is that dimension of the human capable of being touched, stirred, and nourished by the sacred.

The Sacred

In *The Idea of the Holy,* Otto (1923) said that throughout history, humans have had encounters with the sacred. These encounters, mystical in nature, have a profound impact on those who experience them. Otto said that in these experiences, "the soul, held speechless, trembles inwardly to the farthest fiber of its being" (p. 17). Otto, who called these encounters "numinous" experiences, did a careful phenomenological analysis of their nature. He concluded that sacred experiences are characterized by various elements including a feeling of being overwhelmed, a sense of mystical awe, a feeling of fascination, and an experience of intense energy.

Eliade, who served as chair of the Department of the History of Religions at the University of Chicago for 17 years, built on Otto's earlier work. He agreed with Otto that humans always have had encounters with the sacred. For these manifestations, he suggested the word *hierophany,* which literally means "something sacred shows itself to us." In his classic work, *The Sacred and the Profane,* Eliade (1959) defined the sacred as follows:

> The *sacred* is equivalent to a *power,* and, in the last analysis, to *reality.* The sacred is saturated with *being.* Sacred power means reality and at the same time enduringness and efficacy. The polarity sacred-profane is often expressed as an opposition between *real* and *unreal* or pseudo-real. . . . Thus, it is easy to understand that religious man deeply desires *to be,* to participate in *reality,* to be saturated with power. (pp. 12-13)

James also recognized the sacred dimension. His book, *The Varieties of Religious Experience* (James, 1902), is filled with examples of mystical encounters. Discussing the extension of the subconscious self, James (1902) wrote, "The further limits of our being plunge, it seems to me, into an altogether other dimension of existence from the sensible and merely understandable world. Name it the mystical region or the supernatural region, whichever you choose" (pp. 515-516).

Spirituality

The word *spirituality* comes from the Latin *spiritus,* which has to do with "breath" or the animating principle. Kurtz and Ketcham (1992), tracing the history of the word, pointed out that in ancient times it was used in contrast to materialism. Then, the word fell out of general use for 1,600 years. Today, in postmodern times, it has been revived and now often is used in con-trast to religion. Thus, when humanistic psychologists and others say that they are "spiritual but not religious," they are using the word in this contemporary sense.

Most scholars have recognized a difference between religion and spirituality. For example, James (1902) divided religion into institutional and personal. Allport (1961) spoke of extrinsic and intrinsic religion, with extrinsic referring primarily to the public and institutional aspects of religion and intrinsic referring more to one's personal devotion. Maslow (1976) made this same distinction, calling institutional religion "big R" religion and personal spirituality "little r" religion.

It is understandable that some continue to confuse religion and spirituality. For some 2,000 years of Western history, religion held a monopoly on spirituality, and the two were intertwined and almost inseparable. But in our day, this seems to be changing. Millions of people, recognizing that religion and spirituality are not the same, have left organized religion to pursue alternative spiritual paths. Roof (1994), a professor at the University of California, Santa Barbara, documented this trend. Roof surveyed 1,600 baby boomers and found that large numbers of this generation left organized religion during the 1960s and 1970s. Of those with religious backgrounds, 69% of mainline Protestants, 61% of conservative Protestants, 67% of Catholics, and 84% of Jews dropped out. Although 25% of those who dropped out have since returned to church or temple, an estimated 32 million baby boomers show no signs of returning to organized religion. Yet, many of these individuals have turned to Eastern religions, Twelve Step programs, New Age thinking, Native American traditions, Jungian psychology, transpersonal psychology, Greek mythology, shamanic practices, meditation, yoga, massage, and a host of other traditions and practices in an effort to nourish their spiritual lives. There is a growing recognition that religion and spirituality are not the same. The movement away from traditional religion to other forms of spirituality is one of the major sociological changes of our time.

Spirituality, because it manifests in so many different forms around the world, is difficult to define. I am well aware that some warn against looking for universal definitions. Yet, it seems to me that in every culture humans look up in wonder and awe and that somewhere in this universal response to the mystery of existence there is common ground. Huxley (1945/1970) called this universal perspective the "perennial philosophy" that manifests in different forms across time and culture. In my book, *Beyond Religion* (Elkins, 1998), I summarized my own views on spirituality as follows:

First: Spirituality is universal. By this, I mean that spirituality is available to every human being. It is not limited to one religion, one culture, or one group of people. In every part of the world, one finds those who have cultivated their souls and developed their spiritual lives.

Second: Spirituality is a human phenomenon. This does not mean that it has no divine component, but it does mean that spirituality is an inborn, natural potential of the human being. It also means that authentic spirituality is grounded in our humanity; it is not imposed from above or from without.

Third: The common core of spirituality is found at the inner phenomenological level. Spirituality manifests in countless outer forms—from the rain dances of Native Americans to the prayer services of Southern Baptists, from the whirling dervishes of Islam to the meditating monks of Zen Buddhism, from the ecstatic worship services of charismatic churches to the solemn silent meetings of the Quakers. But underneath these outward forms, there is a common longing for the sacred, a universal desire to touch and celebrate the mystery of life. It is in the depths of the soul that one discovers the essential and universal dimensions of spirituality.

Fourth: Spirituality has to do with our capacity to respond to the numinous. The essential character of spirituality is mystical, a fact easily overlooked in a scientific and material age. Spirituality is rooted in the soul and cultivated by experiences of the sacred; it feeds on poignancy, wonder, and awe. Its very nature is an expression of the mystery of life and the unfathomable depths of our own being.

Fifth: There is a certain mysterious energy associated with spirituality. Every culture has recognized a life force that moves through all creation. Mystics, poets, artists, shamans, and others are familiar with this force and have described it through the centuries. The soul comes alive when it is nurtured by this sacred energy, and one's existence becomes infused with passion, power, and depth.

Sixth: The aim of spirituality is compassion. The word *compassion* literally means "to suffer with." Spiritual life springs from the tenderness of the heart, and authentic spirituality expresses itself through loving action toward others. Compassion has always been the hallmark of authentic spirituality and the highest teaching of religion. Loveless spirituality is an oxymoron and an ontological impossibility. (pp. 32-33)

Spiritual Growth: Nourishing the Soul Through Sacred Experiences

These three constructs—the soul, the sacred, and spirituality—provide a foundation for an accessible model of spirituality. In essence, their dynamic relationship is this: When the soul is nourished through regular contact with the sacred, the result is spiritual growth or spirituality.

Spirituality is a process as well as a state of being in which our hearts open to the sacred dimension of life. We grow spiritually when our souls are nourished by sacred experiences. The term *sacred experiences* may sound a bit esoteric, perhaps conjuring up images of the mystics and their intense encounters with the holy. Therefore, it is important to emphasize that sacred experiences exist on a continuum of intensity, the lower end of which is accessible to all of us. In other words, ordinary people can have access to the sacred and its soul-nourishing power. The following diagram illustrates the different levels of intensity of sacred experiences:

Poignant Moments	→	Peak Experiences	→	Mystical Encounters
(low intensity)		(average intensity)		(high intensity)

Poignant moments are the most common sacred experiences. These are not earth-shaking events but rather everyday experiences that touch our hearts and nourish our souls. Perhaps one has been moved by the beauty of a sunset, by the stirring music of a symphony, or by the comforting touch of a friend. Such experiences are poignant moments, times when the sacred brushes against us. Poignant moments are small oases in the desert of our ordinary lives, times that refresh our souls and deepen our spiritual awareness. They often are characterized by feelings of gratitude, humility, and awe.

Peak experiences are more intense than poignant moments. Maslow used this term to apply to the entire range of mystical experiences, but I use it to refer to sacred experiences in the middle of the intensity continuum (see also the chapter by Privette [Chapter 14] in this volume). Compared to poignant moments, peak experiences tend to affect us more strongly, touch our souls more deeply, and often produce significant changes in our lives. Yet, peak experiences lack the overwhelming impact of full-blown mystical encounters. A graduate student told me about the following peak experience. When her baby was born, the doctor placed it gently on her stomach. She said that at that moment, she felt the most profound ecstasy she had ever known. For several minutes, her joy remained so intense that she was hardly aware of the others in the room. This experience had a profound impact on this young woman, and it remains one of her most precious memories.

Mystical encounters are the most powerful sacred experiences. They are characterized by overwhelming impact, sometimes leaving the individual psychologically disorganized for a period of time. Mystical encounters often are "border events" or calls to a new way of life. These are the events described by mystics, prophets, and seers. In fact, the world's religious literature is filled with stories of such encounters. In Western religious literature, two of the most famous are the story of Moses and the burning bush and the conversion of the apostle Paul on the road to Damascus. Although most of us never will experience the shattering intensity of a mystical encounter, we can learn to nourish our souls through poignant moments and perhaps even peak experiences.

CLINICAL APPLICATIONS

The preceding model is quite relevant to the clinical situation. We live in a time of spiritual disorientation, and many clients are spiritually hungry. For example, Frankl (1963) held that meaninglessness is the major existential problem of our time and believed that psychotherapy must address this spiritual issue. Fromm (1950) believed that care of the soul is an important part of psychological healing. Yalom (1980) wrote a comprehensive textbook demonstrating how pathology can rise from struggles with existential issues. The list could go on, but the point is this: Many respected psychologists and psychiatrists agree that psychopathology is not simply the result of problems in the mental and emotional sphere and that some problems are associated with the spiritual dimension.

If we wish to integrate a spiritual perspective into our therapeutic work, the following considerations are important. First, to be helpful to clients in the spiritual arena, the clinician must be in contact with his or her own soul. If we have not done our own spiritual work as therapists, then we will not be able to heal at the level of the soul. Thus, learning to nurture our own souls and develop our own spirituality is central to our work as therapists.

Second, while the therapist provides direct care of clients' souls, it also is important for clients to learn how to do this for themselves. In this sense, therapy is an apprenticeship in which clients learn how to care for their own spiritual lives. As we provide therapeutic guidance, it is important to remember that clients differ in terms of what nourishes them at the spiritual level. Some touch the sacred through music, literature, poetry, and other arts. Others find that daily meditation, journaling, and certain religious or spiritual practices nourish their souls. One of my clients, a woman in her 40s, loved to go camping in the desert. She said that the expanses of the desert and the brilliant night sky touched her at a spiri-

tual level. Another client loved the theater and found that certain plays nourished his soul and gave him a new perspective on life. There are countless activities that can nourish and heal the soul. One of the major therapeutic tasks is to help the client discover those experiences that truly meet the spiritual needs of his or her own unique soul.

Third, once clients have identified activities that nourish them spiritually, it is important for them to begin a regular program of soul care. The word *program* might seem antithetical to spirituality, and it certainly is true that simply going through the motions of a program will not nourish the soul. On the other hand, when clients identify activities that truly nourish their souls and then engage in these experiences on a regular basis, the results can be highly beneficial. In this sense, I believe that clients need a regular program of spiritual development.

Fourth, spiritual interventions should not replace traditional psychotherapy. Although showing clients how to nourish their souls and care for their spiritual lives can be an important part of effective therapy, the therapist must remember that spirituality is only one dimension of clients' lives. Other spheres must not be overlooked. For example, that which a client initially views as sacred and life altering might actually be a protective maneuver against pain or vulnerability. It generally is important, therefore, that the therapist neither discredit nor overly reassure clients about their initial spiritual perceptions; instead, the therapist should empower *them* (i.e., the clients themselves) to evaluate their meaning. Integrating spirituality into traditional therapeutic work can be highly effective, but using spiritual interventions to the neglect of other effective therapeutic approaches might prove to be ineffective and even dangerous to the welfare of clients. Thus, those of us who include a spiritual perspective in our work must proceed with humility and caution.

CONCLUSION

Spirituality always has been an integral part of humanistic psychology and will, no doubt, continue to generate interest as humanistic psychology moves into the future. In this chapter, I gave a brief overview of the topic from a historical perspective and provided a sketch of my own approach to spirituality in the clinical arena. My hope is that this chapter will be another verse in the ongoing poem of humanistic spirituality.

REFERENCES

Allport, G. W. (1961). *The individual and his religion.* New York: Macmillan.

Blake, W. (1977). The marriage of heaven and hell. In A. Ostriker (Ed.), *William Blake: The complete poems* (p. 188). New York: Penguin.

Buber, M. (1970). *I and thou.* New York: Scribner.

Eliade, M. (1959). *The sacred and the profane.* New York: Harper & Row.

Elkins, D. N. (1998). *Beyond religion: A personal program for building a spiritual life outside the walls of traditional religion.* Wheaton, IL: Quest Books.

Elkins, D. N., Lipari, J., & Kozora, C. J. (in press). Attitudes and values of humanistic psychologists: Division 32 survey results. *The Humanistic Psychologist.*

Frager, R. (1989). Transpersonal psychology: Promise and prospects. In R. S. Valle & S. Halling (Eds.), *Existential-phenomenological perspectives in psychology* (pp. 289-309). New York: Plenum.

Frankl, V. E. (1963). *Man's search for meaning.* New York: Simon & Schuster.

Fromm, E. (1950). *Psychoanalysis and religion.* New Haven, CT: Yale University Press.

Hastings, A. (1999). Transpersonal psychology: The fourth force. In D. Moss (Ed.), *Humanistic and transpersonal psychology: A historical and biographical sourcebook* (pp. 192-208). Westport, CT: Greenwood.

Hillman, J. (1975). *Re-visioning psychology.* New York: Harper & Row.

Huxley, A. (1970). *The perennial philosophy.* New York: Harper & Row. (Original work published 1945)

James, W. (1902). *The varieties of religious experience.* New York: Longmans, Green.

Jung, C. G. (1933). *Modern man in search of a soul.* New York: Harcourt Brace & World.

Jung, C. G. (1964). *Man and his symbols.* Garden City, NY: Doubleday.

Kurtz, E., & Ketcham, K. (1992). *The spirituality of imperfection.* New York: Bantam Books.

Maslow, A. H. (1962). *Toward a psychology of being.* New York: Van Nostrand Reinhold.

Maslow, A. H. (1971). *The farther reaches of human nature.* New York: Viking.

Maslow, A. H. (1976). *Religions, values, and peak experiences.* New York: Penguin.

Moore, T. (1992). *Care of the soul.* New York: HarperCollins.

Otto, R. (1923). *The idea of the holy.* London: Oxford University Press.

Roof, W. C. (1994). *A generation of seekers: The spiritual journeys of the baby boomers.* San Francisco: Harper San Francisco.

Schneider, K. J. (1987). A 'centaur' response to Wilber and the transpersonal movement. *Journal of Humanistic Psychology, 27*(2), 196-216.

Schneider, K. (1989). Infallibility is so damn appealing: A reply to Ken Wilber. *Journal of Humanistic Psychology, 29*(4), 470-481.

Sutich, A. (1969). Some considerations regarding transpersonal psychology. *Journal of Transpersonal Psychology, 1*(1), 15-16.

Tart, C. T. (1975a). *States of consciousness.* New York: E. P. Dutton.

Tart, C. T. (1975b). *Transpersonal psychologies.* New York: Harper & Row.

Tart, C. T. (1989). *Open mind, discriminating mind.* New York: Harper & Row.

Taylor, E. (1999). *Shadow culture: Psychology and spirituality in America.* Washington, DC: Counterpoint.

Tillich, P. (1957). *Dynamics of faith.* New York: Harper & Row.

Vaughan, F. (1979). *Awakening intuition.* New York: Doubleday.

Vaughan, F. (1986). *The inward arc.* Boston: Shambhala.

Walsh, R. (1990). *The spirit of shamanism.* Los Angeles: J. P. Tarcher.

Walsh, R. (1995). The problem of suffering: Existential and transpersonal perspectives. *The Humanistic Psychologist, 23,* 345-356.

Washburn, M. (1988). *The ego and the dynamic ground.* Albany: State University of New York Press.

Wilber, K. (1977). *The spectrum of consciousness.* Wheaton, IL: Quest Books.

Wilber, K. (1980). *The Atman Project.* Wheaton, IL: Quest Books.

Wilber, K. (1981). *No boundary.* Boston: Shambhala.

Wilber, K. (1995). *Sex, ecology, spirituality: The spirit of evolution.* Boston: Shambhala.

Wilber, K. (1997). *The eye of the spirit.* Boston: Shambhala.

Yalom, I. D. (1980). *Existential psychotherapy.* New York: Basic Books.

CHAPTER 17

Cognitive Science and Technological Culture

A Humanistic Response

CHRISTOPHER M. AANSTOOS

TO UNDERSTAND anything, it is vital to grasp it in context. Psychology, like all intellectual disciplines, is deeply rooted in its social and cultural milieu (and also is reflective of this larger context). Changes in that larger ground ripple through and influence the course of psychology's own development. Certainly, the rise and dominance of behaviorism during the first two thirds of the 20th century in the United States mirrored the development of industrialization and mass production in this country. The new need for rote, repetitive responses on assembly lines promulgated support for a psychology that promised a technology of manipulation and control of such actions. However, the appeal of the behavioristic paradigm began to wane as we moved into a postindustrial society during the final third of the 20th century. Once the handling of complex information was seen as more important than mechanical performance, competing viewpoints finally were able to gain some ascendancy. One of these was the humanistic approach. Today, it is largely recognized that this humanistic movement became, by the 1960s, a major disputant to behaviorism's hegemony within psychology, a recognition granted even by modern behaviorism's leading advocate, B. F. Skinner. In an evocative end-of-his-life query, "Whatever happened to behaviorism as the science of behavior?" Skinner attributed this loss primarily to "three formidable obstacles" and listed humanistic psychology as the "number one obstacle" (Skinner, 1987).

In the generation since the rise of humanistic psychology during the early 1960s, the sociocultural landscape again has changed significantly, and these changes have had considerable impact on both scientific psychology and the larger prescientific culture in which it is embedded. Probably the most consequential of these changes has been the role of technological developments since the 1960s, epitomized by the increasingly transformational place of the computer in so many facets of life. This role also has been extremely influential within psychology and has resulted in the rise of a new (and now dominant) paradigm, whose legacy is the computational model of the person. It is in relation to this new approach, as well as this new technological culture, that contemporary humanistic psychology now is called on to stand in relationship and dialogue. In this chapter, I examine these new trends in theoretical psychology and in culture. Then, I draw conclusions about the continuing role of humanistic psychology.

TRENDS IN THEORETICAL PSYCHOLOGY

It has become almost axiomatic to understand humanistic psychology as the "third force" in American psychology (Maslow, 1968, p. iii) due to its rise during the early 1960s, at the time when behaviorism and psychoanalysis were the two dominant forces in the field. Behaviorism had come to quite thoroughly dominate academic scientific psychology during the preceding decades, whereas psychoanalysis was the prevailing paradigm for clinical practice. Humanistic psychology's decisive challenge to these mainstream approaches is well documented elsewhere (see, e.g., Aanstoos, 1993a, 1993b, 1999; Aanstoos, Serlin, & Greening, 2000) and is widely acknowledged. Less well understood are the ways in which it also offered some convergences with both of the other approaches. After summarizing some points of comparison and contrast with these dominant traditions of its first generation, I look at how this theoretical dialogue continues in the current generation as contemporary humanistic

psychology confronts a mainstream now dominated by cognitive science.

In reconnoitering the theoretical scene in psychology in 1960, it is important first to realize how revolutionary behaviorism and psychoanalysis actually were vis-à-vis the tradition that had preceded them. With its own self-conscious "founding" during the 1870s as an experimental science allegedly independent of philosophy, psychology conceptualized itself as an epiphenomenon of physiology. Even the title of Wundt's (1873-1874/1904) own magnum opus that started that revolution was *Principles of Physiological Psychology*. In other words, as a late-arriving guest at the rich banquet of scientific prestige during the 19th century, psychology premised its highly desired (and highly leveraged) scientific legitimation on the claim that the reality status of psychological life was underwritten by its presupposed physiological underpinnings. These were regarded as the real targets for psychological analysis, as evidenced not only by Wundt's experiments on sensation but also by the type of mathematical laws of sensation being formulated during that time, for example, by Fechner and Helmholtz.

By contrast, both behaviorism and psychoanalysis advanced the view that it was possible to proceed to develop psychology without first achieving a knowledge of the underlying physiological mechanisms. Early in their careers, the founders of both psychoanalysis and behaviorism explicitly avowed their conviction of a causally determinative underlying physiology (Freud, 1895/1950; Watson, 1913). However, they each eschewed the need for it to be understood prior to work on the specifically psychological level of analysis. In this regard, Freud and Watson both freed their psychologies to focus on the specifically psychological in one way while maintaining a commitment to a theoretical reductionism to physiology in another way. This compromise solution achieved for their psychologies the status of "science" but did so by crippling how far afield they could proceed into the uniquely human realm of experience.

Beginning during the late 1950s, a frontal assault on this constriction began and quickly accelerated, led by a variety of humanistically oriented psychologists. Within the field of professional practice, Rogers (1951, 1961) and May (1953; see also May, Angel, & Ellenberger, 1958) proffered decisive alternatives to the Freudian paradigm. Within the research tradition, Maslow (1954, 1968) and Giorgi (1970; see also Aanstoos, 1996, and Wertz & Aanstoos, 1999) widened the scope of both contents and methods. They fundamentally challenged the basic conceptual foundations of mechanism, reductionism, elementism, and objectivism. Quite suddenly, there now were three paradigms in psychology rather than the preceding duo of behaviorism (in the laboratory) and psychoanalysis (in the clinic). The third entry, known as humanistic psychology by the 1960s, was a new hybrid of both the clinical and research wings of psychology. In curious ways, it also cross-pollinated both sides with allegiances to ideas from either. This infusion was made possible by the return to experience as it actually is lived or, put another way, to the person qua person, as one who is living an experienced situation. On the academic side, this allowed for an odd convergence with behaviorism. As Kvale and Greenness (1967) adroitly showed long ago, the humanistic emphases on actually lived experience, on behavior and action as intentional, and on description all find affinity with behaviorism's own radical rejection of a mentalistic introspective psychology. Likewise, the long lineage of psychoanalytic contributions to humanistic psychology—

from Fromm, Frankl, Binswanger, Boss, May, Laing, and many others—exemplifies that alliance, with an emphasis on psychodynamics and depth psychology. As Merleau-Ponty (1982-1983) showed clearly, both phenomenology and psychoanalysis aim at the same "latency" in experience, that is, its subjectively lived meaningfulness. In both cases, we might conclude that humanistic psychology emphasized what was latent in the two predominant paradigms about the immediacy of the lived and built a psychology around a radical fidelity to that seminal insight while discarding the scaffolding, that is, the reductionistic trappings clung to in psychology's efforts to claim the status of a natural science.

This revolutionary turn had several salubrious effects for the field. Most decisively, it freed psychologists to really attend to human experience, on its own terms, as lived phenomena and without any boundaries of what types of experience were permissible to consider. Its impact was quick and deep, as Skinner (1987) himself subsequently was drawn to acknowledge. The humanistic approach reopened psychology to consciousness as a topic of research and to the significance of relationship and empathy in the clinic. The subsequent developments of object relations and self psychology from within the psychoanalytic tradition reveal how these themes of relationship and empathy have since become more acceptable within the mainstream. Kohut, for example, could almost be counted as a humanistic psychologist given that his compatibility in these matters is so close (Kramer, 1995).

Within the research tradition, cognitive psychology arose as a way of reintegrating mind back into a psychology that had been systematically stripped of it by behaviorism. This development began with a series of brilliant articles by Newell and Simon, laying the foundations for the information processing model (Newell, Shaw, & Simon, 1958; Newell & Simon, 1961; Simon & Newell, 1964), and culminated in their book establishing "human information processing" as the basic premise for an alternative paradigm for psychology (Newell & Simon, 1972). This new psychology was quite quickly successful at reintroducing cognition into mainstream psychology at roughly the same time that humanistic psychology was doing so from the outside. For that reason, Skinner (1987) identified cognitive psychology as "obstacle number two" to behaviorism's failure to control the field.

Newell and Simon were able to persuade psychology to reopen its doors to mental life by means of a key premise, namely, that cognition could be demonstrated mechanistically and, therefore, did not pose a threat to the mechanistic foundation apparently required for psychology's esteemed scientific status. This premise seemingly was well demonstrated by their use of computer models of thinking, in which they showed that programs could be specified sufficiently for computers to perform tasks that had been agreed to involve thinking in humans; chess playing was chosen as the "fruit fly" for this emerging field (Hearst, 1978, p. 197). In this way, the analogy was advanced that people are "information processors" in the same sense that computers are and that, therefore, this computational model could account for human thought as well.

Although humanistic psychologists might revel in Skinner's designation of their field as his number one obstacle (with cognitive psychology number two), it was cognitivism that actually achieved the long-sought paradigm shift in psychology. During the 1970s and 1980s, this new cognitive model became well articulated through a plethora of new books and journals along with gen-

erous government-funded support of its research projects. Soon advertisements for vacant university positions began soliciting cognitive psychologists to replace the retiring behaviorists, and the shift was on. Even within clinical psychology, a cognitive model gained preeminence. Cognitive therapy came to dominate the field of professional practice so quickly and thoroughly that even the new order of managed care, with its retrograde criterion of measurable objectives, effects a "cognitive-behavioral" meld for psychotherapy.

This rapid changing of psychology's palace guard creates both dangers and opportunities for humanistic psychology. The gravest danger is that the fervor for fundamental change—the wave on which humanistic psychology arrived—now has been largely co-opted by cognitivism. It is cognitive psychologists who now reintroduce the field to terms such as *mind, thinking,* and even *consciousness.* Although this new openness offers space where previously it was only taboo, it is atavistic in that the "mind" being reintroduced by cognitivism is a "computational" mind, that is, a mechanism as thoroughly mechanical as the digital computer on which it was modeled. In that substitution, a counterfeit revolution supplants the more foundationally radical alternative of humanistic psychology, as its portrait of a mechanistic consciousness occludes the humanistic view of an intentional one (Aanstoos, 1985, 1986, 1987a, 1987b).

Within cognitive psychology, there has emerged a split. Whereas the computer simulation approach championed by Newell and Simon remains preeminent, Neisser (1967, 1976) developed an alternative cognitivism not based on computer models. Borrowing from the earlier pioneering work of Gibson (1966, 1976), Neisser differentiates his own approach, which seeks more concretely lived manifestations, as the "low road" in contrast to the "high road" of abstraction taken by the computer modelers (Neisser, 1982, p. xi). However, even Neisser's approach is abstract in that it posits certain inferred "schemata" as mediating the perceptual and cognitive relations of person and world. Because these inferred schemata are not given in experience, his theory remains bound to certain assumptions of processing that leave it removed from the realm of immediate experience (Wertz, 1987).

This new cognitive paradigm also offers certain opportunities for humanistic psychology. On the clinical side, its unremitting emphasis on cognition so stridently makes one-sided the previous humanistic insight of the importance of how clients construe their world (Ellis, 1962, 1973) that humanistic psychotherapists now can mark out their contributions to this dialogue by reminding the field of the importance of emotions (for which they initially were branded "touchy-feely"). Even mainstream critics began to accumulate evidence that emotional reactions precede cognitive processing and so are not founded on it (Zajonc, 1980).

On the research side, cognitive psychology has succeeded in reopening the field to the possibility of using verbal protocols of thinking (Ericsson & Simon, 1983). Such use, however, is extremely truncated by presuppositions of underlying computational processes and mechanisms (Aanstoos, 1983). Nevertheless, it does reopen the door to ask research participants what they are thinking and to take these data seriously, itself a tremendous advance over the previous behavioristic dismissal of doing so or the more recent assertion from experimental psychology that research participants do not know their own experience and so any

descriptions from them would be necessarily flawed (Nisbett & Wilson, 1977).

For better and for worse, then, cognitive psychology carried the day and has continued to flourish as the successor to behaviorism. It was able to shatter the constricting taboos that had stultified the field for so long while preserving the essential commitment to mechanism needed to cling to the cloak of deterministic natural science. In addition, its core metaphor of the computer both addressed and reflected the social-cultural changes of the times. Behaviorism had premised its mechanism on the older model of the automatic telephone switchboard in which stimulus automatically incited a response: Dial the number, and the telephone rings at the person's house without the mediation of an operator to connect the caller. By contrast, the newer cognitive model inserted a processing loop, wherein the stimulus became an input and the response an output. In this version, the stimulus alone could not predetermine the response. What emerged would depend on the program whose rules specified the processing to be applied. Inputs of "two" and "three," for example, might yield an output of either "five" or "six" depending on whether the processing was "add" or "multiply." As American corporations were relocating their assembly lines to Asia, the local workers now needed would be processors of information rather than merely unthinking responders to stimuli. The computer model was emerging as the "next big thing," and a psychology that could write the programs would be highly compensated. Indeed, nearly all of Newell and Simon's early research on such models was funded by the defense department. It had no vested interest in psychological models of the person, but it did want very much to develop more powerful computers.

TRENDS IN CULTURE

The emerging technologically driven vision, wrought by the introduction of the computer, affected not only psychology but also the larger society. Computer use has rapidly permeated and changed much of the cultural landscape. Perhaps nowhere is this shift as evident as with the invention and spread of the personal computer and the Internet, in both work and home life, and with the innovations it is continuing to bring. This vastly important change also offers both dangers and opportunities that humanistic psychology is perhaps best positioned to address.

A great danger is the increasing fragmentation of society wrought by this new arrangement. Not only does it fragment our society into even more incommensurable "haves" and "have-nots"—those who have Internet access and those who do not—it also fragments us from each other. As more people work at home, they do not interact in a common workplace. Time spent on the Internet means less time spent with friends and even with families. Research already has shown that increasing computer use results in more loneliness and depression (Kraut et al., 1998). The sad irony is that even though the participants in this research were using the Internet primarily for social contact, its effect was to so reduce their "live" social lives that their experience of loneliness and depression increased with such computer use. Conversely, however, the spread of Internet connectivity also can offer significant opportunities, specifically those that humanistic psychology may well be best positioned to facilitate. Connectivity, after all, is a form of connection, and the various permutations of encounter and self-disclosure required are exactly what humanistic psychologists have long been fostering as the keys to personal develop-

ment. As older forms of civic and social groups and affiliations are being abandoned, the need for newer ways in which to find and grow community can be facilitated by such online "virtual" communities of mutual interests that no longer require geographical proximity. Such dispersed "cybergroups," nevertheless, can offer significant opportunities for collegiality and even for profound fellow-feeling and friendship, empathy, and consolation.

In addition to the computer, other cultural trends now are emerging. Globalization is perhaps the most striking and crucial. Increasingly, production, commerce, and communication are dominated by transnational corporations. This change is true not only for the mass production of goods but also for the mass production of entertainment. For example, the top 10 grossing movies in nearly all countries of the world now are produced by the Hollywood film industry rather than by their own indigenous film industries (Barber, 1996). In general, preferences in tastes are adroitly packaged and sold across the world so that young people especially now are so branded that they are almost interchangeable, all drinking Coca-Cola, smoking Marlboros, wearing Levi's, and eating at McDonald's (Aanstoos, 1997; Ritzer, 2000). Beyond such apparently superficial trends lies the more nefarious way in which this Americanization of even basic facets of life, such as diet and apparel, replaces the indigenous customs of eating and clothing that had evolved for centuries to be optimally suited to their particular place and culture. When locally grown foods are replaced by imports, more than taste in food is changed. When such local practices are lost, the sustainable community is destroyed and is replaced by a colony of the global monoculture. As Rifkin (2000) showed, during this new era of "hypercapitalism," all of life becomes a "paid for experience," and access to it is purchased from giant corporations as social connections and responsibilities are replaced by subscriptions, memberships, private schools, private security forces, private parks, and the like. In such a commodity culture, everything becomes a commodity. But such commodification reduces the person from a citizen, participating in his or her social reality, to a consumer of that social reality whose sole responsibility is simply to consume it more. "Having choices" means having only the trivial choice of Brand A or Brand B.

The resultant discontents of our civilization—loneliness, alienation, boredom, meaninglessness—are the new (yet already almost ubiquitously familiar) forms of malaise of this postmodern era (Aanstoos, 1997; Aanstoos & Puhakka, 1997, Lasch, 1979). Related symptoms include the breakdown of civility, manifested in examples such as the increase in various forms of "rage." Although random shootings or "going postal" may garner the headlines, behind the scenes are demographic trends of startling proportions, showing sharply accelerating increases in phenomena such as "road rage" (by drivers toward other drivers on the road), "air rage" (by passengers in planes toward flight attendants or other passengers), and even "spectator rage" (by parents at coaches or other parents at their children's sporting meets and games). Such outbreaks auger a collapse of civility that expresses the broader collapse of the sense of community. Scholars such as Putnam (2000) have begun to carefully document our growing "social-capital deficit" through statistics showing a decline in participation in social, religious, and work groups—everything from PTAs to bowling leagues, to bridge clubs, to garden clubs, to basic neighborliness. The result is a greater degree of social isolation, animosity, and

unrealistic reliance on materialistic goods to fill the gap.

Regrettably, even our health care, so much more needed in the face of these changes, now also is controlled by this commodity culture as for-profit health centers replace the old version of health care that was not oriented to the bottom line. As "managed care" industries come to dominate the field of "health delivery services," the integrity formerly taken for granted about the advice of one's family doctor now is replaced by a justified skepticism of what that business administration graduate in the health maintenance organization will decide about the course of treatment.

Perhaps most distressing is that this mass consumption society is not ecologically sustainable. Such frenzied production requires depletion of resources and ever-increasing rates of air and water pollution. More than anything else, this eco-cide reveals the shortsightedness and ultimate failure of the technological/consumerist global monoculture (Mander, 1991, see also the chapter by Pilisuk & Joy [Chapter 9] in this volume).

CONCLUSION: THE CONTINUING ROLE OF HUMANISTIC PSYCHOLOGY

These very totalizing tendencies, however, also point the way beyond them. And once again, it is humanistic psychology that can enable that transformative journey. This work will include many facets, from efforts at "resisting McDonaldization" (Smart, 1999) to organizing international meetings devoted to alternatives to consumerism (e.g., the "Alternatives to Consumerism" meeting in Thailand in 1997 organized by Roberts and others; Sivaraksa, 1997). In this regard, three considerations are emerging as most potent: ecopsychology, holistic health, and spirituality. It is in relation to these countertrends especially that the next generation of humanistic psychologists can grow and contribute, and it is there that the new edge of humanism will find a continuing role.

For any field as large, multifarious, and congenitally resistant to definition as humanistic psychology, it would be a gross error of judgment to try to circumscribe its continuing role. There will be many tasks, some foreseen and some not foreseen. Bridging as it does the academic and applied sides of the discipline, humanistic psychology will continue to have a role in both. In the former, its ongoing role will be to recall psychology to the primacy of experience as its own proper subject matter and to devise methodologies appropriate to this domain. This basic recollection of what is human about humans is both timeless and timely. Its envisioning and evocation are particularly crucial as the cybernetic frame of reference comes to exert its totalizing tendencies in our time (Heidegger, 1954/1977). This valuable work is being advanced through many channels. It is being advanced through several journals—the front line in disseminating ideas—such as the *Journal of Humanistic Psychology, The Humanistic Psychologist*, the *Journal of Transpersonal Psychology*, the *Journal of Phenomenological Psychology*, and *Methods*. The work also is being nurtured through organizations and conferences including those sponsored by the Humanistic Psychology division at the American Psychological Association meetings, the Association for Humanistic Psychology, the Association for Transpersonal Psychology, and others (e.g., the recently held Old Saybrook 2 meeting, which sought to redefine humanistic psychology for the new millennium). Perhaps most important of all for the future are the humanistic graduate programs, where the next generation of psychologists are being prepared, in places such as Saybrook Graduate School, Duquesne University, the State University of West Georgia, Sonoma State University, the Institute for Transpersonal Psychology, Seattle University, the California Institute for Integral Studies, and the Center for Humanistic Studies.

On the applied side of the discipline, humanistic psychology has some particularly timely opportunities to effect significant change by supporting those cultural movements in the newly emerging zeitgeist mentioned previously: ecopsychology, holistic health, and spirituality. What all three have in common is a quest for wholeness in human experience. Indeed, they can advance only on this fundamental insight. And advance they will; during the next few decades, our culture will require such momentous change simply to survive. As Houston (2000) recently said, it is now "jump time," that is, the time that our culture prepares to make that quantum leap into the holistic vision needed to confront the otherwise soon to be cataclysmic problems that are the legacy of the past three centuries of mechanistic elementistic thinking. She offered examples of how technological breakthroughs can be used to facilitate the type of increased awareness of our participation in an intermingled culture, fulfilling our deepest spiritual yearnings and leading to the development of a new consciousness. It is precisely this new awareness of our interconnectedness that is needed for the solution to the problems of tribalism, ethnic and economic divisiveness, ecological disasters, and the like. As Norbert-Hodge (1991) showed so clearly in her case study of Ladakh, when an indigenous culture is subjected to a massive and sudden takeover by the global economy, it loses its spiritual bearings and new forms of divisiveness then appear. Differences that had not been problematic before now erupt as if they are age-old fault lines—Buddhist-Hindu, young-old, urban-rural. Norbert-Hodge demonstrated very concretely and poignantly how these are not inherent but rather are created and exploited by new economic realities.

Each of these intersecting fields—ecology, holistic health, and spirituality—has an intrinsic connection with the heart of humanistic psychology. All offer timely new directions for the field, opening doors to its further development as ecopsychology, health psychology, and spiritual psychology. Indeed, all three are already under way. In the first area, we find excellent work being done by many scholars such as Roszak, Metzner, Howard, and Roberts (Clinebell, 1996; Fox, 1995; Roberts, 1998; Roszak, Gomes, & Kanner, 1995; for a synopsis, see also the chapter by Pilisuk & Joy [Chapter 9] in this volume). The field of holistic health got its initial impetus from radical thinking by physicians themselves, such as Siegel (1988) and Chopra (1990), and then was brought to a mass audience through Moyers's (1993) excellent PBS broadcast, *Healing and the Mind*. As more humanistic psychologists begin to form intrinsic melds with other health care providers, this transdiscipline should provide just the advance needed to finally move our society toward a vision of prevention rather than intervention (see the chapter by Criswell [Chapter 43] in this volume). Regarding spirituality, perhaps the clearest example of the cost of modern society is the specifically spiritual thirst evinced by people today. But the very emergence of a distinction between spirituality and religion also offers humanistic psychology the opportunity to help in

this domain as well (see the chapter by Elkins [Chapter 16] in this volume). Certainly, the current infusion of nontheistic spiritual traditions from Asia, particularly Buddhism, provides the model for much subsequent work (Wilber, 2000). In contrast to the first wave of imported Eastern spiritual traditions during the 1960s (by writers such as Watts and Suzuki), this current wave finds the domestic soil now more fertile and ready to support these transplants. Popular writers such as Kabat-Zinn (1994) already have found a wide and sympathetic audience for meditation practices. More scholarly writers also have begun to integrate Buddhism and Western psychotherapy (Brazier, 1995; Epstein, 1995; Rosenbaum, 1999). Other psychologists also are depicting how to integrate Eastern and Western spirituality into our everyday lives (Kornfield, 2000; Welwood, 2000).

In all three areas, these new subfields are emerging even as they are yet groping for foundational bases. Even definitional and methodological questions are quite unsettled. Although such perplexity leaves some bewildered and even discouraged, this very open-endedness also provides significant opportunities to work out these basic issues in the most optimal, rather than the most dogmatic, ways. Doing so will be crucial. Indeed, these foci will be the keys to the next generation, just as the books by May and Frankl during the 1950s on the quest for meaning were to the first generation of humanistic psychologists.

REFERENCES

Aanstoos, C. M. (1983). The think aloud method in descriptive research. *Journal of Phenomenological Psychology, 14,* 150-190.

Aanstoos, C. M. (1985). The structure of thinking in chess. In A. Giorgi (Ed.), *Phenomenology and psychological research* (pp. 86-117). Pittsburgh, PA: Duquesne University Press.

Aanstoos, C. M. (1986). Phenomenology and the psychology of thinking. In P. Ashworth, A. Giorgi, & A. deKoning (Eds.), *Qualitative research in psychology* (pp. 79-116). Pittsburgh, PA: Duquesne University Press.

Aanstoos, C. M. (1987a). A critique of the computational model of thought: The contribution of Merleau-Ponty. *Journal of Phenomenological Psychology, 18,* 187-200.

Aanstoos, C. M. (1987b). Information processing and the phenomenology of thinking. In D. Welton & H. Silverman (Eds.), *Critical and Dialectical Phenomenology* (pp. 250-264). Albany: State University of New York Press.

Aanstoos, C. M. (1993a). Humanism: An overview. In J. Wilson (Ed.), *Magill's survey of social science: Psychology* (6 vols., pp. 1203-1209). Pasadena, CA: Salem.

Aanstoos, C. M. (1993b). Mainstream psychology and the humanistic alternative. In F. Wertz (Ed.), *The humanistic movement in psychology* (pp. 1-12). New York: Gardner.

Aanstoos, C. M. (1996). Reflections and visions: An interview with Amedeo Giorgi. *The Humanistic Psychologist, 24,* 3-27.

Aanstoos, C. M. (1997). Toward a phenomenological psychology of cultural artefacts. *Journal of Phenomenological Psychology, 28,* 66-81.

Aanstoos, C. M. (1999). Pop psychology. In C. Singleton (Ed.), *The Sixties in America* (3 vols., pp. 581-584). Pasadena, CA: Salem.

Aanstoos, C. M., & Puhakka, K. (1997, August). *Exploitable desires: Pseudo-needs and self-forgetfulness in commodity culture.* Invited address presented at the meeting of the American Psychological Association, Chicago.

Aanstoos, C. M., Serlin, I., & Greening, T. (2000). A history of Division 32–Humanistic Psychology. In D. A. Dewsbury (Ed.), *History of the divisions of APA* (pp. 85-112). Washington, DC: American Psychological Association.

Barber, B. R. (1996). *Jihad vs. McWorld.* New York: Random House.

Brazier, D. (1995). *Zen therapy.* New York: John Wiley.

Chopra, D. (1990). *Quantum healing: Exploring the frontiers of mind/body medicine.* New York: Bantam Books.

Clinebell, H. (1996). *Ecotherapy: Healing ourselves, healing the earth.* New York: Haworth.

Ellis, A. (1962). *Reason and emotion in psychotherapy.* Secaucus, NJ: Citadel.

Ellis, A. (1973). *Humanistic psychotherapy: The rational-emotive approach.* New York: McGraw-Hill.

Epstein, M. (1995). *Thoughts without a thinker: Psychotherapy from a Buddhist perspective.* New York: Basic Books.

Ericsson, K. A., & Simon, H. A. (1983). *Protocol analysis: Verbal reports as data.* Cambridge, MA: MIT Press.

Fox, W. (1995). *Toward a transpersonal ecology.* Albany: State University of New York Press.

Freud, S. (1950). Project for a scientific psychology. In *Standard edition of the complete psychological works of Sigmund Freud* (J. Strachey, Trans.). London: Hogarth. (Original work published 1895)

Gibson, J. J. (1966). *The senses considered as perceptual systems.* Boston: Houghton Mifflin.

Gibson, J. J. (1976). *The ecological approach to visual perception.* Boston: Houghton Mifflin.

Giorgi, A. (1970). *Psychology as a human science.* New York: Harper & Row.

Hearst, E. (1978). Man and machine: Chess achievements and chess thinking. In P. Frey (Ed.), *Chess skill in man and machine* (pp. 167-200). New York: Springer-Verlag.

Heidegger, M. (1977). The question concerning technology (W. Lovitt, Trans.). In M. Heidegger (Ed.), *Basic writings* (pp. 287-317). (Original work published 1954)

Houston, J. (2000). *Jump time: Shaping your future in a world of radical change.* Los Angeles: Tarcher.

Kabat-Zinn, J. (1994). *Wherever you go, there you are.* New York: Hyperion.

Kornfield, J. (2000). *After the ecstasy, the laundry: How the heart grows wise on the spiritual path.* New York: Bantam Books.

Kramer, P. (1995). *Introduction.* In C. R. Rogers (Ed.), *On becoming a person* (rev. ed., pp. ix-xv). Boston: Houghton Mifflin.

Kraut, R., Patterson, M., Landmark, V., Kiessler, S., Mukopadhyay, T., & Scherlis, W. (1998). Internet paradox: A social technology that reduces social involvement and psychological well-being? *American Psychologist, 53,* 1017-1031.

Kvale, S., & Greenness, C. (1967). Skinner and Sartre: Toward a radical phenomenology of behavior. *Review of Existential Psychology and Psychiatry, 7,* 128-148.

Lasch, C. (1979). *The culture of narcissism.* New York: Norton.

Mander, J. (1991). *In the absence of the sacred: The failure of technology and the survival of the Indian nations.* San Francisco: Sierra Club Books.

Maslow, A. H. (1954). *Motivation and personality.* New York: Harper & Row.

Maslow, A. H. (1968). *Toward a psychology of being* (2nd ed.). New York: Van Nostrand Reinhold.

May, R. (1953). *Man's search for himself.* New York: Norton.

May, R., Angel, E., & Ellenberger, H. F. (Eds.). (1958). *Existence: A new dimension in psychiatry and psychology.* New York: Basic Books.

Merleau-Ponty, M. (1982-1983). Phenomenology and psychoanalysis: Preface to Hesnard's L'oeuvre de Freud (A. Fisher, Trans.). *Review of Existential Psychology and Psychiatry, 18,* 67-72.

Moyers, B. (1993). *Healing and the mind.* New York: Doubleday.

Neisser, U. (1967). *Cognitive psychology.* New York: Appleton-Century-Crofts.

Neisser, U. (1976). *Cognition and reality.* New York: Freeman.

Neisser, U. (1982). *Memory observed.* New York: Freeman.

Newell, A., Shaw, J. C., & Simon, H. A. (1958). Elements of a theory of human problem solving. *Psychological Review, 65,* 151-166.

Newell, A., & Simon, H. A. (1961). Computer simulation of human thinking. *Science, 134,* 2011-2017.

Newell, A., & Simon, H. A. (1972). *Human information processing.* Englewood Cliffs, NJ: Prentice Hall.

Nisbett, R. E., & Wilson, T. D. (1977). Telling more than we can know: Reports on mental processes. *Psychological Review, 84,* 231-259.

Norbert-Hodge, H. (1991). *Ancient futures: Learning from Ladakh.* San Francisco: Sierra Club Books.

Putnam, R. D. (2000). *Bowling alone: The collapse and revival of American community.* New York: Simon & Schuster.

Rifkin, J. (2000). *The age of access: The new culture of hypercapitalism, where all of life is a paid-for experience.* Los Angeles: Tarcher.

Ritzer, G. (2000). *The McDonaldization of society.* Thousand Oaks, CA: Pine Forge.

Roberts, E. (Ed.). (1998). Humanistic psychology and ecopsychology [Special issue]. *The Humanistic Psychologist, 26.*

Rogers, C. R. (1951). *Client-centered therapy.* Boston: Houghton Mifflin.

Rogers, C. R. (1961). *On becoming a person: A therapist's view of psychotherapy.* Boston: Houghton Mifflin.

Rosenbaum, R. (1999). *Zen and the heart of psychotherapy.* New York: Brunner/Mazel.

Roszak, T., Gomes, M., & Kanner, A. (Eds.). (1995). *Ecopsychology: Restoring the earth, healing the mind.* San Francisco: Sierra Club Books.

Siegel, B. (1988). *Love, medicine, and miracles.* New York: Harper & Row.

Simon, H. A., & Newell, A. (1964). Information processing in computers and man. *American Scientist, 52,* 281-300.

Sivaraksa, S. (1997). *Alternatives to consumerism.* Bangkok, Thailand: Santi Pracha Dhamma Institute.

Skinner, B. F. (1987). Whatever happened to psychology as the science of behavior? *American Psychologist, 42,* 780-786.

Smart, B. (Ed.). (1999). *Resisting McDonaldization.* London: Sage.

Watson, J. B. (1913). Psychology as a behaviorist views it. *Psychological Record, 20,* 158-177.

Welwood, J. (2000). *Toward a psychology of awakening: Buddhism, psychotherapy, and the path of personal and spiritual transformation.* Boston: Shambhala.

Wertz, F. J. (1987). Cognitive psychology and the understanding of perception. *Journal of Phenomenological Psychology, 18,* 103-142.

Wertz, F. J., & Aanstoos, C. M. (1999). Amedeo Giorgi and the project of a human science. In D. Moss (Ed.), *Humanistic and transpersonal psychology: A historical and biographical sourcebook* (pp. 287-300). Westport, CT: Greenwood.

Wilber, K. (2000). *Integral psychology: Consciousness, spirit, psychology, therapy.* Boston: Shambhala.

Wundt, W. (1904). *Principles of physiological psychology* (E. B. Titchner, Trans.). New York: Macmillan. (Original work published 1873-1874)

Zajonc, R. A. (1980, August). *Preferences need no inferences.* Paper presented to the meeting of the American Psychological Association, Montreal.

Part III

HUMANISTIC METHODOLOGY

Introduction to Part III

THIS IS A FERVENT TIME for humanistic research and theory building. As we saw in the previous part of this volume, there is a wealth of humanistic cross-fertilization occurring within psychology, and if trends continue, efforts in that direction will only intensify. The basis for this transitional moment is complex, but there are at least three developments that are fueling it: the general discontent with managed care, the growing disillusionment among both practitioners and practice-oriented researchers with conventional empirical research, and the rising allure of alternative (e.g., postpositivistic) epistemologies and methodologies (Bickman, 1999; Cain & Seeman, in press). The confluence of these trends is highly auspicious for humanistic psychology. In as much as humanistic psychology has long been critical of and supported alternatives to conventional psychological scholarship, it is in a prime position to provide both guidance and concrete assistance in the rebuilding of the discipline.

Humanistic research (also called *human science research methodology*) is poised to take center stage in this heightening conflict. To the extent that theoreticians and practitioners look to fuller, deeper, and more holistic modes to understand and "treat" human experience, the human science research paradigm should provide relevant and critical support. The basis for this contention is that human science research prizes intimacy of understanding as much as, if not more than, concision of understanding. In addition, it favors details, complexity, and plausibility over standardization, linearity, and objectification. Although human science does not reject hypothetico-deductive-inductive methods, it views them as adjunctive and in need of experiential supplementation. That being said, Mihaly Csikszentmihalyi also makes an important point in the Preface to this volume about the risks of obscurantism in human science research and the necessity for critical systematic reflection. Fortunately, there have been a number of attempts to redress this concern, as we shall see in this part of the volume.

The virtue of human science methodology is that it can dramatically revitalize psychology's time-honored inquiries—why people think, feel, and act against their ostensible interests; what motivates people to thrive versus merely exist; why wealth does not automatically buy happiness; why IQ does not necessarily correlate with morality and adjustment does not necessarily equate with passion; and, finally, how psychology is to respond to the radical alteration of human identity wrought by technology. Going beyond the *objective* report or measure, humanistic methodologies can at last return to the subtle and nuanced *contexts* about which reports or measures center; moreover, they can open the door to the reassessment of volumes of inadequate studies—legions of remote nonnaturalistic investigations and scores of anonymous and aggregated findings (Shedler, Maymen, & Manis, 1993).

In short, human science research methodology is poised to turn over a new chapter in empirical psychological inquiry and, indeed, in science itself.

In this part of the volume, we present five representative illustrations of contemporary human science research. In Chapter 18, Fred Wertz sets the table for these illustrations with his magnificent overview of the qualitative research tradition in humanistic psychology. Although the qualitative tradition is by no means exclusive within humanistic research, it generally is considered to be the optimal staging ground within which to situate most person-centered inquiry. Following his historical and conceptual overview of the qualitative tradition, Wertz goes on to elucidate its present and future directions. Of particular note is his eye-opening discussion of Gordon Allport's little-known treatise on qualitative research commissioned by the U.S. government during the 1930s. In this hard-hitting document, Allport formulated one of the most cogent cases for the supplementation of mainstream inquiry with systematic qualitative inquiry ever to be proposed. But tragically, and not surprisingly within the hegemony of American positivistic psychology, Allport's document was quashed and quickly forgotten.

In Chapter 19, which begins the "Contemporary Themes" section, Scott Churchill teams with Wertz to provide a fresh and original distillation of phenomenological research methodology, incorporating both historical and conceptual elements along with clear guidelines for application. Their case illustration, the experience of criminal victimization, is both timely and poignant, and it serves as a superb example of their formulation.

In Chapter 20, Clark Moustakas furnishes a masterful rendering of his pioneering heuristic methodology. In this animated statement, he details the principles of his approach, the steps by which it proceeds, and the fruits that it reaps for both traditional and nontraditional investigators. Moustakas concludes that, regardless of the "facts" derived, discovery is an essential and ongoing element of inquiry.

Humanistic narrative research is the subject of Ruthellen Josselson and Amia Lieblich's commentary in Chapter 21. With incisive clarity, the authors elucidate both the history and development of humanistic narrative research (including its roots in literature), vivify the current controversies surrounding the research, and survey its copious applications.

Leading off the "Emergent Trends" section is the humanizing voice of Stanley Krippner in Chapter 22. Krippner, a prominent consciousness researcher, anatomizes contemporary humanistic research methodology in the light of postmodernity. A highlight of his chapter is his keen analysis of the contrasts and parallels between humanistic and postmodern modalities and their potential for integration. Like others in this volume, Krippner concludes that humanistic and postmodern inquiries are richly linked, provide key counterbalances to each other, and broaden immeasurably psychology's vibrant investigative range.

Psychotherapy outcome research has a long and distinguished humanistic legacy. For a variety of reasons, however, recent humanistic scholars have neglected such research and, ironically, have undermined themselves as a result. Today, this situation is shifting yet again. In the final two chapters of this section, Kirk Schneider and Robert Elliott show that not only can humanistic outcome research be illuminating, it can also be methodologically convincing. In Chapter 23, Schneider presents a novel and highly sensitive case design methodology termed *multiple-case depth research* (MCDR). MCDR combines case study design with depth experiential therapeutic principles. To illustrate the power of MCDR, Schneider presents a hypothetical psychotherapy process and outcome study involving three client cohorts (those who undergo cognitive-behavioral, intersubjective psychoanalytic, or existential-humanistic psychotherapy). He concludes that MCDR, if conducted properly, can provide rich, valid, and unprecedented investigative yields.

In Chapter 24, Elliott offers an overview of the *hermeneutic single-case efficacy design*. With this groundbreaking synthesis, he brings both depth and finely honed logic to the study of clinical outcomes. Elliott poses a challenge: Can we make humanistic inquiry "transparent, systematic, and self-reflective enough to convince ourselves and others" of its validity? Furthermore, he asks, can we "do justice to each client's uniqueness while still" determining whether "(a) . . . the client has changed, (b) . . . the observed changes are credible, and (c) . . . [the] changes have anything to do with our work as therapists"? With these challenges in mind, Elliott responds with deftness and clarity.

REFERENCES

Bickman, L. (1999). Practice makes perfect and other myths about mental health services. *American Psychologist, 54,* 963-965.

Cain, D., & Seeman, J. (in press). *Handbook of research and practice in humanistic psychotherapies.* Washington, DC: American Psychological Association.

Shedler, J., Maymen, M., & Manis, M. (1993). The illusion of mental health. *American Psychologist, 48,* 1117-1131.

CHAPTER 18

Humanistic Psychology and the Qualitative Research Tradition

FREDERICK J. WERTZ

ONE OF THE MOST exciting and promising developments in psychology during the latter part of the 20th century was the proliferation of diverse research methods and the articulation of their scientific and philosophical soundness within a sophisticated methodology that can be called humanistic. This chapter, after spelling out the natural science context in which psychology has developed its disciplinary identity, considers the criteria by which a research method or methodology may be considered humanistic. Next, it takes a sample from the rich tradition of humanistic research in the history of psychology. Then, the chapter focuses on the recent developments in the philosophy of science and psychology itself that have opened the way for the contemporary blossoming of humanistic research methods. Finally, the challenges and contemporary possibilities of employing humanistic research methods are articulated.

PSYCHOLOGY AS A NATURAL SCIENCE

No trend in modern psychology has been more conspicuous or more pervasive than the attempt to make psychology a natural science. With this has come the often witting, and sometimes subtle and unwitting, reduction of the human to the nonhuman. This trend is evident in behaviorism, which attempted to define the subject matter of psychology in terms of physical observables and to explain human behavior using the same principles developed in research on nonhuman animals. This trend is evident in many theoretical orientations such as contemporary evolutionary psychology, which explains human behavior by means of evolutionary biology. In virtually every introductory psychology textbook is a chapter on the biological foundations of psychology in which human behavior is explained by neurophysiology.

This trend of building psychology on a natural science foundation, although not always present in psychological theories (e.g., in cognitive and social psychology), is nowhere more evident than in the area of research methodology. Psychology proudly identifies its founding date with that of the first psychological laboratory by Wilhelm Wundt. At the top of the agenda in virtually every introductory psychology textbook is the assurance that psychology is, first and foremost, a science and that being a science means employing scientific research methods. Based on the model of the physical scientist, research is the testing of hypotheses. These hypotheses ideally postulate causal explanations and would afford prediction and control. To test such hypotheses, the variables postulated must be operationally defined, that is, defined by means of measuring procedures. Within this context, a hierarchy of research methods is delineated, moving up from naturalistic observation to the case study, survey, correlational methods, and the controlled experiment. Naturalistic observation and case study are given descriptions whose brevity reflects their low esteem, and their shortcomings as tests of hypotheses are emphasized. Qualitative methods are considered, at best, useful sources of hypotheses to be used during the early phases of research prior to its establishing the assertions' scientific status, which ideally rests on the experiment. This same view of science is evident in the American Psychological Association's (APA, 2000) criteria for evaluating psychotherapy guidelines. Although the experiences of practicing clinicians, along with case studies and qualitative methods, are acknowledged in the criteria as being of conditional value, the most highly touted method remains the randomized controlled trial.

What Is a Humanistic Research Method?

The core of humanism in classical civilization, the Renaissance, and continuing in modern times is the conviction that humans are different from physical objects and from other animals. Humanists believe that knowledge of humans must reflect those distinctive characteristics. From this, it follows that humans, by virtue of *what they are,* make certain demands on how we know them, demands that are not encountered by the natural sciences.

This point of view was articulated most clearly within the context of modern science by Dilthey (1894/1977). In his view, the primacy of the positivistic approach of "universal theory-hypothesis-exacting test-probabilistic induction" is required of physical sciences by virtue of their subject matter's externality to experience and the relative independence, isolation, and mutual exclusivity of the subject matter's various parts. Because physical objects and their elements occur outside of experience and in mere juxtaposition and succession, their connections, interrelations, and functions are not and cannot be observed directly; instead, they must be hypothesized.

However, Dilthey (1894/1977) thought that it is a fundamental mistake to make this approach primary, let alone the exclusive one in psychology, because the constituents of the psychological order, as well as their interconnections and organization, are given as a real continuum internal to mental life itself. The various phenomena of psychological life, as well as the parts of any single phenomenon, are from the start interrelated and interwoven in a meaningful organization of mutual dependencies, implications, and interior relations that show themselves directly within mental life. Therefore, psychology "has no need of basing itself on the concepts yielded from inferences in order to establish a coherent whole" (p. 28). Relationships are neither added subsequently to the constituents nor deduced; instead, they are concretely lived and immediately available to reflection (p. 35). In his famous dictum, Dilthey proclaimed, "We explain nature, we understand psychic life" (p. 27).

In the *Geisteswissenschaften* (human sciences), description must play a far more profound role than it does in *Naturwissenschaft* (natural science). Methodologically, description provides an "unbiased and unmutilated" view of psychological life in all of its reality. What is necessary beyond description for psychology, in Dilthey's (1894/1977) view, is analysis. One begins with a fully developed, concrete description rather than derived or abstracted elements and processes. Analysis then proceeds to grasp the wholeness as such and the relations of each constituent with the whole and each other. Some of the general characteristics of psychic life found by Dilthey in his analyses of psychological life are its structural unity, its teleological development, the influence of acquired nexus on every single act of consciousness, the centrality of motivation and feelings, a reciprocity and efficacy in relation to the external world, and the fact that each type of constituent (e.g., representation, feeling) cannot be reduced to or be derived from any other (although they always are involved in intrinsic interconnections). Descriptive knowledge such as this is indubitable, according to Dilthey, and objections to this certainty rest on the transference of doubt proper only to the experience of external physical objects.

Dilthey's (1894/1977) critique of what he called *constructive* psychology is not a complete rejection. Dilthey objected only to the primary and exclusive use of hypothesis testing as the orientation in psychology. He believed that after description and analysis carry *Verstehen* (understanding) as far as possible, inference and hypothesis can be used in a supplementary fashion. Note, however, that in his integration of natural science methods within human science, Dilthey reversed the methodological hierarchy currently endorsed by mainstream psychology. He placed qualitative methods first, viewed them as a preferred way of knowing psychological subject matter, and assigned theoretical explanation and hypothesis testing to a subordinate heuristic role. The Continental schools of metascience as developed, for example, by Brentano and Husserl continued through the 20th century to stress the need for a distinctively human science that would employ methods suited for a faithful understanding of personal experience (Radnitzky, 1973).

THE HUMANISTIC RESEARCH PROCEDURES: AN UNDERAPPRECIATED TRADITION IN PSYCHOLOGY

Although the naturalistic model of science has been dominant in American psychology, qualitative human science methods have been present throughout the history of modern psychology and have provided some of the most significant psychological knowledge. There has been a recent revival of interest in Wundt's cultural psychology (Danziger, 1990), which generated volumes of qualitatively based psychological research that Wundt held to be necessary for the study of "higher" psychological processes. Psychoanalysis has had a long and voluminous history of research, from Freud to the present, most of which uses methods quite contrary to the model that has dominated mainstream academic psychology. In developmental psychology, Piaget and some of his followers (e.g., Kohlberg) stand out as having applied highly sophisticated qualitative methods for answering research questions concerning the origins and development of cognition. The Gestalt tradition in perceptual psychology, including the ecological research of Gibson, was primarily qualitative. In social psychology, such work also has been evident, for example, in the very careful research on "groupthink" by Janis.

As we enter the 21st century, we will benefit from remembering the quiet and often unacknowledged tradition of qualitative research in psychology over the past century. To this end, I would like to single out three works that form a part of this tradition. One of the finest psychological studies of all times is William James's investigation of religious experience (James, 1902/1982). A landmark attempt to establish the scientific value of qualitative research was Gordon Allport's advocacy of the use of *personal documents* (Allport, 1942). Finally, Abraham Maslow's study of self-actualization is a classic contribution within the "third force" movement (Maslow, 1954/1987).

James's Investigation of Religious Experience

The context of James's (1902/1982) investigation is his recognition that religious experience is a reality that has eluded scientific study:

The sciences of nature know nothing of spiritual presences. . . . The scientist, so-called, is, during his scientific hour at least, so materialistic that one may well say that on the whole the influence of science goes against the notion that religion should be recognized at all. (p. 490)

This, for James, is part of a larger problem of the scientist in the face of human nature:

Science . . . has ended by utterly repudiating the personal point of view. She catalogs her elements and records her laws indifferent as to what purpose may be shown forth by them, and [she] constructs her theories quite careless of their bearing on human anxieties and fates. (p. 491)

The subtitle of James's volume, *A Study in Human Nature*, indicates that his investigation concerns the distinctively human. James's study sets material existence to one side and dogmatic theology to the other so as to focus methodically on the human experience of religion, what he called "personal religion." To accomplish this, he drew on the most diverse sources of data, such as diaries of mystics and saints from traditions including those of the Christian, Buddhist, Islamic, Hindu, and Emersonian transcendentalist, and he then subjected these data to qualitative analytic procedures.

James's (1902/1982) study is clearly based on an intimate attentiveness to his own personal experience as well as an intense immersion in a staggering array of descriptions of spiritual experiences by other people. His attitude of maximum openness allowed him to see that there is a tremendous variety of religious experiences. He accepted the full spectrum of whatever humans consider to be a contact with "the divine," that is, the divine as they experience it, whether in the moral, physical, or ritual sphere and whether in dependence, fear, sexual connection, or a feeling of the infinite. James concluded that there is no single essence to religious experience and that the boundary between the sacred and the mundane is misty at best. Yet, data of extreme religious experiences enabled James to discern common features through this diversity.

Mystics describe their contact with a mysterious and ineffable presence and are assured of *the reality of the unseen.* James (1902/1982) found three intertwined *beliefs:* that the visible world is part of a more spiritual (indeed, a *loving*) universe from which it draws its significance; that our true end is harmony or unity with this higher universe; and that a communion with this invisible loving reality produces real effects. Because some religious experiences are nearly completely devoid of cognitive content, however, James held that the feeling dimension of the experience is primary—enthusiasm, courage, feeling for the great and wondrous things. There is a new zest, a lyrical enchantment that generates earnestness and perhaps even heroism, an assurance of safety, a temper of peace, and a predominance of loving affections. This experience draws us beyond the physical. "It is the terror and beauty of phenomena, the 'promise' of the dawn and of the rainbow, the 'voice' of thunder, the 'gentleness' of the summer rain, the 'sublimity' of the stars and not their physical laws" (p. 498). Furthermore, this pathic experience entails a sense of uneasiness and solution that there is something wrong with us as we naturally stand and that we may overcome that wrongness through being connected to the higher power, a right that transcends the natural self and world. The conscious self is thereby experienced as continuous with a wider self through which saving experiences occur. In this light, shipwreck and dissolution in the natural world are not absolutely final or definitive, for they may open the way to spiritual fulfillment.

James (1902/1982) found, in the lives of saints, the fruits of religious experience—the charity, devotion, trust, patience, and bravery that result from conversion and grace. In "saintliness," spiritual emotions that are intermittent and fleeting for many, and that James believed are the same in all religions, become the habitual center of a person's psychological life. Saints experience their being in a "wider life"—not only in relation to God but also in relation to moral ideals and inner visions of holiness or right—and the reality of the unseen enlarges their lives. In a friendly continuity between the self and ideal power, there is a self-surrender that engenders elation and freedom as the ego boundaries melt and the emotional center of life shifts to loving and harmonious affections. This self-surrender may take ascetic forms, for example, when pleasure is sacrificed to the higher power. One may develop a strength of soul in which mundane realities such as popularity, ambition, and the falsehoods of daily life become insignificant. Sincerity and truth of expression can prevail regardless of the consequences, and all that is "impure" or inconsistent with the higher sphere is easily given up. The saint is able to love enemies, kiss and intimately care for the sick, and endure pain and suffering in service to the higher good. Martyrdom is the triumph of religious imperturbability. Indeed, it is a grace given in proportion to affliction ("as blows are doubled, happiness swoons within"). James contrasted spiritual morality with mundane morality. The latter is heavyhearted, burdened, and effortful, whereas the good deeds that flow from spiritual experience are light and uplifting. For mundane morality, life is war; the moralist tends the sick with tense muscles, holds his breath, and senses impotence, for well-doing is but the plaster on a sore it cannot cure. Our hour of moral death is our spiritual birthday, a happy relaxation with deep breathing in an eternal present or an effortless well-being.

James's (1902/1982) psychology of spiritual experience is a knowledge that functions evocatively and verges on wisdom. It enriches those to whom the knowledge is given and opens one's heart and mind to the experience as it is lived by oneself and others. Yet, this knowledge is descriptive of the psychological reality under study, rigorously analytical, systematic, and (above all) profoundly empirical. Science unflinchingly confronts the subject matter of human spirituality.

Allport's Case for the Use of Personal Documents

In the course of its efforts to improve the quality of research in the social sciences during the 1930s, the Committee on Appraisal of Research of the Social Science Research Council[1] called for a critical review of works in psychology using personal documents, defined as "account(s) of individual experience which reveal the individual's actions as a human agent and as a participant in social life" (Blumer, cited in Allport, 1942, p. 21). In 1940, Allport volunteered for the task of critically reviewing works in psychology that used documents such as autobiographies, interviews and other recordings, diaries, letters, expressive and projective creations, and questionnaires. Allport's report, published as a monograph in 1942 and now out of print for more than four decades, provided a comprehensive inventory of all research in psychology that used first-person expression. Allport focused on the many and varied uses of such documents in research, the methods employed by researchers, the various types of personal documents, and the value of such documents. Allport's monograph is a passionate, sharp-minded, and intellectually courageous attempt to claim the highest scientific legitimacy for the qualitative analysis of first-person accounts of human experience.

Although Allport recognized the brilliant and fruitful use of these documents by humanistic writers such as James and Hall, he found that most psychologists used first-person accounts in an uncritical manner. He was struck by the contrast between the prevalence and continual increase of first-person documents in clinical case studies and the paucity of sophisticated discussions of the methodology involved. He called for the founding of a journal dedicated wholly to the case study and with special attention to the methodology involved in using personal documents. (Interestingly, such a case study journal is in development now, with potential APA sponsorship.) Allport (1942) marked the advent of critical use in 1920 and reviewed the "motley array of studies, but in every case interesting . . ., centered in the basic problems of method" (p. 36) that emerged between 1920 and 1940, taking on problems such as the reliability and validity of the first-person report and the scientific value of personal documents in classification and prediction. In his inventory of various uses, Allport reported on numerous psychological topics, practical uses, inductive theorizing, interdisciplinary investigations, illustration in scientific reporting, and questionnaire and test construction. Allport argued for an expansion of scientific practice in psychology beyond the usual "nomothetic" outlook (population frequency and aggregate analyses) and into the truly individual or "idiographic" realm, insisting that the personal document is indispensable as data for both approaches.

Concrete psychology using personal documents prevents science from running "an artificial course" and is particularly necessary in the region of subjective meaning; personal documents are the psychologist's "touchstone to reality" (Allport, 1942, p. 184). The usefulness of personal documents is not merely in providing hunches and hypotheses to be tested by behavioral observation and measurement, nor is their use limited to illustrating knowledge validated using statistical procedures.

> Behavioral observation . . . is inferior to the personal document when it comes to the important region of subjective meaning: experiences of love, beauty, [and] religious faith; of pain, ambition, fear, jealousy, [and] frustration; plans, remembrances, fantasies, and friendships; none of these topics comes fully within the horizon of psychologists without the aid of personal reporting. If these regions of experience are excluded, mental science finds itself confined to a shadowy subject matter. (p. 144)

The most important role of qualitative analysis of personal documents resides in the process of discovery, and it provides its own capacity for validation of both inductive generalizations and insights into regularities governing individual cases. The critical tests of scientific method—such as understanding, prediction, and control—are met by personal documents properly handled. Allport outlined and addressed all criticisms that have been advanced against a concrete psychology using personal documents and showed that many are irrelevant, trivial, and/or false. Moreover, the genuine problems that arise in the course of applying such a method can be addressed by its critical and

methodical use, with the genuine limits of the method being no more problematic than those of quantitative and experimental methods.

Allport (1942) elaborated a host of ways in which validity of conceptualizations based on the analysis of personal documents is established and made the interesting point that this validity may rightfully exceed reliability or observer agreement. Allport advocated conceptualizing psychological life using personal documents from different perspectives and argued that various conceptualizations may be equally valid, echoing the theme of humanism that there are many ways of knowing and many legitimate truths. Allport's conclusion was that "bold and radical" innovation in research using personal documents should be encouraged in conjunction with the exploration of alternative ways of writing reports and organizing data as well as alternative means of validation, prediction, and interpretation:

> Strong counter-measures are indicated against theorists who damn the personal document with faint praise, saying that its sole merit lies in its capacity to yield hunches or to suggest hypotheses. . . . They fail to express more than a small part of the value of personal documents for social science. (p. 191)

Maslow's Study of Self-Actualization

One of the most well-known contributions of the third force movement in psychology is Maslow's (1954/1987) groundbreaking study of *self-actualization*. Maslow, writing in a milieu still dominated by behaviorism, was apologetic about his study. He began his presentation by assuring the reader that the study was not planned as ordinary research and was not even begun as a social venture; rather, it was a private way of learning for himself. The findings of this study were so enlightening, exciting, and full of scientifically significant implications that Maslow decided to share the study "in spite of its methodological shortcomings" (p. 125). He acknowledged that however "moot" it might be, the study possessed heuristic value. But then, Maslow stated that the subject matter of this research—the healthy personality, one that is of undeniable importance in psychology—might never yield "conventionally reliable data" (p. 125). He presented his work "with due apologies to those who insist on conventional reliability, validity, sampling, and the like" (p. 125).

One interesting feature of Maslow's (1954/1987) study is the manner in which he combined traditional psychological measuring instruments and qualitative procedures. Reversing the traditional relationship, Maslow used measurement in a purely heuristic manner during the initial phase of the study, for example, to screen out individuals who manifested psychopathology. The positive delineation of self-actualization required qualitative procedures. Maslow's sample of participants were his friends, personal acquaintances, and public and historical figures. Maslow had hoped to also use college students and even characters from fictional works, but as his sense of self-actualization evolved through his encounters with potential participants, those appeared to fall short of his criteria.

Maslow (1954/1987) began with a rather commonsense ("folk") definition including the absence of psychopathology and "self-fulfillment"; "the maximum use of talents, capacities, [and] potentialities"; a sense of safety, belonging, capacity for love, and self-esteem; and philosophical, religious, and axiological bearing (p. 126). Maslow called this technique of selection *iteration* in which

one starts out with a personal or cultural nontechnical definition of the phenomenon as it might be referred to in ordinary speech (the "lexicographic stage"). After modifying this definition to achieve greater internal consistency (a "corrected folk definition"), two groups of participants—one that seems to manifest the subject matter in question and the other that does not—are compared. This comparison yields a "clinical definition" that is more critical in that it may allow the researcher to judge some participants who initially seemed to display the phenomenon as not qualifying and to drop them from the study. Further study of this group of participants allows an even more precise delineation that may disqualify additional participants and specially qualify others for further study. "In this way, an originally vague and unscientific folk concept can become more and more exact . . . [and,] therefore, more scientific" (p. 127).

Maslow (1954/1987) sought not only to measure self-actualization but also to become familiar with its most concrete detail as manifest in spontaneous living, that is, to acquire information as full and satisfactory as that demanded in clinical work. Practical and ethical problems required compromise. For example, the older participants, when informed of the nature of the research, became self-conscious, froze up, or terminated participation, and consequently they were studied "indirectly, almost surreptitiously," by observation rather than by interview. Because living people's names could not be divulged, the usual public availability and repeatability of investigation was not possible, although this was partly overcome by the inclusion of public and historical figures and young people. Maslow finally included nine contemporaries, nine historical and public figures, and five "partial cases" who fell short of the full criteria but still were helpful in the study.

Maslow (1954/1987) likened the data collection to "the slow development of a global and holistic impression of the sort that we form of friends and acquaintances" (p. 128). It was not possible to set up situations as one would an experiment or to do any testing with some participants, and Maslow took advantage of fortuitous opportunities that presented themselves in everyday life and questioned participants to the greatest extent possible. Consequently, data often were incomplete, and standardized quantitative presentation was impossible. Therefore, Maslow presented his findings as "only composite impressions . . . for whatever they are worth" (p. 128). Maslow conducted a holistic analysis of these total impressions and expressed his findings by means of a discussion of interrelated themes that characterize the lives of these most psychologically healthy persons.

Maslow's (1954/1987) findings, which he considered *observational,* are rich and provocative, drawn from and descriptive of his data as they reflect a type of ideal of the self-actualized personality. Maslow's description amounts to an empirically grounded delineation of the essence of self-actualization that he illustrated by means of the empirical details of his cases. The well-known characteristics that Maslow brought to light and clarified in great psychological detail are the perception of reality, acceptant attitude, spontaneous style, problem-centered cognition, comfort in solitude, autonomous self-direction, fresh appreciation of the novel, frequency of peak or mystical experiences, sense of kinship with humanity, humility and respect for others, democratic political stance, close interpersonal relationships, strong ethical standards, intrinsic value orientation, thought-

ful (nonhostile) sense of humor, pervasive creativity, ability to resist social pressure, fallibility, individually based value system, and resolution of dichotomies such as intellect/feelings, selfishness/unselfishness, spiritual/mundane, Dionysian/Appollonian, and masculine/feminine.

Although Maslow (1954/1987) had no doubt about the intrinsic scientific value of his research, he did not view it as ordinary science ("normal science" in Kuhn's sense) because there had been no widespread legitimation of procedures such as his within a fully developed methodology that would provide scientific norms and legitimacy. It is to Maslow's credit that he carried out the research and reported it, albeit apologetically. Although Maslow's research might not be methodologically perfect, no research is. Throughout the project, Maslow's research aimed at revealing the truly human in a holistic way, was carefully and critically conducted, made extensive use of empirical data, provided systematically organized conceptualization that far transcended common sense, and presented an opportunity for critique and challenges of both procedures and findings based on subsequent scholarship and research. It is, in short, bona fide scientific research even if it did not conform to a model of science known to Maslow.

BREAKTHROUGH: FORMALIZATION AND SCIENTIFIC LEGITIMATION OF HUMANISTIC METHODOLOGY

Revisions of the Philosophy of Science

One of the most important developments for the social sciences during the 20th century was the growing recognition of the limits of the positivistic conception of science.

Earlier, this chapter took notice of the continental tradition—including the works of Dilthey, Brentano, and Husserl—that gave rise to the phenomenological, existential, and hermeneutic movements in Europe. In America, however, more impact was felt during the latter part of the 20th century by a movement in British and American philosophy that came to be called *postpositivism* and that has provided probing analyses and critiques of the scientific process.

Popper (1935) asserted convincingly that it is impossible to inductively verify, in any final way, scientific propositions. Kuhn (1962), who studied the changes and revolutions in natural science, demonstrated that progress in science is not continuous or linear but rather involves changes in *paradigms,* that is, basic and unprovable assumptions such as the scientist's basic worldview, methods, values, and a host of social processes. Quine (1951, 1960) added to Popper's critique that even an experiment that does not support a hypothesis is not necessarily falsified, for one could challenge the experiment itself as a proper test, meaning that interpretation, not merely mathematical analysis, animates scientific progress. Wittgenstein (1953) demonstrated the essentially linguistic character of science, which precludes any purely objective observational base. Feyerabend (1975), in examining actual scientific work in detail, argued that scientific advances have involved the use of many methods and that methodological pluralism—indeed, anarchy—is preferable to the hegemony of restrictive methodological norms.

A change in the philosophy of science has taken place. Both Continental and British/American philosophers have devastatingly criticized the positivistic model. In particular, they have questioned its capacity for certainty; its exclusion of subjectivity, values, and larger cultural forces; its ability to mirror reality; and the narrowness of its methodological orientation.

Revolutionary Trends in Psychology

In reviewing the history of psychology since its scientific founding, Giorgi (1970) discovered that during virtually every period, there have been diverse criticisms of psychology that have a common root—the discipline's unquestioned adoption of the natural science approach. Around the same time, Gergen (1973) argued that psychological theory, unlike physics, is limited to particular times and cultures, questioning the appropriateness of seeking universally true propositions and advocating the practice of narrative interpretation that is more similar to studies in literature, history, and journalism in an orientation called *social constructionism.* The emergence of cognitive and humanistic psychologies diminished the domination of behaviorism during the 1960s. Both cognitive and humanistic psychologies emphasized consciousness and the importance of subjectivity in science and human life generally and played important roles in revolutionary movements of the second half of the 20th century.

Fishman (1999) pointed out that changes in the zeitgeist have brought constructionism greater authority and prestige in opposition to the dominant natural science approach. This new zeitgeist, dubbed *postmodernism,* arose during the cultural turmoil of the 1960s and has established a diversification of methods (Fishman, 1999; see also the chapter by Krippner [Chapter 22] in this volume). For example, the cultural forces of feminism that arose during the 1960s and 1970s embraced postmodernism and social constructionism in the questioning of universal laws governing humans, essentialism, and scientific ways of scientific knowing viewed as masculine. By contrast, feminists have emphasized that research involves a human relationship with the subject matter and should involve cooperation, equality, intuition, feeling, and valuing. The growth of multiculturalism as a social movement has contributed in a similar way to overthrowing the hegemony of Anglo-Saxon science.

By the end of the 20th century, there had been a veritable explosion of alternative methods in psychology as well as a reevaluation of standard methods within alternative epistemological contexts. These diversifying trends have self-consciously challenged the hegemony of the natural science approach in psychology. Moustakas (1990; see also his Chapter 20 in this volume) has steadily developed heuristic research, which calls for passionate indwelling and first-person involvement on the part of the researcher, who is viewed as a scientist-artist. Phenomenological methods of research have continued to develop (Giorgi, 1985; Valle & Halling, 1989; von Eckartsberg, 1986; see also the chapter by Churchill & Wertz [Chapter 19] in this volume). Narrative methods have been delineated from a variety of quarters, emphasizing the value of stories as research tools for the generation of psychological knowledge (Bruner, 1986, 1990; Howard, 1991; Josselson & Lieblich, 1993 [see also the chapter by Josselson & Lieblich (Chapter 21) in this volume]; Polkinghorne, 1988; Sarbin, 1986). Schön (1983) articulated a research approach that emerges as a form of reflectivity in the course of practice. Neopragmatism has been suggested as an approach that bases assessments of truth statements on the utility or practical benefits of the knowledge rather than on any presumed correspondence with

reality (Fishman, 1999; Polkinghorne, 1992). Grounded theory has been offered as an approach that begins with no hypothesis and moves toward theory generation by using thick description and inductive analyses (Charmaz, 1995; Glaser & Strauss, 1967). Feminist research has emphasized the relatedness of researcher to participants and the importance of equality, compassion, and sensitivity to the point of view of participants (Aptheker, 1989; Fonow & Cook, 1991; Neilsen, 1990; Riger, 1992). Hermeneutic methods that involve the textual analysis of meaning (drawn from literary and exegetical analyses of sacred texts) offer ways of analyzing meanings implicit in texts of human action in light of historical context, semantics, literary structure, and social conditions (Parker & Addison, 1989; Romanyshyn, 1991). Skolinowski (1994) called *participatory* research an approach that uses empathy, communion, and even identification with research participants and subject matters by the researcher, an approach that has been recognized in the Nobel prize-winning biological research of Barbara McClintock (Keller, 1985). Also drawing on feminist thought is Anderson (1998), who detailed the researcher's use of sympathetic resonance; delight and surprise; reflective listening; "trickstering"; alternative states of consciousness; and artwork, poetry, music, and symbols as data in what she called *intuitive* inquiry. White (1998) advocated the use of what she called exceptional human experiences in psychological science such as dreams, death-related experiences, mystical experiences, encounters, hypnagogic states, hallucinations, and out-of-body experiences. Fagen (1995) reported the use of research that uses graphic creative expressions and intentionally refrained from any verbal or quantitative analysis or interpretation of these expressions in her study of dreams. Braud's (1998) program for establishing the validity of psychological research uses, along with a host of more traditional intellectual methods, procedures including body wisdom, emotional reactions, aesthetic feelings, empathic resonance, and intuitions.

Interview methods have been revisited within a sophisticated phenomenological and hermeneutic approach to science (Kvale, 1996). Case study has been revisited and epistemologically rehabilitated in a manner that addresses concerns about bias and generality of findings (Fishman, 1999; Stake, 1995; Yin, 1994; see also the chapters by Schneider [Chapter 23] and Elliott [Chapter 24] in this volume), and it has been developed within a very sophisticated quasi-judicial framework drawn from case law (Bromley, 1986). Historical and archival methods using documents, oral records, and artifacts have been revived (Tuchman, 1994). Spence (1982) argued that psychoanalytic research does not provide historical truth (i.e., knowledge of the way things really were in the past) but does provide narrative truth, which can be judged only by its practical and aesthetic qualities and by whether it is a good and helpful story. Even the experiment itself has been rudely removed from its privileged seat and former context, as some psychologists doubt whether, and wonder how, it will continue to serve the discipline at all. If it is retained, McGuire (1994) reasoned, the experiment might provide a heuristic function in theory construction rather than be used to test theory. Gergen (1994) contended that experiments might serve as *vivifications* or dramatic rhetorical exhibitions of theory, and Kotre (1992) viewed the truth value of our classic experiments as parables reflecting what history already has taught us but providing a uniquely vivid imagery, a story

line, or an unexpected outcome that he considered the "mythical underpinning" of psychology.

Scholarship in the U.S. and British philosophy of science has shown that it is not necessary, or even appropriate, to subordinate these methods to hypothetico-deductive-inductive ones as the dominant model of science has demanded. With a more widespread and growing sense of their independent scientific legitimacy, and with ever more audibly voiced challenges to the legitimacy of science itself by means of postmodern criticism, the proliferation of alternative methods and the articulation of new methodological norms are growing.

MEANING AS THE DISTINCTIVE THEME OF HUMAN SCIENCE

The challenge now is for humanistic psychologists to draw on the rich tradition of research methods that have been used throughout the history of psychology as well as the many approaches that have been burgeoning during recent years and, in light of a truly sophisticated contemporary philosophy of science, formulate a unified yet diverse methodology in which new norms, progressively expanded in response to the complex challenges of human subject matter, open the horizons of psychological science. Psychology will become faithful to the essentially human rather than remain tied to rigid methods that inauthentically mimic natural science. The central thread running through this movement is the focus on *meaning*. We have come to understand that psychology is not merely the science of behavior or of experience in and of itself but rather a study of *the meaning(s) of experience and behavior for the individual person.* All methodological principles and procedures in psychology must follow from the demands and possibilities of studying the meaning of human life. With a self-conscious and methodical focus on how meanings arise in the lives of individual persons, psychology will form a revitalized relationship with the humanities and other social sciences that converge on the meanings of human life in philosophical, literary/fictional, historical, and cultural contexts.

NOTE

1. The Social Science Research Council was organized in 1923. The Council was composed of representatives from seven constituent professional organizations, including the American Anthropological Association, the American Economic Association, the American Historical Association, the American Political Science Association, the American Psychological Association, the American Sociological Association, and the American Statistical Association with the purpose of planning, fostering, promoting, and developing research in the social field.

REFERENCES

Allport, G. W. (1942). *The use of personal documents in psychological science* (Bulletin No. 49, prepared for the Committee on the Appraisal of Research). New York: Social Science Council.

American Psychological Association. (2000, March). *Criteria for evaluating treatment guidelines* (draft). Washington, DC: Author.

Anderson, R. (1998). Intuitive inquiry: A transpersonal approach. In W. Braud & R. Anderson (Eds.), *Transpersonal research methods for the social sciences: Honoring human experience* (pp. 69-94). Thousand Oaks, CA: Sage.

Aptheker, B. (1989). *Tapestries of life: Women's work, women's consciousness, and meaning of daily experience.* Amherst: University of Massachusetts Press.

Braud, W. (1998). An expanded view of validity. In W. Braud & R. Anderson (Eds.), *Transpersonal research methods for the social sciences: Honoring human experience* (pp. 213-237). Thousand Oaks, CA: Sage.

Bromley, D. B. (1986). *The case study method in psychology and related disciplines.* New York: John Wiley.

Bruner, J. S. (1986). *Actual minds, possible worlds.* Cambridge, MA: Harvard University Press.

Bruner, J. S. (1990). *Acts of meaning.* Cambridge, MA: Harvard University Press.

Charmaz, K. (1995). Grounded theory. In J. Smith, R. Harré, & L. Van Laangerhove (Eds.), *Rethinking methods in psychology* (pp. 27-49). Thousand Oaks, CA: Sage.

Danziger, K. (1990). *Constructing the subject: Historical origins of psychological research.* New York: Columbia University Press.

Dilthey, W. (1977). *Descriptive psychology and historical understanding.* The Hague, The Netherlands: Martinus Nijhoff. (Original work published 1894)

Fagen, N. (1995). *Elaborating dreams through creative expressions: Experiences, accompaniments, and personal effects.* Unpublished doctoral dissertation, Institute of Transpersonal Psychology, Palo Alto, CA.

Feyerabend, P. (1975). *Against method: Outline of an anarchistic theory of knowledge*. London: New Left Books.

Fishman, D. B. (1999). *The case for a pragmatic psychology*. New York: New York University Press.

Fonow, M. M., & Cook, J. A. (1991). *Beyond methodology: Feminist scholarship as lived research*. Bloomington: Indiana University Press.

Gergen, K. J. (1973). Social psychology as history. *Journal of Personality and Social Psychology, 26*, 309-320.

Gergen, K. J. (1994). Social psychology and the phoenix of unreality. In S. Koch & D. E. Leary (Eds.), *A century of psychology as a science* (pp. 528-557). Washington, DC: American Psychological Association.

Giorgi, A. (1970). *Psychology as a human science*. New York: Harper & Row.

Giorgi, A. (1985). *Phenomenology and psychological research*. Pittsburgh, PA: Duquesne University Press.

Glaser, B. G., & Strauss, A. L. (1967). *The discovery of grounded theory*. Chicago: Aldine.

Howard, G. S. (1991). Cultural tales: A narrative approach to thinking, cross-cultural psychology, and psychotherapy. *American Psychologist, 46*, 187-197.

James, W. (1982). *The varieties of religious experience: A study in human nature*. New York: Penguin. (Original work published 1902)

Josselson, R., & Lieblich, A. (1993). *The narrative study of lives*. Newbury Park, CA: Sage.

Keller, E. F. (1985). *Reflections on gender and science*. New Haven, CT: Yale University Press.

Kotre, J. (1992). Experiments as parables. *American Psychologist, 47*, 672-673.

Kuhn, T. S. (1962). *The structure of scientific revolutions*. Chicago: University of Chicago Press.

Kvale, S. (1996). *InterViews: An introduction to qualitative research interviewing*. Thousand Oaks, CA: Sage.

Maslow, A. H. (1987). *Motivation and personality*. New York: Van Nostrand Reinhold. (Original work published 1954)

McGuire, W. J. (1994). Toward social psychology's second century. In S. Koch & D. E. Leary (Eds.), *A century of psychology as a science* (pp. 558-593). Washington, DC: American Psychological Association.

Moustakas, C. (1990). *Heuristic research: Design, methodology, and applications*. Newbury Park, CA: Sage.

Neilsen, J. M. (1990). *Feminist research methods: Exemplary readings in the social sciences*. Boulder, CO: Westview.

Parker, M. J., & Addison, R. B. (1989). *Entering the circle: Hermeneutic investigation in psychology*. Albany: State University of New York Press.

Polkinghorne, D. E. (1988). *Narrative knowing and the human sciences*. Albany: State University of New York Press.

Polkinghorne, D. E. (1992). Postmodern epistemology of practice. In S. Kvale (Ed.), *Psychology and postmodernism* (pp. 146-165). Newbury Park, CA: Sage.

Popper, K. R. (1935). *The logic of scientific discovery*. London: Hutchison.

Quine, W. V. O. (1951). The two dogmas of empiricism. *Philosophical Review, 60*, 20-43.

Quine, W. V. O. (1960). *Word and object*. Cambridge, MA: MIT Press.

Radnitzky, G. (1973). *Contemporary schools of metascience*. Chicago: Henry Regnery.

Riger, S. (1992). Epistemological debates, feminist voices: Science, social values, and the study of women. *American Psychologist, 47*, 730-740.

Romanyshyn, R. (1991). Complex knowing: Towards a psychological hermeneutics. *The Humanistic Psychologist, 19,* 11-29.

Sarbin, T. R. (Ed.). (1986). *Narrative psychology: The storied nature of human conduct.* New York: Praeger.

Schön, D. A. (1983). *The reflective practitioner: How professionals think in action.* New York: Basic Books.

Skolinowski, H. (1994). *The participatory mind: A new theory of knowledge of the universe.* New York: Arkana.

Spence, D. P. (1982). *Narrative truth and historical truth: Meaning and interpretation in psychoanalysis.* New York: Norton.

Stake, R. E. (1995). *The art of case study research.* Thousand Oaks, CA: Sage.

Tuchman, G. (1994). Historical social science: Methodologies, methods, and meanings. In N. K. Denzin & Y. S. Lincoln (Eds.), *Handbook of qualitative research* (pp. 306-323). Thousand Oaks, CA: Sage.

Valle, R. S., & Halling, S. (1989). *Existential-phenomenological perspectives in psychology.* New York: Plenum.

von Eckartsberg, R. (1986). *Life-world experience: Existential-phenomenological research approaches in psychology.* Washington, DC: University Press of America.

White, R. A. (1998). Becoming more human as we work: The reflexive role of exceptional human experience. In W. Braud & R. Anderson (Eds.), *Transpersonal research methods for the social sciences: Honoring human experience* (pp. 128-145). Thousand Oaks, CA: Sage.

Wittgenstein, L. (1953). *Philosophical investigations* (G. E. M. Anscombe, Trans.). New York: Macmillan.

Yin, R. K. (1994). *Case study research.* Thousand Oaks, CA: Sage.

CHAPTER 19

An Introduction to Phenomenological Research in Psychology
Historical, Conceptual, and Methodological Foundations

SCOTT D. CHURCHILL AND FREDERICK J. WERTZ

IN THIS CHAPTER, we begin with the historical and conceptual background of phenomenological psychology. We then highlight some of the major methodological principles that guide phenomenological research in psychology. After a discussion of procedures that typically are involved in empirical research, we illustrate the orientation by describing a particular application of these methods.

HISTORICAL BACKGROUND

During the early 1900s, Edmund Husserl began to develop a "philosophy as rigorous science" called phenomenology. Husserl believed that if science were to fulfill its mission of providing rational knowledge that would enable humanity to freely shape its own destiny, then science must go beyond

an exclusive focus on the physical world and learn to take human experience into consideration with equal rigor. Husserl recognized from the beginning that his work, although primarily philosophical, had important implications for the discipline of psychology, the positive science that studies the experience of individual persons. Husserl believed that psychology, in its efforts to achieve scientific status by imitating the physical sciences, had not secured a proper conceptual foundation and methodology for its unique subject matter. Following Dilthey (1924/1977a), he asserted that description rather than explanation would be the best means for identifying essential constituents of conscious experience. Husserl provided an incisive critique of natural science psychology and delineated a positive alternative of a science that would provide more faithful knowledge of individuals' human experience. Husserl's work, and the 20th-century intellectual movement to which it gave rise, contributed to the larger ongoing effort to offer a science that is truly humanistic in the sense of being designed with a sensitivity to the special qualities of human experience as a subject matter.

On the basis of Husserl's work, European philosophers such as Heidegger, Sartre, and Merleau-Ponty pioneered phenomenological studies of existence (i.e., phenomenological ontology) and, therefore, are known as *existential-phenomenologists.* Psychology continued to occupy a central position in this movement. Sartre's first studies were psychological in nature— on human emotions and imagination— and throughout his career, Sartre continued to produce psychological biographies that he called *existential psychoanalyses*(e.g., Sartre, 1952/1963). Merleau-Ponty, who held the chair of child psychology at the Sorbonne that subsequently was occupied by Piaget, focused on neurophysiology, behavior, perception, intelligence, cognition, sexuality, and other psychological topics (e.g., Merleau-Ponty, 1945/1962, 1942/1963). Although European psychologists— particularly those of the Gestalt orientation—appropriated the phenomenological viewpoint, the European psychiatrists who applied it to clinical psychology were the first to capture the attention of American psychologists.

Even before American figures such as Murray, Allport, Snygg, and Combs would begin to develop what became known as *personalistic* or *personological* approaches during the 1930s and 1940s, psychiatrists in Europe were reading the texts of Dilthey, Husserl, and Heidegger with great care. Jaspers, influenced both by Husserl and by Dilthey's idea of a *verstehende* psychology (based on *understanding* rather than on explanation), developed a "general psychopathology" (Jaspers, 1913/1963) that offered a descriptive phenomenology of hallucinations, delusions, dreams, expressions, motor activity, and gestures as well as a comprehensive approach to characterology and "the person as a whole." Husserl's phenomenology eventually would find its way into the psychiatric writings of Binswanger (1963), Minkowski, (1970), von Gebsattel (1954, 1958), and even Straus (1966). It finally was Heidegger's (1927/1962) analysis of human *Dasein* that gave psychiatry its most radical reorientation by providing a new anthropology on the basis of which to understand both the human person and the pathologies of existence. Psychiatrists had now found a viable paradigm that could take them beyond the description of mental states to the Gestalt "existence" within which consciousness finds its source and origin (for further elaboration, see Binswanger, 1963; Keen, 1970; Spiegelberg, 1972; van den Berg, 1972).

Psychologists such as May, Allport, Rogers, Laing, Szasz, Frankl, Fromm, Moustakas, and Bugental likewise made extensive use of European existential thinking. Concepts such as freedom, alienation, the facticity of death, estrangement of self from other, the falling into "inauthenticity," the possibility of becoming an "authentic self," ontological guilt, and the experience of nothingness were incorporated into their clinical psychology and into their critical analyses of modern Western culture. This trend was associated more with human service than with formal research. Its representatives have devoted themselves to healing the lost souls, that is, the "hollow" men and women of our time who have lost touch with themselves, their fellow men and women, and their sense of wonder about existence (see Churchill, 2000).

Although Van Kaam was a counseling psychologist interested primarily in spiritual formation, he wrote convincingly that all psychology, not just clinical psychology, must acknowledge existential foundations (Van Kaam, 1966). Having developed the first "empirical psychophenomenological method" while conducting doctoral research on "the experience of really feeling understood" (Van Kaam, 1959), he delineated an existential-anthropological framework of understanding that could bring theoretical unity to the fragmented discipline of psychology and helped to set up a program at Duquesne University that aimed to apply phenomenological methods to the full spectrum of psychological subject matter (Van Kaam, 1966, 1987). Giorgi, having been trained to conduct experimental research on perception, played the key role of articulating the need for a "human science" foundation for the entire discipline of psychology and in developing empirical research methods that have been applied to a broad diversity of subject matter (Wertz & Aanstoos, 1999). By the late 1990s, former students and associates of the Duquesne circle were teaching at approximately 50 colleges and universities throughout the United States and Canada. (For prototypic and exemplary research, see Aanstoos, 1984; Churchill, 1984/1993, 1998; Colaizzi, 1973, 1978; Giorgi, 1975, 1985; Giorgi et al., 1971-1983; Fischer, 1974, 1978, 1985; Valle, 1998; Valle & Halling, 1989; Van Kaam, 1959, 1966; von Eckartsberg, 1971, 1986; Wertz, 1982, 1987; Wertz & Aanstoos, 1999; see also Pollio, Henley, & Thompson's [1998] independent yet kindred work.)

CONCEPTUAL BACKGROUND

The contribution of phenomenology to the foundations of the positive sciences fol-lowed from Husserl's (1900/1970) passionate call, "We must go back to the 'things themselves'!" (*zu den Sachen selbst!*). One implication of this statement is that the basic concepts and methodology of each science must rigorously target the essential characteristics of its subject matter. It also means that the concrete affairs *(Sachen)* of everyday life should provide the basis for philosophical reflection. One of the original aims of phenomenology was to complement and contextualize empirical scientific investigations by clarifying the "essence" of regions of study such as nature, animal life, and human psychic life (Husserl, 1952/1989). Such a clarification, Husserl reasoned, would be propaedeutic to any objective inquiries made at the empirical level. Each science must respond to the unique demands of its subject matter. Phenomenologists have insisted that humans are radically different from physical and animal nature and that, therefore, treating humans according to the concepts and methods of natural science is unscientific.

Intentionality

Fundamental for any research that attempts to address everyday life is an adequate conception of consciousness, which Husserl (1913/1962) put forward in the notion of *intentionality.* Whereas a nonhuman thing has a "nature" that resides within itself, consciousness always is consciousness of something other than itself. Experience must be grasped holistically as a relationship in which the subject relates to an object through its *meaning.* In perceiving, a perceiver relates to the perceived; for example, water is presented to the thirsty person as a drink, whereas it is presented to the dishwashing person as a cleaner. These are *objectively experienced meanings* of the water. Intentionality is a relational phenomenon, wherein consciousness and object together constitute one irreducible totality. Phenomenological psychology recognizes the intentionality of all lived experiences including perception, imagination, volition, expectation, remembering, thinking, feeling, and social behavior. These are understood as human potentials or aptitudes for relating to the meanings of our situations.

The concept of intentionality does not imply that the various modes of experience are lived through in a clear and explicit way, let alone reflected on by the person. On the contrary, it acknowledges inexactitude and vagueness in the individual's relations with his or her situations. The concept of intentionality expresses the structural and dynamic relationship of self and world, thereby liberating our conceptions of psychic life from traditional philosophical prejudices that place it "inside" the individual, separate from an "outside" objective reality. Sartre (1947/1970) expressed this point rather dramatically:

> If, impossible though it [may] be, you could enter "into" a consciousness, you would be seized by a whirlwind and thrown back outside, in the thick of the dust, near the tree, for consciousness has no "inside." It is just this being beyond itself . . . this refusal to be a substance which makes it a consciousness. (pp. 3-4)

The Life-World

As we move from simple experiential acts to more extended social, life historical involvements, we continue to find the person's illuminating presence to a meaningful transcendent world. These meanings are different for each unique individual, although they are built on and share many common sociocultural structures such as language. A faithful interrogation of any human experience shows that it is not an isolated event but rather is, according to its immanent structure, a moment of the ongoing social relation between a whole "personality" and the "world" that can be spoken about or revealed through language. The large order unity, outside of which no single human activity can be understood, is referred to by phenomenologists as the *life-world* (*Lebenswelt*), which provides the foundation for all scientific inquiries.

> To return to things themselves is to return to that world which precedes knowledge, of which knowledge always *speaks*, and in relation to which every scientific schematization is an abstract and derivative sign language, as is geography in relation to the countryside in which we have learnt beforehand what a forest, a prairie, or a river is. (Merleau-Ponty, 1945/1962, p. ix)

One of the fundamental characteristics of the life-world is its spatiality, which includes a "referential totality" of equipment, cultural objects, natural objects, other people, and institutions, each of which mutually implies and is inextricably bound up with all the others (Heidegger, 1927/1962). Within this essential context, persons unfold collectively and individually through sharing and each finding and creating his or her own way. This world also always involves temporality, an immanent teleology in which the present, rooted in and retaining a determinate past, determines, acts into, and opens onto an ever uncertain future. From birth to death, humans participate actively in and also are vulnerable to and passively caught up in this world that profoundly transcends them. Yet, each person experiences this world in its meaningful relevance to his or her individual "projects" (i.e., personal goals, interests, and desires), making it one's own world (*Eigenwelt*).

The complexity of the life-world is the basis of the diversity of theories, and in relation to it, each theory is partial. Psychoanalysis emphasizes the rootedness of existence in past affective familial relations, behaviorism emphasizes the instrumentality of embodied comportment and its contingent consequences, cognitive psychology emphasizes the calculatively organizing contribution of the individual, and constructionist theory emphasizes the constitutive role of society and culture. Each of these features of the life-world is significant and powerful enough to give the impression of being a sole determinant, yet holistic phenomenological conceptualization shows that each is implicitly dependent on all of the others and is nothing apart from the whole in which they are equiprimordial and co-essential. Priority must be given to the total life-world over any of the partial aspects stressed by one theory or another. The past cannot operate without a present and a future; the family cannot be understood apart from the culture and the individual; instrumental behavior cannot be understood apart from the meaningful cognition of the situation; calculation cannot be understood apart from embodiment, affect, and conation; and social construction cannot be understood apart form the inherencies of embodied meaning. Phenomenological psychology aims to incorporate those achievements of other schools of psychology that genuinely describe aspects of human existence, thereby integrating the diverse emphases that appear contradictory when theoretically abstracted from the life-world and postulated as mutually exclusive determinants.

AN EMPIRICAL METHODOLOGY FOR PSYCHOLOGY

Phenomenological research consists of four discernible (although not necessarily sequential) moments: formulation of the research question, intuitive contact with the phenomenon, reflective analysis of qualitative data, and psychological description.

Formulation of the Research Question

Like all research, phenomenological research begins with the judgment that our state of knowledge is in some way inadequate or limited. For example, fragmentary or contradictory theories, inconsistent findings, problematic methods, or a scarcity of research about a particular subject matter motivates research. Phenomenological research is appropriate when an assessment of the literature leads to the conclusion that knowledge is *not sufficiently descriptive* or *not sufficiently grounded* in a faithful intimate description of the subject matter and that such a description or grounding will better our knowledge. Husserl contended that *eidetic* inquiry (i.e., investigations of the "essence" of a phenomenon) should come first so as to guide empirical inquiry (i.e., collection and analysis of "facts" about a phenomenon) because a clarified understanding of *what one is studying* is needed so as to target which *variable aspects* require investigation. Phenomenological questions are those that ask about the meaning or essence of something people live through, that is, about its basic constituents and types, how it unfolds or evolves over time, and so on.

Intuitive Contact With the Phenomenon

To engage in phenomenological reflection on a given phenomenon, an *intuitive* relationship is needed between the researcher and the research participant— *direct existential contact*. *Intuitive* means that the phenomenon is directly accessible to the researcher's own consciousness. Evidence for psychological insight can be obtained from all forms of expression—verbal testimony, written protocols, observed behavior, gestures and drawings, artworks, cultural artifacts, and even media representations. In each case, the phenomenological approach brings the researcher into direct personal contact with the psychological event being studied. Only when such personal access has been facilitated can the researcher begin to acquaint himself or herself with the essence of the event.

Early phenomenological investigations consisted of researchers reflecting on their own experience. This method remains invaluable and is encouraged with a full accounting in phenomenological research projects. More recent efforts also have devised procedures for making other people's mental lives systematically accessible in research. For example, the participant may be invited to express an event that he or she already has lived through or to provide a simultaneous description of an ongoing experience. The researcher may indicate a type of life event and ask the participant to provide a descriptive account of an actual example. It is important that such a description discloses the contours of a particular experience as it occurs or may be relived in remembering with a minimum of scientific rubric, generalization, speculation, explanation or anything not immanent to the original concrete event. This becomes part of what Giorgi (1976) referred to as "the ideal of presuppositionless description," which implies that "one does not use language derived from explanatory systems or models in the initial description but [rather] everyday, naive language" (p. 311). An open-ended contact with everyday life is preferred over experiments or questionnaires. The researcher often will explicitly ask for full detail of an event as well as what led up to and followed it. Descriptions may be solicited from the person who lived

through the phenomenon himself or herself or from an "other" who observed someone living through that phenomenon. Descriptions may be simultaneous (as in "think-aloud" protocols) or retrospective. More detailed description may be gained through interviewing, for a description that does not include the whole existential context might conceal the significance of the phenomenon (Kvale, 1983). Ultimately, questions directed toward research participants are intended to obtain enough elaboration of the subtle details of their experience to facilitate the researcher's own imaginative "taking up" and "reliving" of the original experience—a taking up that makes possible a subsequent intuition into the immanent meanings of the experience under investigation.

The researcher's first step is to read and reread the description(s) so as to begin grasping the sense of the whole. This empathic intuition and intensive amplification of the reality of what the participant described, with the researcher calling on all of his or her powers of understanding so as to sensitively share in the participant's living, is the first moment of phenomenological method. "It is one of the most demanding operations, which requires utter concentration on the object intuited without becoming absorbed in it to the point of no longer looking critically" (Spiegelberg, 1983, p. 682). By means of this resonating attunement, one begins to understand the other's position and the rich meanings of the situation described. In "trading places" (Husserl, 1952/1989), the researcher can begin to acquaint himself or herself with the essential meanings and organization of the experience. The phenomenologist aims to make the participant's involvement the phenomenologist's own by co-performing it in the reading. While striving to project himself or herself into the situation described so as to "re-experience" it (Dilthey, 1927/

1977b), the researcher maintains a critical presence, which will serve the subsequent reflective analysis.

Reflective Analysis of Qualitative Data

The analytic phase of the research consists of furthering the intuitive presence to the participant's description by apprehending the individual moments of his or her experience in relation to the whole. In phenomenological reflection, theories, hypotheses, previous explanations, and other preconceptions about the phenomenon are bracketed or held in abeyance. Phenomenology has been defined etymologically by Heidegger (1927/1962) as letting "that which shows itself be seen from itself in the very way in which it shows itself from itself" (p. 58). The researcher's posture in this "letting show itself" also has been described as noninterference, open-minded generosity, wonder, and even *love*. The researcher lets his or her understanding be informed by the protocol rather than be dictated on the basis of assumptions and preconceptions.

The phenomenological researcher brackets questions and concerns about "what really happened" in the situation described and focuses on the *meanings* of the situation as experienced by the participant. There is a turning from "given facts" to "intended meanings"—from the simple "givenness" of the situation in the participant's experience to a reflective apprehension of the meaning of that situation for the person. Descriptive data generally present life situations in a matter-of-fact rendition in which the person's constitutive role and many important meanings may be highly implicit. The phenomenological reduction places into relief what common sense takes for granted (Natanson, 1973, p. 58). The turn from

facts to meanings is a turning from naïve description to a psychological reflection in which co-constituted meanings are brought to light.

The researcher openly reflects on the present data, contemplating the participant's description in a way that allows segments of what is described to be discerned (but not separated) as moments of the participant's experience. Analysis consists of "the distinguishing of the constituents of the phenomenon as well as the exploration of their relations to and connections with adjacent phenomena" (Spiegelberg, 1983, p. 691). The researcher moves dialectically from part to whole, and then back again to individual parts from a sense of the whole, in an effort to discern and comprehend those *relationships* in which one finds the psychological significance that speaks to the researcher's questions in a relevant way.

To the extent that the constituent immanent meanings that fulfill the researcher's interests are not obvious or clearly stated in the original description, the process of analysis involves "explicitation" (Giorgi, 1970). Phenomenological reflection strives to be eidetic, that is, to distinguish essential facts from accidental or incidental facts. It is not just any constituent, implicit dimension, relation among aspects, or pervasive orientation that reflection seeks to apprehend but rather those that constitute the essential or invariant meaning and structure of experience. Each individual protocol is analyzed in its own right, yielding what have been called *individual psychological structures* or descriptions of individual instances of the researched phenomenon. These descriptions, insofar as they are truly structural, involve the researcher's seeing connections among the various moments described within the protocol and formulating an integrative account of the individual's experience.

Phenomenological analysis may strive for varying levels of generality, depending on the aim of the research, ranging from a unique individual to the typical, general, or even universal levels of experience. Constituent meanings essential to a particular experience—say, a particular instance of learning—might not be universal but rather characteristic of one of the types. The attainment of various levels of generality, as well as knowledge of what is unique in a particular case, requires qualitative comparisons of different individual cases, real and imagined, in which the researcher strives to intuit convergences and divergences and, thereby, gains essential insight into relative levels of generality (i.e., a structural understanding of individual, typical, and universal features).

Psychological Description

Having intuited a sense of the research participant's lived experience, and having then gone back to the particulars of the participant's description so as to flesh out a sense of the psychological significance and coherence of the experience, the researcher then proceeds to the final task, psychological description, which expresses the actual findings of the reflections. During this phase, the researcher expresses his or her insights in an integrative statement that conveys the coherent structure of the psychic life under consideration—its various constituents (e.g., temporal phases) and their relations within the whole. The descriptive phase occurs when the researcher is ready to thematize and put into words what has been experienced vicariously, but nonetheless intuitively, within the researcher's taking up of the participant's experience (Dilthey, 1927/1977b, p. 130; see also Merleau-Ponty, 1945/1962, p. 353). Here, the researcher no longer is limited to the partici-

pant's words but rather chooses those that best capture the participant's psychology.

By taking notes as the analysis proceeds, the researcher may keep track of his or her ongoing thoughts, and these informal tentative reflections are the roots of the final understanding expressed in the research report. Ideally, all statements in the descriptions that are relevant to the research problem are represented in the researcher's psychological statements, and all of the researcher's statements have evidence intuitively provided in the data. The implications of the new knowledge may then be drawn out including how it helps to resolve theoretical controversies, empirical questions, and/or practical problems.

AN ILLUSTRATIVE APPLICATION

To illustrate phenomenological research in psychology, we offer a study conducted by the second author with Constance Fischer because it remains one of the most explicit accounts of the use of these methods and little theoretical background is needed to understand the research (Wertz, 1983, 1985). This project, funded by the National Endowment for the Humanities, focused on the experience of crime victims. The research problem was twofold. To date, there had been no thorough, systematic, and descriptive account of the experience of crime victims. Research had focused on victims' attempts to reduce violence in criminals, characteristics that evoked helping behavior by others, the experience of victims by others, and various disparate themes without any integrated understanding of the overall organization and temporal progression of the victims' experience itself. Our research also had the practical goal of providing a series of public forums in which victims, police, justice system personnel, and governmental policy makers would gain greater understanding of the plight of crime victims.

Working with a police department in the greater Pittsburgh area in Pennsylvania, five researchers interviewed a total of 50 individuals who had reported crimes against themselves (excluding rape). These interviews ranged from 40 to 90 minutes, beginning with instructions such as the following: "I would like to understand your experience of the crime you reported. Please begin before it happened and describe the events that occurred, including as much as you can remember." Interviewers used a person-centered listening approach in the collection of data, limiting questions to requests for clarification, filling in gaps, and seeking greater detail. An interview was concluded when the interviewer and participant both agreed that everything the participant lived through in connection with the victimization had been described.

The interviews were prepared for analysis in a series of steps. After an interview was transcribed (ranging from 8 to 30 pages), the researchers read the transcript openly. To be sure that the researchers gave due attention to every bit of data, they differentiated the interview into "meaning units" or portions of the text that pertained to a single theme or moment of the experience. Each tended to be from one to about three sentences in the participant's language. The meaning units then were ordered chronologically, redundancy and irrelevancy were eliminated, and the participant's own words were arranged so that they formed a first-person narrative. Each of these *individual phenomenal descriptions* (ranging from 5 to 20 pages) was a description of the phenomenal experience of an individual instance of victimization. In one of these, for example, a participant whom we called "Marlene" described going home after work as a waitress. Here is a very abbreviated summary of

Marlene's description, which was about 10 pages:

Marlene noticed that a car behind her pulled into the driveway of her apartment building and assumed that it was a neighbor. When she approached her building's steps and looked over her shoulder to see why she hadn't heard the other car's door close, she was assailed by a man who "must have flown" to her from the car, whose door was still open and contained another male passenger. As the man came upon her, Marlene tried to offer him her purse, but he grabbed her and tried to throw her over his shoulder. She imagined being hurt and even killed by him, determined to fight, screamed, and held onto the railing. After a struggle, when a neighbor opened her window and yelled Marlene's name, the assailant released her, ran to the car and drove away. Marlene was terrified for weeks, wondering who the man was, [wondering] whether he knew her, and expecting him to return. Suspecting that he followed her from work and could find her there or even leaving her apartment, she fearfully remained home in bed. Unsatisfied with the care she received from her husband and refusing to let him touch her, Marlene thought her marriage would be ruined and planned to return home to her parents "for the arms." Fortunately, her husband, who had previously lacked sensitivity, "turned it soft" and became her caretaker and protector. He comforted her, installed strong locks, and eventually accompanied her to and from work. Back at work, Marlene stopped flirting with male customers, wore longer skirts, and vigilantly guarded herself against any man who looked at her "the wrong way." To her surprise, her originally continual suspicions never turned into anything, and gradually she became more secure. But her life was changed; she avoided going out alone at night, [she] no longer engaged affectionately with strange male customers, and her husband remained a great deal more nurturing than he had ever been before.

The researchers then began the psychological analysis of each individual instance by reflecting on each meaning unit in order. The basic attitude of the researchers was one of empathy, dwelling with and magnifying each detail of the experience and concentrating on the meaning of the situation as it was experienced by the participant. In considering each meaning unit, the researchers reflected on its relevance for the psychology of the victim's experience as expressed in the protocol, aimed to grasp implicit meanings, distinguished different moments or constituents of meaning, considered the relationship of each meaning unit to each other and to the whole, identified recurrent meanings, imaginatively varied the case so as to discern what was essential to its meaning, and put the findings of these reflections into language. The *individual psychological structure* of each instance of victimization thereby generated was several times longer than the participant's original description.

The individual psychological structure of Marlene's experience was both seen and described as consisting of five temporal phases presented in a highly abbreviated form in the following paragraphs. In this type of research, one often strives for an "isomorphism" between the lived experience and the psychological account of that experience, hence the term *structure*.

1. Before victimization, Marlene experienced the world as safe, meaning that she could pursue her end of going home after work as a free agent. Others were experienced as a relatively harmonious community, as exemplified by her flirting with strangers at work and interpreting the car following her as a neighbor. Victimization in this phase was merely an unthematized possibility.

2. The actual experience of victimization occurred through a very subtle process, beginning with what Marlene called her "fear over my shoulder" that arose when she did not hear the other car's door close. It culminated in a new existential organization involving Marlene's perception of a detrimental other, the absence of any helpful community, and vulnerability—the loss of her own agency in the situation. This new experiential organization initially was fraught with uncertainty, surprise, and shock ("What does he want from me?") but quickly was filled in by Marlene's imagination of being raped, murdered, or "messed up so bad it's not worth living."

3. An active struggle ensued so as to overturn this new existential organization. Marlene tried to overcome her confusion and shock by swift understanding. She saw the car door open and anticipated being kidnapped and never seen again. She tried to offer the other money in lieu of herself, imagined a host of terrible possibilities, and resolved to resist. She held onto the rail and screamed, thereby reasserting her agency, countering the other's detrimentality, and summoning helpful community. This effort, along with her neighbor's response, was successful in bringing the actual victimization to an end as the detrimental other took flight.

4. The experience of victimization, however, was not over. Marlene continued to live through each of its constituents—the detrimentality of others, the absence of helpful community, and the loss of personal power. In this light, many things in her world changed their meanings. The ring of the phone or a knock on the door "sent [her] through the ceiling" because she "was sure

it was him." Her sense of her husband's insensitivity became so heightened that, after dreaming of him raping her, she would not let him touch her. Indeed, she experienced her husband in terms of both "detrimental otherness" and "absence of help." Customers at work whose company she had enjoyed became potential predators. The meanings of victimization spread throughout Marlene's world—in her life at home after the attack, in her contact with the police (who manifested the meaning of absent helpfulness), in her relations with her husband, and in returning to work. By far, the most profound, extensive, and complex experience of victimization occurred after the actual event, through multiple experiential modalities—thinking, imagining, dreaming, perceiving, and anticipating. Correlatively, Marlene's greatest struggle to overcome this new existential structure occurred after the event. Through her active efforts—including vigilant perception, avoidance and curtailment of risky behavior (e.g., flirting), the demanding of sensitivity and protection from her husband—Marlene recovered some lost personal agency and power. Customers at work proved themselves to be friendly, and her husband assured her that "I'm not the guy" and, more important, "turned it soft." These gifts from the world gradually restored the meanings of friendliness and respectful supportive community on the part of others.

5. After the victimization, the world horizon of safety and Marlene's sense of free agency were restored. Even though she no longer thinks of victimization thematically, her psychological life is changed in a host of ways that attest to the meanings of victimization. Marlene's efforts to overcome the possibility of being victimized now are habitual ways of life. She wears longer skirts, does not flirt, avoids the gazes of strange men on the street, and does not go out alone at night. Her husband escorts her often and has become much more caring. She keeps the door locked and does not keep identification in her purse. Although the meaning of these changes (among others) is the negation of victimization, they attest to its existence as an ongoing possibility. In this new order, Marlene has incorporated victimization in transcending it.

Through a series of further analytic operations, the researchers proceeded to attain a more general knowledge of victimization. First, some of the findings in individual psychological structures appeared immediately to be general. For example, the five temporal phases in Marlene's experience noted earlier and the constituents of victimization—detrimentality, loss of agency, and absent community—seemed to be quite general. This is possible because *meanings already go beyond the facts of the individual case*, to which they are not necessarily limited.

Second, explicit comparisons of different individual psychological structures yielded many commonalities. The five stages and three constituents of the core experience were found in all 50. For example, before victimization, all participants experienced events in terms of the horizon of friendly community, as did one family returning home after a vacation who saw their front door ajar and thought that it must be the neighbor's kids playing until, inside, they witnessed their house ransacked. The meaning of *detrimental other* was present in all, whether in the form of muggers, unseen and unknown robbers, or known vandals. All participants reexperienced victimization in a variety of experiential forms throughout their worlds, for example, in *dreaming* (of the "Peeping Tom" appearing one night), *anticipating* (kids on the street snatching her purse), *thinking* (about who might have overturned the car), or *philosophizing* (it is a dog-eat-dog world, and people just let it go on that way).

Third, the researchers moved beyond the 50 instances of victimization provided by their interview data by imagining yet other possible instances of victimization and imaginatively varying the 50 instances they collected so as to arrive at an understanding of what generally is essential to the psychology of victimization. The researchers realized, in this way, that the struggle against victimization is not universal and that neither is the final phase of "recovery and integration"; one can be hurt or even killed without any restoration of agency, helpful community, or removal of detrimentality, as in repeated victimization or kidnapping with endless torture, not to mention murder. They decided to focus their research on the more typical "struggle with victimization" and elaborate how this struggle may be successful rather than to restrict their findings to what evidently is universal. To this extent, the researchers allowed their findings to be limited to the trends of their data that reflected the relatively successful recovery from victimization. Perhaps another type of psychology would be brought to light in the cases of victims who suffered repeatedly and/or were not able to recover or transcend their experience.

The researchers offered general psychological discourse in a two-page summary (Wertz, 1985, pp. 192-193), in greatly elaborated detail with deepening reflections and multiple detailed illustrations from their data (pp. 193-213), and in a form designed to provoke understanding and meaningful discussion among the lay public (Fischer & Wertz, 1979). Because of spatial limitations, here we offer only a very skeletal or distilled version of such general results without any illustrations:

On the ground of a usual situation involving a freely enacted task, in a familiar situation with the meaningful horizon of social harmony and safety, one is shocked by the emergence of victimization—an other detrimental to one's preferred situation has in the absence of helpful community made the victim prey to antithetical purposes, and the vulnerable person is relatively powerless to stop this even though it is against his/her values and will. The victim immediately struggles to overcome the disruptive shock by understanding in order to eliminate the detrimental other, to restore helpful community, and to regain the lost agency/power—thereby to return to his/her preferred situation. When this incident is over, the person continues to live in the horizon of victimization, that is, elaborates the constituent meanings in various situations through recollection, perception, anticipation, imagination, and thinking throughout his/her world. The person struggles to overcome the more broadly elaborated profiles of victimization as they now lurk, as an imminent danger, throughout his/her world at large. Through his/her own active efforts, help from others, and the world's repeated reassertion of noninterference and safety, victimization moves from being an impending actuality to being an unlikely or remote possibility within the newly restored horizon of social harmony. By so elaborating and overcoming victimization, that is, by eliminating the ongoing risk, the former victim shapes a new existence in which victimization is integrated—both conserved and surpassed. Former victims vary from one another according to the particular way victimization was surpassed; for instance, some are more self-reliant, and some are more dependent on helpful others. This new existence is preferred relative to victimization but not necessarily preferred over one's life before victimization. (Wertz, 1985, p. 191)

VALIDITY AND RELIABILITY

Verifiability of phenomenological findings depends on whether another researcher can assume the perspective of the present investigator, review the original protocol data, and see that the proposed insights meaningfully illuminate the situations under study.

> Thus, the chief point to be remembered with this type of research is not so much whether another position could be adopted (this point is granted beforehand) but [rather] whether a reader, adopting the same viewpoints as [those] articulated by the researcher, can also see what the researcher saw, whether or not he/she agrees with it. That is the key criterion for qualitative research. (Giorgi, 1975, p. 96)

Posing the question of validity in absolute terms (i.e., "Is this study valid or invalid?") tends to be unfruitful. All research discloses only a limited truth, that is, a truth limited by the researcher's procedures and perspective. Phenomenological researchers attempt to articulate those limits reflectively and honestly, and additional limits may be discerned by others whose scholarship and reflections bring additional perspectives and procedures to bear. The validity of research findings, therefore, is not contingent on whether they are entirely similar to those of other viewpoints. According to the phenomenological approach, it is not possible to exhaustively know any phenomenon, and different viewpoints can be valid (Churchill, Lowery, McNally, & Rao, 1998; Wertz, 1986). In other words, other perspectives, perhaps rooted in different research interests and their corresponding intuitions, always are possible and contribute in a complementary manner to our knowledge of "the whole." In the end, the value of the findings depends on their ability to help others gain *some* insights into what has been lived unreflectively. Other insights from different viewpoints may then supplement, and thereby extend and possibly even radically decenter, what *always is essentially a partial knowledge* of human life. But this does not imply that "anything goes"; phenomenological findings must be able to be evidenced by concrete prescientific experience of oneself and others. "The main function of phenomenological description is to serve as a reliable guide to the listener's own actual or potential experience of the phenomena" (Spiegelberg, 1983, p. 694). In the end, what makes phenomenological knowledge "true" is its fidelity to experience as it is concretely lived in the life-world.

REFERENCES

Aanstoos, C. M. (Ed.). (1984). *Exploring the lived world: Readings in phenomenological psychology.* Carrollton: West Georgia College.

Binswanger, L. (1963). *Being-in-the-world* (J. Needleman, Ed.). New York: Basic Books.

Churchill, S. D. (1993). Forming clinical impressions: A phenomenological study of psychodiagnostic seeing. In C. Aanstoos (Ed.), *Exploring the lived world: Readings in phenomenological psychology* (West Georgia College Studies in Social

Sciences, Vol. 23, pp. 67-84). Carrollton, GA: Eidos Press. (Original work published 1984)

Churchill, S. D. (1998). The intentionality of psychodiagnostic seeing: A phenomenological investigation of clinical impression formation. In R. Valle (Ed.), *Phenomenological inquiry: Existential and transpersonal dimensions* (pp. 175-207). New York: Plenum.

Churchill, S. D. (2000). Phenomenological psychology. In A. Kazdin (Ed.), *Encyclopedia of psychology* (Vol. 6, pp. 162-168). Washington, DC: American Psychological Association.

Churchill, S. D., Lowery, J., McNally, O., & Rao, A. (1998). The question of reliability in interpretive psychological research: A comparison of three phenomenologically-based protocol analyses. In R. Valle (Ed.), *Phenomenological inquiry: Existential and transpersonal dimensions* (pp. 63-85). New York: Plenum.

Colaizzi, P. F. (1973). *Reflection and research in psychology.* Dubuque, IA: Kendall/ Hunt.

Colaizzi, P. F. (1978). Psychological research as the phenomenologist views it. In R. S. Valle & M. King (Eds.), *Existential-phenomenological alternatives for psychology* (pp. 48-71). New York: Oxford University Press.

Dilthey, W. (1977a). Ideas concerning a descriptive and analytical psychology (R. M. Zaner, Trans.). In W. Dilthey, *Descriptive psychology and historical understanding* (pp. 23-120). The Hague, The Netherlands: Martinus Nijhoff. (Original work published 1924)

Dilthey, W. (1977b). The understanding of other persons and their expressions of life (K. L. Heiges, Trans.). In W. Dilthey, *Descriptive psychology and historical understanding* (pp. 123-144). The Hague, The Netherlands: Martinus Nijhoff. (Original work published 1927)

Fischer, C. T., & Wertz, F. J. (1979). Empirical phenomenological analysis of being criminally victimized. In A. Giorgi, D. Smith, & R. Knowles (Eds.), *Duquesne studies in phenomenological psychology* (Vol. 3, pp. 135-158). Pittsburgh, PA: Duquesne University Press.

Fischer, W. F. (1974). On the phenomenological mode of researching "being anxious." *Journal of Phenomenological Psychology, 4,* 405-423.

Fischer, W. F. (1978). An empirical-phenomenological investigation of being-anxious: An example of the meanings of being-emotional. In R. S. Valle & M. King (Eds.), *Existential-phenomenological alternatives for psychology* (pp. 166-181). New York: Oxford University Press.

Fischer, W. F. (1985). Self-deception: An existential-phenomenological investigation into its essential meanings. In A. Giorgi (Ed.), *Phenomenology and psychological research* (pp. 118-154). Pittsburgh, PA: Duquesne University Press.

Giorgi, A. (1970). *Psychology as a human science: A phenomenologically based approach.* New York: Harper & Row.

Giorgi, A. (1975). An application of phenomenological method in psychology. In A. Giorgi, C. Fischer, & E. Murray (Eds.), *Duquesne studies in phenomenological psychology* (Vol. 2, pp. 82-103). Pittsburgh, PA: Duquesne University Press.

Giorgi, A. (1976). Phenomenology and the foundations of psychology. In J. K. Cole & W. J. Arnold (Eds.), *Nebraska symposium on motivation 1975.* Lincoln: University of Nebraska Press.

Giorgi, A. (Ed.). (1985). *Phenomenology and psychological research.* Pittsburgh, PA: Duquesne University Press.

Giorgi, A., et al. (Eds.). (1971-1983). *Duquesne studies in phenomenological psychology* (4 vols.). Pittsburgh, PA: Duquesne University Press.

Heidegger, M. (1962). *Being and time* (J. MacQuarrie & E. Robinson, Trans.). New York: Harper & Row. (Original work published 1927)

Husserl, E. (1962). *Ideas: General introduction to pure phenomenology* (W. R. B. Gibson, Trans.). New York: Collier Books. (Original work published 1913)

Husserl, E. (1970). *Logical investigations* (J. N. Findlay, Trans.). New York: Humanities Press. (Original work published 1900)

Husserl, E. (1989). *Ideas pertaining to a pure phenomenology and to a phenomenological philosophy, Second Book: Studies in the phenomenology of constitution* (R. Rojcewicz & A. Schuwer, Trans.). Boston: Kluwer. (Original work written 1928 and published posthumously 1952)

Jaspers, K. (1963). *General psychopathology* (J. Hoenig & M. W. Hamilton, Trans.). Chicago: University of Chicago Press. (Original work published 1913)

Keen, E. (1970). *Three faces of being: Toward an existential clinical psychology.* New York: Appleton-Century-Crofts.

Kvale, S. (1983). The qualitative research interview: A phenomenological and hermeneutical mode of understanding. *Journal of Phenomenological Psychology, 14,* 171-196.

Merleau-Ponty, M. (1962). *Phenomenology of perception* (C. Smith, Trans.). London: Routledge and Kegan Paul. (Original work published 1945)

Merleau-Ponty, M. (1963). *The structure of behavior* (A. Fisher, Trans.). Pittsburgh, PA: Duquesne University Press. (Original work written 1938 and published 1942)

Minkowski, E. (1970). *Lived-time: Phenomenological and psychopathological studies.* Evanston, IL: Northwestern University Press.

Natanson, M. (1973). *Edmund Husserl: Philosopher of infinite tasks.* Evanston, IL: Northwestern University Press.

Pollio, H. R., Henley, T., & Thompson, C. B. (1998). *The phenomenology of everyday life.* Cambridge, UK: Cambridge University Press.

Sartre, J.-P. (1963). *Saint Genet: Actor and martyr.* New York: New American Library. (Original work published 1952)

Sartre, J.-P. (1970). Intentionality: A fundamental idea of Husserl's phenomenology (J. P. Fell, Trans.). *Journal of the British Society for Phenomenology, 1,* 4-5. (Original work published 1947)

Spiegelberg, H. (1972). *Phenomenology in psychology and psychiatry.* Evanston, IL: Northwestern University Press.

Spiegelberg, H. (1983). *The phenomenological movement: A historical introduction* (3rd ed.). Hingham, MA: Martinus Nijhoff.

Straus, E. (1966). *Phenomenological psychology: Selected papers* (E. Eng, Trans.). New York: Basic Books.

Valle, R. S. (Ed.). (1998). *Phenomenological inquiry: Existential and transpersonal dimensions.* New York: Plenum.

Valle, R. S., & Halling, S. (Eds.). (1989). *Existential-phenomenological perspectives in psychology: Exploring the breadth and depth of human experience.* New York: Plenum.

van den Berg, J. H. (1972). *A different existence: Principles of phenomenological psychopathology.* Pittsburgh, PA: Duquesne University Press.

Van Kaam, A. (1959). Phenomenal analysis: Exemplified by a study of the experience of really feeling understood. *Journal of Individual Psychology, 15,* 66-72.

Van Kaam, A. (1966). *Existential foundations of psychology.* Pittsburgh, PA: Duquesne University Press.

Van Kaam, A. (1987). *Formative spirituality: Vol. 4. Scientific formation.* New York: Crossroad.

von Eckartsberg, R. (1971). On experiential methodology. In A. Giorgi, W. F. Fischer, & R. von Eckartsberg (Eds.), *Duquesne studies in phenomenological psychology* (Vol. 1, pp. 66-79). Pittsburgh, PA: Duquesne University Press.

von Eckartsberg, R. (1986). *Life-world experience: Existential-phenomenological research approaches in psychology.* Washington, DC: Center for Advanced Research in Phenomenology.

von Gebsattel, V. E. (1954). *Prolegomena zu einer medizinischen Anthropologie* [Prolegomena to a medical anthropology]. Berlin: Springer.

von Gebsattel, V. E. (1958). The world of the compulsive (S. Koppel & E. Angel, Trans.). In R. May, E. Angel, & H. F. Ellenberger (Eds.), *Existence: A new dimension in psychiatry and psychology* (pp. 170-187). New York: Simon & Schuster.

Wertz, F. J. (1982). The findings and value of a descriptive approach to everyday perceptual process. *Journal of Phenomenological Psychology, 13,* 169-195.

Wertz, F. J. (1983). From everyday to psychological description: Analyzing the moments of a qualitative data analysis. *Journal of Phenomenological Psychology, 14,* 197-241.

Wertz, F. J. (1985). Methods and findings in an empirical analysis of "being criminally victimized." In A. Giorgi (Ed.), *Phenomenology and psychological research* (pp. 155-216). Pittsburgh, PA: Duquesne University Press.

Wertz, F. J. (1986). The question of reliability in psychological research. *Journal of Phenomenological Psychology, 17,* 181-205.

Wertz, F. J. (1987). Abnormality from scientific and prescientific perspectives. *Review of Existential Psychology and Psychiatry, 19*(2-3), 205-223.

Wertz, F. J., & Aanstoos, C. M. (1999). Amedeo Giorgi and the project of human science. In D. Moss (Ed.), *Humanistic and transpersonal psychology* (pp. 287-300). Westport, CT: Greenwood.

CHAPTER 20

Heuristic Research
Design and Methodology

CLARK MOUSTAKAS

FROM THE BEGINNING and throughout an investigation, heuristic research involves self-search, self-dialogue, and self-discovery. The research question and methodology flow out of inner awareness, meaning, and inspiration. When I consider an issue, a problem, or a question, I enter into it fully. I focus on it with unwavering attention and interest. I search introspectively, meditatively, and reflectively into its nature and meaning. My primary task is to recognize whatever exists in my consciousness as a fundamental awareness—to receive it, accept it, support it, and dwell inside it. I awaken to it as my question, receptive, open, and with full and unqualified interest in extending my understanding. I begin the heuristic investigation with my own self-awareness and explicate that awareness with reference to a question or problem until an essential insight is achieved, one that will throw a beginning light on a critical human experience.

In the process of heuristic search, I may challenge, confront, or doubt my understanding of a human concern or issue, but when I persist, I ultimately deepen my knowledge of the phenomenon. In the heuristic process, I am personally involved, searching for the qualities, conditions, and relationships that underlie a fundamental question or concern.

I may be entranced by visions, images, and dreams that connect me to my quest. I may come into touch with new regions of myself and discover revealing connections with others. Through the guides of a heuristic design, I am able to see and understand in a different way. If I am investigating the meaning of the delight, then delight hovers nearby and follows me around. It takes me fully into its confidence, and I take it into

AUTHOR'S NOTE: This chapter is adapted from an article of the same title that appeared in the *Person-Centered Review*, Vol. 5, No. 2, pp. 170-190.

mine. Delight becomes a lingering presence. For a while, there is only delight. It opens me to the world in a joyous way and takes me into a richness, a playfulness, and a childlikeness that move freely and effortlessly. I am ready to see, feel, touch, and hear whatever opens me to delight.

In heuristics, an unshakable connection exists between what is out there (in its appearance and reality) and what is within me (in reflective thought, feeling, and awareness). It is "I" who is the person living in a world with others, alone yet inseparable from the community of others; I who sees and understands something, freshly, as if for the first time; and I who comes to know essential meanings inherent in my experience.

In our 1985 article, "Heuristic Inquiry," Douglass and I contrasted heuristic research from the traditional paradigm, noting that traditional empirical investigations presuppose cause-effect relationships, whereas heuristic scientists seek to discover the nature and meaning of phenomena themselves and to illuminate them through direct first-person accounts of individuals who have directly encountered the phenomena in experience (Douglass & Moustakas, 1985). We also contrasted heuristic inquiry from phenomenological research, pointing out the following:

(1) Whereas phenomenology encourages a kind of detachment from the phenomenon being investigated, heuristics emphasizes connectedness and relationship. (2) Whereas phenomenology permits the researcher to conclude with definitive descriptions of the structures of experience, heuristics leads to depictions of essential meanings and portrayal of the intrigue and personal significance that imbue the search to know. (3) Whereas phenomenological research generally concludes with a presen-

tation of the distilled structures of experience, heuristics may involve reintegration of derived knowledge that itself is an act of creative discovery, a synthesis that includes intuition and tacit understanding. (4) Whereas phenomenology loses the persons in the process of descriptive analysis, in heuristics the research participants remain visible in the examination of the data and continue to be portrayed as whole persons. Phenomenology ends with the essence of experience; heuristics retains the essence of the person in experience. (p. 43)

The focus in a heuristic quest is on re-creation of the lived experience, that is, full and complete depictions of the experience from the frame of reference of the experiencing person. The challenge is fulfilled through examples, narrative descriptions, dialogues, stories, poems, artwork, journals and diaries, autobiographical logs, and other personal documents. The heuristic process is congruent with Schopenhauer's (1966) reference to lyric poetry: The depicted is "also at the same time the depicter" (p. 248), requiring vivid perception, description, and illustration of the experience.

A typical way of gathering material is through an "interview," which often takes the form of dialogues with oneself and co-researchers. Ordinarily, such an interview is not ruled by the clock; rather, it is ruled out by inner experiential time. In dialogue, one is encouraged to permit ideas, thoughts, feelings, and images to unfold and be expressed naturally. One completes the quest when one has had an opportunity to tell his or her story to a point of natural closing.

FORMULATING THE QUESTION

The crucial processes in heuristics—once one understands the values, beliefs, and knowledge inherent in the heuristic paradigm—are as follows: concentrated gazing on something that attracts or compels one into a search for meaning; focusing on a topic or formulation of the question; and using methods of preparing, collecting, organizing, analyzing, and synthesizing data.

All heuristic inquiry begins with the internal search to discover, with an encompassing puzzlement, a passionate desire to know, a devotion and commitment to pursue a question that is strongly connected to one's own identity and selfhood. The awakening of such a question comes through an inward clearing and an intentional readiness and determination to discover a fundamental truth regarding the meaning and essence of one's own experience and that of others.

Discovering a significant problem or question that will hold the wondering gaze and the passionate commitment of the researcher is the essential opening of the heuristic process. It means finding a path. The question, as such, will determine whether or not an authentic and compelling path has opened, one that will sustain the researcher's curiosity, involvement, and participation, with full energy and resourcefulness over a lengthy period of time.

The way in which the investigator poses the question—the words and ordering of the words—will determine what activities and materials will bear on the problem and what one will discover. To design a heuristic research study that will reveal the meanings and essences of a particular human experience in an accurate, comprehensive, and vivid way, it is essential that the question be stated in simple, clear, and concrete terms. It is necessary that the key words and phrases be placed in the proper order. The basic elements of the search are found in the primary words stated in the ordering of the question. The question, as such, should reveal itself immediately and evidently, in a way that one knows what one is seeking. The question itself provides the crucial beginning and meaning, the nature of the searcher's quest. The way in which the investigator poses the question will determine what fundamental events, relationships, and activities will bear on the problem.

The question grows out of an intense interest in a particular problem or theme. The researcher's excitement and curiosity inspire the search. Associations multiply as personal experiences bring the core of the problem into focus. As the fullness of the theme emerges, strands and tangents of it may complicate an articulation of a manageable and specific question. Yet, this process of allowing all aspects to come into awareness is essential to the eventual formulation of a clear question.

The heuristic research question has the following definite characteristics:

1. It seeks to reveal more fully the essence or meaning of a phenomenon of human experience.
2. It seeks to discover the qualitative aspects rather than the quantitative dimensions.
3. It engages one's total self and evokes a personal and passionate involvement and active participation in the process.
4. It does not seek to predict or determine causal relationships.
5. It is illuminated through careful descriptions, illustrations, metaphors, poetry, dialogue, and other creative renderings rather than by measurements, ratings, or scores.

The following are suggested steps in formulating the question:

1. List all aspects of particular interests or topics that represent curiosities or

intrigues for you. Do this freely, jotting down questions and thoughts, even if they are not complete.

2. Cluster the related interests or topics into subthemes.

3. Set aside any subthemes that imply causal relationships. Set aside any subthemes that contain inherent assumptions.

4. Look at all of the remaining subthemes and stay with them until one basic theme or question emerges as central, one that passionately awakens your interest, concern, and commitment.

5. Formulate this basic theme or question in a way that specifies clearly and precisely what it is that you want to know.

Then, as Pearce (1971) exclaimed,

If you hold and serve the question, until all ambiguity is erased and you really believe in your question, it will be answered; the break-point will arrive when you will suddenly be "ready." Then you must put your hand to the plow and not look back; walk out onto the water unmindful of the waves. (p. 108)

In heuristic research, the openness of the researcher in elucidating the question, clarifying its terms, and pointing to its directions provides the essential beginnings of the discovery process. From there, as Kierkegaard (1965) stated so aptly, the researcher must strive to be humble and not hold a single presupposition so as to be in a position to learn more.

HEURISTIC METHODOLOGY

Having formulated the question and defined and delineated its primary terms and meanings, the next step is a careful and disciplined organization of methods of preparing to conduct the study. This step is followed by construction of methods and procedures to guide a collection of data that will illuminate an answer to the question. After the data are collected, they must be organized and presented in a way that depicts and illustrates the themes, meanings, and essences of the experience that has been investigated.

Methods of heuristic research are openended. They point to a process of accomplishing something in a thoughtful and orderly way, a manner of proceeding that guides the researcher. There is no exclusive list that would be appropriate for every heuristic investigation; instead, each research process unfolds in its own way. Initially, methods may be envisioned and constructed that will guide the process through preparation for, collection of, and analysis of data. They facilitate the flow of the investigation and aim toward yielding rich, accurate, and complete depictions of the qualities or constituents of the experience. Keen (1975) remarked, "The goal of every technique is to help the phenomenon *reveal itself more completely* than it does in ordinary experience" (p. 41). Every method or procedure must relate to the question and facilitate collection of data that will disclose the nature, meaning, and essence of the experience.

Bridgman (1950) emphasized that "science is what scientists do. . . . There are as many scientific methods as there are individual scientists" (p. 83). The purpose of a method of scientific inquiry is to obtain an answer to the problem in hand. The working scientist, Bridgman observed, "is not consciously following any prescribed course of action but [rather] feels complete freedom to utilize any method or device, whatever which in the particular situation . . .

seems likely to yield the correct answer" (p. 83).

The heuristic researcher constructs methods that will explicate meanings and patterns of experience relevant to the question, procedures that will encourage open expression and dialogue.

METHODS OF PREPARATION

When I began to study loneliness (Moustakas, 1961, 1972, 1975), it became the center of my world. Everything appeared to be connected with loneliness. I found loneliness everywhere in my waking life—a crucial component of hospitalized children separated from their families, an inherent quality of making decisions that importantly affected others' lives. It became a significant focus of the people I met with in therapy—whatever their presenting problems—and of my reflections on my own life. I recognized loneliness as a crucial component of solitude and creativity. My dreams were filled with lonely awakenings and encounters. I walked the streets at night and noticed especially isolated stars, clouds, trees, and flowers. I once was confronted by municipal police and told that I was violating a local ordinance; lonely, middle-of-the-night sojourns were forbidden. If I did not cease these nocturnal walks, I definitely would be arrested. On one occasion, I was escorted home with rotating flaring lights illuminating my every step.

Loneliness, for a while, was the mainstream of my life and colored everything else or influenced the meaning of everything else. This type of autobiographical immersion provides the initial essential preparation for discovering the nature and essence of a particular experience.

Methods of preparation in heuristic research include the following:

1. Developing a set of instructions that will inform potential co-researchers of the nature of the research design, its purpose and process, and what is expected of them

2. Locating and acquiring the research participants and developing a set of criteria for selection of participants such as age, sex, socioeconomic, and education factors; ability to articulate the experience; cooperation; interest; willingness to make the commitment; enthusiasm; and degree of involvement

3. Developing a contract that includes time commitments; place; confidentiality; informed consent; opportunities for feedback; permission to tape-record; permission to use material in a thesis, dissertation, and/or other publications; and verification of the findings

4. Considering ways of creating an atmosphere or climate that will encourage trust, openness, and self-disclosure

5. Using relaxation-meditation activities to facilitate a sense of comfort, relaxation, and at-homeness

6. Constructing a way of apprising co-researchers of the nature of the heuristic design and its process, that is, the importance of immersion and intervals of concentration and respite

Kelly's (1969) guidance is helpful here:

Each person who participates should at some point be apprised of what the "experimenter" thinks he is doing and what he considers evidence of what. It is of equal importance to ask what the "subject" thinks is being done and what he considers evidence of what. Since this can change during the course of the experiment, it is appropriate to ask "subjects" what their perception of the experimental design was at each important juncture in the experience. (p. 56)

METHODS OF COLLECTING DATA

Heuristic research investigations ordinarily employ an informal conversational approach in which both researchers and co-researchers enter into the process fully. Dialogue aims toward encouraging expression, elucidation, and disclosure of the experience being investigated. Jourard (1968) showed that self-disclosure elicits disclosure. There may be moments in the interview process when primary investigators share experiences that will inspire and evoke richer, fuller, and more comprehensive depictions from co-researchers.

The heart of the heuristic interview is dialogue. In *Disclosing Man to Himself,* Jourard (1968) borrowed from Buber's writings to emphasize that "dialogue is like mutual unveiling, where each seeks to be experienced and confirmed by the other. . . . Such dialogue is likely to occur when the two people believe each is trustworthy and of goodwill" (p. 21). Buber (1965) expanded on the values of dialogue:

> Where the dialogue is fulfilled in its being, between partners who have turned to one another in truth, who express themselves without reserve and are free of the desire for semblance, there is brought into being a memorable common fruitfulness which is to be found nowhere else. At such times, at each such time, the world arises in a substantial way between men who have been seized in their depths and opened out by the dynamic of an elemental togetherness. The interhuman opens out what otherwise remains unopened. (p. 86)

In heuristic interviewing, the data generated are dependent on accurate empathic listening; being open to oneself and co-researchers; being flexible and free to vary procedures to respond to what is required in the flow of dialogue; and being skillful in creating a climate that encourages co-researchers to respond comfortably, accurately, comprehensively, and honestly in elucidating the phenomenon.

Questions that might guide a heuristic interview include the following. What does this person know about the experience? What qualities or dimensions of the experience stand out for the person? What examples are vivid and alive? What events, situations, and people are connected with the experience? What feelings and thoughts are generated by the experience? What bodily states or shifts in bodily presence occur in the experience? What time and space factors affect the person's awareness and meaning of the experience? In the process of exploring these questions with co-researchers,

> We cannot and should not be unaffected by what is said. . . . On the contrary, it is only in relating to the other as one human being to another that interviewing is really possible . . . when the interviewer and the participant are both caught up in the phenomenon being discussed. (Weber, 1986, p. 68)

The researcher must keep in mind throughout the process that the material collected must depict the experience in accurate, comprehensive, rich, and vivid terms. In heuristic research, depictions often are presented in stories, examples, conversations, metaphors, and analogies.

The interview should be tape-recorded and later transcribed. The basic data for illuminating the question and providing a basis for analysis of constituents, themes, and essences of the experience come from transcriptions and notes taken immediately following the interview.

To supplement the interview data, the heuristic researcher also may collect personal documents. Diaries, journals, logs, poetry, and artwork offer additional meaning and depth and also supplement depictions of the experience obtained from observations and interviews.

METHODS OF ORGANIZING AND SYNTHESIZING DATA HEURISTICALLY

Immersion and Incubation

The transcriptions, notes, and personal documents are gathered together and organized by the investigator into a sequence that tells the story of each research participant. This may be done in a variety of ways—from the most recent to the most remote event connected with the experience (or vice versa), in the order of actual collection of data, or in whatever way will facilitate full immersion into the material. Essential to the process of heuristic analysis is intimate knowledge of all the material for each participant and for the group of participants collectively. The task involves timeless immersion inside the data, with intervals of resting and returning to the data. The condition of again and again—of repetition—is essential until intimate knowledge is obtained.

Organizing and analyzing heuristic data during the immersion and incubation process may take many forms. Clark (1987), in his study of the psychologically androgynous male, described the process over a period of 5 months. Gradually, the core themes and patterns began to emerge and take shape. To convey a direct contact with the process, I include the following excerpt from Clark's dissertation:

I listened to the interview tapes for several weeks before beginning to take notes on them. Very detailed notes were done on each take including extensive quoting and notes on the affect of the co-researcher as he provided the data.

After immersing in the tape and notes of each co-researcher for some time, I developed a reflective portrait of each and contacted him for feedback on the portrait. I received very positive responses. Three co-researchers added information or emphases on certain aspects of the experience, which were then included in their portraits.

The clustering process utilized to place the data before me in one viewable panorama required many days of painstaking work transferring the essential components of the reflective portraits to a six foot by six foot diagram. This was the androgyny map. . . . This resulted in a diagram of over two hundred components of the experience of the psychologically androgynous male. As the map grew, the color-coding system used to cluster related ideas revealed a system of quadrants. Some individual aspects of the experience appeared in more than one quadrant, but each quadrant represented a unique thematic matrix of closely connected components of psychological androgyny. The process of watching these quadrants take shape was fascinating. When the androgyny map was complete, I spent several weeks alternately immersing myself in studying it and incubating by attending to other interests. During this time, many shifts occurred in my perception of the map, and I began to note themes and relationships between ideas which had not been apparent previously. (pp. 94-96)

Illumination and Explication

Once full knowledge of an experience is ingested and understood, the researcher enters into a process of illumination in which essential qualities and themes are discovered. This is followed by an elucidation and explication of the themes until an *individual depiction* of the meanings and essences of the experience investigated can be constructed. The individual depiction may include descriptive narrative, examples, and verbatim exemplary material drawn from the data. It also may include verbatim conversations, poetry, and artwork. From the individual depictions, a *composite depiction* of the experience is constructed. Then, the heuristic researcher returns to the individual co-researchers. Through immersion and analysis of the individual data, two or three *exemplary portraits* are developed, that is, profiles that are unique yet still embrace and characterize the group as a whole.

The Creative Synthesis

Finally, the heuristic researcher develops a *creative synthesis,* that is, an original integration of the material that reflects the researcher's intuition, imagination, and personal knowledge of the meanings and essences of the experience. The creative synthesis may take the form of a lyric poem, a song, a narrative description, a story, a metaphoric tale, or an artwork.

To sum up, the data are used to develop individual depictions, a composite depiction, exemplary portraits of individual persons, and a creative synthesis of the experience. In this way, the experience is illuminated. A creative vision of the experience is offered, and unlike the case with most research studies, the individual persons remain intact and fully alive in the experience.

Outline Guide of Procedures for Analysis of Data

1. In the first step in organization, handling, and synthesizing, the researcher gathers all of the data from one participant (e.g., recording, transcript, notes, journal, personal documents, poems, artwork).

2. The researcher enters into the material in timeless immersion until it is fully understood. Knowledge of the individual participant's experience, as a whole and in its detail, is comprehensively apprehended by the researcher.

3. The data are set aside for a while, encouraging an interval of rest and return to the data, procedures that facilitate the awakening of fresh energy and perspective. Then, after again reviewing all of the material derived from one individual, the researcher takes notes, identifying the qualities and themes manifested in the data. Further study and review of the data and notes enables the heuristic researcher to construct an individual depiction of the experience. The individual depiction retains the language and includes examples drawn from the individual co-researcher's experience of the phenomenon. It includes qualities and themes that encompass the research participant's experience.

4. The next step requires a return to the original data of the individual co-researcher. Does the individual depiction of the experience fit the data from which it was developed? Does it contain the qualities and themes essential to the experience? If it does, then the researcher is ready to move on to the next co-researcher. If not, then the individual depiction must be revised to include what has been omitted or deleted and what is or is not an essential dimension of the

experience. The individual depiction also may be shared with the research participant for affirmation of its comprehensiveness and accuracy and for suggestions for deletion and addition.

5. When the preceding steps have been completed, the heuristic researcher undertakes the same course of organization and analysis of the data for each research participant until an individual depiction of each co-researcher's experience of the phenomenon has been constructed.

6. The individual depictions, representing each co-researcher's experience, are gathered together. The researcher again enters into an immersion process, with intervals of rest, until the *universal* qualities and themes of the experience are thoroughly internalized and understood. At a timely point in the development of the researcher's knowledge and readiness, the researcher constructs a composite depiction that represents the universal or common qualities and themes that embrace the experience of the co-researchers. The composite depiction (i.e., group depiction reflecting the experience of individual participants) should include exemplary narratives, descriptive accounts, conversations, illustrations, and verbatim excerpts that accentuate the flow, spirit, and life inherent in the experience. The composite depiction should be vivid, accurate, alive, and clear and also should encompass the core qualities and themes inherent in the experience. It should include all of the core meanings of the phenomenon as experienced by the individual participants and by the group as a whole.

7. The heuristic researcher again returns to the raw material derived from each co-researcher's experience and the individual depictions derived from the raw material. From these data, the researcher selects two or three participants who clearly exemplify the group as a whole. The researcher then develops individual portraits of these persons using the raw data, the individual depiction, and autobiographical material that was gathered during preliminary contacts and meetings or that is contained in personal documents or was shared during the interviews. The individual portraits should be presented in such a way that both the phenomenon investigated and the individual persons emerge as real.

8. The final step in heuristic presentation and handling of data is the development of a creative synthesis of the experience. The creative synthesis encourages a wide range of freedom in characterizing the phenomenon. It invites a recognition of tacit intuitive awareness of the researcher, knowledge that has been incubating over months through processes of immersion, illumination, and explication of the phenomenon investigated. The researcher as scientist-artist develops an aesthetic rendition of the themes and essential meanings of the phenomenon. The researcher taps into imaginative and contemplative sources of knowledge and light in synthesizing the experience and in presenting the discovery of essences—peaks and valleys, highlights and horizons. In the creative synthesis, there is a free reign of thought and feeling that supports the researcher's knowledge, passion, and presence. This infuses the work with a personal, professional, and literary value that can be expressed through a narrative, story, poem, artwork, metaphor, analogy, or tale.

This presentation of heuristic research design and methodology has embraced beliefs, values, theory, concepts, processes, and methods that are essential to an understanding and conduct of heuristic research and discovery. Additional parameters of heuristics may be found in my chapter, "Heuristic Research" (Moustakas, 1967);

in my chapter, "Heuristic Methods of Obtaining Knowledge" (Moustakas, 1981); and in our article, "Heuristic Inquiry" (Douglass & Moustakas, 1985).

CREATING THE RESEARCH MANUSCRIPT

Once heuristic interviews have been completed, transcribed, organized, depicted, and synthesized, the research is nearing completion. It is time to present the research process and findings in a form that can be understood and used. I have developed an outline for the manuscript, a guide for presentation of the work of a heuristic investigation. I offer it as one way of bringing together an experience that has profoundly affected the investigator and that holds possibilities for scientific knowledge and social impact and meaning.

Introduction and statement of topic and question. Out of what ground of concerns, knowledge, and experience did the topic emerge? What stands out—one or two critical incidents in your life that created the puzzlement, curiosity, and passion to know? Does the topic have social relevance? How would new knowledge contribute to your profession? To you as a person and as a learner? State your question and elucidate the terms.

Review the literature. Discuss the computer search, databases, descriptors, key words, and years covered. Organize the review to include an *introduction* that presents the topic reviewed and its significance and that provides an overview of the methodological problems; *methods* that describe what induced you to include the published study in your review and how the studies were conducted; *themes* that cluster into patterns and organize the presentation of

findings; and a *summary* of core findings relevant to your research that differentiate your investigation from those in the literature review with regard to the question, model, methodology, and knowledge sought.

Methodology. List and discuss methods and procedures developed in *preparing* to conduct the study; in *collecting* the data; and in *organizing, analyzing, and synthesizing* the data.

Presentation of data. Include verbatim examples that illustrate the collection of data and their analysis and synthesis. Discuss thematic structures and illustrate. Include depictions of the experience as a whole as well as exemplary portraits that are vivid, comprehensive, alive, and accurate. In the presentation of data, include individual depictions, a comprehensive depiction, two or three exemplary individual portraits, and a creative synthesis.

Summary, implications, and outcomes. Summarize your study in brief vivid terms, from its inception to its final synthesis of data. Now that your investigation has been completed, how in fact do your findings differ from findings presented in your literature review? What future studies might you or others conduct as an outcome of your research? Suggest a design for one or two future studies. What implications of your findings are relevant to society? To your profession? To you as a learner and as a person? Write a brief creative conclusion that speaks to the essence of your study and its significance to you and others.

CLOSING REFLECTIONS

This has been a lengthy journey. The heuristic process is rooted in experiential time, not clock time. Once one enters into the quest for knowledge and understanding, once one begins the passionate search for the illumination of a puzzlement, the intensity, wonder, intrigue, and engagement carry one along through ever-growing levels of meaning and excitement. It is as if a new internal time rhythm has awakened, one rooted in a particular absorption and in a sustaining gaze, a rhythm that must take its own course and that will not be satisfied or fulfilled until a natural closing occurs and the rhythm has carried out its intent and purpose.

Heuristic research processes include moments of meaning, understanding, and discovery that the researcher will forever hold onto and savor. Feelings, thoughts, ideas, and images have awakened that will return again and again. A connection has been made that will forever remain unbroken and that will serve as a reminder of a lifelong process of knowing and being. Polanyi (1962) touched on this relationship in the following passage:

> Having made a discovery, I shall never see the world again as before. My eyes have become different; I have made myself into a person seeing and thinking differently. I have crossed a gap, the heuristic gap, which lies between problem and discovery. (p. 142)

REFERENCES

Bridgman, P. (1950). *Reflections of a physicist*. New York: Philosophical Library.

Buber, M. (1965). *The knowledge of man*. New York: Harper & Row.

Clark, J. (1987). *The experience of the psychologically androgynous mate*. Ann Arbor, MI: University Microfilms International.

Douglass, B., & Moustakas, C. (1985). Heuristic inquiry: The intimate search to know. *Journal of Humanistic Psychology, 25*(3), 39-55.

Jourard, S. (1968). *Disclosing man to himself*. New York: Van Nostrand Reinhold.

Keen, E. (1975). *A primer on phenomenological psychology*. New York: Holt, Rinehart & Winston.

Kelly, G. A. (1969). Humanistic methodology in psychological research. *Journal of Humanistic Psychology, 11*(l), 53-65.

Kierkegaard, S. (1965). *The point of view for my work as an author* (B. Nelson, Ed.). New York: Harper & Row.

Moustakas, C. (1961). *Loneliness*. Englewood Cliffs, NJ: Prentice Hall.

Moustakas, C. (1967). Heuristic research. In J. F. T. Bugental (Ed.), *Challenges of humanistic psychology* (pp. 101-107). New York: McGraw-Hill.

Moustakas, C. (1972). *Loneliness and love*. Englewood Cliffs, NJ: Prentice Hall.

Moustakas, C. (1975). *The touch of loneliness*. Englewood Cliffs, NJ: Prentice Hall.

Moustakas, C. (1981). Heuristic methods of obtaining knowledge. In C. Moustakas, *Rhythms, rituals, and relationships* (chap. 4). Detroit, MI: Center for Humanistic Studies.

Pearce, J. C. (1971). *The crack in the cosmic egg*. New York: Julian.

Polanyi, M. (1962). *Personal knowledge*. Chicago: University of Chicago Press.

Schopenhauer, A. (1966). *The world as will and representation* (E. F. J. Payne, Trans.). New York: Dove.

Weber, S. J. (1986). The nature of interviewing. *Phenomenology and Pedagogy, 4*(2), 65-72.

SELECTED HEURISTIC STUDIES*

Cheyne, V. (1988). *Growing up in a fatherless home: The female experience*. Ann Arbor, MI: University Microfilms International.

Craig, E. (1978). *The heart of the teacher: A heuristic study of the inner world of teaching*. Ann Arbor, MI: University Microfilms International.

Hawka, S. (1985). *The experience of feeling unconditionally loved*. Ann Arbor, MI: University Microfilms International.

MacIntyre, M. (1981). *The experience of shyness*. Ann Arbor, MI: University Microfilms International.

McNally, C. (1982). *The experience of being sensitive*. Ann Arbor, MI: University Microfilms International.

Rodriguez, A. (1984). *A heuristic phenomenological investigation of Mexican American ethnic identity*. Ann Arbor, MI: University Microfilms International.

Rourke, P. (1983). *The experience of being inspired*. Ann Arbor, MI: University Microfilms International.

Schultz, D. (1982). *The experience of self-reclamation of former Catholic religious women*. Ann Arbor, MI: University Microfilms International.

Shaw, R. (1989). *Interaction rhythms in intimate relations*. Unpublished dissertation, Union for Experimenting Colleges and Universities, Cincinnati, OH.

Snyder, J. (1988). *The experience of really feeling connected with nature*. Ann Arbor, MI: University Microfilms International.

Snyder, R. (1988). *Rejecting love*. Unpublished dissertation, Union for Experimenting Colleges and Universities, Cincinnati, OH.

Vaughn, L. (1989). *The experience of poetry*. Unpublished dissertation, Union for Experimenting Colleges and Universities, Cincinnati, OH.

*For a more recent list, the reader may wish to consult Moustakas, C. (1990) *Heuristic Research: Design, Methodology, and Applications*. Newbury Park, CA: Sage.

CHAPTER 21

Narrative Research and Humanism

RUTHELLEN JOSSELSON AND AMIA LIEBLICH

THE RECENT burgeoning of interest in narrative inquiry in the social sciences reflects a deep discontent with the sterile legacy of logical positivistic, objectified discourse in relation to human experience. As psychology has evolved into the study of neurological and cognitive processes, personality traits distributed among five factors, and the behavior of undergraduates in contrived situations, consideration of enduring dilemmas of the human condition has been eclipsed. "It seems as if a lot of people have been waking up after a long and strange slumber, asking: Why don't we study people?" (Freeman, 1998, p. 27).

Although rooted in quite a different philosophical tradition, narrative approaches to understanding people share common ground with humanistic psychology and can be seen as a present-day heir to this tradition. Like humanism, narrative psychology attempts to restore the experiencing person to the center of interest and to regard the person as complex, unified, and existing in context.

Although classical approaches in humanistic psychology objected to research, the type of research they found objectionable was that based in objectification of others, exemplified by the laboratory experiment or the forced-choice questionnaire. Humanism necessitated a fundamental change in the approach to research before it could be viewed as consistent with the values and ideals to which a humanistic psychology aspired. In this chapter, we attempt to show that the approach inherent in narrative forms of research, a movement that has been growing throughout the past two decades, provides a means of making the humanistic enterprise empirical.

Narrative psychology and humanism are allied in taking issue with the fragmented, variable-oriented, objectified approaches to understanding that have grown out of psychology's emulation of the philosophy and methodology of 19th-century physics. For both, the aim is greater understanding rather than prediction and control. Fundamentally, narrative approaches stand in opposition to logical positivism and take as a rallying cry the postmodern critique of positivism. Rooted in hermeneutics and phenomenology, narrative psychology regards meaning making as central and requires reflexivity about the process, both within the person being studied and within the person doing the study. Narrative discourse recognizes the contextual nature of all knowing and focuses on the phenomenology of the actor, his or her intentions and self-understanding.

Partly out of disillusion with the often trivializing boundaries of positivistic empirical research, and partly in response to the feminist critique of research that privileges certain cultural positions and excludes the voices of women and others who have been outside the mainstream, psychological researchers have begun to resurrect narrative as a way of trying to grasp the complexity of the individual living in society, culture, and historical time. Within contemporary psychology, Bruner (1986) has most championed the legitimization of what he called "narrative modes of knowing." This mode privileges the particulars of lived experience rather than logical positivistic constructs about variables and classes. It is an effort to approach the understanding of lives in context rather than through a prefigured and narrowing lens. Meaning is not inherent in an act or experience but rather is constructed through social discourse. Meaning is generated by the linkages that the participant makes between aspects of the life he or she is living and by the explicit linkages that the researcher makes between this understanding and interpretation, which is meaning constructed at another level of analysis.

The so-called narrative turn has marked all of the social sciences. Over the past 15 years or so, narrative research and the concepts of narrative and life story have become increasingly prominent in a wide area of human and social sciences—psychology, education, sociology, and history, to name just a few. Besides being used to explore specific topics, narrative studies are flourishing as a means of understanding personal identity, life course development, culture, and the historical world of the narrator.

In psychology, these new paradigms, in contrast to the traditional ones, have as their aims understanding and describing rather than measuring and predicting, focusing on meaning rather than on causation and frequency, interpretation rather than statistical analysis, and recognizing the importance of language and discourse rather than reducing to numerical representation. These approaches are holistic rather than atomistic, concern themselves with particularity rather than with universals, are interested in the cultural context rather than trying to be context free, and give overarching significance to subjectivity rather than questing for some type of objectivity (Smith, Harré, & Langenhove, 1995).

Narrative psychology, being still relatively young as a discipline, is in the early stages of wrestling with problems that humanists have debated for some time. What are the implications of considering the whole person as a unit of analysis? How can we know that our observations are "reliable," and how can we generalize about them to some broader—or more abstract—level of analysis? What are the ethical implications of encountering another person for the purpose of writing about him or her? What are the criteria for a good study within the narrative paradigm? How can we create a theoretical system that is faithful to the particularity of the individual and still offers a systematized replicable form of knowledge?

PHILOSOPHICAL FOUNDATIONS OF NARRATIVE APPROACHES

In opposition to the hegemony of logical positivism, which grounds the authority of science in the presumption of a value-free objective view of empirical phenomena, postmodern hermeneutical approaches to science recognize the relativism of truth claims and the social construction of all aspects of human experience. Psychology, then, is reconceived as "an interpretive science in search of meaning, not an experimental science in search of laws" (Geertz, 1973, p. 5). The hermeneutic school of philosophy and the developing narrative tradition in the social sciences posit a relativistic universe in which all interpretation is inherently grounded in shifting and contestable readings of texts. Broadly conceived, the narrative umbrella covers researchers who work from a variety of interpretive stances including phenomenology, symbolic interactionism, social constructionism, and feminism.

All human social interaction is mediated through language. As Gadamer put it, "Being that can be understood is language" (cited in Gardiner, 1992, p. 113). Hence, all knowledge ultimately is rooted in the apperception and translation of texts that are formed by and constitutive of the world that they seek to portray.

Here is where hermeneutics and humanism are most at odds. Whereas some humanistic theorists regard the human as self-authoring and self-actualizing, a postmodern orientation regards the person and his or her world as inextricably linked and mutually constitutive (Sass, 1988). Thus, there is no pure subjectivity. Human experience is built out of shared contexts for meaning making, all expressed in and transformed by language.

Even if subjectivity is not sui generis, however, it remains central to narrative investigation. Embedded within personal narratives are the threads of culturally derived possibility and individual transformation of these. People are regarded as multilayered, multivocal, and multidetermined. Like humanism, hermeneutics eschews dualities and exclusive categories, focusing instead on the processes of human experi-

ence and their interaction, both internally and externally.

Rather than taking physics as a model, the approaches of narrative analysis have more in common with literary theory and linguistics. It was the Russian literary critic and philosophical anthropologist Mikhail Bakhtin who brought the term *dialogic* to the history of ideas. This term has captured the imaginations of scholars in a multitude of disciplines. The notion of the dialogic as it exists in narratives or texts provides a way of thinking about the foundation of all human knowing in language. In Bakhtin's view, all forms of human interaction are mediated by our dialogic relation to others. Consciousness itself presumes an "otherness" and an "answerability." The self also is a dialogic relation. The dialogic implies a necessary multiplicity in human awareness, all constructed as a polyphonic text (Bakhtin, 1986). Understanding of people, like understanding of literature, becomes a process of textual analysis.

> Is it possible to find any other approach to [man] and his life than through the signifying text that he has created or is creating? . . . Everywhere the actual or possible text and its understanding. Research becomes inquiry and conversation, that is, dialogue. (p. 113)

It was concordant with hermeneutic developments in intellectual history that interest in narrative was renewed in the social sciences. Viewing people as texts allowed for the recognition of the multiple experiences of the self and social reality that constitute human complexity.

THE REACTION AGAINST METHODOLATRY

Whereas logical positivistic science has given rise to a preoccupation with method over meaning, often resulting in obscure trivial investigations that idealize statistical procedures but stray far from concern with the people being studied, narrative approaches have, at least so far, avoided becoming paradigmatic in terms of method. The hope is that "the play of ideas free of authoritative paradigms" (Marcus & Fischer, 1986, pp. 80-81) will lead us to "some new way of producing and legitimating knowledge" (Lather, 1992, p. 96). There continues to be scholarly acceptance of diverse means of producing such knowledge.

What characterizes these approaches is reflexivity, expressed in a public consideration of what one is trying to know and how one is trying to know it and an equally important focus on the characteristics of the knower that affect his or her knowing. Rather than being equipped with a tool box of "instruments" or a prescribed form of "experimentation," narrative researchers attempt to know people in their own frameworks and often include the "observed" as partners in their studies. Interviews, diaries, artworks, and other forms of testimony become the raw data on which narrative researchers attempt to ground their analyses. Narrative researchers reflect on their interactions with the people who participate in their studies and the effect these people might have had on them. The person or people being studied are conceptualized as co-investigators (Hermans & Bonarius, 1991) rather than as people who are being "subjected" to something by faceless investigators.

Within this context, the interview is a primary mode of investigation and draws on humanistic principles for its rationale. Use of the interview is premised on the humanistic belief that people who are unified sovereign subjects contain knowledge that one may have access to by engaging in free and unconstrained conversation. The interviewer attempts to be fully present and in an empathic stance (Josselson, 1995). The interviewer's orientation is phenomenological, with attention focused on the essences of the experiences put forth.

HUMAN LIFE IS LIKE A STORY

Narrative psychology takes as its premise that human experience can be understood only in language and that experience itself is shaped in story form. Events of significance to a person are textualized in a way that employs temporality and causation as well as meaning.

The linguistic emphasis in some branches of narrative inquiry considers the ways in which language organizes both thought and experience. Other researchers recognize the shaping function of language but treat language as transparent as they focus more on the content of meanings that may be created out of life events. Furthermore, within this perspective, there is a continuum between taking the person's narrative at face value as the "narrative truth" and searching for hidden (possibly unconscious) meanings and intentions.

One of the points of concordance between narrative research and humanistic theory is in avoiding having a predetermined theory about the person that the interview or life story is expected to support. Although no one is entirely free of preconceived ideas and expectations, narrative researchers try to come to their narrators as listeners, open to the surprising variations in their social worlds and private lives. In her critique of psychology as a "cruel" field, Apter (1996) deconstructed Freud's Dora case in a manner demonstrating that "Freud tried to inflict his interpretation on her. He heard her own story as a lie, a subterfuge . . . , but in truth he was waiting for sufficient information to prove his own theories" (pp. 4, 24-25). Although narrative researchers try to be as knowledgeable as possible about the themes they are studying so as to be maximally sensitive to nuances of meaning (Kvale, 1996), they are on guard against the "cruel" stance of inflicting meaning in the service of their own ends.

The humanistic focus on the individual as a meaning-making creature is foregrounded in narrative psychology's concern about the way in which the life story is a meaning-creating enterprise. The experience of the self would be impossible without the selection and linkages of moments of life experience that create the life story. Identity is itself a story (McAdams, 1988) of how one has become who one is, the choices one has made, and the various ways in which one has embedded oneself in the social world. Living involves continually constructing and reconstructing stories without knowing their outcomes, that is, revising the plot as new events are added. The self, then, consists of a configuring of "personal events into a historical unity which includes not only what one has been but also anticipations of what one will be" (Polkinghorne, 1988, p. 150). Meaning lies in the contextual interpretations that people give to the various events of their lives, and the goal of narrative psychology is to interpret these interpretations at some higher level of abstraction.

In 1982, Donald Spence rocked the foundations of psychoanalytic thought by raising the question of whether psychoanalysts really were engaged in the archaeological project of unearthing the historical past or, instead, could be better described as pursuing a narrative task—shaping bits of memory, fantasy, and association into a coherent and plausible story. The work of psychoanalysis, in his view, is on meanings communicated and altered through language—a hermeneutic project. Following his argument in *Narrative Truth and Historical Truth* (Spence, 1982), narrative researchers began to rethink the whole enterprise of developmental psychology. Is it the events that shape the person, or are the idiosyncratic and cultural meanings assigned to them even more determinative of the individual's development?

Within this framework, a science of behavior apart from its contexts and intentions is impossible (MacIntyre, 1997). The unity of the individual life resides in a construction of its narrative, a form in which hopes, dreams, despairs, doubts, plans, and emotions all are phrased.

APPROACHES TO NARRATIVE RESEARCH

Within the dominant logical-positivistic research paradigms of their day, both Carl Rogers and Abraham Maslow attempted to devise modes of inquiry that would implement the humanistic agenda. Rogers's research often was qualitative, demonstrating the self-pictures of clients and their changes during therapy by using extracts from their recorded verbalizations while in therapy. Some of the works of Rogers and his students, however, used quantitative content analysis, sorting verbalizations into categories formulated according to the theory and counting their frequencies at various stages of the therapeutic process. Moreover, Rogers adopted the Q-sort technique as a method for systematically studying the notions of the person about himself or herself. Starting from a set of statements to be sorted in prearranged distribution (from most to least descriptive of the self), such data were treated by correlational methods and multivariate analyses. Using the frameworks available, Rogers and his students made heroic efforts to confirm and support his humanistic theory. With the vantage point of hindsight, however, it is doubtful that these quantifying efforts were justified or even suitable to the basic theoretical assumptions underlying this research.

Maslow, who has been more critical of science (Maslow, 1966), produced empirical work in the spirit of narrative research. Philosophically, he objected to the adequacy of mechanical science, as represented by behaviorism, for studying the person as a whole. Humanistic science, which he advocated, was proposed as the only possible approach to questions of value, individuality, consciousness, ethics, and purpose. Accordingly, Maslow's empirical study was a holistic qualitative research of the life courses of healthy people whom he defined as self-actualizers.

Looking generally at Bugental's (1967) original compendium, *Challenges of Humanistic Psychology,* one is struck by the fact that the concepts of narrative or life story are not even part of the discourse of that period of time. Most of the chapters of the book deal with philosophy and therapy, and what attention is given to research still is firmly lodged within the positivistic paradigm. The studies presented as humanistic research were, during that period, very concerned with control, prediction, replicability, and experimental validity. Although there was some effort to think about the effects of the experimenter, writers were quite far from considering the possibility of an open dialogic between researcher and participant that characterizes contemporary narrative research.

The resurgence of interest in language and the poststructural view of people as texts have created space for narrative research to reinvigorate a consideration of the particularity and wholeness of people in the process of living their lives. *Narrative research,* according to our definition, refers to any study based on discourse or on peo-

ple's verbal accounts of their experiences. Such a story need not compose a complete autobiography; it may be short descriptive statements or narratives, formed in the teller's personal language and style, in response to the researcher's open-ended question. Thus, the data may be a complete long monologue provided in response to the instruction, "Please tell me about your life as you remember it," or it may be a much shorter narrative given in response to the question, "What is your earliest memory?" or "What was your experience during the trip [or the war, or your first year at college, etc.]?" Narrative material also can be spontaneous such as the stories children tell their mothers when coming home from nursery school. Narrative data include both oral and written accounts. The common aspect of all these narratives is that the material is offered in the natural language of the teller and is created through his or her individual experience and judgment. Although the researcher may have some previously formed ideas about the topic that naturally provide the rationale for his or her asking and listening, no direct attempt is made to put the verbal responses of the teller in specific form or in predetermined categories. The narrator is free to construct and author his or her stories—the narrator is given the status of expert—while the researcher is there to learn from the narrator's experience.

Narrative researchers employ an empathic stance to gather data. In the spirit of postmodernism, current narrative research assumes that there is neither a single absolute truth in human reality nor one correct reading or interpretation of a life story or text. Instead, the narrative research approach is oriented toward subjectivity, intentionality, pluralism, relativism, holism, and contextuality. Although these aspects are somewhat overlapping and interrelated, they certainly are not identical. The next section attempts to clarify their distinctiveness.

The Empathic Stance

In her analysis of the history of science, Keller (1985) distinguished between the traditions based in a Baconian model of knowing (which is oriented toward prediction and control) and Platonic knowing (which is metaphorically based in eros, union, transcendence, and love). Both humanism and narrative are rooted in the Platonic approach, which regards knowledge as transcendence, that is, the overcoming of distance between the knower and the known. Ideally, a narrative research interview is an "encounter," in which the listener accepts the story with complete respect and refrains from judging or evaluating it. What makes this possible is the empathic stance, in which aspects of what is to be known are invited to permeate the knower, who attempts to "imagine the real" by making the other present (Buber, 1965). Research then becomes a process of overcoming distance rather than creating it—moving what was other, through our understanding of its independent selfhood and experience, into relation with us. Thus, the very indeterminacy between subject and object becomes a resource rather than a threat. Empathy is recruited into understanding precisely because its continuity and receptivity allows for a clearer perception of others. We aim to reach the internal array of an other's experience, always bounded by our shared participation in a matrix of signification (Josselson, 1995).

As both a tool and a goal of psychological research, empathy is premised on continuity, recognizing that kinship between self and other offers an opportunity for a deeper and more articulated understanding. Empathy becomes an attitude of attention to the real world based in an effort to connect ourselves to it rather than to distance ourselves from it. The empathic stance, taking hermeneutics as its epistemological ground, affords the possibility of interpreting others who themselves are engaged in the process of interpreting themselves.

On Subjectivity

Experience as lived, the inner world of a woman or a man—this is the essence of what narrative research tries to reach. In this subjective realm, people may experience freedom and choice—or the absence thereof—without being confronted with the question of whether this really is the case (objectively speaking). The narrator is seen as the author of his or her story and is encouraged to share it for the research purpose as a unique individual creation.

Postmodernism regards subjectivity as neither unified nor fixed but rather as a site for conflicting social forces that continually reshape the sense of identity. Humanism, by contrast, tends to regard subjectivity as a given—a creation of the individual and an expression of his or her freedom. Narrative approaches regard subjectivity in a more inclusive way, privileging the person's experience of subjectivity and analyzing both its personal and sociocultural elements. Thus, the narrative researcher is mindful of, and will present, both what the person studied says about his or her experience (the phenomenology) and the researcher's own interpretation of it.

In this interpretation, the narrative researcher pays particular attention to aspects of the person's experience that relate to his or her socially constructed position in life, a position that might feel self-authored to the person but may actually be a product of the person's place in his or her culturally constituted world. For example, Chase (1995), in a study of women school superintendents, showed how submerged stories of gendered social processes are embedded in the gaps and contradictions of an interview.

Recognizing that people are not fully the authors of their lives in that they are subjected to historical and personal facts of life (e.g., age, nationality, affluence/poverty) and relationally constituted regimes of meaning that attach to their multiple and shifting identity locations (Lather, 1992), narrative research honors the fact that people, nevertheless, are engaged in the process of creating selves out of these experiences within which they can regard themselves as coherent and continuous beings. It is to both of these facets that narrative work turns its attention. In so doing, narrative research recognizes that "the better a person understands the degree to which he is externally determined, the closer he comes to understanding and exercising his real freedom" (Bakhtin, 1986, p. 139).

Narrative approaches to research attempt to grapple with the complexity of subjectivity rather than reducing it to its component parts. This complexity is essential to the hermeneutic enterprise.

> Human subjectivity cannot be understood as an analyzable combination of isolable and fully specifiable mental entities or aspects that either do or do not exist in a determinate fashion (or that exist to a specifiable degree). It is, rather, an interweaving texture of only partially specifiable themes and backgrounds that exist at various levels of implicit and explicit awareness, often merging imperceptibly with one another. (Sass, 1988, p. 245)

Subjectivity, then, is regarded in a holistic fashion.

Intentionality

Narrative research regards the individual as intentional. The focus of research is on what the individual thinks he or she is doing and why the individual thinks he or she is doing so. Behavior, then, always is understood in context—in the individual's context, however he or she may construct it. Even in the production of a life history, the individual is seen as an active agent who chooses the events to include in a web of meaning that links these events (Gergen & Gergen, 1997). This approach is in contrast to the mechanistic view of traditional psychology, which regards the individual as a repository of lawful and determined responses conditioned by reflexes, conditioning, schemata, and so on. From this vantage point, psychology fails to appreciate the individual as a historical entity who creates meaning over time by idiosyncratically linking events. Thus, the experimenter in a traditional psychological research project is armed with carefully observed measurements of behavior but has no capacity to say why a person behaved as he or she did. Individual differences in the construction of meaning around an experiment is what is commonly referred to as *error.*

This significant difference in approach to understanding people obtains even in an experimental procedure as dramatic as the classic Milgram scenario. Undeniably, Milgram, in one of the most memorable and important experimental demonstrations in the history of psychology, raised questions about the abuse of authority. He showed that a frightening number of people would administer potentially lethal shocks when asked to do so, but he left unexplored a deeper understanding of why people thought they were doing what they were doing. To a narrative life history researcher, the interesting question would be to what people attribute their obedient or disobedient actions and what effect taking part in this experiment might have had on the participants' lives.

Relativism

Although postmodern philosophy and epistemology currently is bedeviled by the problems of its relativistic perspective, and because writers are engaged in trying to locate a reality outside the text or to deny its existence (Carr, 1997; Held, 1995; Lather, 1992), most narrative research tends to regard storied life experience as given, disregarding (or at least sidestepping) considerations of its factual worth or reliability.

Our own view of the narrative does not advocate total relativism and does not treat life stories as though they were fictional texts. It is not that we take narratives at face value, that is, as complete and accurate representations of reality. We believe that stories usually are constructed within a certain culture and language and around a core of historical and life events. Taking into consideration these limitations on complete individual freedom, however, there still is a wide canvas for flexibility and creativity in selection of, addition to, emphasis on, and interpretation of these "facts of life" or "cultural givens."

Furthermore, a life story obtained in an interview is regarded as just one instance of the life history, which develops and changes through time and context. "The particular life story is one (or more) instance of the polyphonic versions of the possible constructions or presentations of people's selves and lives, which they use according to specific momentary influences" (Lieblich, Tuval-Mashiach, & Zilber, 1998, p. 8).

A specific aspect of relativism regards the manner in which narrative research approaches the dimension of time. Although many studies ask the narrator to provide a report of past events and experiences, an essential assumption of narrative research methodology is that the past can be viewed only through a window of the present, leading to a selection of "memories" and determining their meanings for the teller today. The past always is understood in the context of the present in which it is remembered. Past events do not exist (or do not interest us as psychologists) separately from the self remembering in the present.

Holism

Although traditional research with verbal texts often used the method of coded content analysis, taking the stories apart and assembling sections by categories, this approach now is criticized by narrative researchers, who prefer to look at a story as a whole and read it in its entirety. Gilligan and her coworkers (Brown et al., 1988) developed a method for reading a narrative for the various voices that tend to appear and disappear in a text of a single interviewee. In following the "private" voice versus the "public" voice in a girl's story, for example, the changing emphases and the interplay of these two dimensions are studied within the whole story, not as separate elements.

The complete verbal product of a research participant can be interpreted by focusing on its major themes or its form and structure (Lieblich et al., 1998). Silences and omissions also are considered (Rosenthal, 1993), and Rogers and colleagues (1999) went so far as to try to develop a "language of the unsayable." Both explicit and implicit themes are analyzed, as is their interrelationship in the text. Thus, an individual story is considered holistically in terms of its themes and patterns before or instead of focusing on between-individual comparisons. When comparisons between people are attempted, an effort is made to preserve the holistic stance rather than reducing people to a single trait or behavioral tendency isolated from the total person.

Contextuality

Life history in narrative research is understood in contextualized terms. The person is assumed to be speaking from a specific position in culture and in historical time. Some of this positionality is reflected in the use of language and concepts with which a person understands his or her life. Other aspects of context are made explicit as the researcher is mindful of the person's experience of himself or herself in terms of gender, race, culture, age, social class, sexual orientation, and so on. A participant is viewed as a unique individual with particularity in terms of social location; a person is not viewed as representative of some universal and interchangeable, randomly selected "subject."

Stories told are embedded in the tellers' cultures and take for their models basic cultural themes, plots, and forms (Gergen & Gergen, 1997). Narrative approaches try to regard a story as told in terms of the possible stories culturally available for telling. Narrative research also is attentive to the context in which the story is narrated. Beyond the fact that different goals or opening questions produce different stories, it is understood in the narrative approach to research that all life stories are highly influenced by the persons to whom the stories are told and by the participants' understanding of what they are doing by telling their stories in those particular circumstances. Put differently, life stories are relational; they are deeply affected by the context of the explicit and implicit relationship between researchers and the researched. No two interviewers will get the same story from an individual interviewee. Therefore, a thoroughly reflexive analysis of the parameters and influences on the interview situation replaces concern with reliability.

Another aspect of contextuality regards avoiding unnecessary generalizations. To become a "body of knowledge," academic fields aim at generalizing to construct laws regarding human development and behavior beyond the single case or story, so the field of traditional psychology abounds with aggregated generalizations of various types. As proposed by Runyan (1984), there are three levels of equally significant generalities in a study of lives: what is true of a particular individual across time and place, what is true of groups (e.g., gender, race, historical period), and what is true of all people. Narrative research and humanistic approaches listen to individual voices in their particular natural context and do not strive to go beyond the two first levels, namely generalizing within the individual or to a group of individuals who might share significant aspects of the same context.

In summary, then, narrative research is conducted through an intense or prolonged contact with the field or life situation, with the researcher/observer attempting to maintain an empathic and nonjudgmental approach to those under study. The aim is to gain a holistic overview of the phenomenon under study by capturing data from the inside of the actors with a view to understanding their meaning-making in the contexts within which they live. Narrative researchers recognize that many interpretations of their observations are possible, and they argue their interpretive framework through careful description of what they have observed.

INTERSUBJECTIVITY AND ETHICS

Because the research dyad is the heart of narrative research, much attention has been given to the nature of this relationship. Knowledge is constructed in the inter-subjective space; what is known is a product of what the teller can and will tell and what the listener can hear. Researchers do not try to experience or present themselves as free of bias; they recognize that they operate within a horizon of understanding (Heidegger, 1962) related to their own situation within history and society. Eschewing notions of "scientific neutrality," they self-consciously reflect on what they are doing as they construct and present otherness in their work (Fine, 1994).

Whenever we encounter the story of another person, we are moving "across a border," to use Ruth Behar's phrase. Good narrative research requires that researchers place themselves in the narration of their texts rather than trying to recount others' stories from the points of view of disembodied observers. But this has yet to become widely accepted practice, as researchers remain shy about acknowledging themselves in written reports as persons of a given gender, class, or cultural background or as persons with evident personality quirks or predilections that are inextricably interwoven in both the hearing and re-presentation of "cases."

Notable exceptions to this view are the works of Behar (1993) and Lieblich (1997), both of whom considered their own stories in parallel to those whose lives they were trying to understand. Behar's (1993) work is a single-case anthropological study of Esperanza, a Mexican woman. As the story of Esperanza unfolds from continuing meetings taking place in her kitchen, Behar is becoming aware that they are more similar than she previously had assumed in both personal and cultural spheres. The later chapters of the book daringly reflect on Behar's past roots and present life issues. Thus, with the researcher included in the written study, not only are the readers presented with a richer and more human picture of the other, but also they are invited to form their own dialogues with both the heroine and the writer. Last but not least, in titling her work *Translated Woman*, Behar makes the point that texts and language have their limitations. As much as a researcher might be empathic and close with his or her subject, there always will be a barrier between the two—the barrier of bringing the other across the space between us into our own world, that is, "translating."

Lieblich's (1997) book is a biographical study of a female Jewish writer, Dvora Baron (1887-1956). The book is written as conversations—which never took place in actuality—between the two women. As the author "visits" the bedridden Baron and asks her about various stages in her life and oeuvre, she also discovers and reveals to the readers a new matrix of similarities and oppositions between the two of them. The author's feelings and attitudes toward her protagonist and the whole process of getting to know her are also shared openly with the readers, something that usually is entirely missing from "conventional" biographies. The outcome is a demonstration of knowledge as a subjective relational enterprise, always created and re-created between individuals rather than in isolation.

It probably is not accidental that both Behar and Lieblich may be considered feminist researchers. Many feminist researchers have made central to their work concern with the power relations inherent in all research, and they try to acknowledge these issues in their research.

Concern about the intersubjective nature of narrative research has led many to ponder the ethical implications of making use of people's ongoing lives in the service of "science." When people's scores are aggregated into some statistic for the purposes of quantitative research, there is little worry about possible harm to be done. But when people's lives are publicly dissected and analyzed for the purpose of scholarship, the research itself becomes an influence—and not always a positive one—in their biographies.

Some researchers have pointed out, however, that participation in narrative research, to the extent that it is an authentic encounter, may itself have healing properties (Miller, 1996). The interview may serve as an "aid to self-reflection" (Habermas, 1993, p. 118) and the discovery of self in the dialogue of the interview (Buber, 1970). Others, however, have pointed out that because the most significant truths about human lives inhere in their stories, people who make their stories available to others must be protected (Bakan, 1996). Doing narrative research—working so close to the core meanings and personal truths of people's lives—is an ethically complex undertaking that must be done with careful self-scrutiny (Josselson, 1996). The researcher must be grounded in deeply humanistic ethics.

THE CONVERSATION BETWEEN NARRATIVE AND HUMANISM

For humanism, the ultimate form of interaction is dialogue (Buber, 1970). Within narrative research, dialogue also is central. Narrative discourse involves respectful and open dialogue among three actors: the narrator (whose life and story provide the essence of the work), the scholar (who assumes final responsibility for the published research), and the readers (who are invited to enter into dialogue with the issues under investigation as a way of enlarging their awareness of themselves and of their world).

Whereas humanism evolved to promote human potential, narrative research has developed as a means of studying whole people in context, partly in hopes that such understanding will lead to means to better the human condition. As allies opposed to fragmented, disembodied, decontextualized representations of people in psychology, both humanistic and narrative psychology may profit from an authentic encounter between their proponents.

REFERENCES

Apter, T. (1996). Expert witness: Who controls the psychologist's narrative? In R. Josselson (Ed.), *The narrative study of lives: Vol. 4. Ethics and process* (pp. 22-44). Thousand Oaks, CA: Sage.

Bakan, D. (1996). Some reflections about narrative research and hurt and harm. In R. Josselson (Ed.), *The narrative study of lives: Vol. 4. Ethics and process* (pp. 3-8). Thousand Oaks, CA: Sage.

Bakhtin, M. M. (1986). *Speech genres and other late essays.* Austin: University of Texas Press.

Behar, R. (1993). *Translated woman.* Boston: Beacon.

Brown, L. M., Argyris, D., Atanucci, J., Bardige, B., Gilligan, C., Johnston, D. K., Miller, B., Osborne, R., Tappan, M., Ward, J., Wiggins, G., & Wilcox, D. (1988). *A guide to reading narratives of conflict and choice for self and relational voice*

(Monograph No. 1). Cambridge, MA: Harvard University, Graduate School of Education.

Bruner, J. (1986). *Actual minds, possible worlds.* Cambridge, MA: Harvard University Press.

Buber, M. (1965). *The knowledge of man.* New York: Harper & Row.

Buber, M. (1970). *I and thou.* New York: Scribner.

Bugental, J. F. T. (1967). *Challenges of humanistic psychology.* New York: McGraw-Hill.

Carr, D. (1997). Narrative and the real world: An argument for continuity. In L. P. Hinchman & S. K. Hinchman (Eds.), *Memory, identity, community: The idea of narrative in the human sciences.* Albany: State University of New York Press.

Chase, S. (1995). Taking narrative seriously: Consequences for method and theory in interview studies. In R. Josselson & A. Lieblich (Eds.), *The narrative study of lives: Vol. 3. Interpreting experience* (pp. 1-26). Thousand Oaks, CA: Sage.

Fine, M. (1994). Working the hyphens: Reinventing self and other in qualitative research. In N. Denzin & Y. Lincoln (Eds.), *Handbook of qualitative research* (pp. 70-82). Thousand Oaks, CA: Sage.

Freeman, M. (1998). Mythical time, historical time, and the narrative fabric of the self. *Narrative Inquiry, 8*(1), 27-50.

Gardiner, M. (1992). *The dialogics of critique.* London: Routledge.

Geertz, C. (1973). *The interpretation of culture.* New York: Basic Books.

Gergen, K. J., & Gergen, M. (1997). Narratives of the self. In L. P. Hinchman & S. K. Hinchman (Eds.), *Memory, identity, community: The idea of narrative in the human sciences.* Albany: State University of New York Press.

Habermas, J. (1993). *Justification and application: Remarks on discourse ethics.* Cambridge, MA: MIT Press.

Heidegger, M. (1962). *Being and time* (J. MacQuarrie & E. Robinson, Trans.). New York: Harper & Row.

Held, B. S. (1995). *Back to reality: A critique of postmodern theory in psychotherapy.* New York: Norton.

Hermans, H. J. M., & Bonarius, H. (1991). The person as co-investigator in personality research. *European Journal of Personality, 5,* 199-216.

Josselson, R. (1995). Imagining the real: Empathy, narrative, and the dialogic self. In R. Josselson & A. Lieblich, (Eds.), *The narrative study of lives: Vol. 3. Interpreting experience* (pp. 27-44). Thousand Oaks, CA: Sage.

Josselson, R. (1996). On writing other people's lives. In R. Josselson (Ed.), *The narrative study of lives: Vol. 4. Ethics and process* (pp. 60-72). Thousand Oaks, CA: Sage.

Keller, E. F. (1985). *Reflections on gender and science.* New Haven, CT: Yale University Press.

Kvale, S. (1996). *Interviews.* Thousand Oaks, CA: Sage.

Lather, P. (1992). Postmodernism and the human sciences. In S. Kvale (Ed.), *Psychology and postmodernism.* London: Sage.

Lieblich, A. (1997). *Conversations with Dvora.* Berkeley: University of California Press.

Lieblich, A., Tuval-Mashiach, R., & Zilber, T. (1998). *Narrative research: Reading, analysis, and interpretation.* Thousand Oaks, CA: Sage.

MacIntyre, A. (1997). The virtues, the unity of a human life, and the concept of a tradition. In L. P. Hinchman & S. K. Hinchman (Eds.), *Memory, identity, community: The idea of narrative in the human sciences.* Albany: State University of New York Press.

Marcus, G. E., & Fischer, M. J. M. (1986). *Anthropology as cultural critique: An experimental moment in the human sciences.* Chicago: University of Chicago Press.

Maslow, A. H. (1966). *The psychology of science.* New York: Harper & Row.

McAdams, D. P. (1988). *Power, intimacy, and the life story.* New York: Guilford.

Miller, M. (1996). Ethics and understanding through interrelationship: I and thou in dialogue. In R. Josselson (Ed.), *The narrative study of lives: Vol. 4. Ethics and Process* (pp. 129-150). Thousand Oaks, CA: Sage.

Polkinghorne, D. E. (1988). *Narrative knowing and the human sciences.* Albany: State University of New York Press.

Rogers, A., Casey, M. E., Ekert, J., Holland, J., Nakkula, V., & Sheinberg, N. (1999). An interpretive poetic of languages of the unsayable. In R. Josselson & A. Lieblich (Eds.), *The narrative study of lives: Vol. 6. Making meaning of narratives.* Thousand Oaks, CA: Sage.

Rosenthal, G. (1993). Reconstruction of life stories: Principles of selection in generating stories for narrative biographical interviews. In R. Josselson & A. Lieblich (Eds.), *The narrative study of lives* (Vol. 1). Newbury Park, CA: Sage.

Runyan, W. M. C. (1984). *Life histories and psychobiography: Explorations in theory and method.* New York: Oxford University Press.

Sass, L. (1988). Humanism, hermeneutics, and the concept of the human subject. In S. B. Messer, L. A. Sass, & R. L. Woolfolk (Eds.), *Hermeneutics and psychological theory.* New Brunswick, NJ: Rutgers University Press.

Smith, J. A., Harré, R., & Langenhove, L. V. (1995). *Rethinking psychology.* London: Sage.

Spence, D. (1982). *Narrative truth and historical truth.* New York: Norton.

CHAPTER 22

Research Methodology in Humanistic Psychology in the Light of Postmodernity

STANLEY KRIPPNER

IN HIS ASSESSMENT of psychology, Koch (1969) concluded that it was unlikely to become a coherent congruent science. His assessment of the humanistic psychologies was sympathetic, yet he feared that the field was at risk of simultaneously hardening into intellectual dogmatism and deteriorating into methodological anarchy. Although there are several approaches to humanistic psychology, that which is common to all humanistic thought is the insistence on a human model distinct from models accounting for animal or mechanical behavior (Wandersman, Poppen, & Ricks, 1976, p. 5). This viewpoint has led humanistic psychologists to emphasize their concern with human growth and self-actualization, their antecedents, their correlates, and their development.

Humanistic thought has made a significant impact on counseling, psychotherapy, and personality theory, and it even has influenced management and education. Humanistic psychologists have expanded the orbit of psychology to include the person's attention to an understanding of the context of his or her action. Hence, humanistic psychology can be defined as the scientific study of behavior, experience, and intentionality (Krippner, Ruttenber, Engelman, & Granger, 1985, p. 105). Nonetheless, humanistic psychologists have been criticized for failing to provide adequate frameworks within which they could evaluate and study their subject matter (p. 113). Rogers (1985) observed that humanistic orientations in psychology have not had a deep impact on mainstream psychology in American colleges and universities, the main reason being "a lack of significant humanistically oriented research" (p. 7).

Although a positivistic methodology permeates most studies of human nature by American psychologists, it would be overly parochial to fail to recognize that there are other methodological avenues to the understanding of human nature. In fact, two methodological paradigms—the experimental and the experiential—always have dominated the history of Western psychology. Those psychological methods that take the experimental disposition imitate the model of the natural sciences and study human nature as a physical or biological phenomenon. The experiential disposition, on the other hand, uses methods that study the unique ontological characteristics of humans. Whereas phenomenological and existential psychologists consider positivism in psychology to be philosophically immature, their own studies of consciousness and subjectivity have been viewed by experimental psychologists as merely poetic pursuits.

Proponents of both paradigms accuse one another of naïvely misunderstanding human nature and the epistemology of psychology. The tension between the experimental and experiential paradigms is exemplified in the works of humanistic psychologists, some of whom have made rare syncretisms of the two methods. Some well-known American psychologists became discontented with behaviorism's mechanistic and atomistic view of human nature, drew on the long tradition linking psychology with the humanities, and institutionally founded the humanistic psychologies in a rebellious manner. They regarded themselves as a "third force," alluding to the fact that they were an alternative to the dominant behavioristic and psychoanalytic orientations in psychology. Several key psychologists of the period became affiliated with the movement in one way or another—Gordon Allport, Henry Murray, Gardner Murphy, Rollo May, Charlotte Bühler, Abraham Maslow, Carl Rogers, and James Bugental, among others. They wrote eloquently on the philosophical tension between the methods that study human nature objectively and those that conduct their investigations subjectively (de Carvalho, 1992).

No other group of American psychologists personally understood and lived the tension between the phenomenological and positivistic epistemologies better than did humanistic psychologists. Although never totally denying the value of experimental studies of behavior, they recognized the restrictions of such studies and methods in the understanding of the unique ontological characteristics of human existence. The proposals for the humanistic psychologies that these individuals helped to establish during the 1960s accommodated the perspectives of both phenomenology and positivism, albeit with different emphases from psychologist to psychologist. In so doing, humanistic psychologists significantly contributed to the dismantling of the positivistic monopoly of behaviorism over midcentury American psychology, thereby paving the way for the rise of the cognitive paradigm. Moreover, by replacing (or at least supplementing) laboratory rats and pigeons with humans, humanistic psychologists rehumanized psychology.

It can be argued that because their mentors either passed away or went into semiretirement, the humanistic psychologies have made no significant epistemological progress and, like behaviorism, have become one more chapter in the history and systems of mid-century American psychology. It can be argued with equal vigor, however, that although the humanistic psychologies have lost some of their significance as distinct schools or systems of psychology, they still remain a viable force. Furthermore, their unique epistemology has been assimilated into other orientations, especially in the newly emerging field of human science.

The humanistic psychologies are scientific approaches to the study of behavior, experience, and intentionality that subsume many of the contributions of other approaches—not only psychoanalysis, behaviorism, and cognitive psychology but also transpersonal psychology and the neurosciences. The humanistic psychologies have departed from the psychological mainstream in many ways, especially in regard to research methods. As a result, they are uniquely positioned to benefit from and incorporate various aspects of postmodern insights, especially those offered by constructive postmodernism that reframes rather than rejects the enterprise of disciplined inquiry.

Like the humanistic psychologies, postmodernity is appalled by the excesses of modernity—its insistence that a single "reality" and "truth" can be obtained by splitting the object being studied from the observing investigator and from values and ethics and that the resulting data can lead to what has been variously called "the Enlightenment Project" and "Walden II." Postmodernity, by contrast, takes the more modest position that language is incapable of providing a completely accurate picture of reality; indeed, the powerful forces that control language explicitly or implicitly manipulate reality to their own ends, whether they be religious dogmatists, scientific authorities, or members of the psychotherapeutic establishment (Lather, 1990; Rosenau, 1992). What is called for is a discourse among competing paradigms, an acknowledgment that truth is local and perhaps different in each time and place. This shift would involve a return to the "radical empiricism" of William James, in which a range of methods of inquiry are employed, given that for James (1902/1958), empiricism including affect was more profound than other types.

What is referred to as the "modern" worldview is responsible for impressive advances in technology, industry, and scientific discovery. However, it has not prevented—and even might have been partially responsible for—unprecedented fragmentation, nihilism, and destruction. As Berman (1984) stated, "Western life seems to be drifting toward increasing entropy, economic and technological chaos, ecological disaster, and ultimately, psychic dismemberment and disintegration" (p. 1). As a corrective to this situation, some postmodern writers hope to preserve the virtues of the modern worldview while replacing its mechanistic and reductionistic assumptions with those that are more organic and holistic in nature.

A number of psychologists (e.g., Sass, 1992; Smith, 1996) appreciate postmodernists' diagnosis of the contemporary social malaise but do not accept prescriptions that might have what Sass (1992) called "dark and troubling" consequences (p. 171). Smith (1996) acknowledged postmodernists' cognizance of the importance of historical and social context in inquiry, as well as their incisive detection of sources of bias, but regarded these contributions as facilitating the improvement of science, not its abandonment. In other words, "the scientific enterprise, fallible as it is, has worked," and the critical "awareness of science's fallibility can help it work better" (p. 153). Schneider (1998) added that experimental research works best "when the boundaries between phenomenon and context are clearly evident, whereas qualitative research is better suited to subtler and more complex phenomena and contexts" (p. 284). In other words, humanistic psychology shares many of the concerns central to the postmodernist critique but prefers solutions that are productive rather than deconstructive.

WORLDVIEWS

During the late 1970s, the philosopher Jean-Francois Lyotard was commissioned by the

Council of Universities of Quebec to undertake a study on the state of knowledge in the Western world (Anderson, 1996, p. 4). His report, published in English in 1984, was titled *The Postmodern Condition* and concluded that all modern systems of knowledge, including science, had been supported by some "meta-narrative" or "grand discourse" (Lyotard, 1984). His examples included Christianity's story of God's will being enacted on earth, the Enlightenment's intellectual story of rational progress, and the Marxists' political story of class conflict and revolution. Lyotard concluded that these meta-narratives usually suppressed differences so as to legitimate their own vision of reality, and he described the postmodern perspective as one of skepticism toward all meta-narratives.

Technically speaking, *postmodernity* refers to the postmodern era or condition, whereas *postmodernism* refers to the various schools, movements, and perspectives that postmodernity has spawned. As Anderson (1996) observed, "Postmodernisms will come and go, but postmodernity—the postmodern condition—will still be here" (p. 7). Anderson identified the "four corners of the postmodern world" as (a) the replacement of "found" identity by "made" identity that is constructed from many cultural sources; (b) the understanding that moral and ethical judgments are made on the basis of socially constructed cultural worldviews; (c) an emphasis on improvisation, variation, parody, and playfulness in art and culture; and (d) The awareness that borders of all types are social constructions of reality that can be crossed, erased, and reconstructed.

The implications of these four corners for scientific research are vast; postmodernists suspect that what scientists take back from nature depends on their way of representing nature. Whether one realizes it or not, humankind's understanding of nature is grasped through language. The postmodern

approach to science involves paradox, irony, and narratives that often employ symbols and metaphors. Postmodern practitioners shift from being detached, theory-testing investigators and onlookers to being involved, interested, interpretive, procedure-testing, critical participants who take an active role in both finding and making information (Anderson, 1990).

Postmodern investigators realize that human phenomena are altered when they are studied, especially if research participants are given feedback about investigations and their roles in them. Postmodern scientists understand that science is not value free; rather, it both produces and reflects implicit or explicit values, especially when its findings become the basis for applied technology (e.g., atomic bombs, space satellites, electronic media). If modern science has a publicly stated value, then it is its quest for *certainty,* a goal that postmodernists regard as futile because of their conviction that knowledge tends to be local rather than universal. In other words, the Enlightenment Project has broken down; the world's diverse people do not think in the same way, much less in a way that modernists would consider rational (Harvey, 1989). Postmodernists would agree with existentialists that existence precedes essence if, indeed, there is any essence at all.

According to postmodernists, the most important human activities can barely be measured, much less predicted and controlled. Rather, the postmodern scientist strives to identify, describe, and understand these activities as deeply and thoroughly as possible. "Truth" is a matter of perspective, and perspectives are a byproduct of social interchange or "discourse." One's language about the world does not necessarily represent the world. The world is not simply something "out there" but rather is interactive; the observer and the observed are in constant dialogue. Modernity tries to hold a mirror to nature, not realizing that the language it uses never can completely represent nature, as linguistic constructs are culturally produced. Postmodernity, to the contrary, asks scientists to realize that its projects engage nature in a discourse, hoping that such an interaction will yield new insights and novel interpretations.

Postmodernists believe that human lives largely revolve around discourse. As humans realize that social utopias are unlikely attainments of scientific investigation, they can take personal responsibility for their actions here and now. They can focus on specific community projects, whether their communities be familial, ethnic, commercial, industrial, spiritual, academic, or something else in nature. For postmodernists, local interactions are the point of departure; community context replaces global ideologies. There is an emphasis on individual, family, and group narratives and on the telling of myths and stories, that is, the ways in which people explain how their world got to be the way it is and what is likely to happen (Anderson, 1990, p. 243).

A hallmark of postmodernity is "deconstruction," which began as a method of literary criticism that reduces the language of a text to a multiplicity of possible meanings rather than to any single meaning such as that supposedly intended by the author. A text can be a story, an event, or a concept. Deconstruction tears the text apart, revealing its contradictions, disclosing its assumptions, and undoing its constructions. People in each culture construct experience in terms of the categories provided by their own linguistic system, coming to terms with a reality that has been filtered through their language. Each culture has a specialized terminology in those aspects of consciousness important for its functioning and survival.

From the position of cultural psychology, the processes of consciousness are not uniform across cultures (Shweder, 1990). For example, Goleman (1993) pointed out that Western culture describes inner experience primarily in psychopathological terms, whereas traditional Eastern cultures have equally intricate vocabularies for describing altered states of consciousness and spiritual experiences. Furthermore, Western psychology equates reality with the world as perceived in the ordinary waking state, denying credibility to realities perceived in other types of awareness. Eastern perspectives, on the other hand, dismiss the physical world as an illusion and see reality as something that cannot be grasped in ordinary waking awareness.

In a scathing rebuttal of postmodernist writers, Matthews (1998), insisted that science never claimed to discover absolute fixed truths about nature; instead, science attempts to make "approximations of truth, based on refutations and challenges of previously held notions" (p. 26). Individual scientists are not objective, but the scientific process itself is objective in its critique, challenge, and refutation of a given theory and, therefore, in its application of the scientific method. "The problem for postmodernists is that while they have identified some problems and have developed a theory, they have no interest in rational criticism" (p. 27). This challenge may serve as a corrective to some postmodernists whose statements are extreme, suggesting that science is merely one of many narratives.

THE HUMANISTIC AND POSTMODERN DISCOURSE

Abraham Maslow

Most of the founders of the humanistic psychologies would be considered modernists. Maslow, for example, proposed a hierarchy of needs that was linear in nature and that supposedly varied little from culture to culture. Early in his career, Maslow advocated experimental studies of human participants employing control groups of apes. During the late 1930s, however, Maslow gradually concentrated on the study of dominance and self-esteem among college women. His suspicion that these human conditions relate to mental health turned out to be a lifelong interest in the study of human motivation and psychological health.

A postmodern flavor entered Maslow's work when he came into contact with the Oriental philosophy of Taoism with its concept of *wu-wei* or noninterference with nature. Maslow (1966) then argued that the organization, classification, and conceptualization methods of Western science abstracted its perceptions to such an extreme that they needed to be balanced by Taoistic nonintrusive receptivity and contemplation of experience, a "getting back to things themselves," as Husserl had argued. Maslow referred to this type of knowledge as "Taoist objectivity," as opposed to the "classical objectivity" of Western psychology.

Maslow was certain that psychology's attempts to imitate outdated models of the physical sciences had led to depersonalization, making psychology atomistic and mechanistic. For Maslow, a science of human nature must be unique because the observer is also the observed. Recognizing that the empiricism of logical positivism and the private subjective world of existential reflection should be balanced, Maslow (1956) proposed a philosophy of psychology that synthesized both methods. He insisted that all knowledge pertaining to human existence is a product of direct and intimate experience and that there is no substitute for experience. Conceptual, abstract,

theoretical knowledge is useful only when people already know experientially. Words fail when there is no experience; words succeed when people share similar experiences. At some point in the process of experiencing, however, one senses the emergence of a pattern, rhythm, or relationship. "Some things just come to mind," according to Maslow (1961, p. 1).

This method assumes fearless respect for the object studied as well as a suspension of judgment. Psychologists should relax, "let it be," melt away with the object of study, and experience it receptively, contemplatively, and Taoistically, not intruding or interfering with the "order of things" (Maslow, 1966, pp. 95-101). Maslow described this first stage as "Taoistic nonintruding receptivity to the experience" (p. 101), that is, as an attitude rather than a technique. At this level of study, experience just happens as it is, not according to psychologists' expectations of control and prediction. However, as researchers begin to organize, classify, and abstract their phenomenological accounts of the object under study, their own constructions determine their perception of experience. The challenge, as a result, is to develop a research methodology that combines the experimental with the experiential but that stays as close as possible to the lived experience.

Carl Rogers

Rogers also advanced a model of personality that is modernistic in nature in that it assumes universal aspects of the so-called self. But even in his earliest psychotherapy studies, Rogers acknowledged that psychotherapists actually combine artistry with science and that experiential—not cognitive—learning is essential in their training. From Rogers' point of view, the proliferation of unchecked theories and techniques has turned psychotherapy into a collection of personality cults and technological cliques. This situation, according to Rogers (1963, pp. 9, 15), made it essential that empirical approaches and objective measurements be implemented but that, at the same time, the subjective aspects of psychotherapy be appraised.

Rogers (1959) proposed that his person-centered psychotherapy provided a simple, clear, and consistent hypothesis of the "if-then" type of paradigm with an operational definition compatible with experimental testing: If the necessary and sufficient conditions of person-centered psychotherapy are fulfilled, then there is a predictable chain of events. More precisely, if the psychotherapist is real and congruent in his or her relationship with the client and provides unconditional positive regard and empathy for the client's condition, then significant personality changes will occur. Because all of the factors in this equation could be operationally defined and measured, Rogers (1961, pp. 225-242) experimentally tested and confirmed his hypothesis with psychotherapy clients.

During the mid-1950s, however, Rogers became increasingly aware of the tension between the tenets of logical positivism and the subjectivism of European existentialism and phenomenology, both of which were forerunners of postmodern perspectives in psychology. Describing the essence of psychotherapy in terms of his personal experience, Rogers explained that when he entered the therapeutic relationship, he made a sincere attempt to understand and unconditionally accept the inner world of the other person, hoping that this would lead to a significant personality change. Rogers contended that in this process, there is a unity of experiencing, a situation in which both therapist and client slip together into a stream of subjective authentic "becoming," that is, an "I-thou" sort of relationship. Once the client learns to dip into his or her subjectivity and the intimacy of the therapeutic encounter, there is a gradual growth of trust and even affection for the awareness of his or her organismic wisdom. This process of self-discovery cannot be taught; it can only be experienced subjectively. Rogers held that even when it is learned, it cannot be symbolized or intellectually recreated; it has value and immediacy only when experienced. Once it is experienced, it also has a significant life-changing effect.

At first, Rogers (1961) thought that the experimental and experiential were two antagonistic but legitimate approaches to the study of psychotherapy, each yielding significant truths yet irreconcilable philosophical points of view. He wrote about this conflict as a growing puzzlement "between the logical empiricism in which I was educated, for which I had a deep respect, and the subjectively oriented existential thinking which was taking root in me because it seemed to fit so well with my therapeutic experience" (p. 99; cf. Rogers, 1959, p. 100). When Rogers resolved this conflict during the mid-1950s, he proposed a humanistic psychology that integrated the objective and subjective modes of knowing, calling it "intersubjective or phenomenological knowledge."

Rollo May

May had more in common with postmodernists than did most of his contemporaries. He granted that the positivistic method had a major role in explaining the biological aspect of the human organism but insisted that it was of little help in understanding the ontological characteristics of human existence (Schneider & May, 1995). People turn to psychotherapy seeking to clarify their problems concerning love, hope, despair, and anxiety, according to May (1967, chap. 1; 1969, p. 18). Many psychologists avoid confronting these human dilemmas, however, explaining love as sexual craving, turning anxiety into physical stress, ruling out hope as mere illusion, explaining away despair as depression, trivializing human passion into the satisfaction of basic needs, and making pleasure a simple release of tension.

Modern psychology, according to May (1967, chap. 1), not only suppresses but also trivializes the most meaningful aspects of human experience. Under the gospel of technique, mainstream psychologists avoid confrontation with the most concrete aspects of being human that somehow are lost in the reductionistic tendencies of objective measurement. In his own proposal for a humanistic psychology, May (1967, chap. 13) stated that psychologists should abandon all pretenses to the manipulation and prediction of behavior, and should stop avoiding human subjectivity merely because it does not have an animal counterpart. A science of human nature, according to May (1967), must follow a human model and study the unique features of humans—what he called "the ontological characteristics of human existence" (pp. 96, 192). These characteristics would include people's capacity to relate to themselves as both subjects and objects; their potential for choice and for ethical actions; their ability to reason; their ability to create myths, metaphors, and symbols; and their ability to participate in the historical development of their communities. Psychology, according to May (1958; see also Schneider & May, 1995), should adopt a phenomenological approach and study people as they really are, not as projections of a psychologist's theories about human nature. Phenomenological knowledge of the person ought to precede other methodological and theoretical presuppositions.

In this context, May (1967) distinguished between "describing what" and "explaining why," taking the position that psychologists should describe rather than explain. Causal explanations of the origins or causes of any particular event fail to describe what the event actually is. To explain how an event such as anxiety came into being does not say what anxiety is as experienced by the person. Psychology should study the phenomenology of the human condition rather than cause-and-effect relationships. The human dilemma arises out of the capacity to experience oneself simultaneously as subject and object, according to May (1967), and psychologists need to focus their investigations on this condition. Students of human nature also should assume from the very beginning that people are centered in themselves and need to preserve their centeredness by self-affirmation, no matter how distorted and conflicted that center might be. They should study myths, symbols, and literature (classical literature in particular given that it is the self-interpretation of humans throughout history; May, 1991). For May, psychology has more affinity with the model of the humanities than with the model of the physical and biological sciences.

Irvin Child and Amedeo Giorgi

The dialectic between behaviorists and humanists has led to many attempts to form a synthesis. Child (1973), for example, observed that cognitive psychology had successfully adapted the methods of the research tradition to studying complex phenomena of the human mind. Child claimed that humanistic psychologists tend to "make statements that are not easily verifiable" (p. 20) and to overly engage in sentimentality and vagueness; hence, many of the research methods used by cognitive psychologists would provide a useful corrective. Child's examples of synthesis include Piaget's work in developmental psychology as well as investigations of moral development, creativity, hypnosis, psychotherapy, and parapsychology.

In other words, Child (1973) gave credit to humanistic psychologists for identifying areas ignored by most schools of psychology and then suggested the adoption of rigorous research methods to obtain data in these areas. For Child, both the humanistic psychologies and the research tradition have been incomplete, but "a new image of psychology" could be established by combining the two because "the first is of the flesh alone, the second is all bones. The two images need to be brought together" (p. v). Child's advice has been seconded by other authors such as Wandersman and colleagues (1976), who predicted a "creative synthesis that can unite the two approaches, or at least large parts of them, into a broader social developmental view of the human being as an active organizer of his own particular environment over time" (pp. 383-384).

One way in which to implement this synthesis would be to apply rigorous research methods to fields of study already pioneered by the humanistic psychologies such as behavioral ecology, human development, life history research, and ecopsychology (i.e., "green psychology"). Metzner (1999) called for a "fundamental reenvisioning of what psychology is . . . , a revision that would take the ecological context of human life into account" (p. 2). Roszak (1992) denounced mainstream psychology for its lack of consideration of the ecological basis of human life in its theories and texts. Ecopsychology has taken its place on the agenda of many humanistic psychologists for the 21st century. Rychlak (1977) also

outlined a program for a psychology that "can be both rigorous and humanistic" (p. 221) and would put humanistic theories to the test in typical experimental fashion, employing validating evidence. "So long as we avoid confounding what is our theory with what is our method, such a rigorous humanism is possible" (p. 222).

For Giorgi (1970), however, such a synthesis is neither necessary nor beneficial. Agreeing with May that the questions of deepest concern in the human realm are the least susceptible to treatment by existing methods, Giorgi (1986) called for a "reform" in the way in which science studies humans. This "human science" would include "phenomenological research, hermeneutic clarifications of meaning, as well as life and case history studies and a variety of studies using qualitative data and/or reconceptualized quasi-experimental designs" (p. 70).

A variant of narrative, single-case research designs is multiple-case studies (Schneider, 1999), an example of what Sass (1988) referred to as "experience-near" research. Multiple-case studies and other types of experience-near research attempt to "intimately elucidate clients' lived or subjective realities . . ., from the verbal to the preverbal and from the personal to the social" (Schneider, 1999, p. 2). Whereas randomized controlled trials and other forms of linear research focus on controllable psychological phenomena, multiple-case designs "address the rich and multifaceted background underlying experimental or survey data" (p. 2). The chief issue in addressing the validity of case research is its plausibility. Are the data plausibly linked to theory? Is the theory plausibly generalizable? Is the conclusion plausibly disconfirmable? Schneider called on multiple-case study investigators to become "critical artists" who can learn to see artistically, feel artistically, and portray experiences artistically but who also can organize, clarify, and summarize data like scientists (p. 4).

Giorgi's (1990) phenomenological method is another example of experience-near research. It obtains descriptions of various experiences and analyzes them for their "lived meanings" using the standard phenomenological procedures of "reduction, imaginative variation, and intuition of essences" (p. 113). Giorgi admitted that the problem of studying human phenomena is complex, especially if the dignity of humans is to be respected. Nevertheless, he identified certain basic interactive features of humans that could form a structure for research. These features were that (a) all humans participate in society, (b) all humans participate in linguistic communication, (c) all humans express experience meaningfully, (d) all humans are capable of transforming the received structures of experience, and (e) all humans participate in groups and communities.

Giorgi's (1990) human science perspective is a way of obtaining methodical, systematic, and critical knowledge about human phenomena, or persons in situations, without distorting the basic characteristics of the phenomena or persons (pp. 125-126). Like May, Giorgi holds that positivistic methods are of little or no use in understanding the ontological characteristics of human existence. Some humanistic psychologists (Barrell, Aanstoos, Richards, & Arons, 1987) would add perceptual psychology, which emphasizes the relationship between an individual's behavior and that individual's experience. It is grounded in the premise that people behave and act in terms of their "perceptual field" (p. 438). Collen (1990) identified systems inquiry as a human science as well. This method involves the study of relationships at each level of a human system such as cells,

organs, organisms, group organizations, societies, and supranational systems as well as the isomorphisms that may exist between levels.

Chaotic Systems Analysis

A form of systems inquiry has emerged that is beginning to demonstrate its utility in describing and understanding processes that undergo continuous change, growth, and evolution of a chaotic nature, such as weather patterns, ecological systems, and a whole array of phenomena that operate in a nonlinear fashion. In accordance with postmodern thought, chaotic systems analysis questions modernists' position that nature can be predicted and controlled. According to Prigogine and Stengers (1984), one of the most highly refined skills in the West is dissection, that is, the reduction of problems into the most simple components. They proposed that the knowledge produced by reductionistic mechanistic science has produced models, theories, and constructs that have become insipid and pragmatically infertile. Chaotic systems inquiry offers a fresh approach that is both process oriented and steeped in evolutionary thought.

Chaotic systems analysis may become an important method of inquiry in both the biological and behavioral sciences (Abraham, Abraham, & Shaw, 1990; Robertson & Combs, 1995). Chaos methodology shifts emphasis from linear relationships of cause and effect to more interactive approaches that stress the importance of defining patterns, form, self-organization, and adaptive qualities of complex processes. Although there exists a rampant debate among postmodernists about the usefulness of any scientific method employing mathematics, its advocates contend that chaotic systems analysis provides a rich and elegant way of describing various psychological processes, such as brain wave patterns, memory retrieval, dynamic fluctuations in sleep, dream content, and complex family interactions. Most experimental methods and their attendant statistical tests are based on linear cause-and-effect assumptions. The nonlinear mathematics of chaos systems analysis may demonstrate its utility for the understanding of complex human phenomena, even though its detractors assert that its derived topological representations, such as attractor reconstructions and fractal dimension estimates, do not represent "true" chaos but rather are mathematical artifacts that are not indicative of the system under scrutiny.

The attempt to study complex systems with linear analysis often yields incomplete data. The effort to use behavioral and psychoanalytic models to study complex human experiences also has been incomplete. An example is human creativity. Creativity was thought by psychoanalysts to be a sublimation of repressed sexual drives. Behaviorists described creativity in terms of a lack of ordinary environmental reinforcement. One psychoanalytic concept was that homeostasis is the end goal of human striving, but humanistic psychologists emphasize the creative processes by which humans go beyond homeostasis. Instead, humans attempt to generate values, whether these values are artistic, technological, social, or spiritual. Indeed, human creativity may have an underlying chaotic process that selectively amplifies small fluctuations and molds them into coherent mental states. These mental states are then experienced as reflection and imagination (Krippner, 1994).

For some psychologists (e.g., Robertson & Combs, 1995), the application of chaos theory to the brain marks a new frontier. Chaos theorists propose that chaotic behav-ior serves as the essential ground state for the brain. The model of brain activity based on chaos theory has greater utility than do brain models that compare brain activity to digital computer activity. The degree of chaos in sleep and wakefulness has been evaluated on the basis of electroencephalographic recordings. As a result, it has been proposed that dreams result from the brain's attempt to bring meaning to the images evoked during the chaotic stimulation of the brain's visual and motor centers, primarily during rapid eye movement sleep.

Hardy (1998) suggested that dreams often depict conflicts between two "chaotic attractors," for example, dominance versus cooperation, helplessness versus competence, activity versus passivity, authenticity versus superficiality. It follows that the "personal myths" that Feinstein and Krippner (1997) detected in dreams may be thought of as chaotic attractors, and a "mythological dialectic" often is necessary to manage or resolve the conflict. Hardy (1998) described a dreamer whose reliance on social interactions based on authority and hierarchy was undermined by a powerful dream about cooperation and synergy. His reflection on hierarchy versus cooperation led him to adopt a new set of values as well as different ways of relating to people at work and in social settings.

The humanistic psychologies include human intention in their domain. Humanistic psychologists assume that humans are able to make choices, search for meaning, and engage in self-reflection. Like chaos theorists, the humanistic psychologists take exception to deterministic models. For example, the French mathematician Laplace (1814) claimed that a superhuman intelligence could predict the whole course of future events, both physical and human. Prediction and control are not the major goals of the humanistic psychologies and chaos theory; instead, both disciplines focus on description and explanation.

RESEARCH AS NARRATIVE

What role can experimental and quasi-experimental methods play in encountering human experiences? Do these methods even have a role, either by themselves or in concert with experiential methods? Perhaps the controversy can only be answered as humanistic psychologists conduct research studies on the topics that they have identified as important in the understanding of human nature. Even if the control and prediction of behavior vanishes from their agenda, the issues of description and understanding will remain. One of the tasks of psychology is to obtain knowledge of human and nonhuman behavior, of individual experience, and of the activities of groups. Humanistic psychologists have flung their net wide. If they can resolve the problem of method, then they bode well to catch some spectacular fish.

Many deconstructive postmodernists believe that modern science should be abandoned altogether. But constructive postmodernists propose that scientific methods, if properly reconstructed and recontextualized, have the ability to provide scholars with powerful and useful tools with valuable metaphors for understanding events that otherwise would elude them. The proposition that modern science is but a vast oversimplification that has no relationship with the outside world cannot be taken seriously. To the contrary, the knowledge that has been derived from modern science has provided numerous approximations of consensual reality. Although these approximations might be imperfect in some ways, they are at least pragmatic approximations.

If the direction of scientific institutions and how they go about obtaining knowledge and constructing truth is to be changed, then science must bridge the gap between the modern and the postmodern. Within this framework, theories, laws, and models can be viewed as metaphors that do not comprise a fixed body of knowledge but rather are a fluid body of ideas that progress and evolve due to the discourses of both researchers and participants. Through this reconstruction, the methodology of the human sciences can take on a socially involved, interactive narration (Polkinghorne, 1992).

Indeed, the scientific experiment can be reframed as a narrative describing an event that occurred in a specific time and place. Experimental methods might not be appropriate for the investigation of certain human problems, but they can be useful in telling other stories, albeit those that lack the profundity of existential crises and peak experiences. The Hawthorne effect and interpersonal expectancy effects demonstrate the impact that the storyteller has on experimental results: A new procedure or story seems to be associated with more dramatic changes than does that same story repeatedly told to the same group. The expectations of the storyteller apparently are perceived in subtle ways by the audience members, who then may perform in ways confirming that story (Harris & Rosenthal, 1988).

Anderson (1990) wrote,

> Testing, experimentation, replication, methodology, and all the apparatus of modern science are just as important in the postmodern world as they ever were. Science is judged, [and] possible explanations compete. Proposed theories are tested for their ability to "fit" with other theories, with intuitive feelings about reality—and also for their ability to fit with any kind of data that can be generated by observation and measurement. (p. 77)

Yet, something is different in postmodernity—an increasing recognition that the foundation of scientific truth ultimately is a social foundation that rests on a network composed of theories, opinions, ideas, words, and cultural traditions.

Postmodernists are suspicious of "metanarratives"; Lyotard (1984) pointed out that these systems of thought "typically suppress differences in order to legitimate their own vision of reality." However, specific narratives can be used as texts in phenomenological and hermeneutic studies. Postmodern psychologists recognize that personal accounts, including those that describe "exceptional human experiences," are to some extent culturally constructed and are loaded with accounts of local significance. The researcher can look for common themes in these narratives, both within a culture and cross-culturally, often obtaining what Hufford (1982) termed "core beliefs." Examples might include "Humans have souls that leave the body" and "There are threatening and frightening spirits." In turn, these core beliefs lead to "core experiences" such as "out-of-body" travel and "demonic possession." This project takes on special importance in studies of the self, a construct central to humanistic psychology but one subjected to considerable deconstruction by postmodernists. Yet, Martin and Sugarman (1996) offered a synthesis that incorporates social constructionist thought with an acknowledgment of the self, creativity, and intentionality, accounting for both the private-individual and public-social domains. This corrective is necessary because the social constructionists often neglect human constructs such as faith, values, convictions, and intentions as well as the cultural and individual differences apparent when each of these constructs is studied.

Cassirer (1954) reminded us that names are not designed to refer to substantial things or to independent entities that exist by themselves. Instead, names and labels are determined by human interests and human purposes, neither of which are fixed and invariable. Foucault (1980) pointed out that language rests midway between nature and discourse and that science needs to shift from a fixed paradigm to a fluid discourse. With these injunctions in mind, one may recall the claim that "exceptional human experiences" cannot be communicated verbally (White, 1991). This assertion has not been welcomed by modern psychology, but it is reasonable from a postmodern viewpoint, considering that language is conceptual and it is only with great difficulty that it can be applied to nonconceptual experience. Furthermore, information acquired in one state of consciousness may be neither dependably recalled nor comprehended in another state.

From the standpoint of modernity, an individual observes and reflects on the world, transforming this experience into words that will express these perceptions and thoughts to others. For postmodernists, language is a system unto itself, a social format that is shaped by a community of participants (Gergen, 1991, p. 110). However, the cultural agencies with power and authority influence not only how conscious events will be communicated but also how they will be experienced (Hess, 1992). Modesty is required when researchers depend on language to convey the experience of a life-changing vision, a dream that came true, an interpersonal adventure, an encounter with nature, a personal loss, a terminal illness, or any other exceptional human experience that is worth studying, albeit with tools that are not completely adequate.

Postmodernity does not speak with a single voice on these topics. Deconstructive postmodernism declares that there is nothing but cultural construction in human experience. Deconstructive postmodernists believe that even the human body image and the organisms that one finds in nature are little more than cultural projections; hence, one's perceptions of them are suspect and unreliable. Ecological postmodernism, on the other hand, sees both the human body and the "earth body" as sources of wisdom and grounding for a humanity trying to effect a transition beyond the failed aspects of modernity (Metzner, 1999; Spretnak, 1991). Constructive postmodernists believe that the constant reexamining of one's beliefs and the dedicated attempt to learn about one's socially constructed reality are the most important learning tasks needed for survival at this time in history (Edge, 1994).

The humanistic psychologies may provide strategies, metaphors, and even applications for assisting in solving some of the critical problems that must be faced both in the present and in whatever postmodern world may emerge in the future. A continuation of the discourse between the humanistic psychologists and the constructive postmodernists, systems and chaos theorists, and students of mythology, narrative, and non-Western thought may well move the humanistic psychologies to the cutting edge of psychological theory, practice, and research.

REFERENCES

Abraham, F. D., Abraham, R. H., & Shaw, C. D. (1990). *A visual introduction to dynamical systems theory for psychology.* Santa Cruz, CA: Aerial Press.

Anderson, W. T. (1990). *Reality isn't what it used to be.* New York: Harper & Row.

Anderson, W. T. (1996). Introduction: What's going on here? In W. T. Anderson (Ed.), *The truth about truth: De-confusing and re-constructing the postmodern world* (pp. 1-11). New York: Tarcher.

Barrell, J. J., Aanstoos, C., Richards, A. C., & Arons, M. (1987). Human science research methods. *Journal of Humanistic Psychology, 27*(4), 424-457.

Berman, M. (1984). *The reenchantment of the world.* New York: Bantam Books.

Cassirer, E. (1954). *An essay on man.* New York, NY: Doubleday.

Child, I. L. (1973). *Humanistic psychology and the research tradition: Their several virtues.* New York: John Wiley.

Collen, A. (1990). Advancing human science. *Saybrook Review, 8*(1), 17-39.

de Carvalho, R. J. (1992). The institutionalization of humanistic psychology. *The Humanistic Psychologist, 20,* 125-135.

Edge, H. L. (1994). *A constructive postmodern perspective on self and community.* Lampeter, Wales: Edwin Mellen.

Feinstein, D., & Krippner, S. (1997). *The mythic path.* New York: Tarcher.

Foucault, M. (1980). *Power/knowledge: Selected interviews and other writings, 1972-1977* (C. Gordon, Ed. and Trans.). New York: Pantheon.

Gergen, K. J. (1991). *The saturated self: Dilemmas of identity in contemporary life.* New York: Basic Books.

Giorgi, A. (1970). *Psychology as a human science.* New York: Harper & Row.

Giorgi, A. (1986). Status of qualitative research in the human sciences: A limited interdisciplinary and international perspective. *Methods: A Journal for Human Science, 1,* 29-62.

Giorgi, A. (1990). Towards an integrated approach to the study of human problems: The parameters of a human science. *Saybrook Review, 8*(1), 111-126.

Goleman, D. (1993). Psychology, reality, and consciousness. In R. Walsh & F. Vaughan (Eds.), *Paths beyond ego: The transpersonal vision* (pp. 13-17). Los Angeles: Tarcher.

Hardy, C. (1998). *Networks of meaning: A bridge between mind and matter.* Westport, CT: Praeger.

Harris, M. J., & Rosenthal, R. (1988). Interpersonal expectancy effects and human performance research. In D. Druckman & J. A. Swets (Eds.), *Enhancing human performance: Issues, theories, and techniques—Background papers* (pp. 1-79). Washington, DC: National Academy Press.

Harvey, D. (1989). *The condition of postmodernity: An enquiry into the origins of cultural change.* Oxford, UK: Basil Blackwell.

Hess, D. (1992). Disciplining heterodoxy, circumventing discipline: Parapsychology, anthropologically. In D. Hess & L. Layne (Eds.), *Knowledge and society: The anthropology of science and technology* (Vol. 9, pp. 223-252). Greenwich, CT: JAI.

Hufford, D. (1982). *The terror that comes in the night.* Philadelphia: University of Pennsylvania Press.

James, W. (1958). *The varieties of religious experience.* New York: New American Library. (Original work published 1902)

Koch, S. (1969, September). Psychology cannot be a coherent science. *Psychology Today,* pp. 47-50.

Krippner, S. (1994). Humanistic psychology and chaos theory: The third revolution and the third force. *Journal of Humanistic Psychology, 34*(3), 48-61.

Krippner, S., Ruttenber, A. J., Engelman, S. R., & Granger, D. L.(1985). Toward the application of general systems theory in humanistic psychology. *Systems Research, 2,* 105-115.

Laplace, P. S. (1814). *Théorie analytique des probabilités* (2nd ed.). Paris: Courcier.

Lather, P. (1990). Postmodernism and the human sciences. *The Humanistic Psychologist, 18,* 64-84.

Lyotard, J.-F. (1984). *The postmodern condition: A report on knowledge* (G. Bennington & B. Massumi, Trans.). Minneapolis: University of Minnesota Press.

Martin, J., & Sugarman, J. (1996). Bridging social constructionism and cognitive constructivism: A psychology of human possibility and constraint. *Journal of Mind and Behavior, 17,* 291-320.

Maslow, A. H. (1956). A philosophy of psychology. In F. T. Severin (Ed.), *Humanistic viewpoints in psychology* (pp. 17-33). New York: McGraw-Hill.

Maslow, A. H. (1961). Some frontier problems in mental health. In A. Combs (Ed.), *Personality theory and counseling practice* (pp. 1-12). Gainesville: University of Florida Press.

Maslow, A. H. (1966). *The psychology of science.* New York: Harper & Row.

Matthews, W. J. (1998). Let's get real: The fallacy of postmodernism. *Journal of Theoretical and Philosophical Psychology, 18,* 16-32.

May, R. (1958). The origins and significance of the existential movement in psychology. In R. May, E. Angel, & H. F. Ellenberger (Eds.), *Existence: A new dimension in psychiatry and psychology* (pp. 3-36). New York: Basic Books.

May, R. (1967). *Psychology and the human dilemma.* New York: Norton.

May, R. (1969). *Love and will.* New York: Norton.

May, R. (1991). *The cry for myth.* New York: Norton.

Metzner, R. (1999). *Green psychology: Transforming our relationship to the earth.* Rochester, VT: Park Street.

Polkinghorne, D. E. (1992). Postmodern epistemology of practice. In S. Kvale (Ed.), *Psychology and postmodernism* (pp. 146-165). Newbury Park, CA: Sage.

Prigogine, I., & Stengers, I. (1984). *Order out of chaos: Man's new dialogue.* Boston: Shambhala.

Robertson, R., & Combs, A. (Eds.). (1995). *Chaos theory in psychology and the life sciences.* Mahwah, NJ: Lawrence Erlbaum.

Rogers, C. R. (1959). A tentative scale for the measurement of process in psychotherapy. In E. A. Rubinstein & M. B. Parloff (Eds.), *Research in psychotherapy* (pp. 96-107). Washington, DC: American Psychological Association.

Rogers, C. R. (1961). *On becoming a person.* Boston: Houghton Mifflin.

Rogers, C. R. (1963). Psychotherapy today. *American Journal of Psychotherapy, 17,* 5-16.

Rogers, C. R. (1985). Toward a more human science of the person. *Journal of Humanistic Psychology, 25*(4), 7-24.

Rosenau, P. M. (1992). *Postmodernism and the social sciences.* Princeton, NJ: Princeton University Press.

Roszak, T. (1992). *The voice of the earth.* New York: Simon & Schuster.

Rychlak, J. F. (1977). *The psychology of rigorous humanism.* New York: John Wiley.

Sass, L. A. (1988). The self in contemporary psychoanalysis: Commentary on Charles Taylor. In S. B. Messer, L. A. Sass, & R. L. Woolfolk (Eds.), *Hermeneutics and psychological theory: Interpretive perspectives on personality, psychotherapy, and psychopathology* (pp. 321-327). New Brunswick, NJ: Rutgers University Press.

Sass, L. A. (1992). The epic of disbelief: The postmodernist turn in contemporary psychoanalysis. In S. Kvale (Ed.), *Psychology and postmodernism* (pp. 166-182). Newbury Park, CA: Sage.

Schneider, K. J. (1998). Toward a science of the heart: Romanticism and the revival of psychology. *American Psychologist, 53,* 277-289.

Schneider, K. J. (1999). Multiple-case depth research: Bringing experience-near closer. *Journal of Clinical Psychology, 55*(12), 1-10.

Schneider, K. J., & May, R. (1995). *The psychology of existence: An integrative, clinical perspective.* New York: McGraw-Hill.

Shweder, R. A. (1990). Cultural psychology: What is it? In J. W. Stigler, R. A. Shweder, & G. Herdt (Ed.), *Cultural psychology: Essays on comparative human development* (pp. 1-43). New York: Cambridge University Press.

Smith, M. B. (1996). Psychology and truth: Human science and the postmodern challenge. *Interamerican Review of Psychology, 30,* 145-158.

Spretnak, C. (1991). *States of grace.* San Francisco: Harper San Francisco.

Wandersman, A., Poppen, P. J., & Ricks, D. F. (Eds.). (1976). *Humanism and behaviorism: Dialogue and growth.* New York: Pergamon.

White, R. A. (1991). Feminist science, postmodern views, and exceptional human experience. *Exceptional Human Experience, 9*(1), 2-11.

CHAPTER 23

Multiple-Case Depth Research

Bringing Experience-Near Closer

KIRK J. SCHNEIDER

INCREASINGLY, clinicians are demanding relevant experience-near research (MacIssac, 1998). Clinicians want to know what is helpful in the natural setting of their work, with the variety of clientele for whom they serve. Mainstream clinical research, on the other hand, often has been at odds with the needs of "frontline" clinicians. Such research tends to be based on hypothetical-deductive-inductive methods and requires strict control of experimental variables. Critics have pointed out the many problems associated with these strict procedures. Among the problems are the latter's remoteness from client realities, their oversimplified formulation of suffering, and their narrow grasp of health and healing (Goldfried & Wolfe, 1996; Schneider, 1998b; Seligman, 1996). For example, the randomized controlled trial (RCT), which

has been hailed as the "gold standard" for psychotherapy outcome evaluation, has been under increasing criticism. These criticisms range from the inability of RCTs to evaluate long-term intensive psychotherapy (Seligman, 1996) to the shortcomings of RCT manualization requirements (Strupp & Anderson, 1997) and from the narrowness of RCT diagnostic formulations (Bohart et al., 1997) to the remoteness of RCT sampling procedures (Goldfried & Wolfe, 1996).

During recent years, there has been a concerted attempt to redress these problematic investigative modalities. The term *experience-near*, for example, has become associated with a variety of alternatives to mainstream clinical research (Kohut, 1978; Sass, 1988). Specifically, experience-near research has one major goal: to intimately elucidate

AUTHOR'S NOTE: This chapter is adapted from an article of the same title that appeared in the *Journal of Clinical Psychology*, Vol. 55, No. 12, pp. 1531-1540, copyright © 1999 John Wiley & Sons.

clients' lived or subjective realities (Hycner & Jacobs, 1995; MacIssac, 1998). Experience-near modalities include phenomenological, hermeneutic, case, heuristic, and observational forms of inquiry.

At the fulcrum of experience-near research is qualitative description. *Qualitative description* refers to the investigation and interpretation of psychological phenomena through words, symbols, and/or gestures. Depth and breadth of understanding are the goals of qualitative description. Although various forms of experience-near research draw on quantitative and even hypothetical-deductive-inductive methodologies, these methodologies are almost exclusively supplemental to the latter.

Traditionally, experience-near research has been confined to verbal transactions, the reports of single individuals, or literal descriptions of therapeutic sequences (e.g., Greenberg, Elliott, & Lietaer, 1994; Kohut, 1978). In this chapter, however, I stretch this traditional formulation of experience-near inquiry. Drawing from my article on romantic psychology (Schneider, 1998b), I propose an experience-near investigation that maximally encompasses clients' lived realities—from the verbal to the preverbal and from the personal to the social. I call this form of inquiry *multiple-case depth research* (MCDR); it combines the benefits of multiple-case design with the insights of experiential depth psychotherapy. First, I summarize the structure and theory of multiple-case design. Then, I summarize experiential depth theory. Finally, I combine the two modes into a multiple-case depth model of inquiry. To concretize my illustration of MCDR, I propose a hypothetical psychotherapy process and outcome study. This study will consist of the evaluation of the experience of three client cohorts who undergo three distinctive therapeutic engagements: cognitive-behavioral, psychoanalytic, and existential-humanistic.

MULTIPLE-CASE RESEARCH DESIGN: A SUMMARY

Multiple-case research is a variant of qualitative . single-case designs (Yin, 1989). According to Yin (1989), qualitative case research is appropriate when the boundaries between the phenomenon under study and its context are not clearly evident. Put another way, qualitative case research addresses complex real-life phenomena. Whereas survey or experimental research tends to address relatively simple, linear, or controllable psychological phenomena, case investigation tends to address the rich and multifaceted background underlying the experimental or survey data. The advantage of multiple- over single-case designs is twofold in that (a) multiple-case designs afford the opportunity for cross-case comparisons and (b) multiple-case designs permit greater latitude for generalizability.

To be valid, case research, as with any qualitative design, must be carried out with care and rigor. Due to the complexity of its subject matter, case research cannot be judged by the scientific criteria associated with experimental designs but rather must be gauged by a broader view of science (Giorgi, 1995; Schneider, 1998b). The chief question for the validity of case research is its plausibility. Are the data plausibly linked to theory? Is the theory plausibly generalizable? Is the conclusion plausibly disconfirmable? (Lukoff, Edwards, & Miller, 1998).

The multiple-case design that I propose in this chapter draws on the following formulas developed by Yin (1993) in conjunction with relevant quantitative data:

the posing of clear questions and the development of a formal research design; the use of theory and reviews of previous research to develop hypotheses and rival hypotheses; the collection of empirical data to test these hypotheses and rival hypotheses; the assembling of a database—independent of any narrative report, interpretations, or conclusions—that can be inspected by third parties; and the conduct of . . . qualitative analyses. (p. xvi)

Furthermore, the multiple-case study will trace a "sequence of interpersonal events over time," describe a "subculture that ha[s] rarely been the topic of previous study," and discover "key phenomena" (Yin, 1989, p. 15).

EXPERIENTIAL DEPTH THEORY: A NECESSARY SUPPLEMENT

As innovative as multiple-case design may be, I propose that it is missing an essential investigative tool—experiential depth. The tradition of experiential depth theory is a long and intricate one. I do not propose to provide a definitive or even exhaustive definition of this theory here, but suffice it to say that it is grounded in both psychodynamic (e.g., Freudian, Jungian, existential-analytic) and experiential therapeutic principles (for a sampling of such frameworks, see Bugental, 1981; 1987; Laing, 1969; Mahrer, 1996; May, 1958, 1983; and Schneider, 1995, 1998a). Experiential depth theory is predicated on one basic tenet: fidelity to phenomena *as lived*. The overarching thrust of experiential depth theory is to attune, at the most core and intimate levels, to given aspects of living. There are four basic dimensions of experiential depth: immediacy, affectivity, kinesthesia, and profundity (Schneider, 1995). These four dimensions guide therapists—and potentially investigators—toward that which is charged in their relations with clients. That which is charged, furthermore, is often understood in experiential depth terms as "process" aspects of the therapeutic work, as differentiated from "content" or verbal aspects. Process dimensions of therapy refer more to *how* clients and therapists communicate than to *what* they explicitly say. Process dimensions are often preverbal, felt, and intuited and possess a type of resonance validity, whereas content aspects are literal and overt. Process dimensions may include how a person holds himself or herself, gestures, or vocalizes in the process of speaking, whereas content aspects refer directly to the ideas of the person's speech. The great value of process attunement is that it opens up rich and hitherto unknown worlds of experience for both therapists and clients alike. It also opens up the possibility for dialogue about these worlds and for vivid elaboration of initial impressions.

MULTIPLE-CASE DEPTH RESEARCH

What then, are the implications of combining a depth experiential perspective with multiple-case research? Let me suggest several. First, a person who combined depth experiential and multiple-case research skills, or a multiple-case depth researcher, would possess several distinct advantages over a traditional case researcher. Among these would be an enhanced ability to both perceive and evoke tacit, symbolic, and subjectively meaningful processes, rather than merely contents, in the investigative dyad. Second, such a researcher would be attuned to the interpersonal field between himself or herself and the participant (hereafter called the co-researcher), not merely to the isolated field of the co-researcher. This form of attunement would permit the researcher to both assess and call attention to mutually influential components of the inquiry. Third, the multiple-case depth researcher would be freed to assess and call attention to relevant literary or symbolic allusions that could advance the inquiry. Finally, a multiple-case depth investigator would be in an optimal position to formulate a clinical as well as literal explication of co-researcher data (for support of this component, see Moustakas, 1990, and Shedler, Maymen, & Manis, 1993).

The thrust of MCDR, then, is to shed maximal light on any given aspect of experience. The task of the multiple-case depth investigator is to elaborate, unpack, and articulate the core dimensions of a given experience for the purpose of both theory development and application. Multiple-case depth researchers, therefore, should be trained in both quantitative and qualitative methodologies. Foremost, however, they should be grounded in three basic principles when they approach their work: the suspension and acknowledgment of biases toward a given phenomenon, maximal attention to all relevant (experiential and symbolic) aspects of the phenomenon, and coherent description or depiction of the phenomenon. From this standpoint, multiple-case depth researchers must develop a wide-ranging ability to be present to themselves and others in a wide variety of modes. They must become what I call *critical artists*. Critical artists learn to see like artists, feel like artists, and even describe and depict experiences like artists, but they can synthesize data like scientists (see also Moustakas, 1990). By *synthesize*, I mean that such investigators can organize, clarify, and summarize data for practical purposes.

MULTIPLE-CASE DEPTH RESEARCH IN ACTION: A HYPOTHETICAL STUDY

One of the most salient questions facing clinicians today is the classic question posed by Paul (1967): What techniques, offered by whom, under what conditions, are helpful to which types of clients? A corollary to this question is the following: What are the best methods to profoundly understand how clients change? The answer to such a question holds enormous potential, not merely for the practicing clinician but for anyone struggling to transform.

In this section, I describe a research model that I believe can profoundly illuminate human transformation. This model not only should help clinicians to improve their practices but also should be of benefit to all who partake in helping relationships. Given the confines of this chapter, I am only able to hint at the latter benefit. However, it should become evident by the close of my illustration.

Consider, then, the following hypothetical study. This study entails a depth experiential case investigation of three therapy client cohorts. The first of these cohorts undergoes a standard 5- to 12-session round of brief cognitive-behavioral therapy (as formulated by Aaron Beck), the second cohort engages in 1 to 6 years (50 to 300 sessions) of existential-humanistic therapy (as developed by James Bugental), and the third cohort enters into a 3- to 5-year (150 to 300 sessions) intersubjective psychoanalysis (as advanced by Robert Stolorow). Let us say further that there is a rough equivalence regarding the composition of each cohort. This equivalence is necessary, according to Yin (1989), to make consistent cross-case comparisons. Each cohort then is composed of five clients; they all derive from the same large American city; and they are similar with respect to gender (e.g., 60% women), age (e.g., 25 to 60 years), ethnic background (e.g., 75% white), economic status (e.g., middle class), and symptomatology (e.g., 75% depression and anxiety). Moreover, none of the cohorts has had any previous therapy, and all are assessed within the same 10-year period.

Significance of the Study/ Literature Review

This study is descriptive-dialogic in nature. Descriptive-dialogic studies are used to "debate conflicting points in existing theory" (Lukoff et al., 1998, p. 47). There are several current theories that are relevant to this proposed study. In light of space considerations, I identify a few of the more prominent ones.

The prevailing theory about psychotherapy outcomes is that, by and large, they are equivalent (Lipsey & Wilson, 1993). Moreover, this assumption of equivalency implies that although short-term systematic therapies (e.g., cognitive-behavioral) and longer term exploratory therapies (e.g., psychoanalysis, existential) are about equally effective, the short-term systematic approach is superior because of its cost-effectiveness (Barlow, 1996). Supporters of longer term exploratory therapies, on the other hand, contend that although the respective modalities might be equivalent with regard to symptom alleviation, the longer term approaches are superior with regard to complex life issues such as issues of meaning, purpose, and values (Bugental & Bracke, 1992; Miller, 1996). The conventional retort to this contention, however, is that there is no compelling evidence to support it and that, in the absence of such evidence, longer term therapy is misguided (Perez, 1999). Longer term theorists reply that the culpability for the paucity of support rests with conventional research (e.g., the RCT) that requires strict control of variables. They argue that if such research were more compatible with the qualitative aims of longer term therapy, then the respective findings might be very different (Schneider, 1999).

Research Questions/Assumptions

This proposed study is one approach to addressing this controversy. If I were to conduct the proposed study, I would concern myself with the following questions:

1. How and in what ways are clients affected by the three therapeutic modalities?
2. To what extent do the three modalities address more than alleviation of symptoms?
3. What can therapists discover about potent change processes?
4. What can be learned about those change processes over time and across social contexts?
5. How do quantitative and qualitative findings compare and contrast?

In keeping with the phenomenological spirit of this study—fidelity to phenomena as lived—I will now reveal my assumptions about the preceding questions. This revelation will help to monitor areas of bias that could jeopardize the integrity of my findings. My first assumption is that each of the three modalities should have major effects on clients' lives. My second assumption is that the longer term approaches—psychoanalysis and existential-humanistic therapy—should have the greatest impact on clients in terms of both symptom reduction and complex life issues. Third, I believe that the evidence will support the superiority of experiential change processes over programmatic ones, even for cognitive-behavioral clients. Fourth, I believe that some new and surprising findings will emerge from this in-depth study; areas of practice such as the physical setting, availability for "small talk," and attention to cultural and political concerns may well be highlighted.

Step 1: Data Collection

The first step in the proposed study is to carefully collect evidence. An important question during this phase concerns construct validity. To what extent does the study assess what it purports to assess (e.g., client changes due to three interventions)? To respond to this question, I will draw on multiple sources of data and corroborating sources of evidence (Lukoff et al., 1998, p. 48). My rationale here is that the more I can learn about clients, the more I can ensure that the changes they undergo are due to therapeutic dimensions, whereas factors such as history, maturation, demand characteristics, and selection bias can be ruled out (p. 51). For the proposed study, then, I will rely on in-depth videotaped interviews with clients, close others, and therapists; archival records (e.g., diaries, medical reports, school and job evaluations); standardized ratings of mental health (e.g., Beck Depression Inventory); and psychophysiological measures of stress (e.g., galvanic skin response). The latter device, to be administered at designated points during interviews, will serve as a stimulus to further both dialogue and exploration.

Data collection will begin at the onset of therapy. I will request that client intakes be videotaped to augment initial interviews, archival inspection, and standardized measures. Following the initial data collection, I will gather data in the same manner at three subsequent points: during, immediately preceding, and 3 years following each of the respective interventions.

In-depth interviews, the core of this investigation, will look something like the following. Clinically and phenomenologically attuned investigators will meet with clients and their intimates (e.g., parents, spouses, friends) in the setting of those clients' and intimates' choice. The atmosphere that is created between investigators and co-investigators will be pivotal. It is essential that co-investigators feel safe with investigators and that an atmosphere of trust is created. Above all, optimal conditions for exploration need to be created. To the degree that co-investigators feel encouraged and inspired to explore, they also are likely to intimately disclose. The bias here is that, once again, lived or embodied data are more directly revealing than rehearsed or intellectualized data and that only in the most warm and accepting atmosphere can lived and embodied data flourish.

Drawing on my formulation of experiential therapy (Schneider, 1995, 1998a), I suggest the following stances for depth interviewers: deep presence, facilitation of such presence in co-researchers, and limited working through of resistance to such presence. By *deep presence,* I mean the capacity of the researcher to "hold" or create a safe space for the intensity of the unfolding inquiry; in addition, I mean the researcher's capacity to illuminate or attune to the salient themes of the inquiry. Put another way, deep presence reflects the degree to which the researcher can hold and illuminate palpably (immediately, affectively, kinesthetically, and profoundly) relevant material both within himself or herself and between the researcher and co-researchers.

The advantage of deep presence, then, is twofold: It creates sanctuary, as Craig (1986) put it, for deeper co-researcher exploration, and it provides the researcher with a type of radar or "infrared map" of salient co-researcher perceptions. This radar and map can be drawn on continually to guide the inquiry. Examples of the impact of researcher presence include a silent sense from co-researchers that they are being "met," that they are being taken seriously, and that they will not be abandoned when intimately disclosing. Presence also clues the researcher in on the feel or tone of co-researcher disclosure. Among the questions that researcher presence might illuminate are the following. To what degree do the co-researchers seem comfortable with their revelations? To what degree are they rushed, circumspect, or ingenuous? How do the co-researchers hold themselves, gesture, or express themselves during the disclosure? To what extent do their bodily expressions (processes) match the content of their speech? What have the co-researchers *not* disclosed? Do they seem to want to reveal more?

My second recommended stance for the researcher is facilitation of deep presence in co-researchers. Put another way, this stance entails the assistance of co-researchers *into* that which is palpably relevant. The more co-researchers can engage that which is palpably relevant, the more their testimony will be salient, experience-near, and valid. Among the means by which such a facilitation can occur are (a) encouraging co-researchers to make "I" statements and to stay with that which personally matters to them, (b) calling attention to co-researchers' nonverbal communication (e.g., body positioning, vocal fluctuations, facial expressions) to spur further exploration, and (c) inviting dialogue about reciprocal influences (within the investigative dyad) that may bear on co-researchers' testimony.

For example, if I suspect an incongruity between a co-researcher's bodily expression and his verbal remarks, then I might ask him to check in with how he feels as he makes his remarks. I might further invite him to stay present to those feelings and to stay open to other associated feelings. To take a further example, let us say that a co-researcher

speaks highly of a given therapist intervention (e.g., cognitive restructuring). Suddenly, a downcast expression appears over her face. From the MCDR point of view, I would want to know immediately what that expression suggests and how it alters (if at all) the co-researcher's initial perceptions about the intervention. As those of us who conduct depth therapy realize, there can be a variety of levels at which clients communicate, and if core perceptions are to be unveiled, then pursuit of those levels is essential. The caveat, of course, is that great care must be taken when assisting clients (or co-researchers) to "unpack" their perceptions. Researchers must follow co-researchers' and not their own leads, in the course of process inquiry; failing to do so risks undermining the chief aim of MCDR—to faithfully record co-researchers' lived experiences.

Another strategy that may facilitate co-researcher disclosure is embodied meditation. For example, at the point where a co-researcher is struggling to clarify how she felt after a key intervention, I might invite her to attend to where she feels that struggle in her body. Upon identifying a bodily region such as her stomach, I might further invite her to place her hand on her stomach and report her experiences. Then, I might ask, "What other feelings, sensations, or images arise as you stay present to that bodily experience?" There are several advantages to taking such a tack. First, the co-researcher is provided with an opportunity to explore and articulate her most intimate perceptions of a given event. Second, experiences can be clarified in their living and immediate richness. Finally, such experiences can provide the researcher with an intensive sense of the tone, scope, and significance of co-researcher data—a sense that can prove critical when the researcher formulates the final interpretations.

A further strategy that may enhance co-researcher exploration is metaphorical allusion. A well-timed cinematic reference can bring forth a wealth of experiential revelation. For example, if a co-researcher refers to himself as a "Jekyll and Hyde," then to further my understanding of him, I would be inclined to reuse the term. Generally, it is best if the researcher reuses the metaphors, images, and "pet" phrases to which co-researchers already have alluded, but occasionally the researcher might want to evoke those stimuli anew. For example, I might suggest to a searching co-researcher, "That image you had of yourself at the beginning of therapy reminds me of Woody Allen. Does that fit?"

Finally, as in depth psychotherapy, the depth researcher must confront the delicate problem of resistance during the course of the interviews. There are numerous reasons why co-researchers, at any number of junctures, might balk at deeper exploration. To address these thorny occasions, the researcher can resort to a variety of means that therapists have also used to optimal effect. Among these are exploration of the possible bases for the resistance, reassurances about interview confidentiality, and gentle reflection or notation of the resistance back to the co-researchers. An illustration of this latter approach might be "I notice that you switched topics as you were speaking about terminating with your therapist" or "Your voice gets quieter as you speak about the changes you see in your husband." Each of these methods of encountering resistance can be seen as a way station, or a pregnant pause, within which further elaboration may be risked.

In the final segment of the data collection phase, client co-researchers will be asked to observe videotaped sessions from the beginning, middle, and end stages of their therapy. Then, they will be asked to comment on their experiences of those sessions, especially where discrepancies exist between the sessions and their interviews. To reconcile other discrepancies, such as between archival material and co-researchers or between significant others and clients, I will check back with these sources, specify the areas in question, and attempt to obtain clarification.

Step 2: Data Reduction

The next step in this proposed study is to "massage" the raw data into coherent and manageable categories. To be valid, these categories must be as free as possible from the selection bias of the researcher (Lukoff et al., 1998). A major area of potential selection bias is the omission of aspects of the material that may be problematic for the researcher. To redress this potential hazard, I will request that co-researchers, as well as independent judges, review my formulations and, if necessary, revise them.

Step 3: Data Interpretation

The final phase of MCDR entails the development of new theory along with the testing or challenging of existing theory. "Validity depends on the quality of the arguments that link data to theory" (Lukoff et al., 1998, p. 49). One of the chief ways in which to ensure the study's (internal) validity at this juncture is to actively search for alternative explanations for my findings. In light of this safeguard, I will compare and contrast my interpretations against a broad range of rival interpretations. I will pay particular attention to negative cases that disconfirm or raise questions about my interpretations, and I will employ independent judges to review and assess my findings. Ultimately, the soundness of my findings will depend on converging lines of evidence—the "weight" of the data—from multiple independent sources (Lukoff et al., 1998). To the extent that these sources corroborate one another and do so repeatedly, I will have plausibly supported my conclusions.

DISCUSSION AND IMPLICATIONS

This chapter has outlined one potential method of enhancing experience-near research. Drawing on multiple-case design and depth therapeutic principles, I formulated a research method (MCDR) that should be of substantial professional and personal value. The more that clinicians and others discover about personal and intimate change processes, the greater will be their ability to serve. If MCDR could be conducted optimally—with sound financing and resources—it could provide unprecedented clarity on a range of issues. Among these are (1) Which therapies, under what conditions, help or hinder which types of clients? (2) What are the respective benefits of symptom alleviation versus personality change? (3) What factors outside of therapy (e.g., family relationships, social networks, economic circumstances) both affect and are affected by therapy? (4) What is the impact of time on therapeutic outcome? and (5) What is perceived suffering; perceived health?

The time for experientially based case research is here. Investigators must not shrink from the task. To the extent they do, they forfeit data about lives for reports, performances, and norms. To be sure, MCDR is a costly and painstaking proposal, but so is quality psychotherapy—and quality helping. It is high time we recognize that association—and strive mightily to address it.

REFERENCES

Barlow, D. H. (1996). Health care policy, psychotherapy research, and the future of psychotherapy. *American Psychologist, 51,* 1050-1058.

Bohart, A. C., O'Hara, M., Leitner, L., Wertz, F. J., Stern, E. M., Schneider, K. J., Serlin, I. A., & Greening, T. C. (1997). Guidelines for the provision of humanistic services. *Humanistic Psychologist, 25,* 64-107.

Bugental, J. F. T. (1981). *The search for authenticity: An existential-analytic approach.* New York: Irvington.

Bugental, J. F. T. (1987). *The art of the psychotherapist.* New York: Norton.

Bugental, J. F. T., & Bracke, P. E. (1992). The future of existential-humanistic psychotherapy. *Psychotherapy, 29,* 28-33.

Craig, P. E. (1986). Sanctuary and presence: An existential view of the therapist's contribution. *The Humanistic Psychologist, 14,* 22-28.

Giorgi, A. (1995). Phenomenological psychology. In J. A. Smith, R. Harre, & L. van Langenhove (Eds.), *Rethinking psychology* (pp. 24-42). London: Sage.

Goldfried, M. R., & Wolfe, B. E. (1996). Psychotherapy practice and research: Repairing a strained alliance. *American Psychologist, 51,* 1007-1016.

Greenberg, L. S., Elliott, R., & Lietaer, G. (1994). Research on experiential psychotherapies. In A. E. Bergin & S. L. Garfield (Eds.), *Handbook of psychotherapy and behavior change* (pp. 509-539). New York: John Wiley.

Hycner, R., & Jacobs, L. (1995). *The healing relationship in Gestalt therapy: A dialogic/self psychology approach.* Highland, NY: Gestalt Journal Press.

Kohut, H. (1978). *The search for the self: Selected writings of Heinz Kohut—1950-1978* (Vol. 1, P. Ornstein, Ed.). Madison, CT: International Universities Press.

Laing, R. D. (1969). *The divided self: An existential study in sanity and madness.* Middlesex, UK: Penguin.

Lipsey, M. W., & Wilson, D. B. (1993). The efficacy of psychological, educational, and behavioral treatments: Confirmation from meta-analysis. *American Psychologist, 48,* 1181-1209.

Lukoff, D., Edwards, D., & Miller, M. (1998). The case study as a scientific method for researching alternative therapies. *Alternative Therapies in Health and Medicine, 4*(2), 44-52.

MacIssac, D. S. (1998). Empathy: Heinz Kohut's contribution. In A. C. Bohart & L. S. Greenberg (Eds.), *Empathy reconsidered: New directions in psychotherapy* (pp. 245-264). Washington, DC: American Psychological Association.

Mahrer, A. R. (1996). *The complete guide to experiential psychotherapy.* New York: John Wiley.

May, R. (1958). Contributions of existential psychotherapy. In R. May, E. Angel, & H. F. Ellenberger (Eds.), *Existence: A new dimension in psychiatry and psychology* (pp. 37-92). New York: Basic Books.

May, R. (1983). *The discovery of being.* New York: Norton.

Miller, I. J. (1996). Managed care is harmful to outpatient mental health services: A call for accountability. *Professional Psychology: Research and Practice, 27,* 349-363.

Moustakas, C. (1990). Heuristic research: Design and methodology. *Person-Centered Review, 5*(2), 170-190.

Paul, G. L. (1967). Strategy of outcome in psychotherapy. *Journal of Consulting Psychology, 31,* 109-118.

Perez, J. E. (1999). Clients deserve empirically supported treatments, not romanticism. *American Psychologist, 54,* 205-206.

Sass, L. A. (1988). The self in contemporary psychoanalysis: Commentary on Charles Taylor. In S. B. Messer, L. A. Sass, & R. L. Woolfolk (Eds.), *Hermeneutics and psychological theory: Interpretive perspectives on personality, psychotherapy, and psychopathology* (pp. 321-327). New Brunswick, NJ: Rutgers University Press.

Schneider, K. J. (1995). Guidelines for an existential-integrative approach. In K. J. Schneider & R. May (Eds.), *The psychology of existence: An integrative, clinical perspective* (pp. 135-183). New York: McGraw-Hill.

Schneider, K. J. (1998a). Existential processes. In L. Greenberg, J. Watson, & G. Lietaer (Eds.), *Handbook of experiential therapy* (pp. 103-120). New York: Guilford.

Schneider. K. J. (1998b). Toward a science of the heart: Romanticism and the revival of psychology. *American Psychologist, 53,* 277-289.

Schneider, K. J. (1999). Clients deserve relationships, not merely "treatments." *American Psychologist, 54,* 206-207.

Seligman, M. E. P. (1996). Science as an ally of practice. *American Psychologist, 51,* 1072-1079.

Shedler, J., Maymen, M., & Manis, M. (1993). The illusion of mental health. *American Psychologist, 48,* 1117-1131.

Strupp, H. H., & Anderson, T. (1997). On the limitations of therapy manuals. *Clinical Psychology Science and Practice, 4,* 76-88.

Yin, R. K. (1989). *Case study research: Design and methods.* Newbury Park, CA: Sage.

Yin, R. K. (1993). *Applications of case study research.* Newbury Park, CA: Sage.

CHAPTER 24

Hermeneutic Single-Case Efficacy Design

An Overview

ROBERT ELLIOTT

THE FIRST systematic studies of therapy process and outcome were carried out by Carl Rogers and his colleagues (Cartwright, Kirtner, & Fiske, 1963; Rogers, 1949; Rogers & Dymond, 1954; Snyder, 1945). From the perspective of some 50 years on, it is unfortunate that this scientific tradition was allowed to largely die out in North America because humanists' abandonment of therapy research now appears to have been a key factor in the declining fortunes of humanistic psychology over the past quarter century (Lietaer, 1990). Today, however, there is no doubt that humanistic therapists once again have begun to study the process and effects of their work with clients (Greenberg, Elliott, & Lietaer, 1994). However, we need to do much more. As I see it, there is a scientific, practical, political, and even moral necessity for us to evaluate the effects that our clients take from our therapies.

Unfortunately, the standard tools for addressing the efficacy of psychotherapy are extremely blunt instruments. The predominant research paradigm, the randomized clinical trial (RCT) design, suffers from a host of scientific difficulties (Cook & Campbell, 1979; Haaga & Stiles, 2000) including poor statistical power, randomization failure, differential attrition, failure to measure important aspects of clients'

AUTHOR'S NOTE: Portions of this chapter were presented at meetings of the Society for Psychotherapy Research, Chicago, June 2000, and the American Psychological Association, Washington, D.C., August 2000. I gratefully acknowledge the inspiration of Art Bohart, on whose initial work the method described here is based, as well as the helpful suggestions of Constance Fischer and David Rennie and the contributions of my students (Helena Jersak, Cristina Magaña, Rhea Partycka, Suzanne Smith, Michelle Urman, John Wagner, and Alan Wright).

functioning, lack of clarity about the actual nature of the therapies offered, and restricted samples leading to poor generalizability.

Not the least of these difficulties are two that are key to humanistic psychology. First, RCTs typically cast clients as passive recipients of standardized treatments rather than as active collaborators and self-healers (Bohart & Tallman, 1999). Thus, the fundamental presuppositions of RCTs are at variance with core humanistic values regarding personal agency and person-to-person relationships.

Second, RCTs do not warrant causal inferences about single cases. This is because they rely on an operational definition of causal influence rather than seeking a substantive understanding of how change actually takes place. In other words, they are "causally empty"; they provide conditions under which inferences can be reasonably made but provide no method for truly understanding the specific nature of the causal relationship. Even when a therapy has been shown to be responsible for change in general (because randomly assigned clients in the active treatment condition show outcomes superior to those of control clients), this overall result does not necessarily apply to particular clients. After all, for any particular client, factors other than therapy actually might have been the source of observed or reported changes or the client's apparent change might have been illusory. Beyond these shortcomings, RCTs leave open questions about which aspects of therapy clients found helpful.

For these reasons, humanistic psychologists are in need of alternatives to RCTs, designs that are consistent with the humanistic perspective while also allowing careful examination of the effects that clients take from therapy. In this chapter, I present a sketch for such a humanistic alternative, a form of systematic case study that I label *hermeneutic single-case efficacy design* (HSCED). (For similar developments, see Bohart, 2000; Fishman, 1999; and Schneider, 1999; see also the second chapter by Schneider [Chapter 23] in this volume.)

Traditionally, systematic case studies have been classified under the traditional design rubric of *single-case pre-post designs* and have been designated as *nonexperimental*, that is, causally uninterpretable (Campbell & Stanley, 1963). Cook and Campbell (1979) noted, however, that such "modus operandi" designs can be interpreted under certain conditions, that is, when there is rich contextual information and what they called "signed causes." Signed causes are influences whose presence is evident in their effects. For example, if a bumper-shaped dent with white paint in it appears in your new car after you have left it parked in a parking lot, then the general nature of the causal agent can be readily inferred, even if the offending vehicle has long since left the scene. Mohr (1993) went further, arguing that the single case is the *best* situation for inferring and generalizing causal influence.

Furthermore, standard suspicions about systematic case studies ignore the fact that skilled practitioners and laypeople in a variety of settings continually use effective but implicit practical reasoning strategies to make causal judgments about single events, ranging from medical illnesses, to lawsuits, to airplane crashes (Schön, 1983). For example, legal and medical practice both are fundamentally systems for developing and testing causal inferences in naturalistic situations.

Thus, the challenge is to explicate a convincing practical reasoning system for judging the influence of therapy on client change. Hermeneutic single-case efficacy designs (HSCEDs) attempt to explicate a set of practical methods that are transparent, systematic, and self-reflective enough to provide an adequate basis for making inferences about therapy efficacy in single cases. The approach outlined here makes use of rich networks of information ("thick" description rather than elegant design) and interpretive (rather than experimental) procedures to develop probabilistic (rather than absolute) knowledge claims. Thus, such an approach is hermeneutic in the sense that it attempts to construct a plausible understanding of the influence processes in complex ambiguous sets of information about a client's therapy.

HSCED uses a mixture of quantitative and qualitative information to create a rich case record that provides both positive and negative evidence for the causal influence of therapy on client outcome. As outlined here, it involves a set of procedures that allow a therapist/researcher to make a reasonable case for claiming that a *client probably improved* and that the client *probably used therapy* to bring about this improvement. Making these inferences requires two things. First, there must be one or more pieces of *positive evidence* linking therapy to observed client change, for example, a plausible report or self-evident association linking a significant within-therapy event to a shift in client problems. Second, *negative evidence* is also required, indicating that plausible nontherapy explanations probably are insufficient to account for apparent client change. The accumulation of negative evidence requires good-faith efforts to show that nontherapy processes can explain apparent client change, including systematic consideration of a set of "competing explanations" for client change (see Cook & Campbell's [1979] account of internal validity).

It is worth noting that humanistic psychologists generally are suspicious of the words *explanation* and *cause*, which they equate with natural science modes of understanding (i.e., mechanical and physicalistic processes) and which they rightly mistrust as reductionistic and dehumanizing. However, thinking causally and searching for explanations is part of what makes us human (Cook & Campbell, 1979), like telling stories. When we describe therapy as *responsible for, bringing about,* or *influencing* change on the part of our clients, we are speaking in explicitly causal terms. Even language such as *facilitating* and *empowering* is implicitly causal. However, in discussing causal influence processes in humans, it is clear that we are not talking about anything like mechanical forces; rather, we are talking about *narrative causality,* which employs a range of modes of explanation including who did something (agentic explanation); what the person's purpose was in acting (intentional explanation); what plan, role, or schema the person was enacting (formal explanation); and what situation allowed the action (opportunity explanation) (Elliott, 1992). At the same time, it is very important for humanistic psychologists to be very careful with their language so as not to fall into the common trap of treating psychological processes as if they were mechanical causes. In other words, therapists do not "cause" their clients to change; rather, clients make use of what happens between them and their therapists so as to bring about (or sometimes to avoid bringing about) desired changes in their lives.

A PRACTICAL REASONING STRATEGY FOR INFERRING CAUSAL INFLUENCE OF THERAPY

In our society, various types of experts must rely on practical reasoning systems in complex circumstances marked by multiple possible causal factors and contradictory evidence. Such circumstances preclude certainty or even near certainty (i.e., $p < .05$) and often require that decisions be made on the basis of "probable cause" or "the weight of the evidence" (i.e., $p < .20$).

The challenge, then, is to make this practical reasoning system transparent, systematic, and self-reflective enough to convince ourselves and others. This requires three things: (a) a rich case record consisting of multiple data sources, both qualitative and quantitative; (b) one or more positive indicators of a direct connection between therapy process and outcome; and (c) a careful assessment leading to the conclusion that nontherapy factors are insufficient to explain apparent client change. This reasoning process is not mechanical and is more like detective work in which available evidence is weighed carefully and contradictory evidence is sought so as to test emerging possible alternative explanations.

Rich Case Record

The first prerequisite for HSCED is a rich comprehensive collection of information about a client's therapy. This collection includes basic facts about the client and his or her presenting problems as well as data about therapy process and outcome using multiple sources or measures. The following are some useful sources of data:

Quantitative outcome measures. Therapy outcome is both descriptive/qualitative (*how* the client changed) and evaluative/quantitative (how *much* the client changed). Thus, it is useful to use selected quantitative outcome measures including standard self-report questionnaires (e.g., Symptom Checklist-90 [Derogatis, 1983]). At a minimum, these measures should be given at the beginning and end of therapy, but it is also a good idea to give them periodically during therapy, for example, every 8 to 10 sessions.

Weekly outcome measure. A key element in HSCED is the administration of a weekly measure of the client's main therapy-related problems or goals. This procedure has two advantages. First, it provides a way of linking important therapy and life events to specific client changes. Second, it ensures that there will be some form of outcome data at whatever point the client stops coming to therapy. (These data are particularly important in naturalistic practice settings.) One such measure is the Simplified Personal Questionnaire (Elliott, Shapiro, & Mack, 1999), a 10-item target complaint measure made up of problems that the client wants to work on in therapy.

Qualitative outcome assessment. As noted previously, therapy outcome is also qualitative or descriptive in nature. Furthermore, it is impossible (and inefficient) to predict and measure every possible way in which a client might change. Therefore, it is essential to ask the client. At a minimum, this inquiry can be conducted at the end of therapy, but it is a good idea to conduct it every 8 to 10 sessions. Because clients are reluctant to be critical of their therapists, qualitative outcome assessment probably is best carried out by a third party, but it can be engaged in by the therapist if necessary. The Change Interview (Elliott, Slatick, & Urman, in press) is one way of obtaining qualitative information about outcome.

Qualitative information about significant events. Because therapeutic change is at least partly an intermittent discrete process, it is a good idea to collect information about important events in therapy. Sometimes, the content of these events can be directly linked to important client changes, making them *signed causes* (e.g., when a client discloses previously unexpressed feelings toward a significant other shortly after a session involving empty chair work with that same significant other). Questions about important therapy events can be included as part of a Change Interview (Elliott et al., in press), but an open-ended weekly post-session client questionnaire such as the Helpful Aspects of Therapy Form (Llewelyn, 1988) can also be very valuable for identifying therapy processes linked with client change.

Assessment of client attributions for change. The client can also be asked about the sources of changes that the client has observed in himself or herself. Both qualitative interviewing and quantitative attribution ratings can be used for this purpose (Elliott et al., in press). However, careful detailed interviewing is essential, for example, asking the client to tell the story of how therapy processes translated into general life changes. Rich descriptions by the client provide information for judging whether attributions are credible.

Direct information about therapy process. Much useful information about change processes occurs within therapy sessions in the form of (a) client narratives and (b) the unfolding interaction between client and therapist. For this reason, it is a very good idea to record all sessions of cases that are going to be used in HSCED research. A shortcut method can be found in the form of brief rating scales or therapist process notes (if they are reasonably detailed). Spence (1986) demonstrated that therapist process notes contain inaccuracies and "narrative smoothing." Therefore, it is a good idea to have an audio (or video) recording against which to check therapist process notes. Lastly, therapist postsession rating scales

can be correlated with weekly outcome so as to test whether particular theoretically important in-session processes or events are linked to extra-therapy change.

Positive Evidence: Clear Links Between Therapy Process and Outcome

As noted previously, making valid causal inferences about the relationship between therapy and client change requires both positive and negative evidence. Positive evidence of a direct or indirect connection between therapy process and outcome is required including one or more of the following:

▶ Client explicitly *attributes* change to therapy.

▶ Client describes *helpful aspects* of therapy linked to changes.

▶ Examination of weekly data reveals covariation between in-therapy processes (e.g., significant therapy events) and week-to-week shifts in client problems, particularly if the nature of the therapy process and the change are logically related to one another (e.g., therapeutic exploration of difficulty followed by change in that difficulty the following week).

A post-therapy Change Interview, a weekly Helpful Aspects of Therapy Form, and a weekly measure of client difficulties or goals (e.g., Simplified Personal Questionnaire) provide the information needed to identify positive connections between therapy processes and client change.

Negative Evidence: Evaluating Competing Explanations for Observed Pre-Post Change

The other basic requirement for causal inference is one of ruling out the major alternative explanations for observed or reported client change. In other words, the therapist is more likely to believe that the client used therapy to make changes if the therapist can eliminate other possible explanations for observed client change. This determination requires, first, a good-faith effort to find nontherapy processes that can account for apparent client change. What are these nontherapy processes that would lead the therapist to discount observed or reported client change? Following is a list of the major nontherapy "competing explanations" (or "internal validity threats" [Cook & Campbell, 1979]) in systematic case study designs such as HSCED:

1. The apparent changes are *negative* (i.e., involve deterioration) or *irrelevant* (i.e., involve unimportant or trivial variables).

2. The apparent changes are due to *statistical artifacts* or random error, including measurement error, experiment-wise error from using multiple change measures, or regression to the mean.

3. The apparent changes reflect *relational artifacts* such as global "hello-goodbye" effects on the part of the client expressing his or her liking for the therapist, wanting to make the therapist feel good, or trying to justify his or her ending therapy.

4. The apparent changes are due to cultural or personal *expectancy artifacts,* that is, expectations or "scripts" for change in therapy.

5. There is credible improvement, but it involves a temporary initial state of distress or dysfunction *reverting to normal baseline* through corrective or self-limiting processes unrelated to therapy.

6. There is credible improvement, but it is due to *extra-therapy life events* such as changes in relationships or work.

7. There is credible improvement, but it is due to *unidirectional psychobiological processes* such as psychopharmacological medications, herbal remedies, and recovery of hormonal balance following biological insult.

8. There is credible improvement, but it is due to the *reactive effects* of being in research.

Space does not allow a full description of these explanatory threats and how they can be evaluated here, but Table 24.1 contains additional information including examples and procedures for assessing their presence.

Note that the first four competing explanations have to do with whether observed or reported client changes are illusory or credible. For this reason, considerable initial attention needs to be paid to documenting and evaluating whether change has actually occurred, that is, whether there was any change to explain in the first place. If this preliminary issue is resolved in favor of convincing demonstration of change having occurred, then the remaining four factors—automatic return to normal functioning, extra-therapy events, psychobiological processes, and effects of research—can be addressed.

Thus, the second task for HSCED is to apply research procedures that address each of these possible alternative explanations for client change. Because the change processes operating in therapy are partial "opportunity causes," mechanistic data collection and analysis procedures will not work. Instead, the researcher must use multiple informants (client and therapist) and

TABLE 24.1 Nontherapy Processes That May Account for Observed Client Change and Methods for Evaluating Them

Nontherapy Process	Examples	Methods for Assessing
1. Nonimprovement	▸ Negative: deterioration ▸ Irrelevant: unimportant, trivial	▸ Analyze for deterioration as well as improvement ▸ Ask about negative changes ▸ Analyze clinical significance of change (Jacobson & Truax, 1991) ▸ Ask client to evaluate importance/significance of changes (Kazdin, 1999)
2. Statistical artifact (random error)	▸ Measurement error ▸ Regression to the mean ▸ Experiment-wise error	▸ Calculate Reliable Change Index (Jacobson & Truax, 1991) ▸ Use multiple pretests (rapid drop vs. stable or worse) ▸ Assess duration of problem (short vs. long) ▸ Assess consistency on multiple measures ▸ Calculate global reliable change (e.g., require reliable change on two out of three measures)
3. Relational artifact (interpersonal dynamics between client and therapist)	▸ "Hello-goodbye" effect: emphasize distress at beginning, positive functioning at end	▸ Measure social desirability ▸ Researcher, not therapist, interviews client ▸ Encourage negative comments ▸ Listen for spontaneous remarks expressing desire to please or evaluation apprehension ▸ Global or vague positive descriptions versus supporting or convincing detail ▸ Presence of both positive and negative descriptions
4. Expectancy artifacts (cultural or personal "scripts")	▸ Client tries to convince self and others that change has occurred when it has not	▸ Ask client to evaluate changes as expected versus surprising ▸ Examine client descriptions for consistency with cultural stereotypes versus plausible detail ▸ Look for spontaneous client attempts to convince self and therapist that change has occurred
5. Self-generated return to baseline	▸ Temporary initial state of distress or dysfunction ▸ Reverts to normal baseline through client's own natural corrective or self-limiting processes ▸ Not caused by therapy; would have happened anyway	▸ Evaluate duration of problems (interview or ratings) ▸ Ask client to evaluate likelihood that change might have occurred without therapy ▸ Use multiple pretests; look for change before therapy starts ▸ Look for client narratives of self-help efforts begun before therapy
6. Extra-therapy events (positive life events)	▸ Improvements in relationships or work ▸ Changes in health status unrelated to therapy (e.g., successful surgery, negative biopsy)	▸ Ask client: qualitative interview ▸ Look for in-session narratives about positive extra-therapy events or changes ▸ Look for extra-therapy events associated with weekly change
7. Unidirectional psychobiological causes	▸ Psychopharmacological medications/herbal remedies ▸ Hormonal stabilization in recovery from stroke or childbirth	▸ Keep track of medications and herbal remedies including changes and dose adjustments ▸ Look for in-session narratives about medical intervention
8. Reactive effects of research	▸ Effects of research activities (e.g., posttraumatic stress disorder assessment) ▸ Relation with research staff (e.g., better than with therapist) ▸ Sense of altruism (e.g., derives meaning from helping others)	▸ Ask client about effects of research (qualitative interview) ▸ Use less obtrusive data collection ▸ Use naturalistic clients rather than recruited ones

data collection strategies, both qualitative and quantitative. These strategies confront the researcher with multiple possible indicators that must be sorted out, typically by looking for points of convergence and interpreting points of contradiction.

In any case, the search for negative evidence can lead to a number of different results:

▶ Some nontherapy processes may be ruled out entirely.

▶ Other nontherapy processes may be found to be present but may fail to provide a full explanation of the observed change.

▶ Nontherapy processes may mediate therapeutic influence on outcome. For example, the client may use therapy to develop a more solid sense of direction, enabling him or her to be more assertive with others.

DISCUSSION AND IMPLICATIONS

This has been a necessarily brief overview of HSCED. To carry out the design, one would need to (a) collect appropriate measures, (b) apply them with a client to construct a rich case record, (c) analyze the information to see whether change occurred, (d) establish whether positive evidence was present linking therapy to client change, (e) analyze the information to assess evidence for each of the nontherapy processes, (f) interpret and weigh the various sets of sometimes conflicting information so as to determine the overall strength and credibility of each nontherapy process, and (g) come to an overall conclusion about the likelihood that therapy was a key influence on client change.

HSCED is a new development and clearly needs testing and elaboration. My team and I have applied HSCED to clients seen in our research and training clinic (Elliott et al., 2000). What we have learned so far can be summarized as follows. First, the question of whether the client improved has turned out to be more complex than we originally thought. Our clients typically presented us with a mixed picture, showing improvement on some measures but not on others or telling us that they had made great strides when the quantitative data contradicted this (or vice versa). It is important not to underestimate the complexity of even this preliminary step.

Second, this experience has convinced us that more work is needed on how to integrate contradictory information. Clearer approaches to determining where the weight of the evidence lies (see the second chapter by Schneider [Chapter 23] in this volume) would help.

Third, we find ourselves in need of additional creative strategies for evaluating nontherapy explanations. For example, to bolster the self-reflective/critical process of examining nontherapy processes, Bohart (2000) proposed a form of HSCED that relies on an adjudication process involving researchers arguing for and against therapy as a primary influence on client change, with final determination made by a "research jury." However, a less involved process might simply make use of two researchers, with one (perhaps the therapist) supporting therapy as an important influence and the other playing "devil's advocate" by trying to support alternative explanations. The researchers might present both sides, leaving the final decision to a scientific review process (see Fishman, 1999).

Fourth, in comparing HSCED to traditional RCT design, we have found that HSCED requires fewer resources but in some ways is more difficult and demanding in that it requires the researchers to address complexities, ambiguities, and contradictions ignored in traditional designs. These complexities are present in all therapy research, but RCTs are able to ignore them by simplifying their data collection and analysis. We argue that every group design is made up of individual clients whose change processes are as rich and contradictory as the clients we have studied. The fact that these complexities are invisible in RCTs is yet another reason to distrust them and to continue working toward viable alternatives that do justice to each client's unique-

ness while still allowing us to determine whether (a) the clients have changed, (b) the observed changes are credible, and (c) these changes have anything to do with our work as therapists. This is a rigorous, highly challenging standard by which to hold ourselves—higher, in fact, than group designs such as RCTs. However, as humanists, we owe it to ourselves, as well as to our clients, to understand our role in providing our clients with opportunities for desired change and growth.

REFERENCES

Bohart, A. C. (2000, June). *A qualitative adjudicational model for assessing psychotherapy outcome*. Paper presented at the meeting of the Society for Psychotherapy Research, Chicago.

Bohart, A. C., & Tallman, K. (1999). *How clients make therapy work: The process of active self-healing*. Washington, DC: American Psychological Association.

Campbell, D. T., & Stanley, J. C. (1963). *Experimental and quasi-experimental designs for research*. Chicago: Rand McNally.

Cartwright, D. S., Kirtner, W. L., & Fiske, D. W. (1963). Method factors in change associated with psychotherapy. *Journal of Abnormal and Social Psychology, 66,* 164-175.

Cook, T. D., & Campbell, D. T. (1979). *Quasi-experimentation: Design and analysis issues for field settings*. Chicago: Rand McNally.

Derogatis, L. R. (1983). *SCL-90-R administration, scoring, and procedures manual—II*. Towson, MD: Clinical Psychometric Research.

Elliott, R. (1992). *Modes of explanation in psychotherapy research*. Unpublished manuscript, University of Toledo, Toledo, OH.

Elliott, R., Shapiro, D. A., & Mack, C. (1999). *Simplified Personal Questionnaire procedure*. Toledo, OH: University of Toledo, Department of Psychology.

Elliott, R., Slatick, E., & Urman, M. (in press). Qualitative change process research on psychotherapy: Alternative strategies. In J. Frommer & D. Rennie (Eds.), *The methodology of qualitative psychotherapy research*. Lengerich, Germany: Pabst Science.

Elliott, R., Smith, S., Magaña, C. G., Germann, J., Jersak, H., Partyka, R., Urman, M., Wagner, J., & Shapiro, D. A. (2000, June). *Hermeneutic single case efficacy design: A pilot project evaluating process-experiential therapy in a naturalistic treatment series*. Panel presented at the meeting of the Society for Psychotherapy Research, Chicago.

Fishman, D. B. (1999). *The case for pragmatic psychology*. New York: New York University Press.

Greenberg, L. S., Elliott, R., & Lietaer, G. (1994). Research on humanistic and experiential psychotherapies. In A. E. Bergin & S. L. Garfield (Eds.), *Handbook of psychotherapy and behavior change* (4th ed., pp. 509-539). New York: John Wiley.

Haaga, D. A. F., & Stiles, W. B. (2000). Randomized clinical trials in psychotherapy research: Methodology, design, and evaluation. In C. R. Snyder & R. E. Ingram (Eds.), *Handbook of psychological change* (pp. 14-39). New York: John Wiley.

Jacobson, N. S., & Truax, P. (1991). Clinical significance: A statistical approach to defining meaningful change in psychotherapy research. *Journal of Consulting and Clinical Psychology, 59,* 12-19.

Kazdin, A. E. (1999). The meaning and measurement of clinical significance. *Journal of Consulting and Clinical Psychology, 67,* 332-339.

Lietaer, G. (1990). The client-centered approach after the Wisconsin Project: A personal view on its evolution. In G. Lietaer, J. Rombauts, & R. Van Balen (Eds.), *Client-centered and experiential psychotherapy in the nineties* (pp. 19-45). Leuven, Belgium: Leuven University Press.

Llewelyn, S. (1988). Psychological therapy as viewed by clients and therapists. *British Journal of Clinical Psychology, 27,* 223-238.

Mohr, L. B. (1993, October). *Causation and the case study.* Paper presented at the National Public Management Research Conference, Madison, WI.

Rogers, C. R. (1949). A coordinated research in psychotherapy: A non-objective introduction. *Journal of Consulting Psychology, 13,* 149-153.

Rogers, C. R., & Dymond, R. F. (Eds.). (1954). *Psychotherapy and personality change.* Chicago: University of Chicago Press.

Schneider, K. J. (1999). Multiple-case depth research. *Journal of Clinical Psychology, 55,* 1531-1540.

Schön, D. A. (1983). *The reflective practitioner: How professionals think in action.* New York: Basic Books.

Snyder, W. U. (1945). An investigation of the nature of nondirective psychotherapy. *Journal of General Psychology, 33,* 193-223.

Spence, D. P. (1986). Narrative smoothing and clinical wisdom. In T. R. Sarbin (Ed.), *Narrative psychology: The storied nature of human conduct* (pp. 211-232). New York: Praeger.

Part IV

HUMANISTIC APPLICATIONS TO PRACTICE

Introduction to Part IV

Humanistic psychology is founded on a dedication to the conviction that life has greater potential than has yet been realized and an openness to a wide range of observations, methods, and practices. In this perspective, we draw humility, challenge, and encouragement from the realization of how much about human beings is yet unknown. Commitment, struggle, successes and failures, and a continually receding frontier await those who would join us.

—James F. T. Bugental, "Rollo May Award," 1997

INNOVATIVE APPROACHES TO PRACTICE have been a hallmark of humanistic psychology from its inception. The current generation of practitioners builds on a rich legacy from the founders of humanistic psychology. These include pioneers such as Charlotte Buhler, Viktor Frankl, Sidney Jourard, Abraham Maslow, Rollo May, Fritz Perls, Carl Rogers, Virginia Stir, and James Bugental, whose contributions to depth psychotherapy span five decades and continue to blaze trails today. The founders were men and women of courage—"heart"—who established an alternative philosophical stance "with [its] own distinctive views of human nature . . . and of psychotherapy" (American Psychological Association, 2000).

Similar courage is required during this era. A challenge for humanistic practitioners is to honor the perspective's ideals and values as formalized in the "Guidelines for the Provision of Humanistic Services," (Bohart et al., 1997) and to respond in keeping with these guidelines to the sociopolitical realities of the time (in the United States)—the influences of the managed care industry, the glamour of the biomedical model, and the pressure to work from positivistic, empirically supported manualized treatment protocols.

In this part of the volume, we first present a sample of contemporary applications to practice that represent the breadth and depth of current interests among humanistic psychotherapists and counselors. Contributors to this section demonstrate the courage and vision of the founders as they open exciting frontiers of practice and, in fresh ways, explore perennial themes in the context of our complex postmodern world.

In Chapter 25, leading off the "Contemporary Themes" section, John Welwood envisions the core process of change in psychotherapy as an unfolding emerging experience that draws on the wisdom of the body-mind connection. The unfolding process, which is "at the heart of all creative discovery," is not a technique in the ordinary sense of the word but rather a capacity latent within the client that can be taught and encouraged to develop in psychotherapy. Welwood identifies the intriguing relationship between the dynamics of unfolding in the context of psychotherapy and our capacity for spiritual awakenings—opening to the farther reaches of our human potential.

The quality of the relationship between therapist and client has long captured the attention of humanistic theorists and therapists. It is recognized as the medium in which the client reclaims his or her wholeness. In a special section, Maurice Friedman and Molly Sterling explore the responsibility of the therapist. In Chapter 26, Friedman begins by defining the essence of responsibility as "responding to the person before you as a person," that is, responding as "I to thou" in each unique therapeutic relationship. Responding means "hearing the unreduced claim of each hour in all its crudeness and disharmony and answering it out of the depths of one's being." In Chapter 27, Sterling's vivid case example invites us to enter into the lived experience of being called to *respond* during the therapy hour. In the process, she underscores the importance of the therapist's presence and deepens our understanding of the responsibilities of both client and therapist.

How do we *be* what we hope to teach others? What does it mean to *be* a humanistic therapist? What are the personal benefits and costs of embracing humanistic values? In Chapter 28, Jeffrey Kottler and Richard Hazler candidly explore these questions and the challenges they present.

Courage, on the part of both the therapist and the client, is a theme that runs throughout the chapters in this section. In Chapter 29, Clemmont Vontress and Lawrence Epp provide an existential model of culture and suggest that everyone is multicultural in the sense that "most people are products of five concentric and intersecting cultures: universal, ecological, national, regional, and racial/ethnic." The counselor is challenged to be a "macroscopic and holistic thinker," that is, to see beyond superficial cultural differences and to help the client identify imbalances among the four spheres of existence. Such counselors are "necessarily artists, who are creative, individualistic, and fluid in their work and who have a spiritual connection with each client"; they are in relationship with their clients as "fellow travelers." Vontress and Epp explore concepts that help counselors to understand the influence of culture in clients' lives and offer practical suggestions for working with "culturally different" clients.

The ability of the therapist to enter into the phenomenological world of the client is also central to the success of the Soteria Project, an innovative and humanizing alternative to psychiatric hospitalization described by Loren Mosher in Chapter 30. The Soteria approach, based on the practice of interpersonal phenomenology, offered a "confiding relationship" to clients diagnosed with schizophrenia and an environment in which recovery from psychosis was expected. Follow-up studies comparing the Soteria method to general psychiatric hospitalization suggests that the former offered highly effective therapeutic interventions and cost-effectiveness. Intriguingly, despite the documented success of Soteria and its replication facilities, it has all but vanished from the consciousness of American psychiatry. Did it threaten the biomedical perspective currently held by the American Psychiatric Association and supported by the pharmaceutical industry? Mosher closes his thought-provoking chapter with a summary of how he prefers to work with his clients and their families along with this poignant statement: "When successful, there is no more schizophrenia, only two or more humans who have been through a shared, awesome, subjective experience."

The next two chapters constitute a special section on awe and terror in humanistic therapy. In Chapter 31, Mark Stern continues the theme of humanizing and demedicalizing psychotherapy. Through the use of riveting dialogue, he enacts a mutually transformative therapeutic relationship with Father Gregory, a man struggling with obsessive thoughts and compulsive rituals, a priest having trouble in "discriminat[ing] between the mercilessness of awe as servile adoration and awe as earnest devotion." We are drawn into the drama of the relationship and experience the therapist's attempt to "embrace the client's awe equally as agony and aspiration."

In Chapter 32, Alvin Mahrer describes another way in which awe is manifested in psychotherapy—the awe-full moment evoked in the context of an experiential session. His chapter is an invitation to take a "baby step" toward having such a session. Mahrer beckons with an in-depth description of the ways in which awe-full moments may occur and the qualitative transformations in one's sense of self that accompany this process.

Humanistic and the postmodern constructivist approaches to psychotherapy share the underlying goal of liberating the individual to live more fully, creatively, and courageously. In Chapter 33, Larry Leitner and Franz Epting provide an overview of constructivism as a "firmly humanistic approach" albeit still relatively overlooked by humanistic practitioners. As the authors highlight constructivist philosophies and approaches to therapy, the compatibility with humanistic theory and practice is clearly evident. The potential power and effectiveness of this perspective in action is revealed by several descriptive examples of constructivist psychotherapy. Leitner and Epting conclude their chapter by stating, "To truly have a rich discipline, we must understand the magnificent creature we call a *person.*" Both constructivist and humanistic therapists seek to understand the experiential worlds of their clients. They do not seek to impose meanings; rather, they seek to understand their clients' "truths" as the basis from which to work together in collaborative relationships.

Searching for meaning in loss is a process that we, as embodied human creatures, are called on to do throughout our lives. In Chapter 34, Myrtle Heery describes the process of searching for meaning in loss—a companion to the existential "givens" of embodiment and finitude—as a journey into uncharted territory for each individual. Her work with people who are bereaved suggests some "stations" typically encountered during the ongoing search process. She invites the reader to explore his or her own losses and to discover the stations of his or her uniquely courageous journey. Heery ends her deeply moving chapter with a question for each of us as therapists: "Can we remain open to accompany our clients into the depths of their hearts?" Are we prepared? Acknowledgment of the spiritual dimensions of the search is among the challenges facing contemporary psychology.

Distinguishing and agreeing on the points of philosophical interface between humanistic and existential approaches to psychotherapy is a long-standing challenge for many who identify with the "third force." In Chapter 35, John Rowan and, with a reply, Ernesto Spinelli provide animated British perspectives and decided opinions on the relationship between humanistic therapy and existential analysis. From our perspective, humansitic psychology is making increasing room for both.

The final three chapters in this part of the volume give a sampling of current trends and considerations in humanistic applications to practice. In Chapter 36, Maureen O'Hara begins the "Emergent Trends" section by providing an enlightening examination of humanistic psychology "in its historical, cultural, philosophical, and marketplace contexts" and argues convincingly that the perspective should not continue to try to justify itself from the bases of an outdated, limited scientific worldview and as part of a powerful, industrialized medical system, however much in vogue at the present time. O'Hara supports the belief that humanistic and transpersonal psychologies "comprise . . . transformative practices with something different and . . . far more timely and relevant to offer an emerging global community in search of its psychological and spiritual bearings." She sounds the clarion call for a postmodern emancipatory humanistic psychology that "draws on the best of its past as well as on constructivist developments in theory and on the newer neurosciences and advances in mind-body studies." Such a theoretically renewed humanistic psychology has a potentially vital role to play in cultural transformation.

In Chapter 37, Will Wadlington also challenges the reader to stretch beyond modernistic conceptualizations of psychotherapy—to "step outside modernism" and expand his or her vision of what constitutes new practices and therapies. Performative social therapy is an example of a new humanistic practice, one that fosters collaborative improvisation as opposed to theory-guided problem solving. Wadlington's description of this revolutionary approach provides an intriguing vision of what is possible as we re-vision humanistic psychology to make it "relevant to the diverse multicultural social context of everyday postmodern life."

In Chapter 38, Jeanne Watson and Arthur Bohart discuss an alternative trend. They present ideas on how experiential therapists can thrive within the current mental health care system without forfeiting the essence of their approaches. Watson and Bohart address the realities of practicing within the time-limited managed care environment and provide specific suggestions for adapting five humanistic-experiential approaches. The authors highlight Bohart and Tallman's (1999) view of clients as "active self-healers" as being compatible with contemporary stances and as offering a meta-theory for working within managed care environments.

REFERENCES

American Psychological Association. (2000). *Position statements on humanistic psychology* [Online]. Available: www.apa.org/divisions/div32/positions.html

Bohart, A. C., O'Hara, M., Leitner, L. M., Wertz, F., Stern, E. M., Schneider, K. J., Serlin, I. A., & Greening, T. (1997). Guidelines for the provision of psychosocial services. *The Humanistic Psychologist, 24,* 64-107.

Bohart, A. C., & Tallman, K. (1999). *How clients make therapy work: The process of active self-healing.* Washington, DC: American Psychological Association.

Bugental, J. F. T. (1997, Winter). Rollo May Award. *Forum,* p. 2. (Saybrook Graduate School)

CHAPTER *25*

The Unfolding of Experience
Psychotherapy and Beyond

JOHN WELWOOD

> *I want to unfold. I don't want to stay folded anywhere because where*
> *I am folded, there I am untrue.*
>
> —R. M. Rilke (*Rilke's Book of Hours*, 1996)

LIFE UNFOLDS, forever giving rise to a freshly emerging flow of discoveries. At least two different types of unfolding operate in human development: (a) a sequential or "horizontal" unfolding in which we evolve through time as new discoveries appear progressively, each one building on those that have preceded it; and beyond that, (b) a more unpredictable type of "vertical" emergence in which something totally fresh and unexpected breaks through, allowing us to move to a deeper level of awareness and see things in a radically new way. Unlike many of the mechanistic metaphors of modern science, the organic metaphor of unfolding helps us to appreciate the emergent open-ended nature of our experience. Understanding the dynamics of unfolding helps to clarify the core process of change in psychotherapy as well as the relationship among therapeutic change, creativity, and more radical types of spiritual awakening.

THE MULTILEVEL TEXTURE OF EXPERIENCING

Human experiencing is a rich fluid tapestry that consists of many interweaving strands of feeling, sensing, and knowing. At every moment, we are processing much more information and sensing many more levels of meaning than we are explicitly aware of at the time. James (1967) eloquently described this holistic tapestry:

> In the pulse of inner life immediately present now in each of us is a little past, a little future, a little awareness of our own body, of each other's persons, of these sublimities we are trying to talk about, of the earth's geography and the direction of history, of

truth and error, of good and bad, and of who knows how much more? (pp. 295-296)

Because we "know" in subtle nonverbal ways much more than we can ever articulate in a logical sequential way, new meanings—new ways of seeing and new things seen—can continually unfold in awareness. Classical depth psychology calls the source of these new meanings *the unconscious*. Yet, despite Jung's laudable attempt to conceive the unconscious in organic terms rather than mechanistic ones, the depth psychology model tends to foster a deterministic view of human behavior in which conscious experience is seen as a derivative of preexisting instincts, repressed drives, object relations, and/or preformatted archetypes. I prefer to understand the emergence of unconscious material into consciousness as an unfolding of relational body/mind patternings that are enfolded in consciousness in the holistic way described in the preceding quote by James (Welwood, 1977a). The unfolding of new meaning is an explication, or a making explicit, of an implicit, already richly patterned field of interrelationship.

For example, a man feels "funny" after a brief conversation with his mother on the telephone without exactly knowing why. At first, he has only a vague sense that something strange just transpired. Yet, his body/mind senses and seems to know *tacitly* the manifold implications of the interaction, while his *surface mind*—which operates through linear focal attention—still is in the dark. His body holds this funny feeling as a hollowness in his chest along with a tightness in his stomach. As he inquires into what is going on inside him, he spends the next hour unfolding a complex tangle of felt meaning—shame, feeling manipulated and controlled, anger, longing to communicate, and helplessness. Some of these feelings are responses to what just transpired on the phone, whereas others relate to his whole relationship with his mother going back 30 years. And all of them were implicit in his initial funny sense. To free up this tangle of feeling, he needed to explicate it through attentive inquiry.

THE HOLOGRAPHIC NATURE OF FELT EXPERIENCE

One analogy that can help us to understand the complexity of implicit experience and how it unfolds is that of the hologram, which Pribram (1971) also used to help explain certain aspects of memory functioning in the brain. A hologram is a photographic plate that records complex interactions of light waves in a way that allows a three-dimensional picture of the object photographed to be projected from it. In a hologram, light wave patterns are scattered evenly throughout the whole photographic plate so that every part of it carries information about the whole. Vast amounts of information are superimposed on each other in a tiny area. As Pribram wrote, "Some ten billion bits of information have been usefully stored holographically in a cubic centimeter" (p. 150). The light waves in a hologram overlap in complex ways (called an *interference pattern*) to form a blurry whole configuration. This holographic blur does not literally resemble the object photographed, nor does it have any recognizable form at all. The complexity of these wave interactions is what gives the holographic image its realistic three-dimensional quality when reproduced from the holographic plate.

The complexity of our inner experiencing is roughly analogous to the structure of a hologram. For example, if you ask yourself how you feel now, then what you get when you first refer inwardly to your felt sensing is a blurry whole. Or, try referring to your felt sense of a person in your life. What is your overall feeling about your father—your whole sense of him? Letting go of any specific memory, thought, or image, let yourself feel the whole quality of your relationship with him. Underneath any image, see whether you can sense the larger blurry whole felt sense of your father and his relationship to you. Notice that the felt sense has a global diffuse feeling texture, feeling color, or feeling tone rather than a definite form that you can readily articulate. Nonetheless, it is still quite distinct from your felt sense of other people, as you can see by comparing it to your felt sense of your mother.

A felt sense contains implicit felt meaning. *Felt* refers to the bodily component, *meaning* implies some type of knowing or patterning (although not of a logical conceptual type here), and *sense* indicates that this meaning is not yet clear. *Implicit* literally means "folded into" or "enfolded." Just as a hologram is blurry because it is a compressed record of many overlapping wave patterns, so too is a felt sense fuzzy or diffuse because it contains a number of overlapping meanings that a given situation has for you based on all of your different ways of interacting with it. Notice that your felt sense of your father includes all the ways in which you ever have experienced him. It is like a holographic record of all your interactions with him (analogous to interference patterns). All of your joys, hurts, disappointments, appreciations, angers—all of your whole experience with him—is holographically compressed in this one felt sense. The felt sense is blurry in that it includes all of this *implicitly*. This implicit is not sharply defined but always functions as a global background. Much of our everyday experience functions in this holistic background way.

THE UNFOLDING PROCESS

Therapeutic unfolding, or the process of making implicit felt meaning explicit, often begins with a diffuse type of receptive attention to the whole felt sense of a situation underneath all of one's different thoughts about it. Clients who cannot tolerate ambiguity, or who cannot let go of a strict reliance on focal attention, usually are more difficult to work with because their speaking tends to repeat what they already have thought about many times before. They talk about their problems without anything new happening.

Yet, when we can tap into and speak *from* a diffusely felt sense rather than from what we think *about* it, this allows a fresh articulation of what is true for us that was not accessible or expressible before. It is only out of the initial blurriness that something fresh can unfold, something that we may have vaguely sensed but not yet fully realized. That is why we usually have to let ourselves *not know* before we can discover anything new. Gendlin (1962, 1964, 1981) developed the Focusing process in response to psychotherapy research suggesting that clients most readily change and move forward if what they say taps into and unfolds presently felt meanings that are concretely experienced in the body as a felt sense (Gendlin, Beebe, Cassens, Klein, & Oberlander, 1968; Rogers, 1967). This research also suggested that therapy does not generally teach clients to draw on diffuse attention, to contact the wider body/mind, and to speak from there (Walker, Rablen, & Rogers, 1959). Focusing was the first major concrete delineation of this process of therapeutic unfolding or "working through."

For example, a client comes in feeling miserable and depressed about his marriage. At first, he speaks about his unhappiness with his wife, giving voice to complaints, guilt, and frustration. But his words are rather lifeless. He is talking "off the top of his head," without any deep inward reference going on. As a therapist, I guide him toward his felt sense of this situation underneath all of his thoughts and emotional reactions. How does the client feel this situation in his body? I might let him feel around inside for a while without saying much. Often, just connecting with it in this way provides some relief and encouragement to delve further into it.

I ask the client about his bodily felt sense. "It's a heavy feeling in my stomach," he responds. Now that he is in touch with this heaviness directly, he can begin to inquire into it and unfold the implicit meaning contained in it. This type of inquiry is a way of holding up a frame to the global heaviness, allowing it to come into sharper relief. Applying a frame to the implicit is somewhat analogous to deblurring a hologram by highlighting major contours so that particular features can emerge from the blur. The frame in this case is a question from me: "What's so heavy about this for you?" Again, he returns to his felt sense, and we wait for something more specific to unfold.

"It's anger, just sitting in my gut," he now says, "weighing me down, eating me out from the inside." With this next step of unfolding, his words start to gather energy and intensity. As he feels into the anger he now has articulated, the next direction appears: "But even more than angry, I feel tremendously disappointed in her [his wife]. She isn' t there for me in the way she used to be." There is a pause. His words have more energy now. We seem to be on the verge of something new emerging. "But I'm also disappointed in myself. Things used to be so good between us, and now we don't even listen to each other." He sighs deeply now as he is getting closer to the core of what he is

feeling. I can tell by his shaky tone of voice that he is close to opening up something larger and more significant. He is no longer talking *about* his felt sense; he is talking *from* it. His next statement really cracks it open: "And you know, I'm just now realizing that I haven't felt my caring for her in a long time. That's what's so heavy; I've locked away my love and sat on it for months now. I'm having a hard time feeling my love for her." Something in his body now is releasing; he breathes more deeply, tears start to form, and the blood is returning to his face. He now is in a much different place from when he first walked in a half hour ago.

Figure 25.1 illustrates this progressive zigzag process of unfolding, with the client alternating between a connection to a vague felt sense—represented by the cloudy circles—and articulation of the meaning implicit in that sense. The content of the realizations reached in this way might seem identical to something that this person could have figured out through intellectual analysis. Yet, more important than the particular discoveries of anger, disappointment, and blocked love was the dynamic movement of unfolding that allowed for a spontaneous felt shift as the client articulated what his body/mind already sensed and felt implicitly.

This type of unfolding process, which moves back and forth between articulation and nonarticulation, is at the heart of all creative discovery, whether in therapy, the arts, or the sciences. In writing this chapter, for example, I started with a global felt sense of what I wanted to say. But I could not know exactly what I would say except by unfolding it word by word and sentence by sentence. Each sentence leads on to the next one, growing and building on what has unfolded already. At the end of this chapter, I should have discovered the full range of

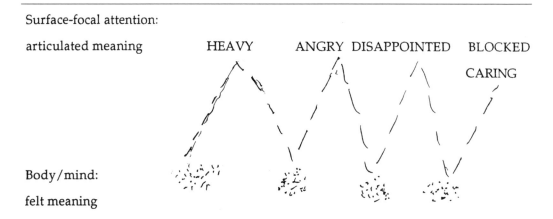

Figure 25.1. Therapeutic Unfolding

my intent (although, of course, there always is more). Similarly, implicit in that whole sense of your father I asked you about earlier, there is probably a whole novel about your relationship with him that could unfold from it. Your whole novel is holographically compressed in your very first diffuse felt sense of him.

As Levinson (1975) observed, "The process of change has its own phenomenology that is no different from the way an artist arrives at a visual concept or a mathematician at a new formulation" (p. 12). Similarly, Bohm (1973) spoke of how a creative physicist should proceed, using language fitting for therapy: "One has to observe the new situation very broadly and tentatively and to 'feel out' the relevant new features" (p. 146). And in words that could apply equally to poetry or psychotherapy, Picard (1952, pp. 173, 36) suggests that speech has potency and depth only when it arises out of a larger undifferentiated space beyond words, moving

> from silence into the word and then back again into the silence and so on, so that the word always comes from the center of silence. . . . Mere verbal noise, on the other hand, moves uninterruptedly along the horizontal line of the sentence. (p. 173) . . . Words that merely come from other words are hard . . . and lonely. (p. 36)

Once an implicit felt sense has opened up, whether in therapy or in developing a new scientific theory, things are never quite the same again. What is creative or healing about the unfolding process is that it allows us to experience ourselves and understand our situations in a much fuller way than was possible before. This fuller way results from the dynamic back-and-forth interaction between two ways of knowing: that of the surface focal mind with that of the wider body/mind. As each step of inquiry brings to light a new facet of an implicit felt sense, the felt sense starts to move and shift like a tangled ball of yarn untangling. As the client pulls loose a given strand, the shape of the bundle changes; the problem no longer feels the same. Pulling each strand not only loosens up the whole tangle but also reveals the next strand to tug. The client's successive ways of articulating a felt implicit alter the shape of the implicit itself.

Although any life problem may have many different angles or many irritating facets, there is usually one central tangle or one central crux (and sometimes two or three). Bringing this central concern into awareness—usually some confused or unresolved way of relating to ourselves, to other people, or to life—is what allows the tangled situation to unravel and release.

Another client of mine explored over the course of many weeks the different ways in which he felt empty and unfulfilled before he finally was able to unfold the crux of the problem. He realized that it was not so much that something particular was missing from his life as that he could not allow himself to acknowledge or consider his heart's true desire. In his words, "That just feels too vulnerable." Many earlier steps of working with the felt sense of emptiness were necessary to lead to this point (just as an artist or scientist has to spend a great deal of time considering the various dimensions of a creative problem before a breakthrough can occur). Finally the client could see that the real issue was not something missing "out there" but rather his own fear of letting himself know what he really wanted. Instead of seeing his life through this distorting lens, he finally could see the lens that was causing the distortions. Realizing that he was not just a victim of circumstance brought a huge sense of relief, allowing him to consider a whole new way of approaching his life.

Therapeutic unfolding has three main stages: widening attention to feel out a global felt sense of a situation; inquiring directly into this felt sense; and by successively articulating it from various angles, discovering its crux, which releases its stuckness and allows new directions to emerge. In this way, confusion gradually moves toward clarity, wrongness toward rightness, and disconnection toward connection. As Gendlin (1981) suggested, every life problem contains in it a sense of a new

direction if only we can let it unfold: "The sense of what is wrong carries with it . . ., inseparably, a sense of the direction toward what is right. . . . Every bad feeling is potential energy toward a more right way of being if you give it space to move toward its rightness" (p. 76).

In facilitating a process of unfolding, a good listener does not fixate or become preoccupied with any particular content that is being articulated. More important than what we say in responding to another is our ability to point to and resonate with the other's (still unclear) felt sense. As Levinson (1975) put it,

> It is clear that the therapist would not have to be correct in his formulations as much as he would have to be in harmony or in resonance with what is occurring in the patient. . . . It might sound outrageous to suggest that it would be possible to do good therapy without ever really understanding what is going on, as long as the therapist is involved in an expansion of awareness and is using his own participation to further elaborate and actualize the patient's world. It is conceivable that this is where therapy actually takes place, whether we like it or not. . . . *The therapist does not explain content; he expands awareness of patterning.* (p. 18)

Often, when a therapy session is transcribed and written out, it makes little sense when reading it. This is because the words that are spoken are not what is most essential. The therapeutic process is not about trying to put feelings into words. Words, in fact, never can be literal snapshots of felt experience any more than a three-dimensional holographic image can literally reproduce the complex wave patterns stored on a holographic plate. Rather, the words the therapist speaks have a transforming effect on the client when they resonate with what that person implicitly feels, thereby helping the feelings to unfold—to reveal new understandings, new depths, and new ways of being and relating.

This understanding of therapeutic working through as a two-way interactive process of unfolding provides a more dynamic and liberating model of therapy than does the one-way street of making the unconscious conscious. The old notion of the unconscious as a separate region of the mind, with its own explicit contents and drives, fostered a deterministic approach to therapy based on bringing to light, through rational analysis, solid problems stored away in the psyche. By failing to recognize or honor the ever-evolving richness and open-endedness of human experiencing, which continually unfolds in surprising and unpredictable ways, deterministic models of therapy only reinforce the split between the surface focal mind and our deeper being, a division that lies at the root of our problems in the first place. As Hillman (1972) pointed out, this type of analysis "is really part of the malady itself and continues to contribute to it. (p. 290) . . . We cannot escape the conclusion that analysis as a therapeutic psychology may well be self-defeating" (p. 294).

VERTICAL EMERGENCE

Discovering, through the unfolding of experience, that psychological problems are not fixed entities stored inside us is a liberating realization that can bring us to the threshold of a new type of awareness altogether. What is it that actually happens when a felt sense unfolds, a frozen feeling thaws, or a tangled life problem unravels? What emerges in a moment of release when an old fixation suddenly shifts?

Often, when an inner knot releases, we breathe deeply, with a sigh of relief, and then go about our business. We might not notice, in such moments, how we gain access to a new quality of presence, energetic aliveness, or beingness. This is perhaps the same energetic force that fuels the process of horizontal unfolding, but in the moment of a problem's dissolution, we can experience it freshly and purely, free of all the personal story lines in which it was cloaked previously. In this gap or opening in our horizontal consciousness, a new awareness of verticality, or depth of being, emerges. I call this a *vertical shift* (Welwood, 1996). In a moment of vertical shift, we move from the realm of personality into a deeper quality of being as the conventional division between observer and observed loosens along with all reactivity, contraction, and/or striving.

The aliveness, expansiveness, and presence that suddenly emerges when a central psychological fixation lets go has a different quality from the incremental horizontal shifts that occur during the gradual unfolding of felt meaning. It is more like the opening of a flower, always fresh and surprising. Here, we encounter our very being as a wide-open spaciousness, where we feel attuned to the larger flow of reality (Welwood, 1977b).

The personal unfolding of felt meaning can be a groundwork that prepares the way for this more radical type of vertical deepening. After all, we cannot let go of anything until we have it first. We cannot go beyond where we are until we have arrived there first. Horizontal unfolding and vertical emergence—finding ourselves and letting go, recognizing where we are and going beyond it—are two aspects of one whole process (Welwood, 2000).

Just as water is a universal element enfolded in all living things, so too is our larger beingness implicit in every aspect of our felt experience. As a felt sense unfolds, it reveals a subtler body/mind knowing underlying the conceptual activity of the surface mind. Similarly, when our larger being emerges, it reveals a ground of openness underlying all of the personal feelings we experience with the body/mind. One term for this larger awareness, using Zen master Suzuki Roshi's words, is *big mind*. Just as we do not see water in the forms in which it is enfolded (in flesh, grass, or wood), so too do we usually fail to recognize this ultimate openheartedness at the root of all our experiences, which in Buddhism is called *bodhicitta* or the heart/mind of enlightenment. The moment when it finally and fully emerges into awareness is, in Zen terms, like "the bottom of the bucket breaking through."

How then can we let the bottom of our lives break through into radical openness without continually having to patch up the bucket because we fear this larger space? Whereas psychological unfolding can provide occasional glimpses of the larger openness at the core of our being, spiritual practice aims at it more directly. If psychological work helps us to find ourselves, then spiritual work takes up from there, helping us to let go of ourselves.

Meditation practice, in particular, is designed to help us let go of the fixations of surface thought and bodily felt meaning by letting them arise without reacting to them and seeing through them to the greater openness of our being. This helps us to give up clinging to mental and emotional contents as well as to moments of opening—to let the play of the mind happen as it will and not get carried away by any of it. Through ongoing practice, the meditator becomes more intimately aware of the nature of his or her mind on all levels—habitual thought patterns, subverbal textures of implicit feeling, and the open ground underlying it all. Instead of attempting to unfold felt meaning, meditation allows a continual return to the unknown so that a deeper awareness can ventilate and permeate the narrow world of self-preoccupation. The ultimate aim of meditation is the direct nonconceptual realization of pure being.

Thus, meditation practice provides a valuable method for helping us to appreciate the larger sacred ground of being underlying all of our thoughts and feelings. It negates neither science (which explains with the surface mind) nor psychotherapy (which inquires into the body/mind); instead, it opens up a larger dimension of awareness that reveals the deep integrity of human existence, allowing us to see how these different levels of human experience make up one whole tapestry.

REFERENCES

Bohm, D. (1973). Quantum theory as an indication of a new order in physics, Part B: Implicate and explicate order in physical law. *Foundations of Physics, 3,* 139-168.

Gendlin, E. T. (1962). *Experiencing and the creation of meaning.* New York: Free Press.

Gendlin, E. T. (1964). A theory of personality change. In P. Worchel & D. Byrne (Eds.), *Personality change.* New York: John Wiley.

Gendlin, E. T. (1981). *Focusing.* New York: Bantam Books.

Gendlin, E. T., Beebe, J., Cassens, J., Klein, M., & Oberlander, M. (1968). Focusing ability in psychotherapy, personality, and creativity. In J. Schlien (Ed.), *Research in psychotherapy* (Vol. 3). Washington, DC: American Psychological Association.

Hillman, J. (1972). *The myth of analysis.* Evanston, IL: Northwestern University Press.

James, W. (1967). The continuity of experience. In J. McDermott (Ed.), *The writings of William James.* New York: Random House.

Levinson. E. (1975). A holographic model of psychoanalytic change. *Contemporary Psychoanalysis, 12*(1), 1-20.

Picard, M. (1952). *The world of silence.* Chicago: Regnery.

Pribram, K. (1971). *Languages of the brain.* Englewood Cliffs, NJ: Prentice Hall.

Rogers, C. R. (1967). *The therapeutic relationship and its impact: A program of research in psychotherapy with schizophrenics.* Madison: University of Wisconsin Press.

Walker, A., Rablen, R., & Rogers, C. R. (1959). Development of a scale to measure process change in psychotherapy. *Journal of Clinical Psychology, 16*, 79-85.

Welwood, J. (1977a). Meditation and the unconscious: A new perspective. *Journal of Transpersonal Psychology, 9*(1), 1-26.

Welwood, J. (1977b). On psychological space. *Journal of Transpersonal Psychology, 9*(2), 97-118.

Welwood, J. (1996). Reflection and presence: The dialectic of self-knowledge. *Journal of Transpersonal Psychology, 28*(2), 107-128.

Welwood, J. (2000). *Toward a psychology of awakening: Buddhism, psychotherapy, and the path of personal and spiritual transformation.* Boston: Shambhala.

CHAPTER 26

Expanding the Boundaries of Theory

MAURICE FRIEDMAN

Love is not a feeling but the responsibility of an I for a thou.

—M. Buber (*I and Thou*, 1958)

RESPONSIBILITY, to Buber (1985), and to me following him, means responding—hearing the un-reduced claim of each hour in all its crudeness and disharmony and answering it out of the depths of one's being. The great character who can awaken responsibility in others is one who acts from the whole of his or her substance and reacts in accordance with the uniqueness of every situation. He or she responds to the new face that each situation wears despite all similarity to others. The situation "demands nothing of what is past. It demands presence, responsibility, it demands you" (p. 14). "Genuine responsibility exists only where there is real responding" (p. 114).

A situation of which we have become aware is never finished with, but we subdue it into the substance of lived life. Only then, true to the moment, do we experience a life that is something other than a sum of moments. We respond to the moment, but at the same time we respond on its behalf, we answer for it. A newly created concrete reality has been laid in our arms; we answer for it. A dog has looked at you, you answer for its glance, a child has clutched your hand, you answer for its touch, a host of men moves about you, you answer for their need. (p. 17)

Only as a partner can a person be perceived as an existing wholeness. To become aware of a person means to perceive his or her wholeness as person defined by spirit—to perceive the dynamic center that stamps on all utterances, actions, and attitudes the recognizable sign of uniqueness. Such an awareness is impossible if, and so long as, the other is for me the detached object of my observation, for that person will not yield his or her wholeness and its center. It is possible only when he or she becomes present for me.

Mutual confirmation is essential to becoming a self, that is, a person who realizes his or her uniqueness precisely through relations to other selves whose distance from him or her is completed by the person's distance from them. This mutual confirmation of persons is most fully realized in "making present," an event that happens partially whenever persons come together but, in its essential structure, only rarely. The other becomes present to me through "inclusion," that is, a bold swinging into the other that demands the most intense action of one's being so as to imagine concretely, to some extent, what the other is thinking, feeling, perceiving, and willing.

THE RESPONSIBILITY OF THE THERAPIST

In his unpublished book on companionship, my old friend George Morgan, author of *The Human Predicament* (Morgan, 1968), made a distinction between *accountability* and *responsibility* that I have found to be particularly helpful in understanding the responsibility of the therapist. Accountability is one's formal obligation according to the laws of the states and the ethical rules of one's profession. Responsibility, on the other hand, means really responding to the person before you as a person. In that sense, it entails mutuality or reciprocity.

If "all real living is meeting," as Buber claims, then all true healing also takes place through meeting. If the psychotherapist is content to "analyze" the patient, that is,

> to bring to light unknown factors from his microcosm and to set to some conscious work in life the energies which have been transformed by such an emergence, then he may be successful in some repair work. At

best, he may help a soul that is diffused and poor in structure to collect and order itself to some extent. But the real matter, the regeneration of an atrophied personal center, will not be achieved. This can only be done by one who grasps the buried latent unity of the suffering soul with the great glance of the doctor, and this can only be attained in the person-to-person attitude of a partner, not by consideration and examination of an object. (Buber, 1958, p. 132)

For the meeting with the patient or client to take place in responsibility, there has to be what Buber called an "I-thou" relationship, that is, a relationship of openness, presence, directness, immediacy, and mutuality. But it is not full mutuality. On the contrary, there is what Buber called a "normative limitation of mutuality" that holds for the therapist as for any helping person. In my terms, there must be mutuality of contact, mutuality of trust (neither therapist nor patient must believe that the other is just making a business out of him or her), and mutuality of concern (both therapist and patient are concerned not only with the problems of the patient but also with the sickness of the family, community, culture, and society from which the patient comes). What there cannot be, however, is mutuality of what Buber called "inclusion" or "imagining the real."

Inclusion, or imagining the real, means a bold swinging to the other with the most intense action of one's being through which one experiences, to some extent, what the other is thinking, feeling, perceiving, and willing. Yet, the therapist must not leave his or her own ground, for it is a bipolar reality. This is how it differs from the much-used term *empathy*. Empathy, in the strict sense, means to leave one's ground so as to go over to the other, just as identification means remaining on one's own side of the relationship and understanding only those experiences of the patient that fit one's own.

The fact that inclusion cannot be mutual in the therapy relationship fits the structure of the relationship (the patient comes to see the therapist) and often also the given of the situation (the patient is enormously interested in the therapist but not for his or her sake). The patient cannot be both in relationship and detached, as the therapist must be. This does not mean that the therapist is primarily an observer, but where the therapist does bring his or her self in, it is for the sake of the therapy and not to claim "equal time."

In his 1957 dialogue with Carl Rogers, Buber would not accept Rogers's insistence that the relationship between therapist and patient should be seen, within the relationship itself, as fully mutual. The patient cannot experience the relationship from the side of the therapist equally well without destroying or fundamentally altering the relationship (Buber, 1988, appendix). This does not mean that the therapist is reduced to treating his or her patient as an object or "it." The one-sided inclusion of therapy still is an I-thou relationship founded on mutuality, trust, and partnership in a common situation, and it is only in this relation that real therapy can take place.

Buber (1990) suggested that there are times when the therapist must put aside his or her professional superiority and method and meet the patient as self to self:

> In a decisive hour, together with the patient entrusted to him, he [the therapist] has left the closed room of psychological treatment in which the analyst rules by means of his systematic and methodological superiority and has stepped forth with him into the air of the world where self is exposed to self. There, in the closed room where one probed and treated the isolated psyche

according to the inclination of the self-encapsulated patient, the patient was referred to ever-deeper levels of his inwardness as to his proper world; here outside, in the immediacy of one human standing over against another, the encapsulation must and can be broken through, and a transformed, healed relationship must and can be opened to the person who is sick in his relationship to otherness—to the world of the other which he cannot remove into his soul. A soul is never sick alone, but there is always a betweenness also, a situation between it and another existing being. The psychotherapist who has passed through the crisis may now dare to touch on this. (p. 142)

Buber wrote this statement as part of his introduction to *Healing Through Meeting*, the posthumously published book of the formerly Jungian Swiss psychotherapist Hans Trüb. In his writings, Trüb described how, in his work, he became aware of the invariable tendency of the primary consciousness to become monological and self-defeating. He also told how this closed circle of the self again and again was forced outward toward relationship through those times when, despite his will, he found himself confronting his patient not as an analyst but as human to human. From these experiences, Trüb came to understand the full meaning of the therapist's responsibility. The therapist takes responsibility for lost and forgotten things, and with the aid of his psychology, he or she helps to bring them to light. But the therapist knows in the depth of his or her self that the secret meaning of these things that have been brought to consciousness first reveals itself *in the outgoing to the other*.

> *Psychology* as science *and psychology* as function know about the soul of man as about something in the third person. . . .

They look down from above into the world of inner things, into the inner world of the individuals. And they deal with its contents as with their "objects," giving names and creating classifications. . . . But the therapist, in his work with the ill, is essentially a human being. . . . Therefore, he seeks and loves the human being in his patients and allows it . . . to come to him ever again. (Trüb, quoted in Friedman, 1991, p. 497; see also Trüb, 1935, p. 550, my translation)

Real guilt is the beginning of ethos or responsibility, wrote Trüb, but before the patient can become aware of it, the patient must be helped by the therapist to become aware of himself or herself in general. The therapist does this by playing the parts of both confidante and big brother or big sister. The therapist gives the patient the understanding that the world has denied him or her and makes it more and more possible for the patient to step out of his or her self-imprisonment into a genuine relation with the therapist. In so doing, according to Trüb, the therapist must avoid the intimacy of a private I-thou relationship with the patient, on the one hand, and the temptation of dealing with the patient as an object, on the other. The therapy relationship cannot become the mutual inclusion of friendship without destroying the therapeutic possibilities of the relationship. But neither can it make the patient into an it. The therapist must be able to risk himself or herself and to participate in the process of individuation.

The therapist must see the illness of the patient as an illness of his or her relations with the world, wrote Trüb (1991). The roots of the suffering lie both in the patient's closing himself or herself off from the world and in the pattern of society itself and its rejection and nonconfirmation of the patient. Consequently, the therapist must, at some point, change from the consoler who takes the part of the patient against the world to the person who puts before the patient the claim of the world. This change is necessary to complete the second part of the healing—that establishment of real relationship with the world that can take place only in the world itself. On the therapist falls the task of preparing the way for the resumption in direct meeting of the interrupted dialogical relationship between the individual and the community. The therapist must test the patient's finding of himself or herself by the criterion of whether the patient's self-realization can be the starting point for a new personal meeting with the world. The patient must go forth whole in himself or herself, but the patient also must recognize that it is not the patient's own self but rather the world with which he or she must be concerned. This does not mean, however, that the patient is simply integrated with or adjusted to the world. The patient does not cease to be a real person responsible for himself or herself, but at the same time, the patient enters into responsible relationship with his or her community (Trüb, 1991, pp. 497-499).

I gave the title "The Problematic of Mutuality" to a chapter in my book, *The Healing Dialogue in Psychotherapy* (Friedman, 1985, pp. 169-194), because the question of how much mutuality is possible and desirable in a "healing through meeting" relationship between therapist and patient is not a problem admitting of a once-and-for-all solution. In that long chapter, in fact, I described approaches of responsible professional therapists ranging from Freud's recommendation of mirrorlike impassivity (which he did not practice himself) to a therapist who encourages her patients to become her friends during the later stages of therapy.

Despite this range of responses to the problematic of mutuality, I do have three conclusions that apply to the whole spectrum. First, the problematic of mutuality goes beyond the intrapsychic reality of transference and countertransference to the real interhuman relationship between therapist and patient. Second, although the therapist and patient share a common situation, this does not mean that each enters from the same or even a similar position. In psychotherapy, the difference in position is not only that of personal stance but also that of role and function, a difference determined by the very difference of purpose that led each to enter the relationship. If the goal is a common one—the healing of the patient—then the relationship to that goal differs radically, as between therapist and patient, and the healing that takes place depends as much on the recognition of this difference as on the mutuality of meeting and trust.

The amount of mutuality possible and desirable in therapy depends not only on the stage of the relationship but also on the unique relationship between this particular therapist and patient and on the style and strength of the therapist. Some therapists testify to bringing their feelings into the therapeutic encounter to a greater or lesser degree, and many testify to themselves being healed through that encounter or at least growing in creativity and wisdom. None of this changes the basic fact—and this is my third conclusion—that the therapist's expression of emotion always is made in the service of the therapy and never in the service of the healing of the therapist, much less mere self-indulgence on the part of the therapist.

A part of the responsibility of the therapist has to do with the nature of the will to heal that he or she brings to the therapeutic task. For the therapist, the distinction between arbitrary and true will rests on a quite real and concrete experiencing of the patient's side of the relationship. Only if the therapist discovers the "otherness" of the patient will the therapist discover his or her own real limits and what is needed to help the patient. The therapist must see the position of the other in that person's concrete actuality yet not lose sight of his or her own. Only this will remove the danger that the will to heal will degenerate into willfulness.

Another part of the therapist's responsibility is caring enough about the patient to wrestle with and for him or her. The therapist should have what Rogers called "unconditional personal regard," certainly. Yet at times, the therapist must contend within the dialogue with the patient while making sure that it remains a dialogue.

If we begin by honoring each person's unique relation to reality, then to say of a person that he or she is "sick" does not imply that the person is outside reality but only that he or she needs help in being brought into the dialogue of "touchstones of reality," to use my own phrase. The terrible dilemma of the sick person is having to choose between giving up one's touchstones of reality in order to communicate with others and giving up communication in order to keep one's touchstones. Such a person needs the help of someone who can glimpse and share the unique reality that has come from this person's life experience and can help this person find a way of bringing it into the common order of existence so that the individual also may raise what he or she has experienced as "I" into the communal reality of "we" (Friedman, 1985, chap. 18). This also is the responsibility of the therapist.

REFERENCES

Buber, M. (1958). *I and thou* (2nd ed., R. G. Smith, Trans., with postscript by M. Buber). New York: Scribner.

Buber, M. (1985). *Between man and man* (R. G. Smith, Trans., with introduction by M. Friedman). New York: Macmillan.

Buber, M. (1988). *The knowledge of man: The philosophy of the interhuman* (M. Friedman, Ed., R. G. Smith & M. Friedman, Trans., with introductory essay by M. Friedman). Atlantic Highlands, NJ: Humanities Press International.

Buber, M. (1990). *A believing humanism* (M. Friedman, Trans., with introduction and explanatory comments by M. Friedman). Amherst, NY: Prometheus Books.

Friedman, M. S. (1985). *The healing dialogue in psychotherapy.* Northvale, NJ: Jason Aronson.

Friedman, M. S. (Ed.). (1991). *The worlds of existentialism: A critical reader* (3rd ed., with updated preface). Atlantic Highlands, NJ: Humanities Press International.

Morgan, G. W. (1968). *The human predicament: Dissolution and wholeness.* Providence, RI: Brown University Press.

Trüb, H. (1935). Individuation, Schuld, und Entscheidung: Über die Grenzen der Psychologie. In Psychologischen Club Zürich (Ed.), *Die kulturelle Bedeutung der Komplexen Psychologie.* Berlin: Springer-Verlag.

CHAPTER 27

Expanding the Boundaries of Practice

MOLLY MERRILL STERLING

MY CLIENT leaned forward, eyes intently on me, voice passionately intense, and said to me, "I just want to be in your kitchen while you cook." Inwardly, I froze. Not one therapist sinew, not one trained muscle of years of practice, flexed into action. Nowhere in me was there a standard response, and I parody our standard psychotherapeutic repertoire a bit here: "Tell me how that would be" or "You would like to be closer to me" or "Our meetings aren't enough for you" or just a genuinely open and quiet waiting for my client to continue. Instead, I reacted viscerally. In my frozen moment, I saw the dishes left as I hurried out early that morning. I felt my pleasure in my own rhythm of my pottering about. I wondered how my family would take to this new person slipped into their lives. These images supplanted my unawareness that I could not sustain my client's intense pressure. I felt, in short, inadequate to her proposition. This seemed to me a concrete request to which I was called to give a concrete answer—not as a therapist following the depth and breadth of our unfolding relatedness but rather as a person, just myself. And so, the gist of my reply carried all of these feelings and many more to which I was then blind: "Oh, you might not like me so much if you were around me more." In one blind stroke, I had cleaved open a chasm of distance, betrayal, shame, fury, and misconstrual.

Sylvia, successful in two careers, is charming, kind, intelligent, and savvy about therapy. She takes care of herself and her life everywhere but in her most private heart, where she hides her shame, guilt, and grief that she neither is loved nor loves (she believes). My blind remark to her plea for abiding acceptance violently broke open her heart and revealed my distance. We were in a situation constructed out of both our needs, and no amount of interpretation would cover over the chasm.

My understanding of the co-created nature of this breach began with my entry into my response to Sylvia. She wanted something from me and had told me so in more than words. She showed herself— naked invitation on her face, intensely leaning toward me, no language to mitigate her longing, no indication that she understood her desire as psychological process. Instead, she was making a direct appeal.

Without any room in my own awareness, I responded to her appeal by drawing away. I refused her deeper demand by refusing her need. On the surface, I like to think that I am compassionate, but during subsequent months, as I became aware that my tendency to withdraw from her level of need could be profound, I came to see that I had not responded to her; I had only responded to myself. We both were engaged actively in a world construed by remaining only within our individual self-referring selves; neither could comprehend the other. Eventually, through my dreams, my consultation, and my therapy, I began taking myself down and into the roots of my reluctance.

I could describe my state as *my* countertransference. I carry in me a shyness about my own ability to be wanted deeply. My history holds some dramatic loss of relationship that is bathed in persistent feelings of inadequacy. However clearly I "know" this history and my characteristic responses, I am not free of this patterned complex being jolted into a present reality as it was here through Sylvia's hope. The very raw expression that Sylvia made of her desire for intimacy with me set into motion my deep sense of what I thought to be my inadequacy as a person that spills over into my ability as a therapist. My reply refused her desire and simultaneously revealed me to her in a way that she herself did not want me to be nor did she expect as an experienced client.

I actually was as unveiled as she was at that moment. My reluctance revealed me, not Sylvia's ideal but rather me with my warts and glitches. Although my response revealed me more intimately than she knew, my reactivity prevented me from recognizing what intimacy was present in the thera-

peutic field of our encounter. She knew the technical violation and felt the emotional reluctance as violation and rejection. Angrily, she immediately accused me of both. In response, I became more flummoxed and unable to gather myself. Let me add that we both, of course, are well versed in her family story and the nature of transference, yet we instinctually knew that any reference to it would have been a gross evasion of our own lived experience, destabilizing our lived moment with irrelevance.

One could say that Sylvia's transference included wanting me to want her wholly, and she would perforce see my inadequacies as terrible rejection. In turn, I felt a resurgence of my personal persistent and old inadequacies, leading me to shy away. But I think that this give-and-take view, seemingly causal through the close link of time and pressure, is not as complete as it could be. I would like to bring forth a description of responsibility from Sylvia's and my arduous ways of meeting—the inner drama of the experience of the ability to respond to one another. To do this, I am indebted to the writings of Levinas (1969, 1991), originally a student of Husserl and Heidegger and a contemporary of Merleau-Ponty (1962) and Buber and, hence, active in the area of philosophy from which existential-humanistic psychotherapy descends (Bugental, 1965/ 1981; Giorgi, 1970; May, Angel, & Ellenberger, 1958; Yalom, 1980).

Levinas's (1969) term for the whole person's impact on the other person in the dyad was *face*. Sylvia's passionate leaning toward me carries Levinas's meaning through dramatic tension, but for Levinas, all meetings call on each person with as much intensity, however subtle. Face, which "exceeds the idea of the other in me" (p. 50), exerts a call, appeal, or demand that is likened to the appeal of a "widow, orphan, stranger, or guest" (pp. 76-77). In other words, the presence of an Other person urges a response of care, of gift, or of responsibility that surpasses anything I can control, and just because I cannot grasp Sylvia's situation and the situation she precipitates for me, I am challenged to grasp that I am obliged to rise to meet her as she is, calling me beyond myself (Peperzak, 1993, pp. 19-30).

The ability to respond is the primary meaning of responsibility. Levinas took this further to show that responsibility also carries the experience of being beholden to the other person, of being dedicated to that person, and of being obligated to him or her. Responsibility, for Levinas, meant that simply by the fact of the face of the other person, one is "taken hostage"—before thought, choice, or action and without reciprocity or bargaining, just within experience that compels and commands us to respond. It is this level of our human condition, brought into presence by our naked encounter, that Sylvia and I have had to reckon with. Humans live within being-for-the-other and, hence, expect it prior to conscious reflection. In the instant of our exchange, we recognized by its absence the fundamental necessity of being ready and available to carry what was being asked by the other. But we knew of its presence only by its absence—by its lack of presence. I failed this structure of experience by my flippant and protective comment that refused her need for dedication. By revealing myself so unconsciously, I put great strain on her capacities, beyond (at that moment) her ability to respond to me as myself. Phenomenologically, her outrage is a just commentary on my failure to complete her appeal for profound care and acceptance (Levinas, 1969, pp. 82-101). I knew that I could not respond to her need of my welcome, and Sylvia knew that I was evading her appeal. She did need to show me her raw desire and have me desire her

deep desire (Kojeve, 1969, p. 7) right then, unmitigated, and unexpurgated. She never expected, in any rational way, that I would take her home.

To return to the lived experience of being called to respond, Sylvia leaned toward me, her eye glinting, and simply yet intensely laid bare her insistent desire: "I just want to be in your kitchen while you cook." A touch of challenge that might have been conscious to her I now registered only in memory. At that moment, I was embedded in the challenge that she exuded. I had no reflective capacity within myself; I was within her demand for entry into my private home, my time, and my heart. Her need was foaming over me like an unpredictable rogue wave. I felt vividly Levinas's conditions of face—of no choice but to respond. I felt compelled by her appeal.

But why? What was this experience of being "compelled"? And what exactly was the "appeal" here? Sylvia's request was unexpected, and I experienced being undone, unhinged, and shocked. In my mind's experiential eye, she descended on me from above and swooped down, more like a falcon than a dove perhaps, but down, "as from a height," another of Levinas's phrases like "widow, orphan, stranger, or guest" to describe phenomenologically the structure of the impact of an Other person. It is descriptively neutral in a way that other language I could use from my clinical vocabulary is not. To say "I felt coerced or subverted" would pathologize this moment, placing responsibility that I could not muster (and knew preconsciously that I should) on Sylvia, who was legitimately revealing her desire for a relational vitality. She literally appealed as a combination of orphan and guest.

As I stumbled into this weakness within my psyche, my reactivity prevented me from being present in two ways: I was not able to hold my experience steady in me until I could use it, as from a reflective distance, for myself and for the work together, nor was I able to speak with completely direct and honest exposure through which I could bring my own experiencing to bear as part of our living actuality. Ironically, at the same time, my response revealed my being, if only my client and I could have discerned it. At that very moment, Sylvia *was* in my kitchen with me—conflicts, mess, hurry, and all. At that moment, she had what she would get in my kitchen in actuality, if not what she wanted in feeling. I was as naked as she was, if only she (and I) could see.

In actuality, neither of us could respond to the other as other. Each of us was responding from her own world and was not yet available to the world of the other, nor was I available to the therapeutically co-created field. In such conditions, neither of us felt the intimacy that was there for the taking. In addition, both of us knew that our relating was not relating (and, certainly, we could not yet see that our nonrelating was revelatory of deeper relating). We each knew phenomenologically, by its lack, that the ability to respond to the other, which we deeply rely on to be present as a structure of relatedness, was absent. We each were locked in an autistic world despite our sentences about living under the same roof. The inability to hear, see, allow, accept, and welcome the other was the betrayal at that moment. And, unfortunately, for our perceived sense of doing therapy well, it was devastating to both of us, although our overt behaviors are different; Sylvia has a temperament that flares in anger, and I have one that hides in fear.

For such response to register with the other person, for Sylvia to have felt received or responded to, I would have needed to perceive, recognize, and draw on my own visceral feelings. Ignoring, denying, or sanitizing my response inside me would not do. Calling on my experience then or later is a literal laying down of my life—my inner life—for the other person. Later, when I was able to clearly and simply declare that Sylvia's insistence or intensity was too much for me as it happened, the atmosphere altered. Overtly, Sylvia would thank me for being steady and clear with her. Covertly, threat of the loss of one another softened and settled down for a time. My appreciation and love for her became more stable in her eyes. Her capacity to reflect and hold her experience of hope and betrayal expanded, releasing my energy to be present. During the time it has taken for these changes to manifest, we were increasingly able to respond to similar failures from our participation together.

As I write this, I see each of us drawing back into her self not as a walled-off separateness but rather as a distinct person, capable of response. We are more attentive, attuned, and kind. Our responsibility as individuals increases as each of us is able to respond more immediately from within, that is, more authentically to the other. Within our encounter, generally we can move among facets of enactment and reflectivity more flexibly. Now, much later, I am able to pick up and carry what she shows me, and she shows me her need from within her awareness of it. Both of us can respond more comprehensively. Through these incremental changes, the phenomenological structure works though our experience of its presence more easily rather than through its lack of presence.

Levinas concluded from his meditation that each of us is more himself or herself as he or she lives for the life of the other. He often quoted Dostoyevsky (1990), "We are all responsible for everything and everyone in the face of everybody and I more than the others" (p. 320), which Levinas paraphrased as being responsible for the responsibility of the other. Said psychologically, as therapist, my authentic experience as myself will be called on by my client beyond what I usually consider to be the bounds of the work. Yet, I must be true to both.

Shifting from emphasis on the transference for its developmental content to participation in a present that holds a living experience of basic structures of relating means shifting toward a recognition of the actual creation of subjectivity in both client and therapist. Sylvia's fury vividly made visible to me her requirement that I meet her need with all of my human capacities. To become responsible for her, I had to release myself. To call her to responsibility for herself, I had to use all of my ability to respond to her in this experience of her above me, exterior to me, appealing as widow, orphan, stranger, or guest. This is not neutral in Levinas's description; it is an offering. Once I had recovered from my initial reluctance and could offer myself to my client, she could

begin to feel my ability to respond and my responsibility for her. The work comes to be about the two of us within this requirement to respond until we can reflect together, even when the experience called forth in us is one of the inability to respond.

When a therapist sets himself or herself aside to attend to a client, the therapist seems to be settling into this behavior of being responsible for the responsibility of the other. But a phenomenological description aims to expose the structure of experience itself, which includes the client. Sylvia demonstrated her responsibility to me for my responsibility when she exploded in hot rage for my vacuous remark. She did not let it pass. She insisted that I know how I was letting her down—not for not saying that I wished she could be in my kitchen but rather for fleeing her intensity, raw need, and anguish that no one, anywhere, wants her in the kitchen, neither past nor present.

REFERENCES

Bugental, J. F. T. (1981). *The search for authenticity: An existential-analytic approach to psychotherapy.* New York: Irvington. (Original work published 1965)

Dostoyevsky, F. (1990). *The brothers Karamazov* (R. Pevear & L. Volokhonsky, Trans.). San Francisco: North Point Press.

Giorgi, A. (1970). *Psychology as a human science: A phenomenologically based approach.* New York: Harper & Row.

Kojeve, A. (1969). *Introduction to the reading of Hegel: Lectures on the phenomenology of the spirit* (A. Bloom, Ed., J. A. Nichols, Trans.). New York: Basic Books.

Levinas, E. (1969). *Totality and infinity: An essay on exteriority* (A. Lingis, Trans.). Pittsburgh, PA: Duquesne University Press.

Levinas, E. (1991). *Otherwise than being or beyond essence.* Dordrecht, The Netherlands: Kluwer.

May, R., Angel, E., & Ellenberger, H. F. (Eds.). (1958). *Existence: A new dimension in psychiatry and psychology.* New York: Basic Books.

Merleau-Ponty, M. (1962). *Phenomenology of perception.* London: Routledge and Kegan Paul.

Peperzak, A. (1993). *To the other: An introduction to the philosophy of Emmanuel Levinas.* West Lafayette, IN: Purdue University Press.

Yalom, I. D. (1980). *Existential psychotherapy.* New York: Basic Books.

CHAPTER 28

The Therapist as a Model of Humane Values and Humanistic Behavior

JEFFREY A. KOTTLER AND RICHARD J. HAZLER

ONE OF THE MOST intriguing challenges of humanistic psychology is for its advocates to practice what they preach. Nothing is more frustrating than to hear stories about "crazy shrinks" or about supposedly humanistic educators and therapists who cannot or do not apply in their own lives the same principles they espouse and teach to their clients and students. At the same time, we can personally vouch for the difficulties of living the values of a humanistic practitioner 24 hours a day.

The facets of humanistic psychology that always have appealed to us most are not only the attention given to the relationships between people but also the emphasis placed on humane values of caring, compassion, authenticity, unconditional regard, respect, and honesty originally described by Maslow (1968), Rogers (1980), Combs (1989), Mahrer (1989), Bugental (1978), and Yalom (1980), among others. There even has been room within this framework to include some of the neglected aspects of nonpossessive love and spirituality (Kelly, 1995) that so often are ignored in other approaches.

Many humanistic practitioners have been encouraged to apply in their personal lives the knowledge and skills they learned for the benefit of their clients. It certainly is a major benefit of our profession that everything learned about therapy can make us more effective humans; more loving and caring toward others; more skilled at communicating our needs and responding to others; more expert at reaching personal goals; and more highly evolved in our moral, spiritual, emotional, and intellectual development (Kottler, 1993).

The benefits of being a humanistic therapist, as positive as they might be, do not come without personal costs that often are burdensome. These personal costs are reflected in many ways including signs and symptoms of therapist impairment (Emerson & Markos, 1996; Kottler & Hazler,

1997; Sussman, 1995). Which part of the human is therapist and which part is humanist? How can these roles be integrated? What is the effect of their interaction on quality of care?

In the first two sections, we present ourselves to you, using the first-person perspective, in a way that accounts for the passionate interest we feel toward *being* what we teach to others.

JEFFREY KOTTLER: SOME UNIVERSAL PRINCIPLES

What first attracted me to this field was the beguiling compassion and formidable expertise of a college counselor who helped me through some difficult times. As I recall, she did not actually *do* very much in our sessions; she just listened a lot, smiled indulgently, and occasionally let me know that I was not alone. Nevertheless, her level of understanding struck me as miraculous, probably because I was not used to having someone's undivided attention.

After completing our work together, I remember trying to make sense of what happened. What had she really done to help me? Again and again, I was drawn not so much to anything specific that she said or did as by her tranquillity and caring. She seemed like such a nice person yet also very powerful. This impressed me a lot.

During the next decade, while I continued to seek out mentors to guide me through my development as a therapist and as a person, I continued to gravitate toward those individuals who seemed to radiate some sort of power. I do not mean this in the conventional sense of being controlling, but rather mean it in the sense that they appeared poised, confident, and grounded.

It occurs to me now that I must seem basically this way to those students, clients, and supervisees who seek me out for guidance. Indeed, I do look quite serene and polished on the outside, especially when I am writing or speaking. This is amazing to me, considering that I have made a whole career out of describing the amount of uncertainty, doubt, and imperfection that I experience internally as I go about my job. The truth, as I have said many times before, is that much of the time I do not have any clear idea of where the heck I am going. I have a hunch that I am not alone in my feelings of being an impostor.

I have been writing for the past several years about the personal dimensions of a therapist's life and work, that is, how a clinician's personal values, attitudes, and characteristics affect therapy outcomes as well as professional satisfaction. This study has included how therapists are affected and influenced by their clients (Kottler, 1993, 1995; Kottler & Markos, 1998), how therapists deal with their imperfections and failures (Kottler, 1999; Kottler & Blau, 1989; Kottler & Hazler, 1997), how practitioners live with the ambiguity and paradoxes of reconciling contradictory principles into an integrated model of helping (Kottler, 1991, 1996), and how therapists struggle with clients who do not meet their expectations or cooperate with their plans for them (Kottler, 1992, 1994b, 1997a). In addition, I have been interested in the interactive nature of conflict in relationships where people disown responsibility for difficulties (Kottler, 1994a, 1997b) as well as the larger theme of what is intrinsically healing about human relationships (Kottler, Montgomery, & Marbley, 1998; Kottler, Sexton, & Whiston, 1994) and novel interaction experiences (Kottler, 1997c).

The clear implication of these findings is that the person of the therapist is intertwined with his or her work. Modeling humanistic values becomes more than a performance at work; it also becomes a belief system to live by each day. This responsibility carries a heavy weight because of limitations placed on us by our bodies, our minds, and society.

RICHARD HAZLER:
THE WEIGHT OF HUMANISM

I love my work and life, but they also weigh heavy on me. I am 53 years old and still looking for new personal growth, new professional challenges, and more ways in which to help others. At the same time, it has become very clear that I need more balance in my life, especially with regard to my emotional and physical health. The humanistic values that have guided my life make it meaningful and worthwhile, but they also create a heavy burden for friends, family, colleagues, and myself. This has not been an easy lesson for me to learn or to face directly. In fact, I often feel exhausted from the effort.

The humanistic environment that I have tried to offer others has not been one that I have applied very successfully to myself. How can I have so much internal struggle around these humanistic values when I believe and act on them? The beginnings of the answer start with working like hell to live these values day to day. My beliefs and experiences lead me to show faith in others and to place my efforts into understanding more about other individuals. I feel directed to help others grow in ways that they choose rather than in ways that I would choose for either their benefit or my own. My humanism does tell me to be myself, but only in the ways that will help other persons when I might really want to say and do things that would give myself more satisfaction or comfort.

Frequently, people will give me variations of what sounds like a simple answer: "Turn your humanist self off away from work."

But I wonder if it does not cheapen my beliefs if I am a humanist during therapy or teaching but less so when I am not doing work. How do I justify turning off my attending reactions, interest in others, trust in others to make their own choices, demonstrations of how I value others' phenomenological worlds, and keeping extra life burdens off of others? How do I avoid providing these humanistic values to people outside of therapy when they are such an important part of who I am as a person as well as a therapist? The reality for me is that as much as I believe in and gain from these beliefs, they also cause me great pain.

My growing awareness of how all life experiences interact to shape both the professional and personal lives of others and myself did not come all at once or in one form. My work always has reflected an interest in how we develop professional skills by means that often are far different from those in any professional curriculum (Hazler, 1991; Hazler & Singer, 1980). This self-felt press to look beyond standard theory and practice produced a need to better understand how humanistic values interact with personal and professional dynamics to affect therapists (Hazler, 1991; Kottler & Hazler, 1997), the resulting dilemmas that demand greater attention to values and beliefs in addition to skills and knowledge (Albright & Hazler, 1995; Carney & Hazler, 1998), and the need of the profession to give more attention to the personal struggles that damage therapists (Hazler & Kottler, 1996). A significant part of my work has been to promote attention to these issues early and often throughout a professional's development (Hazler & Kottler, 1994) by improving formal relationships with personalized methods (Hazler, Stanard, Conkey, & Granello, 1996), drawing on informal relationships for positive professional outcomes (Hazler, 1998b; Hazler & Carney, 1993;

Hazler & Kottler, 1994), and teaching therapists in ways that better reflect personalized professional development stages and needs (Granello & Hazler, 1998; Kottler & Hazler, 1997).

Our exploration of the person inside the therapist has turned up realizations about ourselves and the profession that both inspire us and promote fear and anxiety. The common thread for both of us seems to be the conflicts surrounding how to live up to our humanist values. Trying to live each day as a therapist, educator, and person who is authentic and congruent is a humbling task that demands continuous reflection, evaluation, and evolution. Perhaps as we struggle together with what we consider the greatest challenge of humanistic psychology, we all will come a little closer to living up to the values that we claim are so important to others.

THE CHALLENGE TO MODEL HUMANISTIC VALUES

Several themes appear to run throughout our professional research and life experiences. The first of these gives focus to all of the others by emphasizing that the personal and professional dimensions of the therapist are inseparable. Both the strengths and weaknesses of therapy originate here, and the more we try to separate them, the less humane therapy becomes. The second theme is that we are challenged by our limitations as therapists and humans to balance the polarities of our profession along with our humanistic commitments. A final theme gives recognition to the necessity of seeking the limits of a therapist's humanism. These themes demonstrate both the obstacles in the way of modeling humanistic values and the vehicles available to overcome these challenges.

The scarcity of literature on the pressures of living humanistic values coincides with the reality that therapists are much better prepared for the perils their clients will face than for the perils they will face themselves (Sussman, 1995). Clients are the focus of research and our training. This can be seen as clearly as anywhere in the American Psychological Association's (APA) Task Force on Promotion and Dissemination of Psychological Procedures (1995). This report emphasizing empirical evidence virtually ignores the variability among therapists while focusing almost total attention on the type of therapy performed. This absence of deserved attention seems particularly noticeable for humanists who pride themselves on dealing with people rather than with roles.

THE INSEPARABLE CONNECTION BETWEEN PERSONAL AND PROFESSIONAL DIMENSIONS

Just as we believe that humanistic psychology must be *lived* as well as *practiced* with clients, we see many other interconnections between personal and professional domains. Everything that we learn in life helps us to become more knowledgeable about human existence, that is, the ways in which people live and how they behave. Every movie we see, every novel we read, and every conversation we have helps us to gain a better understanding of why people think, feel, and act the ways in which they do. Similarly, everything we learned in graduate school and life—all of the skills and knowledge—and what we glean from every session with every client increases understanding of ourselves that should allow us to improve all of our personal and professional relationships (Hazler & Kottler, 1994; Kottler & Hazler, 1997; Schneider, 1992). What we do during every workday significantly affects our personal lives, and what we experience at home—during leisure time and travels when we are "off duty"—affects the ways in which we act during our sessions.

Turning our attention to the limited research in this area, one study of group therapy failures found that therapists' personalities and character traits had a profound impact on outcomes (Harpaz, 1994). Group therapy, in particular, increases therapists' anxieties that already are present in individual therapy. Fear of abandonment is a major factor for therapists in that they want to be accepted and want their relationships to be maintained. They also experience, at the same time, the opposite fear of engulfment. When things do not go exactly as planned, guilt and self-blame are common for practitioners.

Therapists also struggle with acknowledging feelings they have toward their clients, whether in the form of sexual attraction, anger, fear, or even hate. In one survey, more than 80% of therapists reported having had strong negative reactions toward their clients, and half of those even had their sleep or eating habits disrupted (Pope & Tabachnick, 1993).

Two therapist characteristics that seem particularly influential are flexibility and empathy (Miller, 1993). This, of course, would be no surprise to humanistic practitioners. Bugental and McBeath (1995), for example, noted, "Empathetically working with the raw stuff of another's life results in one's own life being called into question" (p. 116). It is still more compelling, however, to find that even psychodynamic clinicians do better in their work when they demonstrate high levels of these qualities (Henry, Schacht, Strupp, Butler, & Binder, 1993).

We noted earlier how this empathy comes at a high cost, especially if therapists internalize the burdens they carry. Even in comparison to the medical profession, where life and death hang in the balance on a daily basis, the pressures clearly translate into life-changing and even life-threatening situations for therapists. As only one example, psychiatrists kill themselves at twice the rate that other physicians kill themselves (Zur, 1994).

It is precisely the isolation and privacy that make our work possible that also depletes us emotionally. It is for this reason that many of us are viewed by loved ones as withholding or distant, even though we are supposed to be so warm and compassionate. It is no wonder that we sometimes find it so difficult to practice in our personal lives what we do every day in our offices.

HUMANISTIC PARADOXES

Words used to describe humanistic values seem so straightforward and clean. Using kindly terms such as *caring, compassion, authenticity, respect,* and *honesty* to explain how to be humanistic causes most everyone to nod their heads in agreement and confidence. The struggles come not with these warm words but rather with the paradoxical realities of trying to combine the helpful therapist and the needy human inside to somehow fit into the lives of other individuals and society. These paradoxes produce a never-ending balancing act in which neither the therapist nor the human inside ever is in full control.

Therapists often know, or think they know, what seems to be at the heart of clients' problems. Academic study, experience, attentive listening, and keen observation skills often can provide what seems like viable paths to helping others. Clients expect just such skills and training from the experts they consult for help (Gelatt, 1995). Unfortunately, therapy is not as simple as knowing answers to simple questions. Our clients, as well as the public, may expect us to be omnipotent and omniscient, but we often feel something quite different inside (Kottler, 1995, 1996).

A humanistic model, as well as more contemporary constructivist paradigms, presumes that therapist understanding must start from scratch with each client because every individual brings an entirely different encyclopedia of personal information to be learned and understood. Even this learning and understanding is in question given that the "facts" all rest on isolated and highly biased memories and then are translated through additional communication channels that are often inadequate. The resulting knowledge can perhaps be best characterized as Popper (1974) stated in the most practical of terms: "What the scientist's and the lunatic's theories have in common is that both belong to conjectural knowledge" (p. 1022).

The continuing development of this personalized understanding of a client's phenomenological world is the foundation of humanistic therapists' never-ending search for information (Hazler, 1998a). Every piece of information adds to the knowledge of the person, but it also adds to the complexity of the person and his or her life (Land & Jarman, 1992). The simplest answers are often the ones we see first, and they rarely tell the whole story. Looking at them closely expands our lack of understanding even more than it expands our understanding.

The learning process is one of continual reassessment of the understanding that is developing in the therapist and being actively communicated to the client (Prouty, 1994). We know something, but it is likely wrong or only partially right. When we think we know something to be "absolutely right," then it probably is only a part of our personally developed phenomenological worlds given that only the worlds we individually create for ourselves hold real truth for us.

If balancing knowing and ignorance in relation to clients is difficult, then understanding and seeing the limits of understanding ourselves confuses the situation and adds to the pressures even more. The therapist is part of a relationship directed toward exploration of the client's world. Then, the therapist must decide which part of this personal information should be looked at further (Hazler, 1998a). Making the therapist's genuine self a part of the relationship allows for therapist questions, interpretations, and opinions (Farber, 1996) and other interactions that reflect the person of the therapist more than his or her theory (Boy & Pine, 1990).

Postmodern constructivist models emphasize the importance of identifying the stories that people create around their lives. The therapist's task is to learn clients' individual life narratives and help clients to recognize their personalized stories so that they can accept or modify them for the future (Neimeyer, 1995).

The primary information-gathering position of constructivist therapists is one of *not knowing and needing to be informed* by clients' stories. This can be a difficult position for therapists to take when their training has included lectures, discussions, and books filled with theoretical information that they would like to use directly or pass on to clients. It becomes even more difficult with frequent requirements to authoritatively diagnose clients as though the therapists knew more than the clients about the problems, their origins, and their solutions.

The demands of the day-to-day current world in which we live push us to a "knowing model," where final assessments of the client are expected (Brennan, 1995). The "not knowing model" requires continual adjustments of therapist understanding, where each new piece of information adds a new dimension to the client's story as it is being pieced together by therapist and client (Anderson & Goolishian, 1992). The result is that we must live with both the press to know and the realization that recognizing our ignorance is the most effective model for relating to humans who would move forward in their lives.

GROWTH AND SAFETY

We might have been trained and enculturated to be experts, but we do not often believe we know "truth" or "the answer." In fact, the longer we practice humanistic psychology, the less certain about any static truths we become. What seems like a situation that should cause nothing more than a sense of pride, confidence, and honor also brings what Maslow (1971) first labeled the "fear of one's own greatness.... We fear our highest possibilities (as well as our lowest ones). We are generally afraid to become that which we can glimpse in our most perfect moments, under the most perfect conditions, under conditions of greatest courage" (pp. 35-37). What has become called the "Jonah complex" or the related "impostor phenomenon" (Clance, 1985) is the paradoxical choice between growth and safety (Goud, 1994) that the self-aware humanistic therapist must confront daily.

We rarely can meet our own expectations, much less those of others. Pressures to live up to these expectations as helpers and experts often cause the seeking of the lowest common denominator of success rather than what might be the most growth-producing choice. Rather than risk our greatest potential for success and failure, we can look for a safer path with less to gain and less to lose.

Humanists, in particular, sometimes struggle with taking the safe way out. We ask clients, friends, and colleagues to seek new pieces of themselves, but the challenge to ourselves is a greater one. Do we stay with the behaviors and information we have acquired to lead us through life, or do we seek the unknown about ourselves that lies on the frightening edge of chaos? (Shulman, 1997). The growth choice demands more time filled with personal risk taking with clients, family, and friends, whereas the safe choice provides a respite. It is difficult deciding where and when to ease oneself into the safer personal and interpersonal choices that seem to fit our value system more poorly.

INDIVIDUAL AND COLLECTIVE

The ambiguity of our existence makes it essential that humans find ways in which to organize the little we know and understand. This organization forms the foundation from which to make the conceptualizations and conclusions necessary for taking action in the present. It is a foundation built not on the totality of potential knowledge but rather on what infinitely small amount humanity presently knows, reduced to the much smaller amount that any one person can deal with at any one time. Existentialists from Kelly (1955) to Bugental and McBeath (1995) lean on a self-and-world construct system (SAWC) that recognizes the paradoxical situation and suggests that people must define their own selves and worlds if they are to flourish.

The essence of SAWC gives recognition to the inability of knowing either self or world as ultimate fact and the realization that they appear to be widely different entities. We see through only our own eyes, hear with only our own ears, smell and touch with only our own senses, and think with only our own minds. So, we create a world of our own in which to function while, at the same time, an infinite number of other worlds function simultaneously. The struggle for humanists and therapists, in particular, is to accept the need to create personal SAWCs at the same time that we interact in positive ways with all of the SAWCs that surround us.

The influence that this paradox has on therapists can be seen in a recent study (Kelly, 1995) pointing out the inconsistent values that counselors placed on individualism and collectivism. Clinicians in this study were advocates for their clients, as would be expected. They both were willing to give support and encouraged clients to seek support from themselves and close others. When therapists considered themselves, however, they had a different set of values emphasizing individualism. Unlike the values that they shared for clients, counselors themselves did not want to seek support from close others. Instead, there was an impression of feeling a need to be self-sufficient as therapists and as persons.

The paradox of self and world values places the humanistic therapist in the awkward position of trying to define his or her own world with one set of values while advocating another for everyone else. If the counselor and everyone else division were not enough of a paradox, then there is the reality that all of these people must live in an actual world of which we have no idea of the true organization or limits. Perhaps a final blow to this difficult situation is that reports of genocide, violence, and deadly environmental hazards appear to suggest that our collective ship is sinking (Gergen, 1995). The humanistic therapist is asked to create his or her own world, recognize and understand all others, realize that there is no

final picture of the world, and then make that overall world better somehow. Can there be any wonder why the values of self and others that we carry around can present a highly stressful existence?

CONFLICTING HUMANISTIC COMMITMENTS

Therapists are humans with limited resources both within their environments and within themselves. Clients, friends, colleagues, loved ones, and society as a whole would benefit from people living by humanistic values more consistently, but that is not how the world works right now. Choices need to be made about where, when, how, and to whom therapists will give their most concerted humanistic efforts. The more time given to clients, the less time will be given to family and friends. The more time given to society in forms such as publishing, speaking, and social activism, the less time will be available for both clients and family. The more therapists are providing to all these others for the best of reasons, the less attention they will give to themselves.

Therapists get extensive direction on the amount and type of professional commitment they are to give to their clients. The APA (1992), American Counseling Association (ACA, 1995), and all other legitimate organizations for professional therapists have created extensive ethical guidelines emphasizing therapists' primary responsibility to "respect the dignity and promote the welfare of clients" (ACA, 1995, sec. A.1). It is made perfectly clear in these guides, as well as in casebooks (Herlihy & Corey, 1996; Koocher & Keith-Spiegel, 1998) and textbooks (Corey, Schneider-Corey, & Callanan, 1998; Welfel, 1998), that therapists must make enormous commitments to the people they take into their care.

The amount and clarity provided by training and professional guidelines regarding the therapist's commitment to clients shrinks to virtually nothing when it comes to family and self. The negative results of such inattention show up in a variety of ways, not the least of which are the therapist's own personal problems. In one study, nearly 90% of therapists had gone to personal therapy, and one third of them had gone during the previous year (Mahoney, 1997). Emotional exhaustion and physical fatigue were the most consistent problems, with interpersonal relationship issues, feelings of isolation, disillusionment about the profession anxiety, and depression being common. In fact, these results can be considered "positive" in that they seem to show therapists being more self-supportive at seeking help for themselves than in previous studies.

The confidentiality of the therapeutic setting places honorable therapists in an isolated position when they come home to loved ones. Care must be taken in what is said and what cannot be shared. The pain, frustration, and even the exhilaration of the day can be shown with emotions but rarely with words, stories, and details. The result is helpers coming home with strong feelings and a value that says there is little to share of their origins. Even the best of humanistic therapists can bring themselves home as emotionally drained partners or parents, as persons who are likely to seek dispassionate distance after a day of intenseness, as persons too quick to label and diagnose, as persons who seem to care more for clients than for family, and perhaps as persons whom family members can attract only through developing crises of their own (Zur, 1994). It is little wonder, then, that studies of therapists' interaction with their families can strongly recommend finding opportunities for marital enrichment, education, and

counseling as early as the beginnings of their training programs (Lawson & Gaushell, 1991).

The pressures of dealing with clients, friends, and family might be extreme for the humanistic therapist, but they do not stop there. Schneider (1996) made a strong case for expanding the influence of existential-humanists well beyond individuals to the development of a more humane society. Drawing on others for support, Schneider asked like-minded humanists to commit to incorporating new dimensions into their lives that include greater social and political consciousness (Cushman, 1993; Sipe 1986) as well as more proactive social activism (Schneider, 1998).

These actions would truly reflect the essence of humanistic caring and service. But what is the cost in time, energy, and quality of individual life to one who tries to commit to all of these as well as clients, family, and (perhaps lastly) self?

The decisions that humanistic therapists are pressured to make because of their own value system are enormous, and the implications for their training and profession are equally so. If a social advocacy training model for therapists (Osborne et al., 1998) is desirable to ensure that therapists will take more active social responsibility (Lee & Sirch, 1994), then we must ask where the added time and energy will be found. Will clients, families, or (again) therapists themselves get less time?

There are only so many hours in a therapist's life, no matter how qualified, strong, dedicated, or noble the individual is. No clear line exists to mark where humanistic commitments should begin and where they should end. The criteria for choosing who, where, when, and how to carry out commitments to humanistic values remain vague at a time when the potential need to commit is greatest.

SEEKING THE LIMITS OF A THERAPIST'S HUMANISM

Although we certainly are true believers in the spirit and values of humanism, striving to act as humanistically as we can in our lives and work, we also acknowledge that there are limits to our ability to uphold these beliefs unwaveringly. As we have mentioned several times, it is virtually impossible for any human to be congruent, authentic, and caring to all others and to oneself every minute of his or her life. It is inevitable that, at times, all of us will act hypocritically and not "practice what we preach." This is not exactly a limit of humanism per se, but this orientation does recognize more than most the importance of human qualities in delivering therapeutic services.

The truth is that we are too pragmatic—too steeped in the gritty realities of life—to restrict ourselves to humanistic practices alone. We see too much value in systemic, constructivist, cognitive-behavioral, and the newer brief therapy approaches to remain "monogamous" to any single theory. Furthermore, we recognize that there are times when clients need far more than solid relationships if they are to change. It never ceases to puzzle us how certain therapists, who strike us as essentially cold, withholding, and even mean-spirited or empty inside, still seem to help many clients. At least on the surface, they seem to be the antithesis of anything remotely humanistic in their approach or manner, yet they still are effective. There are many reasons to account for this phenomenon, some of which have been discussed elsewhere (Kottler, 1991). Nevertheless, we do recognize that it is possible, and even desirable, to retain a humanistic orientation to life and therapy while employing a variety of other methodologies embedded in this approach.

We certainly live in a different time than when humanism first enjoyed unparalleled growth. People now are more cynical and more impatient. They want quick cures, and there is a promise from drug companies to get one. Why invest in the hard work of therapy when Prozac will do the job? Why begin marital therapy when Viagra will do the job? And why invest time, effort, and money in a relationship-oriented approach to helping when single-session therapy now is in vogue?

It is difficult to explore new challenges of humanistic psychology without considering those that are faced by all practitioners, regardless of their theoretical orientations. Several trends seem rather obvious (Kottler & Hazler, 1997):

▶ Greater emphasis on eclecticism and integrative theoretical orientations that combine the best features of many different systems

▶ Changing climate in which managed care organizations are regulating the practice of therapy

▶ Increased development of brief therapies that make a difference in a few sessions

▶ More pressure on therapists to abandon value neutrality in favor of moral responsibility

▶ Changing orientation from individual sessions to group and family structures

▶ Increased cultural and gender sensitivity

So, where does humanism fit in? We believe that, among all the theoretical approaches available, humanistic philosophy still provides the best framework for those of us who value human respect, dignity, and caring above all else. We might even go out on a limb and use the "L" word—*love*. It is, after all, the nondemanding, partly conditional (toward certain *behaviors* at least) love that we offer to people in addition to our fancy interventions and strategic techniques.

LOOKING AT OURSELVES AS WELL AS AT OUR CLIENTS

It should come as no surprise to any therapist who has had training in systems thinking that any conflict between two people is most likely the result of obstructive behavior on the part of both participants in the relationship (Wilson & Wilson, 1997). Therefore, we are quite surprised at the attention given to discussing the problem of difficult clients in the literature, in case conferences, and over lunch with colleagues. We speak of these clients as if they are monsters sent to make our lives as miserable as possible. In a perusal of the titles referring to client resistance, we see a number of ugly names that they are called—character disordered, obnoxious, impossible, entitled, abrasive, and so on. The focus usually is on why such miserable folks have to be so difficult, how they got that way, and how we can get them to be more cooperative.

When we get together with colleagues, during informal lunches or formal staff meetings, we often spend our time complaining about the clients we see who are most obnoxious. Sometimes, there is even a competition to see who has the most obstructive or resistant client. To a certain extent, we feel much better after these encounters. We have received support from peers and sometimes even a few helpful suggestions as to how to approach these cases differently.

If, however, we accept the premises stated earlier—that the personal and professional dimensions of therapists' lives are interrelated, that we are humans who are fallible and imperfect as well as skilled professionals, and that difficulties in the therapeutic relationships result from interactive effects—then we must examine our own role and responsibility in creating therapeutic impasses. There are very few difficult clients without difficult therapists who are being unduly rigid. It is for this reason that even before we start looking at these clients' behavior, we should examine what we are doing to make things difficult. What are we expecting of our clients that is unrealistic? What countertransference issues are we acting out? Which of our buttons are being pushed by what our clients are struggling with? What unresolved issues of ours are being triggered? What needs of ours are not being met in these relationships?

When clients do not change as quickly as we might like, when they do not show enthusiastic gratitude for our efforts, when they are significantly different from what we are used to, and when they give us a difficult time because they do not like what we are asking them to do, we are likely to label them as resistant or difficult. If we are feeling especially perturbed, then we might even call them *borderline* or some other name that clearly implies that it is their pathology that is sabotaging treatment.

We do not mean to imply that whether therapy is helpful depends only on the therapist's ability. Clearly, one of the most important variables in predicting positive outcomes is the client's motivation to change. It is just as inaccurate, however, to blame a client for being difficult when therapy is not proceeding according to plan. If we ever hope to work through therapeutic impasses, just as we might resolve any interpersonal conflict, we have to look beyond the client's obstructiveness and also examine what we are doing to contribute to the problem.

IN CLOSING

One of the issues that we have been struggling with the most, and perhaps the greatest challenge we face, is what it really means to *be* a humanist. It seems to us that there are consequences to this choice that transcend what we do in the classroom or office or what we put down on paper. It certainly is not a new challenge for humanistic educators and therapists to live what they teach, that is, to "walk their talk." Nevertheless, one of the reasons why we identify so strongly with a humanistic orientation to work and life is that we feel encouraged to be more effective models of the values we espouse to others. It seems only fair that we practice in our own lives that which we ask of others.

REFERENCES

Albright, D., & Hazler, R. J. (1995). A right to die? Ethical dilemmas of euthanasia. *Counseling and Values, 39,* 177-189.

American Counseling Association. (1995). *Code of ethics and standards of practice.* Alexandria, VA: Author.

American Psychological Association. (1992). *Ethical principles of psychologists and code of conduct.* Washington, DC: Author.

American Psychological Association, Task Force on Promotion and Dissemination of Psychological Procedures. (1995). Training in and dissemination of empirically validated psychological treatments: Report and recommendations. *The Clinical Psychologist, 48,* 2-23.

Anderson, H., & Goolishian, H. (1992). The client is the expert: A not-knowing approach to therapy. In S. McNamee & K. J. Gergen (Eds.), *Therapy as social construction* (pp. 25-39). London: Sage.

Boy, A., & Pine, G. (1990). *A person-centered foundation for counseling and psychotherapy.* Springfield, IL: Charles C Thomas.

Brennan, C. (1995). Beyond theory and practice: A postmodern perspective. *Counseling and Values, 39,* 99-107

Bugental, J. F. T. (1978). *Psychotherapy and process.* Reading, MA: Addison-Wesley.

Bugental, J. F. T., & McBeath, B. (1995). Depth existential therapy: Evolution since World War II. In B. Bongar & L. E. Beutler (Eds.), *Comprehensive textbook of psychotherapy: Theory and practice* (pp. 111-122). New York: Oxford University Press.

Carney, J. V., & Hazler, R. J. (1998). Suicide and cognitive-behavioral therapy: Implications for mental health counselors. *Journal of Mental Health Counseling, 20,* 28-43.

Clance, P. R. (1985). *The impostor phenomenon.* Atlanta, GA: Peachtree.

Combs, A. W. (1989). *A theory of therapy: Guidelines for counseling practice.* Newbury Park, CA: Sage.

Corey, G., Schneider-Corey, M., & Callanan, P. (1998). *Issues and ethics in the helping professions* (5th ed.). Pacific Grove, CA: Brooks/Cole.

Cushman, P. (1993). Psychotherapy as moral discourse. *Journal of Theoretical and Philosophical Psychology, 13*(2), 103-113.

Emerson, S., & Markos, P. A. (1996). Signs and symptoms of the impaired counselor. *Journal of Humanistic Education and Development, 34,* 108-117.

Farber, B. A. (1996). Introduction. In B. A. Farber, D. C. Brink, & P. M. Raskin (Eds.), *The psychotherapy of Carl Rogers* (pp. 1-14). New York: Guilford.

Gelatt, H. B. (1995). Chaos and compassion. *Counseling and Values, 39,* 108-116.

Gergen, K. J. (1995). Postmodernism as a humanism. *The Humanistic Psychologist, 23,* 71-82.

Goud, N. (1994). Jonah complex: The fear of growth. *Journal of Humanistic Education and Development, 32,* 98-111.

Granello, D. H., & Hazler, R. J. (1998). A developmental rationale for curriculum order and teaching styles in counselor education programs. *Counselor Education and Supervision, 38,* 89-105.

Harpaz, N. (1994). Failures in group psychotherapy: The therapist variable. *International Journal of Group Psychotherapy, 44*(1), 3-19.

Hazler, R. J. (1991). Professionalism and human beings: Introduction. *Journal of Humanistic Education and Development, 30,* 1.

Hazler, R. J. (1998a). Client centered theory. In D. Capuzzi & D. R. Gross (Eds.), *Counseling and psychotherapy: Theories and interventions* (2nd ed., pp. 179-202). New York: Macmillan.

Hazler, R. J. (1998b). *Helping in the hallways: Advanced strategies for enhancing school relationships.* Thousand Oaks, CA: Sage.

Hazler, R. J., & Carney, J. (1993). Student-faculty interactions: An underemphasized dimension of counselor education. *Counselor Education and Supervision, 33,* 80-88.

Hazler, R., & Kottler, J. A. (1994).*The emerging professional counselor: Student dreams to professional realities.* Alexandria, VA: American Counseling Association.

Hazler, R. J., & Kottler, J. A. (1996). Following through on the best of intentions: Helping impaired counselors. *Journal of Humanistic Education and Development, 34,* 156-158.

Hazler, R. J., & Singer, M. (1980). *Providing supplemental counseling experiences: Alternatives to role-playing.* (ERIC Document Reproduction Service, No. ED 186 778)

Hazler, R. J., Stanard, B., Conkey, V., & Granello, P. (1996). Mentoring new group leaders. In H. Forrester-Miller & J. A. Kottler (Eds.), *Issues and challenges for group practitioners* (pp. 207-228). Denver: Love.

Henry, W. P., Schacht, T. E., Strupp, H. H., Butler, S. F., & Binder, J. L. (1993). Effects of training in time-limited dynamic psychotherapy: Mediators of therapists' responses to training. *Journal of Consulting and Clinical Psychology, 61,* 441-447.

Herlihy, B., & Corey, G. (1996). *ACA ethical standards casebook* (5th ed.). Alexandria, VA: American Counseling Association.

Kelly, E. W., Jr. (1995). Counselor values: A national survey. *Journal of Counseling and Development, 73,* 648-653.

Koocher, G. P., & Keith-Spiegel, P. (1998). *Ethics in psychology: Professional standards and cases.* New York: Oxford University Press.

Kottler, J. A. (1991). *The compleat therapist.* San Francisco: Jossey-Bass.

Kottler, J. A. (1992). *Compassionate therapy: Working with difficult clients.* San Francisco: Jossey-Bass.

Kottler, J. A. (1993). *On being a therapist* (2nd ed.). San Francisco: Jossey-Bass.

Kottler, J. A. (1994a). *Beyond blame: A new way of resolving conflict in relationships.* San Francisco: Jossey-Bass.

Kottler, J. A. (1994b). Working with difficult group members. *Journal for Specialists in Group Work, 19*(1), 3-10.

Kottler, J. A. (1995). *Growing a therapist.* San Francisco: Jossey-Bass.

Kottler, J. A. (Ed.). (1996). *Finding your way as a counselor.* Alexandria, VA: American Counseling Association.

Kottler, J. A. (1997a). *Succeeding with difficult students.* Thousand Oaks, CA: Corwin.

Kottler, J. A. (1997b). Systemic dysfunction among therapists. *Psychotherapy in Australia, 3*(2).

Kottler, J. A. (1997c). *Travel that can change your life.* San Francisco: Jossey-Bass.

Kottler, J. A. (1999). *The therapist's workbook: Self-assessment, self-care, and self-improvement exercises for mental health professionals.* San Francisco: Jossey-Bass.

Kottler, J. A., & Blau, D. S. (1989). *The imperfect therapist: Learning from failure in therapeutic practice.* San Francisco: Jossey-Bass.

Kottler, J. A., & Hazler, R. J. (1997). *What you never learned in graduate school: A survival guide for therapists.* New York: Norton.

Kottler, J. A., & Markos, P. (1998). Therapist personal reactions to treating sexual offenders. *Sexual Addiction and Compulsivity, 4*(1).

Kottler, J. A., Montgomery, M., & Marbley, A. (1998). Three variations on a theme: The power of being understood. *Journal of Humanistic Education and Development, 37*, 39-46.

Kottler, J. A., Sexton, T., & Whiston, S. (1994). *The heart of healing: Relationships in therapy.* San Francisco: Jossey-Bass.

Land, G., & Jarman, B. (1992). *Breakpoint and beyond.* New York: HarperCollins.

Lawson, D. M., & Gaushell, H. (1991). Intergenerational family characteristics of counselor trainees. *Counselor Education and Supervision, 30*, 309-321.

Lee, C. C., & Sirch, M. L. (1994). Counseling in an enlightened society: Values for a new millennium. *Counseling and Values, 38*, 90-97.

Mahoney, M. J. (1997). Psychotherapists' personal problems and self-care patterns. *Professional Psychology: Research and Practice, 28*(1), 14-16.

Mahrer, A. R. (1989). *The integration of psychotherapies.* New York: Human Sciences Press.

Maslow, A. H. (1968). *Toward a psychology of being.* New York: Van Nostrand Reinhold.

Maslow, A. H. (1971). *The farther reaches of human nature.* New York: Viking.

Miller, L. (1993). Who are the best psychotherapists? Qualities of the effective practitioner. *Psychotherapy in Private Practice, 12*(1), 1-18.

Neimeyer, R. A. (1995). Constructivist psychotherapies: Features, foundations, and future directions. In R. A. Neimeyer & M. J. Mahoney (Eds.), *Constructivism in psychotherapy* (pp. 11-38). Washington, DC: American Psychological Association.

Osborne, J. L., Collison, B. B., House, R. M., Gray, L. A., Firth, J., & Lou, M. (1998). Developing a social advocacy model for counselor education. *Counselor Education and Supervision, 37*, 190-202.

Pope, K. S., & Tabachnick, B. G. (1993). Therapists' anger, hate, fear, and sexual feelings: National survey of therapists' responses, client characteristics, critical events, formal complaints, and training. *Professional Psychology: Research and Practice, 24*(2), 142-152.

Popper, K. (1974). Autobiography and replies to my critics. In P. A. Schilpp (Ed.), *The philosophy of Karl Popper* (pp. 3-181, 961-1197). LaSalle, IL: Open Court.

Prouty, G. (1994). *Theoretical evolutions in person-centered/experiential therapy: Applications to schizophrenic and retarded psychoses*. Westport, CT: Praeger.

Rogers, C. R. (1961). *On becoming a person*. Boston: Houghton Mifflin.

Rogers, C. R. (1980). *A way of being*. Boston: Houghton Mifflin.

Schneider, K. J. (1992). Therapists' personal maturity and effectiveness: How strong is the link? *The Psychotherapy Patient, 8*(3-4), 71-91.

Schneider, K. J. (1996). Jim Bugental's vision: The next step. *Journal of Humanistic Psychology, 36*(4), 67-70.

Schneider, K. J. (1998). Toward a science of the heart: Romanticism and the revival of psychology. *American Psychologist, 53*, 277-289.

Shulman, H. (1997). *Living at the edge of chaos: Complex systems in culture and psyche*. Einsiedeln, Germany: Dainom.

Sipe, R. (1986). Dialectics and method: Reconstructing radical therapy. *Journal of Humanistic Psychology, 26*(2), 52-79.

Sussman, M. E. (Ed.). (1995). *A perilous calling: The hazards of psychotherapy practice*. New York: John Wiley.

Welfel, E. R. (1998). *Ethics in counseling and psychotherapy: Standards, research, and emerging issues*. Pacific Grove, CA: Brooks/Cole.

Wilson, B., & Wilson, L. L. (1997). The multiple selves of the therapist. *Journal of Family Psychotherapy, 8*(2), 73-82.

Yalom, I. (1980). *Existential psychotherapy*. New York: Basic Books.

Zur, O. (1994). Psychotherapists and their families: The effect of clinical practice on individual and family dynamics. *Psychotherapy in Private Practice, 13*(1), 69-95.

CHAPTER 29

Existential Cross-Cultural Counseling

When Hearts and Cultures Share

CLEMMONT E. VONTRESS AND LAWRENCE R. EPP

DURING THE PAST 30 years, counselors have come to recognize the impact of culture on therapeutic relationships, diagnoses, and the techniques they use to help clients. During the 1950s and 1960s, counselors generally considered counseling to be counseling; that is, theories and techniques that worked with one group of clients would work with another group, regardless of cultural background (Jackson, 1995). One indication of how far the helping professions have departed from this position is the *Diagnostic and Statistical Manual of Mental Disorders (DSM-IV)*, which has been prepared to incorporate an awareness that the manual is used in culturally diverse populations in the United States and internationally (American Psychiatric Association, 1994, p. xxiv). Although significant advances have been made in recognizing that clients are reflections of the cultures in which they have been socialized, a theoretical framework still does not exist to help counselors work effec-

tively with culturally different clients who do not fit comfortably within the worldviews of the American psychoanalytic, cognitive-behavioral, and humanistic approaches to counseling. The purpose of this chapter is to offer an existential model of cross-cultural counseling, but the sticky issue of defining the culturally different client will remain a philosophical and practical challenge.

Three or four decades ago, counselors, psychologists, psychiatrists, and social workers began to call attention to the problems they encountered in working with the culturally deprived, the culturally disadvantaged, and African American (or "Negro") clients. During the 1970s, the literature that described the dimensions of the problems presented by such clients increased (Jackson, 1987, 1995). At the same time, some universities introduced graduate courses to enhance the effectiveness of counselors working with the culturally different (Sue, 1981). These courses are now required by the various accreditation bodies in counseling and psychology, but students often complete them feeling more dissimilar from than similar to their culturally different clients because the courses convey reams of factual information on cultural differences that make these seem unbridgeable. Students often come to the faulty conclusion that only persons of like cultures should work together therapeutically. This belief even has become embodied in some Afrocentric counseling theories.

What these courses offer is essentially a group approach. In other words, there is today—as there was during the 1960s—the tendency to generalize about the characteristics of a minority group in graduate classrooms, at professional conferences, and in journal articles and books. Even though Americans of Hispanic, African, Asian, and indigenous descent continue to become total participants in and reflective of the national culture, it often is assumed that cultural differences among ethnic groups are readily distinguishable and easily described. It is our contention that although there are some shared values within ethnic groups, there is a danger of stereotyping ethnic groups if counselors expect too rigidly a given set of behaviors from them. Approaching cross-cultural clients with stereotypes can cause as much misunderstanding as can approaching them with stark ignorance of the cultural values they do hold.

CULTURE

Culture is simultaneously visible and invisible, conscious and unconscious, and cognitive and affective. Although most of it is out of sight and out of mind, it provides humans with their most essential qualities, which are transmitted throughout the life cycle by way of socialization. Culture is the sum total of their beliefs and procedures for negotiating environments at each stage of existence (Vontress, 1986). Most people are products of five concentric and intersecting cultures: universal, ecological, national, regional, and racial/ethnic. The cultures are neither entirely separate nor equal. The most foundational, the universal, is biologically determined and influences all others.

Regardless of the conditions under which people live, they still must adjust to the fact that they are humans. For example, African Americans are, first of all, culturally alike because they are members of the human species. As such, they share biologically dictated behaviors of all members of the human group. Second, they are forced to adjust to the same climatic conditions as are all other Americans. Third, as members of the national culture, they take on the behavior, attitudes, and values of Americans in general. Fourth, they are influenced by the culture of the region in which they live. Thus, Marcus, a native of rural Alabama, is apt to betray his roots by the manner of speech peculiar to that region. Fifth, because of Marcus's African ancestry, Euro-Americans are apt to react to him as if he were inferior, a fact that leaves psychological scars on him and on members of his group (Vontress, 1986).

This perception of culture suggests that everybody is multicultural in the sense of being composed of multiple cultural influences rather than being culturally monolithic. It also limits the groups that may be classified as culturally different to those who share traits that traditionally have been recognized as cultural—ecological, regional, national, or racial/ethnic traits—rather than those who share a universal characteristic. Therefore, women, gay men and lesbians, the physically challenged, and senior citizens are not considered culturally different because they are socialized in the same families and under the same cultural influences as are their male, straight, able-bodied, and younger siblings and relatives.

Although their forced or voluntary segregation from their families or privileged circles gives them the flavor of separate subcultures, we would like to discourage thinking of these groups as culturally different because such a strong label is alienating and not reflective of how these groups think of themselves. To make the stages of human development, gender, disabling condition, or sexual preference into distinct cultural groups is to magnify the natural differences within groups. It would mean looking at all differences through a microscope rather than within their natural contexts.

AN EXISTENTIAL MODEL OF CULTURE

Humans are products of their genetic endowments and life experiences. At conception, their destinies already are determined in part by the DNA helix that exists in every cell. The final shape of that destiny, however, is influenced by individuals' life experiences. Human genetics and life experience intermingle as they are filtered through five cultural layers. The first one is the *universal culture* or the way of life that is indicated by the physiology of the human species. People are conceived in a given way, they must consume nourishment to live, they grow into adulthood, they contribute to the welfare of the group, and they grow old and die. These and other ways of life are invariable dimensions of human existence. Therefore, they may be called *universal culture*.

Human genetic endowment and life experiences also are shaped by the ecosystem and the demands that it makes on people's way of life. The climatic conditions, indigenous vegetation, animal life, seasonal changes, and other factors determine how people interact with nature and themselves. Obviously, people who must use dog sleighs to commute to the grocery store see life differently from those who need only to pluck their nourishment from trees and plants in their backyards. Imagine also what it must be like to live several months of the year in complete darkness and how such an existence affects daily activities. For these and other reasons, it seems tenable to posit the existence of an *ecological culture*, the second ring of the cultural filter.

The third ring of the filter is the *national culture*, which derives from the fact that a stable community of people share the same territory, heritage, language, economic system, government, and allegiance to a way of life for which they are willing to die if necessary. Although people born abroad may join the community, they must fit into the culture already established by earlier generations. In other words, they are expected to become *acculturated* or to take on the culture of their adopted country. In large measure, schools serve as primary institutions of acculturation for young people. However, everybody needs to learn to negotiate the culture of the host country. They must learn its rules and regulations, many of which are sanctioned by law. The social demands and expectations that provide self-direction for individuals in one country usually are inadequate to ensure comfortable adjustment in another country.

The fourth cultural layer that helps to make people into the persons they are is the *regional culture*. Many countries manifest distinct regional differences in terms of language, dress, customs, and other ways of life. Regional differences exist for various reasons. In large countries, different climate zones influence how people negotiate environmental differences. In others, proximity to the borders of neighboring countries contributes to a blending of cultures along the boundaries. Regional cultural differences also often are byproducts of military conquests and political annexations.

The fifth and final ring is called *racial/ethnic,* mainly because racial and ethnic groups usually reside in separate communities where they perpetuate their ways of life. Separatism is especially true in countries where racial attitudes are such that racially and ethnically different people feel unwelcome in the dominant group community. In Paris, for example, there are sections of the city where Africans live, a section where Arabs reside, and other sections where various other ethnic groups settle in their own neighborhoods. In New York City, the same phenomenon is observed. There is not only a Harlem where African Americans reside but also a Spanish Harlem where Spanish-speaking people of color live and perpetuate their culture. It is unnecessary to debate whether people choose voluntarily to live among their own kind or whether they are forced by the larger society to do so. The results are the same—a racial/ethnic culture that is transmitted from one generation to another. Although people may relocate to other communities, their cultural roots usually remain in their communities of origin.

THE CULTURAL DISTILLATE

Individuals are distillates of a cultural filter consisting of five layers. The filtering continues throughout their life spans. At each developmental stage, their genetic endowment interacts with life experiences to determine the nature of their existence. Each human is distinctively different from all others. As Vontress (1979, 1996) pointed out, individuals embody four dynamically interactive "worlds" that can be best described in the language of German existentialists (Binswanger, 1962). First, there is the *Eigenwelt* or that "private realm" of the human personality that cannot be shared with or completely understood by another person. Second, the *Mitwelt* suggests that what people are is a product of their relationships with others. In fact, many would say that no humans really are themselves; rather, they are composites of the other people—primarily their parents and siblings—who shaped their personalities, just as their genes directed their physical characteristics. Third, humans are influenced by the *Umwelt* or the natural environment. How people relate to that environment directly affects the nature of their existence as well as their personalities. Although the natural environment often is taken for granted, it makes the difference between life and death for thousands of species residing in its bosom, which is affectionately called "Mother Nature." Without the natural environment's nourishment and support, none would exist. Fourth, humans relate to the *Überwelt* or the spirit world. They require the respect, direction, love, and affection of parents, elders, departed love ones, and potent spiritual entities. The spirit world connects people with those who, although come and gone, still reside in them due to memories, genetic contributions, and cultural indoctrination (Vontress, 1996). Perhaps this realm also includes intangible feelings of the here and now such as love, empathy, devotion, respect, and altruism that bind the human community together in mutual understanding with a powerful, if unseen, emotional glue.

The existential model of culture presented here highlights the paradoxical complexity and simplicity of human existence. Culture should not be viewed separately from the rest of life; it is the compass of life. Because people cannot live to adulthood without a set of practices and procedures designed to guide their existence, they require a culture for their orientation and survival in the world. The model intends to communicate the notion that acculturation has a purpose. That purpose is to ensure that people live as best as they can while they develop though their life spans.

During existence, humans must maintain a working rapport with themselves; that is, they need to know themselves at all times. Second, they are obliged to establish and maintain a rapport with others because they exist in the world of others and require their love and respect. Third, it is absolutely necessary that individuals recognize that they are a part of the animal kingdom and are governed by biological systems similar to the ones that animate other creatures. Fourth, there is a need for humans to relate to something or somebody greater than themselves. These four needs are dynamic and interactive. Each may demand fulfillment more strongly at one period of life than at others. For example, the need to learn about one's self is urgent during adolescence as one's body quickly changes in the service of developing organs of reproduction. Although the need to relate to others is a powerful force throughout life, it is especially demanding during early adulthood, when individuals prepare to assume adult roles and to initiate intimate and, hopefully, lifelong linkages with members of the opposite or same gender. In many societies, people seem to be more in touch with their spiritual selves toward the end of their lives than at other stages of their existence.

In general, everything that lives manifests a predictable chronology of existence. It is conceived, sprouts, bears fruit, shrivels up, dies, and returns to nature to be recycled. This sobering and inevitable cycle also occurs with humans. The model intends to suggest that human existence is a continuous and changing movement. During youth, human existence flows quickly and abundantly. As people age, the flow of life (genetic expression and life experiences) slows, but the evaporation process continues unabated until the tub of life is empty.

No one escapes from life alive, nor can its flow be slowed or reversed. Considering how our existence ends and evaporates helps to emphasize how precious each moment is.

THE BALANCING OF THE FOUR WORLDS

In recognizing the four worlds of human existence in this model, we outline the expansive outlook of existential cross-cultural counseling. The existential cross-cultural counselor is a macroscopic and holistic thinker who sees beyond superficial cultural differences to find the imbalances among the client's four worlds that produce and maintain his or her emotional disturbances. Viewed as an organic whole, the different worlds are like the developing petals of a flower. For a young sapling to bloom fully, each petal must grow and integrate into the single entity of the flower. As van Deurzen-Smith (1988) applied this notion to counseling,

> It is not possible to work exclusively in one [existential] sphere and neglect all the other aspects. Though clients frequently emphasize their struggle in one particular dimension, it is usually essential to ensure that difficulties in living get worked through on all four dimensions. (p. 88)

Existential cross-cultural counseling recognizes that life is an intricate balancing act. The physical, public, private, and spiritual worlds all require attending or else their neglect will form a hungry vacuum that cries out for emotional nourishment. Individuals must learn how to balance and integrate the various existential spheres of their lives so as to achieve a meaningful synthesis. Due to differing life circumstances, certain individuals will find this task easier than will others. The random meeting of sperm and ova ensures great variations in the intellectual, emotional, and material endowments with which we come into the world. We arrive on different planes, and fate deals us different life spans in which to unfold our existential possibilities. Some will experience long and harmonious lives, whereas others will face brief and nasty struggles ending in unfair deaths. The goal of the existential cross-cultural counselor is to help clients face whatever existence fate bequeaths them with courage, hope, and a striving to find meaning in life's suffering.

However unequal our existence in the four worlds, each of us inevitably moves toward death in which all humans find their ultimate equality. We cannot stop time; the sifting of the hourglass grains is the most rigid and unmerciful aspect of living. Yet, this irrevocable movement enriches life and reminds us of the short chronological boundaries to our existence. Yalom (1980) believed that the striving to transcend death is the creative force behind our monuments, inventions, books, artistic creations, and the like, all of which are conceived to gain individual immortality through the realm of ideas or materials. Some persons, however, become stuck in the past to distract themselves from their movement toward death, with the sad byproduct that this retrospective existence hampers their creativity and enjoyment of the present. It is easy to blame the past for life's unhappiness; it is more difficult to find the courage to move forward and make the best use of the time remaining within the four worlds of existence.

THE CULTURES DEFINING US

Existential cross-cultural counselors realize that cultural groups cannot be understood with fixed principles or stereotypes. Human groups always are changing and possess great diversity among members. Although cultural differences can become sources of cross-cultural misunderstanding, when one scratches off the patina of culture from a human, one finds at the core a humanness that is universal. The existential cross-cultural counselor approaches every culturally different client as a unique human first but uses some of the concepts listed in the following subsections to help understand the influence of culture in the client's life. Each concept is briefly defined, and the implications for existential cross-cultural counseling are discussed.

Acculturation

Acculturation is the process of becoming adapted to a new or different culture with more or less advanced patterns. It usually suggests that the new arrival or socially excluded takes on the language, values, attitudes, dress, and behavior of the host culture. Becoming like the others also implies duration, as Fischer (1965) pointed out. That is, it takes people a while to adjust to a new culture. Young people tend to acculturate more quickly than do their older cultural peers (Turner, 1986). The related concept, *assimilation*, conjures up the image of the human organism unconsciously absorbing surrounding stimuli. Because culture is cumulative, it seems tenable to conclude that young people in a host culture or community are apt to become more like the people in that community more quickly than are their older relatives who have been socialized during their formative years in their native cultures.

An obvious implication is that the more clients are acculturated, the more counselors can feel comfortable using theories and techniques they use generally with American-born clients. However, counselors are faced with the problem of having to make a determination of the level of acculturation presented by each client. There is no single index for doing so. For example, a client may speak perfect English but have little or no understanding of the values, attitudes, or affective dimensions of the host culture. Counselors need to develop an easy yet effective way of finding out the degree to which culturally different clients are similar to people in the host culture. They may require each new counselees to write structured cultural autobiographies in which they reveal dimensions of themselves such as places of birth, schools attended, languages spoken at home, places traveled, any American-born friends, languages spoken, and as many other items as are needed to obtain thumbnail sketches of the new clients.

Collectivism Versus Individualism

Collectivism and individualism are concepts widely discussed and contrasted in social science (Triandis, 1994). *Collectivism* refers to social systems in which individuals submit to the interest of the group, which may be the family, ethnic leaders, community, work colleagues, nation, or other affiliations that provide a sense of belonging for the people. On the other hand, *individualism* suggests societies in which the needs, desires, and aspirations of individuals take precedence over those of groups such as the family, kinship clan, and community at large. Although the concepts often are presented as polarities, it probably is more correct to view them as indicators of general tendencies and inclinations that can coexist in the same individuals depending on the issues or circumstances (Carrithers, 1992; Dube, 1988).

With the intense and constant movement of people from one nation to another, it no longer is tenable to hold to fixed views regarding them. People who are individualistic in one country often become collectivistic in another country, and vice versa, for various reasons. For example, in developing countries where agriculture is the primary means of subsistence, people benefit from being neighborly. In capitalistic societies where individuals often live and work in impersonal environments, others who do not contribute significantly to the fulfillment of one's immediate needs are seen as competitors rather than as compatriots (Fischer, 1965). In collectivistic societies, the heads of families assume a powerful and respected role. In individualistic societies, household heads exert much less influence over family members, especially adults. Existential cross-cultural counselors need to ascertain the extent to which clients are products of individualistic or collectivistic socialization. It is a good practice to ask clients whether there are people at home or elsewhere who should be consulted regarding the presenting problems and their solutions. To enter into counseling without respecting the heads of families may negatively affect the outcomes of counseling. Whatever recommendations are decided on in counseling may be rejected by family authority figures unless they are consulted early in the counseling process.

Cultural Intuition

Cultural intuition is the immediate knowledge, sensation, and rapport that counselors often experience when they relate to clients from their own cultures. It is the empathy that people feel for cultural peers. As a result, there is increased ability to relate to clients and to determine the nature of their presenting problems. This concept should not be interpreted to mean that counselors external to the native cultures of their clients are unable to empathize with them. All people are multicultural in the sense that they share commonalities at some level of experience. For example, the existence of Americans is influenced by a common ecology, economic system, network of bureaucratic procedures, media, and the like. As such, Americans are socialized to respond spontaneously to certain cues to which people reared in other countries do not respond. Therefore, there is a national cultural intuition that enhances the rapport and mutual comprehension of one American for another. Likewise, on the racial/ethnic cultural level, people who grow up in the same racial or ethnic community generally sense the feelings, thoughts, and knowledge of their cultural peers more quickly and spontaneously than do outsiders.

Although cultural intuition is a human phenomenon, the uncanny ability to know what another person thinks, wants, and feels without knowing the origin of the power is especially prevalent among homogeneous groups unaffected by outside influences (Moles, 1967). In such societies, each person is a veritable template of the other. Even so, cross-cultural counselors must guard against countertransference or unconsciously generalizing their own experiences onto clients, who are in fact different from them in many ways because they were socialized in other families. People are alike and different at the same time.

Direct Versus Indirect Intervention

In helping clients, counselors talk to them face to face or interact with others on their behalf. In the United States, counselors usually talk directly with clients who have problems, especially adult clients. On the other hand, in many cultures external to the American society, the head of the family assumes responsibility for all problems in the unit. If a family member has a problem, then the head of the household consults the helper on behalf of the entire family, not just the person who is perceived to be the identified patient. In collectivistic societies, individuals do not have problems; rather, families have problems, and this in turn reflects negatively on the heads of families who feel responsible for their entire units (Triandis, 1994; Vontress, 1991).

Indirectness seems to be more pronounced in traditional collectivistic societies than it is in their individualistic counterparts. In West Africa, for example, parents and other adults in extended families socialize children by reciting fables, riddles, and maxims designed to inculcate important lessons. When the children become adults, they are apt to consult traditional healers who use the same indirect intervention strategies to communicate suggested solutions to problems that clients present (Vontress, 1991). Indirect intervention refers to counselors working through one person to assist another person. It also refers to indirectness in terms of the language and techniques that counselors use to help their clients. In general, American-born people are apt to be up-front in communicating with people. In counseling culturally different clients, direct communication styles might offend them.

Historical Hostility

People are cultural extensions of their forebears (Fischer, 1965; Wade, 1993). Even though much of the past no longer is a conscious part of their present existence, it continues to affect their relationships with others, especially those whose ancestors were participants in the earlier history. For example, because of slavery, many African Americans harbor unrecognized negative feelings toward Euro-Americans (Vontress & Epp, 1997). In a like manner, Native Americans are unable to forgive and forget the atrocities inflicted on their people by European settlers who pushed them off their ancestral lands. The inability of cultural progenies to forgive usually is related to the perception that the people who mistreated their forebears continue to mistreat them (West, 1993). The hostility that they feel has been passed down through generations and, therefore, may be called *historical hostility.*

The phenomenon can be observed in many parts of the world. In Africa, old ethnic rivalries cause parts of the continent to be drenched with blood and set in motion the exodus of thousands of refugees fleeing the murderous attacks of adversaries whose hatred for them goes back many generations. In Europe, the slaughter and displacement of people in the former Yugoslavia is another example of historical hostility being vented against people long removed from the events of the past that first triggered the hostility. In the Middle East, old hostilities continue to simmer and threaten to explode at any time. Therapeutic phenomena such as resistance, transference, and the reluctance of clients to self-disclose often are manifestations of events buried in the cultural histories of counselors and clients.

Holistic Versus Monistic Diagnoses

Societies differ in terms of what people perceive to be problems in life, their causes, and who should be consulted to remedy them (Fischer, 1965). In general, in modern and technologically advanced societies, human problems are categorized into four groups: physical, psychological, social, and spiritual. Each category has its own set of specialists who are trained to relieve individuals of their problems. In the United States, individuals consult physicians for biological problems; they consult counselors, psychologists, and psychiatrists for psychological concerns; they consult social workers and related experts for social difficulties; and they consult ministers, priests, rabbis, and imams for spiritual guidance.

In traditional societies, humans and their problems in living usually are understood holistically. In West Africa, for example, individuals seek the counsel of a single healer for problems ranging from a broken toe to perceived conflict with a deceased relative (Vontress, 1991). They also consult the healer when they are concerned about the yield of their crops. Mainly animists, they perceive problems in holistic terms. Everything in their environment is related. To understand problems presented by clients, healers in traditional Africa seek to understand their relationship with nature, other people, themselves, and the spirits that they consider important in the conduct of their lives. American counselors who focus exclusively on the psychological dimension of their clients' lives must recognize that in many cultures the social, physical, and spiritual dimensions of people's lives are just as important as the psychological ones. Therefore, they are advised to search for ways in which to explore these dimensions with clients from holistic cultures.

Personalism

Personalism is a perspective on life that maintains that the person is the center of intrinsic value (Lavely, 1967). People are more important than what they do to earn a living or the material things they possess. In general, collectivistic societies in which individuals live interdependently in small communities encourage the development of reciprocal interpersonal alliances (Mounier, 1992). Neighbors inquire daily about the well-being of families and the individuals in them. Privacy is not a cherished value as it is in industrialized urban societies. Individuals are less apt to be split into two personas—one private and the other public. Each person is unique, irreplaceable, and worthy of respect and attention.

As a cultural ingredient, personalism has implications for counseling culturally different clients. First, clients may annoy counselors with personal questions that seem inappropriate. For example, they might ask counselors whether they are married, whether they have children, or how old they are. Such questions usually are signs of respect. Clients want to indicate that they value counselors as humans. Second, personalism has implications for diagnosis. Individuals are considered to be more than sets of traits that can be inventoried and added up. Each person is a dynamic presence that responds to the same environments differently at different times. Viewing clients as a static sum-total of inventoried traits and facts is apt to cause many culturally different clients to resist taking tests and accepting the results as indications of who they are.

Introspection and Self-Disclosure

Introspection and self-disclosure are closely related concepts. *Introspection* refers to the self looking within to discover and evaluate the content housed there. In counseling, it is assumed that the content and insights derived from introspection will be shared with the counselor. The revealing of the self to others so that they may know that self is called *self-disclosure* (Chelune & Associates, 1979). Counselors need to recognize that in many collectivistic societies, people are socialized to submerge the self in the interest of the group. In such cultures, it might be considered impolite or unhealthy to focus on the self; the person is a part of the whole. On American college campuses, international students from family-centered

societies often write their family names first and their given names last on official documents.

However, there are other reasons why some clients might not self-disclose. For example, African American lower class males resist revealing personal content unless they perceive their audience to be persons of goodwill. Although most of them can introspect, what they discover about themselves might be so painful that they do not want to share it with anyone. Historical hostility also can keep such clients from self-disclosing with counselors whose ethnicity symbolizes historical oppressors. In fact, clients have been known to generalize the hostility to African American counselors whom they perceive to identify with Euro-Americans.

Cultural Anxiety

Life is a series of events taking place in different venues populated by people and a variety of natural and man-made objects. In large measure, socialization of the young in any culture is designed to teach individuals to manage different problems, situations, and expectations as they move through their life spans. Because parts of the world differ in terms of climate, soil, terrain, and foodstuff, it is understandable that cultural groups develop a variety of patterns of behavior required for survival. Their survival skills put them in good stead so long as they remain in their native cultures. When they travel to strange lands, however, they are likely to experience uneasiness because of their unfamiliarity with role behaviors in the host cultures.

In coming to America, many individuals from collectivistic societies characterized by interdependence among family members are overwhelmed by anxiety. Back home, relatives validate their personalities and statuses in their families and communities. People know where to go, what to do, and who to see when they need information, diversion, support, and objects destined to enhance the quality of life. In living abroad, they may lose the sense of community that is basic to well-being. Being alone in a foreign country for the first time, sojourners often are obliged to make a multitude of unaccustomed daily decisions by themselves, use public transportation, eat strange food, and communicate in a strange language. Although international university students might come from upper class families, on American campuses they are just foreign students who in fact might be treated as simpletons simply because their ability to use English is less than perfect. Therefore, their anxiety is understandable. It is generated by the strangeness of the host culture. It may be referred to as *cultural anxiety.*

The symptoms of cultural anxiety often are misdiagnosed because they are reported as somatic in persons from nonpsychological cultures. That is, individuals often complain of headaches, eye strain, constipation, inability to sleep, and other physical problems. Although living far away from their family members, they often communicate with them by telephone. Counselors who intervene to help them adjust to the United States should ask them about the advice they receive from their parents and other significant adults back home, whom their cultures recognize as the repositories of appropriate advice. Such inquiries enhance the rapport with clients and contribute to the effectiveness of therapeutic interventions with them.

Cultural anxiety approximates the *DSM-IV* diagnostic category of separation anxiety (American Psychiatric Association, 1994). It also resembles homesickness, which many American college students experience. However, it is a much more intense feeling

for individuals residing in a totally new culture where most of the cues and responses acquired during socialization back home serve little purpose. To some degree, racial and ethnic minority group members who are citizens of the United States experience cultural anxiety when they move from the comfort and support of their communities to mainstream cultural environments. Those who have been socialized in integrated settings prior to going away to college usually fit in well on most campuses.

IMPLICATIONS FOR COUNSELING

It is antitherapeutic to stereotype clients who appear to represent national, cultural, or racial groups. People with ancestral roots in Europe, Asia, Africa, the Middle East, the Americas, and other parts of the world defy the simple classifications that their superficial racial characteristics would indicate. Their forebears, in adjusting to the natural and social requirements for living, evolved behavioral differences to adapt to their regions of the continent, but many of these differences can be lost to subsequent generations who are socialized differently. Differences in socioeconomic status, religious beliefs, and educational attainment further confound the ability to stereotype ethnic group members.

American racial and cultural minorities also elude precise definition. For example, wealthy Hispanics, regardless of their countries of origin, are different from those from rural villages in Central and South America. Those who are of the third and fourth generations should not be compared with people who are recent immigrants. In the case of Native Americans, it is unreasonable to consider individuals from different tribes or those who live in cities as similar to people who still reside on reservations. In counseling Asian Americans, it is important to recognize that individuals of Japanese, Chinese, Vietnamese, and Indian descent are apt to be as different from one another as they are from Anglo clients. Although African Americans might have darkly pigmented skin, that is often where the similarity ends. There are cultural differences resulting from educational and economic advantages that set apart upper, middle, and lower class people. Perhaps more important are differences in terms of their identification with or rejection of the white American majority culture. In summary, individually expressed cultural differences, rather than generalizable group differences, risk affecting all three aspects of counseling: the relationship, the diagnosis, and the intervention.

The Relationship

Even though it is untenable to generalize about group similarities and differences as they relate to psychotherapeutic relationships, it is useful to recognize that some clients in all cultural groups respond to counseling differently because of their socialization. For many, the idea of introspecting and self-disclosing is cause for high anxiety. For others, historical hostility or prejudice toward their counselors' cultural or racial groups may impede the establishment of effective rapport. Other clients from countless backgrounds may expect friendly, relaxed, and personal relationships with their helpers, an expectation that might be threatening to counselors who perceive helping as a scientific enterprise demanding a prescribed social distance between interactants. Potential clients present too many perceptions and expectations of helpers to forewarn therapists of each possible cultural pitfall. Instead of relying blindly on therapeutic relationship prescriptions, therapists should realize that the therapeutic relationship, as modeled in Western psychology textbooks, is imbued with cultural assumptions that might need to be altered creatively to serve culturally different clients.

Throughout the history of counseling psychology in the United States, authorities have devoted more attention to the helping relationship than to any other aspect of the therapeutic enterprise. Some writers and theorists have made the relationship the essence of counseling itself. The emphasis on the relationship has highlighted numerous problems in cross-cultural counseling because, in the United States, clients from lower status racial, ethnic, socioeconomic, and national backgrounds are unaccustomed to relating to their higher status counselors as equals. They often feel uncomfortable in cross-cultural counseling relationships because they believe that they are being judged by people who are affluent, more educated, and perhaps unfamiliar with the moral compromises and complexities of a less privileged existence.

In a few instances, culturally different clients might desire unequal relationships with their counselors owing to their cultural belief that professionals are wiser and able to provide accurate advice. Although professionals do possess a wellspring of useful information, and although clients may accord them the deference of respected elders or even gurus, it is important for counselors, irrespective of their clients' attributions, to maintain a posture of philosophical equality with their clients. Culturally different clients might wish to defer to the opinions of their counselors, but there is something detrimental to the human spirit across cultures when counselors do all of the thinking for their clients. Achieving some degree of *individuation*—to borrow a term from Jungian psychology—in personality may be a universal developmental task that is revisited at each of life's stages as choices must be made about the people we are to be. It should be no different in the counseling suite.

The existential cross-cultural counseling relationship strives to approach what Buber (1970) called the "I-thou" rapport, that is, a deep fellowship stressing honest sharing and mutual regard. It would not be an overstatement to characterize this relationship as one that generates a platonic exchange of love akin to what the Greeks called *agape-love,* whereas Boss (1963) chose to label it *psychotherapeutic eros* without intending to imply the romantic element that the word *eros* would suggest. Although underemphasized in other counseling theories, existential counseling sees the sharing and generation of loving feelings as a powerful therapeutic force essential to all significant relationships, not simply therapeutic ones. Satir (1988) expressed the value of love most powerfully: "Without loving and being loved, the human soul and spirit curdle and die" (p. 141).

In the existential cross-cultural counseling relationship, the counselor is not a blank slate awaiting projection in the Freudian schema. In fact, the therapist's interpretation of transference is peripheral to this encounter given that existential counseling assumes that seeking a parental relationship or friendship with a therapist is a natural striving, disguising the very human desire for connection, bonding, and love. To be effective facilitators of such authentic relationships, therapists must be truly willing to help others as a calling and must be at peace with themselves as imperfect and mortal humans who can honestly draw on their own experiences and frailties and be unafraid to share these with their clients.

The existential cross-cultural counseling relationship is spontaneous, unselfish, and respectful, and it shows reverence for the client's culture and uniqueness. Existential cross-cultural counselors love their fellow humans as they love themselves. They are personalistic in the counseling relationship. The person is more important than anything else in life—role, status, class, money, or attractiveness. They do not distance themselves professionally from their clients. Gross (1978) found that psychotherapeutic closeness increases the likelihood of successful counseling. In other words, it is important that clients believe that their counselors appreciate them deeply as fellow humans.

Existential cross-cultural counselors are world citizens who commit themselves to helping their fellow humans through life. They do not allow cultural, national, or racial ideologies or conflicts to loom large in their encounters, for to do so is to encourage cultural defensiveness on the part of their clients. Although it is ironic in a profession that prides itself on its caring and humanism, Vontress noted how radical the notion of a caring therapeutic relationship is to the professional counseling community:

> Over the years, my colleagues have come to see me as an iconoclast because I reject the notions of therapeutic objectivity and professional distance and declare them to be anti-therapeutic. . . . I believe that we must genuinely care about our clients as fellow human beings. I have come to despise the professional games and bureaucracy that we dispense as our means of helping others. No wonder clients often come to hate counseling centers; these organizations often reflect the insensitivity of the clients' world instead of offering a place of refuge and healing. (quoted in Epp, 1998, p. 12)

Being an existential counselor would seem to mean having the courage to be a caring human in an insensitive world.

The Diagnosis

There are several points that therapists should keep in mind when diagnosing clients external to the mainstream culture. First, therapists should ascertain whether assessment tools and procedures normally used with dominant group clients are appropriate for their culturally different counterparts. Second, they should decide whether to diagnose from an "emic" or "etic" perspective or both. That is, should the yardstick for "normal" be based on the expectations of the individual's immediate cultural group (emic) or on those of the community at large, extending beyond the client's racial or cultural neighborhood (etic)? In most cases, people move through several cultural layers in a single day. Therefore, both the emic and etic perspectives might need to be considered at the same time. Even so, the focus of therapy always depends on the nature of the presenting problem. Third, therapists should determine whether a purely psychological assessment is sufficient or whether the diagnosis should be based on social, physical, and spiritual considerations as well. Each client must be viewed individually, not in stereotypical terms.

In choosing diagnoses, therapeutic professionals need to recognize that life consists of opposites and contradictions (Lowen, 1980). That is, to understand and appreciate the negative, it is imperative to experience the positive (Ricken, 1991). Humans are a complex mixture of opposites—sanity and neurosis, rationality and irrationality, good and evil, aggression and compassion, and so on. Due to life circumstances, upbringing, and perhaps biology, some have learned to keep these polarities tilted in the positive direction, but it is a naïve conviction that some live without pathology or evil; all attempt to live managing their negative polarities so that they do not hurt themselves or others. In diagnosing presenting problems and personalities of their clients, counselors should resist temptations to classify people and their struggles with the human condition into simple categories of praise and blame or health and sickness.

The Intervention

Historically, counseling psychology in the United States has placed considerable responsibility on clients to help themselves. The imposition of counselors' own values and expectations on clients has been discouraged. Counselors are taught not to think for clients but rather to help clients think for themselves. However, expecting helpers to solve their problems is normal for people from collectivistic cultures in which authority figures often directly influence the lives of others. Therefore, it is understandable if such people, on their arrival in this country, anticipate the type of intervention to which they have become accustomed. Furthermore, culturally different people may be more comfortable talking to counselors if the clients can bring other family members or friends with them to the consultations. Counselors are advised to determine, during their first interviews with clients, what the clients expect from them in terms of the outcomes and styles of intervention. Do clients prefer (a) to work things out for themselves with a minimum of assistance from counselors, (b) to work cooperatively with counselors, or (c) to be authoritatively directed by counselors in searching for solutions to their presenting problems?

Existential cross-cultural counseling is a voyage to self-discovery not only for clients but also for their counselors, who invariably see a little of themselves in each of their clients. The main goal of therapeutic encounters is to engage individuals in personal struggles to confront the areas of "stuckness" in their lives (Johnson, 1971). To accomplish this goal, counselors should be flexible in style, varying their therapeutic approaches from one client to another and from one phase to another in the treatment of the same clients (May, 1991). The specific technique, approach, or style to be used should be based on the uniqueness of each individual. Existential cross-cultural counselors are necessarily artists who are creative, individualistic, and fluid in their work and who also have a spiritual connection with each client. They reject the notion that psychotherapy is a science embodying facts, principles, and methods that must be memorized and applied in a standardized way to all clients (May, 1991). In fact, Ungersma (1961) indicated that helpers who emphasize techniques too much run the risk of becoming technicians rather than therapists; their clients, in turn, become machines to be manipulated in accordance with prescribed techniques. In a sense, a scientific approach to psychotherapy can often be unwittingly antitherapeutic.

Perhaps the simplest way in which to communicate the existential intervention style is to refer to it as a Socratic dialogue. As the reader may recall, the ancient Greek philosopher Socrates had a knack for getting individuals to discover themselves and to live according to the content of their self-discoveries (Wolff, 1976). He was convinced that the surest way in which to attain reliable knowledge was through the art of disciplined conversation in which he acted as an intellectual midwife (Stumpf, 1975). He would confront people with various points of view on topics under discussion and try to bring into focus their strengths and weaknesses. Out of this experience, he hoped that individuals would develop their own wisdom and resulting directions in life, giving birth to new selves (Johnson, 1977). Socratic dialogues did not always end in clear-cut answers for individuals (Rychlak, 1979). Sometimes, the hard

questioning would trigger ideas in the minds of students that would take time to understand. This approach to knowledge of self was called the *maieutic* or hatching method.

In essence, existential cross-cultural counselors, like Socrates, do not use a bag of tricks to get their clients to explore their existence. If they have a "technique," then it is their focus on the unique existential struggle of each client. As dialecticians, they look for difficulties in impeding the unfolding or becoming of individuals and help them to discover the reasons for their stuckness (Christian, 1977). There is no one way to accomplish this task. How counselors do their work depends on the uniqueness of the interactants. Counselors must ask themselves how they can know and enter the worlds of their clients (May, 1967). Once they are inside, the most important question is what counselors should do next. The answer to this self-inquiry resides in the hearts and minds of counselors, not in a recipe box of techniques. In an interview, Vontress warned,

> I do not know whether all counselors are equipped to be existentialists, however simple this philosophy may sound. Being an intimate friend, in a therapeutic sense, is emotionally draining for the counselor while healing for the client. In my opinion, counseling techniques . . . are not for the client's benefit but [rather] for the counselor's [benefit]. They are a structure for the therapeutic interview as well as the filler, or white noise, to use when the counselor is unsure of what to do. (quoted in Epp, 1998, p. 6)

The central agent of healing in existential cross-cultural counseling is the therapeutic personality of the counselor (Frank, 1961), who relates to the client as a fellow traveler. In graduate schools, many counselors view counseling as a science, justifying their teaching techniques designed to put counselors-in-training in good stead in relating to clients. Unfortunately, culturally different clients often do not see the science or understand the techniques. They see and understand only the helpers there with them—the other humans—who cannot substitute technique for true caring because phoniness, superficiality, and indifference are recognized by members of every human culture.

CONCLUSION

Existential cross-cultural counseling is a rich philosophical approach to psychotherapy that shares many of the same tenets with the world's major cultures and religions as well as both Eastern and Western philosophies. It is this fact that makes it a universally applicable theory of counseling. However, existentialism subtly challenges the other counseling perspectives in its expansive view of life through the four worlds and through its belief that a narrow focus on cognitions, feelings, or psychodynamics in the therapeutic relationship addresses only a narrow slice of existence. Ultimately, the existential cross-cultural counselor wishes to concertedly explore with the client all of life; not simply the random issues that emerge in session—the transient importance of which might only fade into the background of the larger scheme of life that went unexplored.

REFERENCES

American Psychiatric Association. (1994). *Diagnostic and statistical manual of mental disorders* (4th ed.). Washington, DC: Author.

Binswanger, L. (1962). *Existential analysis and psychotherapy.* New York: E. P. Dutton.

Boss, M. (1963). *Psychoanalysis and Dasein analysis.* New York: Basic Books.

Buber, M. (1970). *I and thou.* New York: Scribner.

Carrithers, M. (1992). *Why humans have cultures: Explaining anthropology and social diversity.* New York: Oxford University Press.

Chelune, G. J., & Associates (1979). (Eds.). *Self-disclosure: Origins, patterns, and implications of oneness in interpersonal relations.* San Francisco: Jossey-Bass.

Christian, J. L. (1977). *Philosophy: An introduction to the art of wondering* (2nd ed.). New York: Holt, Rinehart & Winston.

Dube, S. C. (1988). Cultural dimensions of development. *International Social Science Journal, 40,* 505-511.

Epp, L. (1998). The courage to be an existential counselor: An interview of Clemmont Vontress. *Journal of Mental Health Counseling, 20,* 1-12.

Fischer, H. (1965). *Theorie der Kultur* (Cultural theory). Stuttgart, Germany: Seewald-Verlag.

Frank, J. D. (1961). *Persuasion and healing.* Baltimore, MD: Johns Hopkins University Press.

Gross, M. L. (1978). *The psychological society.* New York: Random House.

Jackson, M. L. (1987). Cross-cultural counseling at the crossroads: A dialogue with Clemmont F. Vontress. *Journal of Counseling and Development, 66,* 20-23.

Jackson, M. L. (1995). Multicultural counseling: Historical perspectives. In J. C. Ponterotto, J. M. Casas, L. A. Suzuki, & C. M. Alexander (Eds.), *Handbook of multicultural counseling* (pp. 3-16). Thousand Oaks, CA: Sage.

Johnson, A. H. (1977). *Philosophers in action.* Columbus, OH: Merrill.

Johnson, R. E. (1971). *Existential man: The challenge psychotherapy.* New York: Pergamon.

Lavely, J. H. (1967). Personalism. In P. Edwards (Ed.), *The encyclopedia of philosophy* (Vol. 6, pp. 107-110). New York: Macmillan.

Lowen, A. (1980). *Fear of life.* New York: Macmillan.

May, R. (1967). *Existential psychotherapy.* Toronto: CBC Publications.

May, R. (1991). Existence: A new dimension in psychiatry and psychology. In J. Ehrenwald (Ed.), *The history of psychotherapy* (pp. 388-393). Northvale, NJ: Jason Aronson.

Moles, A. A. (1967). *Sociodynamique de la culture* (Sociodynamics of culture). La Haye, France: Mouton Paris.

Mounier, B. (1992). *Le personnalisme* (Personalism). Paris: Presses Universitaires de France.

Ricken, F. (1991). *Philosophy of the ancients.* Notre Dame, IN: University of Notre Dame Press.

Rychlak, J. F. (1979). *Discovering free will and personal responsibility.* New York: Oxford University Press.

Satir, V. (1988). *The new peoplemaking.* Mountain View, CA: Science and Behavior Books.

Stumpf, S. E. (1975). *Socrates to Sartre: A history of philosophy* (2nd ed.). New York: McGraw-Hill.

Sue, D. W. (1981). *Counseling the culturally different: Theory and practice.* New York: John Wiley.

Triandis, H. C. (1994). *Culture and social behavior.* New York: McGraw-Hill.

Turner, V. M. (1986). Body, brain, and culture. *Cross Currents, 36,* 156-178.

Ungersma, A. J. (1961). *The search for meaning: A new approach in psychotherapy and pastoral psychology.* Philadelphia: Westminster Press.

van Deurzen-Smith, A. (1988). *Existential counseling in practice.* Newbury Park, CA: Sage.

Vontress, C. E. (1979). Cross-cultural counseling: An existential approach. *Personnel and Guidance Journal, 58,* 117-122.

Vontress, C. E. (1986). Social and cultural foundations. In M. D. Lewis, P. Hayes, & J. A. Lewis (Eds.), *An introduction to the counseling profession* (pp. 215-250). Itasca, IL: F. E. Peacock.

Vontress, C. E. (1991). Traditional healing in Africa: Implications for cross-cultural counseling. *Journal of Counseling and Development, 70,* 242-249.

Vontress, C. E. (1996). A personal retrospective on cross-cultural counseling. *Journal of Multicultural Counseling and Development, 24,* 156-166.

Vontress, C. E., & Epp, L. R. (1997). Historical hostility in the African American client: Implications for counseling. *Journal of Multicultural Counseling and Development, 25,* 170-184.

Wade, P. (1993). Race, nature, and culture. *Man, 28,* 17-34.

West, C. (1993). *Race matters.* Boston: Beacon.

Wolff, R. P. (1976). *About philosophy.* Englewood Cliffs, NJ: Prentice Hall.

CHAPTER 30

Treating Madness Without Hospitals
Soteria and Its Successors

LOREN MOSHER

SCHIZOPHRENIA, PSYCHIATRY's "sacred cow" (Szasz, 1976) and longest running conundrum, traditionally is the most medicalized and dehumanized of all the so-called mental illnesses. Besides incarceration, with its known adverse consequences, persons with this label have been subjected to a terrifying array of "treatments"—fever, gold, arsenic, bismuth, tonsillectomy, electroshock, insulin shock, lobotomy, and (most recently) the neuroleptic drugs. When looked at contextually, these interventions seem to be designed to allow the rest of us to avoid having to deal with these persons' humanity— that is, their subjective experience of psychosis and its effect on us. Indeed, persons who are "out of their minds" must, by any means possible, be kept "out of sight," that is, our emotional/psychological sight. Degradation, detribalization, marginalization, and stigmatization are the defining conditions of their subhuman state. How, I asked,

can this process of dehumanization be avoided? The critical elements of the process seemed obvious—medicalization (via labeling), hospitalization, professional treatment, and the use of chemical lobotomy with the neuroleptic drugs. How, in the real world, could care be afforded such persons that at least minimized these psychonoxious elements? The answer: Divert such persons out of the hospital system, involve them in a normalizing context (i.e., a home), allow them to interact with staff who approach them without preconceptions and who are interested in understanding and sharing their experience, and try to avoid drugging their humanity out of them. What came out of this was the Soteria Project.

BACKGROUND

The Soteria Project owes much of its clinical methodology to the phenomenological/ existential thinkers who provided a breath

---

EDITORS' NOTE: The editors are grateful to John Bola for his assistance with this chapter.

of fresh air for many clinicians in a psychoanalytic theory–dominated field (Mosher, 1999). During my psychiatric training, I became interested in the meaningfulness of madness, understanding families and systems, and the conduct of research. In addition, I had an unpleasant "total" institutional experience while in psychiatric training (Goffman, 1961) and had to ask, "If places called *hospitals* are not good for disturbed and disturbing behavior, then what kinds of social environments are?" During 1966-1967, R. D. Laing and his colleagues (all influenced by phenomenological and existential thinking) at the Philadelphia Association's Kingsley Hall in London provided live training in the "do's and don'ts" of the operation of an alternative to psychiatric hospitalization (Laing, 1967). The deconstruction of madness and the madhouse that took place at Kingsley Hall was fertile ground for the development of ideas about how a community-based, supportive, protective, normalizing, relationship-focused environment might facilitate reintegration of psychologically disintegrated persons without artificial institutional disruptions of the process.

The practice of interpersonal phenomenology, as developed and used in the Soteria Project, is a nontheory that can be very helpful in understanding and finding meaningfulness in the experience of being a person labeled as having schizophrenia *once an appropriate context is established.* To wit: Do no harm, treat everyone, and expect to be treated with dignity and respect; provide asylum, quiet, safety, support, protection, containment, and food and shelter; and, perhaps most important, make sure that the atmosphere is imbued with the notion that recovery from psychosis is to be expected. Within this defined and predictable social environment, interpersonal phenomenology can be practiced. Its most basic tenet is "being with," an attentive but nonintrusive and gradual way of getting oneself "into the other person's shoes" so that a shared meaningfulness of the psychotic experience can be established through a relationship. This approach requires unconditional acceptance of the experience of another person as valid and understandable within the historical context of the person's life, even when it cannot be consensually validated. The Soteria approach also included thoughtful attention to the *caregiver's* experience of the situation. This emphasis on the *interpersonal* aspects of phenomenology is relatively new. Although it might seem to be a departure from the traditions of phenomenology, it brings the method more into step with modern concepts of the requirements of interactive fields without sacrificing its basic open-minded, immediate, accepting, nonjudgmental, noncategorizing, "what you see is what you get" core principles. It is in this way that the whole "being" (*Dasein*) in relation to others can be kept in focus. It is not prudent to exclude well-known, seemingly universal ingredients in interpersonal fields; by their very presence and reaction, participants have an effect on the interactions. This application of the Heisenberg principle to interpersonal fields provides us with additional information while preventing us from being uninvolved observers. Basically, the California-based Soteria Project combined Sullivan's (1962) interpersonal focus and phenomenology in developing this unique treatment environment for persons newly labeled as having "schizophrenia."

RESEARCH METHODS

This project's design was a random assignment, 2-year follow-up study comparing the Soteria method of treatment to usual general hospital psychiatric ward interventions for persons *newly diagnosed as having schizophrenia* and deemed in need of hospitalization. We focused on newly diagnosed persons so as to avoid, so far as possible, having to deal with the learned patient role. The Soteria study selected 18- to 30-year-old unmarried participants about whom three independent raters could agree met *Diagnostic and Statistical Manual of Mental Disorders (DSM-II)* criteria for schizophrenia (American Psychiatric Association, 1968) and who were experiencing at least four of seven Bleulerian symptoms of the disorder. The early onset (ages 18 to 30 years) and marital status criteria were designed to identify a subgroup of persons diagnosed with schizophrenia who were at *statistically* high risk for long-term disability, that is, candidates for "chronicity." We believed that an experimental treatment should be provided to those individuals most likely to have high service needs over the long term. All participants were public sector (uninsured or government-insured) clients screened in the psychiatric emergency rooms of two suburban San Francisco Bay Area public general hospitals (N = 179).

The original Soteria House opened in 1971. A replication facility opened in 1974 in another suburban San Francisco Bay Area city. This replication was because clinically we saw, almost from the beginning, that the Soteria method worked. Immediate replication would address the potential criticism that our results were a one-time product of a unique group of charismatic persons and expectation effects. So, there were in fact two geographically separated Soteria-type facilities in California, with the second one called "Emanon." Despite the publication of consistently positive results (Matthews, Roper, Mosher, & Menn, 1979; Mosher & Menn, 1978) for this subgroup of newly diagnosed psychotic persons from the first cohort of participants (1971 to 1976), the Soteria Project ended in 1983. Because of administrative problems and lack of funding, data from the 1976-1983

cohort were not analyzed until 1992. Only recently (Bola & Mosher, 1999, 2000) have combined-cohort 2-year outcome data analyses been conducted.

RESULTS

Briefly summarized, the significant results are described in the following paragraphs.

Admission characteristics. Experimental (N = 82) and control (N = 97) participants were remarkably similar on 10 demographic, 5 psychopathologic, 7 prognostic, and 7 psychosocial preadmission (independent) variables. Because of our selection criteria and the suburban location of the intake facilities, both Soteria-treated and control participants were young (age 21 years), mostly white (10% minority), relatively well-educated (high school graduates) men and women raised in typical lower middle class, blue-collar, suburban American families.

Six-week outcome. In terms of psychopathology, participants in both groups improved significantly and comparably despite only 24% of Soteria participants having received neuroleptic drugs for 2 weeks or more during this initial assessment period. All control participants received adequate antipsychotic drug treatment during their entire hospital stays and were universally discharged on maintenance dosages. More than half stopped them over the 2-year follow-up period (Matthews et al., 1979; Mosher & Menn, 1978; Mosher, Vallone, & Menn, 1995).

Milieu assessment. Because we conceived the Soteria program as a recovery-facilitating social environment, systematic study and comparison to the general hospital psychiatric wards was particularly important. We used the Moos Ward Atmosphere (WAS) and Community Oriented Program Environment Scales (COPES) for this purpose (Moos, 1974, 1975). The differences between the programs were remarkable in their magnitude and stability over 10 years. The Soteria-hospital differences were significant on 8 of the 10 WAS/COPES subscales, with the largest differences on the three "psychotherapy" variables: involvement, support, and spontaneity (Wendt, Mosher, Matthews, & Menn, 1983).

Two-Year Outcomes. The relationship between outcome and neuroleptic drug intake from both cohorts for individuals not lost to follow-up (N = 129) was analyzed and presented recently (Bola & Mosher, 1999). Of all Soteria-treated participants, 43% received *no* neuroleptics during the 2-year study period. Three baseline variables predicted membership in this group: better adolescent social adjustment, low levels of paranoia, and being older. These were predictive despite the homogeneity, and hence little variance, of this specially selected sample. As a group, experimentally treated participants (N = 68) had significantly better outcomes on a composite outcome scale (+0.54 of a standard deviation, p = .024) representing the dimensions of rehospitalization, psychopathology, independent living, and social and occupational functioning; and on three of eight component measures. (The experimental group had markedly better outcomes adjusting for differential attrition, differential length of follow-up, and proportion of individuals with insidious onset). When individuals with *DSM-IV* schizophrenia (i.e. those predicted to have poorer outcomes) were analyzed separately (American Psychiatric Association, 1994), experimental treatment was even more effective on the composite outcome scale (+0.97 of a standard deviation, p = .003) (Bola & Mosher, 2000). These and previous results from the Soteria

study continue to challenge conventional wisdom as to the benefits of early and universal administration of antipsychotic drugs to newly diagnosed psychotic individuals.

Cost. In the first cohort, despite the large differences in lengths of stay during the initial admissions (approximately 1 month vs. 5 months), the cost of the first 6 months of care (in 1976 dollars) for each group was approximately $4,000. Costs were similar because of Soteria's low per diem cost and extensive use of day care as well as group, individual, and medication therapy by the discharged hospital control patients (Matthews et al., 1979; Mosher & Menn, 1978). Data were not available for a cost study of participants studied during the 1976-1982 period.

WHY DID SOTERIA "WORK"?

There is no simple answer to this very important question. The relevant aspects include the setting and milieu characteristics, relationships formed, personal qualities and attitudes of the staff, and the social processes that went on in the facilities. Probably the single most important part of why the program "worked" were the types of relationships established among the participants—staff, clients, volunteers, students, and any individuals who spent a significant amount of time in the facility. It certainly is useful to ask, "How does one establish a confiding relationship with a disorganized psychotic person?" It is in this arena that the contextual constraints or setting characteristics mentioned earlier are so important. A quiet, safe, supportive, protective, and predictable social environment is required. Such environments can be established in a variety of places—a special small homelike facility that sleeps no more than 10 persons including staff (e.g., Soteria), the psychotic person's place of residence including involvement of significant others, and almost anywhere the context can be established in which a 1:1 or 2:1 "being with" contact ratio is offered on a 24-hour basis. Such environments usually *cannot* be established within psychiatric hospitals or on their grounds; the expectation of chronicity for schizophrenia is simply too pervasive in such places, and eventually the dominant biomedical philosophy will prevail.

An important reason why the project worked seemed to depend on the personality characteristics of the staff. The Soteria staff were characterized as psychologically strong, independent, mature, warm, and empathic. *They shared these traits with the staff of the control facilities.* However, Soteria staff were significantly more intuitive, introverted, flexible, and tolerant of altered states of consciousness than were the general hospital psychiatric ward staff (Hirschfeld, Matthews, Mosher, & Menn, 1977; Mosher, Reifman, & Menn, 1973). It is this cluster of cognitive-attitudinal variables that seems to be highly relevant to the Soteria staff's work. Their interactions are best described in the treatment manual (Mosher, Menn, Vallone, & Fort, 1994; Mosher, Vallone, & Menn, 1992). Because they worked 24- or 48-hour shifts, they were afforded the opportunity to be with *residents* (their term for clients/patients) for periods of time that staff of ordinary psychiatric facilities could not. Thus, they were able to experience firsthand complete "disordered" biological cycles. Ordinarily, only family members or significant others have such experiences. Although the official staffing at Soteria was two staff members for six clients, over time it became clear that the optimal ratio was about 50% disorganized persons and 50% more-or-less sane persons. This 1:1 ratio usually was made possible by use of volunteers and recovering clients who knew the territory. We found that these residents could develop very close

supportive relationships with other residents. In this context, it is important to remember that the average length of stay was approximately 5 months. For the most part, at least partial recovery took about 6 to 8 weeks. Hence, many clients were able to be caregivers during the latter parts of their stays. In fact, former residents often returned to Soteria and "adopted" newly admitted clients for whom they subsequently found community resources.

Viewed from an ethnographic/anthropologic perspective, the *basic social processes* differed greatly between the houses and the control facilities (the general hospital psychiatric wards). Five categories were identified in both experimental settings that set them apart from the hospitals:

1. Approaches to social control that avoided codified rules, regulations, and policies
2. Keeping basic administrative time to a minimum so as to allow for a great deal of undifferentiated time
3. Limiting intrusion by unknown outsiders into the settings
4. Working out social order on an emergent face-to-face basis
5. Commitment to a nonmedical model that did not require symptom suppression

By contrast, the control wards were characterized as using a "dispatching process" that involved patching, medical screening, piecing together a story, labeling and sorting, and distributing patients to various other facilities and programs (Wilson, 1978, 1983).

With the passage of time, it has been possible to try to understand why Soteria worked from a variety of overlapping perspectives. The following 12 essential characteristics have been defined (Mosher & Burti, 1994):

1. Small and homelike, sleeping no more than 10 persons including staff
2. Two staff members on duty (a man and a woman) in 24- to 48-hour shifts
3. Ideologically uncommitted staff and program director (to avoid failures of "fit")
4. Peer/fraternal/sororal relationship orientation to mute authority
5. Preservation of personal power and, with it, the maintenance of autonomy
6. Open social system to allow easy access, departure, and return if needed
7. Sharing of day-to-day running of the house by everyone to the extent possible
8. Minimal role differentiation to encourage flexibility
9. Minimal hierarchy to allow relatively structureless functioning
10. Integrated into the local community
11. Encouragement of postdischarge continuity of relationships
12. No formal in-house "therapy" as traditionally defined

A set of interventions (recall that the word *therapy* was eschewed in the Soteria Project) have also been described:

1. An interpersonal phenomenological stance
2. "Being with" and "doing with" without being intrusive
3. Extensive 1:1 contact ratio as needed
4. Living with a temporary family
5. Yoga, massage, art, music, dance, sports, outings, gardening, shopping, cooking, and the like
6. Meetings scheduled to deal with interpersonal problems as they emerged
7. Family mediation provided as needed

It also is likely that Soteria's four explicit rules contributed to its success:

1. No violence to self or others
2. No unknown unannounced visitors (family and friends had easy access, but as a *home* its boundaries to outsiders were like those of usual families)
3. No illegal drugs (there was enough community-noted deviance at Soteria already)
4. No sex between staff and clients (an intergenerational incest taboo)

Note that sex between clients *or* staff was not forbidden. The project's administration introduced the first three rules. The fourth was put in place by staff and clients in a house meeting after the second month of the project's operation. It solved an ongoing potential problem in this relatively easygoing environment.

Although mentioned previously, it is worthwhile to characterize the Soteria milieu's characteristics and functions in one place because they certainly were important ingredients to Soteria's success (Mosher, 1992):

1. Milieu *characteristics:* quiet, stable, predictable, consistent, clear, and accepting
2. Early milieu *functions:* supportive relationships, control of stimulation, provision of respite or asylum, and personal validation
3. Later milieu *functions:* structure, involvement, socialization, collaboration, negotiation, and planning

The early and later functions almost always overlap.

Despite the abundance of outcome-related processes cited, it still must be said that it remains difficult to narrow them down to the few most important ones. With this apology, I provide here a nine-point summary of what I believe to be the critical therapeutic ingredients of the Soteria environment:

1. Positive expectations of recovery, and perhaps learning and growth, from psychosis are important.
2. Flexibility of roles, relationships, and responses on the part of staff is important.
3. Acceptance of the psychotic person's experience of psychosis as real, even if not consensually validatable, is important.
4. Staff's primary duty is to be with the disorganized client. It must be specifically acknowledged that the staff need not *do* anything. If frightened, they should call for help.
5. The experience of psychosis should be normalized and usualized by contextualizing it, framing it in positive terms, and referring to it in everyday language.
6. Extremes of human behavior should be tolerated so long as they do not represent a threat to the person, other clients, or the program.
7. Sufficient time must be spent in the program to allow for relationships to develop that will have a lasting impact through the processes of imitation and identification.
8. These relationships should allow precipitating events to be acknowledged, the usually disavowed painful emotions experienced as a result of them to be discussed until they can be tolerated, and these emotions put into perspective by fitting them into the continuity of the person's life as well as his or her social system's life.
9. A postdischarge peer-oriented social network to provide ongoing community reintegration, rehabilitation (e.g. help with housing, education, work, social life), and support is important.

THE SECOND GENERATION

Although closely involved in the California-based Soteria Project throughout the study's life, I lived in Washington, D.C., while working for the National Institute of Mental Health. In 1972, I became psychiatric consultant to Woodley House, a halfway house founded in Washington in 1958. In consultation, staff often were distressed when describing house residents who went into crises and there was no option but to hospitalize them. They saw recovery from such incarceration as taking nearly 18 months. So, in 1977, a Soteria-like facility (called "Crossing Place") was opened by Woodley House programs that differed from its conceptual parent in that it (a) admitted any non-medically ill client deemed in need of psychiatric hospitalization regardless of diagnosis, length of illness, severity of psychopathology, or level of functional impairment; (b) was an integral part of the local public community mental health system, meaning that most patients who came to Crossing Place were receiving psychotropic medications; and (c) had an informal length-of-stay restriction of about 30 days to make it economically appealing.

So, beginning in 1977, a modified Soteria method was applied to a much broader patient base, the so-called seriously and persistently mentally ill. Although a random assignment study of a Crossing Place model has only recently been published (Fenton, Mosher, Herrell, & Blyler, 1998), it was clear from early on that the Soteria method was effective with this non-research-criteria-derived heterogeneous client group. Because of Crossing Place's location and open admissions, its clients, in comparison to Soteria participants, were older (age 37 years), more nonwhite (70%), multi-admission, 25% HIV-positive, 30% homeless, long-term system users (average of 14 years) who were raised in poor urban ghetto families. From the outset, Crossing Place was able to return 90% or more of its more than 2,000 (by 1997) admissions directly to the community, completely avoiding hospitalization (Kresky-Wolff, Matthews, Kalibat, & Mosher, 1984). In its more than 20 years of operation, there have been no suicides among clients in residence, and no serious staff injuries have occurred. Although the clients were different (as noted previously), the two settings (Soteria and Crossing Place) shared staff selection processes (Hirshfeld et al., 1977; Mosher et al., 1973), philosophies, institutional and social structure characteristics, and the culture of positive expectations.

Descriptively, the two settings can be compared and contrasted as follows. In their presentations to the world, Crossing Place is conventional and Soteria was unconventional. Despite this major difference, the actual in-house interpersonal interactions were similar in their informality, earthiness, honesty, and lack of professional jargon. These similarities arise partially from the fact that neither program ascribed the usual patient role to the clientele. Crossing Place admits long-term system "veterans." Its public funding contains broad length-of-stay standards (1 to 2 months). Soteria's research focus viewed length of stay as a dependent variable, allowing it to vary according to the clinical needs of the newly diagnosed patients. Hence, the initial focus of the Crossing Place staff is on what the clients need to accomplish relatively quickly so that they can resume living in the community. Because

they come from the local public system of care, nearly all Crossing Place clients are *taking one or more psychotropic drugs.* There is a somewhat more formalized social structure than was true at Soteria. Each day, there is a morning meeting on what clients are doing to fix their lives that day as well as one or two evening community meetings.

The two Crossing Place consulting psychiatrists each spend an hour a week with the staff reviewing each client's progress, addressing particularly difficult issues, and helping to develop a consensus on initial and revised treatment plans. Soteria had a variety of ad hoc crisis meetings but only one regularly scheduled house meeting per week. The role of the consulting psychiatrist was more peripheral at Soteria than at Crossing Place; at Soteria, he or she was not ordinarily involved in treatment planning, and no regular treatment meetings were held. Demedicalization was the rule.

A SECOND-GENERATION SIBLING

In 1990, McAuliffe House, a Crossing Place replication, was established in Montgomery County, Maryland. This county borders Washington, D.C., along its southern boundary. Crossing Place helped to train its staff. For didactic instruction, there were numerous articles describing the philosophy, institutional characteristics, social structure, and staff attitudes of Crossing Place and Soteria as well as a treatment manual from Soteria (Mosher et al., 1992, 1994). My own continuing influence as philosopher/clinician/godfather/supervisor is certain to have made replicability of these special social environments easier. In Montgomery County, it was possible to implement the first random assignment study of a residential alternative to hospitalization that was focused on the seriously mentally ill "frequent flyers" in a living, breathing, never before researched, public system of care. Because of this well-funded system's early crisis intervention focus, it hospitalized only about 10% of its more than 1,500 long-term clients each year. Again, because of a well-developed crisis system, less than 10% of hospitalizations were involuntary; hence, our voluntary research sample was representative of even the most difficult multiproblem clients. The study *excluded no one* deemed in need of acute hospitalization except those who had complicating medical conditions or who were acutely intoxicated. The participants were as representative of suburban Montgomery County's public clients as were Crossing Place's participants of urban Washington, D.C., clients—mid-30s, poor, 25% minority, 15% homeless, 10% HIV-positive, long duration of illness, and multiple previous hospitalizations. However, many of the Montgomery County clients came from well-educated, affluent families. The results (Fenton et al., 1998) were not surprising. The alternative and acute general hospital psychiatric wards were clinically equal in effectiveness, but the alternative cost was about 40% less. For a system, this means savings of roughly $19,000 per year for each seriously and persistently mentally ill person who uses acute alternative care exclusively (instead of a hospital). Total costs for the hospital in this study (in 1993 dollars) were about $500 per day (including ancillary costs) and for the alternative were about $150 (including extramural treatment and ancillary costs).

OVERALL THERAPEUTIC INGREDIENTS

Descriptively, the therapeutic ingredients of all these residential alternatives—ones that clearly distinguish them from psychiatric hospitals—in the order they are likely to be experienced by a newly admitted client, are as follows. First, the setting is indistinguishable from other residences in the community, and it interacts with its community.

Second, the facility is small, with space for no more than 10 persons to sleep (6 to 8 clients and 2 staff members), and experienced as homelike. Admission procedures are informal and individualized, based on the client's ability to participate meaningfully.

Third, a primary task of the staff is to understand the immediate circumstances and relevant background that precipitated the crisis necessitating admission. It is anticipated that this will lead to a relationship based on shared knowledge that will, in turn, enable staff to put themselves in the client's shoes. Thus, they will share the client's perception of their social context and what needs to change to enable them to return to it. The relative paucity of paperwork allows time for the interaction necessary to form a relationship.

Fourth, within this relationship, the client will find staff carrying out multiple roles—companion advocate, case worker, and "therapist"—although no therapeutic sessions are held in the house. Staff have the authority to make (in conjunction with the client) and be responsible for on-the-spot decisions. Staff are mostly in their mid-20s, college graduates, and selected on the basis of their interest in working in this special setting with a clientele in psychotic crises. Most use the work as a transitional step on their way to advanced mental health-related degrees. They usually are psychologically tough, tolerant, and flexible and come from lower middle class families with "problem" members (Hirschfeld et al., 1977; Mosher et al., 1973, 1992, 1994). In contrast to psychiatric ward staff, they are trained and closely supervised in the adoption and validation of the clients' perceptions. Problem solving and supervision focus on staff relational difficulties (e.g., transference, countertransference) and are available from fellow staff, on-site program directors, and consulting psychiatrists. Note that the physicians are not in charge of the program.

Fifth, staff are trained to prevent unnecessary dependency and, so far as possible, maintain autonomous decision making on the part of clients. They also encourage clients to stay in contact with their usual treatment and social networks. Clients frequently remark on how different the experience is from that of a hospitalization. This process may result in clients reporting that they feel in control and a sense of security. They also experience a continued connectedness to their usual social environments.

Sixth, access and departure, both initially and subsequently, are made as easy as possible. Short of official readmission, it is an open social system where clients can continue their connection to the program in nearly any way they choose. They can phone in for support, obtain information or advice, make drop-in visits (usually at dinner time), or arrange time with persons with whom they had especially important relationships. All former clients who served in Soteria's successors are invited back to an organized activity one evening each week.

OTHER ALTERNATIVES TO HOSPITALIZATION

During the more than 25 years since the successful implementation of the Soteria Project, a variety of alternatives to psychiatric hospitalization have been developed in the United States. Their results (including those of the Soteria Project) have been reviewed extensively by Braun and colleagues (1981), Kiesler (1982a, 1982b), Straw (1982), and Stroul (1987). Warner (1995) described a subset in greater detail. Each of these reviews found consistently more positive results from descriptive and research data from a variety of alternative interventions than from control groups. Straw (1982), for example, found that in 19 of 20 studies that he reviewed, alternative treatments were as effective as, or more effective than, hospital care and also were 43% less expensive, on average. The Soteria study was noted to be the most rigorous one available in describing a comprehensive treatment approach to a subgroup of persons labeled as having schizophrenia. It was also noted that, for the most part, the effects of various types of hospitalization (e.g., large vs. small, long vs. short) had not been subjected to equally serious scientific scrutiny.

Few true residential alternatives to acute hospitalization have been developed, except in California, where there are a dozen. A recent study of the cost-effectiveness of these alternatives to hospitalization in San Diego (Hawthorne, Green, Lohr, Hough, & Smith, 1999) found results consistent with those of Fenton and colleagues (1998). Unfortunately, it was not a random assignment study. Within the public sector, because of cost concerns, there currently is a movement to develop crisis houses. Their extent or success has not been described completely. However, they *usually* are not viewed or used as alternatives to acute psychiatric hospitalization, although this is subject to local variation. It is surprising that managed care, with its focus on reducing the use of expensive hospitalization, has neither developed nor promoted the use of these cost-effective alternatives. It is truly notable that nearly all residential alternatives to acute psychiatric hospitalization are in the *public* mental health system. Private insurers and health maintenance organizations have been extremely reluctant to pay for care in such facilities (Mosher, 1983).

THE FATE OF SOTERIA

As a clinical program, Soteria closed in 1983. The replication facility, Emanon, had closed in 1980. Despite many publications (40 in all), without an active treatment facility, Soteria disappeared from the consciousness of American psychiatry. Its message was difficult for the field to acknowledge, assimilate, and use. It did not fit into the emerging scientific, descriptive, biomedical character of American psychiatry, and in fact, it called nearly every one of psychiatry's tenets into question. It *demedicalized, dehospitalized, deprofessionalized,* and *deneurolepticized* psychiatry's most persistent, ambivalently held conundrum. So far as mainstream American psychiatry is concerned, it is, to this day, an experiment that either never was conducted or was the object of studied (conspiratorial?) neglect. Taken in concert with the extraordinary power of the pharmaceutical industry over psychiatry and the American Psychiatric Association's alliance with the National Alliance for the Mentally Ill, this should come as no surprise. In support of the studied neglect assertion is the fact that neither of the two recent comprehensive literature reviews and treatment recommendations for schizophrenia references the project (Frances, Docherty, & Kahn, 1996; Lehman & Steinwachs, 1998). This omission happened despite my having reviewed both of those documents in draft form and having brought this remarkable oversight to the authors' attention. There are no new Soteria replications in the United States. It is possible that if a replication were proposed as research, it might not receive internal review board approval for protection of human participants because it would

involve withholding a known effective treatment (neuroleptics) for *a minimum* of 2 weeks.

Surprisingly, Soteria has reemerged in Europe. Luc Ciompi, professor of social psychiatry in Bern, Switzerland, is primarily responsible for its renaissance. Operating since 1984, the Bern-based Soteria has replicated the original Soteria study findings. That is, roughly two thirds of newly diagnosed persons with schizophrenia recovered with little or no drug treatment within 2 to 12 weeks (Ciompi et al., 1992). As original Soteria project papers diffused to Europe and Ciompi began to publish his results, a number of similar projects were developed. At an October 1997 meeting held in Bern, a Soteria Association was formed, headed by Weiland Machleidt of the Hannover University medical faculty. Soteria lives and thrives, admittedly as variations on the original theme, in a number of sites in Germany and one in Stockholm, Sweden.

THE FUTURE

Soteria-type facilities can be very useful for the provision of a temporary artificial social network when a natural one is either absent or dysfunctional. However, common sense would tell us that immediate intervention at the crisis site actually is preferable, when possible, because it avoids medicalization (i.e., locating "the problem" in one person by the labeling and sorting process) of what is actually a social system problem. Dedicated *facilities* cannot, by definition, be where the problem originates. There is no inherent reason why the *special contextual conditions* of Soteria-type programs cannot be created in a family home, in a non-family residence, or in a network meeting held nearly anywhere. This approach has been applied systematically by Alanen and colleagues (1994) in Finland and has spread throughout much of Scandinavia with rather remarkable positive results.

In fact, once the contextual "package" that has been described is established, the simple paradigm within which I prefer to work with clients and their families is (a) to define and acknowledge what happened, (b) to learn to bear the heretofore unbearable emotions associated with the event(s), and (c) to gain a perspective on the experience over time by fitting it into the continuity of the individual's life as well as his or her social system's life. This approach focuses on understanding and trying to find meaningfulness in the subjective experience of psychosis. When successful, there is no more schizophrenia, only two or more humans who have been through a shared, awesome, subjective experience.

REFERENCES

Alanen, Y. O., Rosenbaum, B., Ugelstad, E., Armelius, B., Lehtinen, K., & Sjostrom, R. (1994). *Early treatment of schizophrenic patients: Scandinavian psychotherapeutic approaches.* Oslo, Norway: Scandinavian University Press.

American Psychiatric Association. (1968). *Diagnostic and statistical manual of mental disorders* (2nd ed.). Washington, DC: Author.

American Psychiatric Association. (1994). *Diagnostic and statistical manual of mental disorders* (4th ed.). Washington, DC: Author.

Bola, J., & Mosher, L. R. (1999, August). *Predicting drug free response in acute psychosis from the Soteria project.* Paper presented at the 11th World Congress of Psychiatry, Hamburg, Germany.

Bola, J., & Mosher, L. R. (2000, February). *Treatment of acute psychosis without neuroleptics: Two-year outcomes from the Soteria Project.* Paper presented at the 10th Biennial Winter Workshop on Schizophrenia, Davos, Switzerland.

Braun, P. B., Kochansky, G., Shapiro, R., Greenberg. S., Gudeman, J. E., Johnson, S., & Shore, M. F. (1981). Overview: Deinstitutionalization of psychiatric patients: A critical review of outcome studies. *American Journal of Psychiatry, 138,* 736-749.

Ciompi, L., Duwalder, H.-P., Maier, C., Aebi, E., Trutsch, K., Kupper, Z., & Rutishauser, C. (1992). The pilot project "Soteria Berne": Clinical experiences and results. *British Journal of Psychiatry, 161*(Suppl. 18), 145-153.

Fenton, W., Mosher, L., Herrell, J., & Blyler, C. (1998). A randomized trial of general hospital versus residential alternative care for patients with severe and persistent mental illness. *American Journal of Psychiatry, 155,* 516-522.

Frances, A., Docherty, P., & Kahn, A. (1996). Treatment of schizophrenia. *Journal of Clinical Psychiatry, 57,* 1-59.

Goffman, E. (1961). *Asylums.* New York: Doubleday.

Hawthorne, W. B., Green, E. E., Lohr, J. B., Hough, R., & Smith, P. G. (1999). Comparison of outcomes of acute care in short-term residential treatment and psychiatric hospital settings. *Psychiatric Services, 50,* 401-406.

Hirschfeld, R. M., Matthews, S. M., Mosher, L. R., & Menn, A. Z. (1977). Being with madness: Personality characteristics of three treatment staffs. *Hospital and Community Psychiatry, 28,* 267-273.

Kiesler, C. A. (1982a). Mental hospitals and alternative care: Noninstitutionalization as potential public policy for mental patients. *American Psychologist, 37,* 349-360.

Kiesler, C. A. (1982b). Public and professional myths about mental hospitalization: An empirical reassessment of policy-related beliefs. *American Psychologist, 37,* 1323-1339.

Kresky-Wolff, M., Matthews, S., Kalibat, F., & Mosher, L. R. (1984). Crossing Place: A residential model for crisis intervention. *Hospital and Community Psychiatry, 35,* 72-74.

Laing, R. D. (1967). *The politics of experience.* New York: Random House.

Lehman, A., & Steinwachs, D. M. (1998). Translating research into practice: The schizophrenia patient outcomes research team (PORT) recommendations. *Schizophrenia Bulletin, 24,* 1-11.

Matthews, S. M., Roper, M. T., Mosher, L. R., & Menn, A. Z. (1979). A non-neuroleptic treatment for schizophrenia: Analysis of the two-year post-discharge risk of relapse. *Schizophrenia Bulletin, 5,* 322-333.

Moos, R. H. (1974). *Evaluating treatment environments: A social ecological approach.* New York: John Wiley.

Moos, R. H. (1975). *Evaluating correctional and community settings.* New York: John Wiley.

Mosher, L. R. (1983). Alternatives to psychiatric hospitalization: Why has research failed to be translated into practice? *New England Journal of Medicine, 309,* 1479-1480.

Mosher, L. R. (1992). The social environmental treatment of psychosis: Critical ingredients. In A. Wobart & J. Culberg (Eds.), *Psychotherapy of schizophrenia: Facilitating and obstructive factors* (pp. 254-260). Oslo, Norway: Scandinavian University Press.

Mosher, L. R. (1999). Soteria and other alternatives to acute hospitalization: A personal and professional review. *Journal of Nervous and Mental Diseases, 187,* 142-149.

Mosher, L. R., & Burti, L. (1994). *Community mental health: A practical guide.* New York: Norton.

Mosher, L. R., & Menn, A. Z. (1978). Community residential treatment for schizophrenia: Two-year follow-up. *Hospital and Community Psychiatry, 29,* 715-723.

Mosher, L. R., Menn, A. Z., Vallone, R., & Fort, D. (1994). *Dabeisein: Das Manual zur Praxis in der Soteria.* Bonn, Germany: Psychiatrie-Verlag.

Mosher, L. R., Reifman, A., & Menn, A. (1973). Characteristics of non-professionals serving as primary therapists for acute schizophrenics. *Hospital and Community Psychiatry, 24,* 391-396.

Mosher, L. R., Vallone, R., & Menn, A. Z. (1992). *The Soteria Project: Final progress report* (RO1MH35928, R12MH20123, and R12MH25570). Unpublished report, National Institute of Mental Health. (Available from the author)

Mosher, L. R., Vallone, R., & Menn, A. Z. (1995). The treatment of acute psychosis without neuroleptics: Six-week psychopathology outcome data from the Soteria Project. *International Journal of Social Psychiatry, 41,* 157-173.

Straw, R. B. (1982). *Meta-analysis of deinstitutionalization.* Unpublished doctoral dissertation, Northwestern University, Chicago.

Stroul, B. A. (1987). *Crisis residential services in a community support system.* Rockville, MD: National Institute of Mental Health, Community Support Program.

Sullivan, H. S. (1962). *Schizophrenia as a human process.* New York: Norton.

Szasz, T. (1976). *Schizophrenia: The sacred symbol of psychiatry.* New York: Basic Books.

Warner, R. (Ed.). (1995). *Alternatives to the mental hospital for acute psychiatric treatment.* Washington, DC: American Psychiatric Association.

Wendt, R. J., Mosher, L. R., Matthews, S. M., & Menn, A. Z. (1983). A comparison of two treatment environments for schizophrenia. In J. G. Gunderson, O. A. Will, & L. R. Mosher (Eds.), *The principles and practices of milieu therapy* (pp. 17-33). Northvale, NJ: Jason Aronson.

Wilson, H. S. (1978). Conjoint becoming: Study of Soteria II. In *Current perspectives in psychiatric nursing* (Vol. 2, pp. 135-148). St. Louis, MO: C. V. Mosby.

Wilson, H. S. (1983). Usual hospital treatment in the USA's community mental health system. *International Journal of Nursing Studies, 20,* 176-189.

CHAPTER **31**

Awe Comes Shaking Out of the Bones

E. MARK STERN

THE GREEK TRAGEDIANS contended that grave adversity unveils the most buried varieties of trembling awe. Overcome with ineffable awe, an individual may be left with feelings of shock and bewilderment. The greater share of cringing awe embellishes the unassuming life.

Those awed by a tenacious desire live in a seemingly unending cycle of partially realized cravings. In the extreme, such awe is terror-ridden, inducing torments and finally leaving its prey essentially numb.

Exuberance, too, may be a type of awe, one that often transcends the usual measures of sanity and normality.

Certainly, mystical awe provides the invaluable luminescence often necessary to recognize one's place in an otherwise chaotic universe. Profound awe provides an access to bearing up under these eventualities. Indeed, the persistence of such awe acts as a catalyst to major change.

In the tradition of humanistic psychology, the therapist embraces the client's awe equally as agony and aspiration. A never-ending capacity to learn to discriminate and not discriminate between the mercilessness of awe as servile adoration and awe as earnest devotion is key to the humanistic therapeutic process. Particularly affected by this responsibility are those individuals whom psychiatry labels *obsessive*. The trials and tribulations of the obsessed over love and hate, and over idolatry and affinity, can be touched by the initiation of integrity. Only there can the hopeless burdens of obligation and devotion be met. In these encounters, transformations happen for both therapists and clients.

The vantage point of this chapter involves two people encircled within a therapeutic process. It encompasses 2 years of twice-weekly meetings between these two: the therapist and the client. Because awe, being transpersonal in all its phases, extends beyond the experience of the individual, there is a noticeable blurring of identities in this exposition. Therefore, this obfuscation of boundaries is purposeful. Even as one other states what is, there is, on the part of the other one or more, a necessary cannibalization, a dismantling, and a merger.

A Catholic priest, about 3 years ordained, suffered daily anxiety over the chance happening that bits and pieces of the wafer he had just consecrated at mass might have slipped through his fingers and onto the thick rug below. Father Gregory[1] was, on the surface, amply devoted to the actual presence of Christ in the consecrated bread. Nonetheless, from the day of his ordination, he began to question the authenticity of his devotion. Actual devotion? Or adoration bordering on idolatry?

Gregory lived out his "neglect" as the body of Christ, perhaps by sleight of hand, dismembered. The pain endured was all the more intense as remedies were invoked. Each day following mass, he would feel obligated to return to the altar. Once there, he would get on his hands and knees in search of infinitesimal crumbs. More often than not, fragments turned out to be hardened wax drippings or lint, although sometimes crumbs. He carefully placed the matter on his tongue and consumed "whatever." Adding to his terror was the need to invent excuses for this pantomimic action to the occasional lingering parishioner.

Parishioners made life no easier. Due to overly cautious distractions tethered to their restlessness, Gregory never could be sure that he had pronounced the words of consecration according to strict liturgical rubrics. As a result of these fears of omission, his masses became unusually drawn out.

Gregory, the second son of six children, was his mother's "brightest light" through-

out her life. He was awarded a full scholarship at a prestigious parochial prep school and never failed to rank first in his class. He was accepted by a top-ranking university, where he became a pre-law major.

No sooner than a semester short of completing law school, Gregory abruptly terminated a 2-year engagement to a young woman he was about to marry in favor of joining the incoming class of his diocesan seminary. Although several years older than most of his classmates, he was considered a model seminarian except for a self-imposed reclusiveness.

Gregory's father died months before his ordination. Although he was much attached to his father, it was in an early therapy session that he expressed relief at not yet having been ordained and, therefore, at being "free" not to have to officiate at his father's funeral mass. Concerned about his overarching obsessive traits, Gregory felt helpless to do anything to help himself beyond confessing his sins. And even here, he considered his contrition unworthy and too meager.

Gregory's first parochial assignment was as the assistant pastor of a middle-class parish within walking distance of a contemplative convent. In time, he sought out the chaplain of the convent to be his regular confessor. But "regular" soon became recurrent and habitual. He chastised himself for needing to ring the chaplain's doorbell at all hours requesting that the chaplain hear his urgent confessions. He confided to the elder priest that he believed he had been "irreverent" to the Blessed Sacrament by "allowing" consecrated particles to slide from his hands. The confessor, wise in psychological matters, thought at first that he could deal with Gregory's "scrupulosity."[2]

But the confessor soon realized that he was dealing with a condition beyond his capacity. He advised Gregory to seek psychological counsel.

There was, from the start, an unease about Gregory's being in therapy. So few variations in his early narrative. "Impure thoughts" (sexual or assaultive) were forever eroding. Day after day, he remained convinced that, because of his neglect, the disunited crumbs of the Blessed Sacrament were left undetected and neglected underfoot. His sleep had become erratic, leading to increasing "forgetfulness."

The dialogue between therapist and client moved to another dimension. I became an embodiment of Gregory's deepest emotion and content. Our empathic engagement dissolved the boundaries between the two of us. In the spirit of the meeting, we became functionally indistinguishable. In what follows, the reader is asked to suspend the usual need to mark off which one of us is speaking and/or ruminating. An ideal of humanistic psychotherapy is to disperse identities long enough for them to individuate once again. The reader is left with the task of deciding when or if, within the process, this takes place.

A recurring nightmare: human limbs and parts of torsos hidden underneath the floorboards of an unfamiliar house. Police officers never far away. "Detectives" and "double agents" about to close in.

"Do you think of yourself as a double agent?"

"For someone to be so holy and still be implicated in possible murder!"

"Look carefully into the dream. . . . Look especially for 'telltale' variations."

"Has it ever occurred to you that someone else may be the real killer?"

"That there are accomplices?"

"Let's 'bring the house' into our sessions."

"Describe where we are."

"Familiar surroundings?"

"Point to the floorboards."

Tension grew. "Why would I want to be a double agent?"

"Does a person doubt his own intentions?"

"Foul play? That's possible since nothing ever feels secure."

"I keep asking myself, 'Why me?' "

"What someone else does is their own business."

"But have you ever felt so intertwined with that other person?"

"Who?"

"Whoever."

"Ex-fiancée?"

"People can be unsuited to each other."

"I have my doubts about marriage."

"She knew that?"

"There was no contact after the break."

"Miss her?"

"I think not."

"Never missing anyone?"

"Whatever else, I see you as a shrine keeper."

A conundrum evolved.

"Yeah, the house in the nightmare is kind of like a shrine or a reliquary. . . . Martyrs, saints—who knows, maybe even sacrificial beings?"

". . . Bones can be first-class relics [of saints] in certain circumstances?"

No apparent conscious link to the detached particles of the consecrated Host.

"It feels right to stay with the rummaging."

"The dream house is evidently haunted."

"But haunted by whom?"

"By a murder or by one who consecrates?"

"Or could they be both?"

Some religiously inclined people suffer from spiritual *concupiscence,* a Latin word for obsessive awe or adoration.

An occasional consequence of holy men suffering from spiritual concupiscence is that the vestiges of what had been consecrated come shaking out of one's bones. Breakdowns, in such cases, are not at all unusual. If a brokenhearted person believes that faculties for reaching God are a means of recreating the cosmos by giving it meaning and are wanting, then it becomes all the more necessary to be penitential.

"Gregory always a guardian?"

"A holy man?"

"I feel all the more demeaned."

Weeks later: "The priesthood is about sacrifice."

"Depravity and sacrifice are not always easy to sift through."

"An ax murderer may be his own accomplice."

"Accomplices are either liable to be confederates or stool pigeons."

Attention intensifies. As a teen, Gregory's father had studied in a minor (preparatory) seminary.

"It sometimes comes over me how full of self-pity he was."

"Should he have become the priest?

"[A mother/wife] under these circumstances can feel rejected and [is] likely to infer how sorry he must feel for having married instead of heeding the 'call' by taking priestly vows."

"Then again, if he had taken priestly vows, there would be no *now* for us."

"Was he forever caught up in the conflict between marriage and priesthood?"

"I take it from what you've been saying that you were destined to serve as your father's resolution of *his* conflict."

"The notion of there being an accomplice takes on a poignancy."

"A meaning of its own."

"A bittersweetness with you as the 'alternative'."

"Sounds like you were designated to ease his pain."

"No one ever believed how sick he really was, but I counted him a dead man years before his fatal heart attack."

"And his leaving the preparatory seminary?"

"About two thirds never made it to the major seminary. It was not that unusual."

"Usual may hardly be what counts."

"Among his favorite yarns was one about how one of his 'kids' would eventually latch on to the rope of *his* 'calling.' He often told about the time when, as an adolescent, he was dangerously adrift in the bay due to the defectiveness of an outboard motor. 'Lord,' he prayed, 'if you spare me, I promise . . .,' but just before completing that pledge to give his life to God as a priest, a larger boat approached and tossed him a tow line."

"So it was you who embraced his faith?"

"But hardly with faith."

"Narcissus's reflection?"

"Embodying another's aspiration?"

"Drowning was inevitable?"

"Perpetual terror?"

"As a child growing up where we grew up, I was frightened by backyard sounds."

"Even in the present, there remain distinctive traces of apprehension."

"For example?"

"A fence creaking or a strong wind met at a crossroad."

In the middle of the second year of our meetings, a day came when I found myself threaded to Gregory's steady glance at a tassel on my throw rug. His glance was steady—not steely or calculated, but unwavering. This was a place, an arrival. His shoulders circulated toward me. Minutes created a time to follow and wait. His eyes again moving ever so slightly. Then a brief retreat. The tassel clearly was a nucleus. Eventually: "Something gripping you."

A passing frown. At that instant, he wanted to shut down. Ever so briefly, a glance at his watch. It was about time for the session to end. At last: "Do you mind?" And without waiting for a permissive nod, he leaned over, now brushing his index finger along the ends of the tassel.

"It was nothing." Seconds later, the gesture was repeated. There was an exacting precision. In a flash—index finger and thumb rounding out a speck of lint.

"Could we just stay with what is happening?"

"Just for the moment."

Another minute passed. "And, if at all possible, please bring the house in here so it can be with us."

The doorbell sounds. The next client sits in the waiting room. In context, the rattling sound creeping through the adjoining wall could have been the creaking of floorboards.

"There's time enough."

The briefest of pauses.

He kept his hand in place, rolling a speck of lint ever so barely. It might have been masturbatory. He looked past me. No noticeable eye contact. Then, in extreme shame, "I thought perhaps a particle of the Blessed Sacrament might have become attached to the heel of my shoe."

I suggested that he say no more. "May I bring my own veneration to whatever is between your fingers?"

He had fleeting doubts about whether I would not disrespect this ceremony.

"I'm not sure." Then, as if an "all is well" siren sounded, "It feels like fuzz from your rug."

"Nevertheless."

And almost as a magician, the lint was lost to his fingers. His face only momentarily relaxed.

Gregory could not believe in his passion for sin.

Lewis (1996) gave such passion to the words of the archfiend:

> You will say that these are very small sins;
> like all young tempters, you are anxious to
> be able to report spectacular wickedness. It
> does not matter how small the sins are,
> provided that their cumulative effect is to

edge man . . . into the Nothing. Murder is no better than cards if cards can do the trick. (p. 56)

As bogus as a specter of lint might be, it could not be denied that there was, nonetheless, an innuendo of murder. Had this murder been self-annihilation? Ransom for a derelict father? Was this man sitting across from me a man of awe and faith? Yet inescapably trapped in an inherited obligation?

He had once wanted to be a law enforcement officer. Cloaks and daggers are for the elementally fearful. Those who routinely anticipate exploitation and other assaults are well geared to implicate others of unspeakable crimes (Angyal, 1965).

"Perhaps the FBI or the Secret Service."

These were paths some choose after law school.

"There had been no sharing of these discarded plans?"

"Not even with the woman you thought to marry?"

Suddenly: "Did I mention that her father was a police officer?"

"Had she known that you were considering dropping her after law school?"

"Any which way she *knew*."

"But the 'decision' was obviously underplayed."

"And the effect on her?"

"On you?"

"On me now?"

"How could anyone be content with it?"

"Another's happiness cannot be a major concern."

"One rarely believes that all is always at risk."

"And so little self-protection."

"The priesthood was never far."

"When I was in the ninth grade, I lost my faith. Since that time, I've never stopped ruminating on how to rediscover it."

"Discover?"

"The faith of one generation is the certainty of the next. But how contrary it feels!"

"Don't get me wrong, Sometimes faith comes when least expected."

"But then who's ever truly convinced?"

"If you care enough about it, burdens of maintaining it escalate."

"I continued to attend mass, but can you imagine how empty it was?"

"Still?!"

"I once heard Jesus speak to me. Soon after, I read something about hallucinations. I thought I was going nuts."

"But the voice was real."

"Some things can never be doubted."

"It was him, and he called."

"So confusing to know how to please him."

"How to be the true guardian of the particles and bear great burden of unworthiness."

"Enough to be swept up by a constant sense of sin."

"What is held in awe haunts."

"Do I believe in spite of myself?"

"Do obligations constitute the whole of my belief?"

"It's daunting to live in fear and trembling."

"*And this* God claims to be the true victim."

"Divinity may be killed by unbelief, but then belief is killed as well."

Underhill (1915) portrays a person shackled by belief as one given to a constancy of "violent shattering and rearranging of . . . self" (p. 34).

Awe shakes one's bones and rearranges them.

"Whatever role is played, even in defeat, is ultimately a victory. This greatest mask is more often the greatest truth."

Maslow advised caution about not recognizing innate instinctive needs as quests for identity (cited in Becker, 1969). He told of a man who, in an extraordinary panic of believing himself to be a failure to his wife, flees her and hides away in a hotel room in a distant city. As the man lays awake in dread, a heavy presence bears down on his reclining body. The force is so strong that he surrenders. "This is God," he murmurs. Then he falls into a deep and tranquil sleep. At daybreak, refreshed and renewed, the man vows to serve God by good works. Returning to his wife, the newly infused man rediscovers himself as the redeemed lover.

"How to know I've been 'had' and even so be sanctified?"

Parallel to Maslow's illustration is Gawain in the German epic *Parsifal*. Deep in dream, Gawain forces a knife into the palm of his hand without feeling the slightest pain. Only when a drop of blood appears in the white snow does he become aware of a tear on his wife's cheek. He now is truly humbled and uncommonly free to prevail in battle. His supplications tenderly interweave themselves, first to God and then to his wife. There are no distinctions between power and helplessness.

Maslow and the German epic each engaged what must be the fragmentation necessary to loss and gain. Maslow seemed to defend fragmentation as the urgent "utter anxiety of . . . finitude [in the] lifelong urge to drown out feelings of helplessness and inadequacy in some self-transcending source of sure power" (cited in Becker, 1969, p. 134).

"Wrecked body and fragmented God creates a whole life for me."

From the fear and tremblings of Kierkegaard, in an unbroken pattern through James's luminescent plural flows of consciousness and on through the intrepid candor and personal sufferings of Boisen,

Becker (1969) denoted that any comprehension of obsessiveness "cannot stop short of the ultimate power source in which to ground one's life" (p. 135).

"Perhaps fragmentation is the only way to see your potentialities."

It is by means of being within a totality, made up essentially of shards, that there can ever be authentic closure. Becker noted that the distinction between what have been termed "sick" and "healthy" religion rests with whether the power dilemma is dealt with in an open, free, and critical way or in a despairing, reflexive, deterministic, and ultimately self-defeating manner.

"With all that constitutes it, I accept my vocation as my chosen way of relating."

This is what Erikson (1998) referred to as being "in the center of events" (p. 305).

"A life of repentance for all those who are lost."

Erikson (1998) circumscribed repentance as an "individual decision to become aware of universal sin in one's own personal form" (p. 305).

"There is personal value in what I do, even if I'm anguished about being called to do it."

This, Erikson (1998) noted, is a way of affirming "universal potentials in one's neighbor" (p. 305).

Gregory's impulse to return to the altar so as to check on broken vestiges of the universal body was obsession and, beyond the obsession, activation. His invocation of a true presence surfaced a driving singular vision compounded by disruptive contradiction.

The Jesuit psychiatrist Meissner (1984) contended that any action of any one person necessitates the activation of multiple integrated systems. Beyond that, there are both conscious and unconscious influences that must be counted as necessary to any personal decision to be anything.

"Priesthood invokes a reconstruction of the torn apart."

"My poor guilt-ridden father."

"My poor guilt-ridden mother."

"Poor guilt-ridden believers and nonbelievers."

"The sacrifices are for *them*?"

"Only in part."

"I walk with him along my own lonely path."

Much was gleaned. Fragments finally became not merely murdered limbs but rather building blocks. While in therapy, we came to appreciate in each other the gifts of failure, forgiveness, and unconditional acceptance.

Years have passed. Gregory serves in another locale. More than likely, he continues to hear intermittent unwelcome creaks and whispers. Sometimes, the whispers might have transcendent intentions. He might still, at times, consider bits of fluff to be objects of terror, awe, and devotion. And so they might be.

NOTES

1. The appellation "Father Gregory" is in honor of Saint Gregory of Nazianzuz, who so beautifully portrayed the joy of creation as the risen Lord.

2. Gregory's obsessiveness was perhaps not so uncommon for a religiously zealous person. Church jargon employs the terms *scrupulosity* and *sensitive conscience* almost interchangeably.

REFERENCES

Angyal, A. (1965). *Neurosis and treatment: A holistic theory.* New York: John Wiley.

Becker, E. (1969). *Angel in armor: A post-Freudian perspective on the nature of man.* New York: George Braziller.

Erikson, E. (1998). The Galilean sayings and the sense of "I." In R. Wallerstein & L. Goldberger (Eds.), *Ideas and identities: The life and work of Erik Erikson* (pp. 246-327). Madison, CT: International Universities Press.

Lewis, C. S. (1996). *The Screwtape letters.* New York: Simon & Schuster.

Meissner, W. (1984). *Psychoanalysis and religious experience.* New Haven, CT: Yale University Press.

Underhill, E. (1915). *Practical mysticism.* New York: E. P. Dutton.

CHAPTER 32

If You Are Ready to Undergo These Awe-Full Moments, Then Have an Experiential Session

ALVIN R. MAHRER

I AM GOING TO DESCRIBE a particular type of awe-full moment, a moment that is brief, almost like a flash. It comes and goes in an instant. It can be accompanied with a sense of ecstasy, wonder, amazement, or compelling fascination. It can be accompanied with a sense of dread, terror, primal fear, or frozen nonbeing. These two feelings are like two sides of a coin that is the sense of awe.

The first purpose is to describe this particular type of awe-full moment and the experiential sessions in which it occurs. A case is made that this particular type of awe-full moment can occur outside of experiential sessions, but it is a precious characteristic of most experiential sessions (Mahrer, 1996).

The second purpose is to provide an up-close, in-depth description of three ways in which this particular type of awe-full moment occurs in each experiential session.

A case is made that there are three awe-full moments in each experiential session.

The final purpose is an invitation. If this particular type of awe-full moment is cherished, if it is valued and important to you, and if you truly are ready to undergo these three awe-full moments, then you are invited to take a baby step toward having an experiential session.

THIS PARTICULAR TYPE OF AWE-FULL MOMENT IS A PRECIOUS CHARACTERISTIC OF EXPERIENTIAL SESSIONS

The common notion of awe is large enough, flexible enough, and friendly enough to admit that, even though a sense of awe is rare and is to be treasured, it can happen under a lot of circumstances and in a lot of places. A person can undergo a sense of awe when seeing the birth of a baby, being in the presence of God, opening his or her eyes and truly seeing radiant colors, watching the sun rise, being deeply understood by another, being transfixed by the miraculous change, waking up to the utter beauty of full-some nature, coming to the cataclysmic realization, or being transfixed by the sheer power of a tornado or full eclipse. However, there is a particular type of awe-full moment that is a precious characteristic of experiential sessions.

This Particular Type of Awe-Full Moment Is When You Have Passed the Point of No Return in the Awe-Full Final Leap

The particular type of awe-full moment I am referring to occurs when you have taken that momentous step into the complete and utter commitment of the final leap, when you have gone beyond the point of no return and are in the throes of the final leap into the black abyss, into giving up everything of who and what you are, into a wholesale sacrificing of your entire self, into the bottomless pit of the unseeable unknown, into the cataclysmic ultimate change, into the final oblivion, and into the final leap into the void of absolute death of oneself.

The stakes are about as high as they can be. The risk is the ultimate risk of certain death, eternal nothingness, the end of your existence, or the risked possibility of the becoming of a whole new person, of absolute transformation, of qualitative metamorphosis, and of an entirely new existence. This is the particular type of awe-full moment that perhaps may rarely occur outside of experiential sessions but is a precious characteristic of experiential sessions themselves.

What is so precious is the moment of being in the final leap rather than the accompanying feeling of awe. From the experien-

tial perspective (Mahrer, 1989, 1996), what is so precious, what is celebrated and valued, is having committed yourself to this final leap, the actual undergoing of this final leap, the being in it, and the feeling and experiencing of it. Something is magnificently different in you in this moment. You are committed. You are in the actual throes of the final leap. You no longer are quite the person you had been just before. All of this is what is so precious rather than the accompanying feeling or state of awe.

In this precious moment, there is no one to bathe in this accompanying sense of awe. You would have to stop, turn to the side, and expose yourself to the awe that is nearby. You are not undergoing this awe that is here. You are not facing what can inspire the sense of awe. In this moment, there is little or no appreciation of this sense of awe. The sense, feeling, or state of awe is simply not important in this precious moment. The burst of awe in this awe-full moment is merely a wonderful automatic brief accompaniment of truly being in this final leap. It is an indication, a lovely momentary sign, of actually being in this final leap. You will pass by this puff of awe as you descend in the final leap. Yes, this is an awe-full moment. No, you are not filled with awe.

Most people never know that precious moment of having committed themselves to the final leap. Each experiential session offers you a golden opportunity to undergo the final leap of departing from, of letting go of, the whole person you are and falling headlong into the risked possibility of becoming the person you can become. By stark contrast, most people go through their entire lives without undergoing even a single moment of having committed themselves to that final leap. For nearly every person, living from day to day, year after year, has few (if any) moments when the person actually commits himself or herself to giving up his or her very existence, sacrificing that ever-present sense of self, actively letting go of that sense of "I-ness," letting go of the precious core of who and what the person is, stepping away from the innermost spark of being himself or herself, and resolutely ending the living center of the person's actual existence.

This precious moment is not quite the same as drifting into death. This precious moment comes from actively placing oneself in the position of being ready to undertake the final leap, of then hurling oneself into that final leap, and of knowing the sense of having passed the point of no return. Most people never have known what this tiny moment is like.

There are plenty of fears to protect you from actually undergoing the awe-full final leap. You may come close to the edge. You may even lean perilously forward. But there are plenty of fears that can rescue you from the final leap.

There is a fear of losing control, of giving up that moment-by-moment control that almost always is there. There is a fear of becoming uncivilized, out of control, wild, and animal-like. There is a fear of craziness, lunacy, derangement, and losing your mind. There is a fear that inspires codes of ethics; morality; values; laws; familial, community, and societal recrimination and punishment. There is a fear of the unknown, the empty blackness, and the endless void. There is a fear of death, of the ending of your very existence. Before you commit yourself to the final leap, these fears snap into place and ensure that you never undergo the awe-full final leap.

First there is the lure, the promise, or the goal. Are you really passionate about undergoing wondrous change and becoming all

that you can become? Are you passionate about being free of your hurts and pains, your personal anguishes and sufferings? If your ready answer is *yes*, then all you have to do is undergo the awe-full final leap. Now come the fears. Must you undergo that awe-full final leap? Yes. This is the requirement. It is as if you choose to keep all the hurts and pains, to remain the person with the anguishes and sufferings, and to decline undergoing the wondrous transformation into becoming all that you can become. You choose to remain in this state rather than to succumb to all of the fears that protect you from actually undergoing the awe-full final leap. Isn't this interesting?

The field of psychotherapy protects you from actually undergoing the awe-full final leap. Virtually the entire field of psychotherapy lends its weight to preserving and protecting your self from hurling itself into the final leap. The field uses its resources to enhance your self; to strengthen your self; to feed your self with insight and understanding; to respect your self's ability to know, make decisions, and modify and change its thoughts and actions. Your self is the prized darling of much of what psychotherapy is here to do.

The field of psychotherapy keeps the essential you safely intact while it makes cosmetic changes in things that are nonessential. You can let go of some behavior and can adopt a new one. You can react and respond in some new way. You can revise a way in which you think, an attitude, or an outlook. These are nonessential pieces and bits that can be safely revised and altered. None of them endangers the precious self. None of them requires that you actually undergo the final awe-full leap.

The field of psychotherapy aligns itself on the side of the fears that protect you against the final leap. The field dedicates itself to preserving control, to oppose your losing control, to prevent the outbreak of the awe-fullness of what lies deep inside, to uphold morality and ethics and values, to ensure against craziness and derangement, and to preserve your existence.

The field of psychotherapy rushes away from the promotion of wholesale metamorphosis, deep-seated qualitative change, utter and complete transformation. In these ways and more, the field of psychotherapy effectively guards against your undergoing the awe-full moment of the final leap.

Experiential Sessions Can Occur by Yourself or With an Experiential Teacher-Therapist

Consider two different pictures of what is meant by experiential sessions. In one picture, you are alone in a room. You have the skills to go through an experiential session by yourself. You know what to do and how to do it. You are the "practitioner." Throughout the session, you are in a large comfortable chair with your feet on a large comfortable footrest, or perhaps you are lying on a bed. Your eyes are closed throughout the entire session, which usually lasts for about 1 hour and a half, sometimes 1 hour, sometimes 2 hours. No one is around to disturb you or even to hear you going through the whole session by yourself. This is one picture of an experiential session (Mahrer, 2001).

In a different picture, you are in the office of an experiential teacher-therapist. The office is likely soundproofed. The two chairs are large and comfortable, facing in the same direction, and almost touching one another. Both of you have your eyes closed throughout the entire session, which also lasts for about 1 to 2 hours, ending when the

work is done or when both of you agree that the session is over.

The experiential teacher-therapist guides you through the session, showing you what to do next and how to do it (depending on your proficiency), and also joins right with you in undergoing what you are undergoing as you proceed through the session. The session moves along at your own personal pace, honoring your own personal readiness and willingness to go through each step and baby step. This is the second picture of what is meant by an experiential session (Mahrer, 1996).

Whether the experiential sessions are with yourself or with an experiential teacher-therapist, you can have experiential sessions throughout your life. Picture your having sessions throughout your whole life. If the sessions are by yourself, then you probably have sessions on a rather regular basis, for example, every 1 or 2 weeks (or whenever you want to have a session) over your whole life. If the session is with an experiential teacher-therapist, then you can have sessions whenever you wish, in bunches or spread out, with varying periods in between sessions, and again throughout your whole life. You may start having sessions whenever you wish, as young or as old as you are. I seem to have experiential sessions at least every few weeks.

If you contrast having experiential sessions with being a client or patient to a psychotherapist, then there can be some glaring differences. You start and continue having experiential sessions because you probably want to achieve what the sessions can help you to achieve, not because you "need" to have treatment for some psychological/psychiatric problem, illness, disorder, or condition. You might well have experiential sessions throughout your life rather than have a treatment program of so many sessions with the professional psychotherapist.

This Type of Awe-Full Moment Happens Because of What Happens in Experiential Sessions

Each experiential session offers the person opportunity after opportunity to go beyond the point of no return in hurling himself or herself into the awe-full final leap. Each experiential session has a series of invitations to a series of final leaps. The goals of each experiential session invite the person to take these momentous final leaps. The steps of each session show the person how to take these momentous final leaps.

The goals and the in-session steps are not aimed at putting the person in some type of state of awe or at putting the person through moments of awe. However, if the person has an eye on the goals, and if the person actually walks through the steps, then one of the bonuses or side effects is that the person will undergo this type of awe-full moment.

One goal is to become the qualitatively whole new person you can become. Picture that you begin a session as the person you are, and then picture that you are a qualitatively whole new person by the end of the session. A transformation has happened. It might last only a few minutes or so, or it might last for a long time. You look qualitatively different. The feelings in you are qualitatively new. So is the way in which you think, how you act and behave, and how you are in your world. There is a basic, fundamental, deep-seated qualitative shift in who and what you are. You live and exist in a qualitatively new world. What is "out there" is as different and as new as the person you are inside. The change is awesome.

Nor do you undergo just any change. You become the person you are capable of becoming. Chances are that you ordinarily will spend your entire life without becoming the whole different person you are capable of becoming. Chances are that you have little or no idea of the person you are capable of becoming. As surprising and outlandish as it might seem, a goal of every experiential session is to enable you to undergo this incredible qualitative change into being the whole new person that you are capable of being. This goal sets the stage for your going through this type of awe-full moments.

The other goal is being free of the painful scene and feeling that were front and center for you in the session. By the end of the session, the related other goal is that the qualitatively whole new person no longer has the painful, hurtful, bad feelings in the painful, hurtful, bad scene that was front and center for the person you were when you began the session. Your personal world in which you live now is essentially free of that painful situation, and if the situation still is roughly in your world, it is somehow different, less painful, and less welded to painful feelings in you. You might start the session with a painful scene of being hated, rejected, and shoved away by the one to whom you entrusted yourself. By the end of the session, your world no longer contains such scenes and such feelings in those scenes.

The awe-full moments occur because the session is dedicated to achieving these goals. The awe-full moments also occur because the session proceeds through the following steps.

Step 1: Discover the deeper potential for experiencing. The aim of the first step is to access, to bring forth, to find, and to discover something that is deep down inside you. Picture this as a potentiality for some type of experiencing, a deeper potential for experiencing that typically is outside your awareness. Start by putting yourself in a state of welcoming readiness for undergoing relatively strong feeling. Then find a scene of quite strong feeling, either good or bad feeling, from your current world or from long ago. Let yourself fully enter into, live, and be in this scene, and actively search for the exact instant of peak feeling. The deeper potential for experiencing can be discovered when you enter down inside that precious instant of peak feeling.

Step 2: Welcome, accept, and cherish the deeper potential for experiencing. The purpose of the second step is to achieve a new state of genuinely loving, welcoming, embracing, and cherishing what you had kept sealed off deep down inside, that discovered deeper potential for experiencing.

Step 3: Undergo a qualitative shift into being that deeper potential for experiencing in the context of earlier life scenes. The third step is achieved when you wholly disengage from, and no longer are, the ordinary person you have been, and instead enter wholly and completely into being the utterly new person who is that formerly deeper potential for experiencing. This is accomplished by wholly living and being this qualitatively new person in the context of scenes from the past.

Step 4: Be the qualitatively whole new person in scenes from the forthcoming new post-session world. In the fourth step, the qualitatively whole new person has an ample sample as well as taste, readiness, and commitment to live and be the whole new person in this new person's new world of today, tomorrow, and beyond. This final step provides for trying out, for sampling, for rehearsing, for shaping and refining, and

then for actually experiencing what it is like to be the qualitatively new person in the qualitatively new postsession world.

In an experiential session, one moment of sheer awe occurs as you begin Step 1, a second moment occurs in Step 3, and the third occurs toward the end of Step 4.

Almost any person can have this type of awe-full moment. Although it might seem that some persons ought to have special qualities and characteristics to be able to undergo this type of awe-full moment, in actual practice it seems that almost any person can have this type of awe-full moment. It seems to make no difference whether you are young or old, a tower of strength or a fractured soul, psychologically sophisticated or naïve, a seasoned veteran or a mere beginner in probing the inner world, an old hand or a novice in achieving altered states of consciousness. It does not matter that you have spent your whole life effectively dodging these awe-full moments. Apparently, there are no special qualities, characteristics, talents, or abilities required.

WHAT ARE THE THREE AWE-FULL MOMENTS IN EACH EXPERIENTIAL SESSION?

What are the three awe-full moments in each experiential session, whether the session is with oneself or with an experiential teacher-therapist?

The First Awe-Full Moment Is When You Say Yes and Actually Throw Yourself Into Having an Experiential Session That Can End the Very Existence of the Very Person You Are

The first awe-full moment is when you take the first step of committing yourself to going through a session that can end the very existence of the essential person you are. Once you throw yourself into having a session, there can be no turning back. You have leaned far enough forward that you are about to fall into the abyss. It is too late.

When you stand at the very edge, when you can either hurl yourself into a session or draw safely back, when you stand poised at the edge of the precipice, are you really ready to commit yourself, to submit yourself, to a session that can change you forever, that can put you through a wholesale qualitative wrenching change into being the radically new person you can become, whatever that may be? You know that the two goals are wondrous, precious, and all-powerful. Achieving them means a total commitment. The machinery is ready. Only you can turn it on. Once you say *yes,* once you turn it on, it stays on until the session has done its work, until the session is over. Take your time. The choice is yours.

Picture that you are in a room. You hear the voice of your therapist-teacher or, if you are alone, you hear the voice of the method. The voice says, "Are you truly ready to go through this session, never to turn back until the session is over, no matter what happens and no matter how long it takes? Are you truly ready to commit and dedicate yourself completely? If you are ready, say *yes* loud and clear. If you are ready, say YES . . . NOW!"

If you are, in this instant, fully committed to say *yes,* if you are wholly dedicated to say *yes,* then if we freeze this tiny instant, there almost always is a fraction of a second of awe, of the ecstasy and terror of fully committing and submitting yourself to undergoing a session of wholesale transformation, and of undergoing the qualitative change into becoming a whole new person.

Most people never reach this moment. You spend your life staying safely away from this edge and from the awe-full instant of committing yourself to hurling yourself over the edge and into a session of deepest change.

This is the first moment of sheer awe in a precious experiential session.

The Second Awe-Full Moment Is When You Say Yes and Actually Throw Yourself Into Fully and Completely Being the Qualitatively Whole New Person You Can Be

The second moment comes after you have discovered something deep inside you. It is a hidden deeper quality, a way of being, a possibility for a type of experiencing, and a deeper potentiality for experiencing. It is so deep inside that you rarely, if ever, have felt it, undergone it, or even known that it was there. It is that deep inside you.

But now you do have a clear shot at what it is. You see it up close and in detail. You have discovered a deeply hidden, whole new way of being, a possibility or potentiality for experiencing. Suppose that it is a deeper possibility for experiencing being in charge, in control, and dominating. This is not at all a part of the person you are. This is not part of your daily being or of undergoing, feeling, or experiencing. Once in a rare while, you might touch lightly on a tiny token sample, but this is not you or a part of the person you are. It is sealed off and hidden deep within you.

You also have found a scene, a situation in which you certainly were not this way. You were the way you usually were in that situation—kindly, understanding, gracious, and compromising. The scene happened last night when the whole family was at your place trying to decide what to do with poor old Momma, who is getting more and more gloomy since Daddy died last year. The whole family is politely skating around topics that everyone is astutely complicit in not talking about directly. The scene was explicitly when you did your gracious best to head off the usual confrontation between your explosive older brother and your nasty aunt.

The moment of awe comes when you go back into that scene, just before you actually launched into being the level-headed compromiser between your older brother and your aunt. If we freeze this instant, are you ready for an earth-shattering change, a massive transformation? Are you truly ready, instead of being the person you were, to undergo a truly catastrophic shift into being a qualitative, radical, wholesale new person who is not at all you but rather is the living embodiment of being completely in charge, completely dominating, and in absolute control? You are to undergo being this altogether new and different person fully, with supercharged gusto, in full force, all the way, and with full vigor and intensity. Let yourself be this whole new person totally free of all reality constraints; in total silliness, zaniness, and wildness; and with unbounded exhilaration and excitement.

All right. You are indeed living and being in the scene. It is in that instant when your aunt has just said, "Sam ought to care for Mom. He's got all the money in the family!," and you see your brother Sam's lid about to explode. Right here, in this very frozen instant, are you absolutely ready to throw yourself into being this whole new other person who is the sheer experiencing of wholesale in charge, wholesale control, and wholesale domination? Yes? Then throw yourself into being it . . . NOW!

If we freeze what happens, if you have chosen to say *yes,* and if you have thrown yourself into wholly being this whole new person in this real moment, then there is a fraction of an instant in which you have absolutely let go of every last shred of being the ordinary continuing you; you have passed the point of no return in becoming the qualitatively whole new person who is the pure experiencing of being in absolute change, complete control, and full domination; and you have a flash of awe, of wonder and excitement, of fright and terror.

This is the second moment of awe in a precious session. It is the instant of having passed the point of no return in your wholesale letting go of the very person you have existed as and into actually being the utterly new, radically new, and qualitatively new person who is the deeper potential for experiencing that you had kept hidden and sealed off throughout your whole existence.

The Third Awe-Full Moment Is When You Say Yes and You Continue Being the Qualitatively New Person in the Qualitatively New Postsession World

Now you truly are a whole new person in this session. You have undergone the qualitative switch, the radical conversion, the dramatic transformation. For perhaps the first time in your life, almost certainly in your current life, there is a whole new part to the whole new you. It feels peaceful and exciting to have a sense of being in charge. It feels right and joyful to have a sense of absolute control. It feels natural and alive to have this wonderful sense of domination.

In the final part of the session, you were living and being this whole new person in all types of scenes and situations from the postsession world. You sampled what life can be like as this qualitatively new person who leaves the session and lives and exists in the imminent new world out there, in the whole new world of this whole new person. The new person had a foretaste, a preview, of what life can be like when the door opens and the new you walks into the world of today, tomorrow, and maybe forever.

You are being far more than just the formerly deeper potential for experiencing. You are far more than merely the new experiencing of being in charge, being in absolute control, and experiencing this newly felt domination. This formerly deeper potential now is an integral part of a whole new you. You have become a whole new person that includes this whole new, and integrated, potentiality for experiencing.

What is more, this whole new person lives in a whole new world that is essentially free of those old painful scenes and situations, and the whole new person is essentially free of the painful feelings in those painful situations.

As the session comes to an end, you are this qualitatively whole new person, and you are ready to end the session and enter into a qualitatively whole new world that fits nicely with the qualitatively whole new person you are.

Suppose that we freeze this moment, hold it still. In this very moment, you can remain being this whole new person, and when you open your eyes and walk out of the room, you can live and be in a whole new world out there. Or you can, in this precious moment, switch back into being the ordinary person you always have been, the person you were in the beginning of the session.

This is the third awe-full moment in virtually every experiential session. Who is here? Who is this person you are? Are you the qualitatively new person who opens your eyes, walks out of the room, and lives in a whole new world? Being this whole new person is marvelously available. Or will you, in this frozen awe-full moment, revert back to the ordinary person you almost always have been?

In this frozen moment, there is an instant when the decision has to be made. You must choose one way or the other. Which is it to be? The choice is here. You must choose *yes* to remaining, or you choose *no* and revert back. And your choice is . . .? Here is the moment of awe, filled with excitement and wonder as well as with dread and fright. It all happens in a brief moment.

In this brief moment, perhaps we can appreciate how and why awe can include such a sense of ecstasy, wonder, and fascination. Perhaps it comes from the incredible transformation, from having stepped into being the whole new person. Being this whole new person now, and being able to be this whole new person from now on and forever, can be awe-full. And when awe is accompanied by dread, terror, and primal fear? Perhaps this third awe-full moment allows us to know how easy it is to step back into the ordinary you, how easy it is to see how we actually may choose to step back into a personal world of pain, suffering, hurt, and anguish. We deliberately choose to return to this world of pain and terrible feelings. It is as if the dread, the terror, and the primal fear are from having the choice of becoming and remaining the qualitatively whole new person or of watching our selves clinging to worlds of pain, suffering, hurt, and anguish.

If You Would Like to Undergo These Awe-Full Moments, You Are Invited to Take a Baby Step Toward Having an Experiential Session

Chances are that you never, or rarely, have undergone any of these awe-full moments, and the chances of your having undergone all three are even more remote. Is there now enough of a spark for you to take a first baby step? I hope so.

Take a baby step. Read about baby steps. Attend a workshop. Take a course. Ask a teacher to walk with you through as much of a session as you wish. Reach me in the School of Psychology at the University of Ottawa, Ottawa, Canada K1N 6N5 (amahrer@ uottawa.ca).

The awe-full moments in an experiential session can be precious. Are you ready and willing to take a first baby step?

REFERENCES

Mahrer, A. R. (1989). *Experiencing: A humanistic theory of psychology and psychiatry.* Ottawa, Canada: University of Ottawa Press.

Mahrer, A. R. (1996). *The complete guide to experiential psychotherapy.* New York: John Wiley.

Mahrer, A. R. (2001). *To become the person you can become: The complete guide to self-transformation.* Palo Alto, CA: Bull.

CHAPTER 33

Constructivist Approaches to Therapy

LARRY M. LEITNER AND FRANZ R. EPTING

BEGINNING WITH *The Psychology of Personal Constructs* (Kelly, 1955/ 1991a, 1955/1991b), constructivist theorizing has been an integral aspect of psychology and psychotherapy. A family of theories that assume that reality is in some way created by persons, constructivism both anticipated and benefited from the current interest in postmodern philosophies in psychology. Despite constructivism's powerful influence in helping to shift psychology toward more postmodern understandings of the world, most therapists have little idea of the ways in which constructivist approaches can and do contribute to helping humans solve even the most severe problems. In this chapter, we hope to provide a brief overview of some of the many ways in which constructivist therapies can liberate people to approach life more creatively and courageously. We begin by providing an overview of constructivist assumptions and philosophies. This is followed by a brief dis-

cussion of classic constructivist approaches to therapy. Next, we briefly describe some of the more recent developments of constructivist thought. We conclude with our thoughts on the future of constructivist therapy. Because of space limitations, we focus on individual therapy; however, we provide references for those interested in other approaches.

WHAT IS CONSTRUCTIVISM?

Constructivism is a term for a family of theories starting from a philosophical position that, rather than there being *a* "reality" "out there" to be discovered, persons play an integral role in creating the reality they perceive and grasp experientially. Beginning with Kelly's (1955/1991b) philosophy of constructive alternativism (i.e., the universe is open to an infinite variety of interpretations), constructivists have argued that "objective reality" does not impose its

---

AUTHORS' NOTE: All clinical material has been altered to preserve client anonymity.

meanings on persons. Science, rather than being about discovering truth, is more about theory building or meaning creation. For example, Einstein's fundamental reconstruing of physics rendered many of the "truths" discovered during previous centuries irrelevant. Furthermore, Einstein's theories themselves are not true and eventually will be swept away by a newer way of understanding the world.

The meanings that people create determine what aspects of the universe are grasped as well as the ways in which these aspects are experienced. For example, psychological theorizing assuming the independent autonomous individual had not grasped the sensitivity to context and relationship shown by many women (e.g., Gilligan, 1993). Furthermore, when some meanings (e.g., traditional Freudianism) allowed for women's sensitivity to context, it was understood in pathological ways. It took feminist psychology to create meanings that understood this aspect of women as a rich and viable alternative to the traditional views of morality. In this regard, constructivists are continuously attempting to determine the ways in which hidden assumptions about persons and reality empower or limit the persons we serve.

Thus, constructivist psychology is not about the powerful psychologist imposing reality on the powerless client. Rather, therapy and research are co-created journeys exploring the lived reality of persons. Constructivists believe that meaningful understandings of persons develop when we grasp the unique, personal, and rich realities that humans have created. Most constructivists are concerned more about the process of meaning creation than about the specific meanings created by persons (Leitner, 1985). This emphasis on the process of meaning creation allows the constructivist

therapist to respectfully listen to the client's felt reality without getting into whether the meanings are accurate, realistic, or rational. This more egalitarian view of the relationship between therapist and client can be seen as empowering clients to explore the ways in which they approach the world.

While agreeing that reality never can be known directly, constructivist schools disagree on the exact nature of the relationship between the person and the world. *Radical constructivists* (e.g., Efran, Lukens, & Lukens, 1990) argue that there is no way of even saying that there is a reality outside of the meanings we have created. In a way, then, the real world does not exist given that there is no way in which to see any reality other than the reality of our constructions. Giving primacy to the ways in which we use language (broadly construed such that the term *language* is similar to our use of the term *meaning*), radical constructivists would argue that the language we create totally determines our experience of the world.

Social constructionists, on the other hand, tend to emphasize the meanings that the culture has created and given to its members. In so doing, they critique other schools of psychology as being excessively individualistic. A person is defined for the social constructionists by the culture's way of discussing personhood. Furthermore, as the culture has started to shift ever more rapidly, the self is saturated with so many different social constructions that the very idea of a unified and cohesive sense of self is viewed as an impossibility (Gergen, 1991). Rather, we have multiple "selves," culturally defined, interacting with the multiple selves of others. Interestingly, social constructionism, while agreeing that objective reality cannot be known directly, posits a relativistic cultural reality so powerful that it can impose itself on its members (Burr, 1995).

Critical constructivism occupies a middle ground between these two positions. Critical constructivists assume that there is a real universe that the person engages in the meaning-making process. Meanings are created in interaction between the person and the world. Kelly (1955/1991b) stated that, although we cannot know it directly, the universe is real, integral, and happening all the time. In this regard, critical constructivists are more likely to say that each person's meanings are co-created. The critical constructivist does not reify either the "individual" or the "social" (dividing up psychology into individual vs. social is, in and of itself, a construction that might not be useful [Epting, Pritchard, Leitner, & Dunnett, 1996]) but rather focuses on the powerful "between" as the source of meaning creation.

Constructivism has been criticized by some (e.g., Held, 1995) as being subjective. The gist of the argument is that, without an objective externally true reality, constructivists are excessively relativistic in that they lack any universally true framework for evaluating the meanings that people create. The criticism confuses the position that we never can know *truth* with the position that we cannot develop ways of evaluating meanings. Constructivists have developed numerous ways of evaluating meaning systems without resorting to truth claims (e.g., Leitner, Faidley, & Celentana's [2000] understandings of psychopathology as tied to limited intimacy leading to the experience of emptiness and meaninglessness as well as to the objectification of self and other).

Despite playing a leading-edge role in moving psychology to a more postmodern position as well as being firmly humanistic in its approach, constructivist therapy is relatively ignored by humanistic practitioners. This paradox is related to the abstract theoretical and philosophical nature of much constructivist writing. It can be difficult to see the powerful, concrete, practical implications of such abstract theorizing. We now turn to some of these implications, beginning with some of the classic constructivist approaches to psychotherapy. Many of these approaches involve attitudes of respect, openness, and trust rather than specific techniques. Without creating an atmosphere of reverential caring (Leitner, in press), these illustrations become things done to, rather than ways of being with, the client.

CLASSIC CONSTRUCTIVIST APPROACHES

The Credulous Approach and Contrast

The credulous approach (Kelly, 1955/1991a; Rigdon, Clark, & Hershgold, 1993) involves understanding the client from the assumption that literally everything the client says is "true" (in the sense of communicating important aspects of the client's experience). Viney and Epting (1999) stated that if a client says that he went to the moon, then "he really went to the moon" (p. 4). After all, there are many ways of going to the moon; indeed, there are many moons to which one can go. Therapists can communicate the credulous approach through questions such as "What is it like to . . .?" The therapist's choice of trusting in the reality of the client's reported experience can powerfully contradict the many ways in which persons are told to discount, ignore, and devalue their feelings and beliefs.

Constructivist therapists are also respectful of the ways in which meanings are inherently bipolar (for empirical support of this position, see Rychlak, 1994). For example, someone who contrasts "passive" with "self-confident" should be approached very differently from someone who contrasts "passive" with "murderous." Faidley and Leitner (1993) described a construction of "passive versus murderous" used by a person who shot her spouse when he filed for divorce. Constructivist therapists ask questions such as "How would you be if you were not . . .?" as a way of understanding the potential contrasts in meaning.

A good example of the power of the credulous approach and contrast concerns a client who had a meaning of "depressed versus irresponsible." The credulous approach suggests that we should not ignore this strange duality given that it may reveal important truths about the client's experience. Interestingly enough, this person was referred for therapy after attempting suicide soon after being "rewarded" with a prestigious job promotion (Faidley & Leitner, 1993).

Invitational Mode and Safety

The meanings we create govern our existence and are continually at risk as we encounter a world without certainties and guarantees. Not surprisingly, people often feel great threat as central values are potentially disconfirmed by the world. This threat can be so severe that the very process of meaning creation can be frozen (Leitner, 1999a). Thus, constructivist therapists emphasize making the therapy relationship a safe place, providing the client with a secure base from which to explore the world that he or she has created. Constructivists

may do this by making personal exploration more tentative, experimental, and even playful.

Safety can be emphasized through the invitational mode, that is, the therapist always inviting but never insisting that the client explore certain aspects of experience. Statements such as "Can you tell me more about . . .?" and "I wonder what it is like to . . ." implement the invitational mode. When the client chooses to accept the invitation and explore aspects of his or her experience in more depth, the therapist can be confident that the therapy relationship is experienced as safe enough to handle the material being developed. When the client declines the invitation, the therapist needs to consider the ways in which the client does not trust the safety of the therapy relationship.

Change

Like most humanistic theorists, constructivists assume that people are processes of growth and evolution. Specifically, we assume that people are processes of meaning creation and re-creation (Leitner, 1985). However, many clients cannot see themselves as changing along certain meanings. Because our constructions of the world determine our experience of the world, seeing the self as unchanging sharply limits the prospects of therapeutic growth. Thus, constructivist therapists often work at helping clients to apply constructions of change to the dilemmas they face. (The ability to see a dilemma as changing is the reason why it is easier for "acute" problems to be overcome than for "chronic" ones to be overcome.) Questions such as "Are there times when it is better [or worse or different]?" can help the client to apply a construction of change to the problem. Alert therapists also can make comments when they see the client's experience of the problem shifting, even if ever so slightly.

When the client construes his or her despair as outside of the client's control (e.g., in one's biology or society), the therapist might find it very difficult to help the client see the ways in which changes in his or her meaning system might very well be beneficial. For example, if George is less depressed because he is being "treated better," then he still is not able to take responsibility for the ways in which his meanings have played a role in his depression. If others choose to "treat him worse," for example, then he is back in his old prison. In other words, helping the client to tie changes in symptoms to changes in meaning making is important.

Fixed Role Therapy

Fixed role therapy (Kelly, 1973) can be described as a form of brief psychotherapy applying a self-narrative approach. In its original form, a 2-week invitation is extended to a client to explore some alternative ways of being in the world—alternatives with possibilities for growth and development. The client first writes a self-description that is open and revealing yet sympathetic, as if a character in a play. The therapist and client then co-create (in written form) an alternative character for the client to enact first in the therapy hour and then in the outside world. Over the 2-week period, the client is invited to undertake enactments that initially involve low-risk others (e.g., clerk in a store) and then progress to more important others (e.g., spouse, significant other). At the end of the 2 weeks, the therapist and client assess how things have gone, deciding which experiences were of value and deserve to build on and which to disregard. This procedure is built on the premise that self-consistency can be stultify-

ing at times, and a temporary fragmentation in the form of an alternative role enactment can excite the creative imagination of a client.

Many modifications and elaborations of the procedure have been undertaken. Epting and Nazario (1987) and Viney (1981) showed that very productive work can be accomplished by having clients play out the opposite end of their (bipolar) constructs. For example, a client who self-describes as shy undertakes a rather boisterous alternative role enactment. Many clients cannot wait to jump on the opposite end of their meanings just for the fun of it, even if they later decide to go back to their original positions. In addition, clients have been found to make use of alternative role descriptions long after the 2-week enactment schedule has ended. Fixed role therapy has been used with small groups (Beail & Parker, 1991), families (Procter, 1981, 1985), and the exploration of personal myths (Epting & Pritchard, 1991). Brophy and Epting (1996) used this approach in consulting with junior executives in a large company. Role enactments were used to help employees reinvent themselves in the face of negative evaluations from their seniors.

CONSTRUCTIVISM AND NARRATIVE PSYCHOLOGY

Constructivist theorizing (Mair, 1977, 1988, 1989, 1990) anticipated and shaped many narrative approaches to psychology (Howard, 1991; Polkinghorne, 1988; Terrell & Lyddon, 1995). Many constructivists have used the metaphor of "self-as-storyteller" (Neimeyer, 2000, p. 211) and have described the person as both the author and leading character in a story created to understand meaning in one's life. Narratives *"establish continuity of meaning in the client's lived experience"* (Neimeyer, 1995,

p. 233). Like other narrative therapists, constructivists focus on gaps, incompleteness, and incoherence in the client's life story as indicating problems in living. (Gonçalves, Korman, & Angus [2000] discussed ways of inferring incoherence and incompleteness in narratives.) Because the person is the principal character in the life story, such incoherence implies problems in creating an integrated construction of self-in-the-world.

The reader who is interested in ways in which narratives can be used within constructivist therapy is referred to the rich literature on the topic (Gonçalves, 1995; Moffett & McElheny, 1995; Neimeyer, 2000; White & Epston, 1990). To give one concrete illustration, if the *setting* (e.g., the "where" and "when") of one's narrative is barren, gray, and impoverished, then the narrator could be communicating an important aspect of the experience of self-in-the-world. Gonçalves (1995) described a "moviola" technique in which the therapist's attention moves over the setting like a camera might do in a movie. Often, this focused attention helps the client to create a richer setting for the life story.

FAMILIES AND CHILDREN

There is a rich literature on the application of classic constructivist principles to family therapy (Feixas, 1990a, 1990b, 1992, 1995; Goolishian & Winderman, 1988; Procter, 1981, 1985, 1987). Procter, for example, argued for a family construct system (i.e., a set of meanings shared by members of the family) in addition to each person's personal construct system. Each person in the family has a unique position in this family meaning system. Change for the person involves change along the family's meaning system.

Systemic bow tie diagrams might offer the clearest example of one constructivist technique for family therapy. For example, John and Patsy sought help regarding their inability to communicate around emotionally laden topics (Figure 33.1). John approached these topics with meanings and issues around his fear that Patsy did not love him. These fears led him to be vague and nonresponsive during their conversations. However, Patsy experienced John's vagueness as his not respecting her enough to discuss important issues. Her feelings of not being respected led her to be short and sarcastic with him. John experienced her shortness and sarcasm as confirming his fears about not being loved.

In the bow tie diagram, each person's actions, based on his or her own fears and issues, confirm the fears and issues of the partner. Interventions at any point (at either the level of behavior or the level of the underlying meanings for either partner) could change the entire system. For example, if John could see sarcasm as linked to frustration rather than to lack of love, then he might be less evasive. If he could courageously risk being open and specific even as he feels unloved, then Patsy could feel more respected, thereby decreasing her sarcasm. Patsy could check her sarcastic responses when feeling disrespected, allowing John to feel more loved, thereby reducing his evasiveness. Patsy could experience John's evasiveness as fear more than as disrespect, leading her to be less sarcastic toward John.

Ravenette (1997) is arguably the most creative psychologist using constructivist techniques to understand the inner experience of children. He goes into the assessment session armed with nothing but blank sheets of paper. He invites the child to draw a picture that incorporates a simple structure that he provides (e.g., a bent line drawn in the center of the page). The child then is

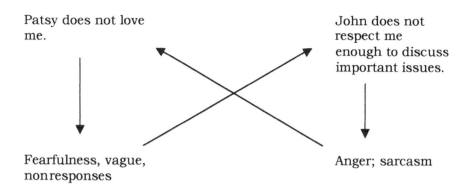

Figure 33.1. Systematic Bow Tie

asked to create the opposite picture of the one just drawn. From there, an engaging dialogue allows the child to share some of his or her personal world. The child also is asked to describe himself or herself as the child imagines a parent would describe him or her (e.g., "What sort of boy would your father say you were?"), setting a rich dialogue into motion. All of Ravenette's numerous techniques have the aim of enabling children to say what they know about their worlds but could not otherwise find words to express.

EXPERIENTIAL PERSONAL CONSTRUCT PSYCHOTHERAPY

Experiential personal construct psychotherapy (EPCP) reveals constructivism's profound relational, experiential, and existential foundations. EPCP sees persons as needing rich and intimate relationships (termed *ROLE relationships*) in which the very being of one another can be experienced and confirmed. At the same time, such relationships are terrifying in that they expose one's very core to potentially devastating disconfirmations. This potential terror often results in the person retreating from intimacy and paying the price through

the experience of emptiness, meaninglessness, and guilt (Leitner, 1985). Often in response to such danger, the client numbs the self to his or her own experience (Leitner, 1999b). EPCP engages the client in this very process of needing to connect deeply (with subsequent richness and terror) versus needing to retreat to protect the self (with subsequent safety yet emptiness).

Because people are relationship seeking, the client brings the desires as well as the terrors associated with deep connections to the therapy room. This allows the client and therapist to use the living relationship of the therapeutic encounter to help the client in self-transformation. Ways in which the client (and therapist) retreat from, minimize, or avoid the therapeutic ROLE relationship are experientially explored to uncover the reasons why the client (and therapist) has created a reality in which retreat and emptiness are the better choice.

EPCP has been used to explore the experience of resistance in psychotherapy (Leitner & Dill-Standiford, 1993), the ways in which therapist interventions are confirmed or disconfirmed by clients (Leitner & Guthrie, 1993), and therapeutic interventions with serious disturbances (Leitner & Celentana, 1997). It has also been used to explore the ways in which clients can act from differing levels of consciousness without resorting to a "therapist-knows-all" position (Leitner, 1999a) and the use of creativity in psychotherapy (Leitner & Faidley, 1999). Leitner and colleagues (2000) proposed a system of diagnosing human meaning making that simultaneously respects the lived experience of the client and opens treatment options for the therapy relationship.

Optimal therapeutic distance, a central aspect of EPCP (Leitner, 1995), is an integration of profound connection and separation. Experientially, optimal distance can be seen when the therapist is close enough to the client to feel the client's experience inside of the therapist while also distant enough such that the therapist can recognize it as the client's experience and not the therapist's own. Optimal distance can be contrasted with *therapeutic strangers* (i.e., the therapist is so distant that he or she cannot experience with the client) and *therapeutic unity* (i.e., when the therapist is so swept up in the client's experience that the feelings are the therapist's more than the client's). In other words, optimal therapeutic distance combines subjectively experiencing the client's experience while, at the same time, professionally understanding the client's experience.

When the therapist is optimally distant, therapy is opened to the possibility of great personal transformations. The therapist simultaneously experiences the overwhelming terror of the client (powerfully affirming its reality for the client) while, through the therapeutic relationship, providing the client with the felt sense that one can approach, grapple with, and learn from the terror. To be optimally distant, however, the therapist has to be aware of his or her very humanity, that is, the ways in which the therapist has retreated from, injured, or

avoided the very ones he or she loves the most (Leitner & Celentana, 1997).

For example, a young man had the delusion that the KGB (the Soviet spy organization) was going to kill his therapist (Leitner, in press). Rather than treating the delusion with neurotoxins or accusations of crazy thinking, the therapist tried to understand the reality of the message behind the delusion. The delusion disappeared when the therapist spoke "from the heart" about knowing what it was like to be so consumed by rage that a person could kill someone as well as being so terrified by life that a person had withdrawn to the point where he or she no longer knew for sure what was real and what was fantasy. At the same time, the therapist talked about such rage being closely tied to a felt injury and hoped that there would come a time when the client would trust the therapy relationship enough to talk about the injury. In other words, the delusion ended when the therapist simultaneously could connect with the client's rage and potential for "psychotic" terror (because the therapist recognized them in himself) while offering an understanding that gave the therapy relationship some hope (see also the chapters by Friedman [Chapter 26] and Sterling [Chapter 27] in this volume).

FUTURE DIRECTIONS

Constructivist therapy continues to evolve and grow. We believe that the future will hold further developments in the area of more focused short-term treatments for mild to moderate disorders. (Ecker & Hulley's [1996, 2000] depth-oriented brief therapy provides one example of a creative use of constructivist principles in this area.) Furthermore, experiential personal construct psychotherapy was developed using constructivist principles to transform the experiences of the most severely disturbed persons being seen in psychotherapy today. Elaboration of this approach into areas of lesser disturbance will be important. Although constructivist principles can be applied to entire communities, little has been done to date in that arena. We find it difficult to predict the exact path of constructivist therapy in the future, but we are optimistic that it will become increasingly important as psychology rediscovers that, to truly have a rich discipline, we must understand the magnificent creature we call *a person*. In so doing, we must honor the meaning-making mystery lying behind the various creations on which psychology has focused in the past.

REFERENCES

Beail, N., & Parker, S. (1991). Group fixed role therapy: A clinical application. *International Journal of Personal Construct Psychology, 4*, 85-96.

Brophy, S., & Epting, F. (1996). Mentoring employees: A role for personal construct psychology. In B. M. Walker, J. Costigan, L. L. Viney, & B. Warren (Eds.), *Personal construct theory: A psychology for the future* (pp. 239-252). Carlton, South Victoria: Australian Psychological Society.

Burr, V. (1995). *An introduction to social constructionism.* London: Routledge.

Ecker, B., & Hulley, L. (1996). *Depth-oriented brief therapy.* San Francisco: Jossey-Bass.

Ecker, B., & Hulley, L. (2000). The order in clinical "disorder": Symptom coherence in depth-oriented brief therapy. In R. Neimeyer & J. Raskin (Eds.), *Constructions of disorder: Meaning making frameworks for psychotherapy* (pp. 63-89). Washington, DC: American Psychological Association.

Efran, J. S., Lukens, M. D., & Lukens, R. J. (1990). *Language, structure, and change: Frameworks of meaning in psychotherapy.* New York: Norton.

Epting, F. R., & Nazario, A., Jr. (1987). Designing a fixed role therapy: Issues, techniques, and modifications. In R. A. Neimeyer & G. J. Neimeyer (Eds.), *Personal construct theory casebook* (pp. 277-289). New York: Springer.

Epting, F. R., & Pritchard, S. (1991, August). *Fixed role as mythology.* Paper presented at the Ninth International Congress on Personal Construct Psychology, Albany, NY.

Epting, F. R., Pritchard, S., Leitner, L. M., & Dunnett, N. G. M. (1996). The case for personal and social constructivism. In D. Kelekin-Fishman & B. Walker (Eds.), *The construction of group realities: Culture, society, and personal construct theory* (pp. 309-322). Melbourne, FL: Krieger.

Faidley, A. J., & Leitner, L. M. (1993). *Assessing experience in psychotherapy: Personal construct alternatives.* Westport, CT: Praeger.

Feixas, G. (1990a). Approaching the individual, approaching the system: A constructivist model for integrative psychotherapy. *Journal of Family Psychology, 4*, 4-35.

Feixas, G. (1990b). Personal construct theory and the systemic therapies: Parallel or convergent trends? *Journal of Marital and Family Therapy, 16*, 1-20.

Feixas, G. (1992). Personal construct approaches to family therapy. In G. Neimeyer & R. Neimeyer (Eds.), *Advances in personal construct psychology* (Vol. 2, pp. 215-255). Greenwich, CT: JAI.

Feixas, G. (1995). Personal constructs in systemic practice. In R. Neimeyer & M. Mahoney (Eds.), *Constructivism in psychotherapy* (pp. 305-337). Washington,

DC: American Psychological Association.

Gergen, K. J. (1991). *The saturated self: Dilemmas of identity in contemporary life.* New York: Basic Books.

Gilligan, C. (1993). *In a different voice: Psychological theory and women's development* (rev. ed.). Cambridge, MA: Harvard University Press.

Gonçalves, O. F. (1995). Cognitive narrative psychotherapy. In M. J. Mahoney (Ed.), *Cognitive and constructivist psychotherapies* (pp. 139-162). New York: Springer.

Gonçalves, O. F., Korman, Y., & Angus, L. (2000). Constructing psychopathology from a cognitive narrative perspective. In R. Neimeyer & J. Raskin (Eds.), *Constructions of disorder: Meaning making frameworks for psychotherapy* (pp. 265-284). Washington, DC: American Psychological Association.

Goolishian, H., & Winderman, L. (1988). Constructivism, autopoiesis, and problem determined systems. *Irish Journal of Psychology, 9,* 130-143.

Held, B. (1995). *Back to reality: A critique of postmodern theory in psychotherapy.* New York: Norton.

Howard, G. S. (1991). Culture tales: A narrative approach to thinking, cross-cultural psychology, and psychotherapy. *American Psychologist, 46,* 187-197.

Kelly, G. A. (1973). Fixed role therapy. In R. M. Jerjevich (Ed.), *Direct psychotherapy: Vol. 28. American originals* (pp. 394-422). Coral Gables, FL: University of Miami Press.

Kelly, G. A. (1991a). *The psychology of personal constructs: A theory of personality.* London: Routledge. (Original work published 1955)

Kelly, G. A. (1991b). *The psychology of personal constructs: Clinical diagnosis and psychotherapy.* London: Routledge. (Original work published 1955)

Leitner, L. M. (1985). The terrors of cognition: On the experiential validity of personal construct theory. In D. Bannister (Ed.), *Issues and approaches in personal construct theory* (pp. 83-103). San Diego, CA: Academic Press.

Leitner, L. M. (1995). Optimal therapeutic distance: A therapist's experience of personal construct psychotherapy. In R. Neimeyer & M. Mahoney (Eds.), *Constructivism in psychotherapy* (pp. 357-370). Washington, DC: American Psychological Association.

Leitner, L. M. (1999a). Levels of awareness in experiential personal construct psychotherapy. *Journal of Constructivist Psychology, 12,* 239-252.

Leitner, L. M. (1999b). Terror, numbness, panic, and awe: Experiential personal constructivism and panic. *The Psychotherapy Patient, 11,* 157-170.

Leitner, L. M. (in press). The role of awe in experiential personal construct psychotherapy. *The Psychotherapy Patient.*

Leitner, L. M., & Celentana, M. A. (1997). Constructivist therapy with serious disturbances. *The Humanistic Psychologist, 25,* 271-285.

Leitner, L. M., & Dill-Standiford, T. J. (1993). Resistance in experiential personal construct psychotherapy: Theoretical and technical struggles. In L. M. Leitner & N. G. M. Dunnett (Eds.), *Critical issues in personal construct psychotherapy* (pp. 135-155). Melbourne, FL: Krieger.

Leitner, L. M., & Faidley, A. J. (1999). Creativity in experiential personal construct psychotherapy. *Journal of Constructivist Psychology, 12,* 273-286.

Leitner, L. M., Faidley, A. J., & Celentana, M. A. (2000). Diagnosing human meaning making: An experiential constructivist approach. In R. Neimeyer & J. Raskin (Eds.), *Constructions of disorder: Meaning making frameworks for psychotherapy* (pp. 175-203). Washington, DC: American Psychological Association.

Leitner, L. M., & Guthrie, A. F. (1993). Validation of therapist interventions in psychotherapy: Clarity, ambiguity, and subjectivity. *International Journal of Personal Construct Psychology, 6,* 281-294.

Mair, J. M. M. (1977). Metaphors for living. In A. W. Landfield & J. K. Cole (Eds.), *Nebraska symposium on motivation* (Vol. 24, pp. 243-290). Lincoln: University of Nebraska Press.

Mair, J. M. M. (1988). Psychology as storytelling. *International Journal of Personal Construct Psychology, 1*, 125-137.

Mair, J. M. M. (1989). *Between psychology and psychotherapy: A poetics of experience.* London: Routledge.

Mair, J. M. M. (1990). Telling psychological tales. *International Journal of Personal Construct Psychology, 3*, 121-135.

Moffett, J., & McElheny, K. R. (Eds.). (1995). *Points of view.* New York: New America Library.

Neimeyer, R. A. (1995). Client-generated narratives in psychotherapy. In R. A. Neimeyer & M. Mahoney (Eds.), *Constructivism in psychotherapy.* Washington, DC: American Psychological Association.

Neimeyer, R. A. (2000). Narrative disruptions in the construction of the self. In R. A. Neimeyer & J. D. Raskin (Eds.), *Constructions of disorder: Meaning-making frameworks for psychotherapy* (pp. 207-242). Washington, DC: American Psychological Association.

Polkinghorne, D. E. (1988). *Narrative knowing and the human sciences.* Albany: State University of New York Press.

Procter, H. (1981). Family construct psychotherapy: An approach to understanding and treating families. In S. Walrond-Skinner (Ed.), *Developments in family therapy* (pp. 350-366). London: Routledge and Kegan Paul.

Procter, H. (1985). A construct approach to family and systems intervention. In E. Button (Ed.), *Personal construct theory and mental health* (pp. 327-350). Cambridge, MA: Brookline Books.

Procter, H. (1987). Change in the family construct system: Therapy of a mute and withdrawn schizophrenic patient. In R. Neimeyer & G. Neimeyer (Eds.), *Personal construct therapy casebook* (pp. 157-170). New York: Springer.

Ravenette, A. T. (1997). *Tom Ravenette: Selected papers—Personal construct psychology and the practice of an educational psychologist.* Farnborough, UK: EPCA Publications.

Rigdon, M., Clark, C., & Hershgold, E. (1993). A case demonstration of two methods for promoting the credulous approach in personal construct psychotherapy. In L. M. Leitner & N. G. M. Dunnett (Eds.), *Critical issues in personal construct psychotherapy* (pp. 157-172). Melbourne, FL: Krieger.

Rychlak, J. F. (1994). *Logical learning theory.* Lincoln: University of Nebraska Press.

Terrell, C. J., & Lyddon, W. J. (1995). Narrative and psychotherapy. *Journal of Constructivist Psychology, 9*, 27-44.

Viney, L. L. (1981). Experimenting with experience: A psychotherapeutic case study. *Psychotherapy: Theory, Research, and Practice, 46*, 287-292.

Viney, L. L., & Epting, F. R. (1999, July). *Towards a personal construct approach to the supervision of counseling.* Paper presented at the International Congress on Personal Psychology, Berlin.

White, M., & Epston, D. (1990). *Narrative means to therapeutic ends.* New York: Norton.

CHAPTER 34

A Humanistic Perspective on Bereavement

Myrtle Heery

THESE REFLECTIONS on loss are particularly poignant for me right now. From start to finish as I have written these words, my dog has been slowly dying. He has been with my family for 14½ years, and he has been at my side throughout this creative process, watching, sleeping, and loving without expectation, as only a dog can do. It is a mystery that his tired body is crying "stop" even as I am writing.

As I hear, smell, and touch this loss, I am searching for meaning. When we experience a loss, meaning may emerge. This possibility does not diminish the pain of loss, but it enriches us as we open to searching. After struggling with his wife's cancer, a client poignantly expressed a meaning he had found after her death: "I appreciate the small things in life so much now. I am grateful for the toilet paper hanging there. I hardly noticed toilet paper before my wife's cancer and her death. I hardly noticed a lot of ordinary things. I notice a lot now."[1]

What does it mean to experience a loss? Some losses are small and have an objective quality such as the loss of house keys, an article of clothing, or a piece of jewelry. Do these objective losses prepare us for more intensely personal and subjective losses such as the loss of a marriage, a parent, a spouse, a child, or a woman's own breast? What happens as we prepare—or fail to prepare—for these more personal losses? What happens to us as we age and continue to lose parts of our lives that are near and dear to us? These questions are part of a search latent in each of us as we age and draw closer to our own deaths.

There are some basic "givens" that are inevitable aspects of the human condition. This chapter addresses the given that Yalom (1980) referred to as "death" and that Bugental (1981, 1987) referred to as "finitude." As humans, we are born with the ultimate and inescapable limit of the death of the physical body. This is the inevitable outcome of another given, that is, embodiment (Bugental, 1981); we are born into a body with all the limitations that bodies are subject to including the fact that one day it will cease to function. Each of us approaches these givens along a number of parameters such as age, gender, social class, cultural/religious beliefs and practices, family, and emotional support systems (including both external and internal support).

This chapter describes the individual's internal support through searching for meaning in loss. Let me stress that this search is not a linear movement that provides definite answers at the end; rather, it is an ongoing process that often takes us into new and uncharted territory. "Spiritual pioneers" (Coles, 1990) are those who have courageously journeyed into this uncharted territory to find meaning in loss. This chapter presents some landmarks of that journey, which I call the "stations" of the search; these are the perceptual stances that we typically encounter as we search for meaning in loss.

A CALL AND RESPONSE

The human potential movement during the 1960s called for enhancement and enrichment of the human. At first, this idealistic call seemed to ignore the limits of the human condition as growth centers such as Esalen expanded and awareness groups flourished across the nation. Those of us who responded to the call of the human potential movement knew that we were going to make great personal and global changes. We *did* and we *did not* make changes. It is the *did not* that I now address.

Responses to the challenge of human potential have not changed the fundamental givens. Each of us has a limited time in this body, and most of us have no idea when this time will end. We live with the certainty and uncertainty of death. The baby boomers in this country, roughly 80 million of us born between 1945 and 1965, now are in midlife or 35 to 55 years of age (Elkins, 1998). More people than ever before, and more people at the same time than ever before, are

looking at mortality and the possible meanings or lack of meaning of this most basic given.

Midlife is a time of profound questioning impelled by deep losses. Most baby boomers have lost at least one significant other to death—spouse, child, friend, or parent. It is no longer "Death never will happen to me" but rather a question of when, where, and how. A major shift of perspective for baby boomers is that we no longer have the luxury of philosophizing about death as something that comes to others and not to ourselves. It is a very different experience to touch, smell, and live with death. One of the significant findings by Yalom and Lieberman (1991) in their research with bereavement and existential awareness is that the death of a spouse often brings one's own death into focus. A participant in their study reported the following:

I realize that everything that's present right now can suddenly stop to be; I know this is very obvious, but somehow it's something I never experienced before. Death can really happen. . . . I see it happening to my friend. . . . My husband's death has made it very clear to me that I was born to die, that death is inevitable. . . . My time will be up eventually. This is obvious; who doesn't know it? But somehow I'm aware of this in a way that I never was really aware of it before. . . . I feel like I could die almost any minute. . . . I'm just more conscious of my mortality. . . . I don't shrug off aches and pains as I have in the past. I think about them. I get a little nervous if I get bronchitis. (p. 337)

As this quote illustrates, a loss that we actually experience heightens our awareness of death. Other contemporary factors heighten our awareness of death including high-risk diseases (e.g., AIDS, cancer) and the increasing uncertainty of life-threatening environmental factors. Psychotherapists are also changing along with the heightened awareness and risk of death, listening with more of an "existential ear" (Bugental & Kleiner, 1993) both to the client and to themselves. We are now responding to our own limitations. Bugental (1981), Frankl (1958), May (1953), and Yalom (1980) have for decades regarded the given of death as essential to psychotherapy.

MEANING AND MEANINGLESSNESS

Meaninglessness has often been perceived as a theological and philosophical concept. Philosophers, artists, writers, historians, and journalists also recognize meaninglessness as an existential concern. For many existential thinkers, such as Camus and Tillich, the anxiety of meaninglessness is part of human existence. Tillich (1952) characterized the anxiety of our times as "the anxiety of doubt and meaninglessness" (p. 73). According to Tillich (1952) and Camus (1942/1955), nothing can take this existential anxiety away; we must accept it as a part of existence.

The existential psychotherapist Frankl, who led groups while living in a concentration camp, wrote that the "will-to-meaning" is the dominant drive of humans. Frankl (1958) emphasized that the human is "dominated neither by the will-to-pleasure nor the will-to-power but [rather] by what I call man's will-to-meaning, that is to say, his deep-seated striving and struggle for a higher and ultimate meaning to his existence" (p. 20). This drive is often frustrated and can lead to a sense of meaninglessness, which Frankl (1959/1963) referred to as an "existential vacuum" (p. 108).

This existential anxiety or existential vacuum becomes the driving force of our search for meaning. The discomfort of that anxiety provides intense motivation. Nowhere do we confront meaninglessness more starkly than when we face the prospect of our own deaths—the loss of our physical bodies, our connections with all those we have loved, all the labors and creations into which we have poured our energies. Perhaps death drives the search in which we might very well find the meaning of living.

There is a range of possible responses to the sense of meaninglessness. Denial certainly is one; the individual may seek to avoid existential anxiety by repressing the sense of meaninglessness. Denial may complement escape as a response in which the individual selectively drowns out the anxiety with an ongoing flurry of activity, often deriving some sense of meaning from accomplishment and the resulting recognition.

One can also respond to existential anxiety with a sense of absurdity (Bugental, 1981) or despair (Tillich, 1952) in which the individual succumbs to the sense of meaninglessness. This might make a search for meaning seem vain; it renders life absurd. The result is self-alienation expressed through an apathetic or self-destructive lifestyle.

One can trivialize life and its experiences through any of these responses. One also can rob it of richness through dogmatism, accepting preset beliefs and answers that offer a sense of comfort and security. Dogmatism might not necessarily trivialize life, but like the other possible responses mentioned so far, it certainly can act as an anesthetic that keeps us from looking at what death and loss mean on a personal level. Through any of these responses, we give away our authenticity, that is, the condition of being true to ourselves.

Another possible response to existential anxiety is what Tillich (1952) referred to as courage. The choice of courage facilitates taking responsibility in spite of the apparent meaninglessness of one's existence (p. 66).

THE COURAGE TO SEARCH

> Courage consists in a confronting of our limitedness within the unlimitedness of being. Courage consists in the exercising of our choice and the taking of our responsibility while recognizing that contingency can overthrow our decision and reverse our best efforts. Courage finds its finest expression in the choice to be. (Bugental, 1981, p. 26)

We often begin looking for meaning in the objective world; for example, focusing on what the doctor should or should not have done can help to resolve feelings about a loved one dying. When we do not feel satisfied with the outer search, we turn to inner searching. In discussing the courage to search, I refer to an inner-directed process (rather than an outer-directed one), that is, to a subjective process that reaches deep into one's inner being. When we search so deeply, we often find ourselves in uncharted waters, and this requires great courage. The inner search is focused on what is happening inside the person—the feelings, awarenesses, and nuances of the depths of the person's inner ocean.

My own courage to search emerged when I nearly drowned in the ocean at around 12 years of age. My girlfriend and I were swept out to sea in a riptide. We were terrified, and our efforts in swimming and screaming for help only exhausted us. My mother heard us and came out to help. She instructed us to float instead of trying to swim and to scream for help periodically. My mother got caught in the riptide as well. I have never forgotten that seemingly endless time of

floating and screaming. As I drifted farther and farther from shore, I found myself imagining what was on the other side of this vast expanse of water, and I realized that I might not live to see it. This only intensified my panic. I remember thinking, "I could die." My mother and friend also were floating out to sea, and I felt tremendous sadness that we all might die.

In the midst of all this, my mother's instructions resonated deeply within me, and no matter how tired I got, they fueled the courage to keep struggling and calling for help, that is, to continue to be. It took great courage for the three of us to float without knowing whether we would be rescued or keep drifting farther from shore. Help finally came. For many days after this experience, I sat at the edge of this vast ocean in awe of my experience and my sense of touching life and death firsthand. The search for meaning in this near-death experience has always brought me deep awareness of my mother's courage and love for me; she risked her life to save mine. I also became aware of a loss—the assumption that my life would go on forever. It was my first wake-up call that life is finite and that death can come at any time and any place.

As theologians such as Tillich and scholars such as May have pointed out for so long, courage is vital to the searching process. My experience in my own psychotherapy practice bears this out. Some people immediately access the courage to search for meaning. They respond to the blank canvas of meaninglessness with inner exploration and creativity, encountering a full range of human experiences. A client who recently had separated from her husband used gardening, and the metaphor of gardening, to explore the meaning of her loss. She said, "My loss reminds me of gardening. When the plants aren't growing for whatever reason, I start over. I see it as an opportunity to plant things completely differently." Her courage sustained her through many hours of therapy in which she searched the depths of sadness, loneliness, and estrangement from her husband. Using her own metaphor, she could creatively transplant these emotions to new places in her inner garden.

Sometimes, inner searching can lead to confirmation of our underlying beliefs about human nature. We see an example of this in a recent interview by Rehak (1999) with diarist and composer Ned Rorem after the death of his partner of 32 years. Rehak asked, "What do you feel grieving has taught you about human nature?" Rorem replied,

> I haven't learned a thing. I haven't learned anything except for the fact that you don't learn anything when people die—and that's already something. Everybody says, "I know just how you feel," and I'm sure they do, but it's like love. Love is very selfish. People who are in love are a bore, usually because all they say is, "How can you possibly understand this great love?" It's the same with death. There's something selfish about love and something selfish about a person dying. I think there is a certain egotism in grief—there has to be. (p. 19)

Rorem gave this reflection on grieving for public reflection. It shows that inner searching does not always deliver sweet answers. In fact, it sometimes brings up hard facts that take courage to face and hold in one's life.

I have been a bereavement counselor for a local hospice for 10 years. I facilitate support groups for those who recently have lost loved ones. I am in awe of the courage of people who first come together as strangers and meet for 8 weeks to plumb the depths of their losses together. It takes courage to attend these groups and even more courage to show up for them emotionally. It is a profound experience to show up for one's own losses and even more so to show up for other people's losses.

SEARCHING FOR MEANING: IMPORTANT CONDITIONS IN THE PSYCHOTHERAPEUTIC SETTING

Bugental (1987) described "searching" as an innate natural capacity that a variety of therapies tap into. Freud's technique of "free association" is an inner searching process, as is Gendlin's (1982) "focusing" and Welwood's (1982) "unfolding." Bugental (1987) said the following of searching: "This innate capacity of human beings is that on which we call whenever we meet a situation to which we need to respond but for which we have no preexisting well-practiced response pathways" (p. 167). This inner searching is vital when one deals with loss.

I recognize three conditions that facilitate the searching process in a psychotherapeutic setting: presence, accompanying the client's subjective search, and caring. It is essential for the client to hold these qualities in order to do any meaningful searching. It is equally crucial for the therapist to hold these qualities during the session because they profoundly affect the client's search.

Presence is accompanied by heightened self-awareness on the part of both therapist and client. With a recent client, I found myself asking, "What is going on in me [the therapist] as my client shares the suicide of her daughter?" I am acutely aware that the depth of my self-awareness directly influences my client's search. If her child's suicide brings up in me an unacknowledged terror concerning my own child, then my lack of presence will limit my client's ability to visit her own terror. The opposite also is true. Consciously experiencing and containing my own terror can create a supportive holding environment that serves my client's search. Being sustained by the therapist's presence often is the turning point for a client (Bugental, 1981, p. 180).

Accompanying the client's subjective search is the second vital condition for searching. My client's daughter committed suicide. It certainly is important for the therapist to know this objective fact, but objective facts are not the focus of the work. The essential work is the willingness and courage of the client and therapist to immerse themselves in the client's subjective world. What is happening inside this woman as she talks about her daughter's suicide? How is her child's death affecting her at this moment? Where does she feel it in her body? These questions, whether or not I ask them aloud, elicit the client's subjective world, the place where she truly lives the tragedy and where she does her inner searching.

Caring is the third vital condition for searching. All care begins with the therapist's courage to recognize a client's suffering and to accept responsibility to be present for this suffering. "Telling a story about suffering gathers together what feels fragmented and injured and leads to feelings of wholeness and presence" (Fredriksson, 1988, p. 29). I have had the experience of caring vividly impressed on me while working with clients whose losses involved physical suffering. On occasion, I have felt physical pain in my breast as a client told and retold the story of her mastectomy. If it feels appropriate, I might share this experience, but generally I hold it within myself.

"Maintaining a holding stance requires a level of attunement that is both deeply satisfying and exhausting" (Slowchower, 1996, p. 332). This ability to maintain a holding stance becomes a deep reservoir from which my caring flows; sometimes, my capacity to

access that holding stance is temporarily exhausted. Caring is an experience shared between therapist and client; at times, it is satisfying to both, and at other times, it is exhausting to both as the pain of loss is slowly transformed into meaning.

COMPASSION: OPENING THE HEART

Jourard (1971) suggested the term *spirit* to the field of psychology, and Bugental (1984) expanded on it to apply to a human who is aware, awake, dynamic, energetic, and involved. In holding a space of spirit and compassion for clients in their searching, the therapist helps clients to hold that same space for themselves. As clients receive that compassion, their hearts are opened and their spirits are enlivened. Welwood (1982) and many Buddhist psychologists have elaborated on the opening of the heart in psychotherapy. Eastern and indigenous traditions have long viewed the opening of the heart as essential to the unfoldment of the individual on the mystical path. The Sufi tradition has described the heart in detail:

> The heart is conceived of as a multi-layered spherical organ, each layer finer than the outer one that envelops it. Each layer has a function which is meant to serve the heart as a whole. The well-being of any layer depends on the well-being of all other layers. Ultimately, all layers are seen as protective sheaths for that which lies at the center. That which lies at the center is the source of light, wisdom, and mystical knowledge. (Sviri, 1997, pp. 5-6)

This emotional and spiritual center holds our capacity for compassion, which takes caring to a new depth. Loss offers the potential gift of opening the spirited heart from a deep level of being. I am reminded of my times with a client whose child had been murdered. We often sat in silence and wept together. I often felt a physical ache in my heart as she recalled the murder of her child. On a subjective nonverbal level, I held her pain close to my being. This closeness stirred my heart to open to the experience of compassion.

How do I know that I am experiencing compassion? Compassion includes caring and the possibility of taking action such as when one cares for a child or someone who is ill. Compassion is often more detached and more universal than caring, and at the same time, it involves a resonance with the suffering of others. Compassion crosses time and space; I feel compassion for the children of Bosnia even if I cannot personally do anything about their plight, and I feel compassion for the victims of a nuclear holocaust that happened more than 50 years ago.

Compassion has a quality of unconditional love and allowance.

In Albom's (1997) interviews with his mentor, Morrie Schwartz, Schwartz spoke of the experience of compassion:

> "Now that I'm suffering, I feel closer to people who suffer than I ever did before. The other night, on TV, I saw people in Bosnia running across the street, getting fired upon, killed, innocent victims . . . , and I just started to cry. I feel their anguish as if it were my own. I don't know any of these people. But—how can I put this?—I'm almost . . . drawn to them." His eyes got moist, and I tried to change the subject, but he dabbed his face and waved me off. "I cry all the time now," he said. "Never mind." (pp. 50-51)

For me, compassion is a way of holding another's experience, that is, a way of being with another and simultaneously separate from him or her. My client whose child was murdered was living every mother's nightmare. I am a mother; I know this nightmare. We are united in the nightmare, yet my client lives the nightmare that for me is a mere possibility rather than a reality. I am separate but not apart. In this union, the compassion of the heart flows. Just as tears produce enzymes that heal the body, compassion produces a felt unity that enlivens the spirit.

This woman's tragic loss has changed both her outer and *inner* lives. My inner life also has been changed by her loss. I have lived the transformative power of compassion. I have accompanied (Doka & Davidson, 1998) this mother through the dark night of her soul with the haunting whispers of my own fears enlivening the flow of compassion between us. I remember once her asking whether I had a child. I said *yes*. She looked at me with compassion and said, "I hope you never have to face a tragedy like this." Guilt and shame filled my being. My child lives. This tragedy has not happened to me but it could.

I returned to the present moment and met her eyes of compassion. She was accompanying me in my unspoken process. She knew that it was her tragedy, yet her compassion for this unspoken vulnerability of being human reached out to me. Our eyes met with this knowledge, and we nodded to one another—heart open to heart. Out of this compassionate stance and the mutual facing of grief, she blossomed and gained personal strength. Charmaz (1997) said the following of this process:

> And that is the paradox of feeling and facing grief. Out of the resolution of grief can come a tremendous blossoming, of confidence, of competence, and of compassion. Through experiencing deep grief, the bereaved may gain amazing strength and wisdom. (p. 240)

SEARCHING FOR MEANING IN LOSS: AN EXERCISE

Inner searching for the meaning of loss can be fostered in bereavement groups. Let me share an exercise that I do with bereavement groups, usually about halfway through the eight weekly group meetings. I explain the structure and purpose of the exercise and invite members of the group to form triads. There are three roles in the exercise: interviewer, interviewee, and secretary. Participants rotate between roles every 10 to 15 minutes, depending on the time that the whole group has decided on.

The interviewer gently and repeatedly asks, "What is the meaning of this loss?" The interviewer's job is to be fully present in asking this question. The interviewer waits for the interviewee to complete his or her response before repeating the question. No matter what the response is, the interviewer stays with that single question, "What is the meaning of this loss?" This continues for the duration of the interviewee's turn.

The interviewee chooses one loss on which to focus his or her full attention and shares this decision with the interviewer. Once the questioning begins, the interviewee may express a wide range of responses including silence, speech, swearing, and expressing emotions nonverbally through crying or laughing.

The secretary writes down the interviewee's answers as accurately as possible, noting both verbal and nonverbal responses. The interviewee receives these notes at the end of the exercise. It is also possible to use audiotapes, which the secretary records and gives to the interviewee.

The group leader assigns participants their roles, keeps time, and answers questions for the triads as they come up. The leader lets participants know that a wide range of responses is possible and that this is desirable. The leader encourages participants to be curious and to remain as open as possible to what comes up in response to the repeated question.

SIGNIFICANT STATIONS VISITED ON THE SEARCH

Each loss is unique, yet participants in this exercise often access similar emotions and perspectives as they respond to the repeated question, "What is the meaning of this loss?" Certain common responses come up repeatedly, both in the exercise and in the larger context of one's grieving process. I call these the stations of the search for meaning in loss. A station is a particular orientation toward loss; when a person is in one of these stations, it is the focus of his or her attention and emotion. Four stations that I have seen most people move through in the course of their grieving process are remembrance, paradox, personal mortality, and mystery.

Remembrance is a very common response to that repeated question as participants remember and describe their losses and the qualities of their loved ones. Responses of remembrance may involve a range of deep emotions including sadness, humor, anger, guilt, regret, longing, and love. When asked "What is the meaning of this loss?" one woman said,

> My meaning in the moment is filled with a lot of guilt. I can't keep my house the way she did. Her house seemed to have an order about it no matter when I came to visit—an order that I loved and respected. I remember the house vividly. I remember every room, the pillows on the beds in the bedrooms, the pots in the kitchen, and the bathroom so clean.

After another repetition of the question, she had an insight: "Ah, organization, the loss has something to do with organization." And she continued her search. After answering several more repetitions of the question, she became clear that organization served to keep her inner chaos in check so that she could avoid looking at it. Without the organized structure, she became more and more aware of her inner chaos. She found the search frightening at first, but she persevered with courage. By the end of the exercise, she was considering the possibility of individual psychotherapy. The loss helped her to make a commitment to herself and to her own growth.

People visit the station of remembrance often. Remembering the deceased supports "a view of human beings as inveterate meaning-makers, weavers of narratives that give thematic significance to the salient plot structure of their lives" (Doka & Davidson, 1998, p. 227). Telling stories of the deceased is natural, and it can signal the beginning of a new relationship with the deceased. When someone telling stories in the station of remembrance is asked about the meaning of their loss, the repetition leads to deeper searching.

This sometimes requires the psychotherapist to sustain a long holding process as the client recounts the same story over and over. For the client, this attention may become focused intention, so that remembrance becomes a vehicle for meaning.

For example, one young woman in the bereavement group kept repeating the story of her deceased brother's hamster. She told how she took over the hamster's care and how she hated the sounds it made running in its cage, but she could not bear to get rid of the hamster because it represented a part of her brother. She was missing her brother deeply and suffered from depression over

his sudden death. As she repeated her frustration with the hamster, she was asked again, "What is the meaning of this loss?" She broke out laughing for the first time in many months. "This is so silly. This bloody animal running around and around on that Ferris wheel. It's really quite funny." Her eyes lit up. She reconnected with her humor, which she had buried at her brother's death. She remembered the humor that she had shared so frequently with her brother. She missed not only her brother but also the humor they had shared. The hamster story opened the door to her latent humor. She started joking with the group, and we all joined in spontaneous laughter. Recovering her humor was an important meaning in the loss of her brother, and it enlivened her relationship with him. What they had shared together came alive in the moment, and she could share it with others.

Another station that many participants visit is *paradox,* which is the experience of simultaneously holding opposites in one's experience of loss. There is meaning and, at the same time, no meaning. There is a void, and there are multiple meanings that emerge like colors washing over an empty canvas. As one participant said,

> There is a void in my life, nothing there, nothing. [long pause] I try to find purpose in the lessons from her, but nothing comes. [long pause] I miss having her plan the wedding with me. The wedding has even more importance now. It feels strange in the moment to realize how important it has become. I am trying to take time out from business to attend to the important things.

The experience of paradox can help the individual to develop deep insights about living. One client who lost an infant shortly after giving birth to him described this experience:

> My child's spirit just flew out of his body after one hour of holding him and singing to him. It was very painful. I was meeting life through birth and then through death. It might sound strange to hear, but what accompanied the pain was a feeling of exhilaration. This was several years ago, and as I say this in the moment, it is still my truth, along with many other experiences this loss has given us. In fact, when I think of this loss, I often cuddle up with my husband. The loss has taken us through many deep places in ourselves, and we are immensely closer than ever before.

Personal mortality is another frequently visited station. The death of a loved one inescapably reminds us of our own mortality. A woman who had lost her husband suddenly in an automobile accident said, "Now I know I will die, and I also get that I do not have any control over when." Another participant lost several family members during a period of 6 months and became acutely aware of her own mortality. In answer to the repeated question, she replied,

> I am so aware of the possibility of my death, and I am more fearful that everyone is going to die. Life is forever changed. It feels like a big hole. Sometimes, the hole is filled with so much kindness and care from others that I weep from amazement. I never knew people cared that much for me, and now I am letting myself care for others. I don't know when they will die. This fact is motivating me to do and say kind things to others now.

The issue of personal mortality is a favorite literary theme: An individual confronts his or her own death and is transformed. Yalom (1998) cited Tolstoy's story, *The Death of Ivan Ilych:*

> Ivan Ilych, a mean-spirited bureaucrat, develops a fatal illness, probably abdominal cancer, and suffers extraordinary pain. His anguish continues relentlessly until, shortly before his death, Ivan Ilych comes upon a stunning truth: *He is dying badly because he has lived badly.* In the few days remaining to him, Ivan Ilych undergoes a dramatic transformation that is difficult to describe in any other terms than personal growth. If Ivan Ilych were a patient, any psychotherapist would beam with pride at the changes in him: He relates more empathically to others; his chronic bitterness, arrogance, and self-aggrandizement disappear. In short, in the last few days of his life, he achieves a far higher level of integration than he has ever reached previously. (pp. 188-189)

Mystery is another station in the search for meaning in loss. As part of that search for meaning, the individual is moved to ask profound questions such as "Why do people die so young?"; "Why would a loving God let this happen?"; and "Is there a God?" Confronting the mystery of life and death often propels individuals into deeper searches. One participant who recently had lost both of her parents to Alzheimer's disease responded to the repeated question as follows:

> My parents were very attached to their minds. They were bright, and they were slowly losing the use of their minds. This loss was a great teaching for everyone. I have always believed the mind is a function of the spirit, but my parents did not hold this belief. In the process of their dying, we

all experienced firsthand that the spirit is still present even when the mind is almost gone. Mercy and kindness became the dominant presence in our home when they died. Shortly before her death, my mother stated clearly, "Don't label us." I responded, "You are still you," and she heard me. I am deeply grateful that in their process of dying a belief I hold dear also became clear to them.

In the station of mystery, that basic question "What is the meaning of this loss?" often goes unanswered. Or rather, the answer is a silence deeper than words or reason. Participants often drop into deep spaces of compassion for each other during group sharings after the exercise. After one participant shared with another, "I cannot find words to convey to you how deeply and profoundly I feel about the loss of your murdered child," there was a long silence. The entire group held the loss in spontaneous silence. It is not a rational response but rather a compassionate holding of the loss. This holding has a mysterious capacity to open the hearts of all participants, with a profoundly transformative effect on the bereaved.

However and whenever an individual visits the mystery of death, it invites the paradox or the mystery of life. Visiting the mystery of life and death touches the mystery of being human. In the mystical paths of many of the world's great religions (Hillman, 1975; Smith, 1976), the secret of humans' being is acknowledged as a mystery. In Sufi mystical psychology, this secret lies at the center of the heart, and it is humans' intimate relationship with God (Sviri, 1997). Through loss and grief, the individual's mysterious relationship with God (or the absence of such a relationship) enters the world of psychotherapy.

SOME PERSPECTIVES ON THE STATIONS OF LOSS

Pioneering work by Kübler-Ross (1982) presented a model of sequential progression through grief including stages of denial, anger, bargaining, and acceptance. A sequential model is based on an overall progression toward some particular stage as a final integration of the experience of loss. By contrast, the stations of loss are not sequential stages. The stations are not sequential because there is no set order to the client's movement through them, and there is no implication of final integration. The stations of loss are a fluid experience. Outside of this group exercise, in one's ongoing daily life, all of these stations are familiar. A person might find over the years, after someone has died, that he or she might remember and might experience mystery. The person might have all of these experiences. They might repeat themselves, and the person might discover new stations to visit.

Our visits to a particular station are not delimited by time. Within the course of a single psychotherapy session, for example, a client may spend 1 or 2 minutes—or the whole hour or anything in between—at a given station. In the longer view, a person's visits to the various stations may be different during the first few months after a loss than they are as more time passes. But there is no set time frame by which we expect a person to move through a given station, such as during the second quarter hour of the psychotherapy session or 2 to 5 years after the loss.

There is no wrong or right way in which to grieve. Each person moves through the stations at a pace and rhythm uniquely determined by his or her own internal needs. It is a life process propelled by searching. This searching can become a function of opening the heart as one visits and revisits the stations over the years, accessing new meanings along the way.

INDIVIDUAL PSYCHOTHERAPY AND THE REPEATED QUESTION: "WHAT IS THE MEANING OF THIS LOSS?"

I have found it helpful to use this question during individual psychotherapy as well as in group settings. In an ongoing therapist-client relationship, the client can explore more freely without the constraints of a set number of meetings and others being present. I typically use this format toward the middle of the session. I explain the structure and take care that the repetition of the question serves the client's inner searching process. My decision to use this question balances intuition and discernment; I do not want to objectify the client's genuine work with a mechanically repeated question. This process has continually deepened clients' inner searching. For example, one client who had lost her grandfather found that she wanted to go to church with her husband and child:

> I've never taken church seriously until now. As I reflect on his death and its meaning, the rituals of the funeral service keep coming to me. I was so profoundly moved by the funeral service. I want this outer form of religion in my family's life.

After the exercise, this woman used the remainder of the session to explore her spiritual beliefs in greater depth.

LIVING THE STATIONS OF LOSS

I now invite the reader to explore his or her own loss. Examine the wheel in Figure 34.1. Think of the stations as the spokes of this wheel. At the center of the wheel is the heart, opening more and more as it visits and revisits the stations. There is no set order or sequence to this process; how often you visit each station and how long you spend there are determined by the unique interplay of your own loss with the makeup of your own being. As you experience your loss on new levels and come to grips with its meaning in your life, you might discover new meanings and new depths to these stations. It is also possible that you will discover new stations on your own unique journey.

IN PASSING

Until the past decade, there had been a tendency in psychology to downplay the exploration of meaning in loss or even the concept of loss itself. "Death is un-American," as Toynbee (1969, p. 131) wrote more than three decades ago. And even when grief is accepted, there are cultural expectations to consider. As Charmaz (1997) observed, "Not all grief is acceptable. Not everyone's grief is acknowledged. Not every survivor copes with grief successfully" (p. 229).

Psychology is on the verge of exploring the mystery of life and death, and this chapter is a contribution to such an exploration. Psychology has come a long way in acknowledging grief and its many dimensions. One of the challenges facing psychology is in acknowledging the spiritual dimensions of the searching process. Can we remain open to accompany our clients into the depths of their hearts? What if this journey becomes a mystical journey? If so, then how are we personally and professionally prepared? I invite the reader to search for his or her own answers to these questions.

I have written this chapter for all of the individuals who have courageously searched for meaning in their losses. In spite of judgment from their selves and others, these

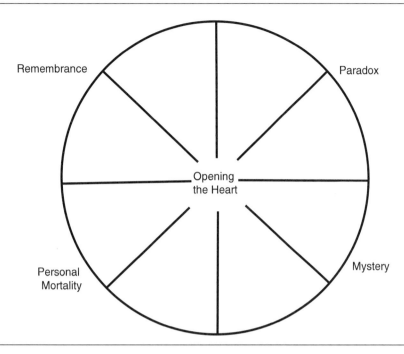

Figure 34.1. Stations of Loss

individuals searched and spoke out so as to be heard. They have gained through their losses, and I thank each and every one of them.

My dog died as I was finishing this chapter. My 13-year-old son, like me and my husband, was overcome with grief. He bent over and covered his face with his hands. I had great compassion for my son, torn between the depth of his loss and the societal admonitions about men and tears, which are particularly powerful for males on the verge of adolescence. I gently took his hands in mine and said, "You love your dog and now he's gone; it's okay to let others see how much you care." So, my son raised his head and wept openly, along with his father and me. All three of us were united in our loss and in our awe of the ancient mystery of life and death. Our dog's presence has touched my heart many times, and his passing has opened it to a new depth of compassion that carries a wealth of meanings, some known and some unknown.

There is never an end to the search for the meaning of loss. There is a continual opening.

NOTE

1. To protect the identities of the clients mentioned in this chapter, all clients are disguised and all statements attributed to them are paraphrased.

REFERENCES

Albom, M. (1997). *Tuesdays with Morrie.* New York, NY: Doubleday.

Bugental, J. F. T. (1981). *The search for authenticity: An existential-analytic approach to psychotherapy* (2nd ed.). New York: Irvington.

Bugental, J. F. T. (1984, October). *Psychotherapy with tragedy survivors: An existential-humanistic perspective.* Paper presented at the meeting of the Association of Pediatric Oncology Social Workers, San Francisco.

Bugental, J. F. T. (1987). *The art of the psychotherapist.* New York: Norton.

Bugental, J. F. T., & Kleiner, R. (1993). Existential psychotherapies. In G. Stricker & J. Gold (Eds.), *Comprehensive handbook of psychotherapy integration* (pp. 101-112). New York: Plenum.

Camus, A. (1955). *An absurd reasoning: The myth of Sisyphus and other essays* (J. O'Brien, Trans.). New York: Vintage. (Original work published 1942)

Charmaz, K. (1997). Grief and loss of self. In K. Charmaz, G. Howarth, & A. Kellehear (Eds.), *The unknown country: Death in Australia, Britain, and the U.S.A.* (pp. 229-241). New York: St. Martin's.

Coles, R. (1990). *Spiritual life of children.* Boston: Houghton Mifflin.

Doka, K., & Davidson, J. (Eds.). (1998). *Living with grief: Who we are, how we grieve.* Philadelphia: Hospice Foundation of America.

Elkins, D. (1998). *Beyond religion.* Wheaton, IL: Theosophical Publishing.

Frankl, V. E. (1958, September 13). The search for meaning. *Saturday Review,* p. 20.

Frankl, V. E. (1963). *Man's search for meaning* (I. Lasch, Trans.). Boston: Beacon. (Original work published 1959)

Fredriksson, L. (1998). The caring conversation: Talking about suffering—A hermeneutic phenomenological study in psychiatric nursing. *International Journal of Human Caring, 2*(1), 24-31.

Gendlin, E. T. (1982). *Focusing.* New York: Bantam Books.

Hillman, J. (1975). *Re-visioning psychology.* New York: Harper & Row.

Jourard, S. M. (1971). *The transparent self: Self-disclosure and well-being* (2nd ed.). New York: John Wiley.

Kübler-Ross, E. (1982). *Living with death and dying.* New York: Macmillan.

May, R. (1953). *Man's search for himself.* New York: Norton.

Rehak, M. (1999, March 14). Elegy: Upon mourning. *The New York Times Sunday Magazine,* p. 19.

Slowchower, J. (1996). Holding and the fate of the analyst's subjectivity. *Psychoanalytic Dialogues, 6,* 323-353.

Smith, H. (1976). *Forgotten truth: The primordial tradition.* New York: Harper & Row.

Sviri, S. (1997). *The taste of hidden things.* Inverness, CA: Golden Sufi Center.

Tillich, P. (1952). *The courage to be.* New Haven, CT: Yale University Press.

Toynbee, A. (1969). Changing attitudes toward death in the modern Western world. In A. Toynbee, A. K. Mann, N. Smart, J. Hinton, S. Yudkin, E. Rhode, R. Hewood, & H. H. Price (Eds.), *Man's concern with death.* New York: McGraw-Hill.

Welwood, J. (1982). The unfolding experience: Psychotherapy and beyond. *Journal of Humanistic Psychology, 22*(1), 91-104.

Yalom, I. D. (1980). *Existential psychotherapy.* New York: Basic Books.

Yalom, I. D. (1998). *The Yalom reader.* New York: Basic Books.

Yalom, I. D., & Lieberman, M. (1991). Bereavement and heightened existential awareness. *Psychiatry, 54,* 334-345.

CHAPTER 35

Existential Analysis
and Humanistic Psychotherapy

JOHN ROWAN

WHAT EXACTLY is the relationship between existential analysis and humanistic psychotherapy? I want to raise this issue because I feel hurt, misunderstood, and even traduced when I see existential writers getting humanistic work wrong. And this they often do. Let me just give one typical quote here and insert other quotes in italic indented form later as illustrations:

> Humanistic approaches perceive humans as basically positive creatures who develop constructively, given the right conditions. The existential position is that people may evolve in any direction, good or bad, and that only reflection on what constitutes good and bad makes it possible to exercise one's choice in the matter. The humanistic

counselor might simply seek to encourage the client in the exploration of her potential. She will feel confident that increased awareness of the internal process will be a gain and will lead to growth and positive change. The existential counselor is less certain of human goodness, and she will count on people's weakness as well as on their strengths. Cultivation of intense emotional release is not an aim of the existential approach. Neither is the frantic reorganization of an individual's living conditions. The existential counselor will be wary of the client's sudden bursts of self-righteous decision making. (van Deurzen-Smith, 1988, pp. 56-57)

This seems to me quite wildly out of keeping with my experience of humanistic approaches,

AUTHOR'S NOTE: An earlier version of this chapter (Rowan's essay and Spinelli's reply) appeared in the *Journal of the Society for Existential Analysis*, Vol. 10, No. 1, pp. 44-71.

and it gets worse as it goes along. I think that any decent therapist would be suspicious of "frantic reorganization of an individual's living conditions" and equally wary of "sudden bursts of self-righteous decision making." This is just prejudicial made-up stuff with no good foundation of which I am aware. But, as can be seen in more detail in the italic indented quotes scattered throughout this chapter, it is typical of an ongoing tendency that, it seems to me, is still growing up among people committed to existentialist philosophy. It seems to say that existentialism gave rise to a perfectly legitimate form of psychotherapy, variously called *Dasein* analysis, existential analysis, existential-phenomenological psychotherapy, and so on. This approach has become enshrined in the work of the Society for Existential Analysis. From this standpoint, humanistic psychotherapy is criticized by such writers as Spinelli (1989, 1994) and van Deurzen-Smith (1988, 1997); indeed, Spinelli has spent many pages critiquing the approaches emanating from humanistic psychology. According to these critics, humanistic psychology is too optimistic and too prone to dilute the pure essence of existentialism with other and baser materials.

HUMANISTIC PSYCHOTHERAPY IS EXISTENTIAL

In this chapter, I endeavor to reverse this critique and say that humanistic psychotherapy, in all its variants (for a brief account, see Rowan, 1992; for a fuller account, see Rowan, 1998) is the real home of existentialism as a praxis, doing justice to all that it has to offer. Existential analysis, on the other hand, is a heresy, a cult, or a sideshow by comparison, cruelly limiting itself by not using the range of interventions made possible by the endeavors of humanistic practitioners. If we were to draw a Venn diagram of the relationship between humanistic psychotherapy and existential analysis, people such as those mentioned, as well as Yalom (1980) and Cohn (1997), would draw two circles side by side with an overlap between them. For them, the overlap would be quite small. But what I want to argue here is that the overlap is so large as to put into question the whole idea of separating the two. In other words, I am suggesting that we should talk all the time about existential-humanistic psychotherapy. Perhaps the reasons why they became so separate are historical; existential writers saw the excesses that humanistic psychology got into during the 1960s and early 1970s and did not want to be tarred with the same brush. Be that as it may, humanistic psychotherapy today is as respectable as any other and can be approached without any qualms. Let me give you 12 reasons why I think this is so.

1. The Heartland of Humanistic Practice

Most of the schools of humanistic psychotherapy claim some use of existentialism or phenomenology or both. Gestalt therapy claims to be a true existential form of therapy, and Clarkson (1989) said that phenomenology is "the philosophical approach which is at the very heart of Gestalt" (p. 13). Psychodrama also has claims to be existential. Brazier (1991) said, "Psychodrama evolved from the existential approach to psychotherapy of Jacob Levi Moreno. Although it is possible to graft psychodramatic methods onto other philosophical approaches, the method is primarily attuned to an existential outlook" (p. 1). Person-centered therapy again has existential roots and important basic statements based in phenomenology, as both du Plock (1996, p. 44) and Spinelli (1990, p. 19) have testified. Perhaps most of all, we can turn to Bugental as an exemplar, as we will see later.

Heidegger's philosophy can give rise to an unjustified optimism, and it could be interpreted as the foundation of an enthusiastic humanism. Indeed, some of the human potential movement is based on simplistic interpretations of Heideggerian and Sartrian notions taken to their most absurd degree of self-assertiveness and voluntarism. (van Deurzen-Smith, 1997, p. 42)

Also much influenced by existentialism is Mahrer, one of the great theoreticians of humanistic psychology but one never mentioned by van Deurzen-Smith or Spinelli, perhaps because Mahrer just published his great masterwork *Experiencing* during the late 1970s (Mahrer, 1978/1989), and they prefer to quote people such as Maslow, who was well dead by then. So, that is my first point—the way in which existentialism and phenomenology are regarded as the heartland of the main approaches within the humanistic milieu. The reason why this identity is so important is well described by Wilber (1981, chap. 8) in his discussion of what he called the Centaur stage of psychospiritual development. He outlined what he called a full-spectrum approach to states of consciousness and theories of the self, and he put the existential and the humanistic in the same bracket. They actually share the same broad worldview, and they both adopt "vision-logic" rather than earlier forms of formal rationality (for a full discussion of vision-logic, see Wilber, 1995, chap. 5).

2. The Poverty of Existential Analysis Alone

Existential analysis without humanistic psychotherapy is robbed of some important resources. It is narrow and dogmatic, as is *Dasein* analysis. To abjure all active interventions is to constrict possibilities too much. Humanistic psychotherapy brings a dimension of experiential depth and aliveness that seems lacking in the rather formalized and psychoanalytically shaded existentialism of Europe. For example, suppose that a client is continually talking about his mother. An immediate humanistic response could be to point to an empty chair and say, "See if you can imagine your mother sitting on that chair, looking the way she looked, breathing the way she breathed, wearing what she used to wear. What would you like to say directly to her?" Another humanistic response could be to pick up one sentence that seemed to carry more emotional weight than the others and invite the client to repeat it several times, perhaps louder than before. Another could be to say something like the following: "I notice that every time you mention your mother, your right foot jerks. See if you can exaggerate that movement. What comes to mind when you do that?" There is nothing unexistential about any of this; in fact, I would argue that it is more existential in the sense of digging deeper into the present moment and making the issue more acutely present. There is a paradox here: Techniques work only when they are not techniques, that is, when they emerge naturally and spontaneously from the work itself. As Walkenstein (1975) put it so well,

> I got close enough, pushed close enough, so that Arthur felt contact with another human being. I was not a robot giving him tried-and-true ready-made formulas, but [I] pushed always toward discovering and then affirming whatever feelings or thoughts were emerging from Arthur. I was often unaware of where I was leading or where he was leading, and I was willing to follow a direction, *to make mistakes*, and to change any direction that seemed to lead to a dead

end—or even to go to the dead end and see what we could discover there. (p. 96)

Nor are these the only types of technique used in humanistic work. There is also the approach of Mahrer and others in the experiential tradition (Greenberg, Watson, & Lietaer, 1998) involving a real attempt to enter much more fully into the psychological world of the other person. Of course, all the usual rules of human intercourse apply, for example, not saying things before the other person is ready to hear them.

Some existential therapists do use humanistic methods from time to time, but they do not talk about these in their theoretical pronouncements. For example, in the case study offered by Strasser about "Bernadette," he said, "After many challenges and reiterating that my advice was not part of our contract, I asked her to put herself in my position and to try to answer her own questions" (cited in du Plock, 1997, p. 32). This is, of course, a typical move in Gestalt therapy, but one that is not often mentioned in expositions of existential-phenomenological theory. Yet, I do not know why it should not be. In Yalom (1991), we find a whole range of techniques, so much so that van Deurzen-Smith (1997) reeled back and accused him of being "psychiatric and behavioral." Yet elsewhere, Deurzen-Smith and others (Milton, 1997; Roberts, 1997) acknowledged that Yalom has made some genuine contributions to the existential understanding of psychotherapy. This double standard also applies to some other writers, such as May and Bugental; sometimes they are in, and sometimes they are out.

3. Not Just Abraham Maslow and Carl Rogers

People involved in existentialism and phenomenology habitually misconstrue and dismiss humanistic psychology as consisting exclusively of the works of Maslow and Rogers. Even then, they generally underestimate Rogers and ignore much of his work. Take Spinelli's (1994) book, for example. His critique of the humanistic approach suffered from being too narrow. He seemed to think that Rogers is about the only humanistic therapist who matters, and he quoted Corey's (1991) book, *Theory and Practice of Counselling and Psychotherapy,* very often in support of his points. I do not know when Corey became an authority on humanistic psychology. What I do know is that it is a mistake to ignore people such as Bohart (1993), Bugental (1987), Mahrer (1996), May (1983), and Schneider (1995, 1999), who have just as much right to be considered part of the heartland of humanistic psychotherapy as does Rogers. Hardly any of Spinelli's (1994) critique applied to these writers, and in fact, all of them work in a way that is close to Spinelli's own. The separation that Spinelli made between the humanistic and the existential-phenomenological was not quite real. The whole school of experiential psychotherapy, an important section of the humanistic camp (Bohart, 1995; Greenberg et al., 1998), is highly compatible with Spinelli's own views, but in his critique he did not seem to have heard of it.

Bugental told me not long ago that he would add some others such as Krippner, Serlin, and Greening. One has only to pick up back copies of the *Journal of Humanistic Psychology* at random to find many such articles making use of existentialism and phenomenology, on the one hand, and humanistic practice, on the other.

While person-centered therapists generally believe that they suspend to a great extent their personal judgments of their clients, they do so against the background of a theory of human being which holds that humans are innately disposed to express their potential and that change in the direction of expressing this potential—of self-actualizing—is central to the therapeutic process. It should be clear on even brief consideration that there are problems with this stance. First, the underlying assumption of person-centered and other humanistic therapies that humans "naturally" grow and develop and struggle to do so, even in the face of adverse environmental conditions, does not stand up to close scrutiny since, while all living things struggle to live, there is no reason to believe that they evince a predisposition of self-actualization. (du Plock, 1996, p. 44)

May is another founding member of the Association for Humanistic Psychology who has made particularly important contributions to our understanding of existential ways of thinking in respect to psychotherapy. His book, *The Discovery of Being* (May, 1983), is full of wisdom on the praxis of psychotherapy. Consider the following:

My thesis here is that we can understand repression, for example, only on the deeper level of the meaning of the human being's potentialities. In this respect, "being" is to be defined as the individual's "pattern of potentialities." These potentialities will be partly shared with other persons but will, in every case, form a unique pattern in each individual. We must ask the questions: What is this person's relation to his own potentialities? What goes on that he chooses or is forced to choose to block off from his awareness something which he

knows, and on another level *knows that he knows?* (p. 17)

I do not know what that sounds like to the reader, but it sounds like existentialism to me. In fact, it is an odd fact that although the existentialist writers (e.g., Spinelli, 1994; van Deurzen-Smith, 1997) often dismiss May as not really being a true existentialist, they often quote him as if he were.

This emphasis on the boundaries of human existence is typical of the existential perspective. It is frequently ignored in the humanistic orientation, which nevertheless prides itself on its existential roots. The humanistic stance puts the accent on human freedom and choice at the expense of a healthy recognition of its counterpart of necessity and determinism. A decidedly existential approach will always include a thorough consideration of realities, limitations, and consequences. A serious analysis of the human condition cannot fail to notice constraints as well as liberties. The humanistic arrogance which believes mankind to be the center of the universe and which encourages a blind pursuit of individual rights and freedom can only lead to disaster. (van Deurzen-Smith, 1988, p. 12)

The point is that self-actualization is an optimistic doctrine in Maslow and Rogers but that it also exists (albeit not as an optimistic doctrine) in May, Mahrer, Bugental, and others. Mahrer (1989) included a 42-page chapter examining the whole notion of actualization in some detail and said things such as the following: "From our perspective, there is nothing of value in 'expressing basic drives.' What is of value is the actualization of deeper potentials which are *integrated*" (p. 563). Making links with other writers in the field, he also said,

> This process of increasing depth and breadth of experiencing has been described as the bringing into being of the person's own complement of motivations (Maslow, 1970) or unique pattern of possibilities (May, 1958). Boss (1963 [p. 15]) speaks of the person's becoming in actuality what is within as a potential. (p. 566)

These are important connections to be making.

4. *James Bugental*

Bugental was the first president of the Association for Humanistic Psychology and still is a member in good standing. Bugental's (1981) statement was as follows: "Phenomenology and existentialism are, to my mind, alternative and supplementing perspectives available to humanistic psychology" (p. 10). He also said,

> For me, the truest existentialism is humanistic, and the soundest humanism is existential. The two are not the same, but their overlap is rich in potential for greater understanding of human experience and for greater effectiveness in the effort to enrich that experience. (p. 10)

Bugental calls his approach *existential-humanistic psychotherapy.* He has written a number of books including *The Search for Existential Identity,* all about patient-therapist dialogue (Bugental, 1976); *Psychotherapy and Process,* his main theoretical book (Bugental, 1978); *The Search for Au-*

thenticity (Bugental, 1981); and *The Art of the Psychotherapist* (Bugental, 1987). In the latter book, he listed his own set of "givens" to compare to those offered by Yalom: *embodiedness* (implying change), *finitude* (implying contingency), *ability to act or not act* (implying responsibility), *choicefulness* (implying relinquishment), and *separate-but-relatedness* (implying being at once a part of and apart from another person). In a later work (Bugental & Sterling, 1995), he added *awareness* (implying self-consciousness). Bugental (1981) said the following:

> The existential point of view speaks of man's condition in a fashion that transcends the dichotomy of pathology and health. Increasingly today, we are recognizing that this dichotomy, while having once served a humane purpose, confounds our thinking and restricts our inventiveness. (p. 17)

Bugental is one of the most important voices in the humanistic field, and we refer to him often. It is intriguing to find that he is on the editorial board of the *Journal of the Society for Existential Analysis* in England as well as the *Journal of Humanistic Psychology* in the United States.

5. *Presence*

Bugental has often referred to the idea of *presence* in psychotherapy. It is actually the nearest thing in the English language to the German word *Dasein* that is so important in existentialism.

> Presence is immensely more than just being there physically, it is obvious. It's being totally in the situation. . . . Presence is being there in body, in emotions, in relating, in thoughts, in every way. . . . Although fun-

damentally presence is a unitary process or characteristic of a person in a situation, accessibility and expressiveness may be identified as its two chief aspects. (Bugental, 1978, pp. 36-37)

He also cautioned, however, that presence is not easy to attain. Certainly, it is not a state to be once achieved and thereafter maintained. "Rather, it is a goal continually sought, often ignored, and always important to the work of psychotherapy" (Bugental & Sterling, 1995, p. 231). He claimed that it is important for any form of psychotherapy but that it is absolutely central for existential work.

May agrees. He drew attention to the way in which Jaspers and Binswanger emphasized the importance of presence and to the way in which Rogers also referred to it quite unmistakably. May (1983) went so far as to say, "Any therapist is existential to the extent that, with all his technical training and his knowledge of transference and dynamisms, he is still able to relate to the patient as 'one existence communicating with another,' to use Binswanger's phrase" (p. 158). And he said that one of the most important things for any therapist is to be aware of whatever blocks the ability to be fully present. This is a real challenge, and one well worth meeting. "The therapist's function is to *be there* (with all of the connotations of *Dasein*), present in the relationship, while the patient finds and learns to live out his own *Eigenwelt*" (p. 163).

6. Gestalt Therapy

People in the field of existential analysis often are ignorant of the recent work in Gestalt, which has roots in existentialism and phenomenology and which lays much more stress on the paradoxical theory of change than it does on techniques as such.

While this [Gestalt therapy] may seem to be a far more directive technique than that associated with phenomenologically derived approaches, the aims of Gestalt therapy—the encouragement of acknowledging responsibility for one's subjective experience, self-acceptance, and reintegration— are essentially the same as those of phenomenological therapies. However, its optimistic stance on human nature, its emphasis on liberation, and the high degree of active intervention on the part of the therapist remain major (if implicit) sources of division between the two approaches. (Spinelli, 1989, pp. 161-162)

The paradoxical theory of change was first brought to my notice in a chapter by Beisser (1972) written when he was director of psychiatric training at the Metropolitan State Hospital. He invited Fritz Perls to demonstrate his work and became very much involved with Gestalt therapy himself. Beisser advanced the theory that change does not happen through a "coercive attempt by the individual or by another person to change him" but does happen if the person puts in the time and effort to be "what he is," that is, "to be fully in his current position" (p. 88). When the therapist rejects the change agent role, change that is orderly and also meaningful is possible. Beisser said, and put in italics, the following summary statement: *"That change occurs when one becomes what he is, not when he tries to become what he is not"* (p. 88). This seems to me to be a good statement of an existential position, and recent Gestaltists such as Yontef endorse it completely.

The view held by many humanistic practitioners that the world is ours to manipulate and that it should, like a machine, be perfectible is anathema to existentialism, which warns against this attitude since it may lead so easily to objectification of human beings and a belief that they can be repaired or perfected by some intervention, whether physical or psychological. (du Plock, 1996, p. 49)

Yontef (1993) himself put it this way:

Gestalt therapy's phenomenological work is done through a relationship based on the existential model of Martin Buber's (1968) *I and Thou.* By that model, a person involves himself fully and intensely with the person or task at hand, each treated as a thou, an end in itself, and not as an 'it', thing, or means to an end. A relationship develops when two people, each with his separate existence and personal needs, contact each other recognizing and allowing the differences between them. (p. 189)

It does not seem to me to be at all true that, as du Plock (1996) rather cruelly put it, "The Gestalt counter to these problems seems to be to have a foot in every theoretical camp and to hop about as required" (p. 46). This can only be the remark of someone who has not kept up with the recent writing on the subject in the Gestalt journals and books.

7. R. D. Laing

An interesting case to look at is that of Laing. Many people think of him as a classic existentialist therapist. Certainly, most people who came into contact with his work seemed to come to the conclusion that he was an amazingly effective therapist, particularly with the most disturbed people. Of course, the existentialist writers in this country have cast doubt on his existentialist credentials. Van Deurzen-Smith (1997) said that Laing was really a Winnicottian, Thompson (1997) said that he was really a skeptic, and Cohn (1997) said that he was really an essentialist (not an existentialist). But all seem to agree that in his work, Laing came across as a classic example of the authentic person, that is, the person who could really be there and who had this quality of presence (as described earlier) that is the key to good psychotherapy. To me, that makes him an existentialist as well as what Spinelli (1989, chap. 7) at least accepts as a phenomenologist. Actually, Laing took the idea of presence much further than most, as the following quotation reveals:

Near the end of his life, Laing often talked about the practice of co-presence. He defined it as the practice of nonintrusive attentiveness, a wholesome concern for each other's life and death. He wrote, "Terror of each other spells the extinction of each other. Communion is mutual extinction of mutual terror. It is joy in, celebration of our co-existence in this world we share, co-presence, our beings being together, completely, as we are." Co-presence, then, is being together lovingly. (Feldmar, 1997, p. 350)

This seems to take existentialist thinking one step further in the field of therapy. It is interesting, therefore, to find that Laing made significant links with humanistic psychology. Laing himself attended several conferences of the European Association for Humanistic Psychology, and at one point he almost became its president. His later work on rebirthing was very close to my own practice in primal integration.

8. *Kurt Goldstein*

One of the most fascinating links between phenomenology and humanistic psychology is a man who is not well known to many. Goldstein was born in 1878 in Upper Silesia of Jewish origins and educated at Breslau and Heidelberg. Here he came into contact with the phenomenological ideas of Husserl, which influenced him very much. He was also familiar with the works of Heidegger and Merleau-Ponty. He became a neurologist and psychiatrist, and in 1914 he joined the staff of the Institute for Brain-Injured Soldiers, which was working on the aftereffects of brain injuries.

In 1926, Perls worked with Goldstein at the institute and was strongly influenced toward the importance of viewing the human organism as a whole rather than as a conglomeration of disparately functioning parts. Goldstein taught Perls that the organism was an indivisible totality, and Gestalt therapy took a great deal from phenomenology. Frieda Fromm-Reichmann, the well-known psychoanalytic psychiatrist, also worked there for a time.

Goldstein then moved on to work at the Frankfurt Neurological Institute, where he met Sigmund Heinrich Foulkes, who was so influential in forming the ideas of group analysis, many of which were also adopted by existential group workers (Cohn, 1997). Goldstein in particular gave him the notion of a network, which he used to such good effect. Goldstein's ideas later were dis-cussed by Spiegelberg (1972) in relation to phenomenology.

In 1927, Goldstein helped to found the International Society for Psychotherapy. In 1934, he brought out a book expounding his mature views on the relations between general and localized brain functions. An English translation of this book was published in 1939 under the title *The Organism* (Goldstein, 1939/1995). In 1935, he emigrated to the United States and taught at Columbia University and Tufts Medical School. During 1938-1939, Goldstein delivered the William James lectures at Harvard University, published in 1940 under the title *Human Nature: In the Light of Psychopathology.*

Goldstein's work substantially influenced Rogers, May, Perls, Mahrer, and Maslow. Maslow met him in New York during the late 1930s and dedicated one of his books to Goldstein. Maslow got from Goldstein much confirmation of an approach that was holistic, functional, dynamic, and purposive rather than atomistic, taxonomic, static, and mechanical. It was Goldstein who first used the term *self-actualization,* using it in his studies of how brain-injured soldiers reorganize their capacities after injury.

Goldstein's key insight was to see that a damaged organism, in its struggle for survival, reorganizes itself into a new unit that incorporates the damage. The organism is active, generating and restoring itself in the direction of self-actualization. Goldstein spoke of a good feeling of increased tension or excitement when actualization is occurring.

Goldstein refused to agree that the body came before the mind. In his view, personality processes enter in fully right from the beginning, so that the initial bodily *reception* to intrusive external agents is itself psychological. So, everything is fully open to psychological description including the amount, location, and type of bodily damage. Later, Mahrer (1989) took up this idea and elaborated on it.

Rogers wrote that Goldstein enriched his thinking, mentioning specifically the "actualizing tendency" or "growth hypothesis" (DeCarvalho, 1991, chap. 7). May interpreted Goldstein's thinking in an existential context, making some criticism of that part of the approach that seemed to be saying that self-actualization was somehow automatic. Bugental referred to Goldstein as a pioneer of humanistic psychology because of his insistence on the uniqueness of the individual at a time when the psychology of behaviorism paid no attention to such things. Mahrer liked Goldstein's emphasis on the wholeness of the person but did not like the assumption that self-actualization was almost bound to happen. Mahrer thought that it required real choice. His most recent book (Mahrer, 1996) showed exactly how this works in the field of experiential psychotherapy. So, Goldstein forms an interesting connection between humanistic psychology in its various forms and phenomenology in its various forms.

9. The Importance of Authenticity

Existential principles are fully embodied in most of the forms of humanistic psychotherapy including person-centered, Gestalt, psychodrama, and experiential therapies; primal integration; radical therapy; feminist therapy; several body therapies; and dream work. They are very much at home there, contributing essentially to the humanistic emphasis on the whole person and the authentic relationship. The humanistic view of authenticity is broader and more inclusive than that found in existential analysis, and this seems to be because those who hold hard to existentialism in an exclusive way

are much too wedded to Heidegger's notions. Van Deurzen-Smith (1997), for example, said, "Being anxious because of our acute awareness of our human limitations and mortality is therefore the key to authenticity and with it the key to true humanity" (p. 39). This one-sided emphasis on death and destruction is just what is wrong with existential analysis in its understanding of authenticity. Compare it to the formulations of Bugental, who has written two books about authenticity. Bugental said that authenticity is a combination of self-respect (we are not just part of an undifferentiated world) and self-enactment (we express our care or involvement in the world in a visible way). Following is a key quotation:

> By authenticity, I mean a central genuineness and awareness of being. Authenticity is that presence of an individual in his living in which he is fully aware in the present moment, in the present situation. Authenticity is difficult to convey in words, but experientially it is readily perceived in ourselves or in others. (Bugental, 1981, p. 102)

In other words, what we in humanistic psychology are saying is that authenticity is an experience.

This is precisely what Cohn (1997) denied, and from this I conclude that Cohn never has experienced authenticity as I understand it. I believe that people who deny the existence or importance of the real self, as Cohn does, are people who never have had experiences of their real selves. This means that they can talk about freedom, but they cannot act freedom. As May (1979) said so well, "Freedom is a quality of action of the centered self" (p. 176). The humanistic view is that action is the acid test of experience.

It is surprising to me that therapists as astute as Carl Rogers appear to have failed to see, much less seriously considered, the directive and potentially abusive features contained in their stance concerning the "real self." In not doing so, they have, however inadvertently, promoted the development of one more model that limits the client's possibilities of being and [that] lumbers important aspects of human-ist[ic] philosophy with an assumption that is difficult to defend. This is particularly galling given the oft-stated claims of humanistic theorists such as Rogers and Perls that their models are founded on existential phenomenology. (Spinelli, 1994, p. 270)

What seems so hard to convey to existential writers is that the real self—the self that is to be actualized in self-actualization—is not a concept but rather an experience. It is not something to be argued at a philosophical level; it is something to be encountered at an experiential level. What we are saying, in effect, is that existential analysis actually is a heresy within humanistic psychotherapy. It tries to deny the existence of the real self. It adopts a notion of authenticity that is flawed in a fundamental way. If it says that authenticity is merely "an openness to existence, an acceptance of what is given, as well as our freedom to respond to it" (Cohn, 1997, p. 127), then there is no way of perceiving authenticity; it becomes an abstract and useless concept. Other existentialists have gone much further, as the following example indicates:

Authenticity consists in having a true and lucid consciousness of the situation, in as-

suming the responsibilities and risks that it involves, in accepting it in pride or humiliation [and] sometimes in horror and hate. There is no doubt that authenticity demands much courage and more than courage. Thus, it is not surprising that one finds it so rarely. (Sartre, 1948, p. 90)

It demands so much because it involves moving beyond the confines of the familiar mental ego, but this is what Heidegger never envisaged. To get away from the abstract argument, let us take a concrete example. It comes from a book by Wheelis titled *The Desert* and was excerpted as follows:

Look at the wretched people huddled in line for the gas chambers at Auschwitz. If they do anything other than move on quietly, they will be clubbed down. Where is freedom?. . . . But wait. Go back in time, enter the actual event, the very moment: They are thin and weak, and they smell; hear the weary shuffling steps, the anguished catch of breath, the clutch of hand. Enter now the head of one hunched and limping man. The line moves slowly; a few yards ahead begin the steps down. He sees the sign, someone whispers "showers," but he knows what happens here. He is struggling with a choice: to shout "Comrades! They will kill you! Run!"—or to say nothing. This option, in the few moments remaining, is his whole life. If he shouts, he dies now, painfully; if he moves on silently, he dies but minutes later. Looking back on him in time and memory, we find the moment poignant but the freedom negligible. It makes no difference in that situation, his election of daring or of inhibition. Both are futile, without consequence. History sees no freedom for him, notes only constraint, labels him victim. But in the consciousness of that one man, it makes great difference whether or not he experiences the choice.

For if he knows the constraint and nothing else, if he thinks "Nothing is possible," then he is living his necessity; but if, perceiving the constraint, he turns from it to a choice between two possible courses of action, then—however he chooses—he is living his freedom. This commitment to freedom can extend to the last breath. (Wheelis, 1972, pp. 286-287)

For humanistic psychotherapy, authenticity is a direct experience of the real self. It is unmistakable and self-authenticating. It is a true experience of freedom and of liberation. We have already heard what Bugental said about it. And that is not all.

The debate between humanists and existentialists on the meaning of "authenticity" is important here. Humanists think it is about self-assertive living—being true to the essential self. Existential therapists consider authenticity to be about being open and truthful to life: accepting its limitations and boundaries and allowing it to manifest as fully as possible through one's own transparency. The result of such an approach as utilized in much humanistic therapy, and especially in the human potential movement, is that everybody loses; those with access to individual therapy become more egotistical, less connected to the wider society, and therefore more isolated from reality, while the poor and otherwise disadvantaged end up labeled as under-achievers. (du Plock, 1996, p. 57)

There is an important link between authenticity and genuineness as described by Rogers.

It is my feeling that congruence is a part of existential authenticity, that the person who is genuinely authentic in his being-in-the-world is congruent within himself; and to the extent that one attains authentic being in his life, to that extent is he congruent. (Bugental, 1981, p. 108)

Again, it takes Bugental to draw our attention to the heartland of the humanistic approach, which is also the heartland of the existential approach. Both Bugental and Rogers are clear that congruence is difficult and demanding, and recent writers such as Mearns (1994, 1996, 1997) have made it clear that it cannot be taught as a skill. It really is very curious to see how someone like Spinelli can go along with all this and then somehow draw back at the last moment. Consider the following quote:

As *authentic* beings, we recognize our individuality. Further, we recognize that this individuality is not a static quality but is, rather, a set of (possibly infinite) potentialities. As such, while in the authentic mode, we maintain an independence of thought and action and subsequently feel "in charge" of the way our [lives are] experienced. Rather than reacting as victims to the vicissitudes of being, we, as authentic beings, acknowledge our role in determining our actions, thought[s], and beliefs and thereby experience a stronger and fuller sense of integration, acceptance, "openness," and "aliveness" to the potentialities of being-in-the-world. (Spinelli, 1989, p. 109)

I could not have put it better myself. It is difficult for me to see how he can go along with so much of the humanistic view of the matter and yet not quite be able to adopt the label of *humanistic*.

10. *The Labeling of Mental Disorders*

Again, there is a great deal of agreement here. It is true that the older existential writers accepted notions of mental illnesses and the nomenclature of mental diseases. But those writing today do not go along with this. I remember Laing being so skeptical about the value of the *Diagnostic and Statistical Manual of Mental Disorders (DSM-IV)* (American Psychiatric Association, 1994) that he gave excruciatingly funny lectures on the subject. Similarly, most humanistic psychotherapists do not give much weight to central notions of mental illness and the standard nomenclature and, indeed, question them quite vigorously. Thus, humanistic psychotherapists adhere to the same existential principles as do the orthodox existential writers. This is brought out well in the work of Cohn (1997), who dealt first with the older writers but then, speaking in his own voice, stated the existential and humanistic case very well in his four points on assessment:

(1) The client you meet as the therapist is the client who meets you. There is no client *as such*. If two therapists meet the same client, it is not the same client. (2) What the client tells you as the therapist, she or he tells only you. She or he may tell another therapist something quite different. (3) There is no "history" to be taken, for there is no history *as such*. A client's history is disclosed in the process of interaction between therapist and client. (4) This means that there cannot be an "assessment" as this would imply an objective situation independent of time, place, and the contribution of the assessing therapist. (pp. 33-34)

This excellent statement of the humanistic view seems to me to be authentic existentialism. And incidentally, it agrees very much with the position taken by Mahrer (1996) in the first chapter of his book. The existential-humanistic view is that one cannot diagnose humans, and using the word *assessment* does not improve matters.

11. *Theory Versus Practice*

Existentialists are very good at describing the principles behind good psychotherapy, but they are not very good at actually carrying them out. Theory yes, practice no. There are some exceptions to this, but not many. If we read the case studies reported by Binswanger or Boss, we find nothing at all impressive—a mountain of theory beside a molehill of actual practice. Only during recent years have we had many cases reported at all. If we count Yalom (1991) as an existential practitioner, then we find in his cases a great deal of self-congratulation, a very wide use of different techniques, and an attitude resembling that of the novelist rather than that of the seasoned practitioner. If we look at the book by Spinelli (1997), then we find one really excellent account of working with a dream, but in the rest we find a disturbingly high proportion of theory to practice. Each case is accompanied by a good deal of theory, so much so that it is almost a textbook of therapy with extended illustrations. Most of the cases are very short, either because some event truncated the process or because the client cut short the therapy. Or, suppose that we look at the recent volume of case histories collected by du Plock (1997). Again, it is notable that most of these studies are short. My stereotype of existential analysis would be that it would continue for a long time, so I was surprised by this. What was also surprising to me was the evident desire for structure that was featured in several of the studies. Two of the therapists felt the need to keep bringing in the division into *Umwelt, Mitwelt, Eigenwelt,* and *Überwelt;* another introduced a structured approach to group work; another worked with a time-limited perspective; another gave his client facts and figures on alcoholism; and another gave specific information on head injuries. Again, the results in the end seemed quite modest and minimal to me. If, on the other hand, I contrast this with the recent book of case studies in the field of Gestalt therapy edited by Feder and Ronall (1996), then I find a freedom of action that is entirely existential in its functioning, with results at the end of the day that are much more impressive to me. I particularly think of the 9-year struggle of the therapist Ruth Wolfert with her client Dora, who came with an eating disorder, who had been sexually abused during childhood, and whose parents had suffered from the Holocaust. At the end, the client wrote,

> Sometimes in the evening as I look across at my husband and children, or in the day [as I look] at my students in school, I feel blessed in my peace and joy and marvel at how far I've come. When I think of how I used to spend all day bingeing and running away from the horrible pain of my life, I feel great love and gratitude to Ruth and the therapy. From the first session to the last, I have been on a journey of discovery,

a journey into life. And I have continued to grow on my own. Now when things bother me, I can usually breathe and get in touch with what is going on and even use it to expand. I am glad for my life, glad to be on a lifelong path of exploration and growth. Thank you, God, and thank you, Ruth! (p. 79)

That seems more like it to me.

12. Existentialists Do Not Have to Be Miserable

This is really so obvious that it should not need to be said. Yet, people in the existential fold keep on emphasizing the black side at the expense of the joy and even ecstasy that can come from adopting an existential position. There are historical reasons for this, of course. Kierkegaard used to be called "the gloomy Dane," Heidegger was not a cheerful person, and Sartre was a serious intellectual during his heyday. When I first came across existentialism during the 1950s, the image was of people dressed all in black having deep discussions in poorly lit cafés on the Left Bank in Paris. The quotation I remember most is one from Sartre—"free and alone, without assistance and without excuse." That does sound pretty bleak. But what I believe is that although we do have to face despair, we can also move through despair; we do not have to rest there. It is not a question of putting a nice face on something nasty. It is facing the despair and moving on through the despair. I remember Macy (1983) telling us that the only valid hope lies on the other side of despair. And that reminds me of Elliott's (1976) way of looking at therapy. Elliott was one of the pioneers of the encounter group, and his model of the human is as a layer cake. In therapy, we go down layer after layer until we touch bottom. Two layers from the bottom, we get feelings of worthlessness, helplessness, and intense pain. One layer from the bottom, we get feelings of aloneness, abandonment, painful loneliness, and isolation. But here there are two sublayers. Sublayer A says, "I'm all I've got, and that's terrible." That is often accompanied by panic. Sublayer B says, "I'm all I've got, and that's okay." The feeling is quite different. And that can lead to the bottom layer of all, which Elliott labeled as freedom, autonomy, independence, self-directedness, groundedness, and centeredness. This seems to me to be a way of looking at the matter that is far away from the gloom and doom of so much existentialist thinking. But even more relevant, because it is an experience rather than a theory, is the following story from May (1983). He was talking about a patient of his who sent him the piece she had written 2 years after the event. This patient, an intelligent 28-year-old woman, was especially gifted in expressing what was occurring within her. She had come for psychotherapy because of serious anxiety spells in closed places, severe self-doubts, and eruptions of rage that sometimes were uncontrollable. Her mother, during periods of anger, often reminded her child of her origin and recounted how she had tried to abort her. During times of trouble, her mother had shouted at the little girl, "If you hadn't been born, we wouldn't have to go through this!" This was the experience she related:

> I remember walking that day under the elevated tracks in a slum area, feeling the thought, "I am an illegitimate child." I recall the sweat pouring forth in my anguish in trying to accept that fact. Then I understood what it must feel like to accept, "I am a Negro in the midst of privileged whites." Or "I am blind in the midst of people who

see." Later on that night, I woke up and it came to me this way: "I accept the fact that I am an illegitimate child." *But* "I am not a child anymore." So it is, "I am illegitimate." That is not so either: "I was born illegitimate." Then what is left? What is left is this: "*I am.*" This act of contact and acceptance with "I am," once gotten hold of, gave me (what I think was for me the first time) the experience, "Since I am, I have the right to be."

What is this experience like? It is a primary feeling—it feels like receiving the deed to my house. It is the experience of my own aliveness not caring whether it turns out to be an ion or just a wave. It is like when [as] a very young child I once reached the core of a peach and cracked the pit, not knowing what I would find and then feeling the wonder of finding the inner seed, good to eat in its bitter sweetness. . . . It is like a sailboat in the harbor being given an anchor so that, being made out of earthly things, it can by means of its anchor get in touch again with the earth, the ground from which its wood grew; it can lift its anchor to sail but always, at times, it can cast its anchor to weather the storm or rest a little. . . . It is my saying to Descartes, "*I am, therefore* I think, I feel, I do."

It is like an axiom in geometry—never experiencing it would be like going through a geometry course not knowing the first axiom. It is like going into my very own Garden of Eden, where I am beyond good and evil and all other human concepts. It is like the experience of the poets of the intuitive world, the mystics, except that instead of the pure feeling of and union with God, it is the finding of and the union with my own being. It is like owning Cinderella's shoe and looking all over the world for the foot it will fit and realizing all of a sudden that one's own foot is the only one it will fit. It is a "matter of fact" in the etymological sense of the expression. It is like a globe before the mountains and oceans and continents have been drawn on it. It is like a child in grammar finding the *subject* of the verb in a sentence—in this case the subject being one's own life span. It is ceasing to feel like a theory toward one's self. (pp. 99-100)

That is her story. And it seems to me that I could not end on a better note.

CONCLUSION

Pulling the threads together, what I have tried to contend for here is that there is much less difference between the existential-phenomenological approach and the various types of humanistic psychotherapy than is usually stated. I think that it would be better to talk about the existential-humanistic tendency within psychotherapy and to admit that we all are tarred with the same brush. It is possible to be a happy existentialist.

REFERENCES

American Psychiatric Association. (1994). *Diagnostic and statistical manual of mental disorders* (4th ed.). Washington, DC: Author.

Beisser, A. (1972). The paradoxical theory of change. In J. Fagan & I. L. Shepherd (Eds.), *Gestalt therapy now* (pp. 88-92). Harmondsworth, UK: Penguin.

Bohart, A. C. (1993). Experiencing: The basis of psychotherapy. *Journal of Psychotherapy Integration, 3*(1), 51-67.

Bohart, A. C. (1995). The person-centered psychotherapies. In A. S. Gurman & S. B. Messer (Eds.), *Essential psychotherapies* (pp. 85-127). New York: Guilford.

Boss, M. (1963). *Psychoanalysis and Daseins analysis.* New York: Basic Books.

Brazier, D. (1991). *A guide to psychodrama.* London: Association for Humanistic Psychology (Britain).

Buber, M. (1968). *I and thou* (2nd ed.). New York: Scribner.

Bugental, J. F. T. (1976). *The search for existential identity.* San Francisco: Jossey-Bass.

Bugental, J. F. T. (1978). *Psychotherapy and process.* New York: McGraw-Hill.

Bugental, J. F. T. (1981). *The search for authenticity* (rev. ed.). New York: Irvington.

Bugental, J. F. T. (1987). *The art of the psychotherapist.* New York: Norton.

Bugental, J. F. T., & Sterling, M. M. (1995). Existential-humanistic psychotherapy: New perspectives. In A. S. Gurman & S. B. Messer (Eds.), *Essential psychotherapies* (pp. 226-260). New York: Guilford.

Clarkson, P. (1989). *Gestalt counselling in action.* London: Sage.

Cohn, H. W. (1997). *Existential thought and therapeutic practice.* London: Sage.

Corey, G. (1991). *Theory and practice of counseling and psychotherapy* (4th ed.). Pacific Grove, CA: Brooks/Cole.

DeCarvalho, R. J. (1991). *The founders of humanistic psychology.* New York: Praeger.

du Plock, S. (1996). The existential-phenomenological movement: 1834-1995. In W. Dryden (Ed.), *Developments in psychotherapy: Historical perspectives* (pp. 29-61). London: Sage.

du Plock, S. (1997). *Case studies in existential psychotherapy and counselling.* Chichester, UK: Wiley.

Elliott, J. (1976). *The theory and practice of encounter group leadership*. Berkeley, CA: Explorations Institute.

Feder, B., & Ronall, R. (Eds.). (1996). *A living legacy of Fritz and Laura Perls: Contemporary case studies*. Bancyfelin, Wales: Anglo-American Books.

Feldmar, A. (1997). [Untitled contribution]. In B. Mullan (Ed.), *R. D. Laing: Creative destroyer* (pp. 340-368). London: Cassell.

Goldstein, K. (1995). *The organism* (with an introduction by O. Sacks). New York: Zone Books. (Original work published 1939)

Greenberg, L. S., Watson, J. C., & Lietaer, G. (1998). *Handbook of experiential psychotherapy*. New York: Guilford.

Macy, J. (1983). *Despair and personal power in the nuclear age*. Philadelphia: New Society.

Mahrer, A. R. (1989). *Experiencing*. Ottawa, Canada: University of Ottawa Press. (Original work published 1978)

Mahrer, A. R. (1996). *The complete guide to experiential psychotherapy*. New York: John Wiley.

Maslow, A. H. (1970). *Motivation and personality* (2nd ed.). New York: Harper & Row.

May, R. (1958). The origins and significance of the existential movement in psychology. In R. May, E. Angel, & H. F. Ellenberger (Eds.), *Existence: A new dimension in psychiatry and psychology*. New York: Basic Books.

May, R. (1979). *Psychology and the human dilemma*. New York: Norton.

May, R. (1983). *The discovery of being*. New York: Norton.

Mearns, D. (1994). *Developing person-centred counselling*. London: Sage.

Mearns, D. (1996). Working at relational depth with clients in person-centred therapy. *Counselling, 7*, 306-311.

Mearns, D. (1997). Achieving the personal development dimension in professional counsellor training. *Counselling, 8*, 113-120.

Milton, M. (1997). Roberto: Living with HIV—Issues of meaning and relationship in HIV-related psychotherapy. In S. du Plock (Ed.), *Case studies in existential psychotherapy and counselling* (pp. 42-58). Chichester, UK: Wiley.

Roberts, J. (1997). Therapy in the latter half of life. In S. du Plock (Ed.), *Case studies in existential psychotherapy and counselling* (pp. 174-189). Chichester, UK: Wiley.

Rowan, J. (1992). What is humanistic psychotherapy? *British Journal of Psychotherapy, 9*(1), 74-83.

Rowan, J. (1998). *The reality game* (2nd ed.). London: Routledge.

Sartre, J.-P. (1948). *Existentialism and humanism*. London: Methuen.

Schneider, K. J., & May, R. (1995). *The psychology of existence: An integrative, clinical perspective*. New York: McGraw-Hill.

Schneider, K. J. (1999). *The paradoxical self: Toward an understanding of our contradictory nature* (2nd ed.). Amherst, NY: Humanity Books.

Spiegelberg, H. (1972). *Phenomenology in psychology and psychiatry: A historical introduction*. Evanston, IL: Northwestern University Press.

Spinelli, E. (1989). *The interpreted world*. London: Sage.

Spinelli, E. (1990). The phenomenological method and client centred therapy. *Journal of the Society for Existential Analysis, 1*, 15-21.

Spinelli, E. (1994). *Demystifying therapy*. London: Constable.

Spinelli, E. (1997). *Tales of un-knowing: Therapeutic encounters from an existential perspective*. London: Duckworth.

Thompson, M. G. (1997). [Untitled contribution]. In B. Mullan (Ed.), *R. D. Laing: Creative destroyer* (pp. 325-339). London: Cassell.

van Deurzen-Smith, E. (1988). *Existential counselling in practice*. London: Sage.

van Deurzen-Smith, E. (1997). *Everyday mysteries: Existential dimensions of psychotherapy.* London: Routledge.

Walkenstein, E. (1975). *Shrunk to fit.* London: Coventure.

Wheelis, A. (1972). How people change. In J. F. Glass & J. R. Staude (Eds.), *Humanistic society* (pp. 276-294). Pacific Palisades, CA: Goodyear.

Wilber, K. (1981). *No boundary.* Boston: Shambhala.

Wilber, K. (1995). *Sex, ecology, spirituality.* Boston: Shambhala.

Yalom, I. (1980). *Existential psychotherapy.* New York: Basic Books.

Yalom, I. (1991). *Love's executioner.* London: Penguin.

Yontef, G. (1993). *Awareness, dialogue, and process: Essays on Gestalt therapy.* Highland, NY: Gestalt Journal Press.

A Reply to John Rowan

Ernesto Spinelli

MY IMMEDIATE RESPONSE to John Rowan's chapter is not dissimilar to that felt sense of misunderstanding and misrepresentation that he refers to as the spur to the writing of his chapter. I also must confess to an additional feeling of anger. Perhaps that is shared by existential psychotherapists as well. Although I define myself as an existential psychotherapist, Rowan's caricature of existential therapists as being miserable, gloomy, and humorless malcontents fails to capture my own lived experience.

On the other hand, I have to say that there is much in Rowan's chapter with which I can agree. He is, for example, quite right, I believe, in pointing to a number of "voices"—that of Kurt Goldstein in particular—that deserve a great deal more attention by existential-phenomenological theorists and practitioners than they have received so far. I am grateful for such stim-

uli and for the overall stimulus of Rowan's chapter. Whatever it might have been that provoked him to offer his views on the relationship between existential and humanistic therapies seems to me to be, ultimately, of far less significance than the fact that the exploration of this relationship has been advanced further such that widely differing perspectives can be considered and criticized in this text and, I hope, elsewhere.

It should come as no surprise to both Rowan and the reader that I strongly disagree with his conclusion that "there is much less difference between the existential-phenomenological approach and the various types of humanistic psychotherapy than usually is stated." I believe that such differences are not, as he emphasizes, so much at the level of practice ("doing"); rather, they are revealed most clearly when examining the underlying assumptions and values (what may broadly be termed as "being qualities") that infuse their practice.

So, for example, whereas Rowan suggests in his opening paragraphs that existential therapy cruelly limits itself "by not using the range of interventions made possible by the endeavors of humanistic practitioners," I would take the view that "cruelty" has nothing to do with the issue in that such restraints follow directly from the philosophical underpinnings and implications of the existential model. To minimize or dismiss the importance of these underpinnings, as I believe Rowan's chapter attempts to do, might allow him to provide some superficial similarities that favor his argument—but only at the cost of glossing over crucial divergences. A number of examples he provides of the humanistic therapist's interventions when dealing with a client who continually speaks of his mother—asking the client to repeat a sentence several times in an increasingly loud voice and suggesting to the client that she exaggerate the movement of her right foot—appear to me to be quite alien to the types of interventions an existential therapist might make. This is so because, rather than seeking to address the "dialogical way of being" of the client *as it is being expressed in the encounter*, these humanistic approaches succeed in shifting the client to another mode of being and, thereby, express an implicit critique of the client's dialogical way of being with the therapist (who, in his or her role as "other" in the client's world relations, might well confirm—however inadvertently—the client's beliefs that the world is as unaccepting of the client as the therapist is, that the world knows better than the client what is the appropriate way for him or her to be, etc.).

Let me state at the outset, however, that the debate in which Rowan and I are engaged has nothing whatsoever to do with

the greater or lesser respectability or validity of one model over another. Nor do I wish to deny humanistic therapy's historical importance or its continuing impact on psychotherapy and counseling as a whole. At a more personal level, I have acknowledged many times the important role that humanistic therapy has played in my own professional development. If what I have gained from it has moved me to question and reject a number of central tenets of humanistic thought, then I do not see this as being any less a gain than if I had continued to accept and advocate these assumptions.

That many humanistic authors *claim* to have been influenced by existential phenomenology is without doubt. That a number of humanistic and existential authors share important points of investigative contact with regard to issues such as the analysis of the therapeutic process and relationship (e.g., Mahrer, 1996) and the "meeting" (or "presence") between humans (e.g., Bugental, 1987) also is without doubt. That a continuing respectful dialogue between such humanistic authors and those who adopt existential-phenomenological perspectives can, and should, take place seems to me to be not only desirable but also necessary. That such a dialogue will be of clarificatory benefit to both views is highly likely. *But claims can be erroneous, just as the existence of shared perspectives does not preclude the existence of divergent views.* And as such, to conclude, as Rowan does, that the views and perspectives of each model are largely one and the same—other than being at times, as he suggests, a heretical "sideshow" (ah, but *whose* heresy and *whose* sideshow?)—seems like questionable logic, to say the least.

A couple of Rowan's arguments rest on a type of "guilt by association" such that, for example, because R. D. Laing was interested in and accepted invitations to speak at humanistic conferences and meetings, he *really* is a humanistic psychotherapist. The fault in such an argument should become evident to Rowan when I place this in the context of my own professional contacts. I have very good relations with a number of American and Australian Gestalt practitioners and organizations—Bob Reznick and Todd Burley at the Gestalt Institute of Los Angeles, Ruth Dunn and Zish Ziembinski at the Melbourne and Perth Gestalt Institutes, respectively, in Australia. My books form part of their training programs, and I continue to be invited to lecture to their members and trainees. Do such associations reveal me to *really* be a Gestalt psychotherapist? Obviously not. But Rowan's argument rests on similar principles.

In like fashion, Rowan raises the case of Rollo May's involvement with both the humanistic and existential approaches. So far as it is presented, Rowan's argument is sound. But what he neglects to mention is May's own ongoing debate with himself and his colleagues as to how best to define his primary theoretical allegiances. In the end, May opted to define himself as an existential therapist rather than a humanistic therapist, basing his decision on a number of philosophical issues and concerns within humanistic psychotherapy regarding matters such as the (non)status of "evil" and the emphasis on technique over encounter. It would seem to me that, rather than assisting Rowan's argument, the example of May contradicts it in that May clearly saw significant differences between the two models such that a compromise of the type suggested by Rowan (i.e., "existential-humanistic") did not, ultimately, make sense to him.

But let us get to the main issue. Rowan's chapter repeats his previous criticism of my use of a quote by Gerald Corey to "encapsulate" the humanistic position. His critique rests on the argument that Corey is not an authority on humanistic therapy. This argument is nothing more than an obvious "red herring." What is at issue is not whether Corey is or is not an authority on humanistic therapy but rather whether what Corey has written of it is or is not accurate and representative of humanistic views in general. In this, I have yet to find anything that Rowan or any other humanistic author has written or stated that would suggest that Corey's summary is not anything less than a succinct and precise synopsis of humanistic thought (Corey, 1991). Furthermore, I would go so far as to say that, on the basis of Rowan's own recent attempt to state the essentials of humanistic theory (Rowan, 1998), Corey's summary does a pretty good job of capturing the main points as he personally understands them.

On the other hand, the reason I chose Corey's description in the first place is because it succeeds very well in laying out what I think are the central underlying issues between humanistic and existential therapies, namely, (a) the issue of actualization in general or self-actualization in particular, (b) the hypothesis of "wholeness" and "integration," and (c) the status of "the self." I have insufficient space here to consider these three critical issues in detail, and in any case, I have made an initial attempt at doing so elsewhere (Spinelli, 1994).

Let me, instead, address another related matter that Rowan raises several times in his chapter (and elsewhere) and that seems to me to be also characteristic of a humanistic perspective. He speaks of *experience* throughout his chapter and, in so doing, suggests its centrality within the humanistic enterprise and of the error that he claims critics such as myself make in ignoring this arena.

I agree with Rowan entirely that the question of experience is crucial. I also agree with him that existential-phenomenological authors have, at times, seemed to lose themselves in a somewhat arid and rarefied linguistic debate whose abstractions bear a tenuous relationship to lived experience. He is correct in highlighting authors such as Mahrer and Bugental for their important contributions. All I can add to this is that similarly important contributions exist in contemporary phenomenological literature focusing on the dilemmas of consciousness (see Varela, 1996, and Chalmers, 1997, among many others). But even here, important divergences arise. Rowan, as well as a number of the authors he mentions, seems to suggest the view that experience can be accessed in some undiluted fashion so that theory (i.e., interpretation) does not get in the way. This, I think, is a characteristic attitude of the great majority of humanistic authors and seems to harken back to an earlier attempt to separate thought from feeling or ideation from emotion.

In contrast to such assumptions, a phenomenologically derived position would not support such schismatic stances (in the same way as it would not support a "split" between so-called subject and so-called object), not merely out of some abstract rationale but, far more important, because structured experientially focused investigations reveal major limitations in this position *at a lived level.*

Instead, existential phenomenology suggests that our experience of experience is intentionally derived, expressive of an "interface" between consciousness and "the world." *For me to note, discern, or speak of "my experience" reveals an interpretive selectivity and reflection that already has taken place. In this way, to suggest some sort of preconceptual "purity" to one's reflective experience is deeply misleading.* I find it strange that such an obvious point

appears to be missed continuously by so many humanistic authors far more intelligent than myself. I can only suppose that it is missed because to accept it leads such authors to radically different experientially derived conclusions from those held by the humanistic model about each of the three issues I highlighted earlier as being crucial to the understanding and exploration of the divergence between humanistic and existential approaches.

So, for example, with regard to the issue of (self-)actualization, it becomes of little import to dispute whether humanistic authors take an optimistic or neutral view on the matter. *What is at issue is whether it is of much (theoretical and experiential) value to speak of (self-)actualization at all and whether, perhaps, existentially derived notions of intersubjective openness, disclosure, and dialogue provide far more adequate attempts to reflect and evoke various features of human experience that the humanistic model has attempted to combine and, thereby, transform into the hypothesis of (self-)actualization.*

In a similar fashion, the humanistic emphasis on wholeness and integration is reconsidered by existential therapy from a standpoint suggesting that, at best, such an emphasis reveals only one aspect of lived experience and permits the opposite and contradictory aspect of the *inevitable incompleteness* in all life experience to also be acknowledged and valued.

The humanistic reinterpretation of Heidegger's philosophical notion of "authenticity" encapsulates this wider dilemma. It seems somewhat rich to me that having changed the original meaning of the term to suit their views on wholeness and integration, some humanistic authors (including Rowan) then criticize existential authors' attempts to convey the original intended meaning to their readers. Although Rowan (or anyone else) has the right to employ the word *authentic* to mean whatever he might want it to mean, it becomes both absurd and arrogant to criticize other authors for employing the term to mean something other than what he prefers. It becomes equally absurd and arrogant to argue that his meaning is the "truer" meaning because it "fits his experience." As another personal example, Rowan recently reviewed my latest book, *Tales of Un-knowing* (Spinelli, 1997) and stated, as he restates in his present chapter, that the case account focusing on dream analysis stands out from all the others for its excellence and value (for which I thank him). I have been lucky enough to have had the book reviewed in quite a number of journals and magazines, and I have to say that in just about every instance, the reviewer has selected a different case as the "stand-out" example such that each of the eight cases has been singled out at least once as being the pivotal case. Now, each experience with regard to which is the stand-out case example is true, and each experience is different. Is any particular reviewer more correct than any other? Is any reviewer's personal experience less worthy or less true than that of any other? Obviously not. So, whatever the accessing of one's experience might have to offer us, it is not going to say much of worth with regard to truth in the manner championed by Rowan. Now, reread his own words in his section on "The Importance of Authenticity": "I believe that people who deny the existence or importance of the real self, as Cohn does, are people who never have had an experience of the real self. This means that they can talk about freedom, but they cannot act freedom." This is misguided—and arrogant—claptrap. Because it is not *my* meaning/experience of freedom, then it

is not freedom at all? What nonsense! That same quote alerts us to the fact that a further concern surfaces, in myriad ways, when considering the humanistic emphasis on a singular, intrapsychic, "real" self. Again, this is not the place for a lengthy debate on the matter. Let me just, once again, quote from the same section of Rowan's chapter: "The real self—the self that is to be actualized in self-actualization—is not a concept but rather an experience. It is not something to be argued at a philosophical level; it is something to be encountered at an experiential level."

But I reiterate that reflective experience is not value free, or concept free or philosophy free, as Rowan suggests. He speaks from a position that denies pivotal variables such as culture and history. The notion of the real self that is being put forward is a relatively recent historical development in Western thought and culture and remains significantly alien to a great many past and current cultures and societies that have no place in their worldviews for a singular, permanent, real self (see, e.g., Kondo's [1990] examination of modern Japanese self-constructs). Existential-phenomenological theorists would argue that a person does not directly experience his or her real self; *rather, a person interprets his or her experience from an a priori biased and value-laden perspective that, in current Western culture, assumes the truth in the belief in a real self and that, in turn, requires that same belief so as to validate the interpretation the person gives to his or her experience.*

I would argue that humanistic theory's greatest weakness (and, significantly, its major divergence with existential-phenomenological theory) lies precisely in its somewhat unquestioning adoption and advocacy of a Western notion of a singular, intrapsychic, real self that can be distinguished from any number of "false selves." I would further suggest that it is this adherence to such a notion that provoked the solipsistic excesses of the 1960s and 1970s to which Rowan refers and that continues to maintain an isolationist divide between "self and other" as understood and practiced by humanistic therapists (Spinelli, 1994).

I am sorry if, in reading my words, Rowan and those who agree with him come to the conclusion that I am merely intellectualizing and not experiencing. Although I cannot convince them of such, I ask them to accept my belief that I am not. The view to which I subscribe is not just some intellectual game I play; it has a direct impact on my very way of engaging with the totality of my experience of being, whether in the personal or professional realm. To attempt to avoid the dualism of real versus false selves not only promotes a less dissociated dialogical stance toward one's self-to-self relations, it also provokes a critical shift in one's sense of engagement with, and responsibility for, his or her relations with others and with the world in general.

Is this way of experiencing more or less valid than the way in which Rowan proposes? I do not think that any of us can say. But instead of validity, we can speak of implications. What are the general and ther-apeutic implications of adopting one experiential perspective over another? A great many, I would argue. For therapy, the very aims and objectives of the enterprise, as well as the types of relational encounters that might be both sought out and avoided, will be reflections of such implications, as numerous existential therapists have begun to explore (Cohn, 1997; Cohn & du Plock, 1995; Spinelli, 1994, 1997; Strasser, 1999; Strasser & Strasser, 1997; van Deurzen-Smith, 1988). For us as humans at least, the existential view challenges the stance of an isolationist, self-centered, self-focused way of being and relating that runs rampant through our culture, and it provides some initial means to assess and consider possibilities that strive to place the self in a self-world intersubjective context.

So, it is because of these differences between the underlying assumptions of the two models/perspectives and their subsequent implications that I remain unconvinced by Rowan's argument. I am afraid that, to employ his terminology, "I just do not experience myself as being a humanistic psychotherapist." And I cannot imagine that Rowan, as a humanistic therapist, would want me to be "inauthentic" and to pretend otherwise.

REFERENCES

Bugental, J. F. T. (1987). *The art of the psychotherapist.* New York: Norton.

Chalmers, D. (1997). Moving forward on the problem of consciousness. *Journal of Consciousness Studies, 4*(1), 3-46.

Cohn, H. W. (1997). *Existential thought and therapeutic practice.* London: Sage.

Cohn, H. W., & du Plock, S. (1995). *Existential challenges to psychotherapeutic theory and practice.* London: Society for Existential Analysis.

Corey, G. (1991). *Theory and practice of counseling and psychotherapy* (4th ed.). Pacific Grove, CA: Brooks/Cole.

Kondo, D. K. (1990). *Crafting selves.* Chicago: University of Chicago Press.

Mahrer, A. R. (1996). *The complete guide to experiential psychotherapy.* Chichester, UK: Wiley.

Rowan, J. (1998). The humanistic approach. *Dialogues, 1*(2), 20-21.

Spinelli, E. (1994). *Demystifying therapy.* London: Constable.

Spinelli, E. (1997). *Tales of un-knowing: Therapeutic encounters from an existential perspective.* London: Duckworth.

Strasser, F. (1999). *The emotions: Experiences in existential psychotherapy and life.* London: Duckworth.

Strasser, F., & Strasser, A. (1997). *Existential time-limited therapy: The wheel of existence.* Chichester, UK: Wiley.

van Deurzen-Smith, E. (1988). *Existential counselling in practice.* London: Sage.

Varela, F. (1996). Neurophenomenology. *Journal of Consciousness Studies, 3,* 330-349.

CHAPTER 36

Emancipatory Therapeutic Practice for a New Era
A Work of Retrieval

MAUREEN O'HARA

NEW MILLENNIUM, new context. Humanistic psychotherapists customarily look at the world from close up—very close up—and mostly from within the inner private worlds of individuals. During changing times, however, sometimes it is important to take a larger view and examine the position of humanistic psychotherapy against the broader contextual landscape. That is what I intend to do in this chapter. I want to take a wider and longer view and look at the humanistic tradition in its historical, cultural, philosophical, and marketplace contexts. I suggest, much as the founders of humanistic psychology did more than 50 years ago, that humanistic psychotherapy and the myriad growth and

healing practices it spawned should cease trying to justify itself as part of a modern industrialized medical system and to argue the case for its legitimacy and usefulness from within an epistemology and scientific worldview that it has long since outgrown. Instead, it must resolve some of its internal theoretical and practice contradictions and clarify its philosophical position, moral vision, and potential role in cultural transformation. It then will be in a position to stake out a role beyond the narrow confines of contemporary psychotherapy professions.

It is time to vigorously press the case that the ideas and practices that have evolved over the past half century loosely collected under the banner of humanistic and trans-

AUTHOR'S NOTE: This chapter is adapted from an article that appeared in the *Journal of Humanistic Psychology,* 37(3), pp. 7-33.
EDITORS' NOTE: The editors thank John Galvin for his editorial assistance with this chapter.

personal psychotherapies not only comprise another form of behavioral engineering but also are transformative practices with something different (and, in my view, far more timely and relevant) to offer an emerging global community in search of its psychological and spiritual bearings. At their best, they are pathways to wholeness and spiritual freedom. If we acknowledge that humanistic psychology is a Western consciousness discipline serving the emancipatory needs of both the well and the suffering, then we can see that it is well placed to take a leadership role in creating new consciousness professions of the future. If it fails to transform itself to respond to the challenges of the new world that is coming into being, then the field, its practitioners, and the graduate programs that educate them will, at best, remain a nostalgic relict of the courageous social experimentation in the North America of the 1960s and, at worst, will become extinct—overtaken by new approaches better suited for life during these pluralistic and turbulent times. If we succeed, as I believe we can, then we should find ample challenges and arenas of opportunity in which to serve.

A HOUSE DIVIDED

Despite its enormous influence in the evolution of the 20th century worldview, and despite concerted efforts to create a single unified "psychological science," clinical psychology and related fields of action remain a house seriously divided (Miller, 1992).

Although an oversimplification, it is possible to identify three more or less distinct domains of theory and practice: the modernistic-objectivistic or biomedical domain (in which the lingua franca is positivistic science), the subjectivistic or psychopoetic romanticist position (which looks to the inner experience of individuals for signs of universal truth), and the postmodernist-constructivist position (which has abandoned truth as a goal of science and instead is comfortable, or even celebratory, of the notion that all knowing is contextual with the interests and cultural biases of knowers irreducibly a part of what is known) (O'Hara, 1995). Although there are many discriminations among the different groups not visible in such a categorization, for the purposes of discussion here, I refer to these groups as the modernistic biomedicalists, the subjectivistic romantics, and the transmodern constructivists, respectively. My choice of the word *transmodern* over the more usual *postmodern* is both to suggest the transformative possibilities of this position and to indicate that this position may be transitional.

After a brief period of pluralistic openness during the late 1960s and early 1970s, the positivistic science-based Boulder model has come to dominate mainstream academic and government psychology. With a few important exceptions (several of them with religious affiliations)—Sonoma State University, the State University of West Georgia, Duquesne University, the University of Dallas, the University of Seattle, and Pepperdine University—by the 1980s humanistic and transpersonal psychologists had become marginalized within departments of psychology (which, over the 1970s, had come to look and sound ever more like departments of medicine, animal behavior, biochemistry, and computer science), had been banished to programs such as counseling and education, or had struck out on their own to create free-standing alternative graduate schools such as Saybrook Graduate School, the Institute for Transpersonal Psychology, the California Institute for Integral Studies, the Center for Humanistic Studies, the Union Institute, the Fielding Institute, and a dozen or so nonaccredited schools.

Outside the academy in the real world of practice, however, the story as lived is quite different. The majority of private mental health practitioners, social service professionals, and the public have remained gloriously pluralistic. They have accommodated the many theoretical and even religious orientations, points of view, and professional roles required to inhabit the multiple worlds in which psychological care is provided. Adherents of each position made their own allowances and adaptations to paradigmatic pluralism. Subjectivistic-romanticist practitioners, for example, resolved the cognitive dissonance engendered when forced to interface with the biomedical culture by convincing themselves that they were only "playing the insurance game," that is, giving objective-sounding medical diagnoses to insurance companies while avoiding them within their actual practices. Conversely, modernistic objectivists supplemented their scientist-practitioner graduate training with postgraduate training, tapping into a vast marketplace of continuing education workshops and growth experiences of all sorts that have offered a rich diet of both romanticist and postmodern growth opportunities and therapeutic training. During the 1970s and 1980s, people favored Gestalt therapy, self-psychology, client-centered therapy, Eriksonian hypnosis, Jungian depth psychology, and transpersonal psychology. The transmodernists, who go by names such as narrative, deconstructionist, constructivist, relational, and contextual therapists, have gained ground during the past decade. In many ways ideally suited to the need to play more than one game, the transmodernists have been particularly visible among marital/family, feminist, and ethnic therapists. Not infrequently moving from world to world—objectivistic diagnosis at the case conference in the morning, transmodern family therapist in the afternoon, and neo-pagan romantic in the evening women's group—many therapists have become comfortably and effectively multi-epistemological.

THE WIDENING CHASM

As the 20th century closes and a new millennium opens, the ground is shifting and such creative "multi-phrenia" is becoming increasingly difficult to sustain. The paradigm wars are heating up, not only on academic and theoretical fronts but also in more concrete arenas of professional practice and business. As third-party payers increasingly insist on short-term drug-based treatment now indistinguishable from biopsychiatric care, and as the American Psychological Association (APA) clamors for prescription privileges for psychologists, the always incoherent center of professional psychological care is threatened with dogmatic schism.

CULTURE WARS

As we enter the second century of psychology, the therapeutic community no longer can deny that it houses multiple theoretical positions about psychological development, suffering, transcendence, and the practice of psychotherapy or that it embraces multiple ways of investigating the fundamental existential questions that psychology must address. Under an ever-widening tent is housed everything from positivistic science to shamanism and ancient myth. To complicate matters even further, there even are multiple views on this multiplicity.

With no coherent and universally accepted meta-story that can make sense of the mental health field's pluralism and help clients to make sense of it, psychology and psychotherapy seem to be undergoing something of a crisis of identity. Mental health professionals find themselves caught up in contradictory and deeply divisive paradigmatic arguments that become all but impossible to reconcile. In October 1996, for example, *American Psychologist* published a special issue on outcome assessment in psychotherapy that included 11 very different points of view on research about psychotherapy, ranging from vigorous defense of experimental "treatment-focused" methods to arguments favoring more contextual "patient-focused" approaches (VandenBos, 1996). No resolution was proposed. More recently, Bickman (1999) argued forcefully for research on psychotherapy that relies less on matching symptoms to intervention and more on attempting to identify "nonspecific factors" such as the quality of the therapeutic alliance. Similar positions have been articulated by Bohart and Tallman (1999) and Miller, Hubble, and Duncan (1995). Nevertheless, momentum in the direction of treatment evaluation research, based on matching symptoms to intervention as a means of establishing universal treatment guidelines and standards of care, continues unabated. Practitioners attempting to straddle more than one discourse community must come to terms with the dawning realization that the grounds for justification of *any* particular clinical approach, ethical consensus, or choice of action are in large part socially constructed.

The situation becomes even more problematic when one considers the fact that some positions are *logically and ethically incommensurate with one another.* As the moral philosopher MacIntyre (1981) observed, when parallel but incommensurate logical, moral, and ethical systems collide, as they increasingly do within the mental health community, ensuing disagreements become divisive, "interminable," and "shrill" (p. 8). The strain that this puts on any community is enormous. In the absence of any universally respected final authority—whether this is science, God, or Truth with a capital "T"—if disagreements are to be resolved at all, then they frequently will be resolved through the exercise of coercive or brute force by the stronger over the weaker.

It is possible to read the recent conservative shift within the APA as an attempt to exert such force. The move away from acceptance of pluralism and toward standardization of treatment, the enthusiastic embrace of the biomedical paradigm, and attempts to limit access to the psychology licensing examination and the right to practice to graduates of APA-accredited graduate programs represent attempts—desperate and shortsighted attempts, in my view—by the governing elites of American psychology to impose paradigmatic orthodoxy on a historically heterodox culture. As Bickman (1999) and Dawes (1994) have said, much of this is being done without any evidence that such moves will help consumers. There is imminent danger of coercive methods being used by modernistic objectivists who represent the powerful majority and who, by denying legitimacy to subjectivists and postmodernists, may force them beyond the margins of acceptability. There are many ways in which the nonmodernistic voices could be silenced. For a therapeutic process to be included by the APA Division 12 task force (Task Force on Promotion and Dissemination of Psychological Procedures, 1995) as a "proven effective treatment" (in contrast to a treatment that is considered "experimental" or "ineffective"), for example, the process must pass muster when held to standards of evaluation derived from biological medicine and drug trials conducted under conditions that bear little or no relationship to the actual practice of psychotherapy. These research protocols involve matching symptoms, diagnoses, and treatments according to specific manualized protocols. Only those therapies that already have been "manualized" (i.e., broken down into clearly delineated, replicable, and quantitatively measurable operational steps) are considered. These criteria for inclusion are based on the proposition that only by comparing psychotherapy outcomes from different therapists, with specific diagnostic populations (e.g., depression, anxiety disorder, sociopathic personality disorder, alcohol dependency) randomly assigned to either no treatment control groups or test groups and with the therapy conducted under specified reproducible clinical conditions, can outcome results be confidently evaluated and effectiveness claims be justified (Barlow, 1996). Context, the degree of experience or other personal dimensions of the therapist, and the unique life circumstances and personal subjective experience of the client have no place in this form of outcome assessment. They are "out of paradigm" (Bohart, O'Hara, & Leitner, 1997). Such strict adherence to abstract standards of formal objectivity and linear and atomistic notions of causality, long abandoned by the biological and physical sciences, has been referred to by some critics as "the cult of empiricism" (Toulmin & Leary, 1994). Regardless of its validity in assessing the effectiveness of some types of behavioral interventions, this type of research protocol effectively eliminates a priori the work of researchers interested in the subjective particularities of individual cases and in the dynamic emergence of creative possibilities that occur within specific client-therapist relationships. Humanistic, transpersonal, and constructivist approaches did not survive the Division 12 cut. Nor did any feminist, depth psychoanalytic, family process, or sociocultural approach. Within the modernistic-objectivistic logic of the task force, such an exclusion is logically and ethically

coherent. But in the world of psychotherapy as is practiced in thousands of therapist offices today, such a narrow view of science is patently absurd.

By all reliable accounts, when we look at therapy as actually experienced by most clients, a far wider range of therapeutic approaches than those that the Division 12 validity criteria would recognize can be shown to have successful outcomes for participants (Bohart & Tallman, 1999, Miller et al., 1995; Seligman, 1995). This absurd situation could place many otherwise successful practitioners in serious professional binds. Because the stated goal of such validation projects is to distinguish those treatments that pass empirical muster from those that do not and, in so doing, endorse one set of methods over others, it is quite clear that methods not "on the list," regardless of the questionable validity of such exclusion, are likely to be seen as substandard. This will leave any practitioner who uses non-endorsed methods, even those who are using tried-and-true methods such as client-centered therapy, open to charges of ethical violations for providing "below standard of care" and vulnerable to malpractice lawsuits. As one of my legal colleagues put it recently, "It is a malpractice attorney's full employment act."

THE NEW HERESY HUNTERS

The threat to psychotherapists is very real, not only for those at the flaky fringe but to all creative and innovative psychotherapists. When paradigms collide, the loser usually is the nondominant voice. Consider a recent case in California brought by the family of a client. The family accused a licensed marriage and family therapist of malpractice for performing what she referred to as "shamanic healing." The therapist had accepted on face value the client's imagery that a giant rat was eating at her brain. The therapist had entered the imaginal world of her client and, using the client's frames of reference, performed an "exorcism" to remove the rat. To the client, the session had made sense; to the therapist's modernist colleagues, such actions seemed weird and irresponsible. The case was settled in favor of the family. The therapist lost her license—and her livelihood. In another case, Thomas Szasz, a longtime antipsychiatry voice, was successfully sued by the family of a deceased physician. The physician had consulted Szasz about depression after having given up treatment with a previous psychiatrist who had prescribed lithium. The physician was fully aware that Szasz was well known for his anti-medication stance. Several months after he had stopped seeing Szasz, the physician killed himself. The family won more than $600,000 in a malpractice settlement against Szasz for not insisting that the patient take medication.

So far, nonphysician psychotherapists have not been required to refer clients for medication, but that time is coming—and fast. If efforts to secure prescription writing power are successful, then psychologists will be expected to insist on medication. If their livelihoods depend on the acceptance of drugs as "standard of care," then we soon will see psychologists appearing as expert witnesses in malpractice suits against other psychologists. This is bound to create even more divisive pressures within the psychology community as prescription writers become differentiated from non-prescription-writing therapists in both training and worldview and as heretics are less and less tolerated.

Examples of professional intolerance can be found already. At the 1995 annual convention of the APA, for example, when *Journal of Humanistic Psychology* editor

Tom Greening expressed his opposition to prescription authority for psychologists, a colleague active in promoting prescription power told Greening that he should resign from the APA because his "type of opposition could undermine and split the organization, which should be united on this issue" (Greening, personal communication, 1996). Similarly, in the August 1996 issue of the *APA Monitor,* Smason (1996) wrote in a letter to the editor,

> We've got PhDs, PsyDs, EdDs, clinical, counseling, and school psychologists, . . . some sociopaths, and God knows what out there as licensed clinicians. . . . Let's establish one method of training and one degree . . . first. Then let's begin requiring adequate pre-doctoral training in psychopharmacological prescription for doctoral students in clinically oriented psychology. (p. 4)

Clearly, this urgency to obtain prescription privileges threatens to narrow the field of clinical psychology and to close off dialogue and support for diversity and creative alternatives, especially for those who do not follow medical models of treatment.

Yet another battle is raging around the recovered memory question, and positivistic psychological researchers with bona fide credentials can be found on both sides of the debate. In my view, the debate has been very productive and has resulted in so-called "false memory syndrome" advocates coming to accept that there is good evidence for amnesia for traumatic events (Freyd, 1993). At the same time, many psychotherapists have become much more circumspect about the epistemic status of what their clients talk to them about. All of this is positive, but the fact that the debate has become so fiercely politicized—taking place in the popular press, in highly publicized court proceedings, and on television talk shows—is part and parcel of the psychological culture wars and has resulted in erosion of public confidence in both psychological research and psychotherapy.

In criminal cases, the role of mental health practitioners as expert witnesses also is hotly contested. Advocates for psychology as an exact and predictive science are challenged frequently by others who deny any such exactitude or objective reliability to psychological testimony.

Nor can therapists turn to the seductive illusion that, as the field progresses and we have more "real data," it will finally be possible to sort out truth from politics in such cases. Arguments on either side of such complex issues as these can always be convincingly bolstered by experimental research, narrative science, phenomenological or hermeneutic science, or (in some cases) all three. Unless and until different ways of knowing and different ways of addressing important existential questions can be accepted for what they are and are not capable of contributing to understandings about human welfare, any attempts to arrive at a "truth" that can be generally applied to all human affairs are bound to lead to interminable acrimonious debates.

FAUST'S THERAPISTS

As if all of these internal doctrinal pressures were not enough to tear apart the fabric of the psychotherapy community, another far greater external threat is barreling down that has begun to alter the practice of psychotherapy beyond recognition—the industrialization of health care.

In many ways, this threat is simply the latest extension into the field of human affairs of the Faustian bargain that modern societies made between stability and progress. No one can deny that positivistic science, the instrumentalist worldview, and the technology based on it brought improvements in the material lives of ordinary people. The average worker in America today lives a longer, more comfortable, and freer life, afflicted with less illness, pain, and tragedy than was any medieval king. Social progress also has been brought about by important (if still imperfectly implemented) cultural innovations such as democracy, abolition of slavery, equal rights, and access to education—all inventions of the modern era. These meant that ordinary people had the opportunity to become emancipated and to make "life, liberty, and the pursuit of happiness" a feasible project for most everyone.

But these gains in individual freedom and the rise of the consumer market economy came with a price, as de Tocqueville already could perceive by the mid-1800s. The psychic losses have been enormous. Alienated from traditional ways of life, displaced from "old world" communities, and brutalized by life in disease-ridden cities and "dark satanic mills," industrialized men and women lost faith in their religions, in each other, in their relationships, and in themselves. Then, as now, large numbers lost hope, and many were driven mad. The mid-1800s witnessed an epidemic of drug use, violence, sexual abuse, destitution, and insanity as people lost touch with the psychic core of their existence.

Psychiatry, or "alienism" as it was then called, was invented as a response to this alienation. And true to the technological optimism of the times, for its first several decades, psychiatry wholeheartedly embraced the "fix it" paradigm of the industrial age. From the start, there was heavy emphasis on technology. Mechanical devices such as physical restraints, brain surgery, and electric shocks, as well as the administration of a range of "miracle" drugs such as opium, chloral hydrate, and cocaine, put the collected armamentarium of modernistic science to the service of deranged minds and civic order. The aim of early psychiatry was to *engineer* satisfactory *adjustment* to the demands of an ordered and mechanistic modern world (Showalter, 1985). Adjustment to normal life in any way possible continued to be a major purpose until the early 1940s. It was then that philosophical movements from war-torn Europe (e.g., existentialism, Gestalt psychology) met up with thinkers such as Adler, Rank, Horney, and Sullivan and the earlier American psychospiritual tradition of James. Out of this potent alchemy, a new humanism began to permeate American psychological thought, and the humanistic revolution in American psychology was born.

Humanistic psychology, as well as its crib-mate transpersonal psychology, was uninterested in and even antipathic to behavioral engineering. Early theorists such as Maslow, Bugental, May, Rogers, Perls, and Watts focused their attention not on what was pathological but rather on what was possible. They were concerned with the expansion and evolution of consciousness as well as the enrichment of experience, and although many of the early pioneers might have been embarrassed by the word, their interests were in "soul-craft" (O'Hara, 1995). Humanistic psychologists were not satisfied with a clinical practice whose ends were adjustment to what they felt were the dehumanizing effects of modernism; instead, they strove to heal the damaged spirit and to restore to their clients the soul, freedom, vitality, and richness of imagination and meaning that had been lost from human experience as a consequence of industrialization.

Practitioners set out explicitly to re-*humanize* psychology in the service of rehumanizing society. Existential, humanistic, and transpersonal psychologists in particu-

lar rejected the reductionistic positions of both Freudian and behavioristic psychology, which they saw as part of the problem rather than the solution to the dehumanization they saw around them given that such positions reduced the complexity of human experience to general interpretive systems, simple formulas, and mechanistic explanations. Instead, the humanists reached back to classical humanism—to Greek and Christian Renaissance and to the romantic transcendentalism of Rousseau, Emerson, and Thoreau—and also reached eastward to the philosophical traditions of Buddhism, Sufism, Hinduism, and the Tao, seeking to create a psychology that could understand us as total beings and help us to break the chains of illusion and to liberate consciousness by aligning itself with the highest aspirations of each human soul. Humanistic psychologists saw the appropriate role or vocation for psychology as facilitating the achievement or evolution of higher levels of consciousness, what Maslow called a "psychology of being." The therapeutic relationship was to be a place where *people*—not patients—were helped to reconnect with their inner worlds; their exuberant (if unruly) passions; and what was best, highest, and most sacred within and between them. In their science, humanistic psychologists sought to explore human life as it is experienced. As Watts (1961) suggested, psychotherapy was to be a means of emancipation, a way of "transformation of consciousness," of inner feelings, of one's own existence as well as "the release of the individual from forms of conditioning imposed upon him by social institutions" (p. 18).

Clients who have been drawn to humanistic and transpersonal psychotherapies over the decades learned awareness techniques imported from Asian meditation practices and participated in emotional psychodramas and powerful Gestalt exercises. They have reached into their depths to reconnect with their passions and dreams. They have confronted their demons and angels; encountered each other in deep and authentic ways; and touched, moved, danced, meditated, experienced rituals, and rediscovered the healing power of art and prayer. They have experienced self-fulfillment, joy, and sometimes even ecstasy. Anything but morally neutral (as the objectivistic scientists claim psychology should be) and certainly not secular (as some Christian fundamentalist critics have charged), humanistic and transpersonal psychology were from the outset *values-based* psychologies, designed to be an antidote to the alienation, ethical corruption, and emptiness of modern aggressively secular, commercial, and industrialized life. Anything but nonempiricist (as positivistic scientists charged) but *radically empiricist* (in the Jamesian or Deweyian sense), humanistic science attempted to return psychological research to the study of actual experience and to place at its center the meaning-making autonomous subject.

ARRIVAL OF THE INDUSTRIAL REVOLUTION IN THE PSYCHOTHERAPY NEIGHBORHOOD

The humanistic revolution in psychotherapy was led by philosophers, psychological thinkers, social critics, and psychotherapists whose cause was human emancipation. They heard in the voices of their patients and clients individual iterations of the age-old struggle to become fully human. They shared a belief that psychotherapy should be a context in which individuals could heal soul wounds inflicted by an excessively materialistic culture and could realize their potential as conscious beings. Both tacitly and explicitly, the founders of the humanistic tradition in psychology considered them-

selves and their new humanistic science to be an antidote to the excessively materialistic culture that reduced persons to objects and reduced everything to the status of a consumable commodity. They represented a paradigm shift in how psychotherapy was understood.

The arrival of managed care to the field represents another paradigmatic shift, only in the opposite direction (Kuhl, 1994). Rapid changes in health care economics such as the rising marketplace power of Health Maintenance Organizations (HMOs), Preferred Provider Organizations, and other forms of managed care as well as the clamor for reduced government spending on entitlement programs such as Medicare and veterans benefits are provoking changes in all mental health practice that, unwittingly or wittingly depending on how paranoid one is, are forcing all schools of therapy—modernistic, romanticist, and constructivist—to adapt themselves to a mechanistic medical model and are attempting to push psychotherapists into employment relationships that have more in common with the industrial production line than with a learned profession. The forces of industrialization are driving changes in university curriculum, practice, and standards of care. This pressure extends all the way to reframing the questions that psychological researchers consider important to address. For the first time, researchers on therapy effectiveness suggest that the corporate health care budgets should be included as a significant variable in outcome assessment (Newman & Tejeda, 1996).

Changes of this magnitude must be regarded as revolutionary, but the managed care revolutionaries have quite a different vision of their brave new world than do most psychotherapists. Most do not come into contact with patients and have no commitment to any emancipatory goals for them. Instead, they are business executives, financiers, bureaucrats, and shareholders looking to make money—lots of it. As part of a political campaign for health care reform, an advertisement in *The New York Times* in September 1996 listed statistics on the stock wealth of some of the chief executive officers of the top three managed care organizations in 1995. For U.S. Healthcare, Columbia/HCA, and Humana, these totals were $795.3 million, $248.6 million, and $232.6 million, respectively. Although the luster is fading now, patients' rights bills are gradually making their way through legislative channels, and the level of public dissatisfaction is rising, the health care industry shows few signs of any fundamental change in its bottom-line focus.

Like all revolutions, this one has an *ideological* base; it encompasses its own worldview or belief system. Managed care spokespeople openly describe their goal as the *industrialization* of health care and, with unconcealed enthusiasm and sometimes open contempt, declare that the days of "therapy as a cottage industry" are over. What has been happening to therapists since the 1990s sometimes is equated with what happened to butchers, bakers, and candlestick makers during the 1800s. Therapists are told to either get on board or get out of business (Kuhl, 1994; Wiley, 1992).

To the managed care industry, psychotherapy is a commodity—indistinguishable from wheelchairs, nurses' uniforms, and open-heart surgery—delivered by interchangeable "service delivery systems." In the early versions of production line industrial processes, it was not thought feasible to have the line workers or consumers make design decisions, and in industrialized mental health care, therapeutic decision making becomes centralized and far removed from the actual therapeutic context. Corporate policy worked out by accountants rather than by independent professional judgment determines to whom, for what, how much, what type, and by whom treatment will be offered. An irony worth mentioning here is that as the health care industry tries to imitate the production line, other large-scale industries are giving up on centralized control. With the help of a new generation of business gurus, many greatly influenced by the values and practices of humanistic psychology, corporate America is discovering that creativity and performance are enhanced when the people closest to the points of any transactions and those most likely to be influenced by their outcomes are the ones who make the decisions about them.

Autonomous professionals—people with the necessary advanced education who practice independently, have demonstrated their competence before their peers, and agree to be bound by ethics and practices of fellow professionals—do not fit well into the managed care framework. Increasingly, the entire practice of psychotherapy is becoming "dumbed down" as higher order knowledge and expertise is replaced with short-term standardized treatment protocols that can be applied by minimally trained workers.

Even more serious is that many of the gains in the direction of autonomy and empowerment of clients, made largely as a consequence of the humanistic revolution, are being lost as clients are told which therapists they must see and what the foci of treatment will be and that they must accept whatever treatment protocols the assessment workers recommend. They might even find themselves coerced into seeing their problems in the company's terms. In July 1995, a memo was sent to providers in a San Diego-based HMO, for which I was a provider briefly, recommending that therapists "set the expectation from the very beginning that therapy is temporary support. . . . Be compassionate and gently steer them toward the short-term model." A utilization reviewer for a national managed care company informed me that my suggestion that a multiply abused woman with whom I was working needed to set the pace of her own therapy was "hand-holding" and had "no place in the new era of health care accountability." When I tried to explain to the utilization reviewer that, in my professional judgment, persons like my client who were badly traumatized and desperately untrusting needed time to establish strong therapeutic alliances, he recommended that I attend a seminar on brief symptom-focused treatment. Similar stories are not hard to come by.

RETURN TO THE FUNDAMENTAL QUESTIONS

Whatever else it does, the managed care revolution is forcing psychotherapists, regardless of their theoretical orientations, to revisit struggles over their core values. Some clinical orientations, particularly those in the biomedical camp, will fit well with the managed care industrialized worldview. Humanistic approaches do not fit nearly as well (for a discussion, see Bugental & Bracke, 1992).

Many mainstream psychotherapists are betting their futures on some version of the industrialized model. As noted earlier, recent actions from the APA's Division 12 appear to coincide with the needs of the managed care industry, as does the APA College of Professional Psychology's move toward certification of specialists in the treatment of specific symptom-defined disorders such as substance abuse. But there is evidence that opinion might not be all that homogeneous even within the APA. Dorothy Cantor, the APA's 1996 president, advocated fighting for psychotherapists' freedom to treat their patients in the ways of their best professional judgment and the clients' own sense of what is effective for them (Cantor, 1990). The APA's 1997 president, Martin Seligman, is a firm advocate for empirical outcome studies but is open to consumer feedback that values longer term, more client-centered therapeutic processes (Seligman, 1995). In addition, the *APA Monitor* prominently featured a research study showing that the active ingredient in the treatment of 225 depressed people was the clients' active participation as well as the strength and duration of the therapeutic bond between therapist and client ("Newsline," 1996).

Nevertheless, graduate schools are rearranging their curricula to produce the line workers for the managed care industry. Professional schools of psychology, believing that part of their mission in the future will be to produce clinicians attractive to HMOs, are dedicating more courses to mastering the medical diagnostic systems, emphasizing brief therapy approaches, and deemphasizing depth approaches (O'Hara, 1996). In 1995, the APA presented its award for educational innovation to a graduate program that had included business courses in its doctoral program. Humanistic psychotherapy, and for that matter psychodynamic, Jungian, family system, transpersonal, and relational psychotherapies, has a very limited place in this brave new world.

A large segment of the American public obviously is not happy with the state of affairs in the contemporary medical world. We know this because of the staggering amounts of money and effort that people are willing to put into alternative medical treatments, many of which are not covered by their health insurance. Also, students continue to apply to graduate psychology programs that permit studies of philosophy, the humanities, political theory, religion, and the arts as well as science-based psychology. Saybrook Graduate School's admissions applications increased nearly 60% during a recent 4-year period. New findings in the neurosciences confirm the holistic, top-down, nonreductionistic paradigms long favored by humanistic psychologists as they undermine the more mechanistic bottom-up cause-and-effect paradigms of behavioral psychology. And clients continue to seek out therapists who will meet them in authentic relation, even if it means making financial sacrifices. Consumers of mental health care who might not know the difference between one school of psychotherapy and another clearly know the difference between being related to as a human and being treated as a "cost to be contained." They know the difference between being confirmed as an empowered agent of their own change and being confirmed as a passive "patient" to be acted on (Bohart & Tallman, 1996, 1999). The American public has come to expect freedom of choice in intimate arenas such as self-care. People already have discovered the important connection among the mind, body, and spirit.

Objections to some of the more egregious problems with managed care—lack of privacy, patient and therapist disempowerment, and lack of freedom of choice—are just now getting rolling, fueled by both professional organizations and public sentiments. Patients' rights and HMO accountability initiatives are working their way through state and federal legislatures. There are also several national coalitions and local consumer groups across the nation organizing to ensure the survival of traditional psychotherapy, and many individual practitioners are refusing to practice under HMO conditions and are seeking to form guilds practicing old-time psychotherapy on a fee-for-service basis, independent of third-party payments (Murray, 1999; O'Hara, 1996).

MENTAL HEALTH COMMUNITY AS MICROCOSM

The field of psychology represents, in microcosmic form, the crisis of values affecting the society at large. In my view, the mainstream of the field, represented by the APA's large practice divisions and the major universities and professional schools, has lost its bearings along with much of the culture it hopes to serve. It has fallen prey to the national obsession with marketplace consumerism and a fetishization of the "techno-fix." The profession seems to have abdicated its role as cultural critic and champion of the sacredness of human experience, bringing eerie echoes of the situation that spurred the creation of humanistic psychology in the first place. As early as 1956, Fromm wrote the culture-transforming volume *The Art of Loving* (Fromm, 1956), in which he argued that the choice for modern people was between relationships based on exploitation and relationships based on love—alienation in one direction, healing and liberation in the other. Fromm believed that much of human psychological and spiritual suffering, then as now, derived from the fact that "all activities are subordinated to economic goals, means have become ends; man is an automaton—well fed, well clad, but without any ultimate concern for that which is his peculiarly human quality and function." Love, he believed, was the "only satisfactory answer to the problem of human existence" (p. 112). Once it is understood that the struggle facing us as we enter the brave new world of the 21st century still is the same struggle for love and meaning that sparked the liberation struggles and the human potential movements during the middle of the 20th century, the only authentic path ahead for humanistic psychology comes into focus.

Contemporary society desperately needs a coherent shared vision. Part of that need, I would submit, is for a psychology based on love. We need a psychology of wellness, of the sacred, and of empowerment; a psychology that gives meaning and significance to individual human lives; a psychology that understands the central importance of stable families, environmental sustainability, and democratic civic institutions that have room for diversity and commonality. These are the values and practices at the core of the humanistic tradition.

From the private lives of individuals to the workings of institutions, governance, and business, the entire world culture must now engage with the question of what will be the guiding myths and core values in the coming global era. I will go out on somewhat of a limb and speculate that, at last, some of the global mythos will have elements in common with the humanistic psychology tradition. On New Year's Eve 1999, as the world celebrated the arrival of the year 2000, it was possible to catch a glimpse of the emerging world story and to see that it is remarkably humanistic. The great global ritual began in New Zealand and Australia and followed the clock across Asia, Europe, and the Americas and then back to the International Date Line. Despite the fact that the year 2000 has religious significance only for Christian societies, images were bounced from satellites and sent around the world that showed people of all nations and creeds, all colors and ages, participating in a celebration of the human spirit. What struck me, as I watched, was how different the new global imagery on display that night was from the heavy-handed imperial iconography that ushered in the 20th century. People in cultures as different as the Easter Islands and England had chosen images that spoke of a shared humanity. The most common images were the faces of individual humans, with the most common symbols those of the Earth from space, wheels, linked hands, and fireworks. Prominent in all of the celebrations were themes of harmony, connection, creativity, and beauty expressed in a common idiom of image, dance, and song. Here was a psychology of love. Nowhere to be seen were military bands, the depersonalized images of faceless soldiers, marching peasants, and bejeweled dignitaries surrounded by waving throngs that have marked other changes in eras. Instead, we saw pictures of individual persons—children, old people, monarchs, singers, musicians, and dancers—joining together in a voluntary expression of solidarity with both humanity and the natural world as a planetary whole.

If psychotherapy is to survive into the new global century and participate as prominently in the development of the 21st century worldview as it did in that of the 20th century, then it will need to rethink whether it wishes to be part of the culture of domination, exploitation, and alienation or of the culture of emancipation and love. If I am right about the themes that infused the millennium celebrations being a harbinger of the values of the emerging global culture, then it is most likely that any successful psychology of the future will draw heavily on the humanistic and transpersonal traditions. When this is woven together with a holistic neuroscience of mind, consciousness disciplines from non-Western cultures, and various mind-body practices, framed in the constructivist terms of postpositivistic contextualist epistemology, it could provide the consciousness-expanding processes for a new global age.

From their beginnings, humanistic psychologists, feminist and ethnic psychologists, and radicals such as Laing and Szasz were unapologetic—even militant—about their rejection of a medicalized psychology of adjustment in favor of a growth-focused psychology of individual and group liberation and self-realization. As the world turns itself inside out, the need for practitioners committed to this emancipatory vision is more important than ever.

ECONOMIC CONSIDERATIONS: THE NEW MARKETPLACE

Noble as such goals might be, can psychotherapists make a living by taking such a position and rejecting the rewards of the industrialized health care system? The answer seems to be *yes*. Times actually may be very promising for mental health professionals with the courage to declare their independence and offer their psychotherapy practices not as a branch of industrialized medicine but as something closer to soul-doctoring or personal development service. Unlike the 1960s, when psychotherapy was something only for the very sick or the very rich, now well over one third of Americans of all classes, ethnicities, and creeds have experienced some form of counseling or therapy, and most would do so again. Each year, more than 30 million people engage in some form of psychotherapy or counseling and buy nearly $1 billion worth of self-help books, tapes, and seminars (the latter without the benefit of third-party payments). Some of this massive expenditure is for severe and debilitating forms of mental distress, and people afflicted by these conditions will require financial assistance from either government or insurance. But when strict criteria of "medical necessity" are applied, a great many equally important but less catastrophic "quality of life" concerns will have to be provided for outside the health care system. Outside the highly bureaucratized and increasingly centralized

health care industry, where the marketplace can act like a real marketplace, people are free to buy what they are looking for from those who wish to provide it. Increasing numbers of psychotherapists are testing the waters outside the medical system. A recent article featured on the front page of *The Wall Street Journal* reported on the formation of a guild among psychotherapists in Connecticut. Organizing to offer psychotherapy on a fee-for-service basis, 57 therapists resigned from managed care panels to create their own association. Although many are not making as much money as they did when they worked for managed care panels, a member reported, "I'm making a living. And guess what, I like going to work in the morning" (Murray, 1999).

As the "dot-com" world continues to heat up and speed up, with all its attendant psychological pressures, demand for de-medicalized psychological services is likely to grow. Most Americans now are aware that there is a deep and important inner life that can seriously hamper or profoundly enrich their experience. People today set higher standards for the quality of their intimate relationships, and of their psychological and spiritual satisfactions, than did any previous population. They have learned that there is help for their pain, and they wish to grow; there are ways in which to address past traumas, anxieties, despairs, and hopes. They understand more about the relationship between the psyche, the soul, and the body than did any Westerners before them, with much of this knowledge being learned from consciousness disciplines with origins beyond Western culture and imported into American popular cultures since the 1960s. Going for counseling no longer carries the stigma it once did, and self-improvement programs have become part of our way of life. In human relations training at work, in their churches, in their women's and men's groups, with their therapists, in abuse recovery programs, in relationship enhancement programs, on spiritual retreats, in self-help groups, and on television talk shows, Americans of all types have enthusiastically embraced the self, relationship, and social evolution agenda of the human potential movement.

There also is an important role to be played by mental health practitioners in prevention, a role that was set aside during the 1970s once lucrative insurance reimbursements became available for individual treatment (Sarason, 1981). The new workplace, with its emphasis on emotional intelligence, successful teamwork, multitasking, diversity, worker empowerment, and responsibility, makes new and higher order mental demands on workers from the executive suite to the shop floor. After a brief period of experimentation during the early 1970s, when humanistic, affective, or confluent education could be found at all levels, American education does not see its role as one of deliberately facilitating the achievement of higher orders of self and relational mastery. This leaves a serious and frequently stress-inducing gap between workplace demands and worker mental capacities (Kegan, 1994). A growth-oriented psychotherapy geared to workplace competence has much to offer at the level of prevention and remediation of workplace pressure. The success of Goleman's emotional intelligence programs give some hint of the enormous market that exists for a growth-focused psychology.

The potential demand for higher order ways of growth is expanding rapidly as Western society prepares itself for life during the 21st century. In a recent survey of Americans, Ray (1996) indicated that he had identified the emergence of a new demographic group within American society—the "culture creatives," who are "seriously involved with psychology, spiritual life, and self-actualization." Although the study appears to have some methodological flaws, Ray's conclusions echoed findings of the study of Bellah, Sullivan, Swidler, and Tipton (1985), from a decade earlier, that an increasing proportion of Americans were actively engaged in a self-development agenda. For many, the values embodied by the human potential movement form the conceptual scaffolding of their pursuit of happiness and fulfillment (Bellah et al., 1985). The quintessential American insistence on individual freedom as a core psychological good renders them characteristically resistant to systems that they find "dehumanizing." We can safely predict that these "self-formers" are the people most likely to reject industrialized mental health care and to want emancipatory, transformational, or integral forms of psychotherapy.

The founders and early proponents of humanistic psychology offered an emancipatory alternative to the mechanistic reductionism of the broader culture including the psychological culture. As the 21st century arrived, the question as to what view of humans would be at the center of its mythos, a profession whose focus is the evolution of consciousness, was never more relevant. A theoretically reinvigorated humanistic psychology that draws on the best of its past, as well as on constructivist developments in theory and on the newer neurosciences and advances in mind-body studies, is well placed to provide the basis of a postmodern emancipatory psychology. The core values of privileging the unique experience of individual human participants; placing human suffering, well-being, and the universal need to search for meaningful answers to existential questions at the center; embracing the need to contain and comfort the high anxiety now endemic on both individual and cultural levels; and committing to both the abatement and prevention of suffering and to the further evolution of human consciousness mean that the humanistic tradition could have much to offer individuals and groups in the embryonic global society. If humanistic psychologists recognize that their work always has stood both as a critique of social institutions that refuse to recognize individual humans as responsible agents of their own change and society's change and as an alternative to those institutions, then they likely recognize that their future is more likely not to be within the industrialized health care settings of today. In the new economy, where entrepreneurial creativity frequently wins out over bureaucratic conventionality, there should be plenty of room for dedicated and enterprising professionals to continue the commitment to the humanistic ideal and to make decent livings without selling their souls to the psychoindustrial complex.

REFERENCES

Barlow, D. H. (1996). Health care policy, psychotherapy research, and the future of psychotherapy. *American Psychologist, 51,* 1050-1059.

Bellah, R. N., Sullivan, W. M., Swidler, A., & Tipton, S. M. (1985). *Habits of the heart: Individualism and commitment in American life.* Berkeley: University of California Press.

Bickman, L. (1999). Practice makes perfect and other myths about mental health services. *American Psychologist, 54,* 963-965.

Bohart, A. C., O'Hara, M., & Leitner, L. M. (1997). Empirically violated treatments: Disenfranchisement of humanistic and other psychotherapies. *Psychotherapy Research, 8,* 141-157.

Bohart, A. C., & Tallman, K. (1996). The active client: Therapy as self-help. *Journal of Humanistic Psychology, 36*(3), 7-30.

Bohart, A. C., & Tallman, K. (1999). *How clients make therapy work.* Washington, DC: American Psychological Association.

Bugental, J. F. T., & Bracke, P. E. (1992). The future of existential-humanistic psychotherapy. *Psychotherapy, 29*(1), 28-33.

Cantor, D. W. (1990). I am not a dinosaur. *Psychotherapy in Private Practice, 8,* 11-19.

Dawes, R. M. (1994). *The house of cards: Psychology and psychotherapy built on myth.* New York: Free Press.

Freyd, P. (Ed.). (1993). *FMS Foundation Newsletter, 2*(7). (Philadelphia: False Memory Sydrome Foundation)

Fromm, E. (1956). *The art of loving.* New York: Harper & Row.

Kegan, R. (1994). *In over our heads: The mental demands of modern life.* Cambridge, MA: Harvard University Press.

Kuhl, V. (1994). The managed care revolution: Implications for humanistic psychotherapy. *Journal of Humanistic Psychology, 34*(2), 62-81.

MacIntyre, A. (1981). *After virtue: A study in moral theory.* Notre Dame, IN: University of Notre Dame Press.

Miller, R. B. (1992). Introduction: Philosophical problems of psychology. In R. B. Miller (Ed.), *The restoration of dialogue: Readings in the philosophy of clinical psychology* (pp. 31-33). Washington, DC: American Psychological Association.

Miller, S., Hubble, M., & Duncan, B. (1995, March-April). No model, no method, no guru, no teacher: A mantra for therapy in the era of accountability. *Family Therapy Networker.*

Murray, S. (1999, November 22). With a guild, therapists flee managed care. *The Wall Street Journal.*

Newman, F. L., & Tejeda, M. J. (1996). The need for research that is designed to support decisions in the delivery of mental health services. *American Psychologist, 51,* 1040-1049.

Newsline. (1996, September). *APA Monitor,* p. 10. (Washington, DC: American Psychological Association)

O'Hara, M. (1995). Carl Rogers: Scientist or mystic? *Journal of Humanistic Psychology, 35*(4), 40-53.

O'Hara, M. (1996, September-October). Divided we stand. *Family Therapy Networker.*

Ray, P. H. (1996, July-August). The integral culture: A study of the emergence of transformational values in America. *AHP Perspective,* pp. 9-14. (Association for Humanistic Psychology)

Sarason, S. B. (1981). An asocial psychology and a misdirected clinical psychology. *American Psychologist, 36,* 827-836.

Seligman, M. E. P. (1995). The effectiveness of psychotherapy: The consumer reports study. *American Psychologist, 50,* 965-974.

Showalter, E. (1985). *The female malady: Women, madness, and English culture, 1830-1980.* New York: Pantheon.

Smason, I. (1996, August). [Letter to the editor]. *APA Monitor,* p. 4. (Washington, DC: American Psychological Association)

Task Force on Promotion and Dissemination of Psychological Procedures, Division of Clinical Psychology of the American Psychological Association (1995). Training and dissemination of empirically-validated psychological treatments: Report and recommendations. *Clinical Psychologist, 48,* 3-23.

Toulmin, S., & Leary, D. (1994). The cult of empiricism in psychology and beyond. In S. Koch & D. Leary (Eds.), *A century of psychology as a science* (pp. 594-617). Washington, DC: American Psychological Association.

VandenBos, G. R. (Ed.). (1996). Outcome assessment of psychotherapy [Special issue]. *American Psychologist, 51*(10).

Watts, A. (1961). *Psychotherapy East and West.* New York: Pantheon.

Wiley, M. S. (1992, March-April). Toeing the bottom line. *Family Therapy Networker,* pp. 30-72.

CHAPTER 37

Performative Therapy
Postmodernizing Humanistic Psychology

WILL WADLINGTON

AN AWARENESS of the implications of postmodernism for contemporary life is crucial for developing new practices, therapies, and forms of social interaction relevant to our chaotic, tumbled-together world.[1] A cultural shift has taken place around us; a new set of problems of everyday living has emerged in what has been variously called our narcissistically detached, decadent, postindustrial, or late capitalist culture. Postmodern thinking, now pervasive across academic disciplines, attempts to document these changes in the cultural environment, challenging traditional conceptions and promoting openness to alternative takes on what is happening. First recognized in the arts, architecture, economics, anthropology, and sociology, postmodernism swept over many fields of cultural study while mainstream psychology slept—and still sleeps. This widespread obliviousness to the postmodern transformation reflects what Kvale (1992) called "the current emptiness and irrelevance of psychological science to culture at large" (p. 52). But humanistic psychologists, who never have been mainstream and always have been aware of deeper and broader cultural concerns, have begun to stir and may awaken others around them to the challenges that postmodernism poses to psychological thinking and practice.

Postmodernism, as both a crucial historical moment[2] and the intellectual critique that describes that moment, coincides with the end of modernism and, with it, the end of the grand "meta-narratives" of Enlightenment rationalism.[3] Postmodernism signals the end of foundations and authority, the end of the ideal of objectivity, and the end of the belief in modern science as the ultimate means to "liberation from superstition and ignorance and the production of wealth, truth, and progress" (Newman & Holzman, 1997, p. 68). But this makes postmodernism sound more coherent than it is. As Kvale (1992) put it, " 'Postmodern' does not designate a systematic theory or a comprehensive philosophy but rather [designates] diverse diagnoses and interpretations of the current culture, a depiction of a multitude of interrelated phenomena" (p. 32). Postmodernism defies categorization as yet another historical episode in a linear sequential story of progressive intellectual accomplishment. A wholesale undermining of foundations and guiding myths, postmodernism poses a threat to most of mainstream psychology, which is a project of modernist science.

Humanistic psychology, itself a reaction to the fundamentalism and positivism of modern science, is less threatened. At its core is a resistance to reductionistic and authoritarian claims of foundational truth, progress through knowledge, and value-free judgment. Humanistic psychology emphasizes freedom, experience, and conscious choice, and it reacts to extreme thinking within modernist science with a spirited and creative alternative vision of humanness. Arising out of a productive dialectic between European existential and phenomenological thinking and American self psychologies (e.g., those of Maslow, Rogers, May, Moustakas, and Bugental [Warmoth, 1996]), humanistic psychology—with its emphasis on holism, human experience, freedom, and moral choice—provides a humanizing alternative to the positivism and scientism that drives behaviorism. It also offers a nonreductionistic version of depth psychological interpretive approaches such as psychoanalysis. Humanistic psychotherapies are creative attempts to add "a wide range of group process, somatic, and nonverbal approaches to the therapist's repertoire" (Warmoth, 1996). These approaches often extend beyond conventional rules and limits to explore the farther reaches of human potential. Humanistic psychotherapists' pioneering work with groups, families, organizations, communi-

ties, and ecologies is consistent with a postmodern shift away from the individual and toward the relational. Explorations of transpersonal realms of being, methodological developments such as qualitative research, and therapeutic innovations such as experiential and constructivist psychotherapies all represent humanistic responses to narrow modernist assumptions.

POSTMODERNIZING HUMANISTIC PSYCHOLOGY

Humanistic psychologists were among the first to acknowledge the importance of postmodernism. A special issue of *The Humanistic Psychologist* was devoted to "Psychology and Postmodernity." Aanstoos (1990), in his preface, wrote of the "eclipse of modernism" as a "crashing of the icons" including traditional psychology and positivistic science. He regarded postmodernism as offering opportunities for humanism[4] and humanistic psychology (p. 5). Similarly, Gergen (1995) discussed the enormous impact on humanistic psychology of various ideological, literary-rhetorical, and social critiques that demarcate the end of the modernist period in intellectual history.[5] He suggested that humanists explore the potential of a postmodern emphasis on the relational "for engendering humane forms of cultural life" (p. 72). Gergen attempted to counter humanistic psychologists' fears that postmodern thought inevitably leads to "rampant relativism."[6] He cautioned against the risks of a "wholesale slide into humanist despair" (p. 72), and he encouraged us to "role-play some of the potentials of postmodern critique" (p. 73) for humanistic psychology in an attempt to invite a new form of intellectual discourse. "Postmodernism," he said, "urges us to create multiple ways of generating integrative conversation in a way that is congenial with the deepest hopes of the humanistic tradition" (p. 71). Gergen tried to reconcile cherished humanistic concerns such as the belief in the embodied self, individual agency, and freedom, with a postmodern orientation toward relational processes and the importance of listening to a diverse and multicultural chorus of voices. Likewise, O'Hara (1992) called for a postmodern humanistic psychology "based in a new relational humanism that understands selves as contextual and relational" (p. 446). These represent important efforts to save humanistic psychology from obsolescence, prodding it out of complacency and provincialism into a more global, and culturally relevant, postmodern awareness.

Recent thinking in humanistic psychology represents a critical questioning stance with regard to the narrow standards of truth and morality into which much of the modernist project of scientific psychology has devolved. In defiance of reductionistic dehumanizing aspects of modernist science, humanistic psychologists have engaged in an important debate against scientism and the medicalization of psychology. For example, humanists have been among the loudest critics of prescription privileges for psychologists and managed mental health care delivery. They also have argued against the imposition of narrowly defined standards of professionalism and demands for rigid credentialing within the psychological community, and they have reacted to the shaming discourse in which those standards and demands are embedded.

Especially with regard to psychotherapy, humanists have held fast. They often are the first to decry "manualized treatments" (Bohart et al., 1997), for example, or to see an insistence on "empirical validation" as an "empirical violation" (Bohart, Leitner, & O'Hara, 1998). In addition, they abhor

what William James called "the psychologist's fallacy" (Schneider, 2000, p. 1) or what also has been described as "methodolatry," that is, the assumption that what is not discoverable by one's chosen method of research does not exist (Bohart et al., 1997). Finally, they steadfastly defend against threats to the privacy and sacredness of the therapeutic relationship. Humanistic psychology was—and continues to be—contrarian, radical, and rigorously anti-authoritarian.

But despite its resistance to the currents of the mainstream, humanistic psychology remains a modernist achievement, a modern romantic or psycho-poetic depth psychological discourse that opposes the modern objectivist or biomedical modernist discourse (see the chapter by O'Hara [Chapter 36] in this volume). Even at its most radical, humanistic psychology never completely steps outside modernism. Humanistic thinkers are engaged in a perpetual debate with powerful political factions of the modernist scientific community about preserving certain historical humanistic values. As a consequence, humanistic thinking is trapped in the linear sequential story of its progress. This is ultimately a tragic story of well-intentioned humanists who fight the good fight against dehumanizing forces of scientism and medicalization within the context of a shaming discourse that treats new therapies as unproven and, therefore, unprofessional.

This story is compelling, and it might be tempting to retell it, emphasizing the need for a reformed humanistic approach that takes the best aspects of the past and applies them to a new set of contemporary problems. Although this effort satisfies the modernistic hope for progress and better techniques, it keeps us locked in an argument about what is worth salvaging from the past rather than attempting new strategies in the present. Resolving this debate would not necessarily further the development of new practices (Holzman, 2000). Neither is it an issue of expanding our definitions of familiar terms (e.g., self, free will, human potential) and attempting to translate our concepts into postmodern parlance. As McNamee (2000) put it, "The attempt is not simply to 'say things differently.' . . . Rather, the attempt is to engage others (theorists, practitioners, researchers, as well as social actors) in activities that broaden our resources for social life" (p. 181).

Ironically, seeking rapprochement between traditional humanistic psychology (as resistance to modernism) and postmodernism (as indifference to modernism) may unduly restrict the development of new generative practices, which invent themselves and proliferate rather than result from linear, progressive, historical processes. Stepping out of a debate with modernist science means forgoing positions on both sides, pro and con. On the one hand, it means relinquishing the need to rationalize and justify humanistic practices either methodologically (as empirically provable) or economically (as low-cost medicine). On the other hand, it means that humanistic psychologists must give up the safety of their defensive posture, their *denial* that they need to rationalize or justify what they do.

Stepping out of the debate also means accepting an invitation to engage in a diverse range of postmodern approaches construed as cultural phenomena rather than as scientific or medical procedures. An alternative to describing practices as applications, treatments, and techniques based on established theories is to think of therapies as having lives of their own or as not-yet-complete, creative, social relationships. Therapies can be seen more as situational and improvisational responses to everyday concerns of people in the diverse contexts they inhabit rather than as solutions or cures. New humanistic practices that emphasize the constructed nature of our experiences, alternative narrations of events, and active performative immersion in the social environment hold promise for postmodernizing humanistic psychology. These new practices encourage action, highlight the power of present-centered awareness, and invite participation in the process of "postmodern psychology-in-the-making" (Holzman, 2000). What matters now are new social experiences, dialogues, conversations, and performances, not new theories. This is a creative challenge more sweeping than *any* of those previously taken on by humanistic psychologists.

A REVOLUTIONARY NEW PRACTICE

Performative social therapy, a postmodern approach to learning, performing, and participating in therapeutic social change, demonstrates what is possible. Performative social therapy is an evolving process of cultural meaning making initially developed by Fred Newman and Lois Holzman and now practiced in several American therapy and training centers. It has sparked both interest and controversy. Emerging out of an ambitious, community-based, noninstitutional effort, it is a dialectical and interactive approach to learning by doing. Performative social therapy is more a way of living one's life than a method applied to life "problems."

The therapeutic task is not only to find a way to live in society but also to work for social change. Performative social therapy is not construed in instrumental terms as applied theory; it is more a creative provocation than a model to be emulated or a technique to be applied. Nor is it regarded epistemologically as another method of knowing oneself or the world. Rather, it is conceived of as a revolutionary way of developing and learning, and of performing in new and unexpected ways, in the real world of social and political action.

Newman and Holzman think of performative social therapy as practical-critical activity that makes things happen. The therapist is engaged with the client in a performance that cannot be scripted or predicted beforehand. Instead of "What's bothering you today?" the therapist's question is more likely to be "What are we going to do today?" Instead of trying to solve "problems," performative social therapists, working with groups and organizations, focus on helping people to create growthful new collaborations. The therapist is not an audience member or critic standing on the outside and interpreting the action. Instead, he or she is a participant with clients in the dialectical process of living their lives. Unlike various theatrical techniques imported into therapy in the past (e.g., role enactment, psychodrama, Gestalt dream work), performing in this new sense is not a means to a therapeutic end but rather an end in itself. By participating in the process of performing, humans do more than merely acquire knowledge; they create new social environments and new ways of interacting with one another.

From the initial interview, a client is likely to be surprised by the nonpathologizing approach of the social therapist, who declines to use diagnostic labels or talk about "symptoms." Because psychological problems are regarded as social in nature, no one person is singled out or excluded because he or she "has" a problem. Individual work is preparatory to group work, where a creative social interaction can take place. Consider, for example, a "depressed" woman who enters a social therapy group. According to Newman and Holzman (1997), the group process involves "creating

something else" out of the depression brought into the room by the client. As they put it,

> Social therapy does not work on the . . . [client's] depression by trying to discover its cause, interpret the reason for it, or provide the . . . [client] or other group members with insights into its roots. . . . Nor does social therapy try to solve the . . . [client's] problem, make her feel better, empathize with her, or get her to give it up. The social therapist works on the depression by working on the conversation. (p. 121)

The performative social therapist's activity "is akin to what a theater director might do. . . . [He or] she relates to the clients' lives (including what they are doing in the therapy group) as an improvisational play (an ongoing conversation) that we as human beings continuously create together" (p. 121).

Like other postmodern thinkers, Newman and Holzman appropriate what is useful. Their work transcends traditional disciplinary boundaries and cuts across domains of discourse. It is not only intellectual but also philosophically informed and practical. From Marx's early work, they draw on the notion that "philosophers have only interpreted the world. . . . The point is to change it" (Marx, cited in Newman & Holzman, 1997, p. 13). They emphasize the importance of doing, of process, and of the present. They see Vygotsky's revolutionary but widely ignored approach to development as "activity-theoretic." In Vygotsky's emphasis on play, and in Wittgenstein's notion of "language games," they see hope for something beyond frozen denotative and representational conceptions of human communication. They challenge psychology's "methodological conservatism" and propose a "tool-and-result . . . dialectical method—in which the 'tool' and the 'result' come into existence together . . . [and] are neither separate nor identical but [rather] elements of a unity (totality, whole)" (Holzman, 1999b, p. 52). Their noninstrumental approach replaces psychology's insistence that "theory and practice are . . . necessarily separate . . . [and that] theories are developed . . . [and] then tested in practice" (Holzman, 1999a, p. 15). Finally, drawing from Vygotsky and their own educational experiments, they advocate a type of learning that is developmental, relational, and performative rather than acquisitional. Learning and developing take place on various "stages" in the world. We learn best by becoming who we are not, by doing things we did not know we could do, and by performing (as Vygotsky said) "a head taller" than ourselves.

LEARNING ENVIRONMENT AS PERFORMANCE SPACE

Newman and Holzman (and numerous others who have helped them) have created a collaborative, evolving, anti-institutional learning community with no fixed membership. Participants are also part of a community of minds linked globally through video and the Internet and through the universal language of drama in the tradition of the Teatro Campesino, Brecht, and other revolutionary forms of theater. In the process of its development, this community has been involved in many activities—a Vygotskian laboratory school, various social projects including a youth antiviolence initiative (the All Stars Talent Show Network), a performance workshop for nonprofessionals, and a weekly radio dialogue. In various cities across the United States, members of the community perform and develop new forms of social therapy. In a space in Soho in New York City, the East Side Institute for Short Term Psychotherapy (a social therapy train-

ing center), the East Side Center for Social Therapy (a therapy setting), and the Castillo Theatre (a performance space for an unpaid acting ensemble committed to political theater) all coexist. There, in one location, Newman and Holzman have created an educational community, a theater space, and a therapy environment. This juxtaposition of activities intentionally blurs distinctions among three powerfully related methods of being in the world based on three existing performance traditions: education, theater, and therapy. At the heart of their active approach is the belief that all three are forms of performance.

The theater/therapy/learning space is contiguous and continuous, allowing each activity to flow freely into the adjacent activity. Access to the therapy space is through the theater space; posters and photos of performances line the walls. In addition to this spatial blurring of boundaries, there is considerable blurring of roles; the actors also are telephone fund-raisers, ushers, and guides. There is no sense of something going on "behind the scenes." Audience members are free to enter the scenery and costume shops. There is no backstage and no proscenium here. The therapy is not spatially separated from the theater either architecturally or conceptually (although doors provide privacy for the therapy rooms). Moving about in this environment, one experiences learning and performance as pervasive rather than as localized functions confined to a designated area. In Newman and Holzman's (1997) view, "The total environment [for learning] is not a place but [rather] an activity" (p. 111).

Newman and Holzman think of their space in the same way as Vygotsky would have thought of it, that is, as a zone of proximal development (ZPD). A ZPD is an environment in which a special type of learning takes place (although Newman and Holzman might object to my reifying the

ZPD even to this extent). This type of learning is not the type we are used to, that is, "acquisitional, knowledge-based learning" (Newman & Holzman, 1997, p. 131). Rather, it is a tripartite learning—of the thing learned, how to learn, and that one is a learner. In this environment, learning is seen as a revolutionary transformative process that liberates by overthrowing existing social relations, abolishing class distinctions, and revoking privilege. There is no failed student of this learning process, no illusion to see through in this theater, no pathological patient to act out, and no healthy norm-setting therapist to interpret that action. The school, theater, and therapy all are developmental in nature. The emphasis is on forming new relationships with one another and moving ahead rather than on being right or knowing more than someone else knows.

The premise is Vygotskian; we all know more than we think we know and more than we give ourselves credit for knowing. Performance is an educational and therapeutic medium. "Human beings become who . . . [they] 'are' by continuously 'being who . . . [they] are not,' " (Newman & Holzman, 1997, p. 110). Newman and Holzman (1997) see Vygotsky's ZPD as a "historical performance space or stage [rather] than [as] a societal scaffold" (p. 110). They view all of us as revolutionaries, as "creators of continuous developmental process" (p. 110). Development "is, significantly, an ensemble—not a solo—performance" (Holzman, 1999b, p. 67). Developmental learning is a lively social process of performing in new ways with one another without privileging one person's knowledge over that of another.

KNOWING AND DOING

Newman and Holzman do more, however, than simply describe a new environment for learning and a new approach to development. They also put forth a revolutionary claim—that knowledge itself, by which they mean the epistemological foundation of modern science, has come to an end. From Marx, Wittgenstein, and Vygotsky again, they appropriate the notion of a "revolutionary ontic shift (not an epistemic alteration) from interpretive cognition to activity" (Newman & Holzman, 1997, p. 26). Vygotsky, for example, held that "all the higher mental functions originate as actual relations between people" (cited in Newman & Holzman, p. 44). Newman and Holzman consider modern philosophy itself as "epistemologized" and positivistic due to its overidentification with the methodology of modern science. They see philosophy as process and speak about "philosophizing" as a dialectical performative activity. Newman and Holzman's work takes the current "end of science" debate further, proclaiming the end of scientifically justified and rationalized psychology. The "revolutionary activity" they advocate is the overthrow of psychology as we know it, especially authoritarian and propagandizing psychology based on foundational claims of proof and truth. In its place, they propose a new method of performed social activity in which the search for certainty is less important and the proof is in the historical relevance of our actions. In other words, they are interested in creating an approach that is more humanistic, takes human cultural meanings into account, and avoids reducing humans to mere objects of scientific scrutiny.

Newman and Holzman call for an acknowledgment of the end of knowing. This is not to imply that some limit of knowledge has been reached; rather, they suggest that knowing is overrated. They see even a postmodernist such as Gergen as falling short by attempting to reform psychology along epistemological lines rather than revolutionizing it by making it more active. Instead of "replacing the dualist epistemology of a knowing mind confronting a material world with a social epistemology" (Gergen, 1994, pp. 128-129), Newman and Holzman advocate doing away with epistemology itself. Therefore, their work pulls for more than congenial conversation about re-visioning humanistic thought or a welcoming of diverse viewpoints. It incites and provokes radically new ways of doing what we do. It asks us to give up knowing and encourages us to perform. It invites us to philosophize with one another, think more dialectically, and change the world rather than to just talk about our unhappiness with the world.

KNOWLEDGE AS AN OBSTACLE TO LEARNING

The invitation to participate in creating a collaborative, developmental, nonepistemological learning environment is, however, surprisingly difficult to accept. This is due in part to the challenge that such activities pose to entrenched cultural attitudes about knowledge, that is, an unshakable belief in epistemology as foundational. The idea that learning requires performing magnifies the challenge, introducing elements of fear and shame. According to the Castillo dramaturge Dan Friedman (1999), performing "involves doing what you don't know how to do. It involves risk. . . . It means living in a perpetual state of uncertainty" (p. 191). It is hard to improvise if one worries too much about looking foolish. Performing in front of others may also involve shame over a self-perceived loss of dignity in not being oneself or in exposing one's hidden self. The attempt to overcome fear and shame—allowing oneself to play, improvise, and perform—is made more difficult if it takes place within a competitive environment that perpetuates intellectual elitism and one-upmanship.

A discourse that invites experimentation and discourages premature criticism helps to counter a widespread shaming discourse within the culture that defends the status quo against threatening new ideas. Forms of practice that avoid blame and that allow doubt and uncertainty (McNamee, 2000) are antidotes to critical "I know more than you know" language often heard in families, schools, and even professional practice settings. In this welcoming discourse, performing is another way in which to invite participation. The emphasis shifts toward new "meaning-making activit[ies]" (Newman & Holzman, 1997, p. 72) such as social projects, theatrical presentations, and the process of performative social therapy.

A vignette described by Holzman in *The End of Knowing* (Newman & Holzman, 1997) illustrates the idea of learning as social performance. It starts with two 8-year-olds at the Barbara Taylor School, a Vygotskian learning environment. "Charles, a new student . . ., begins taunting Alice for being stupid" (p. 130) and for her inability to spell the word *cat*. Rather than shaming Charles for shaming Alice, the learning director at the school helps Charles to engage in a conversation about how *he* learned to spell. (Charles learned in part by watching television game shows.) An improvisational experiment ensues. Soon, all class members are immersed in writing and producing their own "game show spelling performance" (p. 131). In learning more about how they themselves learn, the children transform a potentially shaming and alienating experience into a developmental collaboration. They seem to realize that if Alice cannot spell, then that is not just her problem but also their problem—and our problem as well.

The learning community in which performative therapy is being developed attempts to create an accepting open setting similar to that of a Vygotskian school. But some of what social therapists do provokes strong reactions because they radically overthrow privilege including that of the knower over the nonknower. When it comes to therapy, they challenge the power and privilege of the knowing therapist over the unknowing (or nonknowing) patient. In this regard, they have an affinity with the antipsychiatry of Deleuze and Guattari and with the world-inverting ideas of Laing. They provoke a defensive reaction among those trained in traditional methods of psychotherapy because they challenge one of the fundamental premises of traditional psychotherapy, that is, that there must be an uneven power relationship between the therapist and the patient, either imagined or real. To overthrow the relationship is heretical. To advocate replacing knowing with activity provokes strong resistance and a self-protective grasping for primitive philosophical weapons.

Over the years, the performative social therapy approach has been subject to misunderstandings and ad hominem attacks on its practitioners (see Holzman, 1999a, pp. 19-30). Newman and Holzman typically have reacted to their critics by inviting them to learn more about the approach through attending performances and engaging in dialogue at public talks and conferences. In contrast to many of these critics, who so far have declined participation in a conversation about possible new practices, are thinkers such as Gergen who have accepted the invitation to dialogue, discuss, and even collaborate. For Gergen (1999), it has been apparent that "Newman and his colleagues have surprised, unsettled, and antagonized," yet within their welcoming discourse, Gergen's "voice of difference has neither been ignored nor [been] annihilated. Rather, it has been treated as an integral part of the play" (p. 2).

REHEARSAL

In *Postmodern Psychologies, Societal Practice, and Political Life,* Holzman and Morss (2000) make a powerful and useful distinction between the official performance of opening night and rehearsal. "Performance," they suggest, "is better revealed by the rehearsal" (p. 91). In rehearsal, there is fluid movement between trying things out, meta-communication about what works and what does not work, and everyday conversation. Rehearsal is a time for experimenting and improvising without succumbing to fear and shame. Developing new postmodern humanistic practices will require overcoming self-consciousness and embarrassment and the belief that more knowledge is needed before acting. Rather than passing on knowledge, new collaborations need to be invented, new conversations need to be invited, and new ways of relating to one another need to be developed. Rehearsal begins right now.

But will humanistic psychologists show up for rehearsal? Do they care enough to revolutionize their traditional ways of thinking and practicing psychotherapy? Faced with an undermining of foundations and guiding truths, they may succumb to what Husserl described as a "great weariness" or a profound state of disbelief and despair (cited in Aanstoos, 1990, p. 4); what Lyotard regarded as grief over the loss of "sublime feelings" and "vigorous emotions" (cited in Newman & Holzman, 1997, p. 70); or what Baudrillard saw as the melancholy subjective state of the masses who have "become bored, restless, [and] apathetic" (cited in Newman & Holzman, 1997, p. 66). Postmodernism *is* hard to take.

Performative social therapy, as one example of a postmodern approach to psychotherapy, shows that other performances are possible—performances yet to be created. Active psychotherapies that encourage collaborative improvisation rather than theory-guided problem solving, as well as approaches that welcome developmental social learning rather than the accumulation of knowledge, hold promise for the future.

In rehearsing and developing new practices, it will be important for humanistic psychologists to free themselves even from their own historical traditions. To grow and develop, they must relinquish their claims to more, better, or different knowledge of what it is to be human and allow themselves to improvise new practices relevant to the diverse multicultural social context of everyday postmodern life. Whether or not humanistic psychologists will show up for rehearsal, despite the end of what is known and familiar, remains to be seen.

NOTES

1. In *Works and Lives*, Geertz (1988) said, "The next necessary thing (so at least it seems to me) is neither the construction of a universal Esperanto-like culture, the culture of airports and motor hotels, nor the invention of some vast technology of human management. It is to enlarge the possibility of intelligible discourse between people quite different from one another in interest, outlook, wealth, and power and yet contained in a world where tumbled as they are into endless connection, it is increasingly difficult to get out of each other's way" (p. 147).

2. In his foreword to Lyotard's (1984) important work, *The Postmodern Condition*, Jameson described postmodernism as "a radical break, both with a dominant culture and aesthetic and . . . a new social and economic moment" (p. vii). In *Postmodernism, or, the Cultural Logic of Late Capitalism*, Jameson (1991) noted that "senses of the end of this or that . . ., taken together, . . . perhaps constitute what is increasingly called postmodernism" (p. 1).

3. As the French philosopher Lyotard (1984) put it, "Simplifying to the extreme, I define postmodern as incredulity toward meta-narratives" (p. xxiv).

4. Aanstoos regards humanism as an unbroken tradition leading from the early Renaissance to the present, but one that went underground during much of the modernist era. "Modernity," Aanstoos (1990) said, "over-rode humanism and suppressed its impact on culture" (p. 5).

5. For example, post-Marxist and feminist challenges to claims of objective truth, poststructuralist and deconstructionist attempts to dethrone language in its representational denotative form, and studies of the social psychology of scientific knowledge all contribute to a new sense of what psychology during the postmodern era could be.

6. The question of postmodern relativism is beyond the scope of this chapter. For a fuller exposition on this issue, see Newman and Holzman (1997, pp. 39-46).

REFERENCES

Aanstoos, C. (1990). Preface. *The Humanistic Psychologist, 18,* 3-6.

Bohart, A. C., Leitner, L. M., & O'Hara, M. (1998). Empirically violated treatments: Disenfranchisement of humanistic and other psychotherapies. *Psychotherapy Research, 8,* 141-157.

Bohart, A. C., O'Hara, M., Leitner, L. M., Wertz, F. J., Stern, E. M., Schneider, K. J., Serlin, I. A., & Greening, T. C. (1997). Guidelines for the provision of humanistic services. *The Humanistic Psychologist, 25,* 64-107.

Friedman, D. (1999). Twenty-two weeks of pointless conversation. In L. Holzman (Ed.), *Performing psychology: A postmodern culture of the mind* (pp. 157-196). New York: Routledge.

Geertz, C. (1988). *Works and lives: The anthropologist as author.* Stanford, CA: Stanford University Press.

Gergen, K. J. (1994). *Realities and relationships: Soundings in social construction.* Cambridge, MA: Harvard University Press.

Gergen, K. J. (1995). Postmodernism as a humanism. *The Humanistic Psychologist, 23,* 71-82.

Gergen, K. J. (1999). Foreword. In L. Holzman (Ed.), *Performing psychology: A postmodern culture of the mind* (pp. 1-3). New York: Routledge.

Holzman, L. (1999a). Introduction. In L. Holzman (Ed.), *Performing psychology: A postmodern culture of the mind* (pp. 5-32). New York: Routledge.

Holzman, L. (1999b). Life as performance. In L. Holzman (Ed.), *Performing psychology: A postmodern culture of the mind* (pp. 49-71). New York: Routledge.

Holzman, L. (2000). Performance, criticism, and postmodern psychology. In L. Holzman & J. Morss (Eds.), *Postmodern psychologies, societal practice, and political life* (pp. 79-90). New York: Routledge.

Holzman, L., & Morss, J. (2000). From identity to relationship: Politics and participation. In L. Holzman & J. Morss (Eds.), *Postmodern psychologies, societal practice, and political life* (pp. 91-92). New York: Routledge.

Jameson, F. (1991). *Postmodernism, or, the cultural logic of late capitalism.* Durham, NC: Duke University Press.

Kvale, S. (1992). *Psychology and postmodernism.* Newbury Park, CA: Sage.

Lyotard, J-F. (1984). *The postmodern condition: A report on knowledge.* Minneapolis: University of Minnesota Press.

McNamee, S. (2000). Dichotomies, discourses, and transformative practices. In L. Holzman & J. Morss (Eds.), *Postmodern psychologies, societal practice, and political life* (pp. 179-189). New York: Routledge.

Newman, F., & Holzman, L. (1997). *The end of knowing: A new developmental way of learning.* New York: Routledge.

O'Hara, M. (1992). Relational humanism: A psychology for a pluralistic world. *The Humanistic Psychologist, 20,* 439-446.

Schneider, K. J. (2000). *APA Division 32 executive committee and board response to the revised APA Template* (now Criteria for Evaluating Treatment Guidelines). Unpublished position paper, American Psychological Association.

Warmoth, A. (1996). *Humanistic psychology and humanistic social science* [online]. Available: www.sonoma.edu/classes/psych490/fall96/writings/arthurw/humsoc.html

CHAPTER 38

Humanistic-Experiential Therapies in the Era of Managed Care

JEANNE C. WATSON AND ARTHUR BOHART

SURVIVAL IN AN ERA of managed care and empirically validated therapies has forced humanistic-experiential practitioners to tailor their approaches to market demands. Unable to resist the pull of market forces, practitioners and researchers have been developing ways in which to make humanistic-experiential approaches meaningful during a time of fierce competition and greater regulation. One of the ways in which this concern is manifested is in the greater attention paid to tailoring specific treatments to specific disorders (Greenberg, Watson, & Lietaer, 1998) and to the development of brief therapy approaches. In this chapter, we provide an overview of the works of a number of humanistic-experiential theorists and practitioners and the ways in which their works can be adapted in an environment of managed health care.

Experiential approaches traditionally have focused on facilitating clients' experiencing in sessions and on developing safe therapeutic relationships as important ways of effecting changes in clients' behavior and feelings (Watson, Greenberg, & Lietaer, 1998). The role of the relationship, and more specifically the working alliance, is even more important as we move to developing briefer treatments (Watson, 1997; Watson & Greenberg, 2000). Research has indicated that clients who reach agreement with their therapists on the goals and tasks of therapy early on do better than clients who do not (Watson & Greenberg, 1998). Thus, if we are to be effective in implementing briefer treatment strategies, then we need to know how to formulate a treatment focus early in therapy and make this relevant to clients' goals so that fruitful collaborations can ensue in a shorter time frame.

FACILITATING CLIENTS' EXPERIENCING PROCESS

The work of Greenberg, Rice, and Elliott (1993) and their colleagues proposes the use of markers to guide therapists in the application of moment-to-moment interventions during the session as well as in the formulation and development of short-term treatment plans. These clinicians have spent considerable energy and resources in identifying markers or client statements that indicate when clients are experiencing specific cognitive-affective problems and in developing the appropriate interventions to facilitate resolution of these problems. There are markers to identify conflict splits, self-criticisms (Greenberg & Watson, 1998), unfinished business with significant others (Greenberg & Foerster, 1996; Greenberg & Paivio, 1997), problematic reactions (Rice & Saperia, 1984), an unclear felt sense (Gendlin, 1981; Leijssen, 1998), and loss of meaning (Clarke, 1991). In addition, other markers have been identified for empathic responding (Watson, in press) and for work with victims of post-traumatic stress (Elliott, Davis, & Slatick, 1998; Kennedy-Moore & Watson, 1999). Markers that indicate possible problems with the therapeutic alliance and clients' emotional processing in therapy have also been noted (Kennedy-Moore & Watson, 1999; Watson, in press).

A distinction can be made among habitual markers, task markers, and moment-to-moment processing markers. To facilitate brief treatment approaches, it is essential to identify clients' characteristic ways of behaving in experiential terms and how these are contributing to their current life difficulties. Thus, process-experiential therapists pull together information from multiple levels to develop treatment plans for clients. Each treatment plan is custom tailored to each client's life history, presenting problem, current life issues, and moment-to-moment process in the session.

Clients learn ways of relating to others and themselves from their interactions with caregivers early in life. They learn whether to be watchful, managing, critical, blaming,

neglectful, and destructive as opposed to protective, nurturing, understanding, and supportive of themselves and the people around them (Barrett-Lennard, 1997; Bowlby, 1971; Perls, 1969; Rogers, 1965; van Kessel & Lietaer, 1998). By attending closely to clients' early attachment histories and interactions with significant others, we are able to identify some of their more habitual interpersonal and intrapsychic processes.

This information is important because it provides a context in which to understand clients' presenting issues and the roots of the problems that brought them into therapy. Clients usually reveal how they treat themselves and others in their descriptions of their current problems. The identification of habitual styles of expression is very important in alerting therapists to what is significant and poignant in clients' experiences. If we understand clients' histories and typical ways of responding, then we will be able to identify those markers and the types of microtasks that will be relevant to clients. This procedure is important in developing a good working alliance and facilitates the development of agreement on the tasks and goals of therapy. For example, it is important to identify whether clients invalidate their experiences and whether they are self-critical or neglectful of their own needs and values.

Once clinicians have formulated these characteristic styles, they are in a position to know what is especially poignant and salient for their clients. This enables them to attend to those task markers that are particularly relevant for clients' current concerns. Therapists then are able to know whether to attend to markers that indicate unfinished business, conflict splits, or problematic reactions. Moreover, if they are able to formulate clients' present difficulties in terms of the specific cognitive-affective processes identified by the markers, and if they demonstrate how these are contributing to clients' problems, then they are better positioned to forge positive working alliances and to facilitate clients' improvement in therapy.

The adoption of a specific focus to stimulate and facilitate clients' experiencing is central to brief psychotherapies. Klein, Mathieu-Coughlan, and Kiesler (1986) observed that clients' experiencing process became qualitatively different after they were able to formulate experiential questions and purposefully track them using inner subjective referents. This type of process often resulted in clients' redefining their problems so that there was a distinct shift in the quality of their experiencing.

Experiential therapists facilitate clients' experiencing by responding empathically to clients' inner experiences. This requires that therapists be attuned to their clients' inner worlds and felt senses. One way of remaining attuned is to listen to the poignant aspects of clients' narratives. These are moments when clients use colorful or idiosyncratic language to describe events or their reactions to them. Alternatively, clients may become quite emotional, and it may be obvious from the breaks in their voices or other nonverbal behaviors that they are experiencing intense emotion. At these times, it is important for experiential therapists to respond with empathic affirmation and understanding so that clients feel heard and understood (Greenberg & Elliott, 1997; Watson, in press).

At other times, therapists can stimulate clients' experiencing using evocative and exploratory empathic responses (Rice, 1974). Evocative responses require therapists to use colorful imagistic language or metaphors to bring clients' feelings alive in sessions. At still other times, therapists can respond empathically with an exploratory focus to stimulate clients to examine their perceptions and construals. This approach can help clients to identify salient aspects of their experiences and the idiosyncratic meanings that events might have for them. Sometimes, experiential therapists can further clients' explorations of their inner experiences by offering empathic conjectures on clients' inner states. And on occasion, experiential therapists empathically challenge their clients to think of alternative perspectives and views. Empathic challenging is very supportive and gentle in that therapists, when advancing alternative perspectives, are very careful to respect clients as the experts on their feelings. The alternatives, therefore, are proffered as other possible perspectives and views that clients can try on but should not feel coerced or pressured to adopt (Watson, in press).

In addition to using empathic responses to facilitate clients' experiencing in sessions, experiential therapists use a number of tasks or interventions to arouse clients' emotions in sessions so that these can be processed (Greenberg et al., 1993). These tasks include "chair work" and systematically building the scene. Chair work is useful if clients express chronically negative feelings about significant people in their lives (Greenberg & Foerster, 1996; Paivio & Greenberg, 1995). Having clients imagine their significant others in other chairs can bring those people alive in the room and help clients to access their feelings and needs vis-à-vis the others. The expression of feelings and needs to imagined others provides tremendous relief and enables clients to acknowledge and own the needs that have been frustrated. This shift in orientation frees clients to begin thinking of alternative ways of having their needs met. Clients often are able to reframe earlier perspectives, and they sometimes are able to see the others' perspectives (Watson, 1996), thereby allowing for the integration of affect and reason.

The markers for the two-chair task are clients' statements indicating that they are being self-critical, are undecided about a course of action, or imagine other people as criticizing them. The objective with this task is to have clients voice the negative self-criticisms or the imagined criticisms of others so as to get the clients to react to these statements. When clients voice the critical statements out loud, they usually react with pain, out of which state they can access a need to protect and defend themselves from the hurtful criticisms. Once they have achieved this awareness, they are in a better position to understand the needs of the conflicting sides of their personalities and to begin to negotiate different balances that each side can live with and that are more satisfying to the self overall.

Another technique for helping clients to deal with reactions that take them by surprise, or that seem overwhelming or out of control to them, is systematic evocative unfolding (Rice & Saperia, 1984; Watson, 1996). This technique uses vivid, concrete, imagistic language to help clients retrieve their episodic memories of events. Once the memories of these events have been brought to life in sessions, clients are more easily able to identify the specific triggers that prompted the reactions to better understand the specific meanings or significance of the triggers. Helping clients to rebuild images of different scenes and events using words is very useful in trauma work because it enables clients to reprocess some of the feelings and reactions that they might have suppressed or denied at the time (Elliott et al., 1998; Kennedy-Moore & Watson, 1999).

In summary, experiential therapists have developed a number of different techniques to facilitate clients' experiencing in sessions. These interventions provide models of functioning that enable clinicians to identify clients' habitual styles of treating themselves. With this knowledge, they are able to formulate clients' problems more efficiently and suggest ways of working in brief therapy to help clients resolve certain life difficulties more quickly. The emphasis continues to be on facilitating clients' emotional processing so that they can lead more satisfying lives.

FACILITATING THE RELATIONSHIP IN BRIEF PROCESS-EXPERIENTIAL THERAPY

In short-term and brief therapy approaches, therapists need to be more concentrated on their efforts to establish good working alliances. It is useful to think of the relationship in terms of early, middle, and late phases, with each period having different tasks and goals. At the beginning of therapy, experiential therapists make assessments of how in tune clients are with their inner experiences. Rogers defined *experience* as all that is going on within an individual or organism that is potentially available to awareness. The dictionary defines it as anything observed or lived through as well as feelings and individual reactions to events (Merriam Webster, 1989).

One of the ways in which experiential therapists assess how in touch clients are with their inner experiences is by attending to their vocal quality and the contents of their disclosures (Rice & Wagstaff, 1967; Rice, Watson, & Greenberg, 1996). If clients are able to turn their attention inward, as revealed by changes in their vocal tones such that they soften their voices, their speech patterns become ragged with unusual pauses, and their reactions and descriptions of events become more vivid and idiosyncratic, then it can be assumed that clients are able to be in touch with their inner experiences and use them as reference points in their explorations of themselves and the world. In this case, therapists can move directly to stimulating clients' experiencing process so as to facilitate their explorations and resolutions of negative emotional material.

In cases where clients speak in rehearsed and carefully modulated tones and focus their attention solely on events outside of themselves using conventional well-worn terms, it can be assumed that they are not in touch with their experiences. In these cases, the first task that must be accomplished is for therapists to have clients agree to focus on their inner experiences and to bring them into conscious awareness so that they can be processed. Therapists can explain to their clients that an important task in experiential therapy work is to help them gain access to the parts of their experiencing of which they are unaware. Simultaneously, therapists can be directing their reflections and other interventions toward clients' experiencing as they try to help clients flesh out their feelings and reactions. Therapists also might need to help clients see how attending to their reactions and feelings will help them to feel better so that clients see the task of disclosing their feelings as relevant to their goals in therapy (Watson, in press; Watson & Greenberg, 1998).

Once clients are agreeable to focusing on their inner experiences, therapists and clients move into the middle phase of therapy. During this phase, experiential therapists are alert to the specific cognitive-affective problems that their clients are experiencing, such as self-critical splits, difficulty in accessing their inner experiences, and chronic negative feelings about significant others. This alerts experiential therapists to moments when intervening would be most productive. As they move into this working phase of therapy, experiential therapists

need to be very carefully attuned to the balance between direction and responsiveness (Watson, Kalogerakos, & Enright, 1998).

Therapists need to be attentive to moments when their clients feel overstimulated during this period or when they become overwhelmed by their feelings and need to distance themselves from their experiencing. These moments may be signaled when clients say that they are blank, change the subject, or question their therapists' suggestions. Sometimes, therapists might have to very deliberately help clients to focus on their inner states (Gendlin, 1981; Leijssen, 1996) and help them to develop vocabularies for their inner experiences.

GENDLIN'S FOCUSING-ORIENTED THERAPY

Facilitating experiential change is the core of Gendlin's (1996) focusing-oriented therapy.[1] For Gendlin, experiencing is an ongoing process that includes both cognition and emotion. Experience is more finely ordered and intricate than are any of the words and concepts that we use to describe it. Gendlin (1997) said, "A situation [and the experience of the situation] is so finely ordered that almost anything we say about it is too simple" (p. 32). He held that when one puts experience into words, one does not merely report on something already formed; instead, the very act of putting it into words changes and carries experience forward.

There is always a "more" that lies beyond the words and concepts that we use to represent experience. The experienced complexity that underlies words and concepts implicitly contains the situations in which we live. Experience is concrete and situational. Past learning and words, concepts, philosophies, or rules that have been carried forward into the current situation "cross" with the current situation to both influence our experience of the situation and be influenced, so that their meanings subtly change and are carried forward. Therefore, as we encounter each new situation, there is an implicit potential for new development or the "carrying forward" of old concepts, rules, words, or ways of being. In each situation, we are "making ourselves anew." Gendlin (1997) suggested that "a living body is a self-organizing process" (p. 27) and that one's experience is always "open for further living and action and often demands further steps" (p. 7). There is always room for a new step. Furthermore, and most important to us as therapists, there are situations in which new steps are demanded. These are just the situations where our old rules, concepts, or ways of being are not working, and we must go further. Often implicitly, we know what a next productive step is or will look like. If we try to intellectually manufacture a step and it does not fit, then we can feel our bodies resisting. We know that it is not right, just as we know when we have chosen a word or concept to express an idea and that it is not quite right. When we find the right step, there is a sense of relief or release (Gendlin called it a "felt give"). For Gendlin, the process of change is a creative one of tuning into the implicit experienced complexity of the problem, from which new implications or new steps arise. Psychotherapy is just this process of helping people to "think and experience forward" from where they are to new ways of being and behaving.

Gendlin's focusing-oriented psychotherapy is an integrative therapy designed to facilitate this creative carrying forward process. The basic process is one of facilitating attention to experience in a receptive, inwardly focused manner that helps to carry it forward. Therapists might do nothing but listen in a traditional Rogerian way. For some clients, it is very difficult to represent their inner experiences so that it is particularly difficult for therapists to respond empathically. With these clients, it can be useful to teach them the technique of focusing.

Focusing is an exercise developed by Gendlin (1981) to promote clients' experiencing process in sessions. The steps of focusing ask clients to locate those places in their bodies where they experience their feelings and then to pay attention to those places while they let their feelings take shape in words or images. Leijssen's (1990) research into the steps of focusing identified four components as necessary for the successful resolution of the exercise: a bodily felt sense, an image, a label to describe the felt sense, and a sense of relief. Focusing can be useful for clients who are very distant from their feelings as well as for clients who are overwhelmed by them. In the latter case, focusing on feelings can often diminish them and provide some structure and a way of looking at them. In the case of people who are very distant from their inner experiences, focusing frequently provides them with a way of getting in touch with what is happening even if initially that is limited to an awareness of bodily sensations (Leijssen, 1990).

In addition, Gendlin may use concepts and procedures from many different therapies if they are meaningful and relevant to where clients are experientially. The key difference is that therapists always make sure to help clients check the concepts against their own experiences. They are useful only if they fit experientially. Gendlin (1996) discussed the integrative use of different approaches and procedures within his approach. He suggested that different procedures be thought of as different *avenues* of therapeutic change, and he identified a number of them including the use of imagery, role-play, words, cognitive beliefs, memories, feelings, emotional catharsis, interpersonal interactions, dreams, and habitual behavior. Each can be used in an experiential way. Therapists are not limited to the use of any specific avenue, however Gendlin might advocate learning how to use each avenue. Any avenue can lead to a felt sense, and any avenue can be used to carry it forward. For example, a therapist can engage in a process of challenging dysfunctional beliefs. However, from an experiential perspective, the therapist might also ask what the experiential felt sense says and then use that to work toward change. The cognitive challenge might be to the dysfunctional cognition "I'm no good." This negative evaluation may be challenged by asking for contrary evidence such as memories of times when the client has done good things. Subsequently, the felt sense can be consulted. The therapist might ask "So, how does that feel inside?" and the client might reply "Well, that feels sort of right, but there is more to what I mean by 'I'm no good' than that. It is more like 'I never accomplish anything.'" This further differentiation then can be addressed therapeutically.

Gendlin's focusing-oriented therapy has the potential to be used in a wide range of contexts. What is added to traditional approaches is that nothing is ever tried, nor is any truth ever accepted, unless it is first checked with the client's felt sense. Checking with the client's felt sense is used as a compass for keeping on the right track. In its pure form, the focus is on empathic listening as the primary "technique," with other procedures from other therapies used relatively sparingly.

MAHRER'S EXPERIENTIAL PSYCHOTHERAPY

Mahrer's (1996) experiential psychotherapy postulates that experiencing potential is at the core of human functioning. The goal of experiential therapy is to access the deeper experiencing potential so that it is

possible for the person to become "a qualitatively new person whose potentials for experiencing now include the integrated deeper potential. The person has become a qualitatively new person, perhaps only for a few moments or for a while or from now on." In addition, "the person is now free of the scenes of bad feeling that had been front and center in the beginning of [the] session. These bad-feelinged scenes are no longer a part of the qualitatively new person" (p. 82). Other than this, there is no specified outcome of experiential therapy. It is not meant to specifically reduce anxiety, depression, schizophrenic symptoms, obsessive-compulsive disorder, drinking problems, anorexia, or any other set of symptoms.

Experiential therapy consists of four steps, and the therapist and client go through each of these in all sessions. Each session is considered complete in and of itself. Mahrer (1993) believes that some clients can make major changes in even one session. The four steps are as follows: being in the moment of strong feeling and accessing the inner experiencing, developing an integrative good relationship with inner experiencing, being the inner experiencing in earlier scenes from one's life, and being and behaving as the inner experiencing in the present. In the first step, the client imagines himself or herself in a scene of strong feeling (e.g., a recent conflict with a boss). The therapist tries to allow the client's experiencing to flow through his or her own experiencing. The therapist's job is to "be" the experiencing of the client as much as possible. As the person accesses strong feeling, he or she is stuck within the operating potential. However, the therapist is in a position to access the deeper experiencing. So, for example, while the overly dutiful client is horrified at having cheated on her taxes, the therapist is accessing the deeper experiencing potential, which is the pleasure in getting away with something and defying authority.

In the second step, the goal is to help the client develop an integrative good relationship with the inner experiencing. This includes helping the client to be aware of the inner experiencing, savor the bodily sensation, let it be, and welcome and appreciate it. In the third step, the client is asked to think of an earlier scene when he or she was the inner experiencing, such as enjoying getting away with something and defying authority during childhood, and then to relive it. The second and third steps help the client to accept and incorporate a potential that can enrich his or her personality if integrated in a productive way.

Finally, in the fourth step, the client is to live imaginatively in the present world while being the inner experiencing. For example, the client might rehearse scenes of getting away with something and defying authority in his or her present world. Done in a type of "brainstorming" way, these scenes can be wild and far-fetched. Eventually, the therapist and client narrow it down to a scene that is realistic, for example, a client standing up to his or her boss on an important issue.

This is an existential-humanistic therapy in that the goal is to expand the person's potential for functioning. How the person integrates the new potential into his or her life is up to the person. In one case, for example, a woman came in complaining of neck pains (Mahrer, 1989). Therapy did not explicitly focus on the neck pains; rather, it focused on the client's deep experiencing potential for being "devilish." On the surface, her operating potential was that of being overly responsible. As she accessed and accepted her more devilish side, she made a major career change and, incidentally, the neck pains vanished. This approach to therapy integrates strategies from other therapies for use in carrying out the steps. Mahrer includes psychodynamic elements in the form of reliving earlier scenes as well as behavioral elements in the form of rehearsing new behavior in the extratherapy world. Paradoxical interventions can also be found in some of the things done to help the person appreciate and accept inner experiencing.

Mahrer's approach to therapy is short term insofar as he treats each session as an end in itself, thereby making it very compatible with working in a managed care environment. However, the goal of treatment is not symptom reduction but rather expansion of each client's potential. Consequently, at times it might conflict with the objectives required by managed care providers.

EXISTENTIAL-INTEGRATIVE THERAPY

The basic purpose of existential-integrative therapy is to maximize clients' freedom (Schneider & May, 1995; Schneider, 1998). Freedom is defined as (a) the cultivation of choice within the natural and self-imposed limits of living and (b) the capacity to constrict or expand across a range of conscious and subconscious aspects of human existence. These aspects include the physiological, the behavioral, the cognitive, the psychosexual, the interpersonal, and the "being" or experiential. The existential-integrative framework incorporates a range of therapeutic stances—medical, cognitive-behavioral, psychoanalytic, relational, and experiential—to deal with each of these aspects.

Schneider and May (1995) argued that human experience is organized along a constrictive-expansive continuum. Dread of expansive or constrictive polarities promotes extreme or dysfunctional counterreactions to that dread. Hyperconstriction characterizes dysfunctions such as depression, anxiety, dependency, agoraphobia, paranoia, and obsessive-compulsiveness. Hyperexpansion characterizes disorders such as mania, antisocial personality, hysteria, and narcissism.

Dysfunction involves compulsive (or polarized) expansion and/or constriction in each of the aspects of human existence. For example, at the physiological level, persons may be compulsively constrictive (e.g., inhibited, sedated) or compulsively expansive (e.g., excitable, frenetic). At the environmental level, they may be polarized by their conditioning. At the cognitive level, they may be polarized by constricted dichotomous (either/or) scripts or expansive overgeneralized scripts. At the psychosexual level, they may be polarized by their histories and lack of effective integration of psychosexuality into their personalities. They may be constricted from being physically or sexually abused. Or, they may be expansive in the form of physical or sexual acting out. At the interpersonal level, the issue is one of achieving a balance between being an autonomous self and being able to be interpersonally connected. Finally, at a core experiential/being level, they may feel either unmanageable smallness and obliteration or unmanageable greatness and chaos. The goal of therapy is to maximize access to, and integration of, each of the aspects of being. At the physiological level, the goal may be to help clients become more autonomous by freeing them from substance abuse or by helping them to manage their physiology better. At the environmental level, it may be to alter inappropriately expansive or constrictive reactions to reinforcement contingencies. At the cognitive level, it may be to help them think more discerningly. At the psychosexual level, it may be to help them integrate their affects and drives into adaptive experience and behavior patterns. At

the interpersonal level, it may be to help them become less fearful of people so that they can relate more intimately, or it may be to help them become more sensitive so that they are not overly intrusive. Finally, at the being level, it may be to help them overcome and integrate basic fears of smallness or obliteration or of chaotic expansiveness.

Therapeutic techniques are, accordingly, seen as *liberation strategies*. They are relevant on the basis of deep attunement to clients' desires and capacities for change. The therapist works with the aspects that the client is most comfortable with or that are in accord with his or her particular mode of living. The therapist, therefore, may use physiological procedures such as medication or detoxification (if appropriate), cognitive-behavioral techniques, psychodynamic exploration, and interpersonal techniques to help free the client in the relevant mode of being. The therapist works at the deepest level that he or she can, contingent on (a) what the client wants and needs and (b) what is possible given the therapeutic contract and constraints. Ultimately, however, the existential-integrative therapist attempts to be available to the client at the fuller or being level of his or her experience. (This level is characterized by immediacy, kinesthesia, affect, and profundity.) Some clients might not want to move to the being level. For many, however, it is at this level that fundamental issues of authenticity are addressed.

Existential-integrative therapy can address the needs of a wide range of clients by using procedures and ideas from a variety of perspectives without giving up the dimensions that existential-humanistic therapists value. Therefore, it can be practiced in a diversity of settings. In many settings, however, limits may preclude existential-integrative therapists from pursuing the deepest levels of change even with clients who are capable of and ready for such change. In these cases, it may be necessary for therapists to arrange to continue to see these clients outside of the managed care environment (perhaps for reduced fees) or to make other arrangements.

BOHART AND TALLMAN'S VIEW OF THE CLIENT AS ACTIVE SELF-HEALER

In contrast to the other humanistic and experiential approaches, Bohart and Tallman (1999) provided an empirically supported[2] meta-theoretical perspective that serves as a platform for integrative therapy practice. It is based on the proposition that the client is the real "therapist" in therapy. The therapist is the client's aide or assistant. Therapeutic theories, structures, and procedures are tools that the client uses. Many clients can use virtually any approach to self-heal, and this is why it is so difficult to find differences among different approaches to therapy.

Bohart and Tallman (1999) reviewed a large body of research showing that (a) therapeutic procedures and techniques play only a modest role in producing outcome, (b) different approaches work about equally well on average, (c) self-help procedures work about as well as professionally provided therapy, (d) the relationship between the therapist and client is more important than procedures, (e) client involvement is the single most important predictor of outcome, and (f) there is a considerable body of evidence that humans are resilient and have a capacity for self-healing. These findings suggest that it is the client's involvement that makes therapy work. The therapeutic relationship and procedures contribute primarily to the extent that they invite and sustain involvement and provide some viable structure for learning and problem solving. If the client is actively involved, then he or she can use the structure of many different therapy approaches (or even self-help procedures) to self-heal.

Bohart and Tallman's (1999) thesis of the client as active self-healer provides a meta-perspective in that the therapist and client can choose a procedure from any therapy that is plausible and acceptable to the client. As a meta-perspective, it stands in contrast to the medical model, which significantly influences both therapy research and models of therapy itself. In the medical model, the therapist is the expert on what the client needs. Procedures are "interventions" or "treatments." Both terms imply that healing is generated from an external force (the procedure) that is applied to the client. Research designs equally imply that it is the therapist's interventions that precipitate change *in* clients. The typical model of therapy is as follows:

Therapist Interventions → Operate on Clients → To Produce Effects.

The medical model also dissects the client. Therapy is described as a process that works by operating on dysfunctional parts of the client. Interventions (depending on the orientation) are said to restructure cognitions, modify fear structures, restructure emotion schemes, deepen processing, precipitate insight, strengthen egos, access emotions, eliminate self-criticism, recondition proprioceptive responses, strengthen self-structure, access deep experiencing potential, and/or heighten experiencing. Descriptions of therapy through these lenses typically represent clients as having things done to them, not unlike patients in surgery being operated on.[3]

By contrast, the client as active self-healer perspective assumes that interventions have no power to effect any type of change independently of the client. Interventions have no "life" in themselves; their life, energy, and intelligence come from the client's investment in them. They are more properly viewed as tools that the client can use to shape his or her own outcomes. According to this view, the way in which therapy works is as follows:

Clients → Operate on Therapists'
Interventions → To Produce Effects
and Outcomes.

Clients can creatively use procedures to serve their own productive ends. For example, Bohart and Boyd (1997) found that clients could interpret empathic reflections as providing support and validation (if that is what they needed to grow) or as providing insight (if that is what they needed). Tallman (1990) noted the following after interviews with ex-clients:

> I had taken my interventions and my words much too seriously. Patients reported following suggestions that I could not remember having made. They created their own interpretations, which were sometimes quite different from what I recollected and sometimes more creative and suitable versions of my suggestions. (p. 60)

Therapy is a dialogue between two whole, intelligent humans. Through the dialogue, the therapist and client genuinely collaborate on the best ways for the client to self-heal. The therapist offers ideas. The client offers ideas. Client creativity is prized. Procedures and interventions are not mechanistically "applied to" the client's dysfunction based on some formula or manualized procedure. This view recognizes that the arbitrary application of procedures—even those based on markers—cannot occur without the client's agreement and cooperation. The therapist can use marker information to suggest that a procedure might be helpful to the client at a given point in therapy, but the therapist does not "prescribe" it. Working together, the client and therapist decide on the usefulness of the procedure. The therapist is neither "process directive" nor "content directive" (Greenberg et al., 1993). In fact, the whole issue of whether the therapist should be directive or nondirective is rejected. The very posing of the issue represents the "therapist-centrism" (Bickman & Salzer, 1996) of the field and totally ignores the fact that there is another person present in therapy—the client. Thinking of the client as a genuinely equal partner in a collaborative relationship, the issue becomes one of therapist and client *codirectivity*.

Therefore, therapy is not an operation but rather the provision of a set of *learning opportunities*. The five learning opportunities provided by different therapies include provision of an empathic workspace within which clients can creatively think through their problems (e.g., client-centered therapy), an effective interpersonal learning environment (e.g., therapist as good model as advanced in existential and modern psychodynamic therapy), a context for stimulating dialogue leading to new insights and perspectives (e.g., psychodynamic interpretations, Socratic questioning), exercises to promote creativity (e.g., two-chair work, paradoxical interventions), and programs for teaching new skills and reducing fears (e.g., cognitive-behavioral therapy). Through the collaborative synergy of two intelligent beings working together, in a given session, procedures from therapies as diverse as cognitive-behavioral and experiential might be used.

This meta-perspective allows for a great deal of flexibility in practice based on a fundamental respect and trust in the client's self-healing potential. Different procedures may be used so long as they are offered instead of prescribed and the relationship is genuinely dialogic and collaborative. Because what makes therapy work are clients and not procedures, in a managed care context the therapist would focus on dialogue with the client in regard to whatever procedure is being used, just as a good coach or mentor would dialogue with his or her students on what they are learning. If the therapist feels compelled to use one set of procedures either because of an external review board's directives or because of an agency's requirement to follow empirically validated treatments (Task Force on Promotion and Dissemination of Psychological Procedures, 1995), this is not a problem given that it is *how* the procedure is used that is the issue. If it is a cognitive-behavioral procedure, for example, then the therapist would be interested in the client's reactions to it, the client's possible creative modifications of it, and the client's use of it to learn in ways not officially prescribed by cognitive theory (e.g., exploring experience or the past). Any procedure can be "humanized" once one realizes that it is clients and therapists working together creatively that creates the life and meaning in procedures.

CONCLUSION

We have presented five alternative approaches to treatment under the umbrella of humanistic-experiential psychotherapies. From our review, it can be seen that some approaches are more or less able to be adapted for brief treatments. Process-experiential therapy has been manualized for brief treatment approaches to depression, trauma, and anxiety. Gendlin's focusing approach can be used productively in a short-term treatment setting. Moreover, one of the advantages of this approach is that it is a self-help technique that clients can easily learn and take away with them to use later

when necessary. Like the other experiential approaches, those of Mahrer and the existentialists, although not yet part of the managed care repertoire, could easily be adapted for short-term therapy. The approach put forward by Bohart and Tallman, which views clients as active self-healers, is a more meta-theoretical or philosophical approach that easily embraces treatments provided within a managed care environment.

Irrespective of which approach is used, therapists offering brief treatments need to be aware of the time schedule that is imposed by managed care. To be most effective, it seems important to identify a specific focus early on and to identify a piece of work that can be accomplished in a short period of time. In brief treatments, therapists need to pay special attention to helping their clients resolve specific problems and develop new ways of coping and being in the world prior to termination. They also need to be aware that the short period of time can both enhance their work with clients and detract from it. Some clients respond very favorably to the knowledge that there is a specified time limit to their work. These clients are very goal directed. They are able to focus on their problems and experiencing and are able to resolve personally troubling material quickly. For other clients, however, the short period of time might inhibit them from opening up. These clients would benefit from longer periods of therapy. Their own sense of vulnerability at the prospect of a brief treatment should be trusted and respected. It is important to help these clients to identify and define the problem areas so that they can begin to think of solutions and alternative ways of dealing with them. Exploration of these clients' experiencing process tends to be superficial and their capacity to integrate feelings usually is deliberately shut down as they try to cope with early termination. In these cases, therapists need to come up with alternatives so that clients can continue to work if they so choose once therapy is terminated.

NOTES

1. Parts of this description have been borrowed and reworked from Bohart (1999).

2. There are many ways in which approaches to therapy can be empirically supported besides the "empirically supported treatments" of Division 12 of the American Psychological Association (Task Force on Promotion and Dissemination of Psychological Procedures, 1995). The approach advocated here does not view therapy as a treatment. Therefore, *empirical support* takes on a different meaning. In this case, it means that the basic postulates of the approach all have empirical support.

3. This is despite the acknowledgment by virtually all approaches that the client must be an active participant. In effect, however, such activity consists of compliance with the treatment. But it is the treatment or intervention that does all of the modifying of the particular part of the client that the theory says needs to be modified.

REFERENCES

Barrett-Lennard, G. (1997). The recovery of empathy towards self and others. In A. Bohart & L. S. Greenberg (Eds.), *Empathy reconsidered*. Washington, DC: American Psychological Association.

Bickman, L., & Salzer, M. S. (1996, August). *Dose-response, disciplines, and self-help: Policy implications of* Consumer Reports *findings*. Paper presented at the meeting of the American Psychological Association, Toronto.

Bohart, A. C. (1999). *An implicational view of self-healing and personality change based on Gendlin's theory of experiencing* (No. CG029650). Greensboro, NC: ERIC Counseling and Student Services Clearinghouse.

Bohart, A. C., & Boyd, G. (1997, December). *Clients' construction of the therapy process: A qualitative analysis*. Paper presented at the meeting of the North American Association of the Society for Psychotherapy Research, Tucson, AZ.

Bohart, A. C., & Tallman, K. (1999). *How clients make therapy work: The process of active self-healing*. Washington, DC: American Psychological Association.

Bowlby, J. (1971). *Attachment and loss, Vol: 1. Attachment*. New York: Basic Books.

Clarke, K. (1991). A performance model of the creation of meaning event. *Psychotherapy, 28*, 395-401.

Elliott, R., Davis, K., & Slatick, E. (1998). Process-experiential therapy for post-traumatic stress difficulties. In L. S. Greenberg, J. C. Watson, & G. Lietaer (Eds.), *Handbook of experiential psychotherapy* (pp. 249-271). New York: Guilford.

Gendlin, E. T. (1981). *Focusing*. New York: Bantam Books.

Gendlin, E. T. (1996). *Focusing-oriented psychotherapy: A manual of the experiential method*. New York: Guilford.

Gendlin, E. T. (1997). How philosophy cannot appeal to experience, and how it can. In D. M. Levin (Ed.), *Language beyond postmodernism: Saying and thinking in Gendlin's philosophy* (pp. 3-41). Evanston, IL: Northwestern University Press.

Greenberg, L. S., & Elliott, R. (1997). Varieties of empathic responding. In A. Bohart & L. S. Greenberg (Eds.), *Empathy reconsidered.* Washington, DC: American Psychological Association.

Greenberg, L. S., & Foerster, F. S. (1996). Resolving unfinished business: The process of change. *Journal of Consulting and Clinical Psychology, 64,* 439-446.

Greenberg, L. S., & Paivio, S. C. (1997). *Working with emotions in psychotherapy.* New York: Guilford.

Greenberg, L. S., Rice, L. N., & Elliott, R. (1993). *Facilitating emotional change: The moment-by-moment process.* New York: Guilford.

Greenberg, L. S., & Watson, J. C. (1998). Client-centered and process-experiential psychotherapy in the treatment of depression: A comparative outcome study. *Psychotherapy Research, 8,* 210-224.

Greenberg, L. S., Watson, J. C., & Lietaer, G. (1998). *Handbook of experiential psychotherapy.* New York: Guilford.

Kennedy-Moore, E., & Watson, J. C. (1999). *Expressing emotion: Myths, realities, and therapeutic strategies.* New York: Guilford.

Klein, M. H., Mathieu-Coughlan, P., & Kiesler, D. J. (1986). The experiencing scales. In L. S. Greenberg & W. Pisof (Eds.), *The psychotherapeutic process: A research handbook* (pp. 21-71). New York: Guilford.

Leijssen, M. (1990). On focusing and the necessary conditions of therapeutic change. In G. Lietaer, J. Rombauts, & R. van Balen (Eds.), *Client-centered and experiential psychotherapy in the nineties* (pp. 225-250). Leuven, Belgium: Leuven University Press.

Leijssen, M. (1996). Characteristics of a healing inner relationship. In R. Hutterer, G. Pawlowsky, P. F. Schmid, & R. Stpsits (Eds.), *Client-centered and experiential psychotherapy: A paradigm in motion* (pp. 427-438). Vienna, Austria: Lang.

Leijssen, M. (1998). Focusing microprocesses. In L. S. Greenberg, J. C. Watson, & G. Lietaer (Eds.), *Handbook of experiential psychotherapy* (pp. 121-154). New York: Guilford.

Mahrer, A. R. (1989). *Dreamwork in psychotherapy and self-change.* New York: Norton.

Mahrer, A. R. (1993). Transformational psychotherapy sessions. *Journal of Humanistic Psychology, 33,* 30-37.

Mahrer, A. R. (1996). *The complete guide to experiential psychotherapy.* New York: John Wiley.

Merriam-Webster. (1989). *Webster's new dictionary and thesaurus.* Springfield, MA: Author.

Paivio, S. C., & Greenberg, L. S. (1995). Resolving unfinished business: Experiential therapy using empty-chair dialogue. *Journal of Consulting and Clinical Psychology, 63,* 419-425.

Perls, F. (1969). *Ego, hunger, and aggression.* New York: Random House.

Rice, L. N. (1974). The evocative function of the therapist. In D. Wexler & L. N. Rice (Eds.), *Innovations in client-centered therapy* (pp. 289-311). New York: John Wiley.

Rice, L. N., & Saperia, E. (1984). A task analysis of the resolution of problematic reactions. In L. N. Rice & L. S. Greenberg (Eds.), *Patterns of change: Intensive analysis of psychotherapy process* (pp. 29-66). New York: Guilford.

Rice, L. N., & Wagstaff, A. K. (1967). Client voice quality and expressive style as indexes of productive psychotherapy. *Journal of Consulting Psychology, 31,* 557-563.

Rice, L. N., Watson, J. C., & Greenberg, L. S. (1996). *A measure of client's expressive stance.* Toronto: York University.

Rogers, C. R. (1965). *Client-centered therapy: Its current practice, implications, and theory.* Boston: Houghton Mifflin.

Schneider, K. J., & May, R. (1995). *The psychology of existence: An integrative, clinical perspective.* New York: McGraw-Hill.

Schneider, K. J. (1998). Existential processes. In L. S. Greenberg, J. C. Watson, & G. Lietaer (Eds.), *Handbook of experiential psychotherapy* (pp. 103-120). New York: Guilford.

Tallman, M. (1990). *Single session therapy.* San Francisco: Jossey-Bass.

Task Force on Promotion and Dissemination of Psychological Procedures. (1995) Division of Clinical Psychology of the American Psychological Association. Training and dissemination of empirically validated psychological treatments: Report and recommendations. *The Clinical Psychologist, 48,* 3-23.

van Kessel, W., & Lietaer, G. (1998). Interpersonal processes. In L. S. Greenberg, J. C. Watson, & G. Lietaer (Eds.), *Handbook of experiential psychotherapy.* New York: Guilford.

Watson, J. C. (1996). An examination of clients' cognitive-affective processes during the exploration of problematic reactions. *Journal of Consulting and Clinical Psychology, 63,* 459-464.

Watson, J. C. (1997, April). *Manifesting client's agency in process-experiential psychotherapy.* Paper presented at the meeting of the Society for the Exploration of Psychotherapy Integration, Toronto.

Watson, J. C. (in press). Re-visioning empathy: Theory, research, and practice. In D. Cain & J. Seeman (Eds.), *Handbook of humanistic psychotherapy.* Washington, DC: American Psychological Association.

Watson, J. C., & Greenberg, L. S. (1998). The therapeutic alliance in short-term humanistic and experiential therapies. In J. Safran & C. Muran (Eds.), *The therapeutic alliance in brief psychotherapy* (pp. 123-146). Washington, DC: American Psychological Association.

Watson, J. C., & Greenberg, L. S. (2000). Alliance ruptures and repairs in experiential therapy. *Journal of Clinical Psychology, 56*(2).

Watson, J. C., Greenberg, L. S., & Lietaer, G. (1998). The experiential paradigm unfolding: Relationship and experiencing in therapy. In L. S. Greenberg, J. C. Watson, & G. Lietaer (Eds.), *Handbook of experiential psychotherapy* (pp. 3-27). New York: Guilford.

Watson, J. C., Kalogerakos, F., & Enright, C. (1998, June). *An analysis of the therapeutic alliance in client-centered and process-experiential psychotherapy using SASB.* Paper presented at the meeting of the International Society for Psychotherapy Research, Snowbird, UT.

Part V

HUMANISTIC APPLICATIONS TO BROADER SETTINGS

Introduction to Part V

A MÉLANGE OF CONTEMPORARY humanistic applications and emerging trends is presented in the nine chapters that constitute this part of the volume. They exemplify the broad range of settings in which the humanistic perspective is expressed and those in which it is currently making consequential advances. The central threads that tie them together are the principles that have been at the core of humanistic studies for more than 30 years: "an allegiance to meaningfulness in the selection of problems for study" (Buhler & Bugental, 1965-1966), the "aim to be faithful to the full range of human experience" (American Psychological Association, 2000), and concern "with those aspects of the human experience which have importance in daily life" (Bugental, 1967, p. 7). The reader should keep in mind that although the provocative topics considered in these chapters have long been within the purview of the humanistic perspective, some have not always been welcomed in mainstream academic psychology (e.g., romantic love, psychotherapist as artist, play, somatic medicine, the transpersonal). Even today, some of the topics to come might be considered deliciously nontraditional.

Constance Fischer's engaging chapter opens the "Contemporary Themes" section. In Chapter 39, her fresh view of personality assessment incorporates traditional psychological measures and projective techniques but with a decidedly humanistic twist. Fischer describes the collaborative interpersonal relationships created with her clients in every stage of her approach to the process, from establishing the goals of assessment to interpreting scores. Excerpts from assessment sessions and an example of a portion of a written report further illuminate the potential therapeutic benefits of the collaborative approach. Anticipating commonly asked questions about the approach, she concludes with a clarifying question-and-answer format.

The development of the therapist as a person is central to the preparation of existential-humanistic therapists. In Chapter 40, J. Fraser Pierson and Jeff Sharp present participant-observers' views of The Art of the Psychotherapist (or "Arts") courses, a unique experiential training program designed to explicitly and implicitly teach an existential-humanistic approach to psychotherapy. They describe the philosophy, content, and process of the Arts program and provide highlights from a recent survey of participants. The most prominent themes observed in survey respondents' narrative answers are discussed and illustrated with selected quotations that provide the reader with intimate glimpses of the experience of being an Arts participant. Pierson and Sharp describe a model program that is perceived to strengthen professional identity and the ability to embody, not merely cognize, living existential-humanistic therapeutic principles.

In Chapter 41, Hobart Thomas describes his approach to facilitating creative, experiential, whole person learning within the university class-room. Inspired by Rogers's views on education, and drawing on his own experiences as a faculty member in the experimental interdisciplinary School of Expressive Arts at Sonoma State University during the 1970s, Thomas offers insights and ideas on ways in which a required course may simultaneously stimulate students' emotional and intellectual development and meet the realities of a traditional academic institution. His guiding question is as follows: How can an academic requirement be made to serve the individual, the master within each person who at some deep level knows what is right for that person?

"Play [is] at the heart of life itself," writes O. Fred Donaldson, a man whose playmate-teachers include people of all ages and many other animals including dolphins, wolves, and Beluga whales. In Chapter 42, Donaldson reminds us of the original sense of play we had as children before it was lost in the process of enculturation, a learning process in which play becomes a competitive cultural game with winners and losers and inculcates fear. The stakes are high: "Our contest consciousness makes wisdom and the ecological mind impossible, splintering our consciousness and severing our ties with other life forms." He explores and illustrates what it means to "play by heart," that is, to stop living life as a contest and to allow the absolute kindness of original play to come alive in the world.

In Chapter 43, Eleanor Criswell provides a comprehensive overview of approaches to healing that integrate mental and physical practices. She provides an enlightening examination of the origins of the split between psychological and physical methods, the nature and practice of mind/body medicine, and contributors to this emerging field. Humanistic psychology, with its emphasis on human potential and focus on the whole person, is credited with playing an important role in the development of this contemporary mind/body medical perspective. Actualization of the individual's fullest potential and overall health and well-being is the ultimate goal. In the process, Criswell suggests, the individual patient or client and health care professional enter into a partnership that benefits both; the individual potentially enjoys increased autonomy and responsibility for his or her own health, and medical costs and demands on an overtaxed system are reduced.

"The allure of romance flickers as both an enduring predicament and a recurring opportunity of the human spirit," writes Kenneth Bradford in Chapter 44. Bradford explores the mythic ideal of romantic love, a legacy from the courtly love ethic of the Middle Ages and the conflicts inherent within this idealization—the tensions between erotic desire and security needs. He illuminates a path of genuine romantic love for the 21st century, a path of potential transformation that requires discipline and practice, a path toward deep wholehearted loving where each person in the relationship is liberated and further opened to the awe of being.

Chapter 45 in this panoply is a little different from the others in that it combines a chapter by Roger Walsh with a companion commentary by Kirk Schneider. Walsh begins this thought-provoking chapter by stating that the "existential and transpersonal disciplines have similar concerns and much to offer each other." He then proceeds to compare and contrast the existential and transpersonal perspectives relative to four intriguing topics. In the process, he identifies important distinctions between the traditions. A particularly stimulating point of departure concerns the transpersonal perspective on "transconventional" stages of development. Walsh and Schneider engage in a lively exchange of comments and comparisons that serve to further clarify the philosophical positions of both perspectives. They agree that a more collaborative path would be fruitful. Although Schneider believes that Walsh presents a comparatively balanced view, Schneider takes the opportunity to diffuse an idea often stressed by transpersonal writers: "that transpersonal contexts eclipse or encompass the existential."

In Chapter 46, Arthur Lyons opens the "Emergent Trends" section by challenging those of us who hold humanistic values dear to become more involved in modifying and influencing societal institutions, laws, and customs and to contribute to an emerging trend toward social activism that promotes equal opportunity to live the "good life." He points out that humanistic psychology's historical and philosophical basis has long supported social activism, and he offers inspiring examples of humanistically based grassroots social service programs. Lyons calls on humanistic psychology to "claim its own future" during the 21st century instead of being perceived as a reactionary "third force." To do so is predicated on becoming an increasingly more visible and tangible positive force within the larger social and political arenas that ultimately influence people's lives. It appears that mainstream psychology is beginning to recognize the wisdom of some of the earlier humanistic theorists as the new "positive psychology" embraces a focus on promoting positive qualities at both the individual and cultural levels.

In Chapter 47, Alfonse Montuori and Ron Purser explore trends in humanistic psychology in the workplace. They begin by tracing the history of humanistic psychology's influence on organization development theory and practice, particularly highlighting the contributions of Maslow and Rogers. Although they have witnessed a decrease in humanistic psychology's role within organization development over the past two decades, they foresee valuable contributions yet to be made. Changing social and economic trends augur a resurgence of interest in what the humanistic and existential traditions have to contribute. Montuori and Purser also explore several emerging possibilities for "cross-pollination" between theoretical orientations, spotlighting the work of Pauchant and Associates (1995) on "organizational existentialism" as an especially intriguing development. Montuori and Purser conclude with several suggestions for humanistic psychologists who want to "seize this opportunity" for making more potent contributions in the workplace.

REFERENCES

American Psychological Association. (2000). *History and mission of Division 32* [Online]. Available: www.apa.org/divisions/div32/history.html

Bugental, J. F. T. (1967). *Challenges of humanistic psychology.* New York: McGraw-Hill.

Buhler, C., & Bugental, J. F. T. (Eds.). (1965-1966). *American Association for Humanistic Psychology* [Brochure]. San Francisco: American Association for Humanistic Psychology.

Pauchant, T., & Associates. (Eds.). (1995). *In search of meaning.* San Francisco: Jossey-Bass.

CHAPTER *39*

Collaborative Exploration as an Approach to Personality Assessment

CONSTANCE T. FISCHER

IRST, A SERIES of rhetorical questions. How could it be that a chapter on personality assessment, especially one that makes substantial use of traditional psychological tests and projective techniques, appears in a handbook of humanistic psychology? Aren't testing and assessment tied to logical positivism, and more or less to realism and materialism, as psychology's traditional philosophy of science? Isn't their purpose to classify and explain, from a distanced, laboratory-type pursuit of objectivity? Isn't this framework antithetical to humanistic values?

This chapter does indeed present an approach to psychological assessment that is thoroughly consistent with the values and goals of humanistic psychology. Together, the client and professional formulate the goals of the assessment, and throughout several sessions they explore how the client has gone about aspects of his or her life. The professional shares direct impressions as well as hunches from score patterns, and the

client corrects and refines these offerings and provides examples from his or her life. Mutual specification of contexts and exceptions ("when nots") is essential to the development of individualized understandings; collaborative assessment is about the individual *as a particular individual*. In addition to these activities, with the assessor's encouragement, the client may try out alternative ways of dealing with the assessment tasks and may practice tailored and personally viable ways of dealing with concrete life situations. As is implied, the assessment process is profoundly interpersonal, with each participant's life presenting both limits and resources for productive exploration of presented assessment issues. Both the assessor and client are liable to be surprised at new understandings; both may laugh in delight or mist in sadness at the implications of new understandings.

Although the assessor has made use of test materials, research, and norms that were fashioned primarily within the laboratory tradition of psychology, he or she has utilized these resources from another philosophical frame. Traditional test materials can afford access to tasks that are similar to life-world pursuits. Clients' scores relative to one another, and compared to scores of various groups, can provide useful starting points for exploration of their ways of taking up and moving through their worlds.

INTRODUCTORY EXCERPTS FROM COLLABORATIVE EXPLORATION

This client is a 48-year-old woman referred through her company's employee assistance program in regard to being noncooperative with her supervisor, Mr. Willow. Additional activity and discussion occurred between these excerpts.

Assessor: Mary, you've explained to me how fortunate you've been that your parents were family oriented. And you let me know how much you miss them, even though your dad died 11 years ago and your mom died 6 years ago. [Mary nods several times. We sit quietly, in affirmation, for a moment.] But I was thinking about how complicated families are. Here [sentence completion form, which I place between Mary and myself], where the beginning says "What I wanted but didn't get from my father. . . . ," you wrote "words that I was as capable as my brothers."

Mary: Yes, but for the times—that was quite a while ago—he offered me as much encouragement as most fathers did for their daughters.

Assessor: Yes. And he did seem to have cared a lot about you, even though he didn't say so expressly in words. It would have been nice. . . .

Mary: Yes. . . .

[After Mary's completion of the Bender-Gestalt and some initial discussion]

Assessor: So you're surprised that I think that your copies are quite precise, especially for how quickly you did them?

Mary: Well, yeah. I was pretty self-conscious what with your watching me. I was even a little sweaty.

Assessor: Yes, I was aware of your glancing up at me several times as you worked. I even felt a bit uncomfortable myself, thinking that you might be seeing me as being unfair—not giving you the extra instructions you wanted. I even wondered if you were going to stop and refuse to finish. But you didn't!

Mary: I always do my part, even if others don't.

Assessor: I'm wondering if this is like what happens with Mr. Willow?

Mary: I'm not sure what you mean. . . . But I always do my job, even when he doesn't let me know if I'm doing okay. See, that's where you were different. At least when I finished [the Bender-Gestalt], you discussed with me how I did.

[Later, looking at the Minnesota Multiphasic Personality Inventory-2 (MMPI-2) profile together]

Assessor: This won't surprise you. This scale [L raw score = 7] reflects what you've told me about how you really do try to live by your "morals." And, as you told me, there's no indication that you're "depressed."

Mary: I told you. Yes, I told you that.

Assessor: Help me with this part [pointing to Scale 4 = 69 and Scale 8 = 65]. When these scales are about at this height, it sometimes reflects that a person is pretty vigilant—on guard. I'd guess that that could be so of you, probably being vigilant with yourself that you do things right and at the same time having your radar on to detect anyone being critical?

Mary: Not all the time. [I nod encouragingly.] I'm pretty relaxed with my friend Marion. She understands me, and when she makes a suggestion it's just a suggestion, not a criticism.

Asssessor: Right. And could you tell me some other examples?

Mary: Radar examples come more to mind. My ears are my radar. [Mary provides further examples such as her listening for signs that Mr. Willow is reading her reports in his office or ignoring them to make calls and her listening to a bank teller's tone of voice to determine whether she (Mary) is being respected.]

Assessor: [Returning to MMPI-2 profile, noting that Scale 0 = 50] One other aspect of this profile stands out for me and kind of surprises me. Your score here is similar to that of people who see themselves as kind of self-contained, held back, not particularly outgoing. But with me, you've been very direct. . . .

Mary: People tell me that I'm an introvert, and I guess it's so. But some people don't know that about me because I stand up for what's right. [At my suggestion, Mary gives examples from work.]

Assessor: Mary, I'm beginning to understand something of what it must be like for you to deal with Mr. Willow. You have done your very best to carry out assignments in top-flight form, but he hasn't said much about your performance except to ask some questions. Those questions seem like criticism, like you should have included that material? [Mary nods, questioningly.] I'll bet you must have felt blocked, unappreciated, frustrated [Mary nods in agreement], perhaps like you'd like to show him how angry you are!?

Mary: Well, I'm just angry inside. I would never express it inappropriately.

Assessor: I think we're onto something here! You remember how I felt uncomfortable during the Bender [pointing to the cards in their envelope] and was wondering if you might refuse to finish? As I think of it, I experienced you as becoming angry. [Mary protests that she might have felt angry but would not have walked out—that is not the kind of person she is.] Right. But I felt it anyway. I'll bet Mr. Willow has experienced that too. You and I went ahead and talked about how you had done just fine, even if everything wasn't exactly perfect, and you told me about how you did want more instruction [e.g., how precise to be, whether she could use a straight edge] but that you thought that I didn't want you to ask more. Anyway, I'll bet Mr. Willow picks up your unspoken frustration with him too and may mistakenly feel that you're basically uncooperative.

Mary: Marion says I should go talk to him, but I don't see what I could say that he wouldn't take offense at.

Assessor: Well, maybe you could tell him about our work and say that we discovered that you would be much more comfortable if he would provide you with more instruction—and lots more feedback! [We also talk about how she could tell Mr. Willow that we discovered that Mary is an extremely loyal employee and has not wanted to appear to be challenging his supervisory style.] One more thing I'd like for us to do: Let's right now do a role-play of your sharing with Mr. Willow some of these ideas we've developed. [We do so with false starts, laughter, congratulations, and reminders. Then we role-play Mary going in to ask Mr. Willow about how he liked her last report and whether he has suggestions for the next one.]

Written accounts include descriptions just like these excerpts. For all parties (assessor, client, and other readers), the performance tasks in particular evoke referral-relevant situations at more than verbal/conceptual levels. I hope that the excerpts illustrated that use of formal assessment tools helped both Mary and me to bring more of our explicit and implicit knowledge into the sessions and to move more efficiently than if we had relied on talk alone.

For the reader who is not familiar with traditional personality assessment, let me point out that, for the most part, psychologists' reports still follow the laboratory model of providing objective findings in the form of scores and symptoms and of placing the client within categories and diagnostic systems. However, when we want to know about the *person,* assessments and reports would do well to explore and describe that person's actual life, *regarding scores as tools for accessing that life rather than as "results."* This approach might seem like common sense, but it is not yet all that common.

HUMANISTIC VALUES AND A HUMAN-SCIENCE PSYCHOLOGY FRAMEWORK

I wound up on the faculty of the psychology department at Duquesne University, which during the 1960s came together to develop philosophical foundations, research methods, and clinical practices of a psychology adequate to humans. We named this approach *human-science psychology* in Dilthey's (1894/1977) tradition, in explicit contrast to natural science psychology, which had developed methods appropriate for studying our physical and biological

aspects but had ignored the fuller human. We looked to phenomenology and existentialism for guidance in developing philosophical foundations.

We found the philosophical work of phenomenologists such as Husserl and Heidegger to be especially fruitful, particularly their notion that humans know "truth" only in human ways and always in terms of our various interests in the subject matter, our methods, and so on. We can no longer regard nature as entirely separate from the perceiving, biographical, motivated investigator. Hence, specification of contexts, including researcher involvements, necessarily accompanies "findings," which are always presented as situated understandings. Similarly, as psychologists attempt to understand individuals, they address the individuals' lived worlds. Those worlds include persons' pasts as lived in the present toward futures. Psychologists acknowledge that their understandings of clients are both accessible through and limited by their own lives, assumptions, purposes, and other related contexts. Psychologists do not look for causes or determinants; rather, they look for mutuality and coherence among constituents that are discernible within holistic understandings. An example is the understanding of Mary that unfolded in the preceding excerpts. Mary became understandable in terms of her everyday goals, perceptions, situations, and reactions; we did not have to explain her behavior with Mr. Willow in terms of personality constructs.

The work of the phenomenological psychologist Merleau-Ponty (1945/1962, 1942/1963) was particularly helpful to us in finding ways to address the mutuality of humans being simultaneously physical, biological, and uniquely human. He described these realms as orders, illustrated by a pyramid with the physical order at the base, the biological order growing from there, and the human order from there, with each of the more complex orders influencing those on which it is dependent.

Existential writers helped us to respect individuals as always acting in terms of personal meanings. Faculty member Von Eckartsberg (1971) coined the term "experiaction" to express this condition and to indicate that experience and action are not separate. Existential writers also encouraged us to acknowledge that individuals even actively participate in what "happens to" them. We shape our worlds even as we are shaped by them. We are responsible for acknowledging both constraints ("givens") and choice.

At Duquesne, our empirical-phenomenological research findings are presented as holistic descriptions. The method is hermeneutic; researchers move repeatedly among original descriptions, analyses of each description, emerging general themes, other instances, insights from elsewhere, and evolving understandings, allowing each moment to inform the others and always returning to the original descriptions. The researchers' interests, preknown and discovered assumptions, and accesses to the phenomenon are specified.

So too are human-science assessments hermeneutic, meaning that they are frankly interpretive in this manner. The assessor's formation of clinical impressions is not just inductive/deductive; rather, the assessor cycles in an irregular but disciplined way among direct observation, provided history, diagnostic traditions, validity studies, personality theory, previous clients, one's own life, examples provided by the client, and evolving understandings, always returning to life events. As in qualitative research, the process concludes when understandings are coherent, can be illustrated with life-world data, and are responsive to the initial assessment questions. In both research and assess-ment, although we often cannot pin down the emergence of insight, we are responsible for documenting/illustrating our concluding understandings.

Of course, a humanistic/human-science route is not essential for innovating or using collaborative practices. Many, if not most, assessors have created or incorporated one aspect or another of such practices in their own work, regardless of their theoretical persuasions. Examples are the fine work of Finn (1996; see also Finn & Tonsanger, 1997) and Handler and Hilsenroth (1998).

I do think that a humanistic/human-science framework encourages greater consistency of, and expansion of, individualized collaborative assessment. I have been fortunate to have been at Duquesne, where I could draw from colleagues' philosophically informed pursuits, work with students to expand and refine practices, and write of my ventures. The following sample of my own publications in relation to collaborative individualized assessment variously presents philosophical foundations, teaching exercises, and excerpts: Fischer (1979, 1980, 1989, 1998a, 1998b, 1998c; 2000). "The Testee as Co-evaluator" (Fischer, 1970) was the first article that I know of to call for full collaboration including clients' writing commentary on reports. *Individualizing Psychological Assessment* (Fischer, 1985/1994) is a textbook that includes three chapters of sample reports, tables of examples of wording to enhance individualized description, a chapter comparing Andrew Wyeth's representational art with representational description, and a closing chapter of frequently asked questions.

In short, I think that a human-science approach encourages systematic, philosophically sound practice, whereas humanistic values encourage hopefulness and respect for the client's agency and individuality.

PRACTICES: LIFE-WORLD EXPLORATIONS

The Beginning

When the client is referred by a third party, I ask that party about the concrete issues behind the assessment request. For example, the assessment request, "Differential diagnosis: borderline personality disorder vs. anxiety disorder" turned out to have been formulated in puzzlement about Ms. Trook's frequent, agitated, and sometimes angry outbursts during the initial therapy sessions. When I meet the client, I ask for his or her understanding of what we are going to be doing and offer clarifications. Ms. Trook said, while making our appointment over the phone, that she had no idea. I explained that her therapist was wondering about the outbursts—whether they were a strategy evolved long ago to handle threats or whether they were related to Ms. Trook's currently being anxious. She immediately acknowledged being unusually anxious. When we met, she spontaneously said that she also wondered whether the therapist was afraid that she could not be helped. I replied that, to the contrary, he wanted to know how best to be of help. We then talked of what she knew about her being anxious these days, what aspects she was uncertain about, at what other times she responded with outbursts, and when she did not.

At this point, we have contextualized the referral issue in terms of the client's actual life. And by this time, we have established common ground—mutually developed understandings of our goals and of the client's situation. I think of assessment explorations, which are task oriented, as occurring within a respectful "I-thou" relationship. The client might not be relating to me in that manner, but both of us wind up relating to the client's life in that manner—with respect and with openness to new understandings. We also are aware of our joint responsibility for working toward new understandings; collaborating means *co-laboring!*

Somewhere along our way, I have asked the client what questions about him/herself would be of additional interest to explore as we pursue the third-party questions. After discussion, Ms. Trook and I agreed to look into the question, "How is it that people think I'm angry when I'm just trying to do my part?"

Exploring

As I listened to Ms. Trook's Thematic Apperception Test stories, I noted to myself that she seemed to be putting the main character in a position of waiting for others to provide initiative, direction, or solutions. When I asked Ms. Trook whether she was noticing any themes, her only comment was that the cards seemed to evoke sad stories. I affirmed that many people agreed with her. We went on to the next card, a scene depicting a young man facing away from an older woman, both seeming quiet and serious. Just as Ms. Trook was about to tell her story, I interjected a story, trying to exaggerate her style. I said, "They're in some kind of disagreement. *Why doesn't she just tell him what she wants him to do?!*" Ms. Trook, of course, was taken aback. But then, seeing my grin, she burst into giggles. She corrected me and said that she actually was thinking of the story from the woman's perspective and was seeing her as becoming irritated that he was not fulfilling his role. This led to a brief discussion of friends having told her that she is quite old-fashioned. I went on to ask whether she could tell a different story for the card. Ms. Trook struggled, saying that she could not seem to free herself from her initial perception. I suggested that the woman might ask directly what the man's inclinations were. We were quiet for a while, and then she said, "But what if his inclinations are contrary to what I want? What if he ignores her?" I nodded and gestured for more. After further silence, Ms. Trook said, "You know, I *am* feeling angry with you, even though you did help with a story." Her tone struck me as irritated, but the irritation seemed to be toward both of us.

Ms. Trook: Aren't you allowed to just explain this to me?

Assessor: Well, I'm trying, just like you are, to understand what's going on. I need your help. [long pause] Has something like what's happening with us happened with Dr. Zeller [the therapist]?

Ms. Trook: I was thinking that before. You pay people money to help, and then they just sit there waiting for you to do the work. You probably look pretty stupid to them. I think that's when I do my "outbursts," as Dr. Zeller calls them.

Assessor: Help me with this. Does it seem that you've tended to think that Dr. Zeller, Irene [her supervisor], and I all know answers but just are leaving you on your own on purpose?

Ms. Trook: [irritated, but sad] That really does make me sound stupid. I know you don't have all the answers, but somehow I want you to. And you *do* have *some* answers!

Assessor: But in the past, you've been hesitant to ask directly for opinions or advice? [We then talk about dangers of seeming pushy, of alienating people one needs, and of deeply wanting the other person to just help.]

Finding Landmarks and Pivot Points

The preceding excerpt illustrates that a collaborative assessment intervenes into test giving and into the client's customary style in order to bring that style into focus and to explore alternative ways for the client to reach goals. Most of the enumerated suggestions reviewed at the end of a report are reminders to the client of discovered landmarks that can serve to remind the client that he or she is moving into a problematic situation, and that he or she might want to consider an alternative route (pivoting, like a basketball player, from the current path into another).

Following are further examples of Ms. Trook's exploration that led to later suggestions.

Assessor: [on the Rorschach, noting an active/passive index weighted on the passive side, no cooperative movement responses (COP), and a low level of integrating aspects of a blot ($zd = -5$)] I think the Rorschach, after I scored it, put me in touch with some related possibilities. As you know, I was positively impressed with your level of problem solving with the blocks and with that information subtest [Wechsler Adult Intelligence Scale-III]. We agreed that when you know the standard to be followed, you have been quick, sharp, complete. But here with the inkblots, which provide no standard, it turns out that you held back and didn't really engage the task as fully as I had expected. For example, here [pulling out Card X] you just named animals but never put them into a scene.

Ms. Trook: I guess I did have a general sense of an underwater scene, but it didn't occur to me to pull it together. Was I supposed to? You didn't tell me to.

Assessor: No, I was interested in your own inclinations. But your choice to be sort of passive [Ms. Trook, introjecting: Yes, safe . . .] meant that you didn't make use of as much information as you could have. You certainly didn't try to formulate "the big picture." Say, are you irritated with me now? Would this be a time when you might have "exploded"? Does it seem that I'm criticizing you?

Ms. Trook: No, I don't think so. By now, I'm used to you taking me seriously. But if you were Irene, I'd probably feel criticized. Is it okay to ask you where I should go from here? [We both laugh.]

Assessor: Exactly! What you just did would work with Dr. Zeller and Irene, I'll bet. You found yourself wondering, and you took initiative to ask if I might have some direction for you. I think it's precisely when you find yourself confronted with an ambiguous situation, like the inkblots, or a new task at work, or Dr. Zeller being noncommittal, that you could ask for guidance. I imagine you would feel less criticized and helpless when you initiate discussion instead of waiting dependently. The trick will be to recognize when you've encountered an ambiguous situation and then shift gears or course to be more assertive so you'll be more sure of the situation, of what's wanted. After the shift, you won't feel like you're stuck waiting to be rescued, and you'll be much less likely to be resentful.

Of course there are also points about which the assessor and client agree to disagree or about which they agree that they have not yet reached an adequate understanding. The client knows that there is no secret information that the assessor is withholding, that his or her experiaction pretty much makes sense to both of them, and that

he or she can continue to make sense and to take action after the assessment.

PRACTICES: WRITTEN ACCOUNTS OF ASSESSMENT EXPLORATIONS

General Practices

In the assessment courses at Duquesne, we write in first person and active voice (e.g., "Ms. Trook and I explored these issues through use of the TAT [Thematic Apperception Test] and Rorschach" rather than "The TAT and Rorschach were administered"). We generally write concretely and in past tense to indicate that past comportment can change (e.g., "Jim announced that he wanted to quit working on the block design tasks, saying that they were too difficult" rather than "This boy quits difficult tasks" or "Inferiority feelings interfere with this student's motivation to strive"). We provide an initial visual picture of the client in motion so that readers can picture the descriptions that follow. We stress verbs and adverbs, and we eschew constructs. Reports read much like the preceding excerpts do; they describe by re-presenting representative scenes. All parties (client, assessor, helpers, and decision makers) can read the report, which is written about the client's actual life. All readers are "on the same page" and can use the reported assessment explorations as reference points in their discussions.

Not all assessments require full reports. Sometimes, a brief letter to the client and/or referring party may overview the assessment procedures and then go directly to landmarks/pivot points and related suggestions. Fables or stories may be written for children, their families, and other helpers. Sometimes, the assessor meets with the client and referring party and then writes a summary of that discussion (which was based on the assessment explorations); in such cases, an initial report is not necessary. Where called for, formal diagnoses are provided referencing concrete events. When readers might find technical data (e.g., test profiles, actual TAT stories) helpful, they are attached as an appendix. Clients are invited to write comments directly on a written report that is to be sent to referring parties; they record clarifications, elaborations, corrections, and disagreements. Reports of whatever form are in terms of the client's actual life. A refrain in our Duquesne assessment classes is: "If you can't write it in everyday terms, then you literally do not know 'what in the world' you're talking about."

Excerpts

The following excerpts, from a report written by graduate student Yael Goldman, illustrate re-presentational/representational description as well as the power of exploration through tests to affirm a client's striving. Chantel's written comments on the report indicate that, through the assessment process, she found that her efforts were indeed not just talk and that "after reading my assessment, I have learned even more about when being open to others helps a lot. Thank you." Chantel was a 35-year-old resident of a drug treatment facility. She now was past 6 months in the program, on a second admission.

Introductory Description

Chantel dressed casually in jeans, a plaid button-down shirt, and sneakers. In contrast to her casual dress, she wore large silver hoop earrings and wore her hair ornately arranged in a bun high on her head with strands of dark curls framing her face. On the DAP [human figure drawings], Chantel spent more time on details of her

hair weave than on anything else. The care with which she did her hair suggested a desire for orderliness and beauty.

During the assessment, Chantel leaned all the way back in her chair as she spoke with us [Yael and her graduate student partner, Rebekah]. Her arms rested firmly on the chair, and both feet remained solidly planted on the floor. When Chantel drew or wrote, she leaned forward and rested both arms firmly on the desk. Her posture lent her an appearance of being grounded and straightforward. Chantel is of average height and is sturdy in build, which added to an impression of solidity.

Presented Problem: Feeling Versus Running

For the assessment's focal issue, Chantel chose to concentrate on how to "stay clean" from drugs and alcohol. For Chantel, staying clean—that is, remaining free from abusive substances—was directly related to staying with and working through her feelings, such as loneliness and despair, as opposed to "running" from them. She explained that she ran *from* her uncomfortable feelings *to* drugs and alcohol as an escape. . . . Throughout the assessment situation, Chantel, Rebekah, and I observed and discussed moments when Chantel descended from the surface and opened up and shared her feelings with us. We thus related the here and now of the testing situation to Chantel's focal issue and other aspects of her life. . . .

Chantel as Seen Through the Testing Process

Caring about precision and order. On the Bender-Gestalt, Chantel took her time, (re)counted the dots, and retraced the circles. Her drawings fit neatly on the page. We noted that she was quite careful and precise; on Figure 5, she counted the dots and specified on which dot the line intersected the curve. On the DAP, Chantel drew all three figures in the bottom left corner of the same page. They were roughly the same size, although her self-portrait was slightly larger because the first two drawings portrayed children (the first was fashioned on her daughter). Chantel explained that the reason she drew the first figure in the left corner was because she thought she was going to fill the page, like she did with the Bender-Gestalt. She said she drew figures 2 and 3 in the same fashion so that they would all be uniform. It was important to her to have a unified pattern rather than disarray. She said the other residents considered her a "perfectionist," particularly her roommates because of the care she took cleaning her room. However, when she was using drugs, Chantel cared neither about tidiness nor about order and threw things anywhere. . . . We related the care she took on the Bender-Gestalt to the work she has done at Smithfield House. . . .

Chantel expressing feelings. On the comprehension subtest, Chantel answered in reference to her own beliefs, behaviors, and feelings rather than providing the more standard answers. . . . On Question 6, she replied that she personally would rather borrow money from a friend than from a bank as interest rates would be lower. She prefaced her answers with "for me." . . .

Chantel employed the TAT cards to reveal more about herself and her feelings. For example, Card 3BM portrays a person sitting on the floor hunched over a chair. It reminded Chantel of herself, her mother, and her grandmother. Chantel often found her grandmother collapsed on the floor drunk, hung over, or needing another drink. Chantel also recalled her mother stressed out, tired, and contemplating how to leave her abusive husband. Finally,

Chantel saw a combination of her lineage and an image of herself hung over or depressed. She remarked that it took a long time for her mother to fight back; we agreed that now is Chantel's turn to fight. . . .

Suggestions for Chantel

1. During the testing exercises, you "let go" of many of the issues on your mind, about yourself, your past and future. You did not "run" from us. You mentioned that "last time around" at Smithfield House you might have spoken to us more superficially to avoid going "deep down." Chantel, just as you volunteered for this assessment and fully participated by revealing yourself to us, you can continue taking advantage of such opportunities to discuss your feelings and experiences with others. However, sometimes you may find that relating events to yourself is neither necessary nor appropriate. In the future, *choose* when and when not to express yourself as you deem appropriate. . . .

Even reports utilizing the MMPI, the Rorschach, and other complex instruments with people for whom a referral is about differential diagnosis, suicidality, psychopathy, and so on are written in a similar manner.

CLARIFICATIONS (FREQUENTLY ASKED QUESTIONS)

What Is the Difference Between Collaborative Assessment and Psychotherapy?

The assessment addresses a particular presenting issue in a few sessions, develops understandings of how and when the person contributes to problematic situations, and suggests individualized means for the client to participate differently in those situations. This type of assessment is "therapeutic," first, in the sense of offering a corrective to or transformation of a problem and, second in the sense that the client finds that his or her experience has been affirmed, that his or her agency/power has been demonstrated, and that his or her revised pathways to personal goals have been tried out successfully. The person has developed foundations for continuing growth and deepening through his or her own efforts.

But collaborative assessment is *not* psychotherapy in its older sense of thoroughgoing exploration of a life over an extended time, and especially not when the goal is transformation of personality structure. I suppose that collaborative assessment is similar to some forms of "brief therapy." In assessment, however, we can also provide a printed record for the client and helpers of understandings of test events and their relation to life events along with individualized suggestions for further exploration and trying out.

A caveat: if the assessor focuses on "being therapeutic" rather than on conducting a collaborative, individualized assessment, then the assessment and its potential benefits might be compromised.

Does Individualized Assessment Bypass the Need for Training in Cultural Diversity?

Not at all. It is true that as the assessor explores the other person's life-world, cultural, religious, familial, economic, gender, and age dimensions are likely to arise. However, one should be schooled in the general customs, assumptions, constraints, and attunements of the populations with whom one works (co-labors) as well as with some of the issues in cultural and gender studies (e.g., Butler, 1999). Beyond academic sources, novels can raise awareness (e.g., Naipaul, 1988). Dana (1998a, 1998b), who broadly identifies with humanistic psychol-

ogy, has effectively addressed many aspects of cultural context in regard to assessment.

Conducting a segment of an assessment in a client's home or neighborhood can go a long way toward awakening us to our assumptions and ignorance and toward encouraging fuller appreciation of the person-in-context.

Is Collaborative Assessment Limited to Reflective, Motivated, Fairly Well-Functioning Clients?

This approach, like all others, certainly is most productive with and for those clients who are least restricted. Nevertheless, collaborative exploration with persons we label as mentally retarded, brain-damaged, schizophrenic, and so on, as well as with persons in forensic settings, is as informative as standard assessment while also presenting such persons as individuals, identifying "when nots" of the problematic experiaction, providing tailored suggestions, and often enhancing clients' self-direction.

Why Not Develop Existential Tests Instead of Using Standardized Instruments?

Existential projects and meanings are part of any situation in which we participate, including assessment sessions in which we are clients or assessors. Clients encounter the Wechsler subtests in much the same way as they encounter other similar challenges in life. There have been some efforts to develop life values inventories that might be useful for research, but again, clients' relevant values become apparent in discussions of problems and successes in life, to which we gained access through existing tests.

A Major Purpose of Psychological Assessment Has Been to Provide an Objective Picture of the Client; Isn't Your Approach Awfully Subjective?

Yes, it is decidedly *inter*subjective. The lives of the assessor, readers, and client all come into play in understanding the client and his or her situation. Of course, that is the case for traditional assessment as well, although usually it is not acknowledged. Obviously, an assessment never should be merely subjective in the sense of being just the assessor's personal impressions. The human-science assessor remains rigorously empirical, using directly observed and reported events/contexts as primary data. Personality constructs and diagnostic categories are regarded as tools for reflecting about the client but not as findings. The client is asked for multiple examples of any assessor-offered conceptions, and the examples often lead to revision of those understandings. The assessor's impressions must be both documented as to sources and illustrated through examples.

In addition, the ambiguity that is inherent in many human affairs is respected rather than regarded as deficient knowledge. False precision is eschewed.

Speaking of the Intersubjective Character of Assessment, Shouldn't Assessors' Training Emphasize Interpersonal Sensitivity?

Definitely. Beyond training in test construction, standardized administration, use of norms, and theories of personality and restricted existence, assessors should be trained as therapists. To me, that implies exploring one's own motives, assumptions, and impact as well as developing empathic attunement to others. Moreover, exposure to the arts and humanities broadens and deepens interpersonal presence.

But Don't Tests Get in the Way of the Interpersonal Relationship?

The interpersonal character of the assessment is inevitable; it is not a goal. We should, of course, be mindful of the inherent uneven power in any professional engagement. Working within a humanistic/human-science frame, with its emphasis on understanding rather than on explanation and its emphasis on the life-world rather than on constructs, goes a long way toward maintaining the assessor's integrity. Engaging the client as a responsible participant and asking for concrete examples of issues being discussed also orient the assessment toward the client's world, requiring the assessor to use tests as an access to that world rather than as access to a privileged abstract notion of truth.

How Do You Address the Question of the Validity of Your Assessments?

We bypass the issue of validity of instruments (whether the instrument measures what it is said to measure) by regarding life events as our data and regarding useful revised understandings of them as our results. For me, the validity question shifts to a question of how helpful the assessment proves to be for all parties. Is the client more fully understood? Is the client now more effective in pursuing goals? Do helpers know how to enter the client's world and to work toward mutually desired goals?

When You Are Asked by a Third Party to Conduct an Assessment, Aren't You in a Conflict of Interest When You Also Work With the Client to Develop Less Problematic or More Productive Strategies?

No, not if my reports describe initial ways of functioning and spell out their contexts and then go on to describe my interventions and any ensuing alternatives already available to the client. Of course, the assessor is upfront with the client throughout the assessment about the third party's interests and what will be reported.

Surprisingly, Aren't Many of These Practices Similar to Those of Many Cognitive-Behavioral Therapists?

Yes, insofar as both assist the client to recognize specific situations as being occasions to initiate a change of direction or action. However, I think that working within a humanistic/human-science frame, even when using cognitive-behavioral techniques, encourages a more thoroughgoing respect for the client while simultaneously discouraging adopting a technological attitude toward the client.

CONCLUSION

When an individual's life-world is the focus of psychological assessment and the assessor works within a human-science frame, the work is decidedly humanistic. The assessor-client relationship is interpersonal and collaborative. Scores and test behavior are understood as tools for developing holistic mutual understandings of the client's situations. The client and assessor explore personal meanings and positive options. The process encourages spontaneity, creativity, and personal responsibility.

REFERENCES

Butler, J. (1999). *Gender trouble: Feminism and the subversion of identity.* London: Routledge.

Dana, R. H. (1998a). Personality and the cultural self: Emic and etic contexts as learning resources. In L. Handler & M. Hilsenroth (Eds.), *Teaching and learning personality assessment* (pp. 325-345). Mahwah, NJ: Lawrence Erlbaum.

Dana, R. H. (1998b). *Understanding cultural identity in intervention and assessment.* Thousand Oaks, CA: Sage.

Dilthey, W. (1977). *Descriptive psychology and historical understanding* (R. Zaner & K. Heigas, Trans.). The Hague, The Netherlands: Martinus Nijhoff. (Original work published 1894)

Finn, S. E. (1996). *Manual for using the MMPI-2 as a therapeutic intervention.* Minneapolis: University of Minnesota Press.

Finn, S. E., & Tonsanger, M. E. (1997). Information-gathering and therapeutic models of assessment: Complementary paradigms. *Psychological Assessment, 9,* 374-385.

Fischer, C. T. (1970). The testee as co-evaluator. *Journal of Counseling Psychology, 17,* 70-76.

Fischer, C. T. (1979). Individualized assessment and phenomenological psychology. *Journal of Personality Assessment, 43,* 115-122.

Fischer, C. T. (1980). Phenomenology and psychological assessment: Re-presentational description. *Journal of Phenomenological Psychology, 11,* 79-105.

Fischer, C. T. (1989). A life-centered approach to psychodiagnostics: Attending to the life-world, ambiguity, and possibility. *Person-Centered Review, 4,* 163-170.

Fischer, C. T. (1994). *Individualizing psychological assessment.* Hillsdale, NJ: Lawrence Erlbaum. (Original work published 1985)

Fischer, C. T. (1998a). Being angry revealed as deceptive protest: An empirical-phenomenological analysis. In R. Valle (Ed.), *Phenomenological inquiry in psychology: Existential and transpersonal dimensions* (pp. 111-122). New York: Plenum.

Fischer, C. T. (1998b). Phenomenological, existential, and humanistic foundations for psychology as a human science (pp. 449-472). In M. Hersen & A. Bellack (Eds.), *Comprehensive clinical psychology: Vol. 1. Foundations* (C.E. Walker, Ed.). London: Elsevier Science.

Fischer, C. T. (1998c). The Rorschach and the life-world: Exploratory exercises. In L. Handler & M. Hilsenroth (Eds.), *Teaching and learning personality assessment* (pp. 347-358). Mahwah, NJ: Lawrence Erlbaum.

Fischer, C. T. (2000). Collaborative, individualized assessment. *Journal of Personality Assessment, 74,* 2-14.

Handler, L., & Hilsenroth, M. (Eds.). (1998). *Teaching and learning personality assessment.* Mahwah, NJ: Lawrence Erlbaum.

Merleau-Ponty, M. (1962). *The phenomenology of perception* (C. Smith, Trans.). New York: Humanities Press. (Original work published 1945)

Merleau-Ponty, M. (1963). *The structure of behavior* (A. L. Fisher, Trans.). Boston: Beacon. (Original work published 1942)

Naipaul, V. S. (1988). *The enigma of arrival.* New York: Random House.

von Eckartsberg, R. (1971). On experiential methodology. In A. Giorgi, W. F. Fischer, & R. von Eckartsberg (Eds.), *Duquesne studies in phenomenological psychology* (Vol. 1, pp. 66-79). Pittsburgh, PA: Duquesne University Press.

CHAPTER 40

Cultivating Psychotherapist Artistry
A Model Existential-Humanistic Training Program

J. FRASER PIERSON AND JEFFREY G. SHARP

THE PREPARATION and training of psychotherapists is multifaceted and lifelong, perhaps especially for those who espouse an existential-humanistic orientation. Such an orientation represents a philosophy and value system—a compass rose or point of reference—to navigate through the complexities of psychotherapy and life. Heeding the call to this vocation requires successful completion of a substantial body of formal coursework and supervised field experience consonant with the prevailing scientist-practitioner or professional school models of graduate training in clinical and counseling psychology. In equal measure, it requires an ongoing commitment to personal and professional development as well as the pursuit of meaningful work, relationships, and avocational interests. The existential and humanistic perspectives challenge the practitioner to creatively weave together the science, philosophy, and art of psychotherapy; the capacity to do so is the trademark of the "virtuoso" (Bugental, 1987, p. 264).

The process of fully adopting an existential-humanistic orientation may be fraught with obstacles pertaining to the acquisition of

AUTHORS' NOTE: With deep gratitude, we thank our beloved mentor and friend, James F. T. Bugental, for his vision in creating The Art of the Psychotherapist (Arts) courses and his stoutheartedness in offering them throughout the years to younger colleagues who wish to join him and other luminaries in carrying the torch of existential-humanistic psychotherapy into the future. We thank him for being a courageous trailblazer and for cultivating that pioneering spirit in us. We also thank our friends and colleagues in the Arts community who took part in our survey. Their personal experiences and perceptions enliven our overview of the Arts courses and lend support to our conceptualization of the Arts series serving as a model for experiential training programs. It is with love and much appreciation that we thank our spouses, Jeff Hubbell and Charlie Sharp, for their encouragement and support, which came in many forms throughout this project. We also thank Brook Brown, Myrtle Heery, Mallory Lynch, Bruce Sarbit, and Molly Sterling for their valuable feedback on an earlier draft of this chapter.

education and training. Although humanistic psychologists appear to be represented within academic institutions across the United States, there are relatively few programs leading to master's or doctoral degrees in humanistic psychology (Churchill, 1994).[1] Traditional clinical training programs do not tend to foster "third camp" (or "third force") attitudes such as education of the whole person, exercise of subjectivity, and egalitarianism in the therapeutic relationship (Gendlin, 1994, p. 339). Furthermore, academic textbooks often represent humanistic psychology in limited and historically encapsulated ways (Churchill, 1994). Introductory and survey courses at the undergraduate level might not provide the student with examples of the diversification that exists within the orientation. Graduate-level course offerings in humanistic, existential, phenomenological, and transpersonal psychology are likely to be slim unless the student is enrolled in a program such as those identified by Arons (1996; see also Appendix in this volume) as "centered around a humanistic orientation" (p. 5).

Our experience suggests that faculty members, clinical supervisors, and mentors identified as primarily drawing on an existential-humanistic perspective can be difficult to come by in mainstream psychology graduate programs. To compound the problem, there is a dearth of humanistically oriented practicum and internship cites (Gendlin, 1994). Postgraduate training programs become an essential resource for the psychotherapist who wishes to integrate the humanistic and existential perspectives into clinical practice, teaching, and research. Ensuring the availability of courses and training programs at the graduate and postgraduate levels represents a current challenge for those who support this orientation and its renaissance within the field of psychology.

Another challenge pertains to the nature of psychotherapist preparation programs. As Taylor (2000) suggested, "Therapy is more than linear science, medical procedures, and mechanistic methods. It is also poetry [and] art" (p. 8). He advocated for less emphasis on the science of psychotherapy in training programs and more on the art of psychotherapy because "it is the artistic, creative, spiritual, 'poetic' dimensions of therapy that are most central. . . . " (p. 8). To engage in life-changing psychotherapy, the therapist must "prepare" by cultivating "subjective readiness" in tandem with acquiring traditional academic and applied training (Bugental, 1987, p. 269).

The call for balanced training is supported in a comprehensive review of therapy outcome research conducted by Lambert and Bergin (1994). Studies suggest that the development of the therapist as a person and the acquisition of the skills and techniques of psychotherapy should be given equal emphasis in graduate training programs because the therapist as a person is found to play a significant role in the outcome of treatment.

Psychotherapist preparation from an existential-humanistic perspective is incomplete to the extent that it neglects the development of the therapist as a person—the wellspring and instrument of creativity and artistry. Bugental (1987) posited, "The most mature psychotherapists are more artists than technicians [in that] they bring to bear a wide variety of sensitivities and skills so that their clients can release their latent potentials for fuller living" (p. 264). The seasoned therapist deftly integrates a sound knowledge base acquired through formal academic study and extensive supervised clinical experience with finely tuned perception and intuition. The subjective realm is trusted, and access to this sensitive resource within is increasingly fluid and reflexive (Bugental, 1987). The "intimate journey" (Bugental, 1990) that constitutes life-changing depth psychotherapy requires such artistry.

In this chapter, we describe The Art of the Psychotherapist (or "Arts"), a unique preparation program designed to both explicitly and implicitly teach an existential-humanistic approach to psychotherapy. The courses immerse the maturing psychotherapist in a co-created environment permeated with the humanistic values of compassion, courage, creativity, love, spiritedness, intellectual and personal growth, and "I-thou" relationships as characterized by Buber (1970). It is a learning environment that invites authenticity; cultivates attunement to subjectivity; and stimulates the capacity to be more fully present, moment to moment, to what is most alive within oneself, within the client, and emergent in the therapeutic relationship. We believe that the Arts series provides a valuable model for educators and clinical supervisors interested in designing experientially based psychotherapist preparation programs and for students, interns, and practitioners interested in further developing their artistry as psychotherapists.

The philosophy, content, and process of the Arts courses are described in the next section of the chapter. This summary is followed by highlights of the results of an informal survey of participants conducted to explore the influence of the courses on personal and professional development and to illuminate factors that make the courses attractive on a continuing basis. We then discuss and illustrate the most prominent themes observed in survey respondents' narrative answers to our questions. We conclude with a brief discussion of the relationship of the Arts courses to other institutes and share our reflections on the importance of existential-humanistic training programs in today's world.

Our perspective is one of participant observers. Over the past 5 years, our personal and professional lives have been profoundly influenced by involvement in the Arts courses and in related existential-humanistic organizations. For example, the present collaborative endeavor and envisioned future work is an outgrowth of participation in the Arts program. We met in Arts I, where we began to develop a stimulating friendship. Our basis of mutual respect and trust deepened through the shared experiences of Arts II through IV and now is a platform for launching creative projects.

THE ART OF THE PSYCHOTHERAPIST COURSES

The Arts program is an intensive series of courses based on an existential-humanistic approach to depth psychotherapy. It was conceived of and developed by Jim Bugental and several associates over the course of many years as an outgrowth of, and stimulus to, his research on counseling and psychotherapy processes (J. F. T. Bugental, personal communication, February 2000).[2] Over the years, the courses evolved into a retreat format that allows participants to more fully experience, examine, and learn from their ongoing subjective experiences throughout the trainings. Participants, many of whom are seasoned psychotherapists, come from throughout the United States and Canada. Participants dedicate 6 or more days each year to these trainings. Numerous individuals have done so for more than 10 years. It was our awareness of this ongoing extensive commitment, along with our own personal appreciation of what we have gained from the trainings, that led us to examine more closely the nature and impact of the Arts program.

The Arts program is built on existential-humanistic philosophy and values. But how does one train therapists in such an approach? Existential psychology is notoriously difficult to define, as is humanistic psychology, let alone *existential-humanistic* psychology. And certainly, there is no standard method of conducting existential or humanistic psychotherapy. Prominent theorists have, in fact, emphasized that "existential therapy is not a comprehensive psychotherapeutic system" (May & Yalom, 1995, p. 278). What, then, constitutes training in existential-humanistic psychotherapy?

Reflecting Bugental's ongoing scholarship and clinical practice over the past 40 years, the Arts courses address the training dilemma by incorporating and enhancing values, beliefs, and practices from the rich traditions of existential and humanistic psychology (Bugental & Kleiner, 1993; Bugental & Sterling, 1995; Sharp & Bugental, in press). There is greater emphasis placed on illuminating the subjective experience and attitude of each participant, including one's evolving self-and-world construct system (i.e., "one's implicit vision of one's own identity and the character of one's envisioning world") than on prescribing a rigid set of techniques (Bugental, 1999, p. 109). From humanistic psychology, there is an emphasis placed on possibilities, hope, and potential; from existential traditions, there is an emphasis placed on limits, anxiety, awe, terror, and the tragic aspects of life (Sharp & Bugental, in press). The courses have evolved from Bugental's lifelong practice and study of depth psychotherapy, particularly as elucidated in the following texts: *Psychotherapy and Process: The Fundamentals of an Existential-Humanistic Approach* (Bugental, 1978), *The Art of the Psychotherapist* (Bugental, 1987), and *Psychotherapy Isn't What You Think* (Bugental, 1999). A gifted educator as well as a psychotherapist, Bugental has elegantly translated his reflections on psychotherapy into a highly effective curriculum with original teaching materials and experiential exercises.

Context and Atmosphere

The content, structure, and atmosphere of the Arts courses reflect the philosophy and values described previously. The courses generally take place in retreat settings. These rural settings foster contemplation, reflection, and warm collegiality while also providing a context for conducting focused, intensive clinical exercises. In addition, savory meals are provided in a restful, communal dining area. Participants, many of whom come from busy or even hectic work and home situations, often comment about how luxurious it feels to be nurtured to such an extent—to receive abundantly rather than to be constantly giving. This atmosphere heightens participants' awareness of how demanding and difficult their professional and family worlds are. Acknowledging this—to oneself and to one's colleagues—is in itself unburdening and emancipatory.

The structure of the retreats facilitates focused intensive trainings while also allowing time for reflection, relaxation, hiking, expressive arts, and various group activities that typically fall outside of professional roles. The majority of time is structured around clinical trainings. These trainings may include lectures, demonstrations, role-plays, dyadic or group exercises, reviewing audiotapes and videotapes, and journaling. Again, emphasis is placed on listening closely to one's ongoing subjective experience and one's evolving sense of self, of others, and of possibilities.

A central goal of the Arts program is to create an atmosphere in which participants feel encouraged and safe to explore their own personal subjective reactions to various aspects of clinical work including what it means to be a psychotherapist in our contemporary world (Sharp & Bugental, in press). That is, participants are encouraged to reflect on and share with others far more than their objective opinions about theories or research on psychotherapy. They are encouraged to fully experience and convey to others, as they see fit, the hope, fear, dread, excitement, confusion, frustration, and exhilaration that are inherent aspects of conducting psychotherapy—and that are considered by some to be unprofessional, unacceptable, or unsafe to discuss with colleagues.

Time is also allotted, particularly during the evenings, for singing, dancing, poetry reading, storytelling, presenting slide shows, and (given that the Arts courses evolved in California) relaxing with one's peers in a hot tub. Thus, participants reap the benefits not only of working closely and collaboratively but also of laughing, crying, singing, dancing, playing, and otherwise fully sharing their humanity.

Another powerful element of the Arts courses is the ongoing opportunity to study and work closely with Bugental, a highly respected mentor, elder, and sage. His presence adds an immense richness to the Arts programs. He shares his extensive knowledge of the history of psychology and demonstrates his consummate skills in fostering trust, awareness, and growth. In addition, he discloses aspects of his humanity that stir the heart—his courage, humor, struggles with aging, and ongoing commitment to life as a quest. He is a profound inspiration to the Arts participants as a person and as a man.

Content of Courses

The first course, or Arts I, introduces an existential-humanistic perspective on depth psychotherapy. Through a mixture of didactic presentations and experiential exercises, participants develop greater sensitivity to the process dimension of psychotherapy. Participants extend their range of communication skills, particularly in relation to monitoring, paralleling, and confronting client presence. Therapeutic resistance is described and worked with as an essential obstacle and window to change. Bugental's perspective on fundamental concepts such as presence, subjective awareness, searching, resistance, and the self-and-world construct system is presented (Bugental, 1987). Participants are encouraged to continually reflect on the meaning and impact of these entities in their own work and lives.

Arts II and the ensuing courses build on and enhance the material of Arts I. The ebb and flow between the courses in nonlinear fashion allows material to be expanded and deepened within the context of each presentation. Arts II initially focuses on the primacy of the subjective—the therapist's inner experience, client readiness and reluctance, and intersubjectivity. Familiar difficulties, such as specific client patterns that frequently cause trouble for therapists, are examined. These patterns include the angry client, the injustice collector, the overly dependent client, and the client who seems unwilling to take responsibility for his or her actions or life.

Attention is paid to clarifying and mobilizing implicit elements of psychotherapy such as client concern and intentionality and the therapist's *pou sto* or philosophical stance (Bugental, 1999, p. 85). Core tenets of Bugental's existential-humanistic perspective are expanded on and interwoven throughout the remainder of the Arts courses. The structure and process of the program reflect and enhance understanding of these tenets. It is also emphasized that each therapist must incorporate and amend these ideas in accord with his or her values, beliefs, and cultural-historical context.

Arts III focuses on discovering one's own needs as a therapist and a person and on how these needs affect one's work. This emphasis includes exploration of the therapist's needs and motivations, his or her self-and-world construct system, and his or her unwitting tendencies to keep the work shallow. Participants are encouraged to examine tendencies to objectify clients; to resist being present; and to become preoccupied with theory, technique, or diagnosis. The crucial importance of deepening the therapeutic alliance is addressed, as are client or therapist efforts to collude in sabotaging this process. Participants continually refine and maintain the therapeutic "container" through addressing the ongoing business, legal, and ethical aspects of therapy. Arts III through V may be taken in any order.

Arts IV is more specifically adapted to the needs and interests of the participants. A menu of possible topics is presented to enrollees in advance of the program, and coverage of the various topics is based on participants' requests. The general goals of Arts IV are to explore and extend the scope of an existential-humanistic orientation, to recognize special circumstances in which one's work may require adaptations, and to acknowledge personal limitations. Possible topics include assessing and taking into account client ego function, working with special populations (e.g., children, elders, mandated clients), teaching and supervising, developing shorter term models of existential-humanistic psychotherapy, and working with couples. In addition, technical skills are refined, for example, establishing the therapeutic contract, coping with acting-out impulses, modulating intimacy and eroticism, and preparing for termination.

During Arts V, which is termed the *master course*, an even more significant shift in the teaching orientation occurs. The emphasis of Arts V is on further developing and refining individual styles and interests. Consequently, not only is the content based on the needs and interests of the enrollees, but the participants also do most of the teaching. Participants volunteer to present conceptual materials, learning exercises, or related artistic productions. Current issues in the profession may be the subject of debates or the focus of exercises. One cohort group has incorporated a process group into its training, with the goals of refining participants' skills in leading process groups and of enabling participants to learn from their experiences in the group.

An integral element of Arts V is the acknowledgment and processing of the fundamental change from primarily following the teachings of a revered mentor to taking more initiative and responsibility for the content and direction of the ongoing Arts courses. It is testimony to Bugental's wisdom that he has designed the Arts courses in such a way that autonomy and authority are increasingly transferred to the group. He continues to state his opinions and let his presence be known in all stages of the Arts. Yet, he makes it abundantly clear that a fundamental task at hand in Arts V is to develop an ongoing program that sustains the growth and development of the participants rather than bolstering the authority or power of its creator.

A tremendous sense of community emerges out of participation in the Arts. Cohort groups develop such that the same group of individuals meets once or twice a year. Two groups have been meeting at least once a year for more than 10 years. Participants develop deep friendships and provide mutual support for the growth and emergence of one another. This includes support for ongoing professional development such as providing an opportunity to present a paper in progress, co-teaching, writing for publication (Bugental & Bracke, 1992; Bugental & Heery, 1999; Bugental & Sapienza, 1994), and taking part in peer consultation groups (M. Heery, personal communication, August 2000; M. M. Sterling, personal communication, August 2000). Support is also provided for experiencing and addressing emergent personal issues related to being a psychotherapist.

SURVEY OF
ARTS PARTICIPANTS

Our survey was designed to investigate what it is about participation in the Arts courses that repeatedly beckons friends and colleagues; what participants consider to be their most valuable learning experiences; and how the Arts courses have influenced participants' work as therapists, their overall professional development, and their lives in general. The responses of our "co-researchers" (Rogers, 1985/1989, p. 285) reflect their personal experiences and, as such, provide the reader with an immeasurably enriched view of the courses. They also serve to illuminate important aspects of the courses that others might wish to consider in the design of similar programs for the advanced preparation and continuing education of existential-humanistic psychotherapists.

Method

Everyone (N = 45) who had completed five or more Arts courses by June 1999 was invited to participate in our survey. We developed a questionnaire that consisted of seven open-ended questions and five questions that requested demographic information. E-mail was selected as the primary medium for our survey for several reasons: It is efficient, inexpensive, and (most important) befits the context of our relationships with respondents. We thought that the informality of e-mail would encourage spontaneous reflection and candid narrative answers to the questions. Heuristic and phenomenological methods were employed to analyze survey responses (Pierson & Sharp, 1999).

Results

Participant characteristics. Nearly half (49%, *n* = 22) of those queried responded to our survey. Demographic information provided by the 12 women and 10 men represented in the sample yields a general picture of those who elect to participate in the Arts series and the ongoing autonomous cohort groups that continue to meet on a yearly basis. Respondents ranged in age from 41 to 59 years, with a mean age of 51 years. (Keep in mind that the majority of respondents completed their first Arts course 10 or more years ago.) The highest academic degree completed for half of the group was the Ph.D. and for the other half was the master's. Years of experience as a counselor or psychotherapist ranged from 5 to 32 years, with a mean of 12 years and a median of 18 years. The majority of respondents (73.0%) indicated that they draw on the Arts courses in their work as therapists in private practice settings. Other settings mentioned included social service agencies (18.2%), university counseling centers (13.6%), and academic departments (4.5%). In addition, 1 person indicated work in another profession.

Themes observed. Distillation of the collection of narrative responses to each of the survey questions yielded one or more themes that seemed to capture the essence of what respondents conveyed. For clarity and brevity, in this section we present the most prominent themes observed (Table 40.1) among the answers to three of the survey questions.[3] The three questions were as follows:

1. What compels you to continue to participate in the Arts program?
2. What impact does participation in the Arts program have on your (a) work as a therapist, (b) professional development, and (c) nonprofessional life?
3. What stands out for you as the most significant learning experience that you have had at an Arts training?

In the next section, we explore and synthesize these themes and weave in statements of personal experiences that serve to animate the discussion.

DISCUSSION

Our survey respondents impressed us as being men and women who are demonstrating lifelong commitments to becoming master therapists—artists engaged in "the constant challenge to move past where one is and to explore where one is becoming" (Bugental, 1987, p. 5). They expressed that they deeply value the synergistic company of others on the same quest.

Interestingly, our sample of Arts participants was composed of a seasoned group of therapists in midlife who have been practicing for more than a decade on average. To most, the Arts courses are a form of professional continuing education; to a few, they

are courses taken concurrently with the completion of graduate internships.

Cultivation of Therapist Artistry

The Arts courses are perceived to cultivate the personal qualities and skillful artistry that characterize therapists who seek to effectively practice life-changing psychotherapy from an existential-humanistic perspective. Participants accept the invitation to become immersed in the intimate retreat environment and perceive that it evokes more of what is potential in them as whole persons and more of what is potential in them as psychotherapists. To be sure, skills and techniques are practiced and honed throughout the courses, but accent is given to developing therapists' capacity to be fully present and to have fluid access to their subjectivity in service to clients. Following is a sampling of the ways in which this transformation was expressed:

> I find that I can sit with people with more respect; less judgment; [and] more honesty, hope, and willingness to follow their growth. I also find myself going to places [and] levels of pain and despair that challenge me personally. I really care deeply for my clients. I am challenged to grow constantly in order to match the growth they exhibit in my presence.

> As I am increasingly in touch with deeper, subtler layers of my own experience, I can model that for my client and facilitate the client's deepening awareness as well.

> I am now more aware of and better able to tap the subjective currents both in my client and in myself . . . in a way that was not possible before I took Arts [courses]. I take what Camus calls the path of sympathy,

TABLE 40.1 Prominent Themes Observed Among Arts Participants' Answers to Survey Questions

Question Focus	*Themes*
Motivation to participate	1. Sense of connection and belonging to an intentional community
	2. Opportunity for professional and personal development
	3. Opportunity to learn directly from Jim Bugental
Impact of Arts Courses	1. Increased understanding of the theoretical perspective, its efficacy, and its power
	2. Clarification and solidification of professional identity
	3. Increased confidence in ability to practice from an existential-humanistic perspective
	4. Heightened sensitivity to one's subjective experience in the flow of therapy
	5. Generalization of the sensitivities and skills cultivated in the courses to daily living practices
Significant learning experiences	1. Experiences that stimulated professional and personal development (e.g., brought out potentials, enhanced effectiveness, evoked fresh ways of being)
	2. Experiences that enhanced specific aspects of the therapeutic process and revealed or cultivated qualities related to the self as a therapist-artist
	3. Experiences that occurred in the context of relationship with Jim Bugental

NOTE: Arts = The Art of the Psychotherapist. Refer to the Results section of the text for the actual survey questions posed to participants.

helping clients to push away resistances to searching.

Identification with the perspective. A hallmark of the professional is "a sense of personal identity with the work" (Bugental, 1978, p. 35). Survey respondents expressed that the Arts series helps them to articulate and draw on the existential-humanistic theoretical base on which they ground their work as psychotherapists. This was conveyed in several ways. As one person wrote,

The Arts courses have formed the base of my professional growth from 1987 to the present. Prior to that, I had a rather loosely developed framework. The Arts courses

helped me [to] articulate my basic beliefs and to integrate them more consciously into my professional life.

Another simply typed, "It helps me to place myself both internally and externally in my profession." A third person revealed,

The Arts [series] has always reminded me . . . of the power of this perspective. . . . I have wakened again and again to the vision of presence, individual worth, our own condition. Jim's capacity to elaborate the existential perspective in regard to the many facets of our work always taught me more.

Still another writer confided,

> It deeply informs my own process and way of being with clients. I impart this perspective implicitly in all the teaching and supervising I do. My life perspective has forever changed from all the Arts trainings I have done.

"Before entering the Arts program," wrote a fifth person, "I had the same general approach. But by attending Arts [courses], I have developed a better understanding of what underlies the efficacy and potency of the approach."

Personal outgrowths. The personal dimension of respondents' lives clearly is influenced by participation in the Arts series. Exemplifying this, one woman wrote, "Learnings from my work with Jim Bugental and as part of the [Arts] group transcends psychotherapy in that the art of psychotherapy is also an art for living." Three other examples serve to illustrate this theme:

> I think that this perspective has smoothed my life, [smoothed] my thinking, and has given me tools to be a better family member and community citizen. . . . The emphasis on authenticity seeps into my daily life.

> Arts, being philosophically based in the "lived human experience," has been a large part of how I think, feel, and act in my personal life.

> [The Arts program] reminds me of the importance of keeping the focus on the inner life.

Arts courses provide a nutrient-rich environment for stretching and experiencing oneself and others in fresh ways and for becoming more aware of or enlarging one's self-and-world construct system. Exemplifying this augmentation was the person who wrote,

> My relationships with my wife, daughter, and son have changed in the sense that I am much more willing to be expressive of my feelings. . . . The Arts program has helped me [to] accept and value who I am more than any other life experience. . . . [It has] helped me to see that what I call my "self" is not a static unchangeable aspect of my life experience.

Such understanding also was evident in statements such as the following:

> My sense of self grows stronger.

> [I] understand more about how I relate to myself and others.

> [The Arts program] encourages personal and spiritual growth, provides an intensive adjunct to personal individual therapy, and challenges my habitual resistances.

Significance of Community

In the midst of the increasingly technocratic and often fragmentary discipline of psychology, the Arts courses offer participants a home base or an intentional community. More than half of the men and women who responded to our survey specifically mentioned that the feeling of connection with others in their Arts cohort and of belonging to a larger existential-humanistic community was an important factor in choosing to participate in the Arts courses. One person wrote, "Somehow, even from the very beginning years in the Arts series, I felt a connection with the people who attended, so much so that they have become my 'professional' family." Another person wrote that she continues to be attracted by "the sense of community among participants who have together acquired a perspective on life and our work as therapists that transcends the mundane learning of techniques." A third person, a member of the longest running cohort, articulated the following reasons for returning year after year to take part in Arts courses: "I return each year to the annual gathering . . . because of the deep connections we have formed . . . as an experience of a self-contained community and as a collegium whose personal and professional inspiration is remarkable and sustaining."

To be a member of an extended larger professional community seemed to be especially significant to respondents, whose theoretical viewpoint is in the minority among colleagues in their everyday working environments. One person expressed, "I feel myself to be less of an exile, less existentially isolated." The importance of being in relationship with others who share essential elements of a worldview and value system was underscored in another person's statement: "In many professional circles, I do not speak the same language. It is renewing for me to spend a week once a year with other therapists who speak the same language and value one another."

Participants in the Arts courses develop tremendous group cohesiveness. As is true in the working stages of productive groups, this sense of cohesiveness and the trust on which it is predicated create a climate conducive to profound intrapersonal and interpersonal exploration and to giving and receiving the type of constructive feedback that extends therapist sensitivities and skills. These elements were exemplified in the following statement:

> What compels me to continue is what I learn about myself personally. I was with a group of people who, after only a day or two, were willing and able to see me, help

me see myself, convey this to me, and care about me in the process. This experience is rare in everyday life yet, I think, common in the Arts program.

Compelling for another person was "the intimate level of sharing and training we do together where we can make mistakes and still be accepted."

The environment fosters an ethic of shared commitment to one another's personal and professional development. This experience was particularly pronounced in the survey responses from those who participate in the two longest running cohort groups. It is a remarkable element in these groups and is credited with very positive effects. Members are encouraged to move beyond previously held creative boundaries in areas such as their work as therapists, educators, writers, and workshop presenters. Statements that illustrate this include the following:

> [The Arts program] inspires my professional development. I look at our group as the leaders of the next generation of existential psychotherapists, so it pushes me to contribute on a wider, bigger, broader scale [in the form of] professional writing, presenting, [and so on] to our group and to the public at large.

> The trainings give me a forum to . . . discuss my own perceptions and try out new ideas with a supportive, nonjudgmental group of colleagues. Since it is imperative to try to live the stance I am trying to teach, our Arts meetings are a hothouse in which to practice what I preach. I get to watch people I know and respect try out new material on me, which in turn encourages me to take new risks.

Similarly, another person observed, "We are now a dedicated bunch of colleagues involved in each other's lives professionally and personally. We teach each other, consult with one another, and attend other advanced trainings." Bugental was credited with directly inspiring some respondents to expand professionally, as was noted by a person who wrote, "Jim encouraged us to begin presenting in Arts IV, V, VI, and on. He also supported us in other teaching and writing. He took us [with him] to [American Psychological Association (APA) meetings] as presenters."

The invitation to live more authentically and at one's growing edge is implicit in every activity within the Arts curriculum, from participation in therapeutic skill-building exercises to late-night discussions in the hot tub. As one writer reflected, "Because of some of the self-confrontation that has been my experience of Arts [courses], I feel like I live a bit more existentially in my life, which is to say more authentically." Another person wrote,

> My work deepens and gets more fine-tuned in being with my peers and Jim—just being in their presence in this atmosphere. In a more concrete way, [this occurs] through the informal talks around meals [and so on] and through the formal presentations, demonstrations, and discussions.

Relationship With a Mentor

Bugental's presence as a mentor, teacher, or elder was specifically mentioned as being an essential element of the Arts series for a number of people in our sample. The opportunity to study and work with him was cited as both a compelling reason to participate in the series and the catalyst for outstanding learning experiences. As one member of the longest running cohort group said, "It is . . . a valuable opportunity to work with an elder in our profession, Dr. Jim Bugental,

who has rich wisdom from years of experience."

Learning experiences that occur in relationship with Bugental are expressed in two forms. An example of the first is from a man who wrote, "The most significant integrative experience, a touchstone experience, . . . is [that] after Arts IV, Jim, upon saying goodbye, told me lots of people like his work, [but] he sees I'm really understanding, getting and living it." The significance of being recognized and affirmed by one's mentor is emphasized in his self-disclosure.

Another person indicated that what stands out for him was "Jim's story about paving driveways." That person wrote,

> It is the telling of that story that touches me so much. It is about the life force in nature. How he tells it demonstrates his admiration for that force. Without that belief, what does therapy become? Something very different, I think.

This perception illustrates a second type of learning experience, one in which the power of being affectively touched in the context of the valued relationship with Bugental is central to the learning process.

Bugental is highly esteemed and, frankly, loved by those who participate in the Arts series. This quality of personal regard clearly is reciprocated and permeates the atmosphere at the Arts retreats. The spirit of generativity (Erickson, 1982) is consistently demonstrated in Bugental's way of being in relationship. He offers younger colleagues profound respect for their individuality and individuation processes as psychotherapists—artists on their own heroic journeys.

RELATIONSHIP OF ARTS TO OTHER INSTITUTES

The philosophy and design of the Arts program inspires collaborative professional activities such as teaching, conducting research, and program development. A brief review of a few noteworthy activities undertaken by Arts participants illuminates the influence of the Arts program on other institutions. For example, early in the past decade, several participants conducted training programs in Russia based on the Arts courses. Later, a highly successful program was developed in California to train 19 psychotherapists visiting from Russia (Boyd, 1997-1998). As a result of these trainings, existential-humanistic institutes were created in Moscow and St. Petersburg. These institutes are now affiliated with Moscow State University and the Pedagogical State University of St. Petersburg, respectively. Students in St. Petersburg can receive university credit for Arts trainings (M. Heery, personal communication, June 2000).

The success of these projects led the trainers, most of whom are Arts participants, to envision and create the Existential-Humanistic Institute (EHI), located in the San Francisco Bay Area (Schneider, 1997-1998). EHI is a not-for-profit education, training, and service organization designed to promote the consideration and teaching of existential-humanistic principles in psychology and psychotherapy. It offers workshops and training programs to professionals, students, and the general public, and it publishes a newsletter, *The Existential Humanist*. A panel of seven members, six of whom have been participants in the Arts program for several years, governs EHI. Its advisory board consists of noted scholars from throughout the United States and Canada. A significant number of its members have participated in Arts courses.

EHI provides scholars and practitioners with the opportunity (i.e., a "home") to present evolving work in theory, research, and practice to interested individuals from around the country. Many members of EHI are members of APA's Division 32 and of the Association for Humanistic Psychology. Some members are university faculty members or students, whereas others are active participants in clinical training programs or institutes.

We believe that EHI has created an opportunity for greater dialogue and collaboration between individuals who are concerned with furthering humanistic and existential principles. Creating such an opportunity is, in our view, an important contribution to our field. Furthermore, we believe that the intimacy and cooperation initially fostered in the Arts program have played a substantial role in this cross-fertilization.

CLOSING REFLECTIONS

In this chapter, we have presented the Arts courses as a model existential-humanistic training program. The experienced psychotherapists that contributed to our survey repeatedly underscored the vital role that the Arts series has played in their development as existential-humanistic practitioners. The courses are perceived to strengthen professional identity and, as once articulated in a course flyer, the ability to put "this perspective into clinical actuality" (J. F. T. Bugental, personal communication, April 1996). They also appear to further stimulate participants' capacity for experiential freedom— "the freedom to profoundly feel, sense, and think" (K. J. Schneider, personal communication, September 1999)—the lifeblood of artistic expression.

We have discovered that there is a critical distinction between knowing about an existential-humanistic perspective from a theoretical or scholarly standpoint and "knowing" the perspective because it has been repeatedly modeled and personally experienced and affirmed, not only in one's work as a psychotherapist but also in one's way of being. *Becoming* an existential-humanistic psychotherapist-artist is predicated on such multidimensional comprehension. It is also predicated on an internalized ethic that Bugental (1976) expressed beautifully in *The Search for Existential Identity*:

> Psychotherapy is an art form. An art form seriously practiced by an artist worthy of that name calls for cultivated sensitivity, trained skills, disciplined emotion, and total personal investment. . . . Psychotherapy demands discipline from its responsible practitioners above all else. Only after one has mastered the fundamentals, steeped himself [or herself] in the diversity of human experience, and explored more advanced possibilities can he improvise

and create meaningfully and responsibly. (pp. 297-298)

The mission at the heart of the Arts courses is to facilitate actualization of this ethic. Within a contemporary psychotherapy climate heavily influenced by the managed care industry, the medical model, and the press for positivistic, natural science-based, "empirically supported treatments" (APA, 2000), today, perhaps more than ever, we need psychotherapists who can "create meaningfully and responsibly" in collaborative relationships with their clients. Experiential training programs that honor both the art and science of our profession are essential.[4]

NOTES

1. Currently, the interested graduate student can contact schools included in the informative *West Georgia Directory of Graduate Programs in Humanistic-Transpersonal Psychology in North America* (Arons, 1996) and the Consortium for Diversified Psychology Programs (Taylor, 1999). Excellent resources for postgraduate or continuing education can be found through Division 32 (Humanistic Psychology) of the American Psychological Association, the Association for Humanistic Psychology, and the Existential-Humanistic Institute.

2. Elizabeth Bugental, Myrtle Heery, Molly Sterling, and David Young all have made substantial contributions to the development and implementation of the Arts programs.

3. We have restricted our analysis and discussion to three questions due to space limitations.

4. The Arts courses currently are offered under the direction of Myrtle Heery, Molly Sterling, and David Young, former students of Bugental and Arts co-facilitators for many years. Bugental continues to participate as his health permits. Information about the Arts program may be obtained by contacting The Art of the Psychotherapist, phone: (707) 763-3808; e-mail: mheery@humanstudies.com; snail mail: 4940 Bodega Avenue, Petaluma, CA 94952.

REFERENCES

American Psychological Association. (2000). *Position statements on humanistic psychology* [Online]. Available: www.apa.org/divisions/div32/positions.html

Arons, M. (Ed.). (1996). *West Georgia directory of graduate programs in humanistic-transpersonal psychology in North America* (5th ed.). Carrollton: University of West Georgia, Department of Psychology.

Boyd, K. (1997-1998, Fall-Winter). More Russians on my mind. *The Existential Humanist*, p. 3. (San Francisco: Existential-Humanistic Institute)

Buber, M. (1970). *I and thou*. New York: Scribner.

Bugental, J. F. T. (1976). *The search for existential identity: Patient-therapist dialogues in humanistic psychotherapy*. San Francisco: Jossey-Bass.

Bugental, J. F. T. (1978). *Psychotherapy and process: The fundamentals of an existential-humanistic psychotherapy*. Reading, MA: Addison-Wesley.

Bugental, J. F. T. (1987). *The art of the psychotherapist*. New York: Norton.

Bugental, J. F. T. ((1990). *Intimate journeys: Stories from life-changing psychotherapy*. San Francisco: Jossey-Bass.

Bugental, J. F. T. (1999). *Psychotherapy isn't what you think*. Phoenix, AZ: Zeig, Tucker.

Bugental, J. F. T., & Bracke, P. E. (1992). The future of humanistic-existential psychotherapy. *Psychotherapy, 29*(1), 28-33.

Bugental, J. F. T., & Heery, M. W. (1999). Unearthing the moment. *Self and Society, 27*(3), 26-28.

Bugental, J. F. T., & Kleiner, R. I. (1993). Existential psychotherapies. In G. Stricker & J. R. Gold (Eds.), *Comprehensive handbook of psychotherapy integration* (pp. 101-112). New York: Plenum.

Bugental, J. F. T., & Sapienza, B. G. (1994). The three R's for humanistic psychology: Remembering, reconciling, and re-uniting. In F. Wertz (Ed.), *The humanistic movement: Recovering the person in psychology* (pp. 159-169). Lake Worth, FL: Gardner.

Bugental, J. F. T., & Sterling, M. M. (1995). Existential-humanistic psychotherapy: New perspectives. In A. S. Gurman & S. B. Messar (Eds.), *Essential psychotherapies: Theory and practice* (pp. 226-260). New York: Guilford.

Churchill, S. (1994). The presence of humanistic psychologists in the academy. In F. Wertz (Ed.), *The humanistic movement: Recovering the person in psychology* (pp. 292-305). Lake Worth, FL: Gardner.

Erickson, E. H. (1982). *The life cycle completed*. New York: Norton.

Gendlin, E. (1994). Celebrations and problems of humanistic psychology. In F. Wertz (Ed.), *The humanistic movement: Recovering the person in psychology* (pp. 330-343). Lake Worth, FL: Gardner.

Lambert, M. J., & Bergin, A. E. (1994). The effectiveness of psychotherapy. In A. E. Bergin & S. L. Garfield (Eds.), *Handbook of psychotherapy and behavior change* (4th ed.). New York: John Wiley.

May, R., & Yalom, I. (1995). Existential psychotherapy. In R. Corsini & D. Wedding (Eds.), *Current psychotherapies* (5th ed.). Itasca, IL: F. E. Peacock.

Pierson, J. F., & Sharp, J. G. (1999, August). *Arts retreats: Existentially informed training and community building*. Paper presented at meeting of the American Psychological Association, Boston.

Rogers, C. R. (1989). Toward a more human science of the person. In H. Kirschenbaum & V. L. Henderson (Eds.), *The Carl Rogers reader* (pp. 279-295). Boston: Houghton Mifflin. (Original work published 1985)

Schneider, K. J. (1997-1998, Fall-Winter). An existential-humanistic institute is born. *The Existential-Humanist*, p. 11. (San Francisco: Existential-Humanistic Institute)

Sharp, J., & Bugental, J. F. T. (in press). Existential-humanistic psychotherapy. In R. Corsini (Ed.), *Handbook of innovative therapy* (2nd ed.). New York: John Wiley.

Taylor, E. (1999). An intellectual renaissance of humanistic psychology? *Journal of Humanistic Psychology, 39*(2), 7-25.

Taylor, E. (2000). *The deep poetic soul: An alternative vision of psychotherapy* [Online]. Available: www.sonoma.edu/psychology/os2db/elkins1.html

CHAPTER 41

Keeping Person-Centered Education Alive in Academic Settings

HOBART F. THOMAS

THIS CHAPTER deals with the question of how an academic requirement in a university course can be designed to enhance both the emotional and intellectual development of the learner in ways that transcend typical academic expectations. I describe in detail a method stemming from several years of experience in an alternative educational model that is now employed in the university classroom. I give particular consideration to survival strategies for the person-centered educator operating within institutions that might be disinterested in, or even antithetical toward, person-centered values.

A shift in values occurred in the field of education during the early 1980s. This shift was captured by the University of Notre Dame president, Theodore M. Hesburgh:

We seem to be passing through a time when education is the more cherished as it is the more vocational, when learning how to do something rather than liberal and humanistic learning how to be someone, particularly someone human, is in vogue. Thus we must seriously address the future of liberal education, especially in our day when the most popular course on the American college campus is not literature or history but [rather] accounting. (Hesburgh, 1981, p. 77)

At about the same time that the preceding statement was made, the Spring 1981 issue of the *Journal of Humanistic Psychology* was devoted mostly to a discussion of a number of once flourishing alternative education programs, all basically person centered, that had been phased out of existence.

Rogers (1983) summarized a voluminous body of research to support the effectiveness of the person-centered approach in a variety of learning situations. At the same time, he

AUTHOR'S NOTE: An earlier version of this chapter appeared in *Person-Centered Review*, Vol. 3, No. 3, pp. 337-352.

was frank to report the eventual cessation of the majority of once successful programs and to speculate on some of the reasons for their demise, such as threat to established systems, limited pool of person-centered leaders, creeping bureaucracy and routinization, no codifiable pattern for the operation of a person-centered institution, and unwillingness of leaders to share their power.

For a period of 14 years, I devoted my professional life to a small interdisciplinary experimental school within the California State University system—the School of Expressive Arts at Sonoma State University—that based its curriculum on the fullest possible development of the individual (Thomas, 1981). This program, once highly successful, was phased out of existence in 1984—another "sign of the times."

Those of us who have had the privilege of participating in such unique experiments are now challenged to distill the essence of what has been learned and to share it with others. Thus, we might search together for new procedures and forms that will enable that which is of the highest value to live and flourish anew. It is with such intent that this chapter is written.

SOME IMPORTANT QUESTIONS

In telling the story of how I am attempting to keep person-centered education alive within academic settings, I would like to direct attention to the following questions:

1. Is it possible to provide a climate conducive to the enhancement of personal values and personal integration within a system that often appears disinterested in, or even antithetical toward, such values?

2. How might we redirect an academic requirement to serve the individual's best interests?
3. How can an academic requirement facilitate and enhance qualities in the student such as self-responsibility, eagerness for learning, creativity, affiliation, and cooperation with others?
4. Is it possible to accomplish these goals while still adhering to acceptable academic standards?

BACK TO THE CLASSROOM

In 1986, I made a decision to engage in what for me was a difficult personal challenge. I agreed to teach several sections of an upper division required general education humanities course titled "Written and Oral Analysis." The purpose of the course was to improve students' written and oral communication. What represented a challenge to me was not so much the subject matter of the course itself but rather the fact that students were in the course involuntarily.

Successful completion of this course is required of all students wishing to graduate from the university. For many years, as a psychotherapist and educator, I had been involved in situations where I had assumed that the voluntary participation of clients or students was an essential factor for successful growth to occur. Here, I found myself in a situation that, on the surface at least, appeared to be the very antithesis of what I considered to be person-centered education. Few of these students had asked to be there. Many of them had other priorities—work in their chosen major fields, heavy requirements of other courses, outside employment, family responsibilities, and so on.

Rarely, if ever, are students consulted as to what they want, are interested in, or might feel are meaningful directions to pursue in the educational process. After all, isn't the teacher expected to know what is to be studied and learned, and isn't it ridiculous to expect students to be consulted about these things? When I myself was a student, I was rarely consulted with regard to such matters. Rather, the bulk of my education right through graduate school consisted of following directions, learning what was prescribed for me by a number of different experts, mastering concepts and procedures, meeting others' expectations for me, and finding out how to say the right things and give the correct answers on papers so as to pass examinations and get the coveted degree or credential. In fact, in graduate school, we students used to say, cynically, "If you want to succeed, first study your professor, then study the subject matter."

Long after completing the requirements for my degrees, I decided that I never would be satisfied with teaching and learning that did not in some way make a significant difference in the life of the learner. So, I pursued what often seemed to be an uphill course—the development of the whole person, so far as possible, in the educational setting. I found that the success of this attempt depended on a basic shift from a teacher-centered model of education to a person-centered one.

DEALING WITH THE SYSTEM

I have learned through many years of experience and much trial and error, however, that if person-centered approaches are to survive and flourish within traditional educational settings, then one must be well aware of and not ignore certain fundamental realities. One of the most important of these is the fact that most students within our educational institutions are subject to many external demands. The typical student in our university systems, in addition to facing the demands of his or her personal life, probably is enrolled (at any given time) in five or six different courses of study, each of which requires at least 2 hours outside of class time, on average, for every 1 hour spent in class. In effect, the student has to serve several masters at the same time. As a consequence, all too often the person gets lost in the process. Far too seldom is the student given the opportunity to integrate the vast amount and variety of information within a personal system of values.

On the other hand, the professor who does not require his or her fair share of the student's time will soon find the student's energies drifting elsewhere. The toughest courses that make the most demands on the student get most of his or her attention, often out of fear of failure. In other words, the squeaky wheels get the grease. So, the question becomes one of how to provide the openness and freedom so essential for personal growth within a system that prevents such an opportunity by imposing myriad requirements that far too seldom relate to the personal needs and interests of the individual.

For those of us working on this problem, an important clue existed where we had least expected it—in the requirement itself. We asked ourselves the following questions. How can an academic requirement be made to serve the individual, the master within each person who at some deep level knows what is right for that person? And how is it possible to ensure that each individual is provided with the time necessary to at least get acquainted with the essential process of self-discovery?

Another important reality to be dealt with is the necessity of providing some evidence or product of learning that is demonstrable to others and measures up to reasonable academic standards. Academic degrees and credentials are not (nor do I believe they should be) awarded merely for putting in time or "doing one's own thing," as some people in the heyday of the growth movement believed.

I also would carry the maintenance of standards a step further and challenge myself and my students to always look toward creativity in our productions—toward some unique expression of the self, a new twist, a search for ever-evolving ways of being and expression that offer meaningful contributions to human knowledge and understanding. This, I believe, was the original intent of the Ph.D.—to grant the highest academic award only to those who made original contributions to the pool of human knowledge. Is it too much to ask students, at whatever level, to strive for this quality of creativity rather than merely conforming to existing patterns? I think not. In fact, the more I encourage the development of creativity in my students, the more I am surprised, delighted, and impressed by what they are capable of accomplishing.

To ensure that students may have the opportunity for at least a modicum of self-confrontation, I asked myself the following questions. Why not make the requirement "demon" the servant rather than the master of the person? Can we put this demon to work in helping us to get as much value as possible out of our educational experience? But who determines what is of most value? Traditionally, it has been the professor—the expert in charge. But what if the expert who is supposed to know so much shares the responsibility for determining what is of value with every person in the group? What happens when we focus on the values and concerns of each individual?

AN EXPERIMENTAL MODEL

Following is a description of the tone that I attempt to set in the Written and Oral Analysis course and a general description of the course itself. I usually begin each course with the following quotation attributed to the late Howard Thurman, a well-known San Francisco clergyman: "Ask not what the world needs; rather, ask what makes you come alive and go do that, for what the world needs is people who have come alive." This is followed by these instructions:

The basic requirement for this course is to find what makes you come alive. Try to identify just who you are in terms of your basic values and interests. Get interested in something—anything you deem to be of value. Try to determine what you need to learn to expand and develop this interest. See where it takes you. Try to discover and develop your own style, your own way of expressing, through oral and written presentation to the group, this quest for your deepest and most important values. The sky's the limit. If you are unclear about what is worthy of your time and effort, then your assignment is to search for it and report on the process. Facing openly your blocks and difficulties, whatever they may be, finding the means of expressing them orally, in written form and in dialogue with others, is often the doorway to new learning. This will be your semester's project underlying most of your work in this course.

You will be expected to begin right away the process of discovering, in your own terms, what this project will be and to spend a fair measure of time working on it throughout the semester. What is a fair measure of time? Let's adopt the time-honored academic expectation of 2 hours of study outside of class for every hour spent in class. In this case, since we are spending 3 hours per week in class, you will be expected to spend an additional 6 hours per week devoted to work of your own choosing as it relates to your project for this course.

Somewhat paradoxically—and I realize this may appear strange to some of you—you are being required to devote this period of time to yourself, to ask what you need to become more fulfilled, to achieve more balance or perspective in your life, or perhaps a bit more modestly, at least to investigate and learn something concerning a topic for which you have some curiosity. Since this is a course in written and oral communication, the other aspect of this requirement is to participate with the rest of the group in the continual process of learning about and practicing effective communication, particularly with regard to those matters that are most alive for each of us.

Each of you will be asked to give a minimum of three oral presentations to the class and [to] complete six written papers for the semester. The last of these will be a more comprehensive written and oral presentation to the group of your final project. Regular attendance and participation are expected of everyone. There will be ample opportunity for you to participate actively both in the large group and in smaller subgroups, to both learn from and teach each other.

After setting the tone and providing general instructions and discussion of questions, the first assignment (beginning with the second class session) is for each person to give a 3- to 5-minute oral presentation to the class, accompanied by a written paper, introducing himself or herself to the group. Students are asked to consider questions such as the following. In what ways am I unique? What is there about me that others are most likely to find interesting? What can I share of my interests and values? What makes me come alive? How can I make this course work for me? I encourage people to

have fun and be as creative as they wish with this initial presentation.

I also ask each student, even at this early date, to share some idea of how the student might best use this course for his or her own purposes. I ensure students that I do not expect everyone to be clear or certain about their semester project at this point. What I do request is sort of a position report or a statement of "where I am right now" with regard to this question. Students are asked to try to set some goals that can be modified as we proceed.

I cannot emphasize too strongly the value of constantly encouraging people to recognize and accept what is going on for them at any given moment and to find the means of expressing this experience. I have found that the persistent encouragement of authenticity as the first priority is perhaps the best policy I know. Some of my students' most exciting productions have resulted from their willingness, first, to honestly face the fact that at times they might be feeling ignorant, stupid, inadequate, inept, lost, or worse and to engage themselves with the process of turning these struggles into pieces of creative work. It is extremely important that we acknowledge all feelings and, whenever possible, search for ways of expressing them creatively.

During this introductory session, I also distribute a course syllabus detailing what the course is about. It includes recommended readings, criteria for different grades, and suggestions for actively participating in the evaluative process. To provide a common basis of information, I ask all students to read and give written and oral responses to the same two books. Most recently, I have used Elbow's (1981) *Writing With Power* and Rogers's (1983) *Freedom to Learn for the Eighties*. The former covers important principles of written communication, and the latter provides a conceptual basis for the person-centered approach to learning, something that many students find to be a new and strange experience.

I have found that, after the initial oral presentations followed by discussions and sharing of their written work in groups of three or four people, it seems to work best to concentrate on the two just-mentioned books for the next several weeks and on students' continuing consideration of their special interest projects. I ask for a written response paper to each of the books (average three- to five-page, double-spaced typed paper) emphasizing how they are relating the material to their personal values and their projects for the course. I read these and return them with comments and personal reactions. In addition to establishing an ongoing dialogue between the instructor and students, this process helps me to get some idea of the level at which each student is functioning, his or her strengths and weaknesses, and any areas needing special attention.

A sizable portion of class time throughout the semester is spent in small groups of three or four people where students read each other's work and offer reactions and comments. I purposely encourage the mixing of these groups from time to time so that every student gets to work with every other student at some point in time. At the end of each class session, we devote 15 to 20 minutes in the total group for the purpose of sharing small group experiences with the entire class.

In addition, much class time consists of various exercises involving a variety of types of writing. Typically, this consists of a short presentation by me followed by a writing period of 10 to 20 minutes and then another period of small group discussion (20 to 30 minutes) followed by voluntary sharing with the whole class.

Another technique that seems to work quite well is to devote the first 15 minutes of the class session to student oral reports. We usually limit these to three or four reports with a definite time limit of 5 minutes each. Although these are voluntary, there is the expectation that each student will participate at some point in time. Students are encouraged to talk about anything of importance to them. The talks vary considerably. They may be informative, persuasive, inspirational, entertaining, or merely a statement of what is going on for the person at the time. Some are well planned, whereas others vary from moderately spontaneous to off-the-cuff. Whatever the case, they provide a good opportunity to speak to a group and to practice giving and receiving feedback.

I try to achieve a balance, particularly in the first third to half of the semester, between devoting time to concepts and principles in the two required texts and allowing enough open time and space for pursuit of individual interests. In a way, it seems contradictory to assign readings for everyone while at the same time urging people to use the time for themselves. Frankly, I grappled a lot with this issue and discussed these concerns with the students from time to time. This does not seem to pose too great a difficulty once all the concerns are out on the table. For a number of students, the suggestion of readings at the beginning provides a sort of security blanket, that is, a way of easing into the far more difficult, ambiguous, and often threatening situation of taking an active and responsible role in their own education. Also, the 6 hours a week required outside of class, if not exceeded, can protect students from overworking in this course.

I consider it important, however, for me to maintain a gentle but persistent amount of pressure in reminding and asking people how their basic projects are coming along. Just prior to midterm, each person is required to give an oral position report to the class describing, in as much detail as possible, the progress the student is making and/or the difficulties he or she is having with the project.

It is essential at this point to emphasize that authenticity and honesty in staying true to the process, and describing just what is going on in one's research, is infinitely preferable to presenting a slick product designed just to impress others. I have been most impressed with the energy generated by this process and with the attention and genuine support that students are able to give to each other. The more advanced and creative presentations can inspire, whereas the sometimes awkward but genuine expressions of struggle with works in progress serve to encourage others to be more accepting of themselves and to keep trying. This is a time when individual conferences with students having difficulties often can be of immense benefit in clarifying and removing the blocks to creative expression.

FINDING A SUITABLE PROJECT

The desire to succeed is a double-edged sword. On the one hand, it provides the necessary fuel for each of us to excel in whatever task we undertake. On the other hand, our expectations and standards regarding what constitutes a successful performance or an acceptable product also can become a serious barrier to creative expression.

A bright young woman who had been doing well in the early written assignments and class discussions approached me at mid-semester indicating that she was very distressed over the fact that she did not have the slightest idea of what to do for her semester project. During our discussion, she shared with me a conflict she was having with her parents. She claimed that her parents had threatened to cut off the funds to complete her education if she did not conform to their wishes to spend time at home during her vacation and enroll in what they

considered to be a more prestigious institution. She mentioned that this problem appeared to be consuming most of her time and energy. Finally, I remarked to her, "Do you realize that your project just might be staring you in the face?" This never had occurred to her, but she became interested. "But is this academic? How could something like this be acceptable?" she asked. "I'm not sure," I replied. "That's for you to work on. But whatever the case, you just might have yourself a topic if you want it." As we talked some more, she became clearer about the issues involving the conflict with her parents and the choices that she needed to make. She decided to work more intensely on her problem at the counseling center and to go ahead with the task of turning this whole matter into a class project—a written and oral presentation to be given to the class during the final weeks of the semester.

I wish that it were possible to convey to the reader the delightfully creative manner with which this student gave her final presentation to the group as well as the enthusiastic response she received from her classmates. By taking charge of her own life and facing many crucial issues with her parents, she was in some way speaking for each one of us. With the utmost sensitivity, taste, and humor, she described—complete with childhood photos of herself and her family—artistic sketches and even impromptu dramatization, with a number of clever props, her way of dealing with her conflicts and her resulting choices. To quote a few remarks from her final report:

> For the first time in my life, the type of learning I yearned for was taking place. Oh, humanities class is not the end, merely a delicate taste of a new beginning. One class has not changed me, but it has started the ball rolling within. I am hungry for more similar classes. As it has inspired me, I

don't want to stop now. As the class project allowed me to work on things I deemed important, I governed my own learning process. I directed myself to a goal, one which I eventually achieved. . . . More importantly, the things that I learned in the class extend well beyond the classroom. They affect me personally, and I shall carry this new information with me for a long time.

I consider of most importance her final remarks to the effect that a meaningful process has been set in motion, something that has prospects of continuing in the future.

Another student, a 21-year-old man, gave a different but equally moving and innovative final presentation to the class in the form of a videotape. He dramatized, in very clever and entertaining form, a variety of incidents in his own life, often humorous but with underlying serious intent, that related to his own growing sense of independence and feeling of personal value. A quote from his final report might give a flavor of what the experience was for him:

> In this class, I learned what I was excited about because *I* was the curriculum guide. Since my experience here, I hereby proclaim an end to being led as livestock over the educational pasture. I will, of course, have to follow instructors' guidelines, but preparing my work in a way that motivates me to create, I've found, is like a masonry drill spinning through the writer's block.

I find the process of selecting examples from so many exciting pieces of work a difficult one indeed, but here are a few more. A woman in the class whose sister was dying of cancer used this experience as the basis for her course project. She was able to identify this as her project early in the course. She shared, from time to time, a number of her experiences in dealing with this very difficult emotional task, with regard to both her own personal feelings and her relationship with her dying sister. In addition, she used her time to learn all that she could about the dying process through a fairly systematic study using several resources, relevant literature, tapes, and interviews. Obviously, her motivation was very high, as the following comments indicate:

> This final project has been a wonderful enlightening experience for me and one that doesn't stop with this report or the end of the semester. I am a different person due to this course of study, and I have been able to share the benefits of my learning with others—family and friends—and keep finding opportunities to share this new experience, strength, and hope of mine. I am grateful, too, that I could share this project orally with the class and perhaps diminish the fear of death for others.

Other examples include an art history major, already a competent analytical writer, who for her project developed her creative writing skills; a pre-med student who began writing poetry for the first time and subsequently elected to enroll in a poetry class; and a business student who did a study of the Isle of Rhodes. This latter study, in addition to providing the student with geographical and historical knowledge, resulted in a deep understanding of his family origins and reestablishment of connection with family members. He then culminated the study with a visit to Rhodes. I include a quote from this student's final report to illustrate how the experience of being challenged to assume responsibility for one's own learning may have important ramifications:

> I have seriously taken the questions you had us answer in this class and asked them

for each of my other classes and even the Marketing Association, answering the questions 'How can I make this course work for me? How much do I already know? And what do I want to learn?" This has helped me [to] align my classes with my own interests and goals. I have come to realize that learning happens when you have an inherent interest and a fair amount of time for yourself to study and to devote to the subject.

DOES THIS WORK FOR EVERYONE?

Anonymous end-of-semester evaluations from six classes (totaling 128 students) revealed that the vast majority of students claimed to have had a highly significant learning experience similar in quality to the examples given. As one might expect, there are bound to be exceptions. A few students self-selected out of the course during the beginning weeks of the semester for a variety of unknown reasons. Last year, I advised a couple of students who were falling behind to drop the course. To my surprise, both reenrolled a year later and were taking the course during the semester when this chapter was being written.

A small minority (5% to 7%) claimed not to have derived anything particularly significant from the course, as illustrated by the following comments:

Need more structure; too ambiguous.

I don't want to dig too deeply; all I want is to graduate.

Needed clearer instructions, more clearly stated objectives.

Class moved at too slow a pace. Could have been more challenging.

Complete waste of time.

Need more grading, more specific assignments. I need to be pushed more to perform.

More written analysis; less psychoanalysis.

Finally, a couple of my favorites:

Great instructor in an insignificant class.

More concentration in improving writting [sic] skills.

A number of the negative comments remind me of the continuing need to develop meaningful challenges and structures for those students less able to assume personal responsibility for their own learning. Although I consider myself to be a slow learner in this regard, I am happy to report that the strategies proposed in this chapter have helped to improve my batting average considerably after many years of trial and error.

CONCLUDING REMARKS

As indicated at the beginning of this chapter, I had held a number of reservations about whether person-centered approaches to learning that had worked successfully in alternative educational models could be applied to required academic courses. My experience, from which I have drawn a few representative examples, has convinced me beyond a doubt that beneath the facades lies a crying need for personal relevance on the part of vast numbers of students and teachers in our educational institutions. For me, the following observations of a student speak for many of us who participated in the experience:

I noticed that people worked on subjects that mattered very much to them, and they seemed to benefit personally by doing so. I noticed inner conflicts being at least partially solved, career decisions being made, and in general, a true learning process evolving before my eyes. It was good to see real benefits of school happening instead of rote memorization or abstract generalities. It made me feel good to be at a school where this is going on. If only more classes would emphasize learning for yourself, not for the teacher, much more value would be inherent in our system.

A famous educational leader once remarked that all too often, school becomes a place where we deal only with things that do not matter. I have learned that if I am willing to share what I know and to admit what I do not know, while staying in touch with what my students have to teach me and each other, then indeed this need never be the case.

POSTSCRIPT

After this article was published in 1988, I continued using variants of this model, teaching in both the School of Humanities and Department of Psychology at Sonoma State until my "official" retirement in 1992. Looked at only in terms of time and energy expended, it was some of the hardest work of my professional career. On the other hand, the work also was some of the most personally gratifying. What made it so was largely due to finding that the same quality of personally relevant and transformative educational experiences that characterized our experimental School of Expressive Arts during the 1970s was possible to achieve within more traditional settings.

After my official retirement, I have had the pleasure of occasionally working on a volunteer basis with Arthur Warmoth and his colleagues and students in the Learning Community Program (begun during the late 1980s) in the Department of Psychology at Sonoma State. This program provides psychology students with the opportunity to take charge of their own academic programs while collaborating with others in ongoing support groups.

Block classes (2 to 3 hours each) allow students to deal intensively with both cognitive and experiential learning, with an emphasis on personal integration of whatever constitutes the course curriculum. Also, more advanced students are encouraged to become group facilitators in this program.

Recently, Warmoth and some colleagues in different academic disciplines have combined forces and developed an interdisciplinary learning community model for lower division students (i.e., freshmen and sophomores) working on fulfilling general education requirements. Far too often, in my experience, general education courses are viewed by both students and faculty as primarily meaningless obstacles to be overcome. (My experience with upper division students in a required course certainly convinced me that this need not be the case.) Although this development is still in its early stages, results are very encouraging, according to Warmoth.

I, too, find creative efforts such as these in person-centered humanistic education to be encouraging and too important to be confined just within the walls of psychology departments. I would submit that humanity's perennial love affair with technology, which all too often seems to resemble infatuation, requires an ongoing balancing quest on the part of each of us, wherever we happen to be, for awareness and expression of the deep forces of creativity and love that potentially exist within all of us. It is my hope that what I have found both useful and exciting in my experience as an educator will be of value to the reader in his or her own personal quest wherever the reader happens to be.

REFERENCES

Elbow, P. (1981). *Writing with power.* Oxford, UK: Oxford University Press.

Hesburgh, T. M. (1981). Liberal education: What is its future? *Forum for Correspondence and Contact, 12*(2). (New York: International Center for Integrative Studies)

Rogers, C. R. (1983). *Freedom to learn for the eighties.* Columbus, OH: Merrill.

Thomas, H. F. (1981). Toward a rationale and model for basic education. In E. Bauman, I. B. Brent, L. Piper, & A. Wright (Eds.), *The holistic health lifebook* (pp. 282-293). Berkeley, CA: And/Or Press.

CHAPTER 42

Inklings of Eternity
On the Human Capacity to Play

O. FRED DONALDSON

Everything has been figured out except how to live.

—J.-P. Sartre (cited in Nisker, *Crazy Wisdom*, 1990)

KID STUFF AND GOD'S PLAY

The gift of immaturity itself, which has enabled us to retain, in our best, most human moments the capacity to play. (Campbell, cited in Hyers, 1973, pp. 169-170)

"Once upon a time . . ." childhood and play. Like a daffodil's first push through the early spring earth, I remember running out the screen door of the large white farmhouse into a world full of playmates. I played with an undivided mind, intent on play's demands and pleasures, reconciled to its hardships, not complaining, never believing that I might be doing something better, and certainly not bored. The cornfield, apple orchard, barn, woods, pond, horses, and fox were my tutors as well as the sternest mentors of how well I discharged play's sacred trust. I knew and was known by every field, tree, and animal. I felt my place in the scheme of things. The whole world was a playground, and everything was a playmate. I was living a feeling of belonging as young as infancy and as ancient as all life.

Would I be sent out and play with anything less? No, to come out and play with life in all its forms is our greatest summons and our fullest capacity, revealing an ecological intelligence that animates all living things. In this wisdom, we share the rapture of being alive, that ineffable experience where reality is the same in oneself as in everyone else, where action emerges out of the present moment without reflection, and where one sort of knows how one should relate spontaneously, without thinking, to every moment of life.

Very early in life, this original sense of play is traded away in a Faustian bargain that progressively limits our capacity for the original as we contest with a world we deem to be fearful. In this process, the grace that led me through my earliest years no longer was valid. Life became a battlefield, and play is where I was first taught to fight its contests. And in the end, I no longer questioned the cultural counterfeits, forgetting to dream that my original play was even possible.

Years later, playful children tugged on my pant legs and pulled at my spirit. It was as if they knew my life was missing something that it could not afford to miss. This "something" was so puzzling and undeniable, such a manifestation of an unrecognized power at play in life, that in its light all the old ways, rules, and games would be judged invalid and woefully lacking in their ability to guide me to the heights to which I aspire. I smiled when I read Swimme's (1984) delightful book, *The Universe Is a Green Dragon*. In it, a character, Youth, asks an important question: "Wouldn't it be wonderful if there were schools somewhere that taught humans how to become true masters at the art of play?" (p. 127). I smiled because I knew that I had begun an apprenticeship in just such a school. For 27 years, its masters, children, and animals have mentored me. Our classroom is a playground called Earth.

This chapter is not a substitute (admittedly quite inadequate) for my playmates. Their lessons are revelatory rather than didactic, and their play is proof that nothing conjured by fear, philosophy, or analysis could be as awesome, exhilarating, magical, or battling as a playful encounter. The truth of play is transmitted by touch, laughter, tears, dirt, grass stains, and skinned knees; the rest is hearsay.

Children and animals have changed what I "know" about play, in large part because I began not by observing, analyzing, or thinking about play but rather by playing. I believe that our cultural and biological models of play are like a straitjacket tied over not only our bodies but also our hearts, which we will have to burst if we are to survive. When it comes to play, most adults imitate the caterpillar, which looks up at the butterfly and exclaims, "You're never going to get me up there!" The caterpillar is correct; a metamorphosis is necessary. Likewise, a transformation must occur to become a playmate.

Although I cannot provide a playmate, I can give hints. This chapter is both an inkling and an invitation to come out and play with the world just as it is, in all its wonder and terribleness. Original play is Creation's simplest, oldest, and deepest wisdom, a belonging consciousness and practice more fundamental and far-reaching than we have thought possible. Deep in the human heart is a longing to belong to something more than a shadow and to feel a moment where neither fear nor desire can torture, where no courage is required, and where love holds in the calm core of being. Original play is simply the best way in which to be in touch with ourselves, each other, and the earth.

Play as if your life depends on it. It does!

THE CHILD AS GODSEND: A DIVINE CONSPIRACY

> In this playhouse of infinite forms I have had my play, and here have I caught sight of him that is formless. (Tagore, 1949, p. 35)

Playing With God

> The power of a deity is that it personifies a power that is in Nature and in your nature. When you find that level, then you are in play. (Campbell, cited in Vardey, 1995, p. 507)

Play is the reason why unity exploded into multiplicity and an expression of the desire of the one for the experience of the other in all its manifestations. "This is play" is the universe's message to all of us. To initiate this cosmic play, there is a conspiracy between Creation and childhood called original play. This is the "spring fever" of life when kid stuff and God[1] stuff are the same thing. Play is the enthusiasm of the infinite made manifest, as simple and profound as the tide of spring that rises in a human heart as it does in the rising sap in a maple tree. In this meta-pattern of belonging, we find inklings of eternity in which nothing is excluded and everything is affirmed just as it is, all bound together in the whirling play of the universe.

My playmate, Katie, shares with me an inkling of this conspiracy. When I arrive in the classroom, Katie wanders around the room, stopping momentarily to jump lightly up and down. She vigorously shakes her hand in front of her face. Then she moves a few steps toward me while repeating her self-stimulating motions. She seems disconnected from the other children and staff in the room. Her looks seem to ricochet off of them like so many stray bullets. As I enter the room, I say her name, get down on my hands and knees, and crawl toward her. She smiles, cocks her head, and sends me a delicate blue-eyed play look that hovers and darts in like a hummingbird sucking nectar from a flower. Four-year-old Katie unself-consciously opens her arms to embrace me. We roll over onto a blue and yellow mat. She sits on my tummy and bounces up and down. As I turn over, she slides off and laughs. We lie next to each other, and our eyes connect. Like an arrow, a thought impales my mind: "You know, don't you?" She laughs a tiny bubble of laughter. It seems as though she sent the arrow. "You know," I repeat in my mind. Another bubble of laughter erupts from her. We roll over and continue our play. Katie's bubble of laughter is like a hot spring in my heart on the drive home that day.

What better expression of conspiratorial resonance than a young child's giggle? Katie not only knows the questions that had been rummaging about in my mind like marbles in a tin can; she also knows how to share the answers with me. Like a whack on the back from a Zen master's rod, Katie's laughter and touch is a swift living response to my questions, touching my body, tickling my spirit, and jarring my mind. She does not give me any instructions or discussions. She plays, nothing more.

Katie's giggle is an inkling, a hint of something deeper, an enthusiasm that, when we live it, is Nietzsche's "yea" to a moment that reverberates through all existence. Katie knows that she is God's playmate. She also knows that I am and that so is everyone else. This is not so different from the God connectedness experienced by Mechthild of Magdeburg, Julian of Norwich's looking "with the eye of my understanding," or Saint Catherine of Siena's "life as a miracle of inclusion."

How wonderful this playing with God, and yet it is "nuthin' special." As a child, I spent a lot of time doing nothing. I remember bounding out the door of my uncle's farmhouse on the first day of summer, taking in undeciphered all that lay before me. I disappeared quickly beyond the range of my mother's voice. I did not leave with any plans or expectations; rather, I encountered the day as an adventure. I played with the frogs in the farm pond, chased the horses down the lane, explored the old caboose in the woods, and rested on the top of the hill watching the clouds.

Hours later, I heard the ringing of the large dinner bell that stood on a post outside the kitchen door. I wandered home for dinner, stopping along the way for just one more little visit until finally I was at the mudroom door.

My mother yelled out to me, "Hurry and get washed for dinner. What were you doing all day?"

"Nuthin'," I yelled hack.

Playing with God is utterly down to earth and "nuthin' special." And yet . . . Within this "and yet" lies a profound mystery. Katie and I, for example, act authentically, and in our play we add nothing to life that was not there before. And yet, our play answers Becker's (1973) very important question: "How does one lean on God and give over everything to Him and still stand on his own feet as a passionate human being?" (p. 5). At its simplest and most profound, original play is playing "for God's sake."

VERSUS: COUNTERFEIT PLAY

In the lost childhood of Judas, Jesus was betrayed. (Russell, 1988, p. 71)

Haunted by a vacuum, we may look back in a moment of wistfulness on the innocence of childhood, but having passed through a sort of one-way boundary euphemistically called *maturity,* we are caught like Hamlet between love that beckons us and an archaic sense of cultural duty. Having long since abandoned our original play, we try to protect ourselves from the wisps of childhood as if they bring contagions like winter drafts springing up in an old house, like abandoned hulks of rusty cars left by the roadside. Childhood is in a general state of neglect, condemned not because of anything children do but rather because they have no market value or winning potential in a contest world.

A Faustian Bargain

Little children, watch out for the simulacra! (1 John 5:21)

Early in life, children are presented with a Faustian bargain, a phantom contractual agreement in which the play that began as exploration engaging them in the mystery of the world becomes a cultural game, and their initial sense of all-belonging is replaced with cultural membership.

Abducted by culture and alienated from the belonging of their original play, children abdicate their ecstasy and are exiled from this awareness so as to be educated by those who have been reduced to orphans themselves with faint recall, grieving for the absolute belonging they once knew. Like orphans who are not told about our biological parents, our original feelings and memories of play are replaced with others in such a way that the original is rendered very difficult to access.

This Faustian bargain is a gradual process. At each step of the way, children are coerced into making the bargain because it appears that they have no other choice. In this ruse, for children to be what they might become, they will have to cease to be who they have been.

Each succeeding generation of children grows up with no cultural supports to lean on, no collective myth that makes their original play seem real because it is lived and shared by the adults with whom they live. This is a vicious spiral of adults shortening childhood and pressing adulthood onto younger and younger children, followed by younger and younger children acting out adult contests, followed by cries of frightened adults for adult punishments for younger and younger children. We harvest children too early, grafting onto them the expectations and responsibilities of later years long before their bodies/minds/spirits are designed to carry them. Like land that is overused and undernourished, children are burned out before they have time to develop the skills they bring with them. In so doing, we leach childhood of kindness, wonder, and love; dull the senses; arrest development; and deprive children of belonging. I find, for example, that most children with whom I play around the world lose their sense of original play at around 3 years of age.

The parent generation conveys to its children their own special sense of discord, a discord with roots not in the lives of the children but rather in a life long since gone. Because this contest persists long after the circumstances that created it, it is a source of great confusion and gives the lives of children an emotional content that they cannot properly possess. The result is that although the form of life might be orderly, the content will be chaotic because the trade carries with it a feeling of emptiness at the heart of being.

This profound negation of so many generations turns childhood, potentially our most creative period, into a neglected pastime. The successful child, made to feel happy in his or her grasping, made content in its membership, and made complacent in the face of inner terror, nourishes an environment that thrives on the ruin of childhood.

With the truth of the bargain obscured, children are enticed to be like the fir tree in the fairy tale that wants to be cut down and dressed up with colored lights, bangles, and silvery tinsel, only to be abandoned after the holidays. Memberships and trinkets tell the child that he or she is somebody, a somebody in contest with other somebodies so as not to be a nobody. The binding power of the bribes maintains the delusion that trinkets are the stuff that satisfies the soul. This loss is referred to in the *Upanishads* as no longer experiencing *lila* (divine play) but rather merely vain frivolity (Perry, 1971,

p. 99). We have traded childhood, our birthright, "for a mess of pottage" (Laing, 1967, p. 68).

Duchess's Game

When play becomes contest during childhood, we are stripped of our natural armament and utterly ashamed of childhood's gifts—the life-giving riches that are meant to sustain us in terrible moments of attack and rejection. There is a game played by children in villages throughout Lebanon in which two youngsters stand face to face, and each sticks a finger in the other one's mouth. Both start biting down, and the one who screams and pulls the finger out first is the loser (Nelan, 1996, p. 59).

This game of chicken is just one version of the Duchess's game, which is based on the Duchess's Law from *Alice in Wonderland*, which states, "The more there is of mine, the less there is of yours." This zero-sum game is the organizing principle found in business, government, education, health care, and sports. During the 19th century, for example, Kipling called the struggle between the British and Russian empires the "great game." In 1996, "the whole government would be held hostage while the country waited to see who would blink," Clinton or Gingrich (Gibbs, 1996, p. 23). In August 1998, another "multi-billion-dollar game of chicken was being played out" in Hong Kong (Ramo, 1998, p. 56).

Wherever it is played, the Duchess's game is a painful centrifugal force, scattering and atomizing people. The foundation of the game's relationships is that we forget what we do to each other so as to suppress our awareness of the need for losers.

Because the game's need for losers and bribes is insatiable, it is very difficult to compete just once. At each successive level of contest, there is an increase in the number of losers and a consequent narrowing or restricting of those with whom the winner can identify. For example, "one of the bitterest truths we encounter in these ghetto records [Holocaust] is how easily the concept of 'one's own' shrank into the narrow identity of one's self" (Langer, 1995, p. 155). Unaware, as we are, that fewer and fewer survivors are allowed as the importance of the game increases, we think that if we play by the rules, then we will survive. We pin our well-being to the arbitrariness of the contest order, in whose every action we have something to gain and something to lose. In each turn of the game, we grope uncertainly to the next trinket that might make our eyes shine, just as one might skip from one lover to the next, hoping that he or she will be the fulfillment of the cherished dream. And so we are drawn into an insatiable spiral of life as contest, living with the delusion that contests make us more than who we are.

Humans have assumed and acted as if the Duchess's game is not a cultural rule but rather a natural law. Play as contest becomes a worldview, the fundamental assumptions of which appear so obvious that we do not know what we are assuming because no other way of putting things occurs to us. Lost in the maze, we do not remember how contests start or what they are about; like a nightmare, they are both beginningless and endless. There is no out of bounds. Assuming that this is our natural process of maturation, we contest toward an imagined peace that we cannot achieve.

The result is a person who is visionless yet wholly image, with a storm in his or her heart that rages over the earth. With such a worldview, the wars that begin in the fragmented hearts of people spread to fragment peoples.

Play as contest disrupts our ability for self-integration, our attachment capabilities to others, and our decision-making capacities. The rhythm of living in its fullest sense has been broken, and too often we are incapable of finding it again. Children, for example, who must defend themselves and must increasingly compartmentalize their lives, are quicker to perceive threat in ambiguous situations and respond as though the threat actually was there. They become highly anxious and hypervigilant, always looking for a meaningful form of self-defense or revenge. And when aggression is used "for your own good," the first blow contains the numbing certainty: "You can be beaten; your body and your self are not your own." Self-defense, which destroys the capacity to play, is not an accidental quality of the game but rather its essence.

Nothing stains like blood. In contests, blood acts like a stupefying drug. Every contest in the Duchess's game not only creates a void in the hearts of individuals but also leaves a great cavity in the universe. When we consult the rulebooks rather than our hearts, it is a sign that our hearts have been traded for the trophies of the game. In this trade, there are no genuine inhibitions involved in hurting someone else because one is taught to see clearly that it is not one's own pain that is being felt. That each of us is the somebody else that loses in a contest rarely is grasped, and then only with difficulty.

The Duchess's game is "played for keeps," turning beings into redundant and replaceable things. In its most tragic form, the Duchess's game requires the taking of that which is most valuable, including another's life, because it may be only by dying that the loser can acknowledge the other's victory. This "dying" can take many forms. We are just playing by the rules when we downsize a company and put families out of work, make a devastating hit in a game that disables an opposing player, or participate in a retaliatory drive-by shooting and killing a child. As Langer (1995) pointed out, this rule echoed an axiom of the holocaust universe: "One's own survival almost never could be severed from someone else's death" (p. 6). Exercised to the limit, the "game" turns a human into a corpse in a contest where every victory is a funeral. Our legacy of cultural contests are the means by which children inherit war, practice it, perfect it, and pass it on. In such "play," war and peace become merely phases of a game, like time in and time out.

As a worldview, contest contains from its inception an inherent instability that severely limits our ability to sustain life on earth. Pressed into service not of love but rather of fear, play is stripped of its vitalizing capacity. Our contest consciousness makes wisdom and the ecological mind impossible, splintering our consciousness and severing our ties with other life forms. Separated from the universe, we become frightened of the universe in which we live. Afraid, we do not know how to act. Not knowing how to act, we destroy not only our place in the scheme of things but also the scheme itself.

Contest inflicts a mortal wound on life's spirit, imprisoning us in the chain gang of winning and losing from which life has labored so long and painfully to escape. Neither the meaning of our being nor the possibility of our spirit can be expressed or created by the means that we use to win our way through life. Furthermore, the concepts on which we base our actions are unworthy of the being that clamors to be released. A fearful unloved human remains in silence, the silence that falls when all connection is broken between one and another. The deep-est and most cherished dream of life's first spirit remains just that—a dream unlived.

Failure to Thrive

When we adulterate child's play, we destroy what we cannot make. The bodies and hearts of children are tattered in the long nightfall of the human spirit we call maturity. Children are molded by language, ideas, dreams, and actions—in short, a cultural infrastructure that is totally inadequate for the meaning and possibility inherent in their spirit. Consequently, a child who once glided in play from assurance to assurance now gropes with a poverty of spirit through contests from reassurance to reassurance. We might want to make our children into the people we lack the courage to be, but because there is no model for this, they grow up to be just like us. There is a profound silence that happens when childhood's gifts are set aside and devalued and children become playthings. Then, childhood recedes like an island in the Pacific dropping away behind an outward-bound ship.

THE PLAY WAY: LETTING THE WORLD TICKLE YOUR HEART

We are born into the play school that Swimme's character wondered about, but we are quickly drawn into truancy—to play hooky for the rest of our lives. But like the horse that is ridden too far from the barn, what the human spirit loves to do, above all else, is head for home. Our rehabilitation from contestant to playmate requires wisdom and grace. We must return to play as beginners. To be a beginner is to have an open and compassionate mind, accepting what life presents, however imperfectly, at once and without question, as being the only material with which one can play.

We entered the world unafraid as beginners, with eyes, hands, and hearts wide open. Our innocence was not the naïveté that adults assume but rather a sense of belonging free from fear. Physicists and philosophers tell us that we are made of stardust and that the universe is play; a playmate takes this interpenetration of the universe quite literally. Do you recall what it is like to first discover and play with your toes, a leaf, water, or a star? At such moments, uncluttered by thoughts, we get intimations of the elegant simplicity not only of touching but of being touched by the world. As young children, this mutual touching was simply the way in which we lived. It was "nuthin' special." How else would we enter such a world but by experiencing enthusiasm or, in its original meaning, our "engoddedness."

As young children, we did not go out to "practice" play; we played. After years away, however, we approach what once came so easily with the effort of one who hums because he or she has forgotten the words to the song. We are not even sure what it is that we are supposed to practice. What, for example, are the play skills that we must practice now that we did not practice when we originally played? Who teaches us?

Relearning play is like riding a cutting horse. One has to "get with it" and not try to win or be in control. The collaboration required between horse and rider is so intricate that one must learn to relinquish control of the horse and, instead, learn to control one's own mind. To be comfortable with such a prospect is to play with it, knowing that play's motion is correct because it feels right, not because it conforms to some established standard. This is the sense of integrity embodied in play that expresses an inner wholeness, a congruity between hand and heart that is a result not of control or choreography but rather of a synthesis of centeredness and motion, groundedness and lightness. At some point, we let go of practicing and begin playing. This is what Watts (1994) called not "know how" but rather "no how, that is without any method" (p. 152).

Playing by Heart

Playing by heart expresses a deep and universal intent, something imperishable in the bank of human memory, seeking to surface in the world and the spirit and lives of individuals. Indeed, our great challenge is to express the courage to play with life as it is and the grace to permit it to simply be—a deceptive simplicity that permits itself neither fancy nor artifice. Such a transformation demands a break from living life as a contest and defining grace as table manners.

Original play is absolute kindness come alive in a world of relative relationships. What is required is an action done with one's whole being. An anonymous child in a poem written in 1941 in the Terezin concentration camp expressed this sense of courage beautifully:

> Hey, try to open up your heart
> To beauty: go to the woods someday
> And weave a wreath of memory
>   there.
> Then if the tears obscure your way
> You'll know how wonderful it is to
>   be alive. (Anonymous, n.d., p. 55)

A disappearance of ordinary categories lies at the heart of such play. Like the young child who wrote the poem, Gracie demonstrates in her play the courage to erase such categories. This "erasure" becomes not a product of an act of will or of personal virtue but rather a natural all-compelling expression of a law of nature as real and indestructible as gravity.

Following a workshop with hospital staff, a doctor invited me to come and play with one of her patients. She would tell me about her after my visit. I said that it was fine because I usually do not read files about my playmates.

The doctor took me to a locked ward for elderly patients who were wandering around the room, sitting against the walls, or gazing vacantly at the television blaring loudly in one corner. She pointed across the room to a woman slumped over in her wheelchair and whispered, "That's Gracie." I walked over and knelt down next to her chair. I gave her a "play look" and put my hand on the arm of her wheelchair. Her doctor stood behind me and said, "Gracie, this is Fred. He is here to play with you." Gracie looked up and growled a gruff, "Shut up! Just shut up!" with a vigorous admonishing shake of her finger at the doctor, who smiled and retreated.

I stayed next to her wheelchair. Gracie tilted her head and looked at me with an intense delightful glint in her eye. I was being taken in. She put her finger up toward me as she had done to her doctor. I leaned forward until her fingertip touched my forehead. She smiled and cocked her head to the side as if I truly surprised her. My other hand was in front of her. She softly enclosed my fingers and squeezed for a moment.

The doctor motioned to me that it was time to leave. Gracie and I leaned toward each other. I whispered, "I love you," stood up, and said good-bye. After we left the ward, her doctor told me that Gracie was nearly 96 years old. She had been in the hospital since 1928. During the mid-1950s, she had murdered two people in the hospital and had a lobotomy afterward.

The gentleness of Gracie's touch and the twinkle in her eye are inklings of the deep dynamic childlike principle of play at the heart of life itself. She reminds me that we might live our lives in categories such as man or woman, doctor or patient, but we do not play in them.

Playing by Hand

The future unfolding of the possible human depends on the finishing job done by the human hand. In giving oneself up to be handmade, the playmate fulfills the fundamental promise of life. Through the touch of child's play, we can become delightfully pliable, well made, good to handle and live with, and above all, alive with use. One day, I was playing with a little girl who, because of severe sun sensitivity, cannot be in the sun for very long. Linda was 4 years old and blind. She said, "Fred, rub some sunlight on my face." I reached up into the bright California sun and brought some sunlight down to gently rub on Linda's face. When I finished, she smiled and reached out to touch my face. She gently and slowly moved her hands around my entire head as if she were molding it out of clay. When she finished, she exclaimed, "Oh, Fred, you have a head?"

I did not know what to think. Was I the first person whose head Linda had touched? Was she surprised that I have a head? Or, was she making a statement that now, after her careful finishing touches, I did indeed have a head?

Through the reciprocity of play-touch, Linda and I helped to finish God's handiwork. This is how a human is made and kept alive. Jules Older related a playful encounter between an osteopath and an elderly patient. The patient says, "I've been waiting for you to tell you that it is because of you that I am still alive." The osteopath says, "What are you talking about?" The old man says, "Well, every morning you pinched my toe when the others weren't looking." The physician says, "Yes, but what does that have to do with . . ?" The patient answers, "Nobody plays with the toes of dying men. So, I decided I must not be dying after all" (cited in Field, 1996, p. 2).

To be fully alive, we must be touched into existence. Something literally rubs off, leaving a trace that lingers in me. Sometimes after playing, I feel a kind of all-over rawness, as if my body has been touched, moved, and stretched in every possible way all at once. While part of me feels unable to move, another deeper part is springing to life in an extraordinary fashion. Sometimes, I feel like a piece of marble being chiseled into shape. At other times, I am reminded of the making of a fine Japanese sword that is bent and forged more than a million times. Still at other times, I feel as though I am a mound of clay on which children rub, jump, and pound as if they are trying to soften and make me more pliable so that shaping and refinement may take place. And then there are the times when I feel as if I am being pruned and shaped like a Japanese garden to seem more natural than if I were left to myself. Finally, there are the times when children let me be, as if I were growing like a wildflower.

And all the time it was as if the children were asking me, "What do you want to become? We will help bring you to completion." They are crafting a human—rounding off the edges of my mind, forging my heart's strength, and burnishing my body. Like a hand-polished piece of wood, there is a patina to a well-touched human. This patina is the union of heart and hand in a task elegantly conceived and gracefully done.

There is more. The children know that, with their touch, they craft not only the outside of an inside but an inside as well until an inner glow accompanies the outer patina.

We are, however, never finished pieces to be put in glass cases and admired from afar. Humans are made to be used, not revered. Like a teddy bear, each of us needs to be comfortable and durable enough to withstand a lifetime of use. Play-touch signals an at-homeness that is a tangible bridge connecting human and divine energies, reaching from the ordinary mud of kid stuff to a dwelling place for a higher presence.

RE-CREATION: PLAYING FOR REAL

Quietly the spirit and beauty of the mountains fill my heart
My heart expands and I open to the awe and sense of
discovery offered to me
I feel free and alive and at peace
and nearby just, inside my heart I hear God saying hello
do you want to play? (S. King, personal communication, July 1996)

We are seeking the experience of being alive. The difficulty is that for us to find it, we must not be afraid of life. My playmates often demonstrate that the authentic capacity of play cuts off the psychic and physical roots of fear and clarifies the vast unity of life, enabling us to be fully alive in a playground that Rumi spoke of as being beyond right-doing and wrong-doing. For most of us, even the thought of participating in such play can be as Rilke suggested: "the beginning of terror we're not yet ready to bear" (cited in Cowan, 1989, p. 41). Paul and Stark are two of many of my playmates who were ready to play in the face of their terrors.

Paul was in my kindergarten class. He had leukemia. His doctors and parents were afraid that rambunctious play would hasten his death. So for 6 months, we touched in a variety of other ways: He snuggled in my lap while I read stories, I carried him around the room on my shoulders, and I lay down in the block area when he played with the blocks. But Paul did not join in our roly-poly play.

One day about 6 months into the school year, Paul came to me and asked me to invite his parents to school for a meeting. The four of us met the following afternoon. Paul began quietly, with a sense of urgency: "I want to play with Fred. I know that I'm not going to live as long as the three of you, but I want to live my life as if I were." His sincerity moved us. Through many tears, we agreed that Paul could play with me. When he came to school the following day, he was so excited and his play was so rambunctious, passionate, and uncompromising that he was exhausted by the end of the morning. He stayed home and rested the following day. Because he played so hard when he came to school, Paul could come to school only every other day. About a month later, he died. Paul had made it clear that he chose to play and die rather than live and not play.

*   *   *

Growls, thuds, and deep laughter rumbled from the room. From the sounds, one would think that two bears were rampaging about. It was only us—two grown men rough-and-tumbling around on the floor of a bed-and-breakfast inn at a cancer retreat in Northern California.

Stark often was in intense pain when we met in January 1996. He had been informed just a few weeks earlier that he had pancreatic cancer and was not expected to live more than a couple of months. Between our playtime and his death 7 months later, Stark wrote the poem that introduced this section of the chapter.

We stopped to catch our breath. Stark looked at me and asked, "Fred, what is it that you are really trying to tell me?"

I replied, "This is hard for me to say, Stark, but what I'm trying to tell you is to play with your cancer."

We were quiet for a few moments, just lying on the floor and looking at each other. We smiled, hugged, and continued our roly-poly rambunctiousness like two kids who had wandered far off to play away from the rest of the world.

In such play, there are no enemies, no sides, no fault, no blame, no revenge, no fear, and no self-defense. Contrary to what we might fear, we are left not in an identity crisis but rather in an identity expansion, what Austin (1997) called "not less human but more humane" (p. 51). Raised to a profound and complete level, this is becoming an opening through which others can see God. It is what Zen might call our original face. This might seem foreign at first, but in time we remember an ancestral intelligence, a yearning for this great belonging, a fierce compulsion bubbling to the surface. Like the child who runs out to engage the fullness of the first day of summer, a radical realization shines from our eyes and roars from our hearts. What is involved is a genuine transcendence and not simply a restoration. This difference is described in a Zen poem, "Iron Flute Blown Upside Down":

The bellows blew high the flaming forge;
The sword was hammered on the anvil.

It was the same steel as in the beginning,
But how different was its edge. (Genro,
cited in Hyers, 1973, p. 81)

CONCLUSION: INKLINGS OF ETERNITY

And so Paul and Stark, Katie, and Linda have given you some inklings, and yet . . . Within this "and yet" lies the mystery of play as re-Creation, life's way of first and last resort; nothing less knows the way home. In original play, we are fulfilling the fundamental promise of life as one, not as won. To come out to play is to shed archaic fears of self-preservation, go out of love in search of love, following an invisible compass whose needle maintains a steady true north in the face of human misdirection. When we break this law of life, we inflict a fatal wound on our spirits.

Original play is genuine advance for humankind, a second birth utterly outside the dimensions of relationship we have known. We have lived on earth as if life is an inevitable contest. But in this act of self-defense, we lose sight of the fact that we abandon living so as to stay alive. Play's sense of love and kindness is truly a radical reconfiguration of how we think about and act in the world, transcending not only the parochial and tactical demand to "take sides" but also the seemingly primal demand for self-defense. The true power of our capacity for play, for example, is not survival of the fittest but rather the actual experience of being alive. To play is to return to our true roots where, as Merton (1973) pointed out, we "become able to resist exterior violence with complete success and even, after a certain point, invulnerability" (p. 13). My playmates have shown me that our capacity for living is at its greatest when we play and that, perhaps, our capacity for play is at its greatest when we face trauma and even death. Play is not just about courage in the face of attack or death; it is about courage in the face of life.

What makes my playmates so ordinary and special at the same time is that they are willing to come out to play and love rather than retreat in fear and desperation. Their play is enthusiastic and simple. They do the one thing that most of us seek to avoid at all costs—to act wholeheartedly and put our entire bodies into a situation and to refuse numbness and protection in favor of love and immediacy. In so doing, they add a measure of grace to the world. It is not that they know more; it is that they *are* more. This more is one face of God playing with another face of God.

But such hints are only the beginning. In this quest for aliveness, play must be endlessly lived in one's life. The result is a reverence for life that confirms a direction of spirit that fulfills the pledge given by Rilke (1996):

I live my life in widening circles
that reach out across the world.
I may not ever complete the last one,
but I give myself to it. (p. 48)

NOTE

1. When I use the word "God" throughout this chapter, I refer to the ineffable presence that goes by many names—Creation, Source, the One, Logos, Tao, Brahman, Goddess, Krishna, Allah, Mana, Wakan Takan, the Universal Spirit or Principle, and many others I do not even know.

REFERENCES

Anonymous. (n.d.) *I never saw another butterfly: Children's drawings and poems from Terezin concentration camp.* New York: McGraw-Hill.

Austin J. H. (1997). *Zen and the brain.* Cambridge, MA: MIT Press.

Becker, E. (1973). *The denial of death.* New York: Free Press.

Cowan, J. (1989). *Mysteries and dreamtime.* Dorset, UK: Prism.

Field, T. M. (1996). *Touchpoints, 3*(2), 2. (Touch Research Institute, University of Miami School of Medicine)

Gibbs, N. (1996, January 15). The inner game. *Time*, p. 23.

Hyers, C. (1973). *Zen and the comic spirit.* Philadelphia: Westminster.

Laing, R. D. (1967). *The politics of experience.* New York: Random House.

Langer, L. L. (1995). *Art from the ashes.* New York: Oxford University Press.

Merton, T. (1973). *Ishi means man.* Greensboro, NC: Unicorn Press.

Nelan, B. W. (1996, April 29). Dark with blood. *Time*, p. 59.

Nisker, W. (1990). *Crazy wisdom.* Berkeley, CA: Ten Speed Press.

Perry, W. N. (1971). *A treasury of traditional wisdom.* New York: Harper & Row.

Ramo, J. C. (1998, August 24). When currencies collide. *Time*, pp. 56-57.

Rilke, R. M. (1996). *Rilke's book of hours* (A. Barrows & J. Macy, Trans.). New York: Riverhead Books.

Russell, G. W. (1988). *Child.* Wainscott, NY: Pushcart Press.

Swimme, B. (1984). *The universe is a green dragon.* Santa Fe, NM: Bear.

Tagore, R. (1949). *Collected poems and plays.* New York: Collier.

Vardey, L. (Ed.). (1995). *God in all worlds.* New York: Pantheon.

Watts, A. (1994). *Talking Zen.* New York: Weatherhill.

CHAPTER 43

Humanistic Psychology and Mind/Body Medicine

ELEANOR CRISWELL

IND/BODY MEDICINE is as old as human existence. Archaeological evidence shows shamanic methods in use at least 20,000 years ago (Achterberg, 1985), but one might imagine that the use of mind/body practices to alter oneself and one's environment is much older. It is a natural human tendency, as can be seen in the early developmental stages of childhood. Folk healing methods have persisted over time throughout the world. Alternatively, contemporary mind/body medicine is as recent as the past 30 years. Psychological methods have been combined with modern medicine to form mind/body medicine. Because humanistic psychology has been dedicated to the development of the person's potential—mind, body, and spirit—it has played a key role in the formation of contemporary mind/body medicine. This chapter examines the nature of mind/body medicine; the principles of mind/body medicine; humanistic psychology and mind/body medicine; approaches to mind/body medicine; the contributors to mind/body psychology and mind/body medicine; applications of mind/body medicine; and the future of mind/body medicine and humanistic psychology.

THE NATURE OF MIND/BODY MEDICINE

Mind/body medicine refers to approaches to healing that include mental and physical practices. *Healing* means to return to wholeness, from an Old English word meaning to make whole or sound. Mind/body medicine combines a variety of mental and physical disciplines or approaches. These disciplines draw from clinical practices from different traditions and contemporary research to yield blended medical protocols. Some of the combinations occur as part of an informal treatment team in society. For example, clients engage with practitioners in a variety of disciplines—psychotherapy, medicine, yoga, chiropractic, folk healing, and so forth. At other times, clients experience a variety of therapies and techniques in a clinical or hospital setting. The medical setting combines practices appropriate for the particular presenting complaints, and they are all conducted on-site. For example, the patient in a pain program will receive biofeedback training, physical therapy, medical treatment, psychosocial therapy, recreational therapy, body mechanics training, and stress management classes that also will include a variety of disciplines (e.g., relaxation techniques, visualization, meditation training, stress assessment and management, and yoga). Contemporary mind/body medicine engages the conscious and unconscious mind to mobilize the body's healing capacities. The different approaches have basic principles in common.

THE HISTORY OF MIND/BODY MEDICINE

Mind/body medicine is quite ancient. Shamanistic approaches to healing have existed throughout the nearly 250,000 years of human existence. Shamanistic and other folk approaches exist to this day throughout the world. "Shamanism, an ancient method of healing, is based on the belief that all illness is a result of disharmony between the spirit world and the material world" (Allison, 1999, p. 65). The contemporary use of mind/body techniques frequently was inspired by approaches to healing found in ancient and contemporary cultures throughout the world.

"While the ancient Greek medical practices were originally holistic, ways of viewing the body began to change with the influence of the philosophic pragmatism of Aristotle (c. 384 to c. 332 BCE) and his desire to know and categorize all aspects of the material world" (Allison, 1999, p. 65). This began a separation of mind and body that was reinforced later by the medieval

Christian church. Descartes (1637/1972) wrote about the mind/body split during the 1600s. He was not the only one of his era to speak of this divide, but he is the one credited with having done so. Descartes believed that the soul entered the body though the pineal gland, a small brain structure. This meant that the mind and body were separate; the body was not sacred. The split between the mind and body enabled us to study the body as a non-sacred object. Medical advances were fostered by this consideration of the body. Over the nearly 400 years since, Western culture has considered the mind as separate from the body. This separation allowed psychology to develop and explore its realm and permitted medicine to explore its realm. The separation of mind and body was characteristic of Western culture, but it was not characteristic of the rest of the world. For example, Native Americans and Eastern cultures held a more unified conception of the human.

The discovery of the unconscious by Freud, Jung, and others during the 1800s demonstrated the impact of the mind on the body. Research in anthropology helped us to understand folk healing traditions throughout the world. This research was followed by other evidence of the mind's effect on the body such as the work of Selye (1974) on the effects of stress on the body. Selye defined stress as "the nonspecific response to any demand" (p. 55). The nonspecific response led to a specific syndrome of physiological changes, for example, "evidence of adrenal stimulation, shrinkage of lymphatic organs, gastrointestinal ulcers, and loss of body weight" (p. 55). Selye's research led to numerous studies on the effects of stress on health and the teaching of the principles of stress management to millions of people throughout the world.

Psychophysiology, especially applied psychophysiology, is an important contributor to the development of mind/body medicine. Psychophysiology is an approach to understanding the mind/body functioning of the person through changing psychological states and measuring the resulting physiological changes. Applied psychophysiology uses this information and approach clinically. What is unique about applied psychophysiology is the emphasis on bringing the mind and body together in a clinical or educational setting. Applied psychophysiology is a research-based field and illustrates wonderfully how research can inform the development of the practices. For example, psychophysiological studies of meditation greatly enhanced its acceptance by the general public.

During the late 1960s, the field of biofeedback was born. This domain began with the work of Neal Miller, Joe Kamiya, and others who demonstrated that humans could control physiological functions with information provided about physiological states. Other studies demonstrated the effects of mental practices on physiology such as the studies done to look at the impact of meditation on psychophysiology. Menninger Foundation biofeedback pioneers Elmer and Alyce Green demonstrated that advanced yoga practitioners could voluntarily change physiological functions—brain waves, cardiac function, and temperature. Biofeedback research rapidly expanded, and biofeedback soon began to be used clinically to treat a wide variety of presenting complaints.

Humanistic psychology and the human potential movement helped to popularize biofeedback training, yoga and meditation, psychic or spiritual healing, parapsychology, consciousness research, and other aspects of mind/body medicine because of their emphasis on actualization of full human potential.

The field of psychoneuroimmunology emerged during the 1980s. Numerous studies have demonstrated the connection among psychological states, neurology, and immune system function (Locke & Horning-Rohan, 1983). The fluctuation in immune system function that accompanies psychological states is measurable either by correlational studies or by actual measures of blood chemistry.

Sparked by research findings showing that millions of people are choosing to spend their own "out-of-pocket" money to use what was originally called alternative medicine (now called complementary medicine because of the partnership that has been developing between the alternative approaches and mainstream medicine), mind/body medical programs are emerging in many hospitals and clinics throughout the world. For example, the work of Kabat-Zinn (1990), who teaches mindfulness meditation to patients, has enabled a wealth of mind/body programs to enter into many medical settings.

PRINCIPLES OF MIND/BODY MEDICINE

There are both dualistic and nondualistic approaches to mind/body medicine. The dualistic approach conveys that there is a mind and a body and that the mind can be used to influence the healing tendencies of the body and vice versa. This approach sometimes facilitates a return to a greater sense of wholeness or mind/body integration. The nondualistic approach begins with the understanding that we are already whole and that there is a return to or remembrance of wholeness inherent in mind/body practice. In nondualistic mind/body medicine, the causes of diseases inevitably entail mental, physical, emotional, and environmental factors.

What are the basic principles of mind/body medicine? First, mind/body practitioners and clients/patients believe that there is a connection between the mind and the body.

Second, they hold that the mind influences the body and that the body influences mental states. Third, they contend that changes in mental states can be used to change physical states and vice versa. The mental states and therapies can be either conscious or subconscious. For example, conscious approaches can include cognitive strategies for changing attitudes that have an effect on body states. Biofeedback training is another conscious approach to changing physiology toward homeostasis and healthier functioning. Subconscious approaches include hypnosis or guided visualizations to alter physiology.

Mind/body approaches emphasize the client taking personal responsibility for the healing process. This responsibility begins with the client's informed choice regarding the approach to healing. An understanding of healing processes is important because one can mobilize the healing potential of the client more readily when the client is personally informed and motivated. The relationship between the client and practitioner/educator is important. Rapport between the two is essential. The practitioner needs to relate to the client as a person of worth and dignity at the center of the process. The practitioner helps the client to access his or her inner resources toward healing and health. The contributions of the mind, body, and spirit are honored in the healing process. These principles are inspired by humanistic psychology.

The many approaches to mind/body medicine also include the spiritual dimension. *Spiritual* may be distinguished from *religious* (see the chapter by Elkins [Chapter 16] in this volume). Herbert Benson's group at the Mind/Body Institute of Harvard Medical School report that when we engage in mind/body experiences, we frequently experience the spiritual dimension. This has been observed often by biofeedback trainers and somatics practitioners. The transpersonal dimension, seen by some humanistic psychologists as the farther reaches of human nature, embraces this aspect of human existence.

HUMANISTIC PSYCHOLOGY AND MIND/BODY MEDICINE

Humanistic psychology is concerned with the development of the whole person—body, mind, and spirit. The field of mind/body theory, practice, and research has been aided greatly by humanistic psychology. This support came from the value that humanistic psychology placed on the whole person, and the actualization of potential—which includes the embodied person—was integral to that value. Jourard (1976) contributed to this early appreciation, as did Hanna (1970) and others.

The Association for Humanistic Psychology (AHP) was founded during the early 1960s to provide a meeting ground for psychologists and others who believed that they were not represented in the prevailing preoccupation with psychoanalysis and behaviorism. AHP members included psychologists, educators, philosophers, other professionals, and educated laypersons. Somatics, the integrated mind/body disciplines, was one of the early developments of humanistic psychology. Some AHP members went on to become professionals in the field of somatics. The philosophical stance of the organization was to recognize the worth and dignity of the person and to explore concerns, such as love and creativity, that were left out of mainstream psychology. Some of the founding voices in the AHP who were very concerned with the actualization of human potential included Rogers, Maslow, May, and Jourard.

From the humanistic psychology movement came the realization that it would be valuable to apply humanistic principles to other human endeavors. During the 1970s, the humanistic medicine initiatives emerged. These initiatives had a particular impact on nursing, for example, self-care nursing that draws heavily on humanistic philosophy and practices. Later, the holistic health movement arose. Currently, approaches from this lineage include mind/body medicine and integrative medicine.

The AHP was a spawning ground for somatics. During the early 1970s, the AHP was the first American organization of its kind to embrace the mind/body disciplines. Historically, the AHP's conventions provided a place to demonstrate some of the mind/body techniques. For example, early convention presenters included Moshe Feldenkrais, Ida Rolf, Illana Rubenfeld, and Thomas Hanna. It was the original safe haven for holistic health, humanistic medicine, and alternative/complementary medicine. Many innovations in psychology and related fields began under the AHP umbrella and moved out to form specialized organizations.

Somatics is a term coined by Hanna (1976). He used the term to describe the developing field of mind/body integration disciplines. He used the term *soma,* the Greek word for the living body, to characterize this mind/body combination. He defined the soma as the body experienced from within. It was his brilliant solution for the mind/body problem. Historically, somatology was the name for the field that later was differentiated into anatomy and physiology. This differentiation served to separate the study of the structure of the body from the study of its functions. From the perspective of Hanna's definition of the soma, there is no mind/body split. The soma is process, that is, function rather than structure. It is the result of the original creation of the universe and the evolution over

time to our current expression of that organic foundation (Hanna, 1980). The AHP's Somatics Community helped to carry forward the message.

Somatics practitioners and educators come from different traditions and disciplines. They have common principles and practices. Their concepts have multicultural and multidisciplinary origins. As they pioneer the somatics realm, they discover a language or a vocabulary that is purely somatic. They share a perspective that is very much a sense of a body/mind. The body perceives and responds. It has needs, intentions, and wisdom. Somatics practitioners explore the body wisdom within their own somas and their interactions with others.

Since the 1970s, the field of somatics (the mind/body integration disciplines) was born and has exploded. It now includes Eastern and Western traditions. Any practice that includes mind/body integration as a focus is somatic. Examples of Eastern traditions include martial arts disciplines such as aikido, judo, and karate (Murphy, 1992), yoga (Criswell, 1989), zen, t'ai chi chuan, Tibetan Buddhist practices (Criswell, 1989; Murphy, 1992), and many others. Western traditions include the Alexander Technique (Alexander, 1932), Feldenkrais's Functional Integration® (Rywerant, 1983) and Awareness Through Movement® (Feldenkrais, 1972), Somatic Exercises™ (Hanna, 1988) and Hanna Somatic Education®, Ida Rolf's Structural Integration and related methods (Rolf, 1977), Charlotte Selver's Sensory Awareness (Brooks, 1986), somatically oriented dance and athletics (Murphy, 1992), massage therapy (Knaster, 1996), body-oriented psychotherapy (Kepner, 1987), biofeedback training (Criswell, 1995), and many other disciplines. Medicine, chiropractic, physical therapy, and other disciplines may be considered somatic when they integrate mind and body. (Criswell-Hanna, 1999, p. 47)

APPROACHES TO MIND/BODY MEDICINE

The Western approaches to mind/body medicine have much in common with Eastern disciplines. This commonality is created by the borrowing of techniques between cultures and by working with the natural tendencies of the body. For example, "traditional shamanic practices include trance states and mental focusing techniques similar to those used by hypnotherapy and guided imagery today" (Allison, 1999, p. 65). Mind/body medicine disciplines vary as to the emphasis on mind or body. It is possible to influence the body by way of the mind or by way of the body to the mind. The following approaches illustrate some of the key mind/body medicine approaches: hypnosis, biofeedback, yoga and meditation, visualization, and spiritual approaches.

Hypnosis is the grandparent of all the mind/body medicine approaches. Although hypnosis has probably existed throughout the ages, Anton Mesmer, a German physician, introduced it during the 1700s to Western Europe under the name of "animal magnetism." He passed magnets over the body while he talked to the patient. Mesmer also used conscious and subconscious suggestions. Later, his technique was called hypnosis because it resembled a sleep state. Named for the Greek god of sleep, Hypnosis, we now know that hypnosis is not a sleep state. The brain waves are not characteristic of sleep. Defined as an enhanced state of suggestibility, it may be induced by another person or situation or by oneself. The first step toward a hypnotic state is usually bodily relaxation, although hypnosis

can also be induced during a crisis, for example, in a hospital emergency room. The second step is concentration on a narrow set of stimuli, a restricted focus of attention. When a sufficient trance level is reached, one or more suggestions are made. These suggestions concern changes in attitude, emotion, physiology, or behavior of the patient during the posthypnotic period. Medical hypnosis has been used for relief of a variety of symptoms. There is a rich hypnosis research literature that is full of useful insights for mind/body medicine.

Biofeedback is the feeding back of a biological signal to the person or producer of the signal. "The biological signals are recorded by electronic devices. Through the information provided, you become able to change your physiological state in a desired direction. The information fed back is significant with regard to a predetermined goal" (Criswell, 1995, p. xv). The voluntary control of internal states or self-regulation is the outcome. The field of biofeedback is very solidly research based. A number of presenting complaints have been successfully treated with biofeedback. Because of the nature of biofeedback, humanistic principles are very significant, and their presence is apparent.

The mind/body interface was explored extensively within the field of biofeedback and applied psychophysiology. The field of biofeedback was founded by Joe Kamiya and others. Kamiya was a social scientist who segued over into psychophysiology through dream research electroencephalography. Others joined to explore other psychophysiologies such as electromyograph, skin temperature, and electrodermal activity. This research was supported and encouraged by members of the AHP, the Esalen Institute, and other growth centers at their conventions and conferences. Many humanistic psychologists developed expertise in this area. Biofeedback was developed separately from humanistic psychology, but it also was greatly encouraged by the acceptance by the AHP and institutions such as the Esalen Institute. This contributed to public acceptance. In turn, this acceptance encouraged professionals from different disciplines, as well as a variety of clientele, to spawn the field of biofeedback.

Yoga is a Sanskrit word, *yuj*, meaning yoke or union. It refers to

> the unification or reunification of the self with the universal Self. (This unification seems necessary because we perceive ourselves to be separate.) It means the reunification of the person—mentally, physically, and emotionally. In its ultimate sense, it refers to the reunification of humankind with the universe or cosmic consciousness or the Absolute. (Criswell, 1989, p. 3)

The dualistic approaches to yoga in India fostered the development of the psychotechnology of yoga, that is, the discipline and training of the human's embodiment such that it is capable of Samadhi or union. There is also a nondualistic approach to yoga called Advaita yoga. There are, in fact, many approaches—Hatha, Raja, Jnana, Karma, and Bhakti—that emphasize different practices toward achieving union. Indian yoga therapy is a forerunner of contemporary mind/body medicine. Western versions of yoga therapy have been developing recently. Hatha yoga (the yoga of physical practices) and Raja yoga (the yoga of consciousness and meditation) frequently are part of mind/body medical programs.

Meditation is a valuable part of mind/body medicine. Many cultures have highly developed meditation traditions, for example, Zen Buddhism, other Buddhist traditions, yoga, and many other religious and nonreligious traditions.

Meditation generally includes clearing the mind, quieting the body, concentrating on a central focus, and maintaining that mind/body state for a length of time. It usually includes repetition of a stimulus input. The central focus of concentration can be internal or external. (Criswell, 1995, p. 135)

According to meditation research, one of the benefits of meditation is a shift toward parasympathetic nervous system dominance. The parasympathetic nervous system is the rest, maintenance, and repair system of the body that is so necessary for healing.

Visualization, or the use of the mind to create an image separate from input from the environment, may be verbal (as in visualizing a word) or nonverbal (as in visualizing an image, picture, design, symbol, or scene). Visualization in mind/body medicine can be used in a variety of ways to influence brain function and, therefore, body function. Visualization can be used to listen to the body for information about particular situations. The former approach creates relaxation for healing, whereas the latter approach involves becoming aware of the body's wisdom. Creative visualization is the use of the visualization process to bring new experiences into one's life, for example, anticipating a return to wellness.

The spiritual dimension allows one to experience oneself as related to the larger whole, that is, to experience a sense of connectedness with the all of existence or God. There are different spiritual traditions that foster this experience. It can be engaged outside of a spiritual tradition as well. It is a natural process. In this sense of connectedness, there is a healing process that transcends what the individual is able to do on his or her own. Distant healing is a force that is fostered by the intention of others in the direction of the healing recipient. Dossey (1999) looked at how we influence one another from a distance or nonlocally. The role of spirit in healing has been appreciated by the religions of the world and has a long history of involvement with mind/body medicine.

CONTRIBUTORS TO MIND/BODY MEDICINE

Some of the contributors to the development of contemporary mind/body medicine include the following.

Jeanne Achterberg, author of *Imagery in Healing: Shamanism and Modern Medicine* (Achterberg, 1985), was an associate professor and director of research in rehabilitation science at the University of Texas Health Science Center and codirector of the Professional School of Biofeedback, Dallas, Texas. She is currently on the faculty of Saybrook Graduate School and Research Center. She and her husband, G. Frank Lawlis, gathered together the research and practices in the ancient and modern use of imagery. In addition, they have researched and practiced imagery in healing.

Herbert Benson, a physician specializing in mind/body medicine, began his career in mind/body medicine with a study of the psychophysiology of transcendental meditation during the 1960s (Benson, 1975). The research sparked his awareness of what he later called "the relaxation response." The relaxation response is a shift toward parasympathetic nervous system dominance. The parasympathetic nervous system is the rest, maintenance, and repair system of the body, as compared to the sympathetic nervous system, which is the fight or flight system. He currently is an associate professor of medicine, Mind/Body Medical Institute, Harvard Medical School.

Joan Borysenko expanded on Benson's findings to include psychological well-being, meditation, relaxation, and stress reduction as part of a healing regimen. Her original book, *Minding the Body, Mending the Mind* (Borysenko, 1988), was a bestseller.

Larry Dossey, an authority on spiritual healing, pioneered the return of prayer to healing through research on "the effects of prayer and spirituality" on healing (Dossey, 1999). His latest endeavors are concerned with the nonlocal mind and its therapeutic effects. His books include *Beyond Illness: Discovering the Experience of Health* (Dossey, 1984) and *Space, Time, and Medicine* (Dossey, 1982). His latest book, *Reinventing Medicine: Beyond the Mind-Body to a New Era of Healing* (Dossey, 1999), explored the nonlocal transpersonal dimension of the self.

Dean Ornish, president and director of the Preventive Medicine Research Institute, Sausalito, California, pioneered a combination of stretches (yoga), vegetarian diet, progressive relaxation, breathing techniques, directed and receptive imagery, meditation, and group process (communication skills and group support) with cardiac patients (Ornish, 1990). He calls his regimen the Opening Your Heart Program, and it is an adjunct to conventional medical therapy. Participants in the program are able to demonstrate an improvement in cardiac function by following its procedures and making lifestyle changes. The program also emphasizes opening the heart through expansion of loving feelings and a sense of spiritual connection.

Candace Pert contributed to the discovery of opiate receptors or neuron receptor sites receptive to opiate molecules. She went on to explore the role of peptides and receptor sites throughout the body that communicate messages from our emotional responses. In her book, *Molecules of Emotion* (1997), Pert chronicled the development of her discoveries and their applications.

Rachel Naomi Remen counseled chronically ill and terminal patients for more than 20 years. She is cofounder and medical director of the Commonweal Cancer Help Program, Bolinas, California, and a clinical professor of family and community medicine in the School of Medicine, University of California, San Francisco. Commonweal at Point Reyes National Seashore, California, is a 25-year-old nonprofit foundation specializing in health and environmental research. From her work with patients and her own experiences, she has gained much invaluable wisdom. Her book, *Kitchen Table Wisdom: Stories That Heal* (Remen, 1999), passes that wisdom on to others.

Ilene Serlin, Saybrook Graduate School and Research Center, pioneered an approach to arts medicine. She brings dance/movement therapy together with other expressive arts and kinesthetic imaging to move toward a sense of wholeness among members of breast cancer survivor groups (Serlin, 1996, 1999).

David Spiegal worked in the Stanford University area providing group therapy experiences for breast cancer survivors and noted that the survival rate was higher for those who participated in group therapy combined with their other medical treatments (Spiegal, 1993).

Ian Wickramasekera, Saybrook Graduate School and Research Center, has contributed to the field of hypnosis and biofeedback over the years. He pioneered an approach to integration of mind and body using hypnosis, biofeedback, and psychotherapy (Wickramasekera, 1976). He is a pioneer in biofeedback-assisted psychotherapy. He has participated in numerous studies that show the relationship between mind/body integration and medical status.

There are many more contributors to the development of mind/body medicine—researchers, medical personnel, practitioners of the mind/body disciplines, and courageous patients/clients. The research, practice, and publications of these contributors help to bring mind/body medicine into increasing societal acceptance and availability.

APPLICATIONS OF MIND/BODY MEDICINE

The mind/body medical disciplines have been helpful for

> people suffering from migraine headaches, insomnia, hypertension, asthma and other respiratory conditions, ulcers and other gastrointestinal disorders, incontinence, cardiac and vascular irregularities, muscular problems caused by strokes or accidents, arthritis, anxiety, attention and learning disorders, depression, chemical and emotional addictions, and phobias and other stress-related disorders. (Allison, 1999, p. 67)

Achterberg (1985) reported that she and Lawlis have used their body/mind imagery techniques with patients with "chronic pain, rheumatoid arthritis, cancer, diabetes, severe orthopedic trauma, burn injury, alcoholism, and stress-related disorders such as migraine headaches and hypertension, and during childbirth" (p. 101). Biofeedback has been used effectively with asthma, essential and labile hypertension, insomnia, migraine headaches, Raynaud's disease, cardiac arrhythmias, muscle contraction headaches, addictive behaviors, anxiety disorders, attention deficit disorder with and without hyperactivity, obsessive-compulsive disorder, phobic behaviors, paralysis and stroke rehabilitation, chronic pain, Bell's palsy, and a host of other presenting complaints. The other mind/body medicine approaches have an equally impressive list of applications.

THE FUTURE OF MIND/BODY MEDICINE AND HUMANISTIC PSYCHOLOGY

Although mind/body medicine is ancient, the contemporary field is still young. Continued research, appropriate clinical applications, and motivated medical consumers will help the field to make tremendous progress. The recognition of the role of humanistic psychology in mind/body medicine can greatly enhance both fields. We need to listen to the whole person—body, mind, and spirit. Health is fostered by healthy mind/body interactions. The future of medicine requires greater autonomy on the part of the patient. Medical costs and demands for medical care are taxing our medical systems. For the sake of patients, patients' families, and the community, it is increasingly important that patients be in charge of their health care. This means that patients need to practice preventive health measures that include many of the mind/body medicine disciplines as part of their general lifestyles. When accidents or illnesses occur, patients need to be as knowledgeable as possible (Internet medical resources will play a key role) about their conditions and treatment/training options. They also need to participate fully in the development of treatment plans that include the appropriate blend of mind/body medicine. Mind/body medicine will be used at every step of the way throughout life. Through these means, patients will learn and grow with their health conditions and healthier lifestyles toward the fullest possible actualization of their potentials.

REFERENCES

Achterberg, J. (1985). *Imagery in healing: Shamanism and modern medicine.* Boston: Shambhala.

Alexander, F. M. (1932). *The use of the self: Its conscious direction in relation to diagnosis, function, and the control of reaction* (with an introduction by J. Dewey). New York: E. P. Dutton.

Allison, N. (1999). *The illustrated encyclopedia of body-mind disciplines.* New York: Rosen.

Benson, H. (1975). *The relaxation response.* New York: William Morrow.

Borysenko, J. (1988). *Minding the body, mending the mind.* New York: Bantam Books.

Brooks, C. (1986). *Sensory awareness: Rediscovering of experiencing through the workshops of Charlotte Selver.* Great Neck, NY: Felix Morrow.

Criswell, E. (1989). *How yoga works: An introduction to somatic yoga.* Novato, CA: Freeperson.

Criswell, E. (1995). *Biofeedback and somatics: Toward personal evolution.* Novato, CA: Freeperson.

Criswell-Hanna, E. (1999). Interrelationships between somatic perception and somatic disclosure. In A. C. Richards & T. Schumrum (Eds.), *Invitations to dialogue: The legacy of Sidney M. Jourard.* Dubuque, IA: Kendall/Hunt.

Descartes, R. (1972). *The treatise of man* (T. S. Hall, Trans.). Cambridge, MA: Harvard University Press. (Original work published 1637)

Dossey, L. (1982). *Space, time, and medicine.* Boston: Shambhala.

Dossey, L. (1984). *Beyond illness: Discovering the experience of health*. Boston: Shambhala.

Dossey, L. (1999). *Reinventing medicine: Beyond mind-body to a new era of healing*. New York: HarperCollins.

Feldenkrais, M. (1972). *Awareness through movement: Health exercises for personal growth*. New York: Harper & Row.

Hanna, T. (1970). *Bodies in revolt: A primer in somatic thinking*. New York: Holt, Rinehart & Winston.

Hanna, T. (1976). The field of somatics. *Somatics, 1*(1), 30-34.

Hanna, T. (1980). *The body of life*. New York: Knopf.

Hanna, T. (1988). *Somatics*. Reading, MA: Addison-Wesley.

Jourard, S. M. (1976). Some ways of unembodiment and re-embodiment. *Somatics, 1*(1), 3-7.

Kabat-Zinn, J. (1990). *Full catastrophe living: A practical guide to mindfulness, meditation, and healing*. New York: Delacorte.

Kepner, J. I. (1987). *Body process: Working with the body in psychotherapy*. San Francisco: Jossey-Bass.

Knaster, M. (1996). *Discovering the body's wisdom*. New York: Bantam Books.

Locke, S. E., & Horning-Rohan, M. (1983). *Mind and immunity: Behavioral immunology—An annotated bibliography 1976-1982*. New York: Institute for the Advancement of Health.

Murphy, M. (1992). *The future of the body: Explorations into the further evolution of human nature*. Los Angeles: Tarcher.

Ornish, D. (1990). *Dr. Dean Ornish's program for reversing heart disease*. New York: Random House.

Pert, C. B. (1997). *Molecules of emotion: Why you feel the way you feel*. New York: Scribner.

Remen, R. N. (1999). *Kitchen table wisdom: Stories that heal*. New York: Riverhead.

Rolf, I. (1977). *Rolfing: The integration of human structures*. Santa Monica, CA: Dennis Landman.

Rywerant, Y. (1983). *The Feldenkrais method: Teaching by handling*. New Canaan, CT: Keats.

Selye, H. (1974). *Stress without disress*. Philadelphia: J. B. Lippincott.

Serlin, I. A. (1996). Kinesthetic imaging. *Journal of Humanistic Psychology, 36*(2), 33-35.

Serlin, I. A. (1999). Imagery, movement, and breast cancer. In C. C. Clark, B. Harris, R. J. Gordon, & C. O. Helvie (Eds.), *The encyclopedia of complementary health practice* (pp. 408-410). New York: Springer.

Spiegal, D. (1993). *Living beyond limits*. New York: Times Books.

Wickramasekera, I. (1976). *Biofeedback, behavior therapy, and hypnosis*. Chicago: Nelson-Hall.

CHAPTER 44

Romantic Love as Path
Tensions Between Erotic Desire and Security Needs

G. KENNETH BRADFORD

> *Gamble everything for love if you're a true human being.*
>
> —J. Rumi (*Say I Am You,* 1994)

If one's thoughts toward the Dharma
Were of the same intensity as those
  toward love,
One would become a Buddha
In this very life.

—Sixth Dalai Lama
(cited in Stevens, *Lust for*
Enlightenment, 1999)

Romantic love is one of the most emotionally charged, morally complex, and psychologically challenging issues of our time. More than almost anything, we long to be "in love" and to have our love relationships "work." Romantic love promises a refuge from life's loneliness and the fulfillment of personal happiness through the dream that such love will, paraphrasing the immortal words of Elvis Presley, "make my life complete . . . all my dreams fulfill." At the same time, falling in love carries with it dire threats. The dread of being misunderstood, rejected, betrayed, engulfed, or casually ignored by a beloved can seem worse than death. As much as we want it, we commonly resist the slippage into romance and the vulnerability it brings, disparage it as an "immature" love, and avoid its turbulent waters, choosing instead a safer and more placid course through life.

The profusion of romantic themes in film, literature, art, and music confirms our unremitting entrancement with love's attractions and repulsions as well as its blessings and curses. We are compelled to make sense of love, to exult in it, to shudder and cringe because of it, to be swept away by it, to renounce it in an ascetic gesture, or to avoid it altogether, sweeping love itself away. However it is we respond to the draw of intimacy, sexuality, and the desire for union, one thing is certain: There is no way around it. The allure of romance flickers as both an enduring predicament and a recurring opportunity of the human spirit.

Being in love, we are awakened to an other, an ecstatic otherness, and thereby to the larger vibrancy of life. Senses come alive, colors are more splendid, and the world becomes more inviting and less harsh. Joy and confidence abound as we are enlivened with a "lightness of being" and expansiveness of spirit. Still more, a romantic wildfire may spread beyond the strictly personal to inspired expressions of poetry, artistic creation, or selfless acts of human kindness— to "the grandest cultural achievements," as suggested by Freud (1912/1959, p. 216).

When a love relationship is going well, in addition to ecstatic flight, we are likely to feel a sense of contentment, tranquility, and security that "all shall be well and all manner of thing shall be well" (Eliot, 1971, p. 59). The pacifying side of being in love brings with it the hope that this blissful state will endure. Before we know it, we begin to make plans for the continuation of the relationship. Perhaps we begin to anticipate that we will see each other more often or at least with some predictable regularity. Or, we might imagine how we will move in together and perhaps buy a house or even get married. It is natural to imagine more developed scenarios such as having children and a family, traveling to special or exotic places, or perhaps retiring together in a comfortable companionship. Along with romantic attraction come idyllic hopes that this marvelous relationship will attain a type of permanence and so complete our life in some substantial way. Being in love is not only about the joy of the heart and bliss of sexual exchange; it is also about a deep longing for peace and contentment and for enduring domestic, material, and even spiritual security. As an arena in which we seek stable happiness and existential solace, the romantic urge reaches its completion as the beloved other joins us in feathering a safe cozy nest, however particular lovers define it.

The mythic ideal of romantic love combines the unbound ecstasy of erotic desire with the happy satisfaction of security and dependability. Remarkably, we remain but dimly aware of the inherent conflicts in such a union. However "unromantic" it seems in the current cultural climate, we must recognize that the joyous heights of romance have a corresponding tragic depth. As the 12th-century Sufi poet Rumi (1994) put it,

Love comes with a knife, not some shy question,
and not with fears for its reputation!
(p. 27)

Witness how the overwhelming majority of the world's great romances wind up darkly or at least contain a considerable degree of emotional anguish in the course of their unfolding. Tristan and Iseult, Lancelot and Guinevere, Heloise and Abelard, Romeo and Juliet, Dr. Zhivago and Lara, and Scarlet and Rhett are just a few of the many famous lovers who experience love's ecstatic flight accompanied with a painful descent of some type, that is, a collision with social forces or inner demons that tear them apart. It seems to be the case that the actual experience of falling and being in love brings with it the knife. Just as it makes our spirit soar, falling in love brings us to our knees and wounds us, and perhaps those around us, in ways that we have not bargained for.

THE DIFFERENCE BETWEEN HAPPINESS AND JOY

May (1981) pointed out that differences exist between happiness and joy that must be appreciated before any effort to combine them will be possible. Happiness tends toward a state of *satis*—the Latin root of satisfaction, satiation, and saturation—and the restful peace that comes with having one's needs met. As May put it, "Happiness is a fulfillment of . . . past patterns, hopes, [and] aims," and it is "mediated . . . by the parasympathetic nervous system, which has to do with eating, contentment, resting, [and] placidity" (p. 241). It is a state free of tension and discord, a resting state that is secure and static rather than dynamic. The pursuit of happiness is not different from the pursuit of security, and the fulfillment of happiness occurs as one is sated and comfortably at rest.

Joy, on the other hand, is mediated by the sympathetic nervous system, which tends not toward rest but rather stimulation and is linked with erotic desire. "Joy is a release, an opening up . . ., and leads to awe and wonderment. . . . [It] is living on the razor's edge"(May, 1981, p. 241). Joy is akin to revelation and comes with the breaking of old habits, the dawning of new recognitions, and increasing wakefulness. It is less about satisfying dreams of the past—resulting in some lasting happiness and a restful sleep—than about opening to possibilities beckoning in the present and future. In fact, in breaking free from designs of the past, joy welcomes "discord as the basis of higher harmonies" (p. 242). Where happiness is an expression of the safety and relaxation that arise as one settles securely into one's world, joy comes from the quickening of spirit that stirs as one risks oneself in venturing beyond the known and predictable world.

In the pursuit of conjugal happiness, ecstatic joy is a common casualty. To ensure that our needs for security and satisfaction will be dependably met, we typically want the other to make a firm commitment to us. Having found love, we want to hang onto it. The titles of two popular self-help books, *Getting the Love You Want* (Hendrix, 1988) and *Keeping the Love You Find* (Hendrix, 1992), aptly capture the aggres-

sion ("getting") and possessiveness ("keeping") that are part of the desperate urgency we often feel to secure personal happiness and contentment in a love relationship.[1] At the same time that we feed the hope that a relationship will satisfy our needs for security, we also unwittingly feed corrosive anxieties and fears of losing it. Love freely given and received thereby narrows into an anxious struggle to avoid possible loss. A relationship that feels like heaven can turn into a veritable hell.

It is not the longing for happiness in itself that is the problem. Indeed, the felt need for comfort and security is an inescapable part of our mammalian nature and parasympathetic nervous system. It is not longing that corrodes and frequently destroys relationships; rather, it is the rigid insistence on having things our own way and the fear that we will lose out that give way to a cloying and potentially destructive volatility. The drive to quench longing and attain a happy satisfaction for ourselves can dominate the desire to remain open to the other and to the possibility of renewed joy or deepened poignancy in our relationships. It is the compulsive striving for a particular self-satisfied outcome that is, as the Buddha taught, the essential cause of disappointment in love relationships and in neurotic suffering of all kinds.

The path of romantic love requires that the tension among the desires for ecstasy, release, and transcendence must be acknowledged—and lived—in conjunction with the equally strong needs for safety, satisfaction, and dependability. Even as our hearts pound to be taken higher, to break free of the narrow shells of the self and open tangerine style to the heavens, there is a profound longing for continuity and the earthy settledness of domesticity and psychological security. It turns out not to be enough to simply love and be loved by the other. We also tend to look to that person to meet several of our material and emotional needs, whether or not we admit that to our lover or even to ourselves. Needs that solidify into hopes, calcify into agendas, and become armed as demands can cripple the exhilaration of love freely exchanged.

For example, the attachment that readily grows out of being in love can ignite feelings of possessiveness, jealousy, loathing, and hatred that routinely lead to acts of violence toward others. From classical literature to this week's television fare, we witness how the loss of love or unrequited love can drive a frustrated lover to acts of aggression— from petty acts of bickering or angry withdrawal; to insulting acts of verbal abuse or sexual harassment; to more serious acts of physical violence; or even to the atrocities of aggravated assault, rape, and murder.

In addition, it is all too clear that disappointments in love turn us against ourselves; shake our self-esteem; and evoke feelings of hopelessness, meaninglessness, and self-pity including fits of anxiety and deep despair. When love does not work out, we might believe that there is something substantially missing or wrong with ourselves. This can cause us to retreat from life and to engage in harsh self-criticisms, reckless acts, or even suicide (witness the desperate example of Romeo and Juliet).

To come to a better understanding of the tensions between erotic desire and security needs, we must consider the historic assumptions from the age of chivalry that form and inform our ideas of romance and commitment.

THE KNIGHT AND THE LADY: FOUR MARKS OF ROMANTIC LOVE

Whereas romantic enchantment may be a potentiality for any human in any culture, the relationship of romantic love as an ideal for marriage, and the romantic couple as the ideal imago to which any couple might aspire (and indeed is compelled to aspire), is a peculiarly Western phenomenon. The roots of this ideal and its compelling hold on the Western psyche date from the Middle Ages and come from a spiritual sanction that is now only dimly recognized and most gravely misunderstood. The price of our misunderstanding has been a steady degradation of the true meaning and challenge of romantic love, resulting in considerable confusion and personal misery. Having lost touch with the original purpose of romantic love, we are often discouraged by what seems to be the futility of love affairs. However, once romance as a spiritual path is properly understood and the discipline it demands is rediscovered, love's futility transforms into opportunity.

Contemporary romance is based on the cult of courtly love that emerged in 12th-century Europe. The essential motif of this relationship has a knight, such as Sir Lancelot, and a lady, such as Queen Guinevere, fall for each other. This is no ordinary couple, and what they share is no ordinary love. The knight is in actuality wearing shining armor. Widely revered and respected, he is a virile warrior of exceptional bravery, selflessness, and exemplary moral character. The lady's beauty is ravishing; her demeanor is kind and generous; and she rules with innocence, dignity, and grace. She is widely beloved and admired. Everything about the couple is "so-o-o romantic"—simply extraordinary. Each partner is just perfect or as close to perfection as imagination allows while still remaining human.

So, the first mark of romantic love is that we fall for an *idealized other*. We see what is best in the beloved, at least to our eyes, and fall for those marvelous qualities. At the same time, we see ourselves as the beloved reflected through the eyes of the other, and thereby our own better qualities are evoked.

Self-confidence, patience, attentiveness, joy-fulness, generosity, vivacity, and good humor arise effortlessly. In being loved, we become lovable, desirable, and somehow special. We appear to the other, and thereby to ourselves, at our absolute best.

Not only is each beloved somehow ideal, but the love that dawns between lovers is also is of an ideal sort, defining love's second mark. Romantic love is *unconditional,* that is, free of self-centered agendas that would use the beloved to meet one's own emotional needs and social or economic aspirations. Knight and lady typically are already spoken for, perhaps married to other people and with families and domestic situations of their own. Because they already have some degree of material and emotional security, they place no utilitarian or territorial demands on the relationship. By making no claims on the other, knight and lady bestow on each other the greatest gift in their power to give, and thereby the essence of "true love" is revealed, marking a third characteristic of authentic romance: *delight in the freedom and uniqueness of the other.*

As the poet Paz wrote, "Love is the revelation of the other person's freedom" (cited in Kernberg, 1995, p. 44). Whereas simple lust seeks possession of a sexual object to satisfy itself, true love recognizes the other to be an autonomous free subject with his or her own desires. The recognition of the otherness of the other is a victory of love that "creates the transition from the erotic object to the beloved person" (p. 44). It is an autonomous person who has the freedom to return one's love or not. The courtly lover might be delighted to find that the beloved returns his love, yet he delights still more in her freedom to choose to do so. Even if a beloved should decline one's advances, the courtly lover still is bidden to delight in the freedom and uniqueness that choice reveals. Such a nonpossessive attitude, which may

entail numerous trials of relinquishment and pains of personal loss, is not easy to sustain. It is an attitude adopted and strengthened through engaging in various courtly disciplines such as self-restraint and generosity (*caritas*) of spirit.

The fourth mark that distinguishes romantic love is its nature as a *transcendental discipline* to be engaged in as a decidedly unconventional relationship and unbound by the usual norms and mores of society. For example, the spiritual nature of true love was seen in the medieval court as independent from and incompatible with marriage. Whereas marriage is certified by the conventions of civil or institutional religious authority, true love is convened by a spiritual authority, one that transcends conventional social contracts. The romantic law of the heart was seen as different from and superior to the common law of societal regulation. A famous judgment delivered by a court of the Countess of Champagne in 1174 made this clear:

> Love cannot extend its rights over two married persons. For indeed, lovers grant one another all things mutually and freely, without being impelled by any motive of necessity, whereas husband and wife are held by their duty to submit their will to each other. May this judgment, which we have delivered with extreme caution and after consulting with a great number of other ladies, be for you a constant and unassailable truth. (cited in DeRougemont, 1956, p. 34)

Marriage is the most fundamental social unit on which the family, clan, and all other social groupings depend. It is a cornerstone of the society that convenes it and that it functions to serve and conserve. A fundamentally conservative institution, marriage typically binds the wills of husband and wife to the deployment of those duties defined by sociocultural necessity that function in the service of security arrangements, be they of a material, emotional, or financial nature. True love cannot be "impelled by any motive of necessity"; rather, it is an exercise in unconditional freedom. In this way, true love is bound by its unique purposes, obeys its own laws, and follows its own morality. It cannot be subsumed under conventional roles, privileges, or obligations without losing its singular integrity.

Today, we ask that marriage bridge a gap that was seen as unbridgeable eight centuries ago. Following from the political and social revolutions of the past 200 years, we ask marriage both to fulfill the necessary conventions of the social order and to serve as a relationship of spiritual awakening governed by principles that diverge from that order. This paradox is a principal source of our confusion and the inevitable disappointments in both married life and unmarried love affairs. Whereas it is a reasonable expectation that a committed relationship should meet some of our basic security needs, we do not always appreciate that it is in the nature of romantic love to break free from such necessities so as to serve a transcendental purpose. Thus, there is an underappreciated conflict at the core of committed (marital) relationships based on a lack of understanding of the actual demands that true love makes on us.

THE PRICE OF LOVE

Genuine romantic love serves not to meet our personal needs: it functions less to satisfy passion than to be inspired by it and purified through it. In its ideal form, the courtly love relationship was to remain chaste as the erotic energy between lovers was sublimated into heightened cultural or spiritual pursuits. Being in love inspires the knight in particular to deeds of greatness including the slaying of evil dragons and the undertaking of profound quests. Less is known of how the lady sublimated her desire, although her ardent participation in chivalrous "courtesy" at times found expression in the composing of erotic poetry (e.g., Bly, 1995, p. 142). The crucial point is that knight and lady are not bound to each other by the institutions of marriage and family and the security arrangements that these forms provide; rather, their bond is based on a commitment to eros itself and the commands that eros might make of them. The Indian poetess Mirabai was so bound:

I was going to the river for water,
the gold pitcher balanced with care
upon my head,
and Love's knife entered my heart.
Now God has bound me tightly with
that fine thread,
he takes me wherever he will. (cited in Bly, 1995, p. 187)

In these lines, Mirabai acknowledges the power of love and submits to its call, not to achieve a life of security in a snug home but rather to be led by God on an unforeseen path.

To follow the path of love, it is necessary to willingly open ourselves to love's ecstasy and to be held in its mysterious thrall. Although we may tell ourselves and genuinely feel that it is love that we hunger for, to actually submit to the enchantment of the other can be a bewildering and terrifying experience that is often averted. Being in love can shatter our composure. Knees go weak; words are hard to find; and we can feel exposed, silly, intoxicated, or in other ways "not ourselves." Of course, such rending also may be an ecstatic release, but the price of ecstasy is the breaking open of the safe, familiar, habitual self to which we might have become accustomed. The self here should be understood as the protective covering, the self-image or persona, that insulates us from a more naked encounter with the otherness of the world. The cracking of the ego shell is no light matter, and it is commonplace for us to prefer to "live a quiet life of desperation" than to risk the threat of an emotional upheaval. Acquiescing to a long-term relationship that is without passion or in which passion has become blunted and sexual contact has become routine is not an uncommon occurrence where one or both partners manage to establish a sense of personal safety at the expense of ecstatic aliveness. Of course, avoiding the turbulence of love either by avoiding intimate relationships altogether or by engaging in serial superficial sexual relationships are other ways of maintaining an insulated ego-bound existence.

Whereas the price of avoiding love is the living of a life haunted by that which remains unlived, the price of giving in to love is, to some degree, the loss of one's illusions about oneself and one's world. Love's knife penetrates the illusion that our "I" is the center of the world, ushering us into an increasingly unpredictable, insecure, and selfless existence, one to be lived in the fullness of mortal actuality. Fantasies of permanence and self-centered security give way to a life lived with greater awareness of the transient interrelated nature of things and the blissful and poignant subtleties of being human. Eros serves to heighten the capacity of lovers to be more sensitive and responsive both to each other and to the world. As Saint Augustine put it, "Eros . . . is the power that drives men to God" (cited in May, 1969, p. 72). Through submitting to the ecstasies and undergoing the trials of romance, the ego is decentered, and this is both the price and gift of love's quickening. "[You] discover that you are not master in your own house . . ., and there are spooks about that play havoc with your realities, and that is the end of your monarchy" (Jung, 1996, p. 54).

"Falling" into love means that we lose our footing. Our habitual self-conscious attitude slips as we are slipped up into a less defined, more numinous manner of being in the world. We fall into the joys of love and into our as yet unlived life, which includes "spooky" unintegrated impulses and conflicts. Passionate intimacy penetrates superficiality and cleaves through the insulating layers of self-image, laying bear the core of our subjectivity. In love and naked to the other, and thereby to ourselves, all types of fear, possessiveness, exhilaration, and unreasonable longings are evoked. What has been hidden is exposed, and what has lain dormant is aroused. The trials of chivalry symbolically describe this situation. A state of heightened awareness, being in love can undercut the egocentric attitude, thereby awakening slumbering dragons and beckoning inner quests. Unreasonable moods, aspirations, demands, jealousies, hatreds, confusion, and whatever other emotional knots of the past lay unresolved in our heart are evoked, and we are compelled to address this undigested life.

Although courtly lore depicts the knight as the member of the courtly couple who confronts dragons and undertakes quests, we must not let the gender of the knight distract us. The psychological evocations and inner ordeals of intense love occur to woman and man alike, and the self-discipline and gentleness required by the code of chivalry challenge a lover of either gender. Trials on the path of love enable both knight and lady to more fully embody the chivalric ideal of the "gentleman" or "gentlewoman."

GENTLENESS AND SELF-DISCIPLINE

Because the simple act of falling in love involves little or no effort and might even feel like an act of grace, we naïvely assume that a lasting love should likewise be easy. Yet, poets and sages of many ages knew different. Rilke (1975) stridently declared, "For one human being to love another: that is perhaps the most difficult of all our tasks, the ultimate, the last test and proof, the work for which all other work is but preparation" (p. 31). Fromm (1956) further suggested that this ultimate task is an art that must be learned and practiced so as to develop "mastery" in it. The working of such art takes more than "just a strong feeling" (p. 47); it takes a decisive commitment and resolve to face oneself, especially one's inability to love more fully. Specifically, "the main condition for the achievement of love is the overcoming of one's narcissism" (p. 99).

The "gentleperson" is someone who has subdued, or is on the path of subduing, those possessive, aggressive, and destructive impulses that are rooted in self-interest alone. Becoming "gentle" is not to be understood as becoming passive or "nice" or as avoiding confrontation. It also does not refer to a specifically female attribute, as in the "gentle sex." To be a knight or lady in the chivalrous sense is to become increasingly sensitive (gentle) to the actual condition of oneself, the other, and the living situation of the moment. Through settling into the situation as it is rather than seeking some form of escape, we invariably come up against those aspects of ourselves that have been disowned or unrecognized. Allowing ourselves to be opened by a difficult or appealing life situation challenges the small-minded attitudes and self-limiting beliefs we hold about who we think we are, who we

think the other is, and what we think we "need" in life in general and in a love relationship in particular.

Taming impulsivities and regaining self-composure is an important discipline, valuable in itself and invaluable as a foundation for the increased deepening of love. Certainly, relationships become more satisfying when conflictual issues are resolved; contented relationships are, after all, a worthy ideal for committed relationships in general and for married couples in particular. But for lovers on the mystical path of romance, pacifying the passions alone is not the final goal. It is only one leg of genuine romantic practice. The other leg is a lightning rod. Longing, and the tension it brings, must remain vibrant and alive for a relationship to be romantic.

The path of romance suggests that true love flourishes when the two apparently contradictory impulses of erotic desire and need satisfaction remain intertwined but not necessarily resolved. The longing for union with the beloved must be released to its full flame while the insistence on satisfying that desire is relinquished. Toward this end, lovers of authentic romance deliberately submit to practices of sustaining longing. Rumi (1994) put it succinctly:

Longing is the core of mystery.
Longing itself brings the cure.
The only rule is, Suffer the pain.

Your desire must be disciplined,
and what you want to happen
in time, sacrificed. (p. 72)

This path of the heart invites us to willingly and fully long for our heart's desire while at the same time abandoning our insistence that things turn out the way we want. Longing may emerge from a sense of inner lack as we seek in the other that which we need to make ourselves feel complete and our life secure. We commonly experience a strong enough desire for material comfort or sexual release, but we have a still deeper and more subtle longing for spiritual union and psychological wholeness. The romantic lover deliberately cultivates this more subtle longing, which is not distinct from our more gross desires but rather is essential to them.

Our undisciplined desire seeks to possess that other who we think can put an end to the ache of our longing. We think that to "have" the beloved other will complete us, extinguish our loneliness, and thereby pacify our inner ache of separateness. Indeed, delicious hours spent in the company of the beloved do deliver us from insecurities and fears of all types. Yet, such release is always temporary, and with it comes the threat of losing the divine other on whom we think our freedom and ecstasy depend, hence the desire to hang onto and control the other so as to ensure our own comfort and security. The result is the collapse of love. From the tendency toward possessiveness—and away from longing—are sown seeds of frustration, boredom, and antagonism toward the beloved other. In seeking to overcome our insecurity, we only succeed in suffering the pain of power struggles or unrequited love. Yet, it is the pain of this very misery that also might deliver us from futile longing to a more subtle transcendental desire.

The discipline that the path of romantic love requires of us is to stay open to the lack, insecurity, and unsettledness that gives rise to our longing. But this is not so easy. As Fromm (1956) put it, "The practice of the art of loving requires the practice of faith. (p. 102) . . . To have faith requires courage, the readiness even to accept pain and disappointment. Whoever insists on safety and

security as primary conditions of life cannot have faith" (p. 106). By relaxing our insistence on safety, we stand open to things as they are and thereby risk ourselves on the faith that love will prove greater than fear. In this way, to some extent, we release ourselves from desperate efforts to establish some enduring personal security and face the actuality of our impermanent and mortal existence.

Being present to the actuality of our condition reveals how we are hurdling through time that never will be lived again. With the living awareness of impermanence, our sense of vulnerability in the world is intensified. Not only are our dreams of security shaken, but the preciousness and vivacity of each passing moment become heightened. The heart naturally opens, while the desire to admire and care for the world spontaneously eclipses the need to be adored and taken care of by the world. The sense of not having enough, and so insisting that others fulfill us, gives way to the experience of already being saturated with sensitivity, gratitude, and compassion. The inner emptiness that we might want filled up by a special someone turns out to be a space of genuine freedom revealing an inherent vitality and wholeness. Zen master Sengai came to the point:

> *Falling in love is dangerous,*
> *For passion is the source of illusion;*
> *Yet being in love gives life flavor,*
> *And passions themselves*
> *Can bring one to enlightenment.*
> (cited in Stevens, 1990, p. 108)

Because the way to awakening is found by releasing self-centered demands, these very demands are essential to the path of love. Without the aggressive passions to possess, dominate, manipulate, evade, or ignore the other, there would be nothing to release. And without a gnawing sense of incompleteness, and thereby "neediness," there would be no desire to be completed through being in an intimate love relation. The pain of relationship is not bad news for anyone on this path; neither is it indicative of a lesser or mistaken path. Emotional conflicts are the juice of the journey. As Trungpa (1973) declared, "There's no enlightenment without confusion" (p. 32). Through longing for our deepest desires, we lay bare our deepest attachments, most dreaded fears, and most hidden hypocrisies.

As the grip of personal grasping for or against something is brought into awareness and loosened, we are released into a more essential gratis and satis. Gratification unbound from rigid self-interest blossoms into the feeling of gratitude. We not only become grateful for having a particular need met but also can feel grateful for being part of the vibrancy of life itself and for being opened and made more sensitive by and through this liveliness. Satisfaction so freed may come to be enjoyed as the feeling of being saturated with joy, contentment, and belonging. The beloved may or may not return our love and may or may not gratify us in the way we want. The freedom of the other and the unpredictability of otherness elude our control and return us again and again to an intrinsic emptiness. With this, a type of sadness may be experienced (Trungpa, 1988) exposing the fundamental gentleness and permeability of the human heart. Through accepting love as an art or spiritual discipline, we may come to see that our "completion" lies beyond "us" and our ideas of how it ought to be. The narrowness of our sense of personal deprivation, and thereby insistence on being completed by an other, gives way to a wider awareness and appreciation of our essential relatedness to the otherness of the world.

THE CONNECTION BETWEEN COURTLY LOVE AND TANTRA

Although chivalry provides a general view of love as a path of spiritual transformation, it does not present a coherent set of practices to guide and facilitate the process. It might be that there never was a systematic praxis to courtly love, but in any case, we are left today with only the sketchiest of outlines regarding what practices a courtly lover might undertake to make romantic love an authentic spiritual path. One practice that has endured the ravages of time directs a courtly couple to lie naked in bed and spend the night together without making love (DeRougemont, 1956, pp. 349-351). The lovers are to resist the temptation to "have" each other, even as their desire rises to a fever pitch. Through sustaining the intensity of the longing provoked in this way, the lovers might develop their capacity to tolerate passionate longing.

This type of erotic practice is reminiscent of some aspects of Tantrism, which is not surprising given that it is thought that the tradition of courtly love was imported into Europe from India (DeRougemont, 1956). Still, what developed as chivalry in 12th-century Europe is a far cry from what has been recognizable as the tantric spiritual disciplines of Asia. As might be expected, during the course of such an epic journey, tantra was uprooted from its cultural, philosophical, and religious contexts, and its subtleties probably did not survive the journey intact. Certainly, the medieval European psyche was ill prepared to understand Asian spiritual disciplines in general and the radical tantric principles in particular. In addition, it is widely recognized—in Buddhist,

Taoist, and Hindu traditions alike—that tantric yoga involves advanced practices that require significant meditative preparation in addition to personal instruction from a qualified master (guru). Although it is plausible that knowledge of tantra was carried from India to Europe during the 12th century, there is no record I am aware of indicating that any tantric master made such a journey. Thus, it is not surprising that elements of medieval romance, although retaining a distinct resemblance to tantra, contain only remnants of the principles and practices specific to Tantrism. In any case, whatever tantric/courtly practices that might have existed during the Middle Ages have largely eroded during the intervening centuries and are virtually lost to us today. Even the general suggestion that romance places demands on lovers to be involved in a discipline strikes us as rather odd.

The spiritual potency of chivalry has been reduced to elements of conventional social etiquette. Behaving with civility, politeness, and good manners, which are examples of honoring the specialness of the other, still are bare echoes of what once might have been a rigorous transcendent discipline. We are left with only a vague understanding that it is within the power of erotic love to lead men and women to God and even less understanding of how to address the rigors encountered on such a path. Instead of cultivating a love whose aim is to renounce self-centeredness while practicing gentleness and self-discipline, we are left with a romanticism that has as its dominant goal the finding of emotional and material happiness by finding an ideal mate so as to get one's needs met. This is virtually the opposite of the original focus of courtly love, which aimed not at self-satisfaction but rather at self-transcendence. Therefore, we must reconsider and re-imagine what a practice of true love would be. Thus, a consideration of the fundamental orientation of tantra invites our attention.

Both the principles and praxis of tantra are highly developed, involving a number of yogic and meditative disciplines for training the mind, focusing the energy (*prana* [Sanskrit] or *chi* [Chinese]), and relaxing the body. It might be added that these practices typically involve extensive solitary training. Contrary to popular belief, practicing with a sexual consort and working intimately within an erotic relationship is something reserved for those who either already are well trained or have the requisite capacity for being able to handle the intensity of such a relationship.

In Tantrism, the phenomenon of eros is understood as *kundalini,* a concentrated force of prana that, when not dissipated in mindless distraction, can be aroused to awaken psychic centers, or chakras, thereby dissolving psychic blockages and increasing awareness and bliss. In the tantric relationship, lovers—yogis and yoginis—are bidden to see in their beloveds the embodiment of the divine. In both tantra and the romantic tradition, the beloved other is seen as an emanation of divinity. The passion aroused toward this blessed other is nothing less than the ecstatic love of God or, in Buddhist terms, releasement into the open presence of being (*sunyata*) and its intrinsic cognizance (*rig-pa*).

During the past 20 or 30 years, tantra has become popularized in our culture as a sort of sexual enhancement technology. The emphasis of this popular focus draws on specific yogic techniques aimed at prolonging and intensifying sexual pleasure. Although the benefits of having "better sex" through controlling ejaculation or developing an increased capacity for enjoying and tolerating sexual tension might be considerable, they only scratch the surface of the power of tantric yogas to awaken latent spiritual capacities. As the kundalini ascends the spine during yogic practices, it ignites the chakras, which release neurohormonal secretions often accompanied by great bliss, profound clarity, and pervasive peacefulness. Sovatsky (1998) spoke of kundalini-based psychic awakenings as "postgenital puberties" that inaugurate maturational leaps as kundalini travels from chakra to chakra. He contended that each chakra-awakening puberty is of an experiential magnitude comparable to that of the genital puberty occurring during adolescence.

Western psychology and religion, for the most part, have remained ignorant of the vast psychic potentialities that lie dormant in our human nervous system and that can be activated through erotic encounter. The capability of anyone to not merely "believe" in God but to actually be ignited in God is a possibility typically reserved for mystics, musicians, artists, and lovers. Tantric practice reminds us that our potentiality for being more fully human is far greater than we think and that the recognition of our Buddha nature, freed from pettiness, arrogance, and narcissistic foolishness, is well within reach. We need only practice with diligence disciplines that train our distractible mind and open our insensitive heart. Tantric yoga of both Hindu and Buddhist traditions provides many methods for such practice. However, neither tradition has developed specific intersubjective psychological methods pertinent to what we would recognize today, and cannot avoid recognizing, as the personal relationship aspects of such intimate practices. It is up to contemporary psychological explorers on the path of love, perhaps informed by the sensibilities of the courtly tradition, to integrate the profound clear teachings of Asian tantra into transcendentally focused love relationships of the 21st century.

FROM MYTH TO PATH

Based on the model of courtly love, romance is envisioned as being separate from the domestic relationships of everyday life. Yet, it is precisely this separation that bedevils us. Even the medieval protagonists could not maintain the strict separation commanded by the court. In many cases, it was simply too much for stricken lovers to remain chaste and at a distance from each other, content to channel their libidos into their inner lives alone. The desire to have the beloved and consummate the relationship becomes the seed of planning for ways for the relationship to endure, not only as an inner quest but also as a dependable flesh-and-blood relationship within which to grow one's personal happiness. Falling in love is one thing, but where and how are we to live? The tragedies of Tristan and Iseult, Romeo and Juliet, and others reveal the impossibility of romantic love enduring in an idealized state.

It may be argued that I am overstating the case and that many love affairs do not turn out tragically and might just as well turn out "happily ever after." There is much literature, including Shakespeare's *The Twelfth Night* and *A Midsummer Night's Dream* as well as the legion of contemporary romance novels and Hollywood romantic comedies, that end happily, with each lover satisfied in the arms of the beloved. Yet, as a test and exaltation of romantic love, such an "ending" is, as Eliot reminds us, only the "beginning" of the committed relationship. In most "happy ending" stories, the couple, perhaps against great odds, might get together; but only after coming together do the two begin to face the actual challenges of living with each other and unconditionally loving each other, the outcome of which remains unwritten.

The idyllic fantasy of living "happily ever after" reveals not the path but rather the myth of romantic love. It is this "oh so romantic" myth that distracts us from the true challenge at hand and gives rise to the accurate understanding that romance is an "impossible love" in that it refuses to accord to the idealized fantasy of uninterrupted contentment. Deep love typically does not make life easier; rather, it usually makes it far more difficult. As things do not turn out as we hope, we might find ourselves discouraged, disappointed, and no longer in love. This is a sure sign that we are caught in a passive myth of romance. The way in which to break free from love's myth is to engage love as a path, that is, to open more fully to the tensions—both gross and subtle—of intimate relationship, permitting oneself to be stretched in the process.

It is only as a path, or discipline, that love can be "true" in the ecstatic sense intended when we say "true love." Mitchell (1997) put it the following way:

> Authentic romance, in contrast to its degraded forms, is not split off from a longing for security and predictability but is in a continual dialectical relationship with it. Authentic romance cannot arise where there is a willed, contrived separation between safety and desire, just as authentic spirituality cannot emerge in the context of a willed, contrived separation between the sacred and the profane. (p. 40)

The willingness to be in love and to rejoice in the freedom of the other while simultaneously permitting the emergence of self-centered needs, desires, and impulses creates the crucible within which to realize the nature of a love that is true and whole. Without splitting security needs from erotic desire

or numbing one in favor of the other, we are left in a state of exquisite agony, longing for a completeness that is beyond the power of our will alone to produce. In surrendering to the tensions that remain unresolved in our hearts, we open simultaneously to the other and ourselves, and in those very moments we are released from the inner dividedness through which we feel estranged from the world and incomplete as we are.

It is not by merely tolerating inner and interpersonal tensions, but rather by embracing them wholeheartedly, that love becomes a path. As Welwood (1996) put it, the lover's choice is "to turn toward our true nature or away from it, to live in accord with the soul's desire to awaken or with the ego's tendency to remain entrenched behind its defenses" (p. 96). To open our hearts and minds to what we lack or suffer and so long for is the secret and true essence of romantic love. The willingness to long for our hearts' desire while relaxing the insistence that things turn out in some preconceived way, and to thereby be stretched beyond reason, is in itself the essence of the path of true love. Egotism is thinned as the capacity for selflessness expands.

As the Buddha taught, intentions and actions based on clinging and emotional impulsivities only deepen our confused entanglement in the world. Getting caught up in power struggles, infatuations, and animosities is exhausting and frustrating. Of all the passions, sexual passion is commonly recognized as the most powerful and entangling one. Following a path of renunciation, monks and nuns routinely take vows of celibacy so as to avoid sexual temptation and its inevitable entanglements. By contrast, the genuine path of the romantic is one of transformation, where one embraces passion, confusion, and love's tensions as liberating opportunities. Self-centered tendencies that have remained dormant are evoked through the intense emotional stimulation of erotic intimacy. Once evoked, a lover is in a position to relate to the psychological tensions or conflicts that have arisen and to release them with awareness.

In releasing our preconceptions, limiting beliefs, and petty holds on the other and ourselves, and in allowing ourselves to be moved and claimed by an otherness that returns us to who we most essentially are, a variety of liberated and liberating qualities emerge. With the collapse of our inner dividedness, joyfulness, gratitude, forgiveness, clarity, happiness, and compassion emerge spontaneously. These and other intrinsic qualities of human wakefulness are born from the freedom that comes with being truly in love and loving truly, wholeheartedly, without reserve. Any conditional love has some remnant of bondage in it as some claim or demand is placed on the relationship. Romantic love, properly understood, is a relationship for releasing the bonds we have placed—perhaps inadvertently—on ourselves and others and for

opening, or reopening, ourselves to the unconditioned tremulous wonderment of being. An inspired retranslation of the first Psalm described the victory of the true romantic:

Blessed are the man and the woman
who have grown beyond their greed
and have put an end to their hatred
and no longer nourish illusions.
But they delight in the way things are
and keep their hearts open, day and
night. (cited in Mitchell, 1989, p. 5)

Or, as Eliot (1971) finished his passage,

And all shall be well and
All manner of thing shall be well
When the tongues of flame are in-
folded
Into the crowned knot of fire
And the fire and the rose are one.
(p. 59)[2]

NOTE

1. Whereas the titles of these books reflect our cultural desperation with "getting" and "keeping" love, the contents within them contain much valuable and sage advice for curtailing power struggles and deepening intimate relationships in ways that can lessen relational aggression and possessiveness.

2. Excerpt from "Little Gidding," by T. S. Eliot, in *Four Quartets* (1971), © copyright Harcourt, Inc.

REFERENCES

Bly, R. (1995). *The soul is here for its own joy.* Hopewell, NJ: Ecco.

DeRougemont, D. (1956). *Love in the Western world.* Princeton, NJ: Princeton University Press.

Eliot, T. S. (1971). *Four quartets.* New York: Harcourt Brace Jovanovich.

Freud, S. (1959). *Collected papers* (J. Riviere, Trans.). New York: Basic Books. (Original work published 1912)

Fromm, E. (1956). *The art of loving.* New York: Harper & Row.

Hendrix, H. (1988). *Getting the love you want: A guide for couples.* New York: HarperCollins.

Hendrix, H. (1992). *Keeping the love you find: A personal guide.* New York: Pocket Books.

Jung, C. G. (1996). *The psychology of kundalini yoga: Notes on the seminar given in 1932.* Princeton, NJ: Princeton University Press.

Kernberg, 0. (1995). *Love relations.* New Haven, CT: Yale University Press.

May, R. (1981). *Freedom and destiny.* New York: Norton.

May, R. (1969). *Love and will.* New York: Dell.

Mitchell, S. (1989). *The enlightened heart: An anthology of sacred poetry* (S. Mitchell, Trans.). New York: HarperCollins.

Mitchell, S. (1997). Psychoanalysis and the degradation of romance. *Psychoanalytic Dialogues, 7*(1), 23-41.

Rilke, R. M. (1975). *Rilke on love and other difficulties* (J. Mood, Trans.). New York: Harper & Row.

Rumi, J. (1994). *Say I am you* (J. Moyne & C. Barks, Trans.). Athens, GA: Maypop.

Sovatsky, S. (1998). *Words from the soul: Time, East/West spirituality, and psychotherapeutic narrative.* Albany: State University of New York Press.

Stevens, J. (1990). *Lust for enlightenment: Buddhism and sex.* Boston: Shambhala.

Trungpa, C. (1973). Myth of freedom. In *Garuda 3: Dharmas without blame* (pp. 24-32). Boston: Shambhala.

Trungpa, C. (1988). *Shambhala: The sacred path of the warrior.* Boston: Shambhala.

Welwood, J. (1996). *Love and awakening: Discovering the sacred path of intimate relationship.* New York: HarperCollins.

CHAPTER 45

Authenticity, Conventionality, and Angst
Existential and Transpersonal Perspectives

ROGER WALSH

EXISTENTIAL and transpersonal disciplines have similar concerns and much to offer to each other. Both emphasize a practical focus on those matters of deepest life importance, especially the causes and relief of suffering and what it means to live fully. As such, they pay particular attention to the fundamental nature of our human condition, the ways in which we fall short of our possibilities (especially through entrapment in social illusion), the problem of suffering, and how we can most fully and fundamentally respond to these issues.

In this chapter, I explore four topics that are centrally related to these issues:

▶ The idea that our usual human condition is in some way deficient, lacking, and imbued with suffering

▶ The seduction of conventionality (i.e., the herd or the consensus trance)

▶ The claim that our usual ways of living are somehow inauthentic or somnambulistic

▶ Strategies and responses for authenticity or awakening

In the chapter, I do not summarize the existential and transpersonal movements, nor do I provide the theoretical, phenomenological, contemplative, and experimental data underpinning them. Rather, I simply enunciate and compare their relevant principles and refer the reader to reviews of the two fields (some of the more readable ones include Barrett, 1958; Cooper, 1990; Vaughan, 1995a; Walsh, 1993; Walsh & Vaughan, 1993; Wilber, 1981, 1995, 1996; and Yalom, 1981).

AUTHOR'S NOTE: This is an expansion of my article, "The Problem of Suffering: Existential and Transpersonal Perspectives," that appeared in *The Humanistic Psychologist*, Vol. 23, No. 3, pp. 345-356. I thank James Bugental, Frances Vaughan, and Irv Yalom for inspiration; Kaisa Puhakka and Ken Wilber for helpful suggestions; Bonnie L'Allier for excellent secretarial assistance; and *The Humanistic Psychologist* for permission to use the earlier article as a basis for this chapter.

THE UNSATISFACTORINESS OF OUR USUAL HUMAN CONDITION

Both traditions recognize a bewildering ambiguity and unsatisfactoriness at the heart of everyday life. For Heidegger, we are "thrown" into a situation of ambiguity and alienation, which for Jaspers constitutes "the shipwreck" of our human condition—homeless in an alien world. There, we confront "boundary situations" of aloneness, meaninglessness, responsibility, and death (Yalom, 1981). Consequently, it is no surprise that existentialists claim that our underlying feeling tone is one of angst and that, as Nietzsche (1968) put it, "as deeply as man sees into life, he also sees into suffering" (p. 269).

The transpersonal perspective is in full agreement with the existentialists in acknowledging the pervasiveness of ambiguity and angst, and it suggests that existentialists have made a profound and accurate diagnosis of the fundamental feeling tone of *unenlightened* existence. In fact, transpersonalists have much to learn from the sophisticated accounts that existentialists offer. The two schools differ, however, in their views of origins of this unsatisfactoriness.

At the core of the transpersonal movement, one finds a consistent claim that we suffer from a case of mistaken identity. We see ourselves as "skin-encapsulated egos," to use Alan Watts's somewhat imprecise but picturesque term. This ego or self-sense is, just as existentialists have argued, neither given nor fixed but rather partly chosen and constructed, not substantial and essential but rather illusory and (for transpersonalists) transcendable. Thus, both existentialists and transpersonalists agree that our usual views of the self are erroneous and that careful systematic phenomenology or contemplation reveal these errors.

The two schools differ, however, in their understandings about the nature and neces-

sity of the usual egoic self-sense and about the deeper nature of identity. Existentialists tend to assume that "every experience is 'owned' in that it can and must be attributed to an 'I.' In Kant's terminology, each experience is accompanied by an 'I think' " (Cooper, 1990, pp. 97-98).

Transpersonalists hold a different view based on contemplative experiences. They regard the view that "every experience is owned" as an example of what Buddhists call "wrong view." This is a common process in our usual state of consciousness where imprecise awareness fails to recognize the ego constructive process and mistakenly assumes that there is some self to which experiences are occurring (Engler, 1993; Epstein, 1995).

With meditative training, however, awareness becomes more precise and sensitive, a classic claim now borne out by experimental testing (Shapiro & Walsh, 1984). Then the ego constructive processes begin to be recognized and deconstructed, and the egoic separate self-sense begins to dissolve (Goldstein, 1983). A rapid flux of images, thoughts, and feelings is seen to underlie the assumption of a continuous ego (just as, through the process of flicker fusion, a series of movie frames appears to create continuous images). This recognition was made famous in the West by David Hume, who when looking for his self, could discover "nothing but a bundle or collection of different perceptions, which succeed each other with an inconceivable rapidity and are in a perpetual flux and movement" (Jones, 1969, p. 305). Likewise, in the East, the Buddha proclaimed the doctrine of *anatta* or no-self (Collins, 1982).

The deeper self-senses that are uncovered during meditative training and maturation are said to be increasingly transpersonal, that is, extending beyond the individual or personal to encompass wider aspects of humankind, psyche, and cosmos. The identity that eventually is unveiled has been described variously as the self, mind, spirit, Geist, Atman, Tao, pure consciousness, *sat-chit-ananda,* Buddha nature, and true nature. This identity is said to be experienced as one with, or coessential with, the ground of existence. These claims of a realizable transpersonal identity that is united with the "all" are, of course, central to the perennial philosophy, that common core of wisdom at the contemplative heart of the great religions (Huxley, 1944). What is crucial to recognize, however, is that these claims are not presented as tenets of faith or "mere metaphysics"; rather, they are reports of direct experiences that can, and should, be tested for oneself in meditation. The transpersonal movement has been described as a blending of perennial philosophy and contemporary knowledge, and it is deeply committed to the testing of these and other claims through all appropriate phenomenological, contemplative, intellectual, and scientific means.

In light of these ideas about our usual egoic self-sense and our underlying transpersonal identity, both perennial philosophers and contemporary transpersonalists suggest that our usual condition is one of profound self-alienation (Wilber, 1995). Not surprisingly, transpersonal theorists suggest that this self-alienation is central to understanding our condition and suffering and that growth and awakening to our deeper identity can relieve us of much of our angst, alienation, and Atman project.

The Atman Project

Much of our individual and collective self-inflicted suffering, above and beyond our existential angst, can also be understood in terms of our mistaken identity and the unfortunate motives it spawns (Walsh, 1999; Wilber, 1980). We are said to yearn to recover our true identity, and this yearning is said to be an expression of the eros of Plato, the developmental drive to overcome the alienation of Schelling and Hegel, the pull of the upper chakras of yoga, and the meta-motive of self-transcendence described by Maslow and Wilber.

But when we do not know of our transpersonal nature, the motive to uncover it goes unrecognized and unfostered. This motive then may be denied, distorted, or pathologized. Consequently, we hurl ourselves into a desperate search for substitute gratifications, a search that Wilber (1980) called the Atman project. This is the hopeless quest to find full and enduring satisfaction through the gratification and aggrandizement, rather than the outgrowth and transcendence, of our phase-specifically appropriate, but ultimately stunted and illusory, self-sense.

The Atman project is a hopeless one since ultimately we never can get enough of what we do not really want. Yet billions of lives and countless cultures are driven—and driven insane—by it, and the poisoned, polluted, and plundered earth around us attests to its insatiable fury. Growth and awakening to our deeper identity can relieve us of much of our angst, alienation, and Atman project, although bottomless mystery remains, of course.

In summary, both disciplines have profound concern with, and analyses of, the limitations and unsatisfactoriness of existence. Existentialism seems to have provided an unusually deep account of meaninglessness and unsatisfactoriness. Both disciplines regard alienation as central and see it not simply as a product of cultures or economics (as do social critics and Marxists) but rather as a core element of human existence. However, existentialism and transpersonalism tend to differ in their views of human nature and the self, and hence in their views of self-alienation and possible and appropriate responses.

THE LIMITATIONS AND SEDUCTION OF CONVENTIONALITY AND CONVENTIONAL SLUMBER

Both disciplines recognize and criticize the limitations of conventional worldviews and lifestyles. The existential emphasis is on a critique of unreflective submersion in mass existence and conventional living—"the public" of Kierkegaard, "the herd" of Nietzsche, the "mass existence" of Jaspers, "the masses" of Ortega, and "the they" of Heidegger.

The result is that the usual way of living is regarded as defensive and superficial, a condition that Fromm referred to as "automation conformity" and Heidegger called "everydayness." Everydayness refers to the tendency to look at things superficially, to accept conventional views, and to conceal the truth about ourselves and the world from ourselves. When this drive to conceal becomes prepotent, everydayness exacerbates into full-blown inauthenticity (Zimmerman, 1986).

Transpersonal perspectives agree entirely with this sober assessment of conventional lifestyles and societies. However, they tend to frame this situation, and solutions to it, in terms of states of consciousness and development.

The usual condition is seen as a conventional slumber in which development has proceeded from the preconventional to the conventional but there has ground to a halt in what Maslow (1971) called "the psychopathology of the average." Developmentally, this conventional condition is regarded as a form of collective developmental arrest, with its own stage-specific and stage-limited characteristics such as a conventional worldview, social structure, self-sense, morality, and mores (Walsh & Vaughan, 1993; Wilber, 1980, 1995).

Although the conventional condition or stage represents a significant advance over preconventional magic thinking, it still falls far short of our transconventional transpersonal capacities. Therefore, the conventional condition (and its limitations) has been labeled in many ways. In the East, it has been referred to as *maya*, a dream, and an illusion (Radhakrishnan, 1929). In the West, it has been called a consensus trance, a collective psychosis, a conventional slumber, a shared hypnosis, and a form of unconsciousness (Tart, 1986; Walsh & Vaughan, 1993). However, we do not usually recognize this trance because it is self-masking, we have been hypnotized since infancy, we actively defend it, we all share in it, and we live in the biggest cult of all—culture.

The Seduction of Conventionality

Both existentialists and transpersonalists agree that the power of the conventional majority to control beliefs, attitudes, and desires is awesome. This power can be brutally obvious and coercive as in legal, military, and penal institutions. However, this power usually is more insidious and seductive. For most people, the conventional worldview compels not merely by coercion but also by seduction, and it is this seductive attraction that has been most intriguing and distressing to existentialists and transpersonalists alike.

Because this seduction by the conventional majority is so effective, there must be something in individuals that is strongly attracted. Obviously, this attraction can be analyzed at many levels, for example, in terms of security needs or social belongingness needs. Not surprisingly, however, existentialists focus on existential dynamics as the forces that pressure individuals to succumb to conventional slumber.

Heidegger, in particular, spoke of "falling," which is the almost inescapable tendency to hide from the truth about ourselves and the world. And what is this fearful truth that we go to such lengths to avoid? It is the essential ungroundedness of our existence, values, and choices along with the angst that this generates.

Transpersonalists are in general agreement with this existential view but again tend to add a developmental perspective, in this case coupled with the concept of "coercion to the biosocial mean." This type of coercion was identified in personality research with the finding that people with a strong genetic tendency to deviation from the social mean, such as extreme shyness or assertiveness, tend to be pushed by societal shaping toward the mean. Transpersonalists have suggested that a similar dynamic can occur developmentally such that the average social level of psychological development functions like a magnet, pulling individuals up toward this level but retarding growth beyond it (Walsh & Vaughan, 1993; Wilber, 1995).

Like developmental theorists in several other areas (e.g., faith development, moral development), transpersonalists recognize three major developmental phases: prepersonal, personal, and transpersonal (or preconventional, conventional, and transconventional). Development up to conventional levels is expected and nurtured by society both informally and through formal educational institutions. On the other hand, development beyond conventional levels is an individual matter that can be very threatening to both the individual and conventional society.

Development at any level is rarely all sweetness and light; difficulties exist in all stages. However, there are extra difficulties in transconventional development, and they come from both within and outside of the individual.

In addition to the usual panoply of defenses that work to thwart growth at any stage, there appear to be additional barriers that swing into play at more advanced stages. These barriers, defenses, or meta-defenses have long been recognized in spiritual traditions as, for example, the seduction of the *siddhis* (powers) of yoga or the pseudo-nirvana of Buddhism. More recently, Desoille referred to the "repression of the sublime," and Maslow (1971) described the "Jonah complex" or the fear of our potential and greatness. In addition, people working at these levels must be willing to relinquish attachments to social approval and the consensual worldview because this worldview must be overcome and social approval for doing so is far from likely.

Approval and applause are hardly likely given that transconventional development threatens conventionality and the consensus trance. The conventional worldview, illusion, or maya, together with the values and lifestyles that both express and perpetuate it, are called into question. From the perspective of Becker (1973), this can be seen as a threat to conventional people's immortality projects. Not to share a belief system is to weaken it, and because everyone identifies with his or her belief system, alternate systems are experienced as threatening to one's present (way of) being and future immortality. Herein lies a source of coercion to the biosocial mean and suppression of transpersonal development.

In summary, both existentialism and transpersonalism share a deep concern about the limitations and seductiveness of the usual or conventional worldview, state of consciousness, and lifestyle. Both see unreflective surrender to conventionality as a forfeiture of potential and authenticity, and transpersonal theorists tend to see this seduction and surrender in developmental terms.

Deficiencies of Our Usual Way of Living

Both disciplines acknowledge that our usual ways of living are deficient and that this deficiency includes a moral component.

For existentialists, it is not just that we escape the reality of our individual and human situation through succumbing to mass existence and becoming one of the herd but also that we deliberately deceive ourselves in and about the process. We freely choose to succumb but then obliterate our condition, our freedom, and our choice from awareness.

Enormous amounts of time and energy—indeed, whole lifestyles and social collusions—then go into maintaining our semiconsciousness. For Kierkegaard (1849/ 1954), this is a lifestyle of "Philistinism [that] tranquilizes itself in the trivial," resulting in a state of "shut-upness" and "half-obscurity" (pp. 174-175). Although the full panoply of defenses presumably play their hypnotizing part, it is the twin tranquilizers of habit and diversion that, according to Pascal, are particularly potent and that "are great veils over our existence. As long as they are securely in place, we need not consider what life means" (Barrett, 1958, p. 135).

The net result is inauthenticity or bad faith. This is in part the self-deceiving unacknowledged choice to see ourselves as choiceless victims who fail to live our lives open to both our common existential dilemma and our unique individual situation. The latter failing seems analogous to the trap for Indian yogis of failing to recognize their *svabhava* (unique character or

nature) and to follow their corresponding *svadharma* (unique personal path of practice) (Aurobindo, 1976).

Transpersonalists are in full agreement with this existential view, but again they add a perspective based on development and states of consciousness. Inauthenticity is seen as defensive clinging to conventionality when one could transcend it. Along with bad faith and other forms of moral immaturity, it can be viewed as expressing, stabilizing, and reinforcing our usual distorted consensus trance. For example, unreflective busyness and habits can be seen as forms of "loading stabilization," a process in which a state of consciousness is stabilized and maintained by loading it with input and activity (Tart, 1983).

STRATEGIES AND RESPONSES

Given all of this—our moral immaturities, our deficient ways of living, the limitations and seductive power of conventionality, the unsatisfactoriness and groundlessness of existence—how are we to respond? Both disciplines agree in emphasizing the importance of detribalization and moral heroism, practices that might be essential for any significant degree of psychological maturity.

Detribalization is the process by which we escape from some of the distorting, constricted, and erroneous beliefs of our cultural worldview (Levinson, 1978). Through detribalization, we are able to step back from these beliefs so that we no longer look through and identify with them. Rather, we begin to look at them and, in looking at them, to disidentify from them. In disidentifying from them, we are able to work to transform both them and ourselves.

For existentialists, the central moral recommendation—in fact, perhaps the central recommendation of all existentialism—is the adoption of a heroic attitude (Yalom,

1981). This attitude, together with its corresponding behavior, has been described variously as courage, engagement, resoluteness, and authenticity. It involves an unflinching openness to the reality, ambiguities, and difficulties of life and is accomplished through a clearing away of concealments and obscurities "as a breaking up of the disguises with which *Dasein* bars its own way" (Heidegger, 1962, p. 167, italics added).

These attitudes suggest a decidedly willful and actively heroic stance. Yet, the mature Heidegger hinted at something beyond resoluteness—something less willful, more allowing, and more Taoistic. He called this attitude or way of being "releasement" and described it as standing open to being (Zimmerman, 1986).

Of course, significant parts of Heidegger's thinking seem to include decidedly mystical elements, as is the case with Husserl, the founder of phenomenology (Caputo, 1978; Zimmerman, 1986). Hanna (1993a, 1993b) suggested that this inclination is a natural consequence of profound phenomenological inquiry and that when this method is practiced rigorously and deeply, it will naturally merge into a type of contemplation and begin to yield mystical insights. Careful exploration of the relationship between phenomenology and contemplation/meditation could be very valuable and might open a methodological bridge between existential and transpersonal domains. Clearly, one of the major deficiencies of Western (as opposed to Eastern) philosophy, religion, and psychology has been the lack of a readily available and effective introspective/contemplative discipline.

Although existentialists emphasize a type of moral heroism, it is a far cry from conventional ideas of morality, so much so that there has been debate over whether existentialism can offer any ethical guidelines or moral philosophy (Cooper, 1990). Consider, for example, Kierkegaard's argument for "suspending the ethical" and Nietzsche's "overman," who supposedly was "beyond good and evil."

Yet, the existential arguments make perfect sense from a developmental perspective. The existentialists seem to be arguing for a transconventional morality that goes beyond or transcends conventional views of good and evil, as transconventional morality indeed does (Kohlberg, 1981). Such morality seems to be a means to, as well as an expression of, individual transconventional development.

However, it is primarily an emphasis on *individual* transconventional development. There is some discussion of reciprocal freedom, acknowledging that the quest for freedom and authenticity requires collaboration and "intersubjective solidarity" (Sartre) in which one "frees the other" (Heidegger). However, there is also Nietzsche's idea that "free spirits" need and "live off" the opposition of the herd (Cooper, 1990). Hence, there is little discussion of the establishment of a transconventional community (or *sangha*) or of transpersonal emotions and motives such as encompassing love and compassion. This emphasis on the individual transcender beyond good and evil seems to be one reason why some existentialists have been susceptible to charges of elitism.

A developmental transpersonal perspective, therefore, seems to throw new light on existential ethics (Walsh, 1999). Transpersonalists agree with the necessity for a form of transconventional moral heroism and approve the Buddha's call for a stringent communal ethical life "beyond good and beyond evil" (Byrom, 1976, p. 100). In contemporary developmental terms, the goal is maturation beyond conventional dualism toward Kohlberg's (1981) highest stage (Stage 7), in which morality is grounded in direct unitive experience where others are experienced as part of one's self and are so treated.

Transpersonalists, however, tend to see ethics as but one component of a multipronged discipline designed to foster development to transpersonal/transconventional stages and corresponding states of consciousness. Their language tends to include not only heroic metaphors but also metaphors such as opening, unfolding, awakening, liberation, and enlightenment (Metzner, 1998; Walsh, 1999). It also tends to acknowledge the importance of both communal and individual development (Vaughan, 1995b; Wilber, 1995, 1996).

The preeminent developmental theorist within the transpersonal field has been Wilber (1980, 1995, 1996). He has employed developmental structuralism to compare contemplative traditions across centuries and cultures and has identified six developmental stages beyond the conventional one. Wilber specifically has identified the second of these transconventional stages with the existential perspective and worldview, and he has suggested that existential psychologists may have plumbed aspects of the human condition more deeply than nearly all other Western schools. He has described four further stages and corresponding perspectives beyond the existential one. Not surprisingly, these are increasingly difficult to attain and rarely are realized without the aid of some type of intensive contemplative discipline.

Cross-cultural examination of authentic spiritual disciplines suggests that although they may contain enormous amounts of peculiar cultural baggage, they also may contain common effective processes and practices. To date, seven common elements have been suggested: ethical behavior, attentional stabilization, emotional transformation, perceptual refinement, redirection of motivation, cultivation of wisdom, and service (Walsh, 1999). Almost invari-

ably, authentic disciplines (i.e., disciplines capable of effecting significant transpersonal development) include contemplative or meditative training. This might seem at odds with Heidegger's (1982) warning against "extravagant grubbing about in one's soul" (p. 160), but introspection can involve either obsessive rumination or disciplines of mental development, and the two are light years apart.

These claims for the existence of transpersonal stages and potentials beyond the conventional obviously are of enormous significance. But the obvious question remains: Are they true? Are transpersonal experiences, stages, and capacities valid and valuable potentials within us all? Or, as critics (including some existentialists) have suggested, are they merely the products of pathological, regressed, or deluded minds engaged in desperate defensive maneuvers to avoid the harsh realities of mortality and meaninglessness? A considerable body of theory and research now supports some claims for the value and validity of transpersonal experiences and potentials (Laughlin, McManus, & d'Aquili, 1992; Shapiro & Walsh, 1984; Walsh, 1993; Walsh & Vaughan, 1993; Wilber, 1980, 1995, 1996).

In this arena, however, just as important as laboratory findings and elaborate theories is direct experience. For thousands of years, the great wisdom traditions have argued that the best way in which to assess such claims is to test them oneself through exploring and cultivating one's own mind. On this, existentialists and transpersonalists are in agreement; the most profound and important answers are to be found in one's own life and experience.

COMMENTS AND COMPARISONS

In his reply, Schneider provides thoughtful comments on some of the ideas expressed in this chapter (see also the rejoinder in Schneider, 1996). Although I find a few of his points questionable, for the most part, I am in wholehearted agreement.

Questions

First, to some of the questions. Schneider suggests that transpersonalists critique existentialists erroneously for "being short-sighted about our conscious potential and for being unwarrantedly anxious as a result . . . and for being gloomy and unenlightened." Actually, there is mighty little true enlightenment in either existential or transpersonal circles, and several transpersonalists (myself included) have expressed admiration for the existential openness to the anxiety and dread that an unwavering look at our human condition generates (e.g., Wilber, 1980). The two groups do indeed differ in their estimation of our conscious potential. As mentioned earlier, some transpersonal claims regarding this potential are now supported by research findings, but the most important testing might come from exploring and cultivating one's own mind.

Schneider warns transpersonalists against underestimating and undervaluing "the unfathomability of our condition, awe, and amazement." But the discovery, and even the realization, of transpersonal potentials does not necessarily diminish awe, amazement, and radical mystery. It might even sharpen them because, as Lao Tzu observed,

> From wonder into wonder
> Existence opens. (Bynner, 1944/1980,
>   p. 25)

Agreements

Schneider's central theme is a cry for humility, that is, intellectual and existential humility and awe in the face of the unfathomable infinity and mystery of the universe. Who could not agree?

Schneider also prudently warns against claims for ultimacy. Although I am not sure that one can say that ultimate claims *never* should be made—that would itself be an ultimate claim—Schneider's warning is well taken. Existentialists probably have done better here than have transpersonalists.

Schneider correctly points out the danger of members of one school claiming to fully comprehend another school. In my experience, many examples of internecine psychological warfare actually reflect attacks on *misunderstandings* of other schools. All of us would benefit from deeper study of other perspectives and from becoming skilled in their epistemological methods. Both schools draw on scientific methods and studies where these are appropriate and available, although both are wary of the risks and distortions of scientism, that is, the pseudo-philosophy that holds that science is the best, or even the only, way in which to acquire valid knowledge. The appropriate response to scientism is, "Show us your scientific proof that science is the best or the only way in which to acquire valid knowledge." To this request, there can only be stunned silence.

Many of the differences between the worldviews of existentialists and transpersonalists reflect the divergent effects of their different epistemological methods. For existentialists, the central methods probably are philosophical and psychological reflections: what Saint Bonaventure and (more recently) Wilber have called the "eye of reason." Whereas transpersonalists employ the eye of reason, they also rely on insights provided by meditative and contemplative practices—the "eye of contemplation" (Wilber, 1990). These different epistemologies may underlie many of the existential-transpersonal intellectual differences, given that worldviews reflect episte-mologies.

Both existentialists and transpersonalists, therefore, may benefit from a fuller practice of both epistemological methods. The result may be a more comprehensive, more adequate, and more satisfying understanding of ourselves and our place in the universe as well as a greater convergence between the two schools.

REFERENCES

Aurobindo. (1976). *Essays on the Gita.* Pondicherry, India: Sri Aurobindo Ashram.

Barrett, W. (1958). *Irrational man: A study in existential philosophy.* New York: Doubleday.

Becker, E. (1973). *The denial of death.* New York: Free Press/Macmillan.

Bynner, W. (Trans.). (1980). *The way of life according to Lau Tzu.* New York: Perigee. (Original work published 1944)

Byrom, T. (Trans.). (1976). *The Dhammapada: The sayings of the Buddha.* New York: Random House.

Caputo, J. (1978). *The mystical element in Heidegger's thought.* Athens: Ohio University Press.

Collins, S. (1982). *Selfless persons: Imagery and thought in Theravada Buddhism.* Cambridge, UK: Cambridge University Press.

Cooper, D. (1990). *Existentialism.* Oxford, UK: Basil Blackwell.

Engler, J. (1993). Becoming somebody and nobody: Psychoanalysis and Buddhism. In R. Walsh & F. Vaughan (Eds.), *Paths beyond ego: The transpersonal vision* (pp. 118-121). New York: Tarcher.

Epstein, M. (1995). *Thoughts without a thinker: Psychotherapy from a Buddhist perspective.* New York: Basic Books.

Goldstein, J. (1983). *The experience of insight.* Boston: Shambhala.

Hanna, F. (1993a). Rigorous intuition: Consciousness, being, and the phenomenological method. *Journal of Transpersonal Psychology, 25,* 181-198.

Hanna, F. (1993b). The transpersonal consequences of Husserl's phenomenological method. *The Humanistic Psychologist, 21,* 41-57.

Heidegger, M. (1962). *Being and time.* New York: Harper & Row.

Heidegger, M. (1982). *The basic problems of phenomenology.* Bloomington: Indiana University Press.

Huxley, A. (1944). *The perennial philosophy.* New York: Harper & Row.

Jones, W. (1969). *A history of Western philosophy* (Vol. 3). New York: Harcourt, Brace, Jovanovich.

Kierkegaard, S. (1954). *The sickness unto death* (W. Lowrie, Trans.). New York: Doubleday. (Original work published 1849)

Kohlberg, L. (1981). *Essays on moral development,* Vol. 1: *The philosophy of moral development.* New York: Harper & Row.

Laughlin, C., McManus, J., & d'Aquili, E. (1992). *Brain, symbol, and experience.* New York: Columbia University Press.

Levinson, D. (1978). *The seasons of a man's life.* New York: Random House.

Maslow, A. H. (1971). *The farther reaches of human nature.* New York: Viking.

Metzner, R. (1998). *The unfolding self: Varieties of transformative experience.* Novato, CA: Origin.

Nietzsche, F. (1968). Thus spoke Zarathustra. In W. Kaufmann (Trans.), *The portable Nietzsche.* New York: Viking.

Radhakrishnan, S. (1929). *Indian philosophy* (2 vols.). London: Allen and Unwin.

Schneider, K. (1996). Transpersonal views of existentialism: A rejoinder. *The Humanistic Psychologist, 24,* 145-148.

Shapiro, D., & Walsh, R. (Eds.). (1984). *Meditation: Classic and contemporary perspectives.* Hawthorne, NY: Aldine.

Tart, C. (1983). *States of consciousness.* El Cerrito, CA: Psychological Processes.

Tart, C. (1986). *Waking up: Overcoming the obstacles to human potential.* Boston: New Science Library/Shambhala.

Vaughan, F. (1995a). *The inward arc: Healing in psychotherapy and spirituality* (2nd ed.). Nevada City, CA: Blue Dolphin.

Vaughan, F. (1995b). *Shadows of the sacred: Seeing through spiritual illusions.* Wheaton, IL: Quest.

Walsh, R. (1993). The transpersonal movement: A history and state of the art. *Journal of Transpersonal Psychology, 25,* 123-140.

Walsh, R. (1999). *Essential spirituality: The seven central practices to awaken heart and mind.* New York: John Wiley.

Walsh, R., & Vaughan, F. (1993). *Paths beyond ego: The transpersonal vision.* Los Angeles: Tarcher.

Wilber, K. (1980). *The Atman project.* Wheaton, IL: Quest.

Wilber, K. (1981). *No boundary.* Boston: Shambhala.

Wilber, K. (1990). *Eye to eye* (2nd ed.). Boston: Shambhala.

Wilber, K. (1995). *Sex, ecology, spirituality: The spirit of evolution.* Boston: Shambhala.

Wilber, K. (1996). *A brief history of everything.* Boston: Shambhala.

Yalom, I. (1981). *Existential psychotherapy.* New York: Basic Books.

Zimmerman, M. (1986). *Eclipse of the self: The development of Heidegger's concept of authenticity* (rev. ed.). Athens: Ohio University Press.

A Reply to Roger Walsh

KIRK J. SCHNEIDER

I APPLAUD Roger Walsh's chapter exploring the commonalities between transpersonal and existential perspectives in psychology. It is a welcome presentation, comparatively balanced, and mutually beneficial to the respective positions. However, this case strikes me as an exception in Walsh's, as well as others', writings on these matters, and what follows is my attempt to redress this situation.

Contemporary transpersonal writers stress one major point when comparing their perspective to that of existentialists: that transpersonal contexts eclipse or encompass the existential (Walsh & Vaughan, 1994; Washburn, 1995; Wilber, 1986). As balanced as Walsh's chapter is, even he implies this position when referring to Wilber's developmental stages. In what follows, I attempt to dispel, or at the very least cast doubt on, such a stance.

This entire issue can be framed by one simple question attributed to Albert Einstein: Is the universe friendly (e.g., assimilable, consoling) or unfriendly (e.g., unassimilable, "other")? Transpersonalists such as Walsh and Vaughan (1994), Washburn (1995), and Wilber (1981a, 1981b, 1986) seem confident that the universe is friendly, that is, consciously unifiable and ultimately consoling. They critique existentialists for taking the opposite position, that is, for being shortsighted about our conscious potential and for being unwarrantedly

AUTHOR'S NOTE: This reply is adapted from my article, "Transpersonal Views of Existentialism: A Rejoinder," that appeared in *The Humanistic Psychologist*, Vol. 24, No. 1, pp. 145-148.

anxious as a result. Although it is true that some existential theorists emphasize the unfriendly and absurd dimension of self-cosmic relations, the existential theorists that the former transpersonalists rarely address—the so-called existential-theological thinkers such as Buber (1965a, 1965b), Heschel (1951), and Tillich (1954, 1963)—do not stress the universe's unfriendliness. By contrast, they take the agnostic tack that people do not know whether or not the universe is friendly. Yet, transpersonalists continue to upbraid existentialists for being caught within the dualism of self/not self, for being on a "lower" level of consciousness, and for being gloomy and unenlightened as a result. Transpersonalists accuse existentialists of having a limited understanding of spiritual disciplines (Puhakka, 1991; Walsh & Vaughan, 1994). But transpersonalists themselves claim to fully apprehend the existential view and to assure us of its subordinate understanding of consciousness (Walsh & Vaughan, 1994; Wilber, 1986).

Yet, my thesis here is that such transpersonalists do not fully apprehend the existential worldview given that if they did, then they would see that it is the very uncertainty and ungroundedness of existentialism that lend it its vast breadth (Schneider, 1999). Let me explain.

Existential theology places infinity, indefiniteness, and the *more*, as James (1904/1987, p. 1175) put it, over worldviews that attempt to totalize (or universalize) consciousness. It does this precisely because of the centrality of freedom in existentialists' outlook. To indicate otherwise—to close or dissolve the indefiniteness or to intimate (as has Wilber, 1982) true realities and false realities or erroneous views and correct views—is precisely to delimit freedom (e.g., becoming, emergence). It is precisely to neglect the ongoingness and unencompassable evolution of creation. Moreover, despite what some transpersonalists have suggested, an indefinite worldview does not automatically imply anxiety toward our condition. It does, however, imply a humility toward and fundamental puzzlement about ourselves. It implies a refusal to absolutize, reify, or infer unqualified universality to human experience, and it implies a vivid poignancy to each passing moment. I am moved by life precisely because it is a radical puzzlement to me. I am moved by birth, death, love, and nature precisely because they cannot be completely assimilated, and when they are—momentarily—it is marvelous. But there are always more assimilations possible, more unravelings, and more reconstitutions yet again.

What, then, does it mean to speak of transcending the existential? Does it mean transcending existence? Being? Groundlessness? What is so delimiting about being in awe of existence, about being shaken, stunned, or radically amazed? One could, of course, take the tack of the aforementioned transpersonalists and respond that such expressions are the products of a split self; a self that has yet to encompass otherness and achieve its final blessed state (Washburn, 1995). On the other hand, one could embrace the reverse stance. On this view, awe and amazement unveil the shortsightedness not of those who experience them but rather of those who subordinate such sensibilities. By underscoring the unfathomability of our condition, awe and amazement also, by implication, highlight the constriction, sterility, and blandness associated with minimizing that unfathomability.

Now, it is precisely this latter view—the response of agnosticism to Einstein's query—that has not been explored enough in transpersonal circles. Yet, many of the most respected mystics, including the Buddha, appear to adopt it (Schneider, 1987, 1989, 1993). Such mystics view enlightenment in provisional, eminently pragmatic terms. It is no accident that a respected Buddhist scholar, Batchelor (1990), chose to title his book on the basis of Tillich's credo, *The Faith to Doubt.* There is great courage in this credo *as well as* Walsh's individual and collective "opening, unfolding, awakening, liberation, and enlightenment."

To conclude, if the transpersonal vision culminates in moments, glimpses, and qualified cosmic fusions, then it is subsumable within an existential framework. If, on the other hand, transpersonalism culminates in totalities, ultimates, and unqualified fusions, then *it*, by implication, must overlap the existential. *Either* view may be "correct," and either may be illusory. Only the marketplace of experience, as Walsh prudently notes, will decide this question. In the meantime, it would behoove transpersonal and existential theorists to tread carefully on questions of ultimacy. Einstein's question is far from resolved, and either response to it may be legitimate.

POSTSCRIPT

I am deeply appreciative to Walsh for his thoughtful closing remarks on my reply (see also my rejoinder in Schneider, 1996). I am also in agreement with the thrust of his statement. *Both* existentialists and transpersonalists have much to learn from each other, and there are marvels awaiting us on the collaborative path. The question is, can we look through each other's eyes of reason and contemplation—for they are present in each of our perspectives—and find our mutual way?

REFERENCES

Batchelor, S. (1990). *The faith to doubt.* Berkeley, CA: Parallax.

Buber, M. (1965a). *Between man and man.* New York: Macmillan.

Buber, M. (1965b). *The knowledge of man.* New York: Harper & Row.

Heschel, A. (1951). *Man is not alone: A philosophy of religion.* New York: Farrar, Straus, & Giroux.

James, W. (1987). *William James: Writings 1902-1910.* New York: Literary Classics/Viking. (Original work published 1904)

Puhakka, K. (1991). Review of *The Paradoxical Self* by K. Schneider. *Theoretical and Philosophical Psychology, 11*(2), 134-139.

Schneider, K. J. (1987). A "centaur" response to Wilber and the transpersonal movement. *Journal of Humanistic Psychology, 27*(2), 196-216.

Schneider, K. J. (1989). Infallibility is so damn appealing: A reply to Ken Wilber. *Journal of Humanistic Psychology, 29*(4), 470-481.

Schneider, K. J. (1993). *Horror and the holy: Wisdom-teachings of the monster tale.* Chicago: Open Court.

Schneider, K. J. (1996). Transpersonal views of existentialism: A rejoinder. *The Humanistic Psychologist, 24*, 145-148.

Schneider, K. J. (1999). The fluid center: A third millenium challenge to culture. *The Humanistic Psychologist, 27*(1), 114-130.

Tillich, P. (1954). *The courage to be.* New Haven, CT: Yale University Press.

Tillich, P. (1963). *Systematic theology.* Chicago: University of Chicago Press.

Walsh, R., & Vaughan, F. (1994). The worldview of Ken Wilber. *Journal of Humanistic Psychology, 34*(2), 6-21.

Washburn, M. (1995). *The ego and the dynamic ground: A transpersonal theory of human development.* Albany: State University of New York Press.

Wilber, K. (1981a). *No boundary.* Boston: Shambhala.

Wilber, K. (1981b). *Up from Eden: A transpersonal view of human evolution.* Garden City, NY: Doubleday.

Wilber, K. (1982). The pre/trans fallacy. *Journal of Humanistic Psychology, 22*(2), 5-43.

Wilber, K. (1986). The spectrum of psychopathology. In K. Wilber, D. Brown, & J. Engler (Eds.), *Transformations in consciousness: Conventional and contemplative perspectives on development* (pp. 107-125). Boston: Shambhala.

CHAPTER **46**

Humanistic Psychology and Social Action

ARTHUR LYONS

THE FOCUS of this chapter is to explicitly extend the range of humanistic psychology beyond the scope of healthy individual development. Whereas it is critical to explore what it means to be fully (experientially) human and to study how this perspective informs the vital and fulfilled life, it is also critical that individuals who identify with this way of being become social activists and work at many different levels to modify, improve, and (in some cases) construct social agencies, educational institutions, work environments, correctional facilities, laws, customs, and social values that foster full humanness. The society in which one resides and works has a profound impact on changing the likelihood of an individual accepting the challenge of living life to its fullest.

This chapter examines the criticisms of the humanistic approach as being too "self" focused, examines the philosophical and historical basis for focusing on social action, shows how this revolutionary perspective and challenge put forth by humanistic writ-

ers is now becoming an emerging trend for mainstream psychology, offers examples from different social arenas where such humanistic values are fostered, and provides the reader with the challenge to work toward positive social change.

CRITICISMS OF THE HUMANISTIC APPROACH

Humanistic psychology is often perceived as displaying an excessive preoccupation with enhancing the psychological well-being of only the affluent, that is, those who can afford or who have medical coverage for therapy. Some criticisms go even further and argue that humanistic psychology is primarily a philosophy that fosters excessive self-indulgence. Historically, the criticism goes so far as to give this approach credit for being one of the causal influences of producing the "me" generation of the 1980s. Others (e.g., Csikszentmihalyi & Seligman, 2000) state that in some of its incarnations, the approach has emphasized the self and encouraged a self-centeredness that played down concerns for collective well-being.

The next section responds to these criticisms by offering a different historical perspective. This is not meant to say that these concerns are not valid to at least some degree; rather, the concerns do not accurately reflect the complexity of the humanistic perspective.

HISTORICAL AND PHILOSOPHICAL BASIS FOR FOCUSING ON SOCIAL ACTION

Division 32 (Humanistic Psychology) of the American Psychological Association (APA) was founded in September 1971. It has been an active division of the umbrella organization ever since its inception. It currently has more than 600 active professional members. The division's core values, which motivate its efforts, consist of caring and commitment as well as trust and realistic understanding of the complexity of people as individuals, in groups, in organizations, and in communities. As part of that commitment, the mission statement stresses that humanistic psychologists are particularly concerned about the quality of human welfare and are focused on contributing to fostering social responsibility and change.

Historically, of course, it is important to note that long before Division 32 came into existence, humanistic theorists were writing about these issues. Maslow (1969, 1971, 1962/1968, 1954/1987), in many of his writings, addressed the following distinctions: the "healthy" society versus the "sick" society, the "good" society versus the "poor" society, the society with "high synergy" versus the society with "low synergy," and the society and culture that could be "growth fostering" versus the society or culture that could be "growth inhibiting." Maslow's (1969) basic premise was that the healthy or good society offers all of its members the basic need satisfactions and possibilities of self-actualization and human fulfillment and also exemplifies, values, strives for, and makes possible the attainment of "B-" (or "being") motivation. This involves attending to our highest aspirations and needs. Examples include our aesthetic needs, our appreciation of art and beauty, and our need for higher levels of cognitive understanding. He argued that psychotherapy amounted to fighting against the sickness-producing forces in a society on an individual scale. Maslow (1954/1987) pondered that we could have a healthier society if psychotherapy could be greatly extended. One of the ways in which to extend the benefit of humanistic principles to a larger number of people is through the development of service delivery programs that reach out to many in the community.

In the preface to the second edition of *Toward a Psychology of Being,* Maslow (1962/1968, p. iii) wrote about humanistic psychology as not being purely descriptive or academic but rather suggesting action and implying consequences. He argued that it helped to generate a way of life not only for the individual but also for the same person as a social being or a member of society. Now, more than 40 years since Maslow pondered these thoughts, we are discovering some of the many ways in which those humanistic principles have taken seed, grown, and borne fruit in social programs that reach populations that traditionally would not seek out or be invited to participate in individual psychotherapy.

AN EMERGING TREND FOR MAINSTREAM PSYCHOLOGY

From a seemingly different front, a recent past president of the APA, Martin Seligman, has put forth a vision for a "positive psychology." Csikszentmihalyi and Seligman (2000) challenged psychology to give up its exclusive focus on pathology, which they argued has dominated the discipline and resulted in a model of the human that lacks the positive features that make life worth living. Instead, they proposed that the social and behavioral sciences can play an enormously important role in articulating a vision of the good life that extends beyond individual well-being. Its focus should include the development of work settings that produce worker satisfaction, civic virtues, public policies, and institutions that make people's lives most worth living. A general theme expressed by many of the authors who are contributing to this "new" field is that part of the complexity of psychological development in humans is that it must be examined within the social and cultural context in which it is embedded. This is certainly a theme that is consistent with emerging trends in humanistic psychology.

Ryan and Deci (2000), who researched self-determination theory extensively, focused on three related human needs: the need for competence, the need for belongingness, and the need for autonomy. They claimed that when these three needs are satisfied, personal well-being and social development are optimized. They also argued that the social context needs to be examined with respect to the degree to which it promotes rather than hinders autonomy, competence, and relatedness. There is a strong similarity between these ideas and Maslow's (1968) theorizing of more than 30 years ago. Maslow's theory of motivation called attention to the critical importance of satisfying self-esteem needs and the needs for love and belongingness for psychological health to be attained.

Positive psychologists are laying claim to being the catalysts for changing the focus of psychology from the "negative" to the "positive," that is, from focusing almost exclusively on psychopathology to focusing on building positive qualities in humans. What seems to differentiate this new thrust from previous humanistic writings is that it limits its methods of scientific investigation to those that are conventionally empirical. Regardless, it is refreshing to see the field of psychology begin to mature and to recognize the wisdom of some of the earliest writings of humanistic theorists such as Rogers and Maslow. It should be noted that the final chapter of Maslow's (1954/1987) book, *Motivation and Personality,* was titled "Toward a Positive Psychology," and he could be considered the originator of the theoretical basis for this new mainstream movement.

Psychology is also being challenged by others outside of the field to become more socially relevant. Jackson (2000) and Strickland (2000) both offered a moral imperative for psychology to become a more powerful force for social change. This challenge to the field of psychology is not new. As Jesse Jackson noted in an address to the APA in August 1999, Martin Luther King addressed the same organization in 1967 and expressed the view that the social sciences should be an instrument of social change and should observe and study the complexity of social relations (Jackson, 1999). What is different now is that we are beginning to recognize how multicultural, multiracial, multilingual, and multispiritual our larger society is and that psychological services of a different sort and at a different level of delivery are necessary if we are to adapt in a healthy fashion.

EXAMPLES OF HUMANISTICALLY BASED SOCIAL ACTION PROGRAMS

This section highlights two very different types of social action programs that reflect humanistic values. They are deliberately chosen as examples because they reflect two very different ways in which to influence the social community and they operate in very different fashions. What ties them together is that both reflect humanistic tenets, and both are aimed at improving the quality of life in the communities where they operate. The intent of sharing these examples in some detail is to show two very different ways in which basic humanistic principles are being used successfully to assist the human condition. They are also offered with the express hope of either reinforcing the current humanistically based social involvement of the reader or inspiring such actions in the future. (An introduction to other programs can be found in a special issue of *The Humanistic Psychologist* that was devoted to showing the relationship between humanistic psychology and the promotion of human welfare [Lyons, 1996].)

The first example, the Center for Humanistic Change, illustrates how a local agency can be created, be funded by conventional sources, grow, expand, and have a positive, ongoing impact on many aspects of people's lives within a regional area of northeastern Pennsylvania.

The second example, the National Coalition Building Institute (NCBI), grew out of the work of one individual, Cherie R. Brown, who had a vision that there had to be a better way in which to deal with prejudice, hatred, and bigotry than she had experienced while growing up. There had to be a way for people to recognize the essential humanness within themselves and within the very people whom they treat in bigoted fashion. This example elucidates the development of an institute that has become international in scope and a model that is humanistically based to fight oppression and to promote healing among those who

have been victimized by oppression. The reader will soon see how the NCBI has used Gestalt therapy applications to assist people with individual healing and has expanded its focus to anti-oppression work in the community. This model exemplifies how humans, after experiencing unconditional positive regard, will risk growth. The NCBI model requires its facilitators to trust their participants and invites them to risk, grow, and delight in making mistakes as a basis for further learning. In addition, the NCBI offers a leadership model that challenges people in leadership positions to make courageous growth choices. At the same time, it invites people to acknowledge and experience the inherent fear involved in making such choices and to acknowledge the regressive pull toward playing it safe and not risking.

What is especially exciting about sharing the NCBI program is that it is an example of a very fine project that has grown organically into its present shape by adopting many humanistic tenets, yet its founder was not cognizant of this humanistic heritage.

There are literally hundreds of programs that espouse and apply humanistic psychological and educational principles without labeling them as such. Perhaps this is one of humanistic psychology's greatest contributions to promoting social change. For other examples of social change, the reader may refer to a special issue of *The Humanistic Psychologist* (Autumn 1996) titled "Social Action as Compassionate Heartwork: Humanistic Psychology and the Promotion of Human Welfare." The main thrust of the programs included in that special issue reflect work with populations that differs markedly from the stereotype of humanistic psychology only serving the affluent. The subgroups included, but were not limited to, a prison population, long-term welfare recipients, adolescents, high-risk adolescents, high-risk students (K-12), high-risk low-income women with children, teen parents, young people from dysfunctional backgrounds, mental health patients, and all forms of family.

THE CENTER FOR HUMANISTIC CHANGE

The Center for Humanistic Change came into being in 1975. A small group of individuals including some staff who had been working at Endeavor (a drug treatment center in Bethlehem, Pennsylvania), some board members from the same agency, and some concerned citizens of the local community came together to develop a positive proactive approach to dealing with drug and alcohol problems within the local community. If drugs and alcohol were not going to be primary coping strategies for youths and adults to use for coping with stress in their lives, then social programs had to do more than provide treatment after these coping strategies had become dominant in people's lives. The terminology that was adopted to describe the center's work at that time—prevention—reflected the dominant mode of thinking about treating human suffering. It was still somewhat unusual to allocate drug and alcohol treatment money to prevention of problems rather than to expensive treatment programs after the fact. A quarter of a century later, we can now see that psychology, and in particular humanistic psychology, is focusing more and more on fostering healthy ways of living, which is what this program was established to do. This approach represented a radical departure from the dominant focus of psychology that was primarily centered on the diagnosis and treatment of illness and the study of abnormal and antisocial behavior.

Whereas prevention became the acceptable way of labeling what the center was doing, the center was created to provide a resource for life-skills training and education. At the center, life-skills training included self-esteem and self-confidence training as well as training for effective communication skills (e.g., assertiveness, listening); decision-making skills; conflict resolution and management skills; and establishment of healthy and supportive relationships within families, classrooms, organizations, and communities.

Prevention education has become a key element of the center's mission. Its major themes are self-control, self-responsibility, and connectedness with others. Life-skills education provides a healthy foundation for individuals so that they can grow and reach their highest potentials. The center currently teaches life skills to people of all ages, with special emphasis on the delivery of service to high-risk students (K-12), high-risk low-income women with children, and teen parents. In addition, the center aims to promote primary prevention through interagency collaboration, coalition building, and networking activities (Wright, 1996). Its programs are offered in schools, communities, and workplaces. Its clients include students, teachers, counselors, administrators, parents, social service employees, community groups, business personnel, and individuals interested in personal growth and human relations.

The center's educational philosophy is based on humanistic principles and reflects a concern for the growth of the whole person. The aim is to promote an understanding of the requisites of healthy growth and to help people develop the skills they need to live well. The training sessions and curricula are geared to the development of life skills that aid participants in developing goals, making decisions, communicating effectively, enhancing their self-concepts, and taking charge of their lives in a positive way. The center also develops and implements programs that provide information about alcohol, tobacco, and other drugs (ATOD). The center's ATOD prevention programs provide opportunities and skills training that allow participants to learn about the negative effects of ATOD and examine their attitudes and values about substance use and abuse. The center employs a staff of 12 professionals and paraprofessionals and uses the services of 50 independent contract trainers on an as-needed basis. The organization is funded, in part, by grants from the Northampton County Drug and Alcohol Division, the Lehigh County Office of Drug and Alcohol Abuse, the federal Safe and Drug Free Schools Grants Program, private foundations, donations, and fees for service and gifts.

The current executive director of the center, Shawn Wright, has enumerated several aims of the center. Among these aims is helping individuals to live lives that are rich in alternatives, are intra- and interpersonally healthy, and exclude destructive behaviors and substance abuse dependencies (Wright, 1996). To accomplish these objectives, the center uses a humanistic approach to facilitating education and training. This approach includes cognitive, affective, and behavioral content; directive, facilitative, and creative process; and intrapersonal, interpersonal, and extrapersonal outcomes. The training engages participants experientially on many levels—from their heads, to their hearts, to their hands. The center's philosophy is built on the works of Maslow and Rogers. Displaying attitudes of unconditional positive regard, congruence, and empathy for all clients, the staff at the center provide supportive and healthy relationships reflective of Rogers's principles.

As suggested earlier, the learning strategies that emerged from the humanistic schools of educational philosophy are also major pieces of the center's approach. Humanistic education emphasizes the education of the whole person—cognitive, emotional, and behavioral. The center promotes holistic learning and application of that learning to everyday life (see also the chapter by Thomas [Chapter 41] in this volume). The center offers training in classroom discipline based on firm assertive communication and democratic authority. It also offers workshops that help educators to develop the skills they need to involve students in creating classrooms that are based on respect, self-discipline, and self-motivation.

Much of the center's work revolves around the facilitation of small groups, and all of its trainers are extensively trained in how to do so in a humanistic fashion. Two other arenas in which the center has become extensively involved are curriculum development and the implementation and application of humanistic principles to the workplace. A concrete example of the type of curriculum development that the center creates is CrossRoads, a program aimed at 10th-grade students at risk for dropout. It offers anger management focus groups for students, faculty training in anger management techniques, student life-skills training, and a mentorship component. Like all center programs, CrossRoads aims to help students realize the humanistic goal of self-actualization and is based on many humanistic principles. Students enrolled in the CrossRoads program are encouraged to be open to their own experiences, both positive and negative. They are challenged to see mistakes as a source of learning and to profit from them. They learn skills that will help them to think well of themselves and to feel able and competent while being aware of their own limitations. They also learn to think well of others and to see their relationships with others as an opportunity for self-development.

More than a decade and a half ago, the center developed a separate division, Workplace Associates, to provide employers with resources to help create more productive organizational climates. The same humanistic principles that guide the center are reflected in the format of Workplace Associates. The separate division was established explicitly for marketing purposes. Some of the same criticisms leveled against humanistic psychology discussed earlier in this chapter would have been stumbling blocks to business and industry openly examining the value of the center's programs. Even today, one can note a variety of humanistically based training seminars such as "Executive Coaching," "Mentor Training," and "Effective Listening in the Workplace" that are packaged under nonhumanistic names to avoid this perceived stigma. A concrete example of programming by Workplace Associates is a program that offers expertise in family enhancement training and helps employees to improve their skills in managing their personal and family lives, which in turn makes them more effective employees.

The preceding, then, is a tale about how one small organization, based on humanistic principles, came into existence and has had a significant positive impact on a local community. Since 1975, the center has been a positive presence in the lives of countless individuals and organizations. It has educated thousands of people concerning the value of humanistic approaches to facing life's challenges and maximizing individual and organizational potentials. The center has taken a leadership role in the development and implementation of quality life-skills education and is dedicated to that mission. It represents a model of social change at the micro level. The continued support that it has received from the local community is a validation of its mission.

Remember that this social change organization came about as a direct result of the work of a few individuals acting on their beliefs. None of the originators of the organization currently is affiliated with the center. It has become a social force in its own right.

NATIONAL COALITION BUILDING INSTITUTE

The second example of a humanistically based organization started as a consequence of one person's commitment to make a difference. Its growth into a worldwide organization demonstrates the dedication of its originator and also may be seen as a validation of how much need there is for this type of program.

Cherie Brown cites three early formative influences that helped her to see the need for becoming a community activist interested in combating prejudice. As a 10-year-old growing up in Cleveland, Ohio, she saw the need to build black-Jewish coalitions and organized the Jewish youth group at her synagogue to sponsor a program with the local youth group of a black church. Her family moved to Los Angeles during the summer of 1965, the year that racism exploded into violence in many U.S. cities. At age 15, she participated in black-white dialogues in Watts during a period of massive civil unrest. At age 19, when she came back home from Israel after her first trip there in 1969, she was deeply disturbed by the rising acceptance of a military solution to the Arab-Israeli conflict. She vowed to learn everything she could about how to build bridges across painful group divisions and how to find nonviolent solutions to people's struggles. The NCBI, as it is currently composed 31 years later, represents the culmination of Brown's lifelong efforts to achieve these dreams.

The institute is now an international nonprofit organization that fosters anti-racism coalitions and offers leadership training programs to a broad spectrum of constituents. The NCBI has worked with hundreds of law enforcement agencies, government entities, educational institutions, trade unions, businesses, philanthropies, congregations, and voluntary community organizations. Its principal office is in Washington, D.C., and there are dozens of chapters and affiliates in communities throughout the United States, Canada, England, and Switzerland. Over the past 16 years, the NCBI has developed models for doing effective anti-discrimination work in every imaginable setting, from public schools to police departments, by combining emotional healing work with skills training in community activism.

How did the NCBI come into being? Brown's early work in running workshops with black and Jewish students provided her with two significant insights. First, whenever a black or Jewish student told a specific story that described a painful experience with either racism or anti-Semitism, the grief shared by everyone in the room who heard the story bridged the differences in the group. Empathic listening to another's story led to the development of respect for the other and to unconditional positive regard being expressed for the other. Second, Brown learned that giving students hands-on practical skills for interrupting racist and anti-Semitic behavior empowered them. Providing concrete ways in which to deal with day-to-day encounters with discrimination prompted many students to become activists on their college campuses. Once empowered, they were much more likely to make growth choices rather than playing it safe and not getting involved.

Inspired by the insight of combining emotional healing work with activist training skills, Brown developed an organizational base for doing this work. During the summer of 1984, she launched the NCBI as a leadership training organization that could train thousands of activists worldwide in the necessary skills of prejudice reduction, intergroup conflict resolution, and coalition building. She integrated ideas from the many sensitivity training workshop models in existence at that time with a focus on what was necessary to change entrenched institutional forms of discrimination. The humanistic principles that have governed the NCBI's work against various forms of oppression since its inception can be expressed in two axioms. First, care must be given to individuals so that they may heal the past wounds that prevent them from taking effective grassroots leadership. Second, grassroots political activism, rooted in a spirit of community-based cooperation and teamwork, brings about systemic institutional change (Brown & Mazza, 1996).

A HUMANISTIC CHALLENGE

The need for social action and the need to generate larger scale applications of psychological knowledge and principles are more critical now than ever before. We are faced with significant problems at institutional levels (e.g., dysfunctional schools and work environments), at cultural levels (e.g., racism), and at public policy levels. In addition, we are being challenged to adapt to an increasingly complex, pluralistic, fast-changing, technology-driven world.

It could be argued that the applications of humanistic psychology presented in this chapter do not go far enough in transforming our society. Prilleltensky (1996) argued that we must focus on emancipation as a prerequisite for the good life and the good society. He challenged humanistic psychologists to see that people experience the liberty to make their own choices and to pursue them without oppressive restrictions. In other words, he indicated that a much greater emphasis must be placed on distributive justice and social responsibility. This perspective has much in common with the challenge for promoting social justice that Jackson offered to psychology, as discussed earlier.

Rather than viewing one form of social change as more basic or more essential than another, it is possible to view a world in which social change occurs at both macro and micro levels during the decade ahead. The danger of focusing only on transformative approaches to achieving the good society is that one can easily become overwhelmed and discouraged and even give up trying to effect a positive change. The danger of focusing only on the local applications that primarily affect individuals is that the larger social systems in which they reside evolve only incrementally rather than more dramatically. This chapter has tried to highlight the fact that social change at the local level can be real and significant. It is a call for action and a reminder that humanistic values and tenets can permeate every social arena. Regardless of whether one is a youth volunteer athletic coach, a school board member, a city council member, a union leader, a parent, a student, a teacher, a blue-collar worker, a white-collar worker, a supervisor, a line worker, an employer, an employee, young, or old, the potential to make a difference exists in every social arena of life.

If humanistic psychology is going to make a profound impact on the way in which citizens of the world live their lives during the 21st century, then it must focus on the larger social arena in some fashion. If humanistic psychology is to be perceived as more than a reactionary "third force," then it must claim its own future. And social activism, not merely "consciousness," must become a part of that future.

REFERENCES

Brown, C. R., & Mazza, G. J. (1996). Anti-racism, healing, and community activism. *The Humanistic Psychologist, 24,* 391-402.

Csikszentmihalyi, M., & Seligman, M. (2000). Positive psychology: An introduction. *American Psychologist, 55,* 5-14.

Jackson, J. (1999, August). *Presidential mini-convention on ethnic minorities: Scaling the summit.* Invited address given at the meeting of the American Psychological Association, Boston.

Jackson, J. (2000). What ought psychology to do? *American Psychologist, 55,* 328-330.

Lyons, A. (Ed.). (1996). Social action as compassionate heartwork: Humanistic psychology and the promotion of human welfare [Special issue]. *The Humanistic Psychologist, 24,* 301-406.

Maslow, A. H. (1968). *Toward a psychology of being* (2nd ed.). New York: Van Nostrand Reinhold. (Original work published 1962)

Maslow, A. H. (1969). A theory of meta-motivation: The biological rooting of the value-life. In A. J. Sutich & M. A. Vich (Eds.), *Readings in humanistic psychology* (pp. 153-199). New York: Free Press.

Maslow, A. H. (1971). *The farther reaches of human nature*. New York: Viking.

Maslow, A. H. (1987). *Motivation and personality* (3rd ed.). New York: Harper & Row. (Original work published 1954)

Prilleltensky, I. (1996). Human moral and political values for an emancipatory psychology. *The Humanistic Psychologist, 24,* 307-324.

Ryan, R., & Deci, E. (2000). Self-determination theory and the facilitation of intrinsic motivation, social development, and well-being. *American Psychologist, 55,* 68-78.

Strickland, B. (2000). Misassumptions, misadventures, and the misuse of psychology. *American Psychologist, 55,* 331-338.

Wright, S. (1996). Positive experiences in personal and professional growth. *The Humanistic Psychologist, 24,* 331-340.

CHAPTER 47

Humanistic Psychology in the Workplace

ALFONSO MONTUORI AND RONALD PURSER

HUMANISTIC PSYCHOLOGY has had a considerable influence on the fields of organizational development and management theory. During the 1960s, humanistically oriented values informed the core of organizational development theory and practice (Tannenbaum & Davis, 1967). During this period, organizational development practitioners advocated a normative view of organizations, moving away from the bureaucratic model to design organizations. This view explicitly embodied humanistic and democratic values. Humanistic values were apparent in organizational development interventions that were grounded in normative behaviors such as openness, self-awareness, feedback, and personal growth (Greiner, 1980). Some pioneering theorists of organizational development such as Chris Argyris, Douglas McGregor, Richard Beckhard, Warren Bennis, Herbert Sheperd, and Edgar Schein were heavily influenced by the writings and works of Abraham Maslow, Carl Rogers, Kurt Lewin, and Rollo May. The encounter and training group (or "T-group") movement, what Rogers often called a "therapy for normals," was the precursor to organizational development theory and practice. Like humanistic psychology, the emergence of organizational development as a field could be seen not only as consisting of a set of theories and techniques for intervening in organizations but also as a new philosophy and social movement (Mirvis, 1988).

The pioneering works of Lewin, Argyris, and McGregor were widely influential in disseminating humanistic psychology-based approaches by addressing the relationship between the individual and the institution from a humanistic rather than rational economic perspective. One of Argyris's (1957) first works was titled *Personality and Organization: The Conflict Between System and the Individual.* Earlier, Lewin's work, with his $B = f(p, e)$ formula (i.e., behavior is a function of person and environment), set the stage for an inquiry captured in the subtitle of Argyris's book. Lewin also challenged the view popularized by Frederick Taylor that men in groups (or "gangs," as

Taylor referred to them) were not to be trusted and, therefore, had to be controlled. Lewin looked at the positive dimensions of groups, and his influence in the field of organizational development is extremely far-reaching—from systems change, to teamwork, to participative methods and action research. The democratic focus of Lewin's work was continued in McGregor's famous formulation of Theories X and Y, which drew extensively on Maslow.

Organizational development has depended heavily on humanistic psychology's normative stance that people are ends in themselves and that interventions to change organizations and people are never "value free." In the field of general management as well, other important overviews, such as those of "management psychology" (Leavitt, Pondy, & Boje, 1980) and a special *Harvard Business Review* supplement on management classics, have included contributions of figures in humanistic psychology. Although the influence of humanistic psychology on organizational development and management practice undoubtedly has been extensive, the changing context of the socioeconomic environment beginning during the 1970s, and especially during the 1980s, resulted in what some theorists observed as an erosion of the core humanistic values that have informed and inspired organizational development theory and practice (Margulies & Raia, 1990; Mirvis, 1988; Schein, 1990).

Within the context of a more competitive and turbulent business environment, organizational development practitioners faced clients with pressures to improve the "bottom line." Now, managers wanted not so much a new philosophy but rather practical tools for securing their organizations' economic survival in a turbulent and unpredictable environment. In addition, managers no longer had the luxury of time for reflection,

personal growth, or any other activities that did not have pragmatic utilitarian outcomes. Certainly, by the mid-1970s, T-groups and other "group process"-type interventions were history—denigrated as being too "touchy-feely." More results-oriented interventions came into vogue, such as work redesign, total quality management, and (later) reengineering. Yet, even as the field of organizational development evolved from being a normative managerial philosophy and social movement to a utilitarian set of tools and techniques, the rhetoric of paying attention to the "human side of enterprise," the importance of having good "people skills," and similar humanistic-sounding concerns were mixed in the overall message. Despite the hard-nosed turn in the field, humanistic voices continue to be heard. The roots of organizational development theory and practice still draw their nourishment from the lifeblood of humanistic psychology.

MASLOW'S INFLUENCE

Maslow is unquestionably the central figure in the nexus between organization development and humanistic psychology. His theories on the hierarchy of needs, motivation, synergy, creativity, self-actualization, and "enlightened management" continue to be enormously influential. (See, e.g., *Maslow on Management* [1965/1998; originally titled *Eupsychian Management*] for a recent volume based on notes on his research at Non-Linear Systems during the early 1960s.)

Why is Maslow's work still so popular and relevant? Answering this question may afford us an insight into the future not only of organizational development but also of humanistic psychology. Maslow believed that the industrial situation could serve as the new laboratory for the study of psychodynamics, of high human development, and of the ideal ecology for the human. Early on, Maslow realized that the world of work offered an important locus for both the study of humans and the realization of human potential. The whole prospect of fostering "human potential in the workplace" was a radical dramatic shift from earlier times when workers were treated simply as "cogs in a machine." Under Taylor's so-called scientific management, workers were not expected to think or be creative; rather, they were expected to perform their tasks in a precise and prescribed manner as determined by industrial engineering standards. Since the early 1900s, scientific management (or "Taylorism") was the dominant management philosophy. Hourly workers were viewed as having to adapt to the requirements of the technology. Indeed, humans in the industrialized Taylorized workplace were viewed as extensions of the machine.

In contrast to viewing workers as automatons, Maslow considered that employees aspired to more than simply working for paychecks. After "lower order needs" for security were satisfied, the design and management of the workplace would have to change so as to become a locus for human development and to promote the possibilities for self-actualization. Maslow viewed individuals holistically—as full humans in all their complexity—rather than simply reducing them to interchangeable "hired hands" designed to perform specific tasks and only those tasks. Such a radical reformulation of human needs, and indeed of the nature of the relationship between work and humans, turned the entire Taylorist mentality upside down, creating a major paradigm shift (at least in theory) toward the way in which the workplace was conceptualized. The shift is parallel to the revolution in psychology ushered in by humanistic psychology, which focused away from

pathology and the achievement of "normalcy" to the exploration of the farther reaches of human nature and exceptional functioning.

The inspired focus of Maslow and humanistic psychology can be seen in the attention that has been given recently to enhancing creativity and innovation in industry. *Synergy,* a term that Maslow borrowed from Margaret Mead, is now a popular buzzword and captures the potential of a creative and mutually beneficial collaboration. The importance of listening in managerial communication, a point stressed in an often cited article by Rogers and Roethlisberger (1982), is still at the heart of most work on communication and keeps being resurrected in a variety of forms. Maslow's stress on holistic and organic ways of thinking rather than atomistic ones predates the trend toward "systems thinking" in management.

But whereas these areas of organizational development are still vibrant, the impact of humanistic psychology has been lessened as references to the originators of these concepts have become fewer. Furthermore, fewer original contributions from new generations of humanistic psychologists appear, and the theoretical innovations and contributions in humanistic psychology have diminished considerably since the heyday of Maslow, May, and Rogers. We argue that this reflects the need both to reexplore the contributions of seminal figures such as Maslow, Rogers, and May, addressing both their strengths and weaknesses in the organizational context, and to develop innovative new theoretical perspectives explicitly based in humanistic psychology. As we will see, the concerns addressed by humanistic psychology and the existential-humanistic tradition are very much at the forefront of social and economic trends today, so a vital contribution remains to be made.

Maslow (1965/1998) offered a very important and still neglected insight regarding the importance of searching for "far goals" of the enterprise:

> I've seen very few of these managers or writers on organizational theory who have the courage to think in far terms, in broad-range terms, in utopian terms, in value terms. Generally, they feel they're being hard-headed if they use as the criteria of management success or of healthy organization criteria of smaller labor turnover or less absenteeism or better morale or more profit and the like. But in so doing, they neglect the whole Eupsychian growth and self-actualization and personal development side of the enterprise. (p. 49)

In many respects, Maslow's work on the need to search for these meta-goals for the enterprise was extremely prescient given that a number of progressive organizations are starting to engage their members in developing long-range and shared visions for the enterprises (Porras & Collins, 1997; Senge, 1990). Indeed, Maslow's call for searching for the higher purposes of the enterprise is now actually being practiced through many of the popular "large-group intervention" methods in organizational development (Bunker & Alban, 1996). The "search conference" (Emery & Purser, 1996), for example, is designed to elicit "ideal-seeking" behavior in organizational participants as articulate images of their most desirable futures for their enterprises.

IMPORTING HUMANISTIC PSYCHOLOGY

As we have seen, the works of the pioneers of humanistic psychology, such as those of Maslow and Rogers, have been imported into organizational development theory and practice. But this importation has not been unproblematic. Rogers, for example, was concerned from the start that his work might be trivialized, and Kramer (1995) showed convincingly that it has been. For Rogers, active listening was not a tool to improve productivity; instead, it was a way of establishing a different type of relationship between managers and workers, one that was authentic, nondirective, and a way of releasing the creativity of the relationship rather than a way of exercising supervisory power over someone. As Kramer aptly pointed out, in many cases the idea has been taken to mean that listening can be a way of establishing control, maintaining managerial prerogatives, and engaging in inauthentic "image management." In so doing, it gives the appearance of listening without actually doing so, let alone exploring the profound implications of what Rogers intended.

Although Rogers intended active listening to be a transformative vehicle for moving toward greater democracy, participation, and actualization, in actual practice active listening was reduced to yet another management "tool" in the service of maintaining and upholding existing power relations and bureaucratic organizational structures. Within this context, it became almost impossible to truly practice active listening given that the fundamental presuppositions regarding information flow, roles, and power differentials were not addressed. Active listening, therefore, had implications that went far beyond a mere technique or a psychologizing of relationships. The humanizing aspects of organizational development and human relations programs did not explicitly or even implicitly address the nature of authority, the business environment, organizational structures, and other factors that went beyond the scope of psychology. Even many well-meaning efforts to apply active listening were often ineffective when they occurred within an inhospitable organizational context and in conjunction with inconsistent norms and organizational structures that were antithetical to the idea of developing greater individual creativity and responsibility. It should come as no surprise why so many humanistic organizational development initiatives at the micro level were doomed to failure from the start.

This brings us to the issue of the trivialization of important concepts derived from humanistic psychology. We contend that transformational theories and concepts become trivialized when they are reduced to being merely tools, techniques, or rhetorical slogans, especially when they are used unreflectively within organizational settings. Rather than promoting an honest, reflective, and open inquiry into the nature of organizational problems or human possibilities for self-actualization, the creative fire of transformation is quickly extinguished to the ashes of technique. The technique is encapsulated within the limits and safe boundaries of instrumentalized discourse, which is narrowly concerned with finding the best and most efficient means of achieving some preestablished managerial end.

The implications of Maslow's thinking about organizations, and the implications of the application of humanistic psychology to organizations, go far beyond the application of tools and techniques. They require the development of an entire management philosophy that goes radically against the grain of Taylorism, as we have seen. For humanistic psychology to make any profound inroads into organizations, it also must address the relationship of the human side of enterprise with the technical and bottom-line concerns. But it cannot pit itself against those concerns either. It cannot isolate itself in a separate compartment, with values that are not somehow reconciled with the economic survival of the organization. In other words, "hard" and "soft" values must be coherent so as to avoid the typical pitfall whereby the soft humanistic concern operates within the context of rational-economic strategies that permit the soft only as a form of concession to "the human factor" rather than as an essential part of organizational life and performance. And this stance requires a fundamental rethinking of the nature of the enterprise, one that does not subsume human issues under rational-economic concerns and, therefore, eliminates all organizational development programs, for example, at the first sign of economic trouble.

This situation suggests that the field of organizational development and the implications of humanistic psychology need to move beyond the level of tactical intervention and take on a strategic role as part of a larger integrated management philosophy and organizational theory. This task requires a transdisciplinary approach that is contextual, multidimensional, and transformative in the sense of making explicit and challenging fundamental assumptions. Already, some of the so-called best companies to work for, such as Southwest Airlines, SAS, and Semco (in Brazil), are demonstrating the power of "putting people first" while thriving economically.

RESEARCH

In the realm of organizational development theory and practice, Cooperrider and Srivastva (1987) questioned a fundamental premise of action research, arguing that the behavioral sciences had ignored the potential to tap the "generative capacity" of theory. Inspired by humanistic psychology, they stated,

If we acknowledge Abraham Maslow's (1968) admonition that true science begins and ends in wonder, then we immediately shed light on why action research has failed to produce innovative theory capable of inspiring the imagination, commitment, and passionate dialogue required for consensual re-ordering of social conduct. (p. 131)

They went on to develop a new organizational development intervention method, "appreciative inquiry," in what amounts to an alternative to the traditional problem-finding/problem-solving orientation of the action research method. However, Cooperrider and Srivastva argued that appreciative inquiry is not just another organizational development method or technique but rather is more akin to a "mode of inquiry" that is oriented to eliciting fresh and imaginative possibilities for organizing or, in their words, "images of what might be." Their approach, which pays a great deal of attention to the socially constructed nature of organized meanings, could be seen as an emergent process of dialogical "self-system actualization."

Qualitative research methodologies drawing on humanistic psychology that stress the value of individual experience, subjectivity, and meaning making are making significant inroads. They include collaborative, cooperative, and heuristic research methods, drawing on phenomenology pioneered by Reason, Rowan, Seely-Brown, Torbert, Moustakas, and others. Here, the role of the researcher becomes participative and collaborative rather than that of an outsider manipulating variables "objectively" in imitation of the methods of natural science. The purpose of these methodologies is to gain an understanding of the lived experience of the co-researchers rather than to measure. With the new emphasis on cus-

tomization rather than on mass production, and with an emerging focus on individualized management rather than on generic approaches, an understanding of the subjective experience of managers, workers, and customers will become increasingly important. Qualitative approaches, grounded in humanistic psychology, are set to make an important contribution to the development of new knowledge in business.

THE FUTURE

Humanistic psychology has always focused on organic holistic approaches and understandings of the human. Therefore, it is surprising that there has been little (if any) attempt to reconcile and synergize humanistic psychology with general systems theory and its offshoots (e.g., systems dynamics, critical systems theory, living systems theory, soft systems theory) beyond the work of Krippner, Ruttenber, Engelman, and Granger (1985), who wrote an exploratory article addressing the potential implications of this cross-pollination, and the work of Merry and Brown combining Gestalt theory and systems theory. Given the growing popularity of systems approaches in industry (see Senge, 1990) and their potential compatibility with humanistic psychology, which (through Maslow) already is imbued with an organic holistic approach, this is an area that offers the potential for important work. The tendency has been for systemic concepts and approaches to be borrowed directly from the natural sciences without drawing on the extensive theory and research base provided by holistic approaches in the social sciences that, unlike the natural sciences, have made classic contributions to our understanding of values, meaning, identity, and the like. Indeed, humanistic psychologists have also been quite critical of systems-theoretical approaches precisely because of this and because of their emphasis on social forces and the tradition in humanistic psychology to view the individual as struggling against social and cultural forces to establish authenticity and identity. The opportunity now exists to make the connection between the implicit holism in humanistic psychology and systems approaches and to fully flesh out the theoretical, philosophical, and practical implications.

The emerging interest and impact of feminist perspectives on organizational development and the world of work is also, in many respects, closely aligned with humanistic psychology. The focus on interconnectedness, caring, individual uniqueness, and emotions, and on what have been called stereotypically "feminine" values and concerns, reflects some of the similar issues that humanistic psychology has addressed (e.g., Eisler, 1994). The focus on context, the whole person, the integration of reason and emotion, and real lived experience, as opposed to rational-economic abstraction, offers further opportunities for the development of an alternative, more inclusive perspective on organizational life.

The relationship between the individual and the organization is a further issue that needs to be addressed by humanistic psychology and organizational development. Revisiting this thorny philosophical issue should add important debate and new theoretical developments to humanistic psychology. Historically, humanistic psychology practitioners and some theorists who have been psychologists rather than in the field of organizational development have resisted any attempts to develop a theoretical perspective on the individual that explicitly recognizes social systems as anything but forces militating against the individual's

authenticity and creativity and have viewed the individual as defining himself or herself in opposition to social forces (Montuori & Purser, 1995, 1996). Humanistic psychology theorists would benefit from the lessons learned in organizational development, starting with the work of Lewin, to reassess the nature of this relationship, explore its potential for creativity and human betterment, and develop a theoretical perspective that recognizes the socially embedded nature of the individual without relinquishing the vitally important elements of choice, authenticity, and personal growth. Organizational development would benefit from a closer look at the focus of humanistic psychology on precisely those very elements and from stressing the importance of human dignity in the face of potential manipulation and the trivialization of concepts such as creativity and growth strictly for the benefit of the organization.

The work of Pauchant and Associates (1995) on "organizational existentialism" was a particularly intriguing development. It explicitly grounds thinking about, and acting in, organizations in humanistic-existential psychology and philosophy. In the collection of essays, Pauchant and Associates addressed topics ranging from the legacy of Rank and Frankl to trenchant critiques of the concept of "excellence," which, interestingly enough, they traced back to the influence (and misreading) of Ernest Becker in the classic work by Peters and Waterman (1982). Of particular importance here is challenging fundamental assumptions in the management literature from a humanistic-existentialist perspective, addressing the philosophical underpinnings of the positions, and challenging the humanistic rhetoric. This is a particularly welcome perspective precisely because, as we have seen, there is so much use made of overtly humanistic language in much management literature. In the case of the "excellence myth," it is a rhetoric designed to appeal to "heroic" instincts, to the "be all that you can be" mentality channeled into the workplace, and to the striving for an unattainable "excellence."

The purpose of this critique of excellence is not simply to illustrate a philosophical misreading or, for that matter, to expose the potentially manipulative aspects of the rhetoric. It is also to illustrate how such philosophically problematic positions eventually may be self-defeating and hurt not only the "human side of enterprise" but also the bottom line. Here is the important difference of the thrust of organizational existentialism. As Pauchant and Associates (1995) carefully pointed out, their objective was not only to address the human side of enterprise but also to contextualize it within organizational realities. Their work points to an exciting application of humanistic-existential thought that grounds it fully in its historical and philosophical complexity *and* in the realities of organizational life. This would place it at the heart of an emerging trend in what can only be called "practical philosophy" or the application of philosophical insights to everyday life and, consequently, also to work.

Social trends indicating a renewed interest in meaning and values and a move toward a "postmaterialist" society (see Inglehart, 1997) suggest that the time is right for a new wave of humanistic psychology and existential-humanistic theorizing and practice. In a postmaterialist economy, concepts such as "meaning," particularly in the context of work, become increasingly important and have far-reaching consequences for areas from mental health to motivation but also for the potential emergence of new values and new ways of working and organizing. The new technology

that is having such a huge effect on the economy must also be addressed. Our global interconnectedness, for example, has the potential to create a global village and bring people from different cultures and with different belief systems together in dialogue. At the same time, that very connectivity can be used as a way of ensuring that a worker is never outside the sphere of influence of the organization, with a consequent blurring of spatio-temporal boundaries. Workers can literally be "on call" 24 hours a day, with substantial potential for exploitative practices.

Humanistic psychology, because of its existential-phenomenological tradition, is in a unique position to explore the lived experience of work today during such an incredible period of transition. Because of its strong philosophical roots (e.g., the works of Heidegger and Barrett on technology), humanistic psychology can be interpretive, descriptive, and critical and can offer potential alternatives grounded in humanistic principles.

CONCLUSION

Humanistic psychology has made significant contributions to the discourse and practices of organizational behavior and development. The opportunity has arisen to make further contributions in this area. As we have seen, social and business trends point to a new interest and relevance for the concerns addressed by the humanistic and existential tradition. For these contributions to be made, and for humanistic psychologists to seize this opportunity, we make the following suggestions.

First, reexamine the history of humanistic psychology ideas in the workplace—their applicability and their trivialization. Maslow and Rogers both were concerned with the possibility of trivialization and exclusively experience-focused anti-intellectualism, so we urge organizational development and humanistic psychology theorists and practitioners to study this history and return to the original works of the founders of humanistic psychology—Maslow, Rogers, May, and others—to reacquaint ourselves with the depth and scope of their work. We also suggest the need to go into the philosophical precursors of these authors—Nietzsche, Kierkegaard, Husserl, Heidegger, Camus, Sartre, and others—and assess their contributions in light of the present economic and social environment.

Second, contextualize efforts at organizational change in larger social and economic environments. One of the problems with early human relations efforts was their separation from the economic and organizational structure and bureaucratic dimensions. Following Maslow's stress on organic and systemic thinking, humanistic psychology practitioners and theorists must become transdisciplinary and aware of the embeddedness of individual and psychological change in large systems that may, more often than not, militate against the changes that are being suggested and sought.

Third, inject theoretical innovation explicitly grounded in the roots of humanistic psychology. Much of humanistic psychology's contribution to organizational and behavior and development discourse has been diluted beyond recognition, with little or no recognition of its sources. This suggests not only the extent of humanistic psychology's inroads into the field but also the manner in which it has become marginalized, to some extent, as the sources were discarded. Humanistic psychology needs an injection of new theoretical perspectives that address some of the achievements and shortcomings of humanistic psychology and also some of the inherent tensions in humanistic psychology that have been continually problematic and have prevented it from making more powerful contributions both in psychology and in the workplace.

REFERENCES

Argyris, C. (1957). *Personality and organization: The conflict between the system and the individual.* New York: Harper & Row.

Bunker, B. B., & Alban, B. I. (1996). *Large group change.* San Francisco: Jossey-Bass.

Cooperrider, D., & Srivastva, S. (1987). Appreciative inquiry in organizational life. In R. Woodman & W. A. Pasmore (Eds.), *Research in organizational change and development* (Vol. 1). Greenwich, CT: JAI.

Eisler, R. (1994). From domination to partnership: The hidden subtext for sustainable change. *Journal of Organizational Change Management, 7,* 4.

Emery, M., & Purser, R. (1996). *The search conference.* San Francisco: Jossey-Bass.

Greiner, L. (1980). *OD values and the bottom line.* Unpublished manuscript, University of Southern California, Graduate School of Business, Los Angeles.

Inglehart, R. (1997). *Modernization and postmodernization: Cultural, economic, and social change in 43 countries.* Princeton, NJ: Princeton University Press.

Kramer, R. (1995). Carl Rogers meets Otto Rank: The discovery of relationship. In T. Pauchant & Associates (Eds.), *In search of meaning.* San Francisco: Jossey-Bass.

Krippner, S., Ruttenber, A. J., Engelman, S. R., & Granger, D. L. (1985). Towards the application of general systems theory in humanistic psychology. *Systems Research, 2*, 105-115.

Leavitt, H. R., Pondy, L. R., & Boje, D. M. (1980). *Readings in managerial psychology.* Chicago: University of Chicago Press.

Margulies, N., & Raia, A. (1990). The significance of core values on the theory and practice of organizational development. In F. Massarik (Ed.), *Advances in organization development* (Vol. 1). Norwood, NJ: Ablex.

Maslow, A. H. (1968). *Toward a psychology of being.* New York: Van Nostrand Reinhold.

Maslow, A. H. (1998). *Maslow on management.* New York: John Wiley. (Original work published 1965)

Mirvis, P. (1988). Organization development: Part I—An evolutionary perspective. In W. A. Pasmore & R. Woodman (Eds.), *Research in organizational change and development* (Vol. 2). Greenwich, CT: JAI.

Montuori, A., & Purser, R. (1995). Deconstructing the lone genius myth: Towards a contextual view of creativity. *Journal of Humanistic Psychology, 35*(3), 69-112.

Montuori, A., & Purser, R. (1996). Context and creativity: Beyond social determinism and the isolated genius—A rejoinder to Hale. *Journal of Humanistic Psychology, 36*(2), 34-43.

Pauchant, T., & Associates. (Eds.). (1995). *In search of meaning.* San Francisco: Jossey-Bass.

Peters, T., & Waterman, R. (1982). *In search of excellence.* New York: Warner.

Porras, J. C., & Collins, J. I. (1997). *Built to last.* New York: HarperCollins.

Rogers, C., & Roethlisberger, F. J. (1982). Barriers and gateways to communication. In *Business classics: Fifteen concepts for managerial success.* Boston: Harvard Business Review.

Schein, E. (1990). Back to the future: Recapturing OD vision. In F. Massarik (Ed.), *Advances in organization development* (Vol. 1). Norwood, NJ: Ablex.

Senge, P. (1990). *The fifth discipline.* New York: Doubleday.

Tannenbaum, R., & Davis, S. (1967). Values, man, and organizations. *Industrial Relations, 9*, 197-214.

Part VI

EPILOGUE:
HUMANISTIC
PSYCHOLOGY AT
THE MILLENNIUM

Introduction to Part VI

I N THIS FINAL PART of the volume, we are afforded the chance to pause, take our collective breath, and consider the meaning of the volume in light of the new millennium. The chief questions of this section are as follows. Where is humanistic psychology headed today? What are the major challenges it faces? What are the implications of these challenges for psychology as a whole?

In Chapter 48, Arthur Warmoth provides a detailed commentary on Old Saybrook 2, a landmark humanistic conference held at the State University of West Georgia in May 2000. Old Saybrook 2 is a sequel to the 1964 meeting at Old Saybrook, Connecticut, that is generally considered to be the launching point for organized humanistic psychology. Whereas a handful of luminaries attended the original Old Saybrook conference (e.g., Bugental, May, Maslow, Rogers, Allport), more than 100 such scholars attended Old Saybrook 2. In illuminating fashion, Warmoth reviews the highlights of the conference, considers their relevance to the present volume, and draws out their contemporary significance. For Warmoth, these highlights comprise a "rich" mix of "spiritual ideology, democratic values, and professional aspirations," and they pose timely and urgent challenges to professionals and consumers alike.

In Chapter 49, Michael Mahoney and Sean Mahoney provide an eloquent reflection on the current ambiguities facing both humanistic psychology as well as mainstream psychology. Echoing Warmoth's distillation and drawing liberally from the humanistic-existential tradition, Mahoney and Mahoney make the key point that wherever psychology polarizes, it becomes devitalized. On the other hand, wherever psychology embraces tensions and polarities, it evolves, expands, and renews its potentialities. During an era of quick fixes and pat answers, the question of psychology's encounter with ambiguity is evocative, and despairingly few seem to be raising it. Mahoney and Mahoney, however, challenge psychology—as well as polarizing forces within humanistic psychology—to acknowledge our multifaceted nature and to pioneer what is possible rather than merely resigning to what exists. .

In their closing statements, the editors distill their respective reflections on this volume. James Bugental recognizes the ambitiousness of the humanistic undertaking, challenges the dependency needs of objectified psychology, and calls for the careful building of a profound yet complementary humanistic vision. In her poignant style, J. Fraser Pierson relates the breadth and vibrancy of the humanistic quest. By discovering our selves through others, she concludes, humanistic psychology is becoming a planetary psychology—a psychology for all life. Kirk Schneider closes the volume with a hopeful review of humanistic developments. He perceives the contrails of an emerging personalism in psychology, and he calls on all who resonate with this volume to engage and advance it.

CHAPTER 48

The Old Saybrook 2 Report and the Outlook for the Future

ARTHUR WARMOTH

THE OLD SAYBROOK 2 Conference took place at the State University of West Georgia in Carrollton during May 11-14, 2000. Subtitled "Coming Home to the New Millennium," the conference was hosted by the Department of Psychology and used Harrison Owen's "Open Space" process, which was facilitated by organization development consultant John D. Adams. The aim of the conference, a sequel to the 1964 gathering at Old Saybrook, Connecticut, that formalized humanistic psychology, was to reassess and re-vision contemporary humanistic psychology. In light of this context, there are a number of themes that are found in the present volume that echo the discussions and proceedings of the Old Saybrook 2 Conference (2000). These include the following:

▶ The contemporary relevance of the values and theories of humanistic psychology

▶ The central role of the study of human experience in psychology

▶ The relationship between humanistic psychology's philosophy of science and the varieties of postmodern philosophy

▶ The timeliness of broadening the horizons of humanistic practice

Both the conference and the present volume demonstrate that contemporary humanistic psychology is a rich ragout whose ingredients include a mix of spiritual ideology, democratic values, and professional aspirations.

The spiritual ideology is largely defined by the field of transpersonal psychology. Transpersonal psychology embraces a worldview that incorporates elements of personal mysticism, oriental philosophy, and universal cosmology in proportions that vary among theorists and practitioners. Its views of human potential, wholeness, nature, and the self place it in the intellectual tradition of modern era romanticism, particularly as romanticism has been played out by liberal Judeo-Protestant middle class culture. It can also point to roots in the distinctively American heritage of transcendentalism and the related communal spiritual movements that are documented by Taylor (1999) in his recent book, *Shadow Culture*. Taylor called this the "visionary tradition" in American "folk psychology," but it also might be called a tradition of "personal mysticism" or "cosmic consciousness" (the latter is R. M. Bucke's term and was an important influence on Maslow's concept of the "peak experience").

Humanistic psychology's democratic values and aspirations reflect a broader liberal tradition. These values can be seen as an extension of Rogers's key elements of effective psychotherapy—congruence, unconditional positive regard, and empathic listening—to the larger social-political arena. *Congruence* can be understood as personal integrity, a certain amount of which in politicians and citizens is the sine qua non of the democratic process. *Unconditional positive regard* is a somewhat stilted rephrasing of the democratic values of acceptance, tolerance, and inclusion. *Empathic listening* is the intimate version of the basic democratic processes of dialogue, conversation, and civic discourse. The commitment of the conference participants to democratic principles was evident in value statements that found their way into the conference proceedings (e.g., "deep respect for diversity of every type including contradiction and fragmentation," "prizing of each individual and way of understanding") and a general commitment to inclusion expressed in the following ideal: "One world unified transcends ethnicity, religion, [and] nationality." (Some contradictions inherent in this latter aspiration are discussed later.)

Finally, there was a clear sense of working to expand the professional applications of the field beyond the established arena of psychotherapy. This undoubtedly reflected, in part, the fact that the licensed practice of psychology is under siege as a result of pressures from the managed care industry in concert with the responses to those pressures being orchestrated by professional psychology through organizations such as the American Psychological Association (APA) and state licensing boards. But it also reflected an authentic sense of unfulfilled potential. As many participants pointed out, this potential is suggested by already existing professions such as organization development and humanistic higher education. But as Maureen O'Hara, a member of the planning committee, suggested, "There is a tremendous potential today because everyone knows that our [institutional] systems are broken." She also suggested that this sense of the failure of our institutions was not nearly as widespread during the 1960s and 1970s when humanistic psychology was being developed. It is true that one element of the counterculture of the 1960s was a radical political critique of the aesthetic and moral failures of capitalism. By and large, however, radical politics and the human potential movement kept each other at arm's length. Most of the energy of the human potential movement went into adapting anxious psyches to the realities of what was, for most, objectively (i.e., economically) a reasonably comfortable lifestyle.

The group exploring the question of who the new populations of clients should be came to the conclusion that there are plenty of situations in which traditional humanistic skills are applicable. These skills include active listening, honesty, willingness to take personal risks, and serving as facilitators of dialogue and conversation (particularly where the focus is on conflict resolution and cooperative problem solving). From this perspective, the center of gravity of humanistic practice appears to be close to the basic skills of friendship, love, conviviality and fellowship, and good citizenship. When combined with technical skills and adequate objective information about the parameters of the system in question, these humanistic psychology skills can be useful in a wide variety of organizational and community settings where issues of morale, diversity, and social justice need to be addressed.

In some ways, the most interesting (and longest) report was generated by the group that took on the following questions:

1. How are we shooting ourselves in the foot? What can we do to stop it?
2. What are our biggest known challenges?
3. What opportunities could/should we capitalize on?

The issues the group identified include naïveté about the goodness of human nature, avoidance of rigor, romanticizing of the past, naïveté about realpolitik, being poor at organization and coordination, rationalizing ourselves as "science" ("scientism") and ignoring our roots in the humanist tradition, emphasis on reaction rather than on positive agendas, rejection of other approaches (e.g., positivism) rather than working with them, failure to operationalize the value and practice of prevention, insularity, failure to reach out to the student generation, "camps" within humanistic-existential-transpersonal psychology and failure to articulate a common theory and values, failure to practice listening/respect/compassion, and failure to honor relationships with those who hold other points of view.

I contend that these self-inflicted barriers encountered by organized humanistic psychology orbit primarily around two issues:

▶ An inadequate understanding of the historical and cultural context of our focus on spiritual experience, values, and ideology
▶ Our limited vision, at least in terms of praxis, of the research agenda called for by humanistic theory and values

The insufficient contextualization of our spiritual/cultural identity reflects our failure to transcend the universality assumption received from our Judeo-Protestant heritage. (This assumption is shared by all of the children of Abraham including Islam.) Our too narrow research agenda reflects our failure to transcend the received institutional framework of academic disciplines.

Both of these failures are corollary to the deeper failure of nerve of our economic acquiescence in modernistic versions of medical model psychotherapy and compartmentalized academic disciplines. These are social categorizations that reflect modernism's values of scientism, consumerism, objectification, and cultural universalism. And they account, at least in part, for the divergence of the human potential movement and radical institutional critique during the 1960s mentioned earlier. In the university, the separation of radical politics and the human potential movement was abetted by disciplinary boundaries between sociology and psychology. In the larger community, it was supported by social, racial, and gender differences. Those with status and power tended to emphasize issues of personal choice and competitive competency, and they often channeled their interests into medicalized psychotherapy. Those without status and power tended to focus on the unjust and corrupt characteristics of the dominant system. Perhaps the most successful bridging of these two perspectives has taken place within the women's movement, which, at least in its most comprehensive expressions, seeks institutional changes that will facilitate both personal and social development.

In my view, a more adequate perspective can be gained by adding the postmodern constructionist perspective (Berger & Luckmann, 1966) to the foundational insights of humanistic psychology—the epistemological centrality of the data of human experience and holism or what has come to be called "systems theory" (Warmoth, 1998). Such an approach would be self-reflective about the complexity of the symbolic processes of the social construction of knowledge and, thereby, of social reality. Therefore, it would necessarily be interdisciplinary. It also would be more effective in supporting the humanistic values of inclusion, collaboration, and community (which are also the core values of democratic politics) and in dealing with the realities of a multicultural global society. Furthermore, it would contribute to sophisticated strategies for the advocacy of the ecologically sustainable design of human systems.

TRANSPERSONAL PSYCHOLOGY AS A SPIRITUALITY-BASED SUBCULTURE

It is clear that a large majority of the saving remnant that still identifies with humanistic psychology also identifies in one way or another with transpersonal psychology. There is also a significant segment of American society at large that embraces transpersonal practices, values, and ideas (if not the transpersonal label). Ray (1996) called this group the "cultural creatives," and he estimated them to approach a quarter of the population.

Transpersonal practices include many drawn from Eastern and Native American cultures including meditation, yoga, martial arts, shamanic healing, and vision quests. All of these practices are centered in a belief in personal mysticism and the possibility that personal discipline can lead to universal consciousness or wisdom. The practices also include a range of alternative holistic approaches to healing that are understood from a variety of perspectives ranging from the psychological, to the organic, to the somatic—osteopathy, chiropractic, herbalism, jin shin jyutsu, raiki, acupuncture, biofeedback, somatics, bioenergetics, the methods of Ida Rolf and Moshe Feldenkrais, therapeutic touch, crystal healing, and so forth.

These practices tend to be organized around a set of values historically central to the romantic protest against rationalistic industrial modernism—belief in the goodness of the person and of nature; trust in intuition, the emotions, and personal mysticism (i.e., peak experiences); and an affirmation of the necessity of personal creativity. They also tend to be organized around cosmological ideas, frequently influenced by oriental philosophy, proclaiming cosmic consciousness, universal wisdom, or perennial philosophy. Psychological versions include the collective unconscious of Jung and the evolutionary hierarchy of Wilber. Recent, less universalistic psychologies making room for the tradition of personal mysticism include the romantic psychology of Schneider (1998; see also the first chapter by Schneider [Chapter 6] in this volume) and the personal mythology of Feinstein and Krippner (1997; see also the chapter by Feinstein [Chapter 15] in this volume).

The crucial question that I believe the field has not yet faced is whether the perennial philosophy being proclaimed transcends culture, as many would like to believe, or whether it represents the most recent expression of a particularly American cultural history and identity. Taylor (1999) made a strong case for the second alternative.

To view transpersonal psychology as the heart of a specific cultural or ethnic identity, rather than as a universal religion, does not detract from its value. On the contrary, it reaffirms several specific values *as* values rather than falling into the scientistic messianism of proclaiming them as universal truth. These values include the importance of personal spiritual discipline and insight as well as an affirmation of the value of all human life and of the holistic integrity of nature grounded in our spontaneous aesthetic responses to both life and nature.

However, placing this subculture in its historical context actually deepens its meaning by emphasizing that its values are best realized through civic or social engagement and must embrace, rather than gloss over, the dark side of the human soul. It also suggests that the professional roles that are appropriate for those who identify with this heritage are to be found as much in the humanities—philosophy, literature, and the arts—as in the natural and social sciences.

As Taylor (1999) pointed out, this stream of cultural development has itself been pluralistic. The version that resonates most fully with modern transpersonal psychology was the 19th-century transcendentalism of Emerson, Thoreau, and the Concord group; the authors Hawthorne and Melville; and the naturalists John Muir and John Chapman ("Johnny Appleseed"). But other expressions of this American impulse include the Quakers, Shakers, and Swedenborgians (imported from Europe) as well as Christian Science, Mormonism, and Theosophy (born on American soil). One of the paradoxical characteristics of these

American spiritual movements is that although they share in the Judeo-Protestant tendency to proclaim universal truth, their practical fruits (by which, according to the gospel, "ye shall know them") primarily included Thoreau's philosophy of civil disobedience and a spate of utopian communities that dotted the 19th-century landscape. To me, this suggests that wisdom in this tradition might lie more in the direction of responsible collaborative social action aimed at community building rather than in the direction of the proclamation of a new universal religion.

A dispassionate assessment of our particular cultural tradition suggests that it includes an individualistic bias that emphasizes personal values and beliefs and downplays the importance of shared or intersubjective values, beliefs, and iconographies. Yet, it is these shared symbolic constructions that—along with their objectified projections in texts, art, architecture, and technology—are the basis for all human social organization and institutions, ranging in scale from families and tribes to mighty civilizations. Our tradition has a great deal to say about the emancipation of the individual through the social forms of democracy, and these messages are demonstrating broad cross-cultural appeal in the postmodern world. But other cultures have much to teach us about the structure and dynamics of intersubjectivity and cultural identity, lessons that can be learned only through openness to cross-cultural exploration.

These considerations do not vitiate the value of strivings by humanistic-existential-transpersonal psychologists for definitive philosophical statements in the areas of epistemology (theory of knowledge), ontology (theory of being or of the "nature of things"), and axiology (theory of value). However, they require that our epistemology incorporate the phenomenology of multiple culturally/historically situated worldviews. They also point to an ontology that recognizes a universal human nature that undertakes the construction both of cultural contexts and of individual personalities as well as to an axiology whose respect for all human life includes a valuing of both ethnic and personal identities.

Global integration today is not being propelled by any particular spiritual vision. It is being driven by the economic institutions of capitalism and by technological innovation (particularly in the communications media), sometimes tempered and sometimes propelled by the political forces and institutions of democracy. The intriguing question is whether politics can democratize capitalism before economics capitalizes democracy, devouring the natural and human resources of the planet in the process. In other words, can democracy produce sustainability and social justice in time?

Spiritual intuition and values can play an important role in motivating the needed political action. But the world will be a far more interesting place if the politics is based on an appeal to fairly universal values found in many different cultural contexts (e.g., as respect for life and the integrity of nature) and implemented within a democratic framework of respect for the diversity of religions and cultural traditions than it would be if we count on a universal conversion to the perennial philosophy (Huxley, 1972).[1]

The psychological versions of the perennial philosophy belong to the tradition of romantic protest against our hyperintellectual, print-driven Western civilization. This is an honorable tradition that has offered an essential emotional and aesthetic counterbalance to the dominant culture. But understanding the role of romantic protest

in the larger context of cultural history is essential if we hope to adequately orient ourselves to the complexities of a multicultural global society.

TOWARD PROBLEM-CENTERED INTERDISCIPLINARY RESEARCH AGENDAS

Acknowledging our cultural context and history is the key to not being bound by it. Humanistic psychology began during the 1960s supported by powerful utopian aspirations for emancipation and human fulfillment. Those aspirations today call for humanistic psychology to embrace three complementary missions:

1. Articulate an epistemology adequate for today's circumstances that recognizes the centrality of conscious communication and reflection in human affairs.
2. Participate in healing the wounds inflicted by the hyperintellectualism of the dominant and largely patriarchal worldview (as represented in the United States and other technologically advanced democracies).
3. Develop research strategies and professional roles that are effective in solving human problems.

The effervescent idealism of the founding generation has led to major cultural paradigm shifts in the areas of education, mental health, and management. But much of the organizational energy generated during this period has been channeled into the received social forms of clinical psychology and academic disciplines rather than leading to the creation of the new institutional forms that are called for today.

Humanistic psychology has rightly stood for the centrality of consciousness and personal identity in psychotherapy and the social and behavioral sciences. However, our thinking about the research and professional strategies that grow from this centrality has been constrained by our perceived need to advocate for the phenomena within the received institutional forms of academic discipline and clinical practice. Although this adaptation might represent a commonsensical response to the realities of career politics during the last third of the 20th century, the limitations of strategies based on established social forms are rapidly becoming apparent. It may be a good time to return to the wisdom of Maslow's (1954) "Problem Centering vs. Means Centering in Science" and ask the following question: What are the research strategies that are needed to address the major problems of our time?

There is room to argue about just what the most critical problems are, but I wager that the headings "sustainability," "violence," and "poverty" would include the topics on most of our lists. It is clear that the experience of participants in ecological self-destruction, interpersonal and tribal violence, and the complex dimensions of the cycle of poverty is an important element that needs to be understood in addressing these problems. And these concerns apply not only to the experience of the obvious victims of dysfunctional systems but also to the experience and choices of anyone involved in perpetuating these systems. Therefore, the phenomenological and experiential methods that have been developed by humanistic psychologists clearly are relevant, as are the action research methodologies that have been devised to guide effective organizational and community development.

However, a moment's reflection on the complexity of each of these problems suggests the value of a more imaginative inter-disciplinary approach. None of these problems is likely to be dealt with effectively unless we can mobilize strategies that combine phenomenological insight with objective technical information and intersubjective demographic and sociological systems information and also incorporate the creative imagination of the arts and humanities.

All of these problems share two common characteristics. First, although there are areas where global action is needed (e.g., global warming, currency reform, international terrorism, child labor in manufacturing, the HIV epidemic in Africa), in the advanced industrial democracies, these problems can be solved only at the level of the local community. Second, they all involve an element of the common well-being or public good that requires coalescing political will and community resources into effective public attitudes and policies. This understanding suggests two paths open to humanistic psychologists who are educated in self-awareness and deep reflection on the human condition:

1. Develop proficiency with a broad range of research tools.
2. Develop the ability to facilitate public participation and coordinate interdisciplinary research teams incorporating the broad range of research skills that are needed.

CONCLUSION

It might turn out that humanistic psychology, viewed as the project of the social reconstruction of the modern self, will be primarily identified with a particular historical era during the third quarter of the 20th century, much as classical psychoanalysis as the project of theorizing the erotic unconscious was identified with the first quarter of that century. In this sense, humanistic psychology will be identified with the writings of Maslow, Rogers, May, Bugental, Moustakas, Jourard, and Perls, just as classical psychoanalysis is identified with Freud and a handful of his associates. In both of these cases, the impact of the movement has been larger on the culture as a whole than on the field of academic psychology.

For those of us still identified with the tradition of humanistic psychology, however, the project of constructing a contextualized vision of the psychological foundations of the social construction of social reality offers an abundance of challenges and opportunities. (In fact, based on observations at recent APA conventions, this might be an area where there is significant theoretical convergence with the psychoanalytic tradition.) Reconstructing dysfunctional human systems in the postmodern world in accordance with the emancipatory values of humanistic, existential, and transpersonal psychology is a project that is large enough to keep the next generation of theorists, researchers, and practitioners fully employed.

NOTE

1. See also writers such as Jung, Campbell, Smith, and Wilber. As my colleague Larry Davis suggested, "The attempt to employ Eastern philosophical and psychological practices within the Western cultural context is problematic in that Western cultural transpersonal practices tend to be linked with particular religious practices and notions of a transcendent God. By contrast, Eastern practices are not focused on an external God image but [rather are focused] on the development of the Buddha within, the higher self of one's own being. That is, Eastern mediation practices are directly focused on the growth and development of personal consciousness. Western psychology, somewhat blinded by its own complicity with Western Judeo-Christian religious-cultural views, tends to interpret these Eastern philosophical-meditational practices as if they were a form of Western religion (or at least metaphysical cosmology). This distortion misses the significant recognition that these Eastern meditation practices were explicitly developed as techniques for transforming consciousness" (L. Davis, personal communication, June 2000). Eastern philosophy tends to remain within the framework of expanded consciousness and to avoid making "and therefore" leaps into objectivistic metaphysics. I am grateful to Davis for several helpful suggestions.

REFERENCES

Berger, P. L., & Luckmann, T. (1966). *The social construction of reality.* New York: Doubleday.

Feinstein, D., & Krippner, S. (1997). *The mythic path.* New York: Tarcher/Putnam.

Huxley, A. (1972). *The perennial philosophy.* Freeport, NY: Books for Libraries Press.

Maslow, A. H. (1954). Problem centering vs. means centering in science. In A. H. Maslow, *Motivation and personality* (pp. 13-21). New York: Harper & Row.

Old Saybrook 2 Conference. (2000). *Old Saybrook 2 Conference proceedings* [Online]. Available: www.sonoma.edu/psychology/os2db/proceedings.html

Ray, P. (1996, Spring). The rise of integral culture. *Noetic Sciences Review*, pp. 4-15.

Schneider, K. J. (1998). Toward a science of the heart: Romanticism and the revival of psychology. *American Psychologist, 53*, 277-289.

Taylor, E. (1999). *Shadow culture*. Washington, DC: Counterpoint.

Warmoth, A. (1998). Humanistic psychology and humanistic social science. *Humanity and Society, 22*, 313-319.

CHAPTER 49

Living Within Essential Tensions
Dialectics and Future Development

M ICHAEL J. M AHONEY AND S EAN M AHONEY

T HERE ARE TWO types of people in the world: those who believe that there are two types of people in the world and those who do not. Like kindred koans, this seeming paradox is not meant to be resolved. It invites a recognition that we rely extensively on categories to organize our experience. The object is not to eliminate the categories or to transcend our needs to categorize; rather, it is to become increasingly aware of and informed by the categorical processes in which we are engaged. A theme of this chapter is that a central challenge facing humanistic psychology is a dialectical one, namely, learning to live with and within the essential tensions that pervade all life and development. This theme has run throughout many of the chapters in this volume (e.g., Schneider's reflections on romanticism [Chapter 6], Polkinghorne's analysis of the mysteries of the self [Chapter 8], Greening and Mendelowitz's remarks on literature [Chapters 12 and 13, respectively], and Stern's insights on the experience of awe [Chapter 31]).

The metaphor of the pendulum has often appeared in the rhetoric of psychotherapy, used by both practitioners and clients as a visualization of emotions, patterns, life situations, and the "human condition." This seems to be because we, as humans, possess an innate recognition of the fact that we live within boundaries and are always in flux between edges and centers. This metaphor, simple though it may be, reflects an important and enduring dynamic in the ongoing questioning of psychology and many related disciplines. The future challenges facing humanistic psychology include many of those that face the discipline of psychology, in general, and its attempts to understand and serve humanity, in particular. These challenges include the crisis of hope and the quest for meaning (both of which must address the problems of death and the potential "evil" or "dark sides" of humanity), the complex relations among individual selves and collective systems, and the perennial questions of responsible action. Such challenges can be addressed in terms of the essential tensions that they embrace and the dialectical developments that they make possible. Dialectics refers to the ongoing interaction of contrasts, a process that often generates unprecedented changes in both the contrasts and the systemic contexts in which they are embedded. Tension reduction or the resolution of conflict does not necessarily lead to growth (which, in this context, refers to the development of new patterns of self-organization that are better suited to the ongoing health of the self or organism), and it may in fact retard development by diminishing both the energy and the challenges required for such development.

THE CRISIS OF HOPE

A central challenge for all contemporary visions of humanity and its future is the crisis of hope. Despite popular prose to the contrary, hope is not the same as optimism, nor is it necessarily a reference to a future that will be good or better than a past or present. Rather, hope is an act of engagement. The essential tension invoked, therefore, is not one of optimism and pessimism so much as one of engagement and disengagement. The word *hope* is related to the old English term *hop,* which means a short leap or jump. This is akin to a leap of faith into the present moment or a choice toward authentic engagement and being in the world. For a variety of understandable reasons, many people withdraw from such a leap. The implications, both emotional and practical, of "hoping" oneself into present engagement are frightening and often contain a guarantee of pain or at least a loss of security. Depending on whether their with-

drawal is primarily active or passive, pathognomists have cast the reluctance to make such a leap in hues of either anxiety or depression. As both Kierkegaard and May pointed out, anxiety tends to be expressed as an active and vigilant disengagement from the life-world. Depression, with its etymological connotations of burden, is more of a passive form of withdrawal.

Whatever the motives and expressed forms, disengagement is as daunting a challenge to psychology as engagement is to the individual reaching for a more authentic mode of being in the world. The complexities of this challenge are more easily outlined than are possible responses to it. One such complexity finds a parallel in confusions that often develop around the Buddhist idea of nonattachment, which is importantly different from emotional detachment. Like detachment, hopeless disengagement tends toward a wholesale withdrawal from all dimensions of life (e.g., emotional, intellectual, spiritual, interpersonal). One of the dangers of such disengagement is its tendency to encourage an inertia of isolation and a fragmentation of the fabric of being. As here construed, hope is a continuing engagement with the full, ambiguous, and often distressing spectrum of conscious existence. In Tillich's (1952) words, it is an enacted "courage to be." Choice and agency are central. But how does one engage with a life and a world that seem increasingly chaotic and inevitably painful?

Although the crisis of hope is hardly a new one, it has taken on unprecedented proportions in the wake of 20th-century developments. The relativist turn of postmodernism and the fragility of life after nuclear weaponry have cast new meanings on contemporary crises and our role in their unfolding. The question is not a simple choice between effort and surrender. At least part of the tension suggested here implies that both effort and surrender are styles of being in particular relationships. Moreover, as Renaissance humanists anticipated, human relationships are themselves embedded in bodily experiences of emotions (Lakoff & Johnson, 1999; Magai & McFadden, 1995). A person's relationship with his or her own private emotional life is at the heart of the person's style of relating to others.

A person's relationship with pain is an example. The powerful allure of a pain-free existence is omnipresent in contemporary consciousness. In this context, hope often has come to mean a desperate faith in the possibility of painless consciousness. One of the challenges facing humanism and the contemporary movement toward positive psychology is the problem of pain (Mahoney, in press). Both historically and conceptually, pain has been a central dimension of the problem of evil. Pain is also at the heart of debates about the dark side of human potential. How are we to make sense of our pain, and how shall we conceptualize our capacities to intentionally inflict pain on others? These questions and patterns of thinking are not surprising, but they represent a somewhat limited view of the usefulness of pain and discomfort in that they associate "negative" emotions solely with negative value constructs. May's concept of the daimonic deserves reflection in this context. The term *daimonic* comes from the Greek and can mean both divine and diabolic. For May (1969), the daimonic referred to any dimension of the human that threatened to consume the agentic options of the whole in service of some less holistic balance:

The daimonic is the urge in every being to affirm itself, assert itself, perpetuate and increase itself. The daimonic becomes evil when it usurps the total personality without regard to the integration of the self or to the unique forms and desires of others and their need for integration. It then appears as excessive aggression, hostility, cruelty—the things about ourselves which horrify us most and which we repress whenever we can or, more likely, project on others. But these are the reverse side of the same assertion which empowers our creativity. All life is a flux between these two aspects of the daimonic. (p. 123)

May was not arguing for an essentially negative component of human nature so much as he was suggesting that the capacities for virtues and vices lay delicately nested together in a dynamic balance. Whether accidental or inflicted, human pain is inevitable and essential. But human suffering, although pervasive, is perhaps a less inevitable aspect of the human condition. Regardless, people *do* suffer all over the world and right here in the realms of our own lives. We do what we can, and engagement and presence seem to offer avenues by which we might access our own suffering and that of others, but all too often we end up feeling helpless to do anything about it. The question "Why do we have to suffer?" is derivative of the more fundamental question "What does it mean *that* we suffer?" Our constructions of meaning around the experience of suffering, and of hope itself, play heavily into our ability to deal with the pain we are dealt.

MEANING, SCIENCE, AND HUMAN INQUIRY

The crisis of hope is central to the problem of meaning, which has been perennial to psychology (Baumeister, 1991; Frankl, 1959; Mahoney, 1991). Being engaged with life is inherently an act of ordination or coordination and, hence, an unfolding relationship. Meaning does not reside in symbol systems; rather, meaning is made in acts of relationship—acts that require an ongoing construction of order in the face of relentless chaos or, sometimes, acts that require a construction of chaos amid a painful or unacceptable order (Kauffman, 1993; Masterpasqua & Perna, 1997). Human psychological development always involves changes in meanings. One of the challenges facing humanity is the erosion of meaning that has been accelerating at exponential rates for more than a century. Specific domains of such meaning are legion—the meaning of intimacy, trust, community, work, progress, life, and so on. The quest for meaning is, hence, a quest for relationship. It is an ongoing engagement with the processes that weave such relationship.

Choice, phenomenology, uniqueness, and process are common themes in humanistic-existential descriptions of human experience. In constructivist philosophy, the ongoing construction of meaning—the creation and propagation of an orderly relation with otherness—is paramount in human activity (Neimeyer & Mahoney, 1995). As Buddhists, existentialists, and humanists have agreed, quality of life is relative to mindful and meaningful ways of being. As Epictetus and others have noted, it is not things in themselves that disturb us so much as the meanings we make of them. This is, of course, not to say that the meanings make the things; there *is* furniture in the universe, and often the omnipotent attitude of "I create my own meaning" can become a defense against the realities that do exist rather than a liberating perspective regarding them.

One important expression of the human quest for meaning deserves special commentary. It is the complex endeavor called *science*. The social reconstruction (some would say "deconstruction") of science has spawned renewed exchanges between real-ists and constructionists (Gould, 2000). The emergence of science as a systematic approach to knowledge was followed shortly by dangerous presumptions on the part of some of its proponents. Originally developed as a dialectical integration of reason and experience, science became a new religion of knowledge that presumed to replace all other forms of human inquiry. The central issue on which science elevated itself was that of absolute authority, and its most extreme proponents reduced the problem of meaning to the problem of science and its methods. These extremists came to be called "scientistic" rather than scientific because of their adamant and arrogant denigration of all other approaches to human knowing. Efforts to distinguish science from non-science were, in fact, phrased in terms that conveyed the meaningfulness of science and the meaninglessness of everything beyond its borders (Weimer, 1979).

One of the challenges facing humanistic-existential visions is that of protecting and elaborating the value of inquiry methods that do not fall prey to the narrow strictures of scientistic research. Such problems include fragmentation, reductionism, quantophilia, simplification, strict objectivism, and the illusions of inevitable and limitless progress—illusions that have led to frightening speculations about what a scientistic utopia might look like. But perhaps the most pernicious of these problems is that of intolerance—intolerance for ambiguity, for uncertainty, and for alternative paths and travelers. One can hardly blame a school of thought for defending and trying to multiply itself, but despite its ostensive commitment to community, the power politics of contemporary science has permitted dichotomous polarizations of the form "us-them." These polarizations are apparent in the academy and in the funding policies that influence the survival and growth of different visions of humanity. The continuing debate over "empirical validation," for example, is more than a quest for truth. It is also an indulgence in the perennial processes of selective legitimization, that is, the division of the world into the right and the wrong, the good and the bad, the promising and the pernicious.

One of the tensions that future generations will necessarily encounter is the following: How might mainstream scientists learn to relax their categories enough to appreciate the diversity and value of other ways of knowing? How might humanistic-existential proponents learn to make peace with the fact that some important lessons are learned through mainstream scientific methods? How can needs for power and a distinctive identity be recognized as important sources of learning in future development? Questions such as these again reflect our need to remain engaged in a dialogue of essential tensions.

SELVES AND SYSTEMS

This issue touches on another tension that has already challenged humanistic-existential visions. It is the tension that separates the individual from the collective or selves from systems. Much of the debate in postmodern dialogue deals with this critical mystery. It is a mystery that finds expression throughout many dimensions of time and space. In evolutionary biology, for example, the emergence of the simple cell boundary was a major step in the viability of life as we know it. Boundaries bring both burdens and blessings, of course. The separation that is created permits the storage of energy and some degree of protection for its contents. If the "skin" that forms the boundary is too porous, then these protective functions are lost. If that skin is impermeable, then that which it contains dies an entropic death.

Second only to the importance of the cell membrane in biological evolution was the appearance of the cell nucleus, creating the diverse life form known as eukaryotes. The nucleus came to function as a center—a metaphorical self—in coordinating the activities of the system and its interactions with its surrounds. Still later came the development of sexual reproduction, that is, the exchange of nuclear material in the generation of new life forms. The most recent development in this sequence has been the emergence of symbolic capacities, which allow important exchanges among at least some of those life forms. (We leave it to the reader to determine whether all humans qualify.)

The conceptual limitations of the preceding metaphor are considerable, and yet it may help to convey a critical dilemma facing current and future generations. What lessons can be learned through studies of the mysteries of balance between unity and diversity, stasis and change, identity and otherness? How do parts and wholes coordinate? How do they remain both open and closed? These are among the problems invoked in conjectures about intersubjectivity, the future of the self in an interdependent collective, and the thread of agency in the fabric of being (Anderson, 1997; Goldberger, Tarule, Clinchy, & Belenky, 1996; Guidano, 1987). The existential loneliness of modern life is also entailed. There is considerable irony in the fact that the word *alone* is, in fact, a contraction of two words: *all one*. The poet May Sarton (1994) made a distinction between solitude and loneliness, with solitude being a healing, hopeful, and open realm and loneliness being an empty and dark place. Her dedication to aloneness, whatever its form, is not uncommon among writers and other artists. If we are to begin taking seriously the issues at stake in an existential world, then it seems crucial to open the boundaries of our thinking not only toward the sciences but also toward the arts.

Few thinkers and writers have truly taken up the challenge of "unpacking" the ideas and philosophies of the artistic world for the realm of mainstream academia. Academic artists often remain in their closed worlds not only because that is how they prefer to work but also because they do not receive any validation whatsoever from the so-called real academics. One speculated reason for this is that art is dauntingly attached to perceptions about one's own life and cannot be put away at the end of the day in the same way as can a lecture on history or Freud. Poetry of the 20th century has offered many brilliant insights into the loneliness of our condition and our time, yet for the most part, it has gone unheard (as a valid source of intellectual inquiry) because of its artistic presentation. Artfully rendered or not, the challenges of hope, meaning, and loneliness are perennial and universal, and they ultimately return us to the realm of present action.

TIME AND ACTION

Kant once related his extensive reflections to the following three basic questions. What can one know? What may one hope? What should one do? In relation to some of the questions addressed previously, Kant's queries spoke directly to the challenge of living within essential tensions. Although some forms of knowledge have increased dramatically during recent centuries, we live in a tenuous world that is threatened by presumptions about the known and the knowable. As that world and its boundaries become more changeable and uncertain, demands for certain knowledge and clear distinctions are becoming all the more forceful. It is as if we were systems whose

increasing openness has created a desperately felt need for closure. How will we navigate and nurture these conflicts? Any claim to confident knowledge in response to such questions would belie a deep failure to understand them.

Still, we must do more than question. Or perhaps, we must seek a more active questioning, a form that seeks new inquiries rather than definitive answers. We live in a world that is hungry for hope and desperate for meaning. We live during times when limited abilities to cope with tension threaten the fabric and future of life as we know it. And we live in a context of grave local and global issues that demand present and responsible action. The world's spiritual and wisdom traditions are serving as increasingly popular resources for directions regarding such action. Charity, compassion, humility, love, and responsibility are being encouraged and often enacted in heartening ways. But confusion, cruelty, and suffering remain rampant, and the compassion and authenticity of approaches such as existential-humanism are needed desperately.

In closing, it is important for us to acknowledge that the nature of human nature is not likely to be resolved in any absolute or enduring way during this or any coming century. Nor is it probable that we will eliminate all human suffering, find answers for our pain, or come to terms with every different perspective. Our desire to pin human nature onto some entomological display board is ill aimed. Our nature is our process—and, therefore, an emergent one. Let us not become so entangled in the webs of our languaging that we lose sight of the dynamic complexities whose wings we are presuming to stabilize and preserve for permanent viewing. In embracing our existential choices and expressing our human agency, let us honor the wisdom that recognizes the generativity of essential tensions. Rather than either denying or artificially resolving the tensions in which we find ourselves, it is important for us to learn to live within the tension of opposites in ways that encourage new and more flexible forms to emerge.

REFERENCES

Anderson, W. T. (1997). *The future of the self: Inventing the postmodern person.* New York: Tarcher.

Baumeister, R. F. (1991). *Meanings of life.* New York: Guilford.

Frankl, V. E. (1959). *Man's search for meaning.* New York: Washington Square.

Goldberger, N., Tarule, J., Clinchy, B., & Belenky, M. (Eds.). (1996). *Knowledge, difference, and power: Essays inspired by women's ways of knowing.* New York: Basic Books.

Gould, S. J. (2000). Deconstructing the "science wars" by reconstructing an old mold. *Science, 287,* 253-261.

Guidano, V. F. (1987). *Complexity of the self: A developmental approach to psychopathology and therapy.* New York: Guilford.

Kauffman, S. A. (1993). *The origins of order: Self-organization and selection in evolution.* Oxford, UK: Oxford University Press.

Lakoff, G., & Johnson, M. (1999). *Philosophy in the flesh: The embodied mind and its challenge to Western thought.* New York: Basic Books.

Magai, C., & McFadden, S. H. (1995). *The role of emotions in social and personality development.* New York: Plenum.

Mahoney, M. J. (1991). *Human change processes.* New York: Basic Books.

Mahoney, M. J. (in press). Constructive psychotherapy as a natural home for positive psychology. In C. R. Snyder & S. J. Lopez (Eds.), *Handbook of positive psychology.* Oxford, UK: Oxford University Press.

Masterpasqua, F., & Perna, P. A. (Eds.). (1997). *The psychological meaning of chaos: Translating theory into practice.* Washington, DC: American Psychological Association.

May, R. (1969). *Love and will.* New York: Norton.

Neimeyer, R. A., & Mahoney, M. J. (Eds.). (1995). *Constructivism in psychotherapy.* Washington, DC: American Psychological Association.

Sarton, M. (1994). *From May Sarton's well.* Watsonville, CA: Papier-Mâché Press.

Tillich, P. (1952). *The courage to be.* New Haven, CT: Yale University Press.

Weimer, W. B. (1979). *Notes on the methodology of scientific research.* Hillsdale, NJ: Lawrence Erlbaum.

Closing Statements

JAMES F. T. BUGENTAL, J. FRASER PIERSON, AND KIRK J. SCHNEIDER

F OLLOWING are three intimate reflections on this volume. In keeping with the humanistic spirit, these reflections are personal yet shared, distinctive yet collectively appreciated. Although we hesitated somewhat about how best to close this volume, we ultimately allied with the personal—as we encourage you, the reader, to do as you engage our meditations.

JAMES F. T. BUGENTAL

What does it really mean to be alive? I listen to my friends-teachers-patients as they wrestle with the death that is in them and try to claim more of the life that is also within them. And, of course, I don't come up with The Answer. Yet slowly I come to realize how all of us—if we will but really look and listen—can sense the life pulsing within. (Bugental, 1976, p. 9)

We are in the early stages of one of the major revolutions of the human experience. Once [the person] felt he was at the center of the universe. Then science demonstrated the earth to be far from the center even of our own galaxy, showed the sun to be the center of the solar system, and in countless other ways dispossessed [the person] of his sense of specialness in the cosmos. It was important to our maturity that this occur. But now the time has come for [the person] to point to a new direction to a process that has overcarried. . . .

What I argue for is not a [person]-centered universe but [rather] a [person]-centered [person] in the universe. Let us come home to our own place in our own lives and set about making our destiny our own. (Bugental, 1967, p. 348)

Psychology emerged from the mother of disciplines, philosophy, anxious to join its earlier siblings and to demonstrate its maturity as an adult science. It has done so by avoiding subjectivity that was deemed to be weak and not capable of standing on its own. Instead, persons were treated as interchangeable, and statistics came to match the laboratory as carrying the cachet of truth.

Much useful, interesting, and (to a limited extent) practical has been harvested from the objectified psychology. In this volume, we acknowledge these benefits and trust that they will continue to be attained. Concisely, this is not so much a competitive stance as a complementary one. However, it is a complementation that inevitably must, at times, identify itself by contrasts with the more popularly familiar conception of an impersonal and truly objectified psychology.

Humanistic or personalistic psychology must venture into that long-feared and avoided realm of the subjective. It is our contention that our discipline of psychology is incomplete so long as the actual lived experience of being human is neglected.

To be sure, the methods and values of much that is called psychology cannot be transferred intact to this new and challenging realm. Methods of inquiry, of data processing, and of generalizing all must be reexamined and, in some cases, reinvented.

It is evident that the prospect is a challenging one that will call for all our inventiveness and, importantly, our patience.

The task of any intellectual discipline is to distinguish that which is momentary and superficial from that which is fundamental and abiding. Subjective psychology seems, at first view, to offer few candidates to meet those criteria. It is our belief, however, that such an evaluation is too hasty and takes too little account of how much already is established.

The chief vehicle of inquiring into the personal has been clinical theory and practice. By the very nature of the effort to respond to persons in emotional distress, we have had to attend to the subjective. Out of the wealth of clinical observations, we already have developed an abundant literature and a varied and creative praxis.

The authors of the chapters in this volume write from varied backgrounds but are united in their will to mine the aforementioned—to seek the fundamental and abiding—and to extend the range of our discipline.

REFERENCES

Bugental, J. F. T. (1967). *Challenges of humanistic psychology.* New York: McGraw-Hill.

Bugental, J. F. T. (1976). *The search for existential identity: Patient-therapist dialogues in humanistic psychotherapy.* San Francisco: Jossey-Bass.

J. FRASER PIERSON

In the "Epilogue and Prologue" to *Challenges of Humanistic Psychology,* Bugental (1967) defined the original meaning of *psychology* as "knowledge about the soul" (p. 346). Today, psychology is likely to be defined as "the science of mind and behavior" (Mish, 1988, p. 951), with the accent on modifying behavior or "medicalizing" the mind. The quest for ever-increasing depth and breadth of understanding of the *psyche*—"the human soul, spirit, or mind" (Flexner & Hauck, 1987, p. 1650)— remains at the heart of our discipline but, I believe, is nowhere more eloquently celebrated in theory, research, and practice than among existential and humanistic psychologists. The contributors to the present leading-edge volume give ample evidence of this assertion, as did the founders during the 1960s.

Humanistic psychology once again is at a significant turning point in its development as a uniquely identified perspective within psychology. As Kirk Schneider points out in his closing comments, there are numerous indicators that suggest a renaissance for humanistic psychology—a renewal of interest and activity within the humanistic community and an increased receptivity within the field of psychology. This volume is both a reflection of the vitality of such a potential renaissance and a spur to its flowering. Collectively, the authors of chapters in the volume articulate that which epitomizes humanistic psychology at this time in its history. It is a living perspective and, as such, unfolds in keeping with the global consciousness of our era. We have needed to reassess—to reconsider what we stand for in addition to what we protest. It is my hope that we reunite as a worldwide humanistic community—and discipline of psychol-

ogy—joined by our investment in the study of "human being" and commitment to "human becoming."[1]

Investment in the study of human being and commitment to human becoming is expressed throughout this volume but is particularly apparent in the parts on Humanistic Applications to Practice (Part IV) and Humanistic Applications to Broader Settings (Part V). We now know that conceptualizations of the vital and fulfilled life first bloom within the context of relationship and culture. The universal culture that we share as members of the human species combines with the ecological, national, regional, and racial/ethnic cultures in which we are socialized. All play roles (see the chapter by Vontress & Epp [Chapter 29] in this volume).

I believe that Maslow's (1967) call for "resacralization" (p. 284) is being heard. As he described it, when we are open to sacralization, we see each person we encounter in context and relationship, as unique and intrinsically precious, as woman with a capital W and man with a capital M. We do not forfeit the sacred, poetic, and eternal.

Maslow's (1967) B-motivation, or the "being" values (p. 281; see also Maslow, 1978), guides humanistic psychology now as it did during the early years. A yen to foster the "growth" needs (i.e., meta-needs or actualizing needs) such as aliveness, richness, meaningfulness, playfulness, and lovingness (Goble, 1970, p. 50) radiates throughout the chapters in this volume. The quest is to know humankind "as is" and also to know humankind "under the auspices of eternity" (Spinoza, cited in Maslow, 1967, p. 284).

Some 20 years ago, one aspect of being fully human was "to have concerns that extend beyond self and immediate family to the nation and all humankind" (Simpson, 1977, p. 76). Today, our concerns extend to all sentient creatures and life forms with which we share our planet. This contemporary addendum is not only altruistic but also anchored in our innermost needs to "discover" ourselves through our relations with others. Reflecting on her encounters with free-ranging dolphins, Frohoff (1998) articulated the significant personal dividend resulting from this ethic when she disclosed that "it is from being in the presence of another species that I have learned how to be more 'human' " (p. 79). A similar observation was made by Akerman (1995), who poignantly stated, "There are wonderful creatures that have roamed the earth much longer than we, creatures that not only are worthy of our respect but [also] could teach us about ourselves" (p. xi). More pointedly, Akerman reminded us that we need to take our turns "on morning watch" so that we may save our astoundingly biodiverse planet and ourselves. I am grateful to Pilisuk and Joy (Chapter 9 in this volume) for representing a humanistic perspective in this urgent worldwide human concern. As Campbell put it so cogently, "Today, the planet is the only proper 'in-group' " (cited in Osbon, 1991, p. 25).

Since its coalescence as the "third force" nearly four decades ago, humanistic psychology has identified its central mission as "seek[ing] to bring psychology back to its source, to the *psyche*" (Matson, 1978, p. 23; see also the chapter by Giorgi [Chapter 5] in this volume). It is a mission of almost mythic proportions. Numerous publications, conferences, experiential workshops, and academic courses presently associated with humanistic psychology document our valiant efforts and successes in this direction.

There is yet another way in which we honor and actualize our central mission, and I wish to close by highlighting it. This path draws on the wellspring of the subjective realm within each of us and embraces the feminine.[2] We bring psychology back to its source by how we live our lives (see chapter by Kottler & Hazler [Chapter 28] in this volume), how we choose to be alive on the earth, and how we celebrate our existence (our own and as a species) as well as by our openness to the cosmos.

It is with this awe and reverence that Walt Whitman celebrates existence and the profound mystery of the soul—the animating force in life. Whitman's words and imagery in "Grand Is the Seen" from *Leaves of Grass* resonate within me. They are timeless and convey a passionate sacred sense of soul (psyche) and a powerful way of being alive in the world:

> *Grand is the seen, the light, to me—*
> *grand are the sky and stars,*
> *Grand is the earth, and grand are*
> *lasting time and space,*
> *And grand their laws, so multiform,*
> *puzzling, evolutionary;*
> *But grander far the unseen soul of*
> *me, comprehending, endowing all*
> *those,*
> *Lighting the light, the sky and stars,*
> *delving the earth, sailing the sea,*
> *(What were all those, indeed, without*
> *thee, unseen soul?*
> *Of what amount without thee?)*
> *More evolutionary, vast, puzzling, O*
> *my soul!*
> *More multiform far—more lasting*
> *thou than they.* (Whitman, n.d.,
> p. 422)

Whitman is remembered as a man who had "largeness of view" (Trowbridge, 1902/ 2000, p. 18). He sought to bring nature, "especially nature's living masterpiece" (humankind), into his poetry with unflinching realism yet imbued with optimism, love, and faith (p. 18). Humanistic psychologists also have such "largeness of view," and it is this vision that we celebrate in this volume.

NOTES

1. I have adapted part of this phrase from Matson's (1978) statement, "Humanistic psychology is not just the study of 'human being'; it is a commitment to 'human becoming' " (p. 23).

2. I am inspired by Williams's (1994) concept of "embracing the bear" as embracing the feminine. Her definition of the feminine includes "a reconnection to the self, a commitment to the wildness within" (p. 53).

REFERENCES

Akerman, D. (1995). *The rarest of the rare: Vanishing animals, timeless worlds.* New York: Random House.

Bugental, J. F. T. (1967). *Challenges of humanistic psychology.* New York: McGraw-Hill.

Flexner, S. B., & Hauck, L. C. (Eds.). (1987). *The Random House dictionary of the English language, unabridged* (2nd ed.). New York: Random House.

Frohoff, T. G. (1998). Beyond species. In L. Hogan, D. Metzger, & B. Peterson (Eds.), *Intimate nature: The bond between woman and animals* (pp. 78-84). New York: Fawcett.

Goble, F. G. (1970). *The third force.* New York: Grossman.

Maslow, A. H. (1967). Self-actualization and beyond. In J. F. T. Bugental (Ed.), *Challenges of humanistic psychology* (pp. 279-286). New York: McGraw-Hill.

Maslow, A. H. (1978). Notes on being-psychology. In I. D. Walsh, G. A. Tate, & F. Richards (Eds.), *Humanistic psychology: A source book* (pp. 33-39). New York: Prometheus Books.

Matson, F. W. (1978). Humanistic theory: The third revolution in psychology. In I. D. Welch, G. A. Tate, & F. Richards (Eds.), *Humanistic psychology: A source book* (pp. 23-32). New York: Prometheus Books.

Mish, F. C. (Ed.). (1988). *Webster's ninth new collegiate dictionary.* Springfield, MA: Merriam Webster.

Osbon, D. K. (Ed.). (1991). *Reflections on the art of living: A Joseph Campbell companion.* New York: HarperCollins.

Simpson, E. L. (1977). Humanistic psychology: An attempt to define human nature. In D. D. Nevill (Ed.), *Humanistic psychology: New frontiers* (pp. 67-86). New York: Gardner.

Trowbridge, J. T. (2000, February). Reminiscences of Walt Whitman. *The Atlantic Monthly* [Online]. Available: www.thealantic.com/unbound/poetry/whitman/walt.htm (Original work published 1902)

Whitman, W. (n.d.). *Leaves of grass.* New York: Modern Library.

Williams, T. T. (1994). *An unspoken hunger: Stories from the field.* New York: Random House.

KIRK J. SCHNEIDER

We stand at an incredible threshold in our discipline, and this volume is a direct reflection of that crossing point. The question is, will we coalesce—as many authors of chapters in this volume have done—to forge a generous science of humanity, or will we devolve into a competing anarchy of factions or, worse yet, a monolithic elite?

The term *humanism* in psychology is anachronistic. As this volume suggests, and as many humanists insist, psychology and humanism should be synonymous, just as the "science of persons" should be synonymous with the "science of behavior." Unfortunately, these respective standpoints are not yet interwoven—they are not even compatible in selected quarters—hence the necessity of this volume. Yet, the signs are accumulating that a humanistic revival is brewing, that the courtship with psychological reductionism (or, on the other hand, extreme psychological relativism) is beginning to wane, and that change is afoot. Countertrends notwithstanding, there is a decidedly humanistic flavor to a growing number of developments. Consider, for example, that the flagship journal of the American Psychological Association (APA), the *American Psychologist*, is featuring an increasing number of humanistic critiques (Bevan & Kessel, 1994; Brown, 1997; Goldfried & Wolfe, 1996; Martin & Sugarman, 2000, Packer, 1985; Prilleltensky, 1997; Schneider, 1998; Smith, 1994). Coupled with the increased attention to humanistic themes in mainstream journal articles, an impressive number of humanistic anthologies also have emerged on the scene. Among these are *The Handbook of Experiential Psychotherapy* (Greenberg, Watson, & Lietaer, 1998), *Humanistic and Transpersonal Psychology* (Moss, 1999), *The Humanistic Movement* (Wertz, 1994), *Empathy Reconsidered* (Bohart & Greenberg, 1997), *The Handbook of Research and Practice in Humanistic Psychotherapies* (Cain & Seeman, in press), and *The Handbook of Action Research* (Reason, in press).

With its stress on the exalted, ennobling, and inspiring dimensions of human functioning, positive psychology is forging an unprecedented opportunity for bridge building among humanistic and traditional psychologists. This bridge building could bring powerful new investigative tools to neglected areas of psychological study—areas such as wisdom, creativity, peak performance, peace and ecological psychology, and holistic health (Resnick, Warmoth, & Serlin, 2000).

In the area of psychotherapy practice and research, there has been a particular resurgence of humanistic influence. At the June 2000 meeting of the prestigious Society for Psychotherapy Research, the incoming president, Robert Elliott, introduced his amalgam of humanistic and traditional outcome research, "hermeneutic single-case efficacy design," to a full and captivated audience (Elliott, 2000; see also the chapter by Elliott [Chapter 24] in this volume). There were also a number of well-attended presentations on qualitative research including those on qualitative outcome research, narrative research, adjudication models of research, and multiple-case research. For the past several years, I have had both the privilege and the challenge to act as the APA's Division 32 (Humanistic Psychology) liaison to the Template Implementation Work Group, the APA committee that oversees the development of guidelines for therapeutic practice (APA, 1995). Although I (and others) have had disagreements with this committee over the years, I am encouraged to report that, as of this writing, a significant revision has emerged from our respective dialogues and that this revision has a decidedly humanistic cast (APA, 2000). Moreover, at the APA's August 2000 meeting, its Council of Representatives unanimously approved of this revision, authorizing it as policy. These events, in my view, represent a landmark humanistic advance. Furthermore, they reflect a marked shift within APA policy-making channels, where science does not ipso facto mean experimentalism but can make room for the qualitative and personal as well. Among the highlights of the revision are a broadened view of the criteria that constitute positive therapeutic outcome, a deemphasis on randomized controlled trials as the "gold standard" by which all therapies should be assessed, an increased recognition of the value of alternative outcome methodologies such as quasi-experimental and even rigorous qualitative studies where appropriate, and an increased acknowledgment of the complexity of outcome research and the obligation of guideline makers to address that complexity.

A humanistic transformation also appears to be auguring at the National Institute of Mental Health (NIMH). Under its reform-minded director, Stephen Hyman, the institute now is calling for more relevant, diverse, and in-depth therapy outcome studies. The shift from randomized controlled trials to that which the NIMH terms "effectiveness" research is a pivotal aspect of the aforementioned transition (Foxhall, 2000).

Finally, the Old Saybrook 2 conference, concisely detailed by Warmoth in this volume (Chapter 48), was a timely reflection of the renewed humanistic ethos in psychology. Although there were concerns as well as self-critiques aired at that 4-day gathering, there was an overriding sense of vigor,

urgency, and commitment evident in the work sessions.

To sum, humanistic psychology, as Taylor put it so succinctly, is at a crossroads, but so is the profession that inspired it. The question is, will these fields find ways in which to cooperate, to transcend their parochialism, and to link their traditions, or will they continue to clash, to go their separate ways, and to further subject the profession to impoverishment and eventual co-optation? For humanistic psychology, this question rides on two essential tracks: the willingness to bolster its scholarly output and the willingness to further articulate its scientific perspective (particularly as it relates to social policy). For organized psychology, the question is one of integrity. Will organized psychology return to its original (humanistic) inquiries (what does it mean to be fully experientially human, and how does that understanding illuminate the vital or fulfilled life?), or will it be co-opted by current fashions (e.g., biologism, technicism, nihilism) and atrophy as a result?

I hope that we have shown in this volume that a full and human psychology is an experiential psychology, a psychology that embraces all dimensions of human awareness and subawareness but particularly those that have meaning, impact, and significance for each given person. The challenge is to articulate that meaningful resonance—to weave out of it a rich and subtly nuanced theory, philosophy, or guideline—and to apply that understanding to a diverse and hungering populace. This is a populace that has been bombarded by cosmetic fixes but that yearns, I believe, for existential sustenance. Have we responded to that yearning in this volume? I emphatically believe that we have. Although "sustained good work" needs to continue, as Csikszentmihalyi noted in the Preface to the volume, we have shown that excellent work already has been done and deserves to be acknowledged. Furthermore, we have shown that humanistic psychology is a rich mélange in which joy and sorrow, the personal and interpersonal, and the finite and infinite all have their place and in which "self"-actualization (i.e., the actualization of intimate capacities) is a general ethic.

Can the ideals of humanistic psychology be achieved? Is society ready for those ideals? I do not know. What I do know and share exuberantly with this volume is that they must be engaged.

REFERENCES

American Psychological Association. (1995). *Template for developing guidelines: Interventions for mental disorders and psychosocial aspects of physical disorders.* Washington, DC: Author.

American Psychological Association. (2000, March). *Criteria for evaluating treatment guidelines* [Draft]. Washington, DC: Author.

Bevan, W., & Kessel, F. (1994). Plain truths and home cooking: Thoughts on the making and remaking of psychology. *American Psychologist, 49,* 505-509.

Bohart, A. C., & Greenberg, L. S. (Eds.). (1997). *Empathy reconsidered: New directions in psychotherapy.* Washington, DC: American Psychological Association.

Brown, L. S. (1997). The private practice of subversion: Psychology as Tikkun olam. *American Psychologist, 52,* 449-462.

Cain, D. J., & Seeman, J. (Eds.). (in press). *The handbook of research and practice in humanistic psychotherapies.* Washington, DC: American Psychological Association.

Elliott, R. (2000, June). *Hermeneutic single-case efficacy design.* Paper presented at the meeting of the Society for Psychotherapy Research, Chicago.

Foxhall, K. (2000, July-August). Research for the real world. *APA Monitor,* pp. 28-36. (Washington, DC: American Psychological Association)

Goldfried, M. R., & Wolfe, B. E. (1996). Psychotherapy practice and research: Repairing a strained alliance. *American Psychologist, 51,* 1007-1016.

Greenberg, L. S., Watson, J. C., & Lietaer, G. (1998). *The handbook of experiential psychotherapy.* New York: Guilford.

Martin, J., & Sugarman, J. (2000). *Between the modern and the postmodern: The possibility of self and progressive understanding in psychology, 55,* 397-406.

Moss, D. (Ed.). (1999). *Humanistic and transpersonal psychology: An historical and biographical sourcebook.* Westport, CT: Greenwood.

Packer, M. J. (1985). Hermeneutic inquiry in the study of human conduct. *American Psychologist, 40,* 1081-1093.

Prilleltensky, I. (1997). Values, assumptions, and practices: Assessing the moral implications of psychological discourse and action. *American Psychologist, 52,* 517-535.

Reason, P. (Ed.). (in press). *The handbook of action research: Participative inquiry and practice.* London: Sage.

Resnick, S., Warmoth, A., & Serlin, I. (2000). The humanistic psychology and positive psychology connection: Implications for psychotherapy. *Journal of Humanistic Psychology, 41*(1), 73-101.

Schneider, K. J. (1998). Toward a science of the heart: Romanticism and the revival of psychology. *American Psychologist, 53,* 277-289.

Smith, M. B. (1994). Selfhood at risk: Postmodern perils and the perils of the postmodern. *American Psychologist, 49,* 405-411.

Warmoth, A., Resnick, S., & Serlin, I. (2000). Contributions of humanistic psychology to positive psychology. *Old Saybrook 2* [online]. Available: www.westga.edu/~psydept/os2/current.html

Wertz, F. J. (Ed.). (1994). *The humanistic movement: Recovering the person in psychology.* Lake Worth, FL: Gardner.

Appendix

Regionally Accredited Graduate Schools in Humanistic and Transpersonal Psychology

The following is a limited sample of regionally accredited humanistic and transpersonal graduate programs in psychology. This list is intended to be a resource for the interested reader. It is neither evaluative nor exhaustive. For specific information regarding addresses, programs, and degrees, contact either the individual school or the State University of West Georgia.

Western Region

Antioch University, Marina Del Rey, CA

Antioch University–Seattle, Seattle, WA

California Institute of Integral Studies, San Francisco, CA

Institute in Culture and Creation Spirituality, Oakland, CA

Institute of Transpersonal Psychology, Palo Alto, CA

John F. Kennedy University Graduate School for Holistic Studies, Orinda, CA

John F. Kennedy University Graduate School of Professional Psychology, Orinda, CA

Naropa Institute, Boulder, CO

Pacifica Graduate Institute, Carpinteria, CA

Pepperdine University, Department of Psychology, Culver City, CA

Rosebridge Graduate School of Integrative Psychology, Concord, CA

Saybrook Graduate School and Research Center, San Francisco, CA

Seattle University, Department of Psychology, Seattle, WA

Sonoma State University, Rohnert Park, CA

Southwestern College, Department of Psychology, Santa Fe, NM

Midwestern Region

Center for Humanistic Studies, Detroit, MI

Graduate School of America, Minneapolis, MN

Union Institute Graduate School, Cincinnati, OH

Walden University, Minneapolis, MN

Southern Region

State University of West Georgia, Carrollton, GA

Northeast Region

Duquesne University, Department of Psychology, Pittsburgh, PA

Goddard College, Plainfield, VT

Lesley College, Cambridge, MA

Norwich University, Montpelier, VT

Salve Regina University, Newport, RI

Author Index

Subject Index

About the Editors

Kirk J. Schneider is a psychologist in private practice in San Francisco, where he is a co-founder and current president of the Existential-Humanistic Institute. He serves on the editorial boards of the *Psychotherapy Patient,* the *Journal of Humanistic Psychology,* and the *Review of Existential Psychology and Psychiatry.* He is an adjunct faculty member at Saybrook Graduate School and Research Center (of which he is also an alumnus) and at the California Institute for Integral Studies. His books include *The Paradoxical Self: Toward an Understanding of Our Contradictory Nature* (2nd ed., 1999), *Horror and the Holy: Wisdom-Teachings of the Monster Tale* (1993), and *The Psychology of Existence: An Integrative Clinical Perspective* (co-authored with Rollo May, 1995). He has lectured and published widely and is wholeheartedly committed to restoring depth, romanticism, and awe to 21st century consciousness.

James F. T. Bugental has been a major spokesperson for the humanistic perspective since its coalescence into an influential movement in the field of psychology more than 40 years ago. He is currently an emeritus and adjunct faculty member at Saybrook Graduate School and Research Center and an emeritus and clinical faculty member at Stanford Medical School. He continues to supervise, teach, and write about existential-humanistic psychology and psychotherapy. His major publications include *Psychotherapy Isn't What You Think* (1999), *Intimate Journeys: Stories From Life-Changing Psychotherapy* (1990), *The Art of the Psychotherapist* (1987), *Psychotherapy and Process: The Fundamentals of an*

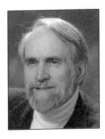

Existential-Humanistic Approach (1978), *The Search for Existential Identity: Patient-Therapist Dialogues in Humanistic Psychotherapy* (1976), *The Search for Authenticity: An Existential-Analytic Approach to Psychotherapy* (1965), and (as editor) *Challenges of Humanistic Psychology* (1967). He also has published more than 80 articles in professional and technical journals as well as 25 original chapters in books edited by others. Translations of his work can be found in French, Finnish, Spanish, German, Dutch, Russian, Italian, Chinese, and Japanese. He serves on the editorial review boards of the *Journal of Humanistic Psychology,* the *Journal of Transpersonal Psychology, The Humanistic Psychologist,* and the *American Journal of Psychotherapy.*

J. Fraser Pierson is a licensed psychologist and Associate Professor of Psychology at Southern Oregon University (SOU), where she teaches a variety of undergraduate and graduate courses within the mental health counseling and human services tracks. She completed her doctoral work at the University of Georgia and an American Psychological Association-approved internship in the Student Services Center at Iowa State University. Prior to coming to SOU, she served as a counselor at the University of West Florida and the Clarion University of Pennsylvania counseling centers. The humanistic and existential perspectives have long inspired and informed her work as a psychotherapist, educator, and counselor-in-training supervisor. Her current scholarly interests include psychotherapist preparation and training, women's self and worldview transformations associated with participation in adventurous sports activities, and the personal meanings associated with experiences and encounters in the natural world. She is a naturalist and mariner by avocation.

About the Contributors

Christopher M. Aanstoos is Professor of Psychology and a member of the graduate faculty at the State University of West Georgia. He received his Ph.D. in phenomenological psychology from Duquesne University. After having previously taught at LaRoche College and Pennsylvania State University, he joined the humanistic psychology program at the State University of West Georgia in 1982. He is a fellow of the American Psychological Association and has served as president of its Division 32 (Humanistic Psychology). He is editor of that division's journal, *The Humanistic Psychologist,* and has edited two books: *Studies in Humanistic Psychology* and *Exploring the Lived World.* He has published more than 70 articles and chapters and has lectured widely.

Mike Arons is Professor Emeritus at the State University of West Georgia. He completed his bachelor of arts degree with a major in psychology at Wayne State University in 1961; completed his doctorate in philosophy at the Sorbonne, Université de Paris, in 1965; and earned a postdoctorate master's degree in psychology at Brandeis University in 1967. Under Paul Ricoeur, he wrote his doctoral dissertation on the subject of creativity and its spur to the emerging cultural revolution, and he later served as a teaching assistant to Abraham Maslow. For a combined 24 years, he chaired and was instrumental in pioneering two humanistically oriented psychology programs: one on Prince Edward Island, Canada, and the other at the State University of West Georgia. He has served as president of Division 32 (Humanistic Psychology) of the American Psychological Association and as president of the Association for

Humanistic Education, and he has twice served on the board of the Association for Humanistic Psychology. He is credited with more than 250 publications in areas including topics such as humanistic-transpersonal psychology, creativity and intuition, values and ethics, and a vision for a new vocation in psychology. He is a recipient of the Division 32 Charlotte Bühler and Abraham H. Maslow Awards.

Arthur Bohart is Professor of Psychology at California State University, Dominguez Hills. He also is an adjunct professor and curriculum consultant at Saybrook Graduate School and Research Center. He received his doctoral degree in clinical psychology from the University of California, Los Angeles. He is coauthor of *How Clients Make Therapy Work: The Process of Active Self-Healing* (1999), co-editor of two other volumes, *Empathy Reconsidered: New Directions in Psychotherapy* (1997) and *Constructive and Destructive Behavior* (2000); and coauthor of a textbook, *Foundations of Clinical and Counseling Psychology* (1999). He fervently believes that therapy is a process of two intelligent beings meeting and creatively dialoging rather than that of a supposed expert (the therapist) changing the client with supposedly potent interventions, and he currently is fighting a rearguard battle to preserve this idea in an era of fascination with technology and purported "empirically supported treatments."

G. Kenneth Bradford is Adjunct Professor at both John F. Kennedy University and the California Institute of Integral Studies. He practices psychotherapy and consultation in the San Francisco Bay Area, working with individuals and couples. His teaching and therapy practice is guided by existential principles and contemplative Buddhist sensibilities. He is a licensed psychologist and obtained his Ph.D. in psychology (clinical concentration) from the Saybrook Institute.

Scott D. Churchill is Chair of Psychology at the University of Dallas, where his professional focus is on the development of phenomenological and hermeneutic methodologies. He is a licensed psychologist who earned his doctorate in clinical phenomenological psychology at Duquesne University. He is an active member of Divisions 24 (Theoretical and Philosophical Psychology) and 32

(Humanistic Psychology) of the American Psychological Association. His recent publications include articles in the *Journal of Phenomenological Psychology* and the *Encyclopedia of Psychology* as well as a chapter in the edited *Phenomenological Inquiry: Existential and Transpersonal Dimensions.* He is editor-in-chief of *Methods: A Journal for Human Science,* serves on several editorial boards, and is a television film critic in his spare time.

Eleanor Criswell is Professor of Psychology and former chair of the Psychology Department at Sonoma State University. She is the founding director of the Humanistic Psychology Institute (now Saybrook Graduate School and Research Center). She is editor of *Somatics Magazine* and director of the Novato Institute for Somatic Research and Training. She is a past president of the Association for Humanistic Psychology and Division 32 (Humanistic Psychology) of the American Psychological Association.

Mihaly Csikszentmihalyi is the C. S. and D. J. Davidson Professor of Psychology in the Peter F. Drucker Graduate School of Management at Claremont Graduate University. He also is director of the Quality of Life Research Center. He is a former professor and chair of the Department of Psychology at the University of Chicago. He is the author of 15 books and more than 200 scholarly articles on creativity and optimal performance. Drawing on years of systematic research, he invented the concept of "flow" as a metaphorical description of the rare mental state associated with feelings of optimal satisfaction and fulfillment. His analysis of the internal and external conditions giving rise to flow show that it almost always is linked to circumstances of high challenge when personal skills are used to the utmost. He has been a visiting professor at the University of Waterloo in Ontario, the University of Illinois, the University of Milan, the University of Alberta, Escola Paulista de Medecina in São Paulo (Brazil), Duquesne University, the University of Maine, the University of Jyvakyla (Finland), and the British Psychological Society.

O. Fred Donaldson is a play specialist internationally recognized for his pioneering use of play as an alternative to competition, abuse, and aggression. For more than 30 years, he has played with children and animals and has trained adults in the significance and use of play. He currently is a play consultant to numerous educational and health institutions in the United States and Sweden. He has written a Pulitzer Prize-nominated book, *Playing by Heart,* and has authored more than 35 articles and book chapters on play.

David N. Elkins is a licensed psychologist and Professor of Psychology in the Graduate School of Education and Psychology at Pepperdine University. He is a past president of Division 32 (Humanistic Psychology) of the American Psychological Association. He is the author of *Beyond Religion: A Personal Program for Building a Spiritual Life Outside the Walls of Traditional Religion* (1998).

Robert Elliott has taught at the University of Toledo since 1978, where he is Professor of Psychology and Director of the Doctoral Program in Clinical Psychology. He received his Ph.D. in clinical psychology from the University of California, Los Angeles, in 1978. He is director of the Center for the Study of Experiential Psychotherapy and president of the Society for Psychotherapy Research and served as coeditor of the journal *Psychotherapy Research* from 1994 to 1998. He is coauthor of *Facilitating Emotional Change* (with Leslie Greenberg and Laura Rice) and *Research Methods for Clinical and Counseling Psychology* (with Chris Barker and Nancy Pistrang).

Lawrence R. Epp is Psychiatric Therapist in the School-Based Mental Health Program at the Johns Hopkins Hospital, one of the nation's most innovative mental health programs. He is the immediate past president of the Maryland Association for Multicultural Counseling and Development. He is an adjunct faculty member at the Johns Hopkins University and at Bowie State University.

Franz R. Epting is Professor of Counseling Psychology in the Department of Psychology at the University of Florida and holds an adjunct appointment within the University Counseling Center. He studied with George Kelly while a graduate student at the Ohio State University. He has been a visiting professor at the University of London, University of Utrecht, and the Ohio State University. He was co-chair of the Fifth International Congress on Personal Construct Psychology and recently was awarded a Lifetime Achievement Award from the North American Personal Construct Theory Network. Active in both constructivist and humanistic psychology, he has published 4 books and more than 80 articles on counseling and personality psychology covering issues in death orientation, optimal functioning, constructivist assessment and psychotherapy, human science methodology, and (more recently) constructivist approaches to sexual orientation and gender. He is a fellow of the American Psychological Association and is most active in Division 32 (Humanistic Psychology), serving as chair of that division's Fellows Committee.

David Feinstein is a clinical/community psychologist who brings mythological perspective to personal, organizational, and community change. He is coauthor of *Personal Mythology: The Mythic Path* and *Rituals for Living and Dying*. He has served on the faculties of the Johns Hopkins University School of Medicine and Antioch College.

Constance T. Fischer is Professor of Psychology and Director of the Psychology Clinic at Duquesne University. She is a diplomate in clinical psychology and engages in a part-time private practice. She is on the editorial boards of *The Humanistic Psychologist,* the *Journal of Humanistic Psychology, Methods: A Journal for Human Science,* and *Clinical Case Studies.* She is currently president of Division 32 (Humanistic Psychology) of the American Psychological Association. Her current projects include editing a volume on qualitative research methods for psychology, preparing a second edition of *Individualizing Psychological Assessment,* and researching the experience of becoming angry through a human-science psychology perspective.

Maurice Friedman is Professor Emeritus of Religious Studies, Philosophy, and Comparative Literature at San Diego State University and is Co-Director of the Institute of Dialogical Psychotherapy. Among his 23 published books are *Martin Buber's Life and Work* (3 vols.), *The Healing Dialogue in Psychotherapy, Encounter on the Narrow Ridge: A Life of Martin Buber,* and *Dialogue and the Human Image: Beyond Humanistic Psychology.*

Amedeo Giorgi is Professor of Psychology at Saybrook Graduate School and Research Center. He also is a former acting dean of that school. He received his Ph.D. in experimental psychology from Fordham University in 1958. He is the author of *Psychology as a Human Science* and was the founder and first editor (25 years) of the *Journal of Phenomenological Psychology.* He has published more than 100 articles on various aspects of the relationship between the phenomenological approach and issues in systematic psychology. Based on the works of Edmund Husserl and Maurice Merleau-Ponty, he is developing a scientific framework for a psychology of human persons as well as a method for researching psychological experiences.

Thomas Greening has been practicing existential-humanistic psychotherapy in the same office for more than four decades. He is on the faculty of Saybrook Graduate School and Research Center and is editor of the *Journal of Humanistic Psychology.* He sometimes reads and writes poems as part of his attempts to become more authentic.

Richard J. Hazler is Professor of Counselor Education at Ohio University. He has years of experience as an instructor and a counselor in schools, prisons, the military, and private practice and as a former editor of the *Journal of Humanistic Education and Development.* He has authored or coauthored numerous humanistically oriented articles and books including *The Therapeutic Environment: Core Conditions for Facilitating Therapy, Helping in the Hallways, What You Never Learned in Graduate School, The Emerging Professional Counselor,* and *Breaking the Cycle of Violence.*

Myrtle Heery is Associate Professor in the Graduate In-Depth Psychology Program at Sonoma State University, Director of the International Institute for Humanistic Studies, and a Teaching Associate with James F. T. Bugental. Some of her publications include an excerpt from her doctoral dissertation, *Hearing Voices, A Non-Psychotic Approach* (translated into five languages), *Mourning the Death of a Loved One, A Cross-Cultural Approach*, and *Food for the Soul, A Psychotherapist's Journey Teaching in Russia*. More recently she has coauthored *Unearthing the Moment* and *Listening to the Listener* (in press). She has lectured at Moscow State University and the State Pedagogical University in St. Petersburg, Russia. In addition to her private psychotherapy practice, she volunteers for hospice as a bereavement counselor and provides trainings in existential-humanistic psychotherapy in Russia, Europe, Mexico, Canada, and the United States.

Adelbert H. Jenkins is Clinical Psychologist and Associate Professor of Psychology at New York University. His scholarly interests include the application of humanistic perspectives on psychological agency to the consideration of people of color in America. The second edition of his book, *Psychology and African Americans: A Humanistic Approach,* was published in 1995. He also has published on topics related to teleologic philosophical issues in clinical psychology and psychoanalytic theory.

Ruthellen Josselson is on the faculty of the Fielding Institute and is Professor of Psychology at the Hebrew University in Jerusalem. She received her Ph.D. in clinical psychology from the University of Michigan. She is a recipient of the Henry A. Murray Award from the American Psychological Association and of a Fulbright Fellowship. She also is a practicing psychotherapist. She is the author of *Revising Herself: The Story of Women's Identity From College to Midlife* and *The Space Between Us: Exploring the Dimensions of Human Relationships*, and she is coeditor of the annual, *The Narrative Study of Lives*. Most recently, she coauthored *Best Friends: The Pleasures and Perils of Girls' and Women's Friendships*.

Melanie Joy is a doctoral student in psychology at Saybrook Graduate School and Research Center, with a concentration in ecological psychology. She has been an activist for animal rights and environmental ethics for more than a decade. She also holds a master's degree from the Harvard Graduate School of Education and conducts classes and workshops on vegetarianism in Boston.

Jeffrey A. Kottler is Chair of the Counseling Department at California State University, Fullerton. He is the author of over 40 books in psychology, counseling, and related fields including *On Being a Therapist, The Imperfect Therapist, Compassionate Therapy: Working With Difficult Clients, Growing a Therapist, Travel That Can Change Your Life, Language of Tears, Learning Group Leadership: An Experiential Approach, Nuts and Bolts of Helping,* and *Doing Good: Passion and Commitment for Helping Others.*

Stanley Krippner is Professor of Psychology at Saybrook Graduate School and Research Center. He has served as president of the Association for the Study of Dreams, the Association for Humanistic Psychology, the Parapsychological Association, and two divisions of the American Psychological Association. He is the coauthor of several books including *Personal Mythology, The Mythic Path, Spiritual Dimensions of Healing,* and *Dream Telepathy.* He is the editor of *Dreamtime and Dreamwork* and eight volumes of *Advances in Parapsychological Research,* and he is coeditor of *Broken Images, Broken Selves: Dissociative Narratives in Clinical Practice* and *Varieties of Anomalous Experience: Examining the Scientific Evidence.*

Larry M. Leitner is Professor of Psychology at Miami University (Ohio). He has published more than 50 books, chapters, and articles dealing with various topics relevant to humanistic psychology. He is on the editorial boards of the *Journal of Constructivist Psychology* and *The Psychotherapy Patient.* He is a fellow of the American Psychological Association (APA) and president-elect of Division 32 (Humanistic Psychology) of the APA.

Amia Lieblich is Professor of Psychology at the Hebrew University in Jerusalem, where she also received her Ph.D. in 1969. She has been a visiting professor at several universities in the United States including the University of California, Los Angeles; the University of California, Berkeley; and the University of Michigan. Her major interests are in the areas of cultural psychology (specifically the impact of the social-political reality in Israel on the lives of men and women in that country), the psychology of gender, and life stories. During recent years, she has done most of her research using narrative approaches. Among her early English publications are *Tin Soldiers on Jerusalem Beach* and *Kibbutz Makom*. More recent publications include *Seasons of Captivity, Conversations With Dvora,* and *Narrative Research: Reading, Analysis, and Interpretation.* Together with Ruthellen Josselson, she is the editor of six volumes of *The Narrative Study of Lives*, published by Sage.

Arthur Lyons is Professor of Psychology at Moravian College in Bethlehem, Pennsylvania, and an evaluation and research consultant with the Davison Group, a humanistically oriented consulting firm. He conducts workshops on diversity, conflict resolution, prejudice reduction, and team building. His applied research topics have included educational reform, benchmarking projects for school districts, high-risk freshman advising programs, youth sports, and work redesign projects in various industrial settings. He also serves as treasurer and membership co-chair for Division 32 (Humanistic Psychology) of the American Psychological Association.

Michael J. Mahoney is Professor of Psychology at the University of North Texas. He also is a distinguished adjunct faculty member at Saybrook Graduate School and Research Center. He is the author of the book *Human Change Processes* and currently serves as editor of the journal *Constructivism in the Human Sciences*.

Sean Mahoney is a poet, playwright, and musician residing in Blacksburg, Virginia. His work reflects an exploration of the intricacies of subjective experience and the trappings of existential being. He currently is examining the growing relationships among self psychology, consciousness studies, and the realm of artistic expression.

Alvin Mahrer is Professor Emeritus in the School of Psychology at the University of Ottawa. He is the author of 12 books and more than 200 publications. He is a former president of Division 32 (Humanistic Psychology) of the American Psychological Association (APA) and is a recipient of the Distinguished Psychologist Award of the APA's Division 29 (Psychotherapy). He probably is best known for his experiential theory of psychology, his experiential psychotherapy and self-transformation, his discovery-oriented research paradigm, and his application of philosophy of science to the field of psychotherapy.

Frederick Martin is a doctoral student at Saybrook Graduate School and Research Center and works with acute psychiatric patients as an intake specialist in a private hospital in Freemont, California. He has a master's degree in public administration. He also is a full-time clinician in the psychiatric emergency room for Alameda County and is a licensed psychiatric technician and hospital administrator. His current interests embrace humanistic psychology's history, meaning, and contemporary significance.

Edward Mendelowitz earned his Ph.D. at the California School of Professional Psychology, where he worked closely with Rollo May. He has presented papers at recent American Psychological Association conferences on individuation and Oedipus, film and postmodernism, ethics and Eastern thought, and the roots of depth psychology. He presently serves on the faculty of the annual film and psychology series sponsored by the Boston Institute of Psychotherapy. His writing gets to the heart of the humanistic-existential-aesthetical bases of our field in its evocation of imagination, transience, possibility, and awe.

Alfonso Montuori is Associate Professor at the California Institute of Integral Studies and a consultant with Lisardco, a leading San Francisco Bay Area executive development firm. He conducts research in the area of creativity and innovation, systems and complexity theories, planetary culture, organizational theory, strategy and strategic thinking, and cultural epistemology. Formally a professional musician with several recordings to his credit and an interpreter for Scotland Yard in London, he has taught at the Saybrook Institute, the College of Notre Dame, and the South-Central University of Technology in Changsha (People's Republic of China). He has published several books including *Evolutionary Competence* (1989), *From Power to Partnership* (with Isabella Conti, 1993), and *Creators on Creating* (with F. A. Barron, 1997) and numerous articles in publications including the *Academy of Management Review*, the *Journal of Management Education*, and the *Journal of Humanistic Psychology*. He has consulted with many international corporations in regard to partnership, creativity and innovation, and systems thinking. He is book series editor of *Advances in Systems Theory, Complexity, and the Human Sciences*, associate editor of *World Futures: The Journal of General Evolution*, a member of the editorial boards of *Pluriverso* (Italy) and *Elites* (Italy), and a reviewer for *Human Relations* and the *Journal of Organizational Change Management*.

Loren Mosher is Director of Soteria Associates, a San Diego-based human service systems consulting firm, and Clinical Professor of Psychiatry in the School of Medicine at the University of California at San Diego. He received his M.D. and psychiatric training at Harvard University. He served as chief of the Center for Studies of Schizophrenia at the National Institute of Mental Health from 1968 to 1980. He designed and directed the Soteria Project (1970 to 1983), from which data still are being analyzed. His 1994 book (with Lorenzo Burti), *Community Mental Health*, provides practical guidelines for the development of user-centered, recovery-oriented, community mental health systems.

Donald Moss is a partner in West Michigan Behavioral Health Services. He serves as adjunct faculty for the Behavioral Medicine Research and Training Foundation in Suquamish, Washington, and mental health director for the humanitarian Trelawny Outreach Project in Western Jamaica. He is president-elect of the Association for Applied Psychophysiology and Biofeedback, editor of the *Biofeedback Newsmagazine,* consulting editor for the *Journal of Neurotherapy,* and a past consulting editor for the *Journal of Phenomenological Psychology.* His third book, *Humanistic and Transpersonal Psychology,* was published in 1998. He is co-editor of the *Handbook of Mind-Body Medicine for Primary Care* (Sage, in press).

Clark Moustakas is the former president of the Center for Humanistic Studies in Detroit, Michigan, and is Senior Consultant and Core Faculty Member in Psychology at the Union Institute in Cincinnati, Ohio. He is the author of several books including *Existential Psychotherapy and the Interpretation of Dreams; Phenomenological Research Methods; Heuristic Research; Psychotherapy With Children; Loneliness and Love; Being-In, Being-For, Being-With;* and *Loneliness.*

Maureen O'Hara is President of Saybrook Graduate School and Research Center. She regularly presents papers on leading-edge issues in relational psychology, client-centered therapy, gender relations, organizational psychology, and the future of consciousness. She has given plenary addresses to the World Future Society, the National League of Nurses, the Association for Humanistic Psychology, the Association for Constructivist Psychology, and the International Gestalt Therapy Association. In July 1999, she was a plenary speaker at the World Psychotherapy Conference in Vienna, Austria. Her published works appear in popular and academic books and journals. She is the founding fellow of the Meridian International Institute on Governance, Leadership, Learning, and the Future, a San Francisco-based futures think tank that consults with leaders in business, government, social service agencies, and the media.

Marc Pilisuk is a clinical and social psychologist. He teaches at Saybrook Graduate School and Research Center and is a professor emeritus of community psychology in the Department of Human and Community Development at the University of California, Davis. He was a founder of the first teach-in; is a past president of the Society for the Study of Peace, Conflict, and Violence; and is a steering committee member of Psychologists for Social Responsibility. He is the author of six books and more than 120 articles and reviews on topics such as social support networks and health, caregiving, community mental health, conflict resolution, military-industrial power, social action, globalization, torture, poverty, and perceptions of a contaminated world. His most recent book (with Susan Parks), *The Healing Web: Social Networks and Human Survival,* deals with the nature of human interdependence. He shares his nonwork time as a caregiver and an activist.

Donald E. Polkinghorne is Professor in the Division of Counseling Psychology at the University of Southern California, where he holds the Attallah Chair in Humanistic Psychology. He is a fellow in Division 12 (Counseling Psychology) of the American Psychological Association (APA) and a fellow and past president of the APA's Division 24 (Theoretical and Philosophical Psychology). His educational background includes an undergraduate degree in religious studies from Washington University (St. Louis) and graduate degrees from Yale University, Hartford Seminary Foundation, and the Union Graduate Institute. His scholarly publications have focused on the epistemological foundations of qualitative research and the implications of Continental philosophy for psychological theory and research. His publications include three books: *An Existential-Phenomenological Approach to Education, Methodology for the Human Sciences,* and *Narrative Knowing and the Human Sciences.* In addition to his scholarly work, he is a licensed psychotherapist and serves as an oral examiner for the California Psychology Licensing Board.

Gayle Privette is Professor of Psychology at the University of West Florida (since 1967), where she teaches theories of individual and group counseling and humanistic psychology, supervises clinical work, does research, and maintains a part-time practice in psychotherapy. She has published numerous articles on peak experience, peak performance, and flow in various publications including the *Journal of Humanistic Psychology,* the *Journal of Personality and Social Psychology,* the *Journal of Social Behavior and Personality,* and *Perceptual and Motor Skills.*

Ronald Purser is Associate Professor of Management in the College of Business at San Francisco State University. He also is an adjunct faculty member at Benedictine University and Saybrook Graduate School and Research Center. He formally was graduate program director of the Center for Organization Development at Loyola University of Chicago. He earned his doctoral degree in organizational behavior from the Weatherhead School of Management at Case Western Reserve University in 1990. He currently is chairperson for the Organization Development and Change division of the National Academy of Management. He is known for his research on workplace participation, social creativity, knowledge work, and environmental management. He is coauthor or coeditor of three books: *The Self-Managing Organization: How Leading Companies Are Transferring the Work of Teams for Real Impact* (with Steve Cabana, 1998), *The Search Conference: A Powerful Method for Planning Organizational Change and Community Action* (with Merrelyn Emery, 1996), and *Social Creativity* (with Alfonso Montuori, Vols. 1-2, 1999).

Ruth Richards is Professor of Psychology at Saybrook Graduate School and Research Center. She also is chair of Concentration in Consciousness and Spirituality. She also is an associate clinical professor in the Department of Psychiatry at the University of California, San Francisco; a research affiliate at McLean Hospital; and a lecturer in psychiatry at Harvard Medical School. She co-edited the book, *Eminent Creativity, Everyday Creativity, and Health* (1997) and was an executive adviser and contributor to the *Encyclopedia of Creativity* (1999). She is on the editorial boards of the *Journal of Humanistic Psychology* and the *Creativity Research Journal*. She draws, writes, and occasionally sings. However, she has learned the most about creativity from her 10-year-old daughter, Lauren.

John Rowan is the author of a number of books including *The Reality Game: A Guide to Humanistic Counselling and Psychotherapy, Ordinary Ecstasy: The Dialectics of Humanistic Psychology, Subpersonalities: The People Inside Us, The Transpersonal in Psychotherapy and Counselling,* and *Healing the Male Psyche: Therapy as Initiation.* He co-edited (with Mick Cooper) *The Plural Self: Multiplicity in Everyday Life* (Sage, 1999). He is on the editorial boards of *Self & Society,* the *Journal of Humanistic Psychology,* the *Counselling Psychology Review,* and the *Transpersonal Psychology Review.* He is a founding member of the Association of Humanistic Psychology Practitioners. He is a past member of the governing board of the U.K. Council for Psychotherapy, representing the Humanistic and Integrative Section. He teaches, supervises, and leads groups at the Minster Centre in London.

Ilene Serlin is Professor of Psychology at Saybrook Graduate School and Research Center. She also is in private practice in San Francisco and Marin County. She is council representative and past president of Division 32 (Humanistic Psychology) of the American Psychological Association. She trained with Laura Perls and was on the faculty of the New York Gestalt Institute. She is on the editorial boards of the *Journal of Humanistic Psychology* and the *American Journal of Dance Therapy.* She has published numerous articles and chapters in existential-humanistic psychology, particularly in the areas of the psychology of women and psychology and the arts.

Jeffrey G. Sharp is a clinical psychologist in private practice in Oakland, California. He also is an adjunct faculty member at Saybrook Graduate School and Research Center and California State University, Hayward. His practice, which includes work with individuals, couples, and families, is informed by humanistic, existential, and systemic principles. He teaches courses on family developmental processes and the art and science of psychotherapy. He is impressed by the crucial role of mentoring in the development of soulful psychotherapists.

Ernesto Spinelli is Academic Dean of the School of Psychotherapy and Counselling at Regent's College in London. His research and writing interests focus principally on the impact on and challenges to psychology and psychotherapy by existential-phenomenological theory and practice. His most recent text is *Tales of Un-Knowing: Therapeutic Encounters From an Existential Perspective* (1997). He is a past chair of the Society for Existential Analysis.

Molly Merrill Sterling is in private practice as co-owner of the James F. T. Bugental Psychology Corporation. She teaches existential-humanistic psychology and psychotherapy at the Community Institute for Psychotherapy and in the intensive workshops developed by James F. T. Bugental titled "Art of the Psychotherapist." Her earlier background is in Asian art and mythology.

E. Mark Stern, a diplomate in Clinical Psychology, is a Fellow of the American Psychological Association and the American Psychological Society. He is a clinical psychologist interested in the intersection of psychological inquiry and practice and religious experience. His edited collections, books, and essays have emphasized the experiential as a means of personal and scientific investigation. He is editor of *The Psychotherapy Patient* series and is senior editor of the Haworth Press. He is a founding editor of the *Journal of Pastoral Counseling* and editor emeritus of *Voices: The Art and Sciences of Psychotherapy.* He was the recipient of the first Carl Rogers Award given by Division 32 (Humanistic Psychology) of the American Psychological Association. He has maintained a practice in clinical psychology and psychotherapy for the past 45 years in New York City and in Clinton Corners in upstate New York.

Thomas Szasz is Professor of Psychiatry Emeritus at the State University of New York Upstate Medical University. He is the author of 25 books including the classic, *The Myth of Mental Illness* (1961), and most recently, *Fatal Freedom: The Ethics and Politics of Suicide* (1999). A forthcoming book is *Pharmacracy: Medicine and Politics in America.* He is widely recognized as the world's foremost critic of psychiatric coercions and excuses. He has received many awards for his defense of individual liberty and responsibility threatened by, in his view, the modern form of totalitarianism masquerading as therapy. A frequent and popular lecturer, he has addressed professional and lay groups and has appeared on radio and television in all of the Americas (North, Central, and South) as well as in Australia, Europe, Japan, and South Africa. His books have been translated into every major language.

Eugene I. Taylor holds an M.A. in general/experimental psychology and Asian studies and a Ph.D. in the history and philosophy of psychology. He is the author of several scholarly studies on William James. His most recent work is *Shadow Culture: Psychology and Spirituality in America* (1999), a historical study of the American visionary tradition. He currently holds an academic appointment at Harvard Medical School as lecturer on psychiatry and is a senior psychologist in the Psychiatry Service at Massachusetts General Hospital. He also is a core faculty member at Saybrook Graduate School and Research Center, where he teaches the history of humanistic and transpersonal psychology.

Hobart F. Thomas is Professor of Psychology Emeritus at Sonoma State University. He is a former chair of the Department of Psychology and Provost of the School of Expressive Arts at that same institution. Trained as a clinical psychologist, he has for many years maintained an active interest in bridging the gap between psychotherapy and academic education and in ways of fostering creativity. He resides in Santa Rosa, California, and as a sideline still plays jazz piano professionally.

John Vasconcellos is a California state senator who has been serving the Silicon Valley for more than 30 years. A longtime supporter of humanistic psychology and humanistic causes, he has been called the "conscience of the legislature." He currently is chair of the Committee on Education, the Committee on Public Safety, the Select Committee on Economic Development, and the Subcommittee on Aging and Long-Term Care. He also co-chairs the Joint Committee on Preparing California for the 21st Century. He is the founder of the California Task Force to Promote Self-Esteem and Personal and Social Responsibility and is the author of *A Liberating Vision: Politics for Growing Humans* (1979) and *Ending Politics as We Know It: Toward a 21st-Century Politics of Healing and Hope* (1999).

Clemmont E. Vontress is Professor Emeritus of Counseling at George Washington University (Washington, D.C.). He was awarded the Life Contribution Award by the American Counseling Association in 1997 and was named Counselor-Educator of the Year by the American Mental Health Counselors Association in 1993. He received his Ph.D. in counseling psychology from Indiana University in 1965. He is a licensed psychologist in the District of Columbia. He is recognized as a pioneer in the field of cross-cultural counseling and has published prolifically in this area. His publications include the books *Counseling Negroes* and *Cross-Cultural Counseling: A Case Book* and the video *Healing and Persuasion: An Interview With Jerome Frank, Ph.D., M.D.*

Will Wadlington is Associate Director of the Center for Counseling and Psychological Services at Pennsylvania State University. He also is in private practice in State College, Pennsylvania. A visual artist and former art professor, he is interested in creativity and contemporary art. His dissertation was on Otto Rank, an early precursor of existential-humanistic psychology who had broad cultural interests and wrote extensively about the artist type.

Roger Walsh is Professor of Psychiatry, Philosophy, and Anthropology at the University of California, Irvine. He graduated from the University of Queensland with degrees in psychology, physiology, neuroscience, and medicine and then passed licensing examinations in psychology, medicine, and psychiatry. Initially, he was a hardcore materialist and reductionistic neuroscientist. His life changed dramatically when, as part of his psychiatry training, he went into therapy with James F. T. Bugental, who introduced him to the inner universe that proved to be as vast, awesome, and mysterious as the outer universe. His interests and research now focus on topics such as meditation, spirituality, and transpersonal psychology. His publications include *Paths Beyond Ego: The Transpersonal Vision* and *Essential Spirituality: The Seven Central Practices to Awaken Heart and Mind.*

Arthur Warmoth is Professor of Psychology at Sonoma State University. He currently is chair of the Consortium for Diversified Psychology Programs, the national organization of graduate programs in humanistic, existential, and transpersonal psychologies. He has been a member of the executive board of Division 32 (Humanistic Psychology) of the American Psychological Association and is a past president of the Association for Humanistic Psychology. He received the Distinguished Service Award from the Saybrook Institute in 1994. In that same year, he and the Sonoma State psychology department received the Charlotte and Karl Bühler Award for pioneering work in graduate education in humanistic psychology from Division 32. He has been involved in humanistic psychology since 1959, when he went to Brandeis University to study with Abraham Maslow.

Jeanne C. Watson is Assistant Professor in the Department of Adult Education, Community Development, and Counselling Psychology, Ontario Institute for Studies in Education, University of Toronto. She is co-author (with Eileen Kennedy-Moore) of *Expressing Emotion: Myths, Realities, and Therapeutic Strategies* and co-editor (with Leslie S. Greenberg and Germain Lietaer) of the *Handbook of Experiential Psychotherapy*. She has written numerous articles on therapy process and outcome. She also has a part-time private practice in Toronto.

John Welwood is a psychotherapist, teacher, and author. He received his Ph.D. in clinical psychology from the University of Chicago, where he also studied and taught existential and Buddhist psychology. He currently trains psychotherapists in "psychotherapy in a spiritual context." He has published more than 50 articles on relationship, psychotherapy, consciousness, and personal change as well as 7 books including *Journey of the Heart: The Path of Conscious Love, Love and Awakening: Discovering the Sacred Path of Intimate Relationships, Awakening the Heart: East/West Approaches to Psychotherapy and the Healing Relationship,* and *Ordinary Magic: Everyday Life as Spiritual Path.* His latest book is *Toward a Psychology of Awakening: Buddhism, Psychotherapy, and the Path of Personal and Spiritual Transformation.*

Frederick J. Wertz is Professor of Psychology at Fordham University. He received his Ph.D. in phenomenological psychology from Duquesne University in 1982. He is editor of the *Journal of Phenomenological Psychology* and also edited *The Humanistic Movement: Recovering the Person in Psychology* and *Advances in Qualitative Research in Psychology: Themes and Variation*. He is a past president of Division 24 (Theoretical and Philosophical Psychology) and of Division 32 (Humanistic Psychology) of the American Psychological Association. His writing has focused on perception, psychopathology, criminal victimization, phenomenological research methodology, psychoanalysis, cognitive psychology, and the philosophical foundations of psychology.